How to Use the Maps in *World History, 4th Edition*

Here are some basic map concepts that will help you to get the most out of the maps in this textbook.

- Always look at the scale, which allows you to determine the distance in miles or kilometers between locations on the map.

- Examine the legend carefully. It explains the colors and symbols used on the map.

- Note the locations of mountains, rivers, oceans, and other geographic features, and consider how these would affect such human activities as agriculture, commerce, travel, and warfare.

- Read the map caption thoroughly. It provides important information, sometimes not covered in the text itself, and poses a thought question to encourage you to think beyond the mere appearance of the map and make connections across chapters, regions, and concepts.

- Several "spot maps" appear in each chapter, to allow you to view in detail smaller areas that may not be apparent in larger maps. For example, a spot map in Chapter 12 lets you zoom in on Charlemagne's Empire.

- Many of the text's maps also carry a globe icon alongside the title, which indicates that the map appears in interactive form on the text's website:

  http://www.wadsworth.com/history_d/special_features/ext/duiker_maps/index.htm

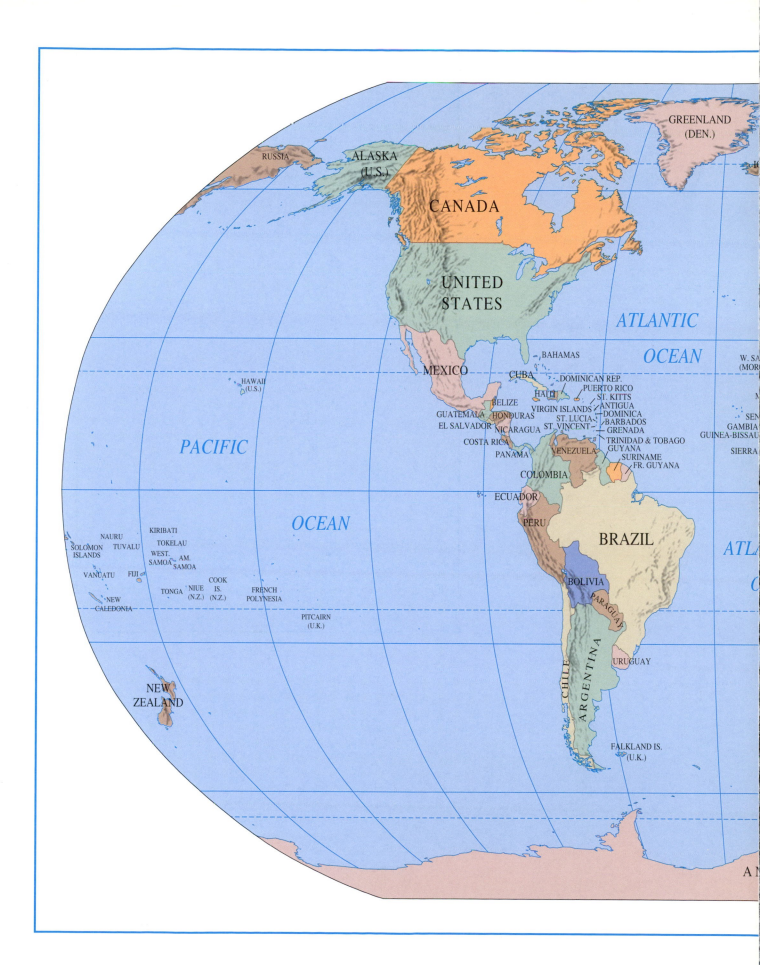

VOLUME I: TO 1800

WORLD HISTORY

4TH EDITION

WILLIAM J. DUIKER
THE PENNSYLVANIA STATE UNIVERSITY

JACKSON J. SPIELVOGEL
THE PENNSYLVANIA STATE UNIVERSITY

THOMSON

WADSWORTH

Australia • Canada • Mexico • Singapore • Spain
United Kingdom • United States

THOMSON

WADSWORTH

Publisher: Clark Baxter
Development Editor: Sue Gleason
Assistant Editor: Julie Yardley
Editorial Assistant: Eno Sarris
Technology Project Manager: Jennifer Ellis
Marketing Manager: Caroline Croley
Marketing Assistant: Mary Ho
Advertising Project Manager: Tami Strang
Project Manager, Editorial Production: Ray Crawford
Print/Media Buyer: Jessica Reed
Permissions Editor: Elizabeth Zuber
Copy Editor: Bruce Emmer
Art Editor: Dovetail Publishing Services, Image Quest

Production Service: Dovetail Publishing Services
Text Designer: Diane Beasley
Photo Researcher: Image Quest
Map Illustrator: Maps.com
Cover Designer: Lisa Devenish
Cover Image: Gozzoli, Benozo di Lese di Sandro (1420–97) *The Journey of the Magi to Bethlehem*, the left hand wall of the chapel, c. 1460 (fresco). Palazzo Medici-Riccardi, Florence, Italy/ The Bridgeman Art Library
Cover Printer: Phoenix Color Corp
Compositor: New England Typographic Service
Printer: R.R. Donnelley & Sons—Willard
Photo credits begin on page xviii

> For more information about our products, contact us at:
> **Thomson Learning Academic Resource Center**
> **1-800-423-0563**
> For permission to use material from this text, contact us by:
> **Phone:** 1-800-730-2214 **Fax:** 1-800-730-2215
> **Web:** http://www.thomsonrights.com

Library of Congress Control Number: 2003107415

Student Edition with InfoTrac College Edition:
ISBN 0-534-60364-5

Instructor's Edition: ISBN 0-534-60388-2

Wadsworth Group/Thomson Learning
10 Davis Drive
Belmont, CA 94002-3098
USA

Asia
Thomson Learning
5 Shenton Way #01-01
UIC Building
Singapore 068808

Australia/New Zealand
Thomson Learning
102 Dodds Street
Southbank, Victoria 3006
Australia

Canada
Nelson
1120 Birchmount Road
Toronto, Ontario M1K 5G4
Canada

Europe/Middle East/Africa
Thomson Learning
High Holborn House
50/51 Bedford Row
London WC1R 4LR
United Kingdom

Latin America
Thomson Learning
Seneca, 53
Colonia Polanco
11560 Mexico D.F.
Mexico

Spain/Portugal
Paraninfo
Calle/Magallanes, 25
28015 Madrid, Spain

Part II NEW PATTERNS OF CIVILIZATION 154

Part III THE EMERGENCE OF NEW WORLD PATTERNS (1400–1800) 350

DOCUMENT CREDITS

PHOTO CREDITS

CHAPTER 9

CHAPTER 10

CHAPTER 11

CHAPTER 12

PART III OPENING

CHAPTER 13

CHAPTER 14

CHAPTER 15

CHAPTER 16

CHAPTER 17

470 © Réunion des Musées Nationaux/Art Resource, NY
475 © Michael Holford, London **477 top** © Réunion des Musées
Nationaux/Art Resource, NY **477 bottom** Courtesy of James R.
Spencer **480 left** © Erich Lessing/Art Resource, NY
480 right Collection of the Earl of Pembroke, Wilton House, Wilts.,

UK/Bridgeman Art Library **481** By courtesy of the National Portrait
Gallery, London **484** © The Granger Collection, NY
488 © Scala/Art Resource, NY **491** © Réunion des Musées
Nationaux/Art Resource, NY **494** © Giraudon/Art Resource, NY
498 © Réunion des Musées Nationaux/Art Resource, NY
505 © Fotomas Archive **507** The Art Archive, London

CHRONOLOGIES

MAPS

PREFACE

For several million years after primates first appeared on the surface of the earth, human beings lived in small communities, seeking to survive by hunting, fishing, and foraging in a frequently hostile environment. Then suddenly, in the space of a few thousand years, there was an abrupt change of direction as human beings in a few widely scattered areas of the globe began to master the art of cultivating food crops. As food production increased, the population in those areas rose correspondingly, and people began to congregate in larger communities. Governments were formed to provide protection and other needed services to the local population. Cities appeared and became the focal point of cultural and religious development. Historians refer to this process as the beginnings of civilization.

For generations, historians in Europe and the United States have pointed to the rise of such civilizations as marking the origins of the modern world. Courses on Western civilization conventionally begin with a chapter or two on the emergence of advanced societies in Egypt and Mesopotamia and then proceed to ancient Greece and the Roman Empire. From Greece and Rome, the road leads directly to the rise of modern civilization in the West.

There is nothing inherently wrong with this approach. Important aspects of our world today can indeed be traced back to these early civilizations, and all human beings the world over owe a considerable debt to their achievements. But all too often this interpretation has been used to imply that the course of civilization has been linear in nature, leading directly from the emergence of agricultural societies in ancient Mesopotamia to the rise of advanced industrial societies in Europe and North America. Until recently, most courses on world history taught in the United States routinely focused almost exclusively on the rise of the West, with only a passing glance at other parts of the world, such as Africa, India, and East Asia. The contributions made by those societies to the culture and technology of our own time were often passed over in silence.

Several reasons have been advanced to justify this approach. Some have argued that students simply are not interested in what is unfamiliar to them. Others have said that it is more important that young minds understand the roots of their own heritage than that of peoples elsewhere in the world. In many cases, however, the motivation for this Eurocentric approach has been the belief that since the time of Socrates and Aristotle Western civilization has been the sole driving force in the evolution of human society.

Such an interpretation, however, represents a serious distortion of the process. During most of the course of human history, the most advanced civilizations have been not in the West, but in East Asia or the Middle East. A relatively brief period of European dominance culminated with the era of imperialism in the late nineteenth century, when the political, military, and economic power of the advanced nations of the West spanned the globe. During recent generations, however, that dominance has gradually eroded, partly as the result of changes taking place within Western societies and partly because new centers of development are emerging elsewhere on the globe—notably in East Asia, where the growing economic strength of Japan and many of its neighbors has led to the now familiar prediction that the twenty-first century will be known as the Pacific Century.

World history, then, is not simply a chronicle of the rise of the West to global dominance, nor is it a celebration of the superiority of the civilization of Europe and the United States over other parts of the world. The history of the world has been a complex process in which many branches of the human community have taken an active part, and the dominance of any one area of the world has been a temporary rather than a permanent phenomenon. It will be our purpose in this book to present a balanced picture of this story, with all respect for the richness and diversity of the tapestry of the human experience. Due attention must be paid to the rise of the West, of course, since that has been the most dominant aspect of world history in recent centuries. But the contributions made by other peoples must be given adequate consideration as well, not only in the period prior to 1500 when the major centers of civilization were located in Asia, but also in our own day, where a multipolar picture of development is clearly beginning to emerge.

Anyone who wishes to teach or write about world history must decide whether to present the topic as an integrated whole or as a collection of different cultures. The world that we live in today, of course, is in many respects an interdependent one in terms of economics as well as culture and communications, a reality that is often expressed by the phrase "global village." The convergence of peoples across the surface of the earth into an integrated world system began in early times and intensified after the rise of capitalism in the early modern era. In growing recognition of this trend, historians trained in global history, as well as instructors in the growing number of world history courses, have now begun to speak and write of a "global approach" that turns attention away from the study of individual civilizations and focuses instead on the "big picture" or, as the world historian Fernand Braudel termed it, interpreting world history as a river with no banks.

On the whole, this development is to be welcomed as a means of bringing the common elements of the evolution of human society to our attention. But there is a problem involved in this approach. For the vast majority of their time on earth, human beings have lived in partial or virtually total isolation from each other. Differences in climate, location, and geographical features have created human societies very different from each other in culture and historical experience. Only in relatively recent times—the commonly accepted date has long been the beginning of the age of European exploration at the end of the fifteenth century, but some would now push it back to the era of the Mongol empire or even further—have cultural interchanges begun to create a common "world system," in which events taking place in one part of the world are rapidly transmitted throughout the globe, often with momentous consequences. In recent generations, of course, the process of global interdependence has been proceeding even more rapidly. Nevertheless, even now the process is by no means complete, as ethnic and regional differences continue to exist and to shape the course of world history. The tenacity of these differences and sensitivities is reflected not only in the rise of internecine conflicts in such divergent areas as Africa, India, and Eastern Europe, but also in the emergence in recent years of such regional organizations as the Organization of African Unity, the Association for the Southeast Asian Nations, and the European Economic Community. Political leaders in various parts of the world speak routinely of "Arab unity," the "African road to socialism," and the "Confucian path to economic development."

The second problem is a practical one. College students today are all too often not well informed about the distinctive character of civilizations such as China and India and, without sufficient exposure to the historical evolution of such societies, will assume all too readily that the peoples in these countries have had historical experiences similar to ours and will respond to various stimuli in a similar fashion to those living in Western Europe or the United States. If it is a mistake to ignore those forces that link us together, it is equally a mistake to underestimate those factors that continue to divide us and to differentiate us into a world of diverse peoples.

Our response to this challenge has been to adopt a global approach to world history while at the same time attempting to do justice to the distinctive character and development of individual civilizations and regions of the world. The presentation of individual cultures will be especially important in Parts I and II, which cover a time when it is generally agreed that the process of global integration was not yet far advanced. Later chapters will begin to adopt a more comparative and thematic approach, in deference to the greater number of connections that have been established among the world's peoples since the fifteenth and sixteenth centuries. Part V will consist of a series of chapters that will center on individual regions of the world while at the same time focusing on common problems related to the Cold War and the rise of global problems such as overproduction and environmental pollution. Moreover, sections entitled "Reflection" at the close of the five major parts of the book will attempt to link events together in a broad comparative and global framework.

We have sought balance in another way as well. Many textbooks tend to simplify the content of history courses by emphasizing an intellectual or political perspective or, most recently, a social perspective, often at the expense of sufficient details in a chronological framework. This approach is confusing to students whose high school social studies programs have often neglected a systematic study of world history. We have attempted to write a well-balanced work in which political, economic, social, religious, intellectual, cultural, and military history have been integrated into a chronologically ordered synthesis.

To enliven the past and let readers see for themselves the materials that historians use to create their pictures of the past, we have included primary sources (boxed documents) in each chapter that are keyed to the discussion in the text. The documents include examples of the religious, artistic, intellectual, social, economic, and political aspects of life in different societies and reveal in a vivid fashion what civilization meant to the individual men and women who shaped it by their actions.

Each chapter has a lengthy introduction and conclusion to help maintain the continuity of the narrative and to provide a synthesis of important themes. Anecdotes in the chapter introductions convey more dramatically the major theme or themes of each chapter. Timelines at the end of each chapter enable students to see the major developments of an era at a glance and within cross-cultural categories, while the more detailed chronologies reinforce the events discussed in the text. An annotated bibliography at the end of each chapter reviews the most recent literature on each period and also gives references to some of the older, "classic" works in each field.

Extensive maps and illustrations serve to deepen the reader's understanding of the text. New to the fourth edition are map captions, designed to enrich students' awareness of the importance of geography to history, and a large number of spot maps, which enable students to see at a glance the region or subject being discussed in the text. The maps have also been revised where needed. To facilitate understanding of cultural movements, illustrations of artistic works discussed in the text are placed next to the discussions. Chapter outlines and focus questions, including analytical questions, at the beginning of each chapter help students with an overview and guide them to the main subjects of each chapter. A glossary of important terms and a pronunciation guide are included to enrich an understanding of the text.

After reexamining the entire book and analyzing the comments and reviews of many colleagues who have found the book to be a useful instrument for introducing their students to world history, we have also made a number of other changes for the fourth edition. In the first place, we have continued our effort to reduce the size of the book without affecting the quality of the material contained therein. As part of this effort, we have reorganized the material of five European chapters into three new chapters. These are Chapter 12, "The Making of Europe in the Middle Ages"; Chapter 13, "Renewal, Reform, and State Building in Europe"; and Chapter 17, "Europe on the Eve of a New World Order." Moreover, Chapters 31 and 32 have been synthesized into a new Chapter 29, "Toward the Pacific Century?" We have also tried to delete excess words while retaining all essential material as well as the narrative thrust of previous editions.

Second, we have sought to strengthen the global framework of the book, but not at the expense of reducing the attention assigned to individual regions of the world. The essays entitled "Reflection" that appear at the end of each of the five parts have been shortened slightly to accommodate the advice of many of our reviewers and to enable us to more concisely draw comparisons and contrasts across geographical, cultural, and chronological lines. Each Reflection section contains two boxed essays, each highlighted with an illustration, to single out issues of particular importance to that period of history. Moreover, additional comparative material has also been added to each chapter to help students be aware of similar developments globally. Among other things, this material includes new comparative sections, such as "Comparison of the Roman and Han Empires" in Chapter 5 and "Europe, China, and Scientific Revolutions" in Chapter 13, as well as comparative illustrations. We hope that these techniques will assist instructors who wish to encourage their students to adopt a comparative approach to their understanding of the human experience.

Third, this new edition contains additional information on the role of women in world history. In conformity with our own convictions, as well as what we believe to be recent practice in the field, we have tried where possible to introduce such material at the appropriate point in the text, rather than to set aside separate sections devoted exclusively to women's issues.

Finally, a number of new illustrations, boxed documents, and maps have been added, and the bibliographies have been revised to take account of newly published material. The chronologies and maps have been fine-tuned as well, to help the reader locate in time and space the multitude of indi-

viduals and place names that appear in the book. To keep up with the ever-growing body of historical scholarship, new or revised material has been added throughout the book on many topics, including early civilizations around the world; the Aryans in India; the Zhou dynasty in China; Sparta; Alexander and the Mauryan Empire in India; Roman trade with China; comparison of Roman and Han Chinese empires; the first Americans; the Maya; first civilizations in South America; Islam; early civilizations in Africa; the spread of Buddhism; the Song dynasty in China; the Mongols; early Japan; the African slave trade; the Ottoman Empire; the Mughals; Ming China; Tokugawa Japan; the impact of Western expansion on indigenous peoples; the impact of the discovery of the Pacific Islands in the eighteenth century; the defeat of Napoleon; slave revolt in Haiti; how industrialized nations limited industrialization in their colonies; Latin America; Canada; the impact of World War I on Africa, East Asia, and the Pacific; the Russian Revolution; and the Asian theater of World War II. In addition, all of the chapters in Part V have been updated to bring our treatment of contemporary events up to the present.

Because courses in world history at American and Canadian colleges and universities follow different chronological divisions, a one-volume comprehensive edition, a two-volume edition of this text, and a volume covering events to 1400 are being made available to fit the needs of instructors. Teaching and learning ancillaries include:

Instructor's Manual with Test Bank   Prepared by Eugene Larson, Los Angeles, Pierce College. Contains Chapter Outlines, Class Lecture/Discussion Topics, Thought/Discussion Questions for Primary Sources (Boxed Documents), Possible Student Projects, and Examination Questions (Essay, Identification, and Multiple Choice).

ExamView®   Create, deliver, and customize tests and study guides (both print and online) in minutes with this easy-to-use assessment and tutorial system. *ExamView®* offers both a Quick Test Wizard and an Online Test Wizard that guide you step-by-step through the process of creating tests, while its unique "WYSIWYG" capability allows you to see the test you are creating on the screen exactly as it will print or display online. You can build tests of up to 250 questions using up to 12 question types. Using *ExamView®*'s complete word processing capabilities, you can enter an unlimited number of new questions or edit existing questions.

Map Acetates and Commentary for World History   Includes more than 100 four-color map images from the text and other sources. Map commentary for each map is prepared by James Harrison, Siena College. Three-hole punched and shrinkwrapped.

History Video Library   Includes Film For Humanities (these are available to qualified adoptions), CNN videos, and Grade Improvement: Taking Charge of Your Learning.

Multimedia Manager for World History: A Microsoft Power Point Link Tool. An advanced PowerPoint presentation tool containing text-specific lecture outlines, figures, and images. In addition, it provides the flexibility to customize each presentation by editing what we have provided or by adding your own collection of slides, videos, and animations. All of the map acetates and selected photos have been incorporated into each lecture. The extensive map commentaries for each map are available through the "Comments" feature of PowerPoint.

Sights and Sounds of History Prepared by David Redles, Cuyahoga Community College. Short, focused video clips, photos, artwork, animations, music, and dramatic readings are used to bring life to historical topics and events which are most difficult for students to appreciate from a textbook alone. For example, students will experience the grandeur of Versailles and the defeat felt by a German soldier at Stalingrad. The video segments, each averaging 4 minutes long, make excellent lecture launchers. Available on Laserdisk or VHS video.

Study Guide Prepared by Dianna Rhyan Kardulias, Columbus State Community College. Contains Chapter Outlines, Terms and Persons to Know, Mapwork, Datework, Primary Sourcework, Artwork, Identifying Important Concepts Behind the Conclusion, and new Multiple Choice questions and Web Resources. Available in two volumes.

Map Exercise Workbook Prepared by Cynthia Kosso, Northern Arizona University. Has been thoroughly revised and improved. Contains over 20 maps and exercises, which ask students to identify important cities and countries. Also includes critical thinking questions for each unit. Available in two volumes.

World History MapTutor This new mapping CD-ROM allows students to learn by manipulating maps through "locate and label" exercises, animations, and critical thinking exercises.

Migrations in Modern World History 1500–2000 CD-ROM An interactive multimedia curriculum on CD-ROM by Patrick Manning and the World History Center. Includes over 400 primary source documents; analytical questions to help the student develop his/her own interpretations of history; timelines; and additional suggested resources, including books, films, and web sites.

CNN Video for Western Civilization and World History Twelve two- to five-minute CNN segments are easy to integrate into classroom discussions or as lecture launchers. Topics range from India's caste system to Pearl Harbor.

Document Exercise Workbooks Prepared by Donna Van Raaphorst, Cuyahoga Community College. Contains a collection of exercises based around primary source documents pertaining to world history.

Journey of Civilizations CD ROM for Windows Prepared by David Redles, Cuyahoga Community College. This CD takes students on 18 interactive journeys through history. Enhanced with QuickTime movies, animations, sound clips, maps, and more, the journeys allow students engage in history as active participants rather than as readers of past events.

Magellan World History Atlas Available to bundle with any history text; contains 44 historical four-color maps, including the conflict in Afghanistan, 2001, and States of the World, 2001.

Internet Guide for History, Third Edition Prepared by John Soares. Provides newly revised and up-to-date Internet exercises by topic. Available at

http://history.wadsworth.com.

Kishlansky, Sources in World History, Second and Third Editions This reader is a collection of documents designed to supplement any world history text. Available in two volumes.

Web Tutor™ This content-rich, Web-based teaching and learning tool helps students succeed by taking the course beyond classroom boundaries to an anywhere, anytime environment. *Web Tutor™* offers real-time access to a full array of study tools, including flashcards (with audio), practice quizzes, online tutorials, and Web links. Web Tutor also provides rich communication tools, including a course calendar, asynchronous discussion, "real-time" chat, and an integrated e-mail system. Available for Blackboard and WebCT.

InfoTrac® College Edition An online university that lets students explore and use full-length articles from more than 900 periodicals for four months. When students log on with their personal ID, they will immediately see how easy it is to search. Students can print out the articles, which date back as far as four years.

Historic Times: The Wadsworth History Resource Center

http://history.wadsworth.com/

Features a career section, forum, and links to museums, historical documents, and other fascinating sites. From the Resource Center you can access the book-specific web site, which contains the following: chapter by chapter tutorial quizzing, *InfoTrac®* activities, Internet activities, interactive maps and timelines, glossary, and hyperlinks for the student, and an online instructor's manual and downloadable PowerPoint files for the Instructor.

ACKNOWLEDGMENTS

Both authors gratefully acknowledge that without the generosity of many others, this project could not have been completed. William Duiker would like to thank Kumkum Chatterjee and On-cho Ng for their helpful comments about unfamiliar issues related to the history of India and premodern China. His long-time colleague Cyril Griffith, now deceased, was a cherished friend and a constant source of information about modern Africa. Art Goldschmidt has been of invaluable assistance in reading several chapters of the manuscript, as well as in unraveling many of the mysteries of Middle Eastern civilization. Finally, he remains profoundly grateful to his wife, Yvonne V. Duiker, Ph.D. She has not only given her usual measure of love and support when this appeared to be an insuperable task, but she has also contributed her own time and expertise to enrich the sections on art and literature, thereby adding life and sparkle to this, as well as the earlier editions of the book. To her, and to his daughters Laura and Claire, he will be forever thankful for bringing joy to his life.

Jackson Spielvogel would like to thank Art Goldschmidt, David Redles, and Christine Colin for their time and ideas and, above all, his family for their support. The gifts of love, laughter, and patience from his daughters, Jennifer and Kathryn, his sons, Eric and Christian, and his daughters-in-law, Liz and Laurie, were invaluable. Diane, his wife and best friend, provided him with editorial assistance, wise counsel, and the loving support that made a project of this magnitude possible.

Thanks to Wadsworth's comprehensive review process, many historians were asked to evaluate our manuscript. We are grateful to the following for the innumerable suggestions that have greatly improved our work:

Najia Aarim
SUNY College at Fredonia

Henry Maurice Abramson
Florida Atlantic University

Charles F. Ames, Jr.
Salem State College

Nancy Anderson
Loyola University

Gloria M. Aronson
Normandale College

Charlotte Beahan
Murray State University

Doris Bergen
University of Vermont

Martin Berger
Youngstown State University

Deborah Biffton
University of Wisconsin-LaCrosse

Charmarie Blaisdell
Northeastern University

Patricia J. Bradley
Auburn University at Montgomery

Dewey Browder
Austin Peay State University

Antonio Calabria
University of Texas at San Antonio

Alice-Catherine Carls
University of Tennessee-Martin

Yuan Ling Chao
Middle Tennessee State University

Mark W. Chavalas
University of Wisconsin

Hugh Clark
Ursinus College

Joan Coffey
Sam Houston State University

John Davis
Radford University

Ross Dunn
San Diego State University

Lane Earn
University of Wisconsin-Oshkosh

Roxanne Easley
Central Washington University

C. T. Evans
Northern Virginia Community College

Edward L. Farmer
University of Minnesota

William W. Farris
University of Tennessee

Ronald Fritze
Lamar University

Joe Fuhrmann
Murray State University

Robert Gerlich
Loyola University

Marc J. Gilbert
North Georgia College

William J. Gilmore-Lehne
Richard Stockton College of New Jersey

Richard M. Golden
University of North Texas

Joseph M. Gowaskie
Rider College

Jonathan Grant
Florida State University

Don Gustafson
Augsburg College

Deanna Haney
Lansing Community College

Ed Haynes
Winthrop College

Linda Kerr
University of Alberta at Edmonton

Zoltan Kramar
Central Washington University

Douglas Lea
Kutztown University

David Leinweber
Emory University

Thomas T. Lewis
Mount Senario College

Craig A. Lockard
University of Wisconsin-Green Bay

George Longenecker
Norwich University

Robert Luczak
Vincennes University

Patrick Manning
Northeastern University

Dolores Nason McBroome
Humboldt State University

John McDonald
Northern Essex Community College

Andrea McElderry
University of Louisville

Jeff McEwen
*Chattanooga State Technical
Community College*

David L. McMullen
*University of North Carolina at
Charlotte*

John A. Mears
Southern Methodist University

Marc A. Meyer
Berry College

Stephen S. Michot
*Mississippi County Community
College*

John Ashby Morton
Benedict College

William H. Mulligan
Murray State University

Henry A. Myers
James Madison University

Marian P. Nelson
University of Nebraska at Omaha

Sandy Norman
Florida Atlantic University

Patrick M. O'Neill
Broome Community College

Norman G. Raiford
Greenville Technical College

Jane Rausch
University of Massachusetts-Amherst

Dianna K. Rhyan
Columbus State Community College

Merle Rife
Indiana University of Pennsylvania

Patrice C. Ross
Columbus State Community College

John Rossi
LaSalle University

Eric C. Rust
Baylor University

Jane Samson
University of Alberta

Keith Sandiford
University of Manitoba

Elizabeth Sarkinnen
Mt. Hood Community College

Bill Schell
Murray State University

Robert M. Seltzer
Hunter College

David Shriver
Cuyahoga Community College

Amos E. Simpson
University of Southwestern Louisiana

Wendy Singer
Kenyon College

Marvin Slind
Washington State University

Paul Smith
Washington State University

John Snetsinger
*California Polytechnic State
University*

George Stow
LaSalle University

Patrick Tabor
Chemeketa Community College

Tom Taylor
Seattle University

John G. Tuthill
University of Guam

Joanne Van Horn
Fairmont State College

Pat Weber
University of Texas-El Paso

Douglas L. Wheeler
University of New Hampshire

David L. White
Appalachian State University

Elmira B. Wicker
Southern University-Baton Rouge

Glee Wilson
Kent State University

Harry Zee
Cumberland County College

The authors are truly grateful to the people who have helped us to produce this book. We especially want to thank Clark Baxter, whose faith in our ability to do this project was inspiring. Sue Gleason thoughtfully guided the overall development of the fourth edition, and Julie Yardley orchestrated the preparation of outstanding teaching and learning ancillaries. Bruce Emmer and Pat Lewis were, as usual, outstanding copy editors. Sarah Evertson provided valuable assistance in obtaining permissions for the illustrations. We are grateful to the staff of New England Typographic Service for providing their array of typesetting and page layout abilities. Jon Peck, of Dovetail Publishing Services, was as cooperative and cheerful as he was competent in matters of production management.

A Note to Students about Languages and the Dating of Time

One of the most difficult challenges in studying world history is coming to grips with the multitude of names, words, and phrases in unfamiliar languages. Unfortunately, this problem has no easy solution. We have tried to alleviate the difficulty, where possible, by providing an English-language translation of foreign words or phrases, a glossary, and a pronunciation guide. The issue is especially complicated in the case of Chinese, since two separate systems are commonly used to transliterate the spoken Chinese language into the Roman alphabet. The Wade-Giles system, invented in the nineteenth century, was the most frequently used until recent years, when the pinyin system was adopted by the People's Republic of China as its own official form of transliteration. We have opted to use the latter, since it appears to be gaining acceptance in the United States, but the initial use of a Chinese word is accompanied by its Wade-Giles equivalent in parentheses for the benefit of those who may encounter the term in their outside reading.

In our examination of world history, we need also to be aware of the dating of time. In recording the past, historians try to determine the exact time when events occurred. World War II in Europe, for example, began on September 1, 1939, when Adolf Hitler sent German troops into Poland, and ended on May 7, 1945, when Germany surrendered. By using dates, historians can place events in order and try to determine the development of patterns over periods of time.

If someone asked you when you were born, you would reply with a number, such as 1984. In the United States, we would all accept that number without question, because it is part of the dating system followed in the Western world (Europe and the Western Hemisphere). In this system, events are dated by counting backward or forward from the birth of Christ (assumed to be the year 1). An event that took place 400 years before the birth of Christ would most commonly be dated 400 B.C. (before Christ). Dates after the birth of Christ are labeled as A.D. These letters stand for the Latin words *anno domini*, which mean "in the year of the Lord" (or the year of the birth of Christ). Thus an event that took place 250 years after the birth of Christ is written A.D. 250, or in the year of the Lord 250. It can also be written as 250, just as you would not give your birth year as A.D. 1984, but simply 1984.

Some historians now prefer to use the abbreviations B.C.E. ("before the common era") and C.E. ("common era") instead of B.C. and A.D. This is especially true of world historians who prefer to use symbols that are not so Western or Christian oriented. The dates, of course, remain the same. Thus, 1950 B.C.E. and 1950 B.C. would be the same year, as would A.D. 40 and 40 C.E. In keeping with the current usage by many world historians, this book will use the terms B.C.E. and C.E.

Historians also make use of other terms to refer to time. A decade is 10 years; a century is 100 years; and a millennium is 1,000 years. The phrase fourth century B.C.E. refers to the fourth period of 100 years counting backward from 1, the assumed date of the birth of Christ. Since the first century B.C.E. would be the years 100 B.C.E. to 1 B.C.E., the fourth century B.C.E. would be the years 400 B.C.E. to 301 B.C.E. We could say, then, that an event in 350 B.C.E. took place in the fourth century B.C.E.

The phrase fourth century C.E. refers to the fourth period of 100 years after the birth of Christ. Since the first period of 100 years would be the years 1 to 100, the fourth period or fourth century would be the years 301 to 400. We could say, then, for example, that an event in 350 took place in the fourth century. Likewise, the first millennium B.C.E. refers to the years 1000 B.C.E. to 1 B.C.E.; the second millennium C.E. refers to the years 1001 to 2000.

The dating of events can also vary from people to people. Most people in the Western world use the Western calendar, also known as the Gregorian calendar after Pope Gregory XIII who refined it in 1582. The Hebrew calendar, on the other hand, uses a different system in which the year one is the equivalent of the Western year 3760 B.C.E., considered by Jews to be the date of the creation of the world. Thus, the Western year 2003 will be the year 5763 on the Jewish calendar. The Islamic calendar begins year 1 on the day Muhammad fled Mecca, which is the year 622 on the Western calendar.

THEMES FOR UNDERSTANDING WORLD HISTORY

*I*n examining the past, historians often organize their material on the basis of themes that enable them to ask and try to answer basic questions about the past. The following ten themes are especially important.

1. *Political systems*. The study of politics seeks to answer certain basic questions that historians have about the structure of a society: How were people governed? What was the relationship between the ruler and the ruled? What people or groups of people (the political elites) held political power? What actions did people take to change their form of government? Historians also examine the causes and results of wars in order to understand the impact of war on human development.

2. *The role of ideas*. Ideas have great power to move people to action. For example, in the twentieth century, the idea of nationalism, which is based on a belief in loyalty to one's nation, helped produce two great conflicts—World War I and World War II. Together these wars cost the lives of more than fifty million people. The spread of ideas from one society to another has also played an important role in world history. From the earliest times, trade has especially served to bring different civilizations into contact with one another, and the transmission of religious and cultural ideas soon followed.

3. *Economics and history*. A society depends for its existence on certain basic needs. How did it grow its food? How did it make its goods? How did it provide the services people needed? How did individual people and governments use their limited resources? Did they spend more money on hospitals or military forces? By answering these questions, historians examine the different economic systems that have played a role in history.

4. *Social life and gender issues*. From a study of social life, we learn about the different social classes that make up a society. But we also examine how people dressed and found shelter, how and what they ate, and what they did for fun. The nature of family life and how knowledge was passed from one generation to another through education are also part of the social life of a society. So, too, are gender issues: What different roles did men and women play in their societies? How and why were those roles different?

5. *The importance of culture*. We cannot understand a society without looking at its culture, or the common ideas, beliefs, and patterns of behavior that are passed on from one generation to another. Culture includes both high culture and popular culture. High culture consists of the writings of a society's thinkers and the works of its artists. A society's popular culture is the world of ideas and experiences of ordinary people. Today the media have embraced the term *popular culture* to describe the most current trends and fashionable styles.

6. *Religion in history*. Throughout history, people have sought to find a deeper meaning to human life. How have the world's great religions, such as Hinduism, Buddhism, Judaism, Christianity, and Islam, influenced people's lives? How have these religions spread to create new patterns of culture?

7. *The role of individuals*. In discussing the role of politics, ideas, economics, social life, cultural developments, and religion, we have dealt with groups of people and forces that often seem beyond the control of any one person. But mentioning the names of Cleopatra, Queen Elizabeth I, Napoleon, and Hitler reminds us of the role of individuals in history. Decisive actions by powerful individuals have indeed played a crucial role in the course of history.

8. *The impact of science and technology*. For thousands of years, people around the world have made scientific discoveries and technological innovations that have changed our world. From the creation of stone tools that made farming easier to the advanced computers that guide our airplanes, science and technology have altered how humans have related to their world.

9. *The environment and history*. Throughout history, peoples and societies have been affected by the physical world in which they live. Climatic changes alone have been an important factor in human history. Peoples and societies, in turn, have also made an impact on their world. Human activities have affected the physical environment and even endangered the very existence of entire societies and species.

10. *The migration of peoples*. One characteristic of world history is an almost constant migration of peoples. Vast numbers of peoples abandoned their homelands and sought to live elsewhere. Sometimes the migration was peaceful. More often than not, however, the migration meant invasion and violent conflict.

Part I

THE FIRST CIVILIZATIONS AND THE RISE OF EMPIRES (PREHISTORY TO 500 C.E.)

For hundreds of thousands of years, human beings lived in small communities, seeking to survive by hunting, fishing, and foraging in an often hostile environment. Then, in the space of a few thousand years, there was an abrupt change of direction as human beings in a few widely scattered areas of the globe began to master the art of cultivating food crops. As food production increased, the population in such areas grew, and people began to congregate in larger communities. Cities appeared and became centers of cultural and religious development. Historians refer to these changes as the beginnings of civilization.

The first civilizations that emerged in Mesopotamia, Egypt, India, and China all shared a number of basic characteristics. Each developed in a river valley that was able to provide the agricultural resources needed to maintain a large population. In each civilization, a part of the population lived in cities, which became the focal points for political, economic, social, cultural, and religious development. All of these early civilizations established some kind of government bureaucracy to meet the administrative demands of the growing population and organized armies for protection and to gain land and power. A new social structure based on economic control arose. While kings and an upper class of priests, political leaders, and warriors dominated, there also existed a large group of free people (farmers, artisans, craftspeople) and, at the very bottom stratum, a class of slaves. Abundant agricultural yields in these regions created opportunities for economic specialization as a surplus of goods enabled artisans and craftspeople to create new products.

The new urban civilizations were also characterized by significant religious and cultural developments. The gods were often deemed critical to a community's success, and professional priestly classes regulated relations with the gods. Rulers, priests, merchants, and artisans used writing to keep records and even create new kinds of literary expression. New forms of artistic activity, including monumental architectural structures, occupied a prominent place in the new urban environments.

By and large, the early river valley civilizations developed independently, grounded in local developments ultimately related to new agricultural practices. But contacts between them did occur and facilitated the exchange of new ideas and technology. Trade was often carried out by nomadic peoples from beyond the frontiers of settled states. Though not as organized as the dwellers in cities, these nomadic peoples also began to play an influential role in the human experience.

From the beginnings of the first civilizations around 3000 B.C.E., there was an ongoing movement toward the creation of larger territorial states with more sophisticated systems of control. This process reached a high point in the first millennium B.C.E. Between 1000 and 500 B.C.E., the Assyrians and Persians amassed empires that encompassed large areas of the ancient Middle East. The conquests of Alexander the Great in the fourth century B.C.E. created an even larger, if short-lived, empire that soon divided into four kingdoms. Later, the western portion of these kingdoms as well as the Mediterranean world and much of western Europe fell subject to the mighty empire of the Romans. At the same time, much of India became part of the Mauryan Empire. Finally, in the last few centuries B.C.E., the Qin and Han dynasties of China created a unified Chinese empire.

© British Museum

THE FIRST CIVILIZATIONS: THE PEOPLES OF WESTERN ASIA AND EGYPT

FOCUS QUESTIONS

- In what areas of the world did systematic agriculture develop during the Neolithic Age, and how did this development affect the lives of men and women?
- What are the characteristics of civilization, and what are some explanations for why early civilizations emerged?
- What effects did geography have on the civilizations that arose in Mesopotamia and Egypt?
- What role did religion play in the early civilizations of western Asia and Egypt, and how did Judaism and Zoroastrianism differ from the other religions of the region?
- What methods and institutions did the Assyrians and Persians use to amass and maintain their respective empires?
- ➤ In what ways were the civilizations of Mesopotamia and Egypt alike? In what ways were they different?

In 1849, a daring young Englishman made a hazardous journey into the deserts and swamps of southern Iraq. Braving high winds and temperatures that reached 120 degrees Fahrenheit, William Loftus led a small expedition southward along the banks of the Euphrates River in search of the roots of civilization. As he said, "From our childhood we have been led to regard this place as the cradle of the human race."

Guided by native Arabs into the southernmost reaches of Iraq, Loftus and his small band of explorers were soon overwhelmed by what they saw. He wrote, "I know of nothing more exciting or impressive than the first sight of one of these great piles, looming in solitary grandeur from the surrounding plains and marshes." One of these piles, known to the natives as the mound of Warka, contained the ruins of Uruk, one of the first cities in the world and part of the world's first civilization.

Southern Iraq, known to ancient peoples as Mesopotamia, was one of the areas in the world where civilization began. In the fertile valleys of large rivers—the Tigris and Euphrates in Mesopotamia, the Nile in Egypt, the Indus in India, and the Yellow River in China—intensive agriculture became capable of supporting large groups of people. In these regions, civilization was born. The first civilizations emerged in western Asia (now known as the Middle East) and Egypt, where people developed organized societies and created the ideas and institutions that we associate with civilization.

Before considering the early civilizations of western Asia and Egypt, however, we must briefly examine our prehistory and observe how human beings made the shift from hunting and gathering to agricultural communities and ultimately to cities and civilization. •

THE FIRST HUMANS

Historians rely mostly on documents to create their pictures of the past, but no written records exist for the prehistory of humankind. In their absence, the story of early humanity depends on archaeological and, more recently, biological information, which anthropologists and archaeologists use to formulate theories about our early past.

Although science has given us more precise methods for examining prehistory, much of our understanding of early humans still relies on considerable conjecture. Given the rate of new discoveries, the following account of the current theory of early human life might well be changed in a few years. As the great British archaeologist Louis Leakey reminded us years ago, "Theories on prehistory and early man constantly change as new evidence comes to light."

The earliest humanlike creatures—known as hominids—lived in Africa some three to four million years ago. Called Australopithecines, or "southern ape-men," by their discoverers, they flourished in eastern and southern Africa and were the first hominids to make simple stone tools. Australopithecines were also bipedal—that is, they walked upright on two legs, a trait that enabled them to move over long distances and make use of their arms and legs for different purposes.

In 1959, Louis and Mary Leakey discovered a new form of hominid in Africa that they labeled *Homo habilis* ("handy

human"). The Leakeys believed that *Homo habilis* was the earliest toolmaking hominid, which had a brain almost 50 percent larger than that of the Australopithecines. Their larger brains and the ability to walk upright allowed these hominids to become more sophisticated in the search for meat, seeds, and nuts for nourishment.

As *Homo habilis* died out, a new phase in early human development occurred around 1.8 million years ago with the emergence of *Homo erectus* ("upright human"). *Homo erectus* made use of larger and more varied tools and was the first hominid to leave Africa and move into Europe and Asia.

Around 250,000 years ago, a third and crucial phase in human development began with the emergence of *Homo sapiens* ("wise human"). By 100,000 B.C.E., two groups of *Homo sapiens* had developed. One type was the Neanderthal, whose remains were first found in the Neander valley in Germany. Neanderthal remains have since been found in both Europe and the Middle East and have been dated to between 100,000 and 30,000 B.C.E. Neanderthals relied on a variety of stone tools and were the first early people to bury their dead. (Some scientists maintain that burial of the dead indicates a belief in an afterlife.) Neanderthals in Europe made clothes from the skins of animals that they had killed for food.

The first anatomically modern humans, known as *Homo sapiens sapiens* ("wise, wise human"), appeared in Africa between 200,000 and 150,000 years ago. Recent evidence indicates that they began to spread outside Africa around 100,000 years ago. Map 1.1 shows probable dates for different movements, although many of these dates are still controversial. By 30,000 B.C.E., *Homo sapiens sapiens* had replaced the Neanderthals, who had largely become extinct.

The movement of the first modern humans was rarely deliberate. Groups of people advanced beyond their old hunting grounds at a rate of only 2 to 3 miles per generation. This was enough, however, to populate the world in some tens of thousands of years. Some scholars have suggested that such advanced human creatures may have emerged independently in different parts of the world, rather than in Africa alone, but the latest genetic evidence strongly supports the out-of-Africa theory as the most likely explanation of human origin. In any case, by 10,000 B.C.E., members of the *Homo sapiens sapiens* species could be found throughout the world. By that time, it was the only human species left. All humans today, be they Europeans, Australian Aborigines, or Africans, belong to the same subspecies of human being.

The Hunter-Gatherers of the Paleolithic Age

One of the basic distinguishing features of the human species is the ability to make tools. The earliest tools were made of stone, and so this early period of human history

THE FIRST HUMANS

Australopithecines	flourished c. 2–4 million years ago
Homo habilis	flourished c. 1–4 million years ago
Homo erectus	flourished c. 100,000–1.8 million years ago
Homo sapiens:	
Neanderthals	flourished c. 100,000–30,000 B.C.E.
Homo sapiens sapiens	emerged c. 200,000 B.C.E.

including buffalo, horses, bison, wild goats, reindeer, and fish.

The hunting of animals and the gathering of wild plants no doubt led to certain patterns of living. Archaeologists and anthropologists have speculated that Paleolithic people lived in small bands of twenty to thirty individuals. They were nomadic (they moved from place to place) because they had no choice but to follow animal migrations and vegetation cycles. Hunting depended on careful observation of animal behavior patterns and required a group effort to have any real degree of success. Over the years, tools became more refined and more useful. The invention of the spear, and later the bow and arrow, made hunting considerably easier. Harpoons and fishhooks made of bone increased the catch of fish.

(c. 2,500,000–10,000 B.C.E.) has been designated the Paleolithic Age (*paleolithic* is Greek for "old stone").

For hundreds of thousands of years, humans relied on hunting and gathering for their daily food. Paleolithic peoples had a close relationship with the world around them, and over a period of time, they came to know which animals to hunt and which plants to eat. They did not know how to grow crops or raise animals, however. They gathered wild nuts, berries, fruits, and a variety of wild grains and green plants. Around the world, they captured and consumed various animals,

Both men and women were responsible for finding food—the chief work of Paleolithic people. Since women bore and raised the children, they generally stayed close to the camps, but they played an important role in acquiring food by gathering berries, nuts, and grains. Men hunted for wild animals, an activity that took them far from camp. Because both men and women played important roles in providing for the band's survival, scientists have argued that a rough equality existed between men and women. Indeed, some speculate that both men and women made the decisions that governed the activities of the Paleolithic band.

MAP 1.1 **The Spread of *Homo sapiens sapiens*.** *Homo sapiens sapiens* spread from Africa beginning about 100,000 years ago. Living and traveling in small groups, these anatomically modern humans were hunter-gatherers. ➤ *Given that some diffusion of humans occurred during ice ages, how would such climate change affect humans and their movements, especially from Asia to Australia and Asia to North America?*

These groups of Paleolithic peoples, especially those who lived in cold climates, found shelter in caves. Over time, they created new types of shelter as well. Perhaps the most common was a simple structure of wood poles or sticks covered with animal hides. Where wood was scarce, Paleolithic hunter-gatherers might use the bones of mammoths for the framework and cover it with animal hides. The systematic use of fire, which archaeologists believe began around 500,000 years ago, made it possible for the caves and human-made structures to have a source of light and heat. Fire also enabled early humans to cook their food, making it taste better, last longer, and in the case of some plants, such as wild grain, easier to chew and digest.

The making of tools and the use of fire—two important technological innovations of Paleolithic peoples—remind us how crucial the ability to adapt was to human survival. Changing physical conditions during periodic ice ages posed a considerable threat to human existence. Paleolithic peoples used their technological innovations—such as the ability to make tools and use fire—to change their physical environment. By working together, they found a way to survive. And by passing on their common practices, skills, and material products to their children, they ensured that later generations, too, could survive in a harsh environment.

But Paleolithic peoples did more than just survive. The cave paintings of large animals found in southwestern France and northern Spain bear witness to the cultural activity of Paleolithic peoples. A cave discovered in southern France in 1994 contains more than three hundred paintings of lions, oxen, owls, panthers, and other animals. Most of these are animals that Paleolithic people did not hunt, which suggests that the paintings were created for religious or even decorative purposes.

The Neolithic Revolution, c. 10,000–4000 B.C.E.

The end of the last ice age around 10,000 B.C.E. was followed by what is called the Neolithic Revolution because it ushered in the New Stone Age (*neolithic* is Greek for "new stone"). The name New Stone Age is misleading, however. Although Neolithic peoples made a new type of polished stone axes, this was not the most significant change they introduced.

A REVOLUTION IN AGRICULTURE

The biggest change was the shift from hunting animals and gathering plants for sustenance to producing food by systematic agriculture (see Map 1.2). The planting of grains and vegetables provided a regular supply of food, while the taming of animals, such as sheep, goats, cattle, and pigs, added a steady source of meat, milk, and fibers such as wool for clothing. Larger animals could also be used as beasts of burden. The growing of crops and the taming of food-producing animals created a new relationship between humans and nature. Historians like to speak of this as an agricultural revolution. Revolutionary change is dramatic and requires great effort, but the ability to acquire food on a regular basis gave humans greater control over their environment. It also enabled them to give up their nomadic ways of life and begin to live in settled communities.

The shift from hunting and gathering to food producing was not as sudden as was once believed, however. The Mesolithic period ("Middle Stone Age," c. 10,000–7000 B.C.E.) saw a gradual transition from a food-gathering and hunting economy to a food-

✧ **PALEOLITHIC CAVE PAINTING.** Cave paintings of large animals provide good examples of the cultural creativity of Paleolithic peoples. One scene is part of a large underground chamber found accidentally in 1940 at Lascaux, France, by some boys looking for their dog. This work is dated around 14,000 B.C.E. Rock paintings found in early Africa, such as the one shown at right, include more human figures and present a more vivid picture of hunting and herding activities.

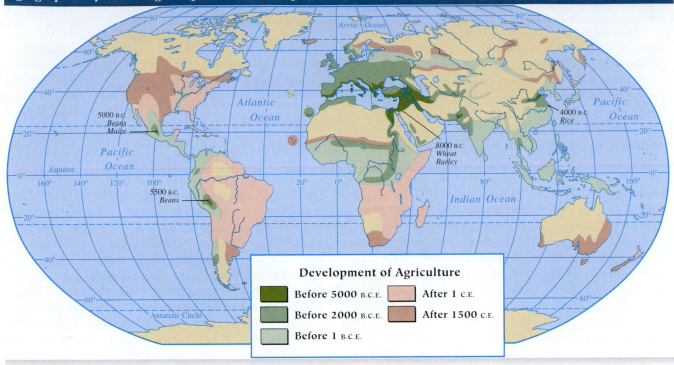

MAP 1.2   The Development of Agriculture.   Agriculture first began between 8000 and 7000 B.C.E. in four different areas. It allowed the establishment of permanent settlements where crops could be grown and domesticated animals that produced meat and milk could be easily tended. ➤ *What human and geographical factors might explain relationships between latitude and the beginning of agriculture?*

producing one and witnessed a gradual domestication of animals as well. Likewise, the movement toward the use of plants and their seeds as an important source of nourishment was also not sudden. Evidence seems to support the possibility that the Paleolithic hunters and gatherers had already grown crops to supplement their traditional sources of food. Moreover, throughout the Neolithic period, hunting and gathering as well as nomadic herding remained ways of life for many people around the world.

Systematic agriculture developed independently in different areas of the world between 8000 and 5000 B.C.E. Inhabitants of the Middle East began cultivating wheat and barley and domesticating pigs, cattle, goats, and sheep by 8000 B.C.E. From the Middle East, farming spread into the Balkans region of Europe by 6500 B.C.E. By 4000 B.C.E., it was well established in the south of France, central Europe, and the coastal regions of the Mediterranean. The cultivation of wheat and barley also spread from western Asia into the Nile valley of Egypt by 6000 B.C.E. and soon spread up the Nile to other areas of Africa, especially the Sudan and Ethiopia. In the woodlands and tropical forests of Central Africa, a separate agricultural system emerged based on the cultivation of tubers or root crops such as yams and tree crops such as bananas. The cultivation of

wheat and barley also eventually moved eastward into the highlands of northwestern and central India, between 7000 and 5000 B.C.E. By 5000 B.C.E., rice was being cultivated in southeastern Asia, from where it spread into southern China. In northern China, the cultivation of millet and the domestication of pigs and dogs seem well established by 6000 B.C.E. In the Western Hemisphere, Mesoamericans (inhabitants of present-day Mexico and Central America) domesticated beans, squash, and maize (corn) as well as dogs and fowl between 7000 and 5000 B.C.E.

CONSEQUENCES OF THE NEOLITHIC REVOLUTION

The growing of crops on a regular basis gave rise to relatively permanent settlements, which historians refer to as Neolithic farming villages or towns. Although Neolithic villages appeared in Europe, India, Egypt, China, and Mesoamerica, the oldest and most extensive ones were located in the Middle East. Jericho, in Palestine near the Dead Sea, was in existence by 8000 B.C.E. and covered several acres by 7000 B.C.E. It had a wall several feet thick that enclosed houses made of sun-dried mudbricks. Çatal Hüyük, located in modern Turkey, was an even larger community. Its walls enclosed 32 acres, and its population probably reached six thousand inhabitants during its high point from 6700 to 5700 B.C.E. People lived in simple mud-brick houses that were built so close to one another that there were few streets. To get to their homes, people would walk along the rooftops and enter the house through a hole in the roof.

Archaeologists have discovered twelve cultivated products in Çatal Hüyük, including fruits, nuts, and three kinds of wheat. People grew their own food and stored it in store-rooms in their homes. Domesticated animals, especially cattle, yielded meat, milk, and hides. Hunting scenes on the walls would indicate that the people of Çatal Hüyük hunted as well, but unlike earlier hunter-gatherers, they no longer relied on hunting to survive. Food surpluses also made it possible for people to do things other than farming. Some people became artisans and made weapons and jewelry that were traded with neighboring peoples, thus connecting the inhabitants of Çatal Hüyük to the wider world around them.

Religious shrines housing figures of gods and goddesses have been found at Çatal Hüyük, as have a number of female statuettes. Molded with noticeably large breasts and buttocks, these "earth mothers" perhaps symbolically represented the fertility of both "our mother" earth and human mothers. Both the shrines and the statues point to the growing role of religion in the lives of these Neolithic peoples.

The Neolithic agricultural revolution had far-reaching consequences. Once people settled in villages or towns, they built houses for protection and other structures for the storage of goods. As organized communities stored food and accumulated material goods, they began to engage in trade. In the Middle East, for example, the new communities exchanged such objects as shells, flint, and semi-precious stones. People also began to specialize in certain crafts, and a division of labor developed. Pottery was made from clay and baked in fire to make it hard. The pots were used for cooking and to store grains. Woven baskets were also used for storage. Stone tools became refined as flint blades were used to make sickles and hoes for use in the fields. In the course of the Neolithic Age, many of the food plants still in use today came to be cultivated. Moreover, vegetable fibers from such plants as flax and cotton were used to make thread that was woven into cloth.

The change to systematic agriculture in the Neolithic Age also had consequences for the relationship between men and women. Men assumed the primary responsibility for working in the fields and herding animals, jobs that kept them away from the home. Women remained behind, caring for the children and weaving cloth, making cheese from milk, and performing other household tasks that required considerable labor. In time, as work outside the home was increasingly perceived as more important than work done in the home, men came to play the more dominant role in human society, a basic pattern that would persist until our own times.

Other patterns set in the Neolithic Age also proved to be enduring elements of human history. Fixed dwellings, domesticated animals, regular farming, a division of labor, men holding power—all of these are part of the human story. For all of our scientific and technological progress, human survival still depends on the growing and storing of food, an accomplishment of people in the Neolithic Age. The Neolithic Revolution was truly a turning point in human history.

Between 4000 and 3000 B.C.E., significant technical developments began to transform the Neolithic towns. The invention of writing enabled records to be kept, while the use of metals marked a new level of human control over the environment and its resources. Already before 4000 B.C.E., artisans had discovered that metal-bearing rocks could be heated to liquefy the metal, which could then be cast in molds to produce tools and weapons that were more useful than stone instruments. Although copper was the first metal to be used for producing tools, after 4000 B.C.E., metalworkers in western Asia discovered that a combination of copper and tin produced bronze, a much harder and more durable metal than copper. Its widespread use has led historians to call the period from around 3000 to 1200 B.C.E. the Bronze Age; thereafter, bronze was increasingly replaced by iron.

At first, Neolithic settlements were hardly more than villages. But as their inhabitants mastered the art of farming, more complex human societies gradually emerged. As wealth increased, these societies sought to protect it from being plundered by outsiders and so began to develop armies and to build walled cities. By the beginning of the Bronze Age, the concentration of larger numbers of people in river valleys was leading to a whole new pattern for human life.

THE EMERGENCE OF CIVILIZATION

As we have seen, early human beings formed small groups that developed a simple culture that enabled them to survive. As human societies grew and developed greater complexity, civilization came into being. A civilization is a complex culture in which large numbers of people share a variety of common elements. Historians have identified a number of basic characteristics of civilization, including the following:

1. *An urban focus*. Cities became the centers for political, economic, social, cultural, and religious development.
2. *A distinct religious structure*. The gods were deemed crucial to the community's success, and professional priestly classes, as stewards of the gods' property, regulated relations with the gods.
3. *New political and military structures*. An organized government bureaucracy arose to meet the administrative

demands of the growing population, and armies were organized to gain land and power.

4. *A new social structure based on economic power.* While kings and an upper class of priests, political leaders, and warriors dominated, there also existed large groups of free common people (farmers, artisans, craftspeople) and, at the very bottom socially, a class of slaves.

5. *The development of writing.* Kings, priests, merchants, and artisans used writing to keep records.

6. *New and significant artistic and intellectual activity.* For example, monumental architectural structures, usually religious, occupied a prominent place in urban environments.

The first civilizations that developed in Mesopotamia and Egypt will be examined in detail in this chapter. But civilizations also developed independently in other parts of the world. Between 3000 and 1500 B.C.E., the valleys of the Indus River in India supported a flourishing civilization that extended hundreds of miles from the Himalayas to the coast of the Arabian Sea (see Chapter 2). This Indus valley civilization carried on extensive trade with city-states in Mesopotamia.

Another river valley civilization emerged along the Yellow River in northern China about four thousand years ago (see Chapter 3). Under the Shang dynasty of kings, which ruled from 1750 to 1122 B.C.E., this civilization contained impressive cities with huge city walls, royal palaces, and large royal tombs. A system of irrigation enabled early Chinese civilization to maintain a prosperous farming society ruled by an aristocratic class whose major concern was war.

Scholars have believed for a long time that civilization emerged only in these four areas—the fertile river valleys of the Tigris and Euphrates, the Nile, the Indus, and the Yellow River. Recently, however, archaeologists have discovered two other early civilizations. One of these flourished in Central Asia (in what are now the republics of Turkmenistan and Uzbekistan) around four thousand years ago. People in this civilization built mudbrick buildings, raised sheep and

Central Asian Civilization

Oxus R.

Caspian Sea

(Uzbekistan)

(Turkmenistan)

0   300   600 Kilometers

0   300 Miles

⊱ **STATUES FROM AIN GHAZAL.**   These life-size statues made of plaster and bitumen date from 6500 B.C.E. and were discovered in 1984 in Ain Ghazal, an archaeological site near Amman, Jordan. They are among the oldest statues ever found of the human figure. Archaeologists are studying the statues to try to understand their purpose and meaning.

Courtesy of the Hashemite Kingdom of Jordan, Dept. of Antiquities

goats, had bronze tools, used a system of irrigation to grow wheat and barley, and had a writing system.

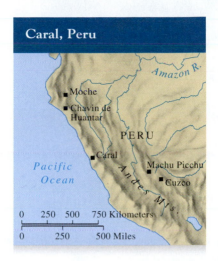

Another early civilization was discovered in the Supe River valley of Peru. At the center of this civilization was the city of Caral, which flourished around 2600 B.C.E. It contained buildings for officials, apartment buildings, and grand residences, all built of stone. The inhabitants of Caral also developed a system of irrigation by diverting a river more than a mile upstream into their fields.

Why early civilizations developed remains difficult to explain. Since civilizations developed independently in different parts of the world, can general causes be identified that would tell us why all of these civilizations emerged? A number of possible explanations of the beginning of civilization have been suggested. A theory of challenge and response maintains that challenges forced human beings to make efforts that resulted in the rise of civilization. Some scholars have adhered to a material explanation. Material forces, such as the accumulation of food surpluses, made possible the specialization of labor and development of large communities with bureaucratic organization. But some areas were not naturally conducive to agriculture. Abundant food could be produced only through a massive human effort to carefully manage the water, an effort that created the need for organization and bureaucratic control and led to civilized cities. Some historians have argued that nonmaterial forces, primarily religious, provided the sense of unity and purpose that made such organized activities possible. Finally, some scholars doubt that we are capable of ever discovering the actual causes of early civilization.

CIVILIZATION IN MESOPOTAMIA

The Greeks spoke of the valley between the Tigris and Euphrates Rivers as Mesopotamia, the land "between the rivers." The region receives little rain, but the soil of the plain of southern Mesopotamia was enlarged and enriched over the years by layers of silt deposited by the two rivers. In late spring, the Tigris and Euphrates overflow their banks and deposit their fertile silt, but since this flooding depends on the melting of snows in the upland mountains where the rivers begin, it is irregular and sometimes cat-astrophic. In such circumstances, farming could be accomplished only with human intervention in the form of irrigation and drainage ditches. A complex system was required to control the flow of the rivers and produce the crops. Large-scale irrigation made possible the expansion of agriculture in this region, and the abundant food provided the material base for the emergence of civilization in Mesopotamia.

The City-States of Ancient Mesopotamia

The creators of the first Mesopotamian civilization were the Sumerians, a people whose origins remain unclear. By 3000 B.C.E., they had established a number of independent cities in southern Mesopotamia, including Eridu, Ur, Uruk, Umma, and Lagash (see Map 1.3). As the cities expanded, they came to exercise political and economic control over the surrounding countryside, forming city-states, which were the basic units of Sumerian civilization.

Sumerian cities were surrounded by walls. Uruk, for example, was encircled by a wall 6 miles long with defense towers located along it every 30 to 35 feet. City dwellings, built of sun-dried bricks, included both the small flats of peasants and the larger dwellings of the civic and priestly officials. Although Mesopotamia had little stone or wood for building purposes, it did have plenty of mud. Mudbricks, easily shaped by hand, were left to bake in the hot sun until they were hard enough to use for building. People in Mesopotamia were remarkably inventive with mudbricks, inventing the arch and the dome and constructing some of the largest brick buildings in the world. Mudbricks are still used in rural areas of the Middle East today.

The most prominent building in a Sumerian city was the temple, which was dedicated to the chief god or goddess of the city and often built atop a massive stepped tower called a ziggurat. The Sumerians believed that gods and goddesses owned the cities, and much wealth was used to build temples as well as elaborate houses for the priests and priestesses who served the deities. Priests and priestesses, who supervised the temples and their property, had much power. The temples owned much of the city land and livestock and served not only as the physical center of the city but also as its economic and political center.

In fact, historians believe that in the early stages of the city-states, priests and priestesses played an important role in ruling. The Sumerians believed that the gods ruled the cities, making the state a theocracy (government by a divine authority). Eventually, however, ruling power passed into the hands of worldly figures, or kings.

Sumerians viewed kingship as divine in origin—kings, they believed, derived their power from the gods and were the agents of the gods. As one person said in a

MAP 1.3   The Ancient Near East. The Fertile Crescent encompassed land with access to water. Employing flood management and irrigation systems, the peoples of the region established civilizations based on agriculture. These civilizations developed writing, law codes, and economic specialization.
➤ *What geographical aspects of the Mesopotamian city-states made conflict between them likely?*

petition to his king: "You in your judgement, you are the son of Anu [god of the sky]; Your commands, like the word of a god, cannot be reversed, Your words, like rain pouring down from heaven, are without number."[1] Regardless of their origins, kings had power—they led armies, supervised the building of public works, and organized workers for the irrigation projects on which Mesopotamian farming depended. The army, the government bureaucracy, and the priests and priestesses all aided the kings in their rule. Befitting their power, Sumerian kings lived in large palaces with their wives and children.

The economy of the Sumerian city-states was primarily agricultural, but commerce and industry became important as well. The people of Mesopotamia produced woolen textiles, pottery, and the metalwork for which they were especially well known. The Sumerians imported copper,

tin, and timber in exchange for dried fish, wool, barley, wheat, and metal goods. Traders traveled by land to the eastern Mediterranean in the west and by sea to India in the east. The invention of the wheel around 3000 B.C.E. led to carts with wheels that made the transport of goods easier.

Sumerian city-states contained three major social groups: nobles, commoners, and slaves. Nobles included royal and priestly officials and their families. Commoners were the nobles' clients, who worked for the palace and temple estates, and other free citizens, who worked as farmers, merchants, fishers, and craftspeople. At least 90 percent of the population was engaged in farming. Slaves belonged to palace officials, who used them in building projects; to temple officials, who used mostly female slaves to weave cloth and grind grain; and to rich landowners, who used them for farming and domestic work.

Empires in Ancient Mesopotamia

As the number of Sumerian city-states grew and the states expanded, new conflicts arose as city-state fought city-state for control of land and water. The fortunes of various city-states rose and fell over the centuries. The constant wars, with their burning and sacking of cities, left many Sumerians in deep despair, as is evident in the words of this Sumerian poem from the city of Ur: "Ur is destroyed, bitter is its lament. The country's blood now fills its holes like hot bronze in a mold. Bodies dissolve like fat in the sun. Our temple is destroyed, the gods have abandoned us, like migrating birds. Smoke lies on our city like a shroud."

Located in the flat land of Mesopotamia, the Sumerian city-states were also open to invasion. To the north of the Sumerian city-states were the Akkadians. We call them a Semitic people because of the type of language they spoke (see Table 1.1). Around 2340 B.C.E., Sargon, leader of the Akkadians, overran the Sumerian city-states and established an empire that included most of Mesopotamia as well as lands westward to the Mediterranean. Attacks from neighboring hill peoples eventually caused the Akkadian empire to fall, and its end by 2100 B.C.E. brought a return to the system of warring city-states. It was not until 1792 B.C.E. that a new empire came to control much of Mesopotamia under Hammurabi, who ruled over the Amorities or Old Babylonians, a large group of Semitic-speaking seminomads.

Hammurabi (1792–1750 B.C.E.) employed a well-disciplined army of foot soldiers who carried axes, spears, and copper or bronze daggers. He learned to divide his opponents and subdue them one by one. Using such methods, he gained control of Sumer and Akkad, creating a new Mesopotamian kingdom. After his conquests, he called himself "the sun of Babylon, the king who has made the four quarters of the world subservient," and established a new capital at Babylon.

Hammurabi, the man of war, was also a man of peace. He followed in the footsteps of previous conquerors by assimilating Mesopotamian culture, with the result that Sumerian ways continued to exist despite the end of the Sumerians as a political entity. A collection of his letters, found by archaeologists, reveals that he took a strong interest in state affairs. He built temples, defensive walls, and irrigation

TABLE 1.1
SOME SEMITIC LANGUAGES
Akkadian
Aramaic
Assyrian
Babylonian
Canaanitic
Phoenician
Syriac
Arabic
Hebrew

Note: Languages in italic type are no longer spoken.

Hammurabi's Empire

THE "ROYAL STANDARD" OF UR. This series of panels is from the "Royal Standard" of Ur, a box dating from c. 2700 B.C.E. and discovered in a stone tomb from the royal cemetery of the Sumerian city-state of Ur. These scenes from the box depict the activities of the king and his court after a military victory. In the top panel, the king and his court drink wine while at the right a musician plays a bull-headed harp. The middle panel shows bulls, rams, and fish being brought to the banquet hall. The bottom panel shows booty from the king's victory.

© British Museum

canals; encouraged trade; and brought an economic revival. After his death, however, a series of weak kings were unable to keep Hammurabi's empire united, and it finally fell to new invaders.

THE CODE OF HAMMURABI

Hammurabi is best remembered for his law code, a collection of 282 laws. For centuries, laws had regulated people's relationships with one another in the lands of Mesopotamia, but only fragments of these earlier codes survive. Hammurabi's collection provides considerable insight into almost every aspect of everyday life there and provides us a priceless glimpse of the values of this early society.

The Code of Hammurabi reveals a society with a system of strict justice. Penalties for criminal offenses were severe and varied according to the social class of the victim. A crime against a member of the upper class (a noble) by a member of the lower class (a commoner) was punished more severely than the same offense against a member of the lower class (see the box on p. 13).

➤➤ **STELE OF HAMMURABI.** Although the Sumerians compiled earlier law codes, Hammurabi's code was the most famous in early Mesopotamian history. The code recognized three social classes in Babylonia (nobles, free commoners, and slaves) and included laws dealing with marriage and divorce, job performance, punishments for crimes, and even sexual relations. The upper section of the stele depicts Hammurabi standing in front of the seated sun god Shamash (who was also the god of justice), who orders the king to record the law. The lower section contains the actual code.

Hammurabi's code took the duties of public officials seriously. Officials were expected to catch burglars. If they failed to do so, officials in the district where the crime was committed had to replace the lost property. If murderers were not found, the officials had to pay a fine to the relatives of the victim.

The law code also furthered the proper performance of work with what amounted to consumer protection laws. Builders were held responsible for the buildings they constructed. If a house collapsed and caused the death of the owner, the builder was put to death. If the collapse caused the death of the son of the owner, the son of the builder was put to death. If goods were destroyed by the collapse, they had to be replaced and the house itself reconstructed at the builder's expense.

The largest category of laws in the Code of Hammurabi focused on marriage and the family. Parents arranged marriages for their children. After marriage, the parties involved signed a marriage contract; without it, no one was considered legally married. While the husband provided a bridal payment, the woman's parents were responsible for a dowry to the new husband.

As in many patriarchal societies, women possessed far fewer privileges and rights in the married relationship than men. A woman's place was in the home, and failure to fulfill her expected duties was grounds for divorce. If she was not able to bear children, her husband could divorce her. Furthermore, a wife who was a "gadabout, . . . neglecting her house [and] humiliating her husband," could be drowned.

Sexual relations were strictly regulated as well. Husbands, but not wives, were permitted sexual activity outside marriage. A wife caught committing adultery was pitched into the river, although her husband could ask the king to pardon her. Incest was strictly forbidden. If a father had incestuous relations with his daughter, he would be banished. Incest between a son and mother resulted in both being burned.

Fathers ruled their children as well as their wives. Obedience was duly expected: "If a son has struck his father, they shall cut off his hand." If a son committed a serious enough offense, his father could disinherit him, although fathers were not permitted to disinherit their sons arbitrarily.

The Culture of Mesopotamia

A spiritual worldview was of fundamental importance to Mesopotamian culture. To the peoples of Mesopotamia, the gods were living realities who affected all aspects of life. It was crucial, therefore, that the correct hierarchies be observed. Leaders could prepare armies for war, but success really depended on a favorable relationship with the gods. This helps explain the importance of the priestly class and is the reason why even the kings took great care to dedicate offerings and monuments to the gods.

THE CODE OF HAMMURABI

Although there were earlier Mesopotamian law codes, Hammurabi's is the most complete. The law code emphasizes the principle of retribution ("an eye for an eye") and punishments that vary according to social status. Punishments could be severe. Marriage and family affairs are also given much attention in the code. The following examples illustrate these concerns.

25. If fire broke out in a free man's house and a free man, who went to extinguish it, cast his eye on the goods of the owner of the house and has appropriated the goods of the owner of the house, that free man shall be thrown into that fire.

129. If the wife of a free man has been caught while lying with another man, they shall bind them and throw them into the water. If the husband of the woman wishes to spare his wife, then the king in turn may spare his subject.

131. If a free man's wife was accused by her husband, but she was not caught while lying with another man, she shall make affirmation by god and return to her house.

196. If a free man has destroyed the eye of a member of the aristocracy, they shall destroy his eye.

198. If he has destroyed the eye of a commoner or broken the bone of a commoner, he shall pay one mina of silver.

199. If he has destroyed the eye of a free man's slave or broken the bone of a free man's slave, he shall pay one-half his value.

209. If a free man struck another free man's daughter and has caused her to have a miscarriage, he shall pay ten shekels of silver for her fetus.

210. If that woman has died, they shall put his daughter to death.

211. If by a blow he has caused a commoner's daughter to have a miscarriage, he shall pay five shekels of silver.

212. If that woman has died, he shall pay one-half mina of silver.

213. If he struck a free man's female slave and has caused her to have a miscarriage, he shall pay two shekels of silver.

214. If that female slave has died, he shall pay one-third mina of silver.

THE IMPORTANCE OF RELIGION

The physical environment had an obvious impact on the Mesopotamian view of the universe. Ferocious floods, heavy downpours, scorching winds, and oppressive humidity were all part of the Mesopotamian climate. These conditions and the resulting famines easily convinced Mesopotamians that this world was controlled by supernatural forces and that the days of human beings "are numbered; whatever he may do, he is but wind," as *The Epic of Gilgamesh* put it. In the presence of nature, Mesopotamians could easily feel helpless, as this poem relates:

> The rampant flood which no man can oppose,
> Which shakes the heavens and causes earth to tremble,
> In an appalling blanket folds mother and child,
> Beats down the canebrake's full luxuriant greenery,
> And drowns the harvest in its time of ripeness.[2]

The Mesopotamians discerned cosmic rhythms in the universe and accepted its order but perceived that it was not completely safe because of the presence of willful, powerful cosmic powers that they identified with gods and goddesses.

With its numerous gods and goddesses animating all aspects of the universe, Mesopotamian religion was polytheistic. The four most important deities were An, god of the sky and hence the most important force in the universe; Enlil, god of wind; Enki, god of the earth, rivers, wells, and canals as well as inventions and crafts; and Ninhursaga, a goddess associated with soil, mountains, and vegetation, who came to be worshiped as a mother goddess, a "mother of all children," who manifested her power by giving birth to kings and conferring the royal insignia on them.

Human relationships with the gods were based on subservience since, according to Sumerian myth, human beings were created to do the manual labor the gods were unwilling to do for themselves. Moreover, humans were insecure because they could never predict the gods' actions. But humans did attempt to relieve their anxiety by discovering the intentions of the gods through divination.

Divination took a variety of forms. A common form, at least for kings and priests who could afford it, involved killing animals, such as sheep or goats, and examining their livers or other organs. Supposedly, features seen in the organs of the sacrificed animals foretold events to come. Thus one handbook states that if the animal organ has shape *x*, then the outcome of the military campaign will be *y*. The Mesopotamian arts of divination arose out of the desire to discover the purposes of the gods. If people could decipher the signs that foretold events, the events would be predictable and humans could act wisely.

THE CULTIVATION OF NEW ARTS AND SCIENCES

The realization of writing's great potential was another aspect of Mesopotamian culture. The oldest Mesopotamian texts date to around 3000 B.C.E. and were written by the Sumerians, who used a cuneiform ("wedge-

Pictographic sign, c. 3100 B.C.									
Interpretation	star	?sun over horizon	?stream	ear of barley	bull's head	bowl	head + bowl	lower leg	?shrouded body
Cuneiform sign, c. 2400 B.C.									
Cuneiform sign c. 700 B.C. (turned through 90°)									
Phonetic value*	dingir, an	u₄, ud	a	še	gu₄	nig₂, ninda	ku₂	du, gin, gub	lu₂
Meaning	god, sky	day, sun	water, seed, son	barley	ox	food, bread	to eat	to walk, to stand	man

*Some signs have more than one phonetic value, and some sounds are represented by more than one sign. U₄ means the fourth sign with the phonetic value u.

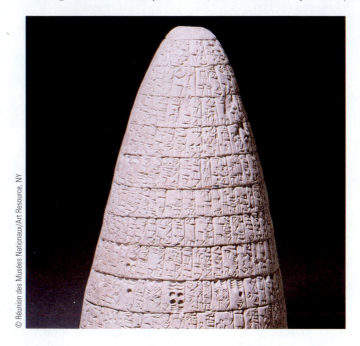

© Réunion des Musées Nationaux/Art Resource, NY

© Michael Holford

➤ **EARLY WRITING.**   Pictured here is the upper part of the cone of Uruinimgina, an example of early cuneiform script from an early Sumerian dynasty. The table shows the development of writing from pictographic signs to the evolution of cuneiform script. The earliest Egyptian writing was also pictographic, as shown in the hieroglyphs from the *Book of the Dead* papyrus of the Lady Anhai during the New Kingdom.

shaped") system of writing. Using a reed stylus, they made wedge-shaped impressions on clay tablets, which were then baked or dried in the sun. Once dried, these tablets were virtually indestructible, and the several hundred thousand that have been found so far have been a valuable source of information for modern scholars. Sumerian writing evolved from pictures of concrete objects to simplified and stylized signs, leading eventually to a phonetic system that made possible the written expression of abstract ideas.

Mesopotamian peoples used writing primarily for record keeping, but cuneiform texts were also used in schools set up to teach the cuneiform system of writing. The primary goal of scribal education was to produce professionally trained scribes for careers in the temples and palaces, the military, and government service. Pupils were male and primarily from wealthy families.

Writing was important because it enabled a society to keep records and maintain knowledge of previous practices and events. Writing also made it possible for people to communicate ideas in new ways, which is especially evident in the most famous piece of Mesopotamian literature, *The Epic of Gilgamesh*, an epic poem that records the exploits of a legendary king of Uruk (see the box on p. 15). Gilgamesh, wise, strong, and perfect in body, part man and part god, befriends a hairy beast named Enkidu. Together they set off in pursuit of heroic deeds. When Enkidu dies, Gilgamesh experiences the pain of mortality and begins a search for the secret of immortality. But his efforts fail. Gilgamesh remains mortal. The desire for immortality, one of humankind's great searches, ends in complete frustration. "Everlasting life," as this Mesopotamian epic makes clear, is only for the gods.

THE GREAT FLOOD

*T*he great epic poem of Mesopotamian literature, The Epic of Gilgamesh, *includes an account by Utnapishtim (a Mesopotamian version of the later biblical Noah), who had built a ship and survived the flood unleashed by the gods to destroy humankind. In this selection, Utnapishtim recounts his story to Gilgamesh, telling how the god Ea advised him to build a boat and how he came to land the boat at the end of the flood.*

THE EPIC OF GILGAMESH

In those days the world teemed, the people multiplied, the world bellowed like a wild bull, and the great god was aroused by the clamor. Enlil heard the clamor and he said to the gods in council, "The uproar of mankind is intolerable and sleep is no longer possible by reason of the babel." So the gods agreed to exterminate mankind. Enlil did this, but Ea [Sumerian Enki, god of the waters] because of his oath warned me in a dream, ". . . Tear down your house and build a boat, abandon possessions and look for life, despise worldly goods and save your soul alive. Tear down your house, I say, and build a boat. . . . then take up into the boat the seed of all living creatures. . . ." [Utnapishtim did as he was told, and then the destruction came.]

For six days and six nights the winds blew, torrent and tempest and flood overwhelmed the world, tempest and flood raged together like warring hosts. When the seventh day dawned the storm from the south subsided, the sea grew calm, the flood was stilled; I looked at the face of the world and there was silence, all mankind was turned to clay. The surface of the sea stretched as flat as a rooftop; I opened a hatch and the light fell on my face. Then I bowed low, I sat down and I wept, the tears streamed down my face, for on every side was the waste of water. I looked for land in vain, but fourteen leagues distant there appeared a mountain, and there the boat grounded; on the mountain of Nisir the boat held fast, she held fast and did not budge. . . . When the seventh day dawned I loosed a dove and let her go. She flew away, but finding no resting place she returned. Then I loosed a swallow, and she flew away but finding no resting place she returned. I loosed a raven, she saw that the waters had retreated, she ate, she flew around, she cawed, and she did not come back. Then I threw everything open to the four winds, I made a sacrifice and poured out a libation on the mountaintop.

Mesopotamians also made outstanding achievements in mathematics and astronomy. In math, the Sumerians devised a number system based on 60, using combinations of 6 and 10 for practical solutions. Geometry was used to measure fields and erect buildings. In astronomy, the Sumerians made use of units of 60 and charted the heavenly constellations. Their calendar was based on twelve lunar months and was brought into harmony with the solar year by adding an extra month from time to time.

EGYPTIAN CIVILIZATION: "THE GIFT OF THE NILE"

"The Egyptian Nile," wrote one Arab traveler, "surpasses all the rivers of the world in sweetness of taste, in length of course and usefulness. No other river in the world can show such a continuous series of towns and villages along its banks." The Nile River was crucial to the development of Egyptian civilization (see the box on p. 16). Egypt, like Mesopotamia, was a river valley civilization.

The Importance of Geography

The Nile is a unique river, beginning in the heart of Africa and coursing northward for thousands of miles. It is the longest river in the world. The Nile was responsible for creating an area several miles wide on both banks of the river that was fertile and capable of producing abundant harvests. The "miracle" of the Nile was its annual flooding. The river rose in the summer from rains in central Africa, crested in Egypt in September and October, and left a deposit of silt that enriched the soil. The Egyptians called this fertile land the "Black Land," because it was dark in color from the silt and the lush crops that grew on it. Beyond these narrow strips of fertile fields lay the deserts (the "Red Land"). About 100 miles before it empties into the Mediterranean, the river splits into two major branches, forming the delta, a triangular-shaped territory called Lower Egypt to distinguish it from Upper Egypt, the land upstream to the south (see Map. 1.4). Egypt's important cities developed at the tip of the delta. Even today, most of Egypt's people are crowded along the banks of the Nile River.

Unlike Mesopotamia's rivers, the flooding of the Nile was gradual and usually predictable, and the river itself was seen as life-enhancing, not life-threatening. Although a system of organized irrigation was still necessary, the small villages along the Nile could create such systems without the massive state intervention that was required in Mesopotamia. Egyptian civilization consequently tended to remain more rural, with many small population centers congregated along a narrow band on both sides of the Nile.

The surpluses of food that Egyptian farmers grew in the fertile Nile valley made Egypt prosperous. But the Nile also served as a unifying factor in Egyptian history. In ancient times, the Nile was the fastest way to travel through the land, making both transportation and communication easier. Winds from the north pushed sailboats south, and the current of the Nile carried them north.

The Significance of the Nile River and the Pharaoh

Two of the most important sources of life for the ancient Egyptians were the Nile River and the pharaoh. Egyptians perceived that the Nile River made possible the abundant food that was a major source of their well-being. This Hymn to the Nile, probably from the nineteenth and twentieth dynasties in the New Kingdom, expresses the gratitude Egyptians felt for the Nile.

HYMN TO THE NILE

Hail to you, O Nile, that issues from the earth and comes to
    keep Egypt alive! . . .
He that waters the meadows which Re created, in order to
    keep every kid alive.
He that makes to drink the desert and the place distant from
    water: that is his dew coming down from heaven. . . .
The lord of fishes, he who makes the marsh-birds to go
    upstream. . . .
He who makes barley and brings emmer into being, that he
    may make the temples festive.
If he is sluggish, then nostrils are stopped up, and everybody
    is poor. . . .
When he rises, then the land is in jubilation, then every belly
    is in joy, every backbone takes on laughter, and every
    tooth is exposed.
The bringer of good, rich in provisions, creator of all good,
    lord of majesty, sweet of fragrance. . . .

He who makes every beloved tree to grow, without lack
    of them.

The Egyptian king, or pharaoh, was viewed as a god and the absolute ruler of Egypt. His significance and the gratitude of the Egyptian people for his existence are evident in this hymn from the reign of Sesotris III (c. 1880–1840 B.C.E.).

HYMN TO THE PHARAOH

He has come unto us that he may carry away Upper Egypt;
    the double diadem [crown of Upper and Lower Egypt]
    has rested on his head.
He has come unto us and has united the Two Lands; he has
    mingled the reed with the bee [symbols of Lower and
    Upper Egypt].
He has come unto us and has brought the Black Land under
    his sway; he has apportioned to himself the Red Land.
He has come unto us and has taken the Two Lands under his
    protection; he has given peace to the Two Riverbanks.
He has come unto us and has made Egypt to live; he has
    banished its suffering.
He has come unto us and has made the people to live; he has
    caused the throat of the subjects to breathe. . . .
He has come unto us and has done battle for his boundaries;
    he has delivered them that were robbed.

Unlike Mesopotamia, which was subject to constant invasion, Egypt had natural barriers that fostered isolation, protected it from invasion, and gave it a sense of security. These barriers included deserts to the west and east; cataracts (rapids) on the southern part of the Nile, which made defense relatively easy; and the Mediterranean Sea to the north. These barriers, however, did not prevent the development of trade. Indeed, there is evidence of very early trade between Egypt and Mesopotamia itself.

The regularity of the Nile floods and the relative isolation of the Egyptians created a sense of security and a feeling of changelessness. To the ancient Egyptians, when the Nile flooded each year, "the fields laugh, and people's faces light up." Unlike people in Mesopotamia, Egyptians faced life with a spirit of confidence in the stability of things. Ancient Egyptian civilization was characterized by a remarkable degree of continuity for thousands of years.

The Old and Middle Kingdoms

Modern historians have divided Egyptian history into three major periods, known as the Old Kingdom, the Middle Kingdom, and the New Kingdom. These were periods of long-term stability characterized by strong monarchical authority, competent bureaucracy, freedom from invasion, much construction of temples and pyramids, and considerable intellectual and cultural activity. But between the periods of stability were times of political chaos known as the Intermediate Periods, which were characterized by weak political structures and rivalry for leadership, invasions, a decline in building activity, and a restructuring of society.

THE OLD KINGDOM

According to the Egyptians' own tradition, their land consisted initially of numerous populated areas ruled by tribal chieftains. Around 3100 B.C.E., the first Egyptian royal dynasty, under a king called Menes, united both Upper and Lower Egypt into a single kingdom. Henceforth, the king would be called "King of Upper and Lower Egypt," and the royal crown would be a double diadem, signifying the unification of all Egypt. Just as the Nile served to unite Upper and Lower Egypt physically, kingship served to unite the two areas politically.

The Old Kingdom encompassed the third through sixth dynasties of Egyptian kings, lasting from around 2686 to 2125 B.C.E. It was an age of prosperity and splendor, made visible in the construction of the greatest and largest

Harvard MFA Expedition. Courtesy, Museum of Fine Arts, Boston

Chronology

THE EGYPTIANS

Early Dynastic Period (Dynasties 1–2)	c. 3100–2686 B.C.E.
Old Kingdom (Dynasties 3–6)	c. 2686–2125 B.C.E.
First Intermediate Period (Dynasties 7–10)	c. 2125–2055 B.C.E.
Middle Kingdom (Dynasties 11–12)	c. 2055–1650 B.C.E.
Second Intermediate Period (Dynasties 13–17)	c. 1650–1550 B.C.E.
New Kingdom (Dynasties 18–20)	c. 1550–1085 B.C.E.
Post-Empire (Dynasties 21–31)	c. 1085–30 B.C.E.

PAIR STATUE OF KING MENKAURE AND HIS QUEEN. The period designated as the Old Kingdom began around 2686 B.C.E., some four centuries after Egypt's unification, and lasted until around 2125 B.C.E. The kings of Egypt (eventually called pharaohs) were regarded as gods, divine instruments who maintained the fundamental order and harmony of the universe and wielded absolute power. This statue depicts King Menkaure and his queen (fourth dynasty).

pyramids in Egypt's history. The capital of the Old Kingdom was located at Memphis, south of the delta.

Kingship was a divine institution in ancient Egypt and formed part of a universal cosmic scheme (see the box on p. 16): "What is the king of Upper and Lower Egypt? He is a god by whose dealings one lives, the father and mother of all men, alone by himself, without an equal."[3] In obeying their king, subjects helped maintain the cosmic order. A breakdown in royal power could only mean that citizens were offending divinity and weakening the universal structure. Among the various titles of Egyptian kings, that of pharaoh (originally meaning "great house" or "palace") eventually came to be the most common.

Although they possessed absolute power, Egyptian kings were not supposed to rule arbitrarily but according to set principles. The chief principle was called *Ma'at*, a spiritual precept that conveyed the ideas of truth and justice but especially right order and harmony. To ancient Egyptians, this fundamental order and harmony had existed throughout the universe since the beginning of time. Pharaohs were the divine instruments who maintained it and were themselves subject to it.

Although theoretically absolute in their power, in practice Egyptian kings did not rule alone. Initially, members of the king's family performed administrative tasks, but by the fourth dynasty, a bureaucracy with regular procedures had developed. Especially important was the office of vizier, "steward of the whole land." Directly responsible to the king, the vizier was in charge of the bureaucracy. For administrative purposes, Egypt was divided into provinces or nomes, as they were later called by the Greeks—twenty-two in Upper Egypt and twenty in Lower Egypt. A governor, called by the Greeks a nomarch, was head of each nome and was responsible to the king and vizier. Nomarchs, however, tended to build up large holdings of land and power within their nomes, creating a potential rivalry with the pharaohs.

THE MIDDLE KINGDOM

Despite the theory of divine order, the Old Kingdom eventually collapsed, ushering in a period of chaos. Finally, a new royal dynasty managed to pacify all Egypt and inaugurated the Middle Kingdom, a period of stability lasting from c. 2055 to 1650 B.C.E. Egyptians later portrayed the Middle Kingdom as a golden age, a clear indication of its stability. Several factors contributed to its vitality. The nome structure was reorganized. The boundaries of each nome were now settled precisely, and the obligations of the nomes to the state were clearly delineated. Nomarchs were confirmed as hereditary officeholders but with the understanding that their duties must be performed faithfully. These included

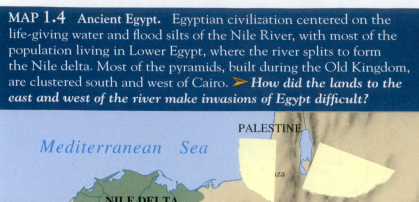

MAP 1.4 Ancient Egypt. Egyptian civilization centered on the life-giving water and flood silts of the Nile River, with most of the population living in Lower Egypt, where the river splits to form the Nile delta. Most of the pyramids, built during the Old Kingdom, are clustered south and west of Cairo. ➤ *How did the lands to the east and west of the river make invasions of Egypt difficult?*

should be done. He appointed me herdsman of this land, for he knew who would keep it in order for him."[4]

Society and Economy in Ancient Egypt

Egyptian society had a simple structure in the Old and Middle Kingdoms; basically, it was organized along hierarchical lines with the god-king at the top. The king was surrounded by an upper class of nobles and priests who participated in the elaborate rituals of life that surrounded the pharaoh. This ruling class ran the government and managed its own landed estates, which provided much of its wealth.

Below the upper classes were merchants and artisans. Merchants engaged in an active trade up and down the Nile as well as in town and village markets. Some merchants also engaged in international trade; they were sent by the king to Crete and Syria, where they obtained wood and other products. Expeditions traveled into Nubia for ivory and down the Red Sea to Punt for incense and spices. Egyptian artisans made an incredible variety of well-built and beautiful goods: stone dishes; painted boxes made of clay; wooden furniture; gold, silver, and copper tools and containers; paper and rope made of papyrus; and linen clothing.

By far the largest number of people in Egypt simply worked the land. In theory, the king owned all the land but granted out portions of it to his subjects. Large sections were in the possession of nobles and the temple complexes. Most of the lower classes were serfs, or common people bound to the land, who cultivated the estates. They paid taxes in the form of crops to the king, nobles, and priests; lived in small villages or towns; and provided military service and forced labor for building projects.

the collection of taxes for the state and the recruitment of labor forces for royal projects, such as stone quarrying.

The Middle Kingdom was characterized by a new concern of the pharaohs for the people. In the Old Kingdom, the pharaoh had been viewed as an inaccessible god-king. Now he was portrayed as the shepherd of his people with the responsibility to build public works and provide for the public welfare. As one pharaoh expressed it: "He [a particular god] created me as one who should do that which he had done, and to carry out that which he commanded

The Culture of Egypt

Egypt produced a culture that dazzled and awed its later conquerors. The Egyptians' technical achievements, especially visible in the construction of the pyramids, demonstrated a measure of skill unequaled in the world at that time. To the Egyptians, all of these achievements were part of a cosmic order suffused with the presence of the divine.

SPIRITUAL LIFE IN EGYPTIAN SOCIETY

The Egyptians had no word for religion because it was an inseparable element of the entire world order to which Egyptian society belonged. The Egyptians were polytheistic and had a remarkable number of gods associated with heavenly bodies and natural forces. Two groups, sun gods and land gods, came to have special prominence, hardly unusual in view of the importance of the sun, the river, and the fertile land along its banks to Egypt's well-being. The sun was the source of life and hence worthy of worship. The sun god took on different forms and names, depending on his specific role. He was worshiped as Atum in human form and also as Re, who had a human body but the head of a falcon. The pharaoh took the title of "Son of Re," since he was regarded as the earthly form of Re. Eventually, Re became associated with Amon, an air god of Thebes, as Amon-Re.

River and land deities included Osiris and Isis with their child Horus, who was related to the Nile and to the sun as well. Osiris became especially important as a symbol of resurrection or rebirth. A famous Egyptian myth told of the struggle between Osiris, who brought civilization to Egypt, and his evil brother Seth, who killed him, cut his body into fourteen parts, and tossed them into the Nile River. Osiris' faithful wife Isis found the pieces and, with help from other gods, restored Osiris to life. As a symbol of resurrection and judge of the dead, Osiris took on an important role for the Egyptians. By identifying with Osiris, one could hope to gain new life just as Osiris had done. The dead, embalmed and mummified, were placed in tombs (in the case of kings, in pyramidal tombs), given the name of Osiris, and by a process of magical identification became Osiris. Like Osiris, they could then be reborn. The flood of the Nile and the new life it brought to Egypt were symbolized by Isis gathering all of Osiris' parts together and were celebrated each spring in the Festival of the New Land.

Later Egyptian spiritual practice began to emphasize morality by stressing Osiris' role as judge of the dead. The dead were asked to give an account of their earthly deeds to show whether they deserved a reward. Other means were also employed to gain immortality. Magical incantations, preserved in the *Book of the Dead*, were used to ensure a favorable journey to a happy afterlife. Specific instructions explained what to do when confronted by the judge of the dead. These instructions had two aspects. The negative confession gave a detailed list of what one had not done:

> What is said on reaching the Broad-Hall of the Two Justices [the place of the next-world judgment], absolving X [the name and title of the deceased] of every sin which he had committed . . .
>
> *I have not committed evil against men.*
> *I have not mistreated cattle.*

> *I have not blasphemed a god. . . .*
> *I have not done violence to a poor man.*
> *I have not done that which the gods abominate.*
> *I have not defamed a slave to his superior.*
> *I have not made anyone sick.*
> *I have not made anyone weep.*
> *I have not killed. . . .*
> *I have not caused anyone suffering. . . .*
> *I have not had sexual relations with a boy.*
> *I have not defiled myself. . . .*[5]

Later the suppliant made a speech listing his good actions: "I have done that which men said and that with which gods are content. . . . I have given bread to the hungry, water to the thirsty, clothing to the naked, and a ferryboat to him who was marooned. I have provided divine offerings for the gods and mortuary offerings for the dead."[6]

At first the Osiris cult was reserved for the very wealthy, who could afford to take expensive measures to preserve the body after death. During the Middle Kingdom, however, the cult became "democratized"—extended to all Egyptians who aspired to an afterlife.

THE PYRAMIDS

One of the great achievements of Egyptian civilization, the building of pyramids, occurred in the time of the Old Kingdom. Pyramids were built as part of a larger complex of buildings dedicated to the dead—in effect, a city of the dead. The area included a large pyramid for the king's burial, smaller pyramids for his family, and mastabas, rectangular structures with flat roofs, as tombs for the pharaoh's noble officials.

The tombs were well prepared for their residents, their rooms furnished and stocked with numerous supplies, including chairs, boats, chests, weapons, games, dishes, and a variety of foods. The Egyptians believed that human beings had two bodies, a physical one and a spiritual one, which they called the *ka*. If the physical body was properly preserved (by mummification) and the tomb was furnished with all the objects of regular life, the *ka* could return, surrounded by earthly comforts, and continue its life despite the death of the physical body.

The largest and most magnificent of all the pyramids was built under King Khufu. Constructed at Giza around 2540 B.C.E., this famous Great Pyramid covers 13 acres, measures 756 feet at each side of its base, and stands 481 feet high. Its four sides are almost precisely oriented to the four points of the compass. The interior included a grand gallery to the burial chamber, which was built of granite with a lidless sarcophagus for the pharaoh's body. The Great Pyramid still stands as a visible symbol of the power of Egyptian kings and the spiritual conviction that underlay Egyptian society. No pyramid built later ever matched its size or splendor. The pyramid was not only the king's tomb; it was also an important symbol of royal

➤➤ **THE PYRAMIDS AT GIZA.** The three pyramids at Giza, across the Nile River from Cairo, are the most famous in Egypt. Pyramids served as tombs for both the king and his immediate family. At the rear is the largest of the three pyramids, the Great Pyramid of Khufu. In the foreground is the smaller pyramid of Menkaure, standing behind the even smaller pyramids for the pharaohs' wives.

power. It could be seen for miles away as a visible reminder of the glory and might of the ruler who was a living god on earth.

ART AND WRITING

Commissioned by kings or nobles for use in temples and tombs, Egyptian art was largely functional. Wall paintings and statues of gods and kings in temples served a strictly spiritual purpose. They were an integral part of the performance of ritual, which was thought necessary to preserve the cosmic order and hence the well-being of Egypt. Likewise, the mural scenes and sculptured figures found in the tombs had a specific function: they were supposed to assist the journey of the deceased into the afterworld.

Egyptian art was also formulaic. Artists and sculptors were expected to observe a strict canon of proportions that determined both form and presentation. This canon gave Egyptian art a distinctive appearance for thousands of years. Especially characteristic was the convention of combining the profile, semiprofile, and frontal views of the human body in relief work and painting in order to represent each part of the body accurately. The result was an art that was highly stylized yet still allowed distinctive features to be displayed.

Writing emerged in Egypt during the first two dynasties. The Greeks later labeled Egyptian writing *hieroglyphics*, meaning "priest-carvings" or "sacred writings." Hieroglyphs were sacred characters used as picture signs that depicted objects and had a sacred value at the same time. Although hieroglyphs were later simplified into two scripts for writing purposes, they never developed into an alphabet. Egyptian hieroglyphs were initially carved in stone, but later the two simplified scripts were written on papyrus, a paper made from the reed that grew along the Nile. Most of the ancient Egyptian literature that has come down to us was written on papyrus rolls and wooden tablets.

Chaos and a New Order: The New Kingdom

The Middle Kingdom came to an end around 1650 B.C.E. with the invasion of Egypt by a people from western Asia known to the Egyptians as the Hyksos. The Hyksos used horse-drawn war chariots and overwhelmed the Egyptian soldiers who fought from donkey carts. For almost a hundred years, the Hyksos ruled much of Egypt, but the conquered took much from their conquerors. From the Hyksos, the Egyptians learned to use bronze in making new farming tools and weapons. They also mastered the military skills of the Hyksos, especially the use of horse-drawn war chariots.

Eventually, a new line of pharaohs—the eighteenth dynasty—made use of the new weapons to throw off Hyksos domination, reunite Egypt, establish the New Kingdom (c. 1550–1085 B.C.E.), and launch the Egyptians along a new militaristic path. During the period of the New Kingdom, Egypt created an empire and became the most powerful state in the Middle East.

Massive wealth aided the power of the New Kingdom pharaohs. The Egyptian rulers showed their wealth by building new temples. Queen Hatshepsut (c. 1503–1480 B.C.E.), in particular, the first woman to become pharaoh in her own right, built a great temple at Deir el Bahri near Thebes. As pharaoh, Hatshepsut sent out military expeditions, encouraged mining, fostered agriculture, and sent a trading expedition up the Nile. Because pharaohs were almost always male, Hatshepsut's official statues show her clothed and bearded like a king. She was addressed as "His Majesty." Hatshepsut was succeeded by her nephew, Thutmosis III (c. 1480–1450 B.C.E.), who led seventeen

AKHENATEN'S HYMN TO ATEN

*A*menhotep IV, more commonly known as Akhenaten, created a religious upheaval in Egypt by introducing the worship of Aten, god of the sun disk, as the sole god. Akhenaten's attitude to Aten is seen in this hymn. Some authorities have noted a similarity in spirit and wording to the 104th Psalm of the Old Testament.

HYMN TO ATEN

Your rays suckle every meadow.
When you rise, they live, they grow for you.
You make the seasons in order to rear all that you have
　made,
The winter to cool them,
And the heat that they may taste you.
You have made the distant sky in order to rise therein,
In order to see all that you do make.
While you were alone,
Rising in your form as the living Aten,
Appearing, shining, withdrawing or approaching,
You made millions of forms of yourself alone.

Cities, towns, fields, road, and river—
Every eye beholds you over against them,
For you are the Aten of the day over the earth. . . .
The world came into being by your hand,
According as you have made them.
When you have risen they live,
When you set they die.
You are lifetime your own self,
For one lives only through you.
Eyes are fixed on beauty until you set.
All work is laid aside when you set in the west.
But when you rise again,
Everything is made to flourish for the king, . . .
Since you did found the earth
And raise them up for your son,
Who came forth from your body:
　the King of Upper and Lower Egypt, . . .
　Akh-en-Aten, . . . and the Chief Wife of the King . . .
　Nefert-iti, living and youthful forever and ever.

---

military campaigns into Syria and Palestine and even reached the Euphrates River. Egyptian forces occupied Palestine and Syria and also moved westward into Libya.

The eighteenth dynasty was not without its troubles, however. Amenhotep IV (c. 1364–1347 B.C.E.) introduced the worship of Aten, god of the sun disk, as the chief god (see the box above) and pursued his worship with great enthusiasm. Changing his own name to Akhenaten ("It is well with Aten"), the pharaoh closed the temples of other gods and especially endeavored to lessen the power of Amon-Re and his priesthood at Thebes. Akhenaten strove to reduce their influence by replacing Thebes as the capital of Egypt with Akhetaten ("dedicated to Aten"), a new city located near modern Tel el Amarna, 200 miles north of Thebes.

Akhenaten's attempt at religious change proved to be a failure. It was too much to ask Egyptians to give up their traditional ways and beliefs, especially since they saw the destruction of the old gods as subversive of the very cosmic order on which Egypt's survival and continuing prosperity depended. Moreover, the priests at Thebes were unalterably opposed to the changes, which had diminished their influence and power. At the same time, Akhenaten's preoccupation with religion caused him to ignore foreign affairs and led to the loss of both Syria and Palestine. Akhenaten's changes were soon undone after his death by those who influenced his successor, the boy-pharaoh Tutankhamun (1347–1338 B.C.E.). Tutankhamun returned the government to Thebes and restored the old gods. The Aten experiment had failed to take hold, and the eighteenth dynasty itself came to an end in 1333.

The nineteenth dynasty managed to restore Egyptian power one more time. Under Rameses II (c. 1279–1213 B.C.E.), the Egyptians regained control of Palestine but were unable to reestablish the borders of their earlier empire. New invasions in the thirteenth century by the "Sea Peoples," as Egyptians called them, destroyed Egyptian power in Palestine and drove the Egyptians back within their old frontiers. The days of Egyptian empire were ended, and the New Kingdom itself expired with the end of the twentieth dynasty in 1085. For the next thousand years, despite periodical revivals of strength, Egypt was dominated by Libyans, Nubians, Persians, and finally Macedonians, after the conquest of Alexander the Great (see Chapter 4). In the first century B.C.E., Egypt became a province in Rome's mighty empire. Egypt continued, however, to influence its conquerors through the richness of its heritage and the awesome magnificence of its physical remains.

Daily Life in Ancient Egypt: Family and Marriage

Ancient Egyptians had a very positive attitude toward daily life on earth and followed the advice of the wisdom literature, which suggested that people marry young and establish a home and family. Monogamy was the general rule, although a husband was allowed to keep additional wives if his first wife was childless. Pharaohs, of course, were entitled to harems. The queen was acknowledged, however, as the Great Wife, with a status higher than that of the other

➢ NUBIANS IN EGYPT.   During the New Kingdom, Egypt expanded to the north, into Palestine and Syria, and to the south, into the African kingdom of Nubia. Nubia had first emerged as an African kingdom around 2300 B.C.E. (see Chapter 8). Shown here in a fourteenth-century B.C.E. painting from an Egyptian official's tomb in Nubia are Nubians arriving in Egypt with bags and rings of gold. Nubia was a rich source of gold for the Egyptians.

wives. The husband was master in the house, but wives were very much respected and in charge of the household and education of the children. From a book of wise sayings (which the Egyptians called "instructions") came this advice:

> If you are a man of standing, you should found your household and love your wife at home as is fitting. Fill her belly; clothe her back. Ointment is the prescription for her body. Make her heart glad as long as you live. She is a profitable field for her lord. You should not contend with her at law, and keep her far from gaining control. . . . Let her heart be soothed through what may accrue to you; it means keeping her long in your house.[7]

Women's property and inheritance remained in their hands, even in marriage. Although most careers and public offices were closed to women, some did operate businesses. Peasant women worked long hours in the fields and at numerous domestic tasks. Upper-class women could function as priestesses, and a few queens, such as Hatshepsut, even became pharaohs in their own right.

Little is known about marital arrangements and ceremonies, although it does appear that marriages were arranged by parents. The primary concerns were family and property, and the chief purpose of marriage was to produce children, especially sons. From the New Kingdom came this piece of wisdom: "Take to yourself a wife while you are [still] a youth, that she may produce a son for you."[8] Only sons could carry on the family name. Daughters were not slighted, however. Numerous tomb paintings show the close and affectionate relationship parents had with both sons and daughters. Although marriages were arranged, some of the surviving love poems from ancient Egypt suggest that some marriages included an element of romance. Here is the lament of a lovesick boy for his "sister" (lovers referred to each other as "brother" and "sister"):

> Seven days to yesterday I have not seen the sister, and a
>   sickness has invaded me;
> My body has become heavy,
> And I am forgetful of my own self.
> If the chief physicians come to me,
> My heart is not content with their remedies. . . .
> What will revive me is to say to me: "Here she is!"
> Her name is what will lift me up. . . .
> My health is her coming in from outside:
> When I see her, then I am well.[9]

Marriages could and did end in divorce, which was allowed, apparently with compensation for the wife. Adultery, however, was strictly prohibited, with stiff punishments—especially for women, who could have their noses cut off or be burned at the stake.

NEW CENTERS OF CIVILIZATION

Our story of civilization so far has been dominated by Mesopotamia and Egypt. But significant developments were also taking place on the fringes of these civilizations. Farming had spread into the Balkan peninsula of Europe by 6500 B.C.E., and by 4000 B.C.E., it was well established in southern France, central Europe, and the coastal regions of the Mediterranean. Although migrating farmers from the Middle East may have brought some farming techniques into Europe, historians now believe that the Neolithic peoples of Europe domesticated animals and began to farm largely on their own.

One outstanding feature of late Neolithic Europe was the building of megalithic structures. *Megalith* is Greek for

Stonehenge and Other Megalithic Sites in Europe

Megalithic sites

"large stone." Radiocarbon dating, a technique that allows scientists to determine the ages of objects, shows that the first megalithic structures were built around 4000 B.C.E., more than a thousand years before the great pyramids were built in Egypt. Between 3200 and 1500 B.C.E., standing stones that were placed in circles or lined up in rows were erected throughout the British Isles and northwestern France. Other megalithic constructions have been found as far north as Scandinavia and as far south as the islands of Corsica, Sardinia, and Malta. Some archaeologists have demonstrated that the stone circles were used as observatories to detect not only such simple astronomical phenomena as midwinter and midsummer sunrises but also such sophisticated phenomena as the major and minor standstills of the moon.

The Impact of the Indo-Europeans

In large part, both the details of construction and the purpose of the megalithic structures of Europe remain a mystery. Also puzzling is the role of the Indo-European peoples. The term *Indo-European* refers to people who used a language derived from a single parent tongue. Indo-European languages include Greek, Latin, Persian, Sanskrit, and the Germanic and Slavic languages (see Table 1.2). It has been suggested that the original Indo-European-speaking peoples were based somewhere in the steppe region north of the Black Sea or in southwestern Asia, in modern Iran or Afghanistan. Although there had been earlier migrations, around 2000 B.C.E. the original Indo-European-speaking peoples began major nomadic movements into Europe (including present-day Italy and Greece), India, and western Asia. One group of Indo-Europeans who moved into Asia Minor and Anatolia (modern Turkey) around 1750 B.C.E. coalesced with the native peoples to form the Hittite kingdom, with its capital at Hattusha (Bogazköy in modern Turkey).

Between 1600 and 1200 B.C.E., the Hittites created their own empire in western Asia and even threatened the power of the Egyptians. The Hittites were the first of the Indo-European peoples to make use of iron, enabling them to construct weapons that were stronger and cheaper to make because of the widespread availability of iron ore. But around 1200 B.C.E., new waves of invading Indo-European peoples destroyed the Hittite empire. The destruction of the Hittite kingdom and the weakening of Egypt around 1200 B.C.E. temporarily left no dominant powers in western Asia, allowing a patchwork of petty kingdoms and city-states to emerge, especially in the area of Syria and Palestine. The Phoenicians were one of these peoples.

© Adam Woolfitt/Robert Harding Picture Library

STONEHENGE. By far the most famous megalithic construction, Stonehenge in England consists of a series of concentric rings of standing stones. Its construction sometime between 2100 and 1900 B.C.E. was no small accomplishment. The eighty bluestones used at Stonehenge weighed 4 tons each and were transported to the site from 135 miles away. Like other megalithic structures, Stonehenge indicates a remarkable awareness of astronomy on the part of its builders, as well as an elaborate coordination of workers.

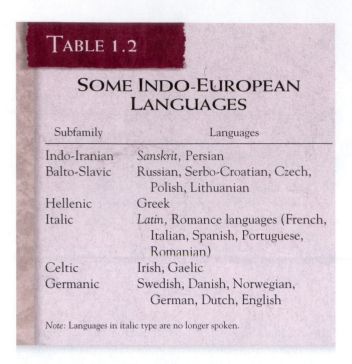

TABLE 1.2

SOME INDO-EUROPEAN LANGUAGES

Subfamily	Languages
Indo-Iranian	*Sanskrit*, Persian
Balto-Slavic	Russian, Serbo-Croatian, Czech, Polish, Lithuanian
Hellenic	Greek
Italic	*Latin*, Romance languages (French, Italian, Spanish, Portuguese, Romanian)
Celtic	Irish, Gaelic
Germanic	Swedish, Danish, Norwegian, German, Dutch, English

Note: Languages in italic type are no longer spoken.

The Phoenicians

A Semitic-speaking people, the Phoenicians lived in the area of Palestine along the Mediterranean coast on a narrow band of land 120 miles long. Their newfound political independence after the demise of Hittite and Egyptian power helped the Phoenicians expand the trade that was already the foundation of their prosperity. The chief cities of Phoenicia—Byblos, Tyre, and Sidon—were ports on the eastern Mediterranean, but they also served as distribution centers for the lands to the east in Mesopotamia. The Phoenicians themselves produced a number of goods for foreign markets, including purple dye, glass, wine, and lumber from the famous cedars of Lebanon. In addition, the Phoenicians improved their ships and became great international sea traders. They charted new routes, not only in the Mediterranean but also in the Atlantic Ocean, where they reached Britain and sailed south along the west coast of Africa. The Phoenicians established a number of colonies in the western Mediterranean, including settlements in southern Spain, Sicily, and Sardinia. Carthage, the Phoenicians' most famous colony, was located on the north coast of Africa.

Culturally, the Phoenicians are best known as transmitters. Instead of using pictographs or signs to represent whole words and syllables as the Mesopotamians and Egyptians did, the Phoenicians simplified their writing by using twenty-two different signs to represent the sounds of their speech. These twenty-two characters or letters could be used to spell out all the words in the Phoenician language. Although the Phoenicians were not the only people to invent an alphabet, theirs would have special significance because it was eventually passed on to the Greeks. From the Greek alphabet was derived the Roman alphabet that we still use today (Table 1.3 shows the derivation of the letters *A* to *F*). The Phoenicians achieved much while independent, but they ultimately fell subject to the Assyrians and Persians.

The Hebrews: The "Children of Israel"

To the south of the Phoenicians lived another group of Semitic-speaking people known as the Hebrews. Although they were a minor factor in the politics of the region, their monotheistic ("one God") religion—known as Judaism—eventually influenced both Christianity and Islam and flourished as a world religion. The Hebrews had a tradition concerning their origins and history that was eventually

TABLE 1.3

THE PHOENICIAN, GREEK, AND ROMAN ALPHABETS

	PHOENICIAN		GREEK			ROMAN	
Phoenician	Phoenician Name	Modern Symbol	Early Greek	Classical Greek	Greek Name	Early Latin	Classical Latin
𐤀	'aleph	'	Λ	A	alpha	A	A
𐤁	beth	b	B	B	beta		B
𐤂	gimel	g	Γ	Γ	gamma		C
𐤃	daleth	d	Δ	Δ	delta	D	D
𐤄	he	h	Ⱶ	E	epsilon	Ⅎ	E
𐤅	waw	w	Ⅎ		digamma	Ⅎ	F

SOURCE: Andrew Robinson, *The Story of Writing* (London, 1995), p. 170.

written down as part of the Hebrew Bible, known to Christians as the Old Testament. Describing them as a nomadic people, the Hebrews' own tradition states that they were descendants of the patriarch Abraham, who had migrated from Mesopotamia to the land of Palestine, where the Hebrews became identified as the "Children of Israel." Moreover, according to tradition, a drought in Palestine caused many Hebrews to migrate to Egypt, where they lived peacefully until they were enslaved by pharaohs who used them as laborers on building projects. The Hebrews remained in bondage until Moses led his people out of Egypt in the well-known "exodus," which some historians have argued would have occurred in the first half of the thirteenth century B.C.E. According to the biblical account, the Hebrews then wandered for many years in the desert until they entered Palestine. Organized into twelve tribes, the Hebrews became embroiled in conflict with the Philistines, a people who had settled in the coastal area of Palestine but were beginning to move into the inland areas.

Many scholars today doubt that the early books of the Hebrew Bible reflect the true history of the early Israelites. They argue that the early books of the Bible, written centuries after the events described, preserve only what the Israelites came to believe about themselves and that recent archaeological evidence often contradicts the details of the biblical account. Some of these scholars have even argued that the Israelites were not nomadic invaders but indigenous peoples in the Palestinian hill country. What is generally agreed, however, is that between 1200 and 1000 B.C.E., the Israelites emerged as a distinct group of people, possibly organized into tribes or a league of tribes, who established a united kingdom known as Israel.

THE UNITED KINGDOM

The first king of the Israelites was Saul (c. 1020–1000 B.C.E.), who initially achieved some success in the ongoing struggle with the Philistines. But after his death in a disastrous battle with this enemy, a brief period of anarchy ensued, until one of Saul's lieutenants, David (c. 1000–970 B.C.E.), reunited the Israelites, defeated the Philistines, and established control over all of Palestine. Among David's conquests was the city of Jerusalem, which he made into the capital of a united kingdom. David centralized Israel's organization and accelerated the integration of the Israelites into a settled community based on farming and urban life.

David's son Solomon (c. 970–930 B.C.E.) did even more to strengthen royal power. He expanded the political and military establishments and was especially active in extending the trading activities of the Israelites. Solomon is known for his building projects, of which the most famous was the Temple in the city of Jerusalem. The Israelites viewed the Temple as the symbolic center of their religion and hence of the kingdom of Israel itself. The Temple now housed the Ark of the Covenant, the holy chest containing the sacred relics of the Hebrew religion

and, symbolically, the throne of the invisible God of Israel. Under Solomon, ancient Israel was at the height of its power, but his efforts to extend royal power throughout his kingdom led to dissatisfaction among some of his subjects.

THE DIVIDED KINGDOM

After Solomon's death, tensions between the northern and southern tribes within Israel led to the establishment of two separate kingdoms—a kingdom of Israel, composed of the ten northern tribes, with its capital eventually at Samaria, and a southern kingdom of Judah, consisting of two tribes, with its capital at Jerusalem (see Map 1.5). In

MAP 1.5 Palestine in the First Millennium B.C.E. United under Saul, David, and Solomon, greater Israel split into two states—Israel and Judah—after the death of Solomon. With power divided, the Israelites could not resist invasions that dispersed many Jews from Palestine. Some, such as the "ten lost tribes," never returned. Others were sent to Babylon but were later allowed to return under the rule of the Persians. ➤ *Why was Israel more vulnerable to the Assyrian Empire than Judah was?*

722 B.C.E., the Assyrians destroyed Samaria, overran the kingdom of Israel, and deported many Hebrews to other parts of the Assyrian Empire. These dispersed Hebrews (the "ten lost tribes") merged with neighboring peoples and gradually lost their identity.

The southern kingdom of Judah was also forced to pay tribute to Assyria but managed to retain its independence as Assyrian power declined. However, a new enemy appeared on the horizon. The Chaldeans defeated Assyria, conquered the kingdom of Judah, and completely destroyed Jerusalem in 586 B.C.E. Many upper-class people from Judah were deported to Babylonia; the memory of their exile is still evoked in the stirring words of Psalm 137:

> By the rivers of Babylon, we sat and wept when we remembered Zion. . . .
> How can we sing the songs of the Lord while in a foreign land?
> If I forget you, O Jerusalem, may my right hand forget its skill.
> May my tongue cling to the roof of my mouth if I do not remember you,
> if I do not consider Jerusalem my highest joy.[10]

But the Babylonian captivity of the people of Judah did not last. A new set of conquerors, the Persians, destroyed the Chaldean kingdom and allowed the people of Judah to return to Jerusalem and rebuild their city and Temple. The revived kingdom of Judah remained under Persian control until the conquests of Alexander the Great in the fourth century B.C.E. The people of Judah survived, even-

⇒ THE KING OF ISRAEL PAYS TRIBUTE TO THE KING OF ASSYRIA. By the end of the ninth century B.C.E., the kingdom of Israel had been forced to pay tribute to the Assyrian Empire. The Assyrians overran the kingdom in 722 B.C.E. and destroyed the capital city of Samaria. In this scene from a black obelisk, Jehu, king of Israel, is shown paying tribute to the king of Assyria.

© British Museum

tually becoming known as the Jews and giving their name to Judaism, the religion of Yahweh, the Jewish God.

THE SPIRITUAL DIMENSIONS OF ISRAEL

According to the Jewish conception, there is but one God, called Yahweh, who is the creator of the world and everything in it. The Jewish God ruled the world; he was subject to nothing. All peoples were his servants, whether they knew it or not. This God was also transcendent. He had created nature but was not in nature. The stars, moon, rivers, wind, and other natural phenomena were not divinities or suffused with divinity, as other peoples of the ancient Near East believed, but God's handiwork. All of God's creations could be admired for their awesome beauty but not worshiped as God.

Nevertheless, this omnipotent creator of the universe was not removed from the life he had created but was a just and good God who expected goodness from his people. If they did not obey his will, they would be punished. But he was also a God of mercy and love: "The Lord is gracious and compassionate, slow to anger and rich in love. The Lord is good to all; he has compassion on all he has made."[11] Despite the powerful dimensions of God as creator of the universe, each person could have a personal relationship with this being. As the psalmist sang: "My help comes from the Lord, the Maker of heaven and earth. He will not let your foot slip—he who watches over you will not slumber."[12]

Three aspects of the Jewish religious tradition had special significance: the covenant, the law, and the prophets. The Israelites believed that during the exodus from Egypt, when Moses had supposedly led his people out of bondage and into the promised land, an unusual event occurred. According to tradition, God entered into a covenant or contract with the tribes of Israel, who believed that Yahweh had spoken to them through Moses (see the box on p. 27). The Israelites promised to obey Yahweh and follow his law. In return, Yahweh promised to take special care of his chosen people, "a peculiar treasure unto me above all people."

THE COVENANT AND THE LAW:
THE BOOK OF EXODUS

According to the biblical account, it was during the exodus from Egypt that the Israelites made their covenant with Yahweh. They agreed to obey their God and follow his law. In return, Yahweh promised to take special care of his chosen people. This selection from the Book of Exodus describes the making of the covenant and God's commandments to the Hebrews.

EXODUS 19:1–8

In the third month after the Israelites left Egypt—on the very day—they came to the Desert of Sinai. After they set out from Rephidim, they entered the desert of Sinai, and Israel camped there in the desert in front of the mountain. Then Moses went up to God, and the Lord called to him from the mountain, and said, "This is what you are to say to the house of Jacob and what you are to tell the people of Israel: 'You yourselves have seen what I did to Egypt, and how I carried you on eagles' wings and brought you to myself. Now if you obey me fully and keep my covenant, then out of all nations you will be my treasured possession. Although the whole earth is mine, you will be for me a kingdom of priests and a holy nation.' These are the words you are to speak to the Israelites." So Moses went back and summoned the elders of the people and set before them all the words the Lord had commanded him to speak. The people all responded together, "We will do everything the Lord has said." So Moses brought their answer back to the Lord.

EXODUS 20:1–3, 7–17

And God spoke all these words, "I am the Lord your God, who brought you out of Egypt, out of the land of slavery. You shall have no other gods before me. . . . You shall not misuse the name of the Lord your God, for the Lord will not hold anyone guiltless who misuses his name. Remember the Sabbath day by keeping it holy. Six days you shall labor and do all your work, but the seventh day is a Sabbath to the Lord your God. On it you shall not do any work, neither you, nor your son or daughter, nor your manservant or maidservant, nor your animals, nor the alien within your gates. For in six days the Lord made the heavens and the earth, the sea, and all that is in them, but he rested on the seventh day. Therefore the Lord blessed the Sabbath day and made it holy. Honor your father and your mother, so that you may live long in the land the Lord your God is giving you. You shall not murder. You shall not commit adultery. You shall not steal. You shall not give false testimony against your neighbor. You shall not covet your neighbor's house. You shall not covet your neighbor's wife, or his manservant or maidservant, his ox or donkey, or anything that belongs to your neighbor."

This covenant between Yahweh and his chosen people could be fulfilled, however, only by obedience to the law of God. Most important were the ethical concerns that stood at the center of the law. Sometimes these took the form of specific standards of moral behavior: "You shall not murder. You shall not commit adultery. You shall not steal."[13] But these concerns were also expressed in decrees that regulated the economic, social, and political life of the community, since God's laws of morality applied to all areas of life. These laws made no class distinctions and emphasized the protection of the poor, widows, orphans, and slaves.

The Israelites believed that certain religious teachers, called prophets, were sent by God to serve as his voice to his people (see the box on p. 28). The golden age of prophecy began in the mid-eighth century and continued during the time when the people of Israel and Judah were threatened by Assyrian and Chaldean conquerors. The "men of God" went through the land warning the Israelites that they had failed to keep God's commandments and would be punished for breaking the covenant: "I will punish you for all your iniquities."

Out of the words of the prophets came new concepts that enriched the Jewish tradition. The prophets embraced a concern for all humanity. All nations would someday come to the God of Israel: "All the earth shall worship thee." This vision encompassed the elimination of war and the establishment of peace for all the nations of the world. In the words of the prophet Isaiah: "He will judge between the nations and will settle disputes for many people. They will beat their swords into plowshares and their spears into pruning hooks. Nation will not take up sword against nation, nor will they train for war anymore."[14]

The prophets also cried out against social injustice. They condemned the rich for causing the poor to suffer, denounced luxuries as worthless, and threatened Israel with prophecies of dire punishments for these sins. God's command was to live justly, share with one's neighbors, care for the poor and the unfortunate, and act with compassion. When God's command was not followed, the social fabric of the community was threatened. These proclamations of Israel's prophets spawned universal ideals of social justice, even if they have never been perfectly realized.

Although the prophets developed a sense of universalism, the demands of the Jewish religion (the need to obey God) eventually encouraged a separation between the Jews and their non-Jewish neighbors. Unlike most other peoples of the Middle East, Jews could not simply be

THREE HEBREW PROPHETS:
MICAH, ISAIAH, AND AMOS

*T*he Hebrew prophets warned the Israelites that they must obey God's commandments or face being punished for breaking their covenant with God. These selections from the prophets Micah, Isaiah, and Amos make clear that God's punishment would fall on the Israelites for their sins. Even the Assyrians, as Isaiah indicated, would be used as God's instrument to punish them.

MICAH 6:9–16

Listen! The Lord is calling to the city—and to fear your name is wisdom—"Heed the rod and the One who appointed it. Am I still to forget, O wicked house, your ill-gotten treasures . . . ? Shall I acquit a man with dishonest scales, with a bag of false weights? Her rich men are violent; her people are liars and their tongues speak deceitfully. Therefore, I have begun to destroy you, to ruin you because of your sins. You will eat but not be satisfied; your stomach will still be empty. You will store up but save nothing, because what you save I will give to the sword. You will plant but not harvest; you will press olives but not use the oil on yourselves, you will crush grapes but not drink the wine. . . . Therefore I will give you over to ruin and your people to derision; you will bear the scorn of the nations."

ISAIAH 10:1–6

Woe to those who make unjust laws, to those who issue oppressive decrees, to deprive the poor of their rights and withhold justice from the oppressed of my people, making widows their prey and robbing the fatherless. What will you do on the day of reckoning, when disaster comes from afar? To whom will you run for help? Where will you leave your riches? Nothing will remain but to cringe among the captives or fall among the slain. Yet for all this, his anger is not turned away, his hand is still upraised. "Woe to the Assyrian, the rod of my anger, in whose hand is the club of my wrath! I send him against a godless nation, I dispatch him against a people who anger me, to seize loot and snatch plunder, and to trample them down like mud in the streets."

AMOS 3:1–2

Hear this word the Lord has spoken against you, O people of Israel—against the whole family I brought up out of Egypt: "You only have I chosen of all the families of the earth; therefore I will punish you for all your sins."

---

amalgamated into a community by accepting the gods of their conquerors and their neighbors. To remain faithful to the demands of their God, they might even have to refuse loyalty to political leaders.

THE RISE OF NEW EMPIRES

A small and independent Israelite state could exist only because there was a power vacuum in western Asia after the destruction of the Hittite kingdom and the weakening of the Egyptian empire. But this condition did not last; new empires soon arose that came to dominate vast stretches of the ancient world.

The Assyrian Empire

The first of these empires was formed in Assyria, located on the upper Tigris River, an area that brought it into both cultural and political contact with Mesopotamia. The Assyrians were a Semitic-speaking people who exploited the use of iron weapons to establish an empire that by 700 B.C.E. included Mesopotamia, parts of the Iranian Plateau, sections of Asia Minor, Syria, Palestine, and Egypt down to Thebes (see Map 1.6). Ashurbanipal (669–626 B.C.E.)

was one of the strongest Assyrian rulers, but during his reign it was already becoming apparent that the Assyrian Empire was greatly overextended. Moreover, subject peoples, such as the Babylonians, greatly resented Assyrian rule and rebelled against it. Soon after Ashurbanipal's reign, the Assyrian Empire began to disintegrate rapidly. The capital city of Nineveh fell to a coalition of Chaldeans and Medes in 612 B.C.E., and in 605 B.C.E., the rest of the empire was finally divided between the two powers.

At its height, the Assyrian Empire was ruled by kings whose power was considered absolute. Under their leadership, the Assyrian Empire came to be well organized. Local officials were directly responsible to the king. The Assyrians also developed an efficient system of communication to administer their empire more effectively. A network of staging posts was established throughout the empire that used relays of horses (mules or donkeys in mountainous terrain) to carry messages. The system was so effective that a provincial governor anywhere in the empire (except Egypt) could send a question and receive an answer from the king in his palace within a week.

The Assyrians' ability to conquer and maintain an empire was due to a combination of factors. Over many years of practice, the Assyrians developed effective military leaders and fighters. They were able to enlist and deploy troops numbering in the hundreds of thousands, although most campaigns were not on such a large scale.

THE ASSYRIAN MILITARY MACHINE

The Assyrians achieved a reputation for possessing a mighty military machine. They were able to use a variety of military tactics and were successful whether they were waging guerrilla warfare, fighting set battles, or laying siege to cities. In these three selections, Assyrian kings boast of their military conquests.

KING SENNACHERIB (704–681 B.C.E.) DESCRIBES A BATTLE WITH THE ELAMITES IN 691

At the command of the god Ashur, the great Lord, I rushed upon the enemy like the approach of a hurricane. . . . I put them to rout and turned them back. I transfixed the troops of the enemy with javelins and arrows. . . . I cut their throats like sheep. . . . My prancing steeds, trained to harness, plunged into their welling blood as into a river; the wheels of my battle chariot were bespattered with blood and filth. I filled the plain with the corpses of their warriors like herbage. . . . As to the sheikhs of the Chaldeans, panic from my onslaught overwhelmed them like a demon. They abandoned their tents and fled for their lives, crushing the corpses of their troops as they went. . . . In their terror they passed scalding urine and voided their excrement into their chariots.

KING SENNACHERIB DESCRIBES HIS SIEGE OF JERUSALEM IN 701

As to Hezekiah, the Jew, he did not submit to my yoke, I laid siege to 46 of his strong cities, walled forts, and the countless small villages in their vicinity, and conquered them by means of well-stamped earth-ramps, and battering-rams brought thus near to the walls combined with the attack by foot soldiers, using mines, breeches, as well as sapper work. I drove out of them 200,150 people, young and old, male and female, horses, mules, donkeys, camels, big and small cattle beyond counting, and considered them booty. Himself I made a prisoner in Jerusalem, his royal residence, like a bird in a cage. I surrounded him with earthwork in order to molest those who were leaving his city's gate.

KING ASHURBANIPAL (669–626 B.C.E.) DESCRIBES HIS TREATMENT OF CONQUERED BABYLON

I tore out the tongues of those whose slanderous mouths had uttered blasphemies against my god Ashur and had plotted against me, his god-fearing prince; I defeated them completely. The others, I smashed alive with the very same statues of protective deities with which they had smashed my own grandfather Sennacherib—now finally as a belated burial sacrifice for his soul. I fed their corpses, cut into small pieces, to dogs, pigs, . . . vultures, the birds of the sky, and also to the fish of the ocean. After I had performed this and thus made quiet again the hearts of the great gods, my lords, I removed the corpses of those whom the pestilence had felled, whose leftovers after the dogs and pigs had fed on them were obstructing the streets, filling the places of Babylon, and of those who had lost their lives through the terrible famine.

Size alone was not decisive, however. The Assyrian army was well organized and disciplined. It included a standing army of infantrymen as its core, accompanied by cavalry and horse-drawn war chariots that were used as mobile platforms for shooting arrows. Moreover, the Assyrians had the advantage of having the first large armies equipped with iron weapons.

Another factor in the army's success was its ability to use different kinds of military tactics (see the box above). The Assyrian army was capable of waging guerrilla warfare in the mountains and set battles on open ground as well as laying siege to cities. The Assyrians were especially renowned for their siege warfare. Some soldiers would hammer a city's walls with heavy, wheeled siege towers and armored battering rams, while others dug tunnels to undermine the walls' foundations and cause them to collapse.

A final factor in the effectiveness of the Assyrian military machine was its use of terror as an instrument of warfare. As a matter of regular policy, the Assyrians laid waste the land in which they were fighting, smashing dams, looting and destroying towns, setting crops on fire, and cutting down trees, particularly fruit trees. The Assyrians were especially known for committing atrocities on their captives. King Ashurnasirpal recorded this account of his treatment of prisoners:

> 3000 of their combat troops I felled with weapons. . . . Many of the captives taken from them I burned in a fire. Many I took alive; from some of these I cut off their hands to the wrist, from others I cut off their noses, ears and fingers; I put out the eyes of many of the soldiers. . . . I burned their young men and women to death.[15]

After conquering another city, the same king wrote: "I fixed up a pile of corpses in front of the city's gate. I flayed the nobles, as many as had rebelled, and spread their skins out on the piles. . . . I flayed many within my land and spread their skins out on the walls."[16] It should be noted that this policy of extreme cruelty to prisoners was not used against all enemies but was primarily reserved for those who were already part of the empire and then rebelled against Assyrian rule.

ASSYRIAN SOCIETY AND CULTURE

Unlike the Hebrews, the Assyrians were not fearful of mixing with other peoples. In fact, Assyrian deportation policies created a polyglot society in which ethnic differences

MAP 1.6   The Assyrian and Persian Empires.   Cyrus the Great united the Persians and led them in a successful conquest of much of the Near East, including most of the lands of the Assyrian Empire. By the time of Darius, the Persian Empire was the largest the world had yet seen. ➤ *How did Persian policies attempt to overcome the difficulties of governing far-flung provinces?*

were not very important. What gave identity to the Assyrians themselves was their language, although even that was akin to the language of their southern neighbors in Babylonia, who also spoke a Semitic language. Religion was also a cohesive force. Assyria was literally "the land of Ashur," a reference to its chief god. The king, as the human representative of the god Ashur, provided a final unifying focus.

Agriculture formed the principal basis of Assyrian life. Assyria was a land of farming villages with relatively few significant cities, especially in comparison to Mesopotamia. Unlike Mesopotamia, where farming required the minute organization of large numbers of people to control irrigation, Assyrian farms received sufficient moisture from regular rainfall.

Trade was second to agriculture in economic importance. For internal trade, metals—such as gold, silver, copper, and bronze—were used as a medium of exchange. Various agricultural products also served as a form of payment or exchange. Because of their geographical location, the Assyrians served as intermediaries and partici-

pated in an international trade in which they imported timber, wine, and precious metals and stones while exporting textiles produced in palaces, temples, and private workshops.

The culture of the Assyrian Empire was essentially a hybrid. The Assyrians assimilated much of Mesopotamian civilization and saw themselves as guardians of Sumerian and Babylonian culture. Assyrian kings also tried to maintain old traditions when they rebuilt damaged temples by constructing the new buildings on the original foundations, not in new locations. Assyrian religion reflected this assimilation of other cultures as well. Although the Assyrians had their own national god (Ashur) as their chief deity, virtually all of their remaining gods and goddesses were Mesopotamian.

Among the best-known objects of Assyrian art are the relief sculptures found in the royal palaces in three of the Assyrian capital cities, Nimrud, Nineveh, and Khorsabad. These reliefs, which were begun in the ninth century and reached their high point in the reign of Ashurbanipal in the seventh century, depicted two different kinds of

KING ASHURBANIPAL'S LION HUNT. This relief, sculpted on alabaster as a decoration for the northern palace in Nineveh, depicts King Ashurbanipal engaged in a lion hunt. The relief sculpture, one of the best-known forms of Assyrian art, ironically reached its high point under Ashurbanipal at the same time that the Assyrian Empire began to disintegrate.

subject matter: ritual or ceremonial scenes revolving around the person of the king and scenes of hunting and war. The latter show realistic action scenes of the king and his warriors engaged in battle or hunting animals, especially lions. These pictures depict a strongly masculine world where discipline, brute force, and toughness are the enduring values—indeed, the very values of the Assyrian military monarchy.

The Persian Empire

After the collapse of the Assyrian Empire, the Chaldeans, under their king Nebuchadnezzar II (605–562 B.C.E.), made Babylonia the leading state in western Asia. Nebuchadnezzar rebuilt Babylon as the center of his empire, giving it a reputation as one of the great cities of the ancient world. But the splendor of Chaldean Babylonia proved to be short-lived when Babylon fell to the Persians in 539 B.C.E.

The Persians were an Indo-European-speaking people who lived in southwestern Iran. Primarily nomadic, the Persians were organized into tribes until the Achaemenid dynasty managed to unify the Persians. One of its members, Cyrus (559–530 B.C.E.), created a powerful Persian state that rearranged the political map of western Asia. In 550 B.C.E., he extended Persian control over the Medes, making Media the first Persian satrapy, or province. Three years later, Cyrus defeated the prosperous Lydian kingdom in western Asia Minor, and Lydia became another Persian satrapy. Cyrus's forces then went on to conquer the Greek city-states that had been established on the Ionian coast. Cyrus then turned eastward, subduing the eastern part of the Iranian Plateau, Sogdia, and even western India. His eastern frontiers secured, Cyrus entered Mesopotamia in 539 and captured Babylon (see Map 1.6). His treatment of Babylonia showed remarkable restraint and wisdom. Babylonia was made into a Persian province under a Persian satrap, but many government officials were kept in their positions. Cyrus took the title "King of All, Great King, Mighty King, King of Babylon, King of the Land of Sumer and Akkad, King of the Four Rims (of the Earth), the Son of Cambyses the Great King, King of Anshan"[17] and insisted that he stood in the ancient, unbroken line of Babylonian kings. By appealing to the vanity of the Babylonians, he won their loyalty. Cyrus also issued an edict permitting the Jews, who had been brought to Babylon in the sixth century B.C.E., to return to Jerusalem with their sacred objects and to rebuild their Temple as well.

To his contemporaries, Cyrus deserved to be called Cyrus the Great. The Greek historian Herodotus recounted that the Persians viewed him as a "father," a ruler who was "gentle, and procured them all manner of goods."[18] Cyrus must have been an unusual ruler for his time, a man who demonstrated considerable wisdom and compassion in the conquest and organization of his empire. He won approval by using not only Persians but also native peoples as government officials in their own states. Unlike the Assyrian rulers of an earlier empire, he had a reputation for mercy. Medes, Babylonians, and Jews all accepted him as their legitimate ruler. Indeed, the Jews regarded him as the anointed one of God: "I am the Lord who says of Cyrus, 'He is my shepherd and will accomplish all that I please'; he will say of Jerusalem, 'Let it be rebuilt'; and of the Temple, 'Let its foundations be laid.' This is what the Lord says to his anointed, to Cyrus, whose right hand I take hold of to subdue nations before him."[19] Cyrus had a genuine respect for ancient civilizations—in building his palaces, he made use of Assyrian, Babylonian, Egyptian, and Lydian practices.

Cyrus's successors extended the territory of the Persian Empire. His son Cambyses (530–522 B.C.E.) undertook a successful invasion of Egypt. Darius (521–486 B.C.E.) added a new Persian province in western India that extended to the Indus River and moved into Europe proper, conquering Thrace and making the Macedonian king a vassal. A revolt of the Ionian Greek cities in 499 B.C.E. resulted in temporary freedom for these communities in western Asia Minor. Aid from the Greek mainland, most notably from Athens, encouraged the Ionians to invade Lydia and burn Sardis, center of the Lydian satrap. This event led to Darius' involvement with the

Chronology

EARLY EMPIRES

The Assyrians

Height of power	700 B.C.E.
Ashurbanipal	669–626 B.C.E.
Fall of Nineveh	612 B.C.E.
Assyrian Empire destroyed	605 B.C.E.

The Persians

Unification under Achaemenid dynasty	600s B.C.E.
Persian control over Medes	550 B.C.E.
Conquests of Cyrus the Great	559–530 B.C.E.
Cambyses and conquest of Egypt	530–522 B.C.E.
Reign of Darius	521–486 B.C.E.

mainland Greeks. After reestablishing control of the Ionian Greek cities, Darius undertook an invasion of the Greek mainland, which culminated in the famous Athenian victory in the Battle of Marathon, in 490 B.C.E. (see Chapter 4).

GOVERNING THE EMPIRE

By the reign of Darius, the Persians had created the largest empire the world had yet seen. It not only included all the old centers of power in Egypt and western Asia but also extended into Thrace and Asia Minor in the west and into India in the east. For administrative purposes, the empire had been divided into approximately twenty provinces called satrapies. Each province was ruled by a governor or satrap, literally a "protector of the kingdom." Satraps collected tributes, were responsible for justice and security, raised military levies for the royal army, and normally commanded the military forces within their satrapies. In terms of real power, the satraps were miniature kings who created courts imitative of the Great King's.

An efficient system of communication was crucial to sustaining the Persian Empire. Well-maintained roads facilitated the rapid transit of military and government personnel. One in particular, the so-called Royal Road, stretched from Sardis, the center of Lydia in Asia Minor, to Susa, the chief capital of the Persian Empire. Like the Assyrians, the Persians established staging posts equipped with fresh horses for the king's messengers.

In this vast administrative system, the Persian king occupied an exalted position. Although not considered to be a god in the manner of an Egyptian pharaoh, he was nevertheless the elect one or regent of the Persian god Ahuramazda (see the next section). All subjects were the king's servants, and he was the source of all justice, possessing the power of life and death over everyone. Persian kings were largely secluded and not easily accessi-

ble. They resided in a series of splendid palaces. Darius in particular was a palace builder on a grand scale. His description of the construction of a palace in the chief Persian capital of Susa demonstrated what a truly international empire Persia was:

> This is the . . . palace which at Susa I built. From afar its ornamentation was brought. . . . The cedar timber was brought from a mountain named Lebanon; the Assyrians brought it to Babylon, and from Babylon the Carians and Ionians brought it to Susa. Teakwood was brought from Gandara and from Carmania. The gold which was used here was brought from Sardis and from Bactria. The stone—lapis lazuli and carnelian—was brought from Sogdiana. . . . The silver and copper were brought from Egypt. The ornamentation with which the wall was adorned was brought from Ionia. The ivory was brought from Ethiopia, from India, and from Arachosia. The stone pillars were brought from . . . Elam. The artisans who dressed the stone were Ionians and Sardians. The goldsmiths who wrought the gold were Medes and Egyptians. . . . Those who worked the baked brick (with figures) were Babylonians. The men who adorned the wall were Medes and Egyptians. At Susa here a splendid work was ordered; very splendid did it turn out.[20]

But Darius was unhappy with Susa. He did not really consider it his homeland, and it was oppressively hot in the summer months. He built another residence at Persepolis, a new capital located to the east of the old one and at a higher elevation.

The policies of Darius also tended to widen the gap between the king and his subjects. As the Great King himself said of all his subjects: "What was said to them by me, night and day it was done."[21] Over a period of time, the Great Kings in their greed came to hoard immense quantities of gold and silver in the various treasuries located in the capital cities. Both their hoarding of wealth and their later overtaxation of their subjects are considered crucial factors in the ultimate weakening of the Persian Empire.

In its heyday, however, the empire stood supreme, and much of its power depended on the military. By the time of Darius, the Persian monarchs had created a standing army of professional soldiers. This army was truly international in character, composed of contingents from the various peoples who made up the empire. At its core was a cavalry force of ten thousand and an elite infantry force of ten thousand Medes and Persians known as the Immortals because they were never allowed to fall below ten thousand in number. When one was killed, he was immediately replaced.

PERSIAN RELIGION

Of all the Persians' cultural contributions, the most original was their religion, Zoroastrianism. According to Persian tradition, Zoroaster was born in 660 B.C.E. After a

ARCHERS OF THE PERSIAN GUARD. This frieze, composed of enamel brick, depicts members of the famous infantry force known as the Immortals, so called because their number was never allowed to drop below ten thousand. Those killed would be replaced immediately. Persian art and architecture were strongly influenced by the earlier work of the Assyrians.

period of wandering and solitude, he experienced revelations that caused him to be revered as a prophet of the "true religion." His teachings were eventually written down in the third century B.C.E. in the *Zend Avesta*, the sacred book of Zoroastrianism.

Like the Hebrews', Zoroaster's spiritual message was monotheistic. To Zoroaster, Ahuramazda was the only god, and the religion he preached was the only perfect one. Ahuramazda (the "Wise Lord") was the supreme deity who brought all things into being. According to Zoroaster, Ahuramazda also possessed qualities that all humans should aspire to, such as good thought, right, and piety. Although Ahuramazda was supreme, he was not unopposed. At the beginning of the world, the good spirit of Ahuramazda was opposed by the evil spirit, later identified as Ahriman.

Humans also played a role in this cosmic struggle between good and evil. Ahuramazda, the creator, gave all humans free will and the power to choose between right and wrong. The good person chooses the right way of Ahuramazda. Zoroaster taught that there would be an end to the struggle between good and evil. Ahuramazda would eventually triumph, and at the last judgment at the end of the world, the final separation of good and evil would occur. Individuals, too, would be judged. Each soul faced a final evaluation of its actions. If a person had performed good deeds, he or she would achieve paradise; if evil deeds, the soul would be thrown into an abyss of torment.

CONCLUSION

The peoples of Mesopotamia and Egypt, like the peoples of India and China, built the first civilizations. They developed cities and struggled with the problems of organized states. They developed writing to keep records and created literature. They constructed monumental architecture to please their gods, symbolize their power, and preserve their culture for all time. They developed new political, military, social, and religious structures to deal with the basic problems of human existence and organization. These first literate civilizations left detailed records that allow us to view how they grappled with three of the fundamental problems that humans have pondered: the nature of human relationships, the nature of the universe, and the role of divine forces in that cosmos. Although other peoples would provide different answers from those of the Mesopotamians and Egyptians, they posed the questions, gave answers, and wrote them down. Human memory begins with the creation of civilizations.

By the middle of the second millennium B.C.E., much of the creative impulse of the Mesopotamian and Egyptian civilizations was beginning to wane. Around 1200 B.C.E., the decline of the Hittites and Egyptians had created a power vacuum that allowed a number of small states to emerge and flourish temporarily. All of them were eventually overshadowed by the rise of the great empires of the Assyrians and Persians. The Assyrian Empire had been the first to unite almost all of the ancient Middle East. Even larger, however, was the empire of the Great Kings of Persia. Although it owed much to the administrative organization created by the Assyrians, the Persian Empire had its own peculiar strengths. Persian rule was tolerant as well as efficient. Conquered peoples were allowed to keep their own religions, customs, and methods of doing business. The many years of peace that the Persian Empire brought to the Middle East facilitated trade and the general well-being of its peoples. It is no wonder that many peoples expressed their gratitude for being subjects of the Great Kings of Persia. Among these peoples were the Jews, who created no empire but nevertheless left an important spiritual legacy. The evolution of monotheism created in Judaism one of the world's greatest religions; moreover, Judaism influenced the development of both Christianity and Islam.

The Persians had also extended their empire to the Indus River, which brought them into contact with another river valley civilization that had developed independently of the civilizations in the Middle East and Egypt. It is to India that we now turn.

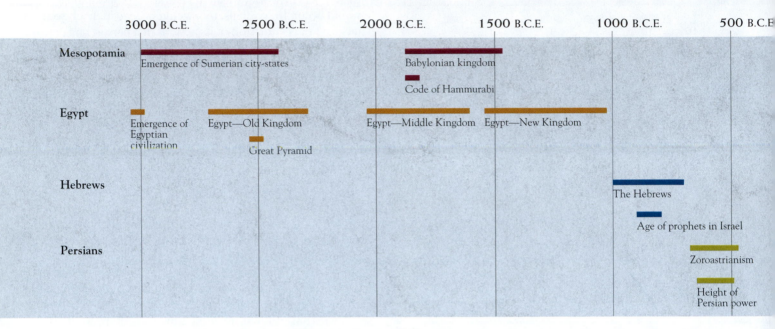

	3000 B.C.E.	2500 B.C.E.	2000 B.C.E.	1500 B.C.E.	1000 B.C.E.	500 B.C.E.

Mesopotamia — Emergence of Sumerian city-states; Babylonian kingdom; Code of Hammurabi

Egypt — Emergence of Egyptian civilization; Egypt—Old Kingdom; Great Pyramid; Egypt—Middle Kingdom; Egypt—New Kingdom

Hebrews — The Hebrews; Age of prophets in Israel

Persians — Zoroastrianism; Height of Persian power

CHAPTER NOTES

1. Quoted in Amélie Kuhrt, *The Ancient Near East, c. 3000–330 B.C.* (London, 1995), vol. 1, p. 68.
2. Quoted in Thorkild Jacobsen, "Mesopotamia," in Henri Frankfort et al., *Before Philosophy* (Baltimore, 1949), p. 139.
3. Quoted in Milton Covensky, *The Ancient Near Eastern Tradition* (New York, 1966), p. 51.
4. Quoted in B. G. Trigger, B. J. Kemp, D. O'Connor, and A. B. Lloyd, *Ancient Egypt: A Social History* (Cambridge, 1983), p. 74.
5. James B. Pritchard, *Ancient Near Eastern Texts*, 3d ed. (Princeton, N.J., 1969), p. 34.
6. Ibid., p. 36.
7. Ibid., p. 413.
8. Ibid., p. 420.
9. Quoted in John A. Wilson, *The Culture of Ancient Egypt* (Chicago, 1956), p. 264.
10. Psalms 137:1, 4–6.
11. Psalms 145:8–9.
12. Psalms 121:2–3.
13. Exodus 20:13–15.
14. Isaiah 2:4.
15. Quoted in H. W. F. Saggs, *The Might That Was Assyria* (London, 1984), p. 261.
16. Ibid., p. 262.
17. Quoted in J. M. Cook, *The Persian Empire* (New York, 1983), p. 32.
18. Herodotus, *The Persian Wars*, trans. George Rawlinson (New York, 1942), p. 257.
19. Isaiah, 44:28, 45:1.
20. Quoted in A. T. Olmstead, *History of the Persian Empire* (Chicago, 1948), p. 168.
21. Quoted in Cook, *The Persian Empire*, p. 76.

SUGGESTED READINGS

For a beautifully illustrated introduction to the ancient world, see *Past Worlds: The Times Atlas of Archaeology* (Maplewood, N.J., 1988), written by an international group of scholars. The following works are of considerable value in examining the prehistory of humankind: R. Leakey, *The Making of Mankind* (London, 1981); R. J. Wenke, *Patterns in Prehistory: Humankind's First Three Million Years*, 4th ed. (New York, 1999); P. Mellars and C. Stringer, *The Human Revolution* (Edinburgh, 1989); and D. O.

Henry, *From Foraging to Agriculture* (Philadelphia, 1989). For a study of the role of women in early human society, see E. Barber, *Women's Work: The First 20,000 Years* (New York, 1994).

An excellent reference tool on the ancient Near East can be found in P. Bienkowski and A. Milward, eds., *Dictionary of the Ancient Near East* (Philadelphia, 2000). A very competent general survey of the political history of Mesopotamia and Egypt is W. W. Hallo and W. K. Simpson, *The Ancient Near East: A History*

(New York, 1971). Also valuable are A. B. Knapp, *The History and Culture of Ancient Western Asia and Egypt* (Chicago, 1987), and W. von Soden, *The Ancient Orient: An Introduction to the Study of the Ancient Near East* (Grand Rapids, Mich., 1994). For a detailed survey, see A. Kuhrt, *The Ancient Near East, c. 3000–330 B.C.*, 2 vols. (London, 1996). H. W. F. Saggs, *Babylonians* (Norman, Okla., 1995) provides an overview of the people of ancient Mesopotamia. On the economic and social history of the ancient Near East, see D. C. Snell, *Life in the Ancient Near East* (New Haven, Conn., 1997). The fundamental collection of translated documents from the ancient Near East is J. B. Pritchard, *Ancient Near Eastern Texts*, 3d ed. (Princeton, N.J., 1969).

General works on ancient Mesopotamia include J. N. Postgate, *Early Mesopotamia: Society and Economy at the Dawn of History* (London, 1992); A. L. Oppenheim, *Ancient Mesopotamia*, 2d ed. (Chicago, 1977); and S. Lloyd, *The Archaeology of Mesopotamia*, rev. ed. (London, 1984). A beautifully illustrated survey can be found in M. Roaf, *Cultural Atlas of Mesopotamia and the Ancient Near East* (New York, 1996). The world of the Sumerians has been well described in S. N. Kramer, *The Sumerians* (Chicago, 1963) and *History Begins at Sumer* (New York, 1959). See also the recent summary of the historical and archaeological evidence by H. Crawford, *Sumer and the Sumerians* (Cambridge, 1991). The fundamental work on the spiritual perspective of ancient Mesopotamia is T. Jacobsen, *The Treasures of Darkness: A History of Mesopotamian Religion* (New Haven, Conn., 1976).

For a good introduction to ancient Egypt, see the beautifully illustrated works by M. Hayes, *The Egyptians* (New York, 1997); J. Baines and J. Málek, *The Cultural Atlas of the World: Ancient Egypt* (Alexandria, Va., 1991); and D. P. Silverman, ed., *Ancient Egypt* (New York, 1997). Other general surveys include N. Grant, *The Egyptians* (New York, 1996); I. Shaw, ed., *The Oxford History of Ancient Egypt* (New York, 2000); and N. Grimal, *A History of Ancient Egypt*, trans. I. Shaw (Oxford, 1992). Egyptian religion is covered in S. Morenz, *Egyptian Religion* (London, 1973). On culture in general, see J. A. Wilson, *The Culture of Ancient Egypt* (Chicago, 1956). The leading authority on the pyramids is I. E. S. Edwards, *The Pyra-*

mids of Egypt, rev. ed. (Harmondsworth, England, 1976). Daily life in ancient Egypt can be examined in E. Strouhal, *Life of the Ancient Egyptians* (Norman, Okla., 1992). An important new study on women is G. Robins, *Women in Ancient Egypt* (Cambridge, Mass., 1993).

On the Sea Peoples, see the standard work by N. Sanders, *The Sea Peoples: Warriors of the Ancient Mediterranean* (London, 1978). A good introductory survey on the Hittites can be found in O. R. Gurney, *The Hittites*, 2d ed. (New York, 1981).

For a good account of Phoenician domestic history and overseas expansion, see D. Harden, *The Phoenicians*, rev. ed. (Harmondsworth, England, 1980). See also M. E. Aubet, *The Phoenicians and the West: Politics, Colonies and Trade* (Cambridge, 1993). There is an enormous literature on ancient Israel. Two good studies on the archaeological aspects are A. Mazar, *Archaeology of the Land of the Bible* (New York, 1992), and A. Ben-Tor, ed., *The Archaeology of Ancient Israel* (New Haven, Conn., 1992). For historical narratives, see especially J. Bright, *A History of Israel*, 3d ed. (Philadelphia, 1981), a fundamental study; the survey by M. Grant, *The History of Ancient Israel* (New York, 1984); and H. Shanks, *Ancient Israel: A Short History from Abraham to the Roman Destruction of the Temple* (Englewood Cliffs, N.J., 1988). For general studies on the religion of the Hebrews, see R. Albertz, *A History of Israelite Religion in the Old Testament Period* (Louisville, Ky., 1994), and W. J. Doorly, *The Religion of Israel* (New York, 1997).

A recent detailed account of Assyrian political, economic, social, military, and cultural history is H. W. F. Saggs, *The Might That Was Assyria* (London, 1984). The Chaldean empire can be examined in H. W. F. Saggs, *Babylonians* (Norman, Okla., 1995).

The classic work on the Persian Empire is A. T. Olmstead, *History of the Persian Empire* (Chicago, 1948), but a recent work by J. M. Cook, *The Persian Empire* (New York, 1983), provides new material and fresh interpretations. Also of value is J. Curtis, *Ancient Persia* (Cambridge, Mass., 1990). On the history of Zoroastrianism, see especially R. C. Zaehner, *The Dawn and Twilight of Zoroastrianism* (London, 1961). Also helpful is M. Boyce, *Zoroastrians: Their Religious Beliefs and Practices* (London, 1979).

INFOTRAC COLLEGE EDITION

For additional reading, go to InfoTrac College Edition, your online research library at
http://web1.infotrac-college.com

Enter the search term "Neolithic" using Keywords.

Enter the search term "Mesopotamia" using Keywords.

Enter the search terms "Sumer or Sumerian" using Keywords.

Enter the search term "antiquities" using the Subject Guide.

Enter the search terms "Egypt history" using the Subject Guide.

Chapter 2

© Freer Gallery of Art, Smithsonian Institution, Washington, D.C.

ANCIENT INDIA

FOCUS QUESTIONS

- What were the chief features of Harappan civilization, and in what ways was it similar to the civilizations that arose in Egypt and Mesopotamia?
- What roles did the caste system and the family play in Indian society?
- What are the main tenets of Hinduism and Buddhism, and how did each religion influence Indian civilization?
- Why was India unable to maintain a unified empire in the first millennium B.C.E., and how was the Mauryan Empire temporarily able to overcome the tendencies toward disunity?
- ➤ What effects did the Aryans have on Indian civilization?

Arjuna was despondent as he prepared for battle. In the opposing army were many of his friends and colleagues, some of whom he had known since childhood. In despair, he turned for advice to Krishna, his chariot driver, who, unknown to Arjuna, was in actuality an incarnation of the Indian deity Vishnu. "Do not despair of your duty," Krishna advised his friend.

> To be born is certain death,
>   to the dead, birth is certain.
> It is not right that you should sorrow
>   for what cannot be avoided. . . .

If you do not fight this just battle
 you will fail in your own law
and in your honor,
 and you will incur sin.

Krishna's advice to Arjuna is contained in the Bhagavadgita, one of India's most sacred classical writings, and reflects one of the key tenets in Indian philosophy—the belief in reincarnation, or rebirth of the soul. It also points up the importance of doing one's duty without regard for the consequences. Arjuna was a warrior, and according to Aryan tribal tradition, he was obliged to follow the code of his class. "There is more joy in doing one's own duty badly," advised Krishna, "than in doing another man's duty well."

In advising Arjuna to fulfill his obligation as a warrior, the author of the Bhagavadgita, writing around the second century B.C.E. about a battle that took place almost a thousand years earlier, was by implication urging all readers to adhere to their own responsibility as members of one of India's major classes. Henceforth, this hierarchical vision of a society divided into groups, each with clearly distinct roles, would become a defining characteristic of Indian history.

The Bhagavadgita is part of a larger work that deals with the early history of the Aryan peoples who entered India from beyond the mountains north of the Khyber Pass between 1500 and 1000 B.C.E. When the Aryans arrived, India had already had a thriving civilization for almost two thousand years. The Indus valley civilization, although not as well known today as the civilizations of Mesopotamia and Egypt, was just as old; and its political, social, and cultural achievements were equally impressive. That civilization, known to historians by the names of its two major cities, Harappa and Mohenjo-Daro, emerged in the late fourth millennium B.C.E., flourished for over one thousand years, and then came to an abrupt end about 1500 B.C.E. It was soon replaced by a new society dominated by the Aryan peoples. The new civilization that emerged represented a rich mixture of the two cultures—Harappan and Aryan—and evolved over the next three thousand years into what we know today as India.

Thus India was and still is a land of diversity. This diversity is evident in its languages and cultures as well as in its physical characteristics. India possesses a bewildering array of languages, few of which are mutually intelligible. It has a deserved reputation, along with the Middle East, as a cradle of religion. Two of the world's major religions, Hinduism and Buddhism, originated in India; and a number of others, including Sikhism and Islam (the latter of which entered the South Asian subcontinent in the ninth or tenth century C.E.), continue to flourish there.

Although today this beautiful mosaic of peoples and cultures has been broken up into a number of separate independent states, the region still possesses a coherent history that despite its internal diversity is recognizably Indian. It is to the origins and early development of that culture that we now turn. •

BACKGROUND TO THE EMERGENCE OF CIVILIZATION IN INDIA

In its size and diversity, India seems more like a continent than a single country. That diversity begins with the geographical environment. The Indian subcontinent, shaped like a spade hanging from the southern ridge of Asia, is composed of a number of core regions. In the far north are the Himalayan and Karakoram mountain ranges, home to the highest mountains in the world. Directly to the south of the Himalayas and the Karakoram range is the rich valley of the Ganges, India's "holy river" and one of the core regions of Indian culture. To the west is the Indus River valley. Today the latter is a relatively arid plateau that forms the backbone of the modern state of Pakistan, but in ancient times it enjoyed a more balanced climate and served as the cradle of Indian civilization.

South of India's two major river valleys lies the Deccan, a region of hills and an upland plateau that extends from the Ganges valley to the southern tip of the Indian subcontinent. The interior of the plateau is relatively hilly and dry, but the eastern and western coasts are occupied by lush plains, which are historically among the most densely populated regions of India. Off the southeastern coast is the island known today as Sri Lanka. Although Sri Lanka is now a separate country quite distinct politically and culturally from India, the island's history is intimately linked with that of its larger neighbor.

In this vast region live a rich mixture of peoples: Dravidians, probably descended from the Indus River culture that flourished at the dawn of Indian civilization, over four thousand years ago; Aryans, descended from the pastoral peoples who flooded southward from Central Asia in the second millennium B.C.E.; and hill peoples, who may have lived in the region prior to the rise of organized societies and thus may have been the earliest inhabitants of all.

HARAPPAN CIVILIZATION: A FASCINATING ENIGMA

In the 1920s, archaeologists discovered the existence of agricultural settlements dating back well over six thousand years in the lower reaches of the Indus River valley in modern Pakistan. Those small mudbrick villages eventually gave rise to the sophisticated human communities that historians call Harappan civilization. Although today the area is relatively arid, during the third and fourth millennia B.C.E., it evidently received much more abundant rainfall, and the valleys of the Indus River and its tributaries supported a thriving civilization that may have covered a total area of over 600,000 square miles, from the Himalayas to the coast of the Indian Ocean. More than seventy sites have been unearthed since the area was first discovered in the 1850s, but the main sites are at the two major cities, Harappa, in the Punjab, and Mohenjo-Daro, nearly 400 miles to the south near the mouth of the Indus River (see Map 2.1).

The origin of the Harappans is still debated, but some scholars have suggested on the basis of ethnographic and linguistic analysis that the language and physical characteristics of the Harappans were similar to those of the Dravidian peoples who live in the Deccan Plateau today. If that is so, Harappa is not simply a dead civilization, whose culture and peoples have disappeared into the sands of history, but a part of the living culture of the Indian subcontinent.

Political and Social Structures

In several respects, Harappan civilization closely resembled the cultures of Mesopotamia and the Nile valley. Like them, it probably began in tiny farming villages scattered throughout the river valley, some dating back to as early as 6500 or 7000 B.C.E. These villages thrived and grew until by the middle of the third millennium B.C.E. they could support a privileged ruling elite living in walled cities of considerable magnitude and affluence. The center of

MAP **2.1**   Ancient Harappan Civilization.   This map shows the location of the first civilization that arose in the Indus River valley, which today is located in the contemporary state of Pakistan. ➤ *What were the names of the two largest urban centers that have so far been excavated?*

power was the city of Harappa, which was surrounded by a brick wall over 40 feet thick at its base and more than $3\frac{1}{2}$ miles in circumference. The city was laid out on an essentially rectangular grid, with some streets as wide as 30 feet. Most buildings were constructed of kiln-dried mudbricks and were square in shape, reflecting the grid pattern. At its height, the city may have had as many as 80,000 inhabitants, as large as some of the most populous urban centers in Sumerian civilization.

Both Harappa and Mohenjo-Daro were divided into large walled neighborhoods, with narrow lanes separating the rows of houses. Houses varied in size,

The City of Mohenjo-Daro

THE CITY OF THE DEAD. Mohenjo-Daro was one of the two major cities of the ancient Indus River civilization. In addition to rows on rows of residential housing, it had a ceremonial center, with a royal palace and a sacred bath that was probably used by the priests as a means of achieving ritual purity. The bath, reminiscent of water tanks in modern Hindu temples, is shown in the center of the photograph here, with the remnants of a Buddhist stupa, constructed centuries later, on the right.

© Borromeo/Art Resource, NY

with some as high as three stories, but all followed the same general plan based on a square courtyard surrounded by rooms. Bathrooms featured an advanced drainage system, which carried wastewater out to drains located under the streets and thence to sewage pits beyond the city walls. But the cities also had the equivalent of the modern slum. At Harappa, tiny dwellings for workers have been found near metal furnaces and the open areas used for pounding grain.

Unfortunately, Harappan writing has not yet been deciphered, so historians know relatively little about the organization of the Harappan state. However, recent archaeological evidence suggests that unlike its contemporaries in Egypt and Sumer, Harappa was not a centralized monarchy with a theocratic base but a collection of over fifteen hundred towns and cities loosely connected by ties of trade and alliance and ruled by a coalition of landlords and rich merchants. There were no royal precincts or imposing burial monuments, and there are few surviving stone or terra-cotta images that might represent kings, priests, or military commanders. There are clear signs, however, that religion had advanced beyond the stage of spirit worship to belief in a single god or goddess of fertility. Presumably, priests at court prayed to this deity to maintain the fertility of the soil and guarantee the annual harvest.

As in Mesopotamia and Egypt, the Harappan economy was based primarily on agriculture. Wheat, barley, rice, and peas were apparently the primary crops. The presence of cotton seeds at various sites suggests that the Harappan peoples may have been the first to master the cultivation of this useful crop and possibly introduced it, along with rice, to other societies in the region. But Harappa also developed an extensive trading network that extended to Sumer and other civilizations to the west. Textiles and foodstuffs were apparently imported from Sumer in exchange for metals such as copper, lumber, precious stones, and various types of luxury goods. Much of this trade was conducted by ship via the Persian Gulf, although some undoubtedly went by land.

Harappan Culture

Archaeological remains indicate that the Indus valley peoples possessed a culture as sophisticated as that of the Sumerians to the west. Although Harappan architecture was purely functional and shows little artistic sensitivity, the aesthetic quality of some of the pottery and sculpture is superb. Harappan painted pottery, wheel-turned and kiln-fired, rivals equivalent work produced elsewhere. Sculpture, however, was the Harappans' highest artistic achievement. Some artifacts possess a wonderful vitality of expression. Fired clay seals show a deft touch in carving animals such as elephants, tigers, rhinoceros, and antelope, and figures made of copper or terra-cotta show a lively sensitivity and a sense of grace and movement that is almost modern.

Unfortunately, the only surviving examples of Harappan writing are the pictographic symbols inscribed on the clay seals. The script contained more than four hundred characters, but most are too stylized to be identified by their shape, and scholars have thus far been unable to decipher them. There are no apparent links with Mesopotamian scripts. Until the script is deciphered, much about the Harappan civilization must remain, as one historian termed it, a fascinating enigma.

© Scala/Art Resource, NY

HARAPPAN SEALS. The Harappan peoples, like their contemporaries in Mesopotamia, developed a writing system to record their spoken language. Unfortunately, it has not yet been deciphered. Most extant examples of Harappan writing are found on fired clay seals depicting human figures and animals. These seals have been found in houses and were probably used to identify the owners of goods for sale. Other seals may have been used as amulets or have had other religious significance. Several depict religious figures or ritualistic scenes of sacrifice.

A Lost Civilization?

Until recently, the area north of the Indus River was presumed to be isolated from the emerging river valley civilizations to the south. But archaeologists have now discovered the remnants of a lost culture there that dates back at least to the late third millennium B.C.E. Bronze Age mudbrick settlements surrounded by irrigated fields have been found along a series of oases that stretch several hundred miles from the Caspian Sea into modern-day Afghanistan. There are also clear indications of the domestication of sheep and goats and of widespread trade with other societies in the region, along with tantalizing hints—in the form of an engraved stone seal found at one site—that the inhabitants of the region were in the process of developing their own form of writing. Although the founders of this mysterious civilization remain unknown, it is now clear that the rudiments of civilization in ancient times were not limited to the great river valleys located on the edges of the African and Asian continents.

THE ARRIVAL OF THE ARYANS

One of the great mysteries of Harappan civilization is how it came to an end. Archaeologists working at Mohenjo-Daro have discovered signs of first a gradual decay and then a sudden destruction of the city and its inhabitants around 1500 B.C.E. Many of the surviving skeletons have been found in postures of running or hiding, reminiscent of the ruins of the Roman city of Pompeii, destroyed by the eruption of Mount Vesuvius in 79 C.E.

These tantalizing signs of flight before a sudden catastrophe have led some scholars to surmise that the city of Mohenjo-Daro (the name was applied by archaeologists and means "city of the dead") and perhaps the remnants of Harappan civilization were destroyed by the Aryans, nomads from the north, who arrived in the subcontinent around the middle of the second millennium B.C.E. Although the Aryans were almost certainly not as sophisticated culturally as the Harappans, like many nomadic peoples, they excelled at the art of war. As in Mesopotamia and the Nile valley, most contacts between pastoral and agricultural peoples proved unstable and ended in armed conflict. Nevertheless, it is doubtful that the Aryan invaders were directly responsible for the final destruction of Mohenjo-Daro. More likely, Harappan civilization had already fallen on hard times, perhaps as a result of climatic change in the Indus valley. Archaeologists have found clear signs of social decay, including evidence of trash in the streets, neglect of public services, and overcrowding in urban neighborhoods. Mohenjo-Daro itself may have been destroyed by an epidemic or by natural phenomena such as floods, an earthquake, or a shift in the course of the Indus River. If that was the case, the Aryans conquered a people whose moment of greatness had already passed.

The Early Aryans

Historians know relatively little about the origins and culture of the Aryans before they entered India, although they were part of the extensive group of Indo-European-speaking peoples who inhabited vast areas in what is now Siberia and the steppes of Central Asia. Whereas other Indo-European-speaking peoples moved westward and eventually settled in Europe, the Aryans moved south across the Hindu Kush into the plains of northern India. Between 1500 and 1000 B.C.E., they gradually advanced eastward from the Indus valley, across the fertile plain of the Ganges, and later southward into the Deccan Plateau until they had eventually extended their political mastery over the entire subcontinent and its Dravidian inhabitants, although Dravidian culture survived to remain a prominent element in the evolution of traditional Indian civilization.

After they settled in India, the Aryans gradually adapted to the geographical realities of their new homeland and abandoned the pastoral life for agricultural pursuits. They were assisted by the introduction of iron, which probably came from the Middle East, where it had first been introduced by the Hittites (see Chapter 1) about 1500 B.C.E. The invention of the iron plow, along with the development of irrigation, allowed the Aryans and their indigenous subjects to clear the dense jungle growth along the Ganges River and transform the Ganges valley into one of the richest agricultural regions in all of South Asia. The Aryans also developed their first writing system and were thus able to transcribe the legends that previously

The Duties of a King

Kautilya, India's earliest known political philosopher, was an adviser to the Mauryan rulers. The Arthasastra, though written down at a later date, very likely reflects his ideas. This passage sets forth some of the necessary characteristics of a king, including efficiency, diligence, energy, compassion, and concern for the security and welfare of the state. In emphasizing the importance of winning popular support as the means of becoming an effective ruler, the author echoes the view of the Chinese philosopher Mencius, who declared that the best way to win the empire is to win the people (see Chapter 3).

THE ARTHASASTRA

Only if a king is himself energetically active do his officers follow him energetically. If he is sluggish, they too remain sluggish. And, besides, they eat up his works. He is thereby easily overpowered by his enemies. Therefore, he should ever dedicate himself energetically to activity. . . .

A king should attend to all urgent business; he should not put it off. For what has been thus put off becomes either difficult or altogether impossible to accomplish.

The vow of the king is energetic activity; his sacrifice is constituted of the discharge of his own administrative duties; his sacrificial fee [to the officiating priests] is his impartiality of attitude toward all; his sacrificial consecration is his anointment as king.

In the happiness of the subjects lies the happiness of the king; in their welfare, his own welfare. The welfare of the king does not lie in the fulfillment of what is dear to him; whatever is dear to the subjects constitutes his welfare.

Therefore, ever energetic, a king should act up to the precepts of the science of material gain. Energetic activity is the source of material gain; its opposite, of downfall.

In the absence of energetic activity, the loss of what has already been obtained and of what still remains to be obtained is certain. The fruit of one's works is achieved through energetic activity—one obtains abundance of material prosperity.

---

had been passed down from generation to generation by memory. Most of what is known about the early Aryans is based on oral traditions passed on in the Rigveda, an ancient work that was written down after the Aryans arrived in India (the Rigveda is one of several Vedas, or collections of sacred instructions and rituals).

As in other Indo-European societies, each of the various Aryan tribes was led by a chieftain, called a *raja* ("prince"), who was assisted by a council of elders composed of other leading members of the tribe; like them, he was normally a member of the warrior class, called the *kshatriya*. The chief derived his power from his ability to protect his tribe from rival groups, an ability that was crucial in the warring kingdoms and shifting alliances that were typical of early Aryan society. Though the *rajas* claimed to be representatives of the gods, they were not gods themselves.

As Aryan society grew in size and complexity, the chieftains began to be transformed into kings, usually called *maharajas* ("great princes"). Nevertheless, the tradition that the ruler did not possess absolute authority remained strong. Like all human beings, the ruler was required to follow the *dharma*, a set of laws that set behavioral standards for all individuals and classes in Indian society (see the box above).

While competing groups squabbled for precedence in India, powerful new empires were rising to the west. First came the Persian Empire of Cyrus and Darius. Then came the Greeks. After two centuries of sporadic rivalry and warfare, the Greeks achieved a brief period of regional dominance in the late fourth century B.C.E. with the rise of Macedonia under Alexander the Great. Alexander had

heard of the riches of India, and in 330 B.C.E., after conquering Persia, he launched an invasion of the east (see Chapter 4). In 326, his armies arrived in the plains of northwestern India. They departed almost as suddenly as they had come, leaving in their wake Greek administrators and a veneer of cultural influence that would affect the area for generations to come.

The Mauryan Empire

The Alexandrian conquest was only a brief interlude in the history of the Indian subcontinent, but it played a formative role, for on the heels of Alexander's departure came the rise of the first dynasty to control much of the region. The founder of the new state, who took the royal title Chandragupta Maurya (324–301 B.C.E.), drove out the Greek occupation forces after the departure of Alexander and solidified his control over the northern Indian plain. He established the capital of his new Mauryan Empire at Pataliputra (modern Patna) in the Ganges valley (see the map on p. 53). Little is known of his origins, although some sources say he had originally fought on the side of the invading Greek forces but then angered Alexander with his outspoken advice.

Little, too, is known of Chandragupta Maurya's empire. Most accounts of his reign rely on a lost work written by Megasthenes, a Greek ambassador to the Mauryan court, in about 302 B.C.E. Chandragupta Maurya was apparently advised by a brilliant court official named Kautilya, whose name has been attached to a treatise on politics called the *Arthasastra*. The work actually dates from a later time, but it may well reflect Kautilya's ideas.

Although the author of the *Arthasastra* follows Aryan tradition in stating that the happiness of the king lies in the happiness of his subjects, the treatise also asserts that when the sacred law of the *dharma* and practical politics collide, the latter must take precedence: "Whenever there is disagreement between history and sacred law or between evidence and sacred law, then the matter should be settled in accordance with sacred law. But whenever sacred law is in conflict with rational law, then reason shall be held authoritative.[1]" The *Arthasastra* also emphasizes ends rather than means, achieved results rather than the methods employed. For this reason, it has often been compared to Machiavelli's

➤ **A HARAPPAN BUST.**   This 4,000-year-old bust found at Mohenjo-Daro displays an elaborate beard, a pair of eyes originally inlaid with shell, and a toga decorated with a trefoil design. Although the trefoil had been used in Egypt and Mesopotamia as a sacred symbol representing stars and deities, little is known about the identity of this Harappan figure or whether the creative execution reflects the influence of other nearby civilizations.

famous political treatise of the Italian Renaissance, *The Prince*, written more than a thousand years later.

As described in the *Arthasastra*, Chandragupta Maurya's government was highly centralized and even despotic: "It is power and power alone which, only when exercised by the king with impartiality, and in proportion to guilt, over his son or his enemy, maintains both this world and the next."[2] The king possessed a large army and a secret police responsible to his orders (according to the Greek ambassador Megasthenes, Chandragupta Maurya was chronically fearful of assassination, a not unrealistic concern for someone who had allegedly come to power by violence). Reportedly, all food was tasted in his presence, and he made a practice of never sleeping twice in the same bed in his sumptuous palace. To guard against corruption, a board of censors was empowered to investigate cases of possible malfeasance and incompetence within the bureaucracy.

The ruler's authority beyond the confines of the capital may often have been limited, however. The empire was divided into provinces that were ruled by governors. At first, most of these governors were appointed by and reported to the ruler, but later the position became hereditary. The provinces themselves were divided into districts, each under a chief magistrate appointed by the governor. At the base of the government pyramid was the village, where the vast majority of the Indian people lived. The village was governed by a council of elders; membership in the council was normally hereditary and was shared by the wealthiest families in the village.

Caste and Class: Social Structures in Ancient India

When the Aryans arrived in India, they already possessed a strong class system based on a ruling warrior class. They apparently held the indigenous peoples in some contempt and assigned them to a lower position in society. The result was a set of social institutions and class divisions that have persisted with only minor changes down to the present day.

THE CASTE SYSTEM

At the base of the social system that emerged from the clash of cultures was the concept of the superiority of the invading peoples over their conquered subjects. In a sense, it became an issue of color, because the Aryan invaders, a primarily light-skinned people, were contemptuous of their subjects, who were dark. Light skin came to imply high status, whereas dark skin suggested the opposite.

The concept of color, however, was only the physical manifestation of a division that took place in Indian society on the basis of economic functions. Indian classes (called *varna*, literally, "color," and commonly known as "castes" in English) did not simply reflect an informal division of labor. Instead, they were a set of rigid social classifications that

Social Classes in Ancient India

The Law of Manu is a set of behavioral norms allegedly prescribed by India's mythical founding ruler, Manu. The treatise was probably written in the first or second century B.C.E. The following excerpt describes the various social classes in India and their prescribed duties.

THE LAW OF MANU

For the sake of the preservation of this entire creation, the Exceedingly Resplendent One [the Creator of the Universe] assigned separate duties to the classes which had sprung from his mouth, arms, thighs, and feet.

Teaching, studying, performing sacrificial rites, so too making others perform sacrificial rites, and giving away and receiving gifts—these he assigned to the [brahmins].

Protection of the people, giving away of wealth, performance of sacrificial rites, study, and nonattachment to sensual pleasures—these are, in short, the duties of a kshatriya.

Tending of cattle, giving away of wealth, performance of sacrificial rites, study, trade and commerce, usury, and agriculture—these are the occupations of a vaisya.

The Lord has prescribed only one occupation [karma] for a sudra, namely, service without malice of even these other three classes.

Of created beings, those which are animate are the best; of the animate, those which subsist by means of their intellect; of the intelligent, men are the best; and of men, the [brahmins] are traditionally declared to be the best.

The code of conduct—prescribed by scriptures and ordained by sacred tradition—constitutes the highest dharma; hence a twice-born person, conscious of his own Self [seeking spiritual salvation], should be always scrupulous in respect of it.

---

determined not only one's occupation but also one's status in society and one's hope for ultimate salvation (see "Escaping the Wheel of Life" later in this chapter). There were five major castes in Indian society in ancient times. At the top were two castes, collectively viewed as the aristocracy, which clearly represented the ruling elites in Aryan society prior to their arrival in India: the priests and the warriors.

The priestly caste, known as the *brahmins*, was usually considered to be at the top of the social scale. Descended from seers who had advised the ruler on religious matters in Aryan tribal society (*brahmin* meant "one possessed of *Brahman*," a term for the supreme god in the Hindu religion), they were eventually transformed into an official class after their religious role declined in importance. Megasthenes described this caste as follows:

> From the time of their conception in the womb they are under the care and guardianship of learned men who go to the mother and . . . give her prudent hints and counsels, and the women who listen to them most willingly are thought to be the most fortunate in their offspring. After their birth the children are in the care of one person after another, and as they advance in years their masters are men of superior accomplishments. The philosophers reside in a grove in front of the city within a moderate-sized enclosure. They live in a simple style and lie on pallets of straw and [deer] skins. They abstain from animal food and sexual pleasures, and occupy their time in listening to serious discourse and in imparting knowledge to willing ears.[3]

The second caste was the *kshatriya*, the warriors. Although often listed below the *brahmins* in social status, many *kshatriyas* were probably descended from the ruling warrior class in Aryan society prior to the conquest of India and thus may have originally ranked socially above the *brahmins*, although they were ranked lower in religious terms. Like the *brahmins*, the *kshatriyas* were originally identified with a single occupation—fighting—but as the character of Aryan society changed, they often switched to other forms of employment. At the same time, new conquering families from other castes were sometimes tacitly accepted into the ranks of the warriors.

The third-ranked caste in Indian society was the *vaisya* (literally, "commoner"). The *vaisyas* were usually viewed in economic terms as the merchant caste. Some historians have speculated that the *vaisyas* were originally guardians of the tribal herds but that after settling in India, many moved into commercial pursuits. Megasthenes noted that members of this caste "alone are permitted to hunt and keep cattle and to sell beasts of burden or to let them out on hire. In return for clearing the land of wild beasts and birds which infest sown fields, they receive an allowance of corn from the king. They lead a wandering life and dwell in tents."[4] Although this caste was ranked below the first two in social status, it shared with them the privilege of being considered "twice-born," a term referring to a ceremony at puberty whereby young males were initiated into adulthood and introduced into Indian society. After the ceremony, male members of the top three castes were allowed to wear the "sacred thread" for the remainder of their lives.

Below the three "twice-born" castes were the *sudras*, who represented the great bulk of the Indian population. The *sudras* were not considered fully Aryan, and the term probably originally referred to the conquered Dravidian population. Most *sudras* were peasants or artisans or worked at other forms of manual labor. They had only limited rights in society (see the box above). In recent years, DNA samples have revealed that most upper-caste South Indians share more genetic characteristics with Europeans than their lower-caste counterparts do, thus tending to confirm the hypothesis that the Aryans established their political and social dominance over the indigenous Dravidian population.

At the lowest level of Indian society, and in fact not even considered a legitimate part of the caste system itself, were the untouchables (also known as outcastes, or *pariahs*). The untouchables probably originated as a slave class consisting of prisoners of war, criminals, ethnic minorities, and other groups considered outside Indian society. Even after slavery was outlawed, the untouchables were given menial and degrading tasks that other Indians would not accept, such as collecting trash, handling dead bodies, or serving as butchers or tanners (handling dead meat). According to the estimate of one historian, they may have accounted for a little more than 5 percent of the total population of India in antiquity.

The life of the untouchables was extremely demeaning. They were not considered human, and their very presence was considered polluting to members of the other *varna*. No Indian would touch or eat food handled or prepared by an untouchable. Untouchables lived in special ghettos and were required to tap two sticks together to announce their presence when they traveled outside their quarters so that others could avoid them.

Technically, the caste divisions were absolute. Individuals supposedly were born, lived, and died in the same caste. In practice, some upward or downward mobility probably took place, and there was undoubtedly some flexibility in economic functions. But throughout most of Indian history, caste taboos remained strict. Members were generally not permitted to marry outside their caste (although in practice, men were occasionally allowed to marry below their caste but not above it). At first, attitudes toward the handling of food were relatively loose, but eventually that taboo grew stronger, and social mores dictated that sharing meals and marrying outside one's caste were unacceptable.

The people of ancient India did not belong to a particular caste as individuals but as part of a larger kin group commonly referred to as the *jati*, a system of extended families that originated in ancient India and still exists in somewhat changed form today. Although the origins of the *jati* system are unknown (there are no indications of strict class distinctions in Harappan society), the *jati* eventually became identified with a specific caste living in a specific area and carrying out a specific function in society. Each caste was divided into thousands of separate *jatis*, each with its own separate economic function.

Caste was thus the basic social organization into which traditional Indian society was divided. Each *jati* was itself composed of hundreds or thousands of individual nuclear families and was governed by its own council of elders. Membership in this ruling council was usually hereditary and was based on the wealth or social status of particular families within the community.

In theory, each *jati* was assigned a particular form of economic activity. Obviously, though, not all families in a given caste could take part in the same vocation, and as time went on, members of a single *jati* commonly engaged in several different lines of work. Sometimes an entire *jati* would have to move its location in order to continue a particular form of activity. In other cases, a *jati* would adopt an entirely new occupation in order to remain in a certain area. Such changes in habitat or occupation introduced the possibility of movement up or down the social scale. In this way, an entire *jati* could sometimes engage in upward mobility, even though it was not possible for individuals, who were tied to their caste identity for life.

The caste system may sound highly constricting, but there were persuasive social and economic reasons why it survived for so many centuries. In the first place, it provided an identity for individuals in a highly hierarchical society. Although an individual might rank lower on the social scale than members of other castes, it was always possible to find others ranked even lower. Caste was also a means for new groups, such as mountain tribal people, to achieve a recognizable place in the broader community. Perhaps equally important, caste was a primitive form of welfare system. Each *jati* was obliged to provide for any of its members who were poor or destitute. Caste also provided an element of stability in a society that all too often was in a state of political anarchy.

DAILY LIFE IN ANCIENT INDIA

Beyond these rigid social stratifications was the Indian family. Not only was life centered around the family, but the family, not the individual, was the most basic unit in society. The ideal was an extended family, with three generations living under the same roof. It was essentially patriarchal, except along the Malabar coast, near the southwestern tip of the subcontinent, where a matriarchal form of social organization prevailed down to modern times. In the rest of India, the oldest male traditionally possessed legal authority over the entire family unit.

The family was linked together in a religious sense by a series of commemorative rites to ancestral members. This ritual originated in the Vedic era and consisted of family ceremonies to honor the departed and to link the living and the dead. The male family head was responsible for leading the ritual. At his death, his eldest son had the duty of conducting the funeral rites.

The importance of the father and the son in family ritual underlined the importance of males in Indian society. Male superiority was expressed in a variety of ways. Women could not serve as priests (although in practice, some were accepted as seers), nor were they normally permitted to study the Vedas. In general, males had a monopoly on education, since the primary goal of learning to read was to carry on family rituals. In high-class families, young men, after having been initiated into the sacred thread, began Vedic studies with a *guru* (teacher). Some then went on to higher studies in one of the major cities. The goal of such an education might be either professional or religious. Such young men were not supposed to marry until after twelve years of study.

In general, only males could inherit property, except in a few cases where there were no sons. According to law, a woman was always considered a minor. Divorce was prohibited, although it sometimes took place. According to the *Arthasastra*, a wife who had been deserted by her husband could seek a divorce. Polygamy was fairly rare and apparently occurred mainly among the higher classes, but husbands were permitted to take a second wife if the first was barren. Producing children was an important aspect of marriage, both because children provided security for their parents in old age and because they were a physical proof of male potency. Child marriage was common for young girls, whether because of the desire for children or because daughters represented an economic liability to their parents. But perhaps the most graphic symbol of women's subjection to men was the ritual of *sati* (often written *suttee*), which required the wife to throw herself on her dead husband's funeral pyre. The Greek visitor Megasthenes reported "that he had heard from some persons of wives burning themselves along with their deceased husbands and doing so gladly; and that those women who refused to burn themselves were held in disgrace."[4] All in all, it was undoubtedly a difficult existence. According to the *Law of Manu*, an early treatise on social organization and behavior in ancient India, probably written in the first or second century B.C.E., women were subordinated to men—first to their father, then to their husband, and finally to their sons:

> She should do nothing independently
>   even in her own house.
> In childhood subject to her father,
>   in youth to her husband,
> and when her husband is dead to her sons,
>   she should never enjoy independence. . . .
>
> She should always be cheerful,
>   and skillful in her domestic duties,
> with her household vessels well cleansed,
>   and her hand tight on the purse strings. . . .
>
> Though he be uncouth and prone to pleasure,
>   though he have no good points at all,
> the virtuous wife should ever
>   worship her lord as a god.[5]

At the root of female subordination to the male was the practical fact that as in most agricultural societies, men did most of the work in the fields. Females were viewed as having little utility outside the home and indeed were considered an economic burden, since parents were obliged to provide a dowry to acquire a husband for a daughter. Female children also appeared to offer little advantage in maintaining the family unit, since they joined the families of their husbands after the wedding ceremony.

Despite all of these indications of female subjection to the male, there are numerous signs that in some ways women often played an influential role in Indian society, and the Hindu code of behavior stressed that they should be treated with respect. Indians appeared to be fascinated by female sexuality, and tradition held that women often used their sexual powers to achieve domination over men. The author of the Mahabharata, a vast epic of early Indian society, complained that "the fire has never too many logs, the ocean never too many rivers, death never too many living souls, and fair-eyed woman never too many men." Despite the legal and social constraints, women often played an important role within the family unit, and many were admired and honored for their talents. It is probably significant that paintings and sculpture from ancient and medieval India frequently show women in a role equal to that of men, and the tradition of the henpecked husband is as prevalent in India as in many Western societies (see the box on p. 46).

Homosexuality was not unknown in India. It was condemned in the law books, however, and generally ignored by literature, which devoted its attention entirely to erotic heterosexuality. The *Kamasutra*, a textbook on sexual practices and techniques dating from the second century C.E. or slightly thereafter, mentions homosexuality briefly and with no apparent enthusiasm.

The Economy

The Aryan conquest did not drastically change the economic character of Indian society. Not only did most Aryans take up farming, but it is likely that agriculture expanded rapidly under Aryan rule with the invention of the iron plow and the spread of northern Indian culture into the Deccan Plateau. One consequence of this process was to shift the focus of Indian culture from the Indus valley farther eastward to the Ganges River valley, which even today is one of the most densely populated regions on earth. The flatter areas in the Deccan Plateau and in the coastal plains were also turned into cropland.

For most Indian farmers, life was harsh. Among the most fortunate were those who owned their own land, although they were required to pay taxes to the state. Many others were sharecroppers or landless laborers. They were subject to the vicissitudes of the market and often paid exorbitant rents to their landlord. Concentration of land in large holdings was limited by the tradition of dividing property among all the sons, but large estates worked by hired laborers or rented out to sharecroppers were not uncommon, particularly in areas where local *rajas* derived much of their wealth from their property.

Another problem for Indian farmers was the unpredictability of the climate. India is in the monsoon zone.

THE HENPECKED MONK

Women were often portrayed in traditional Indian literature as seductresses, luring innocent males from following their higher spiritual nature. This passage is from the Sutrakrtanga, one of the sacred books of the Jain religion. While the object of concern is technically not that familiar figure of ridicule, the henpecked husband, the passage indicates the concern that many men in ancient India felt when exposed to the wiles of their female contemporaries.

THE SUTRAKRTANGA

A celibate monk shouldn't fall in love,
and though he hankers after pleasure he should hold
himself in check,
for these are the pleasures
which some monks enjoy.

If a monk breaks his vows,
and falls for a woman,
she upbraids him and raises her foot to him,
and kicks him on the head.

"Monk, if you won't live with me
as husband and wife,
I'll pull out my hair and become a nun,
for you shall not live without me!"

But when she has him in her clutches
it's all housework and errands!

"Fetch a knife to cut this gourd!"
"Get me some fresh fruit!"

"We want wood to boil the greens,
and for a fire in the evening!"
"Now paint my feet!"
"Come and massage my back!" . . .

"Bring me the chair with the twine seat,
and my wooden-soled slippers to go out walking!"
So pregnant women boss their husbands,
just as though they were household slaves.

When a child is born, the reward of their labors,
she makes the father hold the baby.
And sometimes the fathers of sons
stagger under their burdens like camels.

They get up at night, as though they were nurses,
to lull the howling child to sleep,
and, though they are shamefaced about it,
scrub dirty garments, just like washermen. . . .

So, monks, resist the wiles of women;
avoid their friendship and company.
The little pleasure you get from them
will only lead you into trouble!

The monsoon is a seasonal wind pattern in southern Asia that blows from the southwest during the summer months and from the northeast during the winter. The southwest monsoon is commonly marked by heavy rains. When the rains were late, thousands starved, particularly in the drier areas, which were especially dependent on rainfall. Strong governments attempted to deal with such problems by building state-operated granaries and maintaining the irrigation works, but strong governments were rare, and famine was probably all too common. The staple crops in the north were wheat, barley, and millet, with wet rice common in the fertile river valleys. In the south, grain and vegetables were supplemented by various tropical products, cotton, and spices such as pepper, ginger, cinnamon, and saffron.

By no means were all Indians farmers. As time passed, India became one of the most advanced trading and manufacturing civilizations in the ancient world. After the rise of the Mauryas, India's role in regional trade began to expand, and the subcontinent became a major transit point in a vast commercial network that extended from the rim of the Pacific to the Middle East and the Mediterranean Sea. This regional trade went both by sea and by camel caravan. Maritime trade across the Indian Ocean may have begun as early as the fifth century B.C.E. It extended eastward as far as Southeast Asia and China and southward as far as the straits between Africa and the island of Madagascar. Westward went spices, perfumes, jewels, textiles, precious stones and ivory, and wild animals. In return, India received gold, tin, lead, and wine.

India's expanding role as a manufacturing and commercial hub of the ancient world was undoubtedly a spur to the growth of the state. Under Chandragupta Maurya, the central government became actively involved in commercial and manufacturing activities. It owned mines and vast crown lands and undoubtedly earned massive profits from its role in regional commerce. Separate government departments were established for trade, agriculture, mining, and the manufacture of weapons, and the movement of private goods was vigorously taxed. Nevertheless, a significant private sector also flourished; it was dominated by great caste guilds, which monopolized key sectors of the economy. A money economy probably came into operation during the second century B.C.E., when copper and gold coins

IN THE BEGINNING

*A*s Indians began to speculate about the nature of the cosmic order, they came to believe in the existence of a single monistic force in the universe, a form of ultimate reality called Brahman. Today the early form of Hinduism is sometimes called Brahmanism. In the Upanishads, the concept began to emerge as an important element of Indian religious belief. It was the duty of the individual self—called the Atman—to achieve an understanding of this ultimate reality so that after death the self would merge in spiritual form with Brahman. Sometimes Brahman was described in more concrete terms as a creator god—eventually known as Vishnu—but more often in terms of a shadowy ultimate reality. In the following passage from the Upanishads, the author speculates on the nature of ultimate reality.

THE UPANISHADS

In the beginning . . . , this world was just being, one only, without a second. Some people, no doubt, say: "In the beginning . . . , this world was just nonbeing, one only, without a second; from that nonbeing, being was produced." But how indeed . . . could it be so? How could being be produced from nonbeing? . . .

In the beginning this world was being alone, one only, without a second. Being thought to itself: "May I be many, may I procreate." It produced fire. That fire thought to itself: "May I be many, may I procreate." It produced water. Therefore, whenever a person grieves or perspires, then it is from fire [heat] alone that water is produced. That water thought to itself: "May I be many, may I procreate." It produced food; it is from water alone that food for eating is produced. . . . That divinity (Being) thought to itself: "Well, having entered into these three divinities [fire, water, and food] by means of this living self, let me develop names and forms.

---

were introduced from the Middle East. This in turn led to the development of banking. But village trade continued to be conducted by means of cowry shells (highly polished shells used as a medium of exchange throughout much of Africa and Asia) or barter throughout the ancient period.

ESCAPING THE WHEEL OF LIFE: THE RELIGIOUS WORLD OF ANCIENT INDIA

Like Indian politics and society, Indian religion is a blend of Aryan and Dravidian culture. The intermingling of those two civilizations gave rise to an extraordinarily complex set of religious beliefs and practices, filled with diversity and contrast. Out of this cultural mix came two of the world's great religions, Buddhism and Hinduism, and several smaller ones, including Jainism and Sikhism.

Hinduism

Evidence about the earliest religious beliefs of the Aryan peoples comes primarily from sacred texts such as the Vedas, a set of four collections of hymns and religious ceremonies transmitted by memory through the centuries by Aryan priests. Many of these religious ideas were probably common to all of the Indo-European peoples before their separation into different groups at least four thousand years ago. Early Aryan beliefs were based on the common concept of a pantheon of gods and goddesses representing great forces of nature similar to the immortals of Greek mythology. The Aryan ancestor of the Greek father-god Zeus, for example, may have been the deity known in early Aryan tradition as Dyaus (see Chapter 4).

The parent god Dyaus was a somewhat distant figure, however, who was eventually overshadowed by other, more functional gods possessing more familiar human traits. For a while, the primary Aryan god was the great warrior god Indra. Indra summoned the Aryan tribal peoples to war and was represented in nature by thunder. Later, Indra declined in importance and was replaced by Varuna, lord of justice, who eventually evolved into the modern deity Vishnu. Other gods and goddesses represented various forces of nature or the needs of human beings, such as fire, fertility, and wealth (see the box above).

The concept of sacrifice was a key element in Aryan religious belief in Vedic times. As in many other ancient cultures, the practice may have begun as human sacrifice, but later animals were used as substitutes, although human sacrifice was practiced in some isolated communities down to modern times. The priestly class, the *brahmins*, played a key role in these ceremonies.

Another element of Aryan religious belief in ancient times was the ideal of asceticism. By the sixth century B.C.E., self-sacrifice or even self-mutilation had begun to replace sacrifice as a means of placating or communicating with the gods. Apparently, the original motive for asceticism was to achieve magical powers, but later, in the Upanishads (a set of commentaries on the Vedas compiled in the sixth century B.C.E.), it was seen as a means of spiritual meditation that would enable the practitioner to reach beyond material reality to a world of truth and bliss beyond earthly joy and sorrow: "Those who practice penance and faith in the forest, the tranquil ones, the knowers of truth, living the life of wandering mendicancy—they depart, freed from passion, through the door of the sun, to where dwells, verily . . . the imperishable Soul."[6] It is possible that another motive was to permit those with strong religious convictions to communicate directly with metaphysical reality without having to rely on the priestly class at court.

Asceticism, of course, has been practiced in other religions, including Christianity and Islam, but it seems particularly identified with Hinduism, the religion that emerged from early Indian religious tradition. Eventually, asceticism evolved into the modern practice of body training that we know as *yoga* (union), which is accepted today as a meaningful element of Hindu religious practice.

REINCARNATION

Another new concept also probably began to appear around the time the Upanishads were written—the idea of reincarnation. This is the idea that the individual soul is reborn in a different form after death and progresses through several existences on the wheel of life until it reaches its final destination in a union with the Great World Soul, *Brahman*. Because life is harsh, this final release is the objective of all living souls.

A key element in this process is the idea of *karma*—that one's rebirth in a next life is determined by one's *karma* (actions) in this life. Hinduism places all living species on a vast scale of existence, including the four classes and the untouchables in human society. The current status of an individual soul, then, is not simply a cosmic accident but the inevitable result of actions that that soul has committed in a past existence.

At the top of the scale are the *brahmins*, who by definition are closest to ultimate release from the law of reincarnation. The *brahmins* are followed in descending order by the other castes in human society and the world of the beasts. Within the animal kingdom, an especially high position is reserved for the cow, which even today is revered by Hindus as a sacred beast. Some have speculated that the unique role played by the cow in Hinduism derives from the value of cattle in Aryan pastoral society. But others have pointed

© Scala/Art Resource, NY

out that cattle were a source of both money and food and suggest that the cow's sacred position may have descended from the concept of the sacred bull in Dravidian culture.

The concept of *karma* is governed by the *dharma*, or the law. A law regulating human behavior, the *dharma* imposes different requirements on different individuals depending on their status in society. Those high on the social scale, such as *brahmins* and *kshatriyas*, are held to a more strict form of behavior than are *sudras*. The *brahmin*, for example, is expected to abstain from eating meat, because that would entail the killing of another living being, thus interrupting its *karma*.

How the concept of reincarnation originated is not known, although it was apparently not unusual for early peoples to believe that the individual soul would be reborn in a different form in a later life. In any case, in India the concept may have had practical causes as well as consequences. In the first place, it tended to provide religious sanction for the rigid class divisions that had begun to emerge in Indian society after the Aryan conquest, and it provided moral and political justification for the privileges of those on the higher end of the scale.

At the same time, the concept of reincarnation provided certain compensations for those lower on the ladder of life. For example, it gave hope to the poor that if they behaved properly in this life, they might improve their condition in the next. It also provided a means for unassimilated groups such as ethnic minorities to find a place in Indian society while at the same time permitting them to maintain their distinctive way of life.

The ultimate goal of achieving "good" *karma*, as we have seen, was to escape the cycle of existence. To the sophisticated, the nature of that release was a spiritual union of the individual soul with the Great World Soul, *Brahman*, described in the Upanishads as a form of dreamless sleep, free from earthly desires. Such a

✦ **TRIPLE-HEADED SIVA**   In the first centuries of the first millennium C.E., Hindus began to adopt Buddhist rock art. One of the most outstanding examples is at the Elephanta Caves, near the modern city of Mumbai (Bombay). Dominating the cave is this 18-foot-high triple-headed statue of Siva, representing the Hindu deity in all his various aspects. The central figure presents him in total serenity, enveloped in absolute knowledge. The angry profile on the left portrays him as the destroyer, struggling against time, death, and other negative forces. The right-hand profile shows his loving and feminine side in the guise of his beautiful wife Parvati.

© Royal Smeets Offset, Weert

DANCING SIVA   The Hindu deity Siva is often presented in the form of a bronze statue, performing a cosmic dance in which he simultaneously creates and destroys the universe. While his upper right hand creates the cosmos, his upper left hand reduces it in flames, and the lower two hands offer eternal blessing. Siva's dancing statues present to his followers the visual message of his power and compassion.

concept, however, was undoubtedly too ethereal for the average Indian, who needed a more concrete form of heavenly salvation, a place of beauty and bliss after a life of disease and privation.

It was probably for this reason that the Hindu religion—in some ways so otherworldly and ascetic— came to be peopled with a multitude of very human gods and goddesses. It has been estimated that the Hindu pantheon contains more than 33,000 deities. Only a small number are primary ones, however, notably the so-called trinity of gods: Brahman the Creator, Vishnu the Preserver, and Siva (originally the Vedic god Rudra) the Destroyer. Although Brahman (sometimes in his concrete form called Brahma) is considered to be the highest god, Vishnu and Siva take precedence in the devotional exercises of many Hindus, who can be roughly divided into Vishnuites and Saivites. In addition to the trinity of gods, all of whom have wives with readily identifiable roles and personalities, there are countless minor deities, each again with his or her own specific function, such as bringing good fortune, arranging a good marriage, or guaranteeing a son in childbirth.

The rich variety and earthy character of many Hindu deities are repugnant to many Christians and Muslims, to whom God is an all-seeing and transcendent deity. Many Hindus, however, regard the multitude of gods as simply different manifestations of one ultimate reality. The various deities also provide a useful means for ordinary Indians to personify their religious feelings. Even though some individuals among the early Aryans attempted to communicate with the gods through sacrifice or asceticism, most Indians undoubtedly sought to satisfy their own individual religious needs through devotion, which they expressed through ritual ceremonies and offerings at a Hindu temple. Such offerings were not only a way to seek salvation, but also a means of satisfying all the aspirations of daily life.

Over the centuries, then, Hinduism changed radically from its origins in Aryan tribal society and became a religion of the vast majority of the Indian people. Concern with a transcendental union between the individual soul and the Great World Soul contrasted with practical desires for material wealth and happiness; ascetic self-denial contrasted with an earthy emphasis on the pleasures and values of sexual union between marriage partners. All of these became aspects of Hinduism, the religion of 70 percent of the Indian people.

Buddhism: The Middle Path

In the sixth century B.C.E., a new doctrine appeared in northern India that soon began to rival Hinduism's popularity throughout the subcontinent. This new doctrine was called Buddhism. The historical founder of Buddhism, Siddhartha Gautama, was a native of a small principality in the foothills of the Himalaya Mountains in what is today southern Nepal. He was born in the mid-sixth century B.C.E., the son of a ruling *kshatriya* family. According to tradition, the young Siddhartha was raised in affluent surroundings and trained, like many other members of his class, in the martial arts. On reaching maturity, he married and began to raise a family. However, at the age of twenty-nine he suddenly discovered the pain of illness, the sorrow of death, and the degradation caused by old age in the lives of ordinary people and exclaimed: "Would that sickness, age, and death might be forever bound!" From that time on, he decided to dedicate his life to determining the cause and seeking the cure for human suffering.

To find the answers to these questions, Siddhartha abandoned his home and family and traveled widely. At first he tried to follow the model of the ascetics, but he eventually decided that self-mortification did not lead to a greater understanding of life and abandoned the practice. Then one day after a lengthy period of meditation under a tree, he finally achieved enlightenment as to the meaning of life and spent the remainder of his life preaching it. His conclusions, as embodied in his teachings, became the philosophy (or as some would have it, the religion) of Buddhism. According to legend, the Devil (the Indian term is *Mara*) attempted desperately to tempt him with political power and the company of beautiful girls. But Siddhartha Gautama resisted:

Pleasure is brief as a flash of lightning
Or like an autumn shower, only for a moment. . . .
Why should I then covet the pleasures you speak of?
I see your bodies are full of all impurity:
Birth and death, sickness and age are yours.
I seek the highest prize, hard to attain by men—
The true and constant wisdom of the wise.[7]

How much the modern doctrine of Buddhism resembles the original teachings of Siddhartha Gautama is open to debate, since much time has elapsed since his death and original texts relating his ideas are lacking. Nor is it certain that Siddhartha even intended to found a new religion or doctrine. In some respects, his ideas could be viewed as a reformist form of Hinduism, much as Martin Luther saw Protestantism as a reformation of Christianity. Siddhartha accepted much of the belief system of Hinduism, if not all of its practices. For example, he accepted the concept of reincarnation and the role of *karma* as a means of influencing the movement of individual souls up and down in the scale of life. He followed Hinduism in praising nonviolence and borrowed the idea of living a life of simplicity and chastity from the ascetics. Moreover, his vision of metaphysical reality—commonly known as Nirvana—is closer to the Hindu concept of *Brahman* than it is to the Christian concept of heavenly salvation. Nirvana, which involves an extinction of selfhood and a final reunion with the Great World Soul, is sometimes likened to a dreamless sleep or to a kind of "blowing out" (as of a candle). Buddhists occasionally remark that someone who asks for a description does not understand the concept.

At the same time, the new doctrine differed from existing Hindu practices in a number of key ways. In the first place, Siddhartha denied the existence of an individual soul. To him, the Hindu concept of *Atman*—the individual soul—meant that the soul was subject to rebirth and thus did not achieve a complete liberation from the cares of this world. In fact, Siddhartha denied the ultimate reality of the material world in its entirety and taught that it was an illusion to be transcended. Siddhartha's idea of achieving Nirvana was based on his conviction that the pain, poverty, and sorrow that afflict human beings are caused essentially by their attachment to the things of this world. Once worldly cares are abandoned, pain and sorrow can be overcome. With this knowledge comes *bodhi*, or wisdom (source of the term *Buddhism* and the familiar name for Gautama the Wise: Gautama Buddha).

Achieving this understanding is a key step on the road to Nirvana, which, as in Hinduism, is a form of release

Chronology

ANCIENT INDIA

Harappan civilization	c. 2600–1900 B.C.E.
Arrival of the Aryans	c. 1500 B.C.E.
Life of Gautama Buddha	c. 560–480 B.C.E.
Invasion of India by Alexander the Great	326 B.C.E.
Mauryan dynasty founded	324 B.C.E.
Reign of Chandragupta Maurya	324–301 B.C.E.
Reign of Asoka	269–232 B.C.E.
Collapse of Mauryan dynasty	183 B.C.E.
Rise of Kushan Kingdom	c. first century C.E.

from the wheel of life. According to tradition, Siddhartha transmitted this message in a sermon to his disciples in a deer park at Sarnath, not far from the modern city of Benares (also known as Varanasi). Like so many messages, it is deceptively simple and is enclosed in four noble truths: life is suffering; suffering is caused by desire; the way to end suffering is to end desire; and the way to end desire is to avoid the extremes of a life of vulgar materialism and a life of self-torture and to follow the "Middle Path." This Middle Path, which is also known as the Eightfold Way, calls for right knowledge, right purpose, right speech, right conduct, right occupation, right effort, right awareness, and right meditation (see the box on p. 51).

Buddhism also differed from Hinduism in its relative egalitarianism. Although Siddhartha accepted the idea of reincarnation (and hence the idea that human beings differ as a result of *karma* accumulated in a previous existence), he rejected the Hindu division of humanity into rigidly defined castes based on previous reincarnations and taught that all human beings could aspire to Nirvana as a result of their behavior in this life—a message that likely helped Buddhism win support among people at the lower end of the social scale.

In addition, Buddhism was much simpler than Hinduism. Siddhartha rejected the panoply of gods that had become identified with Hinduism and forbade his followers to worship his person or his image after his death. In fact, many Buddhists view Buddhism as a philosophy rather than a religion.

After Siddhartha Gautama's death in 480 B.C.E., dedicated disciples carried his message the length and breadth of India. Buddhist monasteries were established throughout the subcontinent, and temples and stupas (stone towers housing relics of the Buddha) sprang up throughout the countryside.

HOW TO ACHIEVE ENLIGHTENMENT

One of the most famous passages in Buddhist literature is the sermon at Sarnath, which Siddhartha Gautama delivered to his followers in a deer park outside the holy city of Varanasi (Benares), in the Ganges River valley. Here he set forth the key ideas that would define Buddhist beliefs for centuries to come.

THE SERMON AT BENARES

Thus have I heard: at one time the Lord dwelt at Benares at Isipatana in the Deer Park. There the Lord addressed the five monks:—

"These two extremes, monks, are not to be practiced by one who has gone forth from the world. What are the two? That conjoined with the passions and luxury, low, vulgar, common, ignoble, and useless; and that conjoined with self-torture, painful, ignoble, and useless. Avoiding these two extremes the Tathagata has gained the enlightenment of the Middle Path, which produces insight and knowledge and tends to calm, to higher knowledge, enlightenment, Nirvana.

"And what, monks, is the Middle Path, of which the Tathagata has gained enlightenment, which produces insight and knowledge, and tends to calm, to higher knowledge, enlightenment, Nirvana? This is the noble Eightfold Way: namely, right view, right intention, right speech, right action, right livelihood, right effort, right mindfulness, right concentration. This, monks, is the Middle Path, of which the Tathagata has gained enlightenment, which produces insight and knowledge, and tends to calm, to higher knowledge, enlightenment, Nirvana.

1. Now this, monks, is the noble truth of pain: birth is painful, old age is painful, sickness is painful, death is painful, sorrow, lamentation, dejection, and despair are painful. Contact with unpleasant things is painful, not getting what one wishes is painful. In short the five groups of graspings are painful.
2. Now this, monks, is the noble truth of the cause of pain: the craving, which tends to rebirth, combined with pleasure and lust, finding pleasure here and there; namely, the craving for passion, the craving for existence, the craving for nonexistence.
3. Now this, monks, is the noble truth of the cessation of pain, the cessation without a remainder of craving, the abandonment, forsaking, release, nonattachment.
4. Now this, monks, is the noble truth of the way that leads to the cessation of pain: this is the noble Eightfold Way; namely, right view, right intention, right speech, right action, right livelihood, right effort, right mindfulness, right concentration.

"And when, monks, in these four noble truths my due knowledge and insight with its three sections and twelve divisions was well purified, then, monks, . . . I had attained the highest complete enlightenment. This I recognized. Knowledge arose in me, insight arose that the release of my mind is unshakable; this is my last existence; now there is no rebirth."

Women were permitted to join the monastic order but only in an inferior position. As Siddhartha had explained, women are "soon angered," "full of passion," and "stupid": "That is the reason . . . why women have no place in public assemblies . . . and do not earn their living by any profession." Still, the position of women tended to be better in Buddhist societies than it was elsewhere in ancient India (see the box on p. 52).

During the next centuries, Buddhism began to compete actively with Hindu beliefs, as well as with another new faith known as Jainism. Jainism was founded by Mahavira, a contemporary of Siddhartha Gautama. Resembling Buddhism in its rejection of the reality of the material world, Jainism was more extreme in practice. Where Siddhartha Gautama called for the "middle way" between passion and luxury and pain and self-torture, Mahavira preached a doctrine of extreme simplicity to his followers, who kept no possessions and relied on begging for a living. Some even rejected clothing and wandered through the world naked. Perhaps because of its insistence on a life of poverty, Jainism failed to attract enough adherents to become a major doctrine and never received official support. According to tradition, however, Chandragupta Maurya accepted Mahavira's doctrine after abdicating the throne and fasted to death in a Jain monastery.

ASOKA, A BUDDHIST MONARCH

Buddhism received an important boost when Asoka, the grandson of Chandragupta Maurya, converted to Buddhism in the third century B.C.E. Asoka (269–232 B.C.E.) is widely considered the greatest ruler in the history of India. Reportedly, Asoka began his reign conquering, pillaging, and killing, but after his conversion to Buddhism, he began to regret his bloodthirsty past and attempted to rule benevolently.

Asoka directed that banyan trees and shelters be placed along the road to provide shade and rest for weary travelers. He sent Buddhist missionaries throughout India and ordered the erection of stone pillars with official edicts and Buddhist inscriptions to instruct people in the proper way (see Map 2.2). According to tradition, his son converted the island of Sri Lanka to Buddhism, and the peoples there accepted a tributary relationship with the Mauryan Empire.

THE VOICES OF SILENCE

Most of what is known about the lives of women in ancient India comes from the Vedas or other texts written by men. Classical Sanskrit was the exclusive property of upper-caste males for use in religious and court functions. There are a few examples of women's writings that date from this period. In the first poem quoted here, a Buddhist nun living in the sixth century B.C.E. reflects on her sense of spiritual salvation and physical release from the drudgery of daily life. The other two poems were produced several hundred years later in southern India by anonymous female authors at a time when strict Hindu traditions had not yet been established in the area. Poetry and song were an essential part of daily life, as women sang while working in the fields, drawing water at the well, or reflecting on the hardships of their daily lives. The second poem quoted here breathes the sensuous joy of sex, while the third expresses the simultaneous grief and pride of a mother as she sends her only son off to war.

"A WOMAN WELL SET FREE! HOW FREE I AM"

A woman well set free! How free I am,
How wonderfully free, from kitchen drudgery.
Free from the harsh grip of hunger,
And from empty cooking pots,
Free too of that unscrupulous man,
The weaver of sunshades.
Calm now, and serene I am,
All lust and hatred purged.
To the shade of the spreading trees I go
And contemplate my happiness.

Translated by Uma Chakravarti and Kumkum Roy

"WHAT SHE SAID TO HER GIRLFRIEND"

What she said to her girlfriend:
On beaches washed by seas
older than the earth,
in the groves filled with bird-cries,
on the banks shaded by a punnai
clustered with flowers,
    when we made love
my eyes saw him
and my ears heard him;

my arms grow beautiful
in the coupling
and grow lean
as they come away.
    What shall I make of this?

Translated by A. K. Ramanujan

"HER PURPOSE IS FRIGHTENING, HER SPIRIT CRUEL"

Her purpose is frightening, her spirit cruel.
That she comes from an ancient house is fitting, surely.
In the battle the day before yesterday,
her father attacked an elephant and died there on the field.
In the battle yesterday,
her husband faced a row of troops and fell.
And today,
she hears the battle drum,
and, eager beyond reason, gives him a spear in his hand,
wraps a white garment around him,
smears his dry tuft with oil,
and, having nothing but her one son,
"Go!" she says, sending him to battle.

Translated by George L. Hart III

THE RULE OF THE FISHES: INDIA AFTER THE MAURYAS

After Asoka's death in 232 B.C.E., the Mauryan Empire began to decline. In 183 B.C.E., the last Mauryan ruler was overthrown by one of his military commanders, and India slipped back into disunity. A number of new kingdoms, some of them perhaps influenced by the memory of the Alexandrian conquests, arose along the fringes of the subcontinent in Bactria, known today as Afghanistan. In the first century C.E., Indo-European-speaking peoples fleeing from the nomadic Xiongnu warriors in Central Asia seized power in the area and proclaimed the new Kushan Kingdom (see Chapter 9). For the next two centuries, the Kushanas extended their political sway over northern India as far as the central Ganges valley, while other kingdoms scuffled for predominance elsewhere on the subcontinent. India would not see unity again for another five hundred years.

Several reasons for India's failure to maintain a unified empire have been proposed. Some historians suggest that a decline in regional trade during the first millennium C.E. may have contributed to the growth of small land-based kingdoms, which drew their primary income from agriculture. The tenacity of the Aryan tradition with its emphasis on tribal rivalries may also have contributed. Although the Mauryan rulers tried to impose a more centralized organization, clan loyalties once again came to the fore after the collapse of the Mauryan dynasty. Furthermore, the behavior of the ruling class was characterized by what Indians call the "rule of the fishes," which glorified warfare as the natural activity of the king and the aristocracy. The *Arthasastra*, which set forth a model of a centralized Indian state, assumed that war was the "sport of kings."

THE EXUBERANT WORLD OF INDIAN CULTURE

Few cultures in the world are as rich and varied as that of India. Most societies excel in some forms of artistic and literary achievement and not in others, but India has produced great works in almost all fields of cultural endeavor—art and sculpture, science, architecture, literature, and music.

Literature

The earliest known Indian literature consists of the four Vedas, which were passed down orally from generation to generation until they were finally written down after the Aryan conquest of India. The Rigveda dates from the second millennium B.C.E. and consists of over a thousand hymns that were used at religious ceremonies. The other three Vedas were written considerably later and contain instructions for performing ritual sacrifices and other ceremonies. The Brahmanas and the Upanishads served as commentaries on the Vedas.

The language of the Vedas was Sanskrit, one of the Indo-European family of languages. After the Aryan conquest of India, Sanskrit gradually declined as a spoken language and was replaced in northern India by a simpler tongue known as Prakrit. Nevertheless, Sanskrit continued to be used as the language of the bureaucracy and literary expression for many centuries after that and, like Latin in medieval Europe, served as a common language of communication (*lingua franca*) between various regions of India. In the south, a variety of Dravidian languages continued to be spoken.

As early as the fifth century B.C.E., Indian grammarians had already codified Sanskrit in order to preserve the authenticity of the Vedas for the spiritual edification of future generations. A famous grammar written by the scholar Panini in the fourth century B.C.E. set forth four thousand grammatical rules prescribing the correct usage of the spoken and written language. This achievement is particularly impressive in that Europe did not have a science of linguistics until the nineteenth century, when it was developed partly as a result of the discovery of the works of Panini and later Indian linguists.

After the development of a writing system sometime in the first millennium B.C.E., India's holy literature was probably inscribed on palm leaves stitched together into a book somewhat similar to the bamboo strips used during the

MAP 2.2   The Empire of Asoka. Asoka, the greatest of Indian monarchs, reigned over the Mauryan dynasty in the third century B.C.E. This map shows the extent of his empire, with the location of the pillar edicts that were erected along major trade routes. ➤ *What were the purposes of these pillars?*

Pillar edicts

Rock and minor rock edicts

Asoka Empire, 250 B.C.E.

BACTRIA

HIMALAYAS

Indus R.

Ganges R.

GUJARAT

Varanasi (Benares)

Pataliputra (Patna)

MAGADHA

DECCAN PLATEAU

Arabian Sea

Godavari R.

Bay of Bengal

MALABAR COAST

Indian Ocean

0   250   500   750 Kilometers
0   250   500 Miles

same period in China. Also written for the first time were India's great historical epics, the Mahabharata and the Ramayana. Both of these epics may have originally been recited at religious ceremonies, but they are essentially historical writings that recount the martial exploits of great Aryan rulers and warriors.

The Mahabharata, consisting of more than 90,000 stanzas, was probably written about 100 B.C.E. and describes in great detail a war between cousins for control of the kingdom about 1000 B.C.E. Interwoven in the narrative are many fantastic legends of the Hindu gods. Above all, the Mahabharata is a tale of moral confrontations and an elucidation of the ethical precepts of the *dharma* (see the box

DRAUPADI'S HUMILIATION

*I*n the Mahabharata, the great Indian epic, Draupadi, wife of the five Pandava brothers, is humiliated by both her husbands and their enemies. One of her husbands insults her by betting and losing her in a dice game to their rival cousins, who in turn demand that Draupadi be summoned immediately to be disrobed in public. Furious, she arrives with her hair unbraided, a sign that she is undergoing her monthly cycle. During such periods women were segregated from men to safeguard the latter from menstrual pollution.

Humiliated, Draupadi implores Lord Krishna for assistance in reinstating her honor. As one of the cousins attempts to unravel her sari, all are amazed at the never-ending folds of her garment. Although the disrobing is foiled, Draupadi's humiliation is complete. She vows revenge, refusing to rebraid her hair until it is bathed in the blood of the cousin. The famous scene has remained a favorite and occurs at a pivotal climax of the epic.

THE MAHABHARATA

Then how was it that a woman like me, wife to the Parthas, friend to you, Lord Krishna, sister of Dhristadyumna, came to be dragged into the hall? Subjected to the law of women, stained with blood, shuddering in my sole piece of clothing, I was grievously dragged into the assembly of the Kurus. In the midst of the kings, inside the hall, overrun by my menses, they watched me, the Dhartarastras [the sons of Dhrtarash-tra], and burst out laughing, the foul-minded! ... Am I not ... [Draupadi], by Law the daughter-in-law of Bhisma and Dhrtarashtra? And I was forcibly reduced to a slave!

---

above). The most famous section of the book is the so-called Bhagavadgita, a sermon by the legendary Indian figure Krishna on the eve of a major battle. In this sermon, mentioned at the beginning of this chapter, Krishna sets forth one of the key ethical maxims of Indian society: in taking action, one must be indifferent to success or failure and consider only the moral rightness of the act itself.

The Ramayana, written at about the same time, is much shorter than the Mahabharata. It is an account of a semi-legendary ruler named Rama who, as the result of a palace intrigue, is banished from the kingdom and forced to live as a hermit in the forest. Later, he fights the demon-king of Sri Lanka (Ceylon), who has kidnapped his beloved wife, Sita. Like the Mahabharata, the Ramayana is strongly imbued with religious and moral significance. Rama himself is portrayed as the ideal Aryan hero, a perfect ruler and an ideal son, while Sita projects the supreme duty of female chastity and wifely loyalty to her husband. The Ramayana is a story of the triumph of good over evil, duty over self-indulgence, and generosity over selfishness. It combines filial and erotic love, conflicts of human passion, character analysis, and poetic descriptions of nature (see the box on p. 55).

The Ramayana also has all the ingredients of an enthralling adventure: giants, wondrous flying chariots, invincible arrows and swords, and magic potions and mantras. One of the real heroes of the story is the monkey-king Hanuman, who flies from India to Sri Lanka to set the great battle in motion. It is no wonder that for millennia the Ramayana has remained a favorite among Indians of all age groups, including a hugely popular TV version produced in recent years.

Architecture and Sculpture

After literature, the greatest achievements of early Indian civilization were in architecture and sculpture. Some of the earliest examples of Indian architecture stem from the time of Emperor Asoka, when Buddhism became the religion of the state. Until the time of the Mauryas, Aryan buildings had been constructed of wood. With the rise of the empire, stone began to be used as artisans arrived in India seeking employment after the destruction of the Per-

➤ **ASOKA'S PILLAR.** Stone pillars like this polished sandstone column, which is 32 feet high, were erected during the reign of Emperor Asoka in the third century B.C.E. Commemorating events in the life of the Buddha, announcing official edicts, or marking routes to the holy sites, they were placed on major trunk roads throughout the Indian subcontinent. The massive size of these pillars, some of which weighed up to 50 tons, underscores the engineering skills of the peoples of ancient India.

© Borromeo/Art Resource, NY

RAMA AND SITA

Over the ages, the conclusion of the Indian epic, the *Ramayana*, has been the focus of considerable debate. *After a long period of captivity at the hands of the demon Ravana, Sita is finally liberated by her husband, King Rama. Although the two enjoy a joyful reunion, the people of Rama's kingdom continue to voice suspicions that she has been defiled by her captor, and he is forced to banish her to a forest, where she gives birth to twin sons. The account reflects the tradition, expressed in the Arthasastra, that a king must place the needs of his subjects over his personal desires. Here we read of Rama's anguished decision as he consults with his brother, Lakshmana.*

By accepting banishment, Sita bows to the authority of her husband and the established moral order. Subservient and long-suffering, she has been lauded as the ideal heroine and feminine role model, imitated by generations of Indian women. At the close of the Ramayana, Rama decides to take Sita back "before all my people." She continues to feel humiliated, however, and begs Mother Earth to open up and swallow her.

THE RAMAYANA

"A king must be blameless."

"Such words pierce my heart," said Lakshmana. "Fire himself proved her innocent. She is fired gold, poured into golden fire!"

Rama said, "Lakshmana, consider what is a king. Kings cannot afford blame. Ill fame is evil to kings; they above all men must be beyond reproach. . . . See into what a chasm of sorrow a King may fall. . . ."

Lakshmana said, "Gradually everything seems to change again, and even an Emperor must pay his way through life."

Rama faced his brother. "It must be! It's all the same, can't you see? Where there is growth there is decay; where there is prosperity there is ruin; and where there is birth there is death."

Lakshmana sighed hopelessly. "Well, what will you do?"

"Sita expects to go to the forests tomorrow. Let Sumantra the Charioteer drive you both there, and when you arrive by the river Ganga abandon her."

"She will die. Your child will die!"

"No," said Rama. "I command you! Not a word to anyone."

Lakshmana said, "Surely a king is remote and lonely, and very far from reason. We cannot speak to you. . . ."

Rama said, "Each person can be told what he will understand of the nature of the world, and no more than that—for the rest, take my word." . . .

Sita was forever beautiful. Wearing her ornaments she turned slowly around and looked at every person there. "Rama, let me prove my innocence, here before everyone."

"I give my permission," said Rama.

Then Sita stepped a little away from him and said, "Mother Earth, if I have been faithful to Rama take me home, hide me!"

Earth rolled and moved beneath our feet. With a great rumbling noise the ground broke apart near Sita and a deep chasm opened, lighted from below with bright lights like lightning flashes, from the castles of the Naga serpent kings. . . .

On that throne sat Mother Earth. Earth was not old, she was fair to look on, she was not sad but smiling. She wore flowers and a girdle of seas. Earth supports all life, but she feels no burden in all that. She is patient. She was patient then, under the Sun and Moon and through the rainfalls of countless years. She was patient with seasons and with kings and farmers; she endured all things and bore no line of care from it.

But this was the end of her long patience with Rama. Earth looked at her husband Janaka and smiled. Then she stretched out her arms and took her only child Sita on her lap. She folded her beautiful arms around her daughter and laid Sita's head softly against her shoulder as a mother would. Earth stroked her hair with her fair hands, and Sita closed her eyes like a little girl.

The throne sank back underground and they all were gone; the Nagas dove beneath the ground and the crevice closed gently over them, forever.

---

sian Empire by Alexander. Many of these stone carvers accepted the patronage of Emperor Asoka, who used them to spread Buddhist ideas throughout the subcontinent.

There were three main types of religious structure: the pillar, the stupa, and the rock chamber. During Asoka's reign, many stone columns were erected alongside roads to commemorate the events in the Buddha's life and mark pilgrim routes to holy places. Weighing up to 50 tons each and rising as high as 32 feet, these polished sandstone pillars were topped with a carved capital, usually depicting lions uttering the Buddha's message. Ten remain standing today.

A stupa was originally meant to house a relic of the Buddha, such as a lock of his hair or a branch of the famous Bodhi tree, and was constructed in the form of a burial mound (the pyramids in Egypt also derived from burial mounds). Eventually, the stupa became a place for devotion and the most familiar form of Buddhist architecture. It rose to considerable heights and was surmounted with a spire, possibly representing the stages of existence en route to Nirvana. According to legend, Asoka ordered the construction of 84,000 stupas throughout India to promote the Buddha's message. A few survive today, including the famous stupa at Sanchi, begun under Asoka and completed two centuries later.

The final form of early Indian architecture is the rock chamber carved out of a cliff on the side of a mountain.

⇒ **THE BIRTH OF THE BUDDHA.** As Buddhism evolved, transforming Gautama Buddha from mortal to god, so did Buddhist art change as well. The representation of the Buddha in statuary and in relief panels began to illustrate the story of his life. Reflecting the multicultural influences on the Kushan dynasty, local artists blended Indian with Hellenistic and Central Asian traditions in what is known as the Gandharan style. Here the infant Siddhartha Gautama is seen emerging from his mother's hip, welcomed by the Hindu gods Indra and Brahma. Notice that his mother, Queen Maya, dressed in Greek-style draperies and with wreathed hair, appears in the form of a traditional earth spirit standing under a tree. At this time, both Buddhism and Christianity adopted the halo from earlier traditions as a sign of divinity.

Asoka began the construction of these chambers to provide rooms to house monks or wandering ascetics and to serve as halls for religious ceremonies. The chambers were rectangular in form, with pillars, an altar, and a vault, reminiscent of Roman basilicas in the West. The three most famous chambers of this period are at Bhaja, Karli, and Ajanta; this last one contains twenty-nine rooms.

All three forms of architecture were embellished with decorations. Consisting of detailed reliefs and freestanding statues of deities, other human figures, and animals, these decorations are permeated with a sense of nature and the vitality of life. Many reflect an amalgamation of popular and sacred themes, of Buddhist, Vedic, and pre-Aryan religious motifs, such as male and female earth spirits. Until the second century C.E., Siddhartha Gautama was represented only through symbols, such as the wheel of life, the Bodhi tree, and the footprint, perhaps because artists felt that it was impossible to render a visual impression of the Buddha in the state of Nirvana. After the spread of Mahayana Buddhism in the second century,

when the Buddha was portrayed as a god, his image began to appear in stone.

By this time, India had established its own unique religious art. The art is permeated by sensuousness and exuberance and is often overtly sexual. These scenes are meant to express otherworldly delights, not the pleasures of this world. The sensuous paradise that adorned the religious art of ancient India represented salvation and fulfillment for the ordinary Indian.

Science

Our knowledge of Indian science is limited by the paucity of written sources, but it is evident that ancient Indians had amassed an impressive amount of scientific knowledge in a number of areas. Especially notable was their work in astronomy, where they charted the movements of the heavenly bodies and recognized the spherical nature of the earth at an early date. Their ideas of physics were similar to those of the Greeks; matter was divided into the five

© Robert Harding Picture Library

⇜ SANCHI GATE AND STUPA. First constructed during the reign of Emperor Asoka in the third century B.C.E., the stupa at Sanchi was enlarged over time, eventually becoming the greatest Buddhist monument in the entire Indian subcontinent. Originally intended to house a relic of the Buddha, the stupa became a holy place for devotion and a familiar form of Buddhist architecture. Sanchi's four elaborately carved stone gates, each over 40 feet high, display exciting statues of Buddhist symbolism, including both animals and human figures.

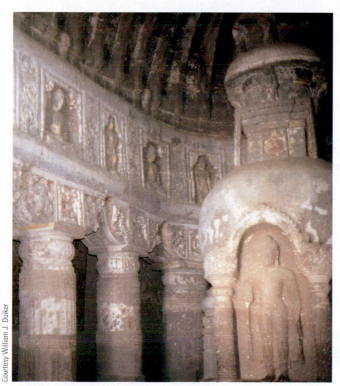

Courtesy William J. Duiker

⇜ A BUDDHIST CHAPEL. Carved out of solid rock cliffs during the Mauryan dynasty, these rock chambers served as small meditation halls for traveling Buddhist monks. Initially, they resembled freestanding shrines of wood and thatch from the Vedic period. Subsequently, chapels such as this fifth-century one at Ajanta evolved into elaborate structures reminiscent of Roman basilicas in the West. Witness the ornate columns, the ribbed vault, and the statue of the Buddha incorporated into the stupa.

elements of earth, air, fire, water, and ether. Many of their technological achievements are impressive, notably the quality of their textiles and the massive stone pillars erected during the reign of Asoka. The pillars weighed up to 50 tons each and were transported many miles to their final destination.

CONCLUSION

While the peoples of North Africa and the Middle East were actively building the first civilizations, a similar process was getting under way in the Indus River valley. Much has been learned about the nature of the Indus valley civilization in recent years, but without written records there are inherent limits to our understanding. How did the Harappan people deal with the fundamental human problems mentioned at the close of Chapter 1? The answers remain tantalizingly elusive.

As often happened elsewhere, however, the collapse of Harappan civilization did not lead to the total disappearance of its culture. The new society that eventually emerged throughout the subcontinent after the coming of the Aryans was clearly an amalgam of two highly distinctive cultures, Aryan and Dravidian, each of which made a significant contribution to the politics, the social institutions, and the creative impulse of ancient Indian civilization.

With the rise of the Mauryan dynasty in the fourth century B.C.E., the distinctive features of a great civilization begin to be clearly visible. It was extensive in its scope, embracing the entire Indian subcontinent and

© Royal Smeets Offset, Weert

✤ **THE IDEAL BUDDHIST COUPLE.** Although originally the Aryans, a pastoral people, espoused a patriarchal religion peopled with male deities preoccupied with conquest and war, after their arrival in India they gradually incorporated female fertility spirits inherited from the local agrarian societies into their pantheon. This stylized couple, who welcome the faithful to the Buddhist rock temple at Karli, symbolize the essence of human life, at harmony with both the temporal and spiritual worlds. This sculpture dates from the first century C.E.

eventually, in the form of Buddhism and Hinduism, spreading to China and Southeast Asia. But the underlying ethnic, linguistic, and cultural diversity of the Indian people posed a constant challenge to the unity of the state. After the collapse of the Mauryas, the subcontinent would not come under a single authority again for several hundred years.

In the meantime, another great experiment was taking place far to the northeast, across the Himalaya Mountains. Like many other civilizations of antiquity, the first Chinese state was concentrated on a major river system. And like them, too, its political and cultural achievements eventually spread far beyond their original habitat. In the next chapter, we turn to the civilization of ancient China.

| 6000 B.C.E. | 3000 B.C.E. | 2000 B.C.E. | 1000 B.C.E. |

Harappan civilization

Founding of Mauryan dynasty

Invasion of Aryans

Reign of Asoka

First agricultural settlements

Trading relations with Middle East begin

Sailors follow monsoon winds across Indian Ocean

Iron Age begins

Invention of writing system

Life of Gautama Buddha

Asoka's pillars erected

Mahabharata

CHAPTER NOTES

1. Quoted in Richard Lannoy, *The Speaking Tree: A Study of Indian Culture and Society* (London, 1971), p. 318.
2. The quotation is from ibid., p. 319. Note also that the *Law of Manu* says that "punishment alone governs all created beings. . . . The whole world is kept in order by punishment, for a guiltless man is hard to find."
3. Strabo's *Geography*, book 15, quoted in Michael Edwardes, *A History of India: From the Earliest Times to the Present Day* (London, 1961), p. 55.
4. Ibid., p. 54.
5. From the *Law of Manu*, quoted in A. L. Basham, *The Wonder That Was India* (London, 1961), pp. 180–181.
6. Mundaka Upanishad 1:2, quoted in William Theodore de Bary et al., eds., *Sources of Indian Tradition* (New York, 1966), pp. 28–29.
7. Quoted in Ananda K. Coomaraswamy, *Buddha and the Gospel of Buddhism* (New York, 1964), p. 34.

SUGGESTED READING

Several standard histories of India provide a good overview of the ancient period. One of the most readable and reliable is S. Wolpert, *New History of India*, 3d ed. (New York, 1989). V. A. Smith's edition of *The Oxford History of India*, 4th ed. (Oxford, 1981), although somewhat out of date, contains a wealth of information on various aspects of early Indian history. Also of note is H. H. Dodwell, ed., *The Cambridge History of India*, 6 vols. (Cambridge, 1922–1953).

By far the most informative and readable narrative on the history of India in premodern times is still A. L. Basham, *The Wonder That Was India* (London, 1961), which contains informative sections on prehistory, economy, language, art and literature, society, and everyday life. Also useful is A. L. Basham, ed., *A Cultural History of India* (Oxford, 1975). For a stimulating analysis of Indian culture and society in general, consult R. Lannoy, *The Speaking Tree: A Study of Indian Culture and Society* (London, 1971). R. Thapar, *Interpreting Early India* (Delhi, 1992), provides a recent view by an Indian historian.

Because of the relative paucity of archaeological exploration in South Asia, evidence for the Harappan period is not as voluminous as for areas such as Mesopotamia and the Nile valley. Some of the best work has been written by scholars who actually worked at the sites. For a recent account, see J. M. Kenoyer, *Ancient Cities of the Indus Valley Civilization* (Karachi, 1998). A somewhat more extensive study is B. Allchin and R. Allchin, *The Birth of Indian Civilization, India and Pakistan Before 500 B.C.* (New York, 1968). For a detailed and well-illustrated analysis, see G. L. Possehl, ed., *The Harappan Civilization: A Contemporary Perspective* (Amherst, N.Y., 1983). Commercial relations between Harappa and its neighbors are treated in S. Ratnagar, *Encounters: The Westerly Trade of the Harappan Civilization* (Oxford, 1981). On the Mauryan period, see D. D. Kosambi, *The Culture and Civilization of Ancient India* (London, 1965), and R. Thapar, *Asoka and the Decline of the Mauryas* (Oxford, 1961).

There are a number of good books on the introduction of Buddhism into Indian society. Buddha's ideals are presented in A. K. Coomaraswamy, *Buddha and the Gospel of Buddhism* (London, 1916; rev. ed., New York, 1964), and E. Conze, *Buddhism: Its Essence and Development* (Oxford, 1951). Also see H. Nakamura and M. B. Dasgupta, *Indian Buddhism: A Survey with Bibliographical Notes* (New Delhi, 1987). H. Akira, *A History of Indian Buddhism: From Sakyamuni to Early Mahayana* (Honolulu, 1990), provides a detailed analysis of early activities by Siddhartha Gautama and his followers. The intimate relationship between Buddhism and commerce is discussed in Liu Hsin-ju, *Ancient India and Ancient China: Trades and Religious Exchanges* (Oxford, 1988).

Hinduism, its origins and development, is the subject of B. Walker, *Hindu World*, 2 vols. (London, 1969). For a more general treatment, see S. N. Dasgupta, *A History of Indian Philosophy*, 5 vols. (Cambridge, 1922–1955), and S. Radhakrishnan, *Indian Philosophy*, rev. ed., 2 vols. (London, 1958).

There are a number of excellent surveys of Indian art, including the comprehensive S. L. Huntington, *The Art of Ancient India: Buddhist, Hindu, Jain* (New York, 1985), and the concise *Indian Art* (London, 1976) by R. Craven. See also V. Dehejia's *Devi: The Great Goddess* (Washington, D.C., 1999) and *Indian Art* (London, 1997).

Few general surveys of Indian literature exist, perhaps because of the magnitude and diversity of India's literature. A good textbook for college students is E. C. Dimock, *The Literatures of India: An Introduction* (Chicago, 1974), which traces Indian literary achievement from the epics to the modern Hindi film.

Many editions of Sanskrit literature are available in English translation. Many are available in the multivolume *Harvard Oriental Series*. For a shorter annotated anthology of selections from the Indian classics, consult S. N. Hay, ed., *Sources of Indian Tradition*, 2 vols. (New York, 1988), or J. B. Alphonso-Karkala, *An Anthology of Indian Literature*, 2d rev. ed. (New Delhi, 1987), put out by the Indian Council for Cultural Relations.

The Mahabharata and Ramayana have been rewritten for 2,500 years. Fortunately, the vibrant versions, retold by William Buck and condensed to 400 pages each, reproduce the spirit of the originals and enthrall today's imagination. See W. Buck, *Mahabharata* (Berkeley, Calif., 1973) and *Ramayana* (Berkeley, Calif., 1976). On the role played by women writers in ancient India, see S. Tharu and K. Lalita, eds., *Women Writing in India: 600 B.C. to the Present*, vol. 1 (New York, 1991).

ℹ INFOTRAC COLLEGE EDITION

For additional reading, go to InfoTrac College Edition, your online research library at
http://web1.infotrac-college.com

Enter the search term "Vedas" using Keywords.

Enter the search term "Hinduism" using the Subject Guide.

Enter the search term "Buddhism" using the Subject Guide.

Enter the search terms "India history" using Keywords.

Enter the search terms "Upanishad or Rigveda or Mahabharata" using Keywords.

Courtesy of William J. Duiker

Chapter 3

CHINA IN ANTIQUITY

FOCUS QUESTIONS

- How did geography influence the civilization that arose in China?
- What were the major tenets of Confucianism, Legalism, and Daoism, and what role did each play in Chinese civilization?
- What were the key aspects of social and economic life in early China?
- What role did nomadic peoples play in early Chinese history?
- ➤ What concepts of kingship and political and governmental institutions characterized each of the major dynasties of early China— the Shang, the Zhou, the Qin, and the Han?

The Master said: "If the government seeks to rule by decree, and to maintain order by the use of punishment, the people will seek to evade punishment and have no sense of shame. But if government leads by virtue and governs through the rules of propriety, the people will feel shame and seek to correct their mistakes."

That statement is from the *Analects*, a collection of remarks by the Chinese philosopher Confucius that were gathered together by his disciples and published after his death in the fifth century B.C.E. Confucius lived at a time when Chinese society was in a state of increasing disarray. The political principles that had governed society since the founding of the Zhou dynasty six centuries earlier were widely ignored, and squabbling principalities scuffled for primacy as the power of the Zhou court steadily declined. The common people groaned under the weight of an oppressive manorial system that left them at the mercy of their feudal lords.

In the midst of this turmoil, Confucius traveled the length of the kingdom observing events and seeking employment as a political counselor. In the process, he attracted a number of disciples, to whom he expounded a set of ideas that in later years served as the guiding principles for the Chinese empire. Some of his ideas are strikingly modern in their thrust. Among them is the revolutionary proposition that government depends on the will of the people.

The civilization that produced Confucius had originated more than fifteen hundred years earlier along the two great river systems of East Asia, the Yellow and the Yangtze. This vibrant new civilization, which we know today as ancient China, expanded gradually over its neighboring areas. By the third century B.C.E., it had emerged as a great empire, as well as the dominant cultural and political force in the entire region.

Like Sumer, Harappa, and Egypt, the civilization of ancient China began as a collection of autonomous villages cultivating food crops along a major river system. Improvements in agricultural techniques led to a food surplus and the growth of an urban civilization characterized by more complex political and social institutions, as well as new forms of artistic and intellectual creativity.

Like its counterparts elsewhere, ancient China faced the challenge posed by the appearance of pastoral peoples on its borders. Unlike Harappa, Sumer, and Egypt, however, ancient China was able to surmount that challenge, and many of its institutions and cultural values survived intact down to the beginning of the twentieth century. For that reason, Chinese civilization is sometimes described as the oldest continuous civilization on earth. •

THE LAND AND PEOPLE OF CHINA

According to Chinese legend, Chinese society was founded by a series of rulers who brought the first rudiments of civilization to the region nearly five thousand years ago. The first was Fu Xi (Fu Hsi), the ox-tamer, who "knotted cords for hunting and fishing," domesticated animals, and introduced the beginnings of family life. The second was Shen Nong (Shen Nung), the divine farmer, who "bent wood for plows and hewed wood for plowshares." He taught the people the techniques of agriculture. Last came Huang Di (Huang Ti), the Yellow Emperor, who "strung a piece of wood for the bow, and whittled little sticks of wood for the arrows." Legend credits Huang Di with creating the Chinese system of writing, as well as with inventing the bow and arrow.[1] Modern historians, of course, do not accept the literal accuracy of such legends but view them instead as part of the process whereby early peoples attempt to make sense of the world and their role in it. Nevertheless, such re-creations of a mythical past often contain an element of truth. Although there is no clear evidence that the "three sovereigns" actually existed, their achievements do symbolize some of the defining characteristics of Chinese civilization: the interaction between nomadic and agricultural peoples, the importance of the family as the basic unit of Chinese life, and the development of a unique system of writing.

Human communities have existed in China for several hundred thousand years. Sometime around the eighth millennium B.C.E., the early peoples living along the riverbanks of northern China began to master the cultivation of crops. A number of these early agricultural settlements were in the neighborhood of the Yellow River, where they gave birth to two Neolithic societies known to archaeologists as the Yangshao and the Longshan cultures (sometimes identified in terms of their pottery as the painted and black pottery cultures). Similar communities have been found in the Yangtze valley in central China and along the coast to the south. The southern settlements were based on the cultivation of rice rather than dry crops such as millet, barley, and wheat, but they were as old as those in the north. Thus agriculture, and perhaps other elements of early civilization, may have developed spontaneously in several areas of China rather than radiating outward from one central region.

At first, these simple Neolithic communities were hardly more than villages, but as the inhabitants mastered the rudiments of agriculture, they gradually gave rise to more sophisticated and complex societies. In a pattern that we have already seen elsewhere, civilization gradually spread from these nuclear settlements in the valleys of the Yellow and Yangtze Rivers to other lowland areas of eastern and central China. The two great river valleys, then, can be considered the core regions in the development of Chinese civilization.

Although these densely cultivated valleys eventually became two of the great food-producing areas of the ancient world, China is more than a land of fertile fields. In fact, only 12 percent of the total land area is arable, compared with 23 percent in the United States. Much of the remainder consists of mountains and deserts that ring the country on its northern and western frontiers.

This often arid and forbidding landscape is a dominant feature of Chinese life and has played a significant role in Chinese history. The geographical barriers served to isolate the Chinese people from advanced agrarian societies in other parts of Asia. The frontier regions in the Gobi Desert, Central Asia, and the Tibetan plateau were sparsely inhabited by peoples of Mongolian, Indo-European, or Turkish extraction. Most were pastoral societies, and like the other river valley civilizations, their contacts with the Chinese were often characterized by mutual distrust and conflict. Although less numerous than the Chinese, many of these peoples possessed impressive skills in war and were sometimes aggressive in seeking

wealth or territory in the settled regions south of the Gobi Desert. Over the next two thousand years, the northern frontier became one of the great fault lines of conflict in Asia as Chinese armies attempted to protect precious farmlands from marauding peoples from beyond the frontier. When China was unified and blessed with capable rulers, it could usually keep the nomadic intruders at bay and even bring them under a loose form of Chinese administration. But in times of internal weakness, China was vulnerable to attack from the north, and on several occasions, nomadic peoples succeeded in overthrowing native Chinese rulers and setting up their own dynastic regimes.

From other directions, China normally had little to fear. To the east lay the China Sea, a lair for pirates and the source of powerful typhoons that occasionally ravaged the Chinese coast but otherwise rarely a source of concern. South of the Yangtze River was a hilly region inhabited by a mixture of peoples of varied language and ethnic stock who lived by farming, fishing, or food gathering. They were gradually absorbed in the inexorable expansion of Chinese civilization.

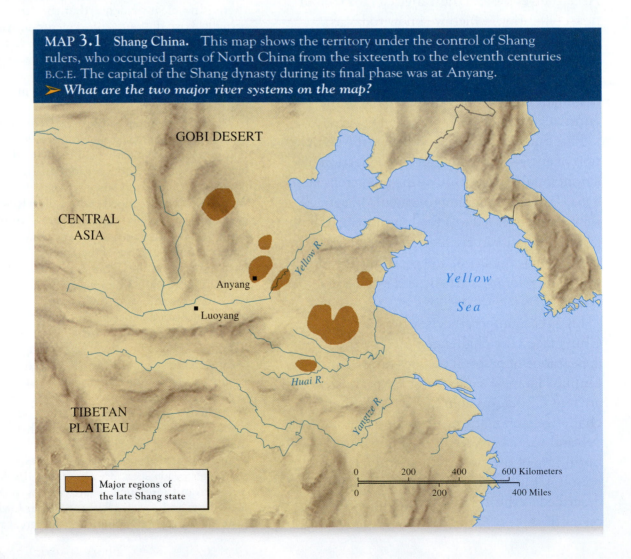

MAP 3.1 Shang China. This map shows the territory under the control of Shang rulers, who occupied parts of North China from the sixteenth to the eleventh centuries B.C.E. The capital of the Shang dynasty during its final phase was at Anyang.
➤ *What are the two major river systems on the map?*

GOBI DESERT

CENTRAL ASIA

Anyang

Luoyang

Yellow R.

Yellow Sea

Huai R.

Yangtze R.

TIBETAN PLATEAU

Major regions of the late Shang state

0   200   400   600 Kilometers
0   200   400 Miles

A Treatise on the Yellow River and Its Canals

Sima Qian (Szu-ma Ch'ien) was a famous historian of the Han dynasty who lived during the second and first centuries B.C.E. In his most famous work, titled Historical Records, he describes the public works projects undertaken during the Xia dynasty to convert the dangerous waters of the Yellow River to human use. Although the identification of irrigation with Yu may be apocryphal, irrigation works were under way in central China at least as early as the sixth century B.C.E., and China later became one of the foremost hydraulic societies in the ancient world.

SIMA QIAN, *HISTORICAL RECORDS*

The documents on the Hsia dynasty tell us that Emperor Yu spent thirteen years controlling and bringing an end to the floods, and during that period, though he passed by the very gate of his own house, he did not take the time to enter. On land he traveled in a cart and on water in a boat; he rode a sledge to cross the mud and wore cleated shoes in climbing the mountains. In this way he marked out the nine provinces, led the rivers along the bases of the mountains, decided what tribute was appropriate for each region in accordance with the quality of its soil, opened up the nine roads, built embankments around the nine marshes, and made a survey of the nine mountains.

Of all the rivers, the Yellow River caused the greatest damage to China by overflowing its banks and inundating the land, and therefore he turned all his attention to controlling it. Thus he led the Yellow River in a course from Chi-shih past Lung-men and south to the northern side of Mount Hua; from there eastward along the foot of Ti-chu Mountain, past the Meng Ford and the confluence of the Lo River to Ta-p'ei. At this point Emperor Yu decided that, since the river was descending from high ground and the flow of the water was rapid and fierce, it would be difficult to guide it over level ground without danger of frequent disastrous breakthroughs. He therefore divided the flow into two channels, leading it along the higher ground to the north, past the Chiang River and so to Ta-lu. There he spread it out to form the Nine Rivers, brought it together again to make the Backward-Flowing River [i.e., tidal river], and thence led it into the Gulf of Pohai. When he had thus opened up the rivers of the nine provinces and fixed the outlets of the nine marshes, peace and order were brought to the lands of the Hsia, and his achievements continued to benefit the Three Dynasties which followed.

The Dawn of Chinese Civilization: The Shang Dynasty

Historians of China have traditionally dated the beginning of Chinese civilization to the founding of the Xia (Hsia) dynasty more than four thousand years ago. Although the precise date for the rise of the Xia is in dispute, recent archaeological evidence confirms its existence. Legend maintains that the founder was a ruler named Yu, who is also credited with introducing irrigation and draining the floodwaters that periodically threatened to inundate the northern China plain (see the box above). The Xia dynasty was replaced by a second dynasty, the Shang, around the sixteenth century B.C.E. (see Map 3.1). The late Shang capital at Anyang, just north of the Yellow River in north-central China, has been excavated by archaeologists. Among the finds were thousands of so-called oracle bones, ox and chicken bones or turtle shells that were used by Shang rulers for divination and to communicate with the gods. The inscriptions on these oracle bones are the earliest known form of Chinese writing and provide much of our information about the beginnings of civilization in China. They describe a culture gradually emerging from the Neolithic to the early Bronze Age.

Political Organization

China under the Shang dynasty was a predominantly agricultural society ruled by an aristocratic class whose major occupation was war. One ancient chronicler complained that "the big affairs of state consist of sacrifice and soldiery."[2] Combat was carried on by means of two-horse chariots. The appearance of chariots in China in the mid-second millennium B.C.E. coincides roughly with similar developments elsewhere, leading some historians to suggest that the Shang ruling class may originally have invaded China from elsewhere in Asia. But items found in Shang burial mounds are similar to Longshan pottery, implying that the Shang ruling elites were linear descendants of the indigenous Neolithic peoples in the area. If that was the case, the Shang may have acquired their knowledge of horse-drawn chariots through contact with the peoples of neighboring regions.

Some recent support for that assumption has come from evidence unearthed in the sandy wastes of Xinjiang, China's far-northwestern province. There archaeologists have discovered corpses dating back as early as the second millennium B.C.E. with physical characteristics that are clearly European. They are also clothed in textiles similar to those worn at the time in Europe, suggesting that they may have been members of an Indo-European migration from areas much farther to the west. If that is the case, they

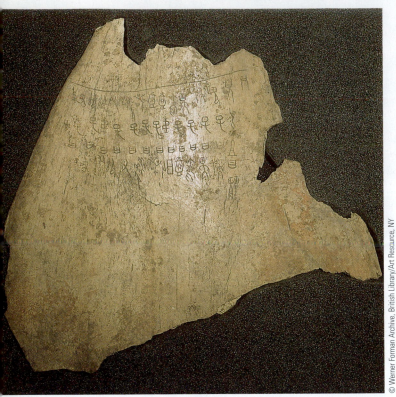

© Werner Forman Archive, British Library/Art Resource, NY

➤ **SHELL AND BONE WRITING.**   The earliest known form of true writing in China dates back to the Shang dynasty and was inscribed on shells or animal bones. Questions for the gods were scratched on bones, which cracked after being exposed to fire. The cracks were then interpreted by sorcerers. The questions often expressed practical concerns: Will it rain? Will the king be victorious in battle? Will he recover from his illness? Originally composed of pictographs and ideographs four thousand years ago, Chinese writing has evolved into an elaborate set of symbols that combine meaning and pronunciation in a single character.

were probably familiar with advances in chariot making that occurred a few hundred years earlier in southern Russia and Kazakstan. By about 2000 B.C.E., spoked wheels were being deposited at grave sites in the Ukraine and also in the Gobi Desert, just north of the great bend of the Yellow River. It is thus likely that the new technology became available to the founders of the Shang dynasty and may have aided their rise to power in northern China.

The Shang king ruled with the assistance of a central bureaucracy in the capital city. His realm was divided into a number of territories governed by aristocratic chieftains, but the king appointed these chieftains and could apparently depose them at will. He was also responsible for the defense of the realm and controlled large armies that often fought on the fringes of the kingdom. The transcendent importance of the ruler was graphically displayed in the ritual sacrifices undertaken at his death, when hundreds of his retainers were buried with him in the royal tomb.

As the inscriptions on the oracle bones make clear, the Chinese ruling elite believed in the existence of super-

natural forces and thought that they could communicate with those forces to obtain divine intervention on matters of this world. In fact, the purpose of the oracle bones was to communicate with the gods. This evidence also suggests that the king was already being viewed as an intermediary between heaven and earth. In fact, an early Chinese character for king (王) consists of three horizontal lines connected by a single vertical line; the middle horizontal line represents the king's place between human society and the divine forces in nature.

The early Chinese also had a clear sense of life in the hereafter. Though some of the human sacrifices discovered in the royal tombs were presumably intended to propitiate the gods, others were meant to accompany the king or members of his family on the journey to the next world. From this conviction would come the concept of the veneration of ancestors (commonly known in the West as "ancestor worship") and the practice, which continues to the present day in many Chinese communities, of burning replicas of physical objects to accompany the departed on their journey to the next world.

Social Structures

In the Neolithic period, the farm village was apparently the basic social unit of China, at least in the core region of the Yellow River valley. Villages were organized by clans rather than by nuclear family units, and all residents probably took the common clan name of the entire village. In some cases, a village may have included more than one clan. At Banpo (Pan P'o), an archaeological site near modern Xian that dates back at least eight thousand years, the houses in the village are separated by a ditch, which some scholars think may have served as a divider between two clans. The individual dwellings at Banpo housed nuclear families, but a larger building in the village was apparently used as a clan meeting hall. The tribal origins of Chinese society may help explain the continued importance of the joint family in traditional China, as well as the relatively small number of family names in Chinese society. Even today there are only about four hundred commonly used family names in a society of more than one billion people.

By Shang times, the classes were becoming increasingly differentiated. It is likely that some poorer peasants did not own their farms but were obliged to work the land of the chieftain and other elite families in the village (see the box on p. 65). The aristocrats not only made war and served as officials (indeed, the first Chinese character for *official* originally meant "warrior"), but they were also the primary landowners. In addition to the aristocratic elite and the peasants, there were a small number of merchants and artisans, as well as slaves, probably consisting primarily of criminals or prisoners taken in battle.

The Shang are perhaps best known for their mastery of the art of bronze casting. Utensils, weapons, and ritual

LIFE IN THE FIELDS

The following passage is from The Book of Songs, a classic written during the early Zhou dynasty. This excerpt describes the calendar of peasant life on an estate in ancient China and indicates the various types of service that peasants provided for their lord.

THE BOOK OF SONGS

In the seventh month the Fire Star passes the meridian;
In the ninth month clothes are given out.
In the days of [our] first month, the wind blows cold;
In the days of [our] second, the air is cold.
Without coats, without garments of hair,
How could we get to the end of the year?
In the days of [our] third month we take our plows in hand;
In the days of [our] fourth we make our way to the fields.
Along with wives and children,
We eat in those south-lying acres.
The surveyor of the fields comes and is glad.

In the seventh month the Fire Star passes the meridian;
In the ninth month clothes are given out.
With the spring days the warmth begins,
And the oriole utters its song.
The young women take their deep baskets
And go along the small paths,
Looking for the tender [leaves of the] mulberry trees
As the spring days lengthen out,
They gather in crowds the white southern wood.
The girl's heart is wounded with sadness,
For she will soon be going with one of the young lords.

. . .

In the eighth month spinning is begun;
We make dark fabrics and yellow,
"With our red dye so bright,
We make robes for our young lords."

In the ninth month we prepare the stockyard,
And in the tenth we bring in the harvest.
The millets, the early and the late,
Together with paddy and hemp, beans and wheat.

. . .

Now we go up to work in the manor.
"In the day you gather the thatch-reeds;
In the evening twist them into rope;
Go quickly on to the roofs;
Soon you are to sow the grain."

In the days of [our] second month we cut the ice with
   tingling blows;
In the days of [our] third month [it is] stored in the
   icehouse.
In the days of [our] fourth month, very early,
A lamb with scallions is offered in sacrifice.
In the ninth month are shrewd frosts;
In the tenth month the stockyard is cleared.
With twin pitchers we hold the feast,
Killed for it is a young lamb.
Up we go into the lord's hall,
Raise the cup of buffalo horn;
"Long life for our lord; may he live forever and ever!"

---

objects made of bronze have been found in royal tombs in urban centers throughout the area known to be under Shang influence (see "Metalwork and Sculpture" later in this chapter). It is also clear that the Shang had achieved a fairly sophisticated writing system that would eventually spread throughout East Asia and evolve into the written language that is still used in China today.

THE ZHOU DYNASTY

In the eleventh century B.C.E., the Shang dynasty was overthrown by an aggressive young state located somewhat to the west of Anyang, the Shang capital, and near the great bend of the Yellow River as it begins to flow directly eastward to the sea. The new dynasty, which called itself the Zhou (Chou), survived for about eight hundred years and was thus the longest-lived dynasty in the history of China. According to tradition, the last of the Shang rulers was a tyrant who oppressed the people (Chinese sources assert that he was a degenerate who built "ponds of wine" and ordered the composing of lustful music that "ruined the morale of the nation"),[3] leading the ruler of the principality of Zhou to revolt and establish a new dynasty.

The Zhou located their capital in their home territory, near the present-day city of Xian. Later they established a second capital city at modern Luoyang, farther to the east, to administer new territories captured from the Shang. This established a pattern of eastern and western capitals that would endure off and on in China for nearly two thousand years.

Political Structures

The Zhou dynasty (1045–221 B.C.E.) adopted the political system of its predecessors, with some changes. The Shang practice of dividing the kingdom into a number of territories governed by officials appointed by the king was continued under the Zhou. At the apex of the government hierarchy was the Zhou king, who was served by a bureaucracy of growing size and complexity. It now included several ministries responsible for rites, education,

MUSIC IN THE CONFUCIAN ERA.   This set of bronze bells was discovered in a recent excavation of the tomb of a Zhou dynasty nobleman. Also found in the pit were several tons of bronze weaponry and ritual vessels, along with the bones of twenty-one attendants, consorts, and musicians, who had presumably been sacrificed to serve their lord in the afterlife. Weighing over 2 tons and covering a range of five octaves, the sixty-five bells required five performers standing on either side. Each bell contained a written inscription, providing the most complete written record of musical systems used in ancient China. Bronze bells have not been found in any other contemporary civilization and are considered one of the great cultural achievements of antiquity. The largest known bell dating from the Roman Empire, for example, is only 6 centimeters high.

law, and public works. Beyond the capital, the Zhou kingdom was divided into a number of principalities, governed by members of the hereditary aristocracy, who were appointed by the king and were at least theoretically subordinated to his authority.

But the Zhou kings also introduced some innovations. According to the *Rites of Zhou,* one of the oldest surviving documents on statecraft, the Zhou dynasty ruled China because it possessed the "mandate of Heaven." According to this concept, Heaven (viewed as an impersonal law of nature rather than as an anthropomorphic deity) maintained order in the universe through the Zhou king, who thus ruled as a representative of Heaven but not as a divine being. The king, who was selected to rule because of his talent and virtue, was then responsible for governing the people with compassion and efficiency. It was his duty to propitiate the gods in order to protect the people from natural calamities or bad harvests. But if the king failed to rule effectively, he could, theoretically at least, be overthrown and replaced by a new ruler. As noted earlier, this idea was used to justify the Zhou conquest of the Shang. Eventually, the concept of the heavenly mandate would become a cardinal principle of Chinese statecraft.[4] Each founder

of a new dynasty would routinely assert that he had earned the mandate of Heaven, and who could disprove it except by overthrowing the king? As a pragmatic Chinese proverb put it: "He who wins is the king; he who loses is the rebel."

By the sixth century B.C.E., the Zhou dynasty began to decline. As the power of the central government disintegrated, bitter internal rivalries arose among the various principalities, where the governing officials had succeeded in making their positions hereditary at the expense of the king. As the power of these officials grew, they began to regulate the local economy and seek reliable sources of revenue for their expanding armies, such as a uniform tax system and government monopolies on key commodities such as salt and iron.

Economy and Society

During the Zhou dynasty, the essential characteristics of Chinese economic and social institutions began to take shape. The Zhou continued the pattern of land ownership that had existed under the Shang: the peasants worked on lands owned by their lord but also had land of their own that they cultivated for their own use. The practice was called the "well field system," since the Chinese character for well (井) resembles a simplified picture of the division of the farmland into nine separate segments. Each peasant family tilled an outer plot for its own use and then joined with other families to work the inner one for the hereditary lord (see the box on p. 65). How widely this system was used is unclear, but it represented an ideal described by Confucian scholars of a later day. As the following poem indicates, life for the average farmer was a difficult one. The "big rat" is probably a reference to the high taxes imposed on the peasants by the government or lord.

> Big rat, big rat
> Do not eat my millet!
> Three years I have served you,
> But you will not care for me.
> I am going to leave you
> And go to that happy land;
> Happy land, happy land,
> Where I will find my place.[5]

Trade and manufacturing were carried out by merchants and artisans, who lived in walled towns under the direct control of the local lord. Merchants did not operate independently but were considered the property of the local lord and on occasion could even be bought and sold like chattels. A class of slaves performed a variety of menial tasks and perhaps worked on local irrigation projects. Most of them were probably prisoners of war captured during conflicts with the neighboring principalities. Scholars do not know how extensive slavery was in ancient times, but slaves probably did not constitute a large portion of the total population.

The period of the later Zhou, from the sixth to the third century B.C.E., was an era of significant economic growth and technological innovation, especially in agriculture. During that time, large-scale water control projects were undertaken to regulate the flow of rivers and distribute water evenly to the fields, as well as to construct canals to facilitate the transport of goods from one region to another (see the box on p. 63). Perhaps the most impressive technological achievement of the period was the construction of the massive water control project on the Min River, a tributary of the Yangtze. This system of canals and spillways, which was put into operation by the state of Qin a few years prior to the end of the Zhou dynasty, diverted excess water from the river into the local irrigation network and watered an area populated by as many as five million people. The system is still in use today, over two thousand years later.

Food production was also stimulated by a number of advances in farm technology. By the mid-sixth century B.C.E., the introduction of iron had led to the development of iron plowshares, which permitted deep plowing for the first time. Other innovations dating from the later Zhou were the use of natural fertilizer, the collar harness, and the technique of leaving land fallow to preserve or replenish nutrients in the soil (see the box on p. 68). By the late Zhou dynasty, the cultivation of wet rice had become one of the prime sources of food in China. Although rice was difficult and time-consuming to produce, it replaced other grain crops in areas with a warm climate because of its good taste, relative ease of preparation, and high nutritious value.

The advances in agriculture, which enabled the population of China to rise as high as twenty million people during the late Zhou era, were also undoubtedly a major factor in the growth of commerce and manufacturing. During the late Zhou, economic wealth began to replace noble birth as the prime source of power and influence. Utensils made of iron became more common, and trade developed in a variety of useful commodities, including cloth, salt, and various manufactured goods.

One of the most important items of trade in ancient China was silk. There is evidence of silkworm raising as early as the Neolithic period. Remains of silk material have been found on Shang bronzes, and a large number of fragments have been recovered in tombs dating from the mid-Zhou era. Silk cloth was used not only for clothing and quilts but also to wrap the bodies of the dead prior to burial. Fragments have been found throughout Central Asia and as far away as Athens, suggesting that the famous "Silk Road" stretching from central China westward to the Middle East and the Mediterranean Sea was in operation as early as the fifth century B.C.E. (see Map 3.4 on p. 79; see also Chapter 10).

With the development of trade and manufacturing, China began to move toward a money economy. The first form of money may have been seashells (the Chinese character for goods or property contains the ideographic symbol for "shell"), but by the Zhou dynasty, pieces of iron shaped like a knife or round coins with a hole in the middle so they could be carried in strings of a thousand were being used. Most ordinary Chinese, however, simply used a system of barter. Taxes, rents, and even the salaries of government officials were normally paid in grain.

The Hundred Schools of Ancient Philosophy

In China, as in other great river valley societies, the birth of civilization was accompanied by the emergence of an organized effort to comprehend the nature of the cosmos and the role of human beings within it. Speculation over such questions began in the very early stages of civilization and culminated at the end of the Zhou era in the "hundred schools" of ancient philosophy, a wide-ranging debate over the nature of human beings, society, and the universe.

The first hint of religious belief in ancient China comes from relics found in royal tombs of Neolithic times. By then, the Chinese had already developed a religious sense

ENVIRONMENTAL CONCERNS IN ANCIENT CHINA

Even in antiquity, China possessed a large population that often stretched the limits of the productive potential of the land. In the following excerpt, the late Zhou philosopher Mencius appeals to his sovereign to adopt policies that will conserve precious resources and foster the well-being of his subjects. Clearly, Mencius was concerned that environmental needs were being neglected. Unfortunately, his advice has not always been followed, and environmental degradation remains a problem in China today. The destruction of the forests, for example, has deprived China of much of its wood resources, and the present government has launched an extensive program to plant trees.

THE BOOK OF MENCIUS

If you do not interfere with the busy season in the fields, then there will be more grain than the people can eat; if you do not allow nets with too fine a mesh to be used in large ponds, then there will be more fish and turtles than they can eat; if hatchets and axes are permitted in the forests on the hills only in the proper seasons, then there will be more timber than they can use. When the people have more grain, more fish and turtles than they can eat, and more timber than they can use, then in the support of their parents when alive and in the mourning of them when dead, they will be able to have no regrets over anything left undone. This is the first step along the Kingly way.

If the mulberry is planted in every homestead of five mu of land, then those who are fifty can wear silk; if chickens, pigs, and dogs do not miss their breeding season, then those who are seventy can eat meat; if each lot of a hundred mu is not deprived of labor during the busy seasons, then families with several mouths to feed will not go hungry. Exercise due care over the education provided by the village schools, and discipline the people by teaching them the duties proper to sons and younger brothers, and those whose heads have turned gray will not be carrying loads on the roads. When those who are seventy wear silk and eat meat and the masses are neither cold nor hungry, it is impossible for their prince not to be a true King.

Now when food meant for human beings is so plentiful as to be thrown to dogs and pigs, you fail to realize that it is time for garnering, and when men drop dead from starvation by the wayside, you fail to realize that it is time for distribution. When people die, you simply say, "It is none of my doing. It is the fault of the harvest." In what way is that different from killing a man by running him through, while saying all the time, "It is none of my doing. It is the fault of the weapon." Stop putting the blame on the harvest and the people of the whole Empire will come to you.

---

beyond the primitive belief in the existence of spirits in nature. The Shang had begun to believe in the existence of one transcendent god, known as Shang Di, who presided over all the forces of nature. As time went on, the Chinese concept of religion evolved from a vaguely anthropomorphic god to a somewhat more impersonal symbol of universal order known as Heaven (*Tian*, or *T'ien*). There was also much speculation among Chinese intellectuals about the nature of the cosmic order. One of the earliest ideas was that the universe was divided into two primary forces of good and evil, light and dark, male and female, called the *yang* and the *yin*, represented symbolically by the sun (*yang*) and the moon (*yin*). According to this theory, life was a dynamic process of interaction between the forces of *yang* and *yin*. Early Chinese could attempt only to understand the process and perhaps to have some minimal effect on its operation. They could not hope to reverse it. It is sometimes asserted that this belief has contributed to the heavy element of fatalism in Chinese popular wisdom. The Chinese have traditionally believed that bad times will be followed by good times, and vice versa.

The belief that there was some mysterious "law of nature" that could be interpreted by human beings led to various attempts to predict the future, such as the Shang oracle bones and other methods of divination. Philosophers invented ways to interpret the will of nature, while shamans, playing a role similar to the *brahmins* in India, were employed at court to assist the emperor in his policy deliberations until at least the fifth century C.E. One of the most famous manuals used for this purpose was the *Yi Jing* (*I Ching*), known in English as the *Book of Changes*.

CONFUCIANISM

Such efforts to divine the mysterious purposes of Heaven notwithstanding, Chinese thinking about metaphysical reality also contained a strain of pragmatism, which is readily apparent in the ideas of the great philosopher Confucius. Confucius (the name is the Latin form of his honorific title, Kung Fuci, or K'ung Fu-tzu, meaning Master Kung) was born in the state of Lu (in the modern province of Shandong) in 551 B.C.E. After reaching maturity, he apparently hoped to find employment as a political adviser in one of the principalities into which China was divided at that time, but he had little success in finding a patron. Nevertheless, he made an indelible mark on history as

THE WAY OF THE GREAT LEARNING

ew texts exist today that were written by Confucius him-self. Most were written or edited by his disciples. The following text, titled The Great Learning, *was probably written two centuries after Confucius' death, but it illustrates his view that good government begins with the cultivation of individual morality and proper human relationships at the basic level. This conviction that to bring peace to the world, you must cultivate your own person continued to win general approval down to modern times. There are interesting similarities between such ideas and the views expressed in the Indian treatise* Arthasastra, *discussed in Chapter 2.*

THE GREAT LEARNING

The Way of the Great Learning consists in clearly exempli-fying illustrious virtue, in loving the people, and in resting in the highest good.

Only when one knows where one is to rest can one have a fixed purpose. Only with a fixed purpose can one achieve calmness of mind. Only with calmness of mind can one attain serene repose. Only in serene repose can one carry on careful deliberation. Only through careful deliberation can one have achievement. Things have their roots and branches; affairs have their beginning and end. He who knows what comes first and what comes last comes himself near the Way.

The ancients who wished clearly to exemplify illustrious virtue throughout the world would first set up good govern-ment in their states. Wishing to govern well their states, they would first regulate their families. Wishing to regulate their families, they would first cultivate their persons. Wishing to cultivate their persons, they would first rectify their minds. Wishing to rectify their minds, they would first seek sincerity in their thoughts. Wishing for sincerity in their thoughts, they would first extend their knowledge. The extension of knowledge lay in the investigation of things. For only when things are investigated is knowledge extended; only when knowledge is extended are thoughts sincere; only when thoughts are sincere are minds rectified; only when minds are rectified are our persons cultivated; only when our persons are cultivated are our families regu-lated; only when families are regulated are states well gov-erned; and only when states are well governed is there peace in the world.

From the emperor down to the common people, all, without exception, must consider cultivation of the indi-vidual character as the root. If the root is in disorder, it is impossible for the branches to be in order. To treat the important as unimportant and to treat the unimportant as important—this should never be. This is called knowing the root; this is called the perfection of knowledge.

---

an independent (and somewhat disgruntled) political and social philosopher.

In conversations with his disciples contained in the *Analects,* Confucius often adopted a detached and almost skeptical view of Heaven. "You are unable to serve man," he commented on one occasion, "how then can you hope to serve the spirits? While you do not know life, how can you know about death?" In many instances, he appeared to advise his followers to revere the deities and the ances-tral spirits but to keep them at a distance. Confucius believed it was useless to speculate too much about meta-physical questions. Better by far to assume that there was a rational order to the universe and then concentrate one's attention on ordering the affairs of this world.[6]

Confucius' interest in philosophy, then, was essentially political and ethical. The universe was constructed in such a way that if human beings could act harmoniously in accordance with its purposes, their own affairs would pros-per. Much of his concern was with human behavior. The key to proper behavior was to behave in accordance with the *Dao* (Way). Confucius assumed that all human beings had their own *Dao,* depending on their individual role in life, and it was their duty to follow it. Even the ruler had his own *Dao,* and he ignored it at his peril, for to do so could mean the loss of the mandate of Heaven. The idea of the *Dao* is reminiscent of the concept of *dharma* in

ancient India and played a similar role in governing the affairs of society.

Two elements in the Confucian interpretation of the *Dao* are particularly worthy of mention. The first is the concept of duty. It was the responsibility of all individuals to subordinate their own interests and aspirations to the broader need of the family and the community. Confucius assumed that if each individual worked hard to fulfill his or her assigned destiny, the affairs of society as a whole would surely prosper as well. In this respect, it was impor-tant for the ruler to set a good example. If he followed his "kingly way," the beneficial effects would radiate throughout society (see the box above).

The second key element is the idea of humanity, some-times translated as "human-heartedness." This concept involves a sense of compassion and empathy for others. It is similar in some ways to Christian concepts, but with a subtle twist. Where Christian teachings call on human beings to "behave toward others as you would have them behave toward you," the Confucian maxim is put in a dif-ferent way: "Do not do unto others what you would not wish done to yourself." To many Chinese, this attitude symbolizes an element of tolerance in the Chinese char-acter that has not always been practiced in other societies.[7]

Confucius may have considered himself a failure because he never attained the position he wanted, but many of his contemporaries found his ideas appealing, and in the generations after his death, his message spread widely throughout China. Confucius was an outspoken critic of his times and lamented the disappearance of what he regarded as the Golden Age of the early Zhou.

In fact, however, Confucius was not just another disgruntled Chinese conservative mourning the passing of the good old days; rather, he was a revolutionary thinker, many of whose key ideas looked forward rather than backward. Perhaps his most striking political idea was that the government should be open to all men of superior quality, not limited to those of noble birth. As one of his disciples reports in the *Analects*: "The Master said, by nature, men are nearly alike; by practice, they get to be wide apart."[8] Confucius undoubtedly had himself in mind as one of those "superior" men, but the rapacity of the hereditary lords must have added strength to his convictions.

The concept of rule by merit was, of course, not an unfamiliar idea in the China of his day; the *Rites of Zhou* had clearly stated that the king himself deserved to rule because of his talent and virtue, rather than as the result of noble birth. In practice, however, aristocratic privilege must often have opened the doors to political influence, and many of Confucius' contemporaries must have regarded his appeal for government by talent as both exciting and dangerous. Confucius did not explicitly question the right of the hereditary aristocracy to play a leading role in the political process, nor did his ideas have much effect in his lifetime. Still, they introduced a new concept that was later implemented in the form of a bureaucracy selected through a civil service examination (see "Confucianism and the State" later in this chapter).

Confucius' ideas, passed on to later generations through the *Analects* as well as through writings attributed to him, had a strong impact on Chinese political thinkers of the late Zhou period, a time when the existing system was in disarray and open to serious question. But as with most great thinkers, Confucius' ideas were sufficiently ambiguous to be interpreted in very contradictory ways. Some, like the philosopher Mencius (370–290 B.C.E.), stressed the humanistic side of Confucian ideas, arguing that human beings were by nature good and hence could be taught their civic responsibilities by example. He also stressed that the ruler had a duty to govern with compassion:

> It was because Chieh and Chou lost the people that they lost the empire, and it was because they lost the hearts of the people that they lost the people. Here is the way to win the empire: win the people and you win the empire. Here is the way to win the people: win their hearts and you win the people. Here is the way to win their hearts: give them and share with them what they like, and do not do to them what they do not like. The people turn to a human ruler as water flows downward or beasts take to wilderness.[9]

Here is a prescription for political behavior that could win wide support in our own day. Other thinkers, however, rejected Mencius' rosy view of human nature and argued for a different approach.

LEGALISM

One school of thought that became quite popular during the "hundred schools" era in ancient China was the philosophy of Legalism. Taking issue with the view of Mencius and other disciples of Confucius that human nature was essentially good, the Legalists argued that human beings were by nature evil and would follow the correct path only if coerced by harsh laws and stiff punishments. These thinkers were referred to as the School of Law because they rejected the Confucian view that government by "superior men" could solve society's problems and argued instead for a system of impersonal laws.

The Legalists also disagreed with the Confucian belief that the universe has a moral core. They therefore believed that only firm action by the state could bring about social order. Fear of harsh punishment, more than the promise of material reward, could best motivate the common people to serve the interests of the ruler. Because human nature was essentially corrupt, officials could not be trusted to carry out their duties in a fair and evenhanded manner, and only a strong ruler could create an orderly society. All human actions should be subordinated to the effort to create a strong and prosperous state subject to his will.

DAOISM

One of the most popular alternatives to Confucianism was the philosophy of Daoism (frequently spelled Taoism). According to Chinese tradition, the Daoist school was founded by a contemporary of Confucius popularly known as Lao Tzu (Lao Zi), or the Old Master. Many modern scholars, however, are skeptical that Lao Tzu actually existed.

Obtaining a clear understanding of the original concepts of Daoism is difficult because its primary document, a short treatise known as the *Dao De Jing* (sometimes translated as *The Way of the Tao*), is an enigmatic book whose interpretation has baffled scholars for centuries. The opening line, for example, explains less what the *Dao* is than what it is not: "The Tao [Way] that can be told of is not the eternal Tao. The name that can be named is not the eternal name."[10]

Nevertheless, the basic concepts of Daoism are not especially difficult to understand. Like Confucianism, Daoism does not anguish over the underlying meaning of the cosmos. Rather, it attempts to set forth proper forms of behavior for human beings here on earth. In most other respects, however, Daoism presents a view of life and its ultimate meaning that is almost diametrically opposed to that of Confucianism. Where Confucian doctrine asserts that it is the duty of human beings to work hard to improve life here on earth, Daoists contend that the

THE DAOIST ANSWER TO CONFUCIANISM

The Dao De Jing (The Way of the Dao) is the great classic of philosophical Daoism (Taoism). Traditionally attributed to the legendary Chinese philosopher Lao Tzu (Old Master), it was probably written sometime during the era of Confucius. This opening passage illustrates two of the key ideas that characterize Daoist belief: it is impossible to define the nature of the universe, and "inaction" (not Confucian "action") is the key to ordering the affairs of human beings.

THE WAY OF THE DAO

The Tao that can be told of is not the eternal Tao;
The name that can be named is not the eternal name.
The Nameless is the origin of Heaven and Earth;
The Named is the mother of all things.

Therefore let there always be nonbeing, so we may see their
    subtlety.
And let there always be being, so we may see their
    outcome.
The two are the same,
But after they are produced, they have different names.
They both may be called deep and profound.

Deeper and more profound,
The door of all subtleties!
When the people of the world all know beauty as beauty,
There arises the recognition of ugliness.
When they all know the good as good,
There arises the recognition of evil.
Therefore:
Being and nonbeing produce each other;
Difficult and easy complete each other;
Long and short contrast each other;
High and low distinguish each other;
Sound and voice harmonize each other;
Front and behind accompany each other.

Therefore the sage manages affairs without action
And spreads doctrines without words.
All things arise, and he does not turn away from them.
He produces them but does not take possession of them.
He acts but does not rely on his own ability.
He accomplishes his task but does not claim credit for it.
It is precisely because he does not claim credit that his
    accomplishment remains with him.

---

true way to interpret the will of Heaven is not action but inaction (*wu wei*). The best way to act in harmony with the universal order is to act spontaneously and let nature take its course (see the box above).

Such a message could be very appealing to those who were uncomfortable with the somewhat rigid flavor of the Confucian work ethic and preferred a more individualistic approach. This image would eventually find graphic expression in Chinese landscape painting, which in its classical form would depict naturalistic scenes of mountains, water, and clouds and underscore the fragility and smallness of individual human beings.

Daoism achieved considerable popularity in the waning years of the Zhou dynasty. It was especially popular among intellectuals, who may have found it appealing as an escapist antidote in a world characterized by growing disorder.

POPULAR BELIEFS

Daoism also played a second role as a loose framework for popular spiritualistic and animistic beliefs among the common people. Popular Daoism was less a philosophy than a religion; it comprised a variety of rituals and forms of behavior that were regarded as a means of achieving heavenly salvation or even a state of immortality on earth. Daoist sorcerers practiced various types of mind- or body-training exercises in the hope of achieving power, sexual prowess, and long life. It was primarily this form of Daoism that survived into a later age.

The philosophical forms of Confucianism and Daoism did not provide much meaning to the mass of the population, for whom philosophical debate over the ultimate meaning of life was not as important as the daily struggle for survival. Even among the elites, interest in the occult and in astrology was high, and magicoreligious ideas coexisted with the interest in natural science and humanistic philosophy throughout the ancient period.

For most Chinese, Heaven was not a vague, impersonal law of nature, as it was for many Confucian and Daoist intellectuals, but a terrain peopled with innumerable gods and spirits of nature, both good and evil, who existed in trees, mountains, and streams as well as in heavenly bodies. As human beings mastered the techniques of farming, they called on divine intervention to guarantee a good harvest. Other gods were responsible for the safety of fishers, transportation workers, or prospective mothers.

Another aspect of popular religion was the belief that the spirits of deceased human beings lived in the atmosphere for a time before ascending to heaven or descending to hell. During that period, surviving family members had to care for the spirits through proper ritual, or they would become evil spirits and haunt the survivors.

Thus in ancient China, human beings were offered a variety of interpretations of the nature of the universe.

Confucianism satisfied the need for a rational doctrine of nation building and social organization at a time when the existing political and social structure was beginning to disintegrate. Philosophical Daoism provided an alternative to Confucianism and a framework for a set of diverse animistic beliefs at the popular level. But neither could satisfy the deeper emotional needs that sometimes inspire the human spirit. Neither could effectively provide solace in a time of sorrow or the hope of a better life in the hereafter. Something else would be needed to fill the gap.

THE RISE OF THE CHINESE EMPIRE: THE QIN AND THE HAN

During the last two centuries of the Zhou dynasty (the fourth and third centuries B.C.E.), the authority of the king became increasingly nominal, and several of the small principalities into which the Zhou kingdom had been divided began to evolve into powerful states that presented a potential challenge to the Zhou ruler himself. Chief among these were Qu (Ch'u) in the central Yangtze valley, Wu in the Yangtze delta, and Yue (Yueh) along the southeastern coast. At first, their mutual rivalries were in check, but by the late fifth century B.C.E., competition intensified into civil war, giving birth to the so-called Period of the Warring States (see the box on p. 73). Powerful principalities vied with each other for preeminence and largely ignored the now purely titular authority of the Zhou court (see Map 3.2). New forms of warfare also emerged with the invention of iron weapons and the introduction of the foot soldier. Cavalry, too, made its first appearance, armed with the powerful crossbow.

Eventually, the relatively young state of Qin, located in the original homeland of the Zhou, became a key player in these conflicts. Benefiting from a strong defensive position in the mountains to the west of the great bend of the Yellow River, as well as from their control of the rich Sichuan

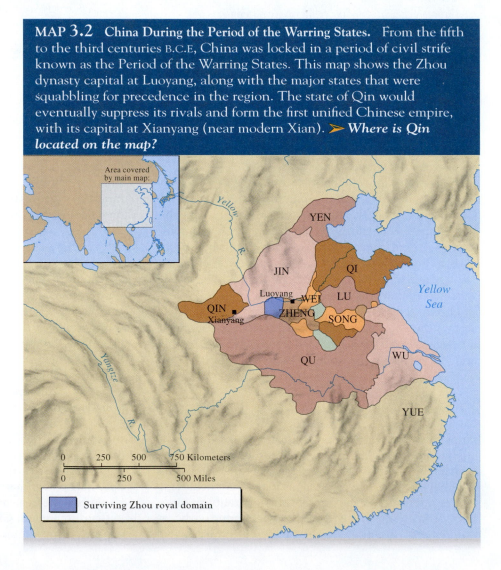

MAP 3.2   China During the Period of the Warring States.   From the fifth to the third centuries B.C.E, China was locked in a period of civil strife known as the Period of the Warring States. This map shows the Zhou dynasty capital at Luoyang, along with the major states that were squabbling for precedence in the region. The state of Qin would eventually suppress its rivals and form the first unified Chinese empire, with its capital at Xianyang (near modern Xian). ➤ *Where is Qin located on the map?*

Surviving Zhou royal domain

THE ART OF WAR

With the possible exception of the nineteenth-century German military strategist Karl von Clausewitz, there is probably no more famous or respected writer on the art of war than the ancient Chinese thinker Sun Tzu. Yet surprisingly little is known about him. Recently discovered evidence suggests that he lived sometime in the fifth century B.C.E., during the chronic conflict of the Period of Warring States, and that he was an early member of an illustrious family of military strategists who advised Zhou rulers for more than two hundred years. But despite the mystery surrounding his life, there is no doubt of his influence on later generations of military planners. Among his most avid followers in our century have been the revolutionary leaders Mao Zedong and Ho Chi Minh, as well as the Japanese military strategists who planned the attacks on Port Arthur and Pearl Harbor.

The following brief excerpt from his classic The Art of War provides a glimmer into the nature of his advice, still so timely today.

SELECTIONS FROM SUN TZU

Sun Tzu said:

"In general, the method for employing the military is this: . . . Attaining one hundred victories in one hundred battles is not the pinnacle of excellence. Subjugating the enemy's army without fighting is the true pinnacle of excellence. . . .

"Thus the highest realization of warfare is to attack the enemy's plans; next is to attack their alliances; next to attack their army; and the lowest is to attack their fortified cities.

"This tactic of attacking fortified cities is adopted only when unavoidable. Preparing large movable protective shields, armored assault wagons, and other equipment and devices will require three months. Building earthworks will require another three months to complete. If the general cannot overcome his impatience but instead launches an assault wherein his men swarm over the walls like ants, he will kill one-third of his officers and troops, and the city will still not be taken. This is the disaster that results from attacking [fortified cities].

"Thus one who excels at employing the military subjugates other people's armies without engaging in battle, captures other people's fortified cities without attacking them, and destroys others people's states without prolonged fighting. He must fight under Heaven with the paramount aim of 'preservation.' . . .

"In general, the strategy of employing the military is this: If your strength is ten times theirs, surround them; if five, then attack them; if double, then divide your forces. If you are equal in strength to the enemy, you can engage him. If fewer, you can circumvent him. If outmatched, you can avoid him. . . .

"Thus there are five factors from which victory can be known:

"One who knows when he can fight, and when he cannot fight, will be victorious.

"One who recognizes how to employ large and small numbers will be victorious.

"One whose upper and lower ranks have the same desires will be victorious.

"One who, fully prepared, awaits the unprepared will be victorious.

"One whose general is capable and not interfered with by the ruler will be victorious.

"These five are the Way (Tao) to know victory. . . .

"Thus it is said that one who knows the enemy and knows himself will not be endangered in a hundred engagements. One who does not know the enemy but knows himself will sometimes be victorious, sometimes meet with defeat. One who knows neither the enemy nor himself will invariably be defeated in every engagement."

---

plains, the Qin gradually subdued their main rivals through conquest or diplomatic maneuvering. In 221 B.C.E., the Qin ruler declared the establishment of a new dynasty, the first truly unified government in Chinese history.

The Qin Dynasty (221–206 B.C.E.)

One of the primary reasons for the triumph of the Qin was probably the character of the Qin ruler, known to history as Qin Shi Huangdi (Ch'in Shih Huang Ti), or the First Emperor of Qin. A man of forceful personality and immense ambition, Qin Shi Huangdi had ascended to the throne of Qin in 246 B.C.E. at the age of thirteen. Described by the famous Han dynasty historian Sima Qian as having "the chest of a bird of prey, the voice of a jackal, and the heart of a tiger," the new king of Qin found the Legalist views of his adviser Li Su (Li Ssu) only too appealing. In 221 B.C.E., Qin Shi Huangdi defeated the last of Qin's rivals and founded a new dynasty with himself as emperor.

The Qin dynasty transformed Chinese politics. Philosophical doctrines that had proliferated during the late Zhou period were prohibited, and Legalism was adopted as the official ideology. Those who opposed the policies of the new regime were punished and sometimes executed, while books presenting ideas contrary to the official orthodoxy were publicly put to the torch, perhaps the first example of book burning in history (see the box on p. 74).

Legalistic theory gave birth to a number of fundamental administrative and political developments, some of

MEMORANDUM ON THE BURNING OF BOOKS

L i Su, the author of the following passage, was a chief minister of the First Emperor of Qin. An exponent of Legalism, Li Su hoped to eliminate all rival theories on government. His recommendation to the emperor on the subject was recorded by the Han dynasty historian Sima Qian. The emperor approved the proposal and ordered all books contrary to the spirit of Legalist ideology to be destroyed on pain of death. Fortunately, some texts were preserved by being hidden or even memorized by their owners and were thus available to later generations. For centuries afterward, the First Emperor of Qin and his minister were singled out for criticism because of their intolerance and their effort to control the very minds of their subjects. Totalitarianism, it seems, is not exclusively a modern concept.

SIMA QIAN, *HISTORICAL RECORDS*

In earlier times the empire disintegrated and fell into disorder, and no one was capable of unifying it. Thereupon the various feudal lords rose to power. In their discourses they all praised the past in order to disparage the present and embellished empty words to confuse the truth. Everyone cherished his own favorite school of learning and criticized what had been instituted by the authorities. But at present Your Majesty possesses a unified empire, has regulated the distinctions of black and white, and has firmly established for yourself a position of sole supremacy. And yet these independent schools, joining with each other, criticize the codes of laws and instructions. Hearing of the promulgation of a decree, they criticize it, each from the standpoint of his own school. At home they disapprove of it in their hearts; going out they criticize it in the thoroughfare. They seek a reputation by discrediting their sovereign; they appear superior by expressing contrary views, and they lead the lowly multitude in the spreading of slander. If such license is not prohibited, the sovereign power will decline above and partisan factions will form below. It would be well to prohibit this.

Your servant suggests that all books in the imperial archives, save the memoirs of Ch'in, be burned. All persons in the empire, except members of the Academy of Learned Scholars, in possession of the *Book of Odes*, the *Book of History*, and discourses of the hundred philosophers should take them to the local governors and have them indiscriminately burned. Those who dare to talk to each other about the *Book of Odes* and the *Book of History* should be executed and their bodies exposed in the marketplace. Anyone referring to the past to criticize the present should, together with all members of his family, be put to death. Officials who fail to report cases that have come under their attention are equally guilty. After thirty days from the time of issuing the decree, those who have not destroyed their books are to be branded and sent to build the Great Wall. Books not to be destroyed will be those on medicine and pharmacy, divination by the tortoise and milfoil, and agriculture and arboriculture. People wishing to pursue learning should take the officials as their teachers.

which would survive the Qin and serve as a model for future dynasties. In the first place, unlike the Zhou, the Qin was a highly centralized state. The central bureaucracy was divided into three primary ministries: a civil authority, a military authority, and a censorate, whose inspectors surveyed the efficiency of officials throughout the system. This would later become standard administrative procedure for future Chinese dynasties.

Below the central government were two levels of administration: provinces and counties. Unlike the Zhou system, officials at these levels did not inherit their positions but were appointed by the court and were subject to dismissal at the emperor's whim. Apparently, some form of merit system was used, although there is no evidence that selection was based on performance in an examination. The civil servants may have been chosen on the recommendation of other government officials. A penal code provided for harsh punishments for all wrongdoers. Officials were watched by the censors, who reported directly to the throne. Those guilty of malfeasance in office were executed.

Qin Shi Huangdi, who had a passion for centralization, unified the system of weights and measures, standardized the monetary system and the written forms of Chinese characters, and ordered the construction of a system of roads extending throughout the empire. He also attempted to eliminate the remaining powers of the landed aristocrats and divided their estates among the peasants, who were now taxed directly by the state. He thus elimi-

The Qin Empire 221–206 B.C.E.

0   250   500   750 Kilometers

0   250   500 Miles

Yellow R.

Xianyang

Yangtze R.

South China Sea

帝 皇 始 秦

QIN SHI HUANGDI. Qin Shi Huangdi, the First Emperor of Qin, who reigned from 221 to 210 B.C.E., was one of the most influential figures in the history of China. Although considered ruthless by many historians, he created the first unified Chinese state, ordered the construction of a system of roads throughout the country, standardized the Chinese currency and written language, and brought together the scattered defensive battlements into what we now know as the Great Wall.

Zhou dynasty, extending the border of China to the edge of the Red River in modern Vietnam. To supply the Qin armies operating in the area, a canal was dug that provided direct inland navigation from the Yangtze River in central China to what is now the modern city of Guangzhou (Canton) in the south.

BEYOND THE FRONTIER: THE NOMADIC PEOPLES AND THE GREAT WALL OF CHINA

The main area of concern for the Qin emperor, however, was in the north, where a nomadic people, known to the Chinese as the Xiongnu (Hsiung-nu) and possibly related to the Huns (see Chapter 5), had become increasingly active in the area of the Gobi Desert. The area north of the Yellow River had been sparsely inhabited since prehistoric times. During the Qin period, the climate of North China was somewhat milder and moister than it is today, and parts of the region were heavily forested. The local population probably lived by hunting and fishing, practicing limited forms of agriculture, or herding animals such as cattle or sheep.

As the climate gradually became drier, people were forced to rely increasingly on animal husbandry as a means of livelihood. Their response was to master the art of riding on horseback and to adopt the nomadic life. Organized loosely into communities consisting of a number of kinship groups, they ranged far and wide in search of pasture for their herds of cattle, goats, or sheep. As they moved seasonally from one pasture to another, they often traveled several hundred miles carrying their goods and their circular felt tents, called *yurts*.

But the new way of life presented its own challenges. Increased food production led to a growing population, which in times of drought outstripped the available resources. Rival groups then competed for the best pastures. After they mastered the art of fighting on horseback sometime during the middle of the first millennium B.C.E., territorial warfare became commonplace throughout the entire frontier region from the Pacific Ocean to Central Asia.

By the end of the Zhou dynasty in the third century B.C.E., the nomadic Xiongnu posed a serious threat to the security of China's northern frontier, and a number of Chinese principalities in the area began to build walls and fortifications to keep them out. But warriors on horseback possessed significant advantages over the infantry of the Chinese.

Qin Shi Huangdi's answer to the problem was to strengthen the walls to keep the marauders out. In Sima Qian's words:

> [The] First Emperor of the Ch'in dispatched Meng T'ien to lead a force of a hundred thousand men north to attack the barbarians. He seized control of all the lands south of the Yellow River and established border defenses along the river, constructing forty-four walled district cities overlooking the river and manning them with convict laborers transported to

nated potential rivals and secured tax revenues for the central government. Members of the aristocratic clans were required to live in the capital city at Xianyang (Hsienyang), just north of modern Xian, so that the court could monitor their activities. Such a system may not have been advantageous to the peasants in all respects, however, since the central government could now collect taxes more effectively and mobilize the peasants for military service and for various public works projects.

The Qin dynasty was equally unsympathetic to the merchants, whom it viewed as parasites. Private commercial activities were severely restricted and heavily taxed, and many vital forms of commerce and manufacturing, including mining, wine making, and the distribution of salt, were placed under a government monopoly.

Qin Shi Huangdi was equally aggressive in foreign affairs. His armies continued the gradual advance to the south that had taken place during the final years of the

the border for garrison duty. Thus he utilized the natural mountain barriers to establish the border defenses, scooping out the valleys and constructing ramparts and building installations at other points where they were needed. The whole line of defenses stretched over ten thousand *li* [a *li* is one-third of a mile] from Lin-t'ao to Liao-tung and even extended across the Yellow River and through Yang-shan and Pei-chia.[11]

Today, of course, we know Qin Shi Huangdi's project as the Great Wall, which extends nearly 4,000 miles from the sandy wastes of Central Asia to the sea. It is constructed of massive granite blocks and is wide enough on top to provide a roadway for horse-drawn chariots. Although the wall that appears in most photographs today was built 1,500 years after the Qin, during the Ming dynasty, some of the walls built by the Qin remain standing. Their construction was a massive project that required the efforts of thousands of laborers, many of whom met their deaths there and, according to legend, are now buried within the wall.

THE FALL OF THE QIN

The Legalist system put in place by the First Emperor of Qin was designed to achieve maximum efficiency as well as total security for the state. It did neither. Qin Shi

➤ **THE GREAT WALL.**   The section of the Great Wall that is often visited by tourists today is not the work of the First Emperor of Qin but was built at the order of a Ming ruler many centuries later. The original walls were often composed of loose stone, dirt, or piled rubble and posed little obstacle to invading nomads from the north. The section illustrated here is located north of the city of Dunhuang in Central Asia.

© Courtesy of William J. Duiker

Huangdi was apparently aware of the dangers of factions within the imperial family and established a class of eunuchs (males whose testicles have been removed) who served as personal attendants for himself and female members of the royal family. The original idea may have been to restrict the influence of male courtiers, and the eunuch system later became a standard feature of the Chinese imperial system. But as confidential advisers to the royal family, eunuchs were in a position of influence. The rivalry between the "inner" imperial court and the "outer" court of bureaucratic officials led to tensions that persisted until the end of the imperial system.

By ruthlessly gathering control over the empire into his own hands, Qin Shi Huangdi had hoped to establish a rule that, in the words of Sima Qian, "would be enjoyed by his sons for ten thousand generations." In fact, his centralizing zeal alienated many key groups. Landed aristocrats and Confucian intellectuals, as well as the common people, groaned under the censorship of thought and speech, harsh taxes, and forced labor projects. "He killed men," recounted the historian, "as though he thought he could never finish, he punished men as though he were afraid he would never get around to them all, and the whole world revolted against him."[12] Shortly after the emperor died in 210 B.C.E., the dynasty quickly descended into factional rivalry, and four years later it was overthrown.

The disappearance of the Qin brought an end to an experiment in absolute rule that later Chinese historians would view as a betrayal of humanistic Confucian principles. But in another sense, the Qin system was a response—though somewhat extreme—to the problems of administering a large and increasingly complex society. Although later rulers would denounce Legalism and enthrone Confucianism as the new state orthodoxy, in practice they would make use of a number of the key tenets of Legalism to administer the empire and control the behavior of their subjects.

The Glorious Han Dynasty (202 B.C.E.–221 C.E.)

The fall of the Qin was followed by a brief period of civil strife as aspiring successors competed for hegemony. Out of this strife emerged one of the greatest and most durable dynasties in Chinese history—the Han (see Map 3.3). The Han dynasty would later become so closely identified with the advance of Chinese civilization that even today the Chinese sometimes refer to themselves as "people of Han" and to their language as the "language of Han."

The founder of the Han dynasty was Liu Bang (Liu Pang), a commoner of peasant origin who would be known historically by his title of Han Gaozu (Han Kao Tsu, or Exalted Emperor of Han). Under his strong rule and that of his successors, the new dynasty quickly moved to consolidate its control over the empire and promote the welfare of its subjects. Efficient and benevolent, at least by the

MAP 3.3   The Han Empire.   This map shows the territory under control of the Han empire at its greatest extent during the first century B.C.E. Note the expansion of Han rule to the west, as Chinese armies penetrated across the Silk Road into Central Asia. ➤ *Where is the Great Wall on the map?*

standards of the time, Gaozu maintained the centralized political institutions of the Qin but abandoned their harsh Legalistic approach to law enforcement. Han rulers also reversed the effort by the First Emperor of Qin to enforce a single ideology and discovered in Confucian principles a useful foundation for the creation of a new state philosophy. Under the Han, Confucianism began to take on the character of an official ideology.

CONFUCIANISM AND THE STATE

The integration of Confucian doctrine with Legalist practice, creating a system generally known as State Confucianism, did not take long to accomplish. Although the founding Han ruler declared his intention to discard the harsh methods adopted by the Qin, he and his successors found it convenient to retain many of the institutions introduced by the First Emperor of Qin. For example, they borrowed the tripartite division of the central government into civilian and military authorities and a censorate. The government was headed by a "grand coun-

cil" including representatives from all three segments of government. The Han also retained the system of local government, dividing the empire into provinces and districts.

Finally, and perhaps most important, the Han continued the Qin system of selecting government officials on the basis of merit rather than birth. Shortly after founding the new dynasty, Emperor Gaozu decreed that local officials would be asked to recommend promising candidates for public service. Thirty years later, in 165 B.C.E., the first known civil service examination was administered to candidates for positions in the bureaucracy. Shortly after that, an academy was established to train candidates. Nevertheless, the first candidates were almost all from aristocratic or other wealthy families, and the Han bureaucracy itself was still dominated by the traditional hereditary elite. Still, the principle of selecting officials on the basis of talent had been established and would eventually become standard practice.

Under the Han dynasty, the population increased rapidly—by some estimates rising from about twenty million to over sixty million at the height of the dynasty—creating a growing need for a large and efficient bureaucracy to maintain the state in proper working order. Unfortunately, the Han were unable to resolve all of the problems left over from the past. Factionalism at court remained a serious problem and undermined the efficiency of the central government. Equally important, despite their efforts, the Han rulers were never able to restrain the great aristocratic families, who continued to play a dominant role in political and economic affairs. The failure to curb the power of the wealthy clans eventually became a major factor in the collapse of the dynasty.

SOCIETY AND ECONOMY IN THE HAN EMPIRE

Han rulers also retained some of the economic and social policies of their predecessors. In particular, they saw that a free peasantry paying taxes directly to the state would both limit the wealth and power of the great noble families and increase the state's revenues. The Han had difficulty preventing the recurrence of the economic inequities that had characterized the last years of the Zhou, however. The land taxes were relatively light, but the peasants also faced a number of other exactions, including military service and forced labor of up to one month annually. Although the use of iron tools brought new lands under the plow and food production increased steadily, the trebling of the population under the Han eventually reduced the average size of the individual farm plot to about one acre per capita, barely enough for survival. As time went on, many poor peasants were forced to sell their land and become tenant farmers, paying rents ranging up to half of the annual harvest. Thus land once again came to be concentrated in the hands of the powerful landed clans, which often owned thousands of acres worked by tenants and mustered their own military forces to bully free farmers into becoming tenants.

Although such economic problems contributed to the eventual downfall of the dynasty, in general the Han era was one of unparalleled productivity and prosperity. The period was marked by a major expansion of trade, both domestic and foreign. This was not necessarily due to official encouragement. In fact, the Han were as suspicious of private merchants as their predecessors had been and levied stiff taxes on trade in an effort to limit commercial activities. Merchants were also subject to severe social constraints. They were disqualified from seeking office, restricted in their place of residence, and viewed in general as parasites providing little true value to Chinese society.

The state itself directed much trade and manufacturing; it manufactured weapons, for example, and operated shipyards, granaries, and mines. The government also moved cautiously into foreign trade, mostly with neighboring areas in Central and Southeast Asia, although trade relations were established with countries as far away as India and the Mediterranean (see Map 3.4). Some of this long-distance trade was carried by sea through southern ports like Guangzhou, but more was transported by overland caravans on the Silk Road (see Chapter 10) and other routes that led westward into Central Asia. Some of the trade was organized in the form of tribute missions, with neighboring countries providing local specialties like tropical products and precious stones in return for Chinese silks, glazed pottery (an early form of porcelain), and various manufactured products. China often gave more than it received to ensure that neighboring monarchs would accept China's benevolent protection and not harbor its enemies.

New technology contributed to the economic prosperity of the Han era. Significant progress was achieved in

© Christopher Lui

⤞ **A PRIZED POSSESSION.**   Horse-drawn chariots were first used by nomadic peoples in the steppes of Central Asia and made their appearance in China late in the second millennium B.C.E. They quickly assured local rulers of military superiority on the battlefield, while their mobility proved useful during big game hunts at a time when the heavily forested plains of northern China were filled with tigers, elephants, and even rhinoceros. Like the pharaohs in Egypt, Chinese rulers filled their tombs with prized possessions deemed useful in the next world. Here we see the remains of a chariot and horses in a burial pit in Hebei province that dates from the early Zhou dynasty.

such areas as textile manufacturing, water mills, and iron casting; skill at ironworking led to the production of steel a few centuries later. Paper was invented under the Han, and the development of the rudder and fore-and-aft rigging permitted ships to sail into the wind for the first time. Thus equipped, Chinese merchant ships carrying heavy cargoes could sail throughout the islands of Southeast Asia and into the Indian Ocean.

Finally, the Han emperors continued the process of territorial expansion and consolidation that had begun under the Zhou and the Qin. Han rulers, notably Han Wudi (Han Wu Ti, or Martial Emperor of Han), successfully completed the assimilation into the empire of the regions south of the Yangtze River, including the Red River delta in what is today northern Vietnam. Han armies also marched westward as far as the Caspian Sea, pacifying nomadic tribal peoples and extending China's boundary far into Central Asia. The Han continued to have problems with the Xiongnu beyond the Great Wall to the north. Nomadic raids on Chinese territory continued intermittently to the end of the dynasty, once reaching almost to the gates of the capital city, now located at Chang'an (Ch'ang An, or Eternal Peace), on the site of modern Xian.

MAP 3.4   Trade Routes of the Ancient World. This map shows the various land and maritime routes that extended from China toward other civilizations that were located to the south and west of the Han empire. The various goods that were exchanged are identified at the bottom of the map.

➤ *What were the major goods exported by China?*

Breakdown of Traded Goods

Region	Imports	Exports
North India		
South India		
China		
Arabia		
East Africa		

Traded goods:

- slaves
- tortoiseshell
- precious stones
- glassware
- ivory
- wine
- coinage
- spices
- metal
- weapons
- incense
- cloth and clothing
- timber
- silks

Chronology

ANCIENT CHINA

Xia (Hsia) dynasty	?–c.1570 B.C.E
Shang dynasty	c.1570–c.1045 B.C.E
Zhou (Chou) dynasty	c.1045–221 B.C.E
Life of Confucius	551–479 B.C.E
Period of the Warring States	403–221 B.C.E
Life of Mencius	370–290 B.C.E
Qin (Ch'in) dynasty	221–206 B.C.E
Life of the First Emperor of Qin	259–210 B.C.E
Formation of Han dynasty	202 B.C.E
Wang Mang interregnum	9–23 C.E.
Collapse of Han dynasty	221 C.E.

THE DECLINE AND FALL OF THE HAN

In 9 C.E., the reformist official Wang Mang, who was troubled by the plight of the peasants, seized power from the Han court and declared the foundation of a new Xin (New) dynasty. The empire had been crumbling for decades. As frivolous or depraved rulers amused themselves with the pleasures of court life, the power and influence of the central government began to wane, and the great noble families filled the vacuum, amassing vast landed estates and transforming free farmers into tenants. Wang Mang tried to confiscate the great estates, restore the ancient well field system, and abolish slavery. In so doing, however, he alienated powerful interests, who conspired to overthrow him. In 23 C.E., beset by administrative chaos and a collapse of the frontier defenses, Wang Mang was killed in a coup d'état.

For a time, strong leadership revived some of the glory of the early Han. The court did attempt to reduce land taxes and carry out land resettlement programs. The growing popularity of nutritious crops like rice, wheat, and soybeans, along with the introduction of new crops such as alfalfa and grapes, helped boost food production. But the monopoly of land and power by the great landed families continued. Weak rulers were isolated within their imperial chambers and dominated by eunuchs and other powerful figures at court. Official corruption and the concentration of land in the hands of the wealthy led to widespread peasant unrest. The population of the empire, which had been estimated at about sixty million in China's first census in the year 2 C.E., had shrunk to less than one-third that number two hundred years later. In the early third century C.E., the dynasty was finally brought to an end when power was seized by Cao Cao (Ts'ao Ts'ao), a general known to later generations as one of the main characters in the famous Chinese epic *The Romance of the Three Kingdoms*. But Cao Cao was unable to consolidate his power, and China entered a period of almost constant anarchy and internal division, compounded by invasions by northern tribal peoples. The next great dynasty did not arise until the beginning of the seventh century, four hundred years later.

DAILY LIFE IN ANCIENT CHINA

Few social institutions have been as closely identified with China as the family. As in most agricultural civilizations, the family served as the basic economic and social unit in society. In traditional China, however, it took on an almost sacred quality as a microcosm of the entire social order.

In Neolithic times, the farm village, organized around the clan, was the basic social unit in China, at least in the core region of the Yellow River valley. Even then, however, the smaller family unit was becoming more important, at least among the nobility, who attached considerable significance to the ritual veneration of their immediate ancestors.

During the Zhou dynasty, the family took on increasing importance, in part because of the need for cooperation in agriculture. The cultivation of rice, which had become the primary crop along the Yangtze River and in the provinces to the south, is highly labor-intensive. The seedlings must be planted in several inches of water in a nursery bed and then transferred individually to the paddy beds, which must be irrigated constantly. During the harvest, the stalks must be cut and the kernels carefully separated from the stalks and husks. As a result, children—and the labor they supplied—were considered essential to the survival of the family, not only during their youthful years but also later, when sons were expected to provide for their parents. Loyalty to family members came to be considered even more important than loyalty to the broader community or the state. Confucius commented that it is the mark of a civilized society that a son should protect his father even if the latter has committed a crime against the community.

At the crux of the concept of family was the idea of filial piety, which called on all members of the family to subordinate their needs and desires to the patriarchal head of the family. More broadly, it created a hierarchical system in which every family member had his or her place. All Chinese learned the "five relationships" that were the key to a proper social order. The son was subordinate to the father, the wife to her husband, the younger brother to the older brother, and all were subject to their king. The final relationship was the proper one between friend and friend.

Courtesy of William J. Duiker

FLOODED RICE FIELDS. Rice, which was first cultivated in China as long as seven or eight thousand years ago, is a very labor-intensive crop that requires many workers to plant the seedlings and organize the distribution of water. Initially, the fields are flooded to facilitate the rooting of the rice seedlings and to add nutrients to the soil. Fish breeding in the flooded fields help keep mosquitoes and other insects in check. As the plants mature, the fields are drained, and the plants complete their four-month growing cycle in dry soil. Shown here is an exmple of terracing on a hillside to preserve water for the nourishment of young seedlings.

Only if all members of the family and the community as a whole behaved in a properly filial manner would society function effectively.

A stable family system based on obedient and hard-working members can serve as a bulwark for an efficient government, but putting loyalty to the family and the clan over loyalty to the state can also present a threat to a centralizing monarch. For that reason, the Qin dynasty attempted to destroy the clan system in China and assert the primacy of the state. Legalists even imposed heavy taxes on any family with more than two adult sons in order to break down the family concept. The Qin reportedly also originated the practice of organizing several family units into larger groups of five and ten families that would exercise mutual control and surveillance. Later dynasties continued the practice under the name of the *Bao-jia* (*Pao-chia*) system.

But the efforts of the Qin to eradicate or at least reduce the importance of the family system ran against tradition and the dynamics of the Chinese economy, and under the Han, the family revived and increased in importance. With official encouragement, the family system began to take on the character that it would possess until our own day. The family was not only the basic economic unit; it was also the basic social unit for education, religious observances, and training in ethical principles.

We know much more about the lifestyle of the elites than that of the common people in ancient China. The first houses were probably constructed of wooden planks, but later Chinese mastered the art of building in tile and brick. By the first millennium B.C.E., most public buildings and the houses of the wealthy were probably constructed in this manner. By Han times, most Chinese probably lived in simple houses of mud, wooden planks, or brick with thatch or occasionally tile roofs. But in some areas, especially the loess (pronounced "less," a type of soil common in North China) regions of North China, cave dwelling remained common down to modern times. The most famous cave dweller of modern times was Mao Zedong, who lived in a cave in Yan'an during his long struggle against Chiang Kai-shek.

Chinese houses usually had little furniture; most people squatted or sat with their legs spread out on the packed mud floor. Chairs were apparently not introduced until the sixth or seventh century C.E. Clothing was simple, consisting of cotton trousers and shirts in the summer and wool or burlap in the winter.

The staple foods were millet in the north and rice in the south. Other common foods were wheat, barley, soybeans, mustard greens, and bamboo shoots. In early times, such foods were often consumed in the form of porridge, but by the Zhou dynasty, stir-frying in a wok was becoming common. When possible, the Chinese family would vary its diet of grain foods with vegetables, fruit (including pears, peaches, apricots, and plums), and fish or meat; but for most, such additions to the daily plate of rice, millet, or soybeans were a rare luxury.

Alcohol in the form of ale was drunk at least by the higher classes and by the early Zhou era had already begun to inspire official concern. According to the *Book of History*, "King Wen admonished . . . the young nobles . . . that they should not ordinarily use spirits; and throughout all the states he required that they should be drunk only on occasion of sacrifices, and that then virtue should preside so that there might be no drunkenness."[13]

Most Chinese, then as now, lived in the countryside. But as time went on, cities began to play a larger role in Chinese society. The first towns were little more than forts for the local aristocracy; they were small in size and limited in population. By the Zhou era, however, larger towns, usually located on the major trade routes, began to combine administrative and economic functions, serving as regional markets or manufacturing centers. Such cities were usually surrounded by a wall and a moat, and a raised platform might be built within the walls to provide a place for ritual ceremonies and housing for the ruler's family.

By the Han, the major city in China was Chang'an, the imperial capital. The city covered a total area of nearly 40 square kilometers and was enclosed by a 12-foot earthen wall surrounded by a moat. Twelve gates provided entry into the city, and eight major avenues ran east-west or north-south. Each avenue was 45 meters wide; a center strip in each avenue was reserved for the emperor, whose palace and gardens occupied nearly half the southern and central part of the city.

The Humble Estate: Women in Ancient China

Female subservience was a key element in the social system of ancient China. As in many traditional societies, the male was considered of transcendent importance because of his role as food procurer or, in the case of farming communities, food producer. In ancient China, men worked in the fields and women raised children and served in the home. The Chinese written language graphically demonstrates how ancient Chinese society regarded the sexes. The character for man (**男**) combines the symbols for strength and a rice field, whereas the character for woman (**女**) represents a person in a posture of deference and respect. The character for peace (**安**) is a woman under a roof. A wife is symbolized by a woman with a broom.

Confucian thought, while not denigrating the importance of women as mothers and homemakers, accepted the dual roles of men and women in Chinese society. Men governed society. They carried on family ritual through the veneration of ancestors. They were the warriors, scholars, and ministers. Their dominant role was firmly enshrined in the legal system. Men were permitted to have more than one wife and to divorce a spouse who did not produce a male child. Women were denied the right to own property, and there was no dowry system in ancient China that would have provided the wife with a degree of financial security from her husband and his family. As the third-century C.E. woman poet Fu Xuan lamented:

> How sad it is to be a woman
> Nothing on earth is held so cheap.
> No one is glad when a girl is born.
> By her the family sets no store.
> No one cries when she leaves her home
> Sudden as clouds when the rain stops.[14]

Not surprisingly women were taught to accept their secondary role in life. Ban Zhao, a prominent female historian of the Han dynasty whose own career was an exception to the rule, described that role as follows:

> To be humble, yielding, respectful and reverential; to put herself after others . . . these qualities are those exemplifying woman's low and humble estate. To retire late and rise early; not to shirk exertion from dawn to dark . . . this is called being diligent. To behave properly and decorously in serving her husband; to be serene and self-possessed, shunning jests and

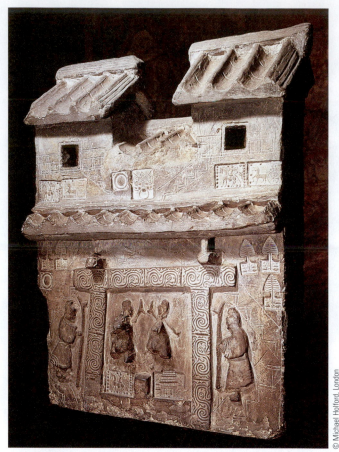

© Michael Holford, London

➤ **HAN POTTERY HOUSE.** During the Han dynasty, the Chinese people thought that even in heaven one could still be surrounded by one's earthly possessions, such as family, servants, and house. Since such material goods could not accompany one directly into the afterworld, pottery models such as the one shown here were made and then placed in tombs with the dead.

laughter . . . this is called being worthy of continuing the husband's lineage. If a woman possess the above-mentioned three qualities, then her reputation shall be excellent.[15]

Some women did become a force in politics, especially at court, where wives of the ruler or other female members of the royal family were often influential in palace intrigues. Such activities were frowned on, however, as the following passage from the *Book of Songs* attests:

> A clever man builds a city,
> A clever woman lays one low;
> With all her qualifications, that clever woman
> Is but an ill-omened bird.
> A woman with a long tongue
> Is a flight of steps leading to calamity;
> For disorder does not come from heaven,
> But is brought about by women.
> Among those who cannot be trained or taught
> Are women and eunuchs.[16]

CHINESE CULTURE

Modern knowledge about artistic achievements in ancient civilizations is limited because often little has survived the ravages of time. Fortunately, many ancient civilizations, such as Egypt and Mesopotamia, were located in relatively arid areas where many artifacts were preserved, even over thousands of years. In more humid regions, such as China and South Asia, the cultural residue left by the civilizations of antiquity has been adversely affected by climate.

As a result, relatively little remains of the cultural achievements of the prehistoric Chinese aside from Neolithic pottery and the relics found at the site of the Shang dynasty capital at Anyang. In recent years, a rich trove from the time of the Qin Empire has been unearthed near the tomb of Qin Shi Huangdi near Xian in central China and at Han tombs nearby. But little remains of the literature of ancient China and almost none of the painting, architecture, and music.

Metalwork and Sculpture

Discoveries at archaeological sites indicate that ancient China was a society rich in cultural achievement. The pottery found at Neolithic sites such as Longshan and Yangshao exhibits a freshness and vitality of form and design, and the ornaments, such as rings and beads, show a strong aesthetic sense.

The pace of Chinese cultural development began to quicken during the Shang dynasty, which ruled in northern China from the sixteenth to the eleventh century B.C.E. At that time, objects cast in bronze began to appear. A variety of bronze vessels were produced for use in preparing and serving food and drink in the ancestral rites. Later vessels were used for decoration or for dining at court.

The method of casting used was one reason for the extraordinary quality of Shang bronze work. Bronze workers in most ancient civilizations used the lost-wax method, where a model was first made in wax. After a clay mold had been formed around it, the model was heated so that the wax would disappear, and the empty space was filled with molten metal. In China, clay molds composed of several sections were tightly fitted together prior to the introduction of the liquid bronze. This technique, which had evolved from ceramic techniques used during the Neolithic period, enabled the artisans to apply the design directly to the mold and thus contributed to the clarity of line and rich surface decoration of the Shang bronzes.

Bronze casting became a large-scale business, and more than ten thousand vessels of an incredible variety of form and design survive today. The art of bronze working continued into the Zhou and the Han dynasties, but the quality and originality declined. The Shang bronzes remain the pinnacle of creative art in ancient China.

One reason for the decline of bronze casting in China was the rise in popularity of iron. Ironmaking developed in China around the ninth or eighth century B.C.E., much later than in the Middle East, where it had been mastered almost a millennium earlier. Once familiar with the process, however, the Chinese quickly moved to the forefront. Ironworkers in Europe and the Middle East, lacking the technology to achieve the high temperatures necessary to melt iron ore for casting, were forced to work with wrought iron, a cumbersome and expensive process. By the fourth century B.C.E., the Chinese had invented the technique of the blast furnace, powered by a person operating a bellows. They were therefore able to manufacture cast-iron ritual vessels and agricultural tools centuries before an equivalent technology appeared in the West.

Another reason for the deterioration of the bronze-casting tradition was the development of cheaper materials such as lacquerware and ceramics. Lacquer, obtained from a resinous

A SHANG WINE VESSEL. Used initially as food containers in royal ceremonial rites during the Shang dynasty, Chinese bronzes were the product of an advanced technology unmatched by any contemporary civilization. This wine vessel displays a deep green patina as well as a monster motif, complete with large globular eyes, nostrils, and fangs, typical of many Shang bronzes. Known as the *taotie*, this fanciful beast is normally presented in silhouette as two dragons face-to-face so that each side forms half of the mask. Although the *taotie* presumably served as a guardian force against evil spirits, scholars are still not aware of its exact significance for early Chinese peoples.

Courtesy of William J. Duiker

QIN SHI HUANGDI'S TOMB.   The First Emperor of Qin ordered the construction of an elaborate mausoleum, an underground palace complex protected by an army of terra-cotta soldiers and horses to accompany him on his journey to the afterlife. This massive formation of six thousand life-size armed soldiers, discovered accidentally by farmers in 1974, reflects Qin Shi Huangdi's grandeur and power.

© Robert Harding Picture Library

substance deposited on trees by the *lac* insect, had been produced since Neolithic times, and by the Han era it had become a popular method of applying a hard coating to objects made of wood or fabric. Pottery, too, had existed since early times, but technological advances during the Han led to the production of a high-quality form of pottery covered with a brown or gray-green glaze, the latter known popularly as celadon. During the Han, both lacquerware and pottery replaced bronze in popularity and value.

In 1974, in a remarkable discovery, farmers digging a well about 35 miles east of Xian unearthed a number of terra-cotta figures in an underground pit about one mile east of the burial mound of the First Emperor of Qin. Chinese archaeologists sent to work at the site discovered a vast terra-cotta army that they believed was a recreation of Qin Shi Huangdi's imperial guard, which was to accompany the emperor on his journey to the next world.

One of the astounding features of the terra-cotta army is its size. The army is enclosed in four pits that were originally encased in a wooden framework, which has since disintegrated. More than a thousand figures have already been unearthed in the first pit, along with horses, wooden chariots, and seven thousand bronze weapons. Archaeologists estimate that there are more than six thousand figures in that pit alone.

Equally impressive is the quality of the work. Slightly larger than life-size, the figures were molded of finely textured clay, then fired and painted. The detail on the uniforms is realistic and sophisticated, but the most striking feature is the individuality of the facial features of the soldiers. Apparently, ten different head shapes were used and

were then modeled further by hand to reflect the variety of ethnic groups and personality types in the army.

The discovery of the terra-cotta army also shows that the Chinese had come a long way from the human sacrifices that had taken place at the death of Shang sovereigns more than a thousand years earlier. But the project must have been ruinously expensive and is additional evidence of the burden the Qin ruler imposed on his subjects. One historian has estimated that one-third of the national income in Qin and Han times may have been spent on preparations for the ruler's afterlife. The emperor's mausoleum has not yet been unearthed, but it is enclosed in a mound nearly 250 feet high and is surrounded by a rectangular wall nearly 4 miles around. According to the Han historian Sima Qian, the ceiling is a replica of the heavens, while the floor contains a relief model of the entire Qin kingdom, with rivers flowing in mercury. According to tradition, traps were set within the mausoleum to prevent intruders, and the workers applying the final touches were buried alive in the tomb with its secrets.

Qin Shi Huangdi's ambitious effort to provide for his immortality became a pattern for his successors during the Han dynasty, although apparently on a somewhat more modest scale. In 1990, Chinese workers discovered a similar underground army for a Han emperor of the second century B.C.E. Like the imperial guard of the First Qin Emperor, the underground soldiers were buried in parallel pits and possessed their own weapons and individual facial features. But they were smaller—only one-third the height of the average human adult—and were armed with wooden weapons and dressed in silk clothing, now decayed. A burial pit nearby indicates that as many as ten thousand workers, probably slaves or prisoners, died in the process of building the emperor's mausoleum, which took an estimated ten years to construct.

Language and Literature

Precisely when writing developed in China cannot be determined, but certainly by Shang times, as the oracle bones demonstrate, the Chinese had developed a simple but functional script. Like many other languages of antiquity, it was primarily ideographic and pictographic in form. Symbols, usually called "characters," were created to represent an idea or to form a picture of the object to be represented. For example, the Chinese characters for mountain (山), the sun (日), and the moon (月) were meant to represent the objects themselves. Other characters, such as "big" (大) (a man with his arms outstretched), represent an idea. The word "east" (東) symbolizes the sun coming up behind the trees.

Each character, of course, would be given a sound by the speaker when pronounced. In other cultures, this process led to the abandonment of the system of ideographs and the adoption of a written language based on phonetic symbols. The Chinese language, however, has never entirely abandoned its original ideographical format, although the phonetic element has developed into a significant part of the individual character. In that sense, the Chinese written language is virtually unique in the world today.

One reason the language retained its ideographic quality may have been the aesthetic quality of the written characters. By the time of the Han dynasty, if not earlier, the written language came to be seen as an art form as well as a means of communication, and calligraphy became one of the most prized forms of painting in China.

Even more important, if the written language had developed in the direction of a phonetic alphabet, it could no longer have served as the written system for all the peoples of an expanding civilization. Although the vast majority spoke a tongue derived from a parent Sinitic language (a system distinguished by its tonal nature, a characteristic that gives Chinese its lilting quality even today), the languages spoken in various regions of the country differed from each other in pronunciation and to a lesser degree in vocabulary and syntax; for the most part, they were (and are today) mutually unintelligible.

The Chinese answer to this problem was to give all the spoken languages the same writing system. Although any character might be pronounced differently in different regions of China, that character would be written the same way (after the standardization undertaken under the Qin) no matter where it was written. This system of written characters could be read by educated

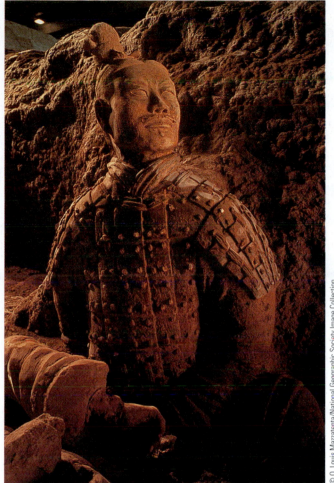

SOLDIER IN QIN SHI HUANGDI'S TOMB. This is one of the six thousand soldiers guarding the underground palace complex of Emperor Qin Shi Huangdi's tomb. Incredibly, each soldier has individualized facial features and expressions. Originally, they carried real weapons, and their uniforms were painted in brilliant colors. They are a most majestic and foreboding sight, individually and collectively.

Chinese from one end of the country to the other. It became the language of the bureaucracy and the vehicle for the transmission of Chinese culture to all Chinese from the Great Wall to the southern border and even beyond. The written language, however, was not identical with the spoken. Written Chinese evolved a totally separate vocabulary and grammatical structure from the spoken tongues. As a result, those who used it required special training.

The earliest extant form of Chinese literature dates from the Zhou dynasty. It was written on silk or strips of bamboo and consisted primarily of historical records such as the *Rites of Zhou*, philosophical treatises such as the *Analects* and *The Way of the Dao*, and poetry, as recorded in *The Book of Songs* and the *Song of the South* (see the box on p. 86). In later years, when Confucian principles had

LOVE SPURNED IN ANCIENT CHINA

The Book of Songs is an anthology of about three hundred poems written during the early Zhou dynasty. According to tradition, they were selected by Confucius from a much larger collection. In later years, many were given political interpretations. The poem reprinted here, however, expresses a very human cry of love spurned.

THE BOOK OF SONGS: THE ODES

You seemed a guileless youth enough,
Offering for silk your woven stuff;
But silk was not required by you;
I was the silk you had in view.
With you I crossed the ford, and while
We wandered on for many a mile
I said, "I do not wish delay,
But friends must fix our wedding-day. . . .
Oh, do not let my words give pain,
But with the autumn come again."

And then I used to watch and wait
To see you passing through the gate;
And sometimes, when I watched in vain,
My tears would flow like falling rain;
But when I saw my darling boy,
I laughed and cried aloud for joy.
The fortune-tellers, you declared,
Had all pronounced us duly paired;
"Then bring a carriage," I replied,
"And I'll away to be your bride."

The mulberry tree upon the ground,
Now sheds its yellow leaves around.

Three years have slipped away from me
Since first I shared your poverty;
And now again, alas the day!
Back through the ford I take my way.

My heart is still unchanged, but you
Have uttered words now proved untrue;
And you have left me to deplore
A love that can be mine no more.

For three long years I was your wife,
And led in truth a toilsome life;
Early to rise and late to bed,
Each day alike passed o'er my head.
I honestly fulfilled my part,
And you—well, you have broke my heart.
The truth my brothers will not know,
So all the more their gibes will flow.
I grieve in silence and repine
That such a wretched fate is mine.

Ah, hand in hand to face old age!—
Instead, I turn a bitter page.
O for the riverbanks of yore;
O for the much-loved marshy shore;
The hours of girlhood, with my hair
Ungathered, as we lingered there.
The words we spoke, that seemed so true,
I little thought that I should rue;
I little thought the vows we swore
Would some day bind us two no more.

---

been elevated to a state ideology, the key works identified with the Confucian school were integrated into a set of so-called Confucian Classics. These works became required reading for generations of Chinese schoolchildren and introduced them to the forms of behavior that would be required of them as adults.

Under the Han dynasty, although poetry and philosophical essays continued to be popular, historical writing became the primary form of literary creativity. Historians such as Sima Qian and Ban Gu (the dynasty's official historian and the older brother of the female historian Ban Zhao) wrote works that became models for later dynastic histories. These historical works combined political and social history with biographies of key figures. Like so much literary work in China, their primary purpose was moral and political—to explain the underlying reasons for the rise and fall of individual human beings and dynasties.

Music

From early times in China, music was viewed not just as an aesthetic pleasure but also as a means of achieving political order and refining the human character. In fact, music may have originated as an accompaniment to sacred rituals at the royal court. According to the *Historical Records*, a history written during the Han dynasty: "When our sage-kings of the past instituted rites and music, their objective was far from making people indulge in the . . . amusements of singing and dancing. . . . Music is produced to purify the heart, and rites introduced to rectify the behavior."[17] Eventually, however, music began to be appreciated for its own sake as well as to accompany singing and dancing.

A wide variety of musical instruments were used, including flutes, various stringed instruments, bells and chimes, drums, and gourds. Bells cast in bronze were first used as musical instruments in the Shang period; they were hung in rows and struck with a wooden mallet. The finest were produced during the mid-Zhou era and are considered among the best examples of early bronze work in China.

By the late Zhou era, bells had begun to give way as the instrument of choice to strings and wind instruments, and the purpose of music shifted from ceremony to entertainment. This led conservative critics to rail against the onset of an age of debauchery.

Ancient historians stressed the relationship between music and court life, but it is highly probable that music, singing, and dancing were equally popular among the common people. The *Book of History,* purporting to describe conditions in the late third millennium B.C.E., suggests that ballads emanating from the popular culture were welcomed at court. Nevertheless, court music and popular music differed in several respects. Among other things, popular music was more likely to be motivated by the desire for pleasure than for the purpose of law and order and moral uplift. Those differences continued to be reflected in the evolution of music in China down to modern times.

CONCLUSION

Of the great classical civilizations discussed in Part I of this book, China was the last to come into full flower. By the time the Shang began to emerge as an organized state, the societies in Mesopotamia and the Nile valley had already reached an advanced level of civilization. Unfortunately, not enough is known about the early stages of these civilizations to allow us to determine why some developed earlier than others, but one likely reason for China's late arrival was that it was virtually isolated from other emerging centers of culture elsewhere in the world and thus was compelled to develop essentially on its own. Only at the end of the first millennium B.C.E. did the Han dynasty come into regular contact with other civilizations in South Asia, the Middle East, and the Mediterranean.

Once embarked on its own path toward the creation of a complex society, however, China achieved results that were in all respects the equal of its counterparts elsewhere. During the glory years of the Han dynasty, China extended the boundaries of its empire far into the sands of Central Asia and southward along the coast of the South China Sea into what is now Vietnam. The doctrine of State Confucianism provided an effective ideology for the state, and Chinese culture appeared unrivaled. In many respects, its scientific and technological achievements were unsurpassed.

One reason for China's striking success was undoubtedly that unlike its contemporary civilizations, it long was able to fend off the danger from nomadic peoples (along the northern frontier). By the end of the second century B.C.E., however, the Xiongnu were looming ominously, and tribal warriors began to nip at the borders of the empire. While the dynasty was strong, the problem was manageable, but when internal difficulties began to corrode the unity of the state, China became increasingly vulnerable to the threat from the north and entered its own time of troubles.

During the glory years of the Han, another great civilization was beginning to take form on the northern shores of the Mediterranean Sea. Unlike China and the other ancient societies discussed thus far, this new civilization in Europe was based as much on trade as on agriculture. Yet the political and cultural achievements of ancient Greece were the equal of any of the great human experiments that had preceded it and soon began to exert a significant impact on the rest of the ancient world.

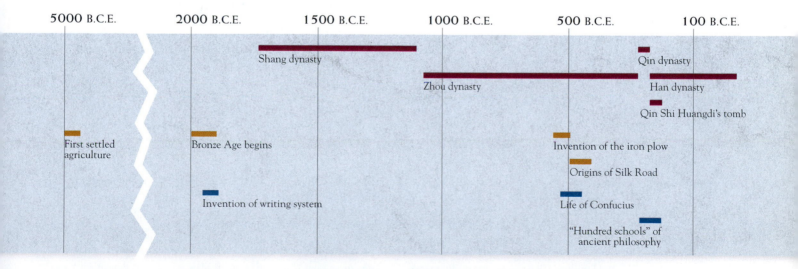

| 5000 B.C.E. | 2000 B.C.E. | 1500 B.C.E. | 1000 B.C.E. | 500 B.C.E. | 100 B.C.E. |

Shang dynasty

Zhou dynasty

Qin dynasty

Han dynasty

Qin Shi Huangdi's tomb

First settled agriculture

Bronze Age begins

Invention of the iron plow

Origins of Silk Road

Invention of writing system

Life of Confucius

"Hundred schools" of ancient philosophy

CHAPTER NOTES

1. *Book of Changes*, quoted in Chang Chi-yun, *Chinese History of Fifty Centuries*, vol. 1, *Ancient Times* (Taipei, 1962), pp. 15, 31, and 65.
2. Ibid., p. 381.
3. Quoted in E. N. Anderson, *The Food of China* (New Haven, Conn., 1988), p. 21.
4. According to Chinese tradition, the *Rites of Zhou* was written by the duke of Zhou himself near the time of the founding of the Zhou dynasty. However, modern historians believe that it was written much later, perhaps as late as the fourth century B.C.E.
5. From *The Book of Songs*, quoted in Sebastian de Grazia, ed., *Masters of Chinese Political Thought: From the Beginnings to the Han Dynasty* (New York, 1973), pp. 40–41.
6. *Confucian Analects* (Lun Yu), ed. James Legge (Taipei, 1963), 11:11 and 6:20.
7. Ibid., 15:23.
8. Ibid., 17:2.
9. *Book of Mencius* (Meng Zi), 4 A:9, quoted in William Theodore de Bary et al., eds., *Sources of Chinese Tradition* (New York, 1960), p. 107.
10. Quoted in de Bary, *Sources of Chinese Tradition*, p. 53.
11. Burton Watson, *Records of the Grand Historian of China* (New York, 1961), vol. 2, pp. 155, 160.
12. Ibid., pp. 32, 53.
13. Clae Waltham, *Shu Ching: Book of History* (Chicago, 1971), p. 154.
14. Arthur Waley, ed., *Chinese Poems* (London, 1983), p. xx.
15. Lloyd E. Eastman, *Family, Fields, and Ancestors: Constancy and Change in China's Social and Economic History, 1550–1949* (New York, 1988), p. 19.
16. Quoted in Herbert A. Giles, *A History of Chinese Literature* (New York, 1923), p. 19.
17. Chang Chi-yun, *Chinese History of Fifty Centuries*, vol. 1, p. 183.

SUGGESTED READING

Several general histories of China provide a useful overview of the period of antiquity. Perhaps the best known is the classic *East Asia: Tradition and Transformation* (Boston, 1973), by J. K. Fairbank, E. O. Reischauer, and A. M. Craig. For an authoritative overview of the ancient period, see M. Loewe and E. L. Shaughnessy, *The Cambridge History of Ancient China from the Origins of Civilization to 221 B.C.* (Cambridge, 1999). Political and social maps of China can be found in A. Herrmann, *A Historical Atlas of China* (Chicago, 1966).

The period of the Neolithic era and the Shang dynasty has received increasing attention in recent years. For an impressively documented and annotated overview, see Kwang-chih Chang, *Shang Civilization* (New Haven, Conn., 1980) and *Studies in Shang Archaeology* (New Haven, Conn., 1982). D. Keightley, *The Origins of Chinese Civilization* (Berkeley, Calif., 1983), presents a number of interesting articles on selected aspects of the period.

The Zhou and Qin dynasties have also received considerable attention. The former is exhaustively analyzed in Cho-yun Hsu and J. M. Linduff, *Western Zhou Civilization* (New Haven, Conn., 1988), and Li Xueqin, *Eastern Zhou and Qin Civilizations* (New Haven, Conn., 1985). The latter is a translation of an original work by a mainland Chinese scholar and is especially interesting for its treatment of the development of the silk industry and the money economy in ancient China. On bronze casting, see E. L. Shaughnessy, *Sources of Eastern Zhou History* (Berkeley, Calif., 1991). Also of value for its treatment of the formation of social classes is Cho-yun Hsu, *Ancient China in Transition* (Stanford, Calif., 1965).

There are a number of useful books on the Han dynasty. Zhong-shu Wang, *Han Civilization* (New Haven, Conn., 1982), presents recent evidence from the mainland on recent excavations from Han tombs and the old imperial capital of Chang'an. M. Loewe, *Everyday Life in Early Imperial China During the Han Period, 202 B.C.–220 A.D.* (London, 1968), contains useful mate-

rial on religious beliefs and the development of social classes during the Han. Also see the lavishly illustrated *Han Civilization of China* (Oxford, 1982) by M. P. Serstevens. For a firsthand view, see B. Watson, *Records of the Grand Historian of China* (New York, 1961), a translation of key passages from Sima Qian's history of the period.

The philosophy of ancient China has attracted considerable attention from Western scholars. Some standard works include A. Waley, *Three Ways of Thought in Ancient China* (New York, 1939); H. G. Creel, *Chinese Thought: From Confucius to Mao Tse-Tung* (Chicago, 1953); Feng Yu-lan, *A Short History of Chinese Philosophy* (New York, 1960); and F. Mote, *Intellectual Foundations of China*, 2d ed. (New York, 1989). On Confucius, see H. G. Creel, *Confucius: The Man and the Myth* (London, 1951), a sympathetic treatment that emphasizes the humanistic side of Confucian philosophy.

For works on general culture and science, consult the illustrated work by R. Temple, *The Genius of China: 3000 Years of Science, Discovery, and Invention* (New York, 1986), and J. Needham, *Science in Traditional China: A Comparative Perspective* (Boston, 1981). See also E. N. Anderson, *The Food of China* (New Haven, Conn., 1988).

The most comprehensive collection of original writings is W. T. de Bary and Irene Bloom, *Sources of Chinese Tradition*, 2d ed. (New York, 1999), which includes excerpts from most of the ancient texts. The complete translations of the Confucian Classics are in J. Legge, *The Chinese Classics*, 5 vols. (Hong Kong, 1960), with critical and exegetical notes. For a modernized edition of the *Book of History*, see C. Waltham, *Shu Ching: Book of History* (Chicago, 1971). For an annotated version of Lao Tzu, see Wing-Tsit Chan, *The Way of Lao Tzu* (Indianapolis, 1963).

For an introduction to classical Chinese literature, consult the three standard anthologies: Liu Wu-Chi, *An Introduction to Chinese Literature* (New York, 1961); V. H. Mair, ed., *The Columbia Anthol-*

ogy of Traditional Chinese Literature (New York, 1994); and S. Owen, ed., *An Anthology of Chinese Literature: Beginnings to 1911* (New York, 1996). For a comprehensive introduction to Chinese art, consult M. Sullivan, *The Arts of China,* 4th ed. (Berkeley, Calif., 1999), with good illustrations in color. Also see M. Tregear, *Chinese Art,* rev. ed. (London, 1997), and *Art Treasures in China* (New York, 1994). Also of interest is P. B. Ebrey, *The Cambridge Illustrated History of China* (Cambridge, 1999). On music, see J. F. So, ed., *Music in the Age of Confucius* (Washington, D. C., 2000).

For additional reading, go to InfoTrac College Edition, your online research library at
http://web1.infotrac-college.com

Enter the search terms "Confucius or Confucian" using Keywords.

Enter the search terms "Taoism or Daoism" using the Subject Guide.

Enter the search terms "Han dynasty" using Keywords.

Enter the search terms "China history" using Keywords.

© Scala/Art Resource, NY

THE CIVILIZATION OF THE GREEKS

FOCUS QUESTIONS

- What was the *polis*, or city-state, and how did the city-states of Athens and Sparta differ?
- What effects did the Persian Wars and the Great Peloponnesian War have on Greek civilization?
- How was Alexander the Great able to amass his empire, and what was his legacy?
- How did the political, economic, and social institutions of the Hellenistic world differ from those of classical Greece?
- In what ways did the schools of philosophy and major religions of the Hellenistic period differ from those of the classical period, and what do those differences suggest about society in the two periods?

During the era of civil war in China known as the Period of the Warring States, a civil war also erupted on the northern shores of the Mediterranean Sea. In 431 B.C.E., two very different Greek city-states—Athens and Sparta— fought for domination of the Greek world. The people of Athens felt secure behind their walls and in the first winter of the war held a public funeral to honor those who had died in battle. On the day of the ceremony, the citizens of Athens joined in a procession, with the relatives of the dead wailing for their loved ones. As was the custom in Athens, one leading citizen was asked to address the crowd, and on this day it was Pericles who spoke to the people. He talked about the greatness of Athens and reminded the Athenians of the strength of their political system: "Our constitution," he said, "is called a democracy because power is in the hands not of a minority but of the whole people. When it is a question of settling private disputes, everyone is equal before the law. . . . Just as our political life is free and open, so is our day-to-day life in our relations with each other. . . . Here each individual is interested not only in his own affairs but in the affairs of the state as well."

In this famous funeral oration, Pericles gave voice to the ideals of democracy and the importance of the individual, ideals that were quite different from those of ancient China, in which the individual was subordinated to a larger order based on obedience to an exalted emperor. The Greeks asked some basic questions about human life: What is the nature of the universe? What is the purpose of human existence? What is our relationship to divine forces? What constitutes a community? What constitutes a state? What is true education? What are the true sources of law? What is truth itself, and how do we realize it? Not only did the Greeks answer these questions, but they also created a system of logical, analytical thought to examine them. Their answers and their system of rational thought laid the intellectual foundation for Western civilization's understanding of the human condition.

The remarkable story of ancient Greek civilization begins with the arrival of the Greeks around 1900 B.C.E. By the eighth century B.C.E., the characteristic institution of ancient Greek life, the *polis*, or city-state, had emerged. Greek civilization flourished and reached its height in the classical era of the fifth century B.C.E., but the inability of the Greek city-states to end their fratricidal warfare eventually left them vulnerable to the Macedonian king Philip II and helped bring an end to the era of independent Greek city-states.

Although the city-states were never the same after their defeat by the Macedonian monarch, this defeat did not bring an end to the influence of the Greeks. Philip's son Alexander led the Macedonians and Greeks on a spectacular conquest of the Persian Empire and opened the door to the spread of Greek culture throughout the Middle East. •

EARLY GREECE

Geography played an important role in Greek history. Compared to the landmasses of Mesopotamia and Egypt, Greece occupied a small area, a mountainous peninsula that encompassed only 45,000 square miles of territory, about the size of the state of Louisiana. The mountains and the sea were especially significant. Much of Greece consists of small plains and river valleys surrounded by mountain ranges 8,000 to 10,000 feet high. The mountains isolated Greeks from one another, causing Greek communities to follow their own separate paths and develop their own way of life. Over a period of time, these communities became so fiercely attached to their independence that they were willing to fight one another to gain advantage. No doubt the small size of these independent Greek communities fostered participation in political affairs and unique cultural expressions, but the rivalry among them also led to the internecine warfare that ultimately devastated Greek society.

The sea also influenced Greek society. Greece had a long seacoast, dotted by bays and inlets that provided numerous harbors. The Greeks also inhabited a number of islands to the west, south, and particularly the east of the Greek mainland. It is no accident that the Greeks became seafarers who sailed out into the Aegean and Mediterranean Seas to make contact with the outside world and later to establish colonies that would spread Greek civilization throughout the Mediterranean.

Greek topography helped determine the major territories into which Greece was ultimately divided (see Map 4.1). South of the Gulf of Corinth was the Peloponnesus, virtually an island attached by a tiny isthmus to the mainland. Consisting mostly of hills, mountains, and small valleys, the Peloponnesus was the location of Sparta, as well as the site of Olympia, where the famous athletic games were held. Northeast of the Peloponnesus was the Attic peninsula (or Attica), the home of Athens, hemmed in by mountains to the north and west and surrounded by the sea to the south and east. Northwest of Attica was Boeotia in central Greece, with its chief city of Thebes. To the north of Boeotia was Thessaly, which contained the largest plains and became a great producer of grain and horses. To the north of Thessaly lay Macedonia, which was not of much importance in Greek history until 338 B.C.E., when the Macedonian king Philip II conquered the Greeks.

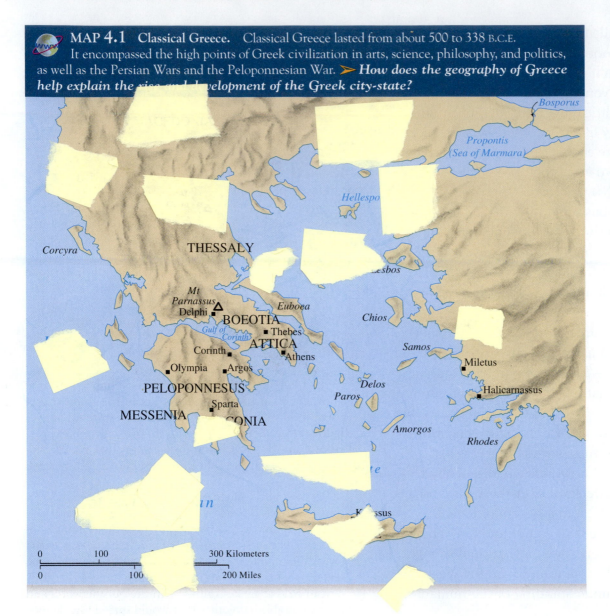

MAP 4.1 Classical Greece. Classical Greece lasted from about 500 to 338 B.C.E. It encompassed the high points of Greek civilization in arts, science, philosophy, and politics, as well as the Persian Wars and the Peloponnesian War. ➤ *How does the geography of Greece help explain the rise and development of the Greek city-state?*

Minoan Crete

The earliest civilization in the Aegean region emerged on Crete, a large island southeast of the Greek mainland. By 2800 B.C.E., a Bronze Age civilization that used metals, especially bronze, in the construction of weapons had been established on Crete. This civilization was discovered at the beginning of the twentieth century by the English archaeologist Arthur Evans, who called it Minoan after Minos, the legendary king of Crete. Evans's excavations on Crete unearthed an enormous palace complex at Knossus, near modern Heracleion. The remains revealed a rich and prosperous culture with Knossus as the apparent center of a far-ranging "sea empire," probably largely commercial in nature. We know from the archaeological remains that the people of Minoan Crete were accustomed to sea travel and had made contact with the more advanced civilization of Egypt. Egyptian products have been found in Crete and Cretan products in Egypt.

Minoan Cretans also had contacts with and exerted influence on the Greek-speaking inhabitants of the Greek mainland.

The Minoan civilization reached its height between 2000 and 1450 B.C.E. The palace at Knossus, the royal seat of the kings, was an elaborate structure that included numerous private living rooms for the royal family and workshops for making decorated vases, ivory figurines, and jewelry. Even bathrooms, with elaborate drains, like those found at Mohenjo-Daro in India, formed part of the complex. The rooms were decorated with brightly colored frescoes showing sporting events and nature scenes. Storerooms in the palace held enormous jars of oil, wine, and grain, paid as taxes in kind to the king.

The centers of Minoan civilization on Crete suffered a sudden and catastrophic collapse around 1450 B.C.E. Some historians believe that a tsunami triggered by a powerful volcanic eruption on the island of Thera was responsible for the devastation. Most historians, how-

⟫ THE MINOAN SPORT OF BULL LEAPING.   Minoan bull games were held on festival days in the great palaces on the island of Crete. In this fresco from the east wing of the palace at Knossus, acrobats of both sexes (the man is in red) somersault over the back of the bull. Another person waits behind the bull to catch the leapers. Some scholars believe that religious festivals featuring the bull may have been imported from the Middle East.

ever, maintain that the destruction was the result of invasion and pillage by mainland Greeks known as the Mycenaeans.

The Mycenaeans

The term *Mycenaean* is derived from Mycenae, a remarkable fortified site excavated by the amateur German archaeologist Heinrich Schliemann starting in 1870. Mycenae was one center in a Mycenaean Greek civilization that flourished between 1600 and 1100 B.C.E. The Mycenaean Greeks were part of the Indo-European family of peoples (see Chapter 1) who spread from their original location into southern and western Europe, India, and Iran. One group entered the territory of Greece from the north around 1900 B.C.E. and eventually managed to gain control of the Greek mainland and develop a civilization.

Mycenaean civilization, which reached its high point between 1400 and 1200 B.C.E., consisted of a number of

Minoan Crete and Mycenaean Greece

Orchomenos
Pylos
Mycenae
Tiryns
GREECE
Thera
Sea of Crete
Knossus
Crete

0 50 100 150 Kilometers
0 50 100 Miles

powerful monarchies based in fortified palace complexes, which were built on hills and surrounded by gigantic stone walls, such as those found at Mycenae, Tiryns, Pylos, Thebes, and Orchomenos. These various centers of power probably formed a loose confederacy of independent states, with Mycenae the strongest.

The Mycenaeans were, above all, a warrior people who prided themselves on their heroic deeds in battle. Archaeological evidence indicates that the Mycenaean monarchies also developed an extensive commercial network. Mycenaean pottery has been found throughout the Mediterranean basin, in Syria and Egypt to the east and Sicily and southern Italy to the west. But some scholars also believe that the Mycenaeans, led by Mycenae itself, spread outward militarily, conquering Crete and making it part of the Mycenaean world. The most famous of all their supposed military adventures has come down to us in the epic poetry of Homer (discussed later in this chapter). Did the Mycenaean Greeks, led by Agamemnon, king of Mycenae, sack the city of Troy on the northwestern coast of Asia Minor around 1250 B.C.E.? Scholars have been debating this question since Schliemann's excavations began. Many believe in the Homeric legend, even if the details have become shrouded in mystery.

By the late thirteenth century, Mycenaean Greece was showing signs of serious trouble. Mycenae itself was torched around 1190 B.C.E., and other Mycenaean centers show a similar pattern of destruction as new waves of Greek-speaking invaders moved into Greece from the north. By 1100 B.C.E., the Mycenaean culture was coming to an end, and the Greek world was entering a new period of considerable insecurity.

THE GREEKS IN A DARK AGE (C. 1100–C. 750 B.C.E.)

After the collapse of Mycenaean civilization, Greece entered a difficult era of declining population and falling food production; not until 850 B.C.E. did farming—and Greece itself—revive. Because of both the difficult conditions and the fact that we have few records to help us reconstruct what happened in this period, historians refer to it as the Dark Age.

During the Dark Age, large numbers of Greeks left the mainland and migrated across the Aegean Sea to various islands and especially to the southwestern shore of Asia Minor, a strip of territory that came to be called Ionia. Two other major groups of Greeks settled in established parts of Greece. The Aeolian Greeks of northern and central Greece colonized the large island of Lesbos and the adjacent territory of the mainland. The Dorians established themselves in southwestern Greece, especially in the Peloponnesus, as well as on some of the south Aegean islands, including Crete.

As trade and economic activity began to recover, iron replaced bronze in the construction of weapons, making them affordable for more people. At some point in the eighth century B.C.E., the Greeks adopted the Phoenician alphabet to give themselves a new system of writing. And near the very end of the Dark Age appeared the work of Homer, who has come to be viewed as one of the great poets of all time.

Homer

The *Iliad* and the *Odyssey*, the first great epic poems of early Greece, were based on stories that had been passed down from generation to generation. It is generally assumed that Homer made use of these oral traditions to compose the *Iliad*, his epic poem of the Trojan War. The war was caused when Paris, a prince of Troy, kidnapped Helen, wife of the king of the Greek state of Sparta, outraging all the Greeks. Under the leadership of the Spartan king's brother, Agamemnon of Mycenae, the Greeks attacked Troy. After ten years of combat, the Greeks finally sacked the city. The *Iliad* is not so much the story of the war itself, however, as it is the tale of the Greek hero Achilles and how the "wrath of Achilles" led to disaster.

The *Odyssey*, Homer's other masterpiece, is an epic romance that recounts the journeys of one of the Greek heroes, Odysseus, after the fall of Troy and his eventual return to his wife, Penelope, after twenty years. But there is a larger vision here as well: the testing of the heroic stature of Odysseus until, by both cunning and patience, he prevails. In the course of this testing, the underlying moral message is "that virtue is a better policy than vice."[1]

© Michael Holford, London

THE SLAYING OF HECTOR. This scene from a late-fifth-century B.C.E. Athenian vase depicts the final battle between Achilles and the Trojan hero Hector. Achilles is shown lunging forward with his spear to deliver the final, deadly blow to the Trojan prince, a scene taken from Homer's *Iliad*. The *Iliad*, together with the *Odyssey*, Homer's other masterpiece, was important to later Greeks as a means of teaching the aristocratic values of courage and honor.

HOMER'S IDEAL OF EXCELLENCE

The Iliad and the Odyssey, which the Greeks believed were both written by Homer, were used as basic texts for the education of Greeks for hundreds of years during antiquity. This passage from the Iliad, describing the encounter between Hector, prince of Troy, and his wife Andromache, illustrates the Greek ideal of gaining honor through combat. At the end of the passage, Homer also reveals what became the Greek attitude toward women: they are supposed to spin and weave and take care of their households and children.

HOMER, *ILIAD*

Hector looked at his son and smiled, but said nothing. Andromache, bursting into tears, went up to him and put her hand in his. "Hector," she said, "you are possessed. This bravery of yours will be your end. You do not think of your little boy or your unhappy wife, whom you will make a widow soon. Some day the Achaeans [Greeks] are bound to kill you in a massed attack. And when I lose you I might as well be dead. . . . I have no father, no mother, now. . . . I had seven brothers too at home. In one day all of them went down to Hades' House. The great Achilles of the swift feet killed them all. . . .

"So you, Hector, are father and mother and brother to me, as well as my beloved husband. Have pity on me now; stay here on the tower; and do not make your boy an orphan and your wife a widow. . . ."

"All that, my dear," said the great Hector of the glittering helmet, "is surely my concern. But if I hid myself like a coward and refused to fight, I could never face the Trojans and the Trojan ladies in their trailing gowns. Besides, it would go against the grain, for I have trained myself always, like a good soldier, to take my place in the front line and win glory for my father and myself. . . ."

As he finished, glorious Hector held out his arms to take his boy. But the child shrank back with a cry to the bosom of his girdled nurse, alarmed by his father's appearance. He was frightened by the bronze of the helmet and the horse-hair plume that he saw nodding grimly down at him. His father and his lady mother had to laugh. But noble Hector quickly took his helmet off and put the dazzling thing on the ground. Then he kissed his son, dandled him in his arms, and prayed to Zeus and the other gods: "Zeus, and you other gods, grant that this boy of mine may be, like me, preeminent in Troy; as strong and brave as I; a mighty king of Ilium. May people say, when he comes back from battle, 'Here is a better man than his father.' Let him bring home the bloodstained armor of the enemy he has killed, and make his mother happy."

Hector handed the boy to his wife, who took him to her fragrant breast. She was smiling through her tears, and when her husband saw this he was moved. He stroked her with his hand and said, "My dear, I beg you not to be too much distressed. No one is going to send me down to Hades before my proper time. But Fate is a thing that no man born of woman, coward or hero, can escape. Go home now, and attend to your own work, the loom and the spindle, and see that the maidservants get on with theirs. War is men's business; and this war is the business of every man in Ilium, myself above all."

Although the *Iliad* and the *Odyssey* supposedly deal with the heroes of the Mycenaean age of the thirteenth century B.C.E., many scholars believe that they really describe the social conditions of the Dark Age. According to the Homeric view, Greece was a society based on agriculture in which a landed warrior-aristocracy controlled much wealth and exercised considerable power. Homer's world reflects the values of aristocratic heroes.

This, of course, explains the importance of Homer to later generations of Greeks. Homer did not so much record history as make it. The Greeks regarded the *Iliad* and the *Odyssey* as authentic history. They gave the Greeks an ideal past with a legendary age of heroes and came to be used as standard texts for the education of generations of Greek males. As one Athenian stated, "My father was anxious to see me develop into a good man . . . and as a means to this end he compelled me to memorize all of Homer."[2] The values Homer inculcated were essentially the aristocratic values of courage and honor (see the box above). It was important to strive for the excellence befitting a hero, which the Greeks called *arete*. In the warrior-aristocratic world of Homer, *arete* is won in struggle or contest. Through his willingness to fight, the hero protects his family and friends, preserves his own honor and his family's, and earns his reputation. In the Homeric world, aristocratic women, too, were expected to pursue excellence. Penelope, for example, the wife of Odysseus, the hero of the *Odyssey*, remains faithful to her husband and displays great courage and intelligence in preserving their household during her husband's long absence. Upon his return, Odysseus praises her for her excellence: "Madame, there is not a man in the wide world who could find fault with you. For your fame has reached heaven itself, like that of some perfect king, ruling a populous and mighty state with the fear of god in his heart, and upholding the right."[3]

To later generations of Greeks, these heroic values formed the core of aristocratic virtue, a fact that explains the tremendous popularity of Homer as an educational tool. Homer gave to the Greeks a single universally accepted model of heroism, honor, and nobility. But in time, as a new world of city-states emerged in Greece, new values of cooperation and community also transformed what the Greeks learned from Homer.

THE GREEK CITY-STATES (C. 750–C. 500 B.C.E.)

During the Dark Age, Greek villages gradually expanded and evolved into independent city-states. By the eighth century B.C.E., the city-state, or what the Greeks called a *polis* (plural, *poleis*), had emerged as a unique and fundamental institution in Greek society.

The Polis

In the most basic sense, a *polis* could be defined as a small but autonomous political unit in which all major political, social, and religious activities were carried out at one central location. The *polis* consisted of a city, town, or village and its surrounding countryside. The city, town, or village was the focus, a central point where the citizens of the *polis* could assemble for political, social, and religious activities. In some *poleis*, this central meeting point was a hill, like the Acropolis at Athens, which could serve as a place of refuge during an attack and later in some sites came to be the religious center on which temples and public monuments were erected. Below the acropolis would be an *agora*, an open place that served both as a market and as a place where citizens could assemble.

Poleis varied greatly in size, from a few square miles to a few hundred square miles. They also varied in population. Athens had a population of more than 300,000 by the fifth century B.C.E. But most *poleis* were much smaller, consisting of only a few hundred to several thousand people.

Although our word *politics* is derived from the Greek term *polis*, the *polis* itself was much more than a political institution. It was a community of citizens in which all political, economic, social, cultural, and religious activities were focused. As a community, the *polis* consisted of citizens with political rights (adult males), citizens with no political rights (women and children), and noncitizens (slaves and resident aliens). All citizens of a *polis* possessed fundamental rights, but these rights were coupled with responsibilities. The Greek philosopher Aristotle argued that the citizen did not just belong to himself: "we must rather regard every citizen as belonging to the state." However, the loyalty that citizens had to their city-states also had a negative side. City-states distrusted one another, and

the division of Greece into fiercely patriotic independent units helped bring about its ruin.

The development of the *polis* was paralleled by the emergence of a new military system. Greek fighting had previously been dominated by aristocratic cavalrymen, who reveled in individual duels with enemy soldiers. But by the end of the eighth century and beginning of the seventh century B.C.E., the hoplite infantry formation came into being. Hoplites were heavily armed infantrymen who wore bronze or leather helmets, breastplates, and greaves (shin guards). Each carried a round shield, a short sword, and a thrusting spear about 9 feet long. Hoplites advanced into battle as a unit, forming a phalanx (a rectangular formation) in tight order, usually eight ranks deep. As long as the hoplites kept their order, were not outflanked, and did not break, they either secured victory or, at the very least, suffered no harm. The phalanx was easily routed, however, if it broke its order. Thus the safety of the phalanx depended, above all, on the solidarity and discipline of its members. As one seventh-century B.C.E. poet noted, a good hoplite was "a short man firmly placed upon his legs, with a courageous heart, not to be uprooted from the spot where he plants his legs."[4]

The hoplite force had political as well as military repercussions. The aristocratic cavalry was now outdated. Since each hoplite provided his own armor, men of property, both aristocrats and small farmers, made up the new phalanx. Those who could become hoplites and fight for the state could also challenge aristocratic control.

Colonization and the Rise of Tyrants

Between 750 and 550 B.C.E., large numbers of Greeks left their homeland to settle in distant lands. The growing gulf between rich and poor, overpopulation, and the development of trade were all factors that spurred the establishment of colonies. Invariably, each colony saw itself as an independent *polis* whose links to the mother *polis* (the *metropolis*) were not political but based on sharing common social, economic, and especially religious practices.

In the western Mediterranean, new Greek settlements were established along the coastline of southern Italy, southern France, eastern Spain, and northern Africa west of Egypt. To the north, the Greeks set up colonies in Thrace, where they sought good agricultural lands to grow grains. Greeks also settled along the shores of the Black Sea and secured the approaches to it with cities on the Hellespont and Bosporus, most notably Byzantium, site of the later Constantinople (Istanbul). In establishing these settlements, the Greeks spread their culture throughout the Mediterranean basin.

Colonization also led to increased trade and industry. The Greeks on the mainland sent their pottery, wine, and olive oil to these areas; in return, they received grains and metals from the west and fish, timber, wheat, metals, and

❧ **THE HOPLITE FORCES.** The Greek hoplites were infantrymen equipped with large round shields and long thrusting spears. In battle, they advanced in tight phalanx formation and were dangerous opponents as long as this formation remained unbroken. This vase painting of the seventh century B.C.E. shows two groups of hoplite warriors engaged in battle. The piper on the left is leading another line of soldiers preparing to enter the fray.

slaves from the Black Sea region. In many *poleis*, the expansion of trade and industry created a new group of rich men who desired political privileges commensurate with their wealth but found such privileges impossible to gain because of the power of the ruling aristocrats.

The aspirations of the new industrial and commercial groups laid the groundwork for the rise of tyrants in the seventh and sixth centuries B.C.E. They were not necessarily oppressive or wicked, as our word *tyrant* connotes. Greek tyrants were rulers who came to power in an unconstitutional way; a tyrant was not subject to the law. Many tyrants were actually aristocrats who opposed the control of the ruling aristocratic faction in their cities. The support for the tyrants, however, came from the new rich who made their money in trade and industry, as well as from poor peasants who were becoming increasingly indebted to landholding aristocrats. Both groups were opposed to the domination of political power by aristocratic oligarchies.

Once in power, the tyrants built new marketplaces, temples, and walls that not only glorified the city but also enhanced their own popularity. Tyrants also favored the interests of merchants and traders. Despite these achievements, however, tyranny was largely extinguished by the end of the sixth century B.C.E. Greeks believed in the rule of law, and tyranny made a mockery of that ideal.

Although tyranny did not last, it played a significant role in the evolution of Greek history by ending the rule of narrow aristocratic oligarchies. Once the tyrants were eliminated, the door was opened to the participation of new and more people in governing the affairs of the community. Although this trend culminated in the development of democracy in some communities, in other states expanded oligarchies of one kind or another managed to remain in power. Greek states exhibited considerable variety in their governmental structures; this can perhaps best be seen by examining the two most famous and most powerful Greek city-states, Sparta and Athens.

Sparta

Located in the southwestern Peloponnesus, Sparta, like other Greek states, faced the need for more land. Instead of sending its people out to found new colonies, the Spartans conquered the neighboring Laconians and later, beginning around 730 B.C.E., undertook the conquest of neighboring Messenia despite its larger size and population. Messenia possessed a large, fertile plain ideal for growing grain. After its conquest in the seventh century B.C.E., the Messenians, like the Laconians earlier, were reduced to serfdom (they were known as *helots*, a name derived from a Greek word for "capture") and made to

THE LYCURGAN REFORMS

In order to maintain their control over the conquered Messenians, the Spartans instituted the reforms that created their military state. In this account of the lawgiver, Lycurgus, the Greek historian Plutarch discusses the effect of these reforms on the treatment and education of boys.

PLUTARCH, LYCURGUS

Lycurgus was of another mind; he would not have masters bought out of the market for his young Spartans, . . . nor was it lawful, indeed, for the father himself to breed up the children after his own fancy; but as soon as they were seven years old they were to be enrolled in certain companies and classes, where they all lived under the same order and discipline, doing their exercises and taking their play together. Of these, he who showed the most conduct and courage was made captain; they had their eyes always upon him, obeyed his orders, and underwent patiently whatsoever punishment he inflicted; so that the whole course of their education was one continued exercise of a ready and perfect obedience. The old men, too, were spectators of their performances, and often raised quarrels and disputes among them, to have a good opportunity of finding out their different characters, and of seeing which would be valiant, which a coward, when they should come to more dangerous encounters. Reading and writing they gave them, just enough to serve their turn; their chief care was to make them good subjects, and to teach them to endure pain and conquer in battle. To this end, as they grew in years, their discipline was proportionately increased; their heads were close-clipped, they were accustomed to go barefoot, and for the most part to play naked.

After they were twelve years old, they were no longer allowed to wear any undergarments; they had one coat to serve them a year; their bodies were hard and dry, with but little acquaintance of baths and unguents; these human indulgences they were allowed only on some few particular days in the year. They lodged together in little bands upon beds made of the rushes which grew by the banks of the river Eurotas, which they were to break off with their hands with a knife; if it were winter, they mingled some thistle-down with their rushes, which it was thought had the property of giving warmth. By the time they were come to this age there was not any of the more hopeful boys who had not a lover to bear him company. The old men, too, had an eye upon them, coming often to the grounds to hear and see them contend either in wit or strength with one another, and this as seriously . . . as if they were their fathers, their tutors, or their magistrates; so that there scarcely was any time or place without someone present to put them in mind of their duty, and punish them if they had neglected it.

[Spartan boys were also encouraged to steal their food.] They stole, too, all other meat they could lay their hands on, looking out and watching all opportunities, when people were asleep or more careless than usual. If they were caught, they were not only punished with whipping, but hunger, too, being reduced to their ordinary allowance, which was but very slender, and so contrived on purpose, that they might set about to help themselves, and be forced to exercise their energy and address. This was the principal design of their hard fare.

work for the Spartans. To ensure control over their conquered Laconian and Messenian helots, the Spartans made a conscious decision to create a military state.

Between 800 and 600 B.C.E., the Spartans instituted a series of reforms that are associated with the name of the lawgiver Lycurgus (see the box above). Although historians are not sure that Lycurgus ever existed, there is no doubt about the result of the reforms that were made: the lives of Spartans were now rigidly organized and tightly controlled (to this day, the word *spartan* means "highly self-disciplined"). Boys were taken from their mothers at the age of seven and put under control of the state. They lived in military-style barracks, where they were subjected to harsh discipline to make them tough and given an education that stressed military training and obedience to authority. At twenty, Spartan males were enrolled in the army for regular military service. Although allowed to marry, they continued to live in the barracks and ate all their meals in public dining halls with their fellow soldiers. Meals were simple; the famous Spartan black broth consisted of a piece of pork boiled in blood,

salt, and vinegar, causing a visitor who ate in a public mess to remark that he now understood why Spartans were not afraid to die. At thirty, Spartan males were recognized as mature and allowed to vote in the assembly and live at home, but they remained in military service until the age of sixty.

While their husbands remained in military barracks until age thirty, Spartan women lived at home. Because of this separation, Spartan women had greater freedom of movement and greater power in the household than was common for women elsewhere in Greece. Spartan women were encouraged to exercise and remain fit to bear and raise healthy children. Like the men, Spartan women engaged in athletic exercises in the nude. Many Spartan women upheld the strict Spartan values, expecting their husbands and sons to be brave in war. The story is told that as a Spartan mother was burying her son, an old woman came up to her and said, "You poor woman, what a misfortune." "No," replied the mother, "because I bore him so that he might die for Sparta, and that is what has happened, as I wished."[5]

The so-called Lycurgan reforms also reorganized the Spartan government, creating an oligarchy. Two kings were primarily responsible for military affairs and served as the leaders of the Spartan army on its campaigns. The two kings shared power with a body called the *gerousia*, a council of elders. It consisted of twenty-eight citizens over the age of sixty, who were elected for life, and the two kings. The primary task of the *gerousia* was to prepare proposals that would be presented to the *apella*, an assembly of all male citizens. The assembly did not debate but only voted on the proposals put before it by the *gerousia*; rarely did the assembly reject these proposals. The assembly also elected the *gerousia* and another body known as the *ephors*, a group of five men who were responsible for supervising the education of youth and the conduct of all citizens.

To make their new military state secure, the Spartans deliberately turned their backs on the outside world. Foreigners, who might bring in new ideas, were discouraged from visiting Sparta. Nor were Spartans, except for military reasons, allowed to travel abroad, where they might pick up new ideas dangerous to the stability of the state. Likewise, Spartan citizens were discouraged from studying philosophy, literature, or the arts—subjects that might encourage new thoughts. The art of war was the Spartan ideal, and all other arts were frowned on.

In the sixth century, Sparta used its military might and the fear it inspired to gain greater control of the Peloponnesus by organizing an alliance of almost all the Peloponnesian states. Sparta's strength enabled it to dominate this Peloponnesian League and determine its policies. By 500 B.C.E., the Spartans had organized a powerful military state that maintained order and stability in the Peloponnesus. Raised from early childhood to believe that total loyalty to the Spartan state was the basic reason for existence, the Spartans viewed their strength as justification for their militaristic ideals and regimented society.

Athens

By 700 B.C.E., Athens had established a unified *polis* on the peninsula of Attica. Although early Athens had been ruled by a monarchy, by the seventh century B.C.E., it had fallen under the control of its aristocrats. They possessed the best land and controlled political and religious life by means of a council of nobles, assisted by a board of nine officials called archons. Although there was an assembly of full citizens, it possessed few powers.

Near the end of the seventh century B.C.E., Athens faced political turmoil because of serious economic problems. Increasing numbers of Athenian farmers found themselves sold into slavery when they were unable to repay loans they had obtained from their aristocratic neighbors, pledging themselves as collateral. Repeatedly, there were cries to cancel the debts and give land to the poor.

The ruling Athenian aristocrats responded to this crisis by choosing Solon, a reform-minded aristocrat, as sole archon in 594 B.C.E. and giving him full power to make changes. Solon canceled all land debts, outlawed new loans based on humans as collateral, and freed people who had fallen into slavery for debts. He refused, however, to carry out land redistribution and hence failed to deal with the basic cause of the economic crisis. This failure, however, was overshadowed by the commercial and industrial prosperity that Athens began to experience in the following decades.

Like his economic reforms, Solon's political measures were also a compromise. Though by no means eliminating the power of the aristocracy, they opened the door to the participation of new people, especially the nonaristocratic wealthy, in the government. But Solon's reforms, though popular, did not truly solve Athens's problems. Aristocratic factions continued to vie for power, and the poorer peasants resented Solon's failure to institute land redistribution. Internal strife finally led to the very institution Solon had hoped to avoid—tyranny. Pisistratus, an aristocrat, seized power in 560 B.C.E. Pursuing a foreign policy that aided Athenian trade, Pisistratus remained popular with the mercantile and industrial classes. But the Athenians rebelled against his son and ended the tyranny in 510 B.C.E. Although the aristocrats attempted to reestablish an aristocratic oligarchy, Cleisthenes, another aristocratic reformer, opposed this plan and, with the backing of the Athenian people, gained the upper hand in 508 B.C.E.

Cleisthenes created a new Council of Five Hundred, chosen by lot by the ten tribes in which all citizens had been enrolled. The Council of Five Hundred was responsible for the administration of both foreign and financial affairs and prepared the business that would be handled by the assembly. This assembly of all male citizens had final authority in the passing of laws after free and open debate; thus Cleisthenes' reforms had reinforced the central role of the assembly of citizens in the Athenian political system.

The reforms of Cleisthenes created the foundations for Athenian democracy. More changes would come in the fifth century, when the Athenians themselves would begin to use the word *democracy* to describe their system (our word *democracy* comes from the Greek words *demos* "people," and *kratia*, "power"). By 500 B.C.E., Athens was more united than it had been and was on the verge of playing a more important role in Greek affairs.

THE HIGH POINT OF GREEK CIVILIZATION: CLASSICAL GREECE

Classical Greece is the name given to the period of Greek history from around 500 B.C.E. to the conquest of Greece by the Macedonian king Philip II in 338 B.C.E. Many of the cultural contributions of the Greeks occurred during this period. The age began with a mighty confrontation between the Greek states and the mammoth Persian Empire.

The Challenge of Persia

As the Greeks spread throughout the Mediterranean, they came into contact with the Persian Empire to the east. The Ionian Greek cities in western Asia Minor had already fallen subject to the Persian Empire by the mid-sixth century B.C.E. An unsuccessful revolt by the Ionian cities in 499 B.C.E.—assisted by the Athenian navy—led the Persian ruler Darius to seek revenge by attacking the mainland Greeks. In 490 B.C.E., the Persians landed an army on the plain of Marathon, only 26 miles from Athens. The Athenians and their allies were clearly outnumbered, but led by Miltiades, one of the Athenian leaders who insisted on attacking, the Greek hoplites charged across the plain of Marathon and crushed the Persian forces.

Xerxes, the new Persian monarch after the death of Darius in 486 B.C.E., vowed revenge and planned to invade. In preparation for the attack, some of the Greek states formed a defensive league under Spartan leadership, while the Athenians pursued a new military policy by developing a navy. By the time of the Persian invasion in 480 B.C.E., the Athenians had produced a fleet of about two hundred vessels.

Xerxes led a massive invasion force into Greece: close to 150,000 troops, almost seven hundred naval ships, and hundreds of supply ships to keep the large army fed. The Greeks

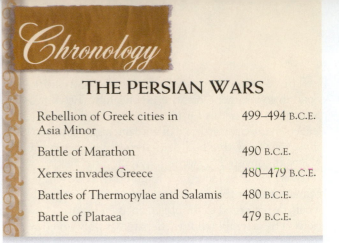

tried to delay the Persians at the pass of Thermopylae, along the main road into central Greece. A Greek force numbering close to nine thousand, under the leadership of the Spartan king, Leonidas, and his contingent of three hundred Spartans, held off the Persian army for two days. The Spartan troops were especially brave. When told that Persian arrows would darken the sky in battle, one Spartan warrior supposedly responded, "That is good news. We will fight in the shade!" Unfortunately for the Greeks, a traitor told the Persians how to use a mountain path to outflank the Greek force. The Spartans fought to the last man.

The Athenians, now threatened by the onslaught of the Persian forces, abandoned their city. While the Persians

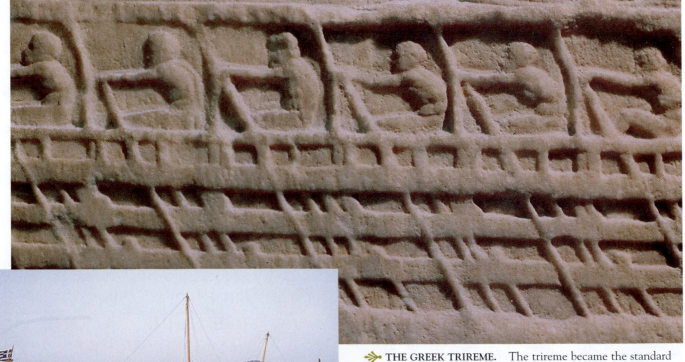

➤ **THE GREEK TRIREME.** The trireme became the standard warship of ancient Greece. Highly maneuverable, fast, and outfitted with metal prows, Greek triremes were especially effective at ramming enemy ships. The strenuous work of the oarsmen aboard a trireme is shown in the relief dating from the fourth century B.C.E. The photo shows the Olympias, a trireme reconstructed by the Greek navy.

Courtesy of William M. Murray

The Art Archive/Acropolis Museum Athens/Dagli Orti

ATHENIAN DEMOCRACY: THE FUNERAL ORATION OF PERICLES

In his History of the Peloponnesian War, *the Greek historian Thucydides presented his reconstruction of the eulogy given by Pericles in the winter of 431–430 B.C.E. to honor the Athenians killed in the first campaigns of the Great Peloponnesian War. It is a magnificent, idealized description of Athenian democracy at its height.*

THUCYDIDES, *HISTORY OF THE PELOPONNESIAN WAR*

Our constitution is called a democracy because power is in the hands not of a minority but of the whole people. When it is a question of settling private disputes, everyone is equal before the law; when it is a question of putting one person before another in positions of public responsibility, what counts is not membership of a particular class, but the actual ability which the man possesses. No one, so long as he has it in him to be of service to the state, is kept in political obscurity because of poverty. And, just as our political life is free and open, so is our day-to-day life in our relations with each other. We do not get into a state with our next-door neighbor if he enjoys himself in his own way, nor do we give him the kind of black looks which, though they do no real harm, still do hurt people's feelings. We are free and tolerant in our private lives; but in public affairs we keep to the law. This is because it commands our deep respect.

We give our obedience to those whom we put in positions of authority, and we obey the laws themselves, especially those which are for the protection of the oppressed, and those unwritten laws which it is an acknowledged shame to break. . . . Here each individual is interested not only in his own affairs but in the affairs of the state as well: even those who are mostly occupied with their own business are extremely well-informed on general politics—this is a peculiarity of ours: we do not say that a man who takes no interest in politics is a man who minds his own business; we say that he has no business here at all. We Athenians, in our own persons, take our decisions on policy or submit them to proper discussions: for we do not think that there is an incompatibility between words and deeds; the worst thing is to rush into action before the consequences have been properly debated. . . . Taking everything together then, I declare that our city is an education to Greece, and I declare that in my opinion each single one of our citizens, in all the manifold aspects of life, is able to show himself the rightful lord and owner of his own person, and do this, moreover, with exceptional grace and exceptional versatility. And to show that this is no empty boasting for the present occasion, but real tangible fact, you have only to consider the power which our city possesses and which has been won by those very qualities which I have mentioned.

---

sacked and burned Athens, the Greek fleet remained offshore near the island of Salamis and challenged the Persian navy to fight. Although the Greeks were outnumbered, they managed to outmaneuver the Persian fleet and utterly defeated it. A few months later, early in 479 B.C.E., the Greeks formed the largest Greek army seen up to that time and decisively defeated the Persian army at Plataea, northwest of Attica. The Greeks had won the war and were now free to pursue their own destiny.

The Growth of an Athenian Empire in the Age of Pericles

After the defeat of the Persians, Athens took over the leadership of the Greek world by forming a defensive alliance against the Persians called the Delian League in the winter of 478–477 B.C.E. Its main headquarters was on the island of Delos, but its chief officials, including the treasurers and commanders of the fleet, were Athenian. Under the leadership of the Athenians, the Delian League pursued the attack against the Persian Empire. Virtually all of the Greek states in the Aegean were liberated from Persian control. Arguing that the Persian threat was now over, some members of the Delian League wished to withdraw. But the Athenians forced them to remain in the league and to pay tribute. In

454 B.C.E., the Athenians moved the treasury of the league from Delos to Athens. By controlling the Delian League, Athens had created an empire.

At home, Athenians favored the new imperial policy, especially after 461 B.C.E., when a political faction, led by a young aristocrat named Pericles, triumphed. Under Pericles, who remained a dominant figure in Athenian politics for more than three decades, Athens embarked on a policy of expanding democracy at home and its new empire abroad. This period of Athenian and Greek history, which historians have subsequently labeled the Age of Pericles, witnessed the height of Athenian power and the culmination of its brilliance as a civilization.

In the Age of Pericles, the Athenians became deeply attached to their democratic system. The sovereignty of the people was embodied in the assembly, which consisted of all male citizens over eighteen years of age. In the 440s, that was probably a group of about 43,000. Not all attended, however, and the number present at the meetings, which were held every ten days on a hillside east of the Acropolis, seldom reached 6,000. The assembly passed all laws and made final decisions on war and foreign policy. Pericles expanded the Athenians' involvement in their democracy (see the box above) by making lower-class citizens eligible for public offices formerly closed to them and introducing state pay for officeholders, including those who served on the large Athenian juries. Poor citizens could now afford to participate in public affairs.

A large body of city magistrates, usually chosen by lot without regard to class, handled routine administrative tasks. The overall directors of policy, a board of ten officials known as generals, were elected by public vote and were usually wealthy aristocrats, even though the people were free to select otherwise. The generals could be reelected, enabling individual leaders to play an important political role. Pericles, for example, was elected to the generalship thirty times between 461 and 429 B.C.E.

Under Pericles, Athens became the leading center of Greek culture. The Persians had destroyed much of the city during the Persian Wars, but Pericles used the treasury money of the Delian League to set in motion a massive rebuilding program. New temples and statues soon made the greatness of Athens more visible. Art, architecture, and philosophy flourished, and Pericles broadly boasted that Athens had become the "school of Greece." But the achievements of Athens alarmed the other Greek states, especially Sparta, and soon all Greece was confronting a new war.

The Great Peloponnesian War and the Decline of the Greek States

During the forty years after the defeat of the Persians, the Greek world came to be divided into two major camps: Sparta and its supporters and the Athenian maritime empire. Sparta and its allies feared the growing Athenian empire. Then, too, Athens and Sparta had created two very different kinds of societies, and neither state was able to tolerate the other's system. A series of disputes finally led to the outbreak of war in 431 B.C.E.

At the beginning of the war, both sides believed they had winning strategies. The Athenians planned to remain behind the protective walls of Athens while the overseas empire and the navy would keep them supplied. Pericles knew that the Spartans and their allies could beat the Athenians in open battles, which was the chief aim of the Spartan strategy. The Spartans and their allies invaded Attica and ravaged the fields and orchards, hoping that the Athenians would send out their army to fight beyond the walls. But Pericles was convinced that Athens was secure behind its walls and stayed put.

In the second year of the war, however, plague devastated the crowded city of Athens and wiped out possibly one-third of the Athenian population. Pericles himself died the following year (429 B.C.E.), a severe loss to Athens. Despite the losses from the plague, the Athenians fought on in a struggle that dragged on for another twenty-seven years. A final crushing blow came in 405 B.C.E., when the Athenian fleet was destroyed at Aegospotami on the Hellespont. Athens was besieged and surrendered in 404. Its walls were torn down, the navy disbanded, and the Athenian empire was no more. The great war was finally over.

The Great Peloponnesian War weakened the major Greek states and destroyed any possibility of cooperation among the Greek states. The next seventy years of Greek history are a sorry tale of efforts by Sparta, Athens, and Thebes, a new Greek power, to dominate Greek affairs. In continuing their petty wars, the Greek states remained oblivious to the growing power of Macedonia to their north and demonstrated convincingly that the genius of the Greeks did not lie in politics. Culture, however, was quite a different story.

The Culture of Classical Greece

Classical Greece saw a period of remarkable intellectual and cultural growth throughout the Greek world, and Periclean Athens was the most important center of classical Greek culture.

THE WRITING OF HISTORY

History as we know it, as the systematic analysis of past events, was introduced to the Western world by the Greeks. Herodotus (c. 484–c. 425 B.C.E.) wrote *History of the Persian Wars*, a work commonly regarded as the first real history in Western civilization. The central theme of Herodotus' work is the conflict between the Greeks and the Persians, which he viewed as a struggle between freedom and despotism. Herodotus traveled extensively and questioned many people to obtain his information. He was a master storyteller and sometimes included considerable fanciful material, but he was also capable of exhibiting a critical attitude toward the materials he used.

Thucydides (c. 460–c. 400 B.C.E.) was a better historian by far; indeed, he is considered the greatest historian of the ancient world. Thucydides was an Athenian and a participant in the Peloponnesian War. He had been elected a general, but a defeat in battle led the fickle Athenian assembly to send him into exile, which gave him the opportunity to write his *History of the Peloponnesian War*.

Unlike Herodotus, Thucydides was not concerned with underlying divine forces or gods as explanatory causal factors in history. He saw war and politics in purely rational terms, as the activities of human beings. He examined the causes of the Peloponnesian War in a clear, methodical, objective fashion, placing much emphasis on accuracy and the precision of his facts. As he stated:

> With regard to my factual reporting of the events of the war I have made it a principle not to write down the first story that came my way, and not even to be guided by my own general impressions; either I was present myself at the events which I have described or else I heard of them from eyewitnesses whose reports I have checked with as much thoroughness as possible.[6]

Thucydides also provided remarkable insight into the human condition. He believed that political situations recur in similar fashion and that the study of history is therefore of great value in understanding the present.

GREEK DRAMA

Drama as we know it in Western culture was invented by the Greeks. Plays were presented in outdoor theaters as part of religious festivals. The form of Greek plays remained rather stable. Three male actors who wore masks acted all the parts. A chorus, also male, spoke lines that explained what was going on. Action was very limited because the emphasis was on the story and its meaning.

The first Greek dramas were tragedies, plays based on the suffering of a hero and usually ending in disaster. Aeschylus (525–456 B.C.E.) is the first tragedian whose plays are known to us. As was customary in Greek tragedy, his plots are simple, and the entire drama focuses on a single tragic event and its meaning. Greek tragedies were supposed to be presented in trilogies (sets of three plays) built around a common theme. The only complete trilogy we possess, called the *Oresteia*, was written by Aeschylus. The theme of this trilogy is derived from Homer. Agamemnon, the king of Mycenae, returns a hero from the defeat of Troy. His wife, Clytemnestra, avenges the sacrificial death of her daughter Iphigenia by murdering Agamemnon, who had been responsible for Iphigenia's death. In the second play of the trilogy, Agamemnon's son Orestes avenges his father by killing his mother. Orestes is now pursued by the avenging Furies, who torment him for killing his mother. Evil acts breed evil acts, and suffering is one's lot, suggests Aeschylus. But Orestes is put on trial and acquitted by Athena, the patron goddess of Athens. Personal vendetta has been eliminated, and law has prevailed. Reason has triumphed over the forces of evil.

Another great Athenian playwright was Sophocles (c. 496–406 B.C.E.), whose most famous play was *Oedipus the King*. In this play, the oracle of Apollo foretells that a man (Oedipus) will kill his own father and marry his mother. Despite all attempts at prevention, the tragic events occur. Although it appears that Oedipus suffered the fate determined by the gods, Oedipus also accepts that he himself as a free man must bear responsibility for his actions: "It was Apollo, friends, Apollo, that brought this bitter bitterness, my sorrows to completion. But the hand that struck me was none but my own."[7]

The third outstanding Athenian tragedian, Euripides (c. 485–406 B.C.E.), moved beyond his predecessors by creating more realistic characters. His plots also became more complex, with a greater interest in real-life situations. Perhaps the greatest of all his plays was *The Bacchae*, which dealt with the introduction of the hysterical rites associated with Dionysus, god of wine. Euripides is often seen as a skeptic who questioned traditional moral and religious values. Euripides was also critical of the traditional view that war was glorious. He portrayed war as brutal and barbaric.

Greek tragedies dealt with universal themes still relevant to our day. They probed such problems as the nature of good and evil, the rights of the individual, the nature of divine forces, and the nature of human beings. Over and over, the tragic lesson was repeated: humans were free and yet could operate only within limitations imposed by the gods. The real task was to cultivate the balance and moderation that led to awareness of one's true position. But the pride in human accomplishment and independence is real. As the chorus chants in Sophocles' *Antigone*: "Is there anything more wonderful on earth, our marvelous planet, than the miracle of man?"[8]

Greek comedy developed later than tragedy. The plays of Aristophanes (c. 450–c. 385 B.C.E.), who used both grotesque masks and obscene jokes to entertain the Athenian audience, are examples of Old Comedy. But comedy in Athens was also more clearly political than tragedy. It was used to attack or savagely satirize both politicians and intellectuals. In *The Clouds*, for example, Aristophanes characterized the philosopher Socrates as the operator of a thought factory where people could learn deceitful ways of handling other people. Later plays gave up the element of personal attack and featured contemporary issues. Of special importance to Aristophanes was his opposition to the Peloponnesian War. *Lysistrata*, performed in 411 B.C.E., at a time when Athens was in serious danger of losing the war, had a comic but effective message against the war (see the box on p. 104).

THE ARTS: THE CLASSICAL IDEAL

The artistic standards established by the Greeks of the classical period have largely dominated the arts of the Western world. Greek art was concerned with expressing eternally true ideals. Its subject matter was basically the human being, expressed harmoniously as an object of great beauty. The classic style, based on the ideals of reason, moderation, symmetry, balance, and harmony in all things, was meant to civilize the emotions.

In architecture, the most important form was the temple dedicated to a god or goddess. At the center of Greek temples were walled rooms that housed the statues of deities and treasuries in which gifts to the gods and goddesses were safeguarded. These central rooms were surrounded by a screen of columns that made Greek temples open structures rather than closed ones. The columns were originally made of wood but were changed to marble in the fifth century B.C.E. The most significant formal element in Greek temples was the shape and size of the columns in combination with the features above and below the column.

ATHENIAN COMEDY: SEX AS AN ANTIWAR INSTRUMENT

Greek comedy became a regular feature of the dramatic presentations at the festival of Dionysus in Athens beginning in 488–487 B.C.E. Aristophanes used his comedies to present political messages, especially to express his antiwar sentiments. The plot of Lysistrata centers on a sex strike by wives in order to get their husbands to end the Peloponnesian War. In this scene from the play, Lysistrata (whose name means "she who dissolves the armies") has the women swear a special oath. The oath involves a bowl of wine offered as a libation to the gods.

ARISTOPHANES, *LYSISTRATA*

LYSISTRATA: Lampito: all of you women: come, touch the bowl, and repeat after me: I WILL HAVE NOTHING TO DO WITH MY HUSBAND OR MY LOVER

KALONIKE: I will have nothing to do with my husband or my lover

LYSISTRATA: THOUGH HE COME TO ME IN PITIABLE CONDITION

KALONIKE: Though he come to me in pitiable condition (Oh, Lysistrata! This is killing me!)

LYSISTRATA: I WILL STAY IN MY HOUSE UNTOUCHABLE

KALONIKE: I will stay in my house untouchable

LYSISTRATA: IN MY THINNEST SAFFRON SILK

KALONIKE: In my thinnest saffron silk

LYSISTRATA: AND MAKE HIM LONG FOR ME.

KALONIKE: And make him long for me.

LYSISTRATA: I WILL NOT GIVE MYSELF

KALONIKE: I will not give myself

LYSISTRATA: AND IF HE CONSTRAINS ME

KALONIKE: And if he constrains me

LYSISTRATA: I WILL BE AS COLD AS ICE AND NEVER MOVE

KALONIKE: I will be as cold as ice and never move

LYSISTRATA: I WILL NOT LIFT MY SLIPPERS TOWARD THE CEILING

KALONIKE: I will not lift my slippers toward the ceiling

LYSISTRATA: OR CROUCH ON ALL FOURS LIKE THE LIONESS IN THE CARVING

KALONIKE: Or crouch on all fours like the lioness in the carving

LYSISTRATA: AND IF I KEEP THIS OATH LET ME DRINK FROM THIS BOWL

KALONIKE: And if I keep this oath let me drink from this bowl

LYSISTRATA: IF NOT, LET MY OWN BOWL BE FILLED WITH WATER.

KALONIKE: If not, let my own bowl be filled with water.

LYSISTRATA: You have all sworn?

MYRRHINE: We have.

Some of the finest examples of Greek classical architecture were built in fifth-century Athens. The most famous building, regarded as the greatest example of the classical Greek temple, was the Parthenon, built between 447 and 432 B.C.E. The master builders Ictinus and Callicrates directed the construction of this temple consecrated to Athena, the patron goddess of Athens. The Parthenon, an expression of Athenian enthusiasm, was also dedicated to the glory of Athens and the Athenians. The Parthenon typifies the principles of classical architecture: the search for calm, clarity, and freedom from superfluous detail.

Greek sculpture also developed a classical style that differed significantly from the artificial stiffness of the figures of an earlier period, which had been influenced by Egyptian sculpture. Statues of the male nude, the favorite subject of Greek sculptors, now exhibited more relaxed attitudes; their faces were self-assured, their bodies flexible and smooth-muscled. Although the figures possessed natural features that made them lifelike, Greek sculptors sought to achieve not realism but a standard of ideal beauty. Polyclitus, a fifth-century sculptor, authored a treatise (now lost) on a canon of proportions that he illus-trated in a work known as the *Doryphoros*. His theory maintained that the use of ideal proportions, based on mathematical ratios found in nature, could produce an ideal human form, beautiful in its perfected and refined features. This search for ideal beauty was the dominant feature of the classical standard in sculpture.

THE GREEK LOVE OF WISDOM

Philosophy is a Greek word that originally meant "love of wisdom." Early Greek philosophers were concerned with the development of critical or rational thought about the nature of the universe and the place of divine forces and souls in it. Many Greeks, however, were simply not interested in such speculations. The Sophists were a group of philosophical teachers in the fifth century B.C.E. who rejected such speculation as foolish; they argued that understanding the universe was beyond the reach of the human mind. It was more important for individuals to improve themselves, so the only worthwhile object of study was human behavior. The Sophists were wandering scholars who sold their services as professional teachers to the young men of Greece, especially those of

Doric

Ionic

Corinthian

© Art Resource, NY

>> **DORIC, IONIC, AND CORINTHIAN ORDERS.**   The Greeks used different shapes and sizes in the columns of their temples. The Doric order, evolved first in the Dorian Peloponnesus, consisted of thick, fluted columns with simple capitals (the decorated tops of the columns). The Greeks considered the Doric order grave, dignified, and masculine. The Ionic style was first developed in western Asia Minor and consisted of slender columns with spiral-shaped capitals. The Greeks characterized the Ionic order as slender, elegant, and feminine in principle. Corinthian columns, with their more detailed capitals modeled after acanthus leaves, came later, near the end of the fifth century B.C.E.

Athens. The Sophists stressed the importance of rhetoric (the art of persuasive oratory) in winning debates and swaying an audience, a skill that was especially valuable in democratic Athens. The Sophists tended to be skeptics who questioned the traditional values of their societies.

>> **THE PARTHENON.**   The arts in classical Greece were designed to express the eternal ideals of reason, moderation, symmetry, balance, and harmony. In architecture, the most important form was the temple, and the classical example of this kind of architecture is the Parthenon, built between 447 and 432 B.C.E. Located on the Acropolis, the Parthenon was dedicated to Athena, the patron goddess of Athens, but it also served as a shining example of the power and wealth of the Athenian empire.

© Michael Holford, London

To the Sophists, there was no absolute right or wrong. True wisdom consisted of being able to perceive and pursue one's own good. Because of these ideas, many people viewed the Sophists as harmful to society and especially dangerous to the values of young people.

In classical Greece, Athens became the foremost intellectual and artistic center. Its reputation is perhaps strongest of all in philosophy. After all, Socrates, Plato, and Aristotle raised basic questions that have been debated for two thousand years; these are still largely the same philosophical questions we wrestle with today.

Socrates (469–399 B.C.E.) left no writing of his own, but we know about him from his pupils, especially his most famous one, Plato. Socrates was a stonemason whose true love was philosophy. He taught a number of pupils, although not for pay, because he believed that the goal of education was to improve the individual. His approach, still known as the Socratic method, employs a question-and-answer technique to lead pupils to see things for themselves using their own reason. Socrates believed that all knowledge is within each person; only critical examination is needed to call it forth. This was the
ophy, since "the unexamined life is no

Socrates questioned authority, ar
into trouble. Athens had had a trad
and inquiry, but defeat in the Pelopo
ated an environment intolerant of
searching. Socrates was accuse

© Scala/Art Resource, NY

⟫ **DORYPHOROS.**   This statue, known as the *Doryphoros*, or spear-carrier, is by the fifth-century B.C.E. sculptor Polyclitus, who believed it illustrated the ideal proportions of the human figure. Classical Greek sculpture moved away from the stiffness of earlier figures but retained the young male nude as the favorite subject matter. The statues became more lifelike, with relaxed poses and flexible, smooth-muscled bodies. The aim of sculpture, however, was not simply realism but rather the expression of ideal beauty.

corrupting the youth of Athens by his teaching. An Athenian jury sentenced him to death.

One of Socrates' disciples was Plato (c. 429–347 B.C.E.), considered by many the greatest philosopher of Western civilization. Unlike his master Socrates, who wrote nothing, Plato wrote a great deal. He was fascinated with the question of reality: How do we know what is real? According to Plato, a higher world of eternal, unchanging Ideas or Forms has always existed. To know these Forms is to know truth. These ideal Forms constitute reality and can

only be apprehended by a trained mind—which, of course, is the goal of philosophy. The objects that we perceive with our senses are simply reflections of the ideal Forms. They are shadows; reality is in the Forms themselves.

Plato's ideas of government were set out in his dialogue titled *The Republic*. Based on his experience in Athens, Plato had come to distrust the workings of democracy. It was obvious to him that individuals could not attain an ethical life unless they lived in a just and rational state. Plato's search for the just state led him to construct an ideal state in *The Republic*, in which the population was divided into three basic groups. At the top was an upper class, a ruling elite, the philosopher-kings: "Unless either philosophers become kings in their countries or those who are now called kings and rulers come to be sufficiently inspired with a genuine desire for wisdom; unless, that is to say, political power and philosophy meet together . . . , there can be no rest from troubles . . . for states . . . [or] for all mankind."[9] The second group were those who showed courage; they would be the warriors who protected the society. All the rest made up the masses, essentially people driven not by wisdom or courage but by desire. They would be the producers of society—the artisans, tradespeople, and farmers. Contrary to common Greek custom, Plato also believed that men and women should have the same education and equal access to all positions.

Plato established a school at Athens known as the Academy. One of his pupils, who studied there for twenty years, was Aristotle (384–322 B.C.E.), who later became a tutor to Alexander the Great. Aristotle did not accept Plato's theory of ideal Forms. Instead he believed that by examining individual objects, we can perceive their form and arrive at universal principles, but that these principles do not exist as a separate higher world of reality beyond material things but are a part of things themselves. Aristotle's interests, then, lay in analyzing and classifying things based on thorough research and investigation. His interests were wide-ranging, and he wrote treatises on an enormous number of subjects: ethics, logic, politics, poetry, astronomy, geology, biology, and physics.

Like Plato, Aristotle wished for an effective form of government that would rationally direct human affairs. Unlike Plato, he did not seek an ideal state based on the embodiment of an ideal Form of justice but tried to find the best form of government by a rational examination of existing governments. For his *Politics*, Aristotle examined the constitutions of 158 states and arrived at general categories for organizing governments. He identified three good forms of government: monarchy, aristocracy, and constitutional government. But based on his examination, he warned that monarchy can easily turn into tyranny, aristocracy into oligarchy, and constitutional government into radical democracy or anarchy. He favored constitutional government as the best form for most people.

Aristotle's philosophical and political ideas played an enormous role in the development of Western thought during the Middle Ages (see Chapter 12). So did his ideas on women. Aristotle maintained that women were biologically inferior to men: "A woman is, as it were, an infertile male. She is female in fact on account of a kind of inadequacy." Therefore, according the Aristotle, women must be subordinated to men, not only in the community but also in marriage: "The association between husband and wife is clearly an aristocracy. The man rules by virtue of merit, and in the sphere that is his by right; but he hands over to his wife such matters as are suitable for her."[10]

Greek Religion

Greek religion was intricately connected to every aspect of daily life; it was both social and practical. Public festivals, which originated from religious practices, served specific functions: boys were prepared to be warriors, girls to be mothers. Because religion was related to every aspect of life, citizens had to have a proper attitude toward the gods. Religion was a civic cult necessary for the well-being of the state. Temples dedicated to a god or goddess were the major buildings in Greek cities.

The poetry of Homer gave an account of the gods that provided Greek religion with a definite structure. Over a period of time, all Greeks came to accept a common religion. There were twelve chief gods who supposedly lived on Mount Olympus, the highest mountain in Greece. Among the twelve were Zeus, the chief deity and father of the gods; Athena, goddess of wisdom and crafts; Apollo, god of the sun and poetry; Aphrodite, goddess of love; and Poseidon, brother of Zeus and god of the seas and earthquakes. Although the twelve Olympian gods were common to all Greeks, each *polis* usually singled out one of the twelve Olympians as a guardian deity for the community. Athena was the patron goddess of Athens, for example.

Greek religion did not have a body of doctrine, nor did it focus on morality. It gave little or no hope of life after death for most people. Because the Greeks wanted the gods to look favorably on their activities, ritual assumed enormous proportions in Greek religion. Prayers were often combined with gifts to the gods based on the principle "I give so that you, the gods, will give in return." Ritual also meant sacrifices of animals or agricultural products. Animal victims were burned on an altar in front of a temple or in front of a home.

Also developed as a way to honor the gods and goddesses were festivals. Some of these (the Panhellenic celebrations) came to have international significance and were held at special locations, such as those dedicated to the worship of Zeus at Olympia or to Apollo at Delphi. Numerous events were held in honor of the gods at the great festivals, including athletic competitions to which all Greeks were invited. The first such games were held at the Olympic festival in 776 B.C.E. and were then held every four years thereafter to honor Zeus. Initially, the Olympic contests consisted of footraces and wrestling, but later boxing, javelin throwing, and various other contests were added.

As another practical side of Greek religion, Greeks wanted to know the will of the gods. To do so, they made use of the oracle, a sacred shrine dedicated to a god or goddess who revealed the future. The most famous was the oracle of Apollo at Delphi, located on the side of Mount Parnassus, overlooking the Gulf of Corinth. At Delphi, a priestess listened to questions while in a state of ecstasy that was believed to be induced by Apollo. Her responses were interpreted by the priests and given in verse form to the person asking questions. Representatives of states and individuals traveled to Delphi to consult the oracle of Apollo. States might inquire whether they should undertake a military expedition; individuals might raise such questions as "Heracleidas asks whether he will have offspring from the wife he has now." Responses were often enigmatic and at times even politically motivated. Croesus, the king of Lydia in Asia Minor who was known for his incredible wealth, sent messengers to the oracle at Delphi, asking whether he should go to war with the Persians. The oracle replied that if Croesus attacked the Persians, he would destroy a mighty empire. Overjoyed to hear these words, Croesus made war on the Persians but was crushed. A mighty empire was indeed destroyed—his own.

Daily Life in Classical Athens

The *polis* was, above all, a male community: only adult male citizens took part in public life. In Athens, this meant the exclusion of women, slaves, and foreign residents, or roughly 85 percent of the total population in Attica. There were probably 150,000 citizens in Athens, of whom about 43,000 were adult males who exercised political power. Resident foreigners, who numbered about 35,000, received the protection of the laws but were also subject to some of the responsibilities of citizens, namely, military service and the funding of festivals. The remaining social group, the slaves, numbered around 100,000. Most slaves in Athens worked in the home as cooks and maids or worked in the fields. Some were owned by the state and worked on public construction projects.

The Athenian economy was largely based on agriculture and trade. Athenians grew grains, vegetables, and fruit for local consumption. Grapes and olives were cultivated for wine and olive oil, which were used locally and also exported. The Athenians raised sheep and goats for wool and dairy products. Because of the size of the population in Attica and the lack of abundant fertile land, Athens had to import 50 to 80 percent of its grain, a staple in the Athenian diet. Trade was thus very important to the Athenian economy.

The Athenian lifestyle was basically simple. Athenian houses were furnished with necessities bought from artisans, such as beds, couches, tables, chests, pottery, stools,

HOUSEHOLD MANAGEMENT AND THE ROLE OF THE ATHENIAN WIFE

In fifth-century Athens, a woman's place was in the home. She had two major responsibilities: the bearing and raising of children and the management of the household. In his dialogue on estate management, Xenophon relates the advice of an Attican gentleman on how to train a wife.

XENOPHON, OECONOMICUS

[Ischomachus addresses his new wife:] For it seems to me, dear, that the gods with great discernment have coupled together male and female, as they are called, chiefly in order that they may form a perfect partnership in mutual service. For, in the first place, that the various species of living creatures may not fail, they are joined in wedlock for the production of children. Secondly, offspring to support them in old age is provided by this union, to human beings, at any rate. Thirdly, human beings live not in the open air, like beasts, but obviously need shelter. Nevertheless, those who mean to win stores to fill the covered place, have need of someone to work at the open-air occupations; since plowing, sowing, planting, and grazing are all such open-air employments; and these supply the needful food. . . . For he made the man's body and mind more capable of enduring cold and heat, and journeys and campaigns; and therefore imposed on him the outdoor tasks. To the woman, since he has made her body less capable of such endurance, I take it that God has assigned the indoor tasks. And knowing that he had created in the woman and had imposed on her the nourishment of the infants, he meted out to her a larger portion of affection for newborn babes than to the man. . . . Now since we know, dear, what duties have been assigned to each of us by God, we must endeavor, each of us, to do the duties allotted to us as well as possible. . . .

Your duty will be to remain indoors and send out those servants whose work is outside, and superintend those who are to work indoors, and to receive the incomings, and distribute so much of them as must be spent, and watch over so much as is to be kept in store, and take care that the sum laid by for a year be not spent in a month. And when wool is brought to you, you must see that cloaks are made for those that want them. You must see too that the dry corn is in good condition for making food. One of the duties that fall to you, however, will perhaps seem rather thankless: you will have to see that any servant who is ill is cared for.

---

baskets, and cooking utensils. Wives and slaves made clothes and blankets at home. The Athenian diet was rather plain and relied on such basic foods as barley, wheat, millet, lentils, grapes, figs, olives, almonds, bread made at home, vegetables, eggs, fish, cheese, and chicken. Olive oil was widely used, not only for eating but also for burning in lamps and rubbing on the body after washing and exercise. Although country houses kept animals, they were used for reasons other than their flesh: oxen for plowing, sheep for wool, and goats for milk and cheese.

The family was a central institution in ancient Athens. It was composed of husband, wife, and children (a nuclear family), although other dependent relatives and slaves were regarded as part of the family economic unit. The family's primary social function was to produce new citizens. Strict laws of the fifth century had stipulated that a citizen must be the offspring of a legally acknowledged marriage between two Athenian citizens whose parents were also citizens.

Adult female citizens could participate in most religious cults and festivals but were otherwise excluded from public life. They could not own property beyond personal items and always had a male guardian. An Athenian woman was expected to be a good wife. Her foremost obligation was to bear children, especially male children who would preserve the family line. A wife was also to take care of her family and her house, either doing the household work herself or supervising the slaves who did the actual work (see the box above).

Women were kept under strict control. Because they were married at fourteen or fifteen, they were taught about their responsibilities early. Although many managed to learn to read and play musical instruments, they were not given any formal education. And women were expected to remain at home out of sight unless attending funerals or festivals. If they left the house, they were to be accompanied. A woman working alone in public was either poverty-stricken or not a citizen.

Male homosexuality was also a prominent feature of Athenian life. The Greek homosexual ideal was a relationship between a mature man and a young male. It is most likely that this was an aristocratic ideal and not one practiced by the common people. While the relationship was frequently physical, the Greeks also viewed it as educational. The older male (the "lover") won the love of his "beloved" through his value as a teacher and the devotion he demonstrated in training his charge. In a sense, this love relationship was seen as a way of initiating young males into the male world of political and military dominance. The Greeks did not feel that the coexistence of homosexual and heterosexual predilections created any special problems for individuals or their society.

The Athenians at last took notice of the new contender. Fear of Philip led them to ally with a number of other Greek states and confront the Macedonians at the Battle of Chaeronea, near Thebes, in 338 B.C.E. The Macedonian army crushed the Greeks, and Philip was now free to consolidate his control over the Greek peninsula. The Greek states were joined together in an alliance that we call the Corinthian League because they met at Corinth. All members took an oath of loyalty: "I swear by Zeus, Earth, Sun, Poseidon, Athena, Ares, and all the gods and goddesses. I will abide by the peace, and I will not break the agreements with Philip the Macedonian, nor will I take up arms with hostile intent against any one of those who abide by the oaths either by land or by sea."[11] Philip insisted that the Greek states end their bitter rivalries and cooperate with him in a war against Persia. Before Philip could undertake his invasion of Asia, however, he was assassinated, leaving the task to his son Alexander.

Alexander the Great

Alexander was only twenty when he became king of Macedonia. He was in many ways prepared to rule by his father, who had taken Alexander along on military campaigns and had given him control of the cavalry at the important battle of Chaeronea. After his father's assassination, Alexander moved quickly to assert his authority, securing the Macedonian frontiers and smothering a rebellion in Greece. He then turned to his father's dream, the invasion of the Persian Empire.

There is no doubt that Alexander was taking a chance in attacking the Persian Empire, which was still a strong state. In the spring of 334 B.C.E., Alexander entered Asia Minor with an army of 37,000 men. About half were Macedonians, the rest Greeks and other allies. The cavalry, which would play an important role as a striking force, numbered about 5,000.

Alexander's first confrontation with the Persians, at a battle at the Granicus River in 334 B.C.E., almost cost him his life but resulted in a major victory. By the following spring, the entire western half of Asia Minor was in Alexander's hands (see Map 4.2). Meanwhile, the Persian king, Darius III, mobilized his forces to stop Alexander's army. Although the Persian troops outnumbered Alexander's, the Battle of Issus was fought on a narrow field that canceled the advantage of superior numbers and resulted in another Macedonian success. After his victory at Issus in 333 B.C.E., Alexander turned south, and by the winter of 332, Syria, Palestine, and Egypt were under his domination. He took the traditional title of pharaoh of Egypt and founded the first of a series of cities named after him (Alexandria) as the Greek administrative capital of Egypt. It became (and remains today) one of Egypt's and the Mediterranean world's most important cities.

WOMEN IN THE LOOM ROOM. In Athens, women were citizens and could participate in religious cults and festivals, but they had no rights and were barred from political activity. Women were thought to belong in the house, caring for the children and the needs of the household. A principal activity of Greek women was the making of clothes. This vase shows two women working on a warp-weighted loom.

THE RISE OF MACEDONIA AND THE CONQUESTS OF ALEXANDER

While the Greek city-states were continuing to fight each other, to their north a new and ultimately powerful kingdom was emerging in its own right. Its people, the Macedonians, were viewed as barbarians by their southern neighbors, the Greeks. The Macedonians were mostly rural folk, organized in tribes, not city-states, and not until the end of the fifth century B.C.E. did Macedonia emerge as an important kingdom. But when Philip II (359–336 B.C.E.) came to the throne, he built an efficient army and turned Macedonia into the strongest power of the Greek world—one that was soon drawn into the conflicts among the Greeks.

ALEXANDER MEETS AN INDIAN KING

In his campaigns in India, Alexander fought a number of difficult battles. At the Battle of the Hydaspes River, he faced a strong opponent in the Indian king Porus. After defeating Porus, Alexander treated him with respect, according to Arrian, Alexander's ancient biographer.

ARRIAN, *THE CAMPAIGNS OF ALEXANDER*

Throughout the action Porus had proved himself a man indeed, not only as a commander but as a soldier of the truest courage. When he saw his cavalry cut to pieces, most of his infantry dead, and his elephants killed or roaming riderless and bewildered about the field, his behaviour was very different from that of the Persian King Darius: unlike Darius, he did not lead the scramble to save his own skin, but so long as a single unit of his men held together, fought bravely on. It was only when he was himself wounded that he turned the elephant on which he rode and began to withdraw. . . . Alexander, anxious to save the life of this great soldier, sent . . . [to him] an Indian named Meroes, a man he had been told had long been Porus's friend. Porus listened to Meroes's message, stopped his elephant, and dismounted; he was much distressed by thirst, so when he had

revived himself by drinking, he told Meroes to conduct him with all speed to Alexander.

Alexander, informed of his approach, rode out to meet him. . . . When they met, he reined in his horse, and looked at his adversary with admiration: he was a magnificent figure of a man, over seven feet high and of great personal beauty; his bearing had lost none of its pride; his air was of one brave man meeting another, of a king in the presence of a king, with whom he had fought honourably for his kingdom.

Alexander was the first to speak. "What," he said, "do you wish that I should do with you?" "Treat me as a king ought," Porus is said to have replied. "For my part," said Alexander, pleased by his answer, "your request shall be granted. But is there not something you would wish for yourself? Ask it." "Everything," said Porus, "is contained in this one request."

The dignity of these words gave Alexander even more pleasure, and he restored to Porus his sovereignty over his subjects, adding to his realm other territory of even greater extent. Thus he did indeed use a brave man as a king ought, and from that time forward found him in every way a loyal friend.

In 331 B.C.E., Alexander renewed his offensive, moved into the territory of the ancient Mesopotamian kingdoms, and fought a decisive battle with the Persians at Gaugamela, not far from Babylon. After his victory, Alexander entered Babylon and then proceeded to the Persian capitals at Susa and Persepolis, where he acquired the Persian treasuries and took possession of vast quantities of gold and silver. By 330, Alexander was again on the march, pursuing Darius. After Darius was killed by one of his own men, Alexander took the title and office of Great King of the Persians. But he was not content to rest with the spoils of the Persian Empire. Over the next three years, he moved east and northeast, as far as modern Pakistan. By the summer of 327 B.C.E., he had entered India, which at that time was divided into a number of warring states. In 326 B.C.E., Alexander and his armies arrived in the plains of northwestern India. At the Battle of the Hydaspes River, Alexander won a brutally fought battle (see the box above). When Alexander made clear his determination to march east to conquer more of India, his soldiers, weary of campaigning year after year, mutinied and refused to go on. Reluctantly, Alexander turned back, leading his men across the arid lands of southern Iran. Conditions in the desert were appalling; the blazing sun and lack of water led to thousands of deaths before Alexander and his remaining troops reached Babylon. Alexander planned still more campaigns, but in June 323 B.C.E., weakened from wounds, fever, and probably

excessive alcohol consumption, he died at the young age of thirty-two.

The Legacy of Alexander

Alexander is one of the most puzzling great figures in history. Historians relying on the same sources give vastly different pictures of him. Some portray him as an idealistic visionary and others as a ruthless Machiavellian. How did Alexander the Great view himself? We know that he sought to imitate Achilles, the warrior-hero of Homer's *Iliad*. Alexander kept a copy of the *Iliad*—and a dagger—under his pillow. He also claimed to be descended from Heracles, the Greek hero who came to be worshiped as a god.

Regardless of his ideals, motives, or views about himself, one fact stands out: Alexander truly created a new age, the Hellenistic era. The word *Hellenistic* is derived from a Greek word meaning "to imitate Greeks." It is an appropriate way, then, to describe an age that saw the extension of the Greek language and ideas to the non-Greek world of the Middle East. Alexander's destruction of the Persian monarchy created opportunities for Greek engineers, intellectuals, merchants, soldiers, and administrators. Those who followed Alexander and his successors participated in a new political unity based on the principle of monarchy. His successors used force to establish military monarchies that dominated the Hellenistic world after his death. Autocratic power became

MAP 4.2   The Conquests of Alexander the Great. In just twelve years, Alexander the Great conquered vast territories. Dominating lands from west of the Nile to east of the Indus, he brought the Persian Empire, Egypt, and much of the Middle East under his control and laid the foundations for the Hellenistic world. ➤ *Approximately how far did he and his troops travel during those twelve years?*

➤ **ALEXANDER THE GREAT.** This bust of Alexander the Great is a Roman copy of the head of a statue, possibly by Lysippus. Although he aspired to be another Achilles, the tragic hero of Homer's *Iliad*, Alexander also sought more divine honors. He claimed to be descended from Heracles, a Greek hero worshiped as a god, and as pharaoh of Egypt, he gained recognition as a living deity.

a regular feature of those Hellenistic monarchies and was part of Alexander's political legacy to the Hellenistic world. His vision of empire no doubt inspired the Romans, who were, of course, the real heirs of Alexander's legacy.

But Alexander also left a cultural legacy. As a result of his conquests, Greek language, art, architecture, and literature spread throughout the Middle East. The urban centers of the Hellenistic age, many founded by Alexander and his successors, became springboards for the diffusion of Greek culture. While the Greeks spread their culture in the east, they were also inevitably influenced by eastern ways. Thus Alexander's legacy created one of the basic characteristics of the Hellenistic world: the clash and fusion of different cultures.

THE RISE OF MACEDONIA AND THE CONQUESTS OF ALEXANDER

Reign of Philip II	359–336 B.C.E.
Battle of Chaeronea; Philip II conquers Greece	338 B.C.E.
Reign of Alexander the Great	336–323 B.C.E.
Alexander invades Asia; Battle of Granicus River	334 B.C.E.
Battle of Issus	333 B.C.E.
Battle of Gaugamela	331 B.C.E.
Fall of Persepolis, the Persian capital	330 B.C.E.
Alexander enters India	327 B.C.E.
Battle of Hydaspes River	326 B.C.E.
Death of Alexander	323 B.C.E.

THE HELLENISTIC KINGDOMS

The united empire that Alexander created by his conquests did not survive his death. All too soon, the most important Macedonian generals were engaged in a struggle for power. By 300 B.C.E., all hope of unity was dead, and eventually four Hellenistic kingdoms emerged as the successors to Alexander: Macedonia under the Antigonid dynasty, Syria and the east under the Seleucids, the Attalid kingdom of Pergamum in western Asia Minor, and Egypt under the Ptolemies (see Map 4.3). All were eventually conquered by the Romans.

The Hellenistic monarchies created a semblance of stability for several centuries, even though Hellenistic kings refused to accept the status quo and periodically engaged in wars to alter it. At the same time, an underlying strain always existed between the new Greco-Macedonian ruling class and the native populations. Together these factors created a certain degree of tension that was never truly ended until the vibrant Roman state to the west stepped in and imposed a new order.

Although Alexander the Great had apparently planned to fuse Greeks and easterners— he used Persians as administrators, encouraged his soldiers to marry easterners, and did so himself—Hellenistic monarchs who succeeded him relied primarily on Greeks and Macedonians to form the new ruling class. Even those easterners who did advance to important administrative posts had learned Greek (all government business was transacted in Greek) and had become Hellenized in a cultural sense. The Greek ruling class was determined to maintain its privileged position.

Since the Hellenizing process was largely an urban phenomenon, the creation of new Greek cities is an especially important topic. In his conquests, Alexander had founded a series of new cities and military settlements, and Hellenistic kings did likewise. The new population centers varied considerably in size and importance. Military settlements were meant to maintain order and might consist of only a few hundred men strongly dependent on the king. But there were also new independent cities with thousands of inhabitants. Alexandria in Egypt was the largest city in the Mediterranean region by the first century B.C.E.

Hellenistic rulers encouraged a massive spread of Greek colonists to the Middle East because of their intrinsic value to the new monarchies. Greeks (and Macedonians) provided not only recruits for the army but also a pool of civilian administrators and workers who contributed to economic development. Even architects, engineers, dramatists, and actors were in demand in the new Greek cities. Many Greeks and Macedonians were quick to see the advantages of moving to the new urban centers and gladly sought their fortunes in the Middle East. The Greek cities of the Hellenistic era were the chief agents in the spread of Greek culture in the Middle East—as far, in fact, as modern Afghanistan and India.

Economic and Social Trends

Agriculture was still of primary importance to both the native populations and the new Greek cities of the Hellenistic world. The Greek cities

➤ **A GREEK-STYLE BUDDHA.**
Alexander's incursion into the Western part of India resulted in some Greek cultural influence on India. Greek accomplishments in astronomy and mathematics influenced some Indian scientists, and Hellenistic artistic styles affected some Indian artists. Especially noticeable, as shown in this stone sculpture of Buddha wearing a Greek-style toga, was the Buddhist Gandharan style, which in the first century B.C.E. combined Indian and Hellenistic artistic traditions.

© Borromeo/Art Resource, NY

MAP 4.3   The Hellenistic Kingdoms.   Alexander died unexpectedly at the age of thirty-two and did not designate a successor. Upon his death, his generals struggled for power, eventually creating four monarchies that spread Hellenistic culture and fostered trade and economic development. ➤ *Which kingdom encompassed most of the old Persian Empire?*

Legend:
- Antigonid kingdom
- Ptolemaic kingdom
- Aetolian League
- Pergamene kingdom
- Seleucid kingdom
- Achaean League
- Mauryan Empire

continued their old agrarian patterns. A well-defined citizen body owned land and worked it with the assistance of slaves. But their farms were isolated units in a vast area of land ultimately owned by the king or assigned to large estate owners and worked by native peasants dwelling in villages.

Commerce experienced considerable expansion in the Hellenistic era. Indeed, trading contacts linked much of the Hellenistic world together. The decline in the number of political barriers encouraged more commercial traffic. Although Hellenistic monarchs still fought wars, the conquests of Alexander and the policies of his successors made possible greater trade between east and west. An incredible variety of products were traded: gold and silver from Spain; salt from Asia Minor; timber from Macedonia; ebony, gems, ivory, and spices from India; frankincense (used on altars) from Arabia; slaves from Thrace, Syria, and Asia Minor; fine wines from Syria and western Asia Minor; olive oil from Athens; and numerous exquisite foodstuffs, such as the famous prunes of Damascus. The greatest trade, however, was in the basic staple of life—grain.

One of the noticeable features of social life in the Hellenistic world was the emergence of new opportunities for women—at least, for upper-class women—especially in the economic realm. Documents show increasing numbers of women involved in managing slaves, selling property, and making loans. Even then, legal contracts in which women were involved had to include their official male guardians. Only in Sparta were women free to control their own economic affairs. Many Spartan women were noticeably wealthy; females owned 40 percent of Spartan land.

Spartan women, however, were an exception, especially on the Greek mainland. Women in Athens, for example, still remained highly restricted and supervised. Although a few philosophers welcomed female participation in men's affairs, many philosophers rejected equality between men and women and asserted that the traditional roles of wives and mothers were most satisfying for women.

But the opinions of philosophers did not prevent upper-class women from making gains in areas other than the economic sphere (see the box on p. 114). New possibili-

A New Autonomy For Women

Upper-class women in Hellenistic society enjoyed noticeable gains, and even in the lives of ordinary women, a new assertiveness came to the fore despite the continuing domination of society by men. The first selection is taken from the letter of a wife to her husband, complaining about his failure to return home. In the second selection, a father complains that his daughter has abandoned him, contrary to an Egyptian law providing that children who have been properly raised should support their parents.

LETTER FROM ISIAS TO HEPHAISTION, 168 B.C.E.

If you are well and other things are going right, it would accord with the prayer that I make continually to the gods. I myself and the child and all the household are in good health and think of you always. When I received your letter from Horos, in which you announce that you are in detention in the Serapeum at Memphis, for the news that you are well I straightway thanked the gods, but about your not coming home, when all the others who had been secluded there have come, I am ill-pleased, because after having piloted myself and your child through such bad times and been driven to every extremity owing to the price of wheat, I thought that now at least, with you at home, I should enjoy some respite, whereas you have not even thought of coming home nor given any regard to our circumstances, remembering how I was in want of everything while you were still here, not to mention this long lapse of time and these critical days, during which you have sent us noth-

ing. As, moreover, Horos who delivered the letter has brought news of your having been released from detention, I am thoroughly ill-pleased. Notwithstanding, as your mother also is annoyed, for her sake as well as for mine please return to the city, if nothing more pressing holds you back. You will do me a favor by taking care of your bodily health. Farewell.

LETTER FROM KTESIKLES TO KING PTOLEMY, 220 B.C.E.

I am wronged by Dionysios and by Nike my daughter. For though I raised her, my own daughter, and educated her and brought her to maturity, when I was stricken with bodily ill-health and was losing my eyesight, she was not minded to furnish me with any of the necessities of life. When I sought to obtain justice from her in Alexandria, she begged my pardon, and in the eighteenth year she swore me a written royal oath to give me each month twenty drachmas, which she was to earn by her own bodily labor. . . . But now corrupted by Dionysios, who is a comic actor, she does not do for me anything of what was in the written oath, despising my weakness and ill-health. I beg you, therefore, O king, not to allow me to be wronged by my daughter and by Dionysios the actor who corrupted her, but to order Diophanes the strategus [a provincial administrator] to summon them and hear us out; and if I am speaking the truth, let Diophanes deal with her corrupter as seems good to him and compel my daughter Nike to do justice to me. If this is done I shall no longer be wronged but by fleeing to you, O king, I shall obtain justice.

ties for females arose when women in some areas of the Hellenistic world were allowed to pursue education in the traditional fields of literature, music, and even athletics. Education, then, provided new opportunities for women: female poets appeared in the third century, and there are instances of women involved in both scholarly and artistic activities.

The creation of the Hellenistic monarchies, which represented a considerable departure from the world of the city-state, also gave new scope to the role played by the monarchs' wives, the Hellenistic queens. In Macedonia, a pattern of alliances between mothers and sons provided openings for women to take an active role in politics, especially in political intrigue. In Egypt, opportunities for royal women were even greater because the Ptolemaic rulers reverted to an Egyptian custom of kings marrying their own sisters. Of the first eight Ptolemaic rulers, four wed their sisters. Ptolemy II and his sister-wife Arsinoë II were both worshiped as gods in their lifetimes. Arsinoë played

an energetic role in government and was involved in the expansion of the Egyptian navy. She was also the first Egyptian queen whose portrait appeared on coins with that of her husband.

CULTURE IN THE HELLENISTIC WORLD

Although the Hellenistic kingdoms encompassed vast territories and many diverse peoples, the Greeks provided a sense of unity as a result of the diffusion of Greek culture throughout the Hellenistic world. The Hellenistic era was a period of considerable cultural accomplishment in many areas—literature, art, science, and philosophy. Although these achievements occurred throughout the Hellenistic world, certain centers, especially the great cities of Alexandria and Pergamum, stood out. In both cities, cultural developments were encouraged by the rulers themselves. Rich Hellenistic kings had considerable resources with which to patronize culture.

New Directions in Literature and Art

The Hellenistic age produced an enormous quantity of literature, most of which has not survived. Hellenistic monarchs, who held literary talent in high esteem, subsidized writers on a grand scale. The Ptolemaic rulers of Egypt were particularly lavish. The combination of their largesse and a famous library with over 500,000 scrolls drew a host of scholars and authors to Alexandria, including a circle of poets. Theocritus (c. 315–250 B.C.E.), originally a native of the island of Sicily, wrote "little poems" or idylls dealing with erotic subjects, lovers' complaints, and pastoral themes expressing his love of nature and his appreciation of nature's beauties.

In the Hellenistic era, Athens remained the theatrical center of the Greek world. While little remained of tragedy, a New Comedy developed, which completely rejected political themes and sought only to entertain and amuse. The Athenian playwright Menander (c. 342–291 B.C.E.) was perhaps the best representative of New Comedy. Plots were simple: typically, a hero falls in love with a not-really-so-bad prostitute, who turns out eventually to be the long-lost daughter of a rich neighbor. The hero marries her, and they live happily ever after.

The Hellenistic period saw a great outpouring of historical and biographical literature. The chief historian of the Hellenistic age was Polybius (c. 203–c. 120 B.C.E.), a Greek who lived for some years in Rome. His major work consisted of forty books narrating the history of the "inhabited Mediterranean world" from 221 to 146 B.C.E. Only the first five books are extant, although long extracts from the rest of the books survive. His history focuses on the growth of Rome from a city-state to a vast empire. It is apparent that Polybius understood the significance of the Romans' achievement. He followed Thucydides in seeking rational motives for historical events. He also approached his sources critically and used firsthand accounts.

In addition to being patrons of literary talent, the Hellenistic monarchs were eager to spend their money to beautify and adorn the cities within their states. The founding of new cities and the rebuilding of old ones provided numerous opportunities for Greek architects and sculptors. The buildings of the Greek homeland—gymnasia, baths, theaters, and of course temples—lined the streets of these cities.

Both Hellenistic kings and rich citizens patronized sculptors. Thousands of statues, many paid for by the people honored, were erected in towns and cities all over the Hellenistic world. Hellenistic sculptors traveled throughout this world, attracted by the material rewards

➤ **OLD MARKET WOMAN.**   Greek architects and sculptors were highly valued throughout the Hellenistic world as kings undertook projects to beautify the cities of their kingdoms. Unlike the sculptors of the classical period, Hellenistic sculptors no longer tried to capture ideal beauty in their sculptures but moved toward a more emotional and realistic art. This statue of an old market woman exemplifies this new trend in art.

offered by wealthy patrons. As a result, Hellenistic sculpture was characterized by a considerable degree of uniformity. While maintaining the technical skill of the classical period, Hellenistic sculptors moved away from the idealism of fifth-century classicism to a more emotional and realistic art, seen in numerous statues of old women, drunks, and little children at play.

A Golden Age of Science

The Hellenistic era witnessed a more conscious separation of science from philosophy. In classical Greece, what we would call the physical and life sciences had been divisions of philosophical inquiry. Nevertheless, by the time of Aristotle, the Greeks had already established an important principle of scientific investigation, empirical research, or systematic observation as the basis for generalization. In the Hellenistic age, the sciences tended to be studied in their own right.

By far the most famous scientist of the period was Archimedes (287–212 B.C.E.) of Syracuse. Archimedes was

THE STOIC IDEAL OF HARMONY WITH GOD

The Stoic Cleanthes (331–232 B.C.E.) succeeded Zeno as head of this school of philosophy. One historian of Hellenistic civilization has called this work by Cleanthes the greatest religious hymn in Greece. Certainly, it demonstrates that Stoicism, unlike Epicureanism, did have an underlying spiritual foundation. This poem has been compared to the great psalms of the Hebrews.

CLEANTHES, HYMN TO ZEUS

Nothing occurs on the earth apart from you, O God, nor in the heavenly regions nor on the sea, except what bad men do in their folly; but you know how to make the odd even, and to harmonize what is dissonant; to you the alien is akin.

And so you have wrought together into one all things that are good and bad,

So that there arises one eternal logos [rationale] of all things,

Which all bad mortals shun and ignore,

Unhappy wretches, ever seeking the possession of good things

They neither see nor hear the universal law of God,

By obeying which they might enjoy a happy life.

---

especially important for his work on the geometry of spheres and cylinders and for establishing the value of the mathematical constant pi. Archimedes was also a practical inventor. He may have devised the so-called Archimedean screw, used to pump water out of mines and to lift irrigation water, as well as a compound pulley for transporting heavy weights. During the Roman siege of Syracuse, he constructed a number of devices to thwart the attackers. According to Plutarch's account, the Romans became so frightened "that if they did but see a little rope or a piece of wood from the wall, instantly crying out, that there it was again, Archimedes was about to let fly some engine at them, they turned their backs and fled."[12] Archimedes' accomplishments inspired a wealth of semilegendary stories. Supposedly, he discovered specific gravity by observing the water he displaced in his bath and became so excited by his realization that he jumped out of the water and ran home naked, shouting, "Eureka!" ("I have found it!"). He is said to have emphasized the importance of levers by proclaiming to the king of Syracuse, "Give me a lever and a place to stand, and I will move the earth." The king was so impressed that he encouraged Archimedes to lower his sights and build defensive weapons instead.

Philosophy: New Schools of Thought

While Alexandria and Pergamum became the renowned cultural centers of the Hellenistic world, Athens remained the prime center for philosophy. After Alexander the Great, the home of Socrates, Plato, and Aristotle continued to attract the most illustrious philosophers from the Greek world, who chose to establish their schools there. New schools of philosophical thought reinforced Athens's reputation as a philosophical center.

Epicurus (341–270 B.C.E.), the founder of Epicureanism, established a school in Athens near the end of the fourth century B.C.E. Epicurus believed that human beings were free to follow self-interest as a basic motivating force. Happiness was the goal of life, and the means to achieve it was the pursuit of pleasure, the only true good. But the pursuit of pleasure was not meant in a physical, hedonistic sense (which is what our word *epicurean* has come to mean). Pleasure was not satisfying one's desire in an active, gluttonous fashion but rather freedom from emotional turmoil, freedom from worry, the freedom that came from a mind at rest. To achieve this kind of pleasure, one had to free oneself from public affairs and politics. But this was not a renunciation of all social life, for to Epicurus, a life could be complete only when it was centered on friendship. Epicurus' own life in Athens was an embodiment of his teachings. He and his friends created their own private community where they could pursue their ideal of true happiness.

Another school of thought was Stoicism, which became the most popular philosophy of the Hellenistic world and later flourished in the Roman Empire as well. It was the product of a teacher named Zeno (335–263 B.C.E.), who came to Athens and began to teach in a public colonnade known as the Painted Portico (the *Stoa Poikile*—hence Stoicism). Like Epicureanism, Stoicism was concerned with how individuals find happiness. But Stoics took a radically different approach to the problem. To them, happiness, the supreme good, could be found only by living in harmony with the will of the gods, by which people gained inner peace (see the box above). Life's problems could not disturb these people, and they could bear whatever life offered (hence our word *stoic*). Unlike Epicureans, Stoics did not believe in the need to separate oneself from the world and politics. Public service was regarded as noble, and the real Stoic was a good citizen and could even be a good government official.

Epicureanism and especially Stoicism focused primarily on the problem of human happiness, and their popularity would suggest a fundamental change in the Greek lifestyle. In the classical Greek world, the happiness of individuals and the meaning of life were closely associated with the life of the *polis*: one found fulfillment within the community. In the Hellenistic kingdoms, the sense that one could find satisfaction and fulfillment through life in the *polis* had weakened. People sought new philosophies that offered personal happiness, and in the cosmopolitan world of the Hellenistic states, with their mixture of peoples, a new openness to thoughts of universality could also emerge. For some people, Stoicism embodied this larger sense of community. The appeal of new philosophies in the Hellenistic era can also be explained by the apparent decline in certain aspects of traditional religion.

Religion in the Hellenistic World

When the Greeks spread throughout the Hellenistic kingdoms, they took their gods with them. Although the construction of temples may have been less important than in classical times, there were still many demonstrations of a lively religious faith. But over a period of time, there was a noticeable decline in the vitality of the traditional Greek Olympian religion, which left Greeks receptive to the numerous religious cults of the eastern world. The eastern religions that appealed most to Greeks, however, were the mystery religions. What was the source of their attraction?

Mystery cults, with their secret initiations and promises of individual salvation, were not new to the Greek world. But the Greeks of the Hellenistic era were also strongly influenced by eastern mystery cults, such as those of Egypt, which offered a distinct advantage over the Greek mystery religions. The latter had usually been connected to specific locations (such as Eleusis), which meant that a would-be initiate had to undertake a pilgrimage in order to participate in the rites. In contrast, the eastern mystery religions were readily available since temples to their gods and goddesses were located throughout the Greek cities of the east. All of the mystery religions were based on the same fundamental premises. Individuals could pursue a path to salvation and achieve eternal life by being initiated into a union with a savior god or goddess who had died and risen again.

The Egyptian cult of Isis was one of the most popular of the mystery religions. Isis was the goddess of women, marriage, and children; as one of her hymns states: "I am she whom women call goddess. I ordained that women should be loved by men: I brought wife and husband together, and invented the marriage contract. I ordained that women should bear children."[13] Isis was also portrayed as the giver of civilization, who had brought laws and letters to all humankind. The cult of Isis offered a precious commodity to its initiates—the promise of eternal life. In many ways, the cult of Isis and the other mystery religions of the Hellenistic era helped to pave the way for the coming and the success of Christianity.

CONCLUSION

Unlike the great centralized empires of the Persians and the Chinese, ancient Greece consisted of a large number of small, independent city-states, most of which had populations of only a few thousand. Despite the small size of their city-states, these ancient Greeks created a civilization that was the fountainhead of Western culture. Socrates, Plato, and Aristotle established the foundations of Western philosophy. Western literary forms are largely derived from Greek poetry and drama. Greek notions of harmony, proportion, and beauty have remained the touchstones for all subsequent Western art. A rational method of inquiry, so important to modern science, was conceived in ancient Greece. Many political terms are Greek in origin, and so are concepts of the rights and duties of citizenship, especially as they were conceived in Athens, the first great democracy. Especially during their classical period, the Greeks raised and debated the fundamental questions about the purpose of human existence, the structure of human society, and the nature of the universe that have concerned thinkers ever since.

All of these achievements came from a group of small city-states in ancient Greece. And yet there remains an element of tragedy about Greek civilization. For all of their brilliant accomplishments, the Greeks were unable to rise above the divisions and rivalries that caused them to fight each other and undermine their own civilization. Of course, their cultural contributions have outlived their political struggles. And the Hellenistic era, which emerged after the Greek city-states had lost their independence, made possible the spread of Greek ideas to larger areas.

The Hellenistic period was a vibrant one. New cities arose and flourished. New philosophical ideas captured the minds of many. Significant achievements were made in art, literature, and science. Greek culture spread throughout the Middle East and made an impact wherever it was carried. But serious problems remained. Hellenistic kings continued to engage in inconclusive wars. Much of the formal culture was the special preserve of the Greek conquerors, whose attitude of superiority kept them largely separated from the native masses of the Hellenistic kingdoms. Although the Hellenistic world achieved a degree of political stability, by the late third century B.C.E. signs of decline were beginning to multiply. Some of the more farsighted perhaps realized the danger the growing power of Rome presented to the Hellenistic world. The Romans would ultimately inherit Alexander's empire and Greek culture, and we now turn to them to try to understand what made them such successful conquerors.

1500 B.C.E. 1000 B.C.E. 750 B.C.E. 500 B.C.E. 250 B.C.E. 100 B.C.E.

Mycenaean Greece
Age of Expansion
Hellenistic kingdoms
Classical Age
Lycurgan reforms in Sparta
Great Peloponnesian War
Battle of Marathon
Conquests of Alexander the Great
Homer
Parthenon
Plato and Aristotle
Flourishing of Hellenistic science
Greek drama (Aeschylus, Sophocles, Euripides)

CHAPTER NOTES

1. Homer, *Odyssey*, trans. E. V. Rieu (New York, 1946), p. 337.
2. Xenophon, *Symposium*, trans. O. J. Todd (New York, 1946), III, 5.
3. Homer, *Odyssey*, trans. E. V. Rieu (New York, 1959), pp. 290–291.
4. Quoted in Thomas R. Martin, *Ancient Greece* (New Haven, Conn., 1996), p. 62.
5. These words from Plutarch are quoted in E. Fantham, H. P. Foley, N. B. Kampen, Sarah B. Pomeroy, and H. A. Shapiro, *Women in the Classical World* (New York, 1994), p. 64.
6. Thucydides, *The Peloponnesian War*, trans. Rex Warner (New York, 1954), p. 24.
7. Sophocles, *Oedipus the King*, trans. David Grene (Chicago, 1959), pp. 68–69.
8. Sophocles, *Antigone*, trans. Don Taylor (London, 1986), p. 146.
9. Plato, *The Republic*, trans. F. M. Cornford (New York, 1945), pp. 178–179.
10. Quotations from Aristotle are in Sue Blundell, *Women in Ancient Greece* (Cambridge, Mass., 1995), pp. 106, 186.
11. Quoted in Sarah B. Pomeroy, Stanley M. Burstein, Walter Donlan, and Jennifer Tolbert Roberts, *Ancient Greece: A Political, Social, and Cultural History* (Oxford, 1999), p. 390.
12. Plutarch, *Life of Marcellus*, trans. John Dryden (New York, n.d.), p. 378.
13. Quoted in W. W. Tarn, *Hellenistic Civilization* (London, 1930), p. 324.

SUGGESTED READING

A standard one-volume reference work for Greek history is J. B. Bury and R. Meiggs, *A History of Greece to the Death of Alexander the Great*, 4th ed. (New York, 1975). Other good general introductions to Greek history include *The Oxford History of the Classical World*, ed. J. Boardman, J. Griffin, and O. Murray (Oxford, 1986), pp. 19–314; T. R. Martin, *Ancient Greece* (New Haven, Conn., 1996); P. Cartledge, *The Cambridge Illustrated History of Ancient Greece* (Cambridge, 1998); and W. Donlan, S. B. Pomeroy, J. T. Roberts, and S. M. Burstein, *Ancient Greece: A Political, Social, and Cultural History* (New York, 1998).

Early Greek history is examined in O. Murray, *Early Greece*, 2d ed. (Cambridge, Mass., 1993), and J. L. Fitton, *The Discovery of the Greek Bronze Age* (Cambridge, 1995).

A good general work on the Greek age of expansion is A. M. Snodgrass, *Archaic Greece* (London, 1980). Economic and social history of the period is covered in C. Starr, *The Economic and Social Growth of Early Greece, 800–500 B.C.* (Oxford, 1977). On colonization, see J. Boardman, *The Greeks Overseas*, rev. ed. (Baltimore, 1980). On tyranny, see J. F. McGlew, *Tyranny and Political Culture in Ancient Greece*

(Ithaca, N.Y., 1993). On Sparta, see W. Forrest, *A History of Sparta, 950–121 B.C.*, 2d ed. (London, 1980), and P. Cartledge, *Spartan Reflections* (Berkeley, Calif., 2001). On early Athens, see the still valuable A. Jones, *Athenian Democracy* (London, 1957), and R. Osborne, *Demos* (Oxford, 1985). The Persian Wars are examined in P. Green, *The Greco-Persian Wars* (Berkeley, Calif., 1996).

A general history of classical Greece can be found in S. Hornblower, *The Greek World, 479–323 B.C.* (London, 1983). Important works on Athens include C. W. Fornara and L. J. Samons II, *Athens from Cleisthenes to Pericles* (Berkeley, Calif., 1991); D. Stockton, *The Classical Athenian Democracy* (Oxford, 1990); and D. Kagan, *Pericles of Athens and the Birth of Democracy* (New York, 1991). On the development of the Athenian Empire, see M. F. McGregor, *The Athenians and Their Empire* (Vancouver, 1987). The best way to examine the Great Peloponnesian War is to read the work of Thucydides, *History of the Peloponnesian War*, trans. R. Warner (Harmondsworth, England, 1954).

A good brief study of Greek art is J. Boardman, *Greek Art* (London, 1985). On sculpture, see A. Stewart, *Greek Sculpture: An Explo-*

ration (New Haven, Conn., 1990). A basic survey of architecture is H. W. Lawrence, *Greek Architecture*, rev. ed. (Harmondsworth, England, 1983). On Greek drama, see the general work by J. De Romilly, *A Short History of Greek Literature* (Chicago, 1985). On Greek philosophy, a detailed study is available in W. K. C. Guthrie, *A History of Greek Philosophy*, 6 vols. (Cambridge, 1962–1981). On Greek religion, see J. N. Bremmer, *Greek Religion* (Oxford, 1994).

On the family and women, see S. C. Humphreys, *The Family, Women and Death* (London, 1983); C. B. Patterson, *The Family in Greek History* (New York, 1998); E. Fantham, H. P. Foley, N. B. Kampen, S. B. Pomeroy, and H. A. Shapiro, *Women in the Classical World* (New York, 1994); and S. Blundell, *Women in Ancient Greece* (Cambridge, Mass., 1995).

The best general surveys of the Hellenistic era are F. W. Walbank, *The Hellenistic World* (London, 1981), and G. Shipley, *The Greek World After Alexander, 323–30 B.C.* (New York, 2000). For a good introduction to the early history of Macedonia, see E. N. Borza, *In the Shadow of Olympus: The Emergence of Macedon* (Princeton, N.J., 1990). Philip II of Macedonia is covered well in N. Hammond and G. Griffith, *A History of Macedonia*, vol. 2, 550–336 B.C. (Oxford, 1979). There are considerable differences of opinion on Alexander the Great. The best biographies include R. L. Fox, *Alexander the Great* (London, 1973); J. R. Hamilton, *Alexander the Great* (London, 1973); and P. Green, *Alexander of Macedon* (Berkeley, Calif., 1991).

The various Hellenistic monarchies can be examined in N. G. L. Hammond and F. W. Walbank, *A History of Macedonia*, vol. 3, *336–167* B.C. (Oxford, 1988); S. Sherwin-White and A. Kuhrt, *From Samarkand to Sardis: A New Approach to the Seleucid Empire* (Berkeley, Calif., 1993); and N. Lewis, *Greeks in Ptolemaic Egypt* (Oxford, 1986). On economic and social trends, see the classic and still indispensable M. I. Rostovtzeff, *Social and Economic History of the Hellenistic World*, 3 vols., 2d ed. (Oxford, 1953). Hellenistic women are examined in two works by S. B. Pomeroy, *Goddesses, Whores, Wives, and Slaves: Women in Classical Antiquity* (New York, 1975) and *Women in Hellenistic Egypt* (New York, 1984).

For a general introduction to Hellenistic culture, see J. Onians, *Art and Thought in the Hellenistic Age* (London, 1979). The best general survey of Hellenistic philosophy is A. A. Long, *Hellenistic Philosophy: Stoics, Epicureans, Skeptics*, 2d ed. (London, 1986). A superb work on Hellenistic science is G. E. R. Lloyd, *Greek Science After Aristotle* (London, 1973). On the entry of Rome into the Hellenistic world, see the basic work by E. S. Gruen, *The Hellenistic World and the Coming of Rome*, 2 vols. (Berkeley, Calif., 1984).

INFOTRAC COLLEGE EDITION

For additional reading, go to InfoTrac College Edition, your online research library at
http://web1.infotrac-college.com

Enter the search terms "Greece history" using Keywords.

Enter the search terms "Peloponnesian War" using Keywords.

Enter the search terms "Greek mythology" using the Subject Guide.

Enter the search terms "Plato or Aristotle or Socrates" using Keywords.

Enter the search terms "Alexander the Great" using Keywords.

Chapter 5

THE WORLD OF THE ROMANS

FOCUS QUESTIONS

- What policies and institutions help explain the Romans' success in conquering and then ruling their empire?
- What problems did Rome face during the last century of the Republic, and how were they ultimately resolved?
- What were the chief features of the Roman Empire at its height in the second century C.E., and what happened to bring it near collapse in the next century?
- What characteristics of Christianity enabled it to grow and ultimately to triumph?
- ➤ In what ways were the Roman Empire and the Han Chinese Empire similar, and in what ways were they different?

lthough the Assyrians, Persians, and Indians under the Mauryan dynasty had created empires, they were neither as large nor as well controlled as the Han Chinese and Roman Empires that flourished at the beginning of the first millennium C.E. These two were the most extensive empires the world had yet seen (the Han Empire, as we saw in Chapter 3, extended from Central Asia to the Pacific Ocean; the Roman Empire encompassed the lands around the Mediterranean as well as parts of the Middle East and western and central Europe).

Roman history is basically the remarkable story of how a group of Latin-speaking people who established a small community on a plain called Latium in central Italy went on to conquer all of Italy and then the entire Mediterranean world. Why were the Romans able to do this? Scholars do not really know all the answers, but the Romans had their own explanation. Early Roman history is filled with legendary tales of the heroes who made Rome great. One of the best known is the story of Horatius at the bridge. Threatened by attack from the neighboring Etruscans, Roman farmers abandoned their fields and moved into the city, where they would be protected by the walls. One weak point in the Roman defenses, however, was a wooden bridge over the Tiber River. Horatius was on guard at the bridge when a sudden assault by the Etruscans caused many Roman troops to throw down their weapons and flee. Horatius urged them to make a stand at the bridge behind him while he held the Etruscans back. Astonished at the sight of a single defender, the confused Etruscans threw their spears at Horatius, who caught them on his shield and barred the way. By the time the Etruscans had regrouped and were about to overwhelm the lone defender, the Roman soldiers brought down the bridge. When Horatius heard the bridge crash into the river behind him, he dived fully armed into the water and swam safely to the other side through a hail of arrows. Rome had been saved by the courageous act of a Roman who knew his duty and was determined to carry it out. Courage, duty, determination—these qualities would serve the many Romans who believed that it was their divine mission to rule nations and peoples. As one writer proclaimed: "By heaven's will my Rome shall be capital of the world." •

THE EMERGENCE OF ROME

Italy is a peninsula extending about 750 miles from north to south (see Map 5.1). It is not very wide, however, averaging about 120 miles across. The Apennines form a ridge

MAP 5.1   Ancient Italy.   Ancient Italy was home to several groups. Both the Etruscans in the north and the Greeks in the south had a major influence on the development of Rome. ➤ *Once Rome conquered the Etruscans, Sabines, Samnites, and other local groups, what aspects of the Italian peninsula helped make it defensible against outside enemies?*

down the middle of Italy that divides west from east. Nevertheless, the peninsula has some fairly large fertile plains ideal for farming. Most important are the Po River valley in the north, probably the most fertile agricultural area; the plain of Latium, on which Rome was located; and Campania to the south of Latium. To the east of the Italian peninsula is the Adriatic Sea and to the west the Tyrrhenian Sea with the nearby large islands of Corsica and Sardinia. Sicily lies just west of the toe of the boot-shaped Italian peninsula.

Geography had an impact on Roman history. Although the Apennines bisected Italy, they were less rugged than the mountain ranges of Greece and did not divide the peninsula into many small isolated communities. Italy also possessed considerably more productive agricultural land than Greece, enabling it to support a large population. Rome's location was favorable from a geographical point of view. Located 18 miles inland on the Tiber River, Rome had access to the sea and yet was far enough inland to be safe from pirates. Built on the famous seven hills, it was easily defended. Because the Tiber could be readily forded, Rome became a natural crossing point for north-south traffic in western Italy. All in all, Rome had a good central location in Italy from which to expand.

Moreover, the Italian peninsula juts into the Mediterranean, making it an important crossroads between the western and eastern portions of the region. Once Rome had unified Italy, involvement in Mediterranean affairs was natural. And after the Romans had conquered their Mediterranean empire, governing it was made considerably easier by Italy's central location.

Early Rome

According to Roman legend, Rome was founded by the twin brothers Romulus and Remus in 753 B.C.E., and archaeologists have found that by that time, a village of huts had indeed been built on the tops of Rome's hills. The early Romans, basically a pastoral people, spoke Latin, which, like Greek, belongs to the Indo-European family of languages (see Table 1.2 in Chapter 1). The Roman historical tradition also maintained that early Rome (to 509 B.C.E.) had been under the control of seven kings and that two of the last three had been Etruscans, people who lived north of Rome in Etruria. Some historians believe that the king list may have historical accuracy. What is certain is that Rome did fall under the influence of the Etruscans for about a hundred years during the period of the kings and that by the beginning of the sixth century B.C.E.,

The City of Rome

SERVIAN WALL

Capitoline
FORUM

VIA SACRA
(Sacred Way)

Rome

VIA APPIA

under Etruscan influence, Rome began to emerge as a city. The Etruscans were responsible for an outstanding building program. They constructed the first roadbed of the chief street through Rome, the Sacred Way, before 575 B.C.E. and oversaw the development of temples, markets, shops, streets, and houses. By 509 B.C.E., the traditionaly accepted date when the monarchy was overthrown and a republican form of government established, a new Rome had emerged, essentially a result of the fusion of Etruscan and native Roman elements.

THE ROMAN REPUBLIC

The transition from monarchy to a republican government was not easy. Rome felt threatened by enemies from every direction and, in the process of meeting these threats, embarked on a military course that led to the conquest of the entire Italian peninsula.

The Roman Conquest of Italy

At the beginning of the Republic, Rome was surrounded by enemies, including the Latin communities on the plain of Latium. If we are to believe Livy, one of the chief ancient sources for the history of the early Roman Republic, Rome was engaged in almost continuous warfare with these enemies for the next hundred years. In his account, Livy provided a detailed narrative of Roman efforts. Many of his stories were legendary in character; writing in the first century B.C.E., he used such stories to teach Romans the moral values and virtues that had made Rome great. These included tenacity, duty, courage, and especially discipline (see the box on p. 123).

ETRUSCAN TOMB MURAL. Like the Egyptians, the Etruscans filled their tombs with furniture, bowls, and other objects of daily life, as well as murals showing diversions experienced in life and awaiting the dead in the afterlife. Shown in this mural found in an Etruscan tomb at Tarquinia are servants and musicians at a banquet. This mural was painted in the first half of the fifth century B.C.E.

© Photo: AKG, London

CINCINNATUS SAVES ROME:
A ROMAN MORALITY TALE

There is perhaps no better account of how the virtues of duty and simplicity enabled good Roman citizens to prevail during the travails of the fifth century B.C.E. than Livy's account of Cincinnatus. He was chosen dictator, supposedly in 457 B.C.E., to defend Rome against the attacks of the Aequi. The position of dictator was a temporary expedient used only in emergencies; the consuls would resign and a leader with unlimited power would be appointed for a limited period (usually six months). In this account, Cincinnatus did his duty, defeated the Aequi, and returned to his simple farm in just fifteen days.

LIVY, *THE EARLY HISTORY OF ROME*

The city was thrown into a state of turmoil, and the general alarm was as great as if Rome herself were surrounded. Nautius was sent for, but it was quickly decided that he was not the man to inspire full confidence; the situation evidently called for a dictator, and, with no dissentient voice, Lucius Quinctius Cincinnatus was named for the post.

Now I would solicit the particular attention of those numerous people who imagine that money is everything in this world, and that rank and ability are inseparable from wealth: let them observe that Cincinnatus, the one man in whom Rome reposed all her hope of survival, was at that moment working a little three-acre farm . . . west of the Tiber, just opposite the spot where the shipyards are today. A mission from the city found him at work on his land—digging a ditch, maybe, or plowing. Greetings were exchanged,

and he was asked—with a prayer for divine blessing on himself and his country—to put on his toga and hear the Senate's instructions. This naturally surprised him, and, asking if all were well, he told his wife Racilia to run to their cottage and fetch his toga. The toga was brought, and wiping the grimy sweat from his hands and face he put it on; at once the envoys from the city saluted him, with congratulations, as Dictator, invited him to enter Rome, and informed him of the terrible danger of Municius's army. A state vessel was waiting for him on the river, and on the city bank he was welcomed by his three sons who had come to meet him, then by other kinsmen and friends, and finally by nearly the whole body of senators. Closely attended by all these people and preceded by his lictors he was then escorted to his residence through streets lined with great crowds of common folk who, be it said, were by no means so pleased to see the new Dictator, as they thought his power excessive and dreaded the way in which he was likely to use it.

[Cincinnatus proceeds to raise an army, march out, and defeat the Aequi.]

In Rome the Senate was convened by Quintus Fabius the City Prefect, and a decree was passed inviting Cincinnatus to enter in triumph with his troops. The chariot he rode in was preceded by the enemy commanders and the military standards, and followed by his army loaded with its spoils. . . . Cincinnatus finally resigned after holding office for fifteen days, having originally accepted it for a period of six months.

By 340 B.C.E., Rome had crushed the Latin states in Latium. During the next fifty years, the Romans waged a fierce struggle with the Samnites, a hill people from the central Apennines, some of whom had settled in Campania, south of Rome. Rome was again victorious. The conquest of the Samnites gave Rome considerable control over a large part of Italy and also brought it into direct contact with the Greek communities. The Greeks had arrived on the Italian peninsula in large numbers during the age of Greek colonization (750–550 B.C.E.; see Chapter 4). Initially, the Greeks settled in southern Italy and then crept around the coast and up the peninsula. They also occupied the eastern two-thirds of Sicily. The Greeks had much influence on Rome. They cultivated olives and grapes, passed on their alphabet, and provided artistic and cultural models through their sculpture, architecture, and literature. Soon after the conquest of the Samnites, the Romans were involved in hostilities with some of these Greek cities and by 267 B.C.E. had completed the conquest of southern Italy. After crushing the remaining Etruscan states to the north in 264 B.C.E., Rome had conquered all of Italy except the extreme north.

To rule Italy, the Romans devised the Roman Confederation. Under this system, Rome allowed some peoples—especially the Latins—to have full Roman citizenship. Most of the remaining communities were made allies. They remained free to run their own local affairs but were required to provide soldiers for Rome. Moreover, the Romans made it clear that loyal allies could improve their status and even have hope of becoming Roman citizens. The Romans had found a way to give conquered peoples a stake in Rome's success.

In the course of their expansion, the Romans had pursued consistent policies that help explain their success. The Romans were superb diplomats who excelled at making the correct diplomatic decisions. While firm and even cruel when necessary—rebellions were crushed without mercy—they were also shrewd in extending their citizenship and allowing autonomy in domestic affairs. In addition, the Romans were not only good soldiers but also persistent ones. The loss of an army or a fleet did not cause them to quit but spurred them on to build new armies and new fleets. Finally, the Romans had a practical sense of strategy. As they conquered, they settled Romans and

Latins in new communities outside Latium. By 264 B.C.E., the Romans had established fortified colonies at strategic locations throughout Italy. By building roads to these settlements and connecting them, the Romans created an impressive military and communications network that enabled them to rule effectively and efficiently. By insisting on military service from its allies in the Roman confederation, Rome essentially mobilized the entire military manpower of Italy for its wars.

The Roman State

The chief executive officers of the Roman Republic were the consuls and praetors. Two consuls, chosen annually, administered the government and led the Roman army into battle. They possessed *imperium*, or "the right to command." In 366 B.C.E., the office of praetor was created. The praetor also possessed *imperium* and could govern Rome when the consuls were away from the city and could also lead armies. The praetor's primary function, however, was the execution of justice. He was in charge of the civil law as it applied to Roman citizens. In 242 B.C.E., reflecting Rome's growth, another praetor was added to judge cases in which one or both people were noncitizens. The Roman state also had a number of administrative officials who handled specialized duties, such as the administration of financial affairs and supervision of the public games of Rome.

The Roman senate came to hold an especially important position in the Roman Republic. The senate or council of elders was a select group of about three hundred men who served for life. The senate could only advise the magistrates, but this advice of the senate was not taken lightly and by the third century B.C.E. had virtually the force of law.

The Roman Republic had a number of popular assemblies. By far the most important was the centuriate assembly. Organized by classes based on wealth, it was structured in such a way that the wealthiest citizens always had a majority. The centuriate assembly elected the chief magistrates and passed laws. Another assembly, the council of the plebs, came into being in 471 B.C.E.

The Roman Republic, then, witnessed the interplay of three major elements. Two consuls and later other elected officials served as magistrates and ran the state. An assembly of adult males (the centuriate assembly), controlled by the wealthiest citizens, elected these officials, while the senate, a small group of large landowners, advised them. The Roman state, then, was an aristocratic republic controlled by a relatively small group of privileged people.

THE STRUGGLE OF THE ORDERS: SOCIAL DIVISIONS IN THE ROMAN REPUBLIC

The most noticeable element in the social organization of early Rome was the division between two groups—the patricians and the plebeians. The patrician class in Rome consisted of families descended from the original senators appointed during the period of the kings. They were great landowners who constituted an aristocratic governing class. Only they could be consuls, other magistrates, and senators. Through their patronage of large numbers of dependent clients, they controlled the centuriate assembly and many other facets of Roman life. The plebeians constituted the considerably larger group of nonpatrician large landowners, less wealthy landholders, artisans, merchants, and small farmers. Although they, too, were citizens, they did not have the same rights as the patricians. Both patricians and plebeians could vote, but only the patricians could be elected to governmental offices. Both had the right to make legal contracts and marriages, but intermarriage between patricians and plebeians was forbidden. At the beginning of the fifth century B.C.E., the plebeians began a struggle to seek both political and social equality with the patricians.

The struggle between the patricians and plebeians dragged on for hundreds of years but led to success for the plebeians. A popular assembly for plebeians only, called the council of the plebs, was created in 471 B.C.E., and new officials, known as tribunes of the plebs, were given the power to protect plebeians. A new law allowed marriages between patricians and plebeians, and in the fourth century B.C.E., plebeians were permitted to become consuls. Finally, in 287 B.C.E., the council of the plebs received the right to pass laws for all Romans.

The struggle between the orders, then, had a significant impact on the development of the Roman state. Plebeians could now hold the highest offices of state, they could intermarry with the patricians, and they could pass laws binding on the entire Roman community. Theoretically, by 287 B.C.E., all Roman citizens were equal under the law, and all could strive for political office. But in reality, as a result of the right of intermarriage, a select number of patrician and plebeian families formed a new senatorial aristocracy that came to dominate the political offices. The Roman Republic had not become a democracy.

THE ROMAN CONQUEST OF THE MEDITERRANEAN (264–133 B.C.E.)

After their conquest of the Italian peninsula, the Romans found themselves face-to-face with a formidable Mediterranean power—Carthage. Founded on the coast of North Africa by Phoenicians around 800 B.C.E., Carthage had flourished and assembled an enormous empire in the western Mediterranean. By the third century B.C.E., the Carthaginian empire included the coast of northern Africa, southern Spain, Sardinia, Corsica, and western Sicily. With its monopoly of western Mediterranean trade, Carthage was the largest and richest state in the area. The presence of Carthaginians in Sicily made the Romans apprehensive about Carthaginian encroachment on the Italian coast. In 264 B.C.E., mutual suspicions drove the two powers into a lengthy struggle for control of the western Mediterranean (see Map 5.2).

The Punic Wars

In the First Punic War (the Latin word for Phoenician was *punicus*), the Romans determined on the conquest of Sicily. The Romans—a land power—realized that they could not win the war without a navy and promptly developed a substantial naval fleet. After a long struggle, a Roman fleet defeated the Carthaginian navy off Sicily, and the war quickly came to an end. In 241 B.C.E., Carthage gave up all rights to Sicily and had to pay an indemnity to Rome. Sicily became the first Roman province.

Carthage vowed revenge and added new lands in Spain to compensate for the loss of Sicily. When the Romans encouraged one of Carthage's Spanish allies to revolt against Carthage, Hannibal, the greatest of the Carthaginian generals, struck back, beginning the Second Punic War (218–201 B.C.E.).

This time the Carthaginian strategy aimed at bringing the war home to the Romans and defeating them in their own backyard. Hannibal crossed the Alps with an army of thirty to forty thousand men and six thousand horses and elephants and inflicted a series of defeats on the Romans. At Cannae in 216 B.C.E., the Romans lost an army of almost forty thousand men. Rome seemed on the brink of disaster but refused to give up, raised yet another army, and began to reconquer some of the Italian cities that had gone over to Hannibal's side. More important, the Romans pursued a strategy aimed at undermining the Carthaginian empire in Spain. By 206 B.C.E., the Romans had pushed the Carthaginians out of Spain.

The Romans then took the war directly to Carthage, forcing the Carthaginians to recall Hannibal from Italy. At the Battle of Zama in 202 B.C.E., the Romans decisively defeated Hannibal's forces, and the war was over. By the peace treaty signed in 201 B.C.E., Carthage lost Spain, which became another Roman province. Rome had become the dominant power in the western Mediterranean.

Fifty years later, the Romans fought their third and final struggle with Carthage. The Carthaginians had technically

MAP 5.2   Roman Conquests in the Mediterranean, 264–133 B.C.E. Beginning with the Punic Wars, Rome expanded its holdings, first in the western Mediterranean at the expense of Carthage and later in Greece and western Asia Minor. ➤ *What aspects of Mediterranean geography, combined with the territorial holdings and aspirations of Rome and the Carthaginians, made the Punic Wars more likely?*

THE DESTRUCTION OF CARTHAGE

The Romans used a technical breach of Carthage's peace treaty with Rome to undertake a third and final war with Carthage (149–146 B.C.E.). Although Carthage posed no real threat to Rome's security, the Romans still remembered the traumatic experiences of the Second Punic War, when Hannibal had ravaged much of their homeland. The hard-liners gained the upper hand in the senate and called for the complete destruction of Carthage. The city was razed, the survivors sold into slavery, and the land turned into a province. In this passage, the historian Appian of Alexandria describes the final destruction of Carthage by the Romans under the command of Scipio Aemilianus.

APPIAN, ROMAN HISTORY

Then came new scenes of horror. The fire spread and carried everything down, and the soldiers did not wait to destroy the buildings little by little, but pulled them all down together. So the crashing grew louder, and many fell with the stones into the midst dead. Others were seen still living, especially old men, women, and young children who had hidden in the inmost nooks of the houses, some of them wounded, some more or less burned, and uttering horrible cries. Still others, thrust out and falling from such a height with the stones, timbers, and fire, were torn asunder into all kinds of horrible shapes, crushed and mangled. Nor was this the end of their miseries, for the street cleaners, who were removing the rubbish with axes, mattocks, and boat hooks, and making the roads passable, tossed with these instruments the dead and the living together into holes in the ground, sweeping them along like sticks and stones or turning them over with their iron tools, and man was used for filling up a ditch. Some were thrown in head foremost, while their legs, sticking out of the ground, writhed a long time. Others fell with their feet downward and their heads above ground. Horses ran over them, crushing their faces and skulls, not purposely on the part of the riders, but in their headlong haste. Nor did the street cleaners either do these things on purpose; but the press of war, the glory of approaching victory, the rush of the soldiery, the confused noise of heralds and trumpeters all round, the tribunes and centurions changing guard and marching the cohorts hither and thither—all together made everybody frantic and heedless of the spectacle before their eyes.

Six days and nights were consumed in this kind of turmoil, the soldiers being changed so that they might not be worn out with toil, slaughter, want of sleep, and these horrid sights. . . .

Scipio, beholding this city, which had flourished 700 years from its foundation and had ruled over so many lands, islands, and seas, as rich in arms and fleets, elephants, and money as the mightiest empires, but far surpassing them in hardihood and high spirit . . . now come to its end in total destruction—Scipio, beholding this spectacle, is said to have shed tears and publicly lamented the fortune of the enemy. After meditating by himself a long time and reflecting on the inevitable fall of cities, nations, and empires, as well as of individuals, upon the fate of Troy, that once proud city, upon the fate of the Assyrian, the Median, and afterwards of the great Persian empire, and, most recently of all, of the splendid empire of Macedon, either voluntarily or otherwise the words of the poet [Homer, *Iliad*] escaped his lips:

> *The day shall come in which our sacred Troy*
> *And Priam, and the people over whom*
> *Spear-bearing Priam rules, shall perish all.*

Being asked by Polybius in familiar conversation (for Polybius had been his tutor) what he meant by using these words, Polybius says that he did not hesitate frankly to name his own country, for whose fate he feared when he considered the mutability of human affairs. And Polybius wrote this down just as he heard it.

---

broken the peace treaty with Rome by going to war against one of Rome's North African allies who had been encroaching on Carthage's home territory. The Romans used this opportunity to carry out the complete destruction of Carthage in 146 B.C.E., a policy advocated by a number of Romans, especially the conservative politician Cato, who ended every speech he made to the senate with the words, "And I think Carthage must be destroyed" (see the box above). The territory of Carthage became a Roman province called Africa.

The Eastern Mediterranean

During the Punic Wars, Rome had become acutely aware of the Hellenistic states of the eastern Mediterranean when the king of Macedonia made an alliance with Hannibal after the Roman defeat at Cannae. But Rome was preoccupied with the Carthaginians, and it was not until after the defeat of Carthage that Rome became involved in the world of Hellenistic politics as an advocate of the freedom of the Greek states. This support of the Greeks brought the Romans into conflict with both Macedonia and the kingdom of the Seleucids. Roman military victories and diplomatic negotiations rearranged the territorial boundaries of the Hellenistic kingdoms and brought the Greek states their freedom in 196 B.C.E. For fifty years, Rome tried to be a power broker in the affairs of the Greeks without assuming direct control of their lands. When these efforts failed, the Romans changed their policy.

In 148 B.C.E., Macedonia was made a Roman province, and when some of the Greek states rose in revolt against

THE ROMAN CONQUEST OF ITALY AND THE MEDITERRANEAN

Rome crushes Latin revolt	340 B.C.E.
Creation of the Roman confederation	338 B.C.E.
Samnite Wars	343–290 B.C.E.
The First Punic War	264–241 B.C.E.
The Second Punic War	218–201 B.C.E.
Battle of Cannae	216 B.C.E.
Rome completes seizure of Spain	206 B.C.E.
Battle of Zama	202 B.C.E.
The Third Punic War	149–146 B.C.E.
Macedonia made a Roman province	148 B.C.E.
Destruction of Carthage	146 B.C.E.
Kingdom of Pergamum deeded to Rome	133 B.C.E.

Rome's restrictive policies, Greece was placed under the control of the Roman governor of Macedonia. In 133 B.C.E., the king of Pergamum deeded his kingdom to Rome, giving Rome its first province in Asia. Rome was now master of the Mediterranean Sea.

The Nature of Roman Imperialism

Rome's empire was built in three stages: the conquest of Italy, the conflict with Carthage and expansion into the western Mediterranean, and the involvement with and eventual domination of the Hellenistic kingdoms in the eastern Mediterranean. The Romans did not possess a master plan for the creation of an empire. Much of their expansion was opportunistic; once involved in a situation that threatened their security, the Romans did not hesitate to act. And the more they expanded, the more threats to their security appeared on the horizon, involving them in yet more conflicts. Indeed, the Romans liked to portray themselves as declaring war only for defensive reasons or to protect allies. That is only part of the story, however. It is likely, as some historians have recently suggested, that at some point a group of Roman aristocratic leaders emerged who favored expansion both for the glory it offered and for the economic benefits it provided. Certainly, by the second century B.C.E., aristocratic senators perceived new opportunities for lucrative foreign commands, enormous spoils of war, and an abundant supply of slave labor for their growing landed estates. By that same time, the destruction of Carthage indicated that Roman imperialism had become more arrogant and brutal as well.

Rome's foreign success also had enormous repercussions for the internal development of the Roman Republic.

THE DECLINE AND FALL OF THE ROMAN REPUBLIC (133–31 B.C.E.)

By the mid-second century B.C.E., Roman domination of the Mediterranean Sea was well established. Yet the process of creating an empire had weakened the internal stability of Rome. This led to a series of crises that plagued Rome for the next hundred years.

Growing Inequality and Unrest

By the second century B.C.E., the senate had become the effective governing body of the Roman state. It consisted of some three hundred men, drawn primarily from the landed aristocracy; they remained senators for life and held the chief magistracies of the Republic. The senate directed the wars of the third and second centuries and took control of both foreign and domestic policy, including financial affairs.

Of course, these aristocrats formed only a tiny minority of the Roman people. The backbone of the Roman state and army had traditionally been the small farmers. But over time, many small farmers had found themselves unable to compete with large, wealthy landowners and had lost their lands. By taking over state-owned land and buying out small peasant owners, these landed aristocrats had developed large estates called *latifundia* that used slave labor. Thus the rise of the *latifundia* contributed to a decline in the number of small farmers. Since the latter group traditionally provided the foundation of the Roman army, the number of men available for military service declined. Moreover, many of these small farmers drifted to the cities, especially Rome, forming a large class of landless poor.

Some aristocrats tried to remedy this growing economic and social crisis. Two brothers, Tiberius and Gaius Gracchus, came to believe that the underlying cause of Rome's problems was the decline of the small farmer. To help the landless poor, they bypassed the senate by having the council of the plebs pass land reform bills that called for the government to reclaim public land held by large landowners and distribute it to landless Romans. Many senators, themselves large landowners whose estates included large areas of public land, were furious. A group of senators took the law into their own hands and killed Tiberius in 133 B.C.E. Twelve years later, Gaius suffered the same fate. The attempts of the Gracchus brothers to bring reforms had opened the door to more instability and further violence. Changes in the Roman army soon brought even worse problems.

A New Role for the Roman Army

In the closing years of the second century B.C.E., a Roman general named Marius began to recruit his armies in a new way. The Roman army had traditionally been a conscript army of small farmers who were landholders. Marius recruited volunteers from both the urban and rural poor who possessed no property. These volunteers swore an oath of loyalty to the general, not the senate, thus inaugurating a professional-type army that might no longer be subject to the state. Moreover, to recruit these men, a general would promise them land, forcing generals to play politics in order to get legislation passed that would provide the land for their veterans. Marius left a powerful legacy. He had created a new system of military recruitment that placed much power in the hands of the individual generals.

Lucius Cornelius Sulla was the next general to take advantage of the new military system. The senate had given him command of a war in Asia Minor, but when the council of the plebs tried to transfer command of this war to Marius, a civil war broke out. Sulla won and seized Rome itself in 82 B.C.E., conducting a reign of terror to wipe out all opposition. Then Sulla restored power to the hands of the senate and eliminated most of the powers of the popular assemblies. Sulla hoped that he had created a firm foundation for the traditional Republic governed by a powerful senate, but his real legacy was quite different from what he had intended. His example of using an army to seize power would prove most attractive to ambitious men.

The Collapse of the Republic

For the next fifty years, Roman history was characterized by two important features: the jostling for power by a number of powerful individuals and the civil wars generated by their conflicts. Three powerful individuals came to hold enormous military and political power—Crassus, Pompey, and Julius Caesar. Crassus, who was known as the richest man in Rome, had successfully put down a major slave rebellion. Pompey had returned from a successful military command in Spain in 71 B.C.E. and been hailed as a hero. Julius Caesar also had a military command in Spain. In 60 B.C.E., Caesar joined with Crassus and Pompey to form a coalition that historians call the first Triumvirate.

The combined wealth and power of these three men was enormous, enabling them to dominate the political scene and achieve their basic aims: Pompey received lands for his veterans and a command in Spain, Crassus was given a command in Syria, and Caesar was granted a special military command in Gaul (modern France), beyond the Rubicon River. When Crassus was killed in battle in 53 B.C.E., his death left two powerful men with armies in direct competition. Caesar had conquered all of Gaul and gained fame, wealth, and military experience as well as an army of seasoned veterans who were loyal to him. When leading senators decided that Pompey would be less harm-

ful to their cause and voted for Caesar to lay down his command and return as a private citizen to Rome, Caesar refused. He chose to keep his army and moved into Italy by crossing the Rubicon, marching on Rome, and defeating Pompey and his allies, leaving Caesar in complete control of the Roman government.

Caesar was officially made dictator in 47 B.C.E. and three years later was named dictator for life. Realizing the need for reforms, he gave land to the poor and increased the size of the senate to nine hundred members. By filling it with many of his supporters and increasing the membership, he effectively weakened the power of the senate. He also reformed the calendar by introducing the Egyptian solar year of 365 days (with later changes in 1582, it became the basis of our own calendar). Caesar planned much more in the way of

➤ **CAESAR.**   Conqueror of Gaul and member of the First Triumvirate, Julius Caesar is perhaps the best-known figure of the late Republic. Caesar became dictator of Rome in 47 B.C.E. and after his victories in the civil war was made dictator for life. Some members of the senate who resented his power assassinated him in 44 B.C.E. Pictured is a marble copy of the bust of Caesar.

© Scala/Art Resource, NY

THE ASSASSINATION OF JULIUS CAESAR

When it became apparent that Julius Caesar had no intention of restoring the Republic as they conceived it, about sixty senators, many of them his friends or pardoned enemies, formed a conspiracy to assassinate the dictator. It was led by Gaius Cassius and Marcus Brutus, who naively imagined that this act would restore the traditional Republic. The conspirators set the Ides of March (March 15), 44 B.C.E., as the date for the assassination. Caesar was in the midst of preparations for a campaign in the eastern part of the empire. Although informed that there was a plot against his life, he chose to disregard the warning. This account of Caesar's death is taken from his biography by the Greek writer Plutarch.

PLUTARCH, LIFE OF CAESAR

Fate, however, is to all appearance more unavoidable than unexpected. For many strange prodigies and apparitions are said to have been observed shortly before this event. . . . One finds it also related by many that a soothsayer bade him [Caesar] prepare for some great danger on the Ides of March. When this day was come, Caesar, as he went to the senate, met this soothsayer, and said to him by way of raillery, "The Ides of March are come," who answered him calmly, "Yes, they are come, but they are not past. . . ."

All these things might happen by chance. But the place which was destined for the scene of this murder, in which the senate met that day, was the same in which Pompey's statue stood, and was one of the edifices which Pompey had raised and dedicated with his theater to the use of the public, plainly showing that there was something of a supernatural influence which guided the action and ordered it to that particular place. Cassius, just before the act, is said to have looked toward Pompey's statue, and silently implored his assistance. . . . When Caesar entered, the senate stood up to show their respect to him, and of Brutus's confederates, some came about his chair and stood behind it, others met him, pretending to add their petitions to those of Tillius Cimber, in behalf of his brother, who was in exile; and they followed him with their joint applications till he came to his seat. When he was sat down, he refused to comply with their requests, and upon their urging him further began to reproach them severely for their importunities, when Tillius, laying hold of his robe with both his hands, pulled it down from his neck, which was the signal for the assault. Casca gave him the first cut in the neck, which was not mortal nor dangerous, as coming from one who at the beginning of such a bold action was probably very much disturbed; Caesar immediately turned about, and laid his hand upon the dagger and kept hold of it. And both of them at the same time cried out, he that received the blow, in Latin, "Vile Casca, what does this mean?" and he that gave it, in Greek to his brother, "Brother, help!" Upon this first onset, those who were not privy to the design were astonished, and their horror and amazement at what they saw were so great that they dared not fly nor assist Caesar, nor so much as speak a word. But those who came prepared for the business enclosed him on every side, with their naked daggers in their hands. Which way soever he turned he met with blows, and saw their swords leveled at his face and eyes, and was encompassed like a wild beast in the toils on every side. For it had been agreed they should each of them make a thrust at him, and flesh themselves with his blood: for which reason Brutus also gave him one stab in the groin. Some say that he fought and resisted all the rest, shifting his body to avoid the blows, and calling out for help, but that when he saw Brutus's sword drawn, he covered his face with his robe and submitted, letting himself fall, whether it were by chance or that he was pushed in that direction by his murderers, at the foot of the pedestal on which Pompey's statue stood, and which was thus wetted with his blood. So that Pompey himself seemed to have presided, as it were, over the revenge done upon his adversary, who lay here at his feet, and breathed out his soul through his multitude of wounds, for they say he received three-and-twenty. And the conspirators themselves were many of them wounded by each other, whilst they all leveled their blows at the same person.

building projects and military adventures in the east, but in 44 B.C.E., a group of leading senators assassinated him (see the box above).

Within a few years after Caesar's death, two men had divided the Roman world between them—Octavian, Caesar's heir and grandnephew, taking the west and Antony, Caesar's ally and assistant, the east. But the empire of the Romans, large as it was, was still too small for two masters, and Octavian and Antony eventually came into conflict. Antony allied himself with the Egyptian queen Cleopatra VII, with whom, like Caesar before him, he fell deeply in love. At the Battle of Actium in Greece in 31 B.C.E., Octavian's forces smashed the army and navy of Antony and Cleopatra. Both fled to Egypt, where, according to the account of the Roman historian Florus, they committed suicide a year later:

Antony was the first to commit suicide, by the sword. Cleopatra threw herself at Octavian's feet, and tried her best to attract his gaze: in vain, for his self-control was impervious to her beauty. It was not her life she was after, for that had already been granted, but a portion of her kingdom. When she realized this was hopeless and that she had been earmarked to feature in Octavian's triumph in Rome, she took advantage of her guard's carelessness to get herself into the mausoleum, as the royal tomb is called. Once there, she put on the royal robes which she was accustomed to wear, and lay down in a richly perfumed coffin beside her Antony. Then she applied poisonous snakes to her veins and slipped into death as though into a sleep.[1]

Chronology

THE DECLINE AND FALL OF THE ROMAN REPUBLIC

Reforms of Tiberius Gracchus	133 B.C.E.
Reforms of Gaius Gracchus	123–121 B.C.E.
Marius: Consecutive consulships	104–100 B.C.E.
Sulla as dictator	82–79 B.C.E.
First Triumvirate (Caesar, Pompey, Crassus)	60 B.C.E.
Caesar as dictator	47–44 B.C.E.
Octavian defeats Antony at Actium	31 B.C.E

© Photo Vatican Museums

Octavian, at the age of thirty-two, stood supreme over the Roman world. The civil wars were ended. And so was the Republic.

THE AGE OF AUGUSTUS (31 B.C.E.–14 C.E.)

In 27 B.C.E., Octavian proclaimed the "restoration of the Republic." He understood that only traditional republican forms would satisfy the senatorial aristocracy. At the same time, Octavian was aware that the Republic could not be fully restored. Although he gave some power to the senate, in fact, Octavian became the first Roman emperor. The senate awarded him the title of Augustus—"the revered one"—a fitting title in view of his power, previously reserved for gods. Augustus proved highly popular, and his continuing control of the army afforded him great power. The senate gave Augustus the title of *imperator,* or commander-in-chief. *Imperator* is Latin for our word *emperor.*

Augustus maintained a standing army of twenty-eight legions, or about 150,000 men (a legion was a military unit of about 5,000 troops). Only Roman citizens could be legionaries, while subject peoples could serve as auxiliary forces, which numbered around 130,000 under Augustus. Augustus was also responsible for setting up a praetorian guard of roughly 9,000 men who had the important task of guarding the person of the emperor. Eventually, the praetorian guard would play a weighty role in making and deposing emperors.

While claiming to have restored the Republic, Augustus inaugurated a new system for governing the provinces. Under the Republic, the senate had appointed the governors of the provinces. Now certain provinces were given to the emperor, who assigned deputies known as legates to govern them. The senate continued to name the governors of the remaining provinces, but the authority of Augustus enabled him to

➤➤ **AUGUSTUS.** Octavian, Caesar's adopted son, emerged victorious from the civil conflict that rocked the Republic after Caesar's assassination. Augustus operated through a number of legal formalities to ensure that control of the Roman state rested firmly in his hands. This marble statue from Prima Porta depicts Augustus.

overrule the senatorial governors and establish a uniform imperial policy.

Augustus also stabilized the frontiers of the Roman Empire. He conquered the central and maritime Alps and then expanded Roman control of the Balkan peninsula up to the Danube River. His attempt to conquer Germany failed when three Roman legions led by a general named Varus were massacred in 9 C.E. by a coalition of German tribes. His defeats in Germany taught Augustus that Rome's power was not unlimited and also devastated him; for months he would beat his head on a door, shouting "Varus, give me back my legions!"

British Museum, Photo © Michael Holford, London

A ROMAN LEGIONARY. The Roman legionaries, famed for their courage and tenacity, made possible Roman domination of the Mediterranean Sea. This tablet, dating from the first half of the third century B.C.E., shows a Roman legionary during the period of the Republic.

Augustan Society

Roman society in the Early Roman Empire was characterized by a system of social stratification, inherited from the Republic, in which Roman citizens were divided into three basic classes: the senatorial, equestrian, and lower classes.

Augustus had accepted the senatorial order as a ruling class for the empire. Senators filled the chief magistracies of the Roman government, held the most important military posts, and governed the provinces. To belong to the senatorial order, one needed to possess property worth 1 million sesterces (an unskilled laborer in Rome received 3 sesterces a day; a Roman legionary, 900 sesterces a year

in pay). The equestrian order was expanded under Augustus and given a share of power in the new imperial state. The equestrian order was open to all Roman citizens of good standing who possessed property valued at 400,000 sesterces. They, too, could now hold military and governmental offices, but the positions open to them were less important than those of the senatorial order.

Citizens not of the senatorial or equestrian orders belonged to the lower classes, who obviously constituted the overwhelming majority of the free citizens. The diminution of the power of the Roman assemblies ended whatever political power they possessed earlier in the Republic. Many of these people were provided with free grain and public spectacles to keep them from creating disturbances. Nevertheless, by gaining wealth and serving as lower officers in the Roman legions, it was sometimes possible for them to advance to the equestrian order.

Augustus died in 14 C.E. after dominating the Roman world for forty-five years. He had created a new order while placating those who yearned for the old by restoring traditional values, a fitting combination for a leader whose favorite maxim was "make haste slowly." By the time of his death, his new order was so well established that few agitated for an alternative. Indeed, as the Roman historian Tacitus pointed out, "Practically no one had ever seen truly Republican government. . . . Political equality was a thing of the past; all eyes watched for imperial commands."[2] The Republic was now only a memory—and given its last century of warfare, an unpleasant one at that. The new order was here to stay.

THE EARLY EMPIRE (14–180)

There was no serious opposition to Augustus' choice of his stepson Tiberius as his successor. By his actions, Augustus established the Julio-Claudian dynasty; the next four successors of Augustus were related either to his own family or that of his wife, Livia.

Several major tendencies emerged during the rule of the Julio-Claudians (14–68 C.E.). In general, more and more of the responsibilities that Augustus had given to the senate tended to be taken over by the emperors, who also instituted an imperial bureaucracy, staffed by talented freedmen, to run the government on a daily basis. As the Julio-Claudian successors of Augustus acted more openly as real rulers rather than as "first citizens of the state," the opportunity for arbitrary and corrupt acts also increased. Nero (54–68) freely eliminated people he wanted out of the way, including his own mother, whom he had murdered. Without troops, the senators proved unable to oppose these excesses; however, Nero's extravagances did provoke a revolt of the Roman legions. Abandoned by his guards, Nero chose to commit suicide by stabbing himself in the throat after uttering his final words, "What an artist the world is losing in me."

The Five Good Emperors (96–180)

At the beginning of the second century, five so-called good emperors presided over a period of peace and prosperity (known as the Pax Romana, the "Roman peace") that lasted almost a hundred years. These rulers treated the ruling classes with respect, cooperated with the senate, ended arbitrary executions, maintained peace throughout the empire, and supported generally beneficial domestic policies. Though absolute monarchs, they were known for their tolerance and diplomacy. By adopting capable men as their successors, the first four good emperors reduced the chances of succession problems.

Under the five good emperors, the powers of the emperor continued to be extended at the expense of the senate. Increasingly, imperial officials appointed and directed by the emperor took over the running of the government. The good emperors also extended the scope of imperial administration to include areas previously untouched by the imperial government. Trajan (98–117) implemented the establishment of a program that provided state funds to assist poor parents in raising and educating their children.

The good emperors were widely praised for their extensive building programs. Trajan and Hadrian (117–138) were especially active in constructing public works—aqueducts, bridges, roads, and harbor facilities—throughout the provinces and in Rome. Trajan built a new forum in Rome to provide a setting for his celebrated victory column. Hadrian's Pantheon, a temple of "all the gods," is one of the grandest ancient buildings surviving in Rome.

The Roman Empire at Its Height: Frontiers and the Provinces

Although Trajan extended Roman rule into Dacia (modern Romania), Mesopotamia, and the Sinai peninsula (see Map 5.3), his successors recognized that the empire was overextended and pursued a policy of retrenchment. Hadrian withdrew Roman forces from much of Meso-

MAP 5.3   The Roman Empire from Augustus to Trajan, 14–117 Augustus and later emperors continued the expansion of the Roman Empire, adding more resources but also increasing the tasks of administration and keeping the peace. Compare this map with Map 5.2. ➤ *Which territories were conquered by Augustus, and which were added by the end of Trajan's reign?*

potamia. Although he retained Dacia and Arabia, he went on the defensive in his frontier policy by reinforcing the fortifications along a line connecting the Rhine and Danube Rivers and building a defensive wall 80 miles long across northern Britain to keep the Scots out of Roman Britain. By the end of the second century, the Roman forces were established in permanent bases behind the frontiers. But when one frontier was attacked, troops had to be drawn from other frontiers, leaving them vulnerable to attack.

At its height in the second century, the Roman Empire was one of the greatest states the world had seen. It covered about 3.5 million square miles and had a population, like that of Han China, estimated at more than fifty million. While the emperors and the imperial administration provided a degree of unity, considerable leeway was given to local customs, and the privileges of Roman citizenship were extended to many people throughout the empire. In 212, the emperor Caracalla completed the process by giving Roman citizenship to every free inhabitant of the empire. Latin was the language of the western part of the empire, while Greek was used in the east. Roman culture spread to all parts of the empire and freely mixed with Greek culture, creating what has been called Greco-Roman civilization.

The administration and cultural life of the Roman Empire depended greatly on cities and towns. A provincial governor's staff was not large, so local city officials were expected to act as Roman agents in carrying out many government functions, especially those related to taxes. Most towns and cities were not large by modern standards. The largest was Rome, but there were also some large cities in the east: Alexandria in Egypt numbered over 300,000 inhabitants, Ephesus in Asia Minor had 200,000, and Antioch in Syria had around 150,000. In the west, cities were usually small, with only a few thousand inhabitants. Cities were important in the spread of Roman culture, law, and the Latin language, and they resembled one another with their temples, markets, amphitheaters, and other public buildings.

The process of Romanization in the provinces was reflected in significant changes in the governing classes of the empire. In the course of the first century, there was a noticeable decline in the number of senators from Italian families. By the end of the second century, Italian senators made up less than 50 percent of the total. Increasingly, the Roman senate was being recruited from wealthy provincial equestrian families. The provinces also provided many of the legionaries for the Roman army and, beginning with Trajan, supplied many of the emperors.

Prosperity in the Early Empire

The Early Empire was a period of considerable prosperity. Internal peace resulted in unprecedented levels of trade. Merchants from all over the empire came to the chief Italian ports of Puteoli on the Bay of Naples and Ostia at the mouth of the Tiber. Trade extended beyond the Roman boundaries and included even goods from China. Chinese merchants traveled across Central Asia, forming part of the Silk Road, a regular, overland route between west and east (see Chapter 3). By the first century C.E., Chinese goods, including silk and lacquerware, were being sent into the eastern part of the Roman Empire, in southwestern Asia, where they were traded for woolen textiles, glass, and precious stones. Moreover, the importation of large quantities of grain to feed the populace of Rome and an incredible quantity of luxury items for the wealthy upper classes in the west led to a steady drain of gold and silver coins from Italy and the west to the eastern part of the empire.

Increased trade helped stimulate manufacturing. The cities of the east still produced the items made in Hellenistic times. The first two centuries of the empire also witnessed the high point of industrial development in Italy.

⇨ THE SHIPPING OF GRAIN. Trade was an important ingredient in the prosperity of the Early Roman Empire. This tomb painting from Ostia, the port of Rome at the mouth of the Tiber, shows workers loading grain onto the *Isis Giminiana*, a small merchant ship, for shipment upriver to Rome. The captain of the ship stands by the rudder. Next to him is Abascantus, the ship's owner.

Some industries became concentrated in certain areas, such as bronze work in Capua and pottery in Arretium in Etruria. Other industries, such as brick making, were pursued in rural areas as by-products of large landed estates.

Despite the profits from trade and commerce, agriculture remained the chief occupation of most people and the underlying basis of Roman prosperity. Although the large landed estates called *latifundia* still dominated agriculture, especially in southern and central Italy, small peasant farms persisted, particularly in Etruria and the Po valley. Although large estates concentrating on sheep and cattle raising used slaves, the lands of some *latifundia* were worked by free tenant farmers who paid rent in labor, produce, or sometimes cash.

The prosperity of the Roman world left an enormous gulf between rich and poor. The development of towns and cities, so important to the creation of any civilization, is based in large degree on the agricultural surpluses of the countryside. In ancient times, the margin of surplus produced by each farmer was relatively small. Therefore, the upper classes and urban populations had to be supported by the labor of a large number of agricultural producers who never found it easy to produce much more than they needed for themselves. In lean years, when there were no surpluses, the townspeople often took what they wanted, leaving little for the peasants.

CULTURE AND SOCIETY IN THE ROMAN WORLD

One of the notable characteristics of Roman culture and society is the enormous influence of the Greeks. Greek ambassadors, merchants, and artists traveled to Rome and spread Greek thought and practices. After the Romans conquered the Hellenistic kingdoms, Roman military commanders shipped Greek manuscripts and artworks back to Rome. Rich Romans hired Greek tutors and sent their sons to Athens to study. As the Roman poet Horace said, "Captive Greece took captive her rude conqueror." Greek thought captivated Roman minds, and the Romans became willing transmitters of Greek culture—with resistance from some Romans who had nothing but contempt for Greek politics and feared that Greek notions would put an end to the old Roman values. Even those who favored Greek culture blamed the Greeks for Rome's new vices, including a taste for luxury and homosexual practices.

Roman Literature

The Latin literature that first emerged in the third century B.C.E. was strongly influenced by Greek models, and it was not until the last century of the Republic that the Romans began to produce poetry in Latin using various Greek forms to express their own feelings about people, social and political life, and love. This evolution can be seen in the work of Catullus (c. 87–54 B.C.E.), the finest lyric poet Rome produced and one of the greatest in world literature.

Catullus became a master at adapting and refining Greek forms of poetry to express his emotions. He wrote poems on a variety of subjects, including political figures, social customs, the use of language, the death of his brother, and the travails of love. Catullus became infatuated with Clodia, the promiscuous wife of a provincial governor, and addressed a number of poems to her (he called her Lesbia), describing his passionate love and hatred for her (Clodia had many other lovers besides Catullus):

> You used to say that you wished to know only Catullus,
>   Lesbia, and wouldn't take even Jove before me!
> I didn't regard you just as my mistress then; I cherished you
>   as a father does his sons or his daughters' husbands.
> Now that I know you, I burn for you even more fiercely,
>   though I regard you as almost utterly worthless.
> How can that be, you ask? It's because such cruelty forces
>   lust to assume the shrunken place of affection.[3]

Catullus' ability to express in simple fashion his intense feelings and curiosity about himself and his world had a noticeable impact on later Latin poets.

The development of Roman prose was greatly aided by the practice of oratory. Romans had great respect for oratory because the ability to persuade people in public debate led to success in politics. Oratory was brought to perfection in a literary fashion by Cicero (106–43 B.C.E.), the best exemplar of the literary and intellectual interests of the senatorial elite of the late Republic and, indeed, the greatest prose writer of that period. For Cicero, oratory was not simply skillful speaking. An orator was a statesman, a man who achieved his highest goal by pursuing an active life in public affairs.

The high point of Latin literature was reached in the Age of Augustus, often called the golden age of Latin literature. The most distinguished poet of the Augustan age was Virgil (70–19 B.C.E.). The son of a small landholder in northern Italy, Virgil welcomed the rule of Augustus and wrote his greatest work in the emperor's honor. Virgil's masterpiece was *The Aeneid*, an epic poem clearly meant to rival the work of Homer. The connection between Troy and Rome is made in the poem when Aeneas, a hero of Troy, survives the destruction of Troy and eventually settles in Latium; hence Roman civilization is linked to Greek history. Aeneas is portrayed as the ideal Roman—his virtues are duty, piety, and faithfulness. Virgil's overall purpose was to show that Aeneas had fulfilled his mission to establish the Romans in Italy and thereby start Rome on its divine mission to rule the world.

> Let others fashion from bronze more lifelike, breathing
>   images—
> For so they shall—and evoke living faces from marble;
> Others excel as orators, others track with their instruments
> The planets circling in heaven and predict when stars will
>   appear.

OVID AND THE ART OF LOVE

*O*vid has been called the last great poet of the Augustan golden age of literature. One of his most famous works was The Art of Love, a guidebook on the seduction of women. Unfortunately for Ovid, the work appeared at a time when Augustus was anxious to improve the morals of the Roman upper class. Augustus considered the poem offensive, and Ovid soon found himself in exile.

OVID, THE ART OF LOVE

Now I'll teach you how to captivate and hold the woman of your choice. This is the most important part of all my lessons. Lovers of every land, lend an attentive ear to my discourse; let goodwill warm your hearts, for I am going to fulfill the promises I made you.

First of all, be quite sure that there isn't a woman who cannot be won, and make up your mind that you will win her. Only you must prepare the ground. Sooner would the birds cease their song in the springtime, or the grasshopper be silent in the summer . . . than a woman resist the tender wooing of a youthful lover. . . .

Now the first thing you have to do is to get on good terms with the fair one's maid. She can make things easy for you. Find out whether she is fully in her mistress's confidence, and if she knows all about her secret dissipations. Leave no stone unturned to win her over. Once you have her on your side, the rest is easy. . . .

In the first place, it's best to send her a letter, just to pave the way. In it you should tell her how you dote on her; pay her pretty compliments and say all the nice things lovers always say. . . . Even the gods are moved by the voice of entreaty. And promise, promise, promise. Promises will cost you nothing. Everyone's a millionaire where promises are concerned. . . .

If she refuses your letter and sends it back unread, don't give up; hope for the best and try again. . . .

Don't let your hair stick up in tufts on your head; see that your hair and your beard are decently trimmed. See also that your nails are clean and nicely filed; don't have any hair growing out of your nostrils; take care that your breath is sweet, and don't go about reeking like a billy goat. All other toilet refinements leave to the women or to perverts. . . .

When you find yourself at a feast where the wine is flowing freely, and where a woman shares the same couch with you, pray to that god whose mysteries are celebrated during the night, that the wine may not overcloud your brain. 'Tis then you may easily hold converse with your mistress in hidden words whereof she will easily divine the meaning. . . .

By subtle flatteries you may be able to steal into her heart, even as the river insensibly overflows the banks which fringe it. Never cease to sing the praises of her face, her hair, her taper fingers and her dainty foot. . . .

Tears, too, are a mighty useful resource in the matter of love. They would melt a diamond. Make a point, therefore, of letting your mistress see your face all wet with tears. Howbeit, if you can't manage to squeeze out any tears— and they won't always flow just when you want them to— put your finger in your eyes.

But, Romans, never forget that government is your medium! Be this your art:—to practice men in the habit of peace, Generosity to the conquered, and firmness against aggressors.[4]

As Virgil expressed it, ruling was Rome's gift.

Ovid (43 B.C.E.–18 C.E.) was the last of the great poets of the golden age. He belonged to a youthful, privileged social group in Rome that liked to ridicule old Roman values. In keeping with the spirit of this group, Ovid wrote a series of frivolous love poems known as the *Amores*. Intended to entertain and shock, they achieved their goal. Another of Ovid's works was *The Art of Love*. This was essentially a takeoff on didactic poems. Whereas authors of earlier didactic poems had written guides to farming, hunting, or some such subject, Ovid's work was a handbook on the seduction of women (see the box above).

The most famous Latin prose work of the golden age was written by the historian Livy (59 B.C.E.–17 C.E.). Livy's masterpiece was the *History of Rome*, which covered the period from the foundation of the city to 9 B.C.E. Only 35 of the original 142 books have survived, although we do possess brief summaries of the whole work from other authors. Livy perceived history in terms of moral lessons. He stated in the preface:

> The study of history is the best medicine for a sick mind; for in history you have a record of the infinite variety of human experience plainly set out for all to see; and in that record you can find for yourself and your country both examples and warnings: fine things to take as models, base things, rotten through and through, to avoid.[5]

For Livy, human character was the determining factor in history.

In the history of Latin literature, the century and a half after Augustus is often labeled the "silver age" to indicate that the literary efforts of the period, while good, were not equal to the high standards of the Augustan "golden age." The popularity of rhetorical training encouraged the use of clever and ornate literary expressions at the expense of original and meaningful content. A good example of this trend can be found in the works of Seneca.

Educated in Rome, Seneca (c. 4 B.C.E.–65 C.E.) became strongly attached to the philosophy of Stoicism. In letters written to a young friend, he expressed the basic tenets of

Stoicism: living according to nature, accepting events dispassionately as part of the divine plan, and a universal love for all humanity. Thus "the first thing philosophy promises us is the feeling of fellowship, of belonging to mankind and being members of a community. . . . Philosophy calls for simple living, not for doing penance, and the simple way of life need not be a crude one."[6] Viewed in retrospect, Seneca displays some glaring inconsistencies. While preaching the virtues of simplicity, he amassed a fortune and was ruthless at times in protecting it. His letters show humanity, benevolence, and fortitude, but his sentiments are often undermined by an attempt to be clever with words.

The greatest historian of the silver age was Tacitus (c. 56–120). His main works included the *Annals* and *Histories*, which presented a narrative account of Roman history from the reign of Tiberius through the assassination of Domitian (14–96). Tacitus believed that history had a moral purpose: "It seems to me a historian's foremost duty is to ensure that merit is recorded, and to confront evil deeds and words with the fear of posterity's denunciations."[7] As a member of the senatorial class, Tacitus was disgusted with the abuses of power perpetrated by the emperors and determined that the "evil deeds" of wicked men would not

be forgotten. His work *Germania* is especially important as a source of information about the early Germans. But it too is colored by Tacitus' attempt to show the Germans as noble savages in comparison to the decadent Romans.

Roman Art

The Romans were also dependent on the Greeks for artistic inspiration. The Romans developed a taste for Greek statues, which they placed not only in public buildings but also in their private houses. Once demand outstripped the supply of original works, reproductions of Greek statues became fashionable. The Romans' own portrait sculpture was characterized by an intense realism that included even unpleasant physical details. Wall paintings and frescoes in the houses of the rich realistically depicted landscapes, portraits, and scenes from mythological stories.

The Romans excelled in architecture, a highly practical art. Although they continued to adapt Greek styles and made use of colonnades and rectangular structures, the Romans were also innovative. They made considerable use of curvilinear forms: the arch, vault, and dome. The Romans were also the first people in antiquity to use con-

⟫ THE PANTHEON. Shown here is the Pantheon, one of Rome's greatest buildings. Constructed of brick, six kinds of concrete, and marble, it was a stunning example of the Romans' engineering skills. The outside porch of the Pantheon contained eighteen Corinthian granite columns, but it was the inside of the temple that amazed onlookers. The interior is a large circular space topped by a huge dome. A hole in the center of the roof was the only source of light. The dome, built up layer by layer, was made of concrete, weighing 5,000 tons. The walls holding the dome are almost 20 feet thick.

CATO THE ELDER ON WOMEN

During the Second Punic War, the Romans enacted the Oppian Law, which limited the amount of gold women could possess and restricted their dress and use of carriages. In 195 B.C.E., an attempt to repeal the law was made, and women demonstrated in the streets on behalf of this effort. According to the Roman historian Livy, the conservative Roman official Cato the Elder spoke against repeal and against the women favoring it. Although the words are probably not Cato's own, they do reflect a traditional male Roman attitude toward women.

LIVY, HISTORY OF ROME

"If each of us, citizens, had determined to assert his rights and dignity as a husband with respect to his own spouse, we should have less trouble with the sex as a whole; as it is, our liberty, destroyed at home by female violence, even here in the Forum is crushed and trodden underfoot, and because we have not kept them individually under control, we dread them collectively. . . . But from no class is there not the greatest danger if you permit them meetings and gatherings and secret consultations. . . .

"Our ancestors permitted no women to conduct even personal business without a guardian to intervene in her behalf; they wished them to be under the control of fathers, brothers, husbands; we (Heaven help us!) allow them now even to interfere in public affairs, yes, and to visit the Forum and our informal and formal sessions. What else are they doing now on the streets and at the corners except urging the bill of the tribunes and voting for the repeal of the law? Give loose rein to their uncontrollable nature and to this untamed creature and expect that they will themselves set bounds to their license; unless you act, this is the least of the things enjoined upon women by custom or law and to which they submit with a feeling of injustice. It is complete liberty or, rather, if we wish to speak the truth, complete license that they desire.

"If they win in this, what will they not attempt? Review all the laws with which your forefathers restrained their license and made them subject to their husbands; even with all these bonds you can scarcely control them. What of this? If you suffer them to seize these bonds one by one and wrench themselves free and finally to be placed on a parity with their husbands, do you think that you will be able to endure them? The moment they begin to be your equals, they will be your superiors. . . .

"Now they publicly address other women's husbands, and, what is more serious, they beg for a law and votes, and from sundry men they get what they ask. In matters affecting yourself, your property, your children, you, Sir, can be importuned; once the law has ceased to set a limit to your wife's expenditures you will never set it yourself. Do not think, citizens, that the situation which existed before the law was passed will ever return."

---

crete on a massive scale. By combining concrete and curvilinear forms, they were able to construct massive buildings—public baths, such as those of Caracalla, and amphitheaters capable of seating fifty thousand spectators. These large buildings were made possible by Roman engineering skills. These same skills were put to use in constructing roads (the Romans built a network of 50,000 miles of roads throughout their empire), aqueducts (in Rome, almost a dozen aqueducts kept a population of one million supplied with water), and bridges.

Roman Law

One of Rome's chief gifts to the Mediterranean world of its day and to later generations was its system of law. The Twelve Tables of 450 B.C.E. was Rome's first code of laws, but it was a product of a simple farming society and proved inadequate for later Roman needs. Nevertheless, from the Twelve Tables the Romans developed a system of civil law that applied to all Roman citizens. As Rome expanded, Romans became involved in problems between Romans and non-Romans as well as between two non-Romans. Although some of their rules of civil law could be used in these cases, special rules were often needed. These rules gave rise to a body of law known as the law of nations, defined by the Romans as "that part of the law which we apply both to ourselves and to foreigners." Under the influence of Stoicism (see Chapter 4), the Romans came to identify their law of nations with natural law, or universal law based on reason. This enabled them to establish standards of justice that applied to all people.

These standards of justice included principles that we would immediately recognize. A person was regarded as innocent until proved otherwise. People accused of wrongdoing were allowed to defend themselves before a judge. A judge was expected to weigh evidence carefully before arriving at a decision. These principles lived on long after the fall of the Roman Empire.

The Roman Family

At the heart of the Roman social structure stood the family, headed by the *paterfamilias*—the dominant male. The household also included the wife, sons with their wives and children, unmarried daughters, and slaves. A family was virtually a small state within the state, and the power of the *paterfamilias* was parallel to that of the state magistrates over the citizens. Like the Greeks, Roman males believed that the weakness of the female sex necessitated male guardians (see the box above). The *paterfamilias*

⤳ A ROMAN LADY. Roman women, especially those of the upper class, developed comparatively more freedom than women in classical Athens despite the persistent male belief that women required guardianship. This mural decoration was found in the remains of a villa destroyed by the eruption of Mount Vesuvius.

twenty-nine, and divorced at thirty-three. She died at thirty-four.

By the second century C.E., significant changes were occurring in the Roman family. The *paterfamilias* no longer had absolute authority over his children; he could no longer sell them into slavery or have them put to death. Moreover, as noted, the husband's absolute authority over his wife also disappeared, and by the late second century, women were no longer required to have guardians.

Upper-class Roman women in the Early Empire had considerable freedom and independence. They had acquired the right to own, inherit, and dispose of property. Unlike the Greeks, Roman wives were not segregated from males in the home but were appreciated as enjoyable company and were at the center of household social life. Upper-class women could attend races, the theater, and events in the amphitheater, although in the latter two places they were forced to sit in separate female sections. Women could not participate in politics, but the Early Empire saw a number of important women who influenced politics through their husbands, including Livia, the wife of Augustus; Agrippina, the mother of Nero; and Plotina, the wife of Trajan.

Slaves and Their Masters

Although slavery was a common institution throughout the ancient world, no people possessed more slaves or relied so much on slave labor as the Romans eventually did. Slaves were used in many ways in Roman society. The rich owned the most and the best. In the late Republic, it became a badge of prestige to be attended by many slaves. Greek slaves were in much demand as tutors, musicians, doctors, and artists. Many slaves of all nationalities were used as menial household workers, such as cooks, valets, waiters, cleaners, and gardeners. Roman businessmen would employ slaves as shop assistants or artisans. Slaves were also used as farm laborers; in fact, huge gangs of slaves worked the large landed estates under pitiful conditions. Cato the Elder argued that it was cheaper to work slaves to death and then replace them than to treat them favorably. In addition, the roads, aqueducts, and public buildings were constructed by contractors using slave labor. The total number of slaves is difficult to judge—estimates range from 20 to 35 percent of the population.

The treatment of Roman slaves varied. There are numerous instances of humane treatment by masters and situations where slaves even protected their owners from danger out of gratitude and esteem. But there are also

exercised that authority; upon his death, sons or nearest male relatives assumed the role of guardians.

Fathers arranged the marriages of their daughters. In the Republic, women married "with legal control" passing from father to husband. By the mid-first century B.C.E., the dominant practice had changed to "without legal control," which meant that married daughters officially remained within the father's legal power. Since the fathers of most married women were dead, not being in the "legal control" of a husband entailed independent property rights that forceful women could translate into considerable power within the household and outside it.

Some parents in upper-class families provided education for their daughters. Some girls had private tutors, and others may have gone to primary schools. However, at the age when boys were entering secondary schools, girls were pushed into marriage. The legal minimum age for marriage was twelve, although fourteen was a more common age in practice. Although some Roman doctors warned that early pregnancies could be dangerous for young girls, early marriages persisted because women often died relatively young. A good example is Tullia, Cicero's beloved daughter. She was married at sixteen, widowed at twenty-two, remarried one year later, divorced at twenty-eight, remarried at

THE ROMAN FEAR OF SLAVES

The lowest stratum of the Roman population consisted of slaves. They were used extensively in households, at the court, as artisans in industrial enterprises, as business managers, and in numerous other ways. Although some historians have argued that slaves were treated more humanely during the Early Empire, these selections by the Roman historian Tacitus and the Roman statesman Pliny indicate that slaves still rebelled against their masters because of mistreatment. Many masters continued to live in fear of their slaves as witnessed by the saying, "As many enemies as you have slaves."

TACITUS, *THE ANNALS OF IMPERIAL ROME*

Soon afterwards the City Prefect, Lucius Pedanius Secundus, was murdered by one of his slaves [61 C.E.]. Either Pedanius had refused to free the murderer after agreeing to a price, or the slave, in a homosexual infatuation, found competition from his master intolerable. After the murder, ancient custom required that every slave residing under the same roof must be executed. But a crowd gathered, eager to save so many innocent lives; and rioting began. The senate-house was besieged. Inside, there was feeling against excessive severity, but the majority opposed any change. Among the latter was Gaius Cassius Longinus, who when his turn came spoke as follows. . . .

"An ex-consul has been deliberately murdered by a slave in his own home. None of his fellow-slaves prevented or betrayed the murderer, though the senatorial decree threatening the whole household with execution still stands. Exempt them from the penalty if you like. But then, if the City Prefect was not important enough to be immune; who will be? Who will have enough slaves to protect him if Pedanius's four hundred were too few? Who can rely on his household's help if even fear for their own lives does not make them shield us?"

[The sentence of death was carried out.]

PLINY THE YOUNGER TO ACILIUS

This horrible affair demands more publicity than a letter—Larcius Macedo, a senator and ex-praetor, has fallen a victim to his own slaves. Admittedly he was a cruel and overbearing master, too ready to forget that his father had been a slave, or perhaps too keenly conscious of it. He was taking a bath in his house at Formiae when suddenly he found himself surrounded; one slave seized him by the throat while the others struck his face and hit him in the chest and stomach and—shocking to say—in his private parts. When they thought he was dead they threw him onto the hot pavement, to make sure he was not still alive. Whether unconscious or feigning to be so, he lay there motionless, thus making them believe that he was quite dead. Only then was he carried out, as if he had fainted with the heat, and received by his slaves who had remained faithful, while his concubines ran up, screaming frantically. Roused by their cries and revived by the cooler air he opened his eyes and made some movement to show that he was alive, it being now safe to do so. The guilty slaves fled, but most of them have been arrested and a search is being made for the others. Macedo was brought back to life with difficulty, but only for a few days; at least he died with the satisfaction of having revenged himself, for he lived to see the same punishment meted out as for murder. There you see the dangers, outrages, and insults to which we are exposed. No master can feel safe because he is kind and considerate; for it is their brutality, not their reasoning capacity, which leads slaves to murder masters.

---

examples of slaves murdering their owners, causing some Romans to live in unspoken fear of their slaves (see the box above). Slaves were also subject to severe punishments, torture, abuse, and hard labor that drove some to run away or even revolt against their owners. The Romans had stringent laws against aiding a runaway slave. The murder of a master by a slave might mean the execution of all the other household slaves.

Near the end of the second century B.C.E., large-scale slave revolts occurred in Sicily, where enormous gangs of slaves were subjected to horrible working conditions on large landed estates. Slaves were branded, beaten, fed inadequately, worked in chains, and housed at night in underground prisons. It took three years (135–132 B.C.E.) to crush a revolt of seventy thousand slaves, and the great revolt on Sicily (104–101 B.C.E.) involved most of the island and took a Roman army of seventeen thousand men to suppress it. The most famous revolt on the Italian peninsula occurred in 73 B.C.E. Led by a Thracian gladiator named Spartacus, the revolt broke out in southern Italy and involved seventy thousand slaves. Spartacus managed to defeat several Roman armies before he was finally trapped and killed in southern Italy in 71 B.C.E. Six thousand of his followers were crucified, the traditional form of execution for slaves.

Imperial Rome

At the center of the colossal Roman Empire was the ancient city of Rome (see Map 5.4). Truly a capital city, Rome had the largest population of any city in the empire—close to one million by the time of Augustus. Only Chang'an, the imperial capital of the Han Chinese empire, had a comparable population during this time. For

THE PUBLIC BATHS OF THE ROMAN EMPIRE

The public baths in Rome and other cities played an important role in urban life. Introduced to Rome in the second century B.C.E. as a result of Greek influence, the number of public baths grew at a rapid pace in the Early Empire as the emperors contributed funds for their construction. The public baths were especially noisy near the end of the afternoon when Romans stopped in after work to use the baths before dinner. The following description is by Lucian, a traveling lecturer who lived in the second century and wrote satirical dialogues in Greek. This selection is taken from Hippias, or the Bath.

LUCIAN, *HIPPIAS, OR THE BATH*

The building suits the magnitude of the site, accords well with the accepted idea of such an establishment, and shows regard for the principles of lighting. The entrance is high, with a flight of broad steps of which the tread is greater than the pitch, to make them easy to ascend. On entering, one is received into a public hall of good size, with ample accommodations for servants and attendants. On the left are the lounging rooms, also of just the right sort for a bath, attractive, brightly lighted retreats. Then, besides them, a hall, larger than need be for the purposes of a bath, but necessary for the reception of richer persons. Next, capacious locker rooms to undress in, on each side, with a very high and brilliantly lighted hall between them, in which are three swimming pools of cold water; it is finished in Laconian marble, and has two statues of white marble in the ancient style. . . .

On leaving this hall, you come into another which is slightly warmed instead of meeting you at once with fierce heat; it is oblong, and has an apse on each side. Next to it, on the right, is a very bright hall, nicely fitted up for massage. . . . Then near this is another hall, the most beautiful in the world, in which one can stand or sit with comfort, linger without danger, and stroll about with profit. It also is refulgent with Phrygian marble clear to the roof. Next comes the hot corridor, faced with Numidian marble. The hall beyond it is very beautiful, full of abundant light and aglow with color like that of purple hangings. It contains three hot tubs.

When you have bathed, you need not go back through the same rooms, but can go directly to the cold room through a slightly warmed chamber. Everywhere there is copious illumination and full indoor daylight. . . . Why should I go on to tell you of the exercising floor and of the cloak rooms? . . . Moreover, it is beautiful with all other marks of thoughtfulness—with two toilets, many exits, and two devices for telling time, a water clock that makes a bellowing sound and a sundial.

anyone with ambitions, Rome was the place to be. People from all over the empire resided there, with entire neighborhoods inhabited by specific groups, such as Greeks and Syrians.

An enormous gulf existed between rich and poor in the city of Rome. While the rich had comfortable villas, the poor lived in apartment blocks called *insulae*, which might be six stories high. Constructed of concrete, they were often poorly built and prone to collapse. The use of wooden beams in the floors and movable stoves, torches, candles, and lamps within the rooms for heat and light made the danger of fire a constant companion. Once started, fires were extremely difficult to put out. The famous conflagration of 64 C.E., which Nero was unjustly accused of starting, devastated a good part of the city. Besides the hazards of collapse and fire, living conditions were also poor. High rents forced entire families into one room. The absence of plumbing, central heating, and open fireplaces made life so uncomfortable that poorer Romans spent most of their time outdoors in the streets.

Fortunately for these people, Rome boasted public buildings unequaled anywhere in the empire. Its temples, forums, markets, baths, theaters, triumphal arches, governmental buildings, and amphitheaters gave parts of the city an appearance of grandeur and magnificence (see the box above).

Though the center of a great empire, Rome was also a great parasite. Beginning with Augustus, the emperors accepted responsibility for providing food for the urban populace, with about 200,000 people receiving free grain. Even with the free grain, conditions were grim for the poor.

In addition to food, entertainment was provided on a grand scale for the inhabitants of Rome. The poet Juvenal said of the Roman masses: "But nowadays, with no vote to sell, their motto is 'Couldn't care less.' Time was when their plebiscite elected generals, heads of state, commanders of legions: but now they've pulled in their horns, there's only two things that concern them: Bread and Circuses."[8] Public spectacles were provided by the emperor and other state officials as part of the great festivals—most of them religious in origin—celebrated by the state. Over one hundred days a year were given over to these public holidays. The festivals included three major types of entertainment. At the Circus Maximus, horse and chariot races attracted hundreds of thousands, while dramatic and other performances were held in theaters. But the most famous of all the public spectacles were the gladiatorial shows.

The Gladiatorial Shows

The gladiatorial shows were an integral part of Roman society. They took place in amphitheaters, the first permanent one having been constructed at Rome in 29 B.C.E. Perhaps the most famous was the Flavian amphitheater, called the Colosseum, constructed at Rome to seat fifty thousand spectators. Amphitheaters were not limited to the city of Rome but were constructed throughout the empire. Considerable resources and ingenuity went into building them, especially in the arrangements for moving wild beasts efficiently into the arena. In most cities and towns, amphitheaters came to be the biggest buildings, rivaled only by the circuses for races and the public baths. Where a society invests its money gives an idea of its priorities. Since the amphitheater was the primary location for the gladiatorial games, it is fair to say that public slaughter was an important part of Roman culture.

Gladiatorial games were held from dawn to dusk. Contests to the death between trained fighters formed the central focus of these games. Most gladiators were slaves or condemned criminals, although some free men lured by the hope of popularity and patronage by wealthy fans participated voluntarily. They were trained for combat in special gladiatorial schools.

Gladiatorial games included other forms of entertainment as well. Criminals of all ages and both sexes were sent into the arena without weapons to face certain death from wild animals who would tear them to pieces. Numerous kinds of animal contests were also staged: wild beasts against each other, such as bears against buffalo; staged hunts with men shooting safely from behind iron bars; and gladiators in the arena with bulls, tigers, and lions. Reportedly, five thousand beasts were killed in one day of games when the Emperor Titus inaugurated the Colosseum in 80 C.E.

These bloodthirsty spectacles were extremely popular with the Roman people. The Roman historian Tacitus

MAP 5.4 Imperial Rome   A large, overcrowded, and dirty city, Rome was the political, economic, social, and cultural hub of the Roman Empire. Squalid and desperate living conditions for the poor contrasted dramatically with the city's magnificent architectural works. ➤ *How did roads from the outside enter Rome, and what might explain this?*

THE GLADIATORIAL GAMES. Although some gladiators were free men enticed by the possibility of rewards, most were condemned criminals, slaves, or prisoners of war who were trained in special schools. A great gladiator could win his freedom through the games. This mosaic, from the fourth century C.E., depicts different aspects of gladiatorial fighting and clearly shows the bloody nature of the gladiatorial games.

said, "Few indeed are to be found who talk of any other subjects in their homes, and whenever we enter a classroom, what else is the conversation of the youths."[9] But the gladiatorial games served a purpose beyond mere entertainment. To the Romans, the games and the other forms of public entertainment fulfilled both a political and a social need. Certainly, they served to divert the idle masses from political unrest. It was said of Emperor Trajan that he understood that although the distribution of grain and money satisfied the individual, spectacles were necessary for the "contentment of the masses."

TRANSFORMATION OF THE ROMAN WORLD: THE DEVELOPMENT OF CHRISTIANITY

The rise of Christianity marked a fundamental break with the dominant values of the Greco-Roman world. To understand the rise of Christianity, we must first examine both the religious environment of the Roman world and the Jewish background from which Christianity emerged.

The Religious World of the Romans

Augustus had taken a number of steps to revive the Roman state religion, which had declined during the turmoil of the late Republic. The official state religion focused on the worship of a pantheon of Greco-Roman gods and goddesses, including Juno, the patron goddess of women; Minerva, the goddess of artisans; Mars, the god of war; and Jupiter Optimus Maximus ("best and greatest"), who became the patron deity of Rome and assumed a central place in the religious life of the city. The Romans believed that observance of proper ritual by state priests brought the Romans into a proper relationship with the gods and guaranteed security, peace, and prosperity. As Cicero, the first-century politician and writer, claimed: "We have overcome all the nations of the world, because we have realized that the world is directed and governed by the gods."[10]

The polytheistic Romans were extremely tolerant of other religions. They allowed the worship of native gods and goddesses throughout their provinces and even adopted some of the local gods. In addition, the imperial cult of Roma and Augustus was developed to bolster support for the emperors. After Augustus, any dead emperors deified by the Roman senate were added to the official imperial cult.

The desire for a more emotional spiritual experience led many people to the mystery religions of the Hellenistic east, which flooded into the western Roman world during the Early Empire. The mystery religions promised their followers an entry into a higher world of reality and the promise of a future life superior to the present one. They also featured elaborate rituals with deep emotional appeal. By participating in their ceremonies and performing their rites, an adherent could achieve communion with spiritual beings and undergo purification that opened the door to life after death.

The Jewish Background

In Hellenistic times, the Jewish people had been granted considerable independence by their Seleucid rulers (see Chapter 4). Roman involvement with the Jews began in 63 B.C.E., and by 6 C.E., Judaea (which embraced the lands of the old Jewish kingdom of Judah) had been made a province and placed under the direction of a Roman procurator. But unrest continued, augmented by divisions among the Jews themselves. The Sadducees favored cooperation with the Romans. The Pharisees, although they wanted Judaea to be free from Roman control, did not advocate violent means to achieve this goal. The Essenes, as revealed in the Dead Sea Scrolls, a collection of documents first discovered in 1947, constituted a Jewish sect that lived in a religious community near the Dead Sea. They, like most other Jews, awaited a Messiah who would save Israel from oppression, usher in the kingdom of God, and establish a true paradise on earth. A fourth group, the Zealots, were militant extremists who advocated the violent overthrow of Roman rule. A Jewish revolt in 66 C.E. was crushed by the Romans four years later. The Jewish Temple in Jerusalem was destroyed, and Roman power once more stood supreme in Judaea.

The Rise of Christianity

It was in the midst of the confusion and conflict in Judaea that Jesus of Nazareth (c. 6 B.C.E.–29 C.E.) began his public preaching. Jesus—a Palestinian Jew—grew up in Galilee, an important center of the militant Zealots. Jesus' message was simple. He reassured his fellow Jews that he did not plan to undermine their traditional religion: "Do not think that I have come to abolish the Law of the Prophets; I have not come to abolish them but to fulfill them."[11] According to Jesus, what was important was not strict adherence to the letter of the law and attention to rules and prohibitions but the transformation of the inner person: "So in everything, do to others what you would have them do to you, for this sums up the Law and the Prophets."[12] God's command was simple—to love God and one another: "Love the Lord your God with all your heart and with all your soul and with all your mind and with all your strength. The second is this: Love your neighbor as yourself."[13] In the Sermon on the Mount (see the box on p. 143), Jesus presented the ethical concepts—humility, charity, and

CHRISTIAN IDEALS: THE SERMON ON THE MOUNT

Christianity was simply one of many religions competing for attention in the Roman Empire during the first and second centuries. The rise of Christianity marked a fundamental break with the value system of the upper-class elites who dominated the world of classical antiquity. As these excerpts from the Sermon on the Mount in the Gospel of Saint Matthew illustrate, Christians emphasized humility, charity, brotherly love, and a belief in the inner being and a spiritual kingdom superior to this material world. These values and principles were not those of classical Greco-Roman civilization as exemplified in the words and deeds of its leaders.

THE GOSPEL ACCORDING TO SAINT MATTHEW

Now when he saw the crowds, he went up on a mountainside and sat down. His disciples came to him, and he began to teach them, saying:

> Blessed are the poor in spirit: for theirs is the kingdom of heaven.
> Blessed are those who mourn: for they will be comforted.
> Blessed are the meek: for they will inherit the earth.
> Blessed are those who hunger and thirst for righteousness: for they will be filled.
> Blessed are the merciful: for they will be shown mercy.
> Blessed are the pure in heart: for they will see God.
> Blessed are the peacemakers: for they will be called sons of God.
> Blessed are those who are persecuted because of righteousness: for theirs is the kingdom of heaven. . . .

You have heard that it was said, "Eye for eye, and tooth for tooth." But I tell you, Do not resist an evil person. If someone strikes you on the right cheek, turn to him the other also. . . .

You have heard that it was said, "Love your neighbor, and hate your enemy." But I tell you, Love your enemies and pray for those who persecute you. . . .

Do not store up for yourselves treasures on earth, where moth and rust destroy, and where thieves break in and steal. But store up for yourselves treasures in heaven, where moth and rust do not destroy, and where thieves do not break in and steal. For where your treasure is, there your heart will be also. . . .

No one can serve two masters. Either he will hate the one and love the other, or he will be devoted to the one and despise the other. You cannot serve both God and Money.

Therefore I tell you, do not worry about your life, what you will eat or drink; or about your body, what you will wear. Is not life more important than food, and the body more important than clothes? Look at the birds of the air; they do not sow or reap or store away in barns, and yet your heavenly Father feeds them. Are you not much more valuable than they? . . . So do not worry, saying, What shall we eat? or What shall we drink? or What shall we wear? For the pagans run after all these things, and your heavenly Father knows that you need them. But seek first his kingdom and his righteousness, and all these things will be given to you as well.

---

brotherly love—that would form the basis for the value system of medieval Western civilization.

Although some Jews welcomed Jesus as the Messiah who would save Israel from oppression and establish God's kingdom on earth, Jesus spoke of a heavenly kingdom, not an earthly one: "My kingdom is not of this world."[14] Consequently, he disappointed the radicals. On the other hand, conservative religious leaders believed Jesus was undermining respect for traditional Jewish religion. To the Roman authorities of Palestine and their local allies, the Nazarene was a potential revolutionary who might transform Jewish expectations of a messianic kingdom into a revolt against Rome. Therefore, Jesus found himself denounced on many sides and was given over to the Roman authorities. The procurator Pontius Pilate ordered his crucifixion. But that did not solve the problem. A few loyal followers of Jesus spread the story that Jesus had overcome death, had been resurrected, and had then ascended into heaven. The belief in Jesus' resurrection became an important tenet of Christian doctrine. Jesus was now hailed "the anointed one" (*Christ* in Greek), the Messiah who would return and usher in the kingdom of God on earth.

Christianity began, then, as a religious movement within Judaism. Although tradition holds that one of Jesus' disciples, Peter, founded the Christian church at Rome, the most important figure in early Christianity after Jesus was Paul of Tarsus (c. 5–c. 67). Paul believed that the message of Jesus should be preached not only to Jews but to Gentiles (non-Jews) as well. Paul was responsible for founding Christian communities throughout Asia Minor and along the shores of the Aegean.

Paul provided a universal foundation for the spread of Jesus' ideas. He taught that Jesus was, in effect, a savior-god, the son of God, who had come to earth to save all humans, who were basically sinners as a result of Adam's original sin of disobedience against God. By his death, Jesus had atoned for the sins of all humans and made possible their reconciliation with God and hence their salvation. By accepting Jesus as their savior, they too could be saved.

Christianity spread slowly at first. Although the teachings of early Christianity were disseminated mostly by the preaching of convinced Christians, written materials also appeared. Among them were a series of letters or epistles written by Paul outlining Christian beliefs for different Christian communities. Some of Jesus' disciples may also have preserved some of the sayings of the master in writing and would have passed on personal memories that became the basis of the written gospels—the "good news" concerning Jesus—which were written down between 50 and 150 and attempted to give a record of Jesus' life and teachings; these texts formed the core of the New Testament.

Although Jerusalem was the first center of Christianity, destruction of the city by the Romans in 70 C.E. dispersed the Christians and left individual Christian churches with considerable independence. By 100, Christian churches had been established in most of the major cities of the east and in some places in the western part of the empire. Many early Christians came from the ranks of Hellenized Jews and the Greek-speaking populations of the east. But in the second and third centuries, an increasing number of followers came from Latin-speaking people. A Latin translation of the Greek New Testament that appeared soon after 200 aided this process.

Initially, the Romans did not pay much attention to the Christians, whom they regarded at first as simply another Jewish sect. As time passed, however, the Roman attitude toward Christianity began to change. The Romans were tolerant of other religions except when they threatened public order or public morals. Many Romans came to view Christians as harmful to the order of the Roman state. Since Christians held their meetings in secret and seemed to be connected to Christian groups in other areas, the government could view them as potentially dangerous to the state.

Some Romans felt that Christians were overly exclusive and hence harmful to the community and public order. The refusal of Christians to recognize other gods meant that they abstained from public festivals that honored these divinities. Finally, Christians refused to participate in the worship of the state gods and imperial cult. Since the Romans regarded these as important to the state, the Christians' refusal undermined the security of the state and hence constituted an act of treason, punishable by death. But to the Christians, who believed that there was only one real god, the worship of state gods and the emperors was idolatry and would endanger their own salvation.

Nevertheless, Roman persecution of Christians in the first and second centuries was only sporadic and local, never systematic. Persecution began during the reign of Nero. After the fire that destroyed much of Rome, the emperor used the Christians as scapegoats, accusing them of arson and hatred of the human race and subjecting them to cruel deaths in Rome. In the second century, Christians were largely ignored as harmless. By the end of the reigns of the five good emperors, Christians still represented a small minority, but one of considerable strength.

The Triumph of Christianity

The sporadic persecution of Christians by the Romans in the first and second centuries had done little to stop the growth of Christianity and had in fact served to strengthen it as an institution in the second and third centuries by causing it to become more organized. Crucial to this change was the emerging role of the bishops, who began to assume more control over church communities. The Christian church was creating a well-defined hierarchical structure in which the bishops and clergy were salaried officers separate from the laity, or regular church members.

Christianity grew slowly in the first century, took root in the second, and by the third had spread widely. Why was Christianity able to attract so many followers? Certainly, the Christian message had much to offer the Roman world. The promise of salvation, made possible by Jesus' death and resurrection, made a resounding impact on a world full of suffering and injustice. Christianity

✧ **JESUS AND HIS APOSTLES.** Pictured is a fourth-century C.E. fresco from a Roman catacomb depicting Jesus and his apostles. Catacombs were underground cemeteries where early Christians buried their dead. Christian tradition holds that in times of imperial repression, Christians withdrew to the catacombs to pray and even hide.

seemed to imbue life with a meaning and purpose beyond the simple material things of everyday reality. Second, Christianity seemed familiar. It was regarded as simply another eastern mystery religion, offering immortality as the result of the sacrificial death of a savior-god. At the same time, it offered more than the other mystery religions did. Jesus had been a human figure, easy to relate to. Moreover, Christianity had universal appeal. Unlike some mystery religions, it was not restricted to men, nor did it require a painful or expensive initiation rite, as other mystery religions did. Initiation was accomplished simply by baptism—a purification by water—through which one entered into a personal relationship with Jesus. In addition, Christianity gave new meaning to life and offered what the Roman state religions could not—a personal relationship with God and connection to higher worlds.

Finally, Christianity fulfilled the human need to belong. Christians formed communities bound to one another in which people could express their love by helping each other and offering assistance to the poor, sick, widows, and orphans. Christianity satisfied the need to belong in a way that the huge, impersonal, and remote Roman Empire could never do.

Christianity proved attractive to all classes. The promise of eternal life was for all—rich, poor, aristocrats, slaves, men, and women. As Paul stated in his Epistle to the Colossians: "And [you] have put on the new self, which is being renewed in knowledge in the image of its Creator. Here there is no Greek nor Jew, circumcised or uncircumcised, barbarian, Scythian, slave or free, but Christ is all, and is in all."[15] Christianity emphasized a sense of spiritual equality for all people.

Many women, in fact, found that Christianity offered them new roles and new forms of companionship with other women. Christian women fostered the new religion in their homes and preached their convictions to other people in their towns and villages. Many also died for their faith. Perpetua (d. 203) was an aristocratic woman who converted to Christianity. Her pagan family begged her to renounce her new faith, but she refused. Arrested by the Roman authorities, she chose instead to die for her faith and was one of a group of Christians who were slaughtered by wild beasts in the arena at Carthage on March 7, 203.

As the Christian church became more organized, some emperors in the third century responded with more systematic persecutions, but their schemes failed to work. The last great persecution was at the beginning of the fourth century, but by that time Christianity had become too strong to be eradicated by force.

In the fourth century, Christianity prospered as never before after Constantine (306–337) became the first Christian emperor. Although he was not baptized until the end of his life, in 313 Constantine issued the Edict of Milan, officially tolerating the existence of Christianity. Under Theodosius "the Great" (378–395), it was made the official religion of the Roman Empire. Christianity had triumphed.

THE DECLINE AND FALL OF THE ROMAN EMPIRE

In the course of the third century, the Roman Empire came near to collapse. Military monarchy under the Severan rulers (193–235), which restored order after a series of civil wars, was followed by military anarchy. For a period of almost fifty years, from 235 to 284, the Roman Empire was mired in the chaos of continual civil war. The imperial throne was occupied by anyone who had the military strength to seize it. In this span of not quite fifty years, there were twenty-two emperors, only two of whom did not meet a violent death. At the same time, the empire was beset by a series of invasions, no doubt exacerbated by the civil wars. In the east, the Sassanid Persians made inroads into Roman territory. Germanic tribes also poured into the empire. The Goths overran the Balkans and moved into Greece and Asia Minor. The Franks advanced into Gaul and Spain. Not until the reign of Aurelian (270–275) were most of the boundaries restored.

Invasions, civil wars, and plague came close to causing an economic collapse of the Roman Empire in the third century. The population declined drastically, possibly by as much as one-third. There was a noticeable decline in trade and small industry. The labor shortage created by the plague affected both military recruiting and the economy. Farm production deteriorated significantly as fields were ravaged by Germanic tribes and even more often by the defending Roman armies. The monetary system began to show signs of collapse as a result of debased coinage and the beginnings of serious inflation. Armies were needed more than ever, but financial strains made it difficult to pay and enlist soldiers. By the mid-third century, the state had to rely on hiring Germans to fight under Roman commanders.

The Reforms of Diocletian and Constantine

At the end of the third century and beginning of the fourth, the Roman Empire gained a new lease on life through the efforts of two strong emperors, Diocletian and Constantine, who restored order and stability. The Roman Empire was virtually transformed into a new state: the so-called Late Empire, which included a new governmental structure, a rigid economic and social system, and a new state religion—Christianity.

Both Diocletian (284–305) and Constantine (306–337) expanded imperial control by strengthening and enlarging the administrative bureaucracies of the Roman Empire. Henceforth, civil and military bureaucracies were sharply separated. Each contained a hierarchy of officials who exercised control at the various levels. The emperor presided over both hierarchies of officials and served as the only link between them. New titles of nobility—such as *illustres* ("illustrious ones") and *illustrissimi* ("the most illustrious ones")—were instituted to dignify the holders of positions in the civil and military bureaucracies.

Additional military reforms were also inaugurated. The army was enlarged to half a million men, including German units. Mobile units were established that could be quickly moved to support frontier troops where the borders were threatened.

Constantine's biggest project was the construction of a new capital city in the east on the site of the Greek city of Byzantium on the shores of the Bosporus. Eventually renamed Constantinople (modern Istanbul), it was developed for defensive reasons: it had an excellent strategic location. Calling it his "New Rome," Constantine endowed the city with a forum, large palaces, and a vast amphitheater.

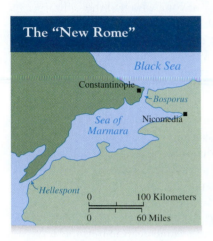

The "New Rome"

The political and military reforms of Diocletian and Constantine greatly enlarged two institutions—the army and civil service—that drained most of the public funds. Though more revenues were needed to pay for the army and bureaucracy, the population was not growing, so the tax base could not be expanded. Diocletian and Constantine devised new economic and social policies to deal with these financial burdens, but like their political policies, these measures were all based on coercion and loss of individual freedom. To fight inflation, Diocletian resorted to issuing a price edict in 301 that established maximum wages and prices for the entire empire, but despite severe penalties, it was unenforceable and failed to work.

Coercion also came to form the underlying basis for numerous occupations in the Late Roman Empire. To ensure the tax base and keep the empire going despite the shortage of labor, the emperors issued edicts that forced people to remain in their designated vocations. Basic jobs, such as baker or shipper, became hereditary. Free tenant farmers continued to decline and soon found themselves bound to the land by large landowners who took advantage of depressed agricultural conditions to enlarge their landed estates.

In general, the economic and social policies of Diocletian and Constantine were based on an unprecedented degree of control and coercion. Though temporarily successful, such authoritarian policies in the long run stifled the very vitality the Late Empire needed to revive its sagging fortunes.

The Fall of the Western Roman Empire

The restored empire of Diocletian and Constantine limped along for more than a century. After Constantine, the empire continued to divide into western and eastern parts.

The west came under increasing pressure from the invading Germanic tribes. The major breakthrough into the Roman Empire came in the second half of the fourth century. Ferocious warriors from Asia, known as Huns (who may have been related to the Xiongnu, the invaders of the Han Empire in China), moved into eastern Europe and put pressure on the Germanic Visigoths, who in turn moved south and west, crossed the Danube into Roman territory, and settled down as Roman allies. But the Visigoths soon revolted, and the Roman attempt to stop them at Adrianople in 378 led to a crushing defeat for Rome.

Increasing numbers of Germans now crossed the frontiers. In 410, the Visigoths sacked Rome. Vandals poured into southern Spain and Africa, Visigoths into Spain and Gaul. The Vandals crossed into Italy from North Africa and ravaged Rome again in 455. Twenty-one years later, the western emperor Romulus Augustulus (475–476) was deposed, and a series of Germanic kingdoms replaced the Roman Empire in the west while an eastern Roman Empire continued with its center at Constantinople.

The end of the Roman Empire has given rise to numerous theories that attempt to provide a single, all-encompassing reason for its decline and fall, including the following: Christianity's emphasis on a spiritual kingdom undermined Roman military virtues and patriotism; traditional Roman values declined as non-Italians gained prominence in the empire; poisoning due to the use of lead water pipes and cups caused a mental decline; plague decimated the population; Rome failed to advance technologically because of slavery; and Rome was unable to achieve a workable political system. There may be an element of truth in each of these theories, but each of them has also been challenged. History is an intricate web of relationships, causes, and effects. No single explanation will ever suffice to explain historical events. One thing is clear: weakened by a shortage of manpower, the Roman army in the west was simply not able to fend off the hordes of people invading Italy and Gaul. In contrast, the eastern Roman Empire, which would survive for another thousand years, remained largely free from invasion (see Chapter 7).

COMPARISON OF THE ROMAN AND HAN EMPIRES

At the beginning of the first millennium C.E., two great empires—the Roman Empire in the West and the Han Empire in the East—dominated large areas of the world. Although there was little contact between them, the Han Empire and the Roman Empire had some remarkable similarities. Both empires lasted for centuries, and both had remarkable success in establishing centralized control. They built elaborate systems of roads in order to rule efficiently and relied on provincial officials and especially

Chronology

THE LATE EMPIRE—CHIEF RULERS AND EVENTS

Military monarchy (Severan dynasty)	193–235
Military anarchy	235–284
Diocletian	284–305
Constantine	306–337
Edict of Milan	313
Theodosius "the Great"	378–395
Visigoths sack Rome	410
Vandals sack Rome	455
Romulus Augustulus is deposed	476

ate after their death, accession to the Roman imperial throne depended less on dynastic principles than on naked military force. As a result, over a period of centuries, Chinese imperial authority was far more stable.

Despite the differences, one major inescapable similarity remains: both empires eventually faced overwhelming problems. Both suffered from overexpansion, and both fortified their long borders with walls, forts, and military garrisons to guard against invasions of nomadic peoples. Both empires were nevertheless eventually overcome by these peoples: the Han dynasty was weakened by the incursions of the Xiongnu, and the western Roman Empire eventually collapsed in the face of invasions by the Germanic peoples.

Nevertheless, one inescapable difference between these two contemporary empires also remained. Although the Han dynasty collapsed, the Chinese imperial tradition, as well as the class structure and set of values that sustained it, continued, and the Chinese empire, under new dynasties, continued well into the twentieth century as a single political entity. In stark contrast, the Roman Empire collapsed and lived on only as an idea.

towns and cities as local centers of administration. Architectural features found in the capital cities of Rome and Chang'an were also transferred on a smaller scale to provincial towns and cities. In both empires, settled conditions led to a high level of agricultural production that sustained large populations, estimated at between fifty and sixty million in each empire. Although both empires expanded into areas that had different languages, ethnic groups, and ways of life, they managed to carry their legal and political institutions, their technical skills, and their languages throughout their empires.

The Roman and Han Empires had similar social and economic structures. The family stood at the heart of the social structure, with the male head of the family as all-powerful. Duty, courage, obedience, and discipline were values inculcated by the family that helped make the empires strong. The wealth of both societies also depended on agriculture. Although a free peasantry was a backbone of strength and stability in each, the gradual conversion of free peasants into tenant farmers by wealthy landowners was common to both societies and ultimately served to undermine the power of their imperial governments.

Of course, there were also significant differences. Social mobility was greater in Rome than in China, and merchants were more highly regarded and allowed more freedom in the West than in the East. Then, too, the dynastic principle in China added a strong element of stability. With the Mandate of Heaven, Chinese rulers had an authority to command, conferred by divine forces, that was easily passed on to other family members. Although Roman emperors were accorded divine status by the Roman sen-

© British Museum

© British Library

EMPERORS, WEST AND EAST. Two great empires with strong central governments dominated much of the ancient world. Shown here are two emperors from these empires. The Roman emperor Hadrian, who ruled from 117 to 138, was the third of the five good emperors. He had been adopted by the emperor Trajan to serve as his successor. Han Gaozu was the first emperor of the Han dynasty, which ruled China for four hundred years. He was responsible for bringing China back under central control by 202 B.C.E. but was killed in a frontier battle in 195 B.C.E.

CONCLUSION

Between 509 and 264 B.C.E., the Latin-speaking community of Rome expanded and brought about the union of almost all of Italy under its control. Even more dramatically, between 264 and 133 B.C.E., Rome expanded to the west and east and became master of the Mediterranean Sea and its surrounding territories, creating one of the largest empires in antiquity. Rome's republican institutions proved inadequate for the task of ruling an empire, however, and after a series of bloody civil wars, Octavian created a new order that would rule the empire in an orderly fashion. His successors established a Roman imperial state.

The Roman Empire experienced a lengthy period of peace and prosperity between 14 and 180. During this Pax Romana, trade flourished and the provinces were governed efficiently. In the course of the third century, however, the Roman Empire came near to collapse due to invasions, civil wars, and economic decline. Although the emperors Diocletian and Constantine brought new life to the so-called Late Empire, their efforts shored up the empire only temporarily. Beginning in 395, the empire divided into western and eastern parts, and in 476, the Roman Empire in the west came to an end.

Although the Roman Empire in the west collapsed and lived on only as an idea, Roman achievements were bequeathed to the future. The Romance languages of today (French, Italian, Spanish, Portuguese, and Romanian) are based on Latin. Western practices of impartial justice and trial by jury owe much to Roman law. As great builders, the Romans left monuments to their skills throughout Europe, some of which, such as aqueducts and roads, are still in use today. Aspects of Roman administrative practices survived in the Western world for centuries. The Romans also preserved the intellectual heritage of the Greco-Roman world of antiquity. Nevertheless, while many aspects of the Roman world would continue, the heirs of Rome created new civilizations—European, Islamic, and Byzantine—that would carry on yet another stage in the development of human society.

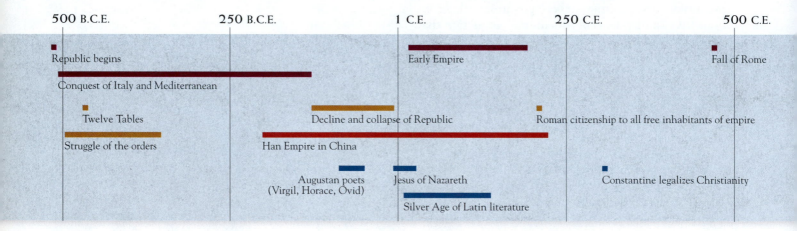

500 B.C.E.	250 B.C.E.	1 C.E.	250 C.E.	500 C.E.

Republic begins — Early Empire — Fall of Rome

Conquest of Italy and Mediterranean

Twelve Tables — Decline and collapse of Republic — Roman citizenship to all free inhabitants of empire

Struggle of the orders — Han Empire in China

Augustan poets (Virgil, Horace, Ovid) — Jesus of Nazareth — Constantine legalizes Christianity

Silver Age of Latin literature

CHAPTER NOTES

1. Florus, *Epitome of Roman History*, trans. E. S. Forster (Cambridge, Mass., 1961), IV, ii, 149–151.
2. Tacitus, *The Annals of Imperial Rome*, trans. Michael Grant (New York, 1956), p. 31.
3. *The Poems of Catullus*, trans. Charles Martin (Baltimore, 1990), p. 109.
4. Virgil, *The Aeneid*, trans. C. Day Lewis (Garden City, N.Y., 1952), p. 154.
5. Livy, *The Early History of Rome*, trans. Aubrey de Sélincourt (New York, 1960), p. 18.
6. Seneca, *Letters from a Stoic*, trans. Robin Campbell (Harmondsworth, England, 1969), let. 5.
7. Tacitus, *The Annals of Imperial Rome*, p. 147.
8. Juvenal, *The Sixteen Satires*, trans. Peter Green (New York, 1967), sat. 10, p. 207.
9. Tacitus, *A Dialogue on Oratory*, in *The Complete Works of Tacitus*, trans. Alfred Church and William Brodribb (New York, 1942), 29, p. 758.
10. Quoted in Chester Starr, *Past and Future in Ancient History* (Lanham, Md., 1987), pp. 38–39.
11. Matthew 5:17.
12. Matthew 7:12.
13. Mark 12:30–31.
14. John 18:36.
15. Colossians 3:10–11.

SUGGESTED READING

For a general account of Roman history, see J. Boardman, J. Griffin, and O. Murray, eds., *The Oxford History of the Roman World* (Oxford, 1991). A standard one-volume reference on the Roman Republic is M. Cary and H. H. Scullard, *A History of Rome down to the Reign of Constantine,* 3d ed. (New York, 1975). Good surveys of the Roman Republic include M. H. Crawford, *The Roman Republic,* 2d ed. (Cambridge, Mass., 1993); H. H. Scullard, *History of the Roman World, 753–146 B.C.,* 4th ed. (London, 1978); M. Le Glay, J.-L. Voisin, and Y. Le Bohec, *A History of Rome,* trans. A. Nevill (Oxford, 1996); and A. Kamm, *The Romans* (London, 1995). For a beautifully illustrated survey, see J. F. Drinkwater and A. Drummond, *The World of the Romans* (New York, 1993). The history of early Rome is well covered in T. J. Cornell, *The Beginnings of Rome: Italy and Rome from the Bronze Age to the Punic Wars (c. 1000–264 B.C.)* (London, 1995).

Aspects of the Roman political structure can be studied in R. E. Mitchell, *Patricians and Plebeians: The Origin of the Roman State* (Ithaca, N.Y., 1990). Changes in Rome's economic life can be examined in A. H. M. Jones, *The Roman Economy* (Oxford, 1974). On the Roman social structure, see G. Alfoeldy, *The Social History of Rome* (London, 1985).

Accounts of Rome's expansion in the Mediterranean world are provided by J.-M. David, *The Roman Conquest of Italy,* trans. A. Nevill (Oxford, 1996), and R. M. Errington, *The Dawn of Empire: Rome's Rise to World Power* (Ithaca, N.Y., 1971). Especially important works on Roman expansion and imperialism include W. V. Harris, *War and Imperialism in Republican Rome* (Oxford, 1979), and E. Badian, *Roman Imperialism in the Late Republic* (Oxford, 1968).

An excellent account of basic problems in the late Republic can be found in M. Beard and M. H. Crawford, *Rome in the Late Republic* (London, 1984). The classic work on the fall of the Republic is R. Syme, *The Roman Revolution* (Oxford, 1960). Also valuable is D. Shotter, *The Fall of the Roman Republic* (London, 1994).

Good surveys of the Early Roman Empire include P. Garnsey and R. Saller, *The Roman Empire: Economy, Society and Culture* (London, 1987); C. Wells, *The Roman Empire,* 2d ed. (London, 1992); and J. Wacher, *The Roman Empire* (London, 1987). A fundamental work on Roman government and the role of the emperor is F. Millar, *The Emperor in the Roman World* (London, 1977).

The Roman army is examined in J. B. Campbell, *The Emperor and the Roman Army* (Oxford, 1984). On the provinces and Roman foreign policy, see E. N. Luttwak, *The Grand Strategy of the Roman Empire from the First Century A.D. to the Third* (Baltimore, 1976), and B. Isaac, *The Limits of Empire: The Roman Empire in the East* (Oxford, 1990).

A good survey of Roman literature can be found in R. M. Ogilvie, *Roman Literature and Society* (Harmondsworth, England, 1980). On Roman art and architecture, see R. Ling, *Roman Painting* (New York, 1991); D. E. Kleiner, *Roman Sculpture* (New Haven, Conn., 1992); and M. Wheeler, *Roman Art and Architecture* (London, 1964). General studies of daily life in Rome include F. Dupont, *Daily Life in Ancient Rome* (Oxford, 1994), and J. P. V. D. Balsdon, *Life and Leisure in Ancient Rome* (London, 1969). On the city of Rome, see O. F. Robinson, *Ancient Rome: City Planning and Administration* (New York, 1992). On the Roman family, see S. Dixon, *The Roman Family* (Baltimore, 1992). Roman women are examined in S. B. Pomeroy, *Goddesses, Whores, Wives, and Slaves: Women in Classical Antiquity* (New York, 1975), and R. Baumann, *Women and Politics in Ancient Rome* (New York, 1995). On slavery, see K. R. Bradley, *Slavery and Society at Rome* (New York, 1994). On the gladiators, see T. Wiedemann, *Emperors and Gladiators* (New York, 1992).

For a general introduction to early Christianity, see J. Court and K. Court, *The New Testament World* (Cambridge, 1990). Useful works on early Christianity include W. A. Meeks, *The First Urban Christians* (New Haven, Conn., 1983); W. H. C. Frend, *The Rise of Christianity* (Philadelphia, 1984); and R. MacMullen, *Christianizing the Roman Empire* (New Haven, Conn., 1984). On Christian women, see D. M. Scholer, ed., *Women in Early Christianity* (New York, 1993), and R. Kraemer, *Her Share of the Blessings: Women's Religion Among the Pagans, Jews and Christians in the Graeco-Roman World* (Oxford, 1995).

The classic work on the demise of the Roman Empire is E. Gibbon, *Decline and Fall of the Roman Empire,* J. B. Bury, ed. (London, 1909–1914). Also valuable are A. Cameron, *The Later Roman Empire* (Cambridge, Mass., 1993), and R. MacMullen, *Corruption and the Decline of Rome* (New Haven, Conn., 1988). On the fourth century, see T. D. Barnes, *The New Empire of Diocletian and Constantine* (Cambridge, Mass., 1982), and M. Grant, *Constantine the Great: The Man and His Times* (New York, 1993). Studies analyzing the aristocratic circles, the barbarian invasions, and the military problem include E. A. Thompson, *Romans and Barbarians* (Madison, Wis., 1982), and A. Ferrill, *The Fall of the Roman Empire: The Military Explanation* (London, 1986).

INFOTRAC COLLEGE EDITION

For additional reading, go to InfoTrac College Edition, your online research library at
http://web1.infotrac-college.com

Enter the search terms "Rome history" using Keywords.

Enter the search terms "Roman Republic" using Keywords.

Enter the search terms "Julius and Caesar" using Keywords.

Enter the search terms "Roman Empire" using Keywords.

Enter the search terms "Roman law" using the Subject Guide.

Reflection

THE FIRST CIVILIZATIONS AND THE RISE OF EMPIRES

*I*n Part I of this book, we have focused our attention on the emergence of the first civilizations during the ancient era. As we have seen, each civilization developed somewhat independently of the others, and we have therefore treated them as distinct entities, each with its own pattern of development. But clearly, these civilizations encountered a number of similar experiences, and contacts between the civilizations and with other nearby peoples sometimes played a significant role in their development. Let us now retrace our steps and evaluate the process in a comparative perspective. How and why did these first civilizations arise? What role did cross-cultural contacts play in their development? What was the nature of the relationship between these permanent settlements and nonagricultural peoples living elsewhere in the world? Finally, what brought about the demise of these early civilizations, and what legacy did they leave for their successors in the region?

An important stimulus behind the rise of all of these early civilizations was the development of settled agriculture, which unleashed a series of changes in the organization of human communities that culminated in the rise of large ancient empires. The exact time and place that crops were first cultivated successfully is uncertain. The first farmers, who may have lived as long as ten thousand years ago, undoubtedly used simple techniques and still relied primarily on other forms of food production, such as hunting, foraging, or pastoralism. The real breakthrough came when farmers began to cultivate crops along the flood plains of river systems. The advantage was that crops grown in such areas were not as dependent on rainfall and therefore produced a more reliable harvest. An additional benefit was that the sediment carried by the river waters deposited nutrients in the soil, thus enabling the farmer to cultivate a single plot of ground for many years without moving to a new location. Thus the first truly sedentary (that is, nonmigratory) societies were born.

The spread of this river valley agriculture in various parts of Asia and Africa was the decisive factor in the rise of the first civilizations. The increase in food production in these regions led to a significant growth in population, while efforts to control the flow of water to maximize the irrigation of cultivated areas and to protect the local inhabitants from hostile forces outside the community provoked the first steps toward cooperative activities on a large scale. The need to oversee the entire process brought about the emergence of an elite that was eventually transformed into a government.

As we have seen, the first clear steps in the rise of the first civilizations took place in the fourth and third millennia B.C.E. in Mesopotamia, northern Africa, India, and China. How the first governments took shape in these areas is not certain, but anthropologists studying the evolution of human communities in various parts of the world have discovered that one common stage in the process is the emergence of what are called "big men" within a single village or a collection of villages. By means of their military prowess, dominant personalities, or political acumen, these people gradually emerge as the leaders of that community.

The appearance of these sedentary societies had a major impact on the social organizations, religious beliefs, and way of life of the peoples living within their boundaries. With the increase in population and the development of centralized authority came the emergence of cities. Within these cities, new forms of livelihood appeared to satisfy the growing need for social services and consumer goods. Some people became artisans or merchants, while others became warriors, scholars, or priests. In some cases, the physical divisions within the first cities reflected the strict hierarchical character of the society as a whole, with a royal palace surrounded by an imposing wall and separate from the remainder of the urban population.

Although the emergence of the first civilizations led to the appearance of major cities, the vast majority of the population undoubtedly consisted of peasants or slaves working on the lands of the wealthy. In general, rural peoples were less affected by the change than their urban counterparts. Most continued to live in simple mud-and-thatch huts and lacked the amenities that were increasingly available to the more affluent residents inside the city walls. Peasants in most societies still faced severe legal restrictions on their freedom of action and movement, and slavery was still commonly practiced in virtually all ancient societies.

Within these civilizations, the nature of social organization and relationships also began to change. As the concept of private property spread, people were less likely to live in large kinship groups, and the concept of the nuclear family became increasingly prevalent. Gender roles came to be differentiated, with men working in the fields or at various specialized occupations and women remaining in the home. Wives were less likely to be viewed as partners and more often as under the control of their husbands.

These new civilizations were also the scene of significant religious and cultural developments. All of them gave birth to new religions as a means of explaining the functioning of the forces of nature. The approval of gods was

RULERS AND GODS

All of the world's earliest civilizations believed that there was a close relationship between rulers and gods. In Egypt, pharaohs were considered gods whose role was to maintain the order and harmony of the universe in their own kingdom. In the words of an Egyptian hymn, "What is the king of Upper and Lower Egypt? He is a god by whose dealings one lives, the father and mother of all men, alone by himself, without an equal." In Mesopotamia, India, and China, rulers were thought to rule with divine assistance. Kings were often seen as rulers who derived their power from the gods and who were the agents or representatives of the gods. In ancient India, rulers claimed to be representatives of the gods because they were descended from Manu, the first man who had been made a king by Brahman, the chief god. Many Romans certainly believed that their success in creating an empire was a visible sign of divine favor. As the Roman statesman Cicero stated, "We have overcome all the nations of the world, because we have realized that the world is directed and governed by the gods."

Their supposed connection to the gods also caused rulers to seek divine aid in the affairs of the world. This led to the art of divination, or an organized method to discover the intentions of the gods. In Mesopotamian and Roman society, one form of divination involved the examination of the livers of sacrificed animals; features seen in the livers were interpreted to foretell events to come. The Chinese used oracle bones to receive advice from supernatural forces that were beyond the power of human beings. Questions to the gods were scratched on turtle shells or animal bones, which were then exposed to fire. Shamans then interpreted the meaning of the resulting cracks on the surface of the shells or bones as messages from supernatural forces. The Greeks divined the will of the gods by use of the oracle, a sacred shrine dedicated to a god or goddess who revealed the future in response to a question.

Underlying all of these divinatory practices was a belief in a supernatural universe, that is, a world in which divine forces were in charge and in which humans were dependent for their own well-being on those divine forces. It was not until the Scientific Revolution of the modern world that many people began to believe in a natural world that was not governed by spiritual forces.

> **VISHNU.** Brahma the Creator, Siva the Destroyer, and Vishnu the Preserver are the three chief Hindu gods of India. Vishnu is known as the Preserver because he mediates between Brahma and Siva and is thus responsible for maintaining the stability of the universe.

Fitzwilliam Museum, University of Cambridge

deemed crucial to a community's chances of success, and a professional class of priests emerged to govern relations with the divine world.

Writing was an important development in the evolution of these new civilizations. In China and Egypt, priests used writing to communicate with the gods. In Mesopotamia and the Indus River civilization, merchants relied on writing to maintain their accounts. Eventually, all of these civilizations used writing as a primary means of communication as well as of creative expression.

At first, these new civilizations had relatively little contact with peoples in the surrounding regions. But there is growing evidence that a pattern of regional trade had begun to develop in the Middle East, and probably in southern and eastern Asia as well, at a very early date. As the population increased, the volume of trade undoubtedly rose with it, and the new civilizations began to move outward to acquire new lands and access to needed resources. As they expanded, they began to encounter peoples along the periphery of their growing empires.

Not much evidence has survived to chronicle the nature of these first encounters, but it is likely that the results varied widely according to time and place. In some cases, the growing civilizations found it relatively easy to absorb isolated communities of agricultural or food-gathering peoples whom they encountered. Such was the case in southern China and in the southern part of the South Asian peninsula. But in other instances, notably among the nomadic or seminomadic peoples in central and northeastern Asia, the problem was more complicated and often resulted in bitter and extended conflict.

Contacts between these nomadic or seminomadic peoples and settled civilizations probably developed gradually over an extended period of time. Often the relationship, at least at the outset, was mutually beneficial, as each needed goods produced by the other. Nomadic peoples in Central Asia also served as an important conduit for goods and ideas between sedentary civilizations transporting goods over long distances as early as 3000 B.C.E. Overland trade throughout southwestern Asia was already well established by the third millennium B.C.E. As we have seen, the Silk Road between China and the Mediterranean became an important avenue of long-distance commerce during the first millennium B.C.E.

Eventually, for reasons that are not always clear, the relationship between the settled peoples and the nomadic peoples became increasingly characterized by conflict. Where conflict occurred, the governments of the sedentary civilizations used a variety of techniques to resolve the problem, including negotiations, conquest, or alliance with

THE USE OF METALS

Around 6000 B.C.E., people in western Asia discovered how to use metals. They soon realized the advantage in using metal rather than stone to make both tools and weapons. Metal could be shaped more exactly, allowing artisans to make more refined tools and weapons with sharp edges and more precise shapes. Copper, silver, and gold, which were commonly found in their elemental form, were the first metals to be used. These were relatively soft and could be easily pounded into different shapes. But an important step was taken when people discovered that a rock that contained metal could be heated to liquefy the metal (a process called smelting). The liquid metal could then be poured into molds of clay or stone to make precisely shaped tools and weapons.

Copper was the first metal to be used in making tools. The first known copper smelting furnace, dated to 3800 B.C.E., was found in the Sinai. At about the same time, however, artisans in Southeast Asia discovered that tin could be added to copper to make bronze. By 3000 B.C.E., artisans in West Asia were also making bronze. Bronze has a lower melting point that makes it easier to cast, but it is also a harder metal than copper and corrodes less. By 1400 B.C.E., the Chinese were making bronze decorative objects as well as battle-axes and helmets. The widespread use of bronze has led historians to speak of the period from around 3000 to 1200 B.C.E. as the Bronze Age, although this is somewhat misleading, in that many peoples continued to use stone tools and weapons even after bronze became available.

But there were limitations to the use of bronze. Tin was not as available as copper, which made bronze tools and weapons expensive. After 1200 B.C.E., bronze was increasingly replaced by iron, which was probably first used around 1500 B.C.E. in western Asia, where the Hittites made new weapons from it. Between 1500 and 600 B.C.E., ironmaking spread across Europe, North Africa, and Asia. Bronze continued to be used, but mostly for jewelry and other domestic purposes. Iron was used to make tools and weapons with sharper edges. Because iron weapons were cheaper than bronze ones, larger numbers of warriors could be armed, and wars could be fought on a larger scale.

Iron was handled differently from bronze: it was heated until it could be beaten into a desired shape. Each hammering produced increased strength for the metal. This wrought iron, as it was called, was typical of iron manufacturing in the West until the late Middle Ages. In China, however, the use of heat-resistant clay in the walls of their blast furnaces raised temperatures to 1,537 degrees Celsius, enabling artisans already in the fourth century B.C.E. to liquefy iron so that it too could be cast in a mold. Europeans would not develop such blast furnaces until the fifteenth century C.E.

© British Museum

➤ **BRONZE AXHEAD.** This axhead was made around 2000 B.C.E. by pouring liquid metal into an ax-shaped mold of clay or stone. Artisans would then polish the surface of the ax to produce a sharp cutting edge.

	6000 B.C.E.	5000 B.C.E.	4000 B.C.E.	3000 B.C.E.	2000 B.C.E.
Middle East	Agriculture and Neolithic towns			Sumerian civilization	
India	First agricultural settlements			Harappan civilization	
China		First settled agriculture			
Egypt and the Mediterranean	Agriculture in the Nile Valley			Flowering of Egyptian civilization	

other pastoral peoples to isolate their primary tormentors. We have seen all of these techniques at work in China, where the Qin and the Han tried a combination of the carrot and the stick to pacify the frontier and bring these unruly peoples under control. The Romans did not hesitate to ally with one Germanic tribe to ward off another.

As it turned out, few of these techniques had any lasting effect. The relationship along the frontier was inherently unstable and in the end was disastrous for the settled empires, all of whom were eventually destroyed or seriously weakened as the result of invasion from beyond the frontier. The first to experience such a fate was the Harappan civilization in the Indus River valley, which may have been brought down at least in part as a result of the intrusion by Indo-European Aryan peoples along the northern frontier. Several hundred years later, the peoples of Mesopotamia fell at the hands of the Assyrians, who were in turn conquered by the Indo-European-speaking Persians. The empire of the pharaohs was conquered by the Hyksos, and the Roman Empire was brought to its knees as the result of constant pressure from the Germanic tribes to the north. Although the empire of the Han was not overthrown by the Xiongnu, pressure along the northern frontier contributed to the weakening of the dynasty, and after its collapse in the early third century B.C.E., the entire northern part of the country was overrun by peoples from beyond the Great Wall.

At the same time, it is also increasingly evident that these early civilizations were brought to their knees not only by nomadic invasions but also by their own weaknesses, which made them increasingly vulnerable to attacks along the frontier. In the Roman Empire, bloated bureaucracies as well as excessive taxation to support them, an inability to achieve a workable political system, the decline of Roman military virtues and a reliance on noncitizen mercenaries, and population decline in part caused by plague all played a role in undermining Rome's ability to protect itself. In China, strains within Han society, more than depredations along the frontier, caused the collapse of Han Empire.

Another possible factor in the decline and collapse of the first civilizations was the role of the environment. Much evidence suggests that ecological changes caused severe difficulties for peoples in the ancient world. Floods or drought may have brought an end to the Harappan empire, and the infestation of salt water may have leached the nutrients from the soils of the Fertile Crescent. Imperial Rome may have suffered food shortages as a result of the desiccation of the wheat fields of northern Africa.

The fall of the ancient empires, of course, did not mark the end of civilization. Although the immediate consequences of the fall of Rome and the Han dynasty were a precipitous drop in world trade and a general decline of prosperity throughout the known world, new societies eventually rose on the ashes of the ancient empires. Although many were different in key respects from those they replaced, they still carried the legacy of their predecessors. In the meantime, the forces that had been unleashed in the civilizations of antiquity sent out strands of influence that were laying the basis for new societies elsewhere in the world: south of the Sahara in western and eastern Africa, where new societies were beginning to take shape; beyond the Alps in central Europe, where the Germanic peoples were in the process of forming a new society; in southeastern Asia, where the influence of India and China was beginning to help shape new societies among the trading and agricultural societies in the region; and across the Sea of Japan in the Japanese islands, where native rulers would import Chinese ideas to form a new civilization uniquely their own. In the meantime, new civilizations were on the verge of creation in the New World, across the oceans in the continents of North and South America.

Part II

NEW PATTERNS OF CIVILIZATION

By the beginning of the first millennium C.E., the great states of the ancient world were in decline; some were even at the point of collapse. On the ruins of these ancient empires, new patterns of civilization began to take shape between 400 and 1400 C.E. In some cases, these new societies were built on the political and cultural foundations of their predecessors. The Tang dynasty in China and the Guptas in India both looked back to the ancient period to provide an ideological model for their own time. The Byzantine Empire carried on parts of the classical Greek tradition while also adopting the powerful creed of Christianity from the Roman Empire. In other cases, new states incorporated some elements of the former classical civilizations while embarking on markedly different directions, as in the new European civilization of the Middle Ages and the Arabic states in the Middle East.

In the meantime, complex societies were also beginning to appear in a number of other parts of the world—in Japan, in Southeast Asia, in sub-Saharan Africa, and in the Americas. Except for the Americas, which were developing in isolation, these civilizations were influenced to a greater or lesser degree by older or more powerful empires in the region and all were increasingly linked by commercial and cultural contacts into the first "global civilization." At the same time, each was able to combine borrowed ideas with indigenous characteristics.

Like their classical predecessors, most of these new states obtained much of their wealth from agriculture. India, China, and medieval Europe were all predominantly agricultural societies. But what is most striking about the period is the growing importance of trade as a factor in national and global development. It was during the first millennium C.E. that the great trade routes of the

Spring Festival on the River; Detail, The Metropolitan Museum of Art, Fletcher Fund, 1947, The A.W. Bahr Collection, (47.18.1)

traditional world—the Silk Road from China to the Middle East and then on to the Mediterranean, the caravan trade route across the Sahara, and the commercial network that stretched across the Indian Ocean—all reached their maturity.

The expanding of regional and global trade also spread ideas. It was commerce that brought Buddhism to China and Southeast Asia and Islam to sub-Saharan Africa and the Indonesian archipelago. At first, the impact of these new ways of thinking was felt primarily in the cities, but eventually it began to spread to the countryside. Kings and princes became converts to the new faiths and provided funds and other forms of patronage in their support.

The spread of religious and cultural ideas sometimes led to conflict. The popularity of Buddhism led eventually to its suppression in China. Tensions between the Islamic and Christian worlds were particularly strong and culminated in the Crusades and the Christian reconquest of Spain and Portugal. But often the assimilation of new religions and cultural ideas took place peacefully, as with the spread of Islam into Africa. Christianity, aided by the zeal of its missionary monks, was an active agent in converting new peoples in central and eastern Europe and transforming their cultures.

Rollout photograph © Justin Kerr, 1997

Chapter 6

THE NEW WORLD

CHAPTER OUTLINE
- THE FIRST AMERICANS
- EARLY CIVILIZATIONS IN CENTRAL AMERICA
- THE FIRST CIVILIZATIONS IN SOUTH AMERICA
- STATELESS SOCIETIES IN THE NEW WORLD
- CONCLUSION

FOCUS QUESTIONS
- Who were the first Americans, and when and how did they arrive?
- What were the main characteristics of the civilizations of the Maya, the Aztecs, and the Inca?
- What role did religion play in the civilizations of the New World?
- What were the main characteristics of the stateless societies in the Americas, and how did they differ from the civilizations that arose in Central America and the Andes?
- In what ways were the civilizations of the New World similar to the early civilizations of the Old World, and in what ways were they different?

*I*n August 1519, five hundred Spanish soldiers of fortune left their anchorage near the modern city of Veracruz and began the long trek from the coast across the dusty plateau of Mexico to the capital of the Aztecs. At their head was Hernán Cortés, a Spanish conquistador who had just burned the ship on which he arrived to ensure that his followers would not launch a mutiny and sail back to Europe. In Tenochtitlán, the Aztec capital located at what is now Mexico City, Emperor Moctezuma received the news of the foreigners' presence and awaited their arrival with anticipation. According to Aztec legend, one of their ancestors, the godlike Quetzalcoatl, had left the area hundreds of years earlier, vowing to return one day to reclaim his heritage. Could this stranger with his band of men be Quetzalcoatl or his representative? When Cortés and his forces, now accompanied by a crowd of people they had encountered en route, reached the vicinity of Moctezuma's capital, the two men met face-to-face. With this encounter, the last barrier between the Old World and the previously unknown civilizations in the Western Hemisphere had been bridged, and a new era dawned.

The Aztecs were only the latest in a series of sophisticated societies that had sprung up at various locations in North and South America since human beings first crossed the Bering Strait several millennia earlier. Most of these early peoples, today often referred to as Amerindians, lived by hunting and fishing or by food gathering. But by the second millennium B.C.E., the first organized societies, based on the cultivation of agriculture, began to take root in Central and South America. One key area of development was on the plateau of central Mexico. Another was in the lowland regions along the Gulf of Mexico and extending into modern Guatemala. A third was in the central Andes Mountains, adjacent to the Pacific coast of South America. Others were just beginning to emerge in the river valleys and great plains of North America.

For the next two thousand years, these societies developed in isolation from their counterparts elsewhere in the world. This lack of contact with other human beings deprived them of access to technological and cultural developments taking place in Africa, Asia, and Europe. They did not know of the wheel, for example, and their written languages were rudimentary compared to equivalents in complex civilizations in other parts of the globe. But in other respects, their cultural achievements were the equal of those realized elsewhere. When the first European explorers arrived in the New World at the turn of the sixteenth century, they described much that they observed in glowing terms.

Unfortunately, one technological development that the peoples of America lacked was a knowledge of firearms. In a few short years, tiny bands of armed Spanish conquistadors were able to demolish the magnificent civilizations of the Aztecs, the Maya, and the Inca. Still, enough archaeological evidence remains to enable us to appreciate their impressive achievements. ●

THE FIRST AMERICANS

When the first human beings arrived in the New World has long been a matter of dispute. In the centuries following the voyages of Christopher Columbus, speculation centered on the possibility that the first settlers to reach the American continents had crossed the Atlantic Ocean. Were they the lost tribes of Israel? Were they Phoenician seafarers from Carthage? Were they refugees from the legendary lost continent of Atlantis? In all cases, the assumption was that they were relatively recent arrivals.

By the mid-nineteenth century, under the influence of the new Darwinian concept of evolution, a new theory developed. It proposed that the peopling of America had taken place much earlier as a result of the migration of small communities across the Bering Strait. Recent evidence, including numerous physical similarities between some early Americans and contemporary peoples living in northeastern Asia, has confirmed this hypothesis. The debate on when the migrations began continues, however. Archaeologist Louis Leakey, one of the pioneers in the search for the origins of humankind in Africa, suggested that the first hominids may have arrived in America as long as 100,000 years ago. Others estimate that the first Americans were members of *Homo sapiens sapiens* who crossed from Asia by foot between 10,000 and 15,000 years ago in pursuit of herds of bison and caribou that moved into the area in search of grazing land at the end of the last ice age. A recently discovered site at Cactus Hill, in central Virginia, shows signs of human habitation as early as 15,000 years ago. Genetic evidence now suggests the possibility of an earlier date, perhaps as early as 29,000 years ago. And other recent discoveries indicate that some early settlers may have originally come from Africa rather than from Asia. The question has not yet been definitively answered.

Nevertheless, it is now generally accepted that human beings were living in the New World at least 15,000 years ago. They gradually spread throughout the North American continent and had penetrated almost to the southern tip of South America by about 10,000 B.C.E. These first Americans were hunters and food gatherers who lived in small nomadic communities close to the source of their food supply. Although it is not known when agriculture was first practiced, beans and squash seeds have been found at sites that date back at least 8,000 years. The cultivation of maize (corn), and perhaps other crops as well, appears to have been under way as early as 5000 B.C.E. in the Tehuacán valley in central Mexico. A similar process may have been under way in the lowland regions near the modern city of Veracruz and in the Yucatán peninsula farther to the east. There, in the region that archaeologists call Mesoamerica, one of the first civilizations in the New World began to appear.

EARLY CIVILIZATIONS IN CENTRAL AMERICA

The first signs of civilization in Mesoamerica appeared in the first millennium B.C.E., with the emergence of what is called Olmec culture in the hot and swampy lowlands along the coast of the Gulf of Mexico south of Veracruz (see Map 6.1). Olmec civilization was characterized by intensive agriculture along the muddy riverbanks in the area and by the carving of stone ornaments, tools, and monuments at sites such as San Lorenzo and La Venta. The site at La Venta includes a ceremonial precinct with a 30-foot-high earthen pyramid, the largest of its date in all Mesoamerica. The Olmec peoples organized a widespread trading network, carried on religious rituals, and devised an as yet undeciphered system of hieroglyphics that is similar in some respects to later Mayan writing (see "Mayan Hieroglyphs" later in this chapter) and may be the ancestor of the first true writing systems in the New World.

Olmec society apparently consisted of several classes, including a class of skilled artisans who produced a series of massive stone heads, some of which are more than 10 feet high. The Olmec peoples supported themselves primarily by cultivating crops, such as corn and beans, but also engaged in fishing and hunting. The Olmec apparently played a ceremonial game on a stone ball court, a ritual that would later be widely practiced throughout the region (see "The Mysterious Maya" later in this chapter).

Eventually, Olmec civilization began to decline and apparently collapsed around the fourth century B.C.E. During its heyday, however, it extended from Mexico City to El Salvador and perhaps to the shores of the Pacific Ocean.

In the meantime, parallel developments were occurring at Monte Albán, on a hillside overlooking the modern city of Oaxaca, in central Mexico. Around the middle of the first millennium B.C.E., the Zapotec peoples created an extensive civilization that flourished for several hundred years in the highlands. Like the Olmec sites, Monte Albán contains a number of temples and pyramids, but they are located in much more awesome surroundings on a massive stone terrace atop a 1,200-foot-high mountain overlooking the Oaxaca valley. The majority of the population, estimated at about twenty thousand, dwelled on terraces cut into the sides of the mountain.

Teotihuacán: America's First Metropolis

The first major metropolis in Mesoamerica was the city of Teotihuacán, capital of an early kingdom about 30 miles northeast of Mexico City that arose around the third century B.C.E. and flourished for nearly a millennium until it collapsed under mysterious circumstances about 800 C.E. Along the main thoroughfare were temples and palaces, all dominated by the massive Pyramid of the Sun, under which archaeologists have discovered the remains of sacrificial victims, probably put to death during the dedication of the structure. In the vicinity are the remains of a large market where goods from distant regions as well as agricultural produce grown by farmers in the vicinity were exchanged. The products traded included cacao, rubber, feathers, and various types of vegetables and meat. Pulque, a liquor extracted

THE PYRAMID OF THE SUN, TEOTIHUACÁN.   The first major metropolis in Central America was Teotihuacán, which was inhabited by as many as 150,000 people during its zenith sometime after 400 C.E. Covering an area of at least 8 square miles, it rivaled its contemporary, the city of Rome, in both size and sophistication. The ceremonial center of Teotihuacán, which contained more than five thousand structures, was laid out along a north-south and east-west axis; it was dominated by the Pyramid of the Sun, rising in four tiers to a height of over 200 feet.

© Richard A. Cooke III

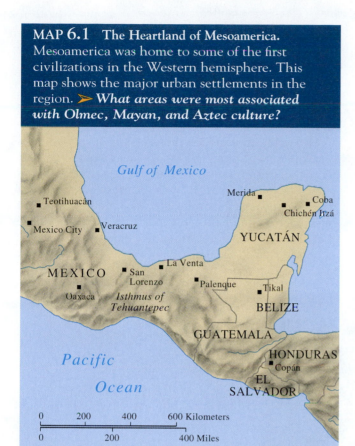

MAP 6.1 **The Heartland of Mesoamerica.**
Mesoamerica was home to some of the first
civilizations in the Western hemisphere. This
map shows the major urban settlements in the
region. ➤ *What areas were most associated
with Olmec, Mayan, and Aztec culture?*

problem was later compounded when peoples from surrounding areas, attracted by the rich farmlands, migrated
into the Valley of Mexico and began to compete for territory with small city-states already established there. As
the local population expanded, farmers began to engage
in more intensive agriculture. They drained the lakes to
build *chinampas*, swampy islands crisscrossed by canals that
provided water for their crops and easy transportation
to local markets for their excess produce.

The Mysterious Maya

Far to the east of the Valley of Mexico, another major civilization had taken form in the Yucatán peninsula. This was
the civilization of the Maya, which was older and just as
sophisticated as the society at Teotihuacán.

Like the Aztecs and the inhabitants of Teotihuacán, the
Maya trace their origins to the parent Olmec civilization
in the lowlands along the Gulf of Mexico. It is not known
when human beings first inhabited the Yucatán peninsula,
but peoples contemporaneous with the Olmecs were
already cultivating such crops as corn, yams, and manioc
in the area during the first millennium B.C.E. As the population increased, an early civilization began to emerge
along the Pacific coast directly to the south of the peninsula and in the highlands of modern Guatemala. Contacts were already established with the Olmecs to the west.

Since the area was a source for cacao trees and obsidian, the inhabitants soon developed relations with other
early civilizations in the region. Cacao trees were the
source of chocolate, which was used as a beverage by the
upper classes, while cocoa beans, the fruit of the cacao tree,
were used as currency in markets throughout the region.

As the population in the area increased, the inhabitants
began to migrate into the central Yucatán peninsula to the
north. The overcrowding forced farmers in the lowland
areas to shift from slash-and-burn cultivation to swamp
agriculture of the type practiced in the lake region of the
Valley of Mexico. By the middle of the first millennium
C.E., the entire area was honeycombed with a patchwork
of small city-states competing for land and resources. The
most important city-states were probably Tikal and Copán,
but it is doubtful that any one was sufficiently powerful
to dominate the area. The largest urban centers such as
Tikal may have had 100,000 inhabitants at their height.

The power of the rulers of the city-states was impressive.
One of the monarchs at Copán—known to scholars as "18
Rabbit" from the hieroglyphs composing his name—ordered
the construction of a grand palace requiring more than
30,000 person-days of labor. Around the ruler was a class of
aristocrats whose wealth was probably based on the ownership of land farmed by their poorer relatives. Eventually,
many of the aristocrats became priests or scribes at the royal
court or adopted honored professions as sculptors or
painters. As the society's wealth grew, so did the role of artisans and traders, who began to form a small middle class.

from the agave plant, was used in religious ceremonies. An
obsidian mine nearby may explain the location of the city;
obsidian is a volcanic glass that was prized in Mesoamerica
for use in tools, mirrors, and the blades of sacrificial knives.

Most of the city consisted of one-story stucco apartment
compounds; some were as large as 35,000 square feet,
sufficient to house more than a hundred people. Each
apartment was divided into several rooms, and the compounds were covered by flat roofs made of wooden beams,
poles, and stucco. The compounds were separated by wide
streets laid out on a rectangular grid and were entered
through narrow alleys.

Living in the fertile Valley of Mexico, an upland plateau
surrounded by magnificent snowcapped mountains, the
inhabitants of Teotihuacán probably obtained the bulk of
their wealth from agriculture. At that time, the valley floor
was filled with swampy lakes containing the water runoff
from the surrounding mountains. The combination of fertile soil and adequate water combined to make the valley one of the richest farming areas in Mesoamerica.

Sometime during the eighth century, for unknown reasons, the wealth and power of the city began to decline,
and eventually its ruling class departed, with the priests
carrying stone images of local deities on their backs. The
next two centuries were a time of troubles throughout the
region as principalities fought over limited farmland. The

The majority of the population on the peninsula, however (estimated at roughly three million at the height of Mayan power), were farmers. They lived on their *chinampa* plots or on terraced hills in the highlands. Houses were built of adobe and thatch and probably resembled the houses of the majority of the population in the area today. There was a fairly clear-cut division of labor along gender lines. The men were responsible for fighting and hunting, the women for homemaking and the preparation of cornmeal, the staple food of much of the population.

Some noblewomen seem to have played important roles in both political and religious life. In the seventh century C.E., for example, Pacal became king of Palenque, one of the most powerful of the Mayan city-states,

through the royal line of his mother and grandmother, thereby breaking the patrilineal descent twice. His mother ruled Palenque for three years and was the power behind the throne for her son's first twenty-five years of rule. Pacal legitimized his kingship by transforming his mother into a divine representation of the "first mother" goddess.

Mayan religion was polytheistic. Although the names were different, Mayan gods shared many of the characteristics of deities of nearby cultures. The supreme god was named Itzamna (Lizard House). Deities were ranked in order of importance, and some, like the jaguar god of night, were evil rather than good. Some scholars believe that many of the nature deities may have been viewed as manifestations of one supreme godhead (see the box

⇛ **A MAYAN BLOODLETTING CEREMONY.** The Mayan elite drew blood at various ritual ceremonies. Here we see Lady Xok, the wife of a king of Yaxchilian, passing a rope pierced with thorns along her tongue in a bloodletting ritual. Above her, the king holds a flaming torch. This vibrant scene from an eighth-century C.E. palace lintel demonstrates the excellence of Mayan stone sculpture as well as the sophisticated weaving techniques shown in the queen's elegant gown.

THE CREATION OF THE WORLD: A MAYAN VIEW

Popul Vuh, a sacred work of the ancient Maya, is an account of Mayan history and religious beliefs. No written version in the original Mayan script is extant, but shortly after the Spanish conquest, it was written down in Quiche (the spoken language of the Maya), using the Latin script, apparently from memory. This version was later translated into Spanish. The following excerpt from the opening lines of Popul Vuh recounts the Mayan myth of the creation.

POPUL VUH: THE SACRED BOOK OF THE MAYA

This is the account of how all was in suspense, all calm, in silence; all motionless, still, and the expanse of the sky was empty.

This is the first account, the first narrative. There was neither man, nor animal, birds, fishes, crabs, trees, stones, caves, ravines, grasses, nor forests; there was only the sky.

The surface of the earth had not appeared. There was only the calm sea and the great expanse of the sky.

There was nothing brought together, nothing which could make a noise, nor anything which might move, or tremble, or could make noise in the sky.

There was nothing standing; only the calm water, the placid sea, alone and tranquil. Nothing existed.

There was only immobility and silence in the darkness, in the night. Only the Creator, the Maker, Tepeu, Gucumatz, the Forefathers, were in the water surrounded with light. They were hidden under green and blue feathers, and were therefore called Gucumatz. By nature they were great sages and great thinkers. In this manner the sky existed and also the Heart of Heaven, which is the name of God and thus He is called.

Then came the word. Tepeu and Gucumatz came together in the darkness, in the night, and Tepeu and Gucumatz talked together. They talked then, discussing and deliberating; they agreed, they united their words and their thoughts.

Then while they meditated, it became clear to them that when dawn would break, man must appear. Then they planned the creation, and the growth of the trees and the thickets and the birth of life and the creation of man. Thus it was arranged in the darkness and in the night by the Heart of Heaven who is called Huracan.

The first is called Caculha Huracan. The second is Chipi-Caculha. The third is Raxa-Caculha. And these three are the Heart of Heaven.

So it was that they made perfect the work, when they did it after thinking and meditating upon it.

---

above). As at Teotihuacán, human sacrifice (normally by decapitation) was practiced to propitiate the heavenly forces. Scenes from paintings and rock carvings depict a society preoccupied with war and the seizure of captives for sacrifice.

Physically, the Mayan cities were built around a ceremonial core dominated by a central pyramid surmounted by a shrine to the gods. Nearby were other temples, palaces, and a sacred ball court. Like many of their modern counterparts, Mayan cities suffered from urban sprawl, with separate suburbs for the poor and the middle class, and even strip malls stretched along transportation routes, where merchants hawked their wares to pedestrians passing by.

The ball court was a rectangular space surrounded by vertical walls with metal rings through which the contestants attempted to drive a hard rubber ball. Although the rules of the game are only imperfectly understood, it apparently had religious significance, and the vanquished players were sacrificed in ceremonies held after the close of the game. Most of the players were men, although there may have been some women's teams. Similar courts have been found at sites throughout Central and South America, with the ear- liest, located near Veracruz, dating back to around 1500 B.C.E.

MAYAN HIEROGLYPHS

In some ways, Mayan culture was more advanced than the later Aztec civilization in the Valley of Mexico. The Mayan writing system was much more sophisticated than the relatively primitive system used by the Aztecs (see the box on p. 162). Unfortunately, when the Spanish conquered the remains of Mayan civilization, they made no attempt to decipher the language with the assistance of natives familiar with the script. The Spanish bishop Diego de Landa, otherwise an astute and sympathetic observer of Mayan culture, remarked: "We found a large number of books in these characters and, as they contained nothing in which there were not to be seen superstition and lies of the devil, we burned them all, which they regretted to an amazing degree, and which caused them much affliction."[1]

The Mayan hieroglyphs remained undeciphered until scholars discovered that many passages contained symbols that recorded dates in the Mayan calendar. This calendar, which measures time back to a particular date in

A SAMPLE OF MAYAN WRITING

*T*he Maya were the only Mesoamerican people to devise a complete written language. Like the Sumerian and Egyptian scripts, the Mayan system was composed of a mixture of ideographs and phonetic symbols, which were written in double columns to be read from left to right and top to bottom. The language was rudimentary in many ways. It had few adjectives or adverbs, and the numbering system used only three symbols: a shell for zero, a dot for one, and a bar for five.

During the classical era from 300 to 900 C.E., the Maya used the script to record dynastic statistics with deliberate precision, listing the date of the ruler's birth, his accession to power, and his marriage and death while highlighting victories in battle, the capture of prisoners, and ritual ceremonies. The symbols were carved on stone panels, stelae, and funerary urns or were painted with a brush on folding screen books made of bark paper; only four of these books from the late period remain extant today.

A sample of Mayan hieroglyphs is shown below.

"birth of . . ."

"death of . . ."

warfare

bloodletting rite

"accession of . . ."

chucah "he captured . . ."   "captor of . . ."

August 3114 B.C.E., required a sophisticated understanding of astronomical events and mathematics to compile. Starting with these known symbols as a foundation, modern scholars have gradually deciphered the script. Like the scripts of the Sumerians and ancient Egyptians, the Mayan hieroglyphs were both ideographic and phonetic and were becoming more phonetic as time passed.

One of the most important repositories of Mayan hieroglyphs is at Palenque, an archaeological site deep in the jungles in the neck of the Mexican peninsula, considerably to the west of the Yucatán. In a chamber located under the Temple of Inscriptions, archaeologists discovered a royal tomb and a massive limestone slab covered with hieroglyphs. By deciphering the message on the slab, archaeologists for the first time identified a historical figure in Mayan history. He was the ruler named Pacal, known from his glyph as "The Shield"; Pacal ordered the construction of the Temple of Inscriptions in the mid-seventh century, and it was his body that was buried in the tomb at the foot of the staircase leading down into the crypt.

As befits their intense interest in the passage of time, the Maya also had a sophisticated knowledge of astronomy and kept voluminous records of the movements of the heavenly bodies. There were practical reasons for their concern. The arrival of the planet Venus in the evening sky, for example, was a traditional time to prepare for war. The Temple of Inscriptions was oriented so that an observer could stand on the platform at the spring equinox and watch the setting of the sun.

THE MYSTERY OF MAYAN DECLINE

Sometime in the eighth or ninth century, the classical Mayan civilization in the central Yucatán peninsula began to decline. At Copán, for example, it ended abruptly in 822 C.E., when work on various stone sculptures ordered by the ruler suddenly ceased. The end of Palenque, a rival state to the west, soon followed. Whether the decline was caused by overuse of the land, invasion, internal revolt, or a natural disaster such as a volcanic eruption is a question that has puzzled archaeologists for decades. Recent evidence supports the theory that overcultivation of the land due to a growing population gradually reduced crop yields. Another theory is that a long drought, which lasted for almost two centuries in the ninth and tenth centuries C.E., may have played a major role. We do know that the period was characterized by an increase in internecine war among the states and the rise of powerful nobles.

© Lee Boltin Picture Library

A BALL COURT.   Throughout Mesoamerica, a dangerous game was played on ball courts such as this one. A large ball of solid rubber was propelled from the hip at such tremendous speed that players had to wear extensive padding. More than an athletic contest, the game had religious significance. The court is thought to have represented the cosmos and the ball the sun, and the losers were sacrificed to the gods in postgame ceremonies.

Whatever the case, cities like Tikal and Palenque were abandoned to the jungles, though newer urban centers in the northern part of the peninsula, like Uxmal and Chichén Itzá, survived and continued to prosper. According to local history, this latter area was taken over by peoples known as the Toltecs, led by a man known as Kukulcan ("feathered serpent"), who migrated to the peninsula from Tula in central Mexico sometime in the tenth century. Some scholars believe this flight was asso-ciated with the legend of the departure of Quetzalcoatl, the feathered serpent who promised that he would someday return to reclaim his homeland.

The Toltecs apparently controlled the upper peninsula from their capital at Chichén Itzá for several centuries, and then they too declined. When the Spaniards arrived, the area was divided into a number of small principalities, and the cities such as Uxmal and Chichén Itzá had been abandoned.

© Otis Imboden/National Geographic Image Collection

THE MAYAN PALACE AT PALENQUE. King Pacal and his eldest son helped create the golden age of Mayan civilization with their innovative architecture and the detailed carvings of glyphs on the many limestone monuments at Palenque. Shown here is the royal palace, which is located adjacent to the Temple of Inscriptions. Pacal was apparently obsessed with the need to legitimize his royal status, since his claim to the throne descended not from his father's line but from that of his mother and grandmother. Some of the temple's glyphs portray the former as the first "mother goddess" of Palenque and thus confirm his own divine provenance as her offspring.

The Aztecs

Among the groups moving into the Valley of Mexico after the fall of Teotihuacán were the Mexica (pronounced "Mesheeca"). No one knows their origins, although folk legend held that their original homeland was an island in a lake called Aztlán. From that legendary homeland comes the name *Aztec*, by which they are known to the modern world. Sometime during the early twelfth century, the Aztecs left their original habitat and, carrying an image of their patron deity, Huitzilopochtli, began a lengthy migration that climaxed with their arrival in the Valley of Mexico sometime late in the century.

Less sophisticated than many of their neighbors, the Aztecs were at first forced to seek alliances with stronger city-states. They were excellent warriors, however, and (like Sparta in ancient Greece and the state of Qin in Zhou dynasty China) had become the leading city-state in the lake region by the early fifteenth century. Establishing their capital at Tenochtitlán, on an island in the middle of Lake Texcoco, they set out to bring the entire region under their domination (see Map 6.2).

For the remainder of the fifteenth century, the Aztecs consolidated their control over much of what is modern Mexico, from the Atlantic to the Pacific Ocean and as far south as the Guatemalan border. The new kingdom was not a centralized state but a collection of semiautonomous territories. To provide a unifying focus for the kingdom, the Aztecs promoted their patron god, Huitzilopochtli, as the guiding deity of the entire population, which now numbered several million.

POLITICS AND SOCIETY

Like all great empires in ancient times, the Aztec state was authoritarian. Power was vested in the monarch, whose authority had both a divine and a secular character. The Aztec ruler claimed descent from the gods and served as an intermediary between the material and the metaphysical worlds. Unlike many of his counterparts in the Old World, however, the monarch did not obtain his position by a rigid law of succession. On the death of the ruler, his successor was selected from within the royal family by a small group of senior officials, who were also members of the family and were therefore eligible for the position. Once placed on the throne, the Aztec ruler was advised by a small council of lords, headed by a prime minister who served as the chief executive of the government, and a bureaucracy. Beyond the capital, the power of the central government was limited. Rulers of territories subject to the Aztecs were allowed considerable autonomy in return for paying tribute, in the form of goods or captives, to the central government. The most important government officials in the provinces were the tax collectors, who collected the tribute. They used the threat of military action against those who failed to carry out their tribute obligations and therefore, understandably, were not popular with the taxpayers. According to Bernal Díaz, a Spaniard who accompanied Hernán Cortés on his expedition to Tenochtitlán in 1519:

> All these towns complained about Montezuma [Moctezuma, the Aztec ruler at the time of the Cortés expedition] and his tax collectors, speaking in private so that the Mexican ambassadors should not hear them, however. They said these officials robbed them of all they possessed, and that if their wives and daughters were pretty they would violate them in front of their fathers and husbands and carry them away. They also said that the Mexicans [that is, the representatives from the capital] made the men work like slaves, compelling them to carry pine trunks and stone and firewood and maize overland and in canoes, and to perform other tasks, such as planting maize fields, and that they took away the people's lands as well for the service of their idols.[2]

Positions in the government bureaucracy were the exclusive privilege of the hereditary nobility, all of whom traced their lineage to the founding family of the Aztec clan. Male children in noble families were sent to temple schools, where they were exposed to a harsh regimen of manual labor, military training, and memorization of information about Aztec society and religion. On reaching adulthood, they would select a career in the military service, the government bureaucracy, or the priesthood. As a reward for their services, senior officials received large estates from the government, and they alone had the right to hire communal labor.

The remainder of the population consisted of commoners, indentured workers, and slaves. Most indentured workers were landless laborers who contracted to work on the nobles' estates, while slaves served in the households of the wealthy. Slavery was not an inherited status, and the children of slaves were considered free citizens. Commoners might sell themselves into slavery when in debt and then later purchase their freedom.

The vast majority of the population were commoners. All commoners were members of large kinship groups called *calpullis*. Each *calpulli*, often consisting of as many as a thousand members, was headed by an elected chief, who ran its day-to-day affairs and served as an intermediary with the central government. Each *calpulli* was responsible for providing taxes (usually in the form of goods) and conscript labor to the state.

Each *calpulli* maintained its own temples and schools and administered the land held by the community. Farmland within the *calpulli* was held in common and could not be sold, although it could be inherited within the family. In the cities, each *calpulli* occupied a separate neighborhood, where its members often performed a particular function, such as metalworking, stonecutting, weaving, carpentry, or commerce. Apparently, a large proportion

MAP **6.2** **The Valley of Mexico Under Aztec Rule.** The Aztecs were one of the most advanced peoples in pre-Columbian Central America. Their capital at Tlaltelolco was located at the site of modern-day Mexico City. Of the five lakes shown here, only Lake Texcoco remains today. ➤ *What was the importance of Teotihucán?*

of the population engaged in some form of trade, at least in the densely populated Valley of Mexico, where an estimated half of the people lived in an urban environment. Many farmers brought their goods to the markets via the canals and sold them directly to retailers (see the box on p. 166).

The *calpulli* compounds themselves were divided into smaller family units. Individual families lived in small flat-roofed dwellings containing one or two rooms. Each house was separate from its neighbors and had direct access to the surrounding streets and canals. The houses of farmers living on the *chinampas* were set on raised dirt platforms built above the surrounding fields to prevent flooding.

Gender roles within the family were rigidly stratified. Male children were trained for war and were expected to

MARKETS AND MERCHANDISE IN AZTEC MEXICO

One of our most valuable descriptions of Aztec civilization is The Conquest of New Spain, *written by Bernal Díaz, a Spaniard who accompanied Hernán Cortés on his expedition to Mexico in 1519. In the following passage, Díaz describes the great market at Tenochtitlán.*

BERNAL DÍAZ, THE CONQUEST OF NEW SPAIN

Let us begin with the dealers in gold, silver, and precious stones, feathers, cloaks, and embroidered goods, and male and female slaves who are also sold there. They bring as many slaves to be sold in that market as the Portuguese bring Negroes from Guinea. Some are brought there attached to long poles by means of collars round their necks to prevent them from escaping, but others are left loose. Next there were those who sold coarser cloth, and cotton goods and fabrics made of twisted thread, and there were chocolate merchants with their chocolate. In this way you could see every kind of merchandise to be found anywhere in New Spain, laid out in the same way as goods are laid out in my own district of Medina del Campo, a center for fairs, where each line of stalls has its own particular sort. So it was in this great market. There were those who sold sisal cloth and ropes and the sandals they wear on their feet, which are made from the same plant. All these were kept in one part of the market, in the place assigned to them, and in another part were skins of tigers and lions, otters, jackals, and deer, badgers, mountain cats, and other wild animals, some tanned and some untanned, and other classes of merchandise.

There were sellers of kidney beans and sage and other vegetables and herbs in another place, and in yet another they were selling fowls, and birds with great dewlaps, also rabbits, hares, deer, young ducks, little dogs, and other such creatures. Then there were the fruiterers; and the women who sold cooked food, flour and honey cake, and tripe, had their part of the market. Then came pottery of all kinds, from big water jars to little jugs, displayed in its own place, also honey, honey paste, and other sweets like nougat. Elsewhere they sold timber too, boards, cradles, beams, blocks, and benches, all in a quarter of their own.

Then there were the sellers of pitch pine for torches, and other things of that kind, and I must also mention, with all apologies, that they sold many canoe loads of human excrement, which they kept in the creeks near the market. This was for the manufacture of salt and the curing of skins, which they say cannot be done without it. I know that many gentlemen will laugh at this, but I assure them it is true. I may add that on all the roads they have shelters made of reeds or straw or grass so that they can retire when they wish to do so, and purge their bowels unseen by passersby, and also in order that their excrement shall not be lost.

serve in the army on reaching adulthood. Women were expected to work in the home, weave textiles, and raise children, although like their brothers they were permitted to enter the priesthood (see the box on p. 167). According to Bernal Díaz, a female deity presided over the rites of marriage. As in most traditional societies, chastity and obedience were desirable female characteristics. Although women in Aztec society enjoyed more legal rights than women in some traditional Old World civilizations, they were still not equal to men. Women were permitted to own and inherit property and to enter into contracts. Marriage was usually monogamous, although noble families sometimes practiced polygyny (the state or practice of having more than one wife at a time). Wedding partners were normally selected from within the lineage group but not the immediate family. As in most societies at the time, parents usually selected their child's spouse, often for purposes of political or social advancement.

Classes in Aztec society were rigidly stratified. Commoners were not permitted to enter the nobility, although some occasionally rose to senior positions in the army or the priesthood as the result of exemplary service. As in medieval Europe, such occupations often provided a route of upward mobility for ambitious commoners. A woman of noble standing would sometimes marry a commoner because the children of such a union would inherit her higher status, and she could expect to be treated better by her husband's family, who would be proud of the marriage relationship.

LAND OF THE FEATHERED SERPENT: AZTEC RELIGION AND CULTURE

The Aztecs, like their contemporaries throughout Mesoamerica, lived in an environment populated by a multitude of gods. Scholars have identified more than a hundred deities in the Aztec pantheon; some of them were nature spirits, like the rain god, Tlaloc, and some were patron deities, like the symbol of the Aztecs themselves, Huitzilopochtli. A supreme deity, called Ometeotl, represented the all-powerful and omnipresent forces of the heavens, but he was rather remote, and other gods, notably the feathered serpent Quetzalcoatl, had a more direct impact on the lives of the people. Representing the forces of creation, virtue, and learning and culture, Quetzalcoatl bears a distinct similarity to Siva in Hindu belief. Accord-

AZTEC MIDWIFE RITUAL CHANTS

*M*ost Aztec women were burdened with time-consuming family chores, such as grinding corn into flour for tortillas and carrying heavy containers of water from local springs. Like their brothers, Aztec girls went to school, but rather than training for war, they learned spinning, weaving, and how to carry out family rituals. In the sixteenth century C.E., the Spanish priest Bernadino de Sahagun interviewed Aztec informants to compile a substantial account of traditional Aztec society. Here we read his narration of ritual chants used by midwives during childhood. For a boy, the highest honor was to shed blood in battle. For a girl, it was to offer herself to the work of domestic life. Compare the gender roles presented here with those of other ancient civilizations in preceding chapters.

BERNADINO DE SAHAGUN, THE FLORENTINE CODEX

My precious son, my youngest one. . . . Heed, hearken: Thy home is not here, for thou art an eagle, thou art an ocelot.

. . . Thou art the serpent, the bird of the lord of the near, of the nigh. Here is only the place of thy nest. Thou hast only been hatched here; thou hast only come, arrived. . . . Thou belongest out there. . . . Thou hast been sent into warfare. War is the desert, thy task. Thou shalt give drink, nourishment, food to the sun, the lord of the earth. . . . Perhaps thou wilt receive the gift, perhaps thou wilt merit death by the obsidian knife, the flowered death by the obsidian knife.

My beloved maiden. . . . Thou wilt be in the heart of the home, thou wilt go nowhere, thou wilt nowhere become a wanderer, thou becomest the banked fire, the hearth stones. Here our Lord planteth thee, burieth thee. And thou wilt become fatigued, thou wilt become tired, thou art to provide water, to grind maize, to drudge; thou art to sweat by the ashes, by the hearth.

➤ **THE ARRANGED MARRIAGE.**   The Maya recorded religious rites, as well as scenes of daily life, on polychrome clay vessels. Used in ritual ceremonies to the gods, these vessels contained a foamy chocolate beverage called *kakaw*, from which we derive the word *cacao*, the tree that produces the cocoa beans from which chocolate is made. The graphs accompanying the scenes normally refer to the cacao as well as the vessel's patron, most often the local lord. Here we see three men presenting an offering for an arranged marriage with a lord's daughter, who is shown kneeling behind her father. Mayan rulers often married their daughters to men of lower rank in order to elevate the latter's status and thereby guarantee their allegiance.

Rollout photograph © Justin Kerr, 1997

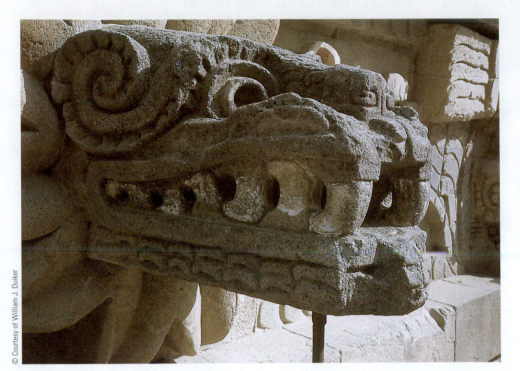

QUETZALCOATL.
Quetzalcoatl was one of the favorite deities of the Central American peoples. His visage of a plumed serpent, as shown here, was prominent in the royal capital of Teotihuacán. According to legend, Quetzalcoatl, the leader of the Toltecs, was tricked into drunkenness and humiliated by a rival god. In disgrace, he left his homeland but promised to return. In 1519, the Aztec monarch Moctezuma welcomed Hernán Cortés, the leader of the Spanish expedition, believing that he was a representative of Quetzalcoatl.

ing to Aztec tradition, this godlike being had left his homeland in the Valley of Mexico in the tenth century, promising to return in triumph (see "The Mystery of Mayan Decline" earlier in this chapter).

Aztec cosmology was based on a belief in the existence of two worlds, the material and the divine. The earth was the material world and took the form of a flat disk surrounded by water on all sides. The divine world, which consisted of both heaven and hell, was the abode of the gods. Human beings could aspire to a form of heavenly salvation but first had to pass through a transitional stage, somewhat like Christian purgatory, before reaching their final destination, where the soul was finally freed from the body. To prepare for the final day of judgment, as well as to help them engage in proper behavior through life, all citizens underwent religious training at temple schools during adolescence and took part in various rituals throughout their lives. The most devout were encouraged to study for the priesthood. Once accepted, they served at temples ranging from local branches at the *calpulli* level to the highest shrines in the ceremonial precinct at Tenochtitlán. In some respects, however, Aztec society may have been undergoing a process of secularization. By late Aztec times, athletic contests at the ball court had apparently lost some of their religious significance. Gambling was increasingly common, and wagering over the results of the matches was widespread. One province reportedly sent sixteen thousand rubber balls to the capital city of Tenochtitlán as its annual tribute to the royal court.

Aztec religion contained a distinct element of fatalism that was inherent in the creation myth, which described an unceasing struggle between the forces of good and evil throughout the universe. This struggle led to the creation and destruction of four worlds, or suns. The world was now living in the time of the fifth sun. But that world, too, was destined to end with the destruction of this earth and all that is within it:

> Even jade is shattered,
> Even gold is crushed,
> Even quetzal plumes are torn. . . .
> One does not live forever on this earth:
> We endure only for an instant![3]

In an effort to postpone the day of reckoning, the Aztecs practiced human sacrifice. The Aztecs believed that by appeasing the sun god, Huitzilopochtli, with sacrifices, they could delay the final destruction of their world. Victims were prepared for the ceremony through elaborate rituals and then brought to the holy shrine, where their hearts were ripped out of their chests and presented to the gods as a holy offering. It was an honor to be chosen for sacrifice, and captives were often used as sacrificial victims, since they represented valor, the trait the Aztecs prized most.

Like the art of the Olmecs, most Aztec architecture, art, and sculpture had religious significance. At the center of the capital city of Tenochtitlán was the sacred precinct, dominated by the massive pyramid dedicated to Huitzilopochtli and the rain god, Tlaloc. According to Bernal Díaz, at its base the pyramid was equal to the plots of six large European town houses and tapered from there to the top, which was surmounted by a platform containing shrines to the gods and an altar for performing human

A DESCRIPTION OF TENOCHTITLÁN

The Aztec capital of Tenochtitlán was built on an island in the Lake of Mexico. After the Spanish conquest, the lake was drained, and the area became the foundation of the modern capital of Mexico, Mexico City. Here Bernal Díaz describes the city as he viewed it from the top of the Temple of the Sun. The Spaniards razed the temple and built a cathedral in its place.

BERNAL DÍAZ, THE CONQUEST OF NEW SPAIN

When we arrived near the great temple and before we had climbed a single step, the great Moctezuma sent six *papas* [priests] and two chieftains down from the top, where he was making his sacrifices, to escort our Captain; and as he climbed the steps, of which there were one hundred and fourteen, they tried to take him by the arms to help him up in the same way as they helped Moctezuma, thinking he might be tired, but he would not let them near him.

The top of the *cue* [pyramid] formed an open square on which stood something like a platform, and it was here that the great stones stood on which they placed the poor Indians for sacrifice. Here also was a massive image like a dragon, and other hideous figures, and a great deal of blood that had been spilled that day. Emerging in the company of two *papas* from the shrine which housed his accursed images, Moctezuma made a deep bow to us all and said: "My lord Malinche, you must be tired after climbing this great *cue* of ours." And Cortés replied that none of us was ever exhausted by anything. Then Moctezuma took him by the hand, and told him to look at his great city and all the other cities standing in the water, and the many others on the land round the lake; and he said that if Cortés had not had a good view of the great marketplace he could see it better from where he now was. So we stood there looking, because that huge accursed *cue* stood so high that it dominated everything. We saw the three causeways that led into Mexico: the causeway of Iztapalapa by which we had entered four days before, and that of Tacuba along which we were afterwards to flee on the night of our great defeat, when the new prince Cuitlahuac drove us out of the city (as I shall tell in due course), and that of Tepeaqualla. We saw the freshwater which came from Chapultepec to supply the city, and the bridges that were constructed at intervals on the causeways so that the water could flow in and out from one part of the lake to another. We saw a great number of canoes, some coming with provisions and others returning with cargo and merchandise; and we saw too that one could not pass from one house to another of that great city and the other cities that were built on the water except over wooden drawbridges or by canoe. We saw *cues* and shrines in these cities that looked like gleaming white towers and castles: a marvelous sight. All the houses had flat roofs, and on the causeways were other small towers and shrines built like fortresses.

Having examined and considered all that we had seen, we turned back to the great market and the swarm of people buying and selling. The mere murmur of their voices talking was loud enough to be heard more than three miles away. Some of our soldiers who had been in many parts of the world, in Constantinople, in Rome, and all over Italy, said that they had never seen a market so well laid out, so large, so orderly, and so full of people.

---

sacrifices (see the box above). The entire pyramid was covered with brightly colored paintings and sculptures.

Although little Aztec painting survives, it was evidently of high quality. Bernal Díaz compared the best work with that of Michelangelo. Artisans worked with stone and with soft metals such as gold and silver, which they cast using the lost-wax technique. They did not have the knowledge for making implements in bronze or iron, however. Stoneworking consisted primarily of representations of the gods and bas-reliefs depicting religious ceremonies. Among the most famous is the massive disk called the Stone of the Sun, carved for use at the central pyramid at Tenochtitlán.

The Aztecs had devised a form of writing based on hieroglyphs that represented an object or a concept. The symbols had no phonetic significance and did not constitute a writing system as such but could give the sense of a message and were probably used by civilian or religious officials as notes or memorandums for their orations. Although many of the notes simply recorded dates in the complex calendar that had evolved since Olmec times, others provide insight into the daily lives of the Aztec peoples. A trained class of scribes carefully painted the notes on paper made from the inner bark of fig trees. Unfortunately, many of these notes were destroyed by the Spaniards as part of their effort to eradicate all aspects of Aztec religion and culture.

THE DESTRUCTION OF AZTEC CIVILIZATION

For a century, the Aztec kingdom dominated much of central Mexico from the Atlantic to the Pacific coast, and its influence penetrated as far south as present-day Guatemala. Most local officials had accepted the sovereignty of the king in Tenochtitlán, but in Tlaxcallan to the east, the authorities were restive under Aztec rule.

In 1519, a Spanish expedition under the command of Hernán Cortés landed at Veracruz, on the Gulf of Mexico (see Chapter 14). Marching to Tenochtitlán at the head of a small contingent of troops, Cortés received a friendly

MOCTEZUMA'S GREETING TO CORTÉS

As his small party arrived in the Aztec capital of Tenochtitlán, Hernán Cortés was greeted by King Moctezuma, who was under the impression that Cortés was the representative of Quetzalcoatl, the Aztec deity who had departed centuries earlier with a promise that he would one day return. In this letter to Queen Isabella of Spain, Cortés describes the welcoming ceremony and King Moctezuma's opening address. As Moctezuma would soon discover, he had been deceived as to his visitor's identity and intentions.

HERNÁN CORTÉS, LETTER FROM MEXICO

Close to the city there is a wooden bridge ten paces wide across a breach in the causeway to allow the water to flow, as it rises and falls. . . .

After we had crossed this bridge, Moctezuma came to greet us and with him some two hundred lords, all barefoot and dressed in a different costume, but also very rich in their way and more so than the others. They came in two columns, pressed very close to the walls of the street, which is very wide and beautiful and so straight that you can see from one end to the other. It is two-thirds of a league long and has on both sides very good and big houses, both dwellings and temples.

[After an exchange of gifts, Moctezuma then] addressed me in the following way:

"For a long time we have known from the writings of our ancestors that neither I, nor any of those who dwell in this land, are natives of it, but foreigners who came from very distant parts; and likewise we know that a chieftain, of whom they were all vassals, brought our people to this region. And he returned to his native land and after many years came again, by which time all those who had remained were married to native women and had built villages and raised children. And when he wished to lead them away again they would not go nor even admit him as their chief; and so he departed. And we have always held that those who descended from him would come and conquer this land and take us as their vassals. So because of the place from which you claim to come, namely, from where the sun rises, and the things you tell us of the great lord or king who sent you here, we believe and are certain that he is our natural lord, especially as you say that he has known of us for some time. So be assured that we shall obey you and hold you as our lord in place of that great sovereign of whom you speak; . . . I know full well of all that has happened to you from Puntunchan to here, and I also know how those of Cempoal and Tascalteca have told you much evil of me; believe only what you see with your eyes, for those are my enemies, and some were my vassals, and have rebelled against me at your coming and said those things to gain favor with you. I also know that they have told you the walls of my houses are made of gold, and that the floor mats in my rooms and other things in my household are likewise of gold, and that I was, and claimed to be, a god; and many other things besides. The houses as you see are of stone and lime and clay."

Then he raised his clothes and showed me his body, saying, as he grasped his arms and trunk with his hands, "See that I am of flesh and blood like you and all other men, and I am mortal and substantial. See how they have lied to you? It is true that I have some pieces of gold left to me by my ancestors; anything I might have shall be given to you whenever you ask. Now I shall go to other houses where I live, but here you shall be provided with all that you and your people require, and you shall receive no hurt, for you are in your own land and your own house."

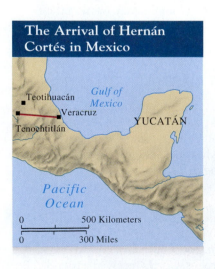

The Arrival of Hernán Cortés in Mexico

welcome from the Aztec monarch Moctezuma Xocoyotzin (often called Montezuma), who initially believed his visitor was a representative of Quetzalcoatl, the godlike "feathered serpent" (see the box above). The king and his subjects were astounded to see men on horseback, for the horse had disappeared from the Americas at least ten thousand years earlier.

But tensions soon erupted between the Spaniards and the Aztecs, provoked in part by demands by Cortés that the Aztecs denounce their native beliefs and accept Christianity. When the Spanish took Moctezuma hostage and began to destroy Aztec religious shrines, the local population revolted and drove the invaders from the city. Receiving assistance from the state of Tlaxcallan, Cortés managed to fight his way back into the city. Meanwhile the Aztecs were beginning to suffer the first effects of the diseases brought by the Europeans, which would eventually wipe out the majority of the local population. In a battle that to many Aztecs must have seemed to symbolize the dying of the legendary fifth sun, the Aztecs were finally vanquished. Within months, their magnificent city and its temples, believed by the conquerors to be the work of Satan, had been destroyed.

THE FIRST CIVILIZATIONS IN SOUTH AMERICA

South America is a vast continent, characterized by extremes in climate and geography. The north is dominated by the mighty Amazon River, which flows through dense tropical jungles carrying a larger flow of water than any other river system in the world (see Map 6.3). Farther to the south, the jungles are replaced by prairies and steppes stretching westward to the Andes Mountains, which extend the entire length of the continent, from the Isthmus of Panama to the Strait of Magellan. Along the Pacific coast, on the western slopes of the mountains, are some of the driest desert regions in the world.

South America has been inhabited by human beings for more than twelve thousand years. Wall paintings discovered at the "cavern of the painted rock" in the Amazon region suggest that Stone Age peoples were living in the area at least eleven thousand years ago, a site at Monte Verde, along the central coast of Chile, has been dated to 10,500 B.C.E., and evidence of human settlement dating back to 9500 B.C.E. has been found on the Tierra del Fuego, at the southern tip of the continent. Early peoples were hunters, fishermen, and food gatherers, but there are indications that irrigated farming was practiced in the northern fringe of the Andes Mountains as early as 2000 B.C.E. Other farming communities of similar age have been discovered in the Amazon River valley and on the western slopes of the Andes, where evidence of terraced agriculture dates back about four thousand years.

By the sixth millennium B.C.E., complex societies had emerged in the central Andes Mountains, in the region of modern Peru, Bolivia, and Ecuador. Archaeologists have discovered the remains of ceremonial precincts, complete with temples, ancestral tombs, and pyramids, similar to those of Mesoamerica. This early Andes civilization may have originated as early as about 2500 B.C.E. (archaeologists have recently discovered the remains of an ancient city in northwestern Peru, with several examples of public architecture and evidence of irrigated agriculture), but it reached its height during the first millennium B.C.E. with the emergence of the Chavin style, named for a site near the modern city of Chavin de Huantar, in the central mountains of modern Peru. The ceremonial precinct at the Chavin site contained an impressive stone temple complete with interior galleries, a stone-block ceiling, and a system of underground canals that probably channeled water into the temple complex for ritualistic purposes. The structure was surrounded by stone figures depicting various deities and two pyramids, possibly dedicated to the sun and the moon.

Moche

Early in the first millennium C.E., another advanced civilization, comprising a total area of over 2,500 square miles, appeared in northern Peru, in the valley of the Moche River, which flows from the foothills of the Andes into the Pacific Ocean. The capital city, large enough in territory to contain over ten thousand people, was dominated by two massive adobe pyramids rising as much as 100 feet high. The largest, known as the Pyramid of the Moon, covered a total of 15 acres and was adorned with painted murals depicting battles, ritual sacrifices, and various local deities.

Artifacts found at Moche, especially the metalwork and stone and ceramic figures, exhibit a high quality of artisanship. They were imitated at river valley sites throughout the surrounding area, which suggests that the authority of the Moche rulers may have extended as far as 400 miles along the coast. The artifacts also indicate that the people at Moche, like those in Central America, were

FANTASTIC CREATURE POT.   Thanks to the elaborate pottery of the Moche valley artists, we have an impressive visual record of the daily lives of the Peruvian peoples living in the sixth to ninth centuries C.E. Many of these colorful pots show scenes from everyday activities, such as hunting, fishing, weaving, cooking, and playing musical instruments. Others display religious ceremonies and sacrifice rituals. As illustrated in the fanged face of this fantastic creature, most probably a jaguar, these potters often blended the natural with the supernatural, which expressed the Moche worldview.

MAP 6.3 **Early Peoples and Cultures of Central and South America.**
This map shows regions of early human settlements in Central and
South America. Urban conglomerations appear in Mesoamerica (see
inset) and along the western coast of South America. ➤ *Why do you
think urban centers appeared in these areas?*

Atlantic
Ocean

SAVANNA
FARMERS

NORTH
ANDEAN
CHIEFDOMS

FARMING TRIBES

(manioc cultivators)
of the Amazon rain forest

Amazon R.

Moche

Chavín
de Huántar

About 500 C.E., farming
introduced from Amazon
Basin into Brazilian
forest and savanna

CENTRAL
ANDEAN
CIVILIZATION

SAVANNA
FARMERS

Immigration of
Tipí-Guariní tribes

Pacific
Ocean

HUNTERS
OF THE
CHACO
SAVANNA

Farming peoples

Chiefdoms

Organized states

Hunters and gatherers

GRASSLAND
STEPPE HUNTERS

Teotihuacán

Chichén Itzá

La Venta

Caribbean Sea

Tikal

Monte Albán

MARITIME
HUNTERS,
SHELLFISH
COLLECTORS

MAIZE AND MANIOC
CULTIVATORS OF
CARIBBEAN LOWLANDS

0   500   1,000   1,500 Kilometers

0   500   1,000 Miles

preoccupied with warfare. Paintings and pottery as well
as other artifacts in stone, metal, and ceramics frequently
portray warriors, prisoners, and sacrificial victims. The
Moche were also fascinated by the heavens, and much of
their art consisted of celestial symbols and astronomical
constellations.

The Moche River valley is extremely arid, receiving
less than an inch of rain annually. The peoples in the
area compensated by building a sophisticated irrigation
system to carry water from the river to the parched fields.
At its zenith, Moche culture was spectacular. By the
eighth century C.E., however, the civilization was in a

state of collapse, the irrigation canals had been abandoned, and the remaining population suffered from severe malnutrition.

What had happened to bring Moche culture to this untimely end? Archaeologists speculate that environmental changes, perhaps brought on by changes in the water temperature known as El Niño, led to major flooding of coastal regions and the advance of sand dunes into the irrigated fields.

Three hundred years later, a new power, the kingdom of Chimor, with its capital at Chanchan, at the mouth of the Moche River, emerged in the area. Built almost entirely of adobe, Chanchan housed an estimated thirty thousand residents in an area of over 12 square miles that included a number of palace compounds surrounded by walls nearly 30 feet high. One compound contained an intricate labyrinth that wound its way progressively inward until it ended in a central chamber, probably occupied by the ruler. Like the Moche before them, the people of Chimor relied on irrigation to funnel the water from the river into their fields. An elaborate system of canals brought the water through hundreds of miles of hilly terrain to the fields near the coast. Nevertheless, by the fifteenth century, Chimor, too, had disappeared, a victim of floods and a series of earthquakes that destroyed the intricate irrigation system that had been the basis of its survival.

These early civilizations in the Andes were by no means isolated from other societies in the region. As early as 2000 B.C.E., local peoples had been venturing into the Pacific Ocean on wind-powered rafts constructed of balsa wood. By the late first millennium C.E., seafarers from the coast of Ecuador had established a vast trading network that extended southward to central Peru and as far north as western Mexico, over 2,000 miles away. Items transported included jewelry, beads, and metal goods. In all likelihood, technological exchanges were an important by-product of the relationship.

The Inca

The Chimor kingdom was eventually succeeded in the late fifteenth century by an invading force from the mountains far to the south. In the late fourteenth century, the Incas were only a small community in the area of Cuzco, a city located at an altitude of 10,000 feet in the mountains of southern Peru. In the 1440s, however, under the leadership of their powerful ruler Pachakuti (sometimes called Pachacutec, or "he who transforms the world"), the Inca peoples launched a campaign of conquest that eventually brought the entire region under their authority. Under Pachakuti and his immediate successors, Topa Inca and Huayna Inca (the word *Inca* means "ruler"), the boundaries of the kingdom were extended as far as Ecuador, central Chile, and the edge of the Amazon basin.

THE FOUR QUARTERS: INCA POLITICS AND SOCIETY

Pachakuti created a highly centralized state (see Map 6.4). With a stunning concern for mathematical precision, he divided his empire, called Tahuantinsuyu, or "the world of the four quarters," into provinces and districts. Each province contained about ten thousand residents (at least in theory) and was ruled by a governor related to the royal family. Excess inhabitants were transferred to other locations. The capital of Cuzco was divided into four quarters, or residential areas, and the social status and economic functions of the residents of each quarter were rigidly defined.

The state was built on forced labor. Often entire communities of workers were moved from one part of the country to another to open virgin lands or engage in massive construction projects. Under Pachakuti, the capital of Cuzco was transformed from a city of mud and thatch into an imposing metropolis of stone. The walls, built of

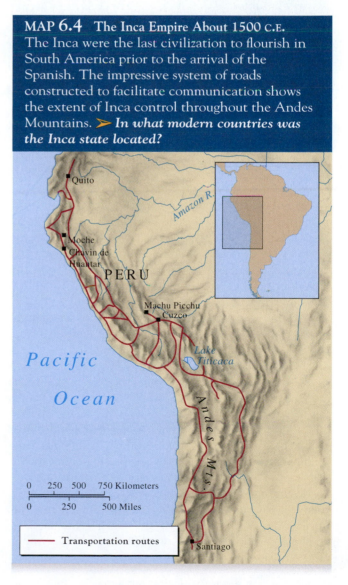

MAP 6.4   The Inca Empire About 1500 C.E. The Inca were the last civilization to flourish in South America prior to the arrival of the Spanish. The impressive system of roads constructed to facilitate communication shows the extent of Inca control throughout the Andes Mountains. ➤ *In what modern countries was the Inca state located?*

VIRGINS WITH RED CHEEKS

A letter from a Peruvian chief to King Philip III of Spain written four hundred years ago gives us a first-hand account of the nature of traditional Incan society. The purpose of author Huaman Poma was both to justify the history and culture of the Incan peoples and to record their sufferings under Spanish domination. In his letter, Poma describes Incan daily life from birth to death in minute detail. He explains the different tasks assigned to men and women, beginning with their early education. Whereas boys were taught to watch the flocks and trap animals, girls were taught to dye, spin and weave cloth, and perform other domestic chores. Most interesting, perhaps, was the emphasis that the Inca placed on virginity, as is witnessed in the document presented here. The Incan tradition of temple virgins is reminiscent of similar practices in ancient Rome, where young girls from noble families were chosen as priestesses to tend the sacred fire in the Temple of Vesta for thirty years. If one lost her virginity, she was condemned to be buried alive in an underground chamber.

HUAMAN POMA, LETTER TO A KING

During the time of the Incas certain women, who were called *accla* or "the chosen," were destined for lifelong virginity. Mostly they were confined in houses and they belonged to one of two main categories, namely sacred virgins and common virgins.

The so-called "virgins with red cheeks" entered upon their duties at the age of twenty and were dedicated to the service of the Sun, the Moon, and the Day-Star. In their whole life they were never allowed to speak to a man.

The virgins of the Inca's own shrine of Huanacauri were known for their beauty as well as their chastity. The other principal shrines had similar girls in attendance. At the less important shrines there were the older virgins who occupied themselves with spinning and weaving the silklike clothes worn by their idols. There was a still lower class of virgins, over forty years of age and no longer very beautiful, who performed unimportant religious duties and worked in the fields or as ordinary seamstresses.

Daughters of noble families who had grown into old maids were adept at making girdles, headbands, string bags, and similar articles in the intervals of their pious observances.

Girls who had musical talent were selected to sing or play the flute and drum at Court, weddings and other ceremonies, and all the innumerable festivals of the Inca year.

There was yet another class of *accla* or "chosen," only some of whom kept their virginity and others not. These were the Inca's beautiful attendants and concubines, who were drawn from noble families and lived in his palaces. They made clothing for him out of material finer than taffeta or silk. They also prepared a maize spirit of extraordinary richness, which was matured for an entire month, and they cooked delicious dishes for the Inca. They also lay with him, but never with any other man.

---

close-fitting stones without the use of mortar, were a wonder to early European visitors. The most impressive structure in the city was a temple dedicated to the sun. According to a Spanish observer, "All four walls of the temple were covered from top to bottom with plates and slabs of gold."[4] Equally impressive are the ruins of the abandoned city of Machu Picchu, built on a lofty hilltop far above the Urubamba River.

Another major construction project was a system of 24,800 miles of highways and roads that extended from the border of modern Colombia to a point south of modern Santiago, Chile. Two major roadways extended in a north-south direction, one through the Andes Mountains and the other along the coast, with connecting routes between them. Rest houses and storage depots were placed along the roads. Suspension bridges made of braided fiber and fastened to stone abutments on opposite banks were built over ravines and waterways. Use of the highways was restricted to official and military purposes. Trained runners carried messages rapidly from one way station to another, enabling information to travel up to 140 miles in a single day.

In rural areas, the population lived mainly by farming. In the mountains, the most common form was terraced agriculture, watered by irrigation systems that carried precise amounts of water into the fields, which were planted with maize, potatoes, and other crops. The plots were tilled by collective labor regulated by the state. Like other aspects of Inca society, marriage was strictly regulated, and men and women were required to select a marriage partner from within the immediate tribal group. For women, there was one escape from a life of domestic servitude. Fortunate maidens were selected to serve as "chosen virgins" in temples throughout the country (see the box above). Noblewomen were eligible to compete for service in the Temple of the Sun at Cuzco, while commoners might hope to serve in temples in the provincial capitals. Punishment for breaking the vow of chastity was harsh, and few evidently took the risk.

INCA CULTURE

Like many other civilizations in pre-Columbian Latin America, the Inca state was built on war. Soldiers for the 200,000-man Inca army, the largest and best armed in the region, were raised by universal male conscription. Military units were moved rapidly along the highway system and were housed in the rest houses located along the road-

MACHU PICCHU. Situated in the Andes in modern Peru, Machu Picchu reflects the glory of Inca civilization. To farm such rugged terrain, the Incas constructed terraces and stone aqueducts. To span vast ravines, they built suspension bridges made of braided fiber and fastened them to stone abutments on the opposite banks. The most revered of the many temples and stone altars at Machu Picchu was the thronelike "hitching post of the sun," so called because of its close proximity to the sun god.

side. Since the Inca had no wheeled vehicles, supplies were carried on the backs of llamas. Once an area was placed under Incan authority, the local inhabitants were instructed in the Quechua language, which became the lingua franca of the state, and were introduced to the state religion. The Inca had no writing system but kept records using a system of knotted strings called *quipu* (see the box on p. 176).

As in the case of the Aztecs and the Maya, the lack of a fully developed writing system did not prevent the Inca from realizing a high level of cultural achievement. Most of what survives was recorded by the Spanish and consists of entertainment for the elites. The Inca had a highly developed tradition of court theater, including both tragic and comic works. There was also some poetry, composed in blank verse and often accompanied by music played on reed instruments.

THE QUIPU. Not having a writing system, the Inca tallied the various data of their kingdom on strands of knotted yarn. Highly skilled and esteemed, official secretaries recorded population census data, crop and household inventories, government inspector reports, crime investigations, taxes, legal decisions and contracts, and all the official statistics of the realm by an intricate system of tying knots on a circular grouping of strings of yarn. One Peruvian chronicler boasted four hundred years ago that these dextrous officials recorded their facts "with such skill that the knots in their cords had the clarity of written letters."[5]

AN INCAN AIDE-MÉMOIRE

The Inca did not possess a written script. To record events and other aspects of their lives that they wished to remember, they used an ingenious system of knotted strings, called quipu. *This description of the process comes from the* Royal Commentaries of the Incas, *an account of Inca civilization and history written by Garcilaso de la Vega. Garcilaso, who was of mixed Inca and Spanish blood, was born shortly before the Spanish conquest of the Incan capital of Cuzco.*

GARCILASO DE LA VEGA, ROYAL COMMENTARIES OF THE INCAS

These men recorded on their knots all the tribute brought annually to the Inca, specifying everything by kind, species, and quality. They recorded the number of men who went to the wars, how many died in them, and how many were born and died every year, month by month. In short they may be said to have recorded on their knots everything that could be counted, even mentioning battles and fights, all the embassies that had come to visit the Inca, and all the speeches and arguments the king had uttered. But the purpose of the embassies or the contents of the speeches, or any other descriptive matter could not be recorded on the knots, consisting as it did of continuous spoken or written prose, which cannot be expressed by means of knots, since these can give only numbers and not words. To supply this want they used signs that indicated historical events or facts or the existence of any embassy, speech, or discussion in time of peace or war. Such speeches were preserved by the *quipucamayus* by memory in a summarized form of a few words: they were committed to memory and taught by tradition to their successors and descendants from father to son. This was especially practiced in the villages or provinces where the event in question had occurred: there naturally such traditions were preserved better than elsewhere, because the natives would treasure them. Another method too was used for keeping alive in the memory of the people their deeds and the embassies they sent to the Inca and the replies he gave them. The *amautas* who were their philosophers and sages took the trouble to turn them into stories, no longer than fables, suitable for telling to children, young people, and the rustics of the countryside: they were thus passed from hand to hand and age to age, and preserved in the memories of all. Their stories were also recounted in the form of fables of an allegorical nature, some of which we have mentioned, while others will be referred to later. Similarly the *harauicus*, who were their poets, wrote short, compressed poems, embracing a history, or an embassy, or the king's reply. In short, everything that could not be recorded on the knots was included in these poems, which were sung at their triumphs and on the occasion of their greater festivals, and recited to the young Incas when they were armed knights. Thus they remembered their history.

THE CONQUEST OF THE INCA

The Inca empire was still in existence when the first Spanish expeditions arrived in the central Andes. The leader of the Spanish invaders, Francisco Pizarro, was accompanied by only a few hundred companions, but like Cortés, he possessed steel weapons, gunpowder, and horses, none of which were familiar to his hosts. In the meantime, internal factionalism, combined with the onset of contagious diseases spread unknowingly by the Europeans, had weakened the ruling elite, and the empire fell rapidly to the Spanish forces in 1532. The last Inca ruler was tried by the Spaniards and executed. Pre-Columbian South America's greatest age was over.

STATELESS SOCIETIES IN THE NEW WORLD

Beyond Central America and the high ridges of the Andes Mountains, on the Great Plains of North America, along the Amazon River in South America, and on the islands of the Caribbean Sea, other communities of Amerindians were also beginning to master the art of agriculture and to build organized societies.

Although human beings had occupied much of the continent of North America during the early phase of human settlement in the New World, the switch to farming as a means of survival did not occur until the third millennium B.C.E. at the earliest, and not until much later in most areas of the continent. Until that time, most Amerindian communities lived by hunting, fishing, or foraging. As the supply of large animals began to diminish, they turned to smaller game and to fishing and foraging for wild plants, fruits, and nuts.

It was probably during the third millennium B.C.E. that peoples in selected parts of North America began to cultivate indigenous plants for food in a systematic way. As wild game and food became scarce, some communities began to place more emphasis on cultivating crops. This shift first occurred in the Mississippi River valley from Ohio, Indiana, and Illinois down to the Gulf of Mexico (see Map 6.5). Among the most commonly cultivated crops were maize, squash, beans, and various grasses.

As the population in the area increased, people began to congregate in villages, and sedentary commu-

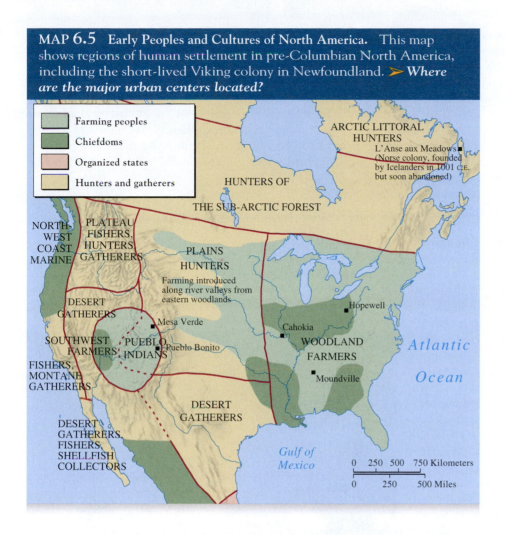

MAP 6.5   Early Peoples and Cultures of North America.   This map shows regions of human settlement in pre-Columbian North America, including the short-lived Viking colony in Newfoundland. ➤ *Where are the major urban centers located?*

nities began to develop in the alluvial lowlands, where the soil could be cultivated for many years at a time because of the nutrients deposited by the river water. Village councils were established to adjudicate disputes, and in a few cases, several villages banded together under the authority of a local chieftain. Urban centers began to appear, some of them inhabited by ten thousand people or more. At the same time, regional trade increased. The people of the Hopewell culture in Ohio ranged from the shores of Lake Superior to the Appalachian Mountains and the Gulf of Mexico in search of metals, shells, obsidian, and manufactured items to support their economic needs and religious beliefs.

At the site of Cahokia, near the modern city of East Saint Louis, Illinois, archaeologists found a burial mound more than 98 feet high with a base larger than that of the Great Pyramid in Egypt. A hundred smaller mounds were also found in the vicinity. The town itself, which covered almost 300 acres and was surrounded by a wooden stockade, was apparently the administrative capital of much of the surrounding territory until its decline in the

thirteenth century C.E. With a population of over twenty thousand, it was reportedly the largest city in North America until Philadelphia surpassed that number in the early nineteenth century. Cahokia carried on extensive trade with other communities throughout the region, and there are some signs of regular contacts with the civilizations in Mesoamerica, such as the presence of ball courts in the Central American style. But wars were not uncommon, leading the Iroquois, who inhabited much of the modern states of Pennsylvania and New York as well as parts of southern Canada, to create a tribal alliance called the League of Iroquois.

West of the Mississippi River basin, most Amerindian peoples lived by hunting or food gathering. During the first millennium C.E., knowledge of agriculture gradually spread up the rivers to the Great Plains, and farming was practiced as far west as southwestern Colorado, where the Anasazi peoples (Navajo for "alien ancient ones") established an extensive agricultural community in an area extending from northern New Mexico and Arizona to southwestern Colorado and parts of southern Utah. Although they apparently never discovered the wheel or used beasts of burden, the Anasazi created a system of roads that facilitated an extensive exchange of technology, products, and ideas throughout the region. By the ninth century, they had mastered the art of irrigation, which allowed them to expand their productive efforts to squash and beans, and had established an important urban center at Chaco Canyon, in southern New Mexico, where they built a walled city with dozens of three-story adobe houses with timbered roofs. Community religious functions were carried out in two large circular chambers called kivas. Clothing was made from hides or cotton cloth. At its height, Pueblo Bonito contained several hundred compounds housing several thousand residents. Another urban community was eventually established along a cliff face at Mesa Verde, in southwestern Colorado.

Sometime during the late twelfth and thirteenth centuries, however, these settlements were suddenly abandoned, and the inhabitants migrated southward. Their descendants, the Zuni and the Hopi, now occupy pueblos in central Arizona and New Mexico. For years, archaeologists surmised that a severe drought was the cause of the migration, but in recent years, new evidence has raised doubts that decreasing rainfall, by itself, was a sufficient explanation. An increase in internecine warfare, perhaps brought about by climatic changes, may also have played a role in the decision to relocate. Some archaeologists point to evidence that cannibalism was practiced at Pueblo Bonito and suggest that migrants from the south may have arrived in the area, provoking bitter rivalries within Anasazi society. In any event, with increasing aridity and the importation of the horse by the Spanish in the sixteenth century, hunting revived, and mounted nomads like the Apache and the Navajo came to dominate much of the Southwest.

East of the Andes Mountains in South America, other Amerindian societies were beginning to make the transition to agriculture. Perhaps the most prominent were the Arawak, a people living along the Orinoco River in modern Venezuela. Having begun to cultivate manioc (a tuber used today in the manufacture of tapioca) along the banks of the river, they gradually migrated down to the coast and then proceeded to move eastward along the northern coast of the continent. Some occupied the islands of the Caribbean Sea. In their new island habitat, they lived by a mixture of fishing, hunting, and cultivating maize, beans, manioc, and squash, as well as other crops such as peanuts, peppers, and pineapples. As the population increased, a pattern of political organization above the village level appeared, along with

recognizable social classes headed by a chieftain whose authority included control over the economy. The Arawak practiced human sacrifice, and some urban centers contained ball courts, suggesting the possibility of contacts with Mesoamerica.

In most such societies, where clear-cut class stratifications had not as yet taken place, men and women were considered of equal status. Men were responsible for hunting, warfare, and dealing with outsiders, while

CLIFF PALACE AT MESA VERDE.   Mesa Verde is one of the best-developed sites of the Anasazi peoples in southwestern North America. At one time they were farmers who tilled the soil atop the mesas, but eventually they were forced to build their settlements in more protected locations. At Cliff Palace, shown here, adobe houses were hidden on the perpendicular face of the mesa. Access was achieved only by a perilous descent via indented finger- and toeholds on the rock face.

EARLY AMERICA

Arrival of human beings in America	At least 15,000 years ago
First organized societies in the Andes	c. 6000 B.C.E.
Agriculture first practiced	c. 5000 B.C.E.
Rise of Olmec culture	First millennium B.C.E.
Origins of Mayan civilization	First millennium C.E.
Teotihuacán civilization	c. 300 B.C.E.–800 C.E.
Moche civilization	c. 150 C.E.–800 C.E.
Decline of the Maya	c. ninth century
Civilization of Chimor	c. 1100–1450
Migration of Mexica to Valley of Mexico	Late twelfth century
Kingdom of the Aztecs	Fifteenth century
Inca takeover in central Andes	Fifteenth century
Arrival of Hernán Cortés in Mexico	1519
Pizarro's conquest of the Inca	1532

women were accountable for the crops, the distribution of food, maintaining the household, and bearing and raising the children. Their roles were complementary and were often viewed as a divine division of labor. In such cases, women in the stateless societies of North America held positions of greater respect than their counterparts in the river valley civilizations of the Old World.

CONCLUSION

The first human beings did not arrive in the New World until quite late in the prehistorical period. For the next several millennia, their descendants were forced to respond to the challenges of the environment in total isolation from other parts of the world. Nevertheless, around 5000 B.C.E., farming settlements began to appear in river valleys and upland areas in both Central and South America. Not long afterward—as measured in historical time—organized communities located along the coast of the Gulf of Mexico and the western slopes of the central Andes Mountains embarked on the long march toward civilization. Along the same path, although perhaps somewhat less advanced in technological

terms, were the emerging societies of North America, which were beginning to expand their commercial and cultural links with civilizations farther to the south and had already laid the foundations for future urbanization. Although the total number of people living in the New World is a matter of debate, some scholars estimate a figure between ten and twenty million.

What is perhaps most striking about the developments in the New World is how closely the process paralleled that in the Old. Although the civilizations in Central and South America were less advanced in terms of technology (the lack of iron and the wheel, for example, and the absence of a sophisticated writing system), in many other respects the states in Central America and the Andes were the equal of those that we will discuss in later chapters. One need only point to the awed comments of early Spanish visitors, who said that the cities of the Aztecs were the equal of Seville and the other great metropolitan centers of Spain.

What was most repugnant to those early European visitors were the religious beliefs and practices of the civilizations that they encountered. They were repelled by the worship of strange idols and even more by the human sacrifices on a massive scale. Before rushing to judgment, however, we should remember that similar practices had been carried out in many societies of the Old World, including the ancient civilizations of Egypt, India, and China. The Spaniards were perhaps most surprised to discover that civilizations that in other respects had achieved such a high degree of culture also practiced human sacrifice.

In recent years, some scholars have speculated that the peoples in the Americas were more peaceful than their counterparts in the Old World. The bulk of the evidence, however, suggests that the Amerindian peoples were every bit as addicted to warfare as those of the ancient empires of Africa and Asia. In the end, military prowess was of little help when the peoples of the Americas encountered the first visitors from overseas. The Europeans' advanced military technology and their mastery of horseback riding gave them a major advantage over the local population. Just as sedentary peoples in ancient Europe were often overwhelmed by nomads migrating westward from the steppes of Central Asia, so the armies of the Aztecs and Incas were no match for the Spanish conquistadors, whose mobility on horseback had been increased through recent European contacts with Arab warriors in North Africa and the Middle East. Yet it should be noted that in the New World as in the Old, many of the first civilizations formed by the human species appear to have been brought to an end as much by environmental changes as by war. In the next chapter, we shall return to the Old World, where new civilizations were in the process of replacing the ancient empires.

CHAPTER NOTES

1. Quoted in Sylvanus Morley and George W. Brainerd, *The Ancient Maya* (Stanford, Calif., 1983), p. 513.
2. Bernal Díaz, *The Conquest of New Spain* (Harmondsworth, England, 1975), p. 210.
3. Michael D. Coe, Dean Snow, and Elizabeth P. Benson, *Atlas of Ancient America* (New York, 1988), p. 149.
4. Garcilaso de la Vega (El Inca), *Royal Commentaries of the Incas and General History of Peru*, pt. 1, trans. Harold V. Livermore (Austin, Tex., 1966), p. 180.
5. Quote from Huaman Poma, *Letter to a King* (New York, 1978), p. 101.

SUGGESTED READING

For a profusely illustrated and informative overview of the early civilizations of the Americas, see M. D. Coe, D. Snow, and E. P. Benson, *Atlas of Ancient America* (New York, 1988). The first arrival of human beings in the New World is discussed in B. Fagan, *The Great Journey: The Peopling of Ancient America* (London, 1987).

For an early classical work on Mayan civilization, see S. G. Morley and G. W. Brainerd, *The Ancient Maya* (Stanford, Calif., 1983). N. Hammond, *Ancient Maya Civilization* (New Brunswick, N.J., 1982), provides a general survey for the nonspecialist. See also M. D. Coe, *The Maya* (London, 1993), and J. Sabloff, *The New Archeology and the Ancient Maya* (New York, 1990).

For a recent overview of Aztec civilization in Mexico, see B. Fagan, *The Aztecs* (New York, 1984). S. D. Gillespie, *The Aztec Kings: The Construction of Rulership in Mexican History* (Tucson, Ariz., 1989), is an imaginative effort to uncover the symbolic meaning in Aztec traditions. For a provocative study of religious traditions in a comparative context, see B. Fagan, *From Black Land to Fifth Sun* (Reading, Mass., 1998). On the Olmecs and the Zapotecs, see E. P. Benson, *The Olmec and Their Neighbors* (Washington, D.C., 1981); M. D. Coe and R. A. Diehl, *In the Land of the Olmec* (Austin, Tex., 1980); and R. E. Blanton, *Monte Alban: Settlement Patterns at the Ancient Zapotec Capital* (New York, 1978).

Much of our information about the lives of the peoples of ancient Central America comes from Spanish writers who visited or lived in the area during the sixteenth and seventeenth centuries. For the original Spanish conquest of Mexico, see H. Cortés, *Letters from Mexico* (New Haven, Conn., 1986), and B. Díaz, *The Conquest of New Spain* (Harmondsworth, England, 1975). See also D. Duran, *The Aztecs: The History of the Indies of New Spain* (New York, 1964).

On the Inca and their predecessors, see R. W. Keatinge, ed., *Peruvian Prehistory: An Overview of Pre-Inca and Inca Society* (Cambridge, 1988); G. Bankes, *Peru Before Pizarro* (Oxford, 1977); and E. P. Lanning, *Peru Before the Incas* (Englewood Cliffs, N.J., 1967). The arrival of the Spanish is chronicled in C. Howard, *Pizarro and the Conquest of Peru* (New York, 1967). For an extended account of Inca civilization, see G. de la Vega (El Inca), *Royal Commentaries of the Incas and General History of Peru* (Austin, Tex., 1966).

On the art and culture of the ancient Americas, see M. E. Miller, *Maya Art and Architecture* (London, 1999); E. Pasztory, *Pre-Columbian Art* (Cambridge, 1998); and L. Schele and M. E. Miller, *The Blood of Kings: Ritual and Dynasty in Maya Art* (New York, 1992). Writing systems are discussed in D. H. Kelley, *Deciphering the Maya Script* (Austin, Tex., 1976), and J. E. S. Thompson, *Maya Hieroglyphic Writing: An Introduction* (Norman, Okla., 1971).

On social issues, see L. Schele and D. Freidel, *A Forest of Kings: The Untold Story of the Ancient Maya* (New York, 1990); R. van Zantwijk, *The Aztec Arrangement: The Social History of Pre-Spanish Mexico* (Norman, Okla., 1985); and N. Shoemaker, *Negotiators of Change: Historical Perspectives on Native American Women* (New York, 1995).

InfoTrac College Edition

For additional reading, go to InfoTrac College Edition, your online research library at
http://web1.infotrac-college.com

Enter the search terms "Inca or Incan" using Keywords.

Enter the search term "Aztec" using Keywords.

Enter the search terms "Maya or Mayan" using Keywords.

Enter the search terms "Machu Picchu" using Keywords.

Enter the search terms "Latin America history" using Keywords.

Chapter 7

Courtesy of William J. Duiker

ISLAM AND BYZANTIUM

CHAPTER OUTLINE

- THE RISE OF ISLAM
- THE ARAB EMPIRE AND ITS SUCCESSORS
- ISLAMIC CIVILIZATION
- THE BYZANTINE EMPIRE
- CONCLUSION

FOCUS QUESTIONS

- What are the main tenets of Islam, and how does the religion compare with Judaism and Christianity?
- Why did the Arabs undergo such a rapid expansion in the seventh and eighth centuries, and why were they so successful in amassing an empire?
- What were the basic political structures of the Arab empire under the Umayyads and the Abbasids, and how did the Seljuk Turks, the Crusades, and the Mongols affect Islamic civilization?
- What were the main features of Islamic society and culture?
- What were the main characteristics of Byzantine and Islamic civilizations, and why and in what ways did they come into conflict?

The collapse of Roman power in the Mediterranean led to the emergence of three new civilizations. In the west, Roman elements combined with German influences and Christianity to form a new Christian European civilization (see Chapter 12). The eastern part of the old Roman Empire, increasingly Greek in culture, continued to flourish as the Christian Byzantine Empire. Although the European civilization of the west and the Byzantine civilization of the east came to share a common bond in Christianity, it proved incapable of keeping them in harmony politically as the two civilizations continued to move apart. The rise of an Islamic Empire, Rome's third heir, resulted in the loss of the southern and eastern Mediterranean worlds of the old Roman Empire to a religious power that was neither Roman nor Christian and brought a conflict between the Islamic and Byzantine worlds in the eastern Mediterranean that lasted for centuries.

In the year 570, in the Arabian city of Mecca, there was born a child named Muhammad whose life changed the course of world history. The son of a merchant, Muhammad grew to maturity in a time of transition. Old empires that had once ruled the entire Middle East were only a distant memory. The region was now divided into many separate states, and the people adhered to many different faiths.

Within a few decades of Muhammad's death, the Middle East was united once again. The initial triumph was primarily political and military. Arab armies marched westward across North Africa and eastward into Mesopotamia and Persia, imposing their authority and creating a new empire that stretched from the Iberian peninsula to the Indus valley. But Arab rule also brought with it a new religion and a new culture—Islam.

Islamic beliefs and culture exerted a powerful influence in all areas occupied by Arab armies. Initially, Arab beliefs and customs, as reflected through the prism of Muhammad's teachings, transformed the societies and cultures of the peoples living in the new empire. But eventually, the distinctive political and cultural forces that had long characterized the region began to reassert themselves. Factional struggles led to the decline and then the destruction of the Arab empire. Invading forces from Central Asia established their control over the great mercantile cities of the region, while Christian crusaders attacked the empire from the west. New states formed in Spain, North Africa, and Persia and began to put their own stamp on the cultures of the region. Like the empires that had preceded it, the Arab empire, with its capital at Baghdad, became a thing of the past.

Still, the Arab conquest left a powerful legacy that survived the decline of Arab political power. The ideological and emotional appeal of Islam remained strong throughout the Middle East and even extended into areas not occupied by Arab armies, such as the Indian subcontinent, Southeast Asia, and sub-Saharan Africa. At the same time, the political unification of the entire region, although temporary, provided an environment conducive to the revival and expansion of long-distance trade and the exchange of culture and ideas that had taken place before the collapse of the classical empires at the beginning of the first millennium C.E. ●

THE RISE OF ISLAM

The Arabs were a Semitic-speaking people of southwestern Asia with a long history. They were mentioned in Greek sources of the fifth century B.C.E. and even earlier in the Old Testament. The Greek historian Herodotus had applied the name *Arab* to the entire peninsula, calling it Arabia. In 106 B.C.E., the Romans extended their authority to the Arabian peninsula, transforming it into a province of their growing empire.

During Roman times, the region was inhabited primarily by the Bedouin Arabs, nomadic peoples who came originally from the northern part of the peninsula. Bedouin society was organized on a tribal basis. The ruling member of the tribe was called the *sheikh* and was selected from one of the leading families by a council of elders called the *majlis*. The *sheikh* ruled the tribe with the consent of the council. Each tribe was autonomous but felt a general sense of allegiance to the larger unity of all the clans in the region. In early times, the Bedouins had supported themselves primarily by sheepherding or by raiding passing caravans, but after the domestication of the camel during the first millennium B.C.E., the Bedouins began to participate in the caravan trade themselves and became major carriers of goods between the Persian Gulf and the Mediterranean Sea.

The Arabs of pre-Islamic times were polytheistic, with a supreme god known as Allah presiding over a community of spirits. It was a communal faith, involving all members of the tribe, and had no priesthood. The supreme deity was symbolized by a sacred stone. Each tribe possessed its own stone, but all worshiped a massive black meteorite, which was located in a central shrine called the Ka'aba in the commercial city of Mecca.

In the fifth and sixth centuries C.E., the economic importance of the Arabian peninsula began to increase. As a result of the political disorder in Mesopotamia—a consequence of the constant wars between the Byzantine and Persian Empires—and in Egypt, the trade routes that ran directly across the peninsula or down the Red Sea became increasingly risky, and a third route, which passed from the Mediterranean through Mecca to Yemen and then by ship across the Indian Ocean, became more popular (see Map 7.1). The communities in that part of the

➤➤ **THE KA'ABA IN MECCA.**   The Ka'aba, a massive black meteorite in the Arabian city of Mecca, is the sacred stone of the Islamic faith. Wherever Muslims pray, they are instructed to face Mecca; each thus becomes a spoke of the Ka'aba, the holy center of the wheel of Islam. If they are able to do so, all Muslims are encouraged to visit the Ka'aba at least once in their lifetime. Called the *hajj,* this pilgrimage to Mecca represents the ultimate in spiritual fulfillment.

peninsula benefited from the change. As a consequence, relations between the Bedouins of the desert and the increasingly wealthy merchants of the towns began to become strained.

The Role of Muhammad

Into this intense world stepped Muhammad (also known as Mohammed), a man whose spiritual visions unified the Arab world with a speed no one would have suspected possible. Born in Mecca to a merchant family and orphaned at the age of six, Muhammad (570–632) grew up to become a caravan manager and eventually married a rich widow, Khadija, who was also his employer. For several years, he lived in Mecca as a merchant but was apparently troubled by the growing gap between the Bedouin values of honesty and generosity (he himself was a member of the local Hashemite clan of the Quraishi tribe) and the acquisitive behavior of the affluent commercial elites in the city. Deeply concerned, he began to visit the nearby hills to meditate in isolation.

On one of these occasions, he experienced visions and heard a voice that he was convinced was inspired by Allah. According to tradition, the message was conveyed by the angel Gabriel, who commanded Muhammad to preach the revelations that he would be given.

Muhammad was acquainted with Jewish and Christian beliefs and came to believe that while Allah had already revealed himself in part through Moses and

Jesus—and thus through the Hebraic and Christian traditions—the final revelations were now being given to him. Out of his revelations, which were eventually dictated to scribes, came the Koran or Qur'an, the holy scriptures of Islam (*Islam* means "submission," implying submission to the will of Allah). The Koran contained the guidelines by which followers of Allah, known as Muslims (practitioners of Islam), were to live. Like the Christians and the Jews, Muslims (also known as Moslems) were a "people of the Book," believers in a faith based on scripture.

After returning home, Muhammad set out to comply with Gabriel's command by preaching to the residents of Mecca about his revelations. At first, many were convinced that he was a madman or a charlatan. Others were undoubtedly concerned that his vigorous attacks on traditional beliefs and the corrupt society around him could severely shake the social and political order. After three years of proselytizing, he had only thirty followers.

Discouraged by the systematic persecution of his followers, which was undertaken with a brutality reminiscent of the cruelties suffered by early Christians, as well as the failure of the Meccans to accept his message, in 622 Muhammad and some of his closest supporters (mostly from his own Hashemite clan) left the city and retreated north to the rival city of Yathrib, later renamed Medina, or "city of the Prophet." That flight, known in history as the Hegira (*Hijrah*), marks the first date on the official calendar of Islam. At Medina, Muhammad failed in his original purpose—to convert the Jewish community in Medina to his beliefs. But he was successful in winning support from many residents of the city as well as from Bedouins in the surrounding countryside. From this mixture, he formed the first Muslim community (the *umma*). Returning to his birthplace at the head of a considerable military force, Muhammad conquered Mecca and converted the townspeople to the new faith. In 630, he made a symbolic visit to the Ka'aba, where he declared it a sacred shrine of Islam and ordered the destruction of the idols of the traditional faith. Two years later, Muhammad died, just as Islam was beginning to spread throughout the peninsula.

The Teachings of Muhammad

Like Christianity and Judaism, Islam is monotheistic. Allah is the all-powerful being who created the universe and everything in it. Islam is also concerned with salvation and offers the hope of an afterlife. Those who hope to achieve it must subject themselves to the will of Allah. Unlike Christianity, Islam makes no claim to the divinity of its founder. Muhammad, like Jesus, Moses, and other figures of the Old Testament, was a prophet, but he was also a man like other men. Because human beings rejected his earlier messengers, Allah sent his final revelation through Muhammad.

MAP 7.1 The Middle East in the Time of Muhammad When Islam began to spread throughout the Middle East in the early seventh century, the dominant states in the region were the Roman Empire in the eastern Mediterranean and the Sassanian Empire in Persia. ➤ *What were the major territorial divisions existing at the time and the key sites connected to the rise of Islam?*

At the heart of Islam is the Koran (meaning "recitation"), with its basic message that there is no God but Allah and Muhammad is his Prophet (see the box on p. 186). Consisting of 114 *suras* (chapters) that were drawn together into an integrated whole by a committee established after Muhammad's death, the Koran is not only the sacred book of Islam but also an ethical guidebook and a code of law and political theory combined.

Islam was a direct and simple faith, emphasizing the need to obey the will of Allah. This meant following a basic ethical code that consisted of what are popularly termed the Five Pillars of Islam: belief in Allah and Muhammad as his Prophet; standard prayer five times a day and public prayer on Friday at midday to worship Allah; observation of the holy month of Ramadan, including fasting from dawn to sunset; making a pilgrimage, if

possible, to Mecca at least once in one's lifetime (see the box on p. 187); and giving alms (called the *zakat*) to the poor and unfortunate. The faithful who observed the law were guaranteed a place in an eternal paradise with the sensuous delights so obviously lacking in the midst of the Arabian desert.

Islam was not just a set of religious beliefs but a way of life as well. After the death of Muhammad, Muslim scholars, known as the *ulama*, drew up a law code, called the *Shari'a*, to provide believers with a set of prescriptions to regulate their daily lives. Much of the *Shari'a* was drawn from the Koran or from the *Hadith*, a collection of the sayings of the Prophet that was used to supplement the revelations contained in the holy scriptures.

Believers were subject to strict behavioral requirements. In addition to the Five Pillars, Muslims were

THE KORAN AND THE
SPREAD OF THE MUSLIM FAITH

The Koran is the sacred book of Islam, holding a place comparable to that of the Bible in Christianity. In this selection from Chapter 47, it is apparent that Islam encourages the spreading of the faith, known to Muslims as jihad. A garden of paradise quite unlike the arid desert homeland of the Arab warriors awaited all believers who died for Allah. In many Islamic countries today, militants are encouraged to battle with their enemies by the promise of entry into paradise as described here.

THE KORAN: CHAPTER 47, "MUHAMMAD, REVEALED AT MEDINA"

Allah will bring to nothing the deeds of those who disbelieve and debar others from His path. As for the faithful who do good works and believe in what is revealed to Muhammad—which is the truth from their Lord—He will forgive them their sins and ennoble their state.

This, because the unbelievers follow falsehood, while the faithful follow the truth from their Lord. Thus Allah coins their sayings for mankind.

When you meet the unbelievers in the battlefield strike off their heads and, when you have laid them low, bind your captives firmly. Then grant them their freedom or take ransom from them, until War shall lay down her armour.

Thus shall you so. Had Allah willed, He could Himself have punished them; but He has ordained it thus that He might test you, the one by the other.

As for those who are slain in the cause of Allah, He will not allow their works to perish. He will vouchsafe them guidance and ennoble their state; He will admit them to the Paradise He has made known to them.

Believers, if you help Allah, Allah will help you and make you strong. But the unbelievers shall be consigned to perdition. He will bring their deeds to nothing. Because they have opposed His revelations, He will frustrate their works.

Have they never journeyed through the land and seen what was the end of those who have gone before them? Allah destroyed them utterly. A similar fate awaits the unbelievers, because Allah is the protector of the faithful; because the unbelievers have no protector.

Allah will admit those who embrace the true faith and do good works to gardens watered by running streams. The unbelievers take their fill of pleasure and eat as the beasts eat: but Hell shall be their home. . . .

This is the Paradise which the righteous have been promised. There shall flow in it rivers of unpolluted water, and rivers of milk forever fresh; rivers of delectable wine and rivers of clearest honey. They shall eat therein of every fruit and receive forgiveness from their Lord. Is this like the lot of those who shall abide in Hell forever and drink scalding water which will tear their bowels? . . .

Know that there is no god but Allah. Implore Him to forgive your sins and to forgive the true believers, men and women. Allah knows your busy haunts and resting places.

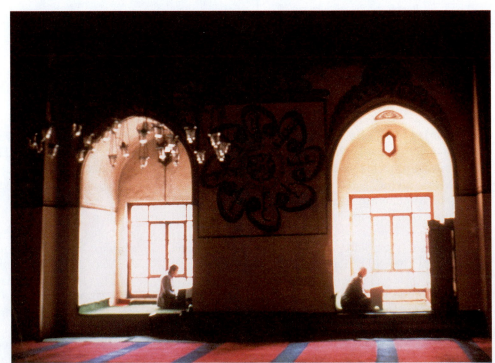

➤ THE QUIET SPIRIT OF A MOSQUE.   For Muslims, the mosque is a revered oasis for worship, reflection, and the reading of the Koran. The practicing Muslim is required to pray to Allah five times a day. While women normally pray at home, men are expected to visit a mosque. If a mosque is not available, they may pray wherever they are at the time of the muezzin's call. At that time, each Muslim stops whatever he is doing and kneels down, facing Mecca, on his portable prayer rug. Above all, the mosque is a place for quiet devotion, a refuge from the bustle of daily life. The artwork in a mosque should reflect motifs from the Koran. In this illustration, two of the faithful pray in a mosque under iron lamps on plush layers of carpets decorated with Koranic symbols.

A Pilgrimage to Mecca

The pilgrimage to Mecca, one of the Five Pillars of Islam, is the duty of every Muslim. Ibn Jubayr, a twelfth-century Spanish Muslim, left a description of his trip in his journal. The work is famous for its vivid and abundant detail. In this almost lyrical passage, Ibn Jubayr tells of reaching his final destination, the Ka'aba at Mecca, containing the Black Stone. The Qarmata were an extremist religious sect in ninth- and tenth-century Mesopotamia.

IBN JUBAYR, TRAVELS

The blessed Black Stone is encased in the corner [of the Ka'aba] facing east. The depth to which it penetrates it is not known, but it is said to extend two cubits into the wall. Its breadth is two-thirds of a span, its length one span and a finger joint. It has four pieces, joined together, and it is said that it was the Qarmata—may God curse them—who broke it. Its edges have been braced with a sheet of silver whose white shines brightly against the black sheen and polished brilliance of the Stone, presenting the observer a striking spectacle which will hold his gaze. The Stone, when kissed, has a softness and moistness which so enchants the mouth that he who puts his lips to it would wish them never to be removed. This is one of the special favors of Divine Providence, and it is enough that the Prophet—may God bless and preserve him—declare it to be a covenant of God on earth. May God profit us by the kissing and touching of it. By His favor may all who yearn fervently for it be brought to it. In the sound piece of the stone, to the right of him who presents himself to kiss it, is a small white spot that shines and appears like a mole on the blessed surface. Concerning this white mole, there is a tradition that he who looks upon it clears his vision, and when kissing it one should direct one's lips as closely as one can to the place of the mole.

---

forbidden to gamble, to eat pork, to drink alcoholic beverages, and to engage in dishonest behavior. Sexual mores were also strict. Contacts between unmarried men and women were discouraged, and ideally marriages were to be arranged by the parents. In accordance with Bedouin custom, polygyny was permitted, but Muhammad attempted to limit the practice by restricting males to four wives.

To what degree the traditional account of the exposition and inner meaning of the Koran can stand up to historical analysis is a matter of debate. The circumstances surrounding the life of Muhammad and his role in founding the religion of Islam have not been exposed to the kind of rigorous scrutiny that has been experienced by the early years of Christianity, and many Muslims are undoubtedly concerned that the consequences of such examination could only undercut many of the key tenets of the Muslim faith. One of the problems connected with such an effort is that the earliest known versions of the Koran available today do not contain the diacritical marks that modern Arabic uses to clarify meaning, thus leaving much of the sacred text ambiguous and open to varying interpretations.

THE ARAB EMPIRE AND ITS SUCCESSORS

The death of Muhammad presented his followers with a dilemma. Although Muhammad had not claimed divine qualities, Muslims saw no separation between political and religious authority. Submission to the will of Allah meant submission to his Prophet Muhammad. According to the Koran, "Whoso obeyeth the messenger obeyeth Allah."[1] Muhammad's charismatic authority and political skills had been at the heart of his success. But he never named a successor, and although he had several daughters, he left no sons. In a male-oriented society, who would lead the community of the faithful?

Shortly after Muhammad's death, a number of his closest followers selected Abu Bakr, a wealthy merchant from Medina who was Muhammad's father-in-law and one of his first supporters, as caliph (*khalifa*, literally "successor"). The caliph was the temporal leader of the Islamic community and was also considered, in general terms, to be a religious leader, or *imam*. Under Abu Bakr's prudent leadership, the movement succeeded in suppressing factional tendencies among some of the Bedouin tribes in the peninsula and began to direct its attention to wider fields. Muhammad had used the Arabic tribal custom of the *razzia* or raid in the struggle against his enemies. Now his successors turned to the same custom to expand the authority of the movement (see the box on p. 186). The Koran called this activity "striving in the way of the Lord," or *jihad*. Although sometimes translated as "holy war," the term is ambiguous and has been subject to varying interpretations.

Creation of an Empire

Once the Arabs had become unified under Muhammad's successor, they began to conduct a *jihad* on a larger scale, directing outward against neighboring peoples the energy they had formerly directed against each other. The Byzantine and Persian Empires were the first to feel the strength of the newly united Arabs, now aroused to a peak of zeal by their common faith. At Yarmuk in 636, the Muslims defeated the Byzantine army. Four years later, they took possession of the Byzantine province of Syria. To the east, the Arabs defeated a Persian force in 637 and then went on to conquer the entire empire of the Sassanids by 650. In the meantime, Egypt and other areas of North Africa were also brought under Arab authority (see Chapter 8).

What accounts for this rapid expansion of the Arabs after the rise of Islam in the early seventh century? Historians have proposed various explanations, ranging from a prolonged drought on the Arabian peninsula to the desire of Islam's leaders to channel the energies of their new converts. Another hypothesis is that the expansion was deliberately planned by the ruling elites in Mecca to extend their trade routes and bring surplus-producing regions under their control. Whatever the case, Islam's ability to unify the Bedouin peoples certainly played a role. Although the Arab triumph was made substantially easier by the ongoing conflict between the Byzantine and Persian Empires, which had weakened both powers, the strength of the Bedouin armies should not be overlooked. Led by a series of brilliant generals, the Arabs put together a large, highly motivated army, whose valor was enhanced by the belief that Muslim warriors who died in battle were guaranteed a place in paradise.

Once the armies had prevailed, Arab administration of the conquered areas was generally tolerant. Sometimes, due to a shortage of trained Arab administrators, government was left to local officials. Conversion to Islam was voluntary in accordance with the maxim in the Koran that "there shall be no compulsion in religion."[2] Those who chose not to convert were required only to submit to Muslim rule and pay a head tax in return for exemption from military service, which was required of all Muslim males. Under such conditions, the local populations often welcomed Arab rule as preferable to Byzantine rule or that of the Sassanid dynasty in Persia. Furthermore, the simple and direct character of the new religion, as well as its egalitarian qualities (all people were viewed as equal in the eyes of Allah), were undoubtedly attractive to peoples throughout the region.

Succession Problems and the Rise of the Umayyads

The main challenge to the growing empire came from within. Some of Muhammad's followers had not agreed with the selection of Abu Bakr as the first caliph and promoted the candidacy of Muhammad Ali, Muhammad's cousin and son-in-law, as an alternative. Ali's claim was ignored by other leaders, however, and after Abu Bakr's death, the office was passed to Umar, another of Muhammad's followers. In 656, Umar's successor, Uthman, was assassinated, and Ali was finally selected for the position. But Ali's rivals were convinced that he had been implicated in the death of his predecessor, and a factional struggle broke out within the Muslim leadership. In 661, Ali himself was assassinated, and Mu'awiya, the governor of

Syria and one of Ali's chief rivals, replaced him in office. Mu'awiya thereupon made the caliphate hereditary in his own family, called the Umayyads, who were a branch of the Quraishi clan. The new caliphate, with its capital at Damascus, remained in power for nearly a century.

The factional struggle within Islam did not bring an end to Arab expansion. At the beginning of the eighth century, new attacks were launched at both the western and the eastern ends of the Mediterranean world (see Map 7.2). Arab armies advanced across North Africa and conquered the Berbers, a primarily pastoral people living along the Mediterranean coast and in the mountains in the interior. Then, around 710, Arab forces, supplemented by Berber allies under their commander, Tariq, crossed the Strait of Gibraltar and occupied southern Spain. The Visigothic kingdom, already weakened by internecine warfare, quickly collapsed, and by 725, most of the Iberian peninsula had become a Muslim state with its center in Andalusia. Seven years later, an Arab force, making a foray into southern France, was defeated by the army of Charles Martel between Tours and Poitiers. Some historians think that internal exhaustion would have forced the invaders to retreat even without their defeat at the hands of the Franks. In any event, the Battle of Tours (or Poitiers) would be the high-water mark of Arab expansion in Europe.

In the meantime, in 717, another Muslim force had launched an attack on Constantinople with the hope of destroying the Byzantine Empire. But the Byzantines' use of Greek fire, a petroleum-based compound containing quicklime and sulfur, destroyed the Muslim fleet, thus saving the empire and indirectly Christian Europe, since the fall of Constantinople would have opened the door to an Arab invasion of eastern Europe. The Byzantine Empire and Islam now established an uneasy frontier in southern Asia Minor.

Arab power also extended to the east, consolidating Islamic rule in Mesopotamia and Persia and northward into Central Asia. But factional disputes continued to plague the empire. Many Muslims of non-Arab extraction resented the favoritism shown by local administrators to Arabs. In some cases, resentment led to revolt, as in Iraq, where Ali's second son, Hussein, disputed the legitimacy of the Umayyads and incited his supporters—to be known in the future as Shi'ites (from the Arabic phrase *shi'at Ali*, "partisans of Ali")—to rise up against Umayyad rule in 680. Hussein's forces were defeated, but a schism between Shi'ite and Sunni (usually translated as "orthodox") Muslims had been created that continues to this day.

Umayyad rule, always (in historian Arthur Goldschmidt's words) "more political than pious," created resentment, not only in Mesopotamia, but also in North Africa, where Berber resistance continued, especially in the mountainous areas south of the coastal plains. The Umayyads contributed to their own demise by their decadent behavior. One caliph allegedly swam in a pool of wine and then imbibed enough of the contents to lower the

MAP 7.2 The Expansion of Islam This map shows the expansion of the Islamic faith from its origins in the Arabian peninsula. Muhammad's followers carried the religion as far west as Spain and southern France and eastward to India and Southeast Asia. ➤ *In which of these areas is the Muslim faith still the dominant religion?*

wine level significantly. Finally, in 750, a revolt led by Abu al-Abbas, a descendant of Muhammad's uncle, led to the overthrow of the Umayyads and the establishment of the Abbasid dynasty (750–1258) in what is now Iraq.

The Abbasids

The Abbasid caliphs brought political, economic, and cultural change to the world of Islam. While stressing religious orthodoxy, they tried to break down the distinctions between Arab and non-Arab Muslims. All Muslims were now allowed to hold both civil and military offices. This change helped open Islamic culture to the influences of the occupied civilizations. Many Arabs now began to intermarry with the peoples they had conquered. In many parts of the Islamic world, notably North Africa and the eastern Mediterranean, most Muslim converts began to consider themselves Arabs. In 762, the Abbasids built a new capital city at Baghdad, on the Tigris River far to the east of the Umayyad capital at Damascus. The new capital was strategically positioned to take advantage of river traffic to the Persian Gulf and also lay astride the caravan route from the Mediterranean

to Central Asia. The move eastward allowed Persian influence to come to the fore, encouraging a new cultural orientation. Under the Abbasids, judges, merchants, and government officials, rather than warriors, were viewed as the ideal citizens.

The new Abbasid caliphate experienced a period of splendid rule well into the ninth century. Best known of the caliphs of the time was Harun al-Rashid (786–809), or Harun "the Upright," whose reign is often described as the golden age of the Abbasid caliphate. His son al-Ma'mun (813–833) was a patron of learning who founded an astronomical observatory and established a foundation for undertaking translations of classical Greek works. This was also a period of growing economic prosperity. The Arabs had conquered many of the richest provinces of the Roman Empire and now controlled the routes to the east (see Map 7.3). Baghdad became the center of an enormous commercial market that extended into Europe, Central Asia, and Africa, greatly adding to the wealth of the Islamic world and promoting an exchange of culture, ideas, and technology from one end of the known world to the other. Paper was introduced from China and eventually passed on to North Africa and Europe. Crops from India

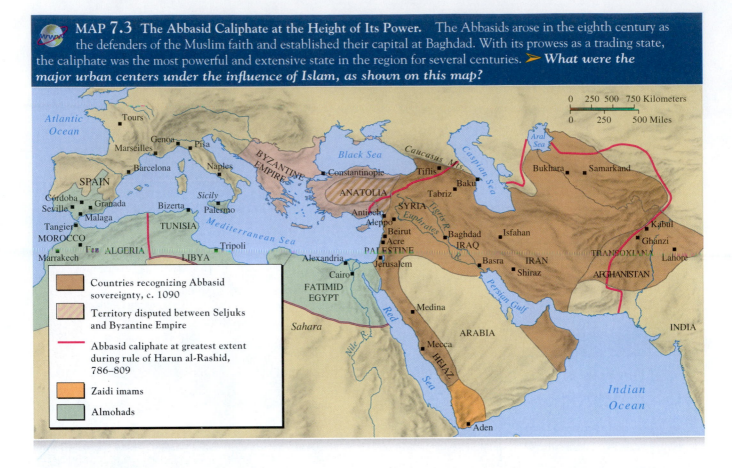

MAP 7.3   The Abbasid Caliphate at the Height of Its Power.   The Abbasids arose in the eighth century as the defenders of the Muslim faith and established their capital at Baghdad. With its prowess as a trading state, the caliphate was the most powerful and extensive state in the region for several centuries. ➤ *What were the major urban centers under the influence of Islam, as shown on this map?*

and Southeast Asia such as rice, sugar, sorghum, and cotton moved toward the west, while glass, wine, and indigo dye were introduced into China.

Under the Abbasids, the caliphs became more regal. More kings than spiritual leaders, described by such august phrases as the "caliph of God," they ruled by autocratic means, hardly distinguishable from the kings and emperors in neighboring civilizations. A thirteenth-century Chinese author, who compiled a world geography based on accounts by Chinese travelers, left the following description of one of the later caliphs:

> The king wears a turban of silk brocade and foreign cotton stuff (buckram). On each new moon and full moon he puts on an eight-sided flat-topped headdress of pure gold, set with the most precious jewels in the world. His robe is of silk brocade and is bound around him with a jade girdle. On his feet he wears golden shoes. . . . The king's throne is set with pearls and precious stones, and the steps of the throne are covered with pure gold.[3]

As the caliph took on more of the trappings of a hereditary autocrat, the bureaucracy assisting him in administering the expanding empire grew more complex as well. The caliph was advised by a council (called a *diwan*) headed by a prime minister, known as a *vizier* (*wazir*). The caliph did not attend meetings of the *diwan* in the normal manner but sat behind a screen and then communi-

cated his divine will to the *vizier*. Some historians have ascribed the change in the caliphate to Persian influence, which permeated the empire after the capital was moved to Baghdad. Persian influence was indeed strong (the mother of the caliph al-Ma'mun, for example, was a Persian), but more likely, the increase in pomp and circumstance was a natural consequence of the growing power and prosperity of the empire.

However, an element of instability lurked beneath the surface. Disputes over the succession to the caliphate were common. At Harun's death, the rivalry between his two sons, Amin and al-Ma'mun, led to civil war and the destruction of Baghdad. As described by the tenth-century Muslim historian al-Mas'udi, "Mansions were destroyed, most remarkable monuments obliterated; prices soared. . . . Brother turned his sword against brother, son against father, as some fought for Amin, others for Ma'mun. Houses and palaces fueled the flames; property was put to the sack."[4]

Vast wealth also contributed to financial corruption. By awarding important positions to court favorites, the Abbasid caliphs began to undermine the foundations of their own power and eventually became mere figureheads. Under Harun al-Rashid, members of his Hashemite clan received large pensions from the state treasury, and his wife, Zubaida, reportedly spent vast sums while shopping on a pilgrimage to Mecca. One powerful family, the Barmakids, amassed vast wealth and power until Harun al-Rashid eliminated the entire clan in a fit of jealousy.

The life of luxury enjoyed by the caliph and other political and economic elites in Baghdad seemingly undermined the stern fiber of Arab society as well as the strict moral code of Islam. Strictures against sexual promiscuity were widely ignored, and caliphs were rumored to maintain thousands of concubines in their harems. Divorce was common, homosexuality was widely practiced, and alcohol was consumed in public despite Islamic law's prohibition against imbibing spirits.

The process of disintegration was accelerated by changes that were taking place within the armed forces and the bureaucracy of the empire. Given the shortage of qualified Arabs for key positions in the army and the administration, the caliphate began to recruit officials from among the non-Arab peoples in the empire, such as Persians and Turks from Central Asia. These people gradually became a dominant force in the army and administration. Eventually, provincial rulers began to break away from central control and establish their own independent dynasties. Spain had already established its own caliphate when a prince of the Umayyad dynasty had escaped execution and fled there in 750. Morocco became independent, and in 973, a new Shi'ite dynasty under the Fatimids was established in Egypt with its capital at Cairo. With increasing disarray in the empire, the Islamic world was held together only by the common commitment to the Koran and the use of Arabic as the prevailing means of communication.

The Seljuk Turks

In the eleventh century, the Abbasid caliphate faced an even more serious threat in the form of the Seljuk Turks. The Seljuk Turks were a nomadic people from Central Asia who had converted to Islam and flourished as military mercenaries for the Abbasid caliphate, where they were known for their ability as mounted archers. Moving gradually into Iran and Armenia as the Abbasids weakened, the Seljuk Turks grew in number until by the eleventh century, they were able to occupy the eastern provinces of the Abbasid empire. In 1055, a Turkish leader captured Baghdad and assumed command of the empire with the title of sultan (the term means "holder of power"). While the Abbasid caliph remained the chief representative of Sunni religious authority, the real military and political power of the state was in the hands of the Seljuk Turks. The latter did not establish their headquarters in Baghdad, which now entered a period of decline.

By the last quarter of the eleventh century, the Seljuks were exerting military pressure on Egypt and the Byzantine Empire. In 1071, when the Byzantines foolishly challenged the Turks, their army was routed at Manzikert, near Lake Van in eastern Turkey, and the victors took over most of the Anatolian peninsula (see Map 7.4). In dire straits,

the Byzantine Empire turned to the west for help, setting in motion the papal pleas that led to the Crusades.

In Europe, and undoubtedly within the Muslim world itself, the arrival of the Turks was regarded as a disaster. The Turks were viewed as barbarians who destroyed civilizations and oppressed populations. In fact, in many respects, Turkish rule in the Middle East was probably beneficial. Converted to Islam, the Turkish rulers temporarily brought an end to the fraternal squabbles between Sunni and Shi'ite Muslims, while supporting the Sunnites. They put their energies into revitalizing Islamic law and institutions and provided much-needed political stability to the empire, which helped restore its former prosperity. In one respect, however, their policies may have been detrimental to the later development of Islam. Adopting a narrow interpretation of the Koran and the *Shari'a,* they encouraged a rigid approach to sacred doctrine that would make it more difficult for the faithful to respond effectively to social changes taking place within Islamic society.

Seljuk political domination over the old Abbasid Empire also provoked resentment on the part of many Iranian Shi'ites, who viewed the Turks as usurping foreigners who had betrayed the true faith of Islam. Among the regime's most feared enemies was Bassan ben Sabbah, a Cairo-trained Persian who formed a rebel group,

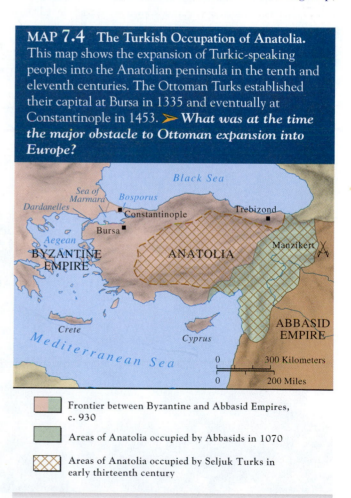

MAP 7.4   The Turkish Occupation of Anatolia. This map shows the expansion of Turkic-speaking peoples into the Anatolian peninsula in the tenth and eleventh centuries. The Ottoman Turks established their capital at Bursa in 1335 and eventually at Constantinople in 1453. ➤ *What was at the time the major obstacle to Ottoman expansion into Europe?*

Frontier between Byzantine and Abbasid Empires, c. 930

Areas of Anatolia occupied by Abbasids in 1070

Areas of Anatolia occupied by Seljuk Turks in early thirteenth century popularly known as "assassins" (guardians), who for several decades terrorized government officials and other leading political and religious figures from their base in the mountains south of the Caspian Sea. Like their modern-day equivalents, the terrorist organization known as al-Qaeda, Sabbah's followers were highly motivated and were adept in infiltrating the enemy's camp in order to carry out their clandestine activities. The organization was finally eliminated by the invading Mongols in the thirteenth century.

The Crusades

Just before the end of the eleventh century, the Byzantine emperor Alexius I desperately called for assistance from other Christian states in Europe to protect his empire against the invading Seljuk Turks. As part of his appeal, he said that the Muslims were desecrating Christian shrines in the Holy Land and also molesting Christian pilgrims en route to the shrines. In actuality, the Muslims had never threatened the shrines or cut off Christian access to them. But tension between Christendom and Islam was on the rise, and the Byzantine

emperor's appeal received a ready response in Europe. Beginning in 1096 and continuing into the thirteenth century, a series of Christian raids on Islamic territories known as the Crusades brought the Holy Land and adjacent areas on the Mediterranean coast from Antioch to the Sinai peninsula under Christian rule (see Chapter 12).

At first, Muslim rulers in the area were taken aback by the invading crusaders, whose armored cavalry presented a new challenge to local warriors, and their response was ineffectual. The Seljuk Turks by that time were preoccupied with events taking place farther to the east and took no action themselves. But in 1169, Sunni Muslims under the leadership of Saladin (Salah al-Din), vizier to the last Fatimid caliph, brought an end to the Fatimid dynasty. Proclaiming himself sultan, Saladin succeeded in establishing his control over both Egypt and Syria, thereby confronting the Christian states in the area with united Muslim power on two fronts. In 1187, Saladin's army invaded the kingdom of Jerusalem and destroyed the Christian forces concentrated there. Further operations reduced Christian occupation in the area to a handful of

⇒ **CASTLE OF THE KNIGHTS.**   Beginning in the eighth century, Muslim rulers erected imposing fortified palaces in the desert. So impressed were the crusaders by the innovative defensive features they saw that they began to incorporate similar ideas into their European castles. In twelfth-century Syria, the crusaders began construction of this imposing citadel, known as the Krak des Chevaliers, on the foundation of a Muslim fort. It housed two thousand fighting monks who, besides defending the premises, chanted Mass in Latin, gossiped in French, and enjoyed Roman baths. Although the fortress was protected by 80-foot-high walls, it was nevertheless captured by Islamic warriors in 1271, the garrison having by then dwindled to two hundred monks.

THE CRUSADES IN MUSLIM EYES

Usamah, an early-twelfth-century Muslim warrior and gentleman, had close associations with the crusaders. When he was ninety years old, he wrote his memoirs including many entertaining observations on the crusaders, or "Franks" as he called them. Here Usamah is astounded at the Franks' rudeness to Muslims and at their assumption of cultural superiority.

USAMAH, BOOK OF REFLECTIONS

1. Everyone who is a fresh emigrant from the Frankish lands is ruder in character than those who have become acclimatized and have held long association with the Moslems. Here is an illustration of their rude character.

Whenever I visited Jerusalem I always entered the Aqsa Mosque, beside which stood a small mosque which the Franks had converted into a church. When I used to enter the Aqsa Mosque, which was occupied by the Templars [an order of crusading knights], who were my friends, the Templars would evacuate the little adjoining mosque so that I might pray in it. One day I entered this mosque, repeated the first formula, "Allah is great," and stood up in the act of praying, upon which one of the Franks rushed on me, got hold of me, and turned my face eastward, saying, "This is the way thou shouldst pray!" A group of Templars hastened to him, seized him, and repelled him from me. I resumed my prayer. The same man, while the others were otherwise busy, rushed once more on me and turned my face eastward,

saying, "This is the way thou shouldst pray!" The Templars again came in to him and expelled him. They apologized to me, saying, "This is a stranger who has only recently arrived from the land of the Franks, and he has never before seen anyone praying except eastward." Thereupon I said to myself, "I have had enough prayer." So I went out, and have ever been surprised at the conduct of this devil of a man, at the change in the color of his face, his trembling, and his sentiment at the sight of one praying toward the qiblah.

2. In the army of King Fulk, son of Fulk, was a Frankish reverend knight who had just arrived from their land in order to make the holy pilgrimage and then return home. He was of my intimate fellowship and kept such constant company with me that he began to call me "my brother." Between us were mutual bonds of amity and friendship. When he resolved to return by sea to his homeland, he said to me:

"My brother, I am leaving for my country and I want thee to send with me thy son (my son, who was then fourteen years old, was at that time in my company) to our country, where he can see the knights and learn wisdom and chivalry. When he returns, he will be like a wise man."

Thus there fell upon my ears words which would never come out of the head of a sensible man; for even if my son were to be taken captive, his captivity could not bring him a worse misfortune than carrying him into the lands of the Franks.

---

fortresses along the northern coast. Unlike the Christians, however, Saladin did not permit a massacre of the civilian population and even tolerated the continuation of Christian religious services in conquered territories.

The Christians returned for another try a few years after the fall of Jerusalem, but the campaign succeeded only in securing some of the coastal cities. Although the Christians would retain a toehold on the coast for much of the thirteenth century (Acre, their last stronghold, fell to the Muslims in 1291), they were no longer a significant force in Middle Eastern affairs. In retrospect, the Crusades had only minimal importance in the history of the Middle East and may even have served to unite the forces of Islam against the foreign invaders, thus creating a residue of distrust toward Christians that continues to resonate through the Islamic world today (see the box above). Far more important in their impact were the Mongols, a pastoral people who swept out of the Gobi Desert in the early thirteenth century to seize control over much of the known world (see Chapter 10). Beginning with the advances of Genghis Khan in northern China, Mongol armies later spread across Central Asia, and in 1258, under the leadership of Hulegu, brother of the more famous Khubilai Khan,

they seized Persia and Mesopotamia, bringing an end to the caliphate at Baghdad.

The Mongols

Unlike the Seljuk Turks, the Mongols were not Muslims, and they found it difficult to adapt to the settled conditions that they found in the major cities in the Middle East. Their treatment of the local population in conquered territories was brutal (according to one historian, after conquering a city, they wiped out not only entire families but also their household pets) and destructive to the economy. Cities were razed to the ground, and dams and other irrigation works were destroyed, reducing prosperous agricultural societies to the point of mass starvation. The Mongols advanced as far as the Red Sea, but their attempt to seize Egypt failed, in part because of the effective resistance posed by the Mamluks (a Turkish military class originally composed of slaves; sometimes written as Mamelukes), who had recently overthrown the administration set up by Saladin and seized power for themselves.

Eventually, the Mongol rulers in the Middle East began to take on the coloration of the peoples that they had conquered. Mongol elites converted to Islam, Persian influence became predominant at court, and the cities began to be rebuilt. By the fourteenth century, the Mongol empire began to split into separate kingdoms and then to disintegrate. In the meantime, however, the old Islamic empire originally established by the Arabs in the seventh and eighth centuries had come to an end. The new center of Islamic civilization was in Cairo, now about to promote a renaissance in Muslim culture under the sponsorship of the Mamluks.

To the north, another new force began to appear on the horizon with the rise of the Ottoman Turks on the Anatolian peninsula. In 1453, Sultan Mehmet II seized Constantinople and brought an end to the decrepit Byzantine Empire. Then the Ottomans began to turn their attention to the rest of the Middle East (see Chapter 15).

ISLAMIC CIVILIZATION

To be a Muslim is not simply to worship Allah but also to live according to his law as revealed in the Koran, which is viewed as fundamental and immutable doctrine, not to be revised by human beings.

As Allah has decreed, so must humans behave. Therefore, Islamic doctrine must be consulted to determine questions of politics, economic behavior, civil and criminal law, and social ethics. In Islamic society, there is no rigid demarcation between church and state, between the sacred and the secular.

The Wealth of Araby: Trade and Cities in the Middle East

As we have noted, this era was probably, overall, one of the most prosperous periods in the history of the Middle East. Trade flourished, not only in the Islamic world but also with China (now in a period of efflorescence during the era of the Tang and the Song dynasties—see Chapter 10), with the Byzantine Empire, and with the trading societies in Southeast Asia (see Chapter 9). Trade goods were carried both by ship and by the "fleets of the desert," the camel caravans that traversed the arid land from Morocco in the far west to the countries beyond the Caspian Sea. From the Sahara came gold and slaves; from China, silk and porcelain; from East Africa, gold, ivory, and rhinoceros horn; and from the lands of South Asia, sandalwood, cotton, wheat, sugar, and spices. Within the empire, Egypt contributed grain; Iraq, linens, dates, and precious stones; Spain, leather goods, olives, and wine; and western India, various textile goods. The exchange of goods was facilitated by the development of banking and the use of currency and letters of credit.

Under these conditions, urban areas flourished. While the Abbasids were in power, Baghdad was probably the greatest city in the empire, but after the rise of the Fatimids in Egypt, the focus of trade shifted to Cairo, described by the traveler Leo Africanus as "one of the greatest and most famous cities in all the whole world, filled with stately and admirable palaces and colleges, and most sumptuous temples."[5] Other great commercial cities included Basra at the head of the Persian Gulf, Aden at the southern tip of the Arabian peninsula, Damascus in modern Syria, and Marrakech in Morocco. In the cities, the inhabitants were generally segregated by religion, with Muslims, Jews, and Christians living in separate neighborhoods. But all were equally subject to the most common threats to urban life—fire, flood, and disease.

The most impressive urban buildings were usually the palace for the caliph or the local governor and the great mosque. Houses were often constructed of stone or brick around a timber frame. The larger houses were often built around an interior courtyard, where the residents could retreat from the dust, noise, and heat of the city streets. Sometimes domestic animals such as goats or sheep would be stabled there. The houses of the wealthy were often multistoried, with balconies and windows covered with latticework to provide privacy for those inside. The poor in both urban and rural areas lived in simpler houses composed of clay or unfired bricks. The Bedouins lived in tents that could be dismantled and moved according to their needs.

Eating habits varied in accordance with economic standing and religious preference. Muslims did not eat pork, but those who could afford it often served other meats such as mutton, lamb, poultry, or fish. Fruit, spices, and various sweets were delicacies. The poor were generally forced to survive on boiled millet or peas with an occasional lump of meat or fat. Bread—white or whole meal—could be found on tables throughout the region except in the deserts, where boiled grain was the staple food.

Islamic Society

In some ways, Arab society was probably one of the most egalitarian of its time. Both the principles of Islam, which held that all were equal in the eyes of Allah, and the importance of trade to the prosperity of the state probably contributed to this egalitarianism. Although there was a fairly well defined upper class, consisting of the ruling families, senior officials, tribal elites, and the wealthiest merchants, there was no hereditary nobility as in many contemporary societies, and the merchants enjoyed a degree of respect that they did not receive in Europe, China, or India.

Though the Arab empire was more urbanized than most other societies at the time, the bulk of the population continued to live in the countryside and supported itself by farming or herding animals. During the early stages, most of the farmland was owned by independent peasants, but later some concentration of land in the hands of wealthy owners began to take place. In river valleys like the Tigris and Euphrates and the Nile, the majority of the farmers probably continued to be independent peasants.

Not all benefited from the high degree of social mobility in the Islamic world, however. Slavery was widespread. Since a Muslim could not be enslaved, the supply came from sub-Saharan Africa or from non-Islamic populations elsewhere in Asia. Most slaves were employed in the army (which was sometimes a road to power, as in the case of the Mamluks) or as domestic servants, who were sometimes permitted to purchase their freedom. The slaves who worked the large estates experienced the worst living conditions and rose in revolt on several occasions.

The Islamic principle of human equality also fell short in the treatment of women. Although the Koran instructed men to treat women with respect, and women did have the right to own and inherit property, in general the male was dominant in Muslim society. Polygyny was permitted, and the right of divorce was in practice restricted to the husband, although some schools of legal thought permitted women to stipulate that their husband could have only one wife or to seek a separation in certain specific circumstances. Adultery and homosexuality were stringently forbidden (although such prohibitions were frequently ignored in practice), and Islamic custom required that women be cloistered in their homes (thus the tradition of the harem) and prohibited from social contacts with males outside their own family. The custom of requiring women to cover virtually all parts of their body when appearing in public was common in urban areas and continues to be practiced in many Islamic societies today. It should be noted, however, that these customs owed more to traditional Arab practice than to Koranic law (see the box on p. 196).

As Islam spread, it assimilated many of the cultural attributes of the peoples it conquered. Consequently, upper-class women in the Arabian peninsula were forced to abandon their freedoms and accept the conditions of a newly imposed patriarchal system. Like women in neighboring regions in the Middle East, they would henceforth don the veil and live in seclusion and submissiveness.

The Culture of Islam

The Arabs were truly heirs to many elements of the remaining Greco-Roman culture of the Roman Empire, and they assimilated Byzantine and Persian culture just as readily. In the eighth and ninth centuries, numerous Greek, Syrian, and Persian scientific and philosophical works were translated into Arabic. As the chief language in the southern Mediterranean and the Middle East, Arabic became an international language. Later, Persian and Turkish also came to be important in administration and culture.

The spread of Islam led to the emergence of a new culture throughout the Arab empire. This was true in all fields of endeavor, from literature to art and architecture. But pre-Islamic traditions were not extinguished and frequently combined with Muslim motifs, resulting in creative works of great imagination and originality.

PHILOSOPHY AND SCIENCE

During the centuries following the rise of the Arab empire, it was the Islamic world that was most responsible for preserving and spreading the scientific and philosophical achievements of ancient civilizations. At a time when ancient Greek philosophy was largely unknown in Europe, key works by Aristotle, Plato, and other Greek philosophers were translated into Arabic and stored in a "house of wisdom" in Baghdad, where they were read and studied by Muslim scholars. Through the writings of the Spanish Muslim philosopher Ibn Rushd (known in the West as Averroës), many of these works eventually became known in Europe and influenced Christian thought. Texts on mathematics and linguistics were brought from India. The process was undoubtedly stimulated by the introduction of paper manufacturing from China in the eighth century. By the end of the century, the first paper factories had been established in Baghdad, and booksellers and libraries soon followed. The first paper mill in Europe appeared in the Pyrenees region of Spain in the twelfth century.

"DRAW THEIR VEILS OVER THEIR BOSOMS"

*P*rior to the Islamic era, many upper-class women greeted men on the street, entertained their husband's friends at home, went on pilgrimages to Mecca, and even accompanied their husbands to battle. Such women were neither veiled nor secluded. Muhammad, however, specified that his own wives, who (according to the Koran) were "not like any other women," should be modestly attired and should be addressed by men from behind a curtain. Over the centuries, Muslim theologians, fearful that female sexuality could threaten the established order, interpreted Muhammad's "modest attire" and his reference to curtains to mean segregated seclusion and body concealment for all Muslim women. In fact, one strict scholar in fourteenth-century Cairo went so far as to prescribe that ideally a woman should be allowed to leave her home only three times in her life: when entering her husband's home after marriage, after the death of parents, and after her own death.

In traditional Islamic societies, veiling and seclusion were more prevalent among urban women than among their rural counterparts. The latter, who worked in the fields and rarely saw people outside their extended family, were less restricted. In this excerpt from the Koran, women are instructed to "guard their modesty" and "draw veils over their bosoms." Nowhere in the Koran, however, does it stipulate that women should be sequestered or covered from head to toe.

THE KORAN: CHAPTER 24

And say to the believing women
That they should lower
Their gaze and guard
Their modesty: that they
Should not display their
Beauty and ornaments except
What [must ordinarily] appear
Thereof: that they should
Draw their veils over
Their bosoms and not display
Their beauty except
To their husbands, their fathers,
Their husbands' fathers, their sons,
Their husbands' sons,
Their brothers or their brothers' sons,
Or their sisters' sons,
Or their women, or the slaves
Whom their right hands
Possess, or male servants
Free of physical needs,
Or small children who
Have no sense of the shame
Of sex; and that they
Should not strike their feet
In order to draw attention
To their hidden ornaments.

Although Islamic scholars are justly praised for preserving much of classical knowledge for the West, they also made considerable advances of their own. Nowhere is this more evident than in mathematics and the natural sciences. Islamic scholars adopted and passed on the numerical system of India, including the use of the zero, and a ninth-century Iranian mathematician created the mathematical discipline of algebra (*al-jebr*). In astronomy, Muslims set up an observatory at Baghdad to study the position of the stars. They were aware that the earth was round and in the ninth century produced a world map based on the tradition of the Greco-Roman astronomer Ptolemy.

Muslim scholars also made many new discoveries in optics and chemistry and, with the assistance of texts on anatomy by the ancient Greek physician Galen (c. 180–200 C.E.), developed medicine as a distinctive field of scientific inquiry. Especially well known was Ibn Sina (980–1037). Known as Avicenna in the West, he compiled a medical encyclopedia that, among other things, emphasized the contagious nature of certain diseases and showed how they could be spread by contaminated water supplies. After its translation into Latin, Avicenna's work

became a basic medical textbook for medieval European university students.

ISLAMIC LITERATURE

Islam brought major changes to the literature of the Middle East. Muslims regarded the Koran as their greatest literary work, but pre-Islamic traditions continued to influence writers throughout the region.

The tradition of Arabic poetry was well established by the time of Muhammad. It extolled Bedouin tribal life, courage in battle, hunting, sports, and respect for the animals of the desert, especially the camel (see the box on p. 197). Because the Arabic language did not possess a written script until the fourth century C.E., poetry was originally passed on by memory. Later, in the eighth and ninth centuries, it was compiled in anthologies.

Pre-Muslim Persia also boasted a long literary tradition, most of it oral and written down in later centuries in the Arabic alphabet. The Persian poetic tradition remained strong under Islam. Rabe'a of Qozdar, Persia's first known woman poet, lived in the second half of the tenth century.

LOVE FOR A CAMEL

*E*arly Arabic poetry focused on simple pleasures, such as wine, women, song, and the faithful camel. This excerpt is from a longer work by the sixth-century Arab poet Tarafah. Tarafah was one of a group of seven poets called the "suspended ones." Their poems, having won a prize in an annual competition, were suspended on a wall for all to read.

THE ODE OF TARAFAH

*Ah, but when grief assails me, straightway I ride it off
    mounted on my swift, lean-flanked camel, night and day
    racing, . . .*

*Her long neck is very erect when she lifts it up, calling to
    mind the rudder of a Tigris-bound vessel. Her skull is
    most like an anvil, the junction of its two halves meeting
    together as it might be on the edge of a file.*

*Her cheek is smooth as Syrian parchment, her split lip
    a tanned hide of Yemen, its slit not bent crooked;
    her eyes are a pair of mirrors, sheltering in the caves of
    her brow-bones, the rock of a pool's hollow, . . .*

*I am at her with the whip, and my she-camel quickens pace
    what time the mirage of the burning stone-tract shimmers;
    elegantly she steps, as a slave-girl at a party will sway,
    showing her master skirts of a trailing white gown.*

*I am not one that skulks fearfully among the hilltops, but
    when the folk seek my succor I gladly give it; if you look
    for me in the circle of the folk you'll find me there, and if
    you hunt me in the taverns there you'll catch me.*

*Come to me when you will, I'll pour you a flowing cup, and
    if you don't need it, well, do without and good luck to
    you!*

*Whenever the tribe is assembled you'll come upon me at the
    summit of the noble House, the oft-frequented; my boon-
    companions are white as stars, and a singing-wench
    comes to us in her striped gown or her saffron robe, wide
    the opening of her collar, delicate her skin to my compan-
    ions' fingers, tender her nakedness.*

*When we say, "Let's hear from you," she advances to us
    chanting fluently, her glance languid, in effortless song.*

Describing the suffering love brings, she wrote: "Beset with impatience I did not know/That the more one seeks to pull away, the tighter becomes the rope."[6]

In the West, the most famous works of Middle Eastern literature are undoubtedly the *Rubaiyat* of Omar Khayyam and *Tales from 1001 Nights* (also called *The Arabian Nights*). Paradoxically, these two works are not as popular with Middle Eastern readers. Both, in fact, were freely translated into Western languages for nineteenth-century European readers, who found themes of wine, women, and hedonistic pleasure more acceptable when set in a quaint foreign disguise.

Unfortunately, very little is known of the life or the poetry of the twelfth-century poet Omar Khayyam. Skeptical, reserved, and slightly contemptuous of his peers, he combined poetry with scientific works on mathematics and astronomy and a revision of the calendar that was more accurate than the Gregorian version devised in Europe hundreds of years later. Omar Khayyam did not write down his poems but composed them orally over wine with friends at a neighborhood tavern. They were recorded later by friends or scribes. Many poems attributed to him were actually written long after his death. Among them is the well-known couplet translated into English in the nineteenth century: "Here with a loaf of bread beneath the bough, a flask of wine, a book of verse, and thou."

Omar Khayyam's poetry is simple and down to earth. Key themes are the impermanence of life, the impossibility of knowing God, and disbelief in an afterlife. Ironically, recent translations of his work appeal to modern attitudes of skepticism and minimalist simplicity that may make him even more popular in the West:

*In youth I studied for a little while;
Later I boasted of my mastery.
Yet this was all the lesson that I learned:
We come from dust, and with the wind are gone.*

*Of all the travelers on this endless road
No one returns to tell us where it leads,
There's little in this world but greed and need;
Leave nothing here, for you will not return. . . .*

*Since no one can be certain of tomorrow,
It's better not to fill the heart with care.
Drink wine by moonlight, darling, for the moon
Will shine long after this, and find us not.*[7]

Like Omar Khayyam's verse, *The Arabian Nights* was loosely translated into European languages and adapted to Western tastes. A composite of folktales, fables, and romances of Indian and indigenous origin, the stories interweave the natural with the supernatural. The earliest stories were told orally and were later transcribed, with many later additions, in Arabic and Persian versions. The famous story of Aladdin and the Magic Lamp, for example, was an eighteenth-century addition. Nevertheless, *The Arabian Nights* has entertained readers for centuries, allowing them to enter a land of wish fulfillment through extraordinary plots, sensuality, comic and tragic situations, and a cast of unforgettable characters.

Sadi (1210–1292), considered the Persian Shakespeare, remains to this day the favorite author in Iran. His *Rose Garden* is a collection of entertaining stories written in prose sprinkled with verse. He is also renowned for his

Sufism was an unorthodox form of Islam that flourished in many parts of the Muslim world. It preached the importance of a highly personal relationship between Allah and the individual believer. Sufi orders began to assume considerable influence by the thirteenth century, perhaps because of the disintegration of the Abbasid empire and the heightened instability throughout the Islamic world. Sufi missionaries played a major role in efforts to spread Islam to India and Central Asia. In this poem, the thirteenth-century Persian poet Rumi describes the mystical relationship achieved by means of passionate music and dance.

RUMI, CALL TO THE DANCE

Come!
But don't join us without music.
We have a celebration here.
Rise and beat the drums.

We are Mansur who said "I am God!"

We are in ecstasy—
Drunk, but not from wine made of grapes.

Whatever your thoughts are about us,
We are far, far from them.

This is the night of the same
When we whirl to ecstasy.

There is light now,
There is light, there is light.

This is true love,
Which means farewell to the mind.
There is farewell today, farewell.

Tonight each flaming heart is a friend of music.
Longing for your lips,
My heart pours out of my mouth.

Hush!
You are made of feeling and thought and passion;
The rest is nothing but flesh and bone.
We are the soul of the world,
Not heavy or sagging like the body.
We are the spirit's treasure,
Not bound to this earth, to time or space.

How can they talk to us of prayer rugs and piety?
We are the hunter and the hunted,
Autumn and spring,
Night and day,
Visible and hidden.
Love is our mother.
We were born of Love.

---

sonnetlike love poems, which set a model for generations to come. Sadi was a master of the pithy maxim:

A cat is a lion in catching mice
But a mouse in combat with a tiger.

He has found eternal happiness who lived a good life,
Because, after his end, good repute will keep his name alive.

When thou fightest with anyone, consider
Whether thou wilt have to flee from him or he from thee.[8]

Some Arabic and Persian literature reflected the deep spiritual and ethical concerns of the Koran. Many writers, however, carried Islamic thought in novel directions. The thirteenth-century poet Rumi, for example, embraced Sufism, a form of religious belief that called for a mystical relationship between Allah and human beings (the term *Sufism* stems from the Arabic word for "wool," referring to the rough wool garments that its adherents wore). Converted to Sufism by a wandering dervish (dervishes, from the word for "poor" in Persian, sought to achieve a mystical union with Allah through dancing and chanting in an ecstatic trance), Rumi abandoned orthodox Islam to embrace God directly through ecstatic love. Realizing that love transcends intellect, he sought to reach God through a trance attained by the whirling dance of the dervish, set to mesmerizing music. As he twirled, the poet extemporized some of the most passionate lyrical verse ever conceived. His faith and art remain an important force in Islamic society today (see the box above).

The Islamic world also made a major contribution to historical writing, another discipline that was stimulated by the introduction of paper manufacturing. The first great Islamic historian was al-Mas'udi. Born in Baghdad in 896, he wrote about both the Muslim and the non-Muslim world, traveling widely in the process. His *Meadows of Gold* is the source of much of our knowledge about the golden age of the Abbasid caliphate. Translations of his work reveal a wide-ranging mind and a keen intellect, combined with a human touch that practitioners of the art in our century might find reason to emulate. Equaling al-Mas'udi in talent and reputation was the fourteenth-century historian Ibn Khaldun. Combining scholarship with government service, Ibn Khaldun was one of the first historians to attempt a philosophy of history.

ISLAMIC ART AND ARCHITECTURE

The art of Islam is a blend of Arab, Turkish, and Persian traditions. Although local influences can be discerned in Egypt, Anatolia, Spain, and other areas and the Mon-

> **MUHAMMAD AND THE SACRED STONE.** In pre-Islamic times, the Arabs were polytheistic, with a supreme deity symbolized by a sacred stone. Although each tribe possessed its own stone, all worshiped the black meteorite stone at a shrine in Mecca called the Ka'aba. In 630 Muhammad proclaimed the Ka'aba to be the sacred shrine of Islam. In this fourteenth-century miniature, we see Muhammad restoring the black stone to its rightful place in the wall of the Ka'aba.

gols introduced an East Asian accent in the thirteenth century, for a long time Islamic art remained remarkably coherent over a wide area. First and foremost, the Arabs, with their new religion and their writing system, served as a unifying force. Fascinated by the mathematics and astronomy they inherited from the Romans or the Babylonians, they developed a sense of rhythm and abstraction that found expression in their use of repetitive geometric ornamentation. The Turks brought abstraction in figurative and nonfigurative designs, and the Persians added their lyrical poetical mysticism. Much Islamic painting, for example, consists of illustrations of Persian texts.

The ultimate expression of Islamic art is to be found in magnificent architectural monuments beginning in the late seventh century. The first great example is the Dome of the Rock, which was built in 691 to proclaim the spiritual and political legitimacy of the new religion to the ancient world. Set in the sacred heart of Jerusalem on Muhammad's holy rock and touching both the Western Wall of the Jews and the oldest Christian church, the Dome of the Rock remains one of the most revered Islamic monuments. Constructed on Byzantine lines with an octagonal shape and marble columns and ornamentation, the interior reflects Persian motifs with mosaics of precious stones. Although rebuilt several times and incorporating influences from both East and West, this first monument to Islam represents the birth of a new art.

At first, desert Arabs, whether nomads or conquering armies, prayed in an open court, shaded along the *kibla* (the wall facing the holy city of Mecca) by a thatched roof supported by rows of palm trunks. There was also a ditch where the faithful could wash off the dust of the desert prior to prayer. As Islam became better established, enormous mosques were constructed, but they were still modeled on the open court, which would be surrounded on all four sides with pillars supporting a wooden roof over the prayer area facing the *kibla* wall. The largest mosque ever built, the Great Mosque of Samarra (848–852), covered 10 acres and contained 464 pillars in aisles surrounding the court. Set in the *kibla* wall was a niche, or *mihrab*, containing a decorated panel pointing to Mecca and representing Allah.

> **AN ENTRANCE PORTAL.** This entrance gate to an Iranian mosque displays the variety and delicacy of the geometrical decorations that often accompanied Islamic architecture. The brilliant blue-and-white mosaic tile shown here eventually evolved into polychromy by the fifteenth century. Note the veiled women in the foreground.

Remains of the massive 30-foot-high outer wall still stand, but the most famous section of the Samarra mosque was its 90-foot-tall minaret, the tower accompanying a mosque from which the *muezzin* (crier) calls the faithful to prayer five times a day.

No discussion of mosques would be complete without mentioning the famous ninth-century mosque at Córdoba in southern Spain, which is still in remarkable condition. Its 514 columns supporting double horseshoe arches transform this architectural wonder into a unique forest of trees pointing upward, contributing to a light and airy effect. The unparalleled sumptuousness and elegance make the Córdoba mosque one of the wonders of world art, let alone Islamic art.

Since the Muslim religion combines spiritual and political power in one, palaces also reflected the glory of Islam. Beginning in the eighth century with the spectacular castles of Syria, the rulers constructed large brick domiciles reminiscent of Roman design, with protective walls, gates, and baths. With a central courtyard surrounded by two-story arcades and massive gate-towers, they resembled fortresses as much as palaces. Characteristic of such "desert palaces" was the gallery over the entrance gate, with holes through which boiling oil could be poured down on the heads of attacking forces. Unfortunately, none of these structures has survived.

The ultimate remaining Islamic palace is the fourteenth-century Alhambra in Spain. The extensive succession of courtyards, rooms, gardens, and fountains created a fairy-tale castle perched high above the city of Granada. Every inch of surface is decorated in intricate floral and semiabstract patterns; much of the decoration is done in carved plasterwork so fine that it resembles lace. The Lion Court in the center of the harem is world renowned for its lion fountain and surrounding arcade with elegant columns and carvings.

One of the most significant contributions of Islamic art is the knotted woolen rug. Originating in the pre-Muslim era, rugs were initially used to insulate stone

➤➤ **THE MOSQUE AT CÓRDOBA.**   Perhaps the most impressive of all Islamic religious structures is the Mosque of Córdoba, in southern Spain, which was built between the eighth and tenth centuries. Shown here is the interior of the mosque, showing some of the columns that give the entire structure an effect of mass as well as lightness.

➤➤ **THE ALHAMBRA IN GRANADA.**   Islamic civilization reached its zenith with the fourteenth-century fairy-tale castle of Alhambra in southern Spain. Perched on a hill high above the city of Granada and framed by snowcapped mountains, the Alhambra is widely considered the most perfect expression of Islamic art. Renowned for its lacelike plaster decorations and imaginative use of reflecting pools and fountains, the Alhambra stands as an exquisite gem of Islam.

© Scala/Art Resource, NY

Courtesy of William J. Duiker

palaces against the cold as well as to warm shepherds' tents. Eventually they were applied to religious purposes, since every practicing Muslim is required to pray five times a day on clean ground. Small rugs served as prayer mats for individual use, while larger and more elaborate ones were given by rulers as rewards for political favors. Bedouins in the Arabian desert covered their sandy floors with rugs to create a cozy environment in their tents.

In villages throughout the Middle East, the art of rug weaving has been passed down from mother to daughter over the centuries. Small girls as young as four years old took part in the process by helping to spin and prepare the wool shorn from the family sheep. By the age of six, girls would begin their first rug, and before adolescence, their slender fingers would be producing fine carpets. Skilled artisanship represented an extra enticement to prospective bridegrooms, and rugs often became an important part of a woman's dowry to her future husband. After the wedding, the wife would continue to make rugs for home use, as well as for sale to augment the family income. Eventually, rugs began to be manufactured in workshops by professional artisans, who reproduced the designs from detailed painted diagrams.

Most decorations on the rugs, as well as on all forms of Islamic art, consisted of Arabic script and natural plant and figurative motifs. Repeated continuously in naturalistic or semiabstract geometrical patterns called arabesques, these decorations completely covered the surface and left no area undecorated. This dense decor was also evident in brick, mosaic, and stucco ornamentation and culminated in the magnificent tile work of later centuries.

No representation of the Prophet Muhammad ever adorned a mosque, in painting or in any other art form. Although no passage of the Koran forbids representational painting, the *Hadith*, an early collection of the Prophet's sayings, warned against any attempt to imitate God through artistic creation or idolatry. From the time of the Dome of the Rock, no figurative representations appear in Islamic religious art.

Human beings and animals could still be represented in secular art, but relatively little survives from the early centuries aside from a very few wall paintings from the royal palaces. Although the Persians used calligraphy and art to decorate their books, the Arabs had no pictorial tradition of their own and only began to develop the art of book illustration in the late twelfth century to illustrate translations of Greek scientific works.

In the thirteenth century, a Mongol dynasty established at Tabriz, west of the Caspian Sea, offered the Middle East its first direct contact with the art of East Asia. Mongol painting, done in the Chinese manner with a full brush and expressing animated movement and intensity (see Chapter 10), freed Islamic painters from traditional confines and enabled them to experiment with new techniques.

Courtesy of William J. Duiker

THE KORAN AS SCULPTURED DESIGN. Muslim sculptors and artists, reflecting the official view that any visual representation of the prophet Muhammad was blasphemous, turned to geometric patterns, as well as to flowers and animals, as a means of fulfilling their creative urge. The predominant motif, however, was the reproduction of Koranic verses in the Arabic script. Calligraphy, which was almost as important in the Middle East as it was in traditional China, used the Arabic script to decorate all of the Islamic arts, from painting to pottery, tile and iron work, and wall decorations such as this carved plaster panel in a courtyard of the Alhambra palace in Spain. Since a recitation from the Koran was an important component of the daily devotional activities for all practicing Muslims, elaborate scriptural panels such as this one perfectly blended the spiritual and the artistic realms.

THE BYZANTINE EMPIRE

In the fourth century, a noticeable separation between the western and eastern parts of the Roman Empire began to develop. In the course of the fifth century, while the Germans moved into the western part of the empire and established various kingdoms, the Roman Empire in the east, centered on Constantinople, continued to exist and even prosper.

The Reign of Justinian (527–565)

In the sixth century, the empire in the east came under the control of one of its most remarkable rulers, the emperor Justinian. As the nephew and heir of the previous emperor, Justinian had been well trained in imperial administration. He married Theodora, daughter of a lower-class circus trainer, who proved to be a remarkably strong-willed woman and played a crucial role in giving Justinian the determination to crush a revolt against his rule in 532. Justinian was determined to reestablish the Roman Empire in the entire Mediterranean world and began his attempt to reconquer the west within a year after the revolt had failed.

Justinian's army under Belisarius, probably the best general of the late Roman world, presented a formidable force. Belisarius sailed to North Africa and quickly destroyed the Vandals in two major battles. From North Africa, he led his forces onto the Italian peninsula after occupying Sicily in 535. But it was not until 552 that the Ostrogoths were finally defeated. Justinian appeared to have achieved his goals. He had restored the imperial Mediterranean world; his empire included Italy, part of Spain, North Africa, Asia Minor, Palestine, and Syria (see Map 7.5). But the conquest of the western empire proved fleeting. Only three years after Justinian's death, the Lombards entered Italy. Although the eastern empire maintained the fiction of Italy as a province, its forces were limited to southern and central Italy, Sicily, and coastal areas, such as the territory around Ravenna.

THE CODIFICATION OF ROMAN LAW

Though his conquests proved short-lived, Justinian made a lasting contribution through his codification of Roman law. The eastern empire was heir to a vast quantity of materials connected to the development of Roman law. These included laws passed by the senate and assemblies, legal commentaries of jurists, decisions of praetors, and the edicts of emperors. Justinian had been thoroughly trained in imperial government and was well acquainted with Roman law. He wished to codify and simplify this mass of materials.

To accomplish his goal, Justinian authorized the jurist Trebonian to make a systematic compilation of imperial edicts. The result was the Code of Law, the first part of the *Corpus Iuris Civilis* (Body of Civil Law), completed in 529. Four years later, two other parts of the *Corpus* appeared: the *Digest*, a compendium of writings of Roman jurists, and the *Institutes*, a brief summary of the chief principles of Roman law that could be used as a textbook on Roman law. The fourth part of the *Corpus* was the *Novels*, a compilation of the most important new edicts issued during Justinian's reign.

Justinian's codification of Roman law became the basis of imperial law in the Byzantine Empire until its end in 1453. More important, however, since it was written in Latin (it was in fact the last product of eastern Roman culture to be written in Latin, which was soon replaced by Greek), it was also eventually used in the West and became the basis of the legal system of all of continental Europe.

LIFE IN CONSTANTINOPLE: THE EMPEROR'S BUILDING PROGRAM

After riots destroyed much of Constantinople in 532, Justinian rebuilt the city and gave it the appearance it would keep for almost a thousand years. With a population estimated in the hundreds of thousands, Constantinople was the largest city in Europe during the Middle Ages. It viewed itself as the center of an empire and a special Christian city.

Until the twelfth century, Constantinople was Europe's greatest commercial center. The city was the chief entrepôt for the exchange of products between West and East. Highly desired in Europe were the products of the East: silk from China, spices from Southeast Asia and India, jewelry and ivory from India (the latter used by artisans for church items), wheat and furs from southern Russia, and flax and honey from the Balkans. Many of these

⤳ **THE EMPEROR JUSTINIAN AND HIS COURT.** As the seat of Byzantine power in Italy, the town of Ravenna became adorned with examples of Byzantine art. The church of San Vitale at Ravenna contains some of the finest examples of sixth-century Byzantine mosaics, in which small pieces of colored glass were attached to the wall to form these figures and their surroundings. The emperor is seen as both head of state (he wears a jeweled crown and a purple robe) and head of the church (he carries a gold bowl symbolizing the body of Jesus).

MAP 7.5 The Byzantine Empire in the Time of Justinian.   The Byzantine emperor Justinian briefly restored much of the Mediterranean portion of the old Roman Empire. His general Belisarius quickly conquered the Vandals in North Africa but wrested Italy from the Ostrogoths only after a long and devastating struggle. ➤ *Examine Map 5.3. What former Roman territories lay outside Justinian's control?*

eastern goods were then shipped to the Mediterranean area and northern Europe. Despite the Germanic incursions, European trade did not entirely end.

Moreover, imported raw materials were used in Constantinople for local industries. During Justinian's reign, two Christian monks smuggled silkworms from China to begin a silk industry. The state had a monopoly on the production of silk cloth, and the workshops themselves were housed in Constantinople's royal palace complex. European demand for silk cloth made it the city's most lucrative product. It is interesting to note that the upper classes, including emperors and empresses, were not discouraged from making money through trade and manufacturing. Indeed, one empress even manufactured perfumes in her bedroom.

Much of Constantinople's appearance in the Early Middle Ages was due to Justinian's program of rebuilding in the sixth century. Earlier, Emperor Theodosius II (408–450) had constructed an enormous defensive wall to protect the city on its land side. The city was dominated by an immense palace complex, a huge arena known as the Hippodrome, and hundreds of churches. No residential district was particularly fashionable; palaces, tenements, and slums ranged alongside one another. Justinian added many new buildings. His public works projects included roads, bridges, walls, public baths, law courts, and colossal underground reservoirs to hold the city's water supply. He also built hospitals, schools, monasteries, and churches. Churches were his special passion, and in Constantinople alone he built or rebuilt thirty-four of them. His greatest achievement was the famous Hagia Sophia, the Church of the Holy Wisdom.

Completed in 537, Hagia Sophia was designed by a Greek architect who did not use the simple, flat-roofed basilica of Western architecture. The center of Hagia Sophia consisted of four huge piers crowned by an enormous dome, which seemed to be floating in space. This effect was emphasized by Procopius, the court historian, who, at Justinian's request, wrote a treatise on the emperor's building projects: "From the lightness of the building, it does not appear to rest upon a solid foundation, but to cover the place beneath as though it were

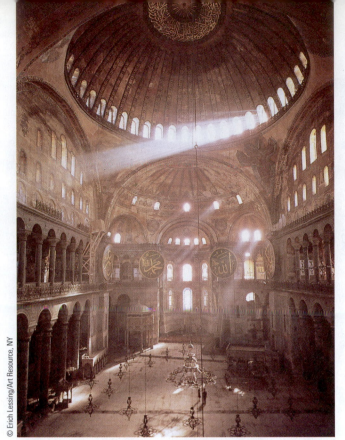

❧ **INTERIOR VIEW OF HAGIA SOPHIA.** Pictured here is the interior of the Church of the Holy Wisdom, constructed under Justinian by Anthemius of Tralles and Isidore of Milan. The pulpits and the great plaques bearing inscriptions from the Koran were introduced when the Turks converted this church into a mosque in the fifteenth century.

suspended from heaven by the fabled golden chain."[9] In part, this impression was created by putting forty-two windows around the base of the dome, which allowed an incredible play of light within the cathedral. Light served to remind the worshipers of God; as Procopius commented:

> Whoever enters there to worship perceives at once that it is not by any human strength or skill, but by the favor of God that this work has been perfected; his mind rises sublime to commune with God, feeling that He cannot be far off, but must especially love to dwell in the place which he has chosen; and this takes place not only when a man sees it for the first time, but it always makes the same impression upon him, as though he had never beheld it before.[10]

As darkness is illumined by invisible light, so too it was believed the world is illumined by invisible spirit.

The royal palace complex, Hagia Sophia, and the Hippodrome were the three greatest buildings in Constantinople. This last was a huge amphitheater, constructed of brick covered by marble, holding between forty and sixty thousand spectators. Although gladiator fights were held there, the main events were the chariot races; twenty-four would usually be presented in one day. The citizens of Constantinople were passionate fans of chariot racing. Successful charioteers were acclaimed as heroes and honored with pub-

lic statues. Crowds in the Hippodrome also took on political significance. Being a member of the two chief factions of charioteers—the Blues or the Greens—was the only real outlet for political expression. Even emperors had to be aware of their demands and attitudes: the loss of a race in the Hippodrome frequently resulted in bloody riots, and rioting could threaten the emperor's power.

From Eastern Roman to Byzantine Empire

Justinian's accomplishments had been spectacular, but when he died, he left the eastern Roman Empire with serious problems: too much distant territory to protect, an empty treasury, a smaller population after a plague, and renewed threats to the frontiers. In the first half of the seventh century, during the reign of Heraclius (610–641), the empire faced attacks from the Persians to the east and the Slavs to the north.

The empire was left exhausted by these struggles. In the midst of them, it had developed a new system of defense by creating a new administrative unit, the *theme*, which combined civilian and military offices in the hands of the same person. Thus the civil governor was also the military leader of the area. Although this innovation helped the empire survive, it also fostered increased militarization. By the mid-seventh century, it had become apparent that a restored Mediterranean empire was simply beyond the resources of the eastern empire, which now increasingly turned its back on the Latin west. A renewed series of external threats in the second half of the seventh century strengthened this development.

The most serious challenge to the eastern empire was presented by the rise of Islam, which, as noted earlier in the chapter, created a powerful new force that swept through the east. The defeat of the eastern Roman army at Yarmuk in 636 meant the loss of the provinces of Syria and Palestine. The Arabs also moved into the old Persian Empire and conquered it. The failed Arab attempt to besiege Constantinople in 717 left Arabs and eastern Roman forces facing each other along a frontier in southern Asia Minor.

Problems also arose along the northern frontier, especially in the Balkans, where an Asiatic people known as the Bulgars had arrived earlier in the sixth century. In 679, the Bulgars defeated the eastern Roman forces and took possession of the lower Danube valley, setting up a strong Bulgarian kingdom.

By the beginning of the eighth century, the eastern Roman Empire was greatly diminished in size, consisting only of the eastern Balkans and Asia Minor. It was now an eastern Mediterranean state. These external challenges had important internal repercussions as well. By the eighth century, the eastern Roman Empire had been transformed into what historians call the Byzantine Empire (sometimes referred to as Byzantium), a civilization with its own unique character that would last until 1453. (Constantinople was built on the site of an older city named Byzantium—hence the term *Byzantine*.)

THE BYZANTINE EMPIRE IN THE EIGHTH CENTURY

The Byzantine Empire was a Greek state. Latin fell into disuse as Greek became not only the common language of the Byzantine Empire but its official language as well.

The Byzantine Empire was also a Christian state, built on a faith in Jesus that was shared in a profound way by almost all its citizens. An enormous amount of artistic talent was poured into church construction, church ceremonies, and church decoration. Spiritual principles deeply permeated Byzantine art. The importance of religion to the Byzantines explains why theological disputes took on an exaggerated form. The most famous of these disputes, the so-called iconoclasic controversy, threatened the stability of the empire in the first half of the eighth century.

Beginning in the sixth century, the use of religious images, especially in the form of icons or pictures of sacred figures, became so widespread that charges of idolatry (the worship of images) began to be heard. The use of images or icons had been justified by the argument that icons were not worshiped but were simply used to help illiterate people understand their religion. This argument failed to stop the iconoclasts, as the opponents of icons were called. Beginning in 730, the Byzantine emperor Leo III (717–741) outlawed the use of icons. Strong resistance ensued, especially from monks. Leo III also used the iconoclastic controversy to add to the prestige of the patriarch of Constantinople, the highest church official in the east and second in dignity only to the bishop of Rome. The Roman popes were opposed to the iconoclastic edicts, and their opposition created considerable dissension between the popes and the Byzantine emperors. Late in the eighth century, the Byzantine rulers reversed their stand on the use of images, but not before considerable damage had been done to the unity of the Christian church. Although the final separation between Roman Catholicism and Greek Orthodoxy (as the Christian church in the Byzantine Empire was called) did not occur until 1054, the iconoclastic controversy was important in moving both sides in that direction.

The emperor occupied a crucial position in the Byzantine state. Portrayed as chosen by God, the Byzantine emperor was crowned in sacred ceremonies, and his subjects were expected to prostrate themselves in his presence. His power was considered absolute and was limited in practice only by deposition or assassination. Because the emperor

The Byzantine Empire, c. 800

appointed the patriarch, he also exercised control over both church and state. The Byzantines believed that God had commanded their state to preserve the true faith—Orthodox Christianity. Emperor, clergy, and civic officials were all bound together in service to this ideal. It can be said that spiritual values truly held the Byzantine state together.

By 750, it was apparent that two of Rome's heirs, the Germanic kingdoms and the Byzantine Empire, were moving in different directions. Nevertheless, Byzantine influence on the medieval Western world was significant. The images of a Roman imperial state that continued to haunt the West had a living reality in the Byzantine state. The legal system of the West came to owe much to Justinian's codification of Roman law. In addition, the Byzantine Empire served in part as a buffer state, protecting the West for a long time from incursions from the east.

The Zenith of Byzantine Civilization

In the seventh and eighth centuries, the Byzantine Empire had lost much of its territory to Slavs, Bulgars, and Muslims. By 750, the empire consisted only of Asia Minor, some lands in the Balkans, and the southern coast of Italy. Although Byzantium was beset with internal dissension and invasions in the ninth century, it was able to deal with them and not only endured but even expanded, reaching its high point in the tenth century, which some historians have called the golden age of Byzantine civilization.

During the reign of Michael III (842–867), the Byzantine Empire began to experience a revival. Iconoclasm was finally abolished in 843, and reforms were made in education, church life, the military, and the peasant economy. There was a noticeable intellectual renewal. But the Byzantine Empire under Michael was still plagued by persistent problems. The Bulgars mounted new attacks, and the Arabs continued to harass the empire. Moreover, a new church problem with political repercussions erupted over differences between the pope as leader of the western Christian church and the patriarch of Constantinople as leader of the eastern (or Orthodox) Christian church. Patriarch Photius condemned the pope as a heretic for accepting a revised form of the Nicene Creed stating that the Holy Spirit proceeded from the Father and the Son instead of "the Holy Spirit, who proceeds from the Father." A council of eastern bishops followed Photius' wishes and excommunicated the pope, creating the so-called Photian schism. Although the differences were later papered over, this controversy served to further the division between the eastern and western Christian churches.

A WESTERN VIEW OF THE BYZANTINE EMPIRE

ishop Liudprand of Cremona undertook diplomatic missions to Constantinople on behalf of two western kings, Berengar of Italy and Otto I of Germany. This selection is taken from his description of his mission to the Byzantine emperor Constantine VII in 949 as an envoy for Berengar, king of Italy from 950 until his overthrow by Otto I of Germany in 964. Liudprand had mixed feelings about Byzantium: admiration, yet also envy and hostility because of its superior wealth.

LIUDPRAND OF CREMONA, ANTAPODOSIS

Next to the imperial residence at Constantinople there is a palace of remarkable size and beauty which the Greeks call Magnavra . . . the name being equivalent to "Fresh breeze." In order to receive some Spanish envoys, who had recently arrived, as well as myself . . . , Constantine gave orders that this palace should be got ready. . . .

Before the emperor's seat stood a tree, made of bronze gilded over, whose branches were filled with birds, also made of gilded bronze, which uttered different cries, each according to its varying species. The throne itself was so marvelously fashioned that at one moment it seemed a low structure, and at another it rose high into the air. It was of immense size and was guarded by lions, made either of bronze or of wood covered over with gold, who beat the ground with their tails and gave a dreadful roar with open mouth and quivering tongue. Leaning upon the shoulders of two eunuchs I was brought into the emperor's presence. At my approach the lions began to roar and the birds to cry out, each according to its kind; but I was neither terrified nor surprised, for I had previously made enquiry about all these things from people who were

well acquainted with them. So after I had three times made obeisance to the emperor with my face upon the ground, I lifted my head, and behold! The man whom just before I had seen sitting on a moderately elevated seat had now changed his raiment and was sitting on the level of the ceiling. How it was done I could not imagine, unless perhaps he was lifted up by some such sort of device as we use for raising the timbers of a wine press. On that occasion he did not address me personally, . . . but by the intermediary of a secretary he enquired about Berengar's doings and asked after his health. I made a fitting reply and then, at a nod from the interpreter, left his presence and retired to my lodging.

It would give me some pleasure also to record here what I did then for Berengar. . . . The Spanish envoys . . . had brought handsome gifts from their masters to the emperor Constantine. I for my part had brought nothing from Berengar except a letter and that was full of lies. I was very greatly disturbed and shamed at this and began to consider anxiously what I had better do. In my doubt and perplexity it finally occurred to me that I might offer the gifts, which on my account I had brought for the emperor, as coming from Berengar, and trick out my humble present with fine words. I therefore presented him with nine excellent cuirasses, seven excellent shields with gilded bosses, two silver gilt cauldrons, some swords, spears, and spits, and what was more precious to the emperor than anything, four carzimasia; that being the Greek name for young eunuchs who have had both their testicles and their penis removed. This operation is performed by traders at Verdun, who take the boys into Spain and make a huge profit.

THE MACEDONIAN DYNASTY

The problems that arose during Michael's reign were effectively dealt with by a new dynasty of Byzantine emperors known as the Macedonians (867–1056), who managed to hold off the external enemies, go over to the offensive, and reestablish domestic order. Supported by the church, the emperors thought of the Byzantine Empire as a continuation of the Christian Roman Empire of late antiquity. Although for diplomatic reasons they occasionally recognized the imperial title of western emperors, such as Charlemagne and Otto I, they still regarded them as little more than barbarian parvenus.

The Macedonian emperors could boast of a remarkable number of achievements in the late

The Byzantine Empire, 1025

ninth and tenth centuries. They worked to strengthen the position of the free farmers, who felt threatened by the attempts of landed aristocrats to expand their estates at the farmers' expense. The emperors were well aware that the free farmers made up the rank and file of the Byzantine cavalry and provided the military strength of the empire. The Macedonian emperors also fostered a burst of economic prosperity by expanding trade relations with western Europe, especially by selling silks and metalwork. Thanks to this prosperity, the city of Constantinople flourished. Foreign visitors continued to be astounded by its size, wealth, and physical surroundings. To western Europeans, it was the stuff of legends and fables (see the box above).

In this period of prosperity, Byzantine cultural influence expanded due to the active missionary efforts of eastern Byzantine Christians. Eastern Orthodox Christianity was spread to eastern European peoples, such as the Bulgars and Serbs. Perhaps the greatest missionary success occurred when the prince of Kiev in Russia converted to Christianity in 987.

Under the Macedonian rulers, Byzantium enjoyed a strong civil service, talented emperors, and military advances. The Byzantine civil service was staffed by well-educated, competent aristocrats from Constantinople who oversaw the collection of taxes, domestic administration, and foreign policy. At the same time, the Macedonian dynasty produced some truly outstanding emperors skilled in administration and law, including Leo VI (886–912) and Basil II (976–1025). In the tenth century, competent emperors combined with a number of talented generals to mobilize the empire's military resources and take the offensive. The Bulgars were defeated, and both the eastern and western parts of Bulgaria were annexed to the empire. The Byzantines went on to add the islands of Crete and Cyprus to the empire and defeat the Muslim forces in Syria, expanding the empire to the upper Euphrates. By the end of the reign of Basil II in 1025, the Byzantine Empire was the largest it had been since the beginning of the seventh century.

New Challenges to the Byzantine Empire

The Macedonian dynasty of the tenth and eleventh centuries had restored much of the power of the Byzantine Empire; its incompetent successors, however, reversed most of the gains. After the Macedonian dynasty was extinguished in 1056, the empire was beset by internal struggles for power between ambitious military leaders and aristocratic families who attempted to buy the support of the great landowners of Anatolia by allowing them greater control over their peasants. This policy was self-destructive, however, because the peasant-warrior was the traditional backbone of the Byzantine state.

The growing division between the Catholic church of the West and the Eastern Orthodox church of the Byzantine Empire also weakened the Byzantine state. The Eastern Orthodox church was unwilling to accept the pope's claim that he was the sole head of the church. This dispute reached a climax in 1054 when Pope Leo IX and Patriarch Michael Cerularius, head of the Byzantine church, formally excommunicated each other, initiating a schism between the two great branches of Christianity that has not been completely healed to this day.

The Byzantine Empire faced external threats to its security as well. The greatest challenge came from the Seljuk Turks who had moved into Asia Minor—the heartland of the empire and its main source of food and manpower. After the Byzantine forces were disastrously defeated at Manzikert by a Turkish army in 1071, the Turks advanced into Anatolia, where many peasants, already disgusted by their

exploitation at the hands of Byzantine landowners, readily accepted Turkish control (see Map 7.4 on p. 191).

A new dynasty, however, soon breathed new life into the Byzantine Empire. The Comneni, under Alexius I Comnenus (1081–1118), were victorious on the Greek Adriatic coast against the Normans, defeated the Pechenegs in the Balkans, and stopped the Turks in Anatolia. Lacking the resources to undertake additional campaigns against the Turks, Emperor Alexius I turned to the West for military assistance. The positive response to the emperor's request led to the Crusades. The Byzantine Empire lived to regret it.

Impact of the Crusades

Ultimately, the Crusades had an enormous impact on the Byzantine Empire. In the First Crusade, the mostly French bands of crusading knights ignored their oath of allegiance and promises to Byzantine Emperor Alexis and organized their own crusader states in Palestine (see Chapter 12). Even more disastrous was the Fourth Crusade. On its way to Palestine, the crusading army became involved in a dispute over the succession to the Byzantine throne. The Venetian leaders of the Fourth Crusade saw an opportunity to neutralize the greatest commercial competitor, the Byzantine Empire. Diverted to Constantinople, the crusaders sacked the great capital city in 1204 and set up the Latin Empire of Constantinople. Some parts of the Byzantine Empire managed to survive under Byzantine princes. In 1259, Michael Paleologus, a Greek military leader, took control of the kingdom of Nicaea in western Asia Minor and led a Byzantine army in recapturing Constantinople two years later.

The Byzantine Empire had been saved, but it was no longer a great Mediterranean power. The restored empire now consisted of the city of Constantinople and its surrounding territory along with some lands in Asia Minor. Though reduced in size, the empire limped along for another two centuries until its weakened condition finally enabled the Ottoman Turks to conquer it in 1453.

 ## CONCLUSION

After the collapse of Roman power in the west, the eastern Roman Empire, centered on Constantinople, continued in the eastern Mediterranean and eventually emerged as the unique Christian civilization known as the Byzantine Empire, which flourished for hundreds of years. One of the greatest challenges to the Byzantine Empire, however, came from a new force—Islam—that blossomed in the Arabian peninsula and spread rapidly throughout the Middle East. In the eyes of some Europeans during the Middle Ages, the Arab empire was a malevolent force that posed a serious threat to the security of Christianity. Their fears were not entirely misplaced, for within half a century after the death of Islam's founder, Muhammad, Arab armies overran Christian states in North Africa and the Iberian peninsula, and Turkish Muslims moved eastward onto the fringes of the Indian subcontinent.

But although the teachings of Muhammad brought war and conquest to much of the known world, they also brought hope and a sense of political and economic stability to peoples throughout the region. Thus for many people in the medieval Mediterranean world, the arrival of Islam was a welcome event. Islam brought a code of law and a written language to societies that had previously not possessed them. Finally, by creating a revitalized trade network stretching from West Africa to East Asia, it established a vehicle for the exchange of technology and ideas that brought untold wealth to thousands and a better life to millions.

Like other empires in the region, the Arab empire did not last. It fell victim to a combination of internal and external pressures, and by the end of the thirteenth century, it was no more than a memory. But it left a powerful legacy in Islam, which remains one of the great religions of the world. In succeeding centuries, Islam began to penetrate into new areas beyond the edge of the Sahara and across the Indian Ocean into the islands of the Indonesian archipelago.

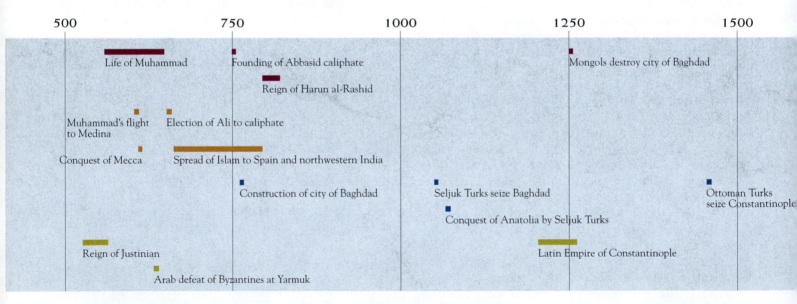

500   750   1000   1250   1500

Life of Muhammad

Founding of Abbasid caliphate

Mongols destroy city of Baghdad

Reign of Harun al-Rashid

Muhammad's flight to Medina

Election of Ali to caliphate

Conquest of Mecca

Spread of Islam to Spain and northwestern India

Construction of city of Baghdad

Seljuk Turks seize Baghdad

Ottoman Turks seize Constantinople

Conquest of Anatolia by Seljuk Turks

Reign of Justinian

Latin Empire of Constantinople

Arab defeat of Byzantines at Yarmuk

CHAPTER NOTES

1. Mohammed Marmaduke Pickthall, trans., *The Meaning of the Glorious Koran* (New York, 1953), p. 89.
2. Quoted in Thomas W. Lippman, *Understanding Islam: An Introduction to the Moslem World* (New York, 1982), p. 118.
3. Friedrich Hirth and W. W. Rockhill, trans., *Chau Ju-kua: His Work on the Chinese and Arab Trade in the Twelfth and Thirteenth Centuries, Entitled Chu-fan-chi* (New York, 1966), p. 115.

4. al-Mas'udi, *The Meadows of Gold: The Abbasids*, ed. Paul Lunde and Caroline Stone (London, 1989), p. 151.

5. Leo Africanus, *The History and Description of Africa and of the Notable Things Therein Contained* (New York, n.d.), pp. 820–821.

6. Ehsan Yarshater, ed., *Persian Literature* (Albany, N.Y., 1988), pp. 125–126.

7. Ibid., pp. 154–159.

8. E. Rehatsek, trans., *The Gulistan or Rose Garden of Sa'di* (New York, 1964), pp. 65, 67, 71.

9. Procopius, *Buildings of Justinian* (London, 1897), p. 9.

10. Ibid., p. 11.

SUGGESTED READING

Standard works on the Arab empire and the rise of Islam include B. Lewis, *The Arabs in History* (New York, 1961), and T. Lippman, *Understanding Islam: An Introduction to the Moslem World* (New York, 1982). More up-to-date is G. E. Perry, *The Middle East: Fourteen Islamic Centuries*, 2d ed. (Englewood Cliffs, N.J., 1992). Worthwhile studies include B. Lewis, *The Middle East: A Brief History of the Last 2,000 Years* (New York, 1986); K. Armstrong, *Islam: A Short History* (New York, 2000); and J. L. Esposito, ed., *The Oxford History of Islam* (New York, 1999). For anthropological background, see D. Bates and A. Rassam, *Peoples and Cultures of the Middle East* (Englewood Cliffs, N.J., 1983).

On Islam, see F. Denny, *An Introduction to Islam* (New York, 1985), and J. L. Esposito, *Islam: The Straight Path* (New York, 1988). Among the various translations of the Koran, two of the best for the introductory student are N. J. Dawood, trans., *The Koran* (Harmondsworth, England, 1990), and M. M. Pickthall, trans., *The Meaning of the Glorious Koran* (New York, 1953). See also R. W. Bulliet, *Conversion to Islam in the Medieval Period: An Essay in Quantitative History* (Cambridge, 1979), and K. Armstrong, *Muhammad: A Biography of the Prophet* (San Francisco, 1993).

Specialized works on various historical periods are numerous. For a view of the Crusades from an Arab perspective, see A. Maalouf, *The Crusades Through Arab Eyes* (London, 1984), and C. Hillenbrand, *The Crusades: Islamic Perspectives* (New York, 2001). On the Mamluks, see R. Irwin, *The Middle East in the Middle Ages: The Early Mamluk Sultanate, 1250–1382* (Carbondale, Ill., 1986). In *God of Battles: Christianity and Islam* (Princeton, N.J., 1998), P. Partner compares the expansionist tendencies of the two great religions.

On the economy, see E. Ashtor, *A Social and Economic History of the Near East in the Middle Ages* (Berkeley, Calif., 1976); K. N. Chaudhuri, *Asia Before Europe: Economy and Civilization of the Indian Ocean from the Rise of Islam to 1750* (Cambridge, 1990); and C.

Issawi, *The Middle East Economy: Decline and Recovery* (Princeton, N.J., 1995). On the crucial role of the camel in Middle Eastern society, see the interesting study by R. W. Bulliet, *The Camel and the Wheel* (Cambridge, 1975).

On women, see F. Hussain, ed., *Muslim Women* (New York, 1984); G. Nashat and J. E. Tucker, *Women in the Middle East and North Africa* (Bloomington, Ind., 1998); S. S. Hughes and B. Hughes, *Women in World History*, vol. 1 (London, 1995); and L. Ahmed, *Women and Gender in Islam* (New Haven, Conn., 1992).

For the best introduction to Islamic literature, consult J. Kritzeck, ed., *Anthology of Islamic Literature* (New York, 1964), with its concise commentaries and introduction. An excellent introduction to Persian literature can be found in E. Yarshater, *Persian Literature* (Albany, N.Y., 1988). For the student, H. Haddawy, trans., *The Arabian Nights* (New York, 1990) is the best version. It presents 271 "nights" in a clear and colorful style.

For the best introduction to Islamic art, consult the concise yet comprehensive work by D. T. Rice, *Islamic Art*, rev. ed. (London, 1975). Also see J. Bloom and S. Blair, *Islamic Arts* (London, 1997). For carpets, a beautifully illustrated source is E. Sakhai, *The Story of Carpets* (London, 1991).

A brief but good introduction to Byzantine history can be found in J. Haldon, *Byzantium: A History* (Charleston, S.C., 2000). The best single political history is G. Ostrogorsky, *A History of the Byzantine State*, 2d ed. (New Brunswick, N.J., 1968). For a comprehensive survey of the Byzantine Empire, see W. Treadgold, *A History of the Byzantine State and Society* (Stanford, Calif., 1997). On Justinian, see J. Moorhead, *Justinian* (London, 1995). The role of the Christian church is discussed in J. Hussey, *The Orthodox Church in the Byzantine Empire* (Oxford, 1986). The zenith of Byzantine civilization is examined in R. Jenkins, *Byzantium: The Imperial Centuries, 610–1071* (New York, 1969).

INFOTRAC COLLEGE EDITION

For additional reading, go to InfoTrac College Edition, your online research library at
http://web1.infotrac-college.com

Enter the search term "Islam" using the Subject Guide.

Enter the search terms "caliph or caliphate" using Keywords.

Enter the search term "Koran" using Keywords.

Enter the search term "Crusades" using Keywords.

Enter the search terms "Sufi or Sufism or Rumi" using Keywords.

Enter the search term "Byzantium" using the Subject Guide.

Chapter 8

EARLY CIVILIZATIONS IN AFRICA

FOCUS QUESTIONS

- What effects did the coming of Islam and the Arabs have on African religion, society, political structures, trade, and culture?
- What were the main characteristics of the West African states of Ghana and Mali?
- What roles did lineage groups, women, and slavery play in African society?
- What are some of the characteristics of African sculpture and carvings, music, and architecture, and what purpose did these forms of creative expression serve in African society?
- What were the main developments in African history before the coming of Islam, and what contacts did early African civilizations and societies have with civilizations outside Africa?

In 1871, the German explorer Karl Mauch began to search southern Africa's central plateau for the colossal stone ruins of a legendary lost civilization. In late August, he found what he had been looking for. According to his diary: "Presently I stood before it and beheld a wall of a height of about 20 feet of granite bricks. Very close by there was a place where a kind of footpath led over rubble into the interior. Following this path I stumbled over masses of rubble and parts of walls and dense thickets. I stopped in front of a towerlike structure. Altogether it rose to a height of about 30 feet." Mauch was convinced that "a civilized nation must once have lived here." Like many other nineteenth-century Europeans, however, Mauch was equally convinced that the Africans who had lived there could never have built such splendid structures like the ones he had found at Great Zimbabwe. To Mauch and other archaeologists, Great Zimbabwe must have been the work of "a northern race closely akin to the Phoenician and Egyptian." It was not until the twentieth century that Europeans could overcome their prejudices and finally admit that Africans south of Egypt had also developed advanced civilizations with spectacular achievements.

The continent of Africa has played a central role in the long evolution of humankind. It was in Africa that the first hominids appeared more than three million years ago. It was probably in Africa that the immediate ancestors of modern human beings—*Homo sapiens*—emerged for the first time. Both the cultivation of crops and the domestication of animals may have occurred first in Africa. Certainly, one of the first states appeared in Africa, in the Nile valley in the northeastern corner of the continent, in the form of the kingdom of the pharaohs. Recent evidence suggests that Egyptian civilization was significantly influenced by cultural developments taking place to the south, in Nubia, in modern Sudan.

After the decline of the Egyptian empire during the first millennium B.C.E., the focus of social change began to shift from the lower Nile valley to other areas of the continent: to West Africa, where a series of major trading states began to take part in the caravan trade with the Mediterranean through the vast wastes of the Sahara; to the region of the upper Nile River, where the states of Kush and Axum dominated trade for several centuries; and to the eastern coast from the Horn of Africa to the straits between the continent and the island of Madagascar, where African peoples began to play an active role in the commercial traffic in the Indian Ocean. In the meantime, a gradual movement of agricultural peoples brought Iron Age farming to the central portion of the continent, leading eventually to the creation of several states in the Congo River basin and the plateau region south of the Zambezi River. When European seafarers began

to round the Cape of Good Hope at the end of the fifteenth century C.E., Western historians would herald their voyages as the beginning of the Age of Discovery. That label was a misnomer, however, for the peoples of Africa had played a significant role in the changing human experience since ancient times. •

THE LAND

After Asia, Africa is the largest of the continents (see Map 8.1). It stretches nearly 5,000 miles from the Cape of Good Hope in the south to the Mediterranean in the north and extends a similar distance from Cape Verde on the west coast to the Horn of Africa on the Indian Ocean. Africa is as diverse as it is vast. The northern coast, washed by the Mediterranean Sea, is mountainous for much of its length. South of the mountains lies the greatest desert on earth, the Sahara, which stretches from the Atlantic to the Indian Ocean. To the east is the Nile River, heart of the ancient Egyptian civilization. Beyond that lies the Red Sea, separating Africa from Asia.

The Sahara acts as a great divide separating the northern coast from the rest of the continent. Africa south of the Sahara is divided into a number of major regions. In the west is the so-called hump of Africa, which juts like a massive shoulder into the Atlantic Ocean. Here the Sahara gradually gives way to grasslands in the interior and then to tropical jungles along the coast. This region, dominated by the Niger River, is rich in natural resources and was the home of many ancient civilizations.

Far to the east, bordering the Indian Ocean, is a very different terrain of snowcapped mountains, upland plateaus, and lakes. Much of this region is grassland populated by wild beasts, which have given it the modern designation of Safari Country. Here, in the East African Rift valley in the lake district of modern Kenya, early hominids began their long trek toward civilization several million years ago.

Farther to the south lies the Congo basin, with its jungles watered by the mighty Congo River. The jungles of equatorial Africa then fade gradually into the hills, plateaus, and deserts of the south. This rich land contains some of the most valuable mineral resources known today.

THE EMERGENCE OF CIVILIZATION

It is not certain when agriculture was first practiced on the continent of Africa. Until recently, historians assumed that crops were first cultivated in the lower Nile valley (the northern part near the Mediterranean) about seven or

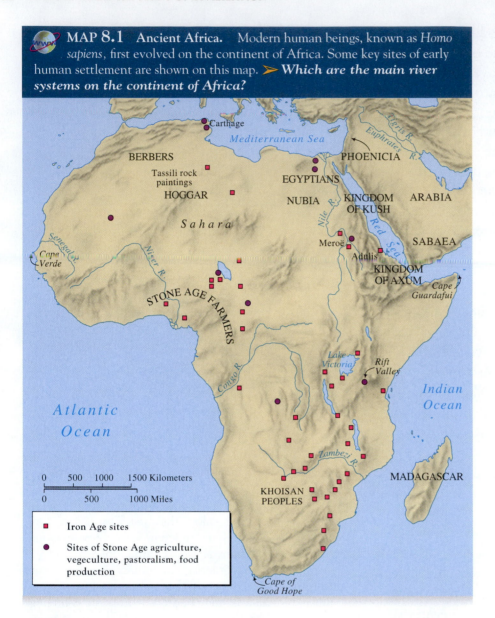

MAP 8.1   Ancient Africa.   Modern human beings, known as *Homo sapiens*, first evolved on the continent of Africa. Some key sites of early human settlement are shown on this map. ➤ *Which are the main river systems on the continent of Africa?*

eight thousand years ago, when wheat and barley were introduced, possibly from the Middle East. Eventually, as explained in Chapter 1, this area gave rise to the civilization of ancient Egypt.

Kush

Recent evidence suggests that this hypothesis may need some revision. South of Egypt, near the junction of the White and the Blue Nile, is an area known historically as Nubia. Some archaeologists suggest that agriculture may have appeared first in Nubia rather than in the lower Nile valley. Stone Age farmers from Nubia may have begun to cultivate local crops such as sorghum and millet along the banks of the upper Nile (the southern part near the river's source) as early as the eleventh millennium B.C.E.

Recent archaeological finds also imply that the first true African kingdom may have been located in Nubia rather than in Egypt. A drawing on an incense burner dated to 3100 B.C.E. or earlier depicts a seated ruler with the falcon motif later adopted by the pharaohs of Egypt. Some scholars suggest that the Nubian concept of kingship may have spread to the north, past the cataracts along the Nile, where it eventually gave birth to the better-known civilization of Egypt.

Whatever the truth of such conjectures, it is clear that contacts between the upper and lower Nile had been established by the late third millennium B.C.E., when Egyptian merchants traveled to Nubia to obtain ivory, ebony, frankincense, and leopard skins. A few centuries later, Nubia had become an Egyptian tributary. At the end of the second millennium B.C.E., Nubia profited from the disintegration of the Egyptian New Kingdom to become

⇶ **THE PYRAMIDS AT MEROË.**   The kingdom of Kush borrowed much of its culture from the Egyptian empire to the north while placing its own imprint on all imports. Kushite rulers, for example, modeled their political institutions after those of the pharaohs, but governmental authority was somewhat more decentralized, and monarchical power was apparently limited by the influence of priests and the local aristocracy. The pyramids at Meroë, on the banks of the Nile River, are another example. Younger, smaller, unpointed at the top, and more standardized in size and shape than their famous counterparts at Giza, they remain a dramatic reminder of the glory of ancient Kush. Some scholars speculate that the idea of erecting pyramids came from the natural hillocks and sand dunes found in the region of the Nile River valley.

the independent state of Kush. Egyptian influence continued, however, as Kushite culture borrowed extensively from Egypt, including religious beliefs, the practice of interring kings in pyramids, and hieroglyphics.

Although its economy was probably founded primarily on agriculture and animal husbandry, Kush developed into a major trading state that endured for hundreds of years. Its commercial activities were stimulated by the discovery of iron ore in a floodplain near the river at Meroë. Strategically located at the point where a land route across the desert to the north intersected the Nile River, Meroë eventually became the capital of the state. In addition to iron products, Kush supplied goods from Central and East Africa, notably ivory, gold, ebony, and slaves (see the box on p. 214) to the Roman Empire, Arabia, and India. At first, goods were transported by donkey caravans to the point where the river north was navigable. By the last centuries of the first millennium B.C.E., however, the donkeys were being replaced by camels, newly introduced from the Arabian peninsula.

Little is known about Kushite society, but it seems likely that it was predominantly urban. Initially, foreign trade was probably a monopoly of the state, but the extensive luxury goods in the numerous private tombs in the vicinity indicate that at one time material prosperity was relatively widespread. This suggests that commercial activities were being conducted by a substantial merchant class.

Axum, Son of Saba

In the first millennium C.E., Kush declined and was eventually conquered by Axum, a new power located in the highlands of modern Ethiopia (see Map 8.2). Axum had been founded during the first millennium B.C.E. as a colony of the kingdom of Saba (popularly known as Sheba) across the Red Sea on the southern tip of the Arabian peninsula. During antiquity, Saba was a major trading state, serving as a transit point for goods carried from South Asia into the lands surrounding the Mediterranean. Biblical sources credited the "queen of Sheba" with vast wealth and

THE SLAVE TRADE IN ANCIENT AFRICA

The practice of slavery was commonplace throughout the African continent from ancient times, but information on the nature of the slave trade is relatively difficult to find. The document below consists of a contract for the purchase of a Nubian slave girl in sixth-century C.E. Egypt. Behind the legal terminology contained in the contract, probably a consequence of the adoption of Roman law in pre-Muslim Egypt, lies the poignant reality of a young Nubian girl, and perhaps her own future children as well, sold into a lifetime of slavery. Tragically, the traffic in slaves continues in the region today as Muslim traders launch periodic raids on Christian villages in the southern Sudan.

SALE OF A NUBIAN SLAVE GIRL

Greeting. We acknowledge that we the aforementioned Pathermuthis and Anatolios, through this our written contract of sale, of our own free will and with voluntary intent and irrevocable and sincere resolution, with steadfast conscience, with correct intention, without any fraud or intimidation or violence or deceit or constraint or any bad faith or deception, that we have sold to you, the aforementioned most well-born Isidora, . . . the girl who belongs to us and who has come to us . . . from the other slave-traders of the Aithiopians, the black slave, Atalous by name, now renamed by you Eutukhia, about twelve years old more or less, an Aloan by race, which afore-mentioned black slave not being previously mortgaged for any principal sum whatsoever or for any business or agreement or afflicted by any old injury or leprosy or beating or concealed ailment, . . . for the mutually agreed, approved, resolved between us, full and just price [of] . . . four gold solidi, of full weight, on the Alexandrian standard, which afore-mentioned price at once we, the vendors, Pathermuthis and Anatolios, have been paid by you . . . for you to possess and to control and to own with every right of ownership, to acquire, to possess, to use her and, with God willing, her children, to manage and to administer concerning her, to sell, to put up as security, to give away, to exchange as dowry and to give . . . and to give to your children and descendants, to leave behind and to transmit to your testamentary heirs, successors, and legal heirs, and in general to do and perform with her all such acts as the laws enjoin upon absolute owners to do with their own property, unhindered and unimpeded, from now for ever, this perpetual warranty and clearance of title and defense of the present sale in regard to every warranty falling on us, the vendors.

resources. In fact, much of that wealth had originated much farther to the east and passed through Saba en route to the countries adjacent to the Mediterranean.

When Saba declined, perhaps because of the desiccation of the Arabian Desert, Axum broke away and survived for centuries as an independent state. Like Saba, Axum owed much of its prosperity to its location on the commercial trade route between India and the Mediterranean, and Greek ships from the Ptolemaic kingdom in Egypt stopped regularly at the port of Adulis on the Red Sea. Axum exported ivory, frankincense, myrrh, and slaves, while its primary imports were textiles, metal goods, wine, and olive oil. For a time, Axum competed for control of the ivory trade with the neighboring state of Kush, and hunters from Axum armed with imported iron weapons scoured the entire region for elephants. Probably

➤ **THE STELE AT AXUM.** Axum was a prosperous trading state by the third century C.E., selling ivory, glass, crystal, brass, copper, and frankincense and myrrh, resins used in burials and as medicines by the peoples of Egypt and the eastern Roman Empire. In the fourth century, the Axumite rulers erected slender columns known as stelae to mark the location of the royal tombs. Shown here is the tallest of the still-standing Axum stelae, in present-day Ethiopia. A slightly taller one, looted by the Italians when they invaded Ethiopia in 1937, now stands in Rome. Note the differences between these pillars and those constructed in India during the reign of Emperor Asoka.

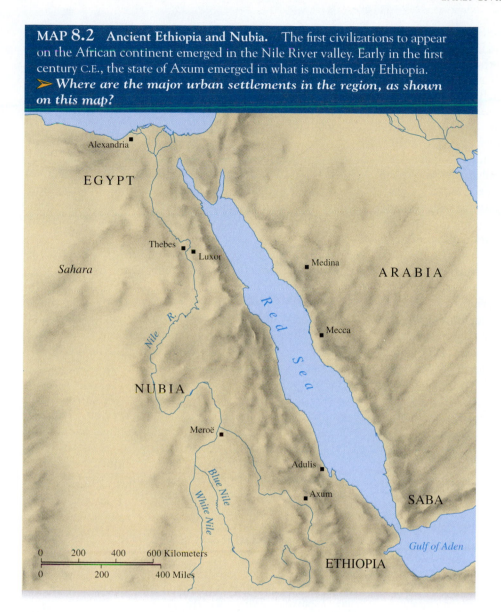

MAP 8.2   Ancient Ethiopia and Nubia.   The first civilizations to appear on the African continent emerged in the Nile River valley. Early in the first century C.E., the state of Axum emerged in what is modern-day Ethiopia.
➤ *Where are the major urban settlements in the region, as shown on this map?*

as a result of this competition, in the fourth century C.E., the Axumite ruler, claiming he had been provoked, launched an invasion of Kush and conquered it.

Perhaps the most distinctive feature of Axumite civilization was its religion. Originally, the rulers of Axum (who claimed descent from King Solomon through the visit of the queen of Sheba to Israel in biblical times) followed the religion of their predecessors in Saba. But in the fourth century C.E., Axumite rulers adopted Christianity from the Egyptians. This commitment to the Egyptian form of Christianity (often called Coptic, from the local language of the day) was retained even after the collapse of Axum and the expansion of Islam through the area in later centuries. Later, Axum (now renamed Ethiopia) would be identified by Europeans as the "hermit kingdom" and the home of Prester John, a legendary Christian king of East Africa.

The Sahara and Its Environs

Kush and Axum were part of the ancient trading network originally established by the Egyptians and were affected in various ways by the cross-cultural contacts that took place throughout that region. Elsewhere in Africa, somewhat different patterns prevailed; they varied from area to area depending on the geography and climate.

At one time, when the world's climate was much colder than it is today, Central Africa may have been one of the few areas that was habitable for the first hominids. Later, from 8000 to 4000 B.C.E., a warm, humid climate prevailed in the Sahara, creating lakes and ponds, as well as vast grasslands (known as savannas) replete with game. Rock paintings found in what are today some of the most uninhabitable parts of the region are a clear indication that the environment was much different several thousand years ago.

By 7000 B.C.E., the peoples of the Sahara were herding animals—first sheep and goats and later cattle. During the sixth and fifth millennia B.C.E., the climate became more arid, however, and the desertification of the Sahara began. From the rock paintings, which for the most part date from the fourth and third millennia B.C.E., we know that by that time the herds were being supplemented by fishing and limited cultivation of crops such as millet, sorghum, and a drought-resistant form of dry rice. After 3000 B.C.E., as the desiccation of the Sahara proceeded and the lakes dried up, farming began to spread into the savannas on the southern fringes of the desert and eventually into the tropical forest areas to the south, where crops were no longer limited to drought-resistant cereals but could include tropical fruits and tubers.

Historians do not know when goods first began to be exchanged across the Sahara in a north-south direction, but during the first millennium B.C.E., the commercial center of Carthage on the Mediterranean had become a focal point of the trans-Saharan trade. The Berbers, a pastoral people of North Africa, served as intermediaries, carrying food products and manufactured goods from Carthage across the desert and exchanging them for salt, gold and copper, skins, various agricultural products, and perhaps slaves.

This trade initiated a process of cultural exchange that would exert a significant impact on the peoples of tropical Africa. Among other things, it may have spread the knowledge of ironworking south of the desert. Although historians once believed that ironworking knowledge reached sub-Saharan Africa from Meroë in the upper Nile valley in the first centuries C.E., recent finds suggest that the peoples along the Niger River were smelting iron five or six hundred years earlier. Some scholars believe that the technique developed independently there, but others believe that it was introduced by the Berbers, who had learned it from the Carthaginians.

Whatever the case, the Nok culture in northern Nigeria eventually became one of the most active ironworking societies in Africa. Excavations have unearthed numerous terra-cotta and iron figures, as well as stone and iron farm implements, dating back as far as 500 B.C.E. The remains of smelting furnaces confirm that the iron was produced locally.

Early in the first millennium C.E., the introduction of the camel provided a major stimulus to the trans-Saharan trade. With its ability to store considerable amounts of food and water, the camel was far better equipped to handle the arduous conditions of the desert than the ox, which had been used previously. The camel caravans of the Berbers became known as the "fleets of the desert."

East Africa

South of Axum, along the shores of the Indian Ocean and in the inland plateau that stretches from the mountains of Ethiopia through the lake district of Central Africa, lived a mixture of peoples, some living by hunting and food gathering and others following pastoral pursuits.

✷ **AN ANCIENT COMMERCIAL CIVILIZATION IN AFRICA.**   Recent exploratory work in the Libyan Desert has revealed the existence of an ancient kingdom that for over a thousand years transported goods between societies along the Mediterranean Sea and sub-Saharan Africa. The Garamantes, as they were known to the Romans, carried salt, glass, metal, olive oil, and wine to Central Africa in return for gold, slaves, and various tropical products. To provide food for their communities in the heart of the desert, they constructed a complex irrigation system consisting of several thousand miles of underground channels. The technique is reminiscent of similar systems in Persia and Central Asia. Shown here is the citadel at Garma, the capital of their empire, which once controlled a territory of over 100,000 square miles. Scholars believe that the kingdom declined as a result of the fall of the Roman Empire and the drying up of the desert.

BEYOND THE PILLARS OF HERCULES

The first suggestion that seafarers could pass from the Atlantic to the Indian Ocean around the southern tip of Africa came from the Greek historian Herodotus. In the following passage from his History of the Persian Wars, Herodotus describes a voyage by Phoenician sailors that was recounted to him during his visit to Egypt. The reference to the position of the sun reflects a phenomenon that could have occurred only if the Phoenicians were sailing south of the equator.

HERODOTUS, *HISTORY OF THE PERSIAN WARS*

Africa proves to be completely surrounded by water except for as much of it as borders on Asia. Of all men of whom we have any knowledge, the Egyptian king Necho was the first to establish this fact. After he had ceased from trying to dig the canal that extends from the Nile to the Arabian Gulf, he dispatched some Phoenicians in ships with orders to sail back into our northern sea by passing through the Pillars of Hercules and so to return to Egypt.

Accordingly these Phoenicians set out and from the Red Sea sailed into the southern ocean. Whenever autumn came, they went ashore wherever in Africa they chanced to be on their voyage, to sow grain in the earth and await the harvest. On reaping the new grain they put again to sea. In this wise, after two years had elapsed, they rounded the Pillars of Hercules and in the third year reached Egypt.

Now, they told a tale that I personally do not believe (though others may, if they choose), how they had the sun on their right hand as they sailed along the African coast.

Beginning in the first millennium B.C.E., new peoples began to migrate into East Africa from the west. Farming peoples speaking dialects of the Bantu family of languages began to move from the region of the Niger River into East Africa and the Congo River basin. They were probably responsible for introducing the widespread cultivation of crops and knowledge of ironworking to much of East Africa, although there are signs of some limited iron smelting in the area before their arrival.

The Bantu settled in rural communities based on subsistence farming. The primary crops were millet and sorghum, along with yams, melons, and beans. The land was often tilled with both iron and stone tools, and the former were usually manufactured in a local smelter. Some people kept domestic animals such as cattle, sheep, goats, or chickens or supplemented their diets by hunting and food gathering. Because the population was minimal and an ample supply of cultivable land was available, most settlements were relatively small; each village formed a self-sufficient political and economic entity.

As early as the era of the New Kingdom in the second millennium B.C.E., Egyptian ships had plied the waters off the East African coast in search of gold, ivory, palm oil, and perhaps slaves. By the first century C.E., the region was an established part of a trading network that included the Mediterranean and the Red Sea. In that century, a Greek seafarer from Alexandria wrote an account of his travels down the coast from Cape Guardafui at the tip of the Horn of Africa to the Strait of Madagascar thousands of miles to the south. Called the *Periplus*, this work provides generally accurate descriptions of the peoples and settlements along the African coast and the trade goods they supplied.

According to the *Periplus*, the port of Rhapta (possibly modern Dar es Salaam) was a commercial metropolis, exporting ivory, rhinoceros horn, and tortoiseshell and importing glass, wine, grain, and metal goods such as weapons and tools. The identity of the peoples taking part in this trade is not clear, but it seems likely that the area was already inhabited by a mixture of local peoples and immigrants from the Arabian peninsula. Out of this mixture would eventually emerge an African-Arabian "Swahili" culture (see "East Africa: The Land of Zanj" later in this chapter) that continues to exist in coastal areas today. Beyond Rhapta was "unexplored ocean." Some contemporary observers believed that the Indian and Atlantic Oceans were connected. Others were convinced that the Indian Ocean was an enclosed sea and that the continent of Africa could not be circumnavigated (see the box above).

Trade across the Indian Ocean and down the coast of East Africa, facilitated by the monsoon winds, would gradually become one of the most lucrative sources of commercial profit in the ancient and medieval worlds. Although the origins of the trade remain shrouded in mystery, traders eventually came by sea from as far away as the mainland of Southeast Asia. Early in the first millennium C.E., Malay peoples bringing cinnamon to the Middle East began to cross the Indian Ocean directly and landed on the southeastern coast of Africa. Eventually, a Malay settlement was established on the island of Madagascar, where the population is still of mixed Malay-African origin. Historians suspect that Malay immigrants were responsible for introducing such Southeast Asian foods as the banana and the yam to Africa. With its high yield and ability to grow in uncultivated rain forest, the banana often became the preferred crop of the Bantu peoples.

Southern Africa

South of the East African plateau and the Congo basin is a vast land of hills, grasslands, and arid desert stretching almost to the Cape of Good Hope at the tip of the continent. As Bantu-speaking farmers spread southward during the final centuries of the first millennium B.C.E., they began to encounter Stone Age peoples in the area who still lived primarily by hunting and foraging. These peoples, many of whom apparently belonged to the Khoisan family of languages (Khoisan languages are distinguished by their numerous "clicking" sounds), were lighter in skin color and generally shorter than the Bantu speakers who were arriving from the north.

Available evidence suggests that early relations between these two peoples were relatively harmonious. Intermarriage between members of the two groups was apparently not unusual, and many of the Khoisan-speaking peoples were gradually absorbed into what became a dominantly Bantu-speaking pastoral and agricultural society that spread throughout much of southern Africa during the first millennium C.E.

THE COMING OF ISLAM

As we saw in Chapter 7, the rise of Islam during the first half of the seventh century C.E. had ramifications far beyond the Arabian peninsula. Arab armies swept across North Africa, incorporating it into the Arab empire and isolating the Christian state of Axum to the south. Although East Africa and West Africa south of the Sahara were not conquered by the Arab forces, Islam eventually penetrated these areas as well.

African Religious Beliefs Before Islam

When Islam arrived, most African societies already had well-developed systems of religious beliefs. Like other aspects of African life, early African religious beliefs varied from place to place, but certain characteristics appear to have been shared by most African societies. One of these common features was a belief in a single creator god. The supreme god of the Bantu, for example, was a pantheistic force from whom all things came. Sometimes, the creator god was accompanied by a whole pantheon of lesser deities. The Ashanti people of Ghana in West Africa believed in a supreme being called Nyame, whose sons were lesser gods. Each son served a different purpose: one was the rainmaker, another the compassionate, and a third was responsible for the sunshine. This heavenly hierarchy paralleled earthly arrangements: worship of Nyame was the exclusive preserve of the king through his priests; lesser officials and the common people worshiped Nyame's sons, who might intercede with their father on behalf of ordinary Africans.

Many African religions also shared a belief in a form of afterlife during which the soul floated in the atmosphere through eternity. Belief in an afterlife was closely connected to the importance of ancestors and the lineage, or clan, in African society. Each lineage group could trace itself back to a founding ancestor or group of ancestors.

These ancestral souls would not be extinguished as long as the lineage group continued to perform rituals in their name. The rituals could also benefit the lineage group on earth, for the ancestral souls, being closer to the gods, had the power to influence, for good or evil, the lives of their descendants.

Such beliefs were challenged but not always replaced by the arrival of Islam. In some ways, the tenets of Islam were in conflict with traditional African beliefs and customs. Although the concept of a single transcendent deity presented no problems in many African societies, Islam's rejection of spirit worship and a priestly class ran counter to the beliefs of many Africans and was often ignored in practice. Similarly, as various Muslim travelers observed, Islam's insistence on the separation of the sexes contrasted with the relatively informal relationships that prevailed in many African societies and was probably slow to take root. In the long run, imported ideas were synthesized with native beliefs to create a unique brand of Africanized Islam.

The Arabs in North Africa

In 641, Arab forces advanced into Egypt, seized the delta of the Nile River, and brought two centuries of Byzantine rule to an end. To guard against attacks from the Byzantine fleet, the Arabs eventually built a new capital at Cairo, inland from the previous Byzantine capital of Alexandria, and began to consolidate their control over the entire region.

The Arab conquerors were probably welcomed by many, if not the majority, of the local inhabitants. Although Egypt had been a thriving commercial center under the Byzantines, the average Egyptian had not shared in this prosperity. Tax rates were generally high, and Christians were subjected to periodic persecution by the Byzantines, who viewed the local Coptic faith and other sects in the area as heresies. Although the new rulers continued to obtain much of their revenue from taxing the local farming population, tax rates were generally lower than they had been under the corrupt Byzantine government, and conversion to Islam brought exemption from taxation. During the next generations, many Egyptians converted to the Muslim faith, but Islam did not move into the upper Nile valley until several hundred years later. As Islam spread southward, it was adopted by many lowland peoples, but it had less success in the mountains of Ethiopia, where Coptic Christianity continued to win adherents (see the next section).

In the meantime, Arab rule was gradually being extended westward along the Mediterranean coast. When the Romans conquered Carthage in 146 B.C.E., they had called their new province Africa, thus introducing a name that would eventually be applied to the entire continent. After the fall of the Roman Empire, much of the area had reverted to the control of local Berber chieftains, but the Byzantines captured Carthage in the mid-sixth century C.E. In 690, the city was seized by the Arabs, who then

A POWER OBJECT.   One of the important aspects of many traditional African religions is the close communion between the worlds of the living and the dead. The artifact shown here (known as a *nkisi*) is a sacred object used by the people of Kongo to harness the power of the spirits to solve problems encountered in their daily lives. Nails were driven into the object (normally a male statue or a two-headed dog) to arouse its inner spirits, who would be activated to identify the source of the problem and resolve it. Over the stomach of this artifact is a container for medicines to assist in the healing ritual.

began to extend their control over the entire area, which they called Al Maghrib ("the west").

At first, the local Berber peoples resisted their new conquerors. The Berbers were tough fighters, and for several generations, Arab rule was limited to the towns and lowland coastal areas. But Arab persistence eventually paid off, and by the early eighth century, the entire North African coast as far west as the Strait of Gibraltar was under Arab rule. The Arabs were now poised to cross the strait and expand into southern Europe and to push south beyond the fringes of the Sahara.

The Kingdom of Ethiopia: A Christian Island in a Muslim Sea

By the end of the sixth century C.E., the kingdom of Axum, long a dominant force in the trade network through the Red Sea, was in a state of decline. Both overexploitation of farmland and a shift in trade routes away from the Red Sea to the Arabian peninsula and Persian Gulf contributed to this decline. By the beginning of the ninth century, the capital had been moved farther into the mountainous interior, and Axum was gradually transformed from a maritime power into an isolated agricultural society.

The rise of Islam on the Arabian peninsula hastened this process, as the Arab world increasingly began to serve as the focus of the regional trade passing through the area. By the eighth century, a number of Muslim trading states had been established on the African coast of the Red Sea, a development that contributed to the transformation of Axum into a landlocked society with primarily agricultural interests. At first, relations between Christian Axum and its Muslim neighbors were relatively peaceful, as the larger and more powerful Axumite kingdom attempted with some success to compel the coastal Islamic states to accept a tributary relationship. Axum's role in the local commercial network temporarily revived, and the area became a prime source for ivory, resins like frankincense and myrrh, and slaves. Slaves came primarily from the south, where Axum had been attempting to subjugate restive tribal peoples living in the Amharic plateau beyond its southern border.

Beginning in the twelfth century, however, relations between Axum and its neighbors deteriorated as the Muslim states along the coast began to move inland to gain control over the growing trade in slaves and ivory. Axum responded with force and at first had some success in reasserting its hegemony over the area. But in the early fourteenth century, the Muslim state of Adal, located at the juncture of the Indian Ocean and the Red Sea, launched a new attack on the Christian kingdom.

Axum also underwent significant internal change during this period. The Zagwe dynasty, which seized control of the country in the mid-twelfth century, centralized the government and extended the Christian faith throughout

THE COAST OF ZANJ

From early times, the people living on the coast of East Africa took an active part in trade along the coast and across the Indian Ocean. The process began with the arrival of Arab traders early in the first millennium C.E. According to local legends, Arab merchants often married the daughters of the local chieftains and then received title to coastal territories as part of their wife's dowry. This description of the area was written by the Arab traveler al-Mas'udi, who visited the "land of Zanj" in 916.

AL-MAS'UDI IN EAST AFRICA

The land of Zanj produces wild leopard skins. The people wear them as clothes, or export them to Muslim countries. They are the largest leopard skins and the most beautiful for making saddles. . . . They also export tortoise shell for making combs, for which ivory is likewise used. . . . The Zanj are settled in that area, which stretches as far as Sofala, which is the furthest limit of the land and the end of the voyages made from Oman and Siraf on the sea of Zanj. . . . The Zanj use the ox as a beast of burden, for they have no horses, mules or camels in their land. . . . There are many wild elephants in this land but no tame ones.

The Zanj do not use them for war or anything else, but only hunt and kill them for their ivory. It is from this country that come tusks weighing fifty pounds and more. They usually go to Oman, and from there are sent to China and India. This is the chief trade route. . . .

The Zanj have an elegant language and men who preach in it. One of their holy men will often gather a crowd and exhort his hearers to please God in their lives and to be obedient to him. He explains the punishments that follow upon disobedience, and reminds them of their ancestors and kings of old. These people have no religious law: their kings rule by custom and by political expediency.

The Zanj eat bananas, which are as common among them as they are in India; but their staple food is millet and a plant called kalari which is pulled out of the earth like truffles. They also eat honey and meat. They have many islands where the coconut grows: its nuts are used as fruit by all the Zanj peoples. One of these islands, which is one or two days' sail from the coast, has a Muslim population and a royal family. This is the island of Kanbulu [thought to be modern Pemba].

---

the kingdom, now known as Ethiopia. Military commanders or civilian officials who had personal or kinship ties with the royal court established vast landed estates to maintain security and facilitate the collection of taxes from the local population. In the meantime, Christian missionaries established monasteries and churches to propagate the faith in outlying areas. Close relations were reestablished with leaders of the Coptic church in Egypt and with Christian officials in the Holy Land. This process was continued by the Solomonids, who succeeded the Zagwe dynasty in 1270. But by the early fifteenth century, the state had become more deeply involved in an expand-

A LOST CITY IN AFRICA. Gedi was founded in the early fourteenth century and abandoned three hundred years later. Its romantic ruins suggest the grandeur of the Swahili civilization that once flourished along the eastern coast of Africa. Located 60 miles north of Mombasa, in present-day Kenya, Gedi once contained several thousand residents but was eventually abandoned after it was attacked by nomadic peoples from the north. Today the ruins of the town, surrounded by a 9-foot wall, seem dwarfed by towering baobab trees populated only by chattering monkeys. Shown here is the entrance to the palace, which probably served as the residence of the chief official in the town. Neighboring houses, constructed of coral stone, contain sumptuous rooms, with separate women's quarters and enclosed lavatories with urinal channels and double-sink washing benches.

Courtesy of William J. Duiker

ing conflict with Muslim Adal to the east, a conflict that lasted for over a century and gradually took on the characteristics of a holy war.

East Africa: The Land of Zanj

The rise of Islam also had a lasting impact on the coast of East Africa, which the Greeks had called Azania and the Arabs called Zanj. During the seventh and eighth centuries, peoples from the Arabian peninsula and the Persian Gulf began to settle at ports along the coast and on the small islands offshore. Then, according to legend, in the middle of the tenth century, a Persian from Shiraz, a city in southern Iran, sailed to the area with his six sons. As his small fleet stopped along the coast, each son disembarked on one of the coastal islands and founded a small community; these settlements eventually grew into important commercial centers such as Mombasa, Pemba, Zanzibar (literally, "the coast of Zanj"), and Kilwa.

Although the legend underestimates the degree to which the area had already become a major participant in local commerce as well as the role of the local inhabitants in the process, it does reflect the importance of Arab and Persian immigrants in the formation of a string of trading ports stretching from Mogadishu (today the capital of Somalia) in the north to Kilwa (south of present-day Dar es Salaam) in the south. Kilwa became especially important as it was near the southern limit for a ship hoping to complete the round-trip journey in a single season. Goods such as ivory, gold, and rhinoceros horn were exported across the Indian Ocean to countries as far away as China, while imports included iron goods, glassware, Indian textiles, and Chinese porcelain. Merchants in these cities often amassed considerable profit, as evidenced by their lavish stone palaces, some of which still stand in the modern cities of Mombasa and Zanzibar. Though now in ruins, Kilwa was one of the most magnificent cities of its day. The fourteenth-century Arab traveler Ibn Battuta described it as "amongst the most beautiful of cities and most elegantly built. All of it is of wood, and the ceilings of its houses are of *al-dis* [reeds]."[1]

Most of the coastal states were self-governing, although sometimes several towns were grouped together under a single dominant authority. Government revenue came primarily from taxes imposed on commerce. Some trade went on between these coastal city-states and the peoples of the interior, who provided gold and iron, ivory, and various agricultural goods and animal products in return for textiles, manufactured articles, and weapons (see the box on p. 220). Relations apparently varied, and the coastal merchants sometimes resorted to force to obtain goods from the inland peoples. A Portuguese visitor recounted that "the men [of Mombasa] are oft-times at war and but seldom at peace with those of the mainland, and they carry on trade with them, bringing thence great store of honey, wax, and ivory."[2]

Chronology

EARLY AFRICA

Origins of agriculture in Africa	c. 7000 B.C.E.
Desiccation of the Sahara	Begins c. 5000 B.C.E.
Kingship appears in the Nile valley	c. 3100 B.C.E.
Kingdom of Kush in Nubia	c. 500 B.C.E.
Iron Age begins	c. sixth century B.C.E.
Beginnings of trans-Saharan trade	c. first millenium B.C.E.
Rise of Axum	First century C.E.
Conquest of Kush by Axum	Fourth century C.E.
Arrival of Bantus in East Africa	Early centuries C.E.
Arrival of Malays on Madagascar	Second century C.E.
Origins of Ghana	Fifth century C.E.
Arab takeover of lower Nile valley	641 C.E.
Development of Swahili culture	c. first millenium C.E.
Spread of Islam across North Africa	Seventh century C.E.
Spread of Islam in Horn of Africa	Ninth century C.E.
Decline of Ghana	Twelfth century C.E.
Establishment of Zagwe dynasty in Ethiopia	c. 1150
Rise of Mali	c. 1250
Kingdom of Zimbabwe	c. 1300–c. 1450
Portuguese ships explore West African coast	Mid-fifteenth century

By the twelfth and thirteenth centuries, a mixed African-Arabian culture, eventually known as Swahili (from the Arabic *sahel* meaning "coast"; thus, "peoples of the coast"), began to emerge throughout the coastal area. Intermarriage between the immigrants and the local population was common, although a distinct Arab community, made up primarily of merchants, persisted in many areas. The members of the ruling class were often of mixed heritage but usually traced their genealogy to Arab or Persian ancestors. By this time, too, many members of the ruling class had converted to Islam. Middle Eastern urban architectural styles and other aspects of Arab culture were implanted within a society still predominantly African. Arabic words and phrases were combined with Bantu grammatical structures to form a mixed language, also known as Swahili; it is the national language of Kenya and Tanzania today.

The States of West Africa

During the eighth century, merchants from the Maghrib began to carry Muslim beliefs to the savanna areas south of the Sahara. At first, conversion took place on an individual basis rather than through official encouragement. The first rulers to convert to Islam were the royal family of Gao at the end of the tenth century. Five hundred years later, most of the population in the grasslands south of the Sahara had accepted Islam.

The expansion of Islam into West Africa had a major impact on the political system. By introducing Arabic as the first written language in the region and Muslim law codes and administrative practices from the Middle East, Islam provided local rulers with the tools to increase their authority and the efficiency of their governments. Moreover, as Islam gradually spread throughout the region, a common religion united previously diverse peoples into a more coherent community.

When Islam arrived in the grasslands south of the Sahara, the region was beginning to undergo significant political and social change. A number of major trading states were in the making, and they eventually transformed the Sahara into one of the leading avenues of world trade, crisscrossed by caravan routes leading to destinations as far away as the Atlantic Ocean, the Mediterranean, and the Red Sea (see Map 8.3).

GHANA

The first of these great commercial states was Ghana, which emerged in the fifth century C.E. in the upper Niger valley, a grassland region between the Sahara and the tropical forests along the West African coast (the modern state of Ghana, which takes its name from the trading society under discussion here, is located in the forest region to the south). The majority of the people in the area were Iron Age farmers living in villages under the authority of a local chieftain. Gradually, these local communities were united to form the kingdom of Ghana.

Although the people of the region had traditionally lived from agriculture, a primary reason for Ghana's growing importance was gold. The heartland of the state was located near one of the richest gold-producing areas in all of Africa. Ghanaian merchants transported the gold to Morocco, whence it was distributed throughout the known world. This trade began in ancient times, as the Greek historian Herodotus relates:

> The Carthaginians also tell us that they trade with a race of men who live in a part of Libya beyond the Pillars of Heracles [the Strait of Gibraltar]. On reaching this country, they unload their goods, arrange them tidily along the beach, and then, returning to their boats, raise a smoke. Seeing the smoke, the natives come down to the beach, place on the ground a certain quantity of gold in exchange for the goods, and go off again to a distance. The Carthaginians then come ashore and take a look at the gold; and if they think it represents a fair price for their wares, they collect it and go away; if, on the other hand, it seems too little, they go back aboard and wait, and the natives come and add to the gold until they

➤ **THE GREAT GATE AT MARRAKECH.** The Moroccan city of Marrakech, founded in the ninth century C.E., was a major northern terminus of the trans-Saharan trade and one of the chief commercial centers in premodern Africa. Widely praised by such famous travelers as Ibn Battuta, the city was an architectural marvel in that all its major public buildings were constructed in red sandstone. Shown here is the Great Gate to the city, through which camel caravans passed en route to and from the vast desert. In the Berber language, Marrakech means "pass without making a noise," a reference to the need for caravan traders to be aware of the danger of thieves in the vicinity.

DESCRIPTION OF A GHANAIAN CAPITAL

After its first appearance in West Africa in the decades following the death of Muhammad, Islam competed with native African religions for followers. Eventually, several local rulers converted to the Muslim faith. This passage by the Arab geographer al-Bakri shows how both religions flourished side by side in the state of Ghana during the eleventh century.

AL-BAKRI'S DESCRIPTION OF GHANA

The king's residence comprises a palace and conical huts, the whole surrounded by a fence like a wall. Around the royal town are huts and groves of thorn trees where live the magicians who control their religious rites. These groves, where they keep their idols and bury their kings, are protected by guards who permit no one to enter or find out what goes on in them.

None of those who belong to the imperial religion may wear tailored garments except the king himself and the heir-presumptive, his sister's son. The rest of the people wear wrappers of cotton, silk or brocade according to their means. Most of the men shave their beards and the women their heads. The king adorns himself with female ornaments around the neck and arms. On his head he wears gold-embroidered caps covered with turbans of finest cotton. He gives audience to the people for the redressing of grievances in a hut around which are placed 10 horses covered in golden cloth. Behind him stand 10 slaves carrying shields and swords mounted with gold. On his right are the sons of vassal kings, their heads plaited with gold and wearing costly garments. On the ground around him are seated his ministers, whilst the governor of the city sits before him. On guard at the door are dogs of fine pedigree, wearing collars adorned with gold and silver. The royal audience is announced by the beating of a drum, called daba, made out of a long piece of hollowed-out wood. When the people have gathered, his coreligionists draw near upon their knees sprinkling dust upon their heads as a sign of respect, whilst the Muslims clap hands as their form of greeting.

---

are satisfied. There is perfect honesty on both sides; the Carthaginians never touch the gold until it equals in value what they have offered for sale, and the natives never touch the goods until the gold has been taken away.[3]

Later, Ghana became known to Arab-speaking peoples in North Africa as "the land of gold." Actually, the name was misleading, for the gold did not come from Ghana, but from a neighboring people, who sold it to merchants from Ghana.

Eventually, other exports from Ghana found their way to the bazaars of the Mediterranean coast and beyond— ivory, ostrich feathers, hides, leather goods, and ultimately slaves. The origins of the slave trade in the area probably go back to the first millennium B.C.E., when Berber tribesmen seized African villagers in the regions south of the Sahara and sold them for profit to buyers in Europe and the Middle East. In return, Ghana imported metal goods (especially weapons), textiles, horses, and salt.

Much of the trade across the desert was still conducted by the nomadic Berbers, but Ghanaian merchants played an active role as intermediaries, trading tropical products such as bananas, kola nuts, and palm oil from the forest states of Guinea along the Atlantic coast to the south. By the eighth and ninth centuries, much of this trade was conducted by Muslim merchants, who purchased the goods from local traders (using iron and copper cash or cowrie shells from Southeast Asia as the primary means of exchange) and then sold them to Berbers, who carried them across the desert. The merchants who carried on this trade often became quite wealthy and lived in splendor in cities like Saleh, the capital of Ghana. So did the king,

of course, who taxed the merchants as well as the farmers and the producers.

Like other West African kings, the king of Ghana ruled by divine right and was assisted by a hereditary aristocracy composed of the leading members of the prominent clans, who also served as district chiefs responsible for maintaining law and order and collecting taxes. The king was responsible for maintaining the security of his kingdom, serving as an intermediary with local deities, and functioning as the chief law officer to adjudicate disputes. The kings of Ghana did not convert to Islam themselves, although they welcomed Muslim merchants and apparently did not discourage their subjects from adopting the new faith (see the box above).

MALI

The state of Ghana flourished for several hundred years, but by the twelfth century, weakened by ruinous wars with Berber tribesmen, it had begun to decline, and it collapsed at the end of the century. In its place rose a number of new trading societies, including large territorial states like Mali and Songhai in the west, Kanem-Bornu in the east, and small commercial city-states like the Hausa states, located in what is today northern Nigeria (see Map 8.4).

The greatest of the states that emerged after the destruction of Ghana was Mali. Extending from the Atlantic coast inland as far as the trading cities of Timbuktu and Gao on the Niger River, Mali built its wealth and power on the gold trade. But the heartland of Mali was situated south of the Sahara in the savanna region,

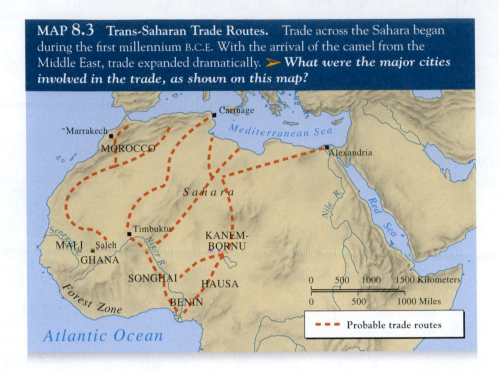

MAP 8.3 Trans-Saharan Trade Routes. Trade across the Sahara began during the first millennium B.C.E. With the arrival of the camel from the Middle East, trade expanded dramatically. ➤ *What were the major cities involved in the trade, as shown on this map?*

where sufficient moisture enabled farmers to grow such crops as sorghum, millet, and rice. The farmers lived in villages ruled by a local chieftain (called a *mansa*), who served as both religious and administrative leader and was responsible for forwarding tax revenues from the village to higher levels of government.

The primary wealth of the country was accumulated in the cities. Here lived the merchants, who were primarily of local origin, although many were now practicing Muslims. Commercial activities were taxed but were apparently so lucrative that both the merchants and the kings prospered. One of the most powerful kings of Mali was Mansa Musa (1312–1337), whose primary contribution to his people was probably not economic prosperity but the Muslim faith. Mansa Musa strongly encouraged the building of mosques and the study of the Koran in his kingdom and imported scholars and books to introduce his subjects to the message of Allah. One visitor from Europe, writing in the late fifteenth century, reported that in Timbuktu "are a great store of doctors, judges, priests, and other learned men, that are bountifully maintained at the king's cost and charges. And hither are brought divers manuscripts of written books out of Barbary [North Africa] which are sold for more money than any other merchandise."[4]

➤ **MANSA MUSA.** Mansa Musa, king of the West African state of Mali, was one of the richest and most powerful rulers of his day. During a famous pilgrimage to Mecca, he arrived in Cairo with a hundred camels laden with gold and gave away so much gold that its value depreciated there for several years. His fame spread to Europe as well, evidenced by this Spanish map of 1375, which depicts Mansa Musa seated on his throne in Mali, holding an impressive gold nugget.

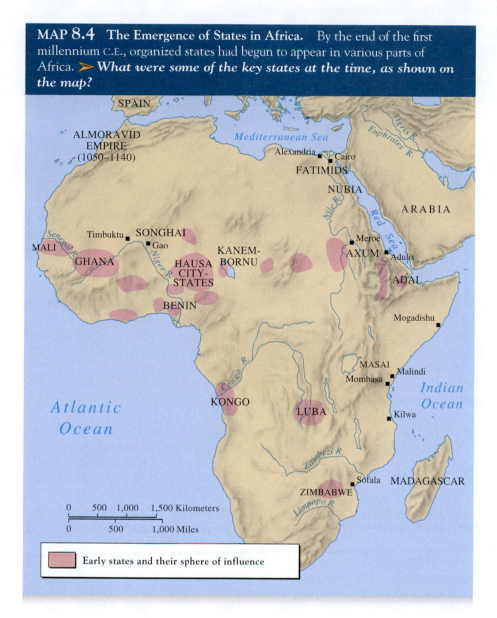

MAP 8.4   The Emergence of States in Africa.   By the end of the first millennium C.E., organized states had begun to appear in various parts of Africa. ➤ *What were some of the key states at the time, as shown on the map?*

SPAIN

ALMORAVID
EMPIRE
(1050–1140)

Mediterranean Sea

Euphrates R.

Tigris R.

Alexandria   Cairo
FATIMIDS

NUBIA

ARABIA

Timbuktu   SONGHAI
Senegal R.   Gao
MALI
GHANA   *Niger R.*   KANEM-
    HAUSA   BORNU
    CITY-
    STATES

Meroë
AXUM   Adulis

ADAL

BENIN

Mogadishu

Congo R.

MASAI
Mombasa   Malindi

KONGO

LUBA

Kilwa

*Atlantic
Ocean*

*Indian
Ocean*

Zambezi R.

Sofala   MADAGASCAR
ZIMBABWE
Limpopo R.

0   500   1,000   1,500 Kilometers

0   500   1,000 Miles

☐ Early states and their sphere of influence

STATES AND STATELESS SOCIETIES IN SOUTHERN AFRICA

In the southern half of the African continent, from the great basin of the Congo River to the Cape of Good Hope, states formed somewhat more slowly than in the north. Until the eleventh century C.E., most of the peoples in this region lived in what are sometimes called "stateless societies," characterized by autonomous villages organized by clans and ruled by a local chieftain or clan head. Beginning in the eleventh century, in some parts of southern Africa, these independent villages gradually began to consolidate. Out of these groupings came the first states.

One area where this process occurred was the Congo River valley, where the combination of fertile land and nearby deposits of copper and iron enabled the inhabitants to enjoy an agricultural surplus and engage in regional commerce. Two new states in particular underwent this transition. Sometime during the fourteenth century, the kingdom of Luba was founded in the center of the continent, in a rich agricultural and fishing area near the shores of Lake Kisale. Luba had a relatively centralized government, in which the king appointed provincial governors, who were responsible for collecting tribute from the village chiefs. At about the same time, the kingdom of Kongo was formed just south of the mouth of the Congo River on the Atlantic coast.

These new states were primarily agricultural, although both had a thriving manufacturing sector and took an active part in the growing exchange of goods throughout the region. As time passed, both began to expand southward to absorb the mixed farming and pastoral peoples in the area of modern Angola. In the drier grassland area to the south, other small communities continued to support themselves by herding, hunting, or food gathering. We know little about these peoples, however, since they possessed no writing system and had few visitors. A Portuguese sailor who encountered them in the late sixteenth century reported, "These people are herdsmen and cultivators. . . . Their main crop is millet, which they grind between two stones or in wooden mortars to make flour. . . . Their wealth consists mainly in their huge number of dehorned cows. . . . They live together in small villages, in houses made of reed mats, which do not keep out the rain."[5]

Zimbabwe

Farther to the east, the situation was somewhat different. In the grassland regions immediately to the south of the Zambezi River, a mixed economy involving farming, cattle herding, and commercial pursuits had begun to develop during the early centuries of the first millennium C.E. Characteristically, villages in this area were constructed inside walled enclosures to protect the animals at night. The most famous of these communities was Zimbabwe, located on the plateau of the same name between the Zambezi and Limpopo Rivers. From the twelfth century to the middle of the fifteenth, Zimbabwe was the most powerful and most prosperous state in the region and played a major role in the gold trade with the Swahili trading communities on the eastern coast.

The ruins of Zimbabwe's capital, known as Great Zimbabwe (the term *Zimbabwe* means "sacred house" in the Bantu language), provide a vivid illustration of the kingdom's power and influence. Strategically situated between substantial gold reserves to the west and a small river leading to the coast, Great Zimbabwe was well placed to benefit from the expansion of trade between the coast and the interior. The town sits on a hill overlooking the river and is surrounded by stone walls, which enclosed an area large enough to hold over ten thousand residents. The houses of the wealthy were built of cement on stone foundations, while those of the common people were of dried mud with thatched roofs. In the valley below is the royal palace, surrounded by a stone wall 30 feet high. Artifacts found at the site include household implements and ornaments made of gold and copper, as well as jewelry and even porcelain imported from China.

Most of the royal wealth probably came from two sources: the ownership of cattle and the king's ability to levy heavy taxes on the gold that passed through the kingdom en route to the coast. By the middle of the fifteenth century, however, the city was apparently abandoned, possibly because of environmental damage caused by overgrazing. With the decline of Zimbabwe, the focus of economic power began to shift northward to the valley of the Zambezi River.

© David Coulson/Robert Estall Photo Library

➤ **GREAT ZIMBABWE.**   Situated on an important trade route and a center for cattle and agriculture, Great Zimbabwe was originally settled by pastoral peoples during the first millennium B.C.E. Later it became the capital of a prosperous state. Its 30-foot walls were the first in Africa to be constructed without the use of mortar. The walled palace shown here indicates why Great Zimbabwe is generally regarded as the most impressive archaeological site in southern Africa.

South of the Limpopo River, pastoralism and hunting continued to be the primary means of livelihood. As we saw earlier, some of these peoples had been absorbed by the Iron Age farming communities that spread southward from Central Africa during the first millennium C.E. Others remained independent in isolated villages or small kingdoms, although they often carried on active trade with the growing states to their north.

One such people were the San, called Bushmen by later Europeans. A hunting and foraging people who spoke a Khoisan language, the San lived in small family communities of twenty to twenty-five members throughout southern Africa from Namibia in the west to the Drakensberg Mountains near the southeastern coast. Scholars have learned about the early life of the San by interviewing their modern descendants and by studying rock paintings found in caves throughout the area. These multicolored paintings, which predate the coming of the Europeans, were drawn with a brush made of small feathers fastened to a reed. They depict various aspects of the San's lifestyle, including their hunting techniques and religious rituals.

When the Europeans arrived in the area, they regarded the San as troublesome pests who raided their cattle. One nineteenth-century European missionary dismissed the San contemptuously, saying: "He has no religion, no laws, no government, no recognized authority, no patrimony, no fixed abode."[6] Over time, as the Europeans constantly encroached on their hunting grounds, the San found it virtually impossible to maintain their way of life. Only a few survive today, most of them in the Kalahari Desert in Botswana.

AFRICAN SOCIETY

Drawing generalizations about social organization, cultural development, and daily life in traditional Africa is difficult because of the diversity of the continent and the absence of written languages in much of the area. Historians must therefore rely on accounts of the occasional visitor, such as al-Mas'udi and the famous fourteenth-century chronicler Ibn Battuta. Such travelers, however, tended to come into contact mostly with the wealthy and the powerful, leaving us to speculate about what life was like for ordinary Africans during this early period.

Urban Life

African towns often began as fortified walled villages and gradually evolved into larger communities serving several purposes. Here, of course, were the center of government and the teeming markets filled with goods from distant regions. Here also were artisans skilled in metal- or woodworking, pottery making, and other crafts. Unlike the rural areas, where a village was usually composed of a single lineage group or clan, the towns drew their residents from several clans, although individual clans usually lived in their own compounds and were governed by their own clan heads.

In the states of West Africa, the focal point of the major towns was the royal precinct. The relationship between the ruler and the merchant class differed from the situation in most Asian societies, where the royal family and the aristocracy were largely isolated from the remainder of the population. In Africa, the chasm between the king and the common people was not so great. Often the ruler would hold an audience to allow people to voice their complaints or to welcome visitors from foreign countries.

This is not to say that the king was not elevated above all others in status. In wealthier states, the walls of the audience chamber would be covered with sheets of beaten silver and gold, and the king would be surrounded by hundreds of armed soldiers and some of his trusted advisers. Nevertheless, the symbiotic relationship between the ruler and merchant class served to reduce the gap between the king and his subjects. The relationship was mutually beneficial, since the merchants received honors and favors from the palace while the king's coffers were filled with taxes paid by the merchants. Certainly, it was to the benefit of the king to maintain law and order in his domain so that the merchants could ply their trade. As Ibn Battuta observed, among the good qualities of the peoples of West Africa was the prevalence of peace in the region. "The traveler is not afraid in it," he remarked, "nor is he who lives there in fear of the thief or of the robber by violence."[7]

Village Life

The vast majority of Africans lived in small rural villages. Their identities were established by their membership in a nuclear family and a lineage group. At the basic level was the nuclear family composed of parents and preadult children; sometimes it included an elderly grandparent and other family dependents as well. They lived in small round huts constructed of packed mud and topped with a conical thatch roof. In most African societies, these nuclear family units would in turn be combined into larger kinship communities known as households or lineage groups.

The lineage group was similar in many respects to the clan in China or the caste system in India in that it was normally based on kinship ties, although sometimes outsiders such as friends or other dependents may have been admitted to membership. Throughout the precolonial era, lineages served, in the words of one historian, as the "basic building blocks" of African society. The authority of the leading members of the lineage group was substantial. As in China, the elders had considerable power over the economic functions of the other people in the group, which provided mutual support for all members.

A village would usually be composed of a single lineage group, although some communities may have consisted of several unrelated families. At the head of the village was the familiar "big man," who was often assisted by a council of representatives of the various households in the community. Often the "big man" was believed to possess supernatural powers, and as the village grew in size and power, he might eventually be transformed into a local chieftain or monarch.

The Role of Women

Although generalizations are risky, we can say that women were usually subordinate to men in Africa, as in most early societies. In some cases, they were valued for the work they could do or for their role in increasing the size of the lineage group. Polygyny was not uncommon, particularly in Muslim societies. Women often worked in the fields while the men of the village tended the cattle or went on hunting expeditions. In some communities, the women specialized in commercial activities. In one area in southern Africa, young girls were sent into the mines to extract gold because of their smaller physiques.

But there were some key differences between the role of women in Africa and elsewhere. In many African societies, lineage was matrilinear rather than patrilinear. In the words of Ibn Battuta, "A man does not pass on inheritance except to the sons of his sister to the exclusion of his own sons."[8] He said he had never encountered this custom before except among the unbelievers of the Malabar coast in India. Women were often permitted to inherit property, and the husband was often expected to move into his wife's house.

WOMEN AND ISLAM IN NORTH AFRICA

In Muslim societies in North Africa, as elsewhere, women were required to cover their bodies to avoid giving temptations to men, but Islam's puritanical insistence on the separation of the sexes contrasted with the relatively informal relationships that prevailed in many African societies. In this excerpt from The History and Description of Africa, *Leo Africanus describes the customs along the Mediterranean coast of Africa. A resident of Spain of Muslim parentage who was captured by Christian corsairs in 1518 and later served under Pope Leo X, Leo Africanus undertook many visits to Africa.*

LEO AFRICANUS, THE HISTORY AND DESCRIPTION OF AFRICA

Their women (according to the guise of that country) go very gorgeously attired: they wear linen gowns dyed black, with exceeding wide sleeves, over which sometimes they cast a mantle of the same color or of blue, the corners of which mantle are very [attractively] fastened about their shoulders with a fine silver clasp. Likewise they have rings hanging at their ears, which for the most part are made of silver; they wear many rings also upon their fingers. Moreover they usually wear about their thighs and ankles certain scarfs and rings, after the fashion of the Africans. They cover their faces with certain masks having only two holes for the eyes to peep out at. If any man chance to meet with them, they presently hide their faces, passing by him with silence, except it be some of their allies or kinsfolks; for unto them they always [uncover] their faces, neither is there any use of the said mask so long as they be in presence. These Arabians when they travel any journey (as they oftentimes do) they set their women upon certain saddles made handsomely of wicker for the same purpose, and fastened to their camel backs, neither be they anything too wide, but fit only for a woman to sit in. When they go to the wars each man carries his wife with him, to the end that she may cheer up her good man, and give him encouragement. Their damsels which are unmarried do usually paint their faces, breasts, arms, hands, and fingers with a kind of counterfeit color: which is accounted a most decent custom among them.

Relations between the sexes were also sometimes more relaxed than in China or India, with none of the taboos characteristic of those societies. Again, in the words of Ibn Battuta, himself a Muslim:

> With regard to their women, they are not modest in the presence of men, they do not veil themselves in spite of their perseverance in the prayers. . . . The women there have friends and companions amongst men outside the prohibited degrees of marriage [i.e., other than brothers, fathers, etc.]. Likewise for the men, there are companions from amongst women outside the prohibited degrees. One of them would enter his house to find his wife with her companion and would not disapprove of that conduct.

When Ibn Battuta asked an African acquaintance about these customs, the latter responded: "Women's companionship with men in our country is honorable and takes place in a good way: there is no suspicion about it. They are not like the women in your country." Ibn Battuta noted his astonishment at such a "thoughtless" answer and did not accept further invitations to visit his friend's house.[9]

Such informal attitudes toward the relationship between the sexes were not found everywhere in Africa and were probably curtailed as many Africans converted to Islam (see the box above). But it is a testimony to the tenacity of traditional customs that the relatively puritanical views about the role of women in society brought by Muslims from the Middle East made little impression even among Muslim families in West Africa.

Slavery

African slavery is often associated with the period after 1500. Indeed, the slave trade did reach enormous proportions in the seventeenth and eighteenth centuries, when European slave ships transported millions of unfortunate victims abroad to Europe or the Americas (see Chapter 14).

Slavery did not originate with the coming of the Europeans, however. It had been practiced in Africa since ancient times and probably originated with prisoners of war who were forced into perpetual servitude. Slavery was common in ancient Egypt and became especially prevalent during the New Kingdom, when slaving expeditions brought back thousands of captives from the upper Nile to be used in labor gangs, for tribute, and even as human sacrifices.

Slavery persisted during the early period of state building, in the first and early second millennia C.E. Berber tribes may have regularly raided agricultural communities south of the Sahara for captives who were transported northward and eventually sold throughout the Mediterranean. Some were enrolled as soldiers, while others, often women, were used as domestic servants in the homes of the well-to-do. The use of captives for forced labor or for sale was apparently also common in African societies farther to the south and along the eastern coast.

Life was difficult for the average slave. The least fortunate were probably those who worked on plantations owned by the royal family or other wealthy landowners.

Those pressed into service as soldiers were sometimes more fortunate, since in Muslim societies in the Middle East, they might at some point win their freedom. Many slaves were employed in the royal household or as domestic servants in private homes. In general, these slaves probably had the most tolerable existence. Although they were not ordinarily permitted to purchase their freedom, their living conditions were often decent and sometimes practically indistinguishable from those of the free individuals in the household. In some societies in North Africa, slaves reportedly made up as much as 75 percent of the entire population. Elsewhere, the percentage was much lower, in some cases less than 10 percent.

AFRICAN CULTURE

In early Africa, as in much of the rest of the world at the time, creative expression, whether in the form of painting, literature, or music, was above all a means of serving religion. Though to the uninitiated a wooden mask or the bronze and iron statuary of southern Nigeria is simply a work of art, to the artist it was often a means of expressing religious convictions. Some African historians reject the use of the term *art* to describe such artifacts because they were produced for religious rather than aesthetic purposes.

Painting and Sculpture

The earliest extant art forms in Africa are rock paintings. The most famous examples are in the Tassili Mountains in the central Sahara, where the earliest paintings may date back as far as 5000 B.C.E., though the majority are a millennium or so younger. Some of the later paintings depict the two-horse chariots used to transport goods prior to the introduction of the camel. Rock paintings are also found elsewhere in the continent, including the Nile valley and in eastern and southern Africa. Those of the San peoples of southern Africa are especially interesting for their illustrations of ritual ceremonies in which village shamans induce rain, propitiate the spirits, or cure illnesses.

More familiar, perhaps, are African wood carvings and sculpture. Wood-carvers throughout the continent produced remarkable masks (actually headpieces) and statuary. The carvings often represent gods, spirits, or ancestral figures and were believed to embody the spiritual powers of the subject in symbolic form. Terra-cotta and metal figurines served a similar purpose.

In the thirteenth and fourteenth centuries C.E., metalworkers at Ife in what is now southern Nigeria produced handsome bronze and iron statues using the lost-wax method, in which melted wax is replaced in a mold by molten metal. The Ife sculptures may in turn have

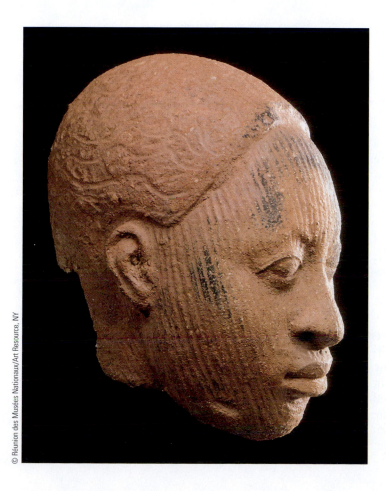

A TERRA-COTTA HEAD.   In addition to metal sculpture, artists from Ife, in southern Nigeria, created exquisite terra-cotta statues. This serene thirteenth-century head represents a servant of the king. Having allegedly descended from the gods, the king rarely showed his own face to his subjects but disguised it behind a veil of glass beads. Because the artist was unable to reproduce a realistic rendering of the king, he transferred the monarch's noble character and divine power onto the servant's face. The vertical lines on the sculpture are probably meant to suggest the beaded veil. The inner serenity and beauty of the head attest to the technical excellence of African clay modeling.

influenced artists in Benin, in West Africa, who produced equally impressive works in bronze during the same period. The Benin sculptures include bronze heads, relief plaques depicting life at court, ornaments, and figures of various animals.

Westerners once regarded African wood carvings and metal sculpture as a form of "primitive art," but the label is not appropriate. The metal sculpture of Benin, for example, is highly sophisticated, and some of the best works are considered masterpieces. Such artistic works were often created by artisans in the employ of the royal court.

Music

Like sculpture and wood carving, African music and dance often served a religious function. With their characteristic heavy rhythmic beat, dances were a means of communicating with the spirits, and the frenzied movements that are often identified with African dance were intended to represent the spirits acting through humans.

African music during the traditional period varied to some degree from one society to another. A wide variety of instruments were used, including drums and other percussion instruments, xylophones, bells, horns and flutes, and stringed instruments like the fiddle, harp, and zither. Still, the music throughout the continent had sufficient common characteristics to justify a few generalizations. In the first place, a strong rhythmic pattern was an important feature of most African music, although the desired effect was achieved through a wide variety of means, including gourds, pots, bells, sticks beaten together, and hand clapping as well as drums.

Another important feature of African music was the integration of voice and instrument into a total musical experience. Musical instruments and the human voice were often woven together to tell a story, and instruments, such as the famous "talking drum," were often used to represent the voice. Choral music and individual voices were frequently used in a pattern of repetition and variation, sometimes known as "call and response." Through this technique, the audience participated in the music by uttering a single phrase over and over as a choral response to the changing call sung by the soloist. Sometimes instrumental music achieved a similar result.

Much music was produced in the context of social rituals, such as weddings and funerals, religious ceremonies, and official inaugurations. It could also serve an educational purpose by passing on to the young people information about the history and social traditions of the community. In the absence of written languages in sub-Saharan Africa (except for the Arabic script, used in Muslim societies in East and West Africa), music served as the primary means of transmitting folk legends and religious traditions from generation to generation.

Storytelling, which was usually undertaken by a priestly class or a specialized class of storytellers, served a similar function.

Architecture

No aspect of African artistic creativity is more varied than architecture. From the pyramids along the Nile to the ruins of Great Zimbabwe south of the Zambezi River, from the Moorish palaces at Zanzibar to the turreted mud mosques of West Africa, African architecture shows a striking diversity of approach and technique that is unmatched in other areas of creative endeavor.

The earliest surviving architectural form found in Africa is the pyramid. The Kushite kingdom at Meroë apparently adopted the pyramidal form from Egypt during the last centuries of the first millennium B.C.E. (see the photo on p. 213). Although used for the same purpose as their earlier counterparts at Giza, the pyramids at Meroë were distinctive in style; they were much smaller and were topped with a flat platform rather than rising to a point. Remains of temples with massive carved pillars at Meroë also reflect Egyptian influence.

Farther to the south, the kingdom of Axum was developing its own architectural traditions. Most distinctive were the carved stone pillars, known as stelae, that were

➣ **A COPTIC CHURCH IN ETHIOPIA.**   In 1200 C.E., Christian monks in Ethiopia began to construct a remarkable series of eleven churches carved out of solid volcanic rock. After a 40-foot trench was formed by removing the bedrock, the central block of stone was hewed into the shape of a Greek cross; then it was hollowed out and decorated. These churches, which are still in use today, testify to the fervor of Ethiopian Christianity.

© Werner Forman/Art Resource, NY

THE MOSQUE AT JENNE, MALI.   With the opening of the gold fields south of Mali, in present-day Ghana, Jenne became an important trading center for gold. Shown here is its distinctive fourteenth-century mosque made of unbaked clay without reinforcements. The projecting timbers offer easy access for repairing the mud exterior, as was regularly required.

used to mark the tombs of dead kings. Some stood as high as 100 feet. The advent of Christianity eventually had an impact on Axumite architecture. During the Zagwe dynasty in the twelfth and thirteenth centuries C.E., churches carved out of solid rock were constructed throughout the country. Stylistically, they combined indigenous techniques inherited from the pre-Christian period with elements borrowed from Christian churches in the Holy Land.

In West Africa, buildings constructed in stone were apparently a rarity until the emergence of states during the first millennium C.E. At that time, the royal palace, as well as other buildings of civic importance, were often built of stone or cement, while the houses of the majority of the population continued to be constructed of dried mud. On his visit to the state of Guinea on the West African coast, the sixteenth-century traveler Leo Africanus noted that the houses of the ruler and other elites were built of chalk with roofs of straw. Even then, however, well into the state-building period, mosques were often built of mud.

Along the east coast, the architecture of the elite tended to reflect Middle Eastern styles. In the coastal towns and islands from Mogadishu to Kilwa, the houses of the wealthy were built of stone and reflected Moorish influence. As elsewhere, the common people lived in huts of mud, thatch, or palm leaves (see the box on p. 232). Mosques were built of stone.

The most famous stone buildings in sub-Saharan Africa are those at Great Zimbabwe. Constructed of carefully cut stones that were set in place without mortar, the great wall and the public buildings at Great Zimbabwe are an impressive monument to the architectural creativity of the peoples of the region.

Literature

Literature in the sense of written works did not exist in sub-Saharan Africa during the early traditional period, except in regions where Islam had brought the Arabic script from the Middle East. But African societies compensated for the absence of a written language with a rich tradition of oral lore. The bard, or professional storyteller, was an ancient African institution by which history was transmitted orally from generation to generation. In many West African societies, bards were highly esteemed and served as counselors to kings as well as protectors of local tradition. Bards were revered for their oratory and singing skills, phenomenal memory, and astute interpretation of history. As one

A CHINESE VIEW OF AFRICA

his passage from Chau Ju-kua's thirteenth-century treatise on geography describes various aspects of life along the eastern coast of Africa in what is now Somalia, including the urban architecture. The author was an inspector of foreign trade in the city of Quanzhou (sometimes called Zayton) on the southern coast of China. His account was compiled from reports of seafarers. Note the varied uses that the local people make of a whale carcass.

CHAU JU-KUA ON EAST AFRICA

The inhabitants of the Chung-li country [the Somali coast] go bareheaded and barefooted; they wrap themselves in cotton stuffs, but they dare not wear jackets, for the wearing of jackets and turbans is a privilege reserved to the ministers and the king's courtiers. The king lives in a brick house covered with glazed tiles, but the people live in huts made of palm leaves and covered with grass-thatched roofs. Their daily food consists of baked flour cakes, sheep's and camel's milk. There are great numbers of cattle, sheep, and camels. . . .

There are many sorcerers among them who are able to change themselves into birds, beasts, or aquatic animals, and by these means keep the ignorant people in a state of terror. If some of them in trading with some foreign ship have a quarrel, the sorcerers pronounce a charm over the ship so that it can neither go forward nor backward, and they only release the ship when it has settled the dispute. The government has formally forbidden this practice.

When one of the inhabitants dies, and they are about to bury him in his coffin, his kinsfolk from near and far come to condole. Each person, flourishing a sword in his hand, goes in and asks the mourners the cause of the person's death. If he was killed by the hand of man, each one says, we will revenge him on the murderer with these swords. Should the mourners reply that he was not killed by any one, but that he came to his end by the will of Heaven, they throw away their swords and break into violent wailing.

Every year there are driven on the coast a great many dead fish measuring two hundred feet in length and twenty feet through the body. The people do not eat the flesh of these fish, but they cut out their brains, marrow, and eyes, from which they get oil. They mix this oil with lime to caulk their boats, and use it also in lamps. The poor people use the ribs of these fish to make rafters, the backbones for door leaves, and they cut off vertebrae to make mortars with.

African scholar wrote, the death of a bard was equivalent to the burning of a library.

Bards served several necessary functions in society. They were chroniclers of history, preservers of social customs and proper conduct, and entertainers who possessed a monopoly over the playing of several musical instruments, which accompanied their narratives. Because of their unique position above normal society, bards often played the role of mediator between hostile families or clans in a community. They were also credited with possessing occult powers and could read divinations and give blessings and curses. Traditionally, bards also served as advisers to the king, sometimes inciting him to action (such as going to battle) through the passion of their poetry. When captured by the enemy, bards were often treated with respect and released or compelled to serve the victor with their art.

One of the most famous West African epics is *The Epic of Son-Jara* (also known as *Sunjata* or *Sundiata*). Passed down orally by bards for more than seven hundred years, it relates the heroic exploits of Son-Jara, the founder and ruler (1230–1255) of Mali's empire. Although Mansa Musa is famous throughout the world because of his flamboyant pilgrimage to Mecca in the fourteenth century, Son-Jara is more celebrated in West Africa because of the dynamic and unbroken oral traditions of the West African peoples (see the box on p. 233).

In addition to the bards, women too were appreciated for their storytelling talents, as well as for their role as purveyors of the moral values and religious beliefs of African societies. In societies that lacked a written tradition, women represented the glue that held the community together. Through the recitation of fables, proverbs, poems, and songs, mothers conditioned the communal bonding and moral fiber of succeeding generations in a way that was rarely encountered in the patriarchal societies of Europe, eastern and southern Asia, and the Middle East. Such activities were not only vital aspects of education in traditional Africa, but they also offered a welcome respite from the drudgery of everyday life and a spark to develop the imagination and artistic awareness of the young. Renowned for its many proverbs, Africa also offers the following: "A good story is like a garden carried in the pocket."

CONCLUSION

Thanks to the dedicated work of a generation of archaeologists, anthropologists, and historians, we now have a much better understanding of the evolution of human societies in Africa than we did a few decades ago. Intensive efforts by archaeologists have demonstrated beyond

A WEST AFRICAN ORAL TRADITION

*I*n this passage from the West African Epic of Son-Jara, Son-Jara's sister, Sugulun Kulunkan, offers to seduce his enemy Sumamuru in order to obtain the Manden secret, or magic spell, needed to control the kingdom of Mali. Sumamuru divulges his all-powerful secret and is rebuked by his mother; both son and mother then disown one another with the trenchant symbols of the slashed breast and cut cloth. After each line of the verse, the bard's assistant would shout the endorsement "true," perhaps the distant origin of today's African American practice of approving each line of religious oratory with "Amen." The subversion of a powerful man by the enticements of a seductive woman is reminiscent of the biblical story of Samson and Delilah.

THE EPIC OF SON-JARA

Son-Jara's flesh-and-blood sister, Sugulun Kulunkan,
She said, "O Magan Son-Jara,
"One person cannot fight this war.
"Let me go seek Sumamuru.
"Were I then to reach him,
"To you I will deliver him,
"So that the folk of the Manden be yours,
"And all the Mandenland you shield."
Sugulun Kulunkan arose,
And went up to the gates of Sumamuru's fortress:
. . .

"Come open the gates, Susu Mountain Sumamuru!
"Come make me your bed companion!"
Sumamuru came to the gates:
"What manner of person are you?"
"It is I Sugulun Kulunkan!"
"Well, now, Sugulun Kulunkan,
"If you have come to trap me,

"To turn me over to some person,
"Know that none can ever vanquish me.
"I have found the Manden secret,
"And made the Manden sacrifice,
"And in five score millet stalks placed it,
"And buried them here in the earth.
"'Tis I who found the Manden secret,
"And made the Manden sacrifice,
"And in a red piebald bull did place it,
"And buried it here in the earth.
"Know that none can vanquish me.
"'Tis I who found the Manden secret
"And made a sacrifice to it,
"And in a pure white cock did place it.
"Were you to kill it,
"And uproot some barren groundnut plants,
"And strip them of their leaves,
"And spread them round the fortress,
"And uproot more barren peanut plants,
"And fling them into the fortress,
"Only then can I be vanquished."
His mother sprang forward at that:
"Heh! Susu Mountain Sumamuru!
"Never tell all to a woman,
"To a one-night woman!
"The woman is not safe, Sumamuru."
Sumamuru sprang towards his mother,
And came and seized his mother,
And slashed off her breast with a knife, magasi!
She went and got the old menstrual cloth.
"Ah! Sumamuru!" she swore.
"If your birth was ever a fact,
"I have cut your old menstrual cloth!"

---

reasonable doubt that the first hominids lived there. Recent evidence suggests that farming may have been practiced in Africa more than twelve thousand years ago, and the concept of kingship may have originated not in Sumer or in Egypt but in the upper Nile valley as long ago as the fourth millennium B.C.E.

Less is known about more recent African history, partly because of the paucity of written records. Still, historians have established that the first civilizations had begun to take shape in sub-Saharan Africa by the first millennium C.E., while the continent as a whole was an active participant in emerging regional and global trade with the Mediterranean world and across the Indian Ocean.

Thus the peoples of Africa were not as isolated from the main currents of human history as was once assumed. Although the state-building process in sub-Saharan

Africa was still in its early stages compared with the ancient civilizations of India, China, and Mesopotamia, in many respects these new states were as impressive and sophisticated as their counterparts elsewhere in the world.

In the fifteenth century, a new factor was added to the equation. Urged on by the tireless efforts of Prince Henry the Navigator, Portuguese fleets began to probe southward along the coast of West Africa. At first, their sponsors were in search of gold and slaves, but at the end of the century, Vasco da Gama's voyage around the Cape of Good Hope signaled Portugal's determination to dominate the commerce of the Indian Ocean in the future. The new situation posed a challenge to the peoples of Africa, whose nascent states and technology would be severely tested by the rapacious demands of the Europeans (see Chapter 14).

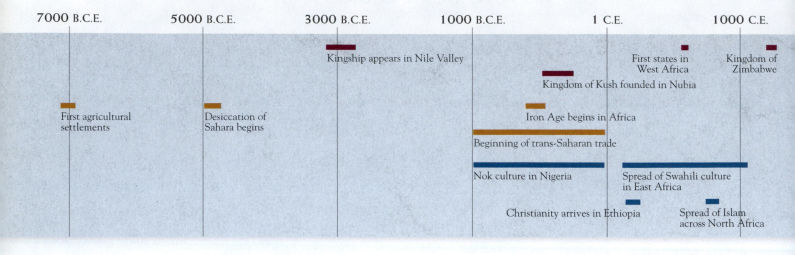

| 7000 B.C.E. | 5000 B.C.E. | 3000 B.C.E. | 1000 B.C.E. | 1 C.E. | 1000 C.E. |

Kingship appears in Nile Valley

First states in West Africa

Kingdom of Zimbabwe

Kingdom of Kush founded in Nubia

First agricultural settlements

Desiccation of Sahara begins

Iron Age begins in Africa

Beginning of trans-Saharan trade

Nok culture in Nigeria

Spread of Swahili culture in East Africa

Christianity arrives in Ethiopia

Spread of Islam across North Africa

CHAPTER NOTES

1. Said Hamdun and Noel King, eds., *Ibn Battuta in Africa* (London, 1975), p. 19.
2. *The Book of Duarte Barbosa* (Nedeln, Liechtenstein, 1967), p. 28.
3. Herodotus, *The Histories*, trans. Aubrey de Sélincourt (Baltimore, 1964), p. 307.
4. Quoted in Margaret Shinnie, *Ancient African Kingdoms* (London, 1965), p. 60.
5. C. R. Boxer, ed., *The Tragic History of the Sea, 1589–1622* (Cambridge, 1959), pp. 121–122.
6. Quoted in Brian Fagan, *New Treasures of the Past: Fresh Finds That Deepen Our Understanding of the Archaeology of Man* (Leicester, England, 1987), p. 154.
7. Hamdun and King, *Ibn Battuta in Africa*, p. 47.
8. Ibid., p. 28.
9. Ibid., pp. 28–30.

SUGGESTED READING

In few areas of world history is scholarship advancing as rapidly as in African history. New information is constantly forcing archaeologists and historians to revise their assumptions about the early history of the continent. Standard texts therefore quickly become out-of-date as their conclusions are supplanted by new evidence.

Still, there are several worthwhile general surveys that provide a useful overview of the early period of African history. The dean of African historians, and certainly one of the most readable, is B. Davidson. For a sympathetic portrayal of the African people, see his *African History* (New York, 1968) and *Lost Cities in Africa*, rev. ed. (Boston, 1970). Other respected accounts are R. Oliver and J. D. Fage, *A Short History of Africa* (Middlesex, England, 1986); J. M. Harris, *Africans and Their History* (New York, 1972); and V. B. Khapoya, *The African Experience: An Introduction* (Englewood Cliffs, N.J., 1994). A more detailed interpretation, by four respected historians, is P. Curtin et al., *African History* (Boston, 1978). For a readable treatment incorporating fairly recent evidence, see K. Shillington, *History of Africa* (New York, 1989). R. O. Collins, ed., *Problems in African History: The Precolonial Centuries* (New York, 1993), provides a useful collection of scholarly articles on key issues in precolonial Africa.

Specialized studies are beginning to appear with frequency on many areas of the continent. For a popular account of archaeological finds, see B. Fagan, *New Treasures of the Past: Fresh Finds That Deepen Our Understanding of the Archaeology of Man* (Leicester, England, 1987). For a more detailed treatment of the early period, see the early volumes in *The Cambridge History of Africa* (Cambridge, 1976–1986). See also R. Oliver and B. Fagan, *Africa in the Iron Age* (Cambridge, 1975); C. Ehret, *An African Classical Age: Eastern and Southern Africa in World History, 1000 B.C. to 400 A.D.* (Charlottesville, Va., 1998), applies historical linguistics to make up for the lack of documentary evidence in the precolonial era. J. D. Clarke and S. A. Brandt, eds., *From Hunters to Farmers* (Berkeley, Calif., 1984), takes an economic approach. Also see D. A. Welsby, *The Kingdom of Kush: The Napataean Meroitic Empire* (London, 1996), and J. Middleton, *Swahili: An African Mercantile Civilization* (New Haven, Conn., 1992). For a fascinating account of trans-Saharan trade, see E. W. Bovill, *The Golden Trade of the Moors: West African Kingdoms in the Fourteenth Century*, 2d ed. (Princeton, N.J., 1995). On the cultural background, see R. Olaniyan, ed., *African History and Culture* (Lagos, Nigeria, 1982), and J. Vansina, *Paths in the Rainforest: Toward a History of Political Tradition in Equatorial Africa* (Madison, Wis., 1990). Although there exist many editions of *The Epic of Son-Jara*, based on recitations of different bards, the most conclusive edition is by F.-D. Sisòkò, translated and thoroughly annotated by J. W. Johnson (Bloomington, Ind., 1992).

On East Africa, see D. Nurse and T. Spear, *The Swahili: Reconstituting the History and Language of an African Society, 800–1500* (Philadelphia, 1985). The maritime story is recounted with documents in G. S. P. Freeman-Grenville, *The East African Coast: Select Documents from the First to the Earlier Nineteenth Century* (Oxford, 1962). For the larger picture, see K. N. Chaudhuri, *Trade and Civilization in the Indian Ocean: An Economic History from the Rise of Islam to 1750* (Cambridge, 1985). On the early history of Ethiopia, see the classic work by S. H. Sellassie, *Ancient and Medieval Ethiopian History* (1972), and J. D. Fage and R. Oliver, eds., *The Cambridge History of Africa*, vol. 4 (Cambridge, 1977–1985).

For useful general surveys of southern Africa, see N. Parsons, *A New History of Southern Africa* (New York, 1983), and K. Shillington, *A History of Southern Africa* (Essex, England, 1987), a profusely illustrated account. For an excellent introduction to African art, see M. B. Visond et al., *A History of Art in Africa* (New York, 2001); R. Hackett, *Art and Religion in Africa* (London, 1996); and S. Adams et al., *Calls and Response: Journeys in African Art* (New Haven, Conn., 2000).

INFOTRAC COLLEGE EDITION

For additional reading, go to InfoTrac College Edition, your online research library at
http://web1.infotrac-college.com

Enter the search term "Africa" using the Subject Guide.

Enter the search terms "slave trade" using Keywords.

Enter the search term "Bantu" using Keywords.

Enter the search terms "Africa history" using Keywords.

Chapter 9

Courtesy of William J. Duiker

THE EXPANSION OF CIVILIZATION IN SOUTHERN ASIA

FOCUS QUESTIONS

- How did Buddhism change in the centuries after Siddhartha Gautama's death, and why did it ultimately decline in popularity in India?
- What impact did Muslim rule have on Indian society?
- What are some of the most important cultural achievements of Indian civilization in the era between the Mauryas and the Mughals?
- What were the main characteristics of Southeast Asian social and economic life, culture, and religion before 1500 C.E.?
- How did Indian civilization influence the civilizations that arose in Southeast Asia?

As the traveler wandered through the length and breadth of the land, he carefully recorded his impressions of the people, from the king down to his most insignificant subject. Their dress, he remarked, was quite different from that of his own country. People wore loose-fitting clothing gathered at the armpits. Most garments were white and were fashioned of cotton, wool, or silk. The robes of the women fell to the ground and completely covered their shoulders. In some areas, the common people wore garments made of leaves or bark or even went naked.

The visitor was especially impressed with the people's personal cleanliness. All wash themselves before eating, he said, and when they complete their meal, they clean their teeth with a willow stick and wash their hands and mouths. After relieving themselves, they wash their bodies and use perfume of sandalwood or turmeric.

The visitor was Xuan Zang (Hsuan Tsang), a Buddhist monk from China who traveled to India in the seventh century C.E. to search for holy scriptures to take back to his own country for translation into Chinese. Because little of the literature of the Indian people from that period survives, Xuan Zang's observations are a valuable resource for our knowledge of the daily lives of the people and show us that the *dhoti* and the *sari*, common forms of Indian dress today, have a long history on the subcontinent. •

INDIA FROM THE MAURYAS TO THE MUGHALS

The India that Xuan Zang visited was no longer the unified land it had been under the Mauryan dynasty. The overthrow of the Mauryas in the early second century B.C.E. had been followed by several hundred years of disunity, when the subcontinent was divided into a number of separate kingdoms and principalities. The dominant force in the north was the Kushan state, established by Indo-European-speaking peoples who had been driven out of what is now China's Xinjiang province by the Xiongnu (see Chapter 3). The Kushans penetrated into the mountains north of the Indus River, where they eventually formed a kingdom with its capital at Bactria, not far from modern Kabul. Over the next two centuries, the Kushans expanded their supremacy along the Indus River and into the central Ganges valley. Then the dynasty began to weaken, and it collapsed sometime in the third century C.E. After the disintegration of the Kushan state, northern India remained divided until the rise of the Gupta dynasty in the early fourth century. The Guptas revived the ancient tradition of the Mauryas for nearly two hundred years until they too were overthrown in about 500 C.E.

Meanwhile, to the south, a number of kingdoms arose among the Dravidian peoples of the Deccan Plateau, which had been only partly under Mauryan rule. The most famous of these kingdoms was Cola (sometimes spelled Chola) on the southeastern coast. Cola developed into a major trading power and sent merchant fleets eastward across the Bay of Bengal, where they introduced Indian culture as well as Indian goods to the peoples of Southeast Asia. In the fourth century C.E., Cola was overthrown by the Pallavas, who ruled from their capital at Kanchipuram (known today as Kanchi), just southwest of modern Madras, for the next four hundred years.

Beginning in the eleventh century, much of northern India fell under the rule of Turkic-speaking peoples who penetrated into the subcontinent from the northwest. Eventually, Turkic dynasties were set up in many areas and introduced the peoples of India to Islamic religion and civilization. These dynasties were able to survive attacks by the forces of Tamerlane (Timur the Lame), but by the end of the fifteenth century, they were coming under severe pressure from the Mughals, a powerful new force from the mountains.

The Kushan Kingdom: Sitting Astride the Silk Road

The Kushan kingdom, with its power base beyond the Khyber Pass in modern Afghanistan, became the dominant political force in northern India in the centuries immediately after the fall of the Mauryas. Sitting astride the main trade routes across the northern half of the subcontinent, the Kushans thrived on the commerce that passed through the area. The bulk of that trade was between the Roman Empire and China and was transported along the route known as the Silk Road, one segment of which passed through the mountains northwest of India (see Chapter 10). From there, goods were shipped to Rome through the Persian Gulf or the Red Sea.

Trade between India and Europe had begun even before the rise of the Roman Empire, but it expanded rapidly in the first century C.E., when sailors mastered the pattern of the monsoon winds in the Indian Ocean (from the southwest in the summer and the northeast in the winter). Commerce between the Mediterranean and the Indian Ocean, as described in the *Periplus*, a first-century C.E. account by a Greek participant, was extensive and often profitable, and it resulted in the establishment of several small Roman settlements along the Indian coast. Rome imported ivory, indigo, textiles, precious stones, and pepper from India and silk from China. The Romans sometimes paid cash for these goods but also exported silver, wine, perfume, slaves, and glass and cloth from Egypt. Overall, Rome appears to have imported much more than it sold to the Far East, leading Emperor Tiberius to grumble that "the ladies and their baubles are transferring our money to foreigners."

The emergence of the Kushan kingdom as a major commercial power was due not only to its role as an intermediary in the Rome-China trade but also to the rising popularity of Buddhism. During the second century C.E. (the precise dates of his reign are unknown), Kanishka, the greatest of the Kushan monarchs, began to patronize Buddhism. Under Kanishka and his successors, an intimate and mutually beneficial relationship was established between Buddhist monasteries and the local merchant community in thriving urban centers like Taxila and Varanasi. Merchants were eager to build stupas and donate money to monasteries in return for social prestige and the implied promise of a better life in this world or the hereafter.

For their part, the wealthy monasteries ceased to be simple communities where monks could find a refuge from the material cares of the world; instead they became major consumers of luxury goods provided by their affluent patrons. Monasteries and their inhabitants became increasingly involved in the economic life of society, and Buddhist architecture began to be richly decorated with precious stones and glass purchased from local merchants

THE GOOD LIFE IN MEDIEVAL INDIA

Much of what we know about life in medieval India comes from the accounts of Chinese missionaries who visited the subcontinent in search of documents recording the teachings of the Buddha. Here the Buddhist monk Fa Xian, who spent several years there in the fifth century C.E., *reports on conditions in the kingdom of Mathura (Mo-tu-lo), a vassal state in western India that was part of the Gupta Empire. Although he could not have been pleased that the Gupta monarchs had adopted the Hindu faith, he found that the people were contented and prosperous except for the outcastes, whom he called Chandalas.*

FA XIAN, *THE TRAVELS OF FA XIAN*

Going southeast from this somewhat less than 80 *joyanas*, we passed very many temples one after another, with some myriad of priests in them. Having passed these places, we arrived at a certain country. This country is called Mo-tu-lo. Once more we followed the Pu-na river. On the sides of the river, both right and left, are twenty *sangharamas*, with perhaps 3,000 priests. The law of Buddha is progressing and flourishing. Beyond the deserts are the countries of western India. The kings of these countries are all firm believers in the law of Buddha. They remove their caps of state when they make offerings to the priests. The members of the royal household and the chief ministers personally direct the food giving; when the distribution of food is over, they spread a carpet on the ground opposite the chief seat (the president's seat) and sit down before it. They dare not sit on couches in the presence of the priests. The rules relating to the almsgiving of kings have been handed down from the time of Buddha till now. Southward from this is the so-called middle country (Madhyadesa). The climate of this country is warm and equable, without frost or snow. The people are very well off, without poll tax or official restrictions. Only those who till the royal lands return a portion of profit of the land. If they desire to go, they go; if they like to stop, they stop. The kings govern without corporal punishment; criminals are fined, according to circumstances, lightly or heavily. Even in cases of repeated rebellion they only cut off the right hand. The king's personal attendants, who guard him on the right and left, have fixed salaries. Throughout the country the people kill no living thing nor drink wine, nor do they eat garlic or onions, with the exception of Chandalas only. The Chandalas are named "evil men" and dwell apart from others; if they enter a town or market, they sound a piece of wood in order to separate themselves; then men, knowing who they are, avoid coming in contact with them. In this country they do not keep swine nor fowls, and do not deal in cattle; they have no shambles [slaughterhouses] or wine shops in their marketplaces. In selling they use cowrie shells. The Chandalas only hunt and sell flesh.

or imported from abroad. The process was highly reminiscent of the changes that occurred in the church in medieval Europe.

It was from the Kushan kingdom that Buddhism began its long journey across the wastes of Central Asia to China and other societies in eastern Asia. As trade between the two regions increased, merchants and missionaries flowed from Bactria over the trade routes snaking through the mountains toward the northeast. At various stopping points on the trail, pilgrims erected statues and decorated mountain caves with magnificent frescoes depicting the life of the Buddha and his message to his followers. One of the most prominent of these centers was at Bamiyan, not far from modern-day Kabul, where believers carved two mammoth statues of the Buddha out of a sheer sandstone cliff. According to the Chinese pilgrim Fa Xian (see the box above), when he visited the area in 400 C.E., over a thousand monks were attending a religious ceremony at the site.

The Gupta Dynasty

The Kushan kingdom came to an end under uncertain conditions sometime in the third century C.E. In 320, a new state was established in the central Ganges valley by a local raja named Chandragupta (no relation to Chandragupta Maurya, the founder of the Mauryan dynasty). Chandragupta located his capital at Pataliputra, the site of the now decaying palace of the Mauryas. Under his successor Samudragupta, the territory under Gupta rule was extended into surrounding areas, and eventually the new kingdom became the dominant political force throughout northern India. It also established a loose suzerainty over the Dravidian state of Pallava to the south, thus becoming the greatest state in the subcontinent since the decline of the Mauryan Empire. Under a succession of powerful, efficient, and highly cultured monarchs, notably Samudragupta and Chandragupta II, India enjoyed a new "classical age" of civilization (see Map 9.1).

The Gupta era was a time of prosperity and thriving commerce with China, Southeast Asia, and the Mediterranean. Great cities, notable for their temples and Buddhist monasteries as well as for their economic prosperity, rose along the main trade routes throughout the subcontinent. The religious trade also prospered, as pilgrims from across India and as far away as China came to visit the major religious centers.

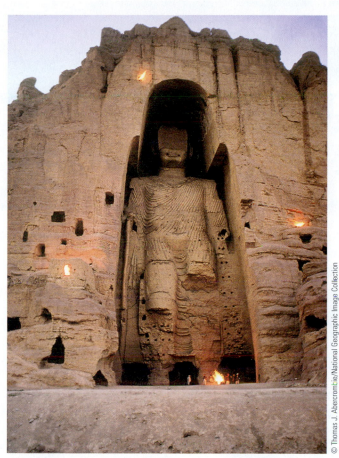

⟫ THE BUDDHAS AT BAMIYAN.   By their sheer size, the two towering Buddhas cut out of a mountain cliff in Afghanistan expressed the builder's perception of the Buddha as encompassing the entire universe. Like the cave complex at Dunhuang in China, the seventh-century C.E. statues at Bamiyan were erected to attract monks and merchants along the Silk Road and to spread the wisdom and compassion of the Buddha. For over a millennium, the extensive cave complex, which contained over a thousand frescoes and statues of various sizes, was a major religious center in Central Asia. The statues were painted and gilded, as in ancient Greece. The drapery on this 175-foot statue reflects the fusion of cultural influences from several regions along the Silk Road, combining Chinese, Indian, Persian, and Greco-Roman styles. Tragically, in 2001, Muslim extremists destroyed the two largest Buddhist statues at the site, as well as everything else in the vicinity, decrying them as "idols of the gods of the infidels."

As in the Mauryan Empire, much of the trade in the Gupta Empire was managed or regulated by the government. The Guptas owned mines and vast crown lands and earned massive profits from their commercial dealings. But there was also a large private sector, dominated by great caste guilds that monopolized key sectors of the economy. A money economy had probably been in operation since the second century B.C.E., when copper and gold coins had been introduced from the Middle East. This in turn led to the development of banking. Nev-

ertheless, there are indications that the circulation of coins was limited. The Chinese missionary Xuan Zang, who visited India early in the seventh century, remarked that most commercial transactions were conducted by barter.[1]

But the good fortunes of the Guptas proved to be relatively short-lived. Beginning in the late fifth century C.E., incursions by nomadic warriors from the northwest gradually reduced the power of the empire. Soon northern India was once more divided into myriad small kingdoms engaged in seemingly constant conflict.

Buddhism at Bay

The Chinese pilgrims who traveled to India during the Gupta era found a Buddhism that had changed in a number of ways in the centuries since the time of Siddhartha Gautama. They also found a doctrine that was beginning to decline in popularity in the face of a resurgent Hinduism.

The transformation in Buddhism had come about in part because the earliest written sources were transcribed two centuries after Siddhartha's death and in part because his message was reinterpreted as it became part of the everyday life of the people. Abstract concepts of a Nirvana that cannot be described began to be replaced, at least in the popular mind, with more concrete visions of heavenly salvation, and Siddhartha was increasingly regarded as a divinity rather than as a sage. The Buddha's teachings that all four classes were equal gave way to the familiar Hindu conviction that some people, by reason of previous reincarnations, were closer to Nirvana than others.

These developments led to a split in the movement. Purists emphasized what they insisted were the original teachings of the Buddha (describing themselves as the school of Theravada, or "the teachings of the elders"). Followers of Theravada considered Buddhism a way of life, not a salvationist creed. Theravada stressed the importance of strict adherence to personal behavior and the quest for understanding as a means of release from the wheel of life.

In the meantime, another interpretation of Buddhist doctrine was emerging in the northwest. Here Buddhist believers, perhaps hoping to compete with other salvationist faiths circulating in the region, began to promote the view that Nirvana could be achieved through devotion and not just through painstaking attention to one's behavior. According to advocates of this school, eventually to be known as Mahayana ("greater vehicle"), Theravada teachings were too demanding or too strict for ordinary people to follow and therefore favored the wealthy, who were more apt to have the time and resources to spend weeks or months away from their everyday occupations. Mahayana Buddhists referred to their rivals as Hinayana, or "lesser vehicle," because in Theravada fewer

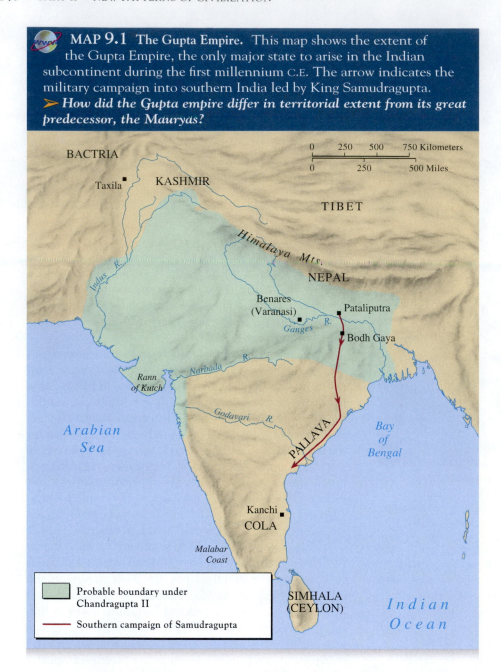

MAP 9.1 The Gupta Empire. This map shows the extent of the Gupta Empire, the only major state to arise in the Indian subcontinent during the first millennium C.E. The arrow indicates the military campaign into southern India led by King Samudragupta.
➤ *How did the Gupta empire differ in territorial extent from its great predecessor, the Mauryas?*

would reach enlightenment. Mahayana thus attempted to provide hope for the masses in their efforts to reach Nirvana, but to the followers of Theravada, it did so at the expense of an insistence on proper behavior.

To advocates of the Mahayana school, salvation could also come from the intercession of a bodhisattva ("he who possesses the essence of Buddhahood"). According to Mahayana beliefs, some individuals who had achieved bodhi and were thus eligible to enter the state of Nirvana after death chose instead, because of their great compassion, to remain on earth in spirit form to help all human beings achieve release from the life cycle. Followers of Theravada, who believed the concept of bodhisattva applied only to Siddhartha Gautama himself,

denounced such ideas as "the teaching of demons." But to their proponents, such ideas extended the hope of salvation to the masses. Mahayana Buddhists revered the saintly individuals who, according to tradition, had become bodhisattvas at death and erected temples in their honor where the local population could pray and render offerings. The most famous bodhisattva was Avalokitesvara, a mythic figure whose name in Sanskrit means "Lord of Compassion." Perhaps because of the identification of Avalokitesvara with the concept of mercy, in China he was gradually transformed into a female figure known as Guan Yin (Kuan Yin).

A final distinguishing characteristic of Mahayana Buddhism was its reinterpretation of Buddhism as a religion rather than as a philosophy. Although Mahayana had philosophical aspects, its adherents increasingly regarded the Buddha as a divine figure, and an elaborate Buddhist cosmology developed. Nirvana was not a form of extinction but a true heaven with many rest stations along the way for the faithful.

Under Kushan rule, Mahayana achieved considerable popularity in northern India and for a while even made inroads in such Theravada strongholds as the island of Sri Lanka. But in the end, neither Mahayana nor Theravada was able to retain its popularity in Indian society. By the seventh century C.E., Theravada had declined rapidly on the subcontinent, although it retained its foothold in Sri Lanka and across the Bay of Bengal in Southeast Asia, where it remained an influential force to modern times. Mahayana prospered in the northwest for centuries, but eventually it was supplanted by a revived Hinduism and later by a new arrival, Islam. But Mahayana too would find better fortunes abroad, as it was carried over the Silk Road or by sea to China and then to Korea and Japan (see Chapters 10 and 11). In all three countries, Buddhism has coexisted with Confucian doctrine and indigenous beliefs to the present.

Why was Buddhism unable to retain its popularity in its native India, although it became a major force elsewhere in Asia? Some have speculated that in denying the existence of the soul, Buddhism ran counter to traditional Hindu belief. Perhaps, too, one of Buddhism's strengths was also a weakness. In rejecting the class divi-sions that defined the Indian way of life, Buddhism appealed to those very groups who lacked an accepted place in Hindu society, such as the untouchables. But at the same time, it represented a threat to those with a higher status. Moreover, by emphasizing the responsibility of each person to seek an individual path to Nirvana, Buddhism undermined the strong social bonds of the Indian caste system.

Perhaps a final factor in the decline of Buddhism was the revival of Hinduism. In its early development, Hinduism had been highly elitist. Not only was observance of court ritual a monopoly of the *brahmin* class (see the box on p. 242), but the major route to individual salvation, asceticism, was hardly realistic for the average Indian. However, in the centuries after the fall of the Mauryas, a growing emphasis on devotion (*bhakti*) as a means of religious observance brought the possibility of improving one's *karma* by means of ritual acts within the reach of Indians of all classes. It seems likely that Hindu devotionalism rose precisely to combat the inroads of Buddhism and reduce the latter's appeal among the Indian population. The Chinese Buddhist missionary Fa Xian, who visited India in the mid-Gupta era, reported that mutual hostility between the Buddhists and the *brahmins* was quite strong:

> Leaving the southern gate of the capital city, on the east side of the road is a place where Buddha once dwelt. Whilst here he bit [a piece from] the willow stick and fixed it in the earth; immediately it grew up seven feet high, neither more nor less.

Courtesy of William J. Duiker

⟫ MAMALLAPURAM SHORE TEMPLE. Mamallapuram ("the city of the great warrior") was so named by one of the powerful kings of the Pallavan kingdom on the eastern coast of South India. From this port, ships embarked on naval expeditions to Sri Lanka and far-off destinations in Southeast Asia. Although the site was originally identified with the Hindu deity Vishnu, in the eighth century C.E. a Pallavan monarch built this shore temple in honor of Vishnu's rival deity, Shiva. It stands as a visual confirmation of the revival of the Hindu faith in southern India at the time. As with many other stone monuments from antiquity, such as the Sphinx in Egypt, centuries of wind and rain have eroded the ornate carvings that originally covered the large granite blocks.

THE EDUCATION OF A BRAHMIN

Although the seventh-century Chinese traveler Xuan Zang was a Buddhist, he faithfully recorded his impressions of the Hindu religion in his memoirs. Here he describes the education of a brahmin, the highest class in Indian society.

XUAN ZANG, RECORDS OF WESTERN COUNTRIES

The Brahmans study the four *Veda Sastras*. The first is called *Shau* [longevity]; it relates to the preservation of life and the regulation of the natural condition. The second is called *Sse* [sacrifice]; it relates to the [rules of] sacrifice and prayer. The third is called *Ping* [peace or regulation]; it relates to decorum, casting of lots, military affairs, and army regulations. The fourth is called *Shue* [secret mysteries]; it relates to various branches of science, incantations, medicine.

The teachers [of these works] must themselves have closely studied the deep and secret principles they contain, and penetrated to their remotest meaning. They then explain their general sense, and guide their pupils in understanding the words that are difficult. They urge them on and skillfully conduct them. They add luster to their poor knowledge, and stimulate the desponding. If they find that their pupils are satisfied with their acquirements, and so wish to escape to attend to their worldly duties, then they use means to keep them in their power. When they have finished their education, and have attained thirty years of age, then their character is formed and their knowledge ripe. When they have secured an occupation they first of all thank their master for his attention. There are some, deeply versed in antiquity, who devote themselves to elegant studies, and live apart from the world, and retain the simplicity of their character. These rise above mundane presents, and are as insensible to renown as to the contempt of the world. Their name having spread afar, the rulers appreciate them highly, but are unable to draw them to the court. The chief of the country honors them on account of their [mental] gifts, and the people exalt their fame and render them universal homage. . . . They search for wisdom, relying on their own resources. Although they are possessed of large wealth, yet they will wander here and there to seek their subsistence. There are others who, whilst attaching value to letters, will yet without shame consume their fortunes in wandering about for pleasure, neglecting their duties. They squander their substance in costly food and clothing. Having no virtuous principle, and no desire to study, they are brought to disgrace, and their infamy is widely circulated.

The unbelievers and Brahmans, filled with jealousy, cut it down and scattered the leaves far and wide, but yet it always sprang up again in the same place as before.[2]

For a while, Buddhism was probably able to stave off the Hindu challenge by its own salvationist creed of Mahayana, which also emphasized the role of devotion, but the days of Buddhism as a dominant faith in the subcontinent were numbered.

Islam on the March

While India was still suffering from the disarray left by the collapse of the Gupta Empire, a new and dynamic force in the form of Islam was arising in the Arabian peninsula to the west. As we have seen, during the seventh and eighth centuries, Arab armies carried the new faith westward to the Iberian peninsula and eastward across the arid wastelands of Persia and into the rugged mountains of the Hindu Kush. Islam first reached India through the Arabs in the eighth century, but a second onslaught in the tenth and eleventh centuries by Turkic-speaking converts had a more lasting effect.

Although Arab merchants had been active along the Indian coasts for centuries, Arab armies did not reach India until the early eighth century. When Indian pirates attacked Arab shipping near the delta of the Indus River, the Muslim ruler in Iraq demanded an apology from the ruler of Sind, a Hindu state in the Indus valley. When the latter refused, Muslim forces conquered lower Sind in 711 and then moved northward into the Punjab, bringing Arab rule into the frontier regions of the subcontinent for the first time.

For the next three centuries, Islam made no further advances into India. But a second phase began at the end of the tenth century with the rise of the state of Ghazni, located in the area of the old Kushan kingdom in present-day Afghanistan. The new kingdom was founded in 962 when Turkic-speaking slaves seized power from the Samanids, a Persian dynasty. When the founder of the new state died in 997, his son, Mahmud of Ghazni (997–1030), succeeded him. Brilliant and ambitious, Mahmud used his patrimony as a base of operations for sporadic forays against neighboring Hindu kingdoms to the southeast. Before his death in 1030, he was able to extend his rule throughout the upper Indus valley and as far south as the Indian Ocean (see Map 9.2). In wealth and cultural brilliance, his court at Ghazni rivaled that of the Abbasid dynasty in neighboring Baghdad. But his achievements had a dark side. Describing Mahmud's conquests in northwestern India, the contemporary historian al-Biruni wrote:

Mahmud utterly ruined the prosperity of the country, and performed wonderful exploits by which the Hindus became like atoms scattered in all directions, and like a tale of old in the mouth of the people. Their scattered remains cherish, of course, the most inveterate aversion towards all Muslims. This is the reason, too, why Hindu sciences have retired far away from those parts of the country conquered by us, and have fled to places which our hand cannot yet reach, to Kashmir, Benares, and other places.[3]

Resistance against the advances of Mahmud and his successors into northern India was led by the Rajputs, aristocratic Hindu clans who were probably descended from tribal groups that had penetrated into northwestern India from Central Asia in earlier centuries. The Rajputs possessed a strong military tradition and fought bravely, but their military tactics, based on infantry supported by elephants, were no match for the fearsome cavalry of the invaders, whose ability to strike with lightning speed contrasted sharply with the slow-footed forces of their adversaries. Moreover, the incessant squabbling among the Rajput leaders put them at a disadvantage against the single-minded intensity and religious fervor of Mahmud's armies. Although the power of Ghazni declined after his death, a successor state in the area resumed the advance

MAP 9.2   India at the Death of Mahmud of Ghazni. Beginning in the tenth century, Turkic-speaking peoples invaded northwestern India and introduced Islam to the peoples in the area. Most famous was the empire of Mahmud of Ghazni. ➤ *Which of the great trading states of southern India are located on the map?*

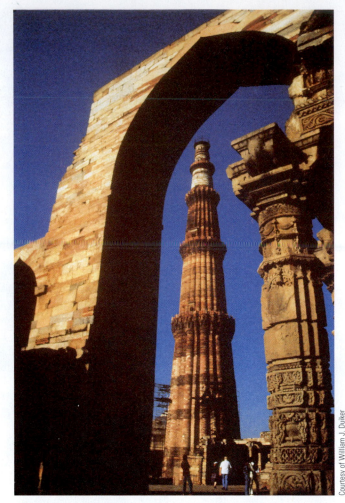

Courtesy of William J. Duiker

KUTUB MINAR. To commemorate their religious victory in 1192, the Muslim conquerors of northern India constructed a magnificent mosque on the site of Delhi's largest Hindu temple. Much of the material for the mosque came from twenty-seven local Hindu and Jain shrines. Adjacent to the mosque soars the Kutub Minar, symbol of the new conquering faith. Originally 238 feet high, the tower's inscription proclaimed its mission to cast the long shadow of God over the realm of the Hindus.

in the late twelfth century, and by 1200, Muslim power, in the form of a new Delhi sultanate, had been extended over the entire plain of northern India.

South of the Ganges River valley, Muslim influence spread more slowly and in fact had little immediate impact. Muslim armies launched occasional forays into the Deccan Plateau, but at first they had little success, even though the area was divided among a number of warring kingdoms, including the Colas along the eastern coast and the Pandyas far to the south.

One reason the Delhi sultanate failed to take advantage of the disarray of its rivals was the threat posed by the Mongols on the northwestern frontier (see Chapter 10). Mongol armies unleashed by the great tribal warrior Genghis Khan occupied Baghdad and destroyed the Abbasid caliphate in the 1250s, while other forces occupied the Punjab around Lahore, from which they threatened Delhi on several occasions. For the next half-century, the attention of the sultanate was focused on the Mongols. That threat finally declined in the early fourteenth century with the gradual breakup of the Mongol Empire, and a new Islamic state emerged in the form of a new Tughluq dynasty (1320–1413), which extended its power into the Deccan Plateau. In praise of his sovereign, the Tughluq monarch Ala-ud-din, the poet Amir Khusrau exclaimed:

Happy be Hindustan, with its splendor of religion,
Where Islamic law enjoys perfect honor and dignity;
In learning Delhi now rivals Bukhara;

Islam has been made manifest by the rulers.
From Ghazni to the very shore of the ocean
You see Islam in its glory.[4]

Such happiness was not destined to endure, however. During the latter half of the fourteenth century, the Tughluq dynasty gradually fell into decline. In 1398, a new military force crossed the Indus River from the northwest, raided the capital of Delhi, and then withdrew. According to some contemporary historians, as many as 100,000 Hindu prisoners were massacred before the gates of the city. Such was India's first encounter with Tamerlane.

Tamerlane (b. 1330s), also known as Timur-i-lang (Timur the Lame), was the ruler of a Mongol khanate based in Samarkand to the north of the Pamir Mountains. His kingdom had been founded on the ruins of the

Courtesy of William J. Duiker

↠ **SAMARKAND, GEM OF AN EMPIRE.**   The city of Samarkand has a long history. Originating during the first millennium B.C.E. as a caravan stop on the Silk Road, it was later occupied by Alexander the Great, the Abbasids, and the Mongols before becoming the capital of Tamerlane's expanding empire. Tamerlane expended great sums in creating a city worthy of his own imperial ambitions. Shown here is the great square, known as the Registan. Site of a mosque, a library, and a Muslim university, all built in the exuberant Persian style, Samarkand was the jumping-off point for trade with China far to the east.

Mongol Empire, which had begun to disintegrate as a result of succession struggles in the thirteenth century. Tamerlane, the son of a local aristocrat, seized power in Samarkand in 1369 and immediately launched a program of conquest. During the 1380s, he brought the entire region east of the Caspian Sea under his authority and then conquered Baghdad and occupied Mesopotamia (see Map 9.3). After his brief foray into northern India, he turned to the west and raided the Anatolian peninsula. Defeating the army of the Ottoman Turks, he advanced almost as far as the Bosporus before withdrawing. "The last of the great nomadic conquerors," as one recent histo-

rian described him, died in 1405 in the midst of a final military campaign.

The passing of Tamerlane removed a major menace from the diverse states of the Indian subcontinent. But the respite from external challenge was not a long one. By the end of the fifteenth century, two new challenges had appeared from beyond the horizon: the Mughals, a newly emerging nomadic power beyond the Khyber Pass in the north, and the Portuguese traders, who arrived by sea from the eastern coast of Africa in search of gold and spices. Both, in different ways, would exert a major impact on the later course of Indian civilization.

THE ISLAMIC CONQUEST OF INDIA

One consequence of the Muslim conquest of northern India was the imposition of many Islamic customs on Hindu society. In this excerpt, the fourteenth-century Muslim historian Zia-ud-din Barani describes the attempt of one Muslim ruler, Ala-ud-din, to forbid the use of alcohol and gambling, two practices expressly forbidden in Muslim society. Ala-ud-din had seized power in Delhi from a rival in 1294.

A MUSLIM RULER SUPPRESSES HINDU PRACTICES

He forbade wine, beer, and intoxicating drugs to be used or sold; dicing, too, was prohibited. Vintners and beer sellers were turned out of the city, and the heavy taxes which had been levied from them were abolished. All the china and glass vessels of the Sultan's banqueting room were broken and thrown outside the gate of Badaun, where they formed a mound. Jars and casks of wine were emptied out there till they made mire as if it were the season of the rains. The Sultan himself entirely gave up wine parties. Self-respecting people at once followed his example; but the ne'er-do-wells went on making wine and spirits and hid the leather bottles in loads of hay or firewood and by various such tricks smuggled it into the city. Inspectors and gatekeepers and spies diligently sought to seize the contraband and the smugglers; and when seized the wine was given to the elephants, and the importers and sellers and drinkers [were] flogged and given short terms of imprisonment. So many were they, however, that holes had to be dug for their incarceration outside the great thoroughfare of the Badaun gate, and many of the wine bibbers died from the rigor of their confinement and others were taken out half-dead and were long in recovering their health. The terror of these holes deterred many from drinking. Those who could not give it up had to journey ten or twelve leagues to get a drink, for at half that distance, four or five leagues from Delhi, wine could not be publicly sold or drunk. The prevention of drinking proving very difficult, the Sultan enacted that people might distill and drink privately in their own homes, if drinking parties were not held and the liquor not sold. After the prohibition of drinking, conspiracies diminished.

ISLAM AND INDIAN SOCIETY

Like their counterparts in other areas that came under Islamic rule, many Muslim rulers in India were quite tolerant of other faiths and used peaceful means, if any, to encourage nonbelievers to convert to Islam. Even the more enlightened, however, could be fierce when their religious zeal was aroused. One ruler, on being informed that a Hindu fair had been held near Delhi, ordered the promoters of the event put to death. Hindu temples were razed, and mosques were erected in their place. Eventually, however, most Muslim rulers realized that not all Hindus could be converted and recognized the necessity of accepting what to them was an alien and repugnant religion. While Hindu religious practices were generally tolerated, non-Muslims were compelled to pay a tax to the state. Some Hindus likely converted to Islam to avoid paying the tax, but they were then expected to make the traditional charitable contribution required of Muslims in all Islamic societies.

Over time, millions of Hindus did turn to the Muslim faith. Some were individuals or groups in the employ of the Muslim ruling class, such as government officials, artisans, or merchants catering to the needs of the court. But many others were probably peasants from the *sudra* class or even untouchables who found in the egalitarian message of Islam a way of removing the stigma of low-class status in the Hindu social hierarchy.

Seldom have two major religions been so strikingly different. Where Hinduism tolerated a belief in the existence of several deities (although admittedly they were all considered by some to be manifestations of one supreme god), Islam was uncompromisingly monotheistic. Where Hinduism was hierarchical, Islam was egalitarian. Where Hinduism featured a priestly class to serve as an intermediary with the ultimate force of the universe, Islam permitted no one to come between believers and their god. Such differences contributed to the mutual hostility that developed between the adherents of the two faiths in the Indian subcontinent, but more mundane issues, such as the Muslim habit of eating beef and the idolatry and sexual frankness in Hindu art, were probably a greater source of antagonism at the popular level (see the box above00).

In other cases, the two peoples borrowed from each other. Some Muslim rulers found the Indian idea of divine kingship appealing. In their turn, Hindu rajas learned by bitter experience the superiority of cavalry mounted on horses instead of elephants, the primary assault weapon in early India. Some upper-class Hindu males were attracted to the Muslim tradition of *purdah* and began to keep their women in seclusion (termed locally "behind the curtain") from everyday society. Hindu sources claimed that one reason for adopting the custom was to protect Hindu women from the roving eyes of foreigners. But it is likely that many Indian families adopted the practice for reasons of prestige or because they were convinced that *purdah* was a prac-

THE PRACTICE OF *SATI*

One of the most distinctive aspects of medieval Indian society was the Hindu custom of sati, whereby a widow was immolated on the funeral pyre of her husband during his cremation. In so doing, she was not only honoring her dead husband but also declaring her allegiance to deeply held community beliefs in the sanctity of the marriage vow. Here the Portuguese adventurer Duarte Barbosa describes such a practice in the southern state of Narsyngua.

DUARTE BARBOSA, ON SATI

In this kingdom of Narsyngua . . . the women are bound by very ancient custom, when their husbands die, to burn themselves alive with their corpses, which are also burnt. This they do to honor the husband. If such a woman is poor and of low estate, when her husband dies she goes with him to the burning ground, "where there is a great pit" in which a pile of wood burns. When the husband's body has been laid therein and begins to burn she throws herself of her own free will into the midst of the said fire, where both their bodies are reduced to ashes. But if she is a woman of high rank, rich, and with distinguished kindred, whether she be a young maid or an old woman, when her husband dies she accompanies the aforesaid corpse of her husband to the aforesaid burning ground, bewailing him; and there they dig a round pit, very wide and deep, which they fill with wood . . . and, when they have kindled it, they lay the man's body therein, and it is burnt while she weeps greatly. Wishing to do all honor to her husband she then causes all his kindred and her own to be called together, that they may come to feast and honor her thereby. . . . Thereafter she attires herself very richly with all the jewels she pos-

sesses, and then distributes to her sons, relatives, and friends all the property that remains. Thus arrayed she mounts on a horse . . . that she may be the better seen of all the people. Mounted on this horse they lead her through the whole city with great rejoicings, until they come back to the very spot where the husband has been burnt, where, they cast a great quantity of wood into the pit itself and on its edge they make a great fire. When it has burnt up somewhat they erect a wooden scaffold with four or five steps where they take her up just as she is. When she is on the top she turns herself round thereon three times, worshipping towards the direction of sunrise, and, this done, she calls her sons, kindred, and friends, and to each she gives a jewel, whereof she has many with her, and in the same way every piece of her clothing until nothing is left except a small piece of cloth with which she is clothed from the waist down. Then she tells the men who are with her on the scaffold to consider what they owe to their wives who, being free to act, yet burn themselves alive for the love of them, and the women she tells to see how much they owe to their husbands, to such a degree as to go with them even to death. Then . . . they place in her hands a pitcher full of oil, and she puts it on her head, and with it she again turns round thrice on the scaffold and again worships towards the rising sun. Then she casts the pitcher of oil into the fire and throws herself after it with as much goodwill as if she were throwing herself on a little cotton, from which she could receive no hurt. The kinsfolk all take part at once and cast into the fire many pitchers of oil and butter which they hold ready for this purpose, and much wood on this, and therewith bursts out such a flame that no more can be seen.

tical means of protecting female virtue. Adult Indian women had already begun to cover their heads with a scarf during the Gupta era.

All in all, Muslim rule probably did not have a significant impact on the lives of most Indian women. *Purdah* was practiced more commonly among high castes than among the lower castes. Though it was probably of little consolation, sexual relations in poor and low-caste families were relatively egalitarian, as men and women worked together on press gangs or in the fields. Muslim customs apparently had little effect on the Hindu tradition of *sati* (see the box above). In fact, in many respects, Muslim women had more rights than their Hindu counterparts. They had more property rights than Hindu women and were legally permitted to divorce under certain conditions and to remarry after the death of their husband. The primary role for Indian women in general, however, was to produce children. Sons were preferred over daughters, not

only because they alone could conduct ancestral rights but also because a daughter was a financial liability. A daughter required that her father provide a costly dowry when she married, yet after the wedding, she would transfer her labor assets to her husband's family. Still, women shared with men a position in the Indian religious pantheon. The cult of the mother-goddess, which had originated in the Harappan era, revived during the Gupta era stronger than ever. The Hindu female deity, known as Devi, was celebrated by both men and women as the source of cosmic power, bestower of wishes, and symbol of fertility.

Overall, the Muslims continued to view themselves as foreign conquerors and generally maintained a strict separation between the Muslim ruling class and the mass of the Hindu population. Although a few Hindus rose to important positions in the local bureaucracy, most high posts in the central government and the provinces were reserved for Muslims. Only with the founding of the

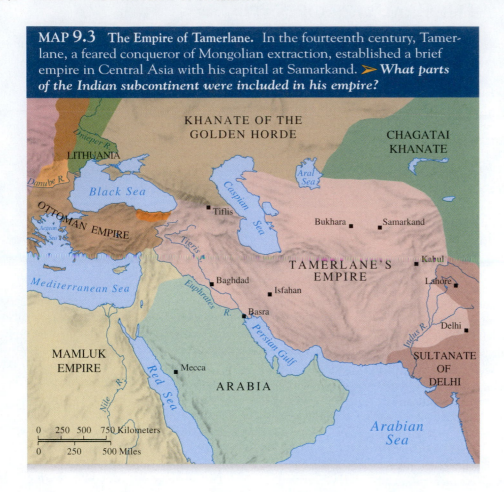

MAP 9.3   The Empire of Tamerlane. In the fourteenth century, Tamerlane, a feared conqueror of Mongolian extraction, established a brief empire in Central Asia with his capital at Samarkand. ➤ *What parts of the Indian subcontinent were included in his empire?*

Mughal dynasty was a serious effort undertaken to reconcile the differences.

One result of this effort was the religion of the Sikhs ("disciples"). Founded by the guru Nanak in the early sixteenth century in the Punjab, Sikhism attempted to integrate the best of the two faiths in a single religion. Sikhism originated in the devotionalist movement in Hinduism, which taught that God was the single true reality. All else is illusion. But Nanak rejected the Hindu tradition of asceticism and mortification of the flesh and, like Muhammad, taught his disciples to participate in the world. Sikhism achieved considerable popularity in northwestern India, where Islam and Hinduism confronted each other directly, and eventually evolved into a militant faith that fiercely protected its adherents against its two larger rivals. In the end, Sikhism did not reconcile Hinduism and Islam but provided an alternative to them.

One complication for both Muslims and Hindus as they tried to come to terms with the existence of a mixed society was the problem of caste. Could non-Hindus form castes, and if so, how were these castes related to the Hindu castes? Where did the Turkic-speaking elites who made up the ruling class in many of the Islamic states fit into the equation?

The problem was resolved in a pragmatic manner that probably followed an earlier tradition of assimilating non-Hindu tribal groups into the system. Members of the Turkic ruling groups formed social groups that were roughly equivalent to the Hindu *brahmin* or *kshatriya* caste. During the Delhi sultanate in the north, members of the local Rajput nobility who converted to Islam were occasionally permitted to join such caste groupings. Ordinary Indians who converted to Islam also formed Muslim castes, although at a lower level on the social scale. Many who did so were probably artisans who converted en masse to obtain the privileges that conversion could bring.

In most of India, then, Muslim rule did not substantially disrupt the caste system. One perceptive European visitor in the early sixteenth century reported that in Malabar, along the southwestern coast, there were separate castes for fishing, pottery making, weaving, carpentry and metalworking, salt mining, sorcery, and labor on the plantations. There were separate castes for doing the laundry, one for the elite and the other for the common people (see the box on p. 249).

Economy and Daily Life

India's landed and commercial elites lived in the cities, often in conditions of considerable opulence. The rulers, of course, possessed the most wealth. One maharaja of a relatively small state in southern India, for example, had over 100,000 soldiers in his pay along with nine hundred

UNTOUCHABLES IN SOUTH INDIA

Some of the best descriptions of Indian society in the late medieval era came from European merchants and missionaries. The following passage was written by the Portuguese traveler Duarte Barbosa and describes an untouchable caste on the southwestern coast of India in the early sixteenth century. The Nayres mentioned in this excerpt were a higher caste in the region.

DUARTE BARBOSA, FROM THE LAND OF MALABAR

And there is yet another caste of Heathen lower than these whom they call Poleas, who among all the rest are held to be accursed and excommunicate; they dwell in the fields and open campaigns [plots] in secret lurking places, whither folk of good caste never go save by mischance, and live in huts very strait and mean. They are tillers of rice with buffaloes and oxen. They never speak to the Nayres save from afar off, shouting so that they may hear them, and when they go along the roads they utter loud cries, that they may be let past, and whosoever hears them leaves the road, and stands in the wood till they have passed by; and if anyone, whether man or woman, touches them his kinsfolk slay him forthwith, and in vengeance therefore they slay Poleas until they weary without suffering any punishment. In certain months of the year they do their utmost to touch some Nayre woman by night as secretly as they can, and this only for the sake of doing evil. They go by in order to get into the houses of the Nayres to touch women, and during these months the women guard themselves carefully, and if they touch any woman, even though none have seen it, and there may be no witnesses, yet she declares it at once, crying out, and she will stay no longer in her house that her caste may not be destroyed; in general she flees to the house of some other low caste folk, and hides herself, that her kinsfolk may not slay her; and that thence she may help herself and be sold to foreigners, which is ofttimes done. And the manner of touching is this, even though no words are exchanged, they throw something at her, a stone or a stick, and if it touches her she is touched and ruined. These people are also great sorcerers and thieves; they are a very evil race.

---

elephants and twenty thousand horses. Another maintained a thousand high-caste women to serve as sweepers of his palace. Each carried a broom and a brass basin containing a mixture of cow dung and water and followed him from one house to another, plastering the path where he was to tread. Most urban dwellers, of course, did not live in such style. Xuan Zang, the Chinese Buddhist missionary who visited India in the early seventh century, left us a description of ordinary homes in urban areas:

> Their houses are surrounded by low walls, and form the suburbs. The earth being soft and muddy, the walls of the towns are mostly built of brick or tiles. The towers on the walls are constructed of wood or bamboo; the houses have balconies and belvederes, which are made of wood, with a coating of lime or mortar, and covered with tiles. The different buildings have the same form as those in China; rushes, or dry branches, or tiles, or boards are used for covering them. The walls are covered with lime and mud, mixed with cow's dung for purity. At different seasons they scatter flowers about. Such are some of their different customs.[5]

The majority of India's population (estimated at slightly more than 100 million in the first millennium C.E.), however, lived on the land. Most were peasants who tilled small plots with a wooden plow pulled by oxen and paid a percentage of the harvest to their landlord. The landlord in turn forwarded part of the payment to the local ruler. In effect, the landlord functioned as a tax collector for the king, who retained ultimate ownership of all farmland in his domain. At best, most peasants lived at the subsistence level. At worst, they were forced into debt and fell victim to moneylenders who charged exorbitant rates of interest.

In the north and in the upland regions of the Deccan Plateau, the primary grain crops were wheat and barley. In the Ganges valley and the southern coastal plains, the main crop was rice. Vegetables were grown everywhere, and southern India produced many spices, fruits, sugarcane, and cotton. The cotton plant apparently originated in the Indus River valley and spread from there. Although some cotton was cultivated in Spain and North Africa by the eighth and ninth centuries, India remained the primary producer of cotton goods. Spices such as cinnamon, pepper, ginger, sandalwood, cardamom, and cumin were also major export products.

Agriculture, of course, was not the only source of wealth in India. Since ancient times, the subcontinent had served as a major entrepôt for trade between the Middle East and the Pacific basin, as well as the source of other goods shipped throughout the known world. Although civil strife and piracy, heavy taxation of the business community by local rulers to finance their fratricidal wars, and increased customs duties between principalities may have contributed to a decline in internal trade, the level of foreign trade remained high, particularly in the Dravidian kingdoms in the south and along the northwestern coast, which were located along the traditional trade routes to the Middle East and the Mediterranean Sea. Much of this foreign trade was carried on by wealthy Hindu castes with close ties to the royal courts. But there were other participants as well, including such non-Hindu minorities as the Muslims, the Parsis, and the Jain community. The Parsis, expatriates from Persia who practiced the Zoroastrian religion, dominated banking and the textile industry in the cities bordering the Rann of Kutch. Later they would become a dominant economic force in the modern city of Mumbai (Bombay). The Jains became prominent in trade and manufacturing even though their faith emphasized simplicity and the rejection of materialism.

According to early European travelers, merchants often lived quite well. One Portuguese observer described the "Moorish" population in Bengal as follows:

> They have girdles of cloth, and over them silk scarves; they carry in their girdles daggers garnished with silver and gold, according to the rank of the person who carries them; on their fingers many rings set with rich jewels, and cotton turbans on their heads. They are luxurious, eat well and spend freely, and have many other extravagances as well. They bathe often in great tanks which they have in their houses. Everyone has three or four wives or as many as he can maintain. They keep them carefully shut up, and treat them very well, giving them great store of gold, silver and apparel of fine silk.[6]

Outside these relatively small, specialized trading communities, most manufacturing and commerce were in the hands of petty traders and artisans, who were generally limited to local markets. This failure to build on the promise of antiquity has led some historians to ask why India failed to produce an expansion of commerce and growth of cities similar to the developments that began in Europe during the High Middle Ages or even in China during the Song dynasty (see Chapter 10). Some have pointed to the traditionally low status of artisans and merchants in Indian society, symbolized by the comment in the *Arthasastra* that merchants were "thieves that are not called by the name of thief."[7] Yet commercial activities were frowned on in many areas in Europe throughout the Middle Ages, a fact that did not prevent the emergence of capitalist societies in much of the West.

Another factor may have been the monopoly on foreign trade held by the government in many areas of India. More important, perhaps, was the impact of the caste system, which reduced the ability of entrepreneurs to expand their activities and have dealings with other members of the commercial and manufacturing community. Successful artisans, for example, normally could not set up as merchants to market their products, nor could merchants compete for buyers outside their normal area of operations. The complex interlocking relationships among the various castes in a given region were a powerful factor inhibiting the development of a thriving commercial sector in medieval India.

The Wonder of Indian Culture

The era between the Mauryas and the Mughals in India was a period of cultural evolution as Indian writers and artists built on the literary and artistic achievements of their predecessors. This is not to say, however, that Indian culture rested on its ancient laurels. To the contrary, it was an era of tremendous innovation in all fields of creative endeavor.

ART AND ARCHITECTURE

At the end of antiquity, the primary forms of religious architecture were the Buddhist cave temples and monasteries. The next millennium witnessed the evolution of religious architecture from underground cavity to monumental structure.

The twenty-eight caves of Ajanta in the Deccan Plateau are one of India's greatest artistic achievements. They are as impressive for their sculpture and painting as for their architecture. Except for a few examples from the second century B.C.E., most of the caves were carved out of solid rock over an incredibly short period of eighteen

⇨ **ROCK PAINTINGS AT SIGIRIYA, SRI LANKA.**   Starting in the third century B.C.E., engineers on the island of Sri Lanka developed a sophisticated irrigation system consisting of dams, reservoirs, water tanks, and canals. One of the most impressive examples was built by the fifth century C.E. kingdom of Sigiriya, in the center of the island. The royal palace, perched for protective purposes on the summit of a 650-foot-high rock mesa, contains extensive water gardens, fountains, and swimming pools to provide royal entertainment. Portraits of serving girls from the king's harem, such as the one shown here, were painted high up along the cliff wall. Many such paintings were destroyed by Buddhist monks when they reclaimed the area after the king's sudden death. Fortunately, a few have survived to captivate viewers over the centuries.

years, from 460 to 478 C.E. In contrast to the early unadorned temple halls, these temples were exuberantly decorated with ornate pillars, friezes, beamed ceilings, and statues of the Buddha and bodhisattvas. Several caves served as monasteries, which by then had been transformed from simple holes in the wall to large complexes with living apartments, halls, and shrines to the Buddha.

All of the inner surfaces of the caves, including the ceilings, sculptures, walls, door frames, and pillars, were painted in vivid colors. Perhaps best known are the wall paintings, which illustrate the various lives and incarnations of the Buddha. These paintings are in an admirable state of preservation, making it possible to reconstruct the customs, dress, house interiors, and physical characteristics of the peoples of fifth-century India. The inner surfaces of the caves were covered with paintings executed in vivid colors and portraying the various lives and incarnations of the Buddha. Similar rock paintings, but focusing on secular subjects, can be found at Sigiriya, a fifth-century royal palace on the island of Sri Lanka.

Among the most impressive rock carvings in southern India are the cave temples at Mamallapuram (also known as Mahabalipuram), south of the modern city of Madras. The sculpture, called *Descent of the Ganges River,* depicts the role played by Siva in intercepting the heavenly waters of the Ganges and allowing them to fall gently on the earth. Mamallapuram also boasts an eighth-century shore temple (see illustration on p. 241), which is one of the earliest surviving freestanding structures in the subcontinent.

From the eighth century until the time of the Mughals, Indian architects built a multitude of magnificent Hindu temples, now constructed exclusively aboveground. Each temple consisted of a central shrine surmounted by a sizable tower, a hall for worshipers, a vestibule, and a porch, all set in a rectangular courtyard that might also contain other minor shrines. Temples became progressively more ornate until the eleventh century, when the sculpture began to dominate the structure itself. The towers became higher and the temple complexes more intricate, some becoming virtual walled compounds set one within the other and resembling a town in themselves.

Among the best examples of temple art are those in the eastern state of Orissa. The Sun Temple at Konarak, standing at the edge of the sea and covered with intricate carvings, is generally considered the masterpiece of its genre. Although now in ruins, the Sun Temple still boasts some of India's most memorable sculptures. Especially renowned are the twelve pairs of carved wheels; each is 10 feet high and represents one of the twelve signs of the zodiac.

The greatest example of medieval Hindu temple art, however, is probably Khajuraho. Of the original eighty temples, dating from the tenth century, twenty remain standing today. All of the towers are buttressed at various levels on the sides, giving the whole a sense of unity and creating a vertical movement similar to Mount Kailasa in the Himalayas, sacred to Hindus. Everywhere the

Courtesy of William J. Duiker

THE KAILASA TEMPLE AT ELLORA.   The greatest example of Indian rock architecture remains the eighth-century temple at Ellora, in central India. Named after Shiva's holy mountain in the Himalayas, the temple is approximately the size of the Parthenon in Athens but was literally carved out of a hillside. The builders dug nearly 100 feet straight down into the top of the mountain to isolate a single block of rock, removing in the process over 3 million cubic feet of stone. Unlike earlier rock-cut shrines, which had been constructed in the form of caves, the Kailasa temple is open to the sky and filled with some of India's finest sculpture. The overall impression is one of massive grandeur.

viewer is entertained by voluptuous temple dancers bringing life to the massive structures. One is removing a thorn from her foot, another is applying eye makeup, and yet another is wringing out her hair.

In the Deccan Plateau, a different style prevailed. The southern temple style was marked by massive oblong stone towers, some as much as 200 feet high. The towers were often covered with a profusion of sculpted figures and were visible for miles. The walls surrounding the temple complex were also surmounted with impressive gate towers, known as *gopuras*.

LITERATURE

During this period, Indian authors produced a prodigious number of written works, both religious and secular. Indian religious poetry was written in Sanskrit and also in the languages of southern India. As Hinduism was transformed from a contemplative to a more devotional religion, its poetry became more ardent and erotic and prompted a sense of divine ecstasy. Much of the religious verse extolled the lives and heroic acts of Siva, Vishnu, Rama, and Krishna by repeating the same themes over and over, which is also a characteristic of Indian art. In the eighth century, a tradition of poet-saints inspired by intense mystical devotion to a deity emerged in southern India. Many were women who sought to escape the drudgery of domestic toil through an imagined sexual union with the god-lover. Such was the case for the twelfth-century mystic whose poem here expresses her sensuous joy in the physical-mystical union with her god:

> It was like a stream
> running into the dry bed
> of a lake,
> like rain pouring on plants
> parched to sticks.
> It was like this world's pleasure
> and the way to the other,
> both walking towards me.
> Seeing the feet of the master,
> O lord white as jasmine
> I was made worthwhile.[8]

The great secular literature of traditional India was also written in Sanskrit in the form of poetry, drama, and prose. Some of the best medieval Indian poetry is found in single-stanza poems, which create an entire emotional scene in just four lines. Witness this poem by the poet Amaru:

> We'll see what comes of it, I thought,
>   and I hardened my heart against her.
> What, won't the villain speak to me? she
>   thought, flying into a rage.
> And there we stood, sedulously refusing to look one
>   another in the face,
> Until at last I managed an unconvincing laugh,
>   and her tears robbed me of my resolution.[9]

One of India's most famous authors was Kalidasa, who lived during the Gupta dynasty. Although little is known of him, including his dates, he probably wrote for the court of Chandragupta II (375–415 C.E.). Even today Kalidasa's hundred-verse poem, *The Cloud Messenger*, remains one of the most popular Sanskrit poems.

In addition to being a poet, Kalidasa was also a great dramatist. He wrote three plays, all dramatic romances that blend the erotic with the heroic and the comic. *Shakuntala*, perhaps the best-known play in all Indian literature, tells the story of a king who, while out hunting, falls in love with the maiden Shakuntala. He asks her to marry him and offers her a ring of betrothal but is suddenly recalled to his kingdom on urgent business. Shakuntala, who is pregnant, goes to him, but the king has been cursed by a hermit and no longer recognizes her. With the help of the gods, the king eventually does recall their love and is reunited with Shakuntala and their son.

Each of Kalidasa's plays is propelled by the magic powers of a goddess, and each ends in affirmation and unity. Another interesting aspect of Kalidasa's plays is that they combine several languages as well as poetry and prose. The language and form of the characters' speeches correspond to their position in the social hierarchy. Thus the king speaks in Sanskrit poetry, while the other characters in the play use prose in three different vernaculars of everyday life.

Kalidasa was one of the greatest Indian dramatists, but he was by no means the only one. Sanskrit plays typically contained one to ten acts. They were performed in theaters in the palaces or in court temples by troupes of actors of both sexes who were trained and supported by the royal family. The plots were usually taken from Indian legends of gods and kings. No scenery or props were used, but costumes and makeup were elaborate. The theaters had to be small because much of the drama was conveyed through intricate gestures and dance conventions. There were many different positions for various parts of the body, including one hundred for the hands alone.

Like poetry, prose developed in India from the Vedic period. The use of prose was well established by the sixth and seventh centuries C.E. This is truly astonishing considering that the novel did not appear until the tenth century in Japan and until the seventeenth century in Europe.

One of the greatest masters of Sanskrit prose was Dandin, who lived during the seventh century. In *The Ten Princes*, he created a fantastic and exciting world that fuses history and fiction. His keen powers of observation, details of low life, and humor give his writing considerable vitality.

MUSIC

Another area of Indian creativity that developed during this era was music. Ancient Indian music had come from the chanting of the Vedic hymns and thus inevitably had a strong metaphysical and spiritual flavor. The actual physical vibrations of music (*nada*) were considered to be related to the spiritual world. An off-key or sloppy rendition of a sacred text could upset the harmony and balance of the entire universe.

In form, Indian classical music is based on a scale, called a *raga*. There are dozens, if not hundreds, of separate scales, which are grouped into separate categories depending on the time of day during which they are to be performed. The performers use a stringed instrument called a *sitar* and various types of wind instruments and drums. The performers select a basic *raga* and then are free to improvise the melodic structure and rhythm. A good performer never performs a particular *raga* the same way twice. As with jazz music in the West, the audience is concerned not so much with faithful reproduction as with the performer's creativity.

THE GOLDEN REGION: EARLY SOUTHEAST ASIA

Between China and India lies the region that today is called Southeast Asia. It has two major components: a mainland region extending southward from the Chinese border down to the tip of the Malay peninsula and an extensive archipelago, most of which is part of present-day Indonesia and the Philippines. Travel between the islands and regions to the west, north, and east was not difficult, so Southeast Asia has historically served as a vast land bridge for the movement of peoples between China, the Indian subcontinent, and the more than 25,000 islands of the South Pacific.

Mainland Southeast Asia consists of several north-south mountain ranges, separated by river valleys that run in a southerly or southeasterly direction. During the first millennium C.E., two groups of migrants—the Thai from southwestern China and the Burmans from the Tibetan highlands—came down these valleys in search of new homelands, as earlier peoples had done before them. Once in Southeast Asia, most of these migrants settled in the fertile deltas of the rivers—the Irrawaddy and the Salween in Burma, the Chao Phraya in Thailand, and the Red River and the Mekong in Vietnam—or in lowland areas in the islands to the south.

Although the river valleys facilitated north-south travel on the Southeast Asian mainland, movement between east and west was relatively difficult. The mountains are densely forested and often infested with malaria-carrying mosquitoes. Consequently, the lowland peoples in the river valleys were often isolated from each other and had only limited contacts with the upland peoples in the mountains. These geographical barriers may help explain why Southeast Asia is one of the few regions in Asia that was never unified under a single government.

Given Southeast Asia's location between China and India, it is not surprising that both civilizations influenced developments in the region. In 111 B.C.E., Vietnam was conquered by the Han dynasty and remained under Chinese control for more than a millennium; it will be discussed in Chapter 11. The Indian states never exerted much political control over Southeast Asia, but their influence was pervasive nevertheless. By the first centuries C.E., Indian merchants were sailing to Southeast Asia; they were soon followed by Buddhist and Hindu missionaries. Indian influence can be seen in many aspects of Southeast Asian culture, from political institutions to religion, architecture, language, and literature.

Paddy Fields and Spices:
The States of Southeast Asia

The traditional states of Southeast Asia can generally be divided between agricultural societies and trading societies. The distinction between farming and trade was a product of the environment. The agricultural societies—notably, Vietnam, Angkor in what is now Cambodia, and the Burman state of Pagan—were situated in rich river deltas that were conducive to the development of a wet rice economy (see Map 9.4). Although all produced some goods for regional markets, none was tempted to turn to commerce as the prime source of national income. In fact, none was situated astride the main trade routes that crisscrossed the region.

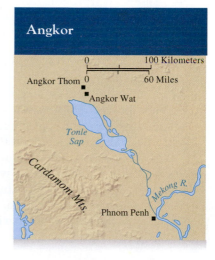

MAP 9.4 Southeast Asia in the Thirteenth Century. This map indicates the major states that arose in Southeast Asia in the early second millennium C.E. Some, like Angkor and Dai Viet, were predominantly agricultural. Others, like Srivijaya and Champa, were commercial. ➤ *Which of these empires were soon to disappear?*

The kingdom of Angkor, which took shape in the ninth century, was the most powerful state to emerge in mainland Southeast Asia before the sixteenth century (see the box on p. 254). The remains of its capital city Angkor Thom give a sense of the magnificence of Angkor civilization. The city formed a square 2 miles

THE KINGDOM OF ANGKOR

Angkor (known to the Chinese as Chon-la) was the greatest kingdom of its time in Southeast Asia. This passage, probably written in the thirteenth century by the Chinese port official Chau Ju-kua, includes a brief description of the capital city, Angkor Thom, which is still one of the great archaeological sites of the region. Angkor was already in decline when Chau Ju-kua described the kingdom, and the capital was abandoned soon afterward, in 1432.

CHAU JU-KUA, RECORDS OF FOREIGN NATIONS

The officials and the common people dwell in houses with sides of bamboo matting and thatched with reeds. Only the king resides in a palace of hewn stone. It has a granite lotus pond of extraordinary beauty with golden bridges, some three hundred odd feet long. The palace buildings are solidly built and richly ornamented. The throne on which the king sits is made of gharu wood and the seven precious substances; the dais is jewelled, with supports of veined wood [ebony?]; the screen [behind the throne] is of ivory.

When all the ministers of state have audience, they first make three full prostrations at the foot of the throne; they then kneel and remain thus, with hands crossed on their breasts, in a circle round the king, and discuss the affairs of state. When they have finished, they make another prostration and retire. . . .

[The people] are devout Buddhists. There are serving [in the temples] some three hundred foreign women; they dance and offer food to the Buddha. They are called *a-nan* or slave dancing girls.

As to their customs, lewdness is not considered criminal; theft is punished by cutting off a hand and a foot and by branding on the chest.

The incantations of the Buddhist and Taoist priests [of this country] have magical powers. Among the former those who wear yellow robes may marry, while those who dress in red lead ascetic lives in temples. The Taoists clothe themselves with leaves; they have a deity called P'o-to-li which they worship with great devotion.

[The people of this country] hold the right hand to be clean, the left unclean, so when they wish to mix their rice with any kind of meat broth, they use the right hand to do so and also to eat with.

The soil is rich and loamy; the fields have no bounds. Each one takes as much as he can cultivate. Rice and cereals are cheap; for every tael of lead one can buy two bushels of rice.

The native products comprise elephants' tusks, the *chan* and *su* [varieties of gharu wood], good yellow wax, kingfisher's feathers, . . . resin, foreign oils, ginger peel, gold-colored incense, . . . raw silk and cotton fabrics.

The foreign traders offer in exchange for these gold, silver, porcelainware, sugar, preserves, and vinegar.

---

on each side. Its massive stone walls were several feet thick and were surrounded by a moat. Four main gates led into the city, which at its height had a substantial population. By the fourteenth century, however, Angkor had begun to decline, and in 1432, Angkor Thom was destroyed by the Thai, who had migrated into the region from southwestern China in the thirteenth century and established their capital at Ayuthaya, in lower Thailand, in 1351.

The islands of the Indonesian archipelago gave rise to two of the region's most notable trading societies—Srivijaya and Majapahit. Both were based in large part on spices. As the wealth of the Arab empire in the Middle East and then of western Europe increased, so did the demand for the products of East Asia. Merchant fleets from India and the Arabian peninsula sailed to the Indonesian islands to buy cloves, pepper, nutmeg, cinnamon, precious woods, and other exotic products coveted by the wealthy. In the eighth century, Srivijaya, located along the eastern coast of Sumatra, became a powerful commercial state that dominated the trade route passing through the Strait of Malacca, at that time the most convenient route from East Asia into the Indian

Ocean. The rulers of Srivijaya had helped bring the route to prominence by controlling the pirates who had previously plagued shipping in the strait. Another inducement was Srivijaya's capital at Palembang, a deepwater port where sailors could wait out the change in the monsoon season before making their return voyage. In 1025, however, Cola, one of the Dravidian kingdoms of southern India and a commercial rival of Srivijaya, inflicted a devastating defeat on the island kingdom. Although Srivijaya survived, it was unable to regain its former dominance, in part because the main trade route had shifted to the east, through the Strait of Sunda and directly out into the Indian Ocean. In the late thirteenth century, this shift in trade patterns led to the founding of a new kingdom of Majapahit on the island of Java. In the mid-fourteenth century, Majapahit succeeded in uniting most of the archipelago and perhaps even part of the Southeast Asian mainland under its rule (see the box on p. 255).

Indian influence was evident in all of these societies to various degrees. Based on models from the Dravidian kingdoms of southern India, Southeast Asian kings were believed to possess special godlike qualities that set

THE LEGENDARY GRANDEUR OF MAJAPAHIT

The Nagarkertagama, written by the court poet Prapanca in 1365, was the national epic of the kingdom of Majapahit. This passage describes the relationship between the kingdom and neighboring countries in the region.

PRAPANCA, NAGARKERTAGAMA

Such is the excellence of His Majesty the Prince who reigns at Majapahit as absolute monarch. His is praised like the moon in autumn, since he fills all the world with joy. The evil-doers are like the red lotus, the good—who love him wholeheartedly—are like the white lotus. His retinue, treasures, chariots, elephants, horses, etc., are [immeasurable] like the sea.

The land of Java is becoming more and more famous for its blessed state throughout the world. "Only Jambudwipa [India] and Java," so people say, "are mentioned for their superiority, good countries as they are, because of the multitude of men experienced in the doctrine . . . ; whatever 'work' turns up, they are very able to handle it."

First comes the Illustrious Brahmaraja, the excellent brahmin, an irreproachable, great poet and expert of the religious traditions; he has complete knowledge of the speculative as well as all the other philosophies, . . . the system of dialectical [logic], etc. And [then] the holy Shamana, very pious, virtuous, experienced in the Vedas and the six pure activities. And also the Illustrious Vishnu, powerful in Samaveda incantations, with which he aims to increase the country's prosperity.

For this reason all kinds of people have continually come from other countries, in multitudes. There are Jambudwipa, Kamboja [Cambodia], China, Yawana [Annam], Champa, Kannataka [in South China], etc., Goda [Gaur] and Siam—these are the places whence they come from. They come by ship with numerous merchants; monks and brahmins are the principal ones who as they come are regaled and are well pleased during their stay.

And in each month of Phalguna [February–March] His Majesty the Prince is honored and celebrated in his residence. Then the high state officials come from all over Java, the heads of districts, and the judicial officials . . . ; also the [people from] other islands, Bali, etc., all come with tributes so numerous that they are uninterrupted, to honor him. Traders and merchants fill the market in dense crowds with all their wares in great variety.

---

them apart from ordinary people. In some societies such as Angkor, the most prominent royal advisers constituted a *brahmin* class on the Indian model. In Pagan and Angkor, some division of the population into separate classes based on occupation and ethnic background seems to have occurred, although these divisions do not seem to have developed the rigidity of Indian castes.

India also supplied Southeast Asians with a writing system. The societies of the region had no written scripts for their spoken languages before the arrival of the Indian merchants and missionaries. Indian phonetic symbols were borrowed and used to record the spoken language. Initially, Southeast Asian literature was written in the Indian Sanskrit but eventually came to be written in the local languages. Southeast Asian authors borrowed popular Indian

Courtesy of William J. Duiker

THE THAI CAPITAL AT AYUTHAYA. The longest-lasting Thai capital was at Ayuthaya, which was one of the finest cities in Asia from the fourteenth century to the eighteenth. After the Burmese invasion in 1767, most of Ayuthaya's inhabitants were killed, and all official Thai records were destroyed. Here the remains of some Buddhist stupas, erected in a ceremonial precinct in the center of the city, remind us of the greatness of Thai civilization.

Chronology

EARLY SOUTHEAST ASIA

Chinese conquest of Vietnam	111 B.C.E.
Arrival of Burman peoples	c. seventh century
Formation of Srivijaya	c. 670
Construction of Borobudur	c. eighth century
Creation of Angkor kingdom	c. ninth century
Thai migrations into Southeast Asia	c. thirteenth century
Rise of Majapahit empire	1292
Fall of Angkor kingdom	1432

themes, such as stories from the Buddhist scriptures and tales from the Ramayana.

A popular form of entertainment among the common people, the *wayang kulit*, or shadow play, may have come originally from India or possibly China, but it became a distinctive art form in Java and other islands of the Indonesian archipelago. In a shadow play, flat leather puppets were manipulated behind an illuminated screen while the narrator recited tales from the Indian classics. The plays were often accompanied by gamelan, a type of music performed by an orchestra composed primarily of percussion instruments such as gongs and drums that apparently originated in Java.

Daily Life

Because of the diversity of ethnic backgrounds, religions, and cultures, making generalizations about daily life in Southeast Asia during the early historical period is difficult. Nevertheless, it appears that Southeast Asian societies did not always apply the social distinctions that were sometimes imported from India. For example, although the local population, as elsewhere, was divided according to a variety of economic functions, the dividing lines between classes were not as rigid and imbued with religious significance as they were in the Indian subcontinent.

Still, traditional societies in Southeast Asia had some clearly hierarchical characteristics. At the top of the social ladder were the hereditary aristocrats, who monopolized both political power and economic wealth and enjoyed a borrowed aura of charisma by virtue of their proximity to the ruler. Most aristocrats lived in the major cities, which were the main source of power, wealth, and foreign influence. Beyond the major cities lived the mass of the population, composed of farmers, fishers, artisans, and merchants. In most Southeast Asian societies, the vast majority were probably rice farmers, living at a bare level of subsistence and paying heavy rents or taxes to a landlord or a local ruler.

The average Southeast Asian peasant was not actively engaged in commerce except as a consumer of various necessities. But accounts by foreign visitors indicate that in the Malay world, some were involved in growing or mining products for export, such as tropical food products, precious woods, tin, and precious gems. Most of the regional trade was carried on by local merchants, who purchased products from local growers and then transported them to the major port cities. During the early state-building era, roads were few and relatively primitive, so most of the trade was transported by small boats down rivers to the major ports along the coast. There the goods were loaded onto larger ships for delivery outside the region. Growers of export goods in areas near the coast were thus indirectly involved in the regional trade network but received few economic benefits from the relationship.

As we might expect from an area of such ethnic and cultural diversity, social structures differed significantly from country to country. In the Indianized states on the mainland, the tradition of a hereditary tribal aristocracy was probably accentuated by the Hindu practice of dividing the population into separate classes, called *varna* in imitation of the Indian model. In Angkor and Pagan, for example, the divisions were based on occupation or ethnic background. Some people were considered free subjects of the king, although there may have been legal restrictions against changing occupations. Others, however, may have been indentured to an employer. Each community was under a chieftain, who in turn was subordinated to a higher official responsible for passing on the tax revenues of each group to the central government.

In the kingdoms in the Malay peninsula and the Indonesian archipelago, social relations were generally less formal. Most of the people in the region, whether farmers, fishers, or artisans, lived in small *kampongs* (Malay for "villages") in wooden houses built on stilts to avoid flooding during the monsoon season. Some of the farmers were probably sharecroppers who paid a part of their harvest to a landlord, who was often a member of the aristocracy. But in other areas, the tradition of free farming was strong. In some cases, some of the poorer land belonged to the village as a collective unit and was assigned for use by the neediest families.

The women of Southeast Asia during this era have been described as the most fortunate in the world. Although most women worked side by side with men in the fields, as in Africa they often played an active role in trading activities. Not only did this lead to a higher literacy rate among women than among their male counterparts, but it also allowed them more financial independence than their counterparts in China and India, a fact that was noticed by the Chinese traveler Zhou Daguan at the end of the thirteenth century: "In Cambodia it is the women who take charge of trade. For this reason a Chinese arriving in the country loses no time in getting himself a mate, for he will find her commercial instincts a great asset."[10]

Although, as elsewhere, warfare was normally part of the male domain, women sometimes played a role as bodyguards as well. According to the Zhou Daguan, women were used to protect the royal family in Angkor, as well as in kingdoms located on the islands of Java and Sumatra. While there is no evidence that such female units ever engaged in battle, they did give rise to wondrous tales of amazon warriors in the writings of foreign travelers such as the fourteenth-century Muslim adventurer Ibn Battuta.

One reason for the enhanced status of women in traditional Southeast Asia is that the nuclear family was more common than the joint family system prevalent in China and the Indian subcontinent. Throughout the region, wealth in marriage was passed from the male to the female, in contrast to the dowry system applied in China and India. In most societies, virginity was usually not a valued commodity in brokering a marriage, and divorce proceedings could be initiated by either party. Still, most marriages were monogamous, and marital fidelity was taken seriously.

The relative availability of cultivable land in the region may help explain the absence of joint families. Joint families under patriarchal leadership tend to be found in areas where land is scarce and individual families must work together to conserve resources and maximize income. With the exception of a few crowded river valleys, few areas in Southeast Asia had a high population density per acre of cultivable land. Throughout most of the area, water was plentiful, and the land was relatively fertile. In parts of Indonesia, it was possible to survive by living off the produce of wild fruit trees—bananas, coconuts, mangoes, and a variety of other tropical fruits.

World of the Spirits: Religious Belief

Indian religions also had a profound effect on Southeast Asia. Traditional religious beliefs in the region took the familiar form of spirit worship and animism that we have seen in other cultures. Southeast Asians believed that spirits dwelled in the mountains, rivers, streams, and other sacred places in their environment. Mountains were probably particularly sacred, since they were considered to be the abode of ancestral spirits, the place to which the souls of all the departed would retire after death.

When Hindu and Buddhist ideas began to penetrate the area early in the first millennium C.E., they exerted a strong appeal among local elites. Not only did the new doctrines offer a more convincing explanation of the nature of the cosmos, but they also provided local rulers with a means of enhancing their prestige and power and conferred an aura of legitimacy on their relations with their subjects. In the Javanese kingdoms and in Angkor, Hindu gods like Vishnu and Siva provided a new and more sophisticated veneer for existing beliefs in nature deities and ancestral spirits. In Angkor, the king's duties included performing sacred rituals on the mountain in the capital city; in time, the ritual became a state cult uniting Hindu gods with local nature deities and ancestral spirits in a complex pantheon.

This state cult, financed by the royal court, eventually led to the construction of temples throughout the country.

Many of these temples housed thousands of priests and retainers and amassed great wealth, including vast estates farmed by local peasants. It has been estimated that there were as many as 300,000 priests in Angkor at the height of its power. This vast wealth, which was often exempt from taxes, may be one explanation for the gradual decline of Angkor in the thirteenth and fourteenth centuries.

Initially, the spread of Hindu and Buddhist doctrines was essentially an elite phenomenon. Although the common people participated in the state cult and helped construct the temples, they did not give up their traditional beliefs in local deities and ancestral spirits. A major transformation began in the eleventh century, however, when Theravada Buddhism began to penetrate the kingdom of Pagan in mainland Southeast Asia from the island of Sri Lanka. From Pagan, it spread rapidly to other areas in Southeast Asia and eventually became the religion of the masses throughout the mainland west of the Annamite Mountains.

Theravada's appeal to the peoples of Southeast Asia is reminiscent of the original attraction of Buddhist thought centuries earlier on the Indian subcontinent. By teaching that individuals could seek Nirvana through their own actions rather than through the intercession of the ruler or a priest, Theravada was more accessible to the masses than the state cults promoted by the rulers. During the next centuries, Theravada gradually undermined the

⟫ **THE BAYON AT ANGKOR.** Whereas Angkor Wat was dedicated to Hindu mythology, the Bayon Temple was a Buddhist structure. In addition to its extraordinary bas-reliefs, which illuminate the everyday life of thirteenth-century Cambodia, the Bayon is known for its huge heads of the Bodhisattva of Mercy. These 172 giant heads, looking in all four cardinal directions for souls to save, are reputedly modeled after the monarch Jayavarman, whose conversion from Hinduism to Buddhism as an adult contributed to the mixture of architectural styles in the temple. The faces are mesmerizing with their haunting smiles, reflecting the mystery of enlightenment.

Courtesy of William J. Duiker

influence of state-supported religions and became the dominant faith in several mainland societies, including Burma, Thailand, Laos, and Cambodia. In the process, however, it was gradually appropriated by local rulers, who portrayed themselves as "immanent Buddhas," higher than ordinary mortals on the scale of human existence.

Theravada did not penetrate far into the Malay peninsula or the Indonesian island chain, perhaps because it entered Southeast Asia through Burma farther to the north. But the Malay world found its own popular alternative to state religions when Islam began to enter the area in the thirteenth and fourteenth centuries. Because Islam's expansion into Southeast Asia took place for the most part after 1500, its emergence as a major force in the region will be discussed in a later chapter.

Not surprisingly, Indian influence extended to the Buddhist and Hindu temples of Southeast Asia. Temple archi-

tecture reflecting Gupta or southern Indian styles began to appear in Southeast Asia during the first centuries C.E. Most famous is the Buddhist temple at Borobudur, in central Java. Begun in the late eighth century at the behest of a king of Sailendra (an agricultural kingdom based in eastern Java), Borobudur is a massive stupa with nine terraces. Sculpted on the sides of each terrace are bas-reliefs depicting the nine stages in the life of Siddhartha Gautama, from childhood to his

THE TEMPLE OF BOROBUDUR. The colossal pyramid temple at Borobudur, on the island of Java, is one of the greatest Buddhist monuments. Constructed in the eighth century, it depicts the path to spiritual enlightenment in stone. The reliefs along the lowest walls depict the world of desire, while the higher levels represent the world of the spirit, culminating at the summit with the empty and closed stupa, signifying the state of Nirvana. Shortly after it was built, Borobudur was abandoned, as a new ruler switched his allegiance to Hinduism and ordered the erection of the Hindu temple of Prambanan nearby. Buried for a thousand years under volcanic ash and jungle, Borobudur was rediscovered in the nineteenth century and was recently restored to its former splendor.

Courtesy of William J. Duiker

final release from the chain of human existence. Surmounted by hollow bell-like towers containing representations of the Buddha and capped by a single stupa, the structure dominates the landscape for miles around.

Second only to Borobudur in technical excellence and even more massive in size are the ruins of the old capital city of Angkor Thom. The temple of Angkor Wat is the most famous and arguably the most beautiful of all the existing structures at Angkor Thom. Built on the model of the legendary Mount Meru (the home of the gods in Hindu tradition), it combines Indian architectural techniques with native inspiration in a structure of impressive delicacy and grace.

In existence for more than six hundred years, Angkor Thom serves as a bridge between the Hindu and Buddhist architectural styles. The last of its great temples, known as the Bayon, followed the earlier Hindu model but was topped with sculpted towers containing four-sided representations of a bodhisattva, searching, it is said, for souls to save. Shortly after the Bayon was built, Theravada Buddhist societies in Burma and Thailand began to create a new Buddhist architecture based on the concept of a massive stupa surmounted by a spire. Most famous, perhaps, is the Shwedagon Pagoda in Yangon (Rangoon), capital of modern Myanmar (Burma), which is covered with gold leaf contributed by devout Buddhists from around the country.

 # CONCLUSION

During the more than fifteen hundred years from the fall of the Mauryas to the rise of the Mughals, Indian civilization faced a number of severe challenges. One challenge was primarily external and took the form of a continuous threat from beyond the mountains in the northwest. A second was generated by internal causes and

ANGKOR WAT.   The Khmer rulers of Angkor constructed a number of remarkable temples and palaces. Devised as either Hindu or Buddhist shrines, the temples also reflected the power and sanctity of the king. This twelfth-century temple known as Angkor Wat is renowned both for its spectacular architecture and for the thousands of fine bas-reliefs relating Hindu legends and Khmer history. Most memorable are the heavenly dancing maidens and the royal processions with elephants and soldiers.

stemmed from the tradition of factionalism and internal rivalry that had marked relations within the aristocracy since the Aryan invasion in the second millennium B.C.E. (see Chapter 2). Despite the abortive efforts of the Guptas, that tradition continued almost without interruption down to the founding of the Mughal Empire in the sixteenth century.

The third challenge was primarily cultural and appeared in the religious divisions between Hindus and Buddhists, and later between Hindus and Muslims, that took place throughout much of this period. It is a measure of the strength and resilience of Hindu tradition that it was able to surmount the challenge of Buddhism and by the late first millennium C.E. had managed to reassert its dominant position in Indian society. But that triumph was short-lived. Like so many other areas in the region of southern Asia, by 1000 C.E., it was now beset by a new challenge presented by nomadic forces from Central Asia. One result of the foreign conquest of northern India was the introduction of Islam into the region. As we shall see later, the new religion was about to become a serious rival to traditional beliefs among the Indian people.

During the same period that Indian civilization faced these challenges at home, it was having a profound impact on the emerging states of Southeast Asia. Situated at the crossroads between two oceans and two great civilizations, Southeast Asia has long served as a bridge linking peoples and cultures, and as complex societies began to develop in the area, it is not surprising that they were strongly influenced by the older civilizations of neighboring China and India. At the same time, the Southeast Asian peoples put their own unique stamp on the ideas that they adopted and eventually rejected those that were inappropriate to local conditions.

The result was a region characterized by an almost unparalleled cultural richness and diversity, reflecting influences from as far away as the Middle East, yet preserving indigenous elements that were deeply rooted in the local culture. Unfortunately, that very diversity posed potential problems for the peoples of Southeast Asia as they faced a new challenge from beyond the horizon. We shall deal with that challenge when we return to the region in a later chapter. In the meantime, we must turn our attention to the other major civilization that spread its shadow over the societies of southern Asia—China.

CHAPTER NOTES

1. Hiuen Tsiang, *Si-Yu-Ki: Buddhist Records of the Western World*, trans. Samuel Beal (London, n.d.), pp. 89–90.
2. "Fo-Kwo-Ki" (Travels of Fa Xian), in ibid., ch. 20, p. xliii.
3. E. C. Sachau, *Alberoni's India* (London, 1914), vol. 1, p. 22, quoted in S. M. Ikram, *Muslim Civilization in India* (New York, 1964), pp. 31–32.
4. Quoted in S. M. Ikram, *Muslim Civilization in India*, p. 68.
5. Hieun Tsiang, *Si-Yu-Ki*, pp. 73–74.
6. Duarte Barbosa, *The Book of Duarte Barbosa* (Nedeln, Liechtenstein, 1967), pp. 147–148.
7. Quoted in Richard Lannoy, *The Speaking Tree: A Study of Indian Culture and Society* (London, 1971), p. 232.
8. Quoted in S. Tharu and K. Lalita, *Women Writing in India*, vol. 1 (New York, 1991), p. 77.
9. Quoted in A. L. Basham, *The Wonder That Was India* (London, 1954), p. 426.
10. Quoted in S. Hughes and B. Hughes, *Women in World History*, vol. 1 (Armonk, N.Y., 1995), p. 217.

SUGGESTED READING

The period from the decline of the Mauryas to the rise of the Mughals in India is not especially rich in terms of materials in English. Still, a number of the standard texts on Indian history contain useful sections on the period. Particularly good are A. L. Basham, *The Wonder That Was India* (London, 1954), and S. Wolpert, *New History of India* (New York, 1989).

A number of studies of Indian society and culture deal with this period. See, for example, R. Lannoy, *The Speaking Tree* (Oxford, 1971), for a sophisticated interpretation of Indian culture during the medieval period. On Buddhism, see H. Nakamura, *Indian Buddhism: A Survey with Bibliographical Notes* (Delhi, 1987), and H. Akira, *A History of Indian Buddhism from Sakyamuni to Early Mahayana* (Honolulu, 1990). For an interesting treatment of the Buddhist influence on commercial activities that is reminiscent of the role of Christianity in Europe, see L. Xinru, *Ancient India and Ancient China: Trade and Religious Changes, A.D. 1–600* (Delhi, 1988).

For a discussion of women's issues, see S. Hughes and B. Hughes, *Women in World History*, vol. 1 (Armonk, N.Y., 1995); S. Tharu and K. Lalita, *Women Writing in India*, vol. 1 (New York, 1991); and V. Dehejia, *Devi: The Great Goddess* (Washington, D.C., 1999).

The most comprehensive treatment of the Indian economy and, in particular, the regional trade throughout the Indian Ocean is K. N. Chaudhuri, *Trade and Civilization in the Indian Ocean: An Economic History from the Rise of Islam to 1750* (Cambridge, 1985), a groundbreaking comparative study. See also his more recent and massive *Asia Before Europe: Economy and Civilization of the Indian Ocean from the Rise of Islam to 1750* (Cambridge, 1990), which owes a considerable debt to F. Braudel's classical work on the Mediterranean Sea.

For an overview of events in Central Asia during this period, see D. Christian, *Inner Eurasia from Prehistory to the Mongol Empire* (Oxford, 1998), and C. E. Bosworth, *The Later Ghaznavids: Splendor and Decay* (New York, 1977). On the career of Tamerlane, see B. F. Manz, *The Rise and Rule of Tamerlane* (Cambridge, 1989).

For Indian art during the medieval period, see S. Huntington, *The Art of Ancient India: Buddhist, Hindu, and Jain* (New York, 1985), and V. Dehejia, *Indian Art* (London, 1997).

For a brief introduction to Indian literature, see E. C. Dimock, *The Literature of India: An Introduction* (Chicago, 1974), and A. K. Warder, *Indian Kavya Literature*, 5 vols. (Delhi, 1972–1988).

The early history of Southeast Asia is not as well documented as that of China or India. Except for Vietnam, where histories written in Chinese appeared shortly after the Chinese conquest, written materials on societies in the region are relatively sparse. Historians were therefore compelled to rely on stone inscriptions and the accounts of travelers and historians from other countries. As a result, the history of precolonial Southeast Asia was presented, as it were, from the outside looking in. A few classic studies, however, presented a useful overview and retain their value. For example, see R. Burling, *Hill Farms and Padi Fields: Life in Mainland Southeast Asia* (Englewood Cliffs, N.J., 1965); P. Wheatley, *The Golden Khersonese: Studies in the Historical Geography of the Malay Peninsula Before A.D. 1500* (Kuala Lumpur, 1961); and G. Coedes, *The Making of Southeast Asia* (Berkeley, Calif., 1966). More recently, some scholars have tended to emphasize the role of indigenous forces in the evolution of the region. See, for example, two works by O. W. Wolters, *Early Indonesian Commerce: A Study of the Origins of Sri Vijaya* (Ithaca, N.Y., 1967) and *The Fall of Srivijaya in Malay History* (Ithaca, N.Y., 1970). For an overview of modern scholarship on the region, see N. Tarling, ed., *The Cambridge History of Southeast Asia*, vol. 1 (Cambridge, 1999).

Impressive advances are now being made in the field of prehistory. See P. Bellwood, *Prehistory of the Indo-Malaysian Archipelago* (Honolulu, 1997), and C. Higham, *The Archaeology of Mainland Southeast Asia* (Cambridge, 1989). Also see C. Higham, *The Bronze Age of Southeast Asia* (Cambridge, 1996).

The role of commerce has recently been highlighted as a key aspect in the development of the region. For two fascinating accounts, see K. R. Hall, *Maritime Trade and State Development in Early Southeast Asia* (Honolulu, 1985), and A. Reid, *Southeast Asia in the Era of Commerce, 1450–1680: The Lands Below the Winds* (New Haven, Conn., 1989). The latter is also quite useful on the role of women.

The nature of kingship has attracted attention from scholars in recent years. K. R. Hall and J. K. Whitmore, eds., *Explorations in Early Southeast Asian History: The Origins of Southeast Asian Statecraft* (Ann Arbor, Mich., 1976), and L. Gesick, ed., *Centers, Symbols, and Hierarchies: Essays on the Classical States of Southeast Asia* (New Haven, Conn., 1983), provide interesting essays on the subject. See also L. Castles and A. Reid, eds., *Pre-Colonial State Systems in Southeast Asia* (Kuala Lumpur, 1975).

INFOTRAC COLLEGE EDITION

For additional reading, go to InfoTrac College Edition, your online research library at
http://web1.infotrac-college.com

Enter the search terms "India history" using Keywords.

Enter the search term "Hinduism" using the Subject Guide.

Enter the search term "Buddhism" using the Subject Guide.

Enter the search term "Tamerlane" using Keywords.

© 2003 Museum of Fine Arts, Boston, Special Chinese and Japanese Fund, 12.886

Chapter 10

FROM THE TANG TO THE MONGOLS: THE FLOWERING OF TRADITIONAL CHINA

CHAPTER OUTLINE

- CHINA AFTER THE HAN
- CHINA REUNIFIED: THE SUI, THE TANG, AND THE SONG
- EXPLOSION IN CENTRAL ASIA: THE MONGOL EMPIRE
- IN SEARCH OF THE WAY
- THE APOGEE OF CHINESE CULTURE
- CONCLUSION

FOCUS QUESTIONS

- How did Chinese historians traditionally view Chinese history, and has this view of China's past been challenged in any way?
- Why were the Mongols able to amass an empire, and what were the main characteristics of their rule in China?
- What roles did Buddhism, Daoism, and Neo-Confucianism play in Chinese intellectual life in the period between the Sui dynasty and the Ming?
- What were the main achievements in Chinese literature and art in the period between the Tang dynasty and the Ming, and what technological innovations and intellectual developments contributed to these achievements?
- What major changes in political structures and social and economic life occurred during the Sui, Tang, and Song dynasties?

O n his first visit to the city, the traveler was mightily impressed. Its streets were so straight and wide that he could see through the city from one end to the other. Along the wide boulevards were beautiful palaces and inns in great profusion. The city was laid out in squares "like a chessboard," and within each square were spacious courts and gardens. Truly, said the visitor, this must be one of the largest and wealthiest cities on earth—a city so splendid that "it is impossible to give a description that should do it justice."[1]

The visitor was Marco Polo, and the city was Khanbaliq (later known as Beijing), capital of the Yuan dynasty (1279–1368) and one of the great commercial centers of the Chinese Empire. Marco Polo was an Italian merchant who had traveled to China in the late thirteenth century and then served as an official at the court of Khubilai Khan.

His diary, published after his return to Italy almost twenty years later, astonished readers with tales of this magnificent but unknown civilization far to the east.

When Marco Polo arrived, China was ruled by the Mongols, a nomadic people from Central Asia who had overthrown the Song (Sung) dynasty and assumed control of the Chinese Empire. The Yuan dynasty, as the Mongol rulers were called, was only one of a succession of dynasties to rule China after the collapse of the Han dynasty in the third century C.E. The end of the Han had led to a period of internal division and civil war that lasted nearly four hundred years and was aggravated by the threat posed by nomadic peoples from the north. This time of troubles ended in the early seventh century, however, when the dynamic Tang dynasty led China to some of its finest achievements.

To this point, Chinese history appeared to be following a pattern similar to that of India. There, as we have seen, the passing of the Mauryan dynasty in the second century B.C.E. unleashed a period of internal division that lasted for several hundred years. Although the Guptas were able to revive the magnificence of India's first golden age, their glorious era soon flickered and died, and it was not until the rise of the Mughal Empire in the early sixteenth century that unity returned to the subcontinent.

But China did not recapitulate the Indian experience. The Tang dynasty collapsed in 907, but after a brief interregnum, China was reunified under the Song, who ruled most of China for nearly three hundred years. The Song were in turn overthrown by the Mongols in the late thirteenth century, and they then gave way to a powerful new native dynasty, the Ming, in 1368. Dynasty followed dynasty, with periods of extraordinary cultural achievement alternating with periods of internal disorder, but in general Chinese society continued to build on the political and cultural foundations of the Zhou and the Han.

Chinese historians, viewing this vast process as it evolved over time, began to hypothesize that Chinese history was cyclical, driven by the dynamic interplay of the forces of good and evil, *yang* and *yin*, growth and decay. Beyond the forces of conflict and change lay the essential continuity of Chinese history, based on the timeless principles established by Confucius and other thinkers during the Zhou dynasty in antiquity. If India often appeared to be a politically and culturally diverse entity, only sporadically knit together by ambitious rulers, China, at least in the eyes of its historians, was a coherent civilization struggling to relive the glories of its ancient golden age while contending against the divisive forces operating throughout the cosmos. In actuality, this picture of a succession of dynasties, each seeking to replicate the glories of China's golden age under the early Zhou dynasty, disguises the reality that under the surface Chinese society was undergoing significant changes and bore scant resemblance to the kingdom that had been founded by the house of Zhou more than twenty centuries earlier. •

CHINA AFTER THE HAN

After the collapse of the Han dynasty at the beginning of the third century C.E., China fell into an extended period of division and civil war. Taking advantage of the absence of organized government in China, nomadic forces from the Gobi Desert penetrated south of the Great Wall and established their own rule over northern China. In the Yangtze valley and farther to the south, native Chinese rule was maintained, but constant civil war and instability led later historians to refer to the period as the "era of the six dynasties."

The collapse of the Han Empire had a marked effect on the Chinese psyche. The Confucian principles that emphasized hard work, the subordination of the individual to community interests, and belief in the essentially rational order of the universe came under severe challenge, and many Chinese began to turn to more messianic creeds that emphasized the supernatural or the promise of earthly or heavenly salvation. Intellectuals began to reject the stuffy moralism and complacency of State Confucianism and sought emotional satisfaction in hedonistic pursuits or philosophical Daoism (see the box on p. 264).

Eccentric behavior and a preference for philosophical Daoism became a common response to a corrupt age. A group of writers known as the "seven sages of the bamboo forest" exemplified the period. Among the best known

A DAOIST CRITIQUE OF CONFUCIANISM

This document is a biting Daoist attack on the type of pompous and hypocritical Confucian "gentleman" who feigned high moral principles while secretly engaging in corrupt and licentious behavior. It was written during the chaotic period following the collapse of the Han dynasty, in the third century C.E.

THE BIOGRAPHY OF A GREAT MAN

What the world calls a gentleman [*chun-tzu*] is someone who is solely concerned with moral law [*fa*], and cultivates exclusively the rules of propriety [*li*]. His hand holds the emblem of jade [authority]; his foot follows the straight line of the rule. He likes to think that his actions set a permanent example; he likes to think that his words are everlasting models. In his youth, he has a reputation in the villages of his locality; in his later years, he is well known in the neighboring districts. Upward, he aspires to the dignity of the Three Dukes; downward, he does not disdain the post of governor of the nine provinces.

Have you ever seen the lice that inhabit a pair of trousers? They jump into the depths of the seams, hiding themselves in the cotton wadding, and believe they have a pleasant place to live. Walking, they do not risk going beyond the edge of the seam; moving, they are careful not to emerge from the trouser leg; and they think they have kept to the rules of etiquette. But when the trousers are ironed, the flames invade the hills, the fire spreads, the villages are set on fire and the towns burned down; then the lice that inhabit the trousers cannot escape.

What difference is there between the gentleman who lives within a narrow world and the lice that inhabit trouser legs?

---

was the poet Liu Ling, whose odd behavior is described in this oft-quoted passage:

> Liu Ling was an inveterate drinker and indulged himself to the full. Sometimes he stripped off his clothes and sat in his room stark naked. Some men saw him and rebuked him. Liu Ling said, "Heaven and earth are my dwelling, and my house is my trousers. Why are you all coming into my trousers?"[2]

But neither popular beliefs in the supernatural nor philosophical Daoism could satisfy deeper emotional needs or provide solace in time of sorrow or the hope of a better life in the hereafter. Instead, Buddhism filled that gap.

Buddhism was brought to China in the first or second century C.E., probably by missionaries and merchants traveling over the Silk Road. The concept of rebirth was probably unfamiliar to most Chinese, and the intellectual hairsplitting that often accompanied discussion of Buddha's message in India was somewhat too esoteric for Chinese tastes. Still, in the difficult years surrounding the decline of the Han dynasty, Buddhist ideas, especially those of the Mahayana school, began to find adherents among intellectuals and ordinary people alike. As Buddhism increased in popularity, it was frequently attacked by supporters of Confucianism and Daoism for its foreign origins. Some even claimed that Gautama Buddha had been a disciple of Lao Tzu. But such sniping did not halt the progress of Buddhism, and eventually the new faith was assimilated into Chinese culture, assisted by the efforts of such tireless advocates as the missionaries Fa Xian and

Courtesy of William J. Duiker

≫ **THE BIG GOOSE PAGODA.** When the Buddhist pilgrim Xuan Zang returned to China from India in the mid-seventh century C.E., he settled in the capital of Chang'an, where, under orders from the Tang emperor, he began to translate Buddhist texts in his possession from Sanskrit into Chinese. The Big Goose Pagoda, shown here, was erected shortly afterward to house them. Originally known as the Pagoda of the Classics, the structure consists of seven stories and is over 240 feet tall.

Xuan Zang and the support of ruling elites in both northern and southern China (see "The Rise and Decline of Buddhism and Daoism" later in this chapter).

CHINA REUNIFIED: THE SUI, THE TANG, AND THE SONG

After nearly four centuries of internal division, China was unified once again in 581 when Yang Jian (Yang Chien), a member of a respected aristocratic family in northern China, founded a new dynasty, known as the Sui (581–618 C.E.). Yang Jian (who is also known by his reign title of Sui Wendi, or Sui Wen Ti) established his capital at the historic metropolis of Chang'an and began to extend his authority throughout the heartland of China.

Like his predecessors, the new emperor sought to create a unifying ideology for the state to enhance its efficiency. But where Liu Bang, the founder of the Han dynasty, had adopted Confucianism as the official doctrine to hold the empire together, Yang Jian turned to Daoism and Buddhism. He founded monasteries for both doctrines in the capital and appointed Buddhist monks to key positions as political advisers.

Yang Jian was a builder as well as a conqueror, ordering the construction of a new canal from the capital to the confluence of the Wei and Yellow Rivers nearly 100 miles to the east. His son, Emperor Sui Yangdi (Sui Yang Ti), continued the process, and the 1,400-mile-long Grand Canal, linking the two great rivers of China, the Yellow and the Yangtze, was completed during his reign. The new canal facilitated the shipment of grain and other commodities from the rice-rich southern provinces to the densely populated north. The canal also served other purposes, such as speeding communications between the two regions and permitting the rapid dispatch of troops to troubled provinces. Sui Yangdi also used the canal as an imperial highway for inspecting his empire. One imperial procession from the capital to the central Yangtze region was described as follows:

> The emperor caused to be built dragon boats, . . . red battle cruisers, multi-decked transports, lesser vessels of bamboo slats. Boatmen hired from all the waterways . . . pulled the vessels by ropes of green silk on the imperial progress to Chiang-tu [Yangzhou]. The Emperor rode in the dragon boat, and civil and military officials of the fifth grade and above rode in the multi-decked transports; those of the ninth grade and above were given the vessels of yellow bamboo. The boats followed one another poop to prow for more than 200 leagues [about 65 miles]. The prefectures and counties through which they passed were ordered to prepare to offer provisions. Those who made bountiful arrangements were given an additional office or title; those who fell short were given punishments up to the death penalty.[3]

Courtesy of William J. Duiker

➤ **THE GRAND CANAL.** Built over centuries, the Grand Canal is one of the wonders of China and a crucial conduit for carrying goods between northern and southern China. After the Song dynasty, when the region south of the Yangtze River became the heartland of the empire, the canal was used to carry rice and other agricultural products to the food-starved northern provinces. Many of the towns and cities located along the canal became famous for their wealth and cultural achievements. Among the most renowned was Suzhou, a center for silk manufacture, which is sometimes described as the "Venice of China" because of its many canals. Shown here is a classical example of a humpback bridge, crossing an arm of the canal in downtown Suzhou.

Despite such efforts to project the majesty of the imperial personage, the Sui dynasty came to an end immediately after Sui Yangdi's death. The Sui emperor was a tyrannical ruler, and his expensive military campaigns aroused widespread unrest. After his return from a failed campaign against Korea in 618, the emperor was murdered in his palace. One of his generals, Li Yuan, took advantage of the instability that ensued and declared the foundation of a new dynasty, known as the Tang (T'ang). Building on the successes of its predecessor, the Tang lasted for three hundred years, until 907.

Li Yuan ruled for a brief period and then was elbowed aside by his son, Li Shimin (Li Shih-min), who assumed the reign title Tang Taizong (T'ang T'ai-tsung). Under his vigorous leadership, the Tang launched a program of internal renewal and external expansion that would make it one of the greatest dynasties in the long history of China (see Map 10.1). Under the Tang, the northwest was pacified and given the name of Xinjiang, or "new region." A long conflict with Tibet led for the first time to the extension of Chinese control over the vast and desolate plateau north of the Himalaya Mountains. The southern provinces below the Yangtze were fully assimilated into the Chinese Empire, and the imperial court established commercial and diplomatic relations with the states of Southeast Asia. With reason, China now claimed to be the foremost power in East Asia, and the emperor demanded fealty and tribute from all his fellow rulers beyond the frontier. Korea accepted tribute status and attempted to adopt the Chinese model, and the Japanese dispatched official missions to China to learn more about its customs and institutions (see Chapter 11).

THE GOOD LIFE IN THE HIGH TANG

At the height of the Tang dynasty, China was at the apex of its power and magnificence. Here the Tang poet Du Fu (Tu Fu) describes a gala festival in the capital of Chang'an (Ch'ang-an) attended by the favored elite. The author's distaste for the spectacle of arrogance and waste is expressed in muted sarcasm.

DU FU, A POEM

Third day of the third month
The very air seems new
In Ch'ang-an along the water
Many beautiful girls . . .
Firm, plump contours,
Flesh and bone proportioned.
Dresses of gauze brocade
Mirror the end of spring
Peacocks crimped in thread of gold
Unicorns in silver. . . .
Some are kin to the imperial favorite
Among them the Lady of Kuo and the Lady of Ch'in [Qin].
Camel-humps of purple meat

Brought in shining pans
The white meat of raw fish
Served on crystal platters
Don't tempt the sated palate.
All that is cut with fancy and
Prepared with care—left untouched.
Eunuchs, reins a-flying
Disturb no dust
Bring the "eight chef d'oeuvres"
From the palace kitchens.
Music of strings and pipes . . .
Accompanying the feasting
Moving the many guests
All of rank and importance.
Last comes a horseman
See him haughtily
Dismount near the screen
And step on the flowery carpet. . . .
The chancellor is so powerful
His mere touch will scorch
Watch you don't come near
Lest you displease him.

Finally, the Tang dynasty witnessed a flowering of Chinese culture. Many modern observers feel that the era represents the apogee of Chinese creativity in poetry and sculpture. One reason for this explosion of culture was the influence of Buddhism, which affected art, literature, and philosophy, as well as religion and politics. Monasteries sprang up throughout China, and (as under the Sui) Buddhist monks served as advisers at the Tang imperial court. The city of Chang'an, now restored to the glory it had known as the capital of the Han dynasty, once again became the seat of the empire. It was possibly the greatest city in the world of its time, with an estimated population of nearly two million. The city was filled with temples and palaces, and its markets teemed with goods from all over the known world (see the box above).

But the Tang, like the Han, sowed the seeds of their own destruction. Tang rulers could not prevent the rise of internal forces that would ultimately weaken the dynasty and bring it to an end. Two ubiquitous problems were court intrigues and official corruption. Xuanzong (Hsuan Tsung, who reigned from 712 to 756), one of the great Tang emperors and a renowned patron of the arts, was dominated in later life by one of his favorite concubines, the beautiful Yang Guifei (Yang Kuei-fei). One of her protégés launched a rebellion in 755 and briefly seized power in the capital of Chang'an. The revolt was eventually suppressed, and Yang Guifei, who is viewed as one of the great villains of Chinese history, was put to death. But the Tang never fully recovered from the catastrophe. The loss of power by the central government led to increased influence by great landed families inside China and chronic instability along the northern and western frontiers, where local military commanders ruled virtually without central government interference. It was an eerie repetition of the final decades of the Han.

The end finally came in the early tenth century, when border troubles with northern nomadic peoples called the Khitan increased, leading to the final collapse of the dynasty in 907. The Tang had followed the classic strategy of "using a barbarian to oppose a barbarian" by allying with a trading people called the Uighurs (a Turkic-speaking people who had taken over many of the caravan routes along the Silk Road) against their old rivals. But yet another nomadic people called the Kirghiz defeated the Uighurs and then turned

Chang'an Under the Sui and the Tang

Forbidden Park

Palace City

Imperial City

Outer City

| 0 | 2 | 4 | 6 | Kilometers |
| 0 | | 2 | 4 | Miles |

MAP 10.1 China Under the Tang.   The era of the Tang dynasty was one of the greatest periods in the long history of China. Tang influence spread from heartland China into neighboring regions, including Central and Southeast Asia. ➤ *Where are the Grand Canal and the Silk Road, as located on the map?*

on the Tang government in its moment of weakness and overthrew it.

China slipped once again into chaos. This time, the period of foreign invasion and division was much shorter. In 960, a new dynasty, known as the Song (960–1279), rose to power. From the start, however, the Song (Sung) rulers encountered more problems than their predecessors. Although the founding emperor, Song Taizu (Sung T'ai-tsu), was able to co-opt many of the powerful military commanders whose rivalry had brought the Tang dynasty to an end, he was unable to reconquer the northwestern part of the country from the nomadic Khitan peoples. The emperor therefore established his capital farther to the east, at Kaifeng, where the Grand Canal intersected the Yellow River. Later, when pressures from the nomads in the north increased, the court was forced to move the capital even farther south, to Hangzhou (Hangchow), on the coast just south of the Yangtze River delta; the emperors who ruled from Hangzhou are known as the southern Song. The Song also lost control over Tibet. Despite its political and military weaknesses, the dynasty nevertheless ruled during a period of economic expansion, pros-

perity, and cultural achievement and is therefore considered among the more successful Chinese dynasties. The population of the empire had risen to an estimated forty million people, slightly more than that of the continent of Europe.

Yet the Song dynasty was never able to surmount the external challenge from the north, and that failure eventually brought about the end of the dynasty. During its final decades, the Song rulers were forced to pay tribute to the Jurchen peoples from Manchuria. In the early thirteenth century, the Song, ignoring precedent and the fate of the Tang, formed an alliance with the Mongols, a new and obscure nomadic people from the Gobi Desert. As under the Tang, the decision proved to be a disaster. Within a few years, the Mongols had become a much more serious threat to China than the Jurchen. After defeating the Jurchen, the Mongols turned their attention to the Song, advancing on Song territory from both the north and the west. By this time, the Song empire had been weakened by internal factionalism and a loss of tax revenues. After a series of river battles and sieges marked by the use of catapults and gunpowder, the Song were defeated, and the conquerors announced the creation of a new Yuan (Mongol) dynasty. Ironically, the Mongols had first learned about gunpowder from the Chinese.

Political Structures: The Triumph of Confucianism

During the nearly seven hundred years from the Sui to the end of the Song, a mature political system based on principles originally established during the Qin and Han dynasties gradually emerged in China. After the Tang dynasty's brief flirtation with Buddhism, State Confucianism became the ideological cement that held the system together. The development of this system took several centuries, and it did not reach its height until the period of the Song dynasty.

EQUAL OPPORTUNITY IN CHINA: THE CIVIL SERVICE EXAMINATION

At the apex of the government hierarchy was the Grand Council, assisted by a secretariat and a chancellery; it included representatives from all three authorities—civil, military, and censorate. Under the Grand Council was the Department of State Affairs, composed of ministries responsible for justice, military affairs, personnel, public works, revenue, and rites (ritual). This department was in effect the equivalent of a modern cabinet.

The Tang dynasty adopted the practice of selecting bureaucrats through civil service examinations but was unable to curb the influence of the great aristocratic clans. The Song were more successful at limiting aristocratic control over the bureaucracy, in part because the power of the nobility had been irreparably weakened during the final years of the Tang dynasty and did not recover during the interregnum that followed its collapse.

One way of strengthening the power of the central administration was to make the civil service examination system the primary route to an official career. To reduce the power of the noble families, relatives of individuals serving in the imperial court, as well as eunuchs, were prohibited from taking the examinations. But if the Song rulers' objective was to make the bureaucracy more subservient to the court, they may have been disappointed. The rising professionalism of the bureaucracy, which numbered about ten thousand in the imperial capital, with an equal number at the local level, provided it with an esprit de corps and an influence that sometimes enabled it to resist the whims of individual emperors.

Under the Song, the examination system attained the form that it would retain in later centuries. In general, three levels of examinations were administered. The first was a qualifying examination given annually at the provincial capital. Candidates who succeeded in this first stage were considered qualified but normally were not given positions in the bureaucracy except at the local level. Many stopped at this level and accepted positions as village teachers to train other candidates. Candidates who wished to go on could take a second examination given at the capital every three years. Successful candidates could apply for an official position. Some went on to take the final examination, which was given in the imperial palace once every three years. Those who passed were eligible for high positions in the central bureaucracy or for appointments as district magistrates.

During the early Tang, the examinations included questions on Buddhist and Daoist as well as Confucian texts, but by Song times, examinations were based entirely on the Confucian classics. Candidates were expected to memorize passages and to be able to define the moral lessons they contained. The system guaranteed that successful candidates—and therefore officials—would have received a full dose of Confucian political and social ethics. Whether they followed those ethics, of course, was another matter. Many students complained about the rigors of memorization and the irrelevance of the process. Others brought crib notes into the examination hall (one enterprising candidate concealed an entire Confucian text in the lining of his cloak). One famous Tang scholar complained that if Mencius and other Confucian worthies had lived in his own day, they would have refused to sit for the examinations.

The Song authorities ignored such criticisms, but they did open the system to more people by allowing all males except criminals or members of certain restricted occupations to take the examinations. To provide potential candidates with schooling, training academies were set up at the provincial and district level. Without such academies, only individuals fortunate enough to receive training in the classics in family-run schools would have had the expertise to pass the examinations. Such policies represented a considerable improvement over earlier times, when most candidates came from the ranks of the elite. According to one historian, more than half of the successful candidates during the mid-Song period came from families that had not previously had a successful candidate for at least three generations. In time, the majority of candidates came from the landed gentry, nonaristocratic landowners who controlled much of the wealth in the countryside. Because the gentry prized education and became the primary upholders of the Confucian tradition, they were often called the scholar-gentry.

But certain aspects of the system still prevented it from truly providing equal opportunity to all. In the first place, only males were eligible. Then again, the Song did not attempt to establish a system of universal elementary education. In practice, only those who had been given a basic education in the classics at home were able to enter the state-run academies and compete for a position in the bureaucracy. The poor had little chance.

Nor could the system guarantee an honest, efficient bureaucracy. Official arrogance, bureaucratic infighting, corruption, and legalistic interpretations of government regulations were as prevalent in medieval China as in bureaucracies the world over. Another problem was that officials were expected to use their positions to help their relatives. As we observed earlier, even Confucius held that filial duty transcends loyalty to the community. What is nepotism in Western eyes was simply proper behavior in China. Chinese rulers attempted to circumvent this problem by assigning officials outside their home region, but this policy met with only limited success.

Despite such weaknesses, the civil service examination system was an impressive achievement for its day and probably provided a more efficient government and more opportunity for upward mobility than were found in any other civilization of its time. Most Western governments, for example, only began to recruit officials on the basis of merit in the nineteenth century. Furthermore, by regulating the content of the examinations, the system helped provide China with a cultural uniformity lacking in empires elsewhere in Asia.

The court also attempted to curb official misbehavior through the censorate. Specially trained officials known as censors were assigned to investigate possible cases of official wrongdoing and report directly to the court. The censorate was supposed to be independent of outside pressures to ensure that its members would feel free to report wrongdoing wherever it occurred. In practice, censors who displeased high court officials were often removed or even subjected to more serious forms of punishment, which reduced the effectiveness of the system.

LOCAL GOVERNMENT

The Song dynasty maintained the local government institutions that it had inherited from its predecessors. At the base of the government pyramid was the district (or county), governed by a magistrate. The magistrate, assisted by his staff of three or four officials and several other menial employees, was responsible for maintaining law and order and collecting taxes within his jurisdiction. A district could exceed 100,000 people. Below the district was the basic unit of Chinese government, the village. Because villages were so numerous in China, the central government did not appoint an official at that level and allowed the villages to administer themselves. Village government was normally in the hands of a council of elders, usually assisted by a chief. The council, usually made up of the heads of influential families in the village, maintained the local irrigation and transportation network, adjudicated local disputes, organized and maintained a militia, and assisted in collecting taxes (usually paid in grain) and delivering them to the district magistrate.

As a rule, most Chinese had little involvement with government matters. When they had to deal with the government, they almost always turned to their village officials. Although the district magistrate was empowered to settle local civil disputes, most villagers preferred to resolve problems among themselves. It was expected that the magistrate and his staff would supplement their income by charging for such services, a practice that reduced the costs of the central government but also provided an opportunity for bribes, a problem that plagued the Chinese bureaucracy down to modern times.

Economy and Society

During the long period between the Sui and the Song, the Chinese economy, like the government, grew considerably in size and complexity. China was still an agricultural society, but major changes were taking place within the economy and the social structure. The urban sector of the economy was becoming increasingly important, new social classes were beginning to appear, and the economic focus of the empire was beginning to shift from the Yellow River valley in the north to the Yangtze River valley in the center—a process that was encouraged both by the expansion of cultivation in the Yangtze delta and by the control exerted over the north by nomadic peoples during the Song.

The economic revival began shortly after the rise of the Tang. During the long period of internal division, land had become concentrated in the hands of aristocratic families, with most peasants reduced to serfdom or slavery. The early Tang tried to reduce the power of the landed nobility and maximize tax revenues by adopting the ancient "equal field" system, in which land was allocated to farmers for life in return for an annual tax payment and three weeks of conscript labor.

At first, the new system was vigorously enforced and led to increased rural prosperity and government revenue. But eventually, the rich and the politically influential learned to manipulate the system for their own benefit and accumulated huge tracts of land. The growing population, caused by a rise in food production and the extended period of social stability, also put steady pressure on the system. Finally, the government abandoned the effort to equalize landholdings and returned the land to private hands while attempting to prevent inequalities through the tax system. The failure to resolve the land problem contributed to the fall of the Tang dynasty in the early tenth century.

The Song tried to resolve the land problem by returning to the successful programs of the early Tang and reducing the power of the wealthy landed aristocrats. During the late eleventh century, the reformist official Wang Anshi (Wang An-shih) attempted to limit the size of landholdings through progressive land taxes and provided cheap credit to poor farmers to help them avoid bankruptcy. His reforms met with some success, but other developments probably contributed more to the general agricultural prosperity under the Song. These included the opening of new lands in the Yangtze River valley, improvements in irrigation techniques such as the chain pump (a circular chain of square pallets on a treadmill that enabled farmers to lift considerable amounts of water or mud to a higher level), and the introduction of a new strain of quick-growing rice from Southeast Asia, which permitted farmers in warmer regions to plant and harvest two crops each year.

Major changes also took place in the Chinese urban economy, which witnessed a significant increase in trade and manufacturing. This process began under the Tang dynasty, but it was not entirely a product of deliberate state policy. In fact, early Tang rulers shared some of the traditional prejudice against commercial activities that had been prevalent under the Han and enacted a number of regulations that restricted trade. As under the Han, the state maintained monopolies over key commodities such as salt.

Despite the restrictive policies of the state, the urban sector grew steadily larger and more complex, helped by several new technological developments. During the Tang, the Chinese mastered the art of manufacturing steel by mixing cast iron and wrought iron. The blast furnace was heated to a high temperature by burning coal, which had been used as a fuel in China from about the fourth century C.E.

The resulting product was used in the manufacture of swords, sickles, and even suits of armor. By the eleventh century, more than 35,000 tons of steel were being produced annually. The introduction of cotton offered new opportunities in textile manufacturing. Gunpowder was invented by the Chinese during the Tang dynasty and used primarily for explosives and a primitive form of flamethrower; it reached the West via the Arabs in the twelfth century.

OCEAN TRADE AND THE SILK ROAD

The nature of trade was also changing. In the past, most long-distance trade had been undertaken by state monopoly. By the time of the Song, private commerce was being actively encouraged, and many merchants engaged in shipping as well as in wholesale and retail trade. Guilds began to appear, along with a new money economy. Paper currency began to be used in the eighth and ninth centuries. Credit (at first called "flying money") also made its first appearance during the Tang. With the increased circulation of paper money, banking began to develop as mer-

TRANSPLANTING RICE SEEDLINGS. The painting shown here is one of a set produced on government commission in the twelfth century to show the various stages in the cultivation of wet rice. As a result of new seed strains and improved irrigation techniques—including water pumps, terracing, and better drainage techniques—rice became the staple food for the Chinese people during the Song dynasty. With its high caloric content and relative ease of preparation, rice has remained the quintessential food in China to this day. Here farmers are transplanting month-old seedlings from the nursery bed to their permanent field, a backbreaking chore indeed.

chants found that strings of copper coins were too cumbersome for their increasingly complex operations. Unfortunately, early issues of paper currency were not backed by metal coinage and led to price inflation. Equally useful, if more prosaic, was the invention of the abacus, an early form of calculator that simplified the calculations needed for commercial transactions.

Long-distance trade, both overland and by sea, expanded under the Tang and the Song. Trade with countries and peoples to the west had been carried on for centuries (see Chapter 3), but it had declined dramatically between the fourth and sixth centuries C.E. as a result of the collapse of the Han and Roman Empires. It began to revive with the rise of the Tang and the simultaneous unification of much of the Middle East under the Arabs. During the Tang era, the Silk Road revived and then reached its zenith. Much of the trade was carried by the Turkic-speaking Uighurs. During the Tang, Uighur caravans of two-humped Bactrian camels (a hardy variety native to Iran and regions to the northeast) carried goods back and forth between China and the countries of South Asia and the Middle East.

In actuality, the Silk Road was composed of a number of separate routes. The first to be used, probably because of the jade found in the mountains south of Khotan, ran along the southern rim of the Taklimakan Desert via Kashgar and thence through the Pamir Mountains into Bactria. The first Buddhist missionaries traveled this route from India to China. Eventually, however, this area began to dry up, and traders were forced to seek other routes. From a climatic standpoint, the best route for the Silk Road was to the north of the Tian Shan (Heavenly Mountains), where moisture-laden northwesterly winds created pastures where animals could graze. But the area was frequently infested by bandits who preyed on unwary travelers. Most caravans therefore followed the southern route, which passed along the northern fringes of the Taklimakan Desert to Kashgar and down into northwestern India. Travelers avoided the direct route through the desert (in the Uighur language, the name means "go in and you won't come out") and trudged from oasis to oasis along the southern slopes of the Tian Shan. The oases were created by the water runoff from winter snows in the mountains, which then dried up in the searing heat of the desert.

The Silk Road was so hazardous that shipping goods by sea became increasingly popular. China had long been engaged in sea trade with other countries in the region, but most of the commerce was originally in the hands of Korean, Japanese, or Southeast Asian merchants. Chinese maritime trade, however, was stimulated by the invention of the compass and technical improvements in shipbuilding such as the widespread use of the sternpost rudder and the lug sail (which enabled ships to sail close to the wind). If Marco Polo's observations can be believed, by the thirteenth century, Chinese junks had multiple sails and weighed up to 2,000 tons, much more than contemporary ships in the West. The Chinese governor of Canton in the early twelfth century remarked:

> According to the government regulations concerning seagoing ships, the larger ones can carry several hundred men, and the smaller ones may have more than a hundred men on board. . . . The ship's pilots are acquainted with the configuration of the coasts; at night they steer by the stars, and in the daytime by the Sun. In dark weather they look at the south-pointing needle. They also use a line a hundred feet long with a hook at the end, which they let down to take samples of mud from the seabottom; by its appearance and smell they can determine their whereabouts.[4]

A wide variety of goods passed through Chinese ports. The Chinese exported tea, silk, and porcelain to the countries beyond the South China Sea, receiving exotic woods, precious stones, and various tropical goods in exchange. Seaports on the southern China coast exported sweet oranges, lemons, and peaches in return for grapes, walnuts, and pomegranates. Along the Silk Road to China came raw hides, furs, and horses. Chinese aristocrats, their appetite for material consumption stimulated by the affluence of Chinese society during much of the Tang and the Song periods, were fascinated by the exotic goods and the flora and the fauna of the desert and the tropical lands of the South Seas. The city of Chang'an became the eastern terminus of the Silk Road and perhaps the wealthiest city in the world during the Tang era. The major port of exit in southern China was Canton, where an estimated 100,000 merchants lived. Their activities were controlled by an imperial commissioner sent from the capital.

Some of this trade was a product of the tribute system, which the Chinese rulers used as an element of their foreign policy. The Chinese viewed the outside world as they viewed their own society—in a hierarchical manner. Rulers of smaller countries along the periphery were viewed as "younger brothers" of the Chinese emperor and owed fealty to him. Foreign rulers who accepted the relationship were required to pay tribute and to promise not to harbor enemies of the Chinese Empire. But the foreign rulers also benefited from the relationship. Not only did it confer legitimacy on them, but they often received magnificent gifts from their "elder brother" as a reward for good behavior. Merchants from their countries also gained access to the vast Chinese market.

DAILY LIFE IN TRADITIONAL CHINA

These political and economic changes affected Chinese society during the Tang and Song era. For one thing, it became much more complex. Whereas previously China had been almost exclusively rural, with a small urban class of merchants, artisans, and workers almost entirely dependent on the state, the cities had now grown into an important, if statistically still insignificant, part of the population. Urban life, too, had changed. Cities were no longer primarily administrative centers dominated by officials and their families but now included a much broader mix of officials, merchants, artisans, touts, and entertainers. Unlike the situation in Europe, however, Chinese cities did not possess special privileges that protected their residents from the rapacity of the central government

In the countryside, equally significant changes were taking place, as the relatively rigid demarcation between the landed aristocracy and the mass of the rural population gave way to a more complex mixture of landed gentry, free farmers, sharecroppers, and landless laborers. There was also a class of "base people," consisting of actors, butchers, and prostitutes, who possessed only limited legal rights and were not permitted to take the civil service examination.

Perhaps the most significant development was the rise of the landed gentry as the most influential force in Chinese society. The gentry class controlled much of the wealth in the rural areas and produced the majority of the candidates for the bureaucracy. By virtue of their possession of land and specialized knowledge of the Confucian classics, the gentry had replaced the aristocracy as the political and economic elite of Chinese society. Unlike the aristocracy, however, the gentry did not form an exclusive class separated by the accident of birth from the remainder of the population. Upward and downward mobility between the scholar-gentry class and the remainder of the population was not uncommon and may have been a key factor in the stability and longevity of the system. A position in the bureaucracy opened the doors to wealth and prestige for the individual and his family, but it was no guarantee of success, and the fortunes of individual families might experience a rapid rise and fall. The soaring ambitions and arrogance of China's landed gentry are vividly described in the following wish list set in poetry by a young bridegroom of the Tang dynasty:

⚜ **SPRING FESTIVAL ON THE RIVER.**   Besides being an artistic masterpiece, this Chinese scroll, known as *Spring Festival on the River,* is one of the most remarkable social documents of early-twelfth-century China. Nearly 33 feet long, it records with encyclopedic detail various aspects of Chinese society, from the imperial court down to the lowliest peasants, as they prepare for the spring festival. The viewer is expected to unfold the scroll slowly from right to left and linger on each segment as the scroll follows the path along the Yellow River to the Song capital of Kaifeng, at the time the most sophisticated city in the world.

Spring Festival on the River; Detail, The Metropolitan Museum of Art, Fletcher Fund, 1947, The A.W. Bahr Collection, (47.18.1)

Chronology

MEDIEVAL CHINA

Arrival of Buddhism in China	c. first century C.E.
Fall of the Han dynasty	220 C.E.
Sui dynasty	581–618
Tang dynasty	618–907
Li Bo (Li Po) and Du Fu (Tu Fu)	700s
Emperor Xuanzong	712–756
Song dynasty	960–1279
Wang Anshi	1021–1086
Southern Song dynasty	1127–1279
Mongol conquest of China	1279
Reign of Khubilai Khan	1260–1294
Fall of the Yuan dynasty	1368
Ming dynasty	1369–1644

Chinese slaves to take charge of treasury and barn,
Foreign slaves to take care of my cattle and sheep.
Strong-legged slaves to run by saddle and stirrup when I ride,
Powerful slaves to till the fields with might and main,
Handsome slaves to play the harp and hand the wine;
Slim-waisted slaves to sing me songs, and dance;
Dwarfs to hold the candle by my dining-couch.[5]

For affluent Chinese in this era, life offered many more pleasures than had been available to their ancestors. There were new forms of entertainment, such as playing cards and chess (brought from India, although an early form had been invented in China during the Zhou dynasty); new forms of transportation, such as the paddle-wheel boat and horseback riding (made possible by the introduction of the stirrup); better means of communication (block printing was first invented in the eighth century C.E.); and new tastes for the palate introduced from lands beyond the frontier. Tea had been introduced from the Burmese frontier by monks as early as the Han dynasty, and brandy and other concentrated spirits produced by the distillation of alcohol made their appearance in the seventh century.

The vast majority of the Chinese people still lived off the land in villages ranging in size from a few dozen residents to several thousand. The life of the farmers was bounded by their village. Although many communities were connected to the outside world by roads or rivers, the average Chinese rarely left the confines of their native village except for an occasional visit to a nearby market town. This isolation was psychological as well as physical, for most Chinese identified with their immediate environment and had difficulty envisioning themselves living beyond the bamboo hedges or mud walls that marked the limit of their horizon.

An even more basic unit than the village in the lives of most Chinese, of course, was the family. The ideal was the joint family with at least three generations under one roof. Because of the heavy labor requirements of rice farming, the tradition of the joint family was especially prevalent in the south. When a son married, he was expected to bring his new wife back to live in his parents' home (see the box on p. 274). Often the parents added a new wing to the house for the new family. If a woman married, she went to live with her husband; women who did not marry remained in the home where they grew up.

Chinese village architecture reflected these traditions. Most family dwellings were simple, consisting of one or at most two rooms. They were usually constructed of dried mud, stone, or brick, depending on available materials and the prosperity of the family. Roofs were of thatch or tile, and the floors were usually of packed dirt. Large houses were often built in a square around an inner courtyard, thus guaranteeing privacy from the outside world.

Within the family unit, the eldest male theoretically ruled as an autocrat. He was responsible for presiding over ancestral rites at an altar, usually in the main room of the house. He had traditional legal rights over his wife, and if she did not provide him with a male heir, he was permitted to take a second wife. She, however, had no recourse to divorce. As the old saying went, "Marry a chicken, follow the chicken; marry a dog, follow the dog." Wealthy Chinese might keep concubines, who lived in a separate room in the house and sometimes competed with the legal wife for precedence.

In accordance with Confucian tradition, children were expected, above all, to obey their parents, who not only determined their children's careers but also selected their marriage partners. Filial piety was viewed as an absolute moral good, above virtually all other moral obligations. Even today, duty to one's parents is considered important in traditional Chinese families, and the tombstones of deceased Chinese are often decorated with tile paintings depicting the filial acts that they performed during their lifetime.

The tradition of male superiority continued from ancient times into the medieval era, especially under the southern Song when it was reinforced by Neo-Confucianism. Female children were considered less desirable than males because they could not undertake heavy work in the fields or carry on the family traditions. Poor families often sold their daughters to wealthy villagers to serve as concubines, and female infanticide was not uncommon in times of famine to ensure there would be food for the remainder of the family. Concubines had few legal rights; female domestic servants, even fewer.

During the Song era, two new practices emerged that changed the equation for women seeking to obtain a successful marriage contract. First, a new form of dowry appeared. Whereas previously the prospective husband offered the bride's family a bride price, now the reverse became the norm, with the bride's parents paying the

The Saintly Miss Wu

The idea that a wife should sacrifice her wants to the needs of her husband and family was deeply embedded in traditional Chinese society. Widows in particular had few rights, and their remarriage was strongly condemned. In this account from a story by Hung Mai, a twelfth-century writer, the widowed Miss Wu wins the respect of the entire community by faithfully serving her mother-in-law.

HUNG MAI, A SONG FAMILY SAGA

Miss Wu served her mother-in-law very filially. Her mother-in-law had an eye ailment and felt sorry for her daughter-in-law's solitary and poverty-stricken situation, so suggested that they call in a son-in-law for her and thereby get an adoptive heir. Miss Wu announced in tears, "A woman does not serve two husbands. I will support you. Don't talk this way." Her mother-in-law, seeing that she was determined, did not press her. Miss Wu did spinning, washing, sewing, cooking, and cleaning for her neighbors, earning perhaps a hundred cash a day, all of which she gave to her mother-in-law to cover the cost of firewood and food. If she was given any meat, she would wrap it up to take home. . . .

Once when her mother-in-law was cooking rice, a neighbor called to her, and to avoid overcooking the rice she dumped it into a pan. Owing to her bad eyes, however, she mistakenly put it in the dirty chamber pot. When Miss Wu returned and saw it, she did not say a word. She went to a neighbor to borrow some cooked rice for her mother-in-law and took the dirty rice and washed it to eat herself.

One day in the daytime neighbors saw [Miss Wu] ascending into the sky amid colored clouds. Startled, they told her mother-in-law, who said, "Don't be foolish. She just came back from pounding rice for someone, and is lying down on the bed. Go and look." They went to the room and peeked in and saw her sound asleep. Amazed, they left.

When Miss Wu woke up, her mother-in-law told her what happened, and she said, "I just dreamed of two young boys in blue clothes holding documents and riding on the clouds. They grabbed my clothes and said the Emperor of Heaven had summoned me. They took me to the gate of heaven and I was brought in to see the emperor, who was seated beside a balustrade. He said 'Although you are just a lowly ignorant village woman, you are able to serve your old mother-in-law sincerely and work hard. You really deserve respect.' He gave me a cup of aromatic wine and a string of cash, saying, 'I will supply you. From now on you will not need to work for others.' I bowed to thank him and came back, accompanied by the two boys. Then I woke up."

There was in fact a thousand cash on the bed, and the room was filled with a fragrance. They then realized that the neighbors' vision had been a spirit journey. From this point on even more people asked her to work for them, and she never refused. But the money that had been given to her she kept for her mother-in-law's use. Whatever they used promptly reappeared, so the thousand cash was never exhausted. The mother-in-law also regained her sight in both eyes.

---

groom's family a dowry. With the prosperity that characterized Chinese society during much of the Song era, affluent parents sought to buy a satisfactory husband for their daughter, preferably one with a higher social standing and good prospects for an official career.

A second source of marital bait during the Song period was the promise of a bride with tiny bound feet. The process of foot binding, carried out on girls aged five to thirteen, was excruciatingly painful, since it bent and compressed the foot to half its normal size by imprisoning it in restrictive bandages. But the procedure was often performed by ambitious mothers intent on assuring their daughters of the best possible prospects for marriage. The zealous mother also wanted her daughter to possess a competitive edge in dealing with the other wives and concubines of her future husband. Bound feet represented submissiveness and self-discipline, two required attributes for the ideal Confucian wife.

Throughout northern China, foot binding became a common practice for women of all social classes. It was less common in southern China, where the cultivation of wet rice could not be carried out with bandaged feet; there it tended to be limited to the scholar-gentry class. Still, most Chinese women with bound feet contributed to the labor force to supplement the family income. Although foot binding was eventually prohibited, the practice lasted into the twentieth century, particularly in rural villages.

As in most traditional societies, there were exceptions to the low status of women in Chinese society. Women had substantial property rights and retained control over their dowries even after divorce or the death of the husband. Wives were frequently an influential force within the home, often handling the accounts and taking primary responsibility for raising the children. Some were active in politics. The outstanding example was Wu Zhao (c. 625–c. 706), popularly known as Empress Wu. Selected by Emperor Tang Taizong as a concubine, after his death she rose to a position of supreme power at court. At first, she was content to rule through her sons, but in 690, she declared herself empress of China. To bolster her claim of legitimacy, she cited a Buddhist sutra to the effect that a woman would rule the world seven hundred years after the death of Gautama Buddha. For her presumption, she has been vilified by later Chinese historians, but she was actually a quite capable ruler. She was responsible for giving meaning to the civil service examination system and was the first to select graduates of the examinations for the highest positions in government. During her last years, she reportedly fell under the influence of courtiers and was deposed in 705, when she was probably around eighty.

EXPLOSION IN CENTRAL ASIA: THE MONGOL EMPIRE

The Mongols, who succeeded the Song as the rulers of China in 1279, rose to power in Asia with stunning rapidity. When Genghis Khan (also known as Chinggis Khan), the founder of Mongol greatness, was born, the Mongols were a relatively obscure pastoral people in the region of modern Outer Mongolia. Like most of the nomadic peoples in the region, they were organized loosely into clans and tribes and even lacked a common name for themselves. Rivalry among the various tribes over pasture, livestock, and booty was intense and increased at the end of the twelfth century as a result of a growing population and the consequent overgrazing of pastures.

Born in 1162, Genghis Khan (his original name was Temuchin, or Temujin) was the son of one of the more impoverished nobles of his tribe. While he was still a child, his father was murdered by a rival, and the youngster was temporarily forced to seek refuge in the wilderness. Nevertheless, through his prowess and the power of his personality, he gradually unified the Mongol tribes. In 1206, he was elected Genghis Khan ("universal ruler") at a massive tribal meeting. From that time on, he devoted himself to military pursuits. Mongol nomads were now forced to pay taxes and were subject to military conscription. "Man's highest joy," Genghis Khan reportedly remarked, "is in victory: to conquer one's enemies, to pursue them, to deprive them of their possessions, to make their beloved weep, to ride on their horses, and to embrace their wives and daughters."[6]

The army that Genghis Khan unleashed on the world was not exceptionally large—less than 130,000 men in 1227, at a time when the total Mongol population numbered between one and two million. But their mastery of military tactics set the Mongols apart

from their rivals. Their tireless flying columns of mounted warriors surrounded their enemies and harassed them like cattle, luring them into pursuit, then ambushing them with flank attacks. John Plano Carpini, a contemporary Franciscan friar, described their tactics:

> As soon as they discover the enemy they charge and each one unleashes three or four arrows. If they see that they can't break him, they retreat in order to entice the enemy to pursue, thus luring him into an ambush prepared in advance. . . . Their military stratagems are numerous. At the moment of an enemy cavalry attack, they place prisoners and foreign auxiliaries in the forefront of their own position, while positioning the bulk of their own troops on the right and left wings to envelop the adversary, thus giving the enemy the impression that they are more numerous than in reality. If the adversary defends himself well, they open their ranks to let him pass through in flight, after which they launch in pursuit and kill as many as possible.[7]

In the years after the election of Temuchin as universal ruler, the Mongols, now in possession of a new type of compound bow, which added both power and distance, defeated tribal groups to their west and then turned their attention to the seminomadic non-Chinese kingdoms in northern China. There they discovered that their adversaries were armed with a weapon called a fire-lance, an early form of flamethrower. Gunpowder had been invented in China during the late Tang period, and by the early thirteenth century, a type of fire-lance had been developed that could spew out a combination of flame and projectiles that could travel 30 or 40 yards and inflict considerable damage on the enemy. By the end of the thirteenth century, the fire-lance had evolved into the much more effective handgun and cannon. These inventions came too late to save China from the Mongols, however, and were transmitted to Europe by the early fourteenth century by foreigners employed by the Mongol rulers of China.

While some Mongol armies were engaged in the conquest of northern China, others traveled farther afield and advanced as far as central Europe (see the box on p. 276). Only the death of the Great Khan may have prevented an all-out Mongol attack on western Europe. In 1231, the Mongols attacked Persia and then defeated the Abbasids at Baghdad in 1258 (see Chapter 7). Mongol forces attacked the Song from the west in the 1260s and finally defeated the remnants of the Song navy in 1279.

By then, the Mongol Empire was quite different from what it had been under its founder. Prior to the conquests of Genghis Khan,

The Mongol Conquest of China

Path of Mongol advance

Yellow R.

Chang'an

Kaifeng

Suzhou

Yangtze R.

Hangzhou

SOUTHERN SONG

Canton

0   250   500   750 Kilometers

0   250   500 Miles

South China Sea

A LETTER TO THE POPE

In 1243, Pope Innocent IV dispatched the Franciscan friar John Plano Carpini to the Mongol headquarters at Karakorum to appeal to the great khan to cease his attacks on Christians. After a considerable wait, Carpini was given the following reply, which could not have pleased the pope. The letter was discovered recently in the Vatican archives.

A LETTER FROM KUYUK KHAN TO POPE INNOCENT IV

By the power of the Eternal Heaven, We are the all-embracing Khan of all the Great Nations. It is our command:

This is a decree, sent to the great Pope that he may know and pay heed.

After holding counsel with the monarchs under your suzerainty, you have sent us an offer of subordination, which we have accepted from the hands of your envoy.

If you should act up to your word, then you, the great Pope, should come in person with the monarchs to pay us homage and we should thereupon instruct you concerning the commands of the Yasak.

Furthermore, you have said it would be well for us to become Christians. You write to me in person about this matter, and have addressed to me a request. This, your request, we cannot understand.

Furthermore, you have written me these words: "You have attacked all the territories of the Magyars and other Christians, at which I am astonished. Tell me, what was their crime?" These, your words, we likewise cannot understand. Jenghiz Khan and Ogatai Khakan revealed the commands of Heaven. But those whom you name would not believe the commands of Heaven. Those of whom you speak showed themselves highly presumptuous and slew our envoys. Therefore, in accordance with the commands of the Eternal Heaven the inhabitants of the aforesaid countries have been slain and annihilated. If not by the command of Heaven, how can anyone slay or conquer out of his own strength?

And when you say: "I am a Christian. I pray to God. I arraign and despise others," how do you know who is pleasing to God and to whom He allots His grace? How can you know it, that you speak such words?

Thanks to the power of the Eternal Heaven, all lands have been given to us from sunrise to sunset. How could anyone act other than in accordance with the commands of Heaven? Now your own upright heart must tell you: "We will become subject to you, and will place our powers at your disposal." You in person, at the head of the monarchs, all of you, without exception, must come to tender us service and pay us homage, then only will we recognize your submission. But if you do not obey the commands of Heaven, and run counter to our orders, we shall know that you are our foe.

That is what we have to tell you. If you fail to act in accordance therewith, how can we foresee what will happen to you? Heaven alone knows.

---

the Mongols had been purely nomadic. They spent their winters in the southern plains, where they found suitable pastures for their cattle, and traveled north in the summer to wooded areas where the waterwas sufficient. They lived in round tents covered with felt (called yurts) that were easily transported. For food, the Mongols depended on milk and meat from their herds and game from hunting.

To administer the new empire, Genghis Khan set up a capital city at Karakorum, in present-day Outer Mongolia, but prohibited his fellow Mongols from practicing sedentary occupations or living in cities. But under his successors, Mongol aristocrats began to enter administrative positions, and commoners took up sedentary occupations as farmers or merchants. As one khan remarked, quoting his Chinese adviser, "Although you inherited the Chinese Empire on horseback, you cannot rule it from that position."[8]

The territorial nature of the empire also changed. Following tribal custom, at the death of the ruling khan, the territory was distributed among his heirs. Genghis Khan's empire was thus divided into several separate khanates, each under the autonomous rule of one of his sons by his principal wife (see Map 10.2). One of his sons was awarded the khanate of Chaghadai in Central Asia with its capital at Samarkand; another ruled Persia from the conquered city of Baghdad; a third took charge of the khanate of Kipchak (commonly known as the Golden Horde). But it was one of his grandsons, named Khubilai Khan (who ruled from 1260 to 1294), who completed the conquest of the Song and established a new Chinese dynasty, called the Yuan (from a phrase in the *Book of Changes* referring to the "original creative force" of the universe). Khubilai moved the capital of China northward to Khanbaliq ("city of the khan"), which was located on a major trunk route from the Great Wall to the plains of northern China. Later the city would be known by the Chinese name Beijing, or Peking ("northern capital").

Mongol Rule in China

At first, China's new rulers exhibited impressive vitality. After a failed attempt to administer their conquest as they had ruled their own tribal society (some advisers reportedly even suggested that the plowed fields be transformed

KHANBALIQ, CAPITAL OF KHUBILAI KHAN

When the Italian merchant and adventurer Marco Polo returned from China to Europe in the late thirteenth century, he wrote a lengthy description of his experiences, later to be popularized in book form as The Travels of Marco Polo. Here he describes the Chinese capital city of Khanbaliq, which he called Cambaluc and would later be known as Peking or Beijing, as it existed during the height of the Mongol dynasty. Although the magnificent gates and palaces that he saw no longer exist today, the layout of modern Beijing is much as it is presented here, with wide streets built at right angles and ending at massive gates that once offered an entryway through the wall that surrounded the imperial city.

THE TRAVELS OF MARCO POLO

Now there was on that spot in old times a great and noble city called Cambaluc, which is as much as to say in our tongue "The city of the emperor." But the great Khan was informed by his astrologers that this city would prove rebellious, and raise great disorders against his imperial authority. So he caused the present city to be built close beside the old one, with only a river between them. And he caused the people of the old city to be removed to the new town that he had founded; and this is called Taidu. However, he allowed a portion of the people which he did not suspect to remain in the old city, because the new one could not hold the whole of them, big as it is.

As regards the size of this new city you must know that it has a compass of twenty-four miles, for each side of it hath a length of six miles, and it is four square. And it is all walled round with walls of earth which have a thickness of full ten paces at bottom, and a height of more than ten paces; but they are not so thick at top, for they diminish in thickness as they rise, so that at top they are only about three paces thick. And they are provided throughout with loop-holed battlements, which are all whitewashed.

There are twelve gates, and over each gate there is a great and handsome palace, so that there are on each side of the square three gates and five palaces; for I ought to mention there is at each angle also a great and handsome palace. In those palaces are vast halls in which are kept the arms of the city garrison.

The streets are so straight and wide that you can see right along them from end to end and from one gate to the other. And up and down the city there are beautiful palaces, and many great and fine hostelries, and fine houses in great numbers. All the plots of ground on which the houses of the city are built are four square, and laid out with straight lines; all the plots being occupied by great and spacious palaces, with courts and gardens of proportionate size. All these plots were assigned to different heads of families. Each square plot is encompassed by handsome streets for traffic; and thus the whole city is arranged in squares just like a chessboard, and disposed in a manner so perfect and masterly that it is impossible to give a description that should do it justice.

Moreover, in the middle of the city there is a great clock—that is to say, a bell—which is struck at night. And after it has struck three times no one must go out in the city, unless it be for the needs of a woman in labor, or of the sick. And those who go about on such errands are bound to carry lanterns with them. Moreover, the established guard at each gate of the city is one thousand armed men; not that you are to imagine this guard is kept up for fear of any attack, but only as a guard of honor for the sovereign, who resides there, and to prevent thieves from doing mischief in the town.

into pasture), Mongol rulers adapted to the Chinese political system and made use of local talents in the bureaucracy, although the highest positions were usually reserved for Mongols. The tripartite division of the administration into civilian, military, and censorate was retained, as were the six ministries. Eventually, even the civil service system was revived, as was the state cult of Confucius, although Khubilai Khan himself was a Buddhist. Some leading Mongols followed their ruler in converting to Buddhism, but most commoners retained their traditional religion. In general, the Mongols remained apart as a separate class with their own laws.

The Mongols' greatest achievement may have been the prosperity they fostered. They continued the relatively tolerant economic policies of the southern Song, and by bringing the entire Eurasian landmass under a single rule, they encouraged long-distance trade, particularly along the Silk Road, now dominated by Muslim merchants from Central Asia. To promote trade, the Grand Canal was extended from the Yellow River to the capital. Adjacent to the canal, a paved highway was constructed that extended all the way from the Song capital of Hangzhou to its Mongol counterpart at Khanbaliq. According to the Italian merchant Marco Polo, who resided there during the reign of Khubilai Khan (see the box above), the new capital was a magnificent city 24 miles in diameter where "so many pleasures may be found that one fancies himself to be in Paradise." The urban area was surrounded by thick walls of earth penetrated by twelve massive gates.

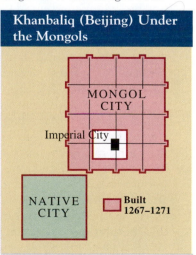

Khanbaliq (Beijing) Under the Mongols

MONGOL CITY

Imperial City

NATIVE CITY

☐ Built 1267–1271

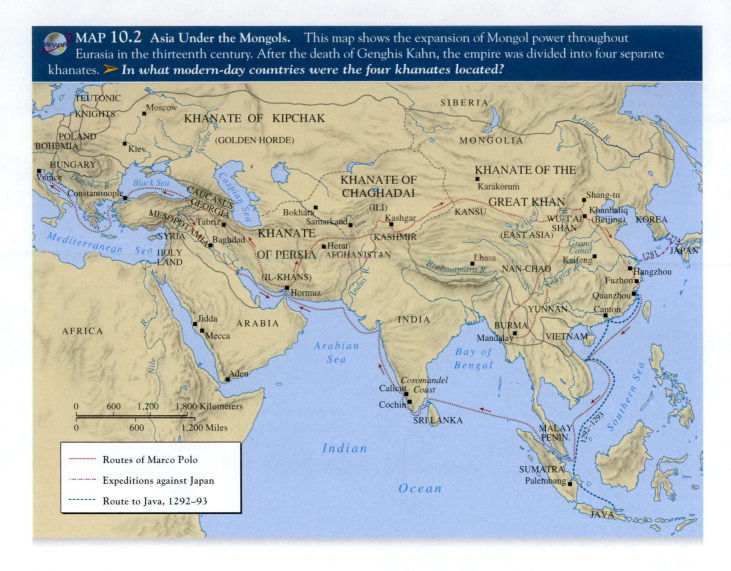

MAP 10.2 Asia Under the Mongols. This map shows the expansion of Mongol power throughout Eurasia in the thirteenth century. After the death of Genghis Kahn, the empire was divided into four separate khanates. ➤ *In what modern-day countries were the four khanates located?*

But the Yuan eventually fell victim to the same fate that had afflicted other powerful dynasties in China. Excessive spending on foreign campaigns, inadequate tax revenues, factionalism and corruption at court and in the bureaucracy, and growing internal instability, brought about in part by a famine in central China in the 1340s, all contributed to the dynasty's demise. Khubilai Khan's successors lacked his administrative genius, and by the middle of the fourteenth century, the Yuan dynasty in China, like the Mongol khanates elsewhere in Central Asia, had fallen into a rapid decline.

The immediate instrument of Mongol defeat was Zhu Yuanzhang (Chu Yuan-chang), the son of a poor peasant in the lower Yangtze valley. After losing most of his family in the famine of the 1340s, Zhu became an itinerant monk and then the leader of a band of bandits. In the 1360s, unrest spread throughout the country, and after defeating a number of rivals, Zhu Yuanzhang put an end to the disintegrating Yuan regime and declared the foundation of a new Ming ("bright") dynasty (1369–1644).

IN SEARCH OF THE WAY

By the time of the Sui dynasty, Buddhism and Daoism had emerged as major rivals of Confucianism as the ruling ideology of the state. But during the last half of the Tang dynasty, Confucianism revived and once again became dominant at court, a position it would retain to the end of the dynastic period in the early twentieth century. Buddhist and Daoist beliefs, however, remained popular at the local level.

The Rise and Decline of Buddhism and Daoism

As noted earlier, Buddhism arrived in China with merchants from India and found its first adherents among the merchant community and intellectuals intrigued by the new ideas. During the chaotic centuries following the collapse of the Han dynasty, Buddhism and Daoism appealed to those who were searching for more emotional and spiritual satisfaction than Confucianism could provide. Both faiths reached beyond the common peo-

THE WAY OF THE GREAT BUDDHA

According to Buddhists, it is impossible to describe the state of nirvana, which is sometimes depicted as an extinction of self. Yet Buddhist scholars found it difficult to avoid trying to interpret the term for their followers. The following passage by the Chinese monk Shen-Hui, one of the leading exponents of Chan Buddhism, dates from the eighth century and attempts to describe the means by which an individual may hope to seek enlightenment. There are clear similarities with philosophical Daoism.

SHEN-HUI, *ELUCIDATING THE DOCTRINE*

"Absence of thought" is the doctrine.

"Absence of action" is the foundation.

True Emptiness is the substance.

And all wonderful things and beings are the function.

True Thusness is without thought; it cannot be known through conception and thought.

The True State is noncreated—can it be seen in matter and mind?

There is no thought except that of True Thusness.

There is no creation except that of the True State.

Abiding without abiding, forever abiding in Nirvana.

Acting without acting, immediately crossing to the Other Shore.

Thusness does not move, but its motion and functions are inexhaustible.

In every instant of thought, there is no seeking; the seeking itself is no thought.

Perfect wisdom is not achieved, and yet the Five Eyes all become pure and the Three Bodies are understood.

Great Enlightenment has no knowledge, and yet the Six Supernatural Powers of the Buddha are utilized and the Four Wisdoms of the Buddha are made great.

Thus we know that calmness is at the same time no calmness, wisdom at the same time no wisdom, and action at the same time no action.

The nature is equivalent to the void and the substance is identical with the Realm of Law.

In this way, the Six Perfections are completed.

None of the ways to arrive at Nirvana is wanting.

Thus we know that the ego and the dharmas are empty in reality and being and nonbeing are both obliterated.

The mind is originally without activity; the Way is always without thought.

No thought, no reflection, no seeking, no attainment; No this, no that, no coming, no going.

With such reality one understands the True Insight [into previous and future mortal conditions and present mortal suffering].

With such a mind one penetrates the Eight Emancipations [through the eight stages of mental concentration].

By merits one accomplishes the Ten Powers of the Buddha.

---

ple and found support among the ruling classes as well. There was even a small Christian church in the capital of Chang'an, introduced to China by Syrian merchants in the sixth century C.E.

As Buddhism attracted more followers, it began to take on Chinese characteristics and divided into a number of separate sects. Some, like the *Chan* (Zen in Japanese) sect, called for mind training and a strict regimen as a means of seeking enlightenment, a technique that reflected Daoist ideas and appealed to many intellectuals (see the box

above). Others, like the Pure Land sect, stressed the role of devotion, an approach that was more appealing to ordinary Chinese, who lacked the time and inclination for strict monastic discipline. Still others were mystical sects, like Tantrism, which emphasized the importance of

> BUDDHIST SHRINE STATUE. The oasis settlement of Jiaohe, located at the confluence of two rivers on a plateau in Chinese Central Asia, had been a stopping point on the Silk Road since the first millennium B.C.E. During the Tang dynasty, when Buddhist merchants carried goods and ideas eastward from India to the Chinese capital at Chang'an, the town's inhabitants were primarily Buddhist. Shown here are the remnants of a Buddhist shrine, with an image of the Buddha set in a niche along the central wall of the building. Like all other structures in the town, the shrine was constructed of sun-dried brick. Eventually the community was occupied by Uighurs, who brought the Muslim faith. Jiaohe was abandoned after the Mongols swept through the area in the thirteenth century, but later a new settlement arose in the nearby Turfan depression, the lowest point in China.

magical symbols and ritual in seeking a preferred way to enlightenment. Some Buddhist groups, like their Daoist counterparts, had political objectives. The White Lotus sect, founded in 1133, often adopted the form of a rebel movement, seeking political reform or the overthrow of a dynasty and forecasting a new era when a "savior Buddha" would come to earth to herald the advent of a new age. Most believers, however, assimilated Buddhism into their daily lives, where it joined Confucian ideology and spirit worship as an element in the highly eclectic and tolerant Chinese worldview.

The burgeoning popularity of Buddhism continued into the early years of the Tang dynasty. Early Tang rulers lent their support to the Buddhist monasteries that had been established throughout the country. Buddhist scriptures were regularly included in the civil service examinations, and Buddhist and Daoist advisers replaced shamans and Confucian scholar-officials as advisers at court. But ultimately, Buddhism and Daoism lost favor at court and were increasingly subjected to official persecution. Part of the reason was xenophobia. Envious Daoists and Confucianists made a point of criticizing the foreign origins of Buddhist doctrines, which one prominent Confucian scholar characterized as nothing but "silly relics." To deflect such criticism, Buddhists attempted to make the doctrine more Chinese, equating the Indian concept of *dharma* (law) with the Chinese concept of *Dao* (the Way). Emperor Tang Taizong ordered the Buddhist monk Xuan Zang to translate Lao Zi's classic *The Way of the Dao* into Sanskrit, reportedly to show visitors from India that China had its own equivalent to the Buddhist scriptures. But another reason for this change of heart may have been financial. The great Buddhist monasteries had accumulated thousands of acres of land and serfs that were exempt from paying taxes to the state. Such wealth contributed to the corruption of the monks and other Buddhist officials and in turn aroused popular resentment and official disapproval. As the state attempted to eliminate the great landholdings of the aristocracy, the large monasteries also attracted its attention. During the later Tang, countless temples and monasteries were destroyed, and over 100,000 monks were compelled to leave the monasteries and return to secular life.

Yet there were probably deeper political and ideological reasons for the growing antagonism between Buddhism and the state. By preaching the illusory nature of the material world, Buddhism was denying the very essence of Confucian teachings—the necessity for filial piety and hard work. By encouraging young Chinese to abandon their rice fields and seek refuge and wisdom in the monasteries, Buddhism was undermining the foundation stones of Chinese society—the family unit and the work ethic. In the last analysis, Buddhism was incompatible with the activist element in Chinese society, an orientation that was most effectively expressed by State Confucianism. In the competition with Confucianism for support by the state, Buddhism, like Daoism, was almost certain to lose, at least in the more this-worldly, secure, and prosperous milieu of late Tang and Song China. The two doctrines continued to win converts at the local level, but official support ceased. In the meantime, Buddhism was under attack in Central Asia as well. In the eighth century, the Uighur kingdom adopted Manichaeanism, an offshoot of the ancient Zoroastrian religion with some influence from Christianity. Manichaeanism spread rapidly throughout the area and may have been a reason for the European belief that a Christian king (the legendary Prester John) ruled some-

Courtesy of William J. Duiker

LONGMEN CAVES BUDDHIST SCULPTURE. The Silk Road, which stretched through Central Asia from the Middle East to China, was an avenue for ideas as well as trade. Over the centuries, Christian, Buddhist, and Muslim teachings came to China across the sandy wastes of the Taklimakan Basin. In the seventh century, the Tang emperor Gaozong commissioned this massive temple carving as part of the large complex of cave art devoted to Buddha at Longmen in central China. Bold and grandiose in their construction, these statues reflect the glory that was the Tang dynasty.

A CONFUCIAN WEDDING CEREMONY

During the twelfth century, the philosopher Zhu Xi attempted to reinvigorate Confucian teachings in a contemporary setting that would be more accessible in its appeal to a broad audience. His goal was militantly Confucian, to combat both popular Buddhist doctrines and the superstitious practices of the common people. With his new moral code, Zhu Xi hoped to put Chinese society back on the Confucian track, with its emphasis on proper behavior. He therefore set forth the proper rituals required to carry out the special days that marked the lives of all Chinese: entry into adolescence, marriage, and funeral and ancestral rites. In the following excerpt, he prescribes the proper protocol for the Confucian wedding ceremony.

4. WELCOMING IN PERSON

On the day before the wedding, the bride's family sends people to lay out the dowry furnishings in the groom's chamber. At dawn the groom's family sets places in the chamber. Meanwhile, the bride's family sets up places outside. As the sun goes down, the groom puts on full attire. After the presiding man makes a report at the offering hall, he pledges the groom and orders him to go to fetch the bride. The groom goes out and mounts his horse. When he gets to the bride's home he waits at his place. The presiding man of the bride's family makes a report at the offering hall, after which he pledges the bride and instructs her. Then he goes out to greet the groom. When the groom enters, he presents a goose. The duenna takes the girl out to climb into the conveyance. The groom mounts his horse and leads the way for the bridal vehicle. When they arrive at his house he leads the bride in and they take their seats. After the eating and drinking are done, the groom leaves the chamber. On reentering, he takes off his clothes and the candles are removed.

5. THE BRIDE IS PRESENTED TO HER PARENTS-IN-LAW

The next day, having risen at dawn, the bride meets her parents-in-law, who entertain her. Then the bride is presented to the elders. If she is the wife of the eldest son, she serves food to her parents-in-law. Then the parents-in-law feast the bride.

6. PRESENTATION AT THE FAMILY SHRINE

On the third day the presiding man takes the bride to be presented at the offering hall.

7. THE GROOM IS PRESENTED TO THE WIFE'S PARENTS

The day after that the groom goes to see his wife's parents. Afterward he is presented to his wife's relatives. The bride's family entertains the groom, as in ordinary etiquette.

---

where in Asia. By the tenth century, Islam was beginning to move east along the Silk Road, posing a severe threat to both Manichaean and Buddhist centers in the area.

Neo-Confucianism: The Investigation of Things

Into the vacuum left by the decline of Buddhism and Daoism stepped a revived Confucianism. But it was a Confucianism that had been significantly altered by its competition with Buddhist and Daoist teachings. Challenged by Buddhist and Daoist ideas about the nature of the universe, Confucian thinkers began to flesh out the spare metaphysical structure of classical Confucian doctrine with a set of sophisticated theories about the nature of the cosmos and humans' place in it. Although the origins of this effort can be traced to the early Tang period, it reached fruition during the intellectually prolific Song dynasty, when it became the dominant ideology of the state.

The fundamental purpose of Neo-Confucianism, as the new doctrine was called, was to unite the metaphysical speculations of Buddhism and Daoism with the pragmatic Confucian approach to society. In response to Buddhism and Daoism, Neo-Confucianism maintained that the world is real, not illusory, and that fulfillment comes from participation, not withdrawal.

The primary contributor to this intellectual effort was the philosopher Zhu Xi (Chu Hsi) (see the box above). Raised during the southern Song era, Zhu Xi accepted the division of the world into a material world and a transcendent world (called by Neo-Confucianists the Supreme Ultimate, or *Tai Ji*). The latter was roughly equivalent to the *Dao*, or Way, in classical Confucian philosophy. To Zhu Xi, this Supreme Ultimate was a set of abstract principles governed by the law of *yin* and *yang* and the five elements.

Human beings served as a link between the two halves of this bifurcated universe. Although human beings live in the material world, each individual has an identity that is linked with the Supreme Ultimate, and the goal of individual action is to transcend the material world in a Buddhist sense to achieve an essential identity with the Supreme Ultimate. According to Zhu Xi and his followers, the means of transcending the material world is self-cultivation, which is achieved by the "investigation of things."

During the remainder of the Song dynasty and into the early years of the Ming, Zhu Xi's ideas became the central core of Confucian ideology and a favorite source of questions for the civil service examinations. But during the mid-Ming era, his ideas came under attack from a Confucian scholar named Wang Yangming. Wang and his supporters disagreed with Zhu Xi's focus on learning through an investigation of the outside world and asserted th correct way to transcend the material world was through an understanding of self. According to this so-called School of Mind, the mind and the universe were a single unit. Knowledge was thus intuitive rather than empirical and was obtained through internal self-searching rather than through an investigation of the outside world. Wang Yangming's ideas attracted many followers during the Ming dynasty, and the school briefly rivaled that of Zhu Xi in popularity among Confucian scholars. Nevertheless, it never won official acceptance, probably because it was too much like Buddhism in denying the importance of a life of participation and social action.

Neo-Confucianism remained the state doctrine until the end of the dynastic system in the twentieth century. Some historians have asked whether the doctrine can help to explain why China failed to experience scientific and industrial revolutions of the sort that occurred in the West. In particular, it has been suggested that Neo-Confucianism tended to encourage an emphasis on the elucidation of moral principles rather than the expansion of scientific knowledge. Though the Chinese excelled in practical technology, inventing gunpowder, the compass (first used by seafarers during the Song dynasty), printing and paper, and cast iron, among other things, they had less interest in scientific theory. Their relative backwardness in mathematics is a good example. Chinese scholars had no knowledge of the principles of geometry and lagged behind other advanced civilizations in astronomy, physics, and optics. Until the Mongol era, they had no knowledge of Arabic numerals and lacked the concept of zero. Even after that time, they continued to use a cumbersome numbering system based on Chinese characters.

Furthermore, intellectual affairs in China continued to be dominated by the scholar-gentry, the chief upholders of Neo-Confucianism, who not only had little interest in the natural sciences or economic change but also viewed them as a threat to their own dominant status in Chinese society. The commercial middle class, who lacked social status and an independent position in society, had little say in intellectual matters. In contrast, in the West, an urban middle class emerged that was a source not only of wealth but also of social prestige, political power, and intellectual ideas. The impetus for the intellectual revolution in the West came from the members of the commercial bourgeoisie, who were interested in the conquest of nature and the development of technology. In China, however, the scholar-gentry continued to focus on the sources of human behavior and a correct understanding of the relationship between humankind and the universe. The result was an intellectual environment that valued continuity over change and tradition over innovation.

THE APOGEE OF CHINESE CULTURE

The period between the Tang and the Ming dynasties was in many ways the great age of achievement in Chinese literature and art. Enriched by Buddhist and Daoist images and themes, Chinese poetry and painting reached the pinnacle of their creativity. Porcelain emerged as the highest form of Chinese ceramics, and sculpture flourished under the influence of styles imported from India and Central Asia.

Literature

The development of Chinese literature was stimulated by two technological innovations: the invention of paper during the Han dynasty and the invention of woodblock printing during the Tang. At first, paper was used for clothing, wrapping material, toilet tissue, and even armor, but by the first century B.C.E., it was being used for writing as well.

MAKING PAPER.   One of China's most important contributions to the world was the invention of paper during the Han dynasty. Although the first known use of paper for writing dates back to the first century B.C.E., paper was also used for clothing, wrapping materials, military armor, and toilet tissue. It was even suggested to a prince in 93 B.C.E. that he use a paper handkerchief. Pounded fibers of hemp and linen were placed on a flat meshed surface and soaked in a large vat. After it dried, the residue was peeled away as a sheet of paper, seen piled at the right in this eighteenth-century painting.

A PASSION FOR BOOKS

*D*uring the Song dynasty, upper-class Chinese women were often encouraged to learn to read in order to enhance their marriageability. They were discouraged from learning to write, however, since the ideal wife was expected to be reserved and modest in order to avoid attracting attention from those outside the family. A prominent exception to the rule was the woman writer Li Qingzhao (Li Ch'ing-chao, 1084–1151 C.E.). Although she was most appreciated for her poetry, this short prose passage, conveying her husband's passion for collecting books, offers rare details of daily life in twelfth-century China, as well as an intimate glimpse into their marriage. Chinese reverence for books, calligraphy, rubbings, and painting is movingly expressed in this excerpt, made all the more poignant by the knowledge that their magnificent collection was eventually destroyed by invading tribal peoples from the north.

EPILOGUE TO RECORDS ON METAL AND STONE

In 1101, in the first year of the Jian-zhong Reign, I came as a bride to the Zhao household. At that time my father was a division head in the Ministry of Rites, and my father-in-law, later a Grand Councilor, was an executive in the Ministry of Personnel. My husband was then twenty-one and a student in the Imperial Academy. In those days our two families, the Zhaos and the Lis, were not well-to-do and we were always frugal. On the first and fifteenth day of every month, my husband would get a short vacation from the Academy; he would "pawn some clothes" for five hundred cash and go to the market at Ziang-guo Temple, where he would buy fruit and rubbings of incriptions. When he brought these home, we would sit facing one another, rolling them out before us, examining and munching. And we thought ourselves persons [living in perfect contentment]. . . .

I happen to have an excellent memory, and every evening after we finished eating, we would sit in the hall called "Return Home" and make tea. Pointing to the heaps of books and histories, we would guess on which line of which page in which chapter of which book a certain passage could be found. Success in guessing determined who got to drink his or her tea first. Whenever I got it right, I would raise the teacup, laughing so hard that the tea would spill in my lap, and I would get up, not having been able to drink any of it at all. I would have been glad to grow old in such a world. Thus, even though we were living in anxiety, hardships, and poverty, our wills were not broken. . . .

In 1126, the first year of the Jing-kang Reign, my husband was governing Ze-chuan when we heard that the Jin Tartars were moving against the capital. He was in a daze, realizing that all those full trunks and overflowing chests, which he contemplated so lovingly and mournfully, would surely soon be his possessions no longer. In the third month of spring in 1127, the first year of the Jian-yan Reign, we hurried south for the funeral of his mother. Since we could not take the overabundance of our possessions with us, we first gave up the bulky printed volumes, the albums of paintings, and the most cumbersome of the vessels. Thus we reduced the size of the collection several times, and still we had fifteen cartloads of books. When we reached Dong-hai, it took a string of boats to ferry them all across the Huai, and again across the Yangzi to Jian-kang. In our old mansion in Qing-zhou we still had more than ten rooms of books and various items locked away, and we planned to have them all brought by boat the next year. But in the twelfth month Jin forces sacked Qing-zhou, and those ten or so rooms I spoke of were all reduced to ashes.

In the seventh century C.E., the Chinese developed the technique of carving an entire page of text into a wooden block, inking it, and then pressing it onto a sheet of paper. Ordinarily, a text was printed on a long sheet of paper like a scroll. Then the paper was folded and stitched together to form a book. The earliest printed book known today is a Buddhist text published in 868 C.E.; it is more than 16 feet long. Although the Chinese eventually developed movable type as well, block printing continued to be used until relatively modern times because of the large number of Chinese characters needed to produce a lengthy text. Even with printing, books remained too expensive for most Chinese, but they did help popularize all forms of literary writing among the educated elite. Although literature was primarily a male occupation, a few women achieved prominence as a result of their creative prowess (see the box above).

During the post-Han era, historical writing and essays continued to be favorite forms of literary activity. Each dynasty produced an official dynastic history of its predecessor to elucidate sober maxims about the qualities of good and evil in human nature, and local gazetteers added to the general knowledge about the various regions. Encyclopedias brought together in a single location information and documents about all aspects of Chinese life.

But it was in poetry, above all, that Chinese of the Tang to the Ming dynasties most effectively expressed their literary talents. Chinese poems celebrated the beauty of nature, the changes of the seasons, the joys of friendship and drink, sadness at the brevity of life, and old age and parting. Given the frequency of imperial banishment and the requirement that officials serve away from their home district, it is little wonder that separation was an important theme. Love poems existed, but were neither as intense as Western verse nor as sensual as Indian poetry.

TWO TANG POETS

Li Bo was one of the great poets of the Tang dynasty. The first selection is probably the best-known poem in China and has been memorized by schoolchildren for centuries. The second poem, titled "Drinking Alone in Moonlight," reflects the poet's carefree attitude toward life.

Du Fu, Li Bo's prime competitor as the greatest poet of the Tang dynasty, was often the more reflective of the two. In the final piece here, the poet has returned to his home in the capital after a rebellion against the dynasty has left the city in ruins.

LI BO, "QUIET NIGHT THOUGHTS"

Beside my bed the bright moonbeams bound
Almost as if there were frost on the ground.
Raising up, I gaze at the Mountain moon;
Lying back, I think of my old hometown.

LI BO, "DRINKING ALONE IN MOONLIGHT"

Among the flowers, with a jug of wine,
I drink all alone—no one to share.
Raising my cup, I welcome the moon.
And my shadow joins us, making a threesome.

Alas! the moon won't take part in the drinking,
And my shadow just does whatever I do.
But I'm friends for a while with the moon and my shadow,
And we caper in revels well suited to spring.
As I sing the moon seems to sway back and forth;
As I dance my shadow goes flopping about.
As long as I'm sober we'll enjoy one another,
And when I get drunk, we'll go our own ways:
Forever committed to carefree play,
We'll all meet again in the Milky Way!

DU FU, "SPRING PROSPECT"

The capital is taken. The hills and streams are left,
And with spring in the city the grass and trees grown dense.
Mourning the times, the flowers trickle their tears;
Saddened with parting, the birds make my heart flutter.
The army beacons have flamed for three months;
A letter from home would be worth ten thousand in gold.
My white hairs I have anxiously scratched ever shorter;
But such disarray! Even hairpins will do no good!

The nature of the Chinese language imposed certain characteristics on Chinese poetry, the first being compactness. The most popular forms were four-line and eight-line poems, with five or seven words in each line. Because Chinese grammar does not rely on case or gender and makes no distinction between verb tenses, five-character Chinese poems were not only brief but often cryptic and ambiguous.

Two Tang poets, Li Bo (Li Po, sometimes known as Li Bai or Li Taibo) and Du Fu (Tu Fu), symbolized the genius of the era as well as the two most popular styles. Li Bo was a free spirit. His writing often centered on nature and shifted easily between moods of revelry and melancholy. Two of his best-known poems are "Resolution on Waking with a Hangover on a Spring Morning" and "Drinking Alone in Moonlight" (see the box above).

Where Li Bo was a carefree Daoist, Du Fu was a sober Confucian. His poems often dealt with historical issues or ethical themes, befitting a scholar-official living during the chaotic times of the late Tang era. Many of his works reflect a concern with social injustice and the plight of the unfortunate rarely to be found in the writings of his contemporaries (see the box above). Neither the poetry nor the prose of the great writers of the Tang and Song dynasties was written for or ever reached the majority of the Chinese population. The millions of Chinese peasants and artisans living in rural villages and market towns acquired their knowledge of Chinese history, Confucian moralisms, and even Buddhist scripture from stories, plays, and songs passed down by storytellers, wandering minstrels, and itinerant monks in a rich oral tradition.

By the Song dynasty, China had sixty million people, one million in Hangzhou alone. With the growth of cities came an increased demand for popular entertainment. Although the Tang dynasty had imposed a curfew on urban residents, the Song did not. The city gates and bridges were closed at dark, but food stalls and entertainment continued through the night. At fairgrounds throughout the year, one could find comedians, musicians, boxers, fencers, wrestlers, acrobats, puppets and marionettes, shadow plays, and especially storytellers. Many of these arts had come from India centuries before and were now the favorite forms of amusement of the Chinese people.

During the Yuan dynasty, new forms of literary creativity, including popular theater and the novel, began to appear. The two most famous novels were *Romance of the Three Kingdoms* and *Tale of the Marshes*. The former had been told orally for centuries, appearing in written form during the Song as a scriptbook for storytellers. It was first printed in 1321 but was not published for mass consumption until 1522. Each new edition was altered in some way, making the final edition a composite effort of generations of the Chinese imagination. The plot recounts the power struggle that took place among competing groups after the fall of the Han dynasty. Packed with court intrigues, descriptions of peasant life, and gripping battles, *Romance of the Three Kingdoms* stands as a magnificent epic, China's counterpart to the Mahabharata.

Tale of the Marshes is an often violent tale of bandit heroes who at the end of the northern Song banded together to oppose government taxes and official oppression. They rob from those in power to share with the poor. *Tale of the Marshes* is the first prose fiction that describes the daily ordeal of ordinary Chinese people in their own language. Unlike the picaresque novel in the West, *Tale of the Marshes* does not limit itself to the exploits of one hero, offering instead 108 different story lines. This multitude of plots is a natural outgrowth of the tradition of the professional storyteller, who attempts to keep the audience's attention by recounting as many adventures as the market will bear.

Art

Although painting flourished in China under the Han and reached a level of artistic excellence under the Tang, little remains from those periods. The painting of the Song and the Yuan, however, is considered the apogee of painting in traditional China.

Like literature, Chinese painting found part of its inspiration in Buddhist and Daoist sources. Some of the best surviving examples of the Tang period are the Buddhist wall paintings in the caves at Dunhuang, in Central Asia. These paintings were commissioned by Buddhist merchants who stopped at Dunhuang and, while awaiting permission to enter China, wished to give thanks for surviving the rigors of the Silk Road. The entrances to the caves were filled with stones after the tenth century, when Muslim zealots began to destroy Buddhist images throughout Central Asia, and have only recently been uncovered. Like the few surviving Tang scroll paintings, these wall paintings display a love of color and refinement that are reminiscent of styles in India and Iran.

Daoism ultimately had a greater influence than Buddhism on Chinese painting. From early times, Chinese artists removed themselves to the mountains to write and paint and find the *Dao*, or Way, in nature. In the fifth century, one Chinese painter, who was too old to travel, began to paint mountain scenes from memory and announced that depicting nature could function as a substitute for contemplating nature itself. Painting, he said, could be the means of realizing the *Dao*. This explains in part the emphasis on nature in traditional Chinese painting. The word *landscape* in Chinese means "mountain-water," and the Daoist search for balance between earth and water, hard and soft, *yang* and *yin*, is at play in the tradition of Chinese painting. To enhance the effect, poems were added to the paintings, underscoring the fusion of poetry and painting in Chinese art. Many artists were proficient in both media, the poem inspiring the painting and vice versa.

To represent the totality of nature, Chinese artists attempted to reveal the quintessential forms of the landscape. Rather than depicting the actual realistic shape of a specific mountain, they tried to portray the idea of "mountain." Empty spaces were left in the paintings because in the Daoist vision, one cannot know the whole truth. Daoist influence was also evident in the tendency to portray human beings as insignificant in the midst of nature. In contrast to the focus on the human body and personality in Western art, Chinese art presented people as tiny figures fishing in a small boat, meditating on a cliff, or wandering up a hillside trail, coexisting with but not dominating nature.

The Chinese displayed their paintings on long scrolls of silk or paper that were attached to a wooden cylindrical bar at the bottom. Varying in length from 3 to 20

LADIES PREPARING SILK. Although the Tang dynasty was a very prolific period in the development of Chinese painting, very few examples survive to the present day. Fortunately, the practice of copying the works of previous masters was a common tradition in China. Here we see a twelfth-century copy of a Tang painting showing ladies preparing newly woven silk. Two women are stretching a bolt of silk while a third irons the cloth with a pan containing burning coals. Silk was a highly prized luxury item in elite circles throughout the imperial period in China.

feet, the paintings were unfolded slowly so that the eye could enjoy each segment, one after the other, beginning at the bottom with water or a village and moving upward into the hills to the mountain peaks and the sky.

By the tenth century, Chinese painters began to eliminate color from their paintings, preferring the challenge of capturing the distilled essence of the landscape in washes of black ink on white silk. Borrowing from calligraphy, now a sophisticated and revered art, they emphasized the brush stroke and created black-and-white landscapes characterized by a gravity of mood and dominated by overpowering mountains.

Other artists turned toward more expressionist and experimental painting. These so-called literati artists were scholars and administrators, highly educated and adept in music, poetry, and painting. Being scholars first and artists second, however, they believed that the purpose of painting was not representation but expression. No longer did painters wish to evoke the feeling of wandering in nature. Instead they tried to reveal to the viewer their own mind and feelings. Like many Western painters in the nineteenth and twentieth centuries, many of these artists were misunderstood by the public and painted only for themselves and one another. They even developed a style of pointillism.

Second only to painting in creativity was the field of ceramics, notably, the manufacture of porcelain. Made of fine clay baked at unusually high temperatures in a kiln, porcelain was first produced during the period after the fall of the Han and became popular during the Tang era. During the Song, porcelain came into its own. Most renowned perhaps are the celadons, in a delicate gray-

National Palace Museum, Taipei, Taiwan, Republic of China

❧ **A MOUNTAIN SCENE.**   As a means of reproducing the totality of nature, Chinese artists often attempted to visualize physical reality. In this famous eleventh-century painting by Fan K'uan, the mountain seems to take on an existence all its own, independent of the interpretation of the artist. Daoist influence is evident here in that human beings play an insignificant role in the grand scheme of nature. The two tiny figures driving mules, a bridge, and a half-hidden temple are eclipsed by the mountain.

Courtesy of William J. Duiker

❧ **TANG TOMB GUARDIAN**   During the Tang dynasty, well-to-do Chinese arranged for their tombs to be stocked with clay figures necessary to satisfy their every need in the afterlife. This practice provides the historian with a visual record of daily court life in imperial China. The more realistic the statue, the more insurance that the deceased would be well served by his musicians, his servants, his horses, and even his favorite dancing girls. Many tomb figures, such as camel drivers from Central Asia, Indian jugglers, and Syrian singers, illustrate the intermingling of peoples along the Silk Road. Shown here is a fierce tomb guardian, stomping on a demon. Painted in brilliant glazes, these ceramic figures are among the most impressive examples of Tang cultural achievement.

green, but Song artists also excelled in other colors and techniques. As in painting, Song delicacy and grace contrasted with the bold and often crude styles popular under the Tang. The translucent character of Chinese porcelain represented the final product of a technique that did not reach Europe until the eighteenth century. During the Yuan and the Ming, new styles appeared. Most notable is the cobalt blue and white porcelain usually identified with the Ming dynasty, which actually originated during the Yuan. The Ming also produced a multicolored porcelain—often in green, yellow, and red—covered with exotic designs.

CONCLUSION

Traditionally, Chinese historians believed that Chinese history tended to be cyclical. The pattern of history was marked by the rise and fall of great dynasties, interspersed with periods of internal division and foreign invasion. Underlying the waxing and waning of dynasties was the essential continuity of Chinese civilization.

This view of the dynamic forces of Chinese history was long accepted as valid by historians in China and in the West and led many to assert that Chinese history was unique and could not be placed in a European or universal framework. Whereas Western history was linear, leading steadily away from the past, China's always returned to its moorings and was rooted in the values and institutions of antiquity.

In recent years, however, this traditional view of a changeless China has come under increasing challenge from historians who see patterns of change that made the China of 1400 a very different place from the country that had existed at the rise of the Tang dynasty in 600. To these scholars, China had passed through its own version of the "middle ages" and was on the verge of beginning a linear evolution into a posttraditional society.

As we have seen, China at the beginning of the Ming had advanced in many ways since the end of the great Han dynasty over a thousand years earlier. The industrial and commercial sector had grown considerably in size, complexity, and technological capacity, while in the countryside the concentration of political and economic power in the hands of the aristocracy had been replaced by a more stable and equitable mixture of landed gentry, freehold farmers, and sharecroppers. In addition, Chinese society had achieved a level of stability and social tranquillity that not only surpassed conditions during the final years of the Han but was the envy of observers from other lands, near and far. The civil service provided an avenue of upward mobility that was unavailable elsewhere in the world, and the state tolerated a diversity of beliefs that responded to the emotional needs and preferences of the Chinese people. In many respects, China's achievements were unsurpassed throughout the world and marked a major advance beyond the world of antiquity.

Yet there were also some key similarities between the China of the Ming and the China of late antiquity. Ming China was still a predominantly agrarian society, with wealth based primarily on the ownership of land. Commercial activities flourished but remained under a high level of government regulation and by no means represented a major proportion of the national income. China also remained a relatively centralized empire based on an official ideology that stressed the virtue of hard work, social conformity, and hierarchy. In foreign affairs, the long frontier struggle with the nomadic peoples along the northern and western frontiers continued unabated.

Thus the significant change that China experienced during its medieval era can probably be best described as change within continuity, an evolutionary working out of trends that had first become visible during the Han dynasty or even earlier. The result was a civilization that was the envy of its neighbors and of the world. It also influenced other states in the region, including Japan, Korea, and Vietnam. It is to these societies along the Chinese rimlands that we now turn.

100   200   300   400   500   600   700   800   900   1000   1100   1200   1300   1400

Era of anarchy and division

Tang dynasty

Song dynasty

Yuan (Mongol) dynasty

Construction of Grand Canal

Reforms of Wang Anshi

Creation of the formal civil service examination

Buddhist penetration of China

Golden age of Tang poetry

Early development of firearms in China

Romance of the Three Kingdoms

Invention of woodblock printing

CHAPTER NOTES

1. *The Travels of Marco Polo* (New York, n.d.), p. 119.
2. Quoted in Arthur F. Wright, *Buddhism in Chinese History* (Stanford, Calif., 1959), p. 30.
3. Quoted in Arthur F. Wright, *The Sui Dynasty* (New York, 1978), p. 180.
4. Chu-yu, *P'ing-chow Table Talks*, quoted in Robert Temple, *The Genius of China: 3,000 Years of Science, Discovery, and Invention* (New York, 1986), p. 150.
5. Quoted in Edward H. Schafer, *The Golden Peaches of Samerkand: A Study of T'ang Exotics* (Berkeley, Calif., 1963), p. 43.
6. Quoted in John K. Fairbank, Edwin O. Reischauer, and Albert M. Craig, *East Asia: Tradition and Transformation* (Boston, 1973), p. 164.
7. Quoted in Rene Grousset, *L'Empire des Steppes* (Paris, 1939), p. 285.
8. A. M. Khazanov, *Nomads and the Outside World* (Cambridge, 1983), p. 241.

SUGGESTED READING

For an authoritative overview of the early imperial era in China, see M. Elvin, *The Pattern of the Chinese Past* (Stanford, Calif., 1973). A global perspective is presented in S. A. M. Adshead, *China in World History* (New York, 1988).

A vast body of material is available on almost all periods of early Chinese history. For the post-Han period, see A. E. Dien, ed., *State and Society in Early Medieval China* (Stanford, Calif., 1990); E. Balazs, *Chinese Civilization and Bureaucracy: Variations on a Theme* (New Haven, Conn., 1964); and D. Twitchett and M. Loewe, *Cambridge History of China*, vol. 3, *Medieval China* (Cambridge, 1986).

For a readable treatment of the brief but tempestuous Sui dynasty, see A. F. Wright, *The Sui Dynasty* (New York, 1978). The Song dynasty has been studied in considerable detail by historians. For a recent interpretation, see J. T. C. Liu, *China Turning Inward: Intellectual Changes in the Early Twelfth Century* (Cambridge, Mass., 1988). Song problems with the northern frontier are chronicled in Tao Jing-shen, *Two Sons of Heaven: Studies in Sung-Liao Relations* (Tucson, Ariz., 1988).

There are a number of good studies on the Mongol period in Chinese history. See, for example, W. A. Langlois, *China Under Mongol Rule* (Princeton, N.J., 1981), and J. W. Dardess, *Conquerors and Confucians: Aspects of Political Change in Late Yuan China* (New York, 1973). M. Rossabi, *Khubilai Khan: His Life and Times* (Berkeley, Calif., 1988), is a recent biography of the dynasty's greatest emperor, while M. Rossabi, ed., *China Among Equals: The Middle Kingdom and Its Neighbors* (Berkeley, Calif., 1983), deals with foreign affairs. For a provocative interpretation of Chinese relations with nomadic peoples, see T. J. Barfield, *The Perilous Frontier: Nomadic Empires and China* (Cambridge, 1989). An analytic account of the dynamics of nomadic society is A. M. Khazanov, *Nomads and the Outside World* (Cambridge, 1983).

The emergence of urban culture during this era is analyzed in C. K. Heng, *Cities of Aristocrats and Bureaucrats: The Development of Medieval Chinese Cityscapes* (Honolulu, 1999).

For an introduction to women's issues during this period, consult P. B. Ebrey, *The Inner Quarters: Marriage and the Lives of Chinese Women in the Sung Period* (Berkeley Calif., 1993); *Chu Hsi's Family Rituals* (Princeton, N.J., 1991); and "Women, Marriage, and the Family in Chinese History," in P. S. Ropp, *Heritage of China: Con-*

temporary Perspectives on Chinese Civilization (Berkeley, Calif., 1990). For an overview of Chinese foot binding, see C. F. Blake, "Foot-Binding in Neo-Confucian China and the Appropriation of Female Labor," *Signs* 19 (Spring, 1994).

On Central Asia, two popular accounts are J. Myrdal, *The Silk Road* (New York, 1979), and N. Marty, *The Silk Road* (Methuen, Mass., 1987). A more interpretive approach is found in S. A. M. Adshead, *Central Asia in World History* (New York, 1993). See also E. T. Grotenhuis, ed., *Along the Silk Road* (Washington, D.C., 2002).

The period from the fall of the Han to the early Ming was an important period in Chinese intellectual history. For developments in Confucianism, see Carsun Chang, *The Development of Neo-Confucian Thought*, 2 vols. (New Haven, Conn., 1963). For a more scholarly study, see W. T. de Bary, *Self and Society in Ming Thought* (New York, 1970). A classic survey of the role of Buddhism in Chinese society is A. F. Wright, *Buddhism in Chinese History* (Stanford, Calif., 1959). See also E. O. Reischauer, *Ennin's Diary: The Record of a Pilgrimage to China in Search of the Law* (New York, 1955). Xuan Zang's journey to India is re-created in R. Bernstein, *Ultimate Journey: Retracing the Path of an Ancient Buddhist Monk Who Crossed Asia in Search of Enlightenment* (New York, 2000).

The classic work on Chinese literature is Liu Wu-Chi, *An Introduction to Chinese Literature* (Bloomington, Ind., 1966). Also consult the more recent and scholarly S. Owen, *An Anthology of Chinese Literature: Beginnings to 1911* (New York, 1996), and V. Mair, *The Columbia Anthology of Traditional Chinese Literature* (New York, 1994). For poetry, see Liu Wu-Chi and I. Yucheng Lo, *Sunflower Splendor: Three Thousand Years of Chinese Poetry* (Bloomington, Ind., 1975), and S. Owen, *The Great Age of Chinese Poetry: The High T'ang* (New Haven, Conn., 1981), the latter presenting poems in both Chinese and English.

For a comprehensive introduction to Chinese art, see the classic M. Sullivan, *The Arts of China*, 4th ed. (Berkeley, Calif., 1999); M. Tregear, *Chinese Art*, rev ed. (London, 1997); and C. Clunas, *Art in China* (Oxford, 1997). The standard introduction to Chinese painting can be found in J. Cahill, *Chinese Painting* (New York, 1985), and Yang Xin et al., *Three Thousand Years of Chinese Painting* (New Haven, Conn., 1997).

INFOTRAC COLLEGE EDITION

For additional reading, go to InfoTrac College Edition, your online research library at
http://web1.infotrac-college.com

Enter the search terms "Tang dynasty or Song dynasty" using Keywords.

Enter the search terms "China history" using Keywords.

Enter the search terms "China and Buddhism" using Keywords.

Enter the search term "Mongol" using Keywords.

Enter the search terms "Taoism or Daoism" using the Subject Guide.

© Kyoto National Museum, Kyoto, Japan with permission from the Kōzan-ji Temple, Kyoto

Chapter 11

THE EAST ASIAN RIMLANDS: EARLY JAPAN, KOREA, AND VIETNAM

CHAPTER OUTLINE
- JAPAN: LAND OF THE RISING SUN
- KOREA: BRIDGE TO THE EAST
- VIETNAM: THE SMALLER DRAGON
- CONCLUSION

FOCUS QUESTIONS
- What centralizing and decentralizing forces were at work in Japan before 1500, and how did they influence the political and governmental structures that arose?
- What were the main characteristics of economic and social life in early Japan?
- What were the most important cultural achievements of early Japan, and how do they illustrate the Japanese ability to blend indigenous and imported elements?
- What were the main developments in Korean and Vietnamese history before 1500?
- ➤ How did Chinese civilization influence the civilizations that arose in Japan, Korea, and Vietnam?

These people, the exasperated official complained, are like birds and beasts. "They wear their hair tied up and go barefoot, while for clothing they simply cut a hole in a piece of cloth for their head or they fasten their garments on the left side [in barbarian style]." Their women are untrustworthy "and promiscuously wander about." In some areas, "men and women go naked without shame" and are little better than bugs.[1]

The speaker was Xue Tong, a Chinese administrator stationed in northern Vietnam at the end of the Han dynasty. His comments vividly reflected the frustration of Chinese bureaucrats faced with what they regarded as the uncivilized behavior of the untutored peoples living along the frontiers of the Chinese Empire. To Xue Tong and other upright Confucian officials like him, it was hopeless to try to civilize these people.

Such comments should not surprise us. During ancient times, China was the most technologically advanced society in East Asia. To the north and west were nomadic

MAP 11.2 Japan's Relations with Korea. This map shows the Japanes̶ time of the Yamato state. Maritime r̶ Japanese traders and missionaries to C̶ indicated. ➤ *What are the four n̶ of Japan?*

Japanese politics. At first, the new̶ trate to the masses, but eventually, p̶ the Pure Land sect, an import from̶ adherents among the common people̶

THE NARA AND HEIAN PERIC̶

Initial efforts to build a new state m̶ the Tang state were successful. Aft̶ death in 622, political influence fel̶

pastoral peoples whose military exploits were often impressive but whose political and cultural attainments were still limited, at least by comparison with the great river valley civilizations of the day. In inland areas south of the Yangtze River were scattered clumps of rice farmers and hill peoples, most of whom had not yet entered the era of state building and certainly had little knowledge of the niceties of Confucian ethics.

But Xue Tong and officials like him were being a little too hasty in their judgments. Along the fringes of Chinese civilization were a number of other agricultural societies that were beginning to follow a pattern of development similar to that of China, although somewhat later in time. One of these was in the islands of Japan, where an organized agricultural society was beginning to take shape just about the time Xue Tong was complaining about the barbarian peoples in the south. These developments may have been hastened by events on the Korean peninsula, where an advanced Neolithic society had begun to develop a few centuries earlier. Even in the Red River valley, where Xue Tong viewed the local inhabitants with such disdain, a relatively advanced civilization had been in existence for several hundred years before the area was conquered by the Han dynasty in the second century B.C.E.

All of these early agricultural societies were eventually influenced to some degree by their great neighbor China. Vietnam remained under Chinese rule for a thousand years. Korea retained its separate existence but was long a tributary state of China and in many ways followed the cultural example of its larger patron. Only Japan retained both its political independence and its cultural uniqueness. Yet even the Japanese were strongly influenced by the glittering culture of their powerful neighbor, and today many Japanese institutions and customs still bear the imprint of several centuries of borrowing from the Middle Kingdom. In this chapter, we will take a closer look at these emerging societies along the Chinese rimlands and consider how

their cultural achievements reflected or contrasted with those of the Chinese Empire. ●

JAPAN: LAND OF THE RISING SUN

The geographical environment helps explain some of the historical differences between Chinese and Japanese society. Whereas China is a continental civilization, Japan is an island country. It consists of four main islands (see Map 11.1): Hokkaido in the north, the main island of Honshu in the center, and the two smaller islands of Kyushu and Shikoku in the southwest. Its total land area is about 146,000 square miles, about the size of the state of Montana. Japan's main islands are at approximately the same latitude as the eastern seaboard of the United States.

Like the eastern United States, Japan is blessed with a temperate climate. It is slightly warmer on the east coast, which is washed by the Pacific Current that sweeps up from the south, and has a number of natural harbors that provide protection from the winds and high waves of the Pacific Ocean. As a consequence, in recent times, the majority of the Japanese people have tended to live along the east coast, especially in the flat plains surrounding the cities of Tokyo, Osaka, and Kyoto. In these favorable environmental conditions, Japanese farmers have been able to harvest two crops of rice annually since early times.

➤ **SIXTH-CENTURY WAREHOUSE.** During the sixth century C.E., an organized society was just beginning to form in the central valley around the modern cities of Kyoto and Osaka. Shown here is a twentieth-century model of a warehouse located in downtown Osaka. On this site, one of Japan's early rulers ordered the construction of sixteen such structures to hold grain and perhaps other foodstuffs. Each warehouse measured about 30 by 35 feet and was supported by several massive wooden posts. Thatched-roof structures built on wooden pilings such as this one were quite common throughout the region.

The following excerpt from the
Chronicles of Japan) is a passa[ge]
article constitution promulgated in 6
opening section reflects Chinese influence i[n]
harmony, there is also a strong focus on
chy. The constitution was put into pract[ice]
the famous Prince Shotoku.

THE CHRONICLES OF JAPAN

Summer, 4th month, 3rd day [12th ye[ar],
604 C.E.]. The Crown Prince persona[lly]
mulgated a constitution consisting o[f]
which are as follows:

I. Harmony is to be cherished, a[nd]
   opposition's sake must be avoi[ded]
   principle. Men are often influe[nced]
   feelings, except a few sagacious
   are some who disobey their lor[ds]
   who dispute with their neighbo[rs]
   above are harmonious and tho[se]
   their discussion will be guided
   conciliation, and reason shall
   There will be nothing that car[not]

II. With all our heart, revere the
    three treasures, consisting of [Buddha,]

to the Tang capital of Chang'an to l[earn]
ical institutions already in use in the
Tang kingdom (see Map 11.2).

EMULATING THE CHINESE M[ODEL]

Shotoku Taishi then launched a ser[ies]
ate a new system based roughly on
In the so-called seventeen-article c[onstitution,]
for the creation of a centralized g[overnment]
supreme ruler and a merit system fo[r]
ing public officials (see the box abov[e]
to limit the powers of the here[ditary]
enhance the prestige and authority
who claimed divine status and was
symbol of the unique character of
In reality, there is evidence that pla[ced the]
Yamato clan on the Korean penins[ula]

After Shotoku Taishi's death in 6[22,]
tinued to introduce reforms based o[n]
to make the government more effic[ient]
called Taika ("great change") refo[rms]
mid-seventh century, the Grand C[ouncil]

Shotoku Taishi	572–622
Era of Taika reforms	Mid-seventh century
Nara period	710–784
Heian (Kyoto) period	794–1185
Murasaki Shikibu	978–c. 1016
Minamoto Yoritomo	1142–1199
Kamakura shogunate	1185–1333
Mongol invasions	Late thirteenth century
Ashikaga period	1333–1600
Onin War	1462–1477

self-sacrifice and were expected to maintain an intense and unquestioning loyalty to their lord. Bonds of loyalty were also quite strong among members of the samurai class, and homosexuality was common. Like the knights of medieval Europe, the samurai fought on horseback (although a samurai carried a sword and a bow and arrows rather than lance and shield) and were supposed to live by a strict warrior code, known in Japan as *Bushido*, or "way of the warrior" (see the box on p. 297). As time went on, they became a major force and almost a surrogate government in much of the Japanese countryside.

© Michael Holford, London

THE KAMAKURA SHOGUNATE AND AFTER

By the end of the twelfth century, as rivalries among noble families led to almost constant civil war, once again centralizing forces asserted themselves. This time the instrument was a powerful noble from a warrior clan named Minamoto Yoritomo (1142–1199), who defeated several rivals and set up his power base on the Kamakura peninsula, south of the modern city of Tokyo. To strengthen the state, he created a more centralized government (the *bakufu*, or "tent government") under a powerful military leader, known as the shogun (general). The shogun attempted to increase the powers of the central government while reducing rival aristocratic clans to vassal status. This "shogunate system," in which the emperor was the titular authority while the shogun exercised actual power, served as the political system in Japan until the second half of the nineteenth century.

The system worked effectively, and it was fortunate that it did, because during the next century, Japan faced the most serious challenge it had confronted yet. The Mongols, who had destroyed the Song dynasty in China, were now attempting to assert their hegemony throughout all of Asia (see Chapter 10). In 1266, Emperor Khubilai Khan demanded tribute from Japan. When the Japanese refused, he invaded with an army of over 30,000 troops. Bad weather and difficult conditions forced a retreat, but the Mongols tried again in 1281. An army nearly 150,000 strong landed on the northern coast of Kyushu. The Japanese were able to contain them for two months until virtually the entire Mongol fleet was destroyed by a massive

⇒ **SAMURAI.** During the Kamakura period, painters began to depict the adventures of the new warrior class. Here is an imposing mounted samurai warrior, the Japanese equivalent of the medieval knight in fief-holding Europe. Like his European counterpart, the samurai was supposed to live by a strict moral code and was expected to maintain an unquestioning loyalty to his liege lord. Above all, a samurai's life was one of simplicity and self-sacrifice.

JAPAN'S WARRIOR CLASS

The samurai was the Japanese equivalent of the medieval European knight. Like the knight, he was expected to adhere to a strict moral code. Although this passage comes from a document dating only to the seventeenth century, it shows the importance of hierarchy and duty in a society influenced by the doctrine of Confucius. Note the similarity with Krishna's discourse on the duties of an Indian warrior in Chapter 2.

THE WAY OF THE SAMURAI

The master once said: . . . Generation after generation men have taken their livelihood from tilling the soil, or devised and manufactured tools, or produced profit from mutual trade, so that peoples' needs were satisfied. Thus the occupations of farmer, artisan, and merchant necessarily grew up as complementary to one another. However, the samurai eats food without growing it, uses utensils without manufacturing them, and profits without buying or selling. . . . The samurai is one who does not cultivate, does not manufacture, and does not engage in trade, but it cannot be that he has no function at all as a samurai. . . .

If one deeply fixes his attention on what I have said and examines closely one's own function, it will become clear what the business of the samurai is. The business of the samurai consists in reflecting on his own station in life, in discharging loyal service to his master if he has one, in deepening his fidelity in associations with friends, and, with due consideration of his own position, in devoting himself to duty above all. . . . The samurai dispenses with the business of the farmer, artisan, and merchant and confines himself to practicing this Way; should there be someone in the three classes of the common people who transgresses against these moral principles, the samurai summarily punishes him and thus upholds proper moral principles in the land. . . . Outwardly he stands in physical readiness for any call to service, and inwardly he strives to fulfill the Way of the lord and subject, friend and friend, father and son, older and younger brother, and husband and wife. Within his heart he keeps to the ways of peace, but without he keeps his weapons ready for use. The three classes of the common people make him their teacher and respect him. By following his teachings, they are enabled to understand what is fundamental and what is secondary.

Herein lies the Way of the samurai, the means by which he earns his clothing, food, and shelter; and by which his heart is put at ease, and he is enabled to pay back at length his obligation to his lord and the kindness of his parents. Were there no such duty, it would be as though one were to steal the kindness of one's parents, greedily devour the income of one's master, and make one's whole life a career of robbery and brigandage. This would be very grievous.

---

typhoon—a "divine wind" (*kamikaze*). Japan would not face a foreign invader again until American forces landed on the Japanese islands in the summer of 1945.

The resistance to the Mongols had put a heavy strain on the system, however, and in 1333, the Kamakura shogunate was overthrown by a coalition of powerful clans. A new shogun, supplied by the Ashikaga family, arose in Kyoto and attempted to continue the shogunate system. But the Ashikaga were unable to restore the centralized power of their predecessors. With the central government reduced to a shell, the power of the local landed aristocracy increased to an unprecedented degree. Heads of great noble families, now called *daimyo* ("great names"), controlled vast landed estates that owed no taxes to the government or to the court in Kyoto. As clan rivalries continued, the daimyo relied increasingly on the samurai for protection, and political power came into the hands of a loose coalition of noble families.

By the end of the fifteenth century, Japan was again close to anarchy. A disastrous civil conflict known as the Onin War (1467–1477) led to the virtual destruction of the capital city of Kyoto and the disintegration of the shogunate. With the disappearance of any central authority, powerful aristocrats in rural areas now seized total control over large territories and ruled as independent great lords. Territorial rivalries and claims of precedence led to almost constant warfare in this period of "warring states," as it is called (in obvious parallel with a similar era during the Zhou dynasty in China). The trend back toward central authority did not begin until the last quarter of the sixteenth century.

Economic and Social Structures

From the time the Yayoi culture was first established on the Japanese islands, Japan was a predominantly agrarian society. Although Japan lacked the spacious valleys and deltas of the river valley societies, its inhabitants were able to take advantage of their limited amount of tillable land and plentiful rainfall to create a society based on the cultivation of wet rice.

As in China, commerce was slow to develop in Japan. During ancient times, each *uji* had a local artisan class, composed of weavers, carpenters, and ironworkers, but trade was essentially local and was regulated by the local clan leaders. With the rise of the Yamato state, a money economy gradually began to develop, although most trade was still conducted through barter until the twelfth century, when metal coins introduced from China became more popular.

LIFE IN THE LAND OF WA

Some of the earliest descriptions of Japan come from Chinese sources. The following passage from the History of the Wei Dynasty was written in the late third century C.E. The term Wa is a derogatory word meaning "dwarf" and was frequently used in China to refer to the Japanese people. The author of this passage, while remarking on the strange habits of the Japanese, writes without condescension.

HISTORY OF THE WEI DYNASTY

The people of Wa make their abode in the mountainous islands located in the middle of the ocean to the southeast of the Taifang prefecture. . . .

All men, old or young, are covered by tattoos. Japanese fishers revel in diving to catch fish and shell-fish. Tattoos are said to drive away large fish and water predators. They are considered an ornament. . . . Men allow their hair to cover both of their ears and wear head-bands. They wear loincloths wrapped around their bodies and seldom use stitches. Women gather their hair at the ends and tie it in a knot and then pin it to the top of their heads. They make their clothes in one piece, and cut an opening in the center for their heads. They plant wet-field rice, China-grass [a type of nettle], and mulberry trees. They raise cocoons and reel the silk off the cocoons. They produce clothing made of China-grass, of coarse silk, and of cotton. In their land, there are no cows, horses, tigers, leopards, sheep, or swan. They fight with halberds, shields, and wooden bows. . . . Their arrows are made of bamboo, and iron and bone points make up the arrowhead.

People . . . live long, some reaching one hundred years of age, and others to eighty or ninety years. Normally men of high echelon have four or five wives, and the plebeians may have two or three. When the law is violated, the light offender loses his wife and children by confiscation, and the grave offender has his household and kin exterminated. There are class distinctions within the nobility and the base, and some are vassals of others. There are mansions and granaries erected for the purpose of collecting taxes. . . .

When plebeians meet the high-echelon men on the road, they withdraw to the grassy area [side of the road] hesitantly. When they speak or are spoken to, they either crouch or kneel with both hands on the ground to show their respect. When responding they say "aye," which corresponds to our affirmative "yes."

Trade and manufacturing began to develop more rapidly during the Kamakura period, with the appearance of trimonthly markets in the larger towns and the emergence of such industries as paper, iron casting, and porcelain. Foreign trade, mainly with Korea and China, began during the eleventh century. Japan exported raw materials, paintings, swords, and other manufactured items in return for silk, porcelain, books, and copper cash. Some Japanese traders were so aggressive in pressing their interests that authorities in China and Korea attempted to limit the number of Japanese commercial missions that could visit each year. Such restrictions were often ignored, however, and encouraged some Japanese traders to turn to piracy.

Significantly, manufacturing and commerce developed rapidly during the more decentralized period of the Ashikaga shogunate and the era of the warring states, perhaps because of the rapid growth in the wealth and autonomy of local daimyo families. Market towns, now operating on a full money economy, began to appear, and local manufacturers formed guilds to protect their mutual interests. Sometimes local peasants would sell products made in their homes, such as clothing made of silk or hemp, household items, or food products, at the markets. In general, however, trade and manufacturing remained under the control of the local daimyo, who would often provide tax breaks to local guilds in return for other benefits. Although Japan remained a primarily agricultural society, it was on the verge of a major advance in manufacturing.

DAILY LIFE

One of the first descriptions of the life of the Japanese people comes from a Chinese dynastic history from the third century C.E. It describes lords and peasants living in an agricultural society that was based on the cultivation of wet rice. Laws had been enacted to punish offenders, local trade was conducted in markets, and government granaries stored the grain that was paid as taxes (see the box above).

Life for the common people probably changed very little over the next several hundred years. Most were peasants, who worked on land owned by their lord or, in some cases, by the state or by Buddhist monasteries. By no means, however, were all peasants equal either economically or socially. Although in ancient times all land was owned by the state and peasants working the land were taxed at an equal rate depending on the nature of the crop, after the Yamato era variations began to develop. At the top were local officials who were often well-to-do peasants. They were responsible for organizing collective labor services and collecting tax grain from the peasants and in turn were exempt from such obligations themselves.

The mass of the peasants were under the authority of these local officials. In general, peasants were free to

Courtesy of the Tokyo National Museum

SCENE OF URBAN LIFE. Although traditional Japan was largely an agricultural society, trade and manufacturing began to develop during the Kamakura period, sparked by the rapid growth of local daimyo families and market towns. Intraregional trade was transported by horse-drawn carts or by boats on rivers or along the coast. Portrayed here is a detail from a thirteenth-century scroll depicting the bustle and general confusion of the city of Edo (now Tokyo).

dispose of their harvest as they saw fit after paying their tax quota, but in practical terms their freedom was limited. Those who were unable to pay the tax sank to the level of *genin*, or landless laborers, who could be bought and sold by their proprietors like slaves along with the land on which they worked. Some fled to escape such a fate and attempted to survive by clearing plots of land in the mountains or by becoming bandits.

In addition to the *genin*, the bottom of the social scale was occupied by the *eta*, a class of hereditary slaves who were responsible for what were considered degrading occupations, such as curing leather and burying the dead. The origins of the *eta* are not entirely clear, but they probably were descendants of prisoners of war, criminals, or mountain dwellers who were not related to the dominant Yamato peoples. As we shall see, the *eta* are still a distinctive part of Japanese society, and although their full legal rights are guaranteed under the current constitution, discrimination against them is not uncommon.

Daily life for ordinary people in early Japan resembled that of their counterparts throughout much of Asia. The vast majority lived in small villages, several of which normally made up a single *shoen*. Housing was simple. Most lived in small two-room houses of timber, mud, or thatch, with dirt floors covered by straw or woven mats (the origin, perhaps, of the well-known *tatami*, or woven-mat

floor, of more modern times). Their diet consisted of rice (if some was left after the payment of the grain tax), wild grasses, millet, roots, and some fish and birds. Life must have been difficult at best; as one eighth-century poet lamented:

> Here I lie on straw
> Spread on bare earth,
> With my parents at my pillow,
> My wife and children at my feet,
> All huddled in grief and tears.
> No fire sends up smoke
> At the cooking place,
> And in the cauldron
> A spider spins its web.[2]

Evidence about the relations between men and women in early Japan presents a mixed picture. The Chinese dynastic history reports that "in their meetings and daily living, there is no distinction between . . . men and women." It notes that a woman "adept in the ways of shamanism" had briefly ruled Japan in the third century C.E. But it also remarks that polygyny was common, with nobles normally having four or five wives and commoners two or three.[3] An eighth-century law code guaranteed the inheritance rights of women, and wives abandoned by their husbands were permitted to obtain a divorce and remarry. A husband could divorce his wife if she did not

SEDUCTION OF
THE AKASHI LADY

*O*ut of the Japanese tradition of female introspective prose
appeared one of the world's truly great novels, The Tale
of Genji, *written around the year 1000 by the diarist and
court author Murasaki Shikibu, known as Lady Murasaki. It is
even today revered for its artistic refinement and sensitivity and
has influenced Japanese writing for a millennium. A panoramic
portrayal of court life in tenth-century Japan, it traces the life and
loves of the courtier Genji as he strives to remain in favor with
those in power while at the same time pursuing his cult of love
and beauty. Truly remarkable is the character of Genji himself,
revealed to the reader through myriad psychological observations.
In this excerpt, Genji has just seduced a lady at court and now
feels misgivings at having betrayed his child bride. A koto is a
Japanese stringed instrument similar to a zither.*

LADY MURASAKI, *THE TALE OF GENJI*

A curtain string brushed against a koto, to tell him that she
had been passing a quiet evening at her music.

"And will you not play for me on the koto of which I
have heard so much?"...

This lady had not been prepared for an incursion and
could not cope with it. She fled to an inner room. How she
could have contrived to bar it he could not tell, but it was
very firmly barred indeed. Though he did not exactly force
his way through, it is not to be imagined that he left matters
as they were. Delicate, slender—she was almost too beautiful. Pleasure was mingled with pity at the thought that he
was imposing himself upon her. She was even more pleasing
than reports from afar had had her. The autumn night, usually so long, was over in a trice. Not wishing to be seen, he
hurried out, leaving affectionate assurances behind.

Genji called in secret from time to time. The two
houses being some distance apart, he feared being seen by
fishers, who were known to relish a good rumor, and sometimes several days would elapse between his visits. . . .

Genji dreaded having Murasaki [his bride] learn of the
affair. He still loved her more than anyone, and he did not
want her to make even joking reference to it. She was a
quiet, docile lady, but she had more than once been
unhappy with him. Why, for the sake of brief pleasure, had
he caused her pain? He wished it were all his to do over
again. The sight of the Akashi lady only brought new longing for the other lady.

He got off a more earnest and affectionate letter than
usual, at the end of which he said: "I am in anguish at the
thought that, because of foolish occurrences for which I
have been responsible but have had little heart, I might
appear in a guise distasteful to you. There has been a
strange, fleeting encounter. That I should volunteer this
story will make you see, I hope, how little I wish to have
secrets from you. Let the gods be my judges.

*"It was but the fisherman's brush with the salty sea pine.
Followed by a tide of tears of longing."*

Her reply was gentle and unreproachful, and at the end of
it she said: "That you should have deigned to tell me a
dreamlike story which you could not keep to yourself calls
to mind numbers of earlier instances.

*"Naive of me, perhaps; yet we did make our vows.
And now see the waves that wash the Mountain of
Waiting!"*

It was the one note of reproach in a quiet, undemanding
letter. He found it hard to put down, and for some nights
he stayed away from the house in the hills.

produce a male child, committed adultery, disobeyed her
parents-in-law, talked too much, engaged in theft, was jealous, or had a serious illness.[4]

When Buddhism was introduced, women were initially
relegated to a subordinate position in the new faith.
Although they were permitted to take up monastic life—
many widows entered a monastery at the death of their
husbands—they were not permitted to visit Buddhist holy
places, nor were they even (in the accepted wisdom) equal
with men in the afterlife. One Buddhist commentary
from the late thirteenth century said that a woman could
not attain enlightenment because "her sin is grievous,
and so she is not allowed to enter the lofty palace of the
great Brahma, nor to look upon the clouds which hover
over his ministers and people."[5] Other Buddhist scholars

were more egalitarian: "Learning the Law of Buddha and
achieving release from illusion have nothing to do with
whether one happens to be a man or a woman."[6] Such
views ultimately prevailed, and women were eventually
allowed to participate fully in Buddhist activities in
medieval Japan.

Although women did not possess the full legal and
social rights of their male counterparts, they played an
active role at various levels of Japanese society. Aristocratic women were prominent at court, and some, such
as the author Lady Murasaki, became renowned for their
artistic or literary talents (see the box above). Though few
commoners could aspire to such prominence, women often
appear in the scroll paintings of the period along with
men, doing the spring planting, threshing and hulling

the rice, and acting as carriers, peddlers, salespersons, and entertainers.

In Search of the Pure Land: Religion in Early Japan

In Japan, as elsewhere, religious belief began with the worship of nature spirits. Early Japanese worshiped spirits, called *kami,* who resided in trees, rivers and streams, and mountains. They also believed in ancestral spirits present in the atmosphere. In Japan, these beliefs eventually evolved into a kind of state religion called Shinto (the Sacred Way or the Way of the Gods) that is still practiced today. Shinto still serves as an ideological and emotional force that knits the Japanese into a single people and nation.

Shinto does not have a complex metaphysical superstructure or an elaborate moral code. It does require certain ritual acts, usually undertaken at a shrine, and a process of purification, which may have originated in primitive concerns about death, childbirth, illness, and menstruation. This traditional concern about physical purity may help explain the strong Japanese concern for personal cleanliness and the practice of denying women entrance to the holy places.

Another feature of Shinto is its stress on the beauty of nature and the importance of nature itself in Japanese life. Shinto shrines are usually located in places of exceptional beauty and are often dedicated to a nearby physical feature. As time passed, such primitive beliefs contributed to the characteristic Japanese love of nature. In this sense, early Shinto beliefs have been incorporated into the lives of all Japanese.

In time, Shinto evolved into a state doctrine that was linked with belief in the divinity of the emperor and the sacredness of the Japanese nation. A national shrine was established at Ise, north of the early capital of Nara, where the emperor annually paid tribute to the sun goddess. But although Shinto had evolved well beyond its primitive origins, like its counterparts elsewhere it could not satisfy all the religious and emotional needs of the Japanese people. For those needs, the Japanese turned to Buddhism.

As we have seen, Buddhism was introduced into Japan from China during the sixth century C.E. and had begun to spread beyond the court to the general population by the eighth century. As in China, most Japanese saw no contradiction between worshiping both the Buddha and their local nature gods, many of whom were considered to be later manifestations of the Buddha. Most of the Buddhist sects that had achieved popularity in China were established in Japan, and many of them attracted powerful patrons at court. Great monasteries were established that competed in wealth and influence with the noble families that had traditionally ruled the country.

Perhaps the two most influential Buddhist sects were the Pure Land (Jodo) sect and Zen (in Chinese, Chan or Ch'an). The Pure Land sect, which taught that devotion alone could lead to enlightenment and release, was very popular among the common people, for whom monastic life was one of the few routes to upward mobility. Among the aristocracy, the most influential school was Zen, which exerted a significant impact on Japanese life and culture during the era of the warring states. In its emphasis on austerity, self-discipline, and communion with nature, Zen complemented many traditional beliefs in Japanese society and became an important component of the samurai warrior's code.

In Zen teachings, there were various ways to achieve enlightenment (*satori* in Japanese). Some stressed that it could be achieved suddenly. One monk, for example, reportedly achieved *satori* by listening to the sound of a bamboo striking against roof tiles, another by carefully watching the opening of peach blossoms in the spring. But other practitioners, sometimes called adepts, said that enlightenment could come only through studying the scriptures and arduous self-discipline (known as *zazen,* or "seated Zen"). Seated Zen involved a lengthy process of meditation that cleansed the mind of extraneous thoughts so that it could concentrate on the essential.

Sources of Traditional Japanese Culture

Nowhere is the Japanese genius for blending indigenous and imported elements into an effective whole better demonstrated than in culture. In such widely diverse fields as art, architecture, sculpture, and literature, the Japanese from early times showed an impressive capacity to borrow selectively from abroad without destroying essential native elements.

Growing contact with China during the period of the rise of the Yamato state stimulated Japanese artists. Missions sent to China and Korea during the seventh and eighth centuries returned with examples of Tang literature, sculpture, and painting, all of which influenced the Japanese.

LITERATURE

Borrowing from Chinese models was somewhat complicated, however, since the early Japanese had no writing system for recording their own spoken language and initially adopted the Chinese written language for writing. But resourceful Japanese soon began to adapt the Chinese written characters so that they could be used for recording the Japanese language. In some cases, Chinese characters were given Japanese pronunciations. But Chinese characters ordinarily could not be used to record Japanese words, which normally contain more than one syllable. Sometimes the Japanese simply used Chinese characters as phonetic symbols that were combined to form Japanese words. Later they simplified the characters into phonetic symbols that were used alongside Chinese characters. This hybrid system continues to be used today.

At first, most educated Japanese preferred to write in Chinese, and a court literature—consisting of essays, poetry, and official histories—appeared in the classical Chinese language. But spoken Japanese never totally disappeared among the educated classes and eventually became the instrument of a unique literature. With the lessening of Chinese cultural influence in the tenth century, Japanese verse resurfaced. Between the tenth and fifteenth centuries, twenty imperial anthologies of poetry were compiled. Initially, they were written primarily by courtiers, but with the fall of the Heian court and the rise of the warrior and merchant classes, all literate segments of society began to produce poetry.

Japanese poetry is unique. It expresses its themes in a simple form, a characteristic stemming from traditional Japanese aesthetics, Zen religion, and the language itself. The aim of the Japanese poet was to create a mood, perhaps the melancholic effect of gently falling cherry blossoms or leaves. With a few specific references, the poet suggested a whole world, just as Zen Buddhism sought enlightenment from a sudden perception. Poets often alluded to earlier poems by repeating their images with small changes, a technique that was viewed not as plagiarism but as an elaboration on the meaning of the earlier poem.

By the fourteenth century, the technique of the "linked verse" had become the most popular form of Japanese poetry. Known as haiku, it is composed of seventeen syllables divided into lines of five, seven, and five syllables. The poems usually focused on images from nature and the mutability of life. Often the poetry was written by several individuals alternately composing verses and linking them together into long sequences of hundreds and even thousands of lines (see the box above).

Poetry served a unique function at the Heian court, where it was the initial means of communication between lovers. By custom, aristocratic women were isolated from all contact with men outside their immediate family and spent their days hidden behind screens. Some amused themselves by writing poetry. When courtship began, poetic exchanges were the only means a woman had to attract her prospective lover, who would be enticed solely by her poetic art.

During the Heian period, male courtiers wrote in Chinese, believing that Chinese civilization was superior and worthy of emulation. Like the Chinese, they viewed prose fiction as "vulgar gossip." Nevertheless, from the ninth century to the twelfth, Japanese women were prolific writers of prose fiction in Japanese. Excluded from school, they learned to read and write at home and wrote diaries and stories to pass the time. Some of the most talented women were invited to court as authors in residence.

In the increasingly pessimistic world of the warring states of Kamakura (1185–1333), Japanese novels typically focused on a solitary figure who is aloof from the refinements of the court and faces battle and possibly death. Another genre, that of the heroic war tale, came out of the new warrior class. These works described the military exploits of warriors, coupled with an overwhelming sense of sadness and loneliness.

The famous classical Japanese drama known as No also originated during this period. No developed out of a variety of entertainment forms, such as dancing and juggling, that were part of the native tradition or had been imported from China and other regions of Asia. The plots were normally based on stories from Japanese history or legend. Eventually, No evolved into a highly stylized drama in which the performers wore masks and danced to the accompaniment of instrumental music. Like much of Japanese culture, *No* was restrained, graceful, and refined.

ART AND ARCHITECTURE

In art and architecture, as in literature, the Japanese pursued their interest in beauty, simplicity, and nature. To some degree, Japanese artists and architects were influenced by Chinese forms. As they became familiar with Chinese architecture, Japanese rulers and aristocrats tried to emulate the splendor of Tang civilization and began constructing their palaces and temples in Chinese style.

During the Heian period (794–1185), the search for beauty was reflected in various art forms, such as narrative hand scrolls, screens, sliding door panels, fans, and lacquer decoration. As in the case of literature, nature themes dominated, such as seashore scenes, a spring rain, moon and mist, or flowering wisteria and cherry blossoms. All were intended to evoke an emotional response on the part of the viewer. Japanese painting suggested the frail beauty of nature by presenting it on a smaller scale. The majestic mountain in a Chinese painting became a more intimate Japanese landscape with rolling hills and a rice field. Faces were rarely shown, and human drama was indicated by a woman lying prostrate or hiding her face in her sleeve. Tension was shown by two people talking at a great distance or with their backs to one another.

During the Kamakura period (1185–1333), the hand scroll with its physical realism and action-packed paintings of the new warrior class achieved great popularity. Reflecting these chaotic times, the art of portraiture flourished, and a scroll would include a full gallery of warriors and holy men in starkly realistic detail, including such unflattering features as stubble, worry lines on a forehead, and crooked teeth. Japanese sculptors also produced naturalistic wooden statues of generals, nobles, and saints. By far the most distinctive, however, were the fierce heavenly "guardian kings," who still intimidate the viewer today.

Zen Buddhism, an import from China in the thirteenth century, also influenced Japanese aesthetics. With its emphasis on immediate enlightenment without recourse to intellectual analysis and elaborate ritual, Zen reinforced the Japanese predilection for simplicity and self-discipline. During this era, Zen philosophy found expression in the Japanese garden, the tea ceremony, the art of flower arranging, pottery and ceramics, and miniature plant display (the famous *bonsai*, literally "pot scenery").

Landscapes served as an important means of expression in both Japanese art and architecture. Japanese gardens were initially modeled on Chinese examples. Early court texts during the Heian period emphasized the importance

🌿 **THE PROTECTIVE DRAGON.**   Viewing Heian culture as an era of decadent aristocratic excess, artists of the Kamakura period (1185–1333) strove to express spiritual purpose in their work. Illustrated narrative hand scrolls, for example, either dramatized the torments of hell or praised the lives of Buddhist saints. Here we see a colorful thirteenth-century painting that depicts a seventh-century Korean monk returning from his travels in China. At his departure from the dock, he rejected the love of a beautiful young woman because of his spiritual dedication. Brokenhearted, she plunges into the ocean, thus transforming herself into a dragon to guide him safely back to Korea. The woman was later recognized as a Buddhist saint whose sacrifice was deemed morally appropriate as a model for Japanese women of the era.

Courtesy of the Freer Gallery of Art, Smithsonian Institution, Washington, D.C. #49.21

© Art Resource, NY

➤ **GUARDIAN KINGS.**   Larger than life and intimidating in its presence, this thirteenth-century wooden statue departs from the refined atmosphere of the Heian court and pulsates with the masculine energy of the Kamakura period. Placed strategically at the entrance to Buddhist shrines, guardian kings such as this one protected the temple and the faithful. In contrast to the refined atmosphere of the Fujiwara court, the Kamakura era was a warrior's world.

➤ **A SEATED BUDDHA.**   Buddhist statuary originated in India and China and evolved as a popular art form in Japan from the seventh century on. Characteristic of these statues are the *mudras*, or hand and body positions by which the Buddha communicated with his followers. Here his connected fingers indicate meditation. Whereas earlier Japanese sculptors worked in bronze, the depletion of metal reserves eventually necessitated the use of wood. This remarkable eleventh-century gilded wood carving, over 10 feet in height, is composed of fifty-three pieces of cypress and exudes a feeling of stability and calm, expressing the Buddha's deep spirituality. He is seated on a bed of lotus leaves, a Buddhist symbol for purity arising out of the mire.

of including a stream or pond when creating a garden. The landscape surrounding the fourteenth-century Golden Pavilion in Kyoto displays a harmony of garden, water, and architecture that makes it one of the treasures of the world. Because of the shortage of water in the city, later gardens concentrated on rock composition, using white pebbles to represent water.

Like the Japanese garden, the tea ceremony represents the fusion of Zen and aesthetics. Developed in the fifteenth

century, it was practiced in a simple room devoid of external ornament except for a *tatami* floor, sliding doors, and an alcove with a writing desk and asymmetrical shelves. The participants could therefore focus completely on the activity of pouring and drinking tea. "Tea and Zen have the same flavor," goes the Japanese saying. Considered the ultimate symbol of spiritual deliverance, the tea ceremony had great aesthetic value and moral significance in traditional times as well as today.

Courtesy of William J. Duiker

Courtesy of Charles Gupton, Tony Stone Images

RYOANJI TEMPLE GARDEN IN KYOTO.   As the result of a water shortage in the fifteenth century, Japanese landscape designers began to make increasing use of rocks and pebbles to represent water. In the Ryoanji Temple in the hills west of Kyoto, seventeen rocks surrounded by wavy raked pebbles are arranged in five groups to suggest mountains emerging from the sea. Here we experience the quintessential Japanese aesthetic expression of allusion, simplicity, restraint, and tranquillity.

THE GOLDEN PAVILION IN KYOTO.   The landscape surrounding the Golden Pavilion displays a harmony of garden, water, and architecture that makes it one of the treasures of the world. Constructed in the fourteenth century as a retreat for the shoguns to withdraw from their administrative chores, the pavilion is named for the gold foil that covered its exterior. Completely destroyed by an arsonist in 1950 as a protest against the commercialism of modern Buddhism, it was rebuilt and reopened in 1987. The use of water as a backdrop is especially noteworthy in Chinese and Japanese landscapes, as well as in the Middle East.

Japan and the Chinese Model

Few societies in Asia have historically been as isolated as Japan. Cut off from the mainland by 120 miles of frequently turbulent ocean, the Japanese had only minimal contact with the outside world during most of their early development.

Whether this isolation was ultimately beneficial to Japanese society cannot be determined. On one hand, the lack of knowledge of developments taking place elsewhere probably delayed the process of change in Japan. On the other hand, the Japanese were spared the destructive invasions that afflicted other ancient civilizations. Certainly, once the Japanese became acquainted with Chinese cul-

ture at the height of the Tang era, they were quick to take advantage of the opportunity. In the space of a few decades, the young state adopted many aspects of Chinese society and culture and thereby introduced major changes into Japanese life.

Nevertheless, Japanese political institutions failed to follow all aspects of the Chinese pattern. Despite Prince Shotoku's effort to make effective use of the imperial traditions of Tang China, the decentralizing forces inside Japanese society remained dominant throughout the period under discussion in this chapter. Adoption of the Confucian civil service examination did not lead to a breakdown of Japanese social divisions; instead, the examination was administered in a manner that preserved and strengthened them. Although Buddhist and Daoist doctrines made a significant contribution to Japanese religious practices, Shinto beliefs continued to play a major role in shaping the Japanese worldview.

Why Japan did not follow the Chinese road to centralized authority has been the subject of some debate among historians. Some argue that the answer lies in differing cultural traditions, while others suggest that Chinese institutions and values were introduced too rapidly to be assimilated effectively by Japanese society. One factor may have been the absence of a foreign threat (except for the Mongols) in Japan. A recent view holds that diseases (such as smallpox and measles) imported inadvertently from China led to a marked decline in the population of the islands, reducing the food output and preventing the population from coalescing in more compact urban centers.

In any event, Japan was not the only society in Asia to assimilate ideas from abroad while at the same time preserving customs and institutions inherited from the past. Across the Sea of Japan to the west and several thousand miles to the south, other Asian peoples were embarked on a similar journey. We now turn to their experience.

KOREA: BRIDGE TO THE EAST

No society in East Asia was more strongly influenced by the Chinese model than Korea. Slightly larger than the state of Minnesota, the Korean peninsula was probably first settled by Altaic-speaking fishing and hunting peoples from neighboring Manchuria during the Neolithic Age. Because the area is relatively mountainous (only about one-fifth of the peninsula is adaptable to cultivation), farming was apparently not practiced until about 2000 B.C.E. The other aspect of Korea's geography that has profoundly affected its history is its proximity to both China and Japan.

In 109 B.C.E., the northern part of the peninsula came under direct Chinese rule. During the next several generations, the area was ruled by the Han dynasty, which divided the territory into provinces and introduced Chinese institutions. With the decline of the Han in the third century C.E., power gradually shifted to local tribal leaders, who drove out the Chinese administrators but continued to absorb Chinese cultural influence. Eventually, three separate kingdoms emerged on the peninsula: Koguryo in the north, Paekche in the southwest, and Silla in the southeast. The Japanese, who had recently established their own state on the Yamato plain, maintained a small colony on the southern coast.

Korea's Three Kingdoms

Yalu R.

Sea of Japan

Pyongyang
KOGURYO

Yellow Sea

SILLA
Kyongju

PAEKCHE

0   300 Kilometers
0   200 Miles

The Three Kingdoms

From the fourth to the seventh centuries, the three kingdoms were bitter rivals for influence and territory on the peninsula. At the same time, all began to absorb Chinese

political and cultural institutions. Chinese influence was most notable in Koguryo, where Buddhism was introduced in the late fourth century C.E. and the first Confucian academy on the peninsula was established in the capital at Pyongyang. All three kingdoms also appear to have accepted a tributary relationship with one or another of the squabbling states that emerged in China after the fall of the Han. The kingdom of Silla, less exposed than its two rivals to Chinese influence, was at first the weakest of the three, but eventually its greater internal cohesion—perhaps a consequence of the tenacity of its tribal traditions—enabled it to become the dominant power on the peninsula. Then the rulers of Silla forced the Chinese to withdraw from all but the area

➤ **KOREAN ROYAL CROWN.**   The Silla dynasty was renowned for the high quality of its gold, jewelry, crowns, and sword sheaths. Shown here is a jewel-inlaid royal crown of the fifth century C.E. that was excavated from a royal tomb in eastern Korea. Although much Silla artwork reflects Chinese influence, royal crowns located in Silla tombs often contain antlerlike motifs, reflecting the animistic traditions of Korea's pre-Chinese past. The comma-shaped jewels symbolize the King's Heaven-sanctioned authority on earth.

adjacent to the Yalu River. To pacify the haughty Chinese, Silla accepted tributary status under the Tang dynasty. The remaining Japanese colonies in the south were eliminated.

With the country unified for the first time, the rulers of Silla attempted to use Chinese political institutions and ideology to forge a centralized state. Buddhism, now rising in popularity, became the state religion, and Korean monks followed the paths of their Japanese counterparts on journeys to the Middle Kingdom. Chinese architecture and art became dominant in the capital at Kyongju and other urban centers, and the written Chinese language became the official means of communication at court. But powerful aristocratic families, long dominant in the southeastern part of the peninsula, were still influential at court. They were able to prevent the adoption of the Tang civil service examination system and resisted the distribution of manorial lands to the poor. The failure to adopt the Chinese model was fatal. Squabbling among noble families steadily increased, and after the assassination of the king of Silla in 780, the country sank into civil war.

Unification

In the early tenth century, a new dynasty called Koryo (the root of the modern word for Korea) arose in the north. The new kingdom adopted Chinese political institutions in an effort to strengthen its power and unify its territory. The civil service examination system was introduced in 958, but as in Japan, the bureaucracy continued to be dominated by influential aristocratic families.

The Koryo dynasty remained in power for four hundred years, protected from invasion by the absence of a strong dynasty in neighboring China. Under the Koryo, industry and commerce slowly began to develop, but as in China, agriculture was the prime source of wealth. In theory, all land was the property of the king, but in actuality, noble families controlled their holdings. The lands were worked by peasants who were subject to burdens similar to those of European serfs. At the bottom of society was a class of "base people" (*chonmin*), composed of slaves, artisans, and other specialized workers.

From a cultural point of view, the Koryo era was one of high achievement. Buddhist monasteries, run by sects

PULGUKSA BELL TOWER. Among the greatest architectural achievements on the Korean peninsula is the Pulguksa (Monastery of the Land of Buddha), built near Kyongju, the ancient capital of Silla, in the eighth century C.E. Shown here is the bell tower, located in the midst of beautiful parklands on the monastery grounds. Young Korean couples often come to this monastery after their weddings to be photographed in the stunning surroundings.

THE FLOWER GARDEN SCRIPTURE

By the eighth century, Buddhism had come to Korea from China, and like their counterparts in Christian Europe, Korean monks could accumulate merit toward salvation by copying the scriptures. In this passage, the eighth-century Master Yongi of Hwangyong monastery has volunteered to copy a scripture as a way of expressing gratitude for the love of his parents and assisting others in following the Buddhist Eightfold Way to wisdom. Note the careful attention to ritual as the process is brought to realization. This scripture, which was discovered in 1979, consisted of two scrolls of thirty white papers joined together, with characters in black ink. Each scroll was 45 feet long.

AN EIGHTH-CENTURY BUDDHIST SCRIPTURE

The scripture is made as follows: First scented water is sprinkled around the roots of a paperbark mulberry tree to quicken its growth; the bark is then peeled and pounded to make paper with a clean surface. The copyists, the artisans who make the centerpiece of the scroll, and the painters who draw the images of buddhas and bodhisattvas all receive the bodhisattva ordination and observe abstinence. After relieving themselves, sleeping, eating, or drinking, they take a bath in scented water before returning to the work. Copyists are adorned with new pure garments, loose trousers, a coarse crown, and a deva crown. Two azure-clad boys sprinkle water on their heads and . . . azure-clad boys and musicians perform music. The processions to the copying site are headed by one who sprinkles scented water on their path, another who scatters flowers, a dharma master who carries a censer, and another dharma master who chants Buddhist verses. Each of the copyists carries incense and flowers and invokes the name of the Buddha as he progresses.

Upon reaching the site, all take refuge in the Three Jewels (the Buddha, the Dharma, and the Order), make three bows, and offer the *Flower Garland Scripture* and others to buddhas and bodhisattvas. Then they sit down and copy the scripture, make the centerpiece of the scroll, and paint the buddhas and bodhisattvas. Thus, azure-clad boys and musicians cleanse everything before a piece of relic is placed in the center.

Now I make a vow that the copied scripture will not break till the end of the future—even when a major chiliocosm is destroyed by the three calamities, this scripture shall be intact as the void. If all living beings rely on this scripture, they shall witness the Buddha, listen to his dharma, worship the relic, aspire to enlightenment without backsliding, cultivate the vows of the Universally Worthy Bodhisattva, and achieve Buddhahood.

---

introduced from China, including Pure Land and Zen (Chan), controlled vast territories, while their monks served as royal advisers at court. At first, Buddhist themes dominated in Korean art and sculpture, and the entire Tripitaka (the "three baskets" of the Buddhist canon) was printed using wooden blocks (see the box above). Eventually, however, with the appearance of landscape painting and porcelain, Confucian themes began to predominate.

Under the Mongols

Like its predecessor in Silla, the kingdom of Koryo was unable to overcome the power of the nobility and the absence of a reliable tax base. In the thirteenth century, the Mongols seized the northern part of the country and assimilated it into the Yuan empire. The weakened kingdom of Koryo became a tributary of the great khan in Khanbaliq (see Chapter 10).

The era of Mongol rule was one of profound suffering for the Korean people, especially the thousands of peasants and artisans who were compelled to perform corvée labor to help build the ships in preparation for Khubilai Khan's invasion of Japan. On the positive side, the Mongols introduced many new ideas and technology from China and farther afield. The Koryo dynasty had managed to survive, but only by accepting Mongol authority, and when the power of the Mongols declined, the kingdom declined with it. With the rise to power of the Ming in China, Koryo collapsed, and power was seized by the military commander Yi Song-gye, who declared the founding of the new Yi dynasty in 1392. Once again, the Korean people were in charge of their own destiny.

VIETNAM: THE SMALLER DRAGON

While the Korean people were attempting to establish their own identity in the shadow of the powerful Chinese empire, the peoples of Vietnam, on China's southern frontier, were trying to do the same. The Vietnamese began to practice irrigated agriculture in the flooded regions of the Red River delta at an early date and entered the Bronze Age sometime during the second millennium B.C.E. By about 200 B.C.E., a young state had begun to form in the area but immediately encountered the expanding power of the Qin empire (see Chapter 3). The Vietnamese were not easy to subdue, however, and the collapse of the Qin dynasty temporarily enabled them to preserve their independence. Nevertheless, a century later, they were absorbed into the Han empire.

At first, the Han were satisfied to rule the delta as an autonomous region under the administration of the local landed aristocracy. But Chinese taxes were oppressive, and in 39 C.E., a revolt led by the Trung Sisters (widows of local nobles who had been executed by the Chinese) briefly brought Han rule to an end. The Chinese soon suppressed the rebellion, however, and began to rule the area directly through officials dispatched from China. In time, however, these foreign officials began to intermarry with the local nobility and form a Sino-Vietnamese ruling class who, though trained in Chinese culture, began to identify with the cause of Vietnamese autonomy.

For nearly a thousand years, the Vietnamese were exposed to the art, architecture, literature, philosophy, and written language of China as the Chinese attempted to integrate the area culturally as well as politically and administratively into their empire. To all intents and purposes, the Red River delta, then known to the Chinese as the "pacified South" (Annam), became a part of China.

The Rise of Great Viet

Despite the Chinese efforts to assimilate Vietnam, the Vietnamese sense of ethnic and cultural identity proved inextinguishable, and in the tenth century, the Vietnamese took advantage of the collapse of the Tang dynasty in China to overthrow Chinese rule.

The new Vietnamese state, which called itself Dai Viet (Great Viet), became a dynamic new force on the Southeast Asian mainland. As the population of the Red River delta expanded, Dai Viet soon came into conflict with Champa, its neighbor to the south. Located along the central coast of modern Vietnam, Champa was a trading society based on Indian cultural traditions. Over the next several centuries, the two states fought on numerous occasions. By the end of the fifteenth century, Dai Viet had conquered Champa. The Vietnamese then resumed their march southward, establishing agricultural settlements in the newly conquered territory. By the seventeenth century, the Vietnamese had reached the Gulf of Siam.

The Kingdom of Dai Viet, 1100

CHINA

Red R.

Thanglong (Hanoi)

DAI VIET

Gulf of Tonkin

HAINAN ISLAND

CHAMPA

0   300 Kilometers
0   200 Miles

The Vietnamese faced an even more serious challenge from the north. The Song dynasty in China, beset with its own problems on the northern frontier, eventually accepted the Dai Viet ruler's offer of tribute status (see the box above), but later dynasties attempted to

➤ **A LOST CIVILIZATION.** Before the spread of Vietnamese settlers into the area early in the second millennium C.E., much of the coast along the South China Sea was occupied by the kingdom of Champa. A trading people who were directly engaged in the regional trade network between China and the Bay of Bengal, the Cham received their initial political and cultural influence from India. This shrine-tower, located on a hill in the modern city of Nha Trang, was constructed in the eleventh century and clearly displays the influence of Indian architecture. Champa finally succumbed to a Vietnamese invasion in the fifteenth century.

reintegrate the Red River delta into the Chinese empire. The first effort was made in the late thirteenth century by the Mongols, who attempted on two occasions to conquer the Vietnamese. After a series of bloody battles, during which the Vietnamese displayed an impressive capacity for guerrilla warfare, the invaders were driven out. A little over a century later, the Ming dynasty tried again, and for twenty years Vietnam was once more under Chinese rule. In 1428, the Vietnamese evicted the Chinese again, but the experience had contributed to the strong sense of Vietnamese identity.

THE CHINESE LEGACY

Despite their stubborn resistance to Chinese rule, after the restoration of independence in the tenth century, Vietnamese rulers quickly discovered the convenience of the Confucian model in administering a river valley society and therefore attempted to follow Chinese practice in forming their own state. The ruler styled himself an emperor like his counterpart to the north (although he prudently termed himself a king in his direct dealings with the Chinese court), adopted Chinese court rituals, claimed the Mandate of Heaven, and arrogated to himself the same authority and privileges in his dealings with his subjects. But unlike a Chinese emperor, who had no particular symbolic role as defender of the Chinese people or Chinese culture, a Vietnamese monarch was viewed, above all, as the symbol and defender of Vietnamese independence.

Like their Chinese counterparts, Vietnamese rulers fought to preserve their authority from the challenges of powerful aristocratic families and turned to the Chinese bureaucratic model, including civil service examinations, as a means of doing so. Under the pressure of strong monarchs, the concept of merit eventually took hold, and the power of the landed aristocracy was weakened if not entirely broken. The Vietnamese adopted much of the Chinese administrative structure, including the six ministries, the censorate, and the various levels of provincial and local administration.

Another aspect of the Chinese legacy was the spread of Buddhist, Daoist, and Confucian ideas, which supplemented the Viets' traditional belief in nature spirits. Buddhist precepts became popular among the local population, who integrated the new faith into their existing belief system by founding Buddhist temples dedicated to the local village deity in the hope of guaranteeing an abundant harvest. Upper-class Vietnamese educated in the Confucian classics tended to follow the more agnostic Confucian doctrine, but some joined Buddhist monasteries. Daoism also flourished at all levels of society and, as in China, provided a structure for animistic beliefs and practices that still predominated at the village level.

During the early period of independence, Vietnamese culture also borrowed liberally from its larger neighbor. Educated Vietnamese tried their hand at Chinese poetry, wrote dynastic histories in the Chinese style, and followed Chinese models in sculpture, architecture, and porcelain. Many

Courtesy of William J. Duiker

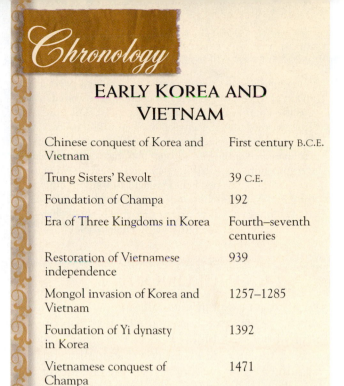

Chronology

EARLY KOREA AND VIETNAM

Chinese conquest of Korea and Vietnam	First century B.C.E.
Trung Sisters' Revolt	39 C.E.
Foundation of Champa	192
Era of Three Kingdoms in Korea	Fourth–seventh centuries
Restoration of Vietnamese independence	939
Mongol invasion of Korea and Vietnam	1257–1285
Foundation of Yi dynasty in Korea	1392
Vietnamese conquest of Champa	1471

THE TEMPLE OF LITERATURE, HANOI. When the Vietnamese regained their independence from China in the tenth century C.E., they retained Chinese institutions that they deemed beneficial. A prime example was the establishment of the Temple of Literature, Vietnam's first university, in 1076. Here the sons of mandarins (officials) were educated in the Confucian classics in preparation for an official career. Beginning in the fifteenth century, those receiving doctorates had stelae erected to identify their achievements. Shown here is the central hall of the temple, where advanced students took the metropolitan examinations for the doctorate.

of the notable buildings of the medieval period, such as the Temple of Literature and the famous One-Pillar Pagoda in Hanoi, are classic examples of Chinese architecture.

But there were signs that Vietnamese creativity would eventually transcend the bounds of Chinese cultural norms. Although most classical writing was undertaken in literary Chinese, the only form of literary expression deemed suitable by Confucian conservatives, an adaptation of Chinese written characters, called *chu nom* ("southern characters"), was devised to provide a written system for spoken Vietnamese. In use by the early ninth century, it eventually began to be used for the composition of essays and poetry in the Vietnamese language. Such pioneering efforts would lead in later centuries to the emergence of a vigorous national literature totally independent of Chinese forms.

Society and Family Life

Vietnamese social institutions and customs were also strongly influenced by those of China. As in China, the introduction of a Confucian system and the adoption of civil service examinations undermined the role of the old landed aristocrats and led eventually to their replacement by the scholar-gentry class. Also as in China, the examinations

were open to most males, regardless of family background, which opened the door to a degree of social mobility unknown in most of the states elsewhere in the region. Candidates for the bureaucracy read many of the same Confucian classics and absorbed the same ethical principles as their counterparts in China. At the same time, they were also exposed to the classic works of Vietnamese history, which strengthened their sense that Vietnam was a distinct culture similar to, but separate from, that of China.

The vast majority of the Vietnamese people, however, were peasants. Most were small landholders or sharecroppers who rented their plots from wealthier farmers, but large estates were rare due to the systematic efforts of the central government to prevent the rise of a powerful local landed elite.

Family life in Vietnam was similar in many respects to that in China. The Confucian concept of family took hold during the period of Chinese rule, along with the related concepts of filial piety and gender inequality. Perhaps the most striking difference between family traditions in China and Vietnam was that Vietnamese women possessed more rights both in practice and by law. Since ancient times, wives had been permitted to own property and initiate divorce proceedings. One consequence of Chinese rule was a growing emphasis on male dominance, but the tradition of women's rights was never totally extinguished and was legally recognized in a law code promulgated in 1460.

Moreover, Vietnam had a strong historical tradition associating heroic women with the defense of the homeland. The Trung Sisters were the first but by no means the only example. In the following passage, a Vietnamese historian of the eighteenth century recounts their story:

The imperial court was far away; local officials were greedy and oppressive. At that time the country of one hundred sons was the country of the women of Lord To. The ladies [the Trung Sisters] used the female arts against their irreconcilable foe; skirts and hairpins sang of patriotic righteousness, uttered a solemn oath at the inner door of the ladies' quarters, expelled the governor, and seized the capital. . . . Were they not grand heroines? . . . Our two ladies brought forward an army of all the people, and, establishing a royal court that settled affairs in the territories of the sixty-five strongholds, shook their skirts over the Hundred Yueh [the Vietnamese people].[7]

 ## CONCLUSION

There are some tantalizing similarities among the three countries we have examined in this chapter. All borrowed liberally from the Chinese model. At the same time, all adapted Chinese institutions and values to the conditions prevailing in their own societies. Though all expressed admiration and respect for China's achievement, all sought to keep Chinese power at a distance.

As an island nation, Japan was the most successful of the three in protecting its political sovereignty and its cultural identity. Both Korea and Vietnam were compelled on various occasions to defend their independence by force of arms. That experience may have shaped their strong sense of national distinctiveness, which we shall discuss further in a later chapter.

The appeal of Chinese institutions can undoubtedly be explained by the fact that Japan, Korea, and Vietnam were all agrarian societies, much like their larger neighbor. But it is undoubtedly significant that the aspect of Chinese political culture that was least amenable to adoption abroad was the civil service examination system. The Confucian concept of meritocracy ran directly counter to the strong aristocratic tradition that flourished in all three societies during their early stage of development. Even when the system was adopted, it was put to quite different uses. Only in Vietnam did the concept of merit eventually triumph over that of birth, as strong rulers of Dai Viet attempted to initiate the Chinese model as a means of creating a centralized system of government.

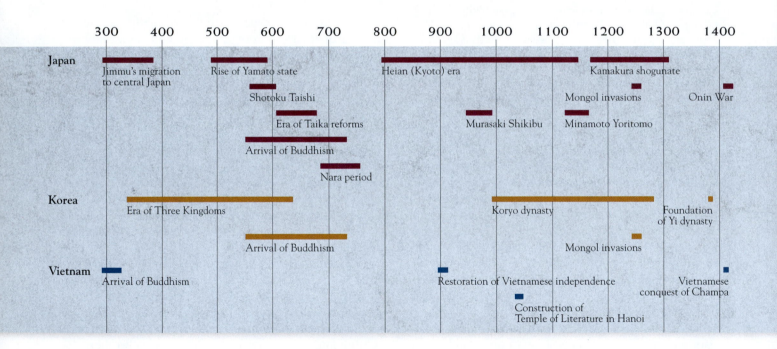

CHAPTER NOTES

1. Keith W. Taylor, *The Birth of Vietnam* (Berkeley, Calif., 1983), p. 75.
2. Quoted in David John Lu, *Sources of Japanese History*, vol. 1 (New York, 1974), p. 7.
3. From "The History of Wei," quoted in ibid., p. 10.
4. From "The Law of Households," quoted in ibid., p. 32.
5. From "On the Salvation of Women," quoted in ibid., p. 127.
6. Quoted in Barbara Ruch, "The Other Side of Culture in Medieval Japan," in Kozo Yamamura, ed., *The Cambridge History of Japan*, vol. 3, *Medieval Japan* (Cambridge, 1990), p. 506.
7. Quoted in Taylor, *The Birth of Vietnam*, pp. 336–337.

SUGGESTED READING

Some of the standard treatments of the rise of Japanese civilization appear in textbooks dealing with the early history of East Asia. Two of the best are J. K. Fairbank, E. O. Reischauer, and A. M. Craig, *East Asia: Tradition and Transformation* (Boston, 1973), and C. Schirokauer, *A Brief History of Chinese and Japanese Civilizations* (San Diego, Calif., 1989). A number of historical works deal specifically with early Japan. G. Sansom, *A History of Japan to 1334* (Stanford, Calif., 1958), is now somewhat out of date but is still informative and very well written. For the latest scholarship on the early period, see the first three volumes of *The Cambridge History of Japan,* ed. J. W. Hall, M. B. Jansen, M. Kanai, and D. Twitchett (Cambridge, 1988).

The best available collections of documents on the early history of Japan are D. J. Lu, ed., *Sources of Japanese History,* vol. 1 (New York, 1974), and Ryusaku Tsunoda et al., eds., *Sources of Japanese Tradition,* vol. 1 (New York, 1958).

For specialized books on the early historical period, see R. J. Pearson, ed., *Windows on the Japanese Past: Studies in Archaeology and Prehistory* (Ann Arbor, Mich., 1986). J. W. Hall, *Government and Local Power in Japan, 500–1700* (Princeton, N.J., 1966), provides a detailed analysis of the development of Japanese political institutions. The relationship between disease and state building is analyzed in W. W. Farris, *Population, Disease, and Land in Early Japan, 645–900* (Cambridge, 1985). The Kamakura period is covered in J. P. Mass, ed., *Court and Bakufu in Japan: Essays in Kamakura History* (New Haven, Conn., 1982). See also H. P. Varley, *The Onin War* (New York, 1977). For Japanese Buddhism, see W. T. de Bary, ed., *The Buddhist Tradition in India, China, and Japan* (New York, 1972).

A concise and provocative introduction to women's issues during this period in Japan, as well as in other parts of the world, can be found in S. S. Hughes and B. Hughes, *Women in World History* (Armonk, N.Y., 1995). For a tenth-century account of daily life for women at the Japanese court, see I. Morris, trans. and ed., *The Pillow Book of Sei Shonagon* (New York, 1991). For the changes that took place from matrilocal and matrilineal marriages to a patriarchal society, consult H. Tonomura, "Black Hair and Red Trousers: Gendering the Flesh in Medieval Japan," in *American Historical Review* 99 (1994).

The best introduction to Japanese literature for college students is still the concise and insightful D. Keene, *Japanese Literature: An Introduction for Western Readers* (London, 1953). The most comprehensive anthology is D. Keene, *Anthology of Japanese Literature* (New York, 1955), while the best history of Japanese literature, also by D. Keene, is *Seeds in the Heart: Japanese Literature from Earlier Times to the Late Sixteenth Century* (New York, 1993).

For the text of *The Tale of Genji,* see the translation by E. Seidensticker (New York, 1976). The most accessible edition for college students is the same author's abridged Vintage Classics edition of 1990, which captures the spirit of the original in 360 pages. Of the many works on the novel, a most stimulating presentation is I. Morris, *The World of the Shining Prince: Court Life in Ancient Japan* (New York, 1964).

For the most comprehensive introduction to Japanese art, consult P. Mason, *History of Japanese Art* (New York, 1993). Also see the concise J. Stanley-Baker, *Japanese Art* (London, 1984). For a stimulating text with magnificent illustrations, see D. Elisseeff and V. Elisseeff, *Art of Japan* (New York, 1985). See also J. E. Kidder Jr., *The Art of Japan* (London, 1985), for an insightful text accompanied by beautiful photographs.

For an informative and readable history of Korea, see Lee Ki-baik, *A New History of Korea* (Cambridge, 1984). P. H. Lee, ed., *Sourcebook of Korean Civilization,* vol. 1 (New York, 1993), is a rich collection of documents dating from the period prior to the sixteenth century.

Vietnam often receives little attention in general studies of Southeast Asia because it was part of the Chinese empire for much of the traditional period. For a detailed investigation of the origins of Vietnamese civilization, see K. W. Taylor, *The Birth of Vietnam* (Berkeley, Calif., 1983). T. Hodgkin, *Vietnam: The Revolutionary Path* (New York, 1981), provides an overall survey of Vietnamese history to modern times. See also J. Buttinger, *The Smaller Dragon: A Political History of Vietnam* (New York, 1966).

INFOTRAC COLLEGE EDITION

For additional reading, go to InfoTrac College Edition, your online research library at
http://web1.infotrac-college.com

Enter the search terms "Asia history" using Keywords.

Enter the search terms "Japan history" using Keywords.

Enter the search term "Shinto" using Keywords.

Enter the search terms "Korea history" using Keywords.

Enter the search terms "Zen Buddhism" using Keywords.

The Art Archive, London, from the collections of the British Library

Chapter 12

THE MAKING OF EUROPE IN THE MIDDLE AGES

CHAPTER OUTLINE

- TRANSFORMATION OF THE ROMAN WORLD
- THE WORLD OF LORDS AND VASSALS
- EVOLUTION OF THE EUROPEAN KINGDOMS
- THE WORLD OF PEASANTS AND TOWNSPEOPLE
- CHRISTIANITY AND MEDIEVAL CIVILIZATION
- THE CULTURE OF THE HIGH MIDDLE AGES
- THE EXPANSION OF MEDIEVAL EUROPE: THE CRUSADES
- THE LATE MIDDLE AGES: A TIME OF TROUBLES IN EUROPE

FOCUS QUESTIONS

- What contributions did the Romans, the Christian church, and the Germanic peoples make to the new civilization that emerged in Europe after the collapse of the western Roman Empire?
- What roles did aristocrats, peasants, and townspeople play in medieval European civilization, and how did their lifestyles differ?
- What were the main aspects of the political, economic, and spiritual revivals that took place in Europe during the High Middle Ages?
- What were the major intellectual and cultural achievements of European civilization in the High Middle Ages?
- ➤ What problems did Europeans face during the fourteenth century, and what impact did they have on European economic, social, and religious life?

In 800, Charlemagne, the king of the Franks, journeyed to Rome to help Pope Leo III, head of the Catholic church, who was barely clinging to power in the face of rebellious Romans. On Christmas Day, Charlemagne and his family, attended by Romans and Franks, crowded into Saint Peter's Basilica to hear Mass. Quite unexpectedly, according to a Frankish writer, "as the king rose from praying before the tomb of the blessed apostle Peter, Pope Leo placed a golden crown on his head." The people in the church shouted, "Long life and victory to Charles Augustus, crowned by God the great and peace-loving Emperor of the Romans." Seemingly, the Roman Empire in the west had been reborn, and Charles had become the first Roman emperor since 476. But this "Roman emperor" was actually a German king, and he had been crowned by the head of the western Christian church. In truth, the coronation of Charlemagne was a sign not of the rebirth of the Roman Empire but of the emergence of a new European civilization that came into being in western Europe after the collapse of the western Roman Empire.

This new civilization—European civilization—was formed by the coming together of three major elements: the legacy of the Romans, the Christian church, and the Germanic peoples who moved in and settled the western empire. European civilization developed during a period that historians call the Middle Ages, or the medieval period, which lasted from about 500 to about 1400. To historians who first used the title, the Middle Ages was a middle period between the ancient world and the modern world. •

TRANSFORMATION OF THE ROMAN WORLD

Already by the third century C.E., Germanic peoples had begun to move into the lands of the Roman Empire. By 500, the western Roman Empire had been replaced politically by a series of states ruled by German kings.

The New Germanic Kingdoms

The fusion of Romans and Germans took different forms in the various Germanic kingdoms. Both the kingdom of the Ostrogoths in Italy and the kingdom of the Visigoths in Spain (see Map 12.1) maintained the Roman structure for the larger native populations, while a Germanic warrior caste came to dominate. Over a period of time, Germans and natives began to fuse. In Britain, however, when the Roman armies abandoned Britain at the beginning of the fifth century, the Angles and Saxons, Germanic tribes from Denmark and northern Germany, moved in and settled there.

THE KINGDOM OF THE FRANKS

Only one of the German states on the European continent proved long-lasting—the kingdom of the Franks. The establishment of a Frankish kingdom was the work of Clovis (c. 482–511), who became a Catholic Christian around 500. Clovis found that his conversion to Catholic Christianity gained him the support of the Roman Catholic church, as the Christian church in Rome had become known, which was only too eager to obtain the friendship of a major ruler in the Germanic states. By 510, Clovis had established a powerful new Frankish kingdom stretching from the Pyrenees in the west to German lands in the east (modern France and western Germany). After Clovis's death, however, as was the Frankish custom, his sons divided his newly created kingdom, and during the sixth and seventh centuries, the once-united Frankish kingdom came to be divided into three major areas: Neustria, Austrasia, and Burgundy.

THE SOCIETY OF THE GERMANIC PEOPLES

As Germans and Romans intermarried and began to create a new society, some of the social customs of the Germanic peoples came to play an important role. The crucial social bond among the Germanic peoples was the family, especially the extended family of husbands, wives, children, brothers, sisters, cousins, and grandparents. The German family structure was quite simple. Males were dominant and made all the important decisions. A woman obeyed her father until she married and then fell under the legal domination of her husband. For most women in the new Germanic kingdoms, their legal status reflected the material conditions of their lives. Most women had life expectancies of only thirty or forty years, and perhaps 15 percent of women died in their childbearing years, no doubt due to complications associated with childbirth. For most women, life consisted of domestic labor: providing food and clothing for the household, caring for the children, and assisting with farming chores.

The German conception of family affected the way Germanic law treated the problem of crime and punishment. In the Roman system, as in our own, a crime such as murder was considered an offense against society or the state and was handled by a court that heard evidence and arrived at a decision. Germanic law was personal. An injury by one person against another could lead to a blood feud in which the family of the injured party took revenge on the family of the wrongdoer. Feuds could lead to savage acts of revenge, such as hacking off hands or feet or gouging out eyes. Because this system could easily get out of control, an alternative system arose that made use of a fine called *wergeld*, which was the amount paid by a wrongdoer to the family of the person injured or killed. *Wergeld*, which means "money for a man," was the value of a person in monetary terms. That value varied considerably according to social status. An offense against a nobleman, for example,

GERMANIC CUSTOMARY LAW: THE ORDEAL

In Germanic customary law, the ordeal was used as a means by which accused persons might clear themselves. Although the ordeal took different forms, all involved a physical trial of some sort, such as holding a red-hot iron. It was believed that God would protect the innocent and allow them to come through the ordeal unharmed. This sixth-century account by Gregory of Tours describes an ordeal by hot water.

GREGORY OF TOURS, AN ORDEAL OF HOT WATER (c. 580)

An Arian presbyter disputing with a deacon of our religion made venomous assertions against the Son of God and the Holy Ghost, as is the habit of that sect [the Arians]. But when the deacon had discoursed a long time concerning the reasonableness of our faith and the heretic, blinded by the fog of unbelief, continued to reject the truth, . . . the former said: "Why weary ourselves with long discussions? Let acts approve the truth; let a kettle be heated over the fire and someone's ring be thrown into the boiling water. Let him who shall take it from the heated liquid be approved as a follower of the truth, and afterward let the other party be converted to the knowledge of the truth. And do you also understand, O heretic, that this our party will fulfill the conditions with the aid of the Holy Ghost; you shalt confess that there is no discordance, no dissimilarity in the Holy Trinity." The heretic consented to the proposition and they separated after appointing the next morning for the trial. But the fervor of faith in which the deacon had first made this suggestion began to cool through the instigation of the enemy. Rising with the dawn he bathed his arm in oil and smeared it with ointment. But neverthe-less he made the round of the sacred places and called in prayer on the Lord. . . . About the third hour they met in the marketplace. The people came together to see the show. A fire was lighted, the kettle was placed upon it, and when it grew very hot the ring was thrown into the boiling water. The deacon invited the heretic to take it out of the water first. But he promptly refused, saying, "You who did propose this trial are the one to take it out." The deacon all of a tremble bared his arm. And when the heretic presbyter saw it besmeared with ointment he cried out: "With magic arts you have thought to protect yourself, that you have made use of these salves, but what you have done will not avail." While they were thus quarreling there came up a deacon from Ravenna named Iacinthus and inquired what the trouble was about. When he learned the truth he drew his arm out from under his robe at once and plunged his right hand into the kettle. Now the ring that had been thrown in was a little thing and very light so that it was thrown about by the water as chaff would be blown about by the wind; and searching for it a long time he found it after about an hour. Meanwhile the flame beneath the kettle blazed up mightily so that the greater heat might make it difficult for the ring to be followed by the hand; but the deacon extracted it at length and suffered no harm, protesting rather that at the bottom the kettle was cold while at the top it was just pleasantly warm. When the heretic beheld this he was greatly confused and audaciously thrust his hand into the kettle saying, "My faith will aid me." As soon as his hand had been thrust in all the flesh was boiled off the bones clear up to the elbow. And so the dispute ended.

cost considerably more than one against a freeman or a slave.

Germanic law also provided a means of determining guilt: the ordeal. The ordeal was based on the idea of divine intervention; divine forces (whether pagan or Christian) would not allow an innocent person to be harmed (see the box above).

The Role of the Christian Church

By the end of the fourth century, Christianity had become the predominant religion of the Roman Empire. As the official Roman state disintegrated, the Christian church played an increasingly important role in the growth of the new European civilization.

THE ORGANIZATION OF THE CHURCH

By the fourth century, the Christian church had developed a system of government. The Christian community in each city was headed by a bishop, whose area of jurisdiction was known as a bishopric, or diocese; the bishoprics of each Roman province were joined together under the direction of an archbishop. The bishops of four great cities—Rome, Jerusalem, Alexandria, and Antioch—held positions of special power in church affairs because the churches in these cities all asserted that they had been founded by the original apostles sent out by Jesus. Soon, however, one of them—the bishop of Rome—claimed that he was the sole leader of the western Christian church. According to church tradition,

MAP 12.1 The New Kingdoms of the Old Western Empire. Germanic tribes filled the power vacuum caused by the demise of the Roman Empire, building states that blended elements of Germanic customs and laws with those of Roman culture, including large-scale conversions to Christianity. The Franks established the most durable of these Germanic states. ➤ *How did the movements of Franks during this period correspond to the borders of present-day France?*

Jesus had given the keys to the kingdom of heaven to Peter, who was considered the chief apostle and the first bishop of Rome. Subsequent bishops of Rome were considered Peter's successors and came to be known as popes (from the Latin word *papa*, meaning "father"). By the sixth century, popes had been successful in extending papal authority over the Christian church in the west and converting the pagan peoples of Germanic Europe. Their primary instrument of conversion was the monastic movement.

THE MONKS AND THEIR MISSIONS

A monk (in Latin, *monachus*, meaning "someone who lives alone") was a man who sought to live a life divorced from the world, cut off from ordinary human society, in order to pursue an ideal of total dedication to God. As the monastic ideal spread, a new form of monasticism based on living together in a community soon became the dominant form. Saint Benedict (c. 480–c. 543), who founded a monastic house for which he wrote a set of rules, established the basic form of monastic life in the western Christian church. The Benedictine rule came to be used by other monastic groups and was crucial to the growth of monasticism in the western Christian world.

Benedict's rule divided each day into a series of activities, with primary emphasis on prayer and manual labor. Physical work of some kind was required of all monks for several hours a day because idleness was "the enemy of the soul." At the very heart of community practice was prayer, the proper "work of God." Although this included private meditation and reading, all monks gathered together seven times during the day for common prayer and chanting of psalms. The Benedictine life was a communal one. Monks ate, worked, slept, and worshiped together.

Each Benedictine monastery was strictly ruled by an abbot, or "father" of the monastery, who had complete authority over his fellow monks. Unquestioning obedience to the will of the abbot was expected of every monk. Each Benedictine monastery held lands that enabled it to be a self-sustaining community, isolated from and independent of the world surrounding it. Within the monastery, however, monks were to fulfill their vow of poverty: "Let all things be common to all, as it is written, lest anyone should say that anything is his own."[1] Only men could be monks, but women, called nuns, also began to withdraw from the world to dedicate themselves to God.

Monasticism played an indispensable role in early medieval civilization. Monks became the new heroes of Christian civilization, and their dedication to God became the highest ideal of Christian life. They were the social workers of their communities: monks provided schools for the young, hospitality for travelers, and hospitals for the sick. Monks also copied Latin works and passed on the legacy of the ancient world to the new European civilization. Monasteries became centers of learning wherever they were located, and monks worked to spread Christianity to all of Europe.

Women played an important role in the monastic missionary movement and the conversion of the Germanic kingdoms. Some served as abbesses (an abbess was the head of a monastery or a convent for nuns); many abbesses came from aristocratic families, especially in Anglo-Saxon England. In the kingdom of Northumbria, for example, Saint Hilda founded the monastery of Whitby in 657. As abbess, she was responsible for making learning an important part of the life of the monastery. Five future bishops were educated under her direction.

Charlemagne and the Carolingians

During the seventh and eighth centuries, as the kings of the Frankish kingdom gradually lost their power, the mayors of the palace—the chief officers of the king's household—

THE CORONATION OF CHARLEMAGNE.   After rebellion in 799 forced Pope Leo III to seek refuge at Charlemagne's court, Charlemagne went to Rome to settle the affair. There, on Christmas Day 800, he was crowned emperor of the Romans by the pope. This manuscript illustration shows Leo III placing a crown on Charlemagne's head.

The Granger Collection

THE ACHIEVEMENTS OF CHARLEMAGNE

Einhard, the biographer of Charlemagne, was born in the valley of the Main River in Germany about 775. Raised and educated in the monastery of Fulda, an important center of learning, he arrived at the court of Charlemagne in 791 or 792. Although he did not achieve high office under Charlemagne, he served as private secretary to Louis the Pious, Charlemagne's son and successor. In this selection, Einhard discusses some of Charlemagne's accomplishments.

EINHARD, *LIFE OF CHARLEMAGNE*

Such are the wars, most skillfully planned and successfully fought, which this most powerful king waged during the forty-seven years of his reign. He so largely increased the Frank kingdom, which was already great and strong when he received it at his father's hands, that more than double its former territory was added to it. . . . He subdued all the wild and barbarous tribes dwelling in Germany between the Rhine and the Vistula, the Ocean and the Danube, all of which speak very much the same language, but differ widely from one another in customs and dress. . . .

He added to the glory of his reign by gaining the good will of several kings and nations; so close, indeed, was the alliance that he contracted with Alfonso, King of Galicia and Asturias, that the latter, when sending letters or ambassadors to Charles, invariably styled himself his man. . . . The Emperors of Constantinople [the Byzantine emperors] sought friendship and alliance with Charles by several embassies; and even when the Greeks [the Byzantines] suspected him of designing to take the empire from them, because of his assumption of the title Emperor, they made a close alliance with him, that he might have no cause of offense. In fact, the power of the Franks was always viewed with a jealous eye, whence the Greek proverb, "Have the Frank for your friend, but not for your neighbor."

This King, who showed himself so great in extending his empire and subduing foreign nations, and was constantly occupied with plans to that end, undertook also very many works calculated to adorn and benefit his kingdom, and brought several of them to completion. Among these, the most deserving of mention are the basilica of the Holy Mother of God at Aix-la-Chapelle [Aachen], built in the most admirable manner, and a bridge over the Rhine River at Mainz, half a mile long, the breadth of the river at this point. . . . Above all, sacred buildings were the object of his care throughout his whole kingdom; and whenever he found them falling to ruin from age, he commanded the priests and fathers who had charge of them to repair them, and made sure by commissioners that his instructions were obeyed. . . . Thus did Charles defend and increase as well as beautify his kingdom. . . .

He cherished with the greatest fervor and devotion the principles of the Christian religion, which had been instilled into him from infancy. Hence it was that he built the beautiful church at Aix-la-Chapelle, which he adorned with gold and silver and lamps, and with rails and doors of solid brass. He had the columns and marbles for this structure brought from Rome and Ravenna, for he could not find such as were suitable elsewhere. He was a constant worshiper at this church as long as his health permitted, going morning and evening, even after nightfall, besides attending mass. . . .

He was very forward in caring for the poor, so much so that he not only made a point of giving in his own country and his own kingdom, but when he discovered that there were Christians living in poverty in Syria, Egypt, and Africa, at Jerusalem, Alexandria, and Carthage, he had compassion on their wants, and used to send money over the seas to them. . . . He sent great and countless gifts to the popes, and throughout his whole reign the wish that he had nearest at heart was to reestablish the ancient authority of the city of Rome under his care and by his influence, and to defend and protect the Church of St. Peter, and to beautify and enrich it out of his own store above all other churches.

assumed more control of the kingdom. One of these mayors, Pepin, finally took the logical step of assuming the kingship of the Frankish state for himself and his family. Upon his death in 768, his son came to the throne of the Frankish kingdom.

This new king was the dynamic and powerful ruler known to history as Charles the Great (768–814), or Charlemagne (from the Latin *Carolus Magnus*). He was determined and decisive, intelligent and inquisitive, a strong statesman, and a

Charlemagne's Empire

FRISIA · SAXONY · Aachen · Verdun · Mainz · TRIBUTARY SLAVIC · BRITTANY · Paris · AUSTRASIA · Loire · ALEMANNI · NEUSTRIA · BURGUNDY · BAVARIA · Bordeaux · Alps · PEOPLES · AQUITAINE · Milan · VENETIA · Pyrenees · PAPAL STATES · Rome · Adriatic Sea

☐ Frankish kingdom, 768
☐ Territories gained by Charlemagne

pious Christian. Himself unable to read or write, he was a wise patron of learning. In a series of military campaigns, he greatly expanded the territory he had inherited and created what came to be known as the Carolingian Empire. At its height, Charlemagne's empire covered much of western and central Europe; not until the time of Napoleon in the nineteenth century would an empire of its size be seen again in Europe (see the box above).

Charlemagne continued the efforts of his father in organizing the Carolingian kingdom. Besides his household staff, Charlemagne's administration of the empire depended on the use of counts as the king's chief representatives in local areas. As an important check on the power of the counts, Charlemagne established the *missi dominici* ("messengers of the lord king"), two men who were sent out to local districts to ensure that the counts were executing the king's wishes.

As Charlemagne's power grew, so did his prestige as the most powerful Christian ruler; one monk even wrote that he ruled the "kingdom of Europe." In 800, Charlemagne acquired a new title: emperor of the Romans. Charlemagne's coronation as Roman emperor demonstrated the strength, even after three hundred years, of the concept of an enduring Roman Empire. More important, it symbolized the fusion of the Roman, Christian, and Germanic elements that formed the base of European civilization. A Germanic king had been crowned emperor of the Romans by the spiritual leader of western Christendom. A new civilization had emerged.

THE WORLD OF LORDS AND VASSALS

The Carolingian Empire began to disintegrate soon after Charlemagne's death in 814, and less than thirty years later, in 843, it was divided among his grandsons into three major sections. At the same time, powerful nobles gained even more power in their own local territories while the Carolingian rulers fought each other. Invasions in different parts of the old Carolingian world added to the process of disintegration.

Invasions of the Ninth and Tenth Centuries

In the ninth and tenth centuries, western Europe was beset by a wave of invasions. Muslims attacked the southern coasts of Europe and sent raiding parties into southern France. The Magyars, a people from western Asia, moved into central Europe at the end of the ninth century and settled on the plains of Hungary, from where they made forays into western Europe. Finally crushed at the Battle of Lechfeld in Germany in 955, the Magyars converted to Christianity and settled down to create the kingdom of Hungary.

The most far-reaching attacks of the time came from the Northmen or Norsemen of Scandinavia, also known to us as the Vikings. The Vikings were warriors whose love of adventure and search for booty and new avenues of trade may have led them to invade other areas of Europe. Viking ships were the best of the period. Long and narrow

with beautifully carved arched prows, the Viking dragon ships carried about fifty men. Their shallow draft enabled them to sail up European rivers and attack places at some distance inland. In the ninth century, Vikings sacked villages and towns, destroyed churches, and easily defeated small local armies. Viking attacks frightened people and led many a clergyman to plead with them to change their behavior and appease God's anger, as is revealed in this sermon in 1014 by an English archbishop:

> Things have not gone well now for a long time at home or abroad, but there has been devastation and persecution in every district again and again, and the English have been for a long time now completely defeated and too greatly disheartened through God's anger; and the pirates [Vikings] so strong with God's consent that often in battle one puts to flight ten, and sometimes less, sometimes more, all because of our sins. . . . We pay them continually and they humiliate us daily; they ravage and they burn, plunder, and rob and carry on board; and lo, what else is there in all these events except God's anger clear and visible over this people?[2]

By the mid-ninth century, the Northmen had begun to build winter settlements in different areas of Europe. By 850, groups of Norsemen from Norway had settled in Ireland, and Danes occupied northeastern England by 878. Beginning in 911, the ruler of the western Frankish lands gave one band of Vikings land at the mouth of the Seine River, forming a section of France that came to be known as Normandy. This policy of settling the Vikings and converting them to Christianity was a deliberate one; by their conversion to Christianity, the Vikings were soon made a part of European civilization.

The Development of Fief-Holding

The disintegration of central authority in the Carolingian world and the invasions by Muslims, Magyars, and Vikings led to the emergence of a new type of relationship between free individuals. When governments ceased to be able to defend their subjects, it became important to find some powerful lord who could offer protection in return for service. The contract sworn between a lord and his subordinate (known as a vassal) is the basis of a form of social organization that later generations of historians viewed as an organized system of government, which they called feudalism. But feudalism was never a system, and many historians today prefer to avoid using the term.

With the breakdown of royal governments, powerful nobles took control of large areas of land. They needed men to fight for them, so the practice arose of giving grants of land to vassals who in return would fight for their lord. The Frankish army had originally consisted of foot soldiers, dressed in coats of mail and armed with

THE VIKINGS ATTACK ENGLAND. This illustration from an eleventh-century English manuscript depicts a group of armed Vikings invading England. Two ships have already reached the shore, and a few Vikings are shown walking down a long gangplank onto English soil. Also shown is a replica of a well-preserved Viking ship found at Oseberg, Norway. The Oseberg ship was one of the largest Viking ships in its day.

swords. But in the eighth century, a military change began to occur when larger horses and the stirrup were introduced. Earlier, horsemen had been throwers of spears. Now they came to be armored in coats of mail (the larger horse could carry the weight) and wielded long lances that enabled them to act as battering rams (the stirrup kept them on their horses). For almost five hundred years, warfare in Europe would be dominated by heavily armored cavalry, or knights, as they came to be called.

Of course, it was expensive to have a horse, armor, and weapons. It also took time and much practice to learn to wield these instruments skillfully from horse-back. Consequently, lords who wanted men to fight for them had to grant each vassal a piece of land that provided for the support of the vassal and his family. In return for the land, the vassal provided his lord with his fighting skills. Each needed the other. In the society of the Early Middle Ages (from 500 to 1000), where there was little trade and wealth was based primarily on land, land became the most important gift a lord could give to a vassal in return for his loyalty and military service.

By the ninth century, the grant of land made to a vassal had become known as a fief. A fief was a piece of land held from the lord by a vassal in return for military service, but vassals who held such grants of land came to exercise rights of jurisdiction or political and legal authority within these fiefs. As the Carolingian world disintegrated politically under the impact of internal dissension and invasions, an increasing number of powerful lords arose who were now responsible for keeping order.

The Practice of Fief-Holding

Fief-holding also became increasingly complicated with the development of subinfeudation. The vassals of a king, who were themselves great lords, might also have vassals who would owe them military service in return for a grant of land taken from their estates. Those vassals, in turn, might likewise have vassals, who at such a level would be simple knights with barely enough land to provide their equipment. The lord-vassal relationship, then, bound together both greater and lesser landowners. At all levels, the lord-vassal relationship was always an honorable relationship between free men and did not imply any sense of servitude.

Fief-holding came to be characterized by a set of practices, known as the feudal contract, that determined the relationship between a lord and his vassal. The major obligation of a vassal to his lord was to perform military service, usually about forty days a year. A vassal was also required to appear at his lord's court when summoned to give advice to the lord. He might also be asked to sit in judgment in a legal case, since the important vassals of a lord were peers and only they could judge each other. Finally, vassals were also responsible for aids, or financial payments to the lord on a number of occasions, among them the knighting of the lord's eldest son, the marriage of his eldest daughter, and the ransom of the lord's person if he were captured.

Under the feudal contract, a lord also had responsibilities toward his vassals. His major obligation was to protect his vassal, either by defending him militarily or by taking his side in a court of law. The lord was also responsible for the maintenance of the vassal, usually by granting him a fief.

The Nobility of the Middle Ages

In the High Middle Ages (the period between 1000 and 1300), European society, like that of Japan during the same period, was dominated by men whose chief concern was warfare. Like the Japanese samurai, many nobles loved war. As one nobleman wrote:

And well I like to hear the call of "Help" and see the
    wounded fall,
Loudly for mercy praying,
And see the dead, both great and small,
Pierced by sharp spearheads one and all.[3]

The men of war were the lords and vassals of medieval society.

The lords were the kings, dukes, counts, barons, and viscounts (and even bishops and archbishops) who had extensive landholdings and wielded considerable political influence. They formed an aristocracy or nobility of people who held real political, economic, and social

➤ **THE TOURNAMENT.** The tournament arose as a socially acceptable alternative to the private warfare that plagued the nobility in the Middle Ages. This fifteenth-century Flemish illustration shows a joust between two heavily armored knights. Shown watching are King Richard II in the middle and the other onlookers at the right. Like the Japanese samurai, European knights were engaged almost constantly in fighting and war.

power. Both the great lords and ordinary knights were warriors, and the institution of knighthood united them. But there were also social divisions among them based on extremes of wealth and landholdings.

ARISTOCRATIC WOMEN

Although women could legally hold property, most women remained under the control of men—their fathers until they married and their husbands after that. Nevertheless, aristocratic women had many opportunities for playing important roles. Because the lord was often away at war or at court, the lady of the castle had to manage the estate. Households could include large numbers of officials and servants, so this was no small responsibility. Maintaining the financial accounts alone took considerable financial knowledge. The lady of the castle was also responsible on a regular basis for overseeing the food supply and maintaining all the other supplies needed for the smooth operation of the household.

Although women were expected to be subservient to their husbands, there were many strong women who advised and sometimes even dominated their husbands. Perhaps most famous was Eleanor of Aquitaine (c. 1122–1204). Married to King Louis VII of France, Eleanor accompanied her husband on a Crusade, but her alleged affair with her uncle during the Crusade led Louis to have their marriage annulled. Eleanor then married Henry, duke of Normandy, who became King Henry II of England (1154–1189). She took an active role in politics, even assisting her sons in rebelling against Henry in 1173 and 1174. Imprisoned for her activities, after Henry's death she again assumed an active political life, providing both military and political support for her sons.

EVOLUTION OF THE EUROPEAN KINGDOMS

The domination of society by the nobility reached its apex in the High Middle Ages. At the same time, kings began extending their power, and out of this growth in the monarchies would eventually come the European states that dominated much of later European history.

England in the High Middle Ages

On October 14, 1066, an army of heavily armed knights under William of Normandy landed on the coast of England and soundly defeated King Harold and his Anglo-Saxon foot soldiers. William was crowned king of England at Christmastime in London and then began the process of combining Anglo-Saxon and Norman institutions to create a new England. Many of the Norman knights were given parcels of land that they held as fiefs from the new English king. William made all nobles swear an oath of loyalty to him as sole ruler of England and insisted that all people owed loyalty to the king. William also took a census and more fully developed the system of taxation and royal courts begun by the Anglo-Saxon kings of the tenth and eleventh centuries. All in all, William of Normandy established a strong, centralized monarchy.

In the twelfth century, the power of the English monarchy was greatly enlarged during the reign of Henry II (1154–1189). The new king was particularly successful in strengthening the power of the royal courts. Henry expanded the number of criminal cases to be tried in the king's court and also devised means for taking property cases from local courts to the royal courts. Henry's goals were clear: expanding the power of the royal courts expanded the king's power and, of course, brought revenues into his coffers. Moreover, since the royal courts were now found throughout England, a body of common law (law that was common to the whole kingdom) began to replace the different law codes that often varied from place to place.

Many English nobles came to resent the ongoing growth of the king's power and rose in rebellion during the reign of King John (1199–1216). At Runnymeade in 1215, John was forced to seal the Magna Carta (the Great Charter) guaranteeing feudal liberties. Feudal custom had always recognized that the relationship between king and vassals was based on mutual rights and obligations. Magna Carta gave written recognition to that fact and was used in later years to support the idea that a monarch's power was limited.

During the reign of Edward I (1272–1307), an institution of great importance in the development of representative government—the English Parliament—also emerged. Originally, the word *parliament* was applied to meetings of the king's Great Council, in which the greater barons and chief prelates of the church met with the king's judges and principal advisers to deal with judicial affairs. But in his need for money, Edward I in 1295 invited two knights from every county and two residents from each town to meet with the Great Council to consent to new taxes. This was the first Parliament.

The English Parliament, then, came to be composed of two knights from every county and two burgesses from every borough as well as the barons and ecclesiastical lords. Eventually, barons and church lords formed the House of Lords; knights and burgesses, the House of Commons. The Parliaments of Edward I approved taxes, discussed politics, passed laws, and handled judicial business. The law of the realm was beginning to be determined not by the king alone but by the king in

MAP 12.2 Europe in the High Middle Ages.   Although the nobility dominated much of European society in the High Middle Ages, kings began the process of extending their power in more effective ways, creating the monarchies that would form the European states. ➤ *Which were the strongest monarchical states by 1300? Why?*

consultation with representatives of various groups that constituted the community.

Growth of the French Kingdom

In 843, the Carolingian Empire had been divided into three major sections. The western Frankish lands formed the core of the eventual kingdom of France. In 987, after the death of the last Carolingian king, the western Frankish nobles chose Hugh Capet as the new king, thus establishing the Capetian dynasty of French kings. Although they carried the title of kings, the Capetians had little real power. They controlled as the royal domain only the lands around Paris known as the Île-de-France. As kings of France, the Capetians were formally the overlords of the great lords of France, such as the dukes of Normandy, Brittany, Burgundy, and Aquitaine. In reality, however, many of the dukes were considerably more powerful than the Capetian kings.

The reign of King Philip II Augustus (1180–1223) was an important turning point in the growth of the French

monarchy. Philip II waged war against the Plantagenet rulers of England, who also ruled the French territories of Normandy, Maine, Anjou, and Aquitaine, and was successful in gaining control of most of these territories, thus enlarging the power of the French monarchy (see Map 12.2). To administer justice and collect royal revenues in his new territories, Philip appointed new royal officials, thus inaugurating a French royal bureaucracy in the thirteenth century.

Capetian rulers after Philip II continued to add lands to the royal domain. Philip IV the Fair (1285–1314) was especially effective in strengthening the French monarchy. He reinforced the royal bureaucracy and also brought a French parliament into being by asking representatives of the three estates, or classes—the clergy (first estate), the nobles (second estate), and the townspeople (third estate)—to meet with him. They did so in 1302, inaugurating the Estates-General, the first French parliament, although it had little real power. By the end of the thirteenth century, France was the largest, wealthiest, and best-governed monarchical state in Europe.

THE EUROPEAN KINGDOMS

England

Norman Conquest	1066
William the Conqueror	1066–1087
Henry II	1154–1189
John	1199–1216
Magna Carta	1215
Edward I	1272–1307
First Parliament	1295

France

Philip II Augustus	1180–1223
Philip IV	1285–1314
First Estates-General	1302

Germany and the Empire

Otto I	936–973
Frederick I Barbarossa	1152–1190
Northern Italian cities defeat Frederick	1176
Frederick II	1212–1250

The Eastern World

Mongol conquest of Russia	1230s
Alexander Nevsky, prince of Novgorod	c. 1220–1263

The Lands of the Holy Roman Empire

In the tenth century, the powerful dukes of the Saxons became kings of the eastern Frankish kingdom (or Germany, as it came to be called). The best known of the Saxon kings of Germany was Otto I (936–973), who intervened in Italian politics and for his efforts was crowned by the pope in 962 as emperor of the Romans, reviving a title that had not been used since the time of Charlemagne. Otto's creation of a new "Roman Empire" in the hands of the eastern Franks (or Germans) added a tremendous burden to the king of Germany, who now took on the onerous task of ruling Italy as well.

In the eleventh century, German kings created a strong monarchy and a powerful empire by leading armies into Italy. The German kings also tried to bolster their power by using their position as emperors to exploit the resources of Italy. But this tended to backfire; many a German king lost armies in Italy in pursuit of a dream of empire, and no German dynasty demonstrates this better than the Hohenstaufens.

The two most famous members of the Hohenstaufen dynasty, Frederick I (1152–1190) and Frederick II (1212–1250), tried to create a new kind of empire. Previous German kings had focused on building a strong German kingdom, to which Italy might be added as an appendage. Frederick I, however, planned to get his chief revenues from Italy as the center of a "holy empire," as he called it (hence the name Holy Roman Empire). But his attempt to conquer northern Italy ran into severe opposition from the pope and the cities of northern Italy. An alliance of these north Italian cities, with the support of the pope, defeated the forces of Emperor Frederick I in 1176.

The main goal of Frederick II was the establishment of a strong centralized state in Italy dominated by the kingdom he had inherited in Sicily. Frederick's major task was to gain control of northern Italy. In attempting to conquer Italy, however, he became involved in a deadly struggle with the popes, who feared that a single ruler of northern and southern Italy meant the end of papal power in central Italy. The north Italian cities were also unwilling to give up their freedom. Frederick waged a bitter struggle in northern Italy, winning many battles but ultimately losing the war.

The struggle between popes and emperors had dire consequences for the Holy Roman Empire. By spending their time fighting in Italy, the German emperors left Germany in the hands of powerful German lords who ignored the emperor and created their own independent kingdoms. This ensured that the German monarchy would remain weak and incapable of maintaining a centralized monarchical state; thus the German Holy Roman Emperor had no real power over either Germany or Italy. Unlike France and England, neither Germany nor Italy created a unified national monarchy in the Middle Ages. Both Germany and Italy consisted of many small, independent states, a situation that changed little until the nineteenth century.

The Slavic Peoples of Central and Eastern Europe

East of the Carolingian Empire lay a spacious plain through which a number of Asiatic nomads, including the Huns, Bulgars, Avars, and Magyars, had pushed their way westward. Eastern Europe was ravaged by these successive waves of invaders who found it relatively easy to create large empires that were in turn overthrown by the next invaders. Over a period of time, the invaders themselves were largely assimilated with the native Slavic peoples of the area.

The Slavic peoples were originally a single people in central Europe, but they gradually divided into three major groups: the western, southern, and eastern Slavs (see Map 12.3). The western Slavs eventually formed the Polish and Bohemian kingdoms. German Christian missionaries converted both the Czechs in Bohemia and the Slavs in Poland by the tenth century. The non-Slavic kingdom of Hungary, which emerged after the Magyars settled down after their defeat in 955, was also converted to Christianity by German missionaries. The Poles,

A MUSLIM'S DESCRIPTION
OF THE RUS

Despite the difficulties that travel presented, early medieval civilization did witness some contact among the various cultures. This might occur through trade, diplomacy, or the conquest and migration of peoples. This document is a description of the Swedish Rus, who eventually merged with the native Slavic peoples to form the principality of Kiev, commonly regarded as the first Russian state. It was written by Ibn Fadlan, a Muslim diplomat sent from Baghdad in 921 to a settlement on the Volga River. His comments on the filthiness of the Rus reflect the Muslim preoccupation with cleanliness.

IBN FADLAN, DESCRIPTION OF THE RUS

I saw the Rus folk when they arrived on their trading mission and settled at the river Atul (Volga). Never had I seen people of more perfect physique. They are tall as date palms, and reddish in color. They wear neither coat nor kaftan, but each man carried a cape which covers one half of his body, leaving one hand free. No one is ever parted from his axe, sword, and knife. Their swords are Frankish in design, broad, flat, and fluted. Each man has a number of trees, figures, and the like from the fingernails to the neck. Each woman carried on her bosom a container made of iron, silver, copper, or gold—its size and substance depending on her man's wealth.

They [the Rus] are the filthiest of God's creatures. They do not wash after discharging their natural functions, neither do they wash their hands after meals. They are as lousy as donkeys. They arrive from their distant lands and lay their ships alongside the banks of the Atul, which is a great river, and there they build big houses on its shores. Ten or twenty of them may live together in one house, and each of them has a couch of his own where he sits and diverts himself with the pretty slave girls whom he had brought along for sale. He will make love with one of them while a comrade looks on; sometimes they indulge in a communal orgy, and, if a customer should turn up to buy a girl, the Rus man will not let her go till he has finished with her.

They wash their hands and faces every day in incredibly filthy water. Every morning the girl brings her master a large bowl of water in which he washes his hands and face and hair, then blows his nose into it and spits into it. When he has finished the girl takes the bowl to his neighbor—who repeats the performance. Thus the bowl goes the rounds of the entire household. . . .

If one of the Rus folk falls sick they put him in a tent by himself and leave bread and water for him. They do not visit him, however, or speak to him, especially if he is a serf. Should he recover he rejoins the others; if he dies they burn him. But if he happens to be a serf they leave him for the dogs and vultures to devour. If they catch a robber they hang him to a tree until he is torn to shreds by wind and weather.

Czechs, and Hungarians all accepted Catholic or western Christianity and became closely tied to the Roman Catholic church and its Latin culture.

The southern and eastern Slavic populations took a different path: the Slavic peoples of Moravia were converted to the Orthodox Christianity of the Byzantine Empire by two Byzantine missionary brothers, Cyril and Methodius, who began their activities in 863. They created the Slavonic (Cyrillic) alphabet, translated the Bible into Slavonic, and developed Slavonic church services. While the southern Slavic peoples accepted Christianity, a split eventually developed between the Croats, who accepted the Roman Catholic church, and the Serbs, who remained loyal to Orthodox Christianity.

Although the Bulgars were originally an Asiatic people who conquered much of the Balkan peninsula, they were eventually absorbed by the larger native south Slavic population. Together, they formed a largely Slavic Bulgarian kingdom that embraced the church services earlier developed by Cyril and Methodius. The acceptance of Eastern Orthodoxy by the southern Slavic peoples, the Serbs and Bulgarians, meant that their cultural life was linked to the Byzantine state.

The eastern Slavic peoples, from whom the modern Russians and Ukrainians are descended, had settled in the territory of present-day Ukraine and European Russia. There, beginning in the late eighth century, they began to encounter Swedish Vikings who moved down the extensive network of rivers into the lands of the eastern Slavs in search of booty and new trade routes (see the box above). These Vikings built trading settlements and eventually came to dominate the native peoples, who called them "the Rus," from which the name *Russia* is derived.

THE DEVELOPMENT OF RUSSIA

A Viking leader named Oleg (c. 873–913) settled in Kiev at the beginning of the tenth century and created the Rus state known as the principality of Kiev. His successors extended their control over the eastern Slavs and expanded the territory of Kiev until it included the territory between the Baltic and Black Seas and the Danube and Volga Rivers. By marrying Slavic wives, the Viking ruling class was gradually assimilated into the Slavic population.

The growth of the principality of Kiev attracted religious missionaries, especially from the Byzantine Empire.

MAP 12.3 The Migrations of the Slavs. Originally from east-central Europe, the Slavic people broke into three groups. The western Slavs converted to Catholic Christianity, while the eastern Slavs and southern Slavs, under the influence of the Byzantine Empire, embraced the Eastern Orthodox faith. ➤ *What connections do these Slavic migrations have with what we today characterize as eastern Europe?*

One Rus ruler, Vladimir (c. 980–1015), married the Byzantine emperor's sister and officially accepted Christianity for himself and his people in 987. From the end of the tenth century, Byzantine Christianity became the model for Russian religious life.

The Kievan Rus state prospered and reached its high point in the first half of the eleventh century. But civil wars and new invasions by Asiatic nomads caused the principality of Kiev to collapse, and the sack of Kiev by north Russian princes in 1169 brought an end to the first Russian state. That first Russian state had remained closely tied to the Byzantine Empire, not to the new Europe. Its Christianity had been Orthodox Christianity, not the Catholicism of Europe. In the thirteenth century, the Mongols conquered Russia and cut it off even more from Europe.

The Mongols had exploded on the scene in the thirteenth century, moving east into China and west into the Middle East and central Europe. Although they conquered Russia, they were not numerous enough to settle the vast Russian lands. They occupied only part of Russia but required Russian princes to pay tribute to them. One Rus-

sian prince soon emerged as more powerful than the others. Alexander Nevsky, prince of Novgorod, defeated a German invading army in northwestern Russia in 1242. His cooperation with the Mongols won him their favor. The khan, leader of the western part of the Mongol Empire, rewarded Alexander Nevsky with the title of grand-prince, enabling his descendants to become the princes of Moscow and eventually leaders of all Russia.

THE WORLD OF PEASANTS AND TOWNSPEOPLE

In the Early Middle Ages, Europe had a relatively small population, but in the High Middle Ages, the number of people nearly doubled, from 38 to 74 million. What accounted for this dramatic increase? For one thing, conditions in Europe were more settled and more peaceful after the invasions of the Early Middle Ages had ended. For another, agricultural production surged after 1000.

The New Agriculture

During the High Middle Ages, Europeans began to farm in new ways. An improvement in climate resulted in better growing conditions, but an important factor in increasing food production was the expansion of cultivated or arable land, accomplished by clearing forested areas. Peasants of the eleventh and twelfth centuries cut down trees and drained swamps until by the thirteenth century, Europeans had more acreage available for farming than at any time before or since.

Technological changes also furthered the development of farming. The Middle Ages saw an explosion of labor-saving devices, many of which were made from iron, which was mined in different areas of Europe. Iron was used to make scythes, axes, and hoes for use on farms as well as saws, hammers, and nails for building purposes. Iron was crucial in making the *carruca*, a heavy, wheeled plow with an iron plowshare pulled by teams of horses, which could turn over the heavy clay soil north of the Alps.

Besides using horsepower, the High Middle Ages harnessed the power of water and wind to do jobs formerly done by humans or animals. Located along streams, mills powered by water were used to grind grains and produce flour. Where rivers were lacking or not easily dammed, Europeans developed windmills to harness the power of the wind. By the end of the twelfth century, windmills dotted the European landscape. Mills turned by water and wind remained the most important devices for generating power until the invention of the steam engine in the eighteenth century.

The shift from a two-field to a three-field system also contributed to the increase in food production. In the Early Middle Ages, peasants planted one field while another of equal size was allowed to lie fallow to regain its fertility. Now estates were divided into three parts. One field was planted in the fall with winter grains, such as rye and wheat, while spring grains, such as oats or barley, and vegetables, such as peas or beans, were planted in the second field. The third was allowed to lie fallow. By rotating their use, only one-third rather than one-half of the land lay fallow at any time. The rotation of crops also kept the soil from being exhausted so quickly, and more crops could now be grown.

The Manorial System

The landholding class of nobles and knights contained a military elite whose ability to function as warriors depended on having the leisure time to pursue the arts of war. Landed estates, located on the fiefs given to a vassal by his lord and worked by a dependent peasant class, provided the economic sustenance that made this way of life possible. A manor or villa was simply an agricultural estate operated by a lord and worked by peasants. Although a large class of free peasants continued to exist, increasing numbers of free peasants became serfs—persons bound to the land and required to provide labor services, pay rents, and be subject to the lord's jurisdiction. By the ninth century, probably 60 percent of the population of western Europe had become serfs.

Labor services consisted of working the lord's demesne, the land retained by the lord, which might consist of one-third to one-half of the cultivated lands scattered throughout the manor. The rest would be used by the peasants for themselves. Building barns and digging ditches were also part of the labor services. Serfs usually worked about three days a week for their lord and paid rents by giving the lord a share of every product they raised.

Serfs were legally bound to the lord's lands and could not leave without his permission. Although free to marry, serfs could not marry anyone outside their manor without the lord's approval. Moreover, lords sometimes exercised public rights or political authority on their lands, which gave them the right to try peasants in their own courts. In fact, the manorial court provided the only law that most peasants knew. Peasants were also required to pay lords for certain services, such as bringing their grain to the lord's mill and paying a fee to have it ground into flour.

➤ PEASANTS IN THE MANORIAL SYSTEM.   In the manorial system, peasants were required to provide labor services for their lord. This thirteenth-century illustration shows a group of English peasants harvesting grain. Overseeing their work is a bailiff, or manager, who supervised the work of the peasants.

AN ITALIAN BANKER DISCUSSES TRADING BETWEEN EUROPE AND CHINA

Working on behalf of a banking guild in Florence, Francesco Balducci Pegolotti journeyed to England and Cyprus. As a result of his contacts with many Italian merchants, he acquired considerable information about long-distance trade between Europe and China. In this account, written in 1340, he provides advice for Italian merchants.

FRANCESCO BALDUCCI PEGOLOTTI, AN ACCOUNT OF TRADERS BETWEEN EUROPE AND CHINA

In the first place, you must let your beard grow long and not shave. And at Tana [modern Rostov] you should furnish yourself with a guide. And you must not try to save money in the matter of guides by taking a bad one instead of a good one. For the additional wages of the good one will not cost you so much as you will save by having him. And besides the guide it will be well to take at least two good menservants who are acquainted with the Turkish tongue. . . .

The road you travel from Tana to China is perfectly safe, whether by day or night, according to what the merchants say who have used it. Only if the merchant, in going or coming, should die upon the road, everything belonging to him will become the possession of the lord in the country in which he dies. . . . And in like manner if he dies in China. . . .

China is a province which contains a multitude of cities and towns. Among others there is one in particular, that is to say the capital city, to which many merchants are attracted, and in which there is a vast amount of trade; and this city is called Khanbaliq [modern Beijing]. And the said city has a circuit of one hundred miles, and is all full of people and houses and of dwellers in the said city. . . .

Whatever silver the merchants may carry with them as far as China, the emperor of China will take from them and put into his treasury. And to merchants who thus bring silver they give that paper money of theirs in exchange . . . and with this money you can readily buy silk and all other merchandise that you have a desire to buy. And all the people of the country are bound to receive it. And yet you shall not pay a higher price for your goods because your money is of paper.

Daily Life of the Peasantry

The lifestyle of the peasants was quite simple. Their cottages consisted of wood frames surrounded by sticks with the space between them filled with straw and rubble and then plastered over with clay. Roofs were simply thatched. The houses of poorer peasants consisted of a single room, but others had at least two rooms—a main room for cooking, eating, and other activities and another room for sleeping. There was little privacy in a medieval peasant household.

Peasant women occupied both an important and difficult position in manorial society. They were expected to carry and bear their children and at the same time fulfill their obligation to labor in the fields. Their ability to manage the household might determine whether a peasant family would starve or survive in difficult times.

Though simple, a peasant's daily diet was adequate when food was available. The staple of the peasant diet, and the medieval diet in general, was bread. Women made the dough for the bread at home, then brought their loaves to be baked in community ovens, which were owned by the lord of the manor. Peasant bread was highly nutritious, containing not only wheat and rye but also barley, millet, and oats, giving it a dark appearance and a very heavy, hard texture. Bread was supplemented by numerous vegetables from the household gardens, cheese from cow's or goat's milk, nuts and berries from woodlands, and fruits, such as apples, pears, and cherries. Chickens provided eggs and sometimes meat.

The Revival of Trade

Medieval Europe was overwhelmingly an agrarian society, with most people living in small villages. In the eleventh and twelfth centuries, however, new elements were introduced that began to transform the economic foundation of European civilization: a revival of trade, the emergence of specialized craftspeople and artisans, and the growth and development of towns.

The revival of trade was a gradual process. During the chaotic conditions of the Early Middle Ages, large-scale trade had declined in western Europe except for Byzantine contacts with Italy and the Jewish traders who moved back and forth between the Muslim and Christian worlds. By the end of the tenth century, however, people were emerging in Europe with both the skills and the products for commercial activity. Cities in Italy took the lead in this revival of trade. Venice, for example, emerged as a town by the end of the eighth century, developed a mercantile fleet, and by the end of the tenth century had become the chief western trading center for Byzantine and Islamic commerce. In the High Middle Ages, Italian merchants became even more daring in their trade activities. They established trading posts in Cairo, Damascus, and a number of Black Sea ports, where they acquired goods brought by Muslim merchants from India, China, and Southeast Asia. A few Italian merchants even journeyed to India and China in search of trade (see the box above).

While the northern Italian cities were busy trading in the Mediterranean, the towns of Flanders were doing

Flanders

likewise in northern Europe. Flanders, the area along the coast of present-day Belgium and northern France, was known for its high-quality woolen cloth. The location of Flanders made it an ideal-center for the traders of northern Europe. Merchants from England, Scandinavia, France, and Germany converged there to trade their goods for woolen cloth. Flanders prospered in the eleventh and twelfth centuries, and such Flemish towns as Bruges and Ghent became centers for the trade and manufacture of woolen cloth.

By the twelfth century, a regular exchange of goods had developed between Flanders and Italy, the two major centers of northern and southern European trade. To encourage this trade, the counts of Champagne in northern France devised a series of six fairs held annually in the chief towns of their territory. At these fairs, northern merchants brought the furs, woolen cloth, tin, and honey of northern Europe and exchanged them for the cloth and swords of northern Italy and the silks, sugar, and spices of the East.

As trade increased, both gold and silver came to be in demand at fairs and trading markets of all kinds. Slowly, a money economy began to emerge. New trading companies and banking firms were set up to manage the exchange and sale of goods. All of these new practices were part of the rise of commercial capitalism, an economic system in which people invested in trade and goods in order to make profits.

The Growth of Cities

The revival of trade led to a revival of cities. Towns had greatly declined in the Early Middle Ages, especially in Europe north of the Alps. Old Roman cities continued to exist but had dwindled in size and population. With the revival of trade, merchants began to settle in these old cities, followed by craftspeople or artisans, people who on manors or elsewhere had developed skills and now saw an opportunity to ply their trade and make goods that could be sold by the merchants. In the course of the eleventh and twelfth centuries, the old Roman cities came alive with new populations and growth.

Beginning in the late tenth century, many new cities or towns were also founded, particularly in northern Europe. Usually, a group of merchants established a settlement near some fortified stronghold, such as a castle or monastery. (This explains why so many place names in Europe end in *borough, burgh, burg,* or *bourg,* which means

"fortress" or "walled enclosure.") Castles were particularly favored because they were generally located along trade routes; the lords of the castle also offered protection. If the settlement prospered and expanded, new walls were built to protect it.

Most towns were closely tied to their surrounding territories because they depended on the countryside for their food supplies. In addition, they were often part of the territory belonging to a lord and were subject to his jurisdiction. Although lords wanted to treat towns and townspeople as they would their vassals and serfs, cities had totally different needs and a different perspective. Townspeople needed mobility to trade. Consequently, these merchants and artisans (who came to be called *burghers* or *bourgeois,* from the same root as *borough* and *burg*) needed their own unique laws to meet their requirements and were willing to pay for them. In many instances, lords and kings saw that they could also make money and were willing to sell to the townspeople the liberties they were beginning to demand, including the right to bequeath goods and sell property, freedom from any military obligation to the lord, and written urban laws that guranteed their freedom. Some towns also obtained the right to govern themselves by choosing their own officials and administering their own courts of law.

As time went on, medieval cities developed their own governments for running the affairs of the community. Only males who were born in the city or had lived there for a particular length of time were defined as citizens. In many cities, these citizens elected members of a city council who served as judges and city officials and passed laws. Elections were carefully rigged to ensure that only members of the wealthiest and most powerful families, who came to be called the patricians, were elected.

Medieval cities remained relatively small in comparison to either ancient or modern cities. A large trading city would number about 5,000 inhabitants. By 1200, London was the largest city in England with 30,000 people. Otherwise, north of the Alps, only a few great urban centers of commerce, such as Bruges and Ghent, had a population close to 40,000. Italian cities tended to be larger, with Venice, Florence, Genoa, Milan, and Naples numbering almost 100,000. Even the largest European city, however, seemed small alongside the Byzantine capital of Constantinople or the Arab cities of Damascus, Baghdad, and Cairo. For a long time to come, Europe remained a rural society, but ultimately, the growth of trade and the rise of towns laid the foundations for the eventual transformation of Europe from a rural agricultural society to an urban, industrial one.

DAILY LIFE IN THE MEDIEVAL CITY

Medieval towns were surrounded by stone walls that were expensive to build, so the space within was precious. Consequently, most medieval cities featured narrow, winding streets with houses crowded against each other and second and third stories extending out over the streets.

Because dwellings were built mostly of wood before the fourteenth century and candles and wood fires were used for light and heat, fire was a constant threat. Medieval cities burned rapidly once a fire started.

Most of the people who lived in cities were merchants involved in trade and artisans engaged in manufacturing of some kind. Generally, merchants and artisans had their own sections within a city. The merchant area included warehouses, inns, and taverns. Artisan sections were usually divided along craft lines, and each craft had its own street where its activity was pursued.

The physical environment of medieval cities was not pleasant. They were often dirty and rife with smells from animal and human waste deposited in backyard privies or on the streets. Air pollution was also a fact of life, not only from the ubiquitous wood fires but also from a cheaper fuel, coal, used industrially by lime-burners, brewers, and dyers, as well as poor people who could not afford to purchase wood. Cities were also unable to stop water pollution, especially from the tanning and animal-slaughtering industries. Butchers dumped blood and all remaining waste products from their butchered animals into the river, while tanners unloaded tannic acids, dried blood, fat, hair, and the other waste products of their operations.

Because of the pollution, cities did not use the rivers for drinking water but relied instead on wells. Private and public baths also existed in medieval towns. Paris, for example, had thirty-two public baths for men and women. City laws did not allow lepers and people with "bad reputations" to use them. This did not, however, prevent public baths from being known for permissiveness due to public nudity. One contemporary commented on what occurred in public bathhouses: "Shameful things. Men make a point of staying all night in the public baths and women at the break of day come in and through 'ignorance' find themselves in the men's rooms."[4]

In medieval cities, women, in addition to supervising the household, purchasing food and preparing meals, raising the children, and managing the family finances, were also often expected to help their husbands in their trades. Some women also developed their own trades to earn extra money. When some master craftspeople died, their widows even carried on their trades. Some women in medieval towns were thus able to lead lives of considerable independence.

INDUSTRY IN MEDIEVAL CITIES

The revival of trade enabled cities and towns to become centers for manufacturing a wide range of goods, such as cloth, metalwork, shoes, and leather goods. From the twelfth century on, craftspeople began to organize themselves into guilds, and by the thirteenth century, there were individual guilds for virtually every craft, such as tanners, carpenters, and bakers, as well as separate guilds for specialized groups of merchants, such as dealers in silk, spices, wool, or banking. Craft guilds directed almost every aspect of the production process. They established standards for the articles produced, specified the methods of production to be used, and even fixed the price at which the finished goods could be sold. Guilds also determined the number of men who could enter a specific trade and the procedure they must follow to do so.

A person who wanted to learn a trade first became an apprentice, usually around the age of ten, to a master craftsperson. Apprentices were not paid but did receive room and board from their masters. After five to seven years of service, in which they learned their craft, apprentices became journeymen (or journeywomen, although most were male) who then worked for wages for other masters. Journeymen aspired to become masters as well. To do so, they were expected to produce a "masterpiece," a finished piece in their craft that allowed the master craftsmen of the guild to judge whether the journeymen were qualified to become masters and join the guild.

➤ SHOPS IN A MEDIEVAL TOWN.   Most urban residents were merchants involved in trade and artisans who manufactured a wide variety of products. Master craftsmen had their workshops in the ground-level rooms of their houses. In this illustration, two well-dressed burghers are touring the shopping district of a French town. Tailors, furriers, a barber, and a grocer (from left to right) are visible at work in their shops.

Bibliotheque Nationale, Paris

CHRISTIANITY AND MEDIEVAL CIVILIZATION

Christianity was an integral part of the fabric of European society and the consciousness of Europe. Papal directives affected the actions of kings and princes alike, and Christian teachings and practices touched the lives of all Europeans.

The Papal Monarchy

Since the fifth century, the popes of the Catholic church had reigned supreme over the affairs of the church. They had also come to exercise control over the territories in central Italy that came to be known as the Papal States, which kept the popes involved in political matters, often at the expense of their spiritual obligations. At the same time, the church became increasingly entangled in the evolving feudal relationships. High officials of the church, such as bishops and abbots, came to hold their offices as fiefs from nobles. As vassals, they were obliged to carry out the usual duties, including military service. Of course, lords assumed the right to choose their vassals and thus came to appoint bishops and abbots. Because lords often chose their vassals from other noble families for political reasons, these bishops and abbots were often worldly figures who cared little about their spiritual responsibilities.

REFORM OF THE PAPACY

By the eleventh century, church leaders realized the need to free the church from the interference of lords in the appointment of church officials. Lay investiture was the practice by which secular rulers both chose nominees to church offices and invested them with the symbols of their office. Pope Gregory VII (1073–1085) decided to fight this practice. Elected pope in 1073, Gregory was convinced that he had been chosen by God to reform the church. To pursue this aim, Gregory claimed that he—the pope—was God's "vicar on earth" and that the pope's authority extended over all of Christendom, including its rulers. Gregory sought nothing less than the elimination of lay investiture. Only in this way could the church regain its freedom, by which Gregory meant the right of the church to appoint clergy and run its own affairs. If rulers did not accept this, they could be deposed by the pope.

Gregory VII soon found himself in conflict with the king of Germany over these claims. King Henry IV (1056–1106) of Germany was also a determined man who had appointed high-ranking clerics, especially bishops, as his vassals in order to use them as administrators. In 1075, Pope Gregory issued a decree forbidding high-ranking clerics from receiving their investiture from lay leaders: "We decree that no one of the clergy shall receive the investiture with a bishopric or abbey or church from the hand of an emperor or king or of any layperson. . . ."[5] Henry had no intention of obeying a decree that challenged the very heart of his administration.

The struggle between Henry IV and Gregory VII, which is known as the Investiture Controversy, was one of the great conflicts between church and state in the High Middle Ages. It dragged on until a new German king and a new pope reached a compromise in 1122 called the Concordat of Worms. Under this agreement, a bishop in Germany was first elected by church officials. After election, the nominee paid homage to the king as his lord, who then invested him with the symbols of temporal office. A representative of the pope, however, then invested the new bishop with the symbols of his spiritual office.

THE CHURCH SUPREME

The popes of the twelfth century did not abandon the reform ideals of Pope Gregory VII, but they were more inclined to consolidate their power and build a strong administrative system. During the papacy of Pope Innocent III (1198–1216), the Catholic church reached the height of its power. At the beginning of his pontificate, in a letter to a priest, the pope made a clear statement of his views on papal supremacy:

> As God, the creator of the universe, set two great lights in the firmament of heaven, the greater light to rule the day, and the lesser light to rule the night, so He set two great dignities in the firmament of the universal church, . . . the greater to rule the day, that is, souls, and the lesser to rule the night, that is, bodies. These dignities are the papal authority and the royal power. And just as the moon gets her light from the sun, and is inferior to the sun . . . so the royal power gets the splendor of its dignity from the papal authority.[6]

Innocent III's actions were those of a man who believed that he, the pope, was the supreme judge of European affairs. To achieve his political ends, he did not hesitate to use the spiritual weapons at his command, especially the interdict, which forbade priests to dispense the sacraments of the church in the hope that the people, deprived of the comforts of religion, would exert pressure against their ruler. Apparently Pope Innocent's interdicts worked: for example, one of them forced the king of France, Philip Augustus, to take back his wife and queen after Philip had tried to have his marriage annulled.

New Religious Orders and New Spiritual Ideals

Between 1050 and 1150, a wave of religious enthusiasm seized Europe, leading to a spectacular growth in the number of monasteries and the emergence of new monastic orders. Most important was the Cistercian order, founded in 1098 by a group of monks dissatisfied with the lack of a strict discipline at their own Benedictine monastery. The Cistercians were strict. They ate a simple diet and possessed only a single robe apiece. More time for prayer and manual labor was provided by shortening the number of hours spent at religious services. The Cistercians played a major role in developing a new, activist spiritual model for twelfth-century Europe. A Benedictine monk often spent hours in prayer to honor God. The Cistercian ideal had a different emphasis: "Arise, soldier of Christ, arise! Get up off the ground and

A MIRACLE OF SAINT BERNARD

Saint Bernard of Clairvaux has been called "the most widely respected holy man of the twelfth century." He was an outstanding preacher, wholly dedicated to the service of God. His reputation reportedly influenced many young men to join the Cistercian order. He also inspired a myriad of stories dealing with his miracles.

A MIRACLE OF SAINT BERNARD

A certain monk, departing from his monastery . . . , threw off his habit, and returned to the world at the persuasion of the Devil. And he took a certain parish living; for he was a priest. Because sin is punished with sin, the deserter from his Order lapsed into the vice of lechery. He took a concubine to live with him, as in fact is done by many, and by her he had children.

But as God is merciful and does not wish anyone to perish, it happened that many years after, the blessed abbot [Saint Bernard] was passing through the village in which this same monk was living, and went to stay at his house. The renegade monk recognized him, and received him very reverently, and waited on him devoutly . . . but as yet the abbot did not recognize him.

On the morrow, the holy man said Matins and prepared to be off. But as he could not speak to the priest, since he had got up and gone to the church for Matins, he said to the priest's son "Go, give this message to your master." Now the boy had been born dumb. He obeyed the command and feeling in himself the power of him who had given it, he ran to his father and uttered the words of the Holy Father clearly and exactly. His father, on hearing his son's voice for the first time, wept for joy, and made him repeat the same words . . . and he asked what the abbot had done to him. "He did nothing to me," said the boy, "except to say, 'Go and say this to your father.'"

At so evident a miracle the priest repented, and hastened after the holy man and fell at his feet saying, "My Lord and Father, I was your monk so-and-so, and at such-and-such a time I ran away from your monastery. I ask your Paternity to allow me to return with you to the monastery, for in your coming God has visited my heart." The saint replied unto him, "Wait for me here, and I will come back quickly when I have done my business, and I will take you with me." But the priest, fearing death (which he had not done before), answered, "Lord, I am afraid of dying before then." But the saint replied, "Know this for certain, that if you die in this condition, and in this resolve, you will find yourself a monk before God."

The saint [eventually] returned and heard that the priest had recently died and been buried. He ordered the tomb to be opened. And when they asked him what he wanted to do, he said, "I want to see if he is lying as a monk or a clerk in his tomb." "As a clerk," they said; "we buried him in his secular habit." But when they had dug up the earth, they found that he was not in the clothes in which they had buried him; but he appeared in all points, tonsure and habit, as a monk. And they all praised God.

return to the battle from which you have fled! Fight more boldly after your flight, and triumph in glory!"[7] These were the words of Saint Bernard of Clairvaux (1090–1153), who more than any other person embodied the new spiritual ideal of Cistercian monasticism (see the box above).

Women were also actively involved in the spiritual movements of the age. The number of women joining religious houses grew dramatically in the High Middle Ages. Most nuns were from the ranks of the landed aristocracy. Convents were convenient for families unable or unwilling to find husbands for their daughters and for aristocratic women who did not wish to marry. Female intellectuals found them a haven for their activities. Most of the learned women of the Middle Ages were nuns.

© Bibliotheque royale Albert ler (Ms IV 119, fol.72 verso)

➤ **A GROUP OF NUNS.** Although still viewed by the medieval church as inferior to men, women were as susceptible to the spiritual fervor of the twelfth century as men, and female monasticism grew accordingly. This miniature shows a group of Flemish nuns listening to the preaching of an abbot, Gilles li Muisis. The nun wearing a white robe at the far left is a novice.

In the thirteenth century, two new religious orders emerged that had a profound impact on the lives of ordinary people. Like their founder, Saint Francis of Assisi (1182–1226), the Franciscans lived among the people, preaching repentance and aiding the poor. Their calls for a return to the simplicity and poverty of the early church, reinforced by their own example, were especially effective and made them very popular.

Dominicans arose out of the desire of a Spanish priest, Dominic de Guzmán (1170–1221), to defend church teachings from heresy—beliefs contrary to official church doctrine. Unlike Francis, Dominic was an intellectual who was appalled by the growth of heresy within the church. He came to believe that a new religious order of men who lived lives of poverty but were learned and capable of preaching effectively would best be able to attack heresy. The Dominicans became especially well known for their roles as the inquisitors of the papal Inquisition.

The Holy Office, as the papal Inquisition was formally called, was a court that had been established by the church to find and try heretics. Gradually, the Holy Office developed a regular procedure to deal with heretics. If an accused heretic confessed, he or she was forced to perform public penance and was subjected to punishment, such as flogging. The heretic's property was then confiscated and divided between the secular authorities and the church. Beginning in 1252, those not confessing voluntarily were tortured. Those who refused to confess and were still considered guilty were turned over to the state for execution. So also were relapsed heretics—those who confessed, did penance, and then reverted to heresy again. To the Christians of the thirteenth century, who believed that there was only one path to salvation, heresy was a crime against God and against humanity. In their minds, force should be used to save souls from damnation.

THE CULTURE OF THE HIGH MIDDLE AGES

The High Middle Ages was a time of extraordinary intellectual and artistic vitality. It witnessed the birth of universities and a building spree that left Europe bedecked with churches and cathedrals.

The Rise of Universities

The university as we know it—with faculty, students, and degrees—was a product of the High Middle Ages. The word *university* is derived from the Latin word *universitas*, meaning a corporation or guild, and referred to either a corporation of teachers or a corporation of students. Medieval universities were educational guilds or corporations that produced educated and trained individuals.

The first European university appeared in Bologna, Italy, where a great teacher named Irnerius (1088–1125), who taught Roman law, attracted students from all over Europe. Most of them were laymen, usually older individuals who were administrators for kings and princes and were eager to learn more about law to apply it in their own jobs. To protect themselves, students at Bologna formed a guild or *universitas*, which was recognized by Emperor Frederick Barbarossa and given a charter in 1158.

The first university in northern Europe was the University of Paris. In the second half of the twelfth century, a number of students and masters left Paris and started their own university at Oxford, England. Kings, popes, and princes soon competed to found new universities, and by the end of the Middle Ages, there were eighty universities in Europe, most of them in England, France, Italy, and Germany.

University students (all men—women did not attend universities in the Middle Ages) began their studies with the traditional liberal arts curriculum, which consisted of grammar, rhetoric, logic, arithmetic, geometry, music, and astronomy. Teaching was done by the lecture method. The word *lecture* is derived from the Latin verb for "read." Before the development of the printing press in the fifteenth century, books were expensive and few students could afford them, so teachers read from a basic text (such as a collection of laws if the subject was law) and then added their explanations. No exams were given after a series of lectures, but when a student applied for a degree, he was given a comprehensive oral examination by a committee of teachers. The exam was taken after a four- or six-year period of study. The first degree a student could earn was a bachelor of arts; later he might receive a master of arts.

After completing the liberal arts curriculum, a student could go on to study law, medicine, or theology. This last was the most highly regarded subject at the medieval university. The study of law, medicine, or theology could take a decade or more. A student who passed his final oral examinations was granted a doctor's degree, which officially enabled him to teach his subject. Students who received degrees from medieval universities could pursue other careers besides teaching that proved to be much more lucrative. A law degree was necessary for those who wished to serve as advisers to kings and princes. The growing administrative bureaucracies of popes and kings also demanded a supply of clerks with a university education who could keep records and draw up official documents. Universities provided the teachers, administrators, lawyers, and doctors for medieval society.

The Development of Scholasticism

The importance of Christianity in medieval society made it certain that theology would play a central role in the European intellectual world. Theology, the formal study of religion, was "queen of the sciences" in the new universities.

Beginning in the eleventh century, the effort to apply reason or logical analysis to the church's basic theological doctrines had a significant impact on the study of theology. The word *scholasticism* is used to refer to the philosophical and theological system of the medieval schools. Scholasticism tried to reconcile faith and reason, to demonstrate that what was accepted on faith was in harmony with what could be learned by reason.

The overriding task of scholasticism was to harmonize Christian teachings with the work of the Greek philosopher Aristotle. In the twelfth century, due largely to the work of Muslim and Jewish scholars, western Europe was introduced to a large number of Greek scientific and philosophical works, including the works of Aristotle. However, Aristotle's works threw many theologians into consternation. Aristotle was so highly regarded that he was called "the philosopher," yet he had arrived at his conclusions by rational thought, not by faith, and some of his doctrines contradicted the teachings of the church. The most famous attempt to reconcile Aristotle and the doctrines of Christianity was that of Saint Thomas Aquinas.

Thomas Aquinas (1225–1274) is best known for his *Summa Theologica* (*A Summa of Theology*—a summa was a compendium of knowledge that attempted to bring together all the received learning of the preceding centuries on a given subject). Aquinas's masterpiece was organized according to the dialectical method of the scholastics. Aquinas first posed a question, cited sources that offered opposing opinions on the question, and then resolved the matter by arriving at his own conclusions. In this fashion, Aquinas raised and discussed some six hundred articles.

Aquinas's reputation derives from his masterful attempt to reconcile faith and reason. He took it for granted that there were truths derived by reason and truths derived by faith. He was certain, however, that the two truths could not be in conflict. The natural mind, unaided by faith, could arrive at truths concerning the physical universe. Without the help of God's grace, however, reason alone could not grasp spiritual truths, such as the Trinity (the manifestation of God in three separate yet identical persons—Father, Son, and Holy Spirit) or the Incarnation (Jesus' simultaneous identity as God and human).

Romanesque Architecture

The eleventh and twelfth centuries witnessed an explosion of building, both private and public. The construction of castles and churches absorbed most of the surplus resources of medieval society and at the same time reflected its basic preoccupations, God and warfare. The churches were by far the most conspicuous of the public buildings. Hundred of new cathedrals, abbeys, and pilgrimage churches, as well as thousands of parish churches in rural villages, were built in the eleventh and twelfth centuries. The building spree was a direct reflection of a revived religious culture and the increased wealth of the period.

The cathedrals of the eleventh and twelfth centuries were built in the Romanesque style, prominent examples of which can be found in Germany, France, and Spain. Romanesque churches were normally built in the basilica shape used in the construction of churches in the Late Roman Empire. Basilicas were rectangular churches with flat wooden roofs. Romanesque builders made a significant innovation by replacing the flat wooden roof with a long, round stone vault called a barrel vault or a cross vault where two barrel vaults intersected. The latter was used when a transept was added to create a church plan in the shape of a cross. Although barrel and cross vaults were technically difficult to create, they were considered aesthetically more pleasing than the flat wooden roofs and were also less apt to catch fire.

Because stone roofs were extremely heavy, Romanesque churches required massive pillars and walls to hold them up. This left little space for windows, and Romanesque churches were correspondingly dark on the inside. Their massive walls and pillars gave Romanesque churches a sense of solidity and almost the impression of a fortress.

BARREL VAULTING.   The eleventh and twelfth centuries witnessed an enormous amount of church construction. Utilizing the basilica shape, master builders replaced flat wooden roofs with long, round stone vaults, known as barrel vaults. As this illustration of a Romanesque church in Vienne, France, indicates, the barrel vault limited the size of a church and left little room in the walls for windows.

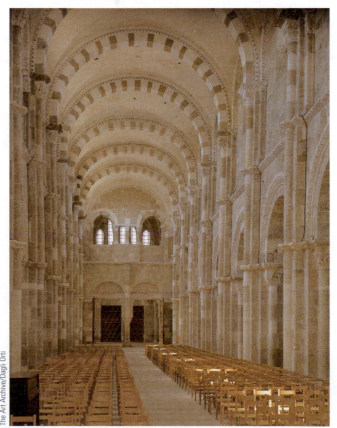

The Art Archive/Dagli Orti

The Gothic Cathedral

Begun in the twelfth century and brought to perfection in the thirteenth, the Gothic cathedral remains one of the greatest artistic triumphs of the High Middle Ages. Soaring skyward, as if to reach heaven, it was a fitting symbol for medieval people's preoccupation with God.

Two fundamental innovations of the twelfth century made Gothic cathedrals possible. The combination of ribbed vaults and pointed arches replaced the barrel vault of Romanesque churches and enabled builders to make Gothic churches higher than their Romanesque counterparts. The use of pointed arches and ribbed vaults created an impression of upward movement, a sense of weightless upward thrust that implied the energy of God. Another technical innovation, the flying buttress, basically a heavy arched pier of stone built onto the outside of the walls, made it possible to distribute the weight of the church's vaulted ceilings outward and down and thus eliminate the heavy walls used in Romanesque churches to hold the weight of the massive barrel vaults. Thus Gothic cathedrals could be built with thin walls containing magnificent stained-glass windows, which created a play of light inside that varied with the sun at different times of the day. This preoccupation with colored light in Gothic cathedrals was not accidental but was executed by people who believed that natural light was a symbol of the divine light of God.

The first fully Gothic church was the abbey of Saint-Denis near Paris, inspired by its famous Abbot Suger (1122–1151) and built between 1140 and 1150. Although the Gothic style was a product of northern France, by the mid-thirteenth century, French Gothic architecture had spread to virtually all of Europe. By the mid-thirteenth century, French Gothic architecture was seen most brilliantly in cathedrals in Paris (Notre-Dame), Reims, Amiens, and Chartres.

A Gothic cathedral was the work of the entire community. All classes contributed to its construction. Master masons, who were both architects and engineers, designed them, and stonemasons and other craftspeople were paid a daily wage and provided the skilled labor to build them. A Gothic cathedral symbolized the chief preoccupation of a medieval Christian community, its dedication to a spiritual ideal. As we have observed before, the largest buildings of an era reflect the values of its society. The Gothic cathedral, with its towers soaring toward heaven, gave witness to an age when a spiritual impulse underlay most aspects of its existence.

THE EXPANSION OF MEDIEVAL EUROPE: THE CRUSADES

As it developed, European civilization remained largely confined to one geographical area. Some Europeans, especially merchants, had contacts with parts of Asia and Africa, and Viking explorers even reached the eastern

❧ THE GOTHIC CATHEDRAL. The Gothic cathedral was one of the great artistic triumphs of the High Middle Ages. Seen here is the cathedral of Notre-Dame in Paris. Begun in 1163, it was not completed until the beginning of the fourteenth century.

fringes of North America in the tenth and eleventh centuries. But at the end of the eleventh century, Europeans began their first concerted attempt to expand beyond the frontiers of Europe by conquering the land of Palestine.

The First Crusades

The Crusades were based on the idea of a holy war against the infidels or unbelievers. The wrath of Christians was directed against the Muslims, and at the end of the eleventh century, Christian Europe found itself with a glorious opportunity to attack them. The immediate impetus for the Crusades came when the Byzantine emperor, Alexius I, asked Pope Urban II for help against the Seljuk Turks, who were Muslims. The pope saw a golden opportunity to provide papal leadership for a great cause: to rally the warriors of Europe for the liberation of Jerusalem and the Holy Land (Palestine) from the infidel. At the Council of Clermont in southern France near the end of 1095, Urban II challenged Christians to take up their weapons and join in a holy war to recover the Holy Land. The pope promised remission of sins: "All who die by the way, whether by land or by sea,

THE SIEGE OF JERUSALEM: CHRISTIAN AND MUSLIM PERSPECTIVES

During the First Crusade, Christian knights laid seige to Jerusalem in June 1099. The first excerpt is taken from an account by Fulcher of Chartres, who accompanied the crusaders to the Holy Land. The second selection is by a Muslim writer, Ibn al-Athir, whose account of the First Crusade can be found in his history of the Muslim world.

FULCHER OF CHARTRES, CHRONICLE OF THE FIRST CRUSADE

Then the Franks entered the city magnificently at the noon-day hour on Friday, the day of the week when Christ redeemed the whole world on the cross. With trumpets sounding and with everything in an uproar, exclaiming: "Help, God!" they vigorously pushed into the city, and straightway raised the banner on the top of the wall. All the heathen, completely terrified, changed their boldness to swift flight through the narrow streets of the quarters. The more quickly they fled, the more quickly they put to flight.

Count Raymond and his men, who were bravely assailing the city in another section, did not perceive this until they saw the Saracens [Muslims] jumping from the top of the wall. Seeing this, they joyfully ran to the city as quickly as they could, and helped the others pursue and kill the wicked enemy.

Then some, both Arabs and Ethiopians, fled into the Tower of David; others shut themselves in the Temple of the Lord and of Solomon, where in the halls a very great attack was made on them. Nowhere was there a place where the Saracens could escape swordsmen.

On the top of Solomon's Template, to which they had climbed in fleeing, many were shot to death with arrows and cast down headlong from the roof. Within this Temple, about ten thousand were beheaded. If you had been there, your feet would have been stained up to the ankles with the blood of the slain. What more shall I tell? Not one of them was allowed to live. They did not spare the women and children.

ACCOUNT OF IBN AL-ATHIR

In fact Jerusalem was taken from the north on the morning of Friday 22 Sha'ban 492/15 July 1099. The population was put to the sword by the Franks, who pillaged the area for a week. A band of Muslims barricaded themselves into the Oratory of David and fought on for several days. They were granted their lives in return for surrendering. The Franks honored their word, and the group left by night for Ascalon. In the Masjid al-Aqsa the Franks slaughtered more than 70,000 people, among them a large number of Imams and Muslim scholars, devout and ascetic men who had left their homelands to live lives of pious seclusion in the Holy Place. The Franks stripped the Dome of the Rock of more than forty silver candelabra, each of them weighing 3,600 drams, and a great silver lamp weighing forty-four Syrian pounds, as well as a hundred and fifty smaller candelabra and more than twenty gold ones, and a great deal more booty. Refugees from Syria reached Baghdad in Ramadan, among them the qadi Abu sa'd al-Harawi. They told the Caliph's ministers a story that wrung their hearts and brought tears to their eyes. On Friday they went to the Cathedral Mosque and begged for help, weeping so that their hearers wept with them as they described the sufferings of the Muslims in the Holy City: the men killed, the women and children taken prisoner, the homes pillaged. Because of the terrible hardships they had suffered, they were allowed to break the fast.

---

or in battle against the pagans, shall have immediate remission of sins. This I grant them through the power of God with which I am invested."[8] The enthusiastic crowd cried out in response: "It is the will of God, it is the will of God."

Three organized crusading bands of noble warriors, most of them French, made their way eastward. The crusading army probably numbered several thousand cavalry and as many as ten thousand infantry. After the capture of Antioch in 1098, much of the crusading host proceeded down the Palestinian coast, evading the well-defended coastal cities, and reached Jerusalem in June 1099. After a five-week siege, the Holy City was taken amid a horrible massacre of the inhabitants—men, women, and children (see the box above).

After further conquest of Palestinian lands, the crusaders ignored the wishes of the Byzantine emperor and organized four Latin crusader states. Because the crusader kingdoms were surrounded by Muslims hostile to them, they grew increasingly dependent on the Italian commercial cities for supplies from Europe. Some Italian cities, such as Genoa, Pisa, and above all, Venice, grew rich and powerful in the process.

But it was not easy for the crusader kingdoms to maintain themselves. Already by the 1120s, the Muslims had begun to strike back. The fall of one of the Latin kingdoms in 1144 led to renewed calls for another Crusade, especially from the monastic firebrand Saint Bernard of Clairvaux. He exclaimed: "Now, on account of our sins, the enemies of the cross have begun to show their faces. . . . What are you doing, you servants of the cross? Will you throw to the dogs that which is most holy? Will you cast pearls before swine?"[9] Bernard even managed to enlist two powerful rulers, but their Second Crusade proved to be a total failure.

The Third Crusade was a reaction to the fall of the Holy City of Jerusalem in 1187 to the Muslim forces under Saladin. Now all of Christendom was ablaze with calls for a new

Crusade. Three major monarchs agreed to lead their forces in person: Emperor Frederick Barbarossa of Germany (1152–1190), Richard I the Lionhearted of England (1189–1199), and Philip II Augustus, king of France (1180–1223). Some of the crusaders finally arrived in the East by 1189 only to encounter problems. Frederick Barbarossa drowned while swimming in a local river, and his army quickly disintegrated. The English and French arrived by sea and met with success against the coastal cities, where they had the support of their fleets, but when they moved inland, they failed miserably. Eventually, after Philip went home, Richard the Lionhearted negotiated a settlement whereby Saladin agreed to allow Christian pilgrims free access to Jerusalem.

The Later Crusades

After the death of Saladin in 1193, Pope Innocent III initiated the Fourth Crusade. On its way to the East, the crusading army became involved in a dispute over the succession to the Byzantine throne. The Venetian leaders of the Fourth Crusade saw an opportunity to neutralize their greatest commercial competitor, the Byzantine Empire. Diverted to Constantinople, the crusaders sacked the great capital city of Byzantium in 1204 and set up the new Latin Empire of Constantinople. Not until 1261 did a Byzantine army recapture Constantinople. In the meantime, additional Crusades were undertaken to reconquer the Holy Land. All of them were largely disasters, and by the end of the thirteenth century, the European military effort to capture Palestine was recognized as a complete failure.

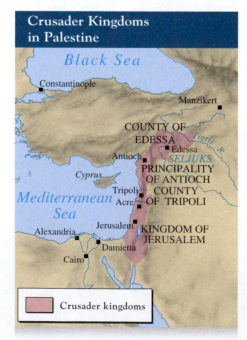

Crusader Kingdoms in Palestine

Black Sea

Constantinople

Manzikert

COUNTY OF EDESSA

Edessa

Antioch

SELJUKS

Cyprus

PRINCIPALITY OF ANTIOCH

Tripoli

COUNTY OF TRIPOLI

Mediterranean Sea

Acre

Alexandria

Jerusalem

KINGDOM OF JERUSALEM

Damietta

Cairo

Tigris R.

Crusader kingdoms

THE LATE MIDDLE AGES: A TIME OF TROUBLES IN EUROPE

At the beginning of the fourteenth century, changes in weather patterns in Europe ushered in what has been called a "little ice age." Shortened growing seasons and disastrous weather conditions, including heavy storms and constant rain, led to widespread famine and hunger. Soon an even greater catastrophe struck.

The Black Death

The Black Death of the mid-fourteenth century was the most devastating natural disaster in European history, ravaging Europe's population and causing economic, social, political, and cultural upheaval. Contemporary chroniclers lamented how parents abandoned their children; one related the words: "Oh father, why have you abandoned me? ... Mother, where have you gone?"[10] People were horrified by an evil force they could not understand and by the subsequent breakdown of all normal human relations.

Bubonic plague was the most common and most important form of plague in the diffusion of the Black Death and was spread by black rats infested with fleas who were host to the deadly bacterium *Yersinia pestis*. This great plague originated in Asia. After disappearing from Europe and the Middle East in the Middle Ages, bubonic plague continued to haunt areas of southwestern China. Rats accompanying Mongol troops spread the plague into central and northwestern China and into Central Asia in the mid-thirteenth century. From there, trading caravans brought the plague to Caffa, on the Black Sea, in 1346.

The plague reached Europe in October 1347 when Genoese merchants brought it from Caffa to the island of Sicily off the coast of Italy. It quickly spread to southern Italy and southern France by the end of 1347 (see Map 12.4). Diffusion of the Black Death followed commercial trade routes. In 1348, it spread through Spain, France, and the Low Countries and into Germany. By the end of that year, it had moved to England, ravaging it in 1349. By the end of 1349, the plague had reached northern Europe and Scandinavia. Eastern Europe and Russia were affected by 1351.

MAP 12.4 Spread of the Black Death.   The plague started in Sicily in 1347 and within three years had killed between one-quarter and one-half of Europe's population. Outbreaks continued into the early eighteenth century, and it took Europe two hundred years to return to the population level it had before the Black Death. ➤ *Is there a general pattern between distance from Sicily and the elapsed time before a region was infected with the plague?*

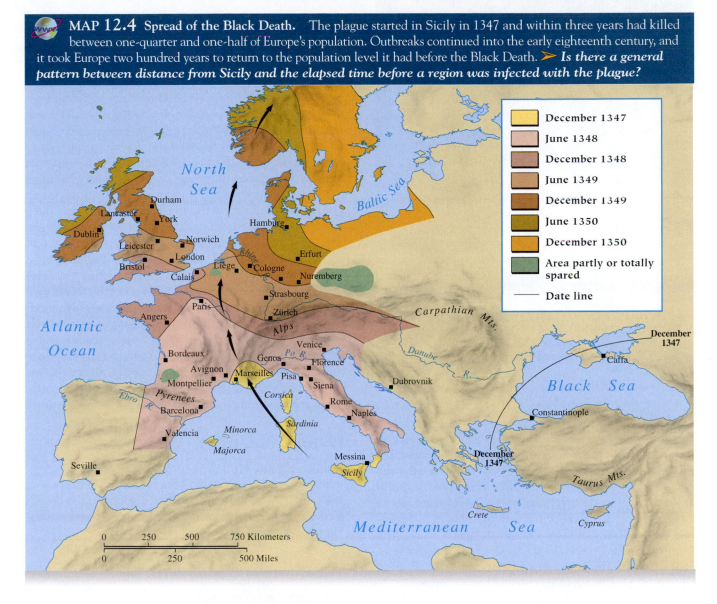

Mortality figures for the Black Death were incredibly high. Especially hard hit were Italy's crowded cities, where 50 to 60 percent of the people died. One citizen of Florence wrote, "A great many breathed their last in the public streets, day and night; a large number perished in their homes, and it was only by the stench of their decaying bodies that they proclaimed their deaths to their neighbors. Everywhere the city was teeming with corpses."[11] In England and Germany, entire villages simply disappeared. In Germany, of approximately 170,000 inhabited locations, only 130,000 were left by the end of the fourteenth century. It has been estimated that out of a total European population of 75 million, as many as 38 million people may have died of the plague between 1347 and 1351. Not until the mid-sixteenth century did Europe begin to reattain its thirteenth-century population levels.

The attempt of contemporaries to explain the Black Death and mitigate its harshness led to extreme sorts of behavior. To many, either the plague had been sent by God as a punishment for humans' sins, or it had been caused by the devil. Some, known as the flagellants, resorted to extreme measures to gain God's forgiveness. Groups of flagellants, both men and women, wandered from town to town, flogging each other with whips to beg the forgiveness of a God who, they felt, had sent the plague to punish humans for their sinful ways. One contemporary chronicler described their activies:

The penitents went about, coming first out of Germany. They were men who did public penance and scourged themselves with whips of hard knotted leather with little iron spikes. Some made themselves bleed very badly between the shoulder blades and some foolish women had cloths ready to catch the blood and smear it on their eyes, saying it was miraculous blood. While they were doing penance, they sang very mournful songs about the nativity and the passion of Our Lord. The object of this penance was to put a stop to the mortality, for in that time . . . at least a third of all the people in the world died.[12]

⇒ THE FLAGELLANTS.   Reactions to the plague were extreme at times. Believing that asceticism could atone for humanity's sins and win God's forgiveness, flagellants wandered from town to town flogging themselves and each other with whips, as in this illustration.

The flagellants created mass hysteria wherever they went, and authorities worked overtime to crush the movement.

An outbreak of virulent anti-Semitism also accompanied the Black Death. Jews were accused of causing the plague by poisoning town wells. The worst pogroms against this minority were carried out in Germany, where more than sixty major Jewish communities in Germany had been exterminated by 1351 (see the box on p. 341). Many Jews fled eastward to Russia and especially to Poland, where the king offered them protection. Eastern Europe became home to large Jewish communities.

Economic Dislocation and Social Upheaval

The death of so many people in the fourteenth century also had severe economic consequences. Trade declined, and some industries suffered greatly. Florence's woolen industry, one of the giants, had produced 70,000 to 80,000 pieces of cloth in 1338; in 1378, it was yielding only 24,000 pieces.

Both peasants and noble landlords were also affected. A shortage of workers caused a dramatic rise in the price of labor, while the decline in the number of people lowered the demand for food, resulting in falling prices. Landlords were now paying more for labor at the same time that their rental income was declining. Concurrently, the decline in the number of peasants after the Black Death made it easier for some to convert their labor services to rent, thus freeing them from serfdom. But there were limits to how much the peasants could advance. They faced the same economic hurdles as the lords, who also attempted to impose wage restrictions and reinstate old forms of labor service. New governmental taxes also hurt. Peasant complaints became widespread and soon gave rise to rural revolts.

The English Peasants' Revolt of 1381 was the most prominent of all. After the Black Death, the English peasants had enjoyed improved conditions with greater freedom and higher wages or lower rents. Aristocratic landlords had fought back with legislation to depress wages and an effort to reimpose old feudal dues. The most immediate cause of the revolt, however, was the monarchy's attempt to raise revenues by imposing a poll tax, a flat charge on each adult member of the population. Peasants in eastern England refused to pay the tax and expelled the collectors forcibly from their villages. Rebellion spread as peasants burned down the manor houses of aristocrats, lawyers, and government officials. Soon, however, the young king, Richard II (1377–1399), with the assistance of aristocrats, arrested hundreds of the rebels and ended the revolt.

Although the peasant revolts sometimes resulted in short-term gains for the participants, the uprisings were relatively easily crushed and their gains quickly lost. Accustomed to ruling, the established classes easily combined and stifled dissent. Nevertheless, the revolts of the fourteenth century had introduced a new element to European life; henceforth, social unrest would be a characteristic of European history.

Political Instability

Famine, plague, economic turmoil, and social upheaval were not the only problems of the fourteenth century. War and political instability must also be added to the list. Of all the struggles that ensued in the fourteenth century, the Hundred Years' War was the most violent.

THE HUNDRED YEARS' WAR

In the thirteenth century, the English king, Henry III, still held one small possession in France known as the duchy of Gascony. As duke of Gascony, the English king pledged loyalty as a vassal to the French king, but when King Philip VI of France (1328–1350) seized Gascony in 1337, the duke of Gascony—King Edward III of England (1327–1377)—declared war on Philip. The attack on Gascony was a convenient excuse; Edward III had already laid claim to the throne of France after the senior branch of the Capetian dynasty had become extinct in 1328.

The Hundred Years' War began in a burst of knightly enthusiasm. The French army of 1337 still relied largely on heavily armed noble cavalrymen, who looked with contempt on foot soldiers and crossbowmen, whom they regarded as social inferiors. The English, too, used heavily armed cavalry, but they relied even more on large numbers of paid foot soldiers. Armed with pikes, many of these soldiers had also adopted the longbow, invented by the Welsh. The longbow had greater striking power, longer range, and more rapid speed of fire then the crossbow.

A MEDIEVAL HOLOCAUST: THE CREMATION OF THE STRASBOURG JEWS

In their attempt to explain the widespread horrors of the Black Death, medieval Christian communities looked for scapegoats. As at the time of the Crusades, the Jews were accused of poisoning wells and hence spreading the plague. This selection by a contemporary chronicler, written in 1349, gives an account of how Christians in the town of Strasbourg in the Holy Roman Empire dealt with their Jewish community. It is apparent that financial gain was also an important factor in killing the Jews.

JACOB VON KÖNIGSHOFEN, "THE CREMATION OF THE STRASBOURG JEWS"

In the year 1349 there occurred the greatest epidemic that ever happened. Death went from one end of the earth to the other. . . . And from what this epidemic came, all wise teachers and physicians could only say that it was God's will. . . . This epidemic also came to Strasbourg in the summer of the above-mentioned year, and it is estimated that about sixteen thousand people died.

In the matter of this plague the Jews throughout the world were reviled and accused in all lands of having caused it through the poison which they are said to have put into the water and the wells—that is what they were accused of—and for this reason the Jews were burnt all the way from the Mediterranean into Germany. . . .

[The account then goes on to discuss the situation of the Jews in the city of Strasbourg.]

On Saturday . . . they burnt the Jews on a wooden platform in their cemetery. There were about two thousand people of them. Those who wanted to baptize themselves were spared. [Some say that about a thousand accepted baptism.] Many small children were taken out of the fire and baptized against the will of their fathers and mothers. And everything that was owed to the Jews was canceled, and the Jews had to surrender all pledges and notes that they had taken for debts. The council, however, took the cash that the Jews possessed and divided it among the workingmen proportionately. The money was indeed the thing that killed the Jews. If they had been poor and if the feudal lords had not been in debt to them, they would not have been burnt. . . .

Thus were the Jews burnt at Strasbourg, and in the same year in all the cities of the Rhine, whether Free Cities or Imperial Cities or cities belonging to the lords. In some towns they burnt the Jews after a trial; in others, without a trial. In some cities the Jews themselves set fire to their houses and cremated themselves.

It was decided in Strasbourg that no Jew should enter the city for a hundred years, but before twenty years had passed, the council and magistrates agreed that they ought to admit the Jews again into the city for twenty years. And so the Jews came back again to Strasbourg in the year 1368 after the birth of our Lord.

The first major battle of the Hundred Years' War occurred in 1346 at Crécy, just south of Flanders. The larger French army followed no battle plan but simply attacked the English lines in a disorderly fashion. The arrows of the English archers decimated the French cavalry. As the chronicler Froissart described it, "[with their longbows] the English continued to shoot into the thickest part of the crowd, wasting none of their arrows. They impaled or wounded horses and riders, who fell to the ground in great distress, unable to get up again without the help of several men."[13] It was a stunning victory for the English and the foot soldier.

The Battle of Crécy was not decisive, however. The English simply did not possess the resources to subjugate all of France, but they continued to try. The English king, Henry

THE BATTLE OF CRÉCY. This fifteenth-century manuscript illustration depicts the Battle of Crécy, the first of several military disasters suffered by the French in the Hundred Years' War, and shows why the English preferred the longbow to the crossbow. At the left, the French crossbowmen stop shooting and prime their weapons by cranking the handle, while English archers continue to shoot their longbows (a skilled archer could launch ten arrows a minute).

Bibliotheque Nationale, Paris, France/Bridgeman Art Library

V (1413–1422), was especially eager to achieve victory. At the Battle of Agincourt in 1415, the heavy, armor-plated French knights attempted to attack across a field turned to mud by heavy rain; the result was a disastrous French defeat and the death of fifteen hundred French nobles. Henry went on to forge an alliance with the duke of Burgundy, making the English masters of northern France.

The seemingly hopeless French cause fell into the hands of the dauphin Charles, the heir to the throne, who governed the southern two-thirds of French lands. Charles's cause seemed doomed until a French peasant woman quite unexpectedly saved the timid monarch. Born in 1412, the daughter of well-to-do peasants, Joan of Arc was a deeply religious person who came to believe that her favorite saints had commanded her to free France. In February 1429, Joan made her way to the dauphin's court and persuaded Charles to allow her to accompany a French army to Orléans. Apparently inspired by the faith of the peasant girl called "the Maid of Orléans" the French armies found new confidence in themselves and liberated Orléans. Within a few weeks, the entire Loire valley had been freed of the English. Joan had brought the war to a decisive turning point.

But she did not live to see the war concluded. Captured by the Burgundian allies of the English in 1430, Joan was turned over by the English to the Inquisition on charges of witchcraft. In the fifteenth century, spiritual visions were thought to be inspired by either God or the devil. Joan was condemned to death as a heretic and burned at the stake in 1431. To the end, as the flames rose up around her, she declared "that her voices came from God and had not deceived her." Twenty-five years later, a new ecclesiastical court exonerated her of these charges, and five centuries later, in 1920, she was made a saint of the Roman Catholic church.

Joan of Arc's accomplishments proved decisive. Although the war dragged on for another two decades, defeats of English armies in Normandy and Aquitaine led to French victory by 1453. Important to the French success was the use of the cannon, a new weapon made possible by the invention of gunpowder. The Chinese had invented gunpower in the eleventh century and devised a simple cannon by the thirteenth century. The Mongols greatly improved this technology, developing more accurate cannons and cannonballs; both spread to the Middle East in the thirteenth century and to Europe by the fourteenth. The use of gunpowder eventually brought drastic changes to European warfare by making castles, city walls, and armored knights obsolete.

POLITICAL DISINTEGRATION

By the fourteenth century, the feudal order had begun to break down. With money from taxes, kings could now hire professional soldiers, who tended to be more reliable than feudal knights anyway. Fourteenth-century kings had their own problems as well. Many dynasties in Europe were unable to produce male heirs, while the founders of new dynasties had to fight for their positions as groups of nobles, trying to gain advantages for themselves, supported opposing candidates. Rulers encountered financial problems too. Hiring professional soldiers left them always short of cash, adding yet another element of uncertainty and confusion to fourteenth-century politics.

The Decline of the Church

The papacy of the Roman Catholic church reached the height of its power in the thirteenth century. But problems in the fourteenth century led to a serious decline for the church. By that time, the monarchies of Europe were no longer willing to accept papal claims of temporal supremacy, as is evident in the struggle between Pope Boniface VIII (1294–1303) and King Philip IV (1285–1314) of France. In his desire to acquire new revenues, Philip expressed the right to tax the clergy of France, but Boniface VIII claimed that the clergy of any state could not pay taxes to their secular ruler without the pope's consent. In no uncertain terms he argued that popes were supreme over both the church and the state (see the box on p. 343).

Philip IV refused to accept the pope's position and sent a small contingent of French forces to capture Boniface and bring him back to France for trial. The pope escaped but soon died from the shock of his experience. Philip's strong-arm tactics had produced a clear victory for the national monarchy over the papacy, since no later pope dared renew the extravagant claims of Boniface VIII. To ensure his position and avoid any future papal threat, Philip IV engineered the election of a Frenchman, Clement V (1305–1314), as pope. Using the excuse of turbulence in the city of Rome, the new pope took up residence in Avignon on the east bank of the Rhone River.

THE PAPACY AT AVIGNON (1305–1378)

The residency of the popes in Avignon for almost three-quarters of the fourteenth century led to a decline in papal prestige and an increase in antipapal sentiment. The city of Rome was the traditional capital of the universal church. The pope was the bishop of Rome, and his position was based on being the successor to the apostle Peter, the first bishop of Rome. It was unseemly that the head of the Catholic church should reside in Avignon instead of Rome. In the 1330s, the popes began to construct a stately palace in Avignon, a clear indication that they intended to stay for some time.

Many contemporaries believed, somewhat questionably, that the popes at Avignon were captives of the French monarchy. Although Avignon did not belong to the French monarchy, it was easy to believe in view of the city's proximity to French lands. Moreover, during the seventy-three years of the Avignonese papacy, of the 134 new cardinals created by the popes, 113 of them were French. Finally, the splendor in which the pope and car-

Boniface VIII's Defense of Papal Supremacy

One of the most remarkable documents of the fourteenth century was the exaggerated statement of papal supremacy issued by Pope Boniface VIII in 1302 in the heat of his conflict with the French king Philip IV. Ironically, this strongest statement ever made of papal supremacy was issued at a time when the rising power of the secular monarchies made it increasingly difficult for the premises to be accepted. Not long after issuing it, Boniface was taken prisoner by the French. Although freed by his fellow Italians, the humiliation of his defeat brought his death a short time later.

POPE BONIFACE VIII, UNAM SANCTAM

We are compelled, our faith urging us, to believe and to hold—and we do firmly believe and simply confess—that there is one holy catholic and apostolic church, outside of which there is neither salvation nor remission of sins. . . . In this church there is one Lord, one faith, and one baptism. . . . Therefore, of this one and only church there is one body and one head . . . Christ, namely, and the vicar of Christ, St. Peter, and the successor of Peter. For the Lord himself said to Peter, feed my sheep. . . .

We are told by the word of the gospel that in this His fold there are two swords—a spiritual, namely, and a temporal. . . .

Both swords, the spiritual and the material, therefore, are in the power of the church; the one, indeed, to be wielded for the church, the other by the church; the one by the hand of the priest, the other by the hand of kings and knights, but at the will and sufferance of the priest. One sword, moreover, ought to be under the other, and the temporal authority to be subjected to the spiritual. . . .

Therefore if the earthly power err it shall be judged by the spiritual power; but if the lesser spiritual power err, by the greater. But if the greatest, it can be judged by God alone, not by man, the apostle bearing witness. A spiritual man judges all things, but he himself is judged by no one. This authority, moreover, even though it is given to man and exercised through man, is not human but rather divine, being given by divine lips to Peter and founded on a rock for him and his successors through Christ himself whom he has confessed; the Lord himself saying to Peter: "Whatsoever thou shalt bind, etc." Whoever, therefore, resists this power thus ordained by God, resists the ordination of God. . . .

Indeed, we declare, announce, and define that it is altogether necessary to salvation for every human creature to be subject to the Roman pontiff.

---

dinals were living in Avignon led to a highly vocal criticism of both clergy and papacy in the fourteenth century. At last, Pope Gregory XI, perceiving the disastrous decline in papal prestige, returned to Rome in 1377.

THE GREAT SCHISM AND CRIES FOR REFORM

Gregory XI (1370–1378) died in Rome the spring after his return. When the college of cardinals met to elect a new pope, the citizens of Rome, fearful that the French majority would choose another Frenchman who would move the papacy back to Avignon, threatened that the cardinals would not leave Rome alive unless a Roman or an Italian were elected pope. Wisely, the terrified cardinals duly elected the Italian archbishop of Bari as Pope Urban VI (1378–1389). Five months later, a group of dissenting cardinals—the French ones—declared Urban's election invalid and chose one of their number, a Frenchman, who took the title of Clement VII and promptly returned to Avignon. Because Urban remained in Rome, there were now two popes, beginning what has been called the Great Schism of the church.

The Great Schism divided Europe. France and its allies supported the pope in Avignon, whereas France's enemy England and its allies supported the pope in Rome. The Great Schism was also damaging to the faith of Chris-

tian believers. The pope was widely believed to be the true leader of Christendom; when both lines of popes denounced the other as the Antichrist, people's faith in the papacy and the church were undermined. Finally, a church council met at Constance, Switzerland, in 1417. After the competing popes resigned or were deposed, a new pope was elected who was acceptable to all parties.

By the mid-fifteenth century, as a result of these crises, the church had lost much of its temporal power. The popes no longer had any hope of asserting supremacy over temporal governments as the medieval papacy had. Even worse, the papacy and the church had also lost much of their moral prestige.

CONCLUSION

The collapse of the Han dynasty in China in the third century C.E. led to nearly four centuries of internal chaos. The fall of the Roman Empire in the fifth century brought a quite different result as three new civilizations emerged out of the collapse of Roman power in the Mediterranean. Islam emerged in the east; its adherents occupied large parts of the old Roman Empire, preserved much of Greek culture, and created their own flourishing civilization. The eastern part of the old Roman Empire, increasingly Greek in culture, continued to survive as the Christian Byzantine Empire. And a new Christian European civilization was establishing its roots in the west.

The coronation of Charlemagne, the descendant of a Germanic tribe converted to Christianity, as Roman emperor in 800 symbolized the fusion of the three chief components of the new European civilization: the German tribes, the Roman legacy, and the Christian church. Charlemagne's Carolingian Empire fostered the idea of a distinct European identity. With the disintegration of that empire, power fell into the hands of many different lords, who came to constitute a powerful group of nobles that dominated the political, economic, and social life of Europe. But quietly and surely, within this world of castles and private power, kings gradually began to extend their public power and laid the foundations for the European kingdoms that in one form or another have dominated European politics ever since.

European civilization began to flourish in the High Middle Ages. The revival of trade, the expansion of towns and cities, and the development of a money economy did not mean the end of a predominantly rural European society, but they did open the door to new ways to make a living and new opportunities for people to expand and enrich their lives. At the same time, the High Middle Ages also gave birth to an intellectual and spiritual revival that transformed European society.

Fourteenth-century European society, however, was challenged by an overwhelming number of disintegrative forces. Devastating plague, decline in trade and industry, bank failures, peasant revolts pitting the lower classes against the upper classes, seemingly constant warfare, and even the spectacle of two popes condemning each other as the Antichrist all seemed to overpower Europeans in this "calamitous century." To some people, it appeared that the last days of the world were at hand. European society, however, proved remarkably resilient, and as we shall see, in the next chapter, elements of recovery would make the fifteenth century a period of significant political, economic, artistic, and intellectual change.

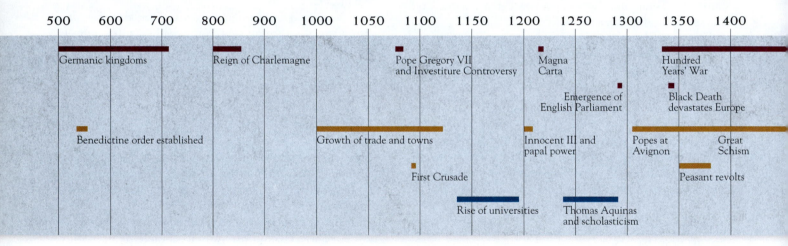

| 500 | 600 | 700 | 800 | 900 | 1000 | 1050 | 1100 | 1150 | 1200 | 1250 | 1300 | 1350 | 1400 |

Germanic kingdoms

Reign of Charlemagne

Pope Gregory VII and Investiture Controversy

Magna Carta

Hundred Years' War

Emergence of English Parliament

Black Death devastates Europe

Benedictine order established

Growth of trade and towns

Innocent III and papal power

Popes at Avignon

Great Schism

First Crusade

Peasant revolts

Rise of universities

Thomas Aquinas and scholasticism

CHAPTER NOTES

1. Norman F. Cantor, ed., *The Medieval World, 300–1300* (New York, 1963), p. 104.
2. Quoted in Simon Keynes, "The Vikings in England, c. 790–1016," in Peter Sawyer, ed., *The Oxford Illustrated History of the Vikings* (Oxford, 1997), p. 81.
3. Quoted in Marvin Perry, Joseph Peden, and Theodore Von Laue, *Sources of the Western Tradition*, vol. 1(Boston, 1987), p. 218.
4. Quoted in Jean Gimpel, *The Medieval Machine* (Harmondsworth, England, 1977), p. 92.
5. Ernest F. Henderson, ed., *Select Historical Documents of the Middle Ages* (London, 1892), p. 365.
6. Oliver J. Thatcher and Edgar H. McNeal, eds., *A Source Book for Medieval History* (New York, 1905), p. 208.
7. Quoted in R. H. C. Davis, *A History of Medieval Europe from Constantine to Saint Louis*, 2d ed. (New York, 1988), p. 252.
8. Thatcher and McNeal, *Source Book for Medieval History*, p. 517.
9. Quoted in Hans E. Mayer, *The Crusades*, trans. John Gillingham (New York, 1972), pp. 99–100.
10. Quoted in David J. Herlihy, *The Black Death and the Transformation of the West*, ed. Samuel K. Cohn Jr. (Cambridge, Mass., 1997), p. 9.
11. Giovanni Boccaccio, *The Decameron*, trans. Frances Winwar (New York, 1955), p. xiii.
12. Jean Froissart, *Chronicles*, ed. and trans. Geoffrey Brereton (Harmondsworth, England, 1968), p. 111.
13. Froissart, *Chronicles*, p. 89.

SUGGESTED READING

Good general histories of the medieval period can be found in B. Tierney and S. Painter, *Western Europe in the Middle Ages, 300–1475* (New York, 1983); E. Peters, *Europe and the Middle Ages*, 2d ed. (Englewood Cliffs, N.J., 1989); and D. Nicholas, *The Evolution of the Medieval World: Society, Government, and Thought in Europe, 312–1500* (London, 1993). A brief history of the Early Middle Ages can be found in R. Collin, *Early Medieval Europe, 300–1000* (New York, 1991).

Surveys of Carolingian Europe include P. Riche, *The Carolingians: A Family Who Forged Europe* (Philadelphia, 1993), and R. McKitterick, *The Frankish Kingdoms Under the Carolingians, 751–987* (London, 1983). On Charlemagne, see H. R. Loyn and J. Percival, *The Reign of Charlemagne* (New York, 1976).

Two introductory works on fief-holding are J. R. Strayer, *Feudalism* (Princeton, N.J., 1985), and the classic work by M. Bloch, *Feudal Society* (London, 1961). For an important revisionist view, see S. Reynolds, *Fiefs and Vassals* (Oxford, 1994).

There are numerous works on the various medieval states. On England, see R. Frame, *The Political Development of the British Isles, 1100–1400* (Oxford, 1990). On Germany, see H. Fuhrmann, *Germany in the High Middle Ages, c. 1050–1250* (Cambridge, 1986), an excellent account, and B. Arnold, *Princes and Territories in Medieval Germany* (Cambridge, 1991). On France, see J. Dunbabib, *France in the Making, 843–1180* (Oxford, 1985). On Italy, see D. J. Herlihy, *Cities and Society in Medieval Italy* (London, 1980). On eastern Europe, see N. Davies, *God's Playground: A History of Poland*, vol. 1 (Oxford, 1981), and S. Franklin and J. Shephard, *The Emergence of Rus, 750–1200* (New York, 1996).

On economic conditions in the Middle Ages, see N. J. G. Pounds, *An Economic History of Medieval Europe* (New York, 1974), and R. S. Lopez, *The Commercial Revolution of the Middle Ages, 950–1350* (Englewood Cliffs, N.J., 1971). Urban history is covered in D. Nicholas, *The Growth of the Medieval City: From Late Antiquity to the Early Fourteenth Century* (New York, 1997). On women in general, see L. Bitel, "Women in Early Medieval Northern Europe," in R. Bridenthal, S. M. Stuard, and M. E. Wiesner, *Becoming Visible*, 3d ed. (New York, 1998), and D. J. Herlihy, *Opera Muliebria: Women and Work in Medieval Europe* (New York, 1990). On peasant life, see R. Fossier, *Peasant Life in the Medieval West* (New York, 1988).

For a general survey of church life, see R. W. Southern, *Western Society and the Church in the Middle Ages*, rev. ed. (New York, 1990). On the papacy in the High Middle Ages, see C. Morris, *The Papal Monarchy* (Oxford, 1989), and I. S. Robinson, *The Papacy* (Cambridge, 1990). The papacy of Innocent III is covered in J. E. Sayers, *Innocent III, Leader of Europe, 1198–1216* (New York, 1994). Good works on monasticism include B. Bolton, *The Medieval Reformation* (London, 1983); C. H. Lawrence, *Medieval Monasticism* (London, 1984), a good general account; and H. Leyser, *Hermits and the New Monasticism* (London, 1984). On the Inquisition, see B. Hamilton, *The Medieval Inquisition* (New York, 1981). A good general study of the church in the fourteenth century is F. P. Oakley, *The Western Church in the Later Middle Ages* (Ithaca, N.Y., 1980). On the Avignonese papacy, see Y. Renouard, *The Avignon Papacy, 1305–1403* (London, 1970).

The development of universities is covered in S. Ferruolo, *The Origin of the University* (Stanford, Calif., 1985), and the brief, older work by C. H. Haskins, *The Rise of Universities* (Ithaca, N.Y., 1957). A good introduction to Romanesque style is A. Petzold, *Romanesque Art* (New York, 1995). On the Gothic movement, see M. Camille, *Gothic Art: Glorious Visions* (New York, 1996), and C. Wilson, *The Gothic Cathedral* (London, 1990).

Two good general surveys on the Crusades are H. E. Mayer, *The Crusades*, 2d ed. (New York, 1988), and J. Riley-Smith, *The Crusades: A Short History* (New Haven, Conn., 1987). Other works of value are J. Riley-Smith, ed., *The Oxford Illustrated History of the Crusades* (New York, 1995), and R. C. Smail, *Crusading Warfare, 1097–1193*, 2d ed. (New York, 1995).

On the Black Death, see P. Ziegler, *The Black Death* (New York, 1969), and D. J. Herlihy, *The Black Death and the Transformation of the West*, ed. S. K. Cohn Jr. (Cambridge, Mass., 1997).

Worthy accounts of the Hundred Years' War include A. Curry, *The Hundred Years' War* (New York, 1993), and R. H. Neillands, *The Hundred Years' War* (New York, 1990). On Joan of Arc, see M. Warner, *Joan of Arc: The Image of Female Heroism* (New York, 1981). On the political history of the fourteenth century, see B. Guenée, *States and Rulers in Later Medieval Europe*, trans. J. Vale (Oxford, 1985).

INFOTRAC COLLEGE EDITION

For additional reading, go to InfoTrac College Edition, your online research library at
http://web1.infotrac-college.com

Enter the search term "Charlemagne" using the Keywords.

Enter the search terms "early Christianity" using the Keywords.

Enter the search term "Feudalism" or "Feudal" using the Subject Guide.

Enter the search terms "Cities and Towns, Medieval" using the Subject Guide.

Enter the search terms "Middle Ages" using the Subject Guide.

Enter the search terms "Black Death" using Keywords.

Enter the search terms "Medieval England" using Keywords.

NEW PATTERNS OF CIVILIZATION

In Part II of this book, we examined the period that followed the collapse of the civilizations of antiquity down to the end of the fourteenth century. During this period, a number of significant forces were at work in human society. The concept of civilization gradually spread from such heartland regions as the Middle East, the Mediterranean basin, the South Asian subcontinent, and China into new areas of the world—to sub-Saharan Africa, to central and western Europe, to Southeast Asia, and even to the islands of Japan, off the eastern edge of the Eurasian landmass. Across the oceans, unique but advanced civilizations began to take shape in the Americas. In the meantime, the vast migration of peoples continued, leading not only to bitter conflicts but also to increased interchanges of technology and ideas. The result was the transformation of separate and distinct cultures and civilizations into an increasingly complex and vast world system embracing not only technology and trade but also ideas and religious beliefs.

What explains this explosion in human activity? One answer is advances in technology. Improved irrigation methods, the introduction of new crops, and the increased use of the iron plow led to a substantial rise in food production, thus creating wealth that could be used for the purchase of other goods. Advances were made in ship construction and navigational techniques. Other factors were the mastery of monsoon patterns in the Indian Ocean, the domestication of the camel in North Africa and the Middle East, and increased trade. During the first millennium C.E., the great trade routes of the traditional world—the Silk Road from China to the Middle East and then on to the Mediterranean, the caravan trade across the Sahara, and the maritime network that stretched across the Indian Ocean—all reached their maturity.

As had been the case during antiquity, the Middle East was the heart of this activity. The Arab Empire, which took shape after the death of Muhammad in the early seventh century, provided the key link in the revived trade routes through the region. Muslim traders—both Arab and Berber—opened contacts with West African societies south of the Sahara, while their ships followed the monsoon winds eastward as far as the Spice Islands in Southeast Asia. Nomads from Central Asia carried goods back and forth along the Silk Road between the Middle East and China. For the next several hundred years, the great cities of the Middle East— Mecca, Damascus, and Baghdad—became among the wealthiest in the known world. The great Chinese city of Chang'an lay at the eastern extremity of the Silk Road as it snaked eastward across Central Asia.

Islam's contributions to the human experience during this period were cultural and technological as well as economic. Muslim philosophers preserved the works of the ancient Greeks for posterity, Muslim scientists and mathematicians made new discoveries about the nature of the universe and the human body, and Arab cartographers and historians mapped the known world and speculated about the fundamental forces in human society.

But the Middle East was not the only or necessarily even the primary contributor to world trade and civilization during this period. While the Arab Empire became the linchpin of trade between the Mediterranean and eastern and southern Asia, a new center of primary importance in world trade was emerging in East Asia, focused on China. China had been a major participant in regional trade during the Han dynasty, when its silks were already being transported to Rome via Central Asia, but its role had declined after the fall of the Han. Now, with the rise of the great Tang and Song dynasties, China reemerged as a major commercial power in East Asia, trading by sea with Southeast Asia and Japan and by land with the nomadic peoples of Central Asia. In general, overland trade was carried on by non-Chinese peoples in Central Asia, but the Chinese themselves became directly involved in the maritime trade with the countries in the South Seas.

By now, China was not only a regional economic power but a global one as well. The Silk Road through Turkestan became one of the most important trade routes of the era, and during the Ming dynasty, Chinese fleets briefly sailed across the Indian Ocean as far as the Red Sea and the eastern coast of Africa.

Like the Middle East, China was also a prime source of new technology. From China came paper, printing, the compass, and gunpowder. The double-hulled Chinese junks that entered the Indian Ocean during the Ming dynasty were slow and cumbersome but extremely seaworthy and capable of carrying substantial quantities of goods over long distances. Among China's other contributions were porcelain, chess, the mechanical clock, and the iron stirrup. Many such inventions arrived in Europe by way of India or the Middle East, and their Chinese origins were therefore unknown in the West.

Increasing trade on a regional or global basis also led to the exchange of ideas. Buddhism was brought to China by merchants, and Islam first arrived in sub-Saharan Africa and the Indonesian archipelago in the same manner. In their new environments, these religions initially had an impact mainly on merchants and other city-dwellers, but in some cases they gradually gained favor in the countryside.

Merchants were not the only means by which religious and cultural ideas spread, however. Sometimes migration, conquest, or relatively peaceful processes played a part. The case of the Bantu-speaking peoples in Central Africa is apparently an example of peaceful expansion; and while Islam sometimes followed the path of Arab warriors, they rarely imposed their religion by force on the local population. In some instances, as with the Mongols, the conquerors made no effort to convert others to their own religions. By contrast, Christian monks, motivated by missionary fervor, converted many of the peoples of central and eastern Europe. Roman Catholic monks brought Latin Christianity to the Ger-

manic and western Slavic peoples, and monks from the Byzantine Empire largely converted the southern and eastern Slavic populations to Eastern Orthodox Christianity.

Another characteristic of the period between 500 and 1400 C.E. was the almost constant migration of nomadic and seminomadic peoples. Dynamic forces in the Gobi Desert, Central Asia, the Arabian peninsula, and Central Africa provoked vast numbers of peoples to abandon their homelands and seek their livelihood elsewhere. Sometimes the migration was peaceful. More often, however, migration produced violent conflict and sometimes invasion and subjugation. As had been the case during antiquity, the most active source of migration was Central Asia. From here, Turkic-speaking peoples spilled over the Hindu Kush into northern India, southwest into Persia, and farther west into the Balkans

TRADE AND CIVILIZATION

Between 500 and 1400, the level of interdependence among human societies began to intensify as three major trade routes—the Indian Ocean, the Silk Road, and the trans-Saharan caravan route—began to create the framework for a single world trade system. New technology, new crops, and new ideas crossed from one end of the known world to the other. Contacts occurred in the realm of technology as in that of ideas, including inventions such as paper, the compass, and gunpowder; crops such as sugar, cotton, and spices; and great religious systems such as Buddhism, Hinduism, Christianity, and Islam. One interesting aspect of this process was the close relationship between missionary activities and trade. Buddhist merchants first brought the teachings of Siddhartha Gautama to China, and Muslim traders carried the words of the prophet Muhammad to Southeast Asia and sub-Saharan Africa. At the same time, Christian missionaries may have brought the first accurate knowledge of silk manufacturing from China to the Mediterranean.

What were the major causes of the rapid expansion of trade dur-

> **ARAB MERCHANTS IN A CARAVAN.** By land or by sea, Arab trade routes extended over half the globe. The world of Islam and the camel, both portrayed in this thirteenth-century miniature, were essential components of Muslim commercial ventures.

© Bibliothèque Nationale, Paris, Paris Arabe 5847, FOL 138, RcC1230

ing this period? One key factor was the introduction of new technology in the field of transportation. The development of the compass, improved techniques in mapmaking and shipbuilding, and greater knowledge of wind patterns all contributed to the expansion of maritime trade far from familiar shores. Caravan trade, once carried by wheeled chariots or on the backs of oxen, now used the camel as the preferred beast of burden through the parched deserts of Africa and the Middle East.

Another factor in the expansion of commerce during this period was the appearance of several multinational empires that created zones of stability and affluence in key areas from North Africa eastward toward the Pacific. Central to the process was the emergence of the empire of the Abbasids in the Middle East. China reached a zenith of prosperity during the Tang and Song dynasties as Europe was slowly emerging from the collapse of the Roman Empire. In the thirteenth century, the Mongol invasions brought this era to an end but then created a new era of peace and stability that lasted for over a century and fostered long-distance trade throughout the known world.

FEUDAL ORDERS AROUND THE WORLD

When we use the word *feudalism*, we usually think of European knights on horseback clad in iron coats and armed with sword and lance. However, between 800 and 1500, a form of social organization that a later generation of historians called feudalism developed in different parts of the world. By the term *feudalism*, these historians meant a decentralized political order in which local lords owed loyalty and provided military service to a king or more powerful lord. In Europe, a feudal order based on lords and vassals arose between 800 and 900 and flourished for the next four hundred years.

In Japan, a feudal order much like that found in Europe developed between 800 and 1500. By the end of the ninth century, powerful nobles in the countryside, while owing a loose loyalty to the Japanese emperor, began to exercise political and legal power in their own extensive lands. To protect their property and security, these nobles retained samurai, warriors who owed loyalty to the nobles and provided military service for them. Like knights in Europe, the samurai followed a warrior code and fought on horseback, clad in iron. However, they carried a sword and bow and arrow rather than a sword and lance.

➤ **A KNIGHT'S EQUIPMENT.** Pictured here is a charging European knight with his equipment. The introduction of the high saddle, stirrups, and larger horses allowed horsemen to wear heavier armor and to wield long lances. Compare the equipment of the European knight to that of the samurai warrior on page 296.

© Leiden, University Library, BPL 20, f.60r

In some respects, the political relationships among the Indian states beginning in the fifth century took on the character of the feudal system that emerged in Europe in the Middle Ages. Like medieval European lords, local Indian rajas were technically vassals of the king, but unlike in European feudalism, the relationship was not a contractual one. Still, the Indian model became highly complex, with "inner" and "outer" vassals, depending on their physical or political proximity to the king, and "greater" or "lesser" vassals, depending on their power and influence. As in Europe, the vassals themselves often had vassals.

In the Valley of Mexico, the Aztecs developed a political system between 1300 and 1500 that bore some similarities to the Japanese, Indian, and European feudal orders. Although the Aztec king was a powerful, authoritarian ruler, the local rulers of lands outside the capital city were allowed considerable freedom. However, they did pay tribute to the king and also provided him with military forces. Unlike the knights and samurai of Europe and Japan, however, Aztec warriors were armed with sharp knives made of stone and spears of wood fitted with razor-sharp blades cut from stone.

	300 C.E.	400 C.E.	500 C.E.	600 C.E.	700 C.E.	800 C.E.	900 C.E.
India and the Middle East	Gupta dynasty in India			Life of Muhammad	Foundation of Abbasid caliphate		Arrival of Islam
Africa	Conquest of Kush by Axum	First states appear in West Africa		Spread of Islam across North Africa / Arab takeover of lower Nile valley			
East and Southeast Asia			Rise of Yamato state in Japan	Tang dynasty in China	Golden Age of the Silk Road	Rise of the kingdom of Angkor	
Americas	Teotihuacán civilization / Moche culture in South America					Decline of the Maya	
Europe			Germanic kingdoms		Charlemagne and the Carolingian Empire / Growth of feudalism		

in southeastern Europe. Later, Central Asia gave birth to an even more fearsome force in the form of the Mongols. Mongol expansion began with the unification of Mongol tribes in the Gobi Desert by Genghis Khan and culminated in the advance of Mongolian armies to the gates of central Europe and the conquest of China in the thirteenth century. Wherever they went, they left a train of enormous destruction and loss of life. Inadvertently, the Mongols were also the source of a new wave of epidemics that swept through much of Europe and the Middle East in the fourteenth century. The spread of the plague—known at the time as the Black Death—took much of the population of Europe to an early grave.

But there was another side to the era of nomadic expansion. Often, as historian Thomas J. Barfield has noted, the nomadic peoples had a symbiotic relationship with the sedentary societies, propping up governments like the Tang dynasty in China in order to protect their source of income. Once nomadic warriors completed their conquests, they settled down to become administrators. Often the results were constructive. German migrations and Viking incursions contributed to the creation of dynamic new societies in Europe, and Turkish invasions led to the rise of states in the Anatolian peninsula and northern India.

Even the invasions of the Mongols—the "scourge of God," as Europeans of the thirteenth and fourteenth centuries called them—had constructive as well as destructive consequences. After their initial conquests, for a brief period of three generations, the Mongols provided an avenue for trade throughout the most extensive empire (known as the Pax Mongolica) the world had yet seen. When the pope dispatched envoys to the imperial court in Mongolia in the mid-thirteenth century, it was the first time Europeans had traveled the entire distance by land to East Asia.

The millennium following the destruction of the ancient empires brought about enormous changes in human society. During the era of Mongol expansion, there was widespread death and suffering throughout the known world. At the same time, the world had witnessed a significant expansion in the technological and material capacity of human societies and in the depth of contact among them. The era of widespread peace brought about as the result of the Mongol conquests also inaugurated what one scholar has described as the "idea of the unified conceptualization of the globe," creating a "basic information circuit" that spread commodities, ideas, and inventions from one end of the Eurasian supercontinent to the other. The way was prepared for a new stage of world history.

900 C.E. 1000 C.E. 1100 C.E. 1200 C.E. 1300 C.E. 1400 C.E. 1500 C.E.

in northern India

Conquest of Baghdad by the Mongols

Ottoman Turks seize Constantinople

Portuguese ships explore West African coast

Kingdom of Zimbabwe

Spread of Mongols across East Asia

Beginning of Ming dynasty in China

Civilization of Chimor

Kingdom of the Aztecs

Rise of European kingdoms

Black Death

Part III

THE EMERGENCE OF NEW WORLD PATTERNS

(1400–1800)

Beginning in the fifteenth century, a new force entered the world scene in the form of a revived Europe. The period of history known as the early modern era (1400–1800) was marked in Europe by an explosion of scientific knowledge and the appearance of a new secular ideology that emphasized the power of human beings to dominate nature and improve their material surroundings. After the breakdown of Christian unity in the Reformation era, Europeans engaged in a vigorous period of state building that resulted in the creation of independent monarchies in western and central Europe, which formed the basis for a new European state system.

The rise of early modern Europe had an immediate as well as a long-term impact on the rest of the world. The first stage began with the discovery of the Americas by Christopher Columbus in 1492 and the equally important voyages of Vasco da Gama and Ferdinand Magellan into the Indian and Pacific Oceans. These voyages and those that followed in this so-called Age of Discovery or Age of Exploration not only injected European sea power into new areas of the world but also vastly extended the maritime trade network until for the first time it literally encircled the globe. Some historians have characterized this period as the beginning of an era of European dominance.

Significant as it was, however, the emergence of Europe as a major player on the world stage was by no means the only important feature of this period. An excessive emphasis on the expanding European civilization tends to overlook the fact that other areas of the world were realizing impressive achievements of their own. Two great new Islamic empires founded by the Ottomans in Turkey and the Safavids in Persia, arose in the Middle East, while a third, that of the Mughals, unified the Indian subcontinent for the first time in nearly two thousand years. Islam was now firmly established in Africa south of the Sahara and in Asia as far east as the Indonesian archipelago.

In most of Asia, the European revival had only minimal effects. Portuguese merchants reached the coast of China in the early sixteenth century and landed on the islands of Japan a generation later. Merchants and missionaries from various European countries were active in both countries by the end of the century. But the ruling authorities in China and Japan, like their counterparts in the mainland states in Southeast Asia, became increasingly wary of the impact of Europeans' activities on their own societies, and by the eighteenth century, the Western presence in the region had markedly declined.

The first thrust of European expansion, then, significantly changed the face of the world, but it did not firmly establish European dominance. China remained, in the eyes of many, the most advanced and most sophisticated civilization on earth, and its achievements were imitated by its neighbors and admired by philosophers in far-off Europe. The era of Muslim dominance over the seas had come to an end, but Islam was still a force to be reckoned with. The bulk of Africa remained essentially outside the purview of European influence.

Chapter 13

RENEWAL, REFORM, AND STATE BUILDING IN EUROPE

CHAPTER OUTLINE

- THE RENAISSANCE
- THE REFORMATION OF THE SIXTEENTH CENTURY
- EUROPE IN CRISIS: WAR, REVOLUTION, AND SOCIAL DISINTEGRATION, 1560–1650
- RESPONSE TO CRISIS: THE PRACTICE OF ABSOLUTISM
- ENGLAND AND THE EMERGENCE OF CONSTITUTIONAL MONARCHY
- EUROPEAN CULTURE
- CONCLUSION

FOCUS QUESTIONS

- What were the main features of the Renaissance, and how did it differ from the Middle Ages?
- What were the main tenets of Lutheranism, Calvinism, and Anabaptism, and how did they differ from each other and from Catholicism?
- Why is the period between 1560 and 1650 in Europe called an age of crisis, and how did the turmoil contribute to the artistic and intellectual developments of the period?
- What was absolutism, and what were the main characteristics of the absolute monarchies that merged in France, Prussia, Austria, and Russia? Why did England follow a different path?
- ➤ What did Copernicus, Kepler, Galileo, and Newton contribute to a new vision of the universe, and how did their vision differ from the Ptolemaic conception of the universe? What was the significance of this new vision?

After the disintegrative patterns of the fourteenth century, Europe began a remarkable recovery that encompassed a revival of arts and letters in the fifteenth century, known as the Renaissance, and a religious renaissance in the sixteenth century, known as the Reformation. The religious division of Europe (Catholics versus Protestants) that was a result of the Reformation was instrumental in beginning a series of wars that dominated much of European history from 1560 to 1650 and exacerbated the economic and social crises that were besetting the region.

One of the responses to the crises of the seventeenth century was a search for order. The most general trend was an extension of monarchical power as a stabilizing force. This development, which historians have called absolutism or absolute monarchy, was most evident in France during the flamboyant reign of Louis XIV, regarded by some as the perfect embodiment of an absolute monarch. In his memoirs, the duc de Saint-Simon, who had firsthand experience of French court life, said that Louis was "the very figure of a hero, so imbued with a natural but most imposing majesty that it appeared even in his most insignificant gestures and movements." The king's natural grace gave him a special charm: "He was as dignified and majestic in his dressing gown as when dressed in robes of state, or on horseback at the head of his troops." He spoke well and learned quickly. He was naturally kind, and "he loved truth, justice, order, and reason." His life was orderly: "Nothing could be regulated with greater exactitude than were his days and hours." His self-control was impeccable: "He did not lose control of himself ten times in his whole life, and then only with inferior persons." But even absolute monarchs had faults, and Saint-Simon had the courage to point them out: "Louis XIV's vanity was without limit or restraint," which led to his "distaste for . . . all independence of character and sentiment in others," as well as his "mistakes of judgment in matters of importance."

The seventeenth century in Europe also witnessed the Scientific Revolution, which brought to Europeans a new way of viewing the universe and their place in it. In time, the Scientific Revolution would add to Europe's growing sense of power as changes in government, the economy, and the military enabled Europeans to move out into the global stage in a dramatic fashion. •

THE RENAISSANCE

People who lived in Italy between 1350 and 1550 or so believed that they had witnessed a rebirth of classical antiquity—the world of the Greeks and Romans. To them, this marked a new age, which historians later called the Renaissance (French for "rebirth") and viewed as a distinct period of European history, which began in Italy and then spread to the rest of Europe.

Renaissance Italy was largely an urban society. The city-states became the centers of Italian political, economic, and social life. Within this new urban society, a secular spirit emerged as increasing wealth created new possibilities for the enjoyment of worldly things.

The Renaissance was also an age of recovery from the disasters of the fourteenth century, including the Black Death, political disorder, and economic recession. In pursuing that recovery, Italian intellectuals became intensely interested in the glories of their own past, the Greco-Roman culture of antiquity.

A new view of human beings emerged as people in the Italian Renaissance began to emphasize individual ability. The fifteenth-century Florentine architect Leon Battista Alberti expressed the new philosophy succinctly: "Men can do all things if they will."[1] This high regard for human worth and for individual potentiality gave rise to a new social ideal of the well-rounded personality or "universal person" (*l'uomo universale*) who was capable of achievements in many areas of life.

Renaissance Society

After the severe economic reversals and social upheavals of the fourteenth century, the European economy gradually recovered as manufacturing and trade increased in volume. The Italians and especially the Venetians expanded their wealthy commercial empire, rivaled only by the increasingly powerful Hanseatic League, a commercial and military alliance of north German coastal towns. Not until the sixteenth century, when overseas discoveries gave new importance to the states facing the Atlantic, did the Italian city-states begin to suffer from the competitive advantages of the more powerful national territorial states.

In the Middle Ages, society was divided into three estates: the clergy, or first estate, whose preeminence was grounded in the belief that people should be guided to spiritual ends; the nobility, or second estate, whose privileges rested on the principle that nobles provided security and justice for society; and the peasants and inhabitants of the towns and cities, the third estate. Although this social order continued into the Renaissance, some changes also became evident.

THE NOBILITY

Throughout much of Europe, the landholding nobles faced declining real incomes during most of the fourteenth and fifteenth centuries. Many members of the old nobility survived, however, and new blood also infused its ranks. By 1500, the nobles, old and new, who constituted between 2 and 3 percent of the population in most countries, managed to dominate society, as they had done in the

Middle Ages, holding important political posts and serving as advisers to the king.

By 1500, certain ideals came to be expected of the noble, or aristocrat. These were best expressed in *The Book of the Courtier*, by the Italian Baldassare Castiglione (1478–1529). Castiglione described the three fundamental attributes of the perfect courtier. First, nobles are born, not made, and they should exhibit impeccable character, grace, and talents. Second, the perfect noble must participate in military and bodily exercises, because the principal profession of a courtier was arms; however, unlike the medieval knight, who was primarily concerned with military skill, the Renaissance noble must also seek a classical education and adorn his life with the arts. Third, the noble was expected to follow a certain standard of conduct. Nobles should not hide their accomplishments but show them with grace. The aim of the perfect noble was to serve his prince in an effective and honest way.

PEASANTS AND TOWNSPEOPLE

Except in the heavily urban areas of northern Italy and Flanders, peasants made up the overwhelming mass of the third estate—they constituted 85 to 90 percent of the total European population. Serfdom decreased as the manorial system continued its decline. Increasingly, the labor dues owed by a peasant to his lord were converted into rents paid in money. By 1500, especially in western Europe, more and more peasants were becoming legally free.

The remainder of the third estate were inhabitants of towns and cities, originally merchants and artisans. But by the fifteenth century, the Renaissance town or city had become more complex. At the top of urban society were the patricians, whose wealth from capitalistic enterprises in trade, industry, and banking enabled them to dominate their urban communities economically, socially, and politically. Below them were the petty burghers—the shopkeepers, artisans, guildmasters, and guildsmen—who were largely concerned with providing goods and services for local consumption. Below these two groups were the propertyless workers earning pitiful wages and the unemployed, living squalid and miserable lives. These poor city-dwellers constituted 30 to 40 percent of the urban population.

FAMILY AND MARRIAGE IN RENAISSANCE ITALY

The family bond was a source of great security in the urban world of Renaissance Italy. To maintain the family, parents carefully arranged marriages, often to strengthen business or family ties. Details were worked out well in advance, sometimes when children were only two or three, and reinforced by a legally binding marriage contract (see the box on p. 355). The important aspect of the contract was the size of the dowry, a sum of money presented by the wife's family to the husband upon marriage.

The father-husband was the center of the Italian family. He gave it his name, managed all finances (his wife had no share in his wealth), and made the crucial decisions that determined his children's lives. A father's authority over his children was absolute until he died or formally freed his children. In Renaissance Italy, children did not become adults on reaching a certain age; adulthood came only when the father went before a judge and formally emancipated them. The age of emancipation varied from early teens to late twenties.

The wife managed the household, a position that gave women a certain degree of autonomy in their daily lives. Most wives, however, also knew that their primary function was to bear children. Upper-class wives were frequently pregnant; Alessandra Strozzi of Florence, for example, who had been married at the age of sixteen, bore eight children in ten years. For women in the Renaissance, childbirth was a fearful occasion. Not only was it painful, but it could be deadly; possibly as many as one woman in ten died in childbirth.

The Intellectual Renaissance

The emergence and growth of individualism and secularism as characteristics of the Italian Renaissance are most noticeable in the intellectual and artistic realms. The most important literary movement associated with the Renaissance is humanism.

ITALIAN RENAISSANCE HUMANISM

Renaissance humanism was an intellectual movement based on the study of the classics, the literary works of Greece and Rome. Humanists studied the liberal arts—grammar, rhetoric, poetry, moral philosophy or ethics, and history—all based on the writings of ancient Greek and Roman authors. We call these subjects the humanities.

Petrarch (1304–1374), who has often been called the father of Italian Renaissance humanism, did more than any other individual in the fourteenth century to foster the development of Renaissance humanism. Petrarch sought to find forgotten Latin manuscripts and set in motion a ransacking of monastic libraries throughout Europe. He also began the humanist emphasis on the use of pure classical Latin. Humanists used the works of Cicero as a model for prose and those of Virgil for poetry. As Petrarch said, "Christ is my God; Cicero is the prince of the language."

In Florence, the humanist movement took a new direction at the beginning of the fifteenth century. Fourteenth-century humanists such as Petrarch had described the intellectual life as one of solitude. They rejected family and a life of action in the community. However, the humanists who worked as secretaries for the city council of Florence took a new interest in civic life. They came to believe that it was the duty of an intellectual to live an active life for one's state. Humanists came to believe that their study of

MARRIAGE NEGOTIATIONS

*M*arriages were so important in maintaining families in Renaissance Italy that much energy was put into arranging them. Parents made the choices for their children, for considerations that had little to do with the modern notion of love. This selection is taken from the letters of a Florentine matron of the illustrious Strozzi family to her son Filippo in Naples. The family's considerations were complicated by the fact that the son was in exile.

ALESSANDRA STROZZI TO HER SON FILIPPO IN NAPLES

[April 20, 1464] Concerning the matter of a wife [for Filippo], it appears to me that if Francesco di Messer Tanagli wishes to give his daughter, that it would be a fine marriage. . . . Now I will speak with Marco [Parenti, Alessandra's son-in-law], to see if there are other prospects that would be better, and if there are none, then we will learn if he wishes to give her [in marriage]. . . . Francesco Tanagli has a good reputation, and he has held office, not the highest, but still he has been in office. You may ask: "Why should he give her to someone in exile?" There are three reasons. First, there aren't many young men of good family who have both virtue and property. Secondly, she has only a small dowry, 1,000 florins, which is the dowry of an artisan [although not a small sum, either—senior officials in the government bureaucracy earned 300 florins a year]. . . . Third, I believe that he will give her away, because he has a large family and he will need help to settle them. . . .

[July 26, 1465] Francesco is a good friend of Marco and he trusts him. On S. Jacopo's day, he spoke to him discreetly and persuasively, saying that for several months he had heard that we were interested in the girl and . . . that when we had made up our minds, she will come to us willingly. [He said that] you were a worthy man, and that his family had always made good marriages, but that he had only a small dowry to give her, and so he would prefer to send her outside of Florence to someone of worth, rather than to give her to someone here, from among those who were available, with little money. . . . We have information that she is affable and competent. She is responsible for a large family (there are twelve children, six boys and six girls), and the mother is always pregnant and isn't very competent. . . .

[August 31, 1465] I have recently received some very favorable information [about the Tanagli girl] from two individuals. . . . They are in agreement that whoever gets her will be content. . . . Concerning her beauty, they told me what I had already seen, that she is attractive and well-proportioned. Her face is long, but I couldn't look directly into her face, since she appeared to be aware that I was examining her . . . and so she turned away from me like the wind. . . . She reads quite well . . . and she can dance and sing. . . .

So yesterday I sent for Marco and told him what I had learned. And we talked about the matter for a while, and decided that he should say something to the father and give him a little hope, but not so much that we couldn't withdraw, and find out from him the amount of the dowry. . . . May God help us to choose what will contribute to our tranquility and to the consolation of us all. . . .

[September 13, 1465] Marco came to me and said that he had met with Francesco Tanagli, who had spoken very coldly, so that I understand that he had changed his mind.

[Filippo Strozzi eventually married Fiametta di Donato Adimari in 1466.]

---

the humanities should be put to the service of the state. It is no accident that humanists served as secretaries in Italian city-states or at courts of princes or popes.

Also evident in the humanism of the first half of the fifteenth century was a growing interest in classical Greek civilization. One of the first Italian humanists to gain a thorough knowledge of Greek was Leonardo Bruni, who became an enthusiastic pupil of the Byzantine scholar Manuel Chrysoloras, who taught in Florence from 1396 to 1400.

THE IMPACT OF PRINTING

The Renaissance witnessed the development of printing, which made an immediate impact on European intellectual life and thought. Printing from hand-carved wooden blocks had been done in the West since the twelfth century and in China even before that. What was new in the fifteenth century in Europe was multiple printing with movable metal type. The development of printing from movable type was a gradual process that culminated some time between 1445 and 1450; Johannes Gutenberg of Mainz played an important role in bringing the process to completion. Gutenberg's Bible, completed in 1455 or 1456, was the first true book produced from movable type.

By 1500, there were more than a thousand printers in Europe, who collectively had published almost forty thousand titles (between eight and ten million copies). Probably 50 percent of these books were religious—Bibles and biblical commentaries, books of devotion, and sermons. Next in importance were the Latin and Greek classics, medieval grammars, legal handbooks, and works on philosophy.

The printing of books encouraged the development of scholarly research and the desire to attain knowledge. Printing also stimulated the development of an ever-expanding lay reading public, a development that had an enormous impact on European society. Printing allowed European civilization to compete for the first time with the civilization of China.

The Artistic Renaissance

Renaissance artists sought to imitate nature in their works of art. Their search for naturalism became an end in itself: to persuade onlookers of the reality of the object or event they were portraying. At the same time, the new artistic standards reflected the new attitude of mind in which human beings became the focus of attention, the "center and measure of all things," as one artist proclaimed.

The frescoes by Masaccio (1401–1428) in Florence have long been regarded as the first masterpieces of Early Renaissance art. With his use of monumental figures, a more realistic relationship between figures and landscape, and the visual representation of the laws of perspective, a new realistic style of painting was born. Onlookers became aware of a world of reality that appeared to be a continuation of their own.

This new Renaissance style was absorbed and modified by other Florentine painters in the fifteenth century. Especially important were two major developments. One emphasized the technical side of painting —understanding the laws of perspective and the geometrical organization of outdoor space and light. The second development was the investigation of movement and anatomical structure. The realistic portrayal of the human nude became one of the foremost preoccupations of Italian Renaissance art. By the end of the fifteenth century, Italian painters had created a new artistic environment. Many artists had mastered the new techniques for a scientific observation of the world around them and were now ready to move into new forms of creative expression. This marked the shift to the High Renaissance.

The High Renaissance was dominated by the work of three artistic giants, Leonardo da Vinci (1452–1519), Raphael (1483–1520), and Michelangelo (1475–1564). Leonardo carried on the fifteenth-century experimental tradition by studying everything and even dissecting human bodies in order to see how nature worked. But Leonardo stressed the need to advance beyond such realism and initiated the high Renaissance's preoccupation with the idealization of nature, an attempt to generalize from realistic portrayal to an ideal form.

At twenty-five, Raphael was already regarded as one of Italy's best painters. He was acclaimed for his numerous madonnas, in which he attempted to achieve an ideal of beauty far surpassing human standards. He is well known

LEONARDO DA VINCI, *THE LAST SUPPER*. Leonardo da Vinci was the impetus behind the High Renaissance concern for the idealization of nature, moving from a realistic portrayal of the human figure to an idealized form. Evident in Leonardo's *Last Supper* is his effort to depict a person's character and inner nature through gesture and movement. Unfortunately, Leonardo used an experimental technique in this fresco, which soon led to its physical deterioration.

◆ **RAPHAEL, *SCHOOL OF ATHENS*.** Raphael arrived in Rome in 1508 and began to paint a series of frescoes commissioned by Pope Julius II for the papal apartments at the Vatican. In *School of Athens*, painted about 1510–1511, Raphael created an imaginary gathering of ancient philosophers. In the center stand Plato and Aristotle. At the left is Pythagoras, showing his system of proportions on a slate. At the right is Ptolemy, holding a celestial globe.

for his frescoes in the Vatican Palace; his *School of Athens* reveals a world of balance, harmony, and order—the underlying principles of the art of the classical world of Greece and Rome.

Michelangelo, an accomplished painter, sculptor, and architect, was fiercely driven by a desire to create, and he worked with great passion and energy on a remarkable number of projects. Michelangelo was influenced by Neoplatonism, especially evident in his figures on the ceiling of the Sistine Chapel. These muscular figures reveal an ideal type of human being with perfect proportions. In good Neoplatonic fashion, their beauty is meant to be

◆ **MICHELANGELO, *CREATION OF ADAM*.** In 1508, Pope Julius II recalled Michelangelo to Rome and commissioned him to decorate the ceiling of the Sistine Chapel. This colossal project was not completed until 1512. Michelangelo attempted to tell the story of the Fall of Man by depicting nine scenes from the biblical Book of Genesis. In this scene, the well-proportioned figure of Adam, meant by Michelangelo to be a reflection of divine beauty, awaits the divine spark.

a reflection of divine beauty; the more beautiful the body, the more God-like the figure.

THE NORTHERN ARTISTIC RENAISSANCE

In trying to provide an exact portrayal of their world, the artists of the north (especially the Low Countries) and Italy took different approaches. In Italy, the human form became the primary vehicle of expression as Italian artists sought to master the technical skills that allowed them to portray humans in realistic settings. The large wall spaces of Italian churches had given rise to the art of fresco painting, but in the north, the prevalence of Gothic cathedrals with their stained-glass windows resulted in more emphasis on illuminated manuscripts and wooden panel painting for altarpieces. The space available in these works was limited, and great care was put into depicting each object, leading northern painters to become masters at rendering details.

The most influential northern school of art in the fifteenth century was centered in Flanders. Jan van Eyck (c. 1380–1441) was among the first to use oil paint, a medium that enabled the artist to use a varied range of colors and create fine details. In *Giovanni Arnolfini and His Bride,* van Eyck's attention to detail is staggering. Nevertheless, van Eyck's comprehension of perspective was still uncertain. His work is indicative of northern Renaissance painters, who, in their effort to imitate nature, did so not by mastery of the laws of perspective and proportion but by empirical observation of visual reality and the accurate portrayal of details. By the end of the fifteenth century, however, artists from the north began to study in Italy and were more and more influenced by what artists were doing there.

The State in the Renaissance

In the second half of the fifteenth century, attempts were made to reestablish the centralized power of monarchical governments after the political disasters of the fourteenth century. Some historians called these states the "new monarchies," especially those of France, England, and Spain (see Map 13.1).

WESTERN EUROPE

The Hundred Years' War left France prostrate. But the war had also developed a degree of French national feeling toward a common enemy that the kings could use to reestablish monarchical power. The development of a French territorial state was greatly advanced by King Louis XI (1461–1483), known as the Spider because of his wily and devious ways. Louis strengthened the use of the *taille*—an annual direct tax usually on land or property— as a permanent tax imposed by royal authority, giving him

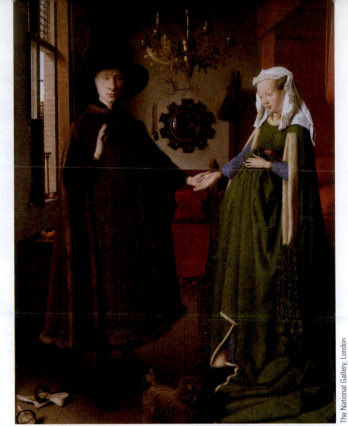

JAN VAN EYCK, *GIOVANNI ARNOLFINI AND HIS BRIDE.* Northern painters took great care in depicting each object and became masters at rendering details. This emphasis on a realistic portrayal is clearly evident in this oil painting, supposedly a portrait of Giovanni Arnolfini, an Italian merchant who had settled in Bruges, and his wife, Giovanna Cenami.

a sound, regular source of income, which created the foundations of a strong French monarchy.

The Hundred Years' War had also strongly affected the English. The cost of the war in its final years and the losses to the labor force strained the English economy. At the end of the war, England faced even greater turmoil when a civil war, known as the War of the Roses, erupted and aristocratic factions fought over the monarchy until 1485, when Henry Tudor established a new dynasty.

As the first Tudor king, Henry VII (1485–1509) worked to establish a strong monarchical government. Henry ended the private wars of the nobility by abolishing their private armies. He was also very thrifty. By not overburdening the nobility and the middle class with taxes, Henry won their favor, and they provided him much support.

Spain, too, experienced the growth of a strong national monarchy by the end of the fifteenth century. During the Middle Ages, several independent Christian kingdoms had emerged in the course of the long reconquest of the Iberian peninsula from the Muslims. Two of the strongest were Aragon and Castile. When Isabella of Castile (1474–1504) married Ferdinand of Aragon (1479–1516) in 1469, it was a major step toward unifying Spain. The two rulers worked to strengthen royal control of government.

MAP 13.1 Europe in the Fifteenth Century. By the second half of the fifteenth century, states in western Europe, particularly France, Spain, and England, had begun the process of modern state building. With varying success, they reined in the power of the church and nobles, increased the ability to levy taxes, and established effective government bureaucracies. ➤ *What aspects of Europe's political boundaries help explain why France and the Holy Roman Empire were often at war with each other?*

Ferdinand and Isabella also pursued a policy of strict religious uniformity. Spain possessed two large religious minorities, the Jews and the Muslims, both of which had been largely tolerated in medieval Spain. Increased persecution in the fourteenth century, however, led most Spanish Jews to convert to Catholicism. In 1492, Ferdinand and Isabella took the drastic step of expelling all professed Jews from Spain. Muslims, too, were then "encouraged" to convert to Catholicism, and in 1502, Isabella issued a decree expelling all professed Muslims from her kingdom.

CENTRAL AND EASTERN EUROPE

Unlike France, England, and Spain, the Holy Roman Empire failed to develop a strong monarchical authority. The failure of the German emperors in the thirteenth cen-

tury ended any chance of centralized monarchical authority, and Germany became a land of hundreds of virtually independent states. After 1438, the position of Holy Roman emperor was held in the hands of the Habsburg dynasty. Having gradually acquired a number of possessions along the Danube, known collectively as Austria, the house of Habsburg had become one of the wealthiest landholders in the empire and by the mid-fifteenth century had begun to play an important role in European affairs.

In eastern Europe, rulers struggled to achieve the centralization of the territorial states. Religious differences troubled the area, as Roman Catholics, Eastern Orthodox Christians, and other groups, including the Mongols, confronted each other. In Poland, the nobles gained the upper hand and established the right to elect their kings, a policy that drastically weakened royal authority. In Hungary, King Matthias Corvinus (1458–1490) broke the power of the wealthy lords and created a well-organized central administration. After his death, his work was largely undone.

Since the thirteenth century, Russia had been under the domination of the Mongols. Gradually, the princes of Moscow rose to prominence by using their close relationship to the Mongol khans to increase their wealth and expand their possessions. During the reign of the great Prince Ivan III (1462–1505), a new Russian state was born. Ivan III annexed other Russian principalities and took advantage of dissension among the Mongols to throw off their yoke by 1480.

THE ITALIAN STATES

During the Middle Ages, Italy had failed to develop a centralized monarchical state. Papal opposition to the Hohenstaufens in the thirteenth century had virtually guaranteed that. Moreover, the kingdom of Naples in the south was dominated by the French house of Anjou,

Sicily was ruled by the Spanish house of Aragon, and the papacy remained in shaky control of much of central Italy as rulers of the Papal States. Lack of centralized authority had enabled numerous city-states in northern and central Italy to remain independent of any political authority. Three of them—Milan, Venice, and Florence—managed to become fairly well centralized territorial states (see Map 13.2).

Milan, located at the crossroads of the main trade routes from Italian coast cities to the Alpine passes, was one of the richest city-states in Italy. In the fourteenth century, members of the Visconti family established themselves as dukes of Milan and extended their power over all of Lombardy. After the death of the last Visconti ruler of Milan in 1447, a *condottiere* (leader of a mercenary band) named Francesco Sforza turned on his Milanese employers, conquered the city, and became its new duke. Both Visconti and Sforza rulers worked to create the institutions of a strongly centralized territorial state.

MAP 13.2   Renaissance Italy.   Italy in the late fourteenth century was a land of five major states and numerous independent city-states. Increased prosperity and a supportive intellectual climate helped create the atmosphere for the middle and upper classes to "rediscover" Greco-Roman culture. Modern diplomacy was also a product of Renaissance Italy. ➤ *Could the presence of several other powers within easy marching distance make a ruler recognize the importance of diplomacy?*

The other major northern Italian state was the republic of Venice, which had grown rich from trade throughout the eastern Mediterranean and into northern Europe. A small oligarchy of merchant-aristocrats, who had become extremely wealthy through their commercial activities, ran the Venetian government on behalf of their own interests. Venice's commercial empire brought in enormous revenues and gave it the status of an international power. At the end of the fourteenth century, Venice embarked on the conquest of a territorial state in northern Italy to protect its overland trade routes.

The republic of Florence dominated the region of Tuscany. In the course of the fourteenth century, a small but wealthy merchant oligarchy established control of the Florentine government, led the Florentines in a series of successful wars against their neighbors, and established Florence as a major territorial state in northern Italy. In 1434, Cosimo de' Medici (1434–1464) took control of the ruling oligarchy. Although the wealthy Medici family maintained republican forms of government for appearance's sake, it ran the government from behind the scenes. Through lavish patronage and the careful courting of political allies, the Medici were successful in dominating the city at a time when Florence was the cultural center of Italy.

The growth of powerful monarchical states led to trouble for the Italians and brought an end to the independence of the Italian states. Attracted by the riches of Italy, the French king Charles VIII (1483–1498) led an army of thirty thousand men into Italy and occupied the kingdom of Naples. Other Italian states turned for help to the Spanish, who gladly complied. For the next thirty years, the French and Spanish competed to dominate Italy. The terrible sack of Rome in 1527 by the armies of the Spanish king Charles I brought a temporary end to the Italian wars. Thereafter, the Spaniards dominated Italy.

MACHIAVELLI AND THE NEW STATECRAFT

No one gave better expression to the Italians' preoccupation with political power than Niccolò Machiavelli (1469–1527), who wrote *The Prince* (1513), one of the most influential works on political power in the Western world. Machiavelli's major concerns in *The Prince* were the acquisition, maintenance, and expansion of political power as the means to restore and maintain order in his time. In the Middle Ages, many political theorists stressed the ethical side of a prince's activity—how a ruler ought to behave based on Christian moral principles. Machiavelli bluntly contradicted this approach: "For the gap between how people actually behave and how they ought to behave is so great that anyone who ignores everyday reality in order to live up to an ideal will soon discover he had been taught how to destroy himself, not how to preserve himself."[2] Machiavelli considered his approach far more realistic than that of his medieval forebears. Politi-

cal activity, therefore, could not be restricted by moral considerations. The prince acts on behalf of the state and for the sake of the state must be willing to let his conscience sleep. Machiavelli was among the first to abandon morality as the basis for the analysis of political activity.

THE REFORMATION OF THE SIXTEENTH CENTURY

The Protestant Reformation is the name given to the religious reform movement that divided the western church into Catholic and Protestant groups. Although Martin Luther began the Reformation in the early sixteenth century, several earlier developments had set the stage for religious change.

Prelude to Reformation

During the second half of the fifteenth century, the new classical learning of the Italian Renaissance spread to the European countries north of the Alps and spawned a movement called Christian humanism or Northern Renaissance humanism, whose major goal was the reform of Christendom. The Christian humanists believed in the ability of human beings to reason and improve themselves and thought that through education in the sources of classical, and especially Christian, antiquity, they could instill an inner piety or an inward religious feeling that would bring about a reform of the church and society. To change society, they must first change the human beings who compose it.

The most influential of all the Christian humanists was Desiderius Erasmus (1466–1536), who formulated and popularized the reform program of Christian humanism. He called his conception of religion "the philosophy of Christ," by which he meant that Christianity should be a guiding philosophy for the direction of daily life rather than the system of dogmatic beliefs and practices that the medieval church seemed to stress. In other words, he emphasized inner piety and deemphasized the external forms of religion (such as the sacraments, pilgrimages, fasts, and relics). To Erasmus, the reform of the church meant spreading an understanding of the philosophy of Jesus Christ, providing enlightened education in the sources of early Christianity, and criticizing the abuses in the church. No doubt his work helped prepare the way for the Reformation; as contemporaries proclaimed, "Erasmus laid the egg that Luther hatched."

Church and Religion on the Eve of the Reformation

Corruption in the Catholic church was another factor that encouraged people to want reform. Between 1450 and 1520, a series of popes—called the Renaissance popes—failed to meet the church's spiritual needs. The popes were supposed to be the spiritual leaders of the Catholic church but as leaders of the Papal States were all too often involved in worldly interests. Julius II (1503–1513), the fiery "warrior-pope," personally led armies against his enemies, much to the disgust of pious Christians, who viewed the pope as a spiritual leader. As one intellectual wrote, "How, O bishop standing in the room of the Apostles, dare you teach the people the things that pertain to war?" Many high church officials were also concerned with money and used their church offices as opportunities to advance their careers and their wealth, and many ordinary parish priests seemed ignorant of their spiritual duties.

While the leaders of the church were failing to meet their responsibilities, ordinary people were clamoring for meaningful religious expression and certainty of salvation. As a result, for some the process of salvation became almost mechanical. Collections of relics grew as more and more people sought certainty of salvation through veneration of these relics. Frederick the Wise, elector of Saxony and Martin Luther's prince, had amassed over five thousand relics to which were attached indulgences that could reduce one's time in purgatory by 1,443 years. (An indulgence is a remission, after death, of all or part of the punishment due to sin.)

Martin Luther and the Reformation in Germany

Martin Luther was a monk and a professor at the University of Wittenberg, where he lectured on the Bible. Probably sometime between 1513 and 1516, through his study of the Bible, he arrived at an answer to a problem—the assurance of salvation—that had disturbed him since his entry into the monastery.

Catholic doctrine had emphasized that both faith and good works were required of a Christian to achieve personal salvation. In Luther's eyes, human beings, weak and powerless in the sight of an almighty God, could never do enough good works to merit salvation. Through his study of the Bible, Luther came to believe that humans are not saved through their good works but through faith in the promises of God, made possible by the sacrifice of Jesus on the cross. This doctrine of salvation, or justification by grace through faith alone, became the primary doctrine of the Protestant Reformation. Because Luther had arrived at this doctrine from his study of the Bible, the Bible became for Luther as for all other Protestants the chief guide to religious truth.

Luther did not see himself as a rebel, but he was greatly upset by the widespread selling of indulgences. Especially offensive in his eyes was the monk Johann Tetzel, who hawked indulgences with the slogan: "As soon as the coin in the coffer [money box] rings, the soul from purgatory springs." Greatly angered, he issued in 1517 a stunning indictment of the abuses in the sale of indulgences, the Ninety-Five Theses (see the box on p. 363). Thousands of copies were printed and quickly spread to all parts of Germany.

By 1520, Luther had begun to move toward a more definite break with the Catholic church and called on the German princes to overthrow the papacy in Germany and establish a reformed German church. Through all his calls for change, Luther expounded more and more on his new doctrine of salvation. It is faith alone, he said, not good works, that justifies and brings salvation through Christ.

Unable to accept Luther's ideas, the church excommunicated him in January 1521. He had also been summoned in 1520 to appear before the imperial diet or Reichstag of the Holy Roman Empire, convened by the newly elected Emperor Charles V (1519–1556). Ordered to recant the heresies he had espoused, Luther refused and made the famous reply that became the battle cry of the Reformation:

Unless I am convicted by Scripture and plain reason—I do not accept the authority of popes and councils, for they have contradicted each other—my conscience is captive to the Word of God. I cannot and I will not recant anything, for to go against conscience is neither right nor safe. Here I stand, I cannot do otherwise. God help me. Amen.[3]

LUTHER AND THE NINETY-FIVE THESES

*T*o most historians, the publication of Luther's Ninety-Five Theses marks the beginning of the Reformation. To Luther, they were simply a response to what he considered to be the blatant abuses committed by sellers of indulgences. Although written in Latin, the theses were soon translated into German and disseminated widely across Germany. They made an immense impression on Germans already dissatisfied with the ecclesiastical and financial policies of the papacy.

MARTIN LUTHER, SELECTIONS FROM THE NINETY-FIVE THESES

5. The Pope has neither the will nor the power to remit any penalties beyond those he has imposed either at his own discretion or by canon law.

20. Therefore the Pope, by his plenary remission of all penalties, does not mean "all" in the absolute sense, but only those imposed by himself.

21. Hence those preachers of Indulgences are wrong when they say that a man is absolved and saved from every penalty by the Pope's Indulgences.

27. It is mere human talk to preach that the soul flies out [of purgatory] immediately [when] the money clinks in the collection box.

28. It is certainly possible that when the money clinks in the collection box greed and avarice can increase; but the intercession of the Church depends on the will of God alone.

50. Christians should be taught that, if the Pope knew the exactions of the preachers of Indulgences, he would rather have the basilica of St. Peter reduced to ashes than built with the skin, flesh, and bones of his sheep [the indulgences that so distressed Luther were being sold to raise money for the construction of the new St. Peter's Basilica in Rome].

81. This wanton preaching of pardons makes it difficult even for learned men to redeem respect due to the Pope from the slanders or at least the shrewd questionings of the laity.

82. For example: "Why does not the Pope empty purgatory for the sake of most holy love and the supreme need of souls? This would be the most righteous of reasons, if he can redeem innumerable souls for sordid money with which to build a basilica, the most trivial of reasons."

86. Again: "Since the Pope's wealth is larger than that of the crassest Crassi of our time, why does he not build this one basilica of St. Peter with his own money, rather than with that of the faithful poor?"

90. To suppress these most conscientious questionings of the laity by authority only, instead of refuting them by reason, is to expose the Church and the Pope to the ridicule of their enemies, and to make Christian people unhappy.

94. Christians should be exhorted to seek earnestly to follow Christ, their Head, through penalties, deaths, and hells.

95. And let them thus be more confident of entering heaven through many tribulations rather than through a false assurance of peace.

Staatliche Museen Bildarchiv Preussischer Kulturbesitz, Kupferstichkabinett, Berlin (West), Photo: Jorg P. Anders

> **WOODCUT: LUTHER VERSUS THE POPE.** In the 1520s, after Luther's return to Wittenberg, his teachings began to spread rapidly, ending ultimately in a reform movement supported by state authorities. Pamphlets containing picturesque woodcuts were important in the spread of Luther's ideas. In the woodcut shown here, the crucified Jesus attends Luther's service on the left, while on the right the pope is at a table selling indulgences.

Members of the Reichstag were outraged and demanded that Luther be captured and delivered to the emperor. But Luther's ruler, Elector Frederick of Saxony, stepped in and protected him.

During the next few years, Luther's religious movement became a revolution. Luther was able to gain the support of many of the German rulers among the three hundred or so states that made up the Holy Roman Empire. These rulers quickly took control of the churches in their territories. The Lutheran churches in Germany (and later in Scandinavia) quickly became territorial or state churches in which the state supervised the affairs of the church. As part of the development of these state-dominated churches, Luther also instituted new religious services to replace the Catholic Mass. These focused on Bible reading, preaching of the word of God, and song.

Politics and Religion in the German Reformation

From its very beginning, the fate of Luther's movement was closely tied to political affairs. In 1519, Charles I, king of Spain and the grandson of Emperor Maximilian, was elected Holy Roman emperor as Charles V. Charles V ruled over an immense empire, consisting of Spain and its overseas possessions, the traditional Austrian Habsburg lands, Bohemia, Hungary, the Low Countries, and the kingdom of Naples in southern Italy. Politically, Charles wanted to maintain his enormous empire; religiously, he hoped to preserve the unity of his empire in the Catholic faith. However, a number of problems kept him preoccupied and cost him both his dream and his health.

The chief political concern of Charles V was his rivalry with the king of France, Francis I (1515–1547). Their conflict over disputed territories led to four wars that lasted more than twenty years. At the same time, Charles faced opposition from Pope Clement VII (1523–1534), who, guided by political considerations, joined the side of Francis I. The advance of the Ottoman Turks (see Chapter 15) into the eastern part of Charles's empire forced the emperor to divert forces there as well.

Finally, the internal political situation in the Holy Roman Empire was also not in Charles's favor. Germany was a land of several hundred territorial states. Although all owed loyalty to the emperor, in the Middle Ages these states had become quite independent of imperial authority. By the time Charles V was able to bring military forces to Germany in 1546, Lutheranism had become well established and the Lutheran princes were well organized. Unable to defeat them, Charles was forced to negotiate a truce. An end to religious warfare in Germany came in 1555 with the Peace of Augsburg. The division of Christianity was formally acknowledged; Lutheran states were to have the same legal rights as Catholic states. Although the German states were now free to choose between Catholicism and Lutheranism, the peace settlement did not recognize the principle of religious toleration for individuals. The right of each German ruler to determine the religion of his subjects was accepted, but not the right of the subjects to choose their own religion.

The Spread of the Protestant Reformation

With the Peace of Augsburg, what had at first been merely feared was now certain: the ideal of Christian unity was forever lost. The rapid spread of new Protestant groups made this a certainty.

CALVIN AND CALVINISM

John Calvin (1509–1564) was educated in his native France but after his conversion to Protestantism was forced to flee for the safety of Switzerland. In 1536, he published the first edition of the *Institutes of the Christian Religion*, a masterful synthesis of Protestant thought that immediately secured Calvin's reputation as one of the new leaders of Protestantism.

On most important doctrines, Calvin stood very close to Luther. He adhered to the doctrine of justification by faith alone to explain how humans achieved salvation. But Calvin also placed much emphasis on the absolute sovereignty of God or the all-powerful nature of God—what Calvin called the "power, grace, and glory of God." One of the ideas derived from his emphasis on the absolute sovereignty of God—predestination—gave a unique cast to Calvin's teachings. This "eternal decree," as Calvin called it, meant that God had predestined some people to be saved (the elect) and others to be damned (the reprobate). According to Calvin, "He has once for all determined, both whom He would admit to salvation, and whom He would condemn to destruction."[4] Although Calvin stressed that there could be no absolute certainty of salvation, his followers did not always make this distinction. The practical psychological effect of predestination was to give later Calvinists an unshakable conviction that they were doing God's work on earth, making Calvinism a dynamic and activist faith.

In 1536, Calvin began working to reform the city of Geneva. He was able to fashion a tightly organized church order that employed both clergy and laymen in the service of the church. The Consistory, a special body for enforcing moral discipline, functioned as a court to oversee the moral life, daily behavior, and doctrinal orthodoxy of Genevans and to admonish and correct deviants. Citizens in Geneva were punished for such varied "crimes" as dancing, singing obscene songs, drunkenness, swearing, and playing cards.

Calvin's success in Geneva enabled the city to become a vibrant center of Protestantism. Following Calvin's lead, missionaries trained in Geneva were sent to all parts of Europe. Calvinism became established in France, the Netherlands, Scotland, and central and eastern Europe, and by the mid-sixteenth century, Calvin's Geneva stood as the fortress of the Reformation.

THE ENGLISH REFORMATION

The English Reformation was rooted in politics, not religion. King Henry VIII (1509–1547) had a strong desire to divorce his first wife, Catherine of Aragon, with whom the king had a daughter, Mary, but no male heir. He wanted to marry Anne Boleyn, with whom the king had fallen in love. Impatient with the pope's unwillingness to grant him an annulment of his marriage, Henry turned to England's own church courts. As archbishop of Canterbury and head of the highest church court in England, Thomas Cranmer ruled in May 1533 that the king's marriage to Catherine was "absolutely void." At the beginning of June, Anne was crowned queen, and three months later a child was born, a girl (the future queen Elizabeth I), much to the king's disappointment.

In 1534, at Henry's request, Parliament moved to finalize the break of the Church of England with Rome. The Act of Supremacy of 1534 declared that the king was "the only supreme head on earth of the Church of England," a position that gave him control of doctrine, clerical appointments, and discipline. Although Henry VIII had broken with the papacy, little change occurred in matters of doctrine, theology, and ceremony. Some of his supporters, including Archbishop Cranmer, sought a religious reformation as well as an administrative one, but Henry was unyielding. But he died in 1547 and was succeeded by his son, the underage and sickly Edward VI (1547–1553), and during Edward's reign, Cranmer and others inclined toward Protestant doctrines were able to move the Church of England (or Anglican church) in a more Protestant direction. New acts of Parliament gave the clergy the right to marry and created a new Protestant church service.

Edward VI was succeeded by Mary (1553–1558), a Catholic who attempted to return England to Catholicism. Her actions aroused much anger, however, especially when "bloody Mary" burned more than three hundred Protestant heretics. By the end of Mary's reign, England was more Protestant than it had been at the beginning.

THE ANABAPTISTS

The Anabaptists were the radical reformers of the Protestant Reformation. To Anabaptists, the true Christian church was a voluntary association of believers who had undergone spiritual rebirth and had then been baptized into the church. Anabaptists advocated adult rather than infant baptism. They also wanted to return to the practices and spirit of early Christianity and considered all believers to be equal. Each church chose its own minister, who might be any member of the community since all Christians were considered priests (though women were often excluded).

Finally, unlike the Catholics and other Protestants, most Anabaptists believed in the complete separation of church and state. Government was to be excluded from the realm of religion and could not exercise political jurisdiction over real Christians. Anabaptists refused to hold political office or bear arms because many took the commandment "Thou shall not kill" literally. Their political beliefs as much as their religious beliefs caused the Anabaptists to be regarded as dangerous radicals who threatened the very fabric of sixteenth-century society. Indeed, the chief thing Protestants and Catholics could agree on was the need to persecute Anabaptists.

The Social Impact of the Protestant Reformation

The Protestants were especially important in developing a new view of the family. Because Protestantism had eliminated any idea of special holiness for celibacy and had abolished both monasticism and a celibate clergy, the family could be placed at the center of human life, and a new stress on "mutual love between man and wife" could be extolled.

But were doctrine and reality the same? Most often, reality reflected the traditional roles of husband as the ruler and wife as the obedient servant whose chief duty was to please her husband. Luther stated it clearly:

> The rule remains with the husband, and the wife is compelled to obey him by God's command. He rules the home and the state, wages war, defends his possessions, tills the soil, builds, plants, etc. The woman on the other hand is like a nail driven into the wall . . . so the wife should stay at home and look after the affairs of the household, as one who has been deprived of the ability of administering those affairs that are outside and that concern the state. She does not go beyond her most personal duties.[5]

Obedience to her husband was not a wife's only role; her other important duty was to bear children. To Calvin and Luther, this function of women was part of the divine plan, and for most Protestant women, family life was their only destiny (see the box on p. 366). Overall, the Protestant Reformation did not noticeably transform women's subordinate place in society.

The Catholic Reformation

By the mid-sixteenth century, Lutheranism had become established in Germany and Scandinavia and Calvinism in Switzerland, France, the Netherlands, and eastern Europe. In England, the split from Rome had resulted in

A PROTESTANT WOMAN

*I*n the initial zeal of the Protestant Reformation, women were frequently allowed to play unusual roles. Catherine Zell of Germany (c. 1497–1562) first preached beside her husband in 1527. After the death of her two children, she devoted the rest of her life to helping her husband and their Anabaptist faith. This selection is taken from one of her letters to a young Lutheran minister who had criticized her activities.

CATHERINE ZELL TO LUDWIG RABUS OF MEMMINGEN

I, Catherine Zell, wife of the late lamented Mathew Zell, who served in Strasbourg, where I was born and reared and still live, wish you peace and enhancement in God's grace. . . .

From my earliest years I turned to the Lord, who taught and guided me, and I have at all times, in accordance with my understanding and His grace, embraced the interests of His church and earnestly sought Jesus. Even in youth this brought me the regard and affection of clergymen and others much concerned with the church, which is why the pious Mathew Zell wanted me as a companion in marriage; and I, in turn, to serve the glory of Christ, gave devotion and help to my husband, both in his ministry and in keeping his house. . . . Ever since I was ten years old I have been a student and a sort of church mother, much given to attending sermons. I have loved and frequented the company of learned men, and I conversed much with them, not about dancing, masquerades, and worldly pleasures but about the kingdom of God. . . .

Consider the poor Anabaptists, who are so furiously and ferociously persecuted. Must the authorities everywhere be incited against them, as the hunter drives his dog against wild animals? Against those who acknowledge Christ the Lord in very much the same way we do and over which we broke with the papacy? Just because they cannot agree with us on lesser things, is this any reason to persecute them and in them Christ, in whom they fervently believe and have often professed in misery, in prison, and under the torments of fire and water?

Governments may punish criminals, but they should not force and govern belief, which is a matter for the heart and conscience not for temporal authorities. . . . When the authorities pursue one, they soon bring forth tears, and towns and villages are emptied.

---

the creation of a national church. The situation in Europe did not look particularly favorable to the Roman Catholic church (see Map 13.3). However, the Catholic church also underwent a revitalization in the sixteenth century, giving it new strength. There were three chief pillars of the Catholic Reformation: the Jesuits, a reformed papacy, and the Council of Trent.

The Society of Jesus, known as the Jesuits, was founded by a Spanish nobleman, Ignatius of Loyola (1491–1556). Loyola gathered together a small group of individuals who were recognized as a religious order by the pope in 1540. The new order was grounded on the principles of absolute obedience to the papacy, a strict hierarchical order for the society, the use of education to achieve its goals, and a dedication to engage in "conflict for God." A special vow of absolute obedience to the pope made the Jesuits an important instrument for papal policy. Jesuit missionaries proved singularly successful in restoring Catholicism to parts of Germany and eastern Europe.

A reformed papacy was another important factor in the development of the Catholic Reformation. The involvement of Renaissance popes in dubious finances and Italian political and military affairs had created numerous sources of corruption. It took the jolt of the Protestant Reformation to bring about serious reform. Pope Paul III (1534–1549) perceived the need for change and took the audacious step of appointing a reform commission to ascertain the church's ills. The commission's report in 1537 blamed the church's problems on the corrupt policies of

➤ **IGNATIUS OF LOYOLA.** The Jesuits became the most important new religious order of the Catholic Reformation. Shown here in a sixteenth-century painting by an unknown artist is Ignatius of Loyola, founder of the Society of Jesus. Loyola is seen kneeling before Pope Paul III, who officially recognized the Jesuits in 1540.

© Scala/Art Resource, NY

MAP 13.3 Catholics and Protestants in Europe by 1560. The Reformation continued to evolve beyond the basic split of the Lutherans from the Catholics. Several Protestant sects broke away from the teachings of Martin Luther, each with a separate creed and different ways of worship. In England, Henry VIII broke with the Catholic church for political and dynastic reasons. ➤ *Which areas of Europe were solidly Catholic, which were solidly Lutheran, and which were neither?*

popes and cardinals. It was also Paul III who formally recognized the Jesuits and began the Council of Trent.

In March 1545, a group of high church officials met in the city of Trent on the border between Germany and Italy and initiated the Council of Trent, which met intermittently from 1545 to 1563 in three major sessions. The final decrees of the Council of Trent reaffirmed traditional Catholic teachings in opposition to Protestant beliefs.

Scripture and tradition were affirmed as equal authorities in religious matters; only the church could interpret Scripture. Both faith and good works were declared necessary for salvation. Belief in purgatory and in the use of indulgences was strengthened, although the selling of indulgences was prohibited.

After the Council of Trent, the Roman Catholic church possessed a clear body of doctrine and a unified church under the acknowledged supremacy of the popes. The Roman Catholic church had become one Christian denomination among many. With a new spirit of confidence, the Catholic church entered a militant phase, as well prepared as the Calvinists to do battle for the Lord. An era of religious warfare was about to unfold.

EUROPE IN CRISIS: WAR, REVOLUTION, AND SOCIAL DISINTEGRATION, 1560–1650

Between 1560 and 1650, Europe experienced religious wars, revolutions and constitutional crises, economic and social disintegration, and a witchcraft craze. It was truly an age of crisis.

Politics and the Wars of Religion in the Sixteenth Century

By 1560, Calvinism and Catholicism had become militant religions dedicated to spreading the word of God as they interpreted it. Although their struggle for the minds and hearts of Europeans was at the heart of the religious wars of the sixteenth century, economic, social, and political forces also played an important role in these conflicts.

THE FRENCH WARS OF RELIGION (1562–1598)

Religion was central to the French civil wars of the sixteenth century. The growth of Calvinism had led to persecution by the French kings, but the latter did little to stop the spread of Calvinism. Huguenots (as the French Calvinists were called) constituted only about 7 percent of the population, but 40 to 50 percent of the French nobility became Huguenots, including the house of Bourbon, which stood next to the Valois in the royal line of succession. The conversion of so many nobles made the Huguenots a potentially dangerous political threat to monarchical power. Still, the Calvinist minority was greatly outnumbered by the Catholic majority, and the Valois monarchy was staunchly Catholic. At the same time, an extreme Catholic party, known as the ultra-Catholics, favored strict opposition to the Huguenots.

The religious issue was not the only factor that contributed to the French civil wars. Towns and provinces, which had long resisted the growing power of monarchical centralization, were only too willing to join a revolt against the monarchy. So were the nobles, and the fact that so many of them were Calvinists created an important base of opposition to the crown.

For thirty years, battles raged in France between Catholic and Calvinist parties. Finally, in 1589, Henry of Navarre, the political leader of the Huguenots and a member of the Bourbon dynasty, succeeded to the throne as Henry IV (1589–1610). Realizing, however, that he would never be accepted by Catholic France, Henry converted to Catholicism. With his coronation in 1594, the Wars of Religion had finally come to an end. The Edict of Nantes in 1598 solved the religious problem by acknowledging Catholicism as the official religion of France while guaranteeing the Huguenots the right to worship and to enjoy all political privileges, including the holding of public offices.

PHILIP II AND THE CAUSE OF MILITANT CATHOLICISM

The greatest advocate of militant Catholicism in the second half of the sixteenth century was King Philip II of Spain (1556–1598), the son and heir of Charles V. Philip's reign ushered in an age of Spanish greatness, both politically and culturally. Philip II had inherited from his father Spain, the Netherlands, and possessions in Italy and the New World. To strengthen his control, Philip insisted on strict conformity to Catholicism and strong, monarchical authority. Achieving the latter was not an easy task, because each of the lands of his empire had its own structure of government.

The Catholic faith was crucial to the Spanish people and their ruler. Driven by a heritage of crusading fervor, Spain saw itself as a nation of people chosen by God to save Catholic Christianity from the Protestant heretics. Philip II, the "most Catholic king," became the champion of Catholicism throughout Europe. Spain's leadership of a "holy league" against Turkish encroachments in the Mediterranean resulted in a stunning victory over the Turkish fleet in the Battle of Lepanto in 1571. But Philip's problems with the Netherlands and the English Queen Elizabeth led to his greatest misfortunes.

Philip's attempt to strengthen his control in the Spanish Netherlands, which consisted of seventeen provinces (modern Netherlands and Belgium), soon led to a revolt. The nobles, who stood to lose the most politically, strongly opposed Philip's efforts. Religion also became a major catalyst for rebellion when Philip attempted to crush Calvinism. Violence erupted in 1566, when Calvinists—especially nobles—began to destroy statues and stained-glass windows in Catholic churches. Philip responded by sending ten thousand veteran Spanish and Italian troops to crush the rebellion. But the revolt became organized, especially in the northern provinces, where the Dutch, under the leadership of William of Nassau, the prince of Orange, offered growing resistance. The struggle dragged on for decades until 1609, when a twelve-year truce ended the war, virtually recognizing the independence of the northern provinces. These seven northern provinces, which called themselves the United Provinces of the Netherlands, became the core of the modern Dutch state.

To most Europeans, Spain still seemed the greatest power of the age at the beginning of the seventeenth century, but the reality was quite different. The treasury was empty; Philip II went bankrupt in 1596 from excessive expenditures on war; and his successor did the same in 1607 by spending a fortune on his court. The armed forces were obsolescent, and the government was inefficient. Spain continued to play the role of a great power, but real power had shifted to England.

THE ENGLAND OF ELIZABETH

When Elizabeth Tudor, the daughter of Henry VIII and Anne Boleyn, ascended the throne in 1558, England was home to fewer than four million people. Yet during her reign, the small island kingdom became leader of the Protestant nations of Europe and laid the foundations for a world empire.

Intelligent, cautious, and self-confident, Elizabeth moved quickly to solve the difficult religious problem she inherited from her half-sister, Queen Mary. Elizabeth's religious policy was based on moderation and compromise. She repealed the Catholic laws of Mary's reign, and a new Act of Supremacy designated Elizabeth as "the only supreme governor" of both church and state. The Church of England under Elizabeth was basically Protestant, but it was of a moderate bent that kept most people satisfied.

Caution and moderation also dictated Elizabeth's foreign policy. Gradually, however, Elizabeth was drawn into conflict with Spain. Having resisted for years the idea of invading England as too impractical, Philip II of Spain was finally persuaded to do so by advisers who assured him that the people of England would rise against their queen when the Spaniards arrived. A successful invasion of England would mean the overthrow of heresy and the return of England to Catholicism. Philip ordered preparations for a fleet of warships, the Armada, to spearhead the invasion of England.

The Armada was a disaster. The Spanish fleet that finally set sail had neither the ships nor the manpower that Philip had planned to send. Battered by a number of encounters with the English, the Spanish fleet sailed back to Spain by a northward route around Scotland and Ireland, where it was further pounded by storms. Although the English and Spanish would continue their war for another sixteen years, the defeat of the Armada guaranteed for the time being that England would remain a Protestant country.

Economic and Social Crises: Witchcraft Mania

The period of European history from 1560 to 1650 witnessed severe economic and social crises as well as political upheaval. Economic contraction began to be evident in some parts of Europe by the 1620s. In the 1630s and 1640s, as imports of silver from the Americas declined, economic recession intensified, especially in the Mediterranean area. Once the industrial and financial center of Europe in the age of the Renaissance, Italy was now becoming an economic backwater.

Population trends of the sixteenth and seventeenth centuries also reveal Europe's worsening conditions. The population of Europe increased from 60 million in 1500 to 85 million by 1600, the first major recovery of European population since the devastation of the Black Death in the mid-fourteenth century. However, records also indicate a decline of the population by 1650, especially in central and southern Europe. Europe's longtime adversaries—war, famine and plague—continued to affect population levels. Europe's entry into another "little ice age" after the middle of the sixteenth century, when average temperatures fell, affected harvests and gave rise to famines. Europe's problems created social tensions, some of which became manifested in an obsession with witches.

Hysteria over witchcraft affected the lives of many Europeans in the sixteenth and seventeenth centuries. Neighbors accused neighbors of witchcraft, leading to widespread trials of witches. Perhaps more than 100,000 people were prosecuted throughout Europe on charges of witchcraft. As more and more people were brought to trial, the fear of witches, as well as the fear of being accused of witchcraft, escalated to frightening levels (see the box on p. 370).

Common people—usually those who were poor and without property—were more likely to be accused of witchcraft. Indeed, where lists are given, those mentioned most often are milkmaids, peasant women, and servant girls. In the witchcraft trials of the sixteenth and seventeenth centuries, more than 75 percent of the accused were women, most of them single or widowed and many over fifty years old.

That women should be the chief victims of witchcraft trials was hardly accidental. Nicholas Rémy, a witchcraft judge in France in the 1590s, found it "not unreasonable

A WITCHCRAFT TRIAL IN FRANCE

Persecutions for witchcraft reached their high point in the sixteenth and seventeenth centuries, when tens of thousands of people were brought to trial. In this excerpt from the minutes of a trial in France in 1652, we can see why the accused witch stood little chance of exonerating herself.

THE TRIAL OF SUZANNE GAUDRY

28 May, 1652. . . . Interrogation of Suzanne Gaudry, prisoner at the court of Rieux. . . . During interrogations on May 28 and May 29, the prisoner confessed to a number of activities involving the devil.

Deliberation of the Court—June 3, 1652

The undersigned advocates of the Court have seen these interrogations and answers. They say that the aforementioned Suzanne Gaudry confesses that she is a witch, that she had given herself to the devil, that she had renounced God, Lent, and baptism, that she has been marked on the shoulder, that she has cohabited with the devil and that she has been to the dances, confessing only to have cast a spell upon and caused to die a beast of Philippe Cornié. . . .

Third Interrogation, June 27

This prisoner being led into the chamber, she was examined to know if things were not as she had said and confessed at the beginning of her imprisonment.

—Answers no, and that what she has said was done so by force.

Pressed to say the truth, that otherwise she would be subjected to torture, having pointed out to her that her aunt was burned for this same subject.

—Answers that she is not a witch. . . .

She was placed in the hands of the officer in charge of torture, throwing herself on her knees, struggling to cry, uttering several exclamations, without being able, nevertheless, to shed a tear. Saying at every moment that she is not a witch.

The Torture

On this same day, being at the place of torture.

This prisoner, before being strapped down, was admonished to maintain herself in her first confessions and to renounce her lover.

—Says that she denies everything she has said, and that she has no lover. Feeling herself being strapped down, says that she is not a witch, while struggling to cry. . . and upon being asked why she confessed to being one, said that she was forced to say it.

Told that she was not forced, that on the contrary she declared herself to be a witch without any threat.

—Says that she confessed it and that she is not a witch, and being a little stretched [on the rack] screams ceaselessly that she is not a witch.

Asked if she did not confess that she had been a witch for twenty-six years.

—Says that she said it, that she retracts it, crying that she is not a witch.

Asked if she did not make Philippe Cornié's horse die, as she confessed.

—Answers no, crying Jesus-Maria, that she is not a witch.

The mark having been probed by the officer, in the presence of Doctor Bouchain, it was adjudged by the aforesaid doctor and officer truly to be the mark of the devil.

Being more tightly stretched upon the torture rack, urged to maintain her confessions.

—Said that it was true that she is a witch and that she would maintain what she had said.

Asked how long she has been in subjugation to the devil.

—Answers that it was twenty years ago that the devil appeared to her, being in her lodgings in the form of a man dressed in a little cowhide and black breeches. . . .

Verdict

July 9, 1652. In the light of the interrogations, answers, and investigations made into the charge against Suzanne Gaudry, . . . seeing by her own confessions that she is said to have made a pact with the devil, received the mark from him, . . . and that following this, she had renounced God, Lent, and baptism and had let herself be known carnally by him, in which she received satisfaction. Also, seeing that she is said to have been a part of nocturnal carols and dances.

For expiation of which the advice of the undersigned is that the office of Rieux can legitimately condemn the aforesaid Suzanne Gaudry to death, tying her to a gallows, and strangling her to death, then burning her body and burying it here in the environs of the woods.

---

that this scum of humanity, i.e., witches, should be drawn chiefly from the feminine sex." To another judge, it came as no surprise that witches would confess to sexual experiences with Satan: "The Devil uses them so, because he knows that women love carnal pleasures, and he means to bind them to his allegiance by such agreeable provocations."[6]

By the mid-seventeenth century, the witchcraft hysteria had begun to subside. As governments grew stronger, fewer magistrates were willing to accept the unsettling and divisive conditions generated by the trials of witches. Moreover, by the end of the seventeenth and beginning of the eighteenth centuries, more and more people were questioning altogether their old attitudes toward religion and found it especially contrary to reason to believe in the old view of a world haunted by evil spirits.

Seventeenth-Century Crises: Revolution and War

Although many Europeans responded to the upheavals of the second half of the sixteenth century with a desire for peace and order, the first fifty years of the seventeenth century continued to be a period of crisis. A series of rebellions and civil wars rocked the domestic stability of many European governments. A devastating war that affected much of Europe also added to the sense of crisis.

THE THIRTY YEARS' WAR (1618–1648)

The Thirty Years' War began in 1618 in the Germanic lands of the Holy Roman Empire as a struggle between Catholic forces, led by the Habsburg Holy Roman Emperors, and Protestant—primarily Calvinist—nobles in Bohemia who rebelled against Habsburg authority (see Map 13.4). What began as a struggle over religious issues soon became a wider conflict perpetuated by political motivations as both minor and major European powers—Denmark, Sweden, France, and Spain—entered the war. The competition for European leadership between the Bourbon dynasty of France and the Habsburg dynasties of Spain and the Holy Roman Empire was an especially important factor. Nevertheless, most of the battles were fought on German soil.

The war in Germany was officially ended in 1648 by the Peace of Westphalia, which proclaimed that all German states, including the Calvinist ones, were free to determine their own religion. The major contenders gained new territories, and France emerged as the dominant nation in Europe. The more than three hundred states that made up the Holy Roman Empire were recognized as independent states, and each was given the power to conduct its own foreign policy; this brought an end to the Holy Roman Empire as a political entity and ensured German disunity for another two hundred years. The Peace of Westphalia made it clear that political motives, not religious convictions, had become the guiding force in public affairs.

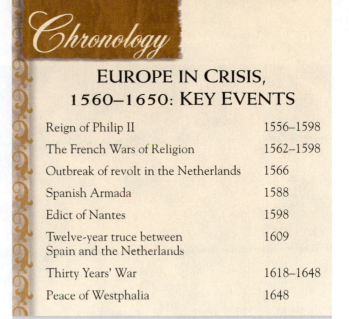

Chronology

EUROPE IN CRISIS, 1560–1650: KEY EVENTS

Reign of Philip II	1556–1598
The French Wars of Religion	1562–1598
Outbreak of revolt in the Netherlands	1566
Spanish Armada	1588
Edict of Nantes	1598
Twelve-year truce between Spain and the Netherlands	1609
Thirty Years' War	1618–1648
Peace of Westphalia	1648

RESPONSE TO CRISIS: THE PRACTICE OF ABSOLUTISM

Many people responded to the crises of the seventeenth century by searching for order. An increase in monarchical power became an obvious means for achieving stability. The result was what historians have called absolutism or absolute monarchy. Absolutism meant that the sovereign power or ultimate authority in the state rested in the hands of a king who claimed to rule by divine right—the idea that kings received their power from God and were responsible to no one except God. Late sixteenth-century political theorists believed that sovereign power consisted of the authority to make laws, tax, administer justice, control the state's administrative system, and determine foreign policy.

France Under Louis XIV

France during the reign of Louis XIV (1661–1715) has traditionally been regarded as the best example of the practice of absolute monarchy in the seventeenth century. French culture, language, and manners reached into all levels of European society. French diplomacy and wars overwhelmed the political affairs of western and central Europe. The court of Louis XIV seemed to be imitated everywhere in Europe.

One of the keys to Louis's power was his control of the central policy-making machinery of government because it was part of his own court and household. The royal court located at Versailles served three purposes simultaneously: it was the personal household of the king, the location of central governmental machinery, and the place where powerful subjects came to find favors and offices for themselves and their clients. The greatest danger to Louis's personal rule came from the very high nobles and princes of the blood (the royal princes), who considered it their natural role to assert the policy-making role of royal ministers. Louis eliminated this threat by removing them from the royal council, the chief administrative body of the king, and enticing them to his court, where he could keep them preoccupied with court life and out of politics. Instead of the high nobility and royal princes, Louis relied for his ministers on nobles who came from relatively new aristocratic families. His ministers were expected to be subservient; "I had no intention of sharing my authority with them," Louis said.

Louis's domination of his ministers and secretaries gave him control of the central policy-making machinery of government and thus authority over the traditional areas of monarchical power: the formulation of foreign policy, the making of war and peace, the assertion of the secular power

⟡▶ **SUN KINGS, WEST AND EAST.**   At the end of the seventeenth century, two powerful rulers dominated the affairs of their regions and saw themselves as sun kings—the sources of light for their people. On the left, Louis XIV, who ruled France from 1643 to 1715, is seen in a portrait by Hyacinth Rigaud that captures the king's sense of royal dignity and grandeur. On the right, Kangxi, who ruled China from 1661 to 1722, is seen in a nineteenth-century portrait that shows the ruler seated in majesty on his imperial throne.

of crown against any religious authority, and the ability to levy taxes to fulfill these functions. However, Louis had considerably less success with the internal administration of the kingdom. The traditional groups and institutions of French society—the nobles, officials, town councils, guilds, and representative estates in some provinces—were simply too powerful for the king to have direct control over the lives of his subjects. As a result, the control of the central government over the provinces and the people was carried out largely by the careful bribery of the important people to see that the king's policies were executed.

The cost of building palaces, maintaining his court, and pursuing his wars made finances a crucial issue for Louis XIV. He was most fortunate in having the services of Jean-Baptiste Colbert (1619–1683) as controller general of finances. Colbert sought to increase the wealth and power of France by general adherence to mercantilism, a set of principles that dominated economic thought in the seventeenth century. According to the mercantilists, the prosperity of a nation depended on a plentiful supply of bullion (gold and silver). For this reason, it was desirable to achieve

a favorable balance of trade in which goods exported were of greater value than those imported, promoting an influx of gold and silver payments that would increase the quantity of bullion. Mercantilism focused on the role of the state, believing that state intervention in the economy was desirable for the sake of the national good.

Colbert was an avid practitioner of mercantilism. To decrease imports and increase exports, he granted subsidies to individuals who established new industries. To improve communications and the transportation of goods internally, he built roads and canals. To decrease imports directly, Colbert raised tariffs on foreign goods.

The increase in royal power that Louis pursued led the king to develop a professional army numbering 100,000 men in peacetime and 400,000 in time of war. To achieve the prestige and military glory befitting an absolute king as well as to ensure the domination of his Bourbon dynasty over European affairs, Louis waged four wars between 1667 and 1713. His ambitions roused much of Europe to form coalitions that were determined to prevent the certain destruction of the European balance of power by Bourbon

MAP 13.4 Europe in the Seventeenth Century. This map shows Europe at the time of the Thirty Years' War (1618–1648). Although the struggle began in Bohemia and much of the fighting took place in the Germanic lands of the Holy Roman Empire, the conflict became a Europe-wide struggle. ➤ *Compare this map with Map 13.3. Which countries engaged in the war were predominantly Protestant, which were Catholic, and which were mixed?*

hegemony. Although Louis added some territory to France's northeastern frontier and established a member of his own Bourbon dynasty on the throne of Spain, he also left France impoverished and surrounded by enemies.

Absolutism in Central and Eastern Europe

During the seventeenth century, a development of great importance for the modern Western world took place with the appearance in central and eastern Europe of three new powers: Prussia, Austria, and Russia.

Frederick William the Great Elector (1640–1688) laid the foundation for the Prussian state. Realizing that the land he had inherited, known as Brandenburg-Prussia, was a small, open territory with no natural frontiers for defense, Frederick William built an army of forty thousand men, making it the fourth largest in Europe. To sustain the army, Frederick William established the General War Commissariat to levy taxes for the army and oversee its growth. The Commissariat soon evolved into an agency for civil government as well. The new bureaucratic machine became the elector's chief instrument to govern the state. Many of its officials were members of the Prussian landed aristocracy, the Junkers, who also served as officers in the all-important army.

In 1701, Frederick William's son Frederick officially gained the title of king. Elector Frederick III became King Frederick I, and Brandenburg-Prussia simply Prussia. In the eighteenth century, Prussia emerged as a great power in Europe.

PETER THE GREAT DEALS
WITH A REBELLION

During his first visit to the West, in 1697–1698, Peter received word that the Streltsy, an elite military unit stationed in Moscow, had revolted against his authority. Peter hurried home and crushed the revolt in a very savage fashion. This selection is taken from an Austrian account of how Peter dealt with the rebels.

PETER AND THE STRELTSY

How sharp was the pain, how great the indignation, to which the tsar's Majesty was mightily moved, when he knew of the rebellion of the Streltsy, betraying openly a mind panting for vengeance! He was still tarrying at Vienna, quite full of the desire of setting out for Italy; but, fervid as was his curiosity of rambling abroad, it was, nevertheless, speedily extinguished on the announcement of the troubles that had broken out in the bowels of his realm. Going immediately to Lefort . . . , he thus indignantly broke out: "Tell me, Francis, how I can reach Moscow by the shortest way, in a brief space, so that I may wreak vengeance on this great perfidy of my people, with punishments worthy of their abominable crime. Not one of them shall escape with impunity. Around my royal city, which, with their impious efforts, they planned to destroy, I will have gibbets and gallows set upon the walls and ramparts, and each and every one of them will I put to a direful death." Nor did he long delay the plan for his justly excited wrath; he took the quick post, as his ambassador suggested, and in four weeks' time he had got over about three hundred miles without accident, and arrived the 4th of September, 1698—a monarch for the well disposed, but an avenger for the wicked.

His first anxiety after his arrival was about the rebellion—in what it consisted, what the insurgents meant, who dared to instigate such a crime. And as nobody could answer accurately upon all points, and some pleaded their own ignorance, others the obstinacy of the Streltsy, he began to have suspicions of everybody's loyalty. . . . No day, holy or profane, were the inquisitors idle; every day was deemed fit and lawful for torturing. There were as many scourges as there were accused, and every inquisitor was a butcher. . . . The whole month of October was spent in lacerating the backs of culprits with the knout and with flames; no day were those that were left alive exempt from scourging or scorching; or else they were broken upon the wheel, or driven to the gibbet, or slain with the ax. . . .

To prove to all people how holy and inviolable are those walls of the city which the Streltsy rashly meditated scaling in a sudden assault, beams were run out from all the embrasures in the walls near the gates, in each of which two rebels were hanged. This day beheld about two hundred and fifty die that death. There are few cities fortified with as many palisades as Moscow has given gibbets to her guardian Streltsy.

The Austrian Habsburgs had long played a significant role in European politics as Holy Roman emperors. By the end of the Thirty Years' War, the Habsburg hopes of creating an empire in Germany had been dashed. In the seventeenth century, the house of Austria created a new empire in eastern and southeastern Europe.

The nucleus of the new Austrian Empire remained the traditional Austrian hereditary possessions: Lower and Upper Austria, Carinthia, Carniola, Styria, and Tyrol. To these had been added the kingdom of Bohemia and parts of northwestern Hungary. After the defeat of the Turks in 1687 (see Chapter 15), Austria took control of all of Hungary, Transylvania, Croatia, and Slovenia, thus establishing the Austrian Empire in southeastern Europe. By the beginning of the eighteenth century, the house of Austria had assembled an empire of considerable size.

The Austrian monarchy, however, never became a highly centralized, absolutist state, primarily because it contained so many different national groups. The Austrian Empire remained a collection of territories held together by the Hapburg emperor, who was archduke of Austria, king of Bohemia, and king of Hungary. Each of these regions, however, had its own laws and political life.

FROM MOSCOW TO RUSSIA

A new Russian state had emerged in the fifteenth century under the leadership of the principality of Moscow and its grand dukes. In the sixteenth century, Ivan IV (1533–1584) became the first ruler to take the title of *tsar* (the Russian word for *Caesar*). Ivan expanded the territories of Russia eastward and crushed the power of the Russian nobility. He was known as Ivan the Terrible because of his ruthless deeds, among them stabbing his son to death in a heated argument. When Ivan's dynasty came to an end in 1598, it was followed by a period of anarchy that did not end until the Zemsky Sobor (national assembly) chose Michael Romanov as the new tsar, establishing a dynasty that lasted until 1917. One of its most prominent members was Peter the Great.

Peter the Great (1689–1725) was an unusual character. A towering, strong man at 6 feet 9 inches tall, Peter enjoyed a low kind of humor—belching contests and crude jokes—and vicious punishments, including floggings, impalings, and roastings (see the box above). Peter received a firsthand view of the West when he made a trip there in 1697–1698 and returned to Russia with a firm determination to westernize or Europeanize Russia. He was especially eager to borrow European technology in order to give him the army and navy he needed to make Russia a great power.

As could be expected, one of his first priorities was the reorganization of the army and the creation of a navy. Employing both Russians and Europeans as officers, he conscripted peasants for twenty-five-year stints of service to build a standing army of 210,000 men. Peter has also been given credit for forming the first Russian navy.

To impose the rule of the central government more effectively throughout the land, Peter divided Russia into provinces. Although he hoped to create a "police state," by which he meant a well-ordered community governed in accordance with law, few of his bureaucrats shared his concept of duty to the state. Peter hoped for a sense of civic duty, but his own forceful personality created an atmosphere of fear that prevented it.

The object of Peter's domestic reforms was to make Russia into a great state and military power. His primary goal was to "open a window to the west," meaning an ice-free port easily accessible to Europe. This could only be achieved on the Baltic, but at that time, the Baltic coast was controlled by Sweden, the most important power in northern Europe. A long and hard-fought war with Sweden won Peter the lands he sought. In 1703, Peter began the construction of a new city, Saint Petersburg, his window to the west and a symbol that Russia was looking westward to Europe. Under Peter, Russia became a great military power and, by his death in 1725, an important European state.

ENGLAND AND THE EMERGENCE OF CONSTITUTIONAL MONARCHY

Not all states were absolutist in the seventeenth century. One of the most prominent examples of resistance to absolute monarchy came in England, where king and Parliament struggled to determine the roles each should play in governing England.

Revolution and Civil War

With the death of Queen Elizabeth I in 1603, the Tudor dynasty became extinct, and the Stuart line of rulers was inaugurated with the accession to the throne of Elizabeth's cousin, King James VI of Scotland, who became James I (1603–1625) of England. James espoused the divine right of kings, a viewpoint that alienated Parliament, which had grown accustomed under the Tudors to act on the premise that monarch and Parliament together ruled England as a "balanced polity." Then, too, the Puritans—Protestants within the Anglican church who, inspired by Calvinist theology, wished to eliminate every trace of Roman Catholicism from the Church of England—were alienated by the king's strong defense of the Anglican church. Much of England's gentry, mostly well-to-do landowners, had become Puritans, and this Puritan gentry formed an important and substantial part of the House of Commons, the lower house of Parliament. It was not wise to alienate these men.

The conflict that had begun during the reign of James came to a head during the reign of his son Charles I (1625–1649). Charles also believed in divine-right monarchy, and religious differences also added to the hostility between Charles I and Parliament. The attempt of Charles to impose more ritual on the Anglican church struck the Puritans as a return to Catholic practices. When Charles tried to force the Puritans to accept his religious policies, thousands of them went off to the "howling wildernesses" of America.

Grievances mounted until England finally slipped into a civil war (1642–1648) won by the parliamentary forces, due largely to the New Model Army of Oliver Cromwell, the only real military genius of the war. The New Model Army was composed primarily of more extreme Puritans known as the Independents, who, in typical Calvinist fashion, believed they were doing battle for God. As Cromwell wrote in one of his military reports, "Sir, this is none other but the hand of God; and to Him alone belongs the glory." We might give some credit to Cromwell; his soldiers were well trained in the new military tactics of the seventeenth century.

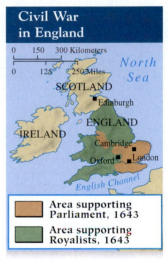

Civil War in England

North Sea

SCOTLAND
Edinburgh

ENGLAND
IRELAND
Cambridge
Oxford   London

English Channel

0   150   300 Kilometers
0   125   250 Miles

■ Area supporting Parliament, 1643
■ Area supporting Royalists, 1643

After the execution of Charles I on January 30, 1649, Parliament abolished the monarchy and the House of Lords and proclaimed England a republic or commonwealth. But Cromwell and his army, unable to work effectively with Parliament, dispersed it by force and established a military dictatorship. After Cromwell's death in 1658, the army decided that military rule was no longer feasible and restored the monarchy in the person of Charles II, the son of Charles I.

Restoration and a Glorious Revolution

Charles was sympathetic to Catholicism, and Parliament's suspicions were aroused in 1672 when Charles took the audacious step of issuing the Declaration of Indulgence, which suspended the laws that Parliament had passed against Catholics and Puritans after the restoration of the monarchy. Parliament forced the king to suspend the declaration.

THE BILL OF RIGHTS

In 1688, the English experienced yet another revolution, a bloodless one in which the Stuart king James II was replaced by Mary, James's daughter, and her husband, William of Orange. After William and Mary had assumed power, Parliament passed a Bill of Rights that specified the rights of Parliament and laid the foundation for a constitutional monarchy.

THE BILL OF RIGHTS

Whereas the said late King James II having abdicated the government, and the throne being thereby vacant, his Highness the prince of Orange (whom it hath pleased Almighty God to make the glorious instrument of delivering this kingdom from popery and arbitrary power) did (by the device of the lords spiritual and temporal, and diverse principal persons of the Commons) cause letters to be written to the lords spiritual and temporal, being Protestants, and other letters to the several counties, cities, universities, boroughs, and Cinque Ports, for the choosing of such persons to represent them, as were of right to be sent to parliament, to meet and sit at Westminster upon the two and twentieth day of January, in this year 1689, in order to such an establishment as that their religion, laws, and liberties might not again be in danger of being subverted; upon which letters elections have been accordingly made.

And thereupon the said lords spiritual and temporal and Commons, pursuant to their respective letters and elections, being now assembled in a full and free representation of this nation, taking into their most serious consideration the best means for attaining the ends aforesaid, do in the first place (as their ancestors in like case have usually done), for the vindication and assertion of their ancient rights and liberties, declare:

1. That the pretended power of suspending laws, or the execution of laws, by regal authority, without consent of parliament is illegal.

2. That the pretended power of dispensing with the laws, or the execution of law by regal authority, as it hath been assumed and exercised of late, is illegal.

3. That the commission for erecting the late court of commissioners for ecclesiastical causes, and all other commissions and courts of like nature, are illegal and pernicious.

4. That levying money for or to the use of the crown by pretense of prerogative, without grant of parliament, for longer time or in other manner than the same is or shall be granted, is illegal.

5. That it is the right of the subjects to petition the king, and all commitments and prosecutions for such petitioning are illegal.

6. That the raising or keeping a standing army within the kingdom in time of peace, unless it be with consent of parliament, is against law.

7. That the subjects which are Protestants may have arms for their defense suitable to their conditions, and as allowed by law.

8. That election of members of parliament ought to be free.

9. That the freedom of speech, and debates or proceedings in parliament, ought not to be impeached or questioned in any court or place out of parliament.

10. That excessive bail ought not to be required, nor excessive fines imposed, nor cruel and unusual punishments inflicted.

11. That jurors ought to be duly impaneled and returned, and jurors which pass upon men in trials for high treason ought to be freeholders.

12. That all grants and promises of fines and forfeitures of particular persons before conviction are illegal and void.

13. And that for redress of all grievances, and for the amending, strengthening, and preserving of the laws, parliament ought to be held frequently.

The accession of James II (1685–1688) to the crown virtually guaranteed a new constitutional crisis for England. An open and devout Catholic, his attempt to further Catholic interests made religion once more a primary cause of conflict between king and Parliament. James named Catholics to high positions in the government, army, navy, and universities. Parliamentary outcries against James's policies stopped short of rebellion because members knew that he was an old man and that his successors were his Protestant daughters Mary and Anne, born to his first wife. But on June 10, 1688, a son was born to James II's second wife, also a Catholic. Suddenly the specter of a Catholic hereditary monarchy loomed large. A group of prominent English noblemen invited the Dutch chief executive, William of Orange, husband of James's daughter Mary, to invade England. William and Mary raised an army and invaded England while James, his wife, and their infant son fled to France. With little bloodshed, England had undergone its "Glorious Revolution."

In January 1689, Parliament offered the throne to William and Mary, who accepted it along with the provisions of a bill of rights (see the box above). The Bill of Rights affirmed Parliament's right to make laws and levy taxes. The rights of citizens to keep arms and have a jury trial were also confirmed. By deposing one king and establishing another, Parliament had destroyed the divine-right theory of kingship (William was, after all, king by grace of Parliament, not God) and asserted its right to participate

ABSOLUTE AND LIMITED MONARCHY

France	
Louis XIV	1643–1715
Brandenburg-Prussia	
Frederick William the Great Elector	1640–1688
Elector Frederick III (King Frederick I)	1688–1713
Russia	
Ivan IV the Terrible	1533–1584
Peter the Great	1689–1725
First trip to the West	1697–1698
Construction of Saint Petersburg begins	1703
England	
Civil wars	1642–1648
Commonwealth	1649–1653
Charles II	1660–1685
Declaration of Indulgence	1672
James II	1685–1688
Glorious Revolution	1688
Bill of Rights	1689

© Réunion des Musées Nationaux/Art Resource, NY

PETER PAUL RUBENS, *THE LANDING OF MARIE DE' MEDICI AT MARSEILLES*. Peter Paul Rubens played a key role in spreading the Baroque style from Italy to other parts of Europe. In *The Landing of Marie de' Medici at Marseilles*, Rubens made a dramatic use of light and color, bodies in motion, and luxurious nudes to heighten the emotional intensity of the scene. This was one of a cycle of twenty-one paintings dedicated to the queen mother of France.

in the government. Parliament did not have complete control of the government, but it now had the right to participate in affairs of state. Over the next century, it would gradually prove to be the real authority in the English system of constitutional monarchy.

EUROPEAN CULTURE

Art and intellectual activity experienced dramatic changes in the sixteenth and seventeenth centuries. Especially important in developing a new view of the world was the Scientific Revolution.

Art: The Baroque

The artistic movement known as the Baroque dominated the Western artistic world for a century and a half. The Baroque began in Italy in the last quarter of the sixteenth century and spread to the rest of Europe and Latin America. Baroque artists sought to harmonize the classical ideals of Renaissance art with the spiritual feelings of the sixteenth-century religious revival. In large part, Baroque art and architecture reflected the search for power that was characteristic of much of the seventeenth century. Baroque churches and palaces featured richly ornamented facades, sweeping stair-

cases, and an overall splendor meant to impress people. Kings and princes wanted not only their subjects but also other kings and princes to be in awe of their power.

Baroque painting was known for its use of dramatic effects to arouse the emotions, especially evident in the works of Peter Paul Rubens (1577–1640), a prolific artist and an important figure in the spread of the Baroque from Italy to other parts of Europe. In his artistic masterpieces, bodies in violent motion, heavily fleshed nudes, a dramatic use of light and shadow, and rich sensuous pigments converge to express intense emotions.

A Golden Age of Literature in England

In England, writing for the stage reached new heights between 1580 and 1640. The golden age of English literature is often called the Elizabethan Era because much of the English cultural flowering occurred during her reign. Of all the forms of Elizabethan literature, none expressed the energy and intellectual versatility of the era better than drama. And no dramatist is more famous or more accomplished than William Shakespeare (1564–1614).

WILLIAM SHAKESPEARE: IN PRAISE OF ENGLAND

William Shakespeare is one of the most famous play-wrights in the Western world. He was a universal genius, outclassing all others in his psychological insights, depth of characterization, imaginative skills, and versatility. His historical plays reflected the patriotic enthusiasm of the English in the Elizabethan Era, as this excerpt from Richard II illustrates.

WILLIAM SHAKESPEARE, RICHARD II

This royal throne of kings, this sceptered isle,
This earth of majesty, this seat of Mars,
This other Eden, demi-Paradise,
This fortress built by Nature for herself
Against infection and the hand of war,
This happy breed of men, this little world,
This precious stone set in the silver sea,
Which serves it in the office of a wall
Or as a moat defensive to a house
Against the envy of less happier lands—
This blessed plot, this earth, this realm, this England,
This nurse, this teeming womb of royal kings,
Feared by their breed and famous by their birth,
Renowned for their deeds as far from home,
For Christian service and true chivalry,
As is the sepulcher in stubborn Jewry [the Holy Sepulcher in Jerusalem]
Of the world's ransom, blessed Mary's Son—
This land of such dear souls, this dear dear land,
Dear for her reputation through the world,
Is now leased out, I die pronouncing it,
Like a tenement or pelting farm.
England, bound in with the triumphant sea,
Whose rocky shore beats back the envious siege
Of watery Neptune, is now bound in with shame,
With inky blots and rotten parchment bonds.
That England, that was wont to conquer others,
Hath made a shameful conquest of itself.
Ah, would the scandal vanish with my life,
How happy then were my ensuing death!

Shakespeare was a "complete man of the theater." Although best known for writing plays, he was also an actor and a shareholder in the chief acting company of the time, the Lord Chamberlain's Company, which played in various London theaters. Shakespeare is to this day hailed as a genius. A master of the English language, he imbued its words with power and majesty. And his technical proficiency was matched by incredible insight into human psychology. Whether writing tragedies or comedies, Shakespeare exhibited a remarkable understanding of the human condition (see the box above).

The Scientific Revolution

In the Middles Ages, many educated Europeans took an intense interest in the world around them. But these "natural philosophers," as medieval scientists were known, relied on a few ancient authorities, especially Aristotle, and preferred refined logical analysis to systematic observations of the natural world. A number of changes and advances in the fifteenth and sixteenth centuries may have played a major role in helping "natural philosophers" abandon their old views and develop new ones.

The Renaissance humanists mastered Greek and Latin and made available new works of Galen, Ptolemy, Archimedes, and Plato. These writings made it apparent that some ancient thinkers had disagreed with Aristotle and other accepted authorities of the Middle Ages.

Other developments also encouraged new ways of thinking. Technical problems, such as calculating the tonnage of ships accurately, served to stimulate scientific activity because they required careful observations and precise measurements. The invention of new instruments and machines, such as the telescope and the microscope, made fresh scientific discoveries possible. And the printing press played a crucial role in spreading innovative ideas quickly and easily.

The study of mathematics, which spurred the scientific achievements of the sixteenth and seventeenth centuries, was promoted in the Renaissance by the rediscovery of the works of ancient mathematicians. Copernicus, Kepler, Galileo, and Newton were all great mathematicians who believed that the secrets of nature would be revealed through the language of mathematics. The mention of these names also reminds us that the Scientific Revolution was largely the work of a few great intellectuals.

TOWARD A NEW HEAVEN: A REVOLUTION IN ASTRONOMY

The philosophers of the Middle Ages had used the ideas of Aristotle, Ptolemy (the greatest astronomer of antiquity, who lived in the second century C.E.), and Christianity to construct the Ptolemaic or geocentric conception of the universe. In this conception, the universe was seen as a series of concentric spheres with a fixed or

Courtesy of the Lilly Library, Indiana University, Bloomington, Indiana

Courtesy of the Lilly Library, Indiana University, Bloomington, Indiana

MEDIEVAL CONCEPTION OF THE UNIVERSE. As this sixteenth-century illustration shows, the medieval cosmological view placed the earth at the center of the universe, surrounded by a series of concentric spheres. The earth was imperfect and constantly changing, while the heavenly bodies that surrounded it were perfect and incorruptible. Beyond the tenth and final sphere was heaven, where God and all the saved souls were located.

THE COPERNICAN SYSTEM. The Copernican system was presented in *On the Revolutions of the Heavenly Spheres*, published shortly before Copernicus's death. As shown in this illustration from the first edition of the book, Copernicus maintained that the sun was the center of the universe while the planets, including the earth, revolved around it. Moreover, the earth rotated daily on its axis.

motionless earth at its center. Composed of material substance, the earth was imperfect and constantly changing. The spheres that surrounded the earth were made of a crystalline, transparent substance and moved in circular orbits around the earth. These heavenly bodies, pure orbs of light, were embedded in the moving, concentric spheres and in 1500 numbered ten. Working outward from the earth, the first eight spheres contained the moon, Mercury, Venus, the sun, Mars, Jupiter, Saturn, and the fixed stars. The ninth sphere imparted to the eighth sphere of the fixed stars its daily motion, while the tenth sphere was frequently described as the prime mover that moved itself and imparted motion to the other spheres. Beyond the tenth sphere was the Empyrean Heaven—the location of God and all the saved souls. God and the saved souls were at one end of the universe, then, and humans were at the center. They had power over the earth, but their real purpose was to achieve salvation.

Nicholas Copernicus (1473–1543), a native of Poland, was a mathematician who felt that Ptolemy's geocentric system failed to accord with the observed motions of the heavenly bodies and hoped that his heliocentric (sun-centered) conception would offer a more accurate explanation. Copernicus argued that the sun was motionless at the center of the universe. The planets revolved around the sun in the order of Mercury, Venus, the earth, Mars, Jupiter, and Saturn. The moon, however, revolved around the earth. Moreover, what appeared to be the movement of the sun around the earth was really explained by the daily rotation of the earth on its axis and the journey of the earth around the sun each year. But Copernicus did not reject the idea that the heavenly spheres moved in circular orbits, and his system did not work considerably better than the Ptolemaic system.

The next step in destroying the geocentric conception and supporting the Copernican system was taken by Johannes Kepler (1571–1630). A brilliant German mathematician and astronomer, Kepler arrived at laws of planetary motion that confirmed Copernicus's heliocentric theory. In his first law, however, he contradicted Copernicus by showing that the orbits of the planets around the sun were not circular but elliptical, with the sun at one focus of the ellipse rather than at the center.

Kepler's work destroyed the basic structure of the Ptolemaic system. People could now think in new terms of the actual paths of planets revolving around the sun in elliptical orbits. But important questions remained unanswered. What were the planets made of? And how does

THE STARRY MESSENGER

The Italian Galileo Galilei was the first European to use a telescope to make systematic observations of the heavens. His observations, as reported in The Starry Messenger *in 1610, stunned European intellectuals by revealing that the celestial bodies were not perfect and immutable, as had been believed, but were apparently composed of materials similar to the earth. In this selection, Galileo describes how he devised a telescope and what he saw with it.*

GALILEO GALILEI, THE STARRY MESSENGER

About ten months ago a report reached my ears that a certain Fleming had constructed a spyglass by means of which visible objects, though very distant from the eye of the observer, were distinctly seen as if nearby. Of this truly remarkable effect several experiences were related, to which some persons gave credence while others denied them. A few days later the report was confirmed to me in a letter from a noble Frenchman at Paris, Jacques Badovere, which caused me to apply myself wholeheartedly to inquire into the means by which I might arrive at the invention of a similar instrument. This I did shortly afterwards, my basis being the theory of refraction. First I prepared a tube of lead, at the ends of which I fitted two glass lenses, both plane on one side while on the other side one was spherically convex and the other concave. Then placing my eye near the concave lens I perceived objects satisfactorily large and near, for they appeared three times closer and nine times larger than when seen with the naked eye alone. Next I constructed another one, more accurate, which represented objects as enlarged more than sixty times. Finally, sparing neither labor nor expense, I succeeded in constructing for myself so excellent an instrument that objects seen by means of it appeared nearly one thousand times larger and over thirty times closer than when regarded with our natural vision.

It would be superfluous to enumerate the number and importance of the advantages of such an instrument at sea as well as on land. But forsaking terrestrial observations, I turned to celestial ones, and first saw the moon from as near at hand as if it were scarcely two terrestrial radii. After that I observed often with wondering delight both the planets and the fixed stars, and since I saw these latter to be very crowded, I began to seek (and eventually found) a method by which I might measure their distances apart. . . .

Now let us review the observations made during the past two months, once more inviting the attention of all who are eager for true philosophy to the first steps of such important contemplations. Let us speak first of that surface of the moon which faces us. For greater clarity I distinguish two parts of this surface, a lighter and a darker; the lighter part seems to surround and to pervade the whole hemisphere, while the darker part discolors the moon's surface like a kind of cloud, and makes it appear covered with spots. . . . From observation of these spots repeated many times I have been led to the opinion and conviction that the surface of the moon is not smooth, uniform, and precisely spherical as a great number of philosophers believe it (and the other heavenly bodies) to be, but is uneven, rough, and full of cavities and prominences, being not unlike the face of the earth, relieved by chains of mountains and deep valleys.

---

one explain motion in the universe? An Italian scientist achieved the next important breakthrough to a new cosmology by answering the first question.

Galileo Galilei (1564–1642) taught mathematics and was the first European to make systematic observations of the heavens by means of a telescope, inaugurating a new age in astronomy. Galileo turned his telescope to the skies and made a remarkable series of discoveries: mountains on the moon, four moons revolving around Jupiter, and sunspots. Galileo's observations seemed to destroy yet another aspect of the traditional cosmology in that the universe seemed to be composed of material similar to that of earth rather than a perfect and unchanging substance.

Galileo's revelations, published in *The Starry Messenger* in 1610, made Europeans aware of a new picture of the universe (see the box above). But in the midst of his newfound acclaim, Galileo found himself under increasing suspicion by the authorities of the Catholic church. The Catholic church condemned Copernicanism and ordered Galileo to abandon the Copernican thesis. The church attacked the Copernican system because it threatened not only Scripture but also an entire conception of the universe. The heavens were no longer a spiritual world but a world of matter.

By the 1630s and 1640s, most astronomers had come to accept the new heliocentric conception of the universe. Nevertheless, the problem of explaining motion in the universe and tying together the ideas of Copernicus, Galileo, and Kepler had not yet been done. This would be the work of an Englishman who has long been considered the greatest genius of the Scientific Revolution.

Born in 1642, Isaac Newton attended Cambridge University, where he later accepted a chair in mathematics and wrote his major work, *Mathematical Principles of Natural Philosophy*, known simply as the *Principia* by the first word of its Latin title. In the first book of the *Principia*, Newton defined the three laws of motion that govern the planetary bodies, as well as objects on earth. Crucial to his whole argument was the universal law of gravitation, which explained why the planetary bodies did not go off in straight lines but continued in elliptical orbits about the sun. In mathematical terms, Newton explained that every object in the universe is attracted to every other object by a force called gravity.

Newton had demonstrated that one mathematically proven universal law could explain all motion in the universe. At the same time, the Newtonian synthesis created a new cosmology in which the universe was seen as one huge, regulated machine that operated according to natural laws in absolute time, space, and motion. Newton's world-machine concept dominated the modern worldview until the twentieth century, when Albert Einstein's concept of relativity created a new picture of the universe.

WOMEN IN THE ORIGINS OF MODERN SCIENCE

Women as well as men were involved in the Scientific Revolution. One of the most prominent female scientists of the seventeenth century, Margaret Cavendish (1623–1673), came from an aristocratic background. Cavendish was a participant in the crucial scientific debates of her time. She wrote a number of works on scientific matters, including *Observations upon Experimental Philosophy* and *Grounds of Natural Philosophy*. In these works, she was especially critical of the growing belief that humans through science were the masters of nature: "We have no power at all over natural causes and effects. . . . For man is but a small part, . . . his powers are but particular actions of Nature, and he cannot have a supreme and absolute power."[7]

In Germany, many of the women interested in science were astronomers. The most famous was Maria Winkelmann (1670–1720). She was educated by her father and uncle and received training in astronomy from a nearby self-taught astronomer. Her opportunity to be a practicing astronomer came when she married Gottfried Kirch, Germany's foremost astronomer. She became his assistant at the astronomical observatory operated in Berlin by the Academy of Science. She made some original contributions, including a hitherto undiscovered comet, as her husband related:

> Early in the morning (about 2:00 A.M.) the sky was clear and starry. Some nights before, I had observed a variable star, and my wife (as I slept) wanted to find and see it for herself. In so doing, she found a comet in the sky. At which time she woke me, and I found that it was indeed a comet. . . . I was surprised that I had not seen it the night before.[8]

When her husband died in 1710, Winkelmann applied for a position as assistant astronomer at the Berlin Academy, for which she was highly qualified. As a woman—with no university degree—she was denied the post by the academy's members, who feared that it would establish a precedent by hiring a woman ("mouths would gape").

Winkelmann's difficulties with the Berlin Academy reflect the obstacles women faced in being accepted in scientific work, which was considered a male preserve. All of these women scientists were exceptional women because a life devoted to any kind of scholarship was still viewed as at odds with the domestic duties women were expected to perform.

TOWARD NEW EARTH: DESCARTES AND RATIONALISM

The new conception of the universe contained in the cosmological revolution of the sixteenth and seventeenth centuries inevitably had an impact on the Western view of humankind. Nowhere is this more evident than in the work of the French philosopher René Descartes (1596–1650). The starting point for Descartes's new system was doubt. As Descartes explained at the beginning of his most famous work, *Discourse on Method*, written in 1637, he decided to set aside all that he had learned and begin again. One fact seemed to Descartes beyond doubt—his own existence:

> But I immediately became aware that while I was thus disposed to think that all was false, it was absolutely necessary that I who thus thought should be something; and noting that this truth *I think, therefore I am*, was so steadfast and so assured that the suppositions of the skeptics, to whatever extreme they might all be carried, could not avail to shake it, I concluded that I might without scruple accept it as being the first principle of the philosophy I was seeking.[9]

With this emphasis on the mind, Descartes asserted that he would accept only things that his reason said were true.

From his first postulate, Descartes deduced an additional principle, the separation of mind and matter. Descartes argued that since "the mind cannot be doubted but the body and material world can, the two must be radically different." From this came an absolute dualism between mind and matter, or what has also been called Cartesian dualism. Using mind or human reason and its best instrument, mathematics, humans can understand the material world because it is pure mechanism, a machine that is governed by its own physical laws because it was created by God—the great geometrician.

Descartes's separation of mind and matter allowed scientists to view matter as dead or inert, as something that was totally separate from themselves and could be investigated independently by reason. The split between mind and body led Westerners to equate their identity with mind and reason rather than with the whole organism. Descartes has rightly been called the father of modern rationalism.

THE SPREAD OF SCIENTIFIC KNOWLEDGE

In the course of the Scientific Revolution, attention was paid to the problem of establishing the proper means to examine and understand the physical realm. The result was the creation of a scientific method—a way to examine and understand nature—that was crucial to the evolution of science in the modern world. Curiously enough, it was an Englishman with few scientific credentials who developed a scientific method that became widely used. Francis Bacon (1561–1626), a lawyer, believed that a correct scientific method should be built on inductive principles, which means that scientists should proceed from the particular to the general. Carefully organized experiments and systematic, thorough observations would lead to correct general principles.

Bacon was clear about what he believed his scientific method could accomplish. He stated that "the true and lawful goal of the sciences is none other than this: that human life be endowed with new discoveries and power." He wanted science to contribute to the "mechanical arts" by creating devices that would benefit industry, agriculture, and trade. Bacon was prophetic when he said that "I am laboring to lay the foundation, not of any sect or doctrine, but of human utility and power." And how would this "human power" be used? To "conquer nature in action."[10] The control and domination of nature became a central proposition of modern science and the technology that accompanied it.

The spread of scientific ideas to a wide public was greatly aided by the new scientific societies. The English Royal Society evolved out of informal gatherings of scientists at London and Oxford in the 1640s. It received little government support, and its fellows simply co-opted new members. The French Royal Academy of Sciences, in contrast, received abundant state support and remained under government control. Both the English and French societies showed that science should proceed along the lines of a cooperative venture.

EUROPE, CHINA, AND SCIENTIFIC REVOLUTIONS

An interesting question that arises is why the Scientific Revolution occurred in Europe and not in China. In the Middle Ages, China had been the most technologically advanced civilization in the world. After 1500, that distinction passed to the West. Historians are not sure why.

LOUIS XIV AND COLBERT VISIT THE ACADEMY OF SCIENCES. In the seventeenth century, individual scientists received royal and princely patronage, and a number of learned societies were established. In France, Louis XIV, urged on by his minister Colbert, gave formal recognition to the French Academy in 1666. In this painting by Henri Testelin, Louis XIV is shown seated, surrounded by Colbert and members of the French Royal Academy of Sciences.

Some have compared the sense of order in Chinese society to the competitive spirit existing in Europe. Others have emphasized China's ideological viewpoint that favored living in harmony with nature rather than trying to dominate it. One historian has even suggested that China's civil service system drew the "best and the brightest" into government service, to the detriment of other occupations.

CONCLUSION

In the next chapter, we will examine how the movement of Europeans outside of Europe began to change the shape of world history. But what had made this development possible? After all, the religious division of Europe had led to almost a hundred years of religious warfare complicated by serious political, economic, and social issues before Europeans finally admitted that they would have to accept different ways to worship God.

At the same time, the concept of a united Christendom, held as an ideal since the Middle Ages, had been irrevocably destroyed by the religious wars, enabling a system of nation-states to emerge in which power politics took on increasing significance. Within those states slowly emerged some of the machinery that made possible a growing centralization of power. In those states called absolutist, strong monarchs with the assistance of their aristocracies took the lead in providing the leadership for greater centralization. In all the major European states, a growing concern for power led to larger armies and greater conflict, stronger economies, and more powerful governments. From a global point of view, the political and economic power of Europeans was beginning to slowly outstrip that of other peoples.

The Scientific Revolution also represents a major turning point in modern civilization. With a new conception of the universe came a new conception of humankind. The work of Descartes and Bacon left Europeans with the separation of mind and matter and the belief that by using only reason they could understand and dominate the world of nature. Combined with the eighteenth-century Enlightenment (see Chapter 17) the Scientific Revolution gave the West an intellectual boost that contributed to the increased confidence of Western civilization. Europeans—with their strong governments, prosperous economies, and strengthened military forces—began to dominate other parts of the world, leading to a growing belief in the superiority of their civilization.

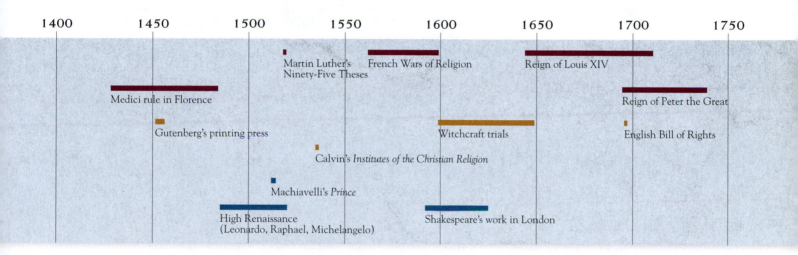

| 1400 | 1450 | 1500 | 1550 | 1600 | 1650 | 1700 | 1750 |

Martin Luther's Ninety-Five Theses

French Wars of Religion

Reign of Louis XIV

Medici rule in Florence

Reign of Peter the Great

Gutenberg's printing press

Witchcraft trials

English Bill of Rights

Calvin's *Institutes of the Christian Religion*

Machiavelli's *Prince*

High Renaissance
(Leonardo, Raphael, Michelangelo)

Shakespeare's work in London

CHAPTER NOTES

1. Quoted in Jacob Burckhardt, *The Civilization of the Renaissance in Italy*, trans. S. G. C. Middlemore (London, 1960), p. 81.
2. Niccolò Machiavelli, *The Prince*, trans. David Wootton (Indianapolis, Ind., 1995), p. 48.
3. Quoted in Roland Bainton, *Here I Stand: A Life of Martin Luther* (New York, 1950), p. 144.
4. John Calvin, *Institutes of the Christian Religion*, trans. John Allen (Philadelphia, 1936), vol. 1, p. 228; vol. 2, p. 181.
5. Quoted in Bonnie S. Anderson and Judith P. Zinsser, *A History of Their Own: Women in Europe from Prehistory to the Present* (New York, 1988), vol. 1, p. 259.
6. Quoted in Joseph Klaits, *Servants of Satan: The Age of Witch Hunts* (Bloomington, Ind., 1985), p. 68.
7. Quoted in Londa Schiebinger, *The Mind Has No Sex? Women in the Origins of Modern Science* (Cambridge, Mass., 1989), pp. 52–53.

8. Ibid., p. 85.
9. René Descartes, *Philosophical Writing*, ed. and trans. Norman K. Smith (New York, 1958), pp. 118–119.

10. Francis Bacon, *The Great Instauration*, trans. Jerry Weinberger (Arlington Heights, Ill., 1989), pp. 2, 8, 2, 16, 21.

SUGGESTED READING

The classic study of the Italian Renaissance is J. Burckhardt, *The Civilization of the Renaissance in Italy* (London, 1960), first published in 1860. General works on the Renaissance in Europe include D. L. Jensen, *Renaissance Europe*, 2d ed. (Lexington, Mass., 1991); P. Burke, *The European Renaissance: Centres and Peripheries* (Oxford, 1998); J. R. Hale, *The Civilization of Europe in the Renaissance* (New York, 1994); and the classic work by M. P. Gilmore, *The World of Humanism, 1453–1517* (New York, 1962). For a good summary of recent literature on the Renaissance, see P. Burke, *The Renaissance* (New York, 1997). For beautifully illustrated introductions to the Renaissance, see G. Holmes, *Renaissance* (New York, 1996), and M. Aston, ed., *The Panorama of the Renaissance* (New York, 1996).

Numerous facets of social life in the Renaissance are examined in J. R. Hale, *Renaissance Europe: The Individual and Society* (London, 1971). On family and marriage, see D. Herlihy, *The Family in Renaissance Italy* (St. Louis, Mo., 1974), and the valuable C. Klapisch-Zuber, *Women, Family, and Ritual in Renaissance Italy* (Chicago, 1985). Women are examined in M. L. King, *Women of the Renaissance* (Chicago, 1991).

Brief introductions to Renaissance humanism can be found in D. Kelley, *Renaissance Humanism* (Boston, 1991), and C. G. Nauert Jr., *Humanism and the Culture of Renaissance Europe* (Cambridge, 1995). The impact of printing is exhaustively examined in E. Eisenstein, *The Printing Press as an Agent of Change*, 2 vols. (New York, 1978). Good surveys of Renaissance art include R. Turner, *Renaissance Florence: The Invention of a New Art* (New York, 1997); F. Hartt, *History of Italian Renaissance Art*, 4th ed. (Englewood Cliffs, N.J., 1994); and L. Murray, *The High Renaissance* (New York, 1967).

For a general work on the political development of Europe in the Renaissance, see J. H. Shennan, *The Origins of the Modern European State, 1450–1725* (London, 1974). On France, see D. Potter, *A History of France, 1460–1560* (London, 1995). Early Renaissance England is examined in J. R. Lander, *Crown and Nobility, 1450–1509* (London, 1976). Good coverage of Renaissance Spain can be found in J. N. Hillgarth, *The Spanish Kingdoms, 1250–1516*, vol. 2, *Castilian Hegemony, 1410–1516* (New York, 1978). The best overall study of the Italian states is L. Martines, *Power and Imagination: City-States in Renaissance Italy* (New York, 1979). Machiavelli's life can be examined in Q. Skinner, *Machiavelli* (Oxford, 1981).

Basic surveys of the Reformation period include H. J. Grimm, *The Reformation Era, 1500–1650*, 2d ed. (New York, 1973); D. L. Jensen, *Reformation Europe*, 2d ed. (Lexington, Mass., 1990); G. R. Elton, *Reformation Europe, 1517–1559* (Cleveland, Ohio, 1963); C. Lindberg, *The European Reformations* (Cambridge, Mass., 1996); and E. Cameron, *The European Reformation* (New York, 1991). Also see the interesting and useful book by S. Ozment, *Protestants: The Birth of a Revolution* (New York, 1992).

The classic account of Martin Luther's life is R. Bainton, *Here I Stand: A Life of Martin Luther* (New York, 1950). More recent works include J. M. Kittelson, *Luther the Reformer: The Story of the Man and His Career* (Minneapolis, Minn., 1986), and H. A. Oberman, *Luther: Man Between God and the Devil* (New York, 1992). The most comprehensive account of the various groups and individuals who are called Anabaptist is G. H. Williams, *The Radical Reformation*, 2d ed. (Kirksville, Mo., 1992). Two worthwhile surveys of the English Reformation are A. G. Dickens, *The English Reformation*, 2d ed. (New York, 1989), and G. R. Elton, *Reform and Reformation: England, 1509–1558* (Cambridge, Mass., 1977). On John Calvin, see A. McGrath, *A Life of John Calvin: A Study in the Shaping of Western Culture* (Cambridge, Mass., 1990), and W. J. Bouwsma, *John Calvin* (New York, 1988).

On the impact of the Reformation on the family, see J. F. Harrington, *Reordering Marriage and Society in Reformation Germany* (New York, 1995). A good introduction to the Catholic Reformation can be found in M. R. O'Connell, *The Counter-Reformation, 1559–1610* (New York, 1974).

On the French Wars of Religion, see M. P. Holt, *The French Wars of Religion, 1562–1629* (New York, 1995), and R. J. Knecht, *The French Wars of Religion, 1559–1598*, 2d ed. (New York, 1996). A good biography of Philip II is G. Parker, *Philip II*, 3d ed. (Chicago, 1995). Elizabeth's reign can be examined in C. Haigh, *Elizabeth I*, 2d ed. (New York, 1998). On the Thirty Years' War, see G. Parker, *The Thirty Years' War*, 2d ed. (London, 1997), and R. G. Asch, *The Thirty Years' War: The Holy Roman Empire and Europe, 1618–1648* (New York, 1997). A good general work on the period of the English Revolution is M. A. Kishlansky, *A Monarchy Transformed* (London, 1996).

Witchcraft hysteria can be examined in J. B. Russell, *A History of Witchcraft* (London, 1980), and B. P. Levack, *The Witch-Hunt in Early Modern Europe* (London, 1987).

For brief accounts of seventeenth-century French history, see R. Briggs, *Early Modern France, 1560–1715* (Oxford, 1977), and J. B. Collins, *The State in Early Modern France* (Cambridge, 1995). A solid and very readable biography of Louis XIV is J. B. Wolf, *Louis XIV* (New York, 1968). For a brief study, see P. R. Campbell, *Louis XIV, 1661–1715* (London, 1993). On the creation of an Austrian state, see R. J. W. Evans, *The Making of the Habsburg Monarchy, 1550–1700* (Oxford, 1979), and C. Ingrao, *The Habsburg Monarchy, 1618–1815* (Cambridge, 1994). F. L. Carsten, *The Origins of Prussia* (Oxford, 1954), remains an outstanding study of early Prussian history. Works on Peter the Great include M. S. Anderson, *Peter the Great*, 2d ed. (New York, 1995), and L. Hughes, *Russia in the Age of Peter the Great* (New Haven, Conn., 1998). On England, see W. A. Speck, *The Revolution of 1688* (Oxford, 1988).

For a general survey of Baroque culture, see J. S. Held, *Seventeenth and Eighteenth Century Art: Baroque Painting, Sculpture, Architecture* (New York, 1971). The literature on Shakespeare is enormous. For a biography, see A. L. Rowse, *The Life of Shakespeare* (New York, 1963).

Four general surveys of the Scientific Revolution are A. G. R. Smith, *Science and Society in the Sixteenth and Seventeenth Centuries* (London, 1972); J. R. Jacob, *The Scientific Revolution: Aspirations and* *Achievements, 1500–1700* (Atlantic Highlands, N.J., 1998); S. Shapin, *The Scientific Revolution* (Chicago, 1996); and J. Henry, *The Scientific Revolution and the Origins of Modern Science* (New York, 1997).

INFOTRAC COLLEGE EDITION

For additional reading, go to InfoTrac College Edition, your online research library at
http://web1.infotrac-college.com

Enter the search term "Renaissance" using the Subject Guide.

Enter the search term "Reformation" using the Subject Guide.

Enter the search term "Machiavelli" using Keywords.

Enter the search terms "Martin and Luther not King" using Keywords.

Enter the search terms "Thirty Years' War" using Keywords.

Enter the search terms "Louis XIV" using Keywords.

The Art Archive, London

Chapter 14

NEW ENCOUNTERS: THE CREATION OF A WORLD MARKET

CHAPTER OUTLINE

- AN AGE OF EXPLORATION AND EXPANSION
- AFRICA IN TRANSITION
- SOUTHEAST ASIA IN THE ERA OF THE SPICE TRADE
- CONCLUSION

FOCUS QUESTIONS

- Why did Europeans begin to embark on voyages of discovery and expansion at the end of the fifteenth century?
- How did Portugal and Spain acquire their overseas empires, and how did their empires differ?
- How and why did the Europeans expand into Africa, and what were the main consequences of their presence there?
- What were the main features of the African slave trade, and what effects did it have on Africa?
- ➤ What were the main characteristics of Southeast Asian civilization, and how was it affected by the coming of Islam and the Europeans?

When, in the spring of 1498, a local official asked the Portuguese explorer Vasco da Gama why he had come all the way to India from his homeland in Europe, he replied simply, "Christians and spices." Da Gama might have been more accurate if he had reversed the order of his objectives. As it turned out, God was probably much less important than gold and glory to Europeans like himself who participated in the Age of Exploration that was already under way. Still, da Gama's comments at Calicut were an accurate forecast of the future, for his voyage inaugurated an extended period of European expansion into Asia, led by merchant adventurers and missionaries, that lasted several hundred years and had effects that are still felt today. Eventually, it resulted in a Western takeover of existing trade routes in the Indian Ocean and the establishment of colonies throughout Asia, Africa, and Latin America. So complete did Western dominance seem that some historians assumed that the peoples of the non-Western world were mere passive recipients in this process, absorbing and assimilating the advanced knowledge of the West and offering nothing in return. Historians writing about the period after 1500 often talked metaphorically about the "impact of the West" and the "response" of non-Western peoples.

That image of impact and response, however, is not an entirely accurate description of what took place between the end of the fifteenth century and the end of the eighteenth. Although European rule was firmly established in Latin America and the island regions of Southeast Asia, traditional governments and institutions elsewhere remained largely intact and in some areas, notably South Asia and the Middle East, displayed considerable vitality. Moreover, although da Gama and his contemporaries are deservedly famous for their contribution to a new era of maritime commerce that circled the globe, they were not alone in extending the world trade network and transporting goods and ideas from one end of the earth to the other. Islam, too, was on the march, blazing new trails into Southeast Asia and across the Sahara to the civilizations that flourished along the banks of the Niger River. In this chapter, we turn our attention to the stunning expansion in the scope and volume of commercial and cultural contacts that took place in the generations preceding and following da Gama's historic voyage to India, as well as to the factors that brought about this expansion. •

AN AGE OF EXPLORATION AND EXPANSION

The voyage of Vasco da Gama has customarily been seen as a crucial step in the opening of trade routes to the East. In the sense that the voyage was a harbinger of future European participation in the spice trade, this view undoubtedly has merit. In fact, however, as has been pointed out in earlier chapters, the Indian Ocean had been a busy thoroughfare for centuries. The spice trade had been carried on by sea in the region since the days of the legendary Queen of Sheba, and Chinese junks had sailed to the area in search of cloves and nutmeg since the Tang dynasty. Then, during the early fifteenth century, Chinese fleets sailed into the Indian Ocean and all the way to the coast of East Africa in search of trade and alliances (see Chapter 16).

Islam and the Spice Trade

By the fourteenth century, a growing percentage of the spice trade was being transported in Muslim ships sailing from ports in India or the Middle East. Muslims, either Arabs or Indian converts, had taken part in the Indian Ocean trade for centuries, and by the thirteenth century, Islam had established a presence in seaports on the islands of Sumatra and Java and was gradually moving inland. In 1292, the Venetian traveler Marco Polo observed that Muslims were engaging in missionary activity in northern Sumatra: "This kingdom is so much frequented by the Saracen merchants that they have converted the natives to the Law of Mahomet—I mean the townspeople only, for the hill people live for all the world like beasts, and eat human flesh, as well as other kinds of flesh, clean or unclean."[1]

But the major impact of Islam came in the early fifteenth century with the rise of the new sultanate at Malacca, whose founder was a Muslim convert. With its strategic location astride the strait of the same name (see Map 14.1), Malacca "is a city that was made for commerce; . . . the trade and commerce between the different nations for a thousand leagues on every hand must come to Malacca,"[2] said a sixteenth-century Portuguese visitor. Within a few years, Malacca had surpassed the old Hindu state of Majapahit on the island of Java and become the leading power in the region.

Unfortunately for the Muslim traders who had come to Southeast Asia for the spice trade, others would also covet that trade. Although China's interest in the area would soon come to an end, the arrival of Vasco da Gama's fleet was a sure sign that others would soon follow. Southeast Asia was on the verge of a new era in which outside forces would compete aggressively to exploit the region's vast riches.

A New Player: Europe

For almost a millennium, Catholic Europe had been confined to one area. Its one major attempt to expand beyond those frontiers, the Crusades, had largely failed. Of course, Europe had never completely lost contact with the outside world: the goods of Asia and Africa made their way into medieval castles, the works of Muslim philosophers were read in medieval universities, and the Vikings in the ninth and tenth centuries had even explored the eastern fringes of North America. Nevertheless, Europe's contacts with non-European civilizations remained limited until the fifteenth century, when Europeans began to embark on a remarkable series of overseas journeys. What caused European seafarers to undertake such dangerous voyages to the ends of the earth?

Europeans had long been attracted to the East. In the Middle Ages, myths and legends of an exotic land of great riches and magic were widespread. Although Muslim

MAP 14.1 European Voyages and Possessions in the Sixteenth and Seventeenth Centuries. This map indicates the most important voyages launched by Europeans during their momentous Age of Exploration in the sixteenth and seventeenth centuries. ➤ *Why did Vasco da Gama sail so far into the South Atlantic on his voyage to Asia?*

Principal Voyages of Exploration

A Portuguese expeditions, 1430s–1480s
B Dias, 1487–1488
C da Gama, 1497–1499
D Portuguese voyages to the Orient, 1509–1514
E Columbus's first voyage, 1492

F Columbus's three successive voyages, 1493–1504
G Voyages attended by Vespucci, 1499–1502
H Magellan–del Cano, 1519–1522
I Cabot, 1497

Areas under Spanish control
Areas under Portuguese control

Spanish trading cities
Portuguese trading cities
Independent trading cities

Spanish routes
Portuguese routes
Other routes

control of Central Asia cut Europe off from the countries farther east, the Mongol conquests in the thirteenth century had reopened the doors. The most famous medieval travelers to the East were the Polos of Venice. In 1271, Nicolò and Maffeo, merchants from Venice, accompanied by Nicolò's son Marco, undertook the lengthy journey to the court of the great Mongol ruler Khubilai Khan (see Chapter 10). As one of the great Khan's ambassadors, Marco traveled to Japan as well and did not return to Italy until 1295. An account of his experiences, the *Travels*, proved to be the most informative of all the descriptions of Asia by medieval European travelers. Others, like the Franciscan friar John Plano Carpini, had preceded the Polos, but in the fourteenth century the conquests of the Ottoman Turks and then the breakup of the Mongol Empire reduced Western traffic to the East. With the clos-

ing of the overland routes, a number of people in Europe became interested in the possibility of reaching Asia by sea. Christopher Columbus had a copy of Marco Polo's *Travels* in his possession when he began to envision his epoch-making voyage across the Atlantic Ocean.

An economic motive thus looms large in Renaissance European expansion (see Chapter 13). The rise of capitalism in Europe was undoubtedly a powerful spur to the process. Merchants, adventurers, and government officials had high hopes of finding precious metals and expanding the areas of trade, especially for the spices of the East. Spices continued to be transported to Europe via Arab intermediaries but were outrageously expensive. Adventurous Europeans did not hesitate to express their desire to share in the wealth. As one Spanish conquistador explained, he and his kind went to the New World to "serve God and His Majesty, to give light to those who were in darkness, and to grow rich, as all men desire to do."[3]

This statement expresses another major reason for the overseas voyages—religious zeal. A crusading mentality was particularly strong in Portugal and Spain, where the Muslims had largely been driven out in the Middle Ages. Contemporaries of Prince Henry the Navigator of Portugal said that he was motivated by "his great desire to make increase in the faith of our Lord Jesus Christ and to bring him all the souls that should be saved." The naval academy established by the prince to promote overseas exploration was subsidized in part by a militantly anti-Muslim Christian brotherhood. Although most scholars believe that the religious motive was secondary to economic considerations, it would be foolish to overlook the genuine desire on the part of both explorers and conquistadors, let alone missionaries, to convert the heathen to Christianity. Hernán Cortés, the conqueror of Mexico, asked his Spanish rulers if it was not their duty to ensure that the native Mexicans "are introduced into and instructed in the holy Catholic faith."[4] Spiritual and secular affairs were closely intertwined in the sixteenth century. No doubt,

grandeur and glory as well as plain intellectual curiosity and a spirit of adventure also played some role in European expansion.

If "God, glory, and gold" were the primary motives, what made the voyages possible? First of all, the expansion of Europe was a state enterprise, tied to the growth of centralized monarchies during the Renaissance. By the second half of the fifteenth century, European monarchies had increased both their authority and their resources and were in a position to turn their energies beyond their borders. That meant the invasion of Italy for France, but for Portugal, a state not strong enough to pursue power in Europe, it meant going abroad. The Spanish scene was more complex, since the Spanish monarchy was strong enough by the sixteenth century to pursue power both on the Continent and beyond.

At the same time, by the end of the fifteenth century, European states had a level of knowledge and technology that enabled them to achieve a regular series of voyages beyond Europe. Although the highly schematic and symbolic medieval maps were of little help to sailors, the *portolani*, or detailed charts made by medieval navigators

A SIXTEENTH-CENTURY MAP OF AFRICA. Advances in mapmaking also contributed to the European Age of Exploration. Here a section of a world map by the early-sixteenth-century Spanish cartographer Juan de la Cosa shows the continent of Africa. Note the drawing of the legendary Prester John, mentioned in Chapter 8, at the right, and the Portuguese caravels with their lateen sails in the South Atlantic Ocean.

and mathematicians in the thirteenth and fourteenth centuries, were more useful. With details on coastal contours, distances between ports, and compass readings, they proved of great value for voyages in European waters. But because the *portolani* were drawn on a flat scale and took no account of the curvature of the earth, they were of little use for longer overseas voyages. Only when seafarers began to venture beyond the coasts of Europe did they begin to accumulate information about the actual shape of the earth. By the end of the fifteenth century, cartography had developed to the point that Europeans possessed fairly accurate maps of the known world.

In addition, Europeans had developed remarkably seaworthy ships as well as new navigational techniques. European shipmakers had mastered the use of the sternpost rudder (an import from China) and had learned how to combine the use of lateen sails with a square rig. With these innovations, they could construct ships mobile enough to sail against the wind and engage in naval warfare and also large enough to mount heavy cannon and carry a substantial amount of goods over long distances. Previously, sailors had used a quadrant and their knowledge of the position of the polestar to ascertain their latitude. Below the equator, however, this technique was useless. Only with the assistance of new navigational aids such as the compass (a Chinese invention) and the astrolabe (an astronomical instrument used to measure the altitude of the sun and the stars above the horizon) were they able to explore the high seas with confidence.

A final spur to exploration was the growing knowledge of the wind patterns in the Atlantic Ocean (see Map 14.4 on p. 411). The first European fleets sailing southward along the coast of West Africa had found their efforts to return hindered by the strong winds that blew steadily from the north along the coast. By the late fifteenth cen-

THE CARAVEL, WORKHORSE OF THE AGE OF EXPLORATION.   Prior to the fifteenth century, most European ships were either small craft with lateen sails used in the Mediterranean or slow, unwieldy square-rigged vessels operating in the North Atlantic. By the sixteenth century, European naval architects began to build ships that combined the maneuverability and speed offered by lateen sails (widely used by sailors in the Indian Ocean) with the carrying capacity and seaworthiness of the square-riggers. For a century, caravels were the feared "sea-raiders" of the oceans.

tury, however, sailors had learned to tack out into the ocean, where they were able to catch westerly winds in the vicinity of the Azores islands that brought them back to the coast of western Europe. Christopher Columbus used this technique in his voyages to the Americas, and others relied on their new knowledge of the winds to round the continent of Africa in search of the Spice Islands.

The Portuguese Maritime Empire

Portugal took the lead in exploration when it began exploring the coast of Africa under the sponsorship of Prince Henry the Navigator (1394–1460). Prince Henry's motives were a blend of seeking a Christian kingdom as an ally against the Muslims, acquiring new trade opportunities for Portugal, and extending Christianity. In 1419, he founded a school for navigators on the southwestern coast of Portugal. Shortly thereafter, Portuguese fleets began probing southward along the western coast of Africa in search of gold, which had for centuries been carried northward from south of the Atlas Mountains in central Morocco. In 1441, Portuguese ships reached the Senegal River, just north of Cape Verde, and brought home a cargo of black Africans, most of whom were sold as slaves to wealthy buyers elsewhere in Europe. Within a few years, an estimated thousand slaves were shipped annually from the area back to Lisbon. Inadvertently, the Portuguese had found a way to circumvent the traditional trans-Saharan slave route from Central Africa to the Mediterranean.

Continuing southward, in 1471 the Portuguese discovered a new source of gold along the southern coast of the hump of West Africa (an area that would henceforth be known to Europeans as the Gold Coast). A few years later, they established contact with the state of Bakongo, near the mouth of the Congo River in Central Africa, and with the inland state of Benin, north of the Gold Coast. To facilitate trade in gold, ivory, and slaves (some slaves were brought back to Lisbon and others were bartered to local merchants for gold), the Portuguese leased land from local rulers and built stone forts along the coast.

Hearing reports of a route to India around the southern tip of Africa, Portuguese sea captains continued their probing. In 1487, Bartolomeu Dias took advantage of westerly winds in the South Atlantic to round the Cape of Good Hope, but he feared a mutiny from his crew and returned home without continuing onward. Ten years later, a fleet under the command of Vasco da Gama rounded the cape and stopped at several ports controlled by Muslim merchants along the coast of East Africa, including Sofala, Kilwa, and Mombasa. Then, having located a Muslim navigator who was familiar with seafaring in the region, da Gama's fleet crossed the Arabian

Courtesy of William J. Duiker

➤ **MALINDI, GATEWAY TO ASIA** The seaport of Malindi, located on the eastern coast of present-day Kenya, was Vasco da Gama's jumping-off point for his historic voyage to India. It was here that he located a navigator willing to guide his fleet eastward across the Indian Ocean. In later years, merchant vessels often stopped at the port en route to the Spice Islands. Shown here is the graveyard of a Christian church built by early Portuguese missionaries as they wended their way to Asia in search of souls to save. Reportedly the church was erected under the direction of Francis Xavier, later to achieve renown for his missionary efforts in China and Japan.

Sea and arrived off the port of Calicut on the southwestern coast of India, on May 18, 1498. The Portuguese crown had sponsored da Gama's voyage with the clear objective of destroying the Muslim monopoly over the spice trade, a monopoly that had been intensified by the Ottoman conquest of Constantinople in 1453 (see Chapter 15). Calicut was a major entrepôt on the long route from the Spice Islands to the Mediterranean Sea, but the ill-informed Europeans believed it was the source of the spices themselves. They had also heard there was a Christian community in the area, supposedly established by the apostle Thomas in the first century C.E.

On arriving in Calicut, da Gama announced to his surprised hosts that he had arrived in search of "Christians and spices." He did not find the first, but he did find the second. Although he lost two ships en route, da Gama's remaining vessels returned to Europe with their holds filled with ginger and cinnamon, a cargo that earned the investors a profit of several thousand percent.

During the next years, the Portuguese set out to gain control of the spice trade. In 1510, Admiral Afonso de Albuquerque established his headquarters at Goa, on the western coast of India south of present-day Bombay. From there the Portuguese raided Arab shippers, provoking the

THE PORTUGUESE CONQUEST
OF MALACCA

In 1511, a Portuguese fleet led by Afonso de Albuquerque attacked the Muslim sultanate at Malacca, on the west coast of the Malay peninsula. Occupation of the port gave the Portuguese control over the strategic Strait of Malacca and the route to the Spice Islands. In this passage, Albuquerque tells his men the reasons for the attack. Note that he sees control of Malacca as a way to reduce the power of the Muslim world. The relevance of economic wealth to military power continues to underlie conflicts among nations today. The Pacific War in the 1940s, for example, began as a result of a conflict over control of the rich resources of Southeast Asia.

THE COMMENTARIES OF THE GREAT AFONSO DE ALBUQUERQUE, SECOND VICEROY OF INDIA

Although there be many reasons which I could allege in favor of our taking this city and building a fortress therein to maintain possession of it, two only will I mention to you, on this occasion. . . .

The first is the great service which we shall perform to Our Lord in casting the Moors out of this country. . . . If we can only achieve the task before us, it will result in the Moors resigning India altogether to our rule, for the greater part of them—or perhaps all of them—live upon the trade of this country and are become great and rich, and lords of extensive treasures. . . . For when we were committing ourselves to the business of cruising in the Straits (of the Red Sea), where the King of Portugal had often ordered me to go (for it was there that His Highness considered we could cut down the commerce which the Moors of Cairo, of Mecca, and of Judah, carry on with these parts), Our Lord for his service thought right to lead us hither, for when Malacca is taken the places on the Straits must be shut up, and they will never more be able to introduce their spiceries into those places.

And the other reason is the additional service which we shall render to the King D. Manuel in taking this city, because it is the headquarters of all the spiceries and drugs which the Moors carry every year hence to the Straits without our being able to prevent them from so doing; but if we deprive them of this their ancient market there, there does not remain for them a single port, nor a single situation, so commodious in the whole of these parts, where they can carry on their trade in these things. . . . I hold it as very certain that if we take this trade of Malacca away out of their hands, Cairo and Mecca are entirely ruined, and to Venice will no spiceries be conveyed except that which her merchants go and buy in Portugal.

---

following comment from an Arab source: "[The Portuguese] took about seven vessels, killing those on board and making some prisoner. This was their first action, may God curse them."[5] In 1511, Albuquerque attacked Malacca itself.

For Albuquerque, control of Malacca would serve two purposes. It could help to destroy the Arab spice trade network by blocking passage through the Strait of Malacca, and it could also provide the Portuguese with a way station en route to the Spice Islands and other points east (see the box above). After a short but bloody battle, the Portuguese seized the city and put the local Arab population to the sword. They then proceeded to erect the normal accoutrements of the day—a fort, a factory (a common term at the time for a warehouse), and a church.

The Spice Islands

0 — 500 Kilometers
0 — 300 Miles

Molucca Sea
Tidor — Halmahera
Pacific Ocean
Ceram
Island of New Guinea
Banda Sea — Banda Islands

From Malacca, the Portuguese launched expeditions farther east, to China and the Moluccas, then known as the Spice Islands. There they signed a treaty with a local sultan for the purchase and export of cloves to the European market. Within a few years, they had managed to seize control of the spice trade from Muslim traders and had garnered substantial profits for the Portuguese monarchy.

Why were the Portuguese so successful? Basically, their success was a matter of guns and seamanship. The first Portuguese fleet to arrive in Indian waters was relatively modest in size. It consisted of three ships and twenty guns, a force sufficient for self-defense and intimidation but not for serious military operations. Sixteenth-century Portuguese fleets were more heavily armed and were capable of inflicting severe defeats if necessary on local naval and land forces. The Portuguese by no means possessed a monopoly on the use of firearms and explosives, but they used the maneuverability of their light ships to maintain their distance while bombarding the enemy with their powerful cannons. Such tactics gave them a military superiority over lightly armed rivals that they were able to exploit until the arrival of other European forces several decades later.

Courtesy of William J. Duiker

➤ **AN EARLY JEWISH COMMUNITY IN INDIA.** When Vasco de Gama arrived in the port city of Cochin, along the western coast of India, in 1498, he was surprised to discover the presence of a Jewish community that had been in the area since as early as the first century C.E. Jewish merchants from the Middle East had settled there to take part in the trading network that stretched westward from the Indian Ocean all the way to the Mediterranean Sea. Shown here is the entrance gate to the Jewish quarter in Cochin. Inside the gates are a number of commercial establishments and a synagogue that dates back to the fourteenth century.

Voyages to the "New World"

While the Portuguese were seeking access to the spice trade of the Indies by sailing eastward through the Indian Ocean, the Spanish attempted to reach the same destination by sailing westward across the Atlantic. Although the Spanish came to overseas discovery and exploration later than the Portuguese, their greater resources enabled them to establish a far grander overseas empire.

An important figure in the history of Spanish exploration was an Italian from Genoa, Christopher Columbus (1451–1506). Knowledgeable Europeans were aware that the world was round but had little understanding of its circumference or the extent of the continent of Asia. Convinced that the circumference of the earth was smaller than contemporaries believed and that Asia was larger, Columbus felt that Asia could be reached by sailing due west instead of eastward around Africa. After being rejected by the Portuguese, he persuaded Queen Isabella of Spain to finance his exploratory expedition, which reached the Americas in October 1492 and explored the coastline of Cuba and the northern shores of the neighboring island of Hispaniola. Columbus believed that he had reached Asia and in three subsequent voyages (1493, 1498, and 1502) sought in vain to find a route through the outer islands to the Asian mainland. In his four voyages, Columbus reached all the major islands of the Caribbean, which he called the Indies, as well as Honduras in Central America.

Although Columbus clung to his belief until his death, other explorers soon realized that he had discovered a new frontier altogether. State-sponsored explorers joined the

© North Wind Picture Archives

➤ **COLUMBUS LANDS IN THE NEW WORLD.** In the log that he wrote during his first voyage to the Americas, Christopher Columbus noted that the peoples of the New World were intelligent and friendly, and relations between them and the Spanish were amicable at first. Later, however, the conquistadors began to mistreat the local people. Here is a somewhat imaginative painting of the first encounter from a European perspective. Note the upturned eyes on Columbus and several of his companions, suggesting that their motives were spiritual rather than material.

race to the New World. A Venetian seafarer, John Cabot, explored the New England coastline of the Americas under a license from King Henry VII of England. The continent of South America was discovered accidentally by the Portuguese sea captain Pedro Cabral in 1500. Amerigo Vespucci, a Florentine, accompanied several voyages and wrote a series of letters describing the geography of the New World. The publication of these letters led to the use of the name "America" (after Amerigo) for the new lands.

The newly discovered territories were referred to as the New World, even though they possessed flourishing civilizations populated by millions of people when the Europeans arrived. But the Americas were new to the Europeans, who quickly saw opportunities for conquest and exploitation. The Spanish, in particular, were interested because in 1494 the Treaty of Tordesillas had divided the newly discovered world into separate Portuguese and Spanish spheres of influence. Thereafter, the route east around the Cape of Good Hope was to be reserved for the Portuguese, while the route across the Atlantic (except for the eastern hump of South America) was assigned to Spain. The Spanish conquistadors were a hardy lot of mostly upper-class individuals motivated by a typical sixteenth-century blend of glory, greed, and religious crusading zeal. Although sanctioned by the Castilian crown, these groups were financed and outfitted privately, not by the government.

Their superior weapons, organizational skills, and determination brought the conquistadors incredible success. Beginning in 1519 with a small band of men, Hernán Cortés took three years to overthrow the mighty Aztec empire in central Mexico, led by the chieftain Moctezuma (see Chapter 6). By 1550, the Spanish had gained control of northern Mexico. Between 1531 and 1536, another expedition led by a hardened and somewhat corrupt soldier, Francisco Pizarro (1470–1541), took control of the

Inca empire high in the Peruvian Andes. The Spanish conquests were undoubtedly facilitated by the previous arrival of European diseases, which had decimated the local population. Although it took another three decades before the western part of Latin America was brought under Spanish control (the Portuguese took over Brazil), already by 1535, the Spanish had created a system of colonial administration that made the New World an extension of the old—at least in European eyes.

Administration of the Spanish Empire in the New World

Spanish policy toward the inhabitants of the New World, whom the Europeans called Indians, was a combination of confusion, misguided paternalism, and cruel exploitation. Confusion arose over the nature of the Indians. Unsure whether these strange creatures were "full men" or not, Spanish doctors of law debated how to fit them into currently existing European legal patterns. While the conquistadors made decisions based on expediency and their own interests, Queen Isabella declared the Indi-

Courtesy of William J. Duiker

HAVANA, SPAIN'S LIFELINE TO THE NEW WORLD. After the conquest of Mexico by Hernán Cortés, trade between Spain and its new possession flourished. Spanish navigators soon discovered that the Bay of Havana, on the north shore of the island of Cuba, was an ideal stopping point for fleets en route to and from the New World, and a city sprang up along the banks of its harbor. To protect the population from the ravages of enemy fleets—notably the English—Spanish authorities erected a number of fortifications along the coast near the city. Shown here is El Moro castle, an early fortification located at the entrance to the bay. It has long served as a visual symbol of the city of Havana.

LAS CASAS AND THE SPANISH TREATMENT OF THE AMERICAN NATIVES

artolomé de Las Casas (1474–1566) was a Dominican monk who participated in the conquest of Cuba and received land and Indians in return for his efforts. But in 1514, he underwent a radical transformation that led him to believe that the Indians had been cruelly mistreated by his fellow Spaniards. He spent the remaining years of his life (he lived to the age of ninety-two) fighting for the Indians. This section is taken from his most influential work, Brevísima Relación de la Destrucción de las Indias, *known to English readers as* The Tears of the Indians. *This work was largely responsible for the legend of the Spanish as inherently "cruel and murderous fanatics." Many scholars today feel that Las Casas may have exaggerated his account to shock his contemporaries into action.*

BARTOLOMÉ DE LAS CASAS, THE TEARS OF THE INDIANS

There is nothing more detestable or more cruel than the tyranny which the Spaniards use toward the Indians for the getting of pearl. Surely the infernal torments cannot much exceed the anguish that they endure, by reason of that way of cruelty; for they put them under water some four or five ells deep, where they are forced without any liberty of respiration, to gather up the shells wherein the Pearls are; sometimes they come up again with nets full of shells to take breath, but if they stay any while to rest themselves, immediately comes a hangman row'd in a little boat, who as soon as he hath well beaten them, drags them again to their labor. Their food is nothing but filth, and the very same that contains the Pearl, with small portion of that bread which that Country affords; in the first whereof there is little nourishment; and as for the latter, it is made with great difficulty, besides that they have not enough of that neither for sustenance; they lie upon the ground in fetters, lest they should run away; and many times they are drown'd in this labor, and are never seen again till they swim upon the top of the waves; oftentimes they also are devoured by certain sea monsters, that are frequent in those seas. Consider whether this hard usage of the poor creatures be consistent with the precepts which God commands concerning charity to our neighbor, by those that cast them so undeservedly into the dangers of a cruel death, causing them to perish without any remorse or pity, or allowing them the benefit of the Sacraments, or the knowledge of Religion; it being impossible for them to live any time under the water; and this death is so much the more painful, by reason that by the coarctation of the breast, while the lungs strive to do their office, the vital parts are so afflicted that they die vomiting the blood out of their mouths. Their hair also, which is by nature black, is hereby changed and made of the same color with that of the sea Wolves; their bodies are also so besprinkled with the froth of the sea, that they appear rather like monsters than men.

---

ans to be subjects of Castile and instituted the *encomienda* system, which permitted the conquering Spaniards to collect tribute from the natives and use them as laborers. In return, the holders of an *encomienda* were supposed to protect the Indians and supervise their spiritual and material needs. In practice, this meant that the settlers were free to implement the system as they pleased. Three thousand miles from Spain, Spanish settlers largely ignored their government and brutally used the Indians to pursue their own economic interests. Indians were put to work on sugar plantations and in the lucrative gold and silver mines. Forced labor, starvation, and especially disease took a fearful toll of Indian lives. With little or no natural resistance to European diseases, the Indians of America were ravaged by smallpox, measles, and typhus brought by the explorers and the conquistadors. Although scholarly estimates of native populations vary drastically, a reasonable guess is that at least half of the natives died of European diseases. On Hispaniola alone, out of an initial population of 100,000 natives when Columbus arrived in 1493, only 300 Indians survived by 1570. In 1542, largely in response to the publications of Bartolomé de Las Casas, a Dominican monk who championed the Indians (see the box above), the government abolished the *encomienda* system and provided more protection for the natives.

A board of trade known as the *Casa de Contratación* supervised all economic matters related to the New World, but the chief organ of colonial administration was the Council of the Indies. The council nominated colonial viceroys, oversaw their activities, and kept an eye on ecclesiastical affairs in the colonies. Spanish possessions in the New World were initially divided between New Spain (Mexico, Central America, and the Caribbean islands), with its center in Mexico City, and Peru (western South America), with its capital at Lima. Each area was governed by a viceroy who served as the king's chief civil and military officer and was aided by advisory groups called *audiencias*, which also functioned as supreme judicial bodies.

By papal agreement, the Catholic monarchs of Spain were given extensive rights over ecclesiastical affairs in the New World. They could nominate church officials, build churches, collect fees, and supervise the various religious orders that conducted missionary activities. Catholic

AN AZTEC'S LAMENT

*I*n an earlier chapter, we observed the Spanish conquest of Mexico from the point of view of the invaders. Here we present an Aztec account. Aztec memoirs of the battle were collected by the Spanish a few years after the seizure of Tenochtitlán and were later translated from the original Nahuatl into Spanish or other European languages. In this passage, an Aztec observer describes the enormous sense of sorrow he felt at the tragedy that had befallen his compatriots. Note that the writer concludes that the defeat was ordained by the "Giver of Life" because of his displeasure with the Aztec people.

FLOWERS AND SONGS OF SORROW

Nothing but flowers and songs of sorrow
are left in Mexico and Tlatelolco,
where once we saw warriors and wise men.

We know it is true
that we must perish,

for we are mortal men.
You, the Giver of Life,
you have ordained it.

We wander here and there
in our desolate poverty.
We are mortal men.
We have seen bloodshed and pain
where once we saw beauty and valor.

We are crushed to the ground;
we lie in ruins.
There is nothing but grief and suffering
in Mexico and Tlatelolco,
where once we saw beauty and valor.

Have you grown weary of your servants?
Are you angry with your servants,
O Giver of Life?

---

monks had remarkable success converting and baptizing hundreds of thousands of Indians in the early years of the conquest. Soon after the missionaries came the establishment of dioceses, parishes, schools, and hospitals—all the trappings of a European society.

The Impact of European Expansion

The arrival of the Europeans had an enormous impact on both the conquerors and the conquered. The native American civilizations, which (as we discussed in Chapter 6) had their own unique qualities and a degree of sophistication rarely appreciated by the conquerors, were virtually destroyed, while the native populations were ravaged by diseases introduced by the Europeans. Ancient social and political structures were ripped up and replaced by European institutions, religion, language, and culture (see the box above).

How does one evaluate the psychological impact of colonization on the colonizers? The relatively easy European success in dominating native peoples undoubtedly reinforced the conviction of Europeans in the inherent superiority of their civilization. The Scientific Revolution of the eighteenth century, to be followed by the era of imperialism a century later, then served to strengthen the Eurocentric perspective that has long pervaded Western civilization in its relationship with the rest of the world.

European expansion also affected the conquerors in the economic arena. Wherever they went in the Americas, Europeans sought gold and silver. One Aztec observer commented that the Spanish conquerors "longed and lusted for gold. Their bodies swelled with greed, and their hunger was ravenous; they hungered like pigs for that gold."[6] Rich silver deposits were found and exploited in Mexico and southern Peru (modern Bolivia). When the mines at Potosí in Peru were opened in 1545, the value of precious metals imported into Europe quadrupled. It has been estimated that between 1503 and 1650, some 16 million kilograms of silver and 185,000 kilograms of gold entered the port of Seville, fueling a price revolution that affected the Spanish economy.

But gold and silver were only two of the products sent to Europe from the New World. Into Seville flowed sugar, dyes, cotton, vanilla, and hides from livestock raised on the South American pampas. New agricultural products native to the Americas, such as potatoes, coffee, corn, manioc, and tobacco, were also imported. Because of its trading posts in Asia, Portugal soon challenged the Italian states as the chief entry point of the eastern trade in spices, jewels, silk, carpets, ivory, leather, and perfumes, although the Venetians clung tenaciously to a portion of the spice trade until they lost out to the Dutch in the seventeenth century. Economic historians believe that the increase in the volume and area of European trade and the rise in fluid capital due to this expansion were crucial factors in producing a new era of commercial capitalism that represented the first step toward the world economy that has characterized the modern era.

European expansion, which was in part a product of European rivalries, also deepened those rivalries and increased the tensions among European states. Bitter conflicts arose over the cargoes coming from the New World and Asia. Although the Spanish and Portuguese were first in the competition, by the end of the sixteenth

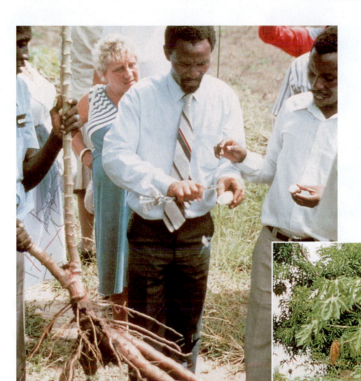

Courtesy of William J. Duiker

▶ MANIOC, FOOD FOR THE MILLIONS.
One of the plants native to the Americas that European adventurers would take back to the Old World was manioc (also known as cassava or yuca). A tuber like the potato, manioc is a prolific crop that grows well in poor, dry soils, but it lacks the high nutrient value of grain crops such as wheat and rice and for that reason never became popular in Europe (except as the source of tapioca). It was introduced to Africa in the seventeenth century and eventually became a staple food for up to one-third of the population of the continent. Shown here (inset) is a manioc plant growing in east Africa.

century, new competitors were entering the scene and beginning to challenge the dominance of the Iberian powers. The first to arrive were the English and the Dutch.

Why did Europeans risk their lives to explore new lands far from friendly shores? For some, expansion abroad brought hopes for land, riches, and social advancement. One Spaniard commented in 1572 that many "poor young men" left Spain for Mexico, where they might hope to acquire landed estates and call themselves "gentlemen." Although some wives accompanied their husbands abroad, many ordinary European women found new opportunities for marriage in the New World because of the lack of white women. In the violence-prone world of early Spanish America, a number of women also found themselves rich after their husbands were killed unexpectedly. In one area of Central America, women owned about 25 percent of the landed estates by 1700.

New Rivals

Portugal's efforts to dominate the trade of the Indian Ocean were never totally successful. The Portuguese lacked both the numbers and the wealth to overcome local resistance and colonize the Asian regions. Moreover, their massive investments in ships and laborers for their empire (hundreds of ships and hundreds of thousands of workers in shipyards and overseas bases) proved very costly. Only half of the ships involved in the India trade survived for a second journey. Disease, shipwreck, and battles took a heavy toll of life. The empire was simply too large and Portugal too small to maintain it, and by the end of the century, the Portuguese were being severely challenged by rivals.

The Spanish had established themselves in Asia in the early 1520s, when Ferdinand Magellan, seeking a western route to the Spice Islands across the Pacific Ocean, had sailed around the southern tip of South America, crossed the Pacific, and landed on the island of Cebu in the Philippine Islands. Although Magellan and some forty of his crew were killed in a skirmish with the local population, one of the two remaining ships, now under the command of the Spanish navigator Sebastian del Cano, sailed on to Tidor, in the Moluccas, and thence around the world via the Cape of Good Hope. In the words of a contemporary historian, they arrived in Cádiz "with precious cargo and fifteen men surviving out of a fleet of five sail."[7]

As it turned out, the Spanish could not follow up on Magellan's accomplishment, and in 1529 they sold their rights in Tidor to the Portuguese. But Magellan's voyage was not a total loss. In the absence of concerted resistance from the local population, the Spanish managed to consolidate their control over the Philippines, which eventually became a major Spanish base in the carrying trade across the Pacific. Spanish galleons carried silk and other luxury goods to Acapulco in exchange for silver from the mines of Mexico.

The primary threat to the Portuguese toehold in Southeast Asia, however, came from the English and the Dutch, both of whom were now strongly influenced by mercantilist theory (see Chapter 13). In 1591, the first English expedition to the Indies through the Indian Ocean arrived in London with a cargo of pepper. Nine years later, a private joint-stock company, the East India Company, was founded to provide a stable source of capital for future voyages. In 1608, an English fleet landed at Surat, on the northwestern coast of India. Eventually, a commercial treaty was signed, and a permanent English representative was assigned to the Mughal imperial court. Trade with Southeast Asia soon followed.

The Dutch were quick to follow suit. Dutch sailors had managed to obtain Portuguese maps of the Indian coast, and the first Dutch fleet arrived in India in 1595. In 1602,

Cape Horn and the Strait of Magellan

the Dutch East India Company was established under government sponsorship and was soon actively competing with the English and the Portuguese in the region.

The Dutch, the French, and the English also began to make inroads on Spanish and Portuguese possessions in the Americas. War and steady pressure from their Dutch and English rivals eroded Portuguese trade in both the West and the East, although Portugal continued to profit from its large colonial empire in Brazil. A formal administration system had been instituted in Brazil in 1549, and Portuguese migrants had established massive plantations there to produce sugar for export to the Old World. The Spanish also maintained an enormous South American empire, but Spain's importance as a commercial power declined rapidly in the seventeenth century because of a drop in the output of the silver mines, the poverty of the Spanish monarchy, and the stifling hand of the Spanish aristocracy as well as the pressure of its English rival.

The Dutch formed their own Dutch West India Company in 1621 to compete with Spanish and Portuguese interests in the Americas. But although it made some inroads in Portuguese Brazil and the Caribbean, the company's profits were never large enough to compensate for the expenditures. Dutch settlements were also established on the North American continent. The main-

Courtesy of William J. Duiker

PASSAGE TO THE UNKNOWN. During its historic first voyage around the world in the early sixteenth century, Ferdinand Magellan's fleet passed through this passage near the southern tip of South America. Now known as the Strait of Magellan, this narrow body of water between the mainland and the nearby island of Tierra del Fuego remains to sailors one of the most terrifying in the world, with 100-mile-per-hour winds gusting regularly through this passage between the Pacific and the Atlantic Oceans.

MAP 14.2 **European Possessions in the West Indies.** After the first voyage of Christopher Columbus, other European adventurers followed on his trail, seeking their share of the alleged riches of the New World. ➤ *Where were the major settlements established by European countries in the sixteenth century?*

land colony of New Netherlands stretched from the mouth of the Hudson River as far north as Albany, New York. In the meantime, French colonies appeared in the Lesser Antilles, and in Louisiana, at the mouth of the Mississippi River.

In the second half of the seventeenth century, however, rivalry and years of warfare with the English and the French (who had also become active in North America) brought the decline of the Dutch commercial empire in the New World. In 1664, the English seized the colony of New Netherlands and renamed it New York, and the Dutch West India Company soon went bankrupt. In 1663, Canada became the property of the French crown and was administered like a French province. But the French failed to provide adequate men or money, allowing their continental wars to take precedence over the conquest of the North American continent. By the early eighteenth cen-

tury, the French began to cede some of their American possessions to their English rival.

The English, meanwhile, had proceeded to create a colonial empire in the New World along the Atlantic seaboard of North America. The failure of the Virginia Company made it evident that colonizing American lands was not necessarily conducive to quick profits. But the desire to escape from religious oppression combined with economic interests did make successful colonization possible, as the Massachusetts Bay Company demonstrated. The Massachusetts colony had only four thousand settlers in its early years, but by 1660 their number had swelled to forty thousand. Although the English had established control over most of the eastern seaboard by the end of the seventeenth century, the North American colonies still remained of minor significance to the English economy.

AFRICA IN TRANSITION

Although the primary objective of the Portuguese in rounding the Cape of Good Hope was to find a sea route to the Spice Islands, they soon discovered that profits were to be made en route, along the eastern coast of Africa. In the early sixteenth century, a Portuguese fleet commanded by Francisco de Almeida seized a number of East African port cities, including Kilwa, Sofala, and Mombasa, and built forts along the coast in an effort to control the trade in the area. Above all, the Portuguese wanted to monopolize the trade in gold, which was mined by Bantu workers in the hills along the upper Zambezi River and then shipped to Sofala on the coast (see Chapter 8). For centuries, the gold trade had been monopolized by local Shona peoples at Zimbabwe. In the fifteenth century, it had come under the control of a Shona dynasty known as the Mwene Metapa. The Mwene Metapa had originally controlled the region south of the Zambezi River and may have been the builders of the impressive city known today as Great Zimbabwe, but sometime in the fifteenth century, they moved northeastward to the valley of the Zambezi. Here they encountered the arriving Portuguese, who had begun to move inland to gain access to the lucrative gold trade and had established ports on the Zambezi River. The Portuguese opened treaty relations with the Mwene Metapa, and Jesuit priests were eventually posted to the court in 1561. At first, the Mwene Metapa found the Europeans useful as an ally against local rivals, but by the end of the sixteenth century, the Portuguese had established a protectorate and forced the local ruler to grant title to large tracts of land to European officials and private individuals living in the area. Eventually, those lands would be integrated into the colony of Mozambique. The Portuguese, however, lacked the personnel, the capital, and the expertise to dominate local trade and in the late seventeenth century, a vassal of the Mwene Metapa succeeded in driving them from the plateau; his descendants maintained control of the area for the next two hundred years.

North of the Zambezi River, Bantu peoples were coming under pressure not only from the Portuguese but also from pastoralists migrating southward from the southern Sudan. The latter were frequently aggressive and began to occupy the rift valley and parts of the lake district that had previously been controlled by Bantu farmers. In some cases, the conflict between farmers and pastoralists was fairly clear-cut. In Rwanda and Burundi, immediately west of Lake Victoria, farming Hutu peoples (Bantu speakers) defended their hilltop communities against roving Tutsi pastoralists occupying the surrounding lowlands.

The first Europeans to settle in southern Africa were the Dutch. After an unsuccessful attempt to seize the Portuguese settlement on the island of Mozambique off the

FORT JESUS AT MOMBASA. Mombasa, a port city on the eastern coast of Africa, was a jumping-off point for the Portuguese as they explored the lands bordering on the Indian Ocean. Erected in the early sixteenth century atop a bluff overlooking the harbor, Fort Jesus remained an imposing symbol of European power until 1698, when the Portuguese were expelled by the Arabs. Castles built in this style are situated along the sea routes to the Spice Islands, but the European presence has now departed.

East African coast, in 1652 the Dutch set up a way station at the Cape of Good Hope to serve as a base for their fleets en route to the East Indies. At first, the new settlement was meant simply to provide food and other provisions to Dutch ships, but eventually it developed into a permanent colony. Dutch farmers, known as Boers and speaking a Dutch dialect that evolved into Afrikaans, began to settle in the sparsely occupied areas outside the city of Cape Town. The temperate climate and the absence of tropical diseases made the territory near the cape practically the only land south of the Sahara that the Europeans had found suitable for habitation.

West Africa had been penetrated from across the Sahara since ancient times, and contact undoubtedly increased after the establishment of Muslim control over the Mediterranean coastal regions. Muslim traders crossed the desert carrying Islamic values, political culture, and legal traditions along with their goods. The early stage of state formation had culminated with the kingdom of Mali, symbolized by the renowned Mansa Musa, whose pilgrimage to Mecca in the fourteenth century had left an indelible impression on observers.

After Mali's decline, it was succeeded by the kingdom of Songhai. Under King Askia Mohammed (1493–1528), the leader of a pro-Islamic faction who had seized power from members of the original founding family, the state increasingly relied on Islamic institutions and ideology to strengthen national unity and centralize authority (see the box on p. 401). Askia Mohammed himself embarked on a pilgrimage to Mecca and was recognized by

KING OF SONGHAI

The Epic of Askia Mohammed is an oral history passed down through generations of West Africans. It relates the heroic deeds of the famous monarch who led the kingdom of Songhai to the zenith of its power in the early sixteenth century. In the epic, the young hero, called Mamar Kassaye, becomes chieftain by killing his evil uncle Si (Sonni Ali Ber, who ruled Songhai from 1463 to 1492). Once in power, Mamar consolidated the expanding Songhai kingdom and ruled it until his death in 1528. He was revered for his piety, his patronage of scholarship at Timbuktu, and his celebrated pilgrimage to Mecca. The following passage describes his assumption of power and the means he used to convert his subjects to Islam.

THE EPIC OF ASKIA MOHAMMED

> His father gave him a white stallion, really white, really,
>   really, really, really, really, really white like, like
>   percale.
> He gave him all the things necessary.
> He gave him two lances.
> He gave him a saber, which he wore.
> He gave him a shield.
> He bid him good-bye.
> …
> The horse gallops swiftly, swiftly, swiftly, swiftly, swiftly,
>   swiftly he is approaching.
> He comes into view suddenly, leaning forward on his mount.
> Until, until, until, until, until, until, until he touches the
>   prayer skin of his uncle, then he reins his horse there.
> …
> As he approaches the prayer skin of his uncle,
> He reins his horse.
> He unslung his lance, and pierced his uncle with it until the
>   lance touched the prayer skin.

> Until the spear went all the way to the prayer skin.
> …
> They took away the body, and Mamar came to sit down on
>   the prayer skin of his uncle.
> They prayed.
> They took away the body to bury it.
> That is how Mamar took the chieftaincy.
> …
> He ruled then, he ruled, he ruled, he ruled, he converted.
> Throughout Mamar's reign, what he did was to convert
>   people.
> Any village that he hears is trying to resist,
> That is not going to submit,
> He gets up and destroys the village.
> If the village accepts, he makes them pray.
> If they resist, he conquers the village, he burns the village.
> Mamar made them convert, Mamar made them convert,
>   Mamar made them convert.
> Until, until, until, until, until, until he got up and said he
>   would go to Mecca.
> …
> They build a mosque before his arrival.
> When he arrives, he and his people,
> He teaches the villagers prayers from the Koran.
> He makes them pray.
> They—they learn how to pray.
> After that, in the morning, he continues on.
> Every village that follows his orders, that accepts his wishes,
> He conquers them, he moves on.
> Every village that refuses his demand,
> He conquers it, he burns it, he moves on.
> Until the day—Mamar did that until, until, until, until the
>   day he arrived at the Red Sea.

the caliph of Cairo as the Muslim ruler of the Niger River valley. On his return from Mecca, he tried to revive Timbuktu as a major center of Islamic learning but had little success in converting his subjects. He did preside over a significant increase in trans-Saharan trade, which provided a steady source of income to Songhai and other kingdoms in the region. Despite the efforts of Askia Mohammed and his successors, centrifugal forces within Songhai eventually led to its breakup after his death.

The period of Songhai's decline was also a time of increased contact with Europeans. The English, the French, and the Dutch all became active in the West African trade in the mid-sixteenth century. The Dutch, in particular, encroached on the Portuguese spheres of influence. During the mid-seventeenth century, the Dutch seized a number of Portuguese forts along the West African coast while at the same time taking over the bulk of the Portuguese trade across the Indian Ocean.

The Slave Trade

The European exploration of the African coastline had little apparent significance for most peoples living in the interior of the continent, except for a few who engaged in direct or indirect trade with the foreigners. But for peoples living on or near the coast, the impact was often great indeed. As the trade in slaves increased during the sixteenth through the eighteenth centuries, thousands, and then millions, were removed from their homes and forcibly exported to plantations in the New World.

Traffic in slaves had existed for centuries before the arrival of Portuguese fleets along African shores. West African states like the kingdoms of Mali and Songhai routinely used slaves (mostly captured in battles with neighboring rivals) as agricultural laborers. In East Africa and the upper Nile valley, slavery had been practiced since ancient times and continued at a fairly steady level during the fifteenth century, with the major trade routes snaking across the Sahara and up the Nile River. The primary market for African slaves was the Middle East, where most were used as domestic servants. Slavery also existed in many European countries, where a few slaves from Africa or war captives from the regions north of the Black Sea were used for domestic purposes or as agricultural workers in the lands adjacent to the Mediterranean.

At first, the Portuguese simply replaced European slaves with African ones. During the second half of the fifteenth century, about a thousand slaves were taken to Portugal each year; the vast majority were apparently destined to serve as domestic servants for affluent families throughout Europe. But the discovery of the New World in the 1490s and the subsequent planting of sugarcane in South America and the islands of the Caribbean changed the situation. Cane sugar was native to Indonesia and had first been introduced to Europeans from the Middle East during the Crusades. By the fifteenth century, it was grown (often by slaves from Africa or the region of the Black Sea) in modest amounts on Cyprus, Sicily, and southern regions of the Iberian peninsula. But when the Ottoman Empire seized much of the eastern Mediterranean (see Chapter 15), the Europeans needed to seek out new areas suitable for cultivation. In 1490, the Portuguese established sugar plantations worked by African laborers at São Tomé, an island in the Bay of Biafra off the central coast of Africa. Demand increased as sugar gradually replaced honey as a sweetener, especially in northern Europe.

But the primary impetus to the sugar industry came from the colonization of the Americas. During the sixteenth century, plantations were established along the eastern coast of Brazil and on several islands in the Caribbean.

Because the cultivation of cane sugar is an arduous process demanding both skill and large quantities of labor, the new plantations required more workers than could be provided by the Indian population in the New World, many of whom had died of diseases imported from the Old World. Since the climate and soil of much of West Africa were not especially conducive to the cultivation of sugar, African slaves began to be shipped to Brazil and the Caribbean to work on the plantations. The first were sent from Portugal, but in 1518, a Spanish ship carried the first boatload of African slaves directly from Africa to the New World.

During the next two centuries, the trade in slaves increased by massive proportions (see Map 14.3). An estimated 275,000 enslaved Africans were exported to other countries during the sixteenth century, with 2,000 going annually to the Americas alone. During the next century, the total climbed to over a million and jumped to six million in the eighteenth century, when the trade spread from West and Central Africa to East Africa. Even during the nineteenth century, when Great Britain and a number of other European countries attempted to end the slave trade, nearly two million were exported. It has been estimated that altogether as many as ten million African slaves were transported to the Americas between the early sixteenth and the late nineteenth centuries. As many as two million were exported to other areas during the same period.

One reason for these astonishing numbers, of course, was the tragically high death rate. Though figures on the number of slaves who died on the journey are almost entirely speculative, a high proportion undoubtedly died on the voyage before arriving at their destination. We know that mortality rates for Europeans in the West Indies were ten to twenty times higher than in Europe,

➤ A SLAVE SHIP.   Beginning in the sixteenth century, European traders began to ship native Africans to the Americas to be used as slave labor on the plantations. During the first shipments, up to one-third of the human cargo died of disease. (Even among crew members, mortality rates were sometimes as high as one in four.) Later merchants became more efficient and reduced losses to about 10 percent. As this sketch shows, the victims were still crammed together in an inhumane manner.

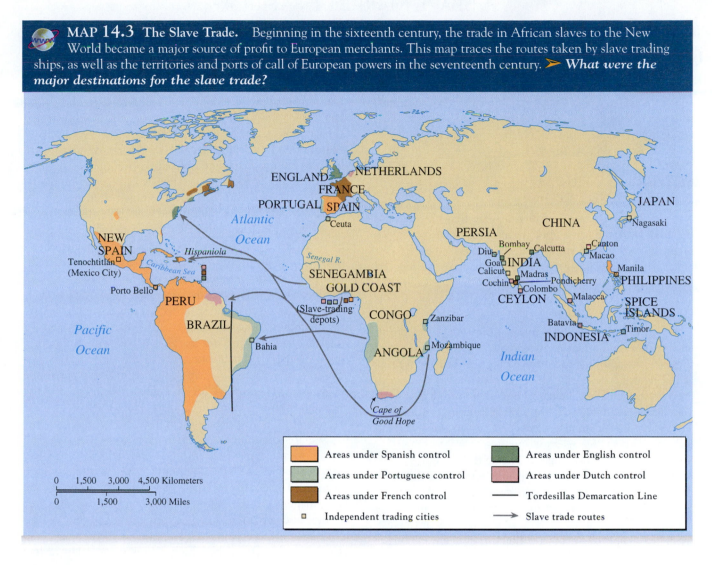

MAP 14.3 The Slave Trade. Beginning in the sixteenth century, the trade in African slaves to the New World became a major source of profit to European merchants. This map traces the routes taken by slave trading ships, as well as the territories and ports of call of European powers in the seventeenth century. ➤ *What were the major destinations for the slave trade?*

and a European arriving in the West Indies had a life expectancy of five to ten years (in Africa, where yellow fever was prevalent, the average life expectancy for an arriving European was only about one year). Ironically, African slaves who survived the brutal voyage fared somewhat better than whites: death rates for newly arrived Europeans in the West Indies averaged more than 125 per 1,000 annually, but the figure for Africans was only about 30 per 1,000.

The reason for these staggering death rates was clearly more than maltreatment, although that was certainly a factor. As we have seen, the transmission of diseases from one continent to another brought high death rates among those lacking immunity. African slaves were somewhat less susceptible to European diseases than the American Indian populations. Indeed, they seem to have possessed a degree of immunity, perhaps because their ancestors had developed antibodies to "white people's diseases" owing to the trans-Saharan trade. The Africans would not have had immunity to native American diseases, however.

The mortality rates, of course, were higher for immigrants than for those born in the New World, who as children gradually developed at least a partial immunity to many of the more fatal diseases. Death rates for native-born slaves tended to be significantly lower than for recent arrivals, which raises the question of why the slave population did not begin to rise after the initial impact of settlement had worn off. The answer appears to be a matter of economics. In the first place, only half as many women were enslaved as men, birthrates for women living in slavery were low, and infant mortality was high. In the second place, as long as the price of slaves was low, many slave owners in the West Indies apparently believed that purchasing a new slave was less expensive than raising a child from birth to working age at adolescence. After the price of slaves began to rise during the eighteenth century, plantation owners started to devote more efforts to replenishing the supply of workers by natural means.

Slaves were obtained by traditional means. Before the coming of the Europeans in the fifteenth century, most

A SLAVE MARKET IN AFRICA

Traffic in slaves had been carried on in Africa since the kingdom of the pharaohs in ancient Egypt. But the slave trade increased dramatically after the arrival of European ships off the coast of West Africa. The following passage by a Dutch observer describes a slave market in Africa and the conditions on the ships that carried the slaves to the New World. Note the difference in tone between this account and the far more critical views expressed in Chapter 22.

SLAVERY IN AFRICA: A FIRSTHAND REPORT

Not a few in our country fondly imagine that parents here sell their children, men their wives, and one brother the other. But those who think so deceive themselves, for this never happens on any other account but that of necessity, or some great crime; most of the slaves that are offered to us are prisoners of war, who are sold by the victors as their booty.

When these slaves come to Fida, they are put in prison all together; and when we treat concerning buying them, they are brought out into a large plain. There, by our surgeons, whose province it is, they are thoroughly examined, even to the smallest member, and that naked too, both men and women, without the least distinction or modesty. Those that are approved as good are set on one side; and the lame or faulty are set by as invalids. . . .

The invalids and the maimed being thrown out, . . . the remainder are numbered, and it is entered who delivered them. In the meanwhile, a burning iron, with the arms or name of the companies, lies in the fire, with which ours are marked on the breast. This is done that we may distinguish them from the slaves of the English, French, or others (which are also marked with their mark), and to prevent the Negroes exchanging them for worse, at which they have a good hand.

I doubt not but this trade seems very barbarous to you, but since it is followed by mere necessity, it must go on; but we take all possible care that they are not burned too hard, especially the women, who are more tender than the men.

When we have agreed with the owners of the slaves, they are returned to their prison. There from that time forward they are kept at our charge, costing us two pence a day a slave; which serves to subsist them, like our criminals, on bread and water. To save charges, we send them on board our ships at the very first opportunity, before which their masters strip them of all they have on their backs so that they come aboard stark naked, women as well as men. In this condition they are obliged to continue, if the master of the ship is not so charitable (which he commonly is) as to bestow something on them to cover their nakedness.

You would really wonder to see how these slaves live on board, for though their number sometimes amounts to six or seven hundred, yet by the careful management of our masters of ships, they are so regulated that it seems incredible. And in this particular our nation exceeds all other Europeans, for the French, Portuguese and English slave ships are always foul and stinking; on the contrary, ours are for the most part clean and neat.

The slaves are fed three times a day with indifferent good victuals, and much better than they eat in their own country. Their lodging place is divided into two parts, one of which is appointed for the men, the other for the women, each sex being kept apart. Here they lie as close together as it is possible for them to be crowded.

We are sometimes sufficiently plagued with a parcel of slaves which come from a far inland country who very innocently persuade one another that we buy them only to fatten and afterward eat them as a delicacy. When we are so unhappy as to be pestered with many of this sort, they resolve and agree together (and bring over the rest to their party) to run away from the ship, kill the Europeans, and set the vessel ashore, by which means they design to free themselves from being our food.

I have twice met with this misfortune; and the first time proved very unlucky to me, I not in the least suspecting it, but the uproar was quashed by the master of the ship and myself by causing the abettor to be shot through the head, after which all was quiet.

---

slaves in Africa were prisoners or war captives or had inherited their status. Many served as domestic servants or as wageless workers for the local ruler, and some were permitted to purchase their freedom under certain conditions. When Europeans first began to take part in the slave trade, they would normally purchase slaves from local African merchants at the infamous slave markets in exchange for gold, guns, or other European manufactured goods such as textiles or copper or iron utensils (see the box above). At first, local slave traders obtained their supply from immediately surrounding regions, but as demand increased, they had to move farther inland to locate their

victims. In a few cases, local rulers became concerned about the impact of the slave trade on the political and social well-being of their societies. In a letter to the king of Portugal in 1526, King Affonso of Congo (Bakongo) complained that "so great, Sire, is the corruption and licentiousness that our country is being completely depopulated."[8] As a general rule, however, local monarchs viewed the slave trade as a source of income, and many launched forays against defenseless villages in search of unsuspecting victims.

Historians once thought that Europeans controlled the terms of the slave trade and were able to obtain victims

THE PENETRATION OF AFRICA

Life of Prince Henry the Navigator	1394–1460
Portuguese ships reach the Senegal River	1441
Bartolomeu Dias sails around the tip of Africa	1487
First Portuguese sugar plantation at São Tomé	1490
First boatload of slaves to the Americas	1518
Dutch way station established at Cape of Good Hope	1652
Ashanti kingdom established in West Africa	1680
Portuguese expelled from Mombasa	1728

at bargain prices. Recently, however, it has become clear that African intermediaries—private merchants, local elites, and trading state monopolies—were very active in the process and were often able to dictate the price, volume, and availability of slaves to European purchasers. The majority of the slaves sold to European buyers were males; females, who were in great demand in Africa and on the trans-Saharan trade, tended to be reserved for those markets. The slave merchants were often paid in various types of imported goods, including East Asian textiles (highly desired for their bright colors and durability), furniture, and other manufactured products. Until the end of the seventeenth century, the Portuguese preferred gold to slaves and would sometimes pay for the gold by selling slaves to African kingdoms that were short of labor. In fact, not until the beginning of the eighteenth century did slaves surpass gold and ivory as the continent's leading exports.

The effects of the slave trade varied from area to area. It might be assumed that apart from the tragic effects on the lives of individual victims and their families, the practice would have led to the depopulation of vast areas of the continent. This did occur in some areas, notably in modern Angola, south of the Congo River basin, and in thinly populated areas in East Africa, but it was less true in West Africa. There high birthrates were often able to counterbalance the loss of able-bodied adults, and the introduction of new crops from the New World, such as maize, peanuts, and manioc, led to an increase in food production that made it possible to support a larger population. One of the many cruel ironies of history is that while the institution of slavery was a tragedy for many, it benefited others.

Still, there is no denying the reality that from a moral point of view, the slave trade represented a tragic loss for millions of Africans, not only for the individual victims, but also for their families. One of the more poignant aspects of the trade is that as many as 20 percent of those sold to European slavers were children, a statistic that may be partly explained by the fact that many European countries had enacted regulations that permitted more children than adults to be transported aboard the ships.

How did Europeans justify cruelty of such epidemic proportions? In some cases, they rationalized that slave traders were only carrying on a tradition that had existed for centuries throughout the Mediterranean and African world. In others, they eased their consciences by noting that slaves brought from Africa would now be exposed to the Christian faith and would be able to replace American Indian workers, many of whom were considered too physically fragile for the heavy human labor involved in cutting sugarcane.

Political and Social Structures in a Changing Continent

Of course, the Western economic penetration of Africa had other dislocating effects. As in other parts of the non-Western world, the importation of manufactured goods from Europe undermined the foundations of local cottage industry and impoverished countless families. The demand for slaves and the introduction of firearms intensified political instability and civil strife. At the same time, the impact of the Europeans should not be exaggerated. Only in a few isolated areas, such as South Africa and Mozambique, were permanent European settlements established. Elsewhere, at the insistence of African rulers and merchants, European influence generally did not penetrate beyond the coastal regions.

Nevertheless, inland areas were often affected by events taking place elsewhere. In the western Sahara, for example, the diversion of trade routes toward the coast led to the weakening of the old Songhai trading empire and its eventual conquest by a vigorous new Moroccan dynasty in the late sixteenth century. Morocco had long hoped to expand its influence into the Sahara in order to seize control over the commerce in gold and salt, and in 1590 Moroccan forces defeated Songhai's army at Gao, on the Niger River, and then occupied the great caravan center of Timbuktu. Even after the departure of the invaders, Songhai was beyond recovery, and the next two centuries were marked by civil disorder among tribal groups and intense competition between Muslims in the cities and towns and adherents of traditional African religions in rural areas.

European influence had a more direct impact along the coast of West Africa, especially in the vicinity of European forts such as Dakar and Sierra Leone, but no European colonies were established there before 1800. Most of the numerous African states in the area from

Cape Verde to the delta of the Niger River were sufficiently strong to resist Western encroachments, and they often allied with each other to force European purchasers to respect their monopoly over trading operations. Some, like the powerful Ashanti kingdom, established in 1680 on the Gold Coast, profited substantially from the rise in seaborne commerce. Some states, particularly along the so-called Slave Coast, in what is now Dahomey and Togo, or in the densely populated Niger River delta, took an active part in the slave trade. The demands of slavery and the temptations of economic profit, however, also contributed to the increase in conflict among the states in the area.

This was especially true in the region of the Congo River, where Portuguese activities eventually led to the splintering of the Congo Empire and two centuries of rivalry and internal strife among the successor states in the area. A similar pattern developed in East Africa, where Portuguese activities led to the decline and eventual collapse of the Mwene Metapa. Northward along the coast, in present-day Kenya and Tanzania, African rulers, assisted by Arab forces from Oman and Muscat in the Arabian peninsula, expelled the Portuguese from Mombasa in 1728. Swahili culture now regained some of the dynamism it had possessed before the arrival of Vasco da Gama and his successors. But with much shipping now diverted southward to the route around the Cape of Good Hope, the commerce of the area never completely recovered and was increasingly dependent on the export of slaves and ivory obtained through contacts with African states in the interior.

SOUTHEAST ASIA IN THE ERA OF THE SPICE TRADE

In Southeast Asia, the encounter with the West that began with the arrival of Portuguese fleets in the Indian Ocean at the end of the fifteenth century eventually resulted in the breakdown of traditional societies and the advent of colonial rule. The process was a gradual one, however. By 1700, although the Dutch retained their hold on the islands, Europeans had generally abandoned the Southeast Asian mainland. As we will see in a later chapter, though, the mainland's reprieve was only temporary.

The Arrival of the West

As we have seen, the Spanish soon followed the Portuguese into Southeast Asia. By the seventeenth century, the Dutch, English, and French had begun to join the scramble for rights to the lucrative spice trade.

Chronology

THE SPICE TRADE

Vasco da Gama lands at Calicut in southwestern India	1498
Portuguese seize Malacca	1511
Portuguese ships land in southern China	1514
Magellan's voyage around the world	1519–1522
East India Company established	1600
Vereenigde Oost-Indische Compagnie (VOC) established	1602
English arrive at Surat in northwestern India	1608
Dutch fort established at Batavia	1619
Dutch seize Malacca from the Portuguese	1641
Burmese sack of Ayuthaya	1767
British seize Malacca from the Dutch	1795

Within a short time, the Dutch, through the aggressive and well-financed Dutch East India Company (Vereenigde Oost-Indische Compagnie, or VOC, which possessed ten times the capital of the English East India Company), had not only succeeded in elbowing their rivals out of the spice trade but had also begun to consolidate their political and military control over the area. On the island of Java, where they established a fort at Batavia (today's Jakarta) in 1619, the Dutch found that it was necessary to bring the inland regions under their control to protect their position. Rather than establishing a formal colony, however, they tried to rule as much as possible through the local landed aristocracy. On Java and the neighboring island of Sumatra, the VOC established pepper plantations, which soon became the source of massive profits for Dutch merchants in Amsterdam. Elsewhere they attempted to monopolize the clove trade by limiting cultivation of the crop to one island. By the end of the eighteenth century, the Dutch had succeeded in bringing almost the entire Indonesian archipelago under their control.

The arrival of the Europeans had somewhat less impact on mainland Southeast Asia, where cohesive monarchies in Burma, Thailand, and Vietnam resisted foreign encroachment. In addition, the coveted spices did not thrive on the mainland, so the Europeans' efforts there were far

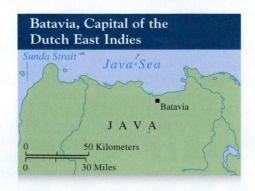

Batavia, Capital of the Dutch East Indies

Sunda Strait

Java Sea

Batavia

JAVA

0   50 Kilometers

0   30 Miles

⚜ BATAVIA, CAPITAL OF THE DUTCH EAST INDIES. After seizing control of the spice trade from European and Islamic rivals, the Dutch established their headquarters at Batavia, on the northern coast of Java, in 1619. Eventually, the canals shown in this photograph became breeding grounds for malaria-bearing mosquitos, forcing the Dutch to move a few miles to the south, the site of modern-day Jakarta.

The Art Archive, London

less determined than in the islands. The Portuguese did establish limited trade relations with several mainland states, including the Thai kingdom at Ayuthaya, Burma, Vietnam, and the remnants of the old Angkor kingdom in Cambodia. By the early seventeenth century, other nations had followed and had begun to compete actively for trade and missionary privileges. As was the case elsewhere, the Europeans soon became involved in local factional disputes as a means of obtaining political and economic advantages. In Burma, the English and the French supported rival groups in the internal struggles of the monarchy until a new dynasty emerged and threw the foreigners out. A similar process took place at Ayuthaya, where the French were forced to evacuate the area in the late seventeenth century.

In Vietnam, the arrival of Western merchants and missionaries coincided with a period of internal conflict among ruling groups in the country. After their arrival in the mid-seventeenth century, the European powers characteristically began to intervene in local politics, with the Portuguese and the Dutch supporting rival factions. By the end of the century, when it became clear that economic opportunities were limited, most European states abandoned their factories (trading stations) in the area. French missionaries attempted to remain, but their efforts were hampered by the local authorities, who viewed the Catholic insistence that converts give their primary loyalty to the pope as a threat to the legal status and prestige of the Vietnamese emperor (see the box on p. 408).

State and Society in Precolonial Southeast Asia

Between 1400 and 1800, Southeast Asia experienced the last flowering of traditional culture before the advent of European rule in the nineteenth century. Although the coming of the Europeans had an immediate and direct impact in some areas, notably the Philippines and parts of the Malay world, in most areas Western influence was still relatively limited. Europeans occasionally dabbled in local politics and modified regional trade patterns, but they generally were not a decisive factor in the evolution of local political or social systems.

Nevertheless, Southeast Asian societies were changing in several subtle ways—in their trade patterns, their means of livelihood, and their religious beliefs. In some ways, these changes accentuated the differences between individual states in the region. Yet beneath these differences was an underlying commonality of life for most people.

AN EXCHANGE OF ROYAL CORRESPONDENCE

In 1681, King Louis XIV of France wrote a letter to the "king of Tonkin" (the Trinh family head, then acting as viceroy to the Vietnamese ruler) requesting permission for Christian missionaries to proselytize in Vietnam. The latter politely declined the request on the grounds that such activity was prohibited by ancient custom. In fact, Christian missionaries had been active in Vietnam for years, and their intervention in local politics had aroused the anger of the court in Hanoi.

A LETTER TO THE KING OF TONKIN FROM LOUIS XIV

Most high, most excellent, most mighty, and most magnanimous Prince, our very dear and good friend, may it please God to increase your greatness with a happy end!

We hear from our subjects who were in your Realm what protection you accorded them. We appreciate this all the more since we have for you all the esteem that one can have for a prince as illustrious through his military valor as he is commendable for the justice which he exercises in his Realm. We have even been informed that you have not been satisfied to extend this general protection to our subjects but, in particular, that you gave effective proofs of it to Messrs. Deydier and de Bourges. We would have wished that they might have been able to recognize all the favors they received from you by having presents worthy of you offered you; but since the war which we have had for several years, in which all of Europe had banded together against us, prevented our vessels from going to the Indies, at the present time, when we are at peace after having gained many victories and expanded our Realm through the conquest of several important places, we have immediately given orders to the Royal Company to establish itself in your kingdom as soon as possible, and have commanded Messrs. Deydier and de Bourges to remain with you in order to maintain a good relationship between our subjects and yours, also to warn us on occasions that might present themselves when we might be able to give you proofs of our esteem and of our wish to concur with your satisfaction as well as with your best interests.

By way of initial proof, we have given orders to have brought to you some presents which we believe might be agreeable to you. But the one thing in the world which we desire most, both for you and for your Realm, would be to obtain for your subjects who have already embraced the law of the only true God of heaven and earth, the freedom to profess it, since this law is the highest, the noblest, the most sacred, and especially the most suitable to have kings reign absolutely over the people.

We are even quite convinced that, if you knew the truths and the maxims which it teaches, you would give first of all to your subjects the glorious example of embracing it. We wish you this incomparable blessing together with a long and happy reign, and we pray God that it may please Him to augment your greatness with the happiest of endings.

Written at Saint-Germain-en-Laye, the 10th day of January, 1681,

Your very dear and good friend,
Louis

ANSWER FROM THE KING OF TONKIN TO LOUIS XIV

The King of Tonkin sends to the King of France a letter to express to him his best sentiments, saying that he was happy to learn that fidelity is a durable good of man and that justice is the most important of things. Consequently practicing of fidelity and justice cannot but yield good results. Indeed, though France and our Kingdom differ as to mountains, rivers, and boundaries, if fidelity and justice reign among our villages, our conduct will express all of our good feelings and contain precious gifts. Your communication, which comes from a country which is a thousand leagues away, and which proceeds from the heart as a testimony of your sincerity, merits repeated consideration and infinite praise. Politeness toward strangers is nothing unusual in our country. There is not a stranger who is not well received by us. How then could we refuse a man from France, which is the most celebrated among the kingdoms of the world and which for love of us wishes to frequent us and bring us merchandise? These feelings of fidelity and justice are truly worthy to be applauded. As regards your wish that we should cooperate in propagating your religion, we do not dare to permit it, for there is an ancient custom, introduced by edicts, which formally forbids it. Now, edicts are promulgated only to be carried out faithfully; without fidelity nothing is stable. How could we disdain a well-established custom to satisfy a private friendship? . . .

We beg you to understand well that this is our communication concerning our mutual acquaintance. This then is my letter. We send you herewith a modest gift, which we offer you with a glad heart.

This letter was written at the beginning of winter and on a beautiful day.

Despite the diversity of cultures and religious beliefs in the area, Southeast Asians were in most respects closer to each other than they were to peoples outside the region. For the most part, the states and peoples of Southeast Asia were still in control of their own destiny.

RELIGION AND KINGSHIP

During the early modern era, both Buddhism and Islam became well established in Southeast Asia, and Christianity began to attract some converts, especially in the Philippines. Buddhism was dominant in lowland areas on the mainland, from Burma to Vietnam. At first, Muslim influence was felt mainly on the Malay peninsula and along the northern coast of Java and Sumatra, where local merchants encountered their Muslim counterparts from foreign lands on a regular basis. At the same time, traditional religious beliefs continued to survive, especially in inland areas, where the local populations either ignored the new doctrines or integrated them into their traditional forms of spirit worship. Buddhists in rural Burma and Thailand, for example, might also believe in nature spirits. On Java and Sumatra, where Islam was slow to penetrate into the interior, the result was a division between devout Muslims in the cities and essentially animist peasants in the rural villages that persists to this day.

Both Buddhism and Islam brought other changes in their train—temple education for Buddhists and schools for Islamic scholars and new religious and moral restrictions on human behavior such as refraining from eating pork and drinking wine for Muslims (though some foreign Muslims complained that the latter rule was not always followed). Because Islam discouraged the traditional tattooing of the body, Muslim converts turned to the technique of decorating textiles called *batik*.

Buddhism and Islam also helped shape Southeast Asian political institutions. As the political systems began to mature, they evolved into four main types: Buddhist kings, Javanese kings, Islamic sultans, and Vietnamese emperors (for the case of Vietnam, which was strongly influenced by China, see Chapter 11). In each case, institutions and concepts imported from abroad were adapted to local circumstances.

The Buddhist style of kingship took shape between the eleventh and the fifteenth centuries, as Theravada Buddhism spread throughout the area. It became the predominant political system in the Buddhist states of mainland Southeast Asia—Burma, Ayuthaya, Laos, and Cambodia. Perhaps the dominant feature of the Buddhist model was the godlike character of the monarch, who was considered by virtue of his karma to be innately superior to other human beings and served as a link between human society and the cosmos. Court rituals stressed the sacred character of the monarch, and even the palace was modeled after the symbolic design of the Hindu universe. In its center was an architectural rendering of sacred Mount Meru, the legendary home of the gods.

The Javanese model was a blend of Buddhist and Islamic political traditions. Like their Buddhist counterparts, Javanese monarchs possessed a sacred quality and maintained the balance between the sacred and the material world, but as Islam penetrated the Indonesian islands in the fifteenth and sixteenth centuries, the monarchs began to lose their semidivine quality.

The Islamic model was found mainly on the Malay peninsula and along the coast of the Indonesian archipelago. In this pattern, the head of state was a sultan, who was viewed as a mortal, although he still possessed some magical qualities. The sultan served as a defender of the faith and staffed his bureaucracy mainly with aristocrats, but he also frequently relied on the Muslim community of scholars—the *ulama*—and was expected, at least in theory, to rule according to the *Shari'a* (see the box on p. 410).

ECONOMY AND SOCIETY

During the early period of European penetration, the economy of most Southeast Asian societies was based on agriculture, as it had been for thousands of years. Still, by the sixteenth century, commerce was beginning to affect daily life, especially in the cities that were beginning to proliferate along the coasts or on navigable rivers. In part, this was because agriculture itself was becoming more commercialized as cash crops like sugar and spices replaced subsistence farming in rice or other cereals in some areas.

Regional and interregional trade were already expanding before the coming of the Europeans. The central geographical location of Southeast Asia enabled it to become a focal point in a widespread trading network. Spices, of course, were the mainstay of the interregional trade, but Southeast Asia exchanged other products as well. The region exported tin (mined in Malaya since the tenth century), copper, gold, tropical fruits and other agricultural products, cloth, gems, and luxury goods in exchange for manufactured goods, ceramics, and high-quality textiles such as silk from China. Although on balance the region was an importer of manufactured goods, it produced some high-quality goods of its own. The ceramics of Vietnam and Thailand, though not made with the high-firing techniques used in China, were still of good quality. The Portuguese traveler Duarte Barbosa observed that the Javanese were skilled cabinetmakers, weapons manufacturers, shipbuilders, and locksmiths. The royal courts were both the main producers and the primary consumers of luxury goods, most of which were produced by highly skilled slaves in the employ of the court.

In general, Southeast Asians probably enjoyed a somewhat higher living standard than most of their contemporaries elsewhere in Asia. Although most of the population was poor by modern Western standards, hunger was not a widespread problem. Several factors help explain this relative prosperity. In the first place, most of Southeast Asia has been blessed by a salubrious climate. The uniformly high temperatures and the abundant rainfall enable

THE TIMELY END OF
SULTAN ZAINAL-'ABIDIN

Acheh, on the northern tip of the island of Sumatra, was one of the first areas in Southeast Asia to be converted to Islam. This passage from the History of Acheh *describes the cruel habits of Sultan Zainal-'Abidin, who ruled in the early seventeenth century. Note the understated way in which the author describes his deposition.*

HISTORY OF ACHEH

Then Sultan Seri'Alam was deposed and Sultan Zainal was installed.

The former had occupied the throne for one year before passing away. He passed away in the year 995 (A.H.) [1617 C.E.]. . . .

After the kingdom of Acheh Dar as-Salam and all its subject territories had been handed over to Sultan Zainal-'Abidin, he would always go out on to the arena and would have rutting elephants as well as ones which were not rutting charge each other, and as a result several people were gored to death by them, and the Bunga Setangkai palace was rammed and then collapsed in ruins together with its annexes. . . . He would order men to beat each other and to duel with staves and shields, and would order Achehnese champion fencers to compete with Indian ones, so that several of the Achehnese and Indian fencers were killed and some were wounded. . . .

If the Sultan were holding audience in a certain place all the chiefs were instructed to sit in homage in the hot sun or in the rain without distinction between the good or the evil. . . .

When the chiefs noticed these habits of the Sultan, and observed that they were growing worse day by day, they said to each other, "What should we do about our lord, for if his oppression of us is like this while he is still young, what will it be like when he is older? According to us, if he continues to be ruler everything will certainly fall in ruins about our ears." Then Sharif al-Muluk Maharaja Lela said, "If that is how it is, it would be best for us to depose our lord the Sultan."

After the chiefs had reached agreement on this matter, one evening the Sultan summoned persons to recite texts in praise of God, and the chiefs were summoned along with them. On that occasion they were reciting texts in the Friday annex. The Sultan was then put on an elephant and was taken to Makota 'Alam. When he arrived at Makota 'Alam [where he was put to death] . . . the Sultan had occupied the throne for two years when he passed away. He passed away in the year 997. In that same year Sultan 'Ala ad-Din Ri'ayat Shah Marhum Sayyid al-Mukkamil was installed.

---

as many as two or even three crops to be grown each year. Second, although the soil in some areas is poor, the alluvial deltas on the mainland are fertile, and the volcanoes of Indonesia periodically spew forth rich volcanic ash that renews the mineral resources of the soil of Sumatra and Java. Finally, with some exceptions, most of Southeast Asia was relatively thinly populated. According to one estimate, the population of the entire region in 1600 was about twenty million, or about 5.5 persons per square kilometer, well below levels elsewhere in Asia. Only in a few areas such as the Red River delta in northern Vietnam was overpopulation a serious problem.

Social institutions tended to be fairly homogeneous throughout Southeast Asia. Compared with China and India, there was little social stratification, and the nuclear family predominated. In general, women fared better in

Courtesy of William J. Duiker

➤ THE JAPANESE BRIDGE AT HOI AN. The Europeans were not the only people who sailed far from native shores in the pursuit of commercial profit during the Age of Exploration. Even prior to the arrival of the first Portuguese fleets in eastern Asia, merchants from within the region as well as from the Middle East had established a vigorous trading network stretching from Japan into the Indian Ocean. Among the active participants were the Japanese. Shown here is a bridge erected in the port city of Hoi An, along the coast of Vietnam south of present-day Da Nang. The bridge spanned a creek entering the harbor and separated the Japanese section of town from other neighborhoods inhabited by Chinese merchants or Europeans. Japanese merchants shipped a variety of tropical goods from the area, as well as local porcelain.

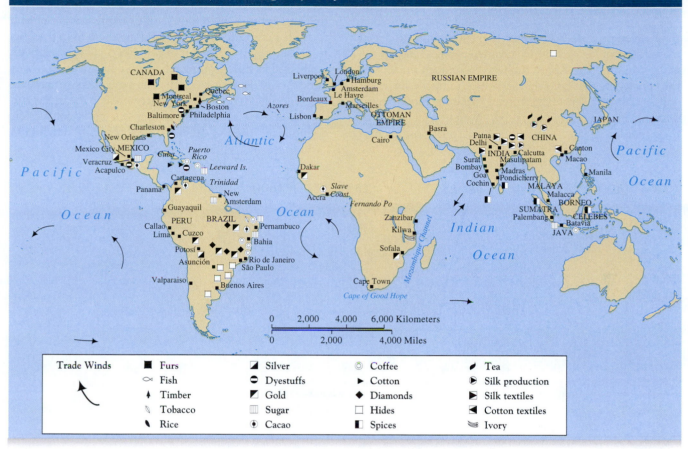

MAP 14.4   The Pattern of World Trade from the Sixteenth to the Eighteenth Centuries.   This map shows the major products that were traded by European merchants throughout the world during the era of European exploration. Prevailing wind patterns in the oceans are shown on the map. ➤ *What were the primary sources of gold and silver, so sought after by Columbus and his successors?*

Trade Winds					
■ Furs	◢ Silver	◉ Coffee	⬧ Tea		
⤬ Fish	◓ Dyestuffs	► Cotton	◗ Silk production		
▲ Timber	◨ Gold	◆ Diamonds	◣ Silk textiles		
◌ Tobacco	▥ Sugar	▫ Hides	◀ Cotton textiles		
◣ Rice	◉ Cacao	◪ Spices	≋ Ivory		

the region than anywhere else in Asia. Daughters often had the same inheritance rights as sons, and family property was held jointly between husband and wife. Wives were often permitted to divorce their husbands, and monogamy was the rule rather than the exception. In some cases, the family of the groom provided the dowry in marriage, and married couples often went to live in the wife's village. Although women were usually restricted to specialized work, such as making ceramics, weaving, or transplanting the rice seedlings into the main paddy fields, and rarely possessed legal rights equal to those of men, they enjoyed a comparatively high degree of freedom and status in most societies in the region and, as we saw in Chapter 9, were sometimes involved in commerce. In the Indonesian islands, for example, women apparently devised a simple fourteen-character alphabet based on the Indian script to record their business transactions. This written language was often passed on to their daughters, while their sons were trained to read sacred works in religious schools.

CONCLUSION

During the fifteenth century, Europeans burst onto the world scene. Beginning with the seemingly modest ventures of the Portuguese ships that sailed southward along the West African coast, the process accelerated with the epoch-making voyages of Christopher Columbus to the Americas and Vasco da Gama to the Indian Ocean in the 1490s. Soon a number of other European states had entered the scene, and by the end of the eighteenth century, they had created a global trade network dominated by Western ships and Western power that distributed foodstuffs, textile goods, spices, and precious minerals from one end of the globe to the other (see Map 14.4).

In less than three hundred years, the European Age of Exploration changed the face of the world. In some areas, such as the Americas and the Spice Islands, it led to the destruction of indigenous civilizations and the establishment of European colonies. In others, as in Africa, South Asia, and mainland Southeast Asia, it left native regimes intact but had a strong impact on local societies and regional trade patterns.

At the time, many European observers viewed the process in a favorable light. Not only did it expand world trade and foster the exchange of new crops and discoveries between the Old and the New Worlds (a process that will be discussed in the Reflection at the end of Part III), but it also introduced the message of Jesus Christ to "heathen peoples" around the globe. Most modern historians have been much more critical, concluding that European activities during the sixteenth and seventeenth centuries created a "tributary mode of production" based on European profits from unequal terms of trade that foreshadowed the exploitative relationship char-

acteristic of the later colonial period. Other scholars have questioned that contention, however, and argue that although Western commercial operations had a significant impact on global trade patterns, they did not—at least not before the eighteenth century—freeze out non-European participants. Muslim merchants, for example, were long able to evade European efforts to eliminate them from the spice trade, and the trans-Saharan caravan trade was relatively unaffected by European merchant shipping along the West African coast. In some cases, the European presence may even have encouraged new economic activity, as in the Indian subcontinent (see Chapter 16). If there was an "age of Western dominance," then, it did not take shape until much later.

CHAPTER NOTES

1. Harry J. Benda and John A. Larkin, eds., *The World of Southeast Asia: Selected Historical Readings* (New York, 1967), p. 13.
2. J. H. Parry, *The European Reconnaissance: Selected Documents* (New York, 1968), p. 113, quoting from Armando Cortesão, *The Summa Oriental of Tomé Pires* (London, 1944), vol. 2, pp. 283–287.
3. Quoted in J. H. Parry, *The Age of Reconnaissance: Discovery, Exploration, and Settlement, 1450 to 1650* (New York, 1963), p. 33.
4. Quoted in Richard B. Reed, "The Expansion of Europe," in Richard DeMolen, ed., *The Meaning of the Renaissance and Reformation* (Boston, 1974), p. 308.
5. K. N. Chaudhuri, *Trade and Civilization in the Indian Ocean: An Economic History from the Rise of Islam to 1750* (Cambridge, 1985), p. 65.
6. Miguel Leon-Portilla, ed., *The Broken Spears: The Aztec Account of the Conquest of Mexico* (Boston, 1969), p. 51.
7. Quoted in Parry, *Age of Reconnaissance*, pp. 176–177.
8. Quoted in Basil Davidson, *Africa in History: Themes and Outlines* (London, 1968), p. 137.

SUGGESTED READING

Classic works on the period of European expansion include J. H. Parry, *The Age of Reconnaissance: Discovery, Exploration, and Settlement, 1450 to 1650* (New York, 1963); B. Penrose, *Travel and Discovery in the Renaissance, 1420–1620* (New York, 1962); and the brief work by J. H. Parry, *The Establishment of European Hegemony, 1415–1715* (New York, 1961). Also see K. M. Panikkar, *Asia and Western Dominance* (London, 1959), and H. Furber, *Rival Empires of Trade in the Orient, 1600–1800* (Minneapolis, Minn. 1976). For a more critical interpretation, see E. Wolf, *Europe and the People Without History* (Berkeley, Calif., 1982), and A. G. Frank, *World Accumulation, 1492–1789* (New York, 1978).

On the technological aspects, see C. M. Cipolla, *Guns, Sails, and Empires: Technological Innovation and the Early Phases of European Expansion, 1400–1700* (New York, 1965); F. Fernandez-Armesto, ed., *The Times Atlas of World Exploration* (New York, 1991); and R. C. Smith, *Vanguard of Empire: Ships of Exploration in the Age of Columbus* (Oxford, 1993); also see A. Pagden, *Lords of All the World: Ideologies of Empire in Spain, Britain, and France, c. 1500–c. 1800* (New Haven, Conn., 1995). For an overview on the impact of European expansion in the Indian Ocean, see K. N. Chaudhuri, *Trade and Civilization in the Indian Ocean: An Economic History from the Rise of Islam to 1750* (Cambridge, 1985). For a series of stimulating essays reflecting modern scholarship, see J. D. Tracy, *The Rise of Merchant Empires: Long-Distance Trade in the Early Modern World, 1350–1750* (Cambridge, 1990).

On European expansion in the Americas, see S. E. Morison, *The European Discovery of America: The Southern Voyages, 1492–1616* (New York, 1974). For a fundamental work on Spanish colonization, see J. H. Parry, *The Spanish Seaborne Empire* (New York, 1966). The most recent work on the conquistadors is H. Thomas, *Conquest: Montezuma, Cortés, and the Fall of Old Mexico* (New York, 1993). See also the richly illustrated H. Innes, *The Conquistadors* (New York, 1969). The human effects of the interaction of New and Old World cultures are examined thoughtfully in A. W. Crosby, *The Columbian Exchange: Biological and Cultural Consequences of 1492* (Westport, Conn., 1972).

On Portuguese expansion, the fundamental work is C. R. Boxer, *The Portuguese Seaborne Empire, 1415–1825* (New York, 1969). For a more recent interpretation, see W. B. Diffie and G. D. Winius, *Foundations of the Portuguese Empire, 1415–1580* (Minneapolis, Minn., 1979). On the Dutch, see J. I. Israel, *Dutch Primacy in World Trade, 1585–1740* (Oxford, 1989). The effects of European trade in Southeast Asia are discussed in A. Reid, *Southeast Asia in the Age of Commerce, 1450–1680* (New Haven, Conn., 1989).

On the African slave trade, the standard work is P. Curtin, *The African Slave Trade: A Census* (Madison, Wis., 1969). For more recent treatments, see P. Lovejoy, *Transformations in Slavery: A History of Slavery in Africa* (1983), and P. Manning, *Slavery and African Life* (Cambridge, 1990); H. Thomas, *The Slave Trade* (New York, 1997), provides a useful overview. Also see C. Palmer, *Human Cargoes: The British Slave Trade to Spanish America, 1700–1739* (Urbana, Ill., 1981), and K. F. Kiple, *The Caribbean Slave: A Biological History* (Cambridge, 1984).

For a brief introduction to women's experiences during the Age of Exploration and global trade, see S. Hughes and B. Hughes, *Women in World History*, vol. 2 (Armonk, N.Y., 1997). For a more theoretical discussion of violence and gender in the early modern period, consult R. Trexler, *Sex and Conquest: Gendered Violence, Political Order, and the European Conquest of the Americas* (Ithaca, N.Y., 1995). The native American female experience with the European encounter is presented in R. Gutierrez, *When Jesus Came the Corn Mothers Went Away: Marriage, Sexuality and Power in New Mexico, 1500–1846* (Stanford, Calif., 1991), and K. Anderson, *Chain Her by One Foot: The Subjugation of Women in Seventeenth Century New France* (London, 1991).

INFOTRAC COLLEGE EDITION

For additional reading, go to InfoTrac College Edition, your online research library at http://web1.infotrac-college.com

Enter the search terms "Vasco da Gama" using Keywords.

Enter the search terms "Christopher Columbus" using the Subject Guide.

Enter the search term "mercantilism" using the Subject Guide.

Enter the search terms "Africa history" using Keywords.

Chapter 15

THE MUSLIM EMPIRES

CHAPTER OUTLINE
- THE OTTOMAN EMPIRE
- THE SAFAVIDS
- THE GRANDEUR OF THE MUGHALS
- CONCLUSION

FOCUS QUESTIONS
- Why are the Ottoman, Safavid, and Mughal Empires sometimes called "gunpowder empires," and how accurate is that characterization?
- What were the main characteristics of each of the Muslim empires, and in what ways were they similar?
- What contact did each of the Muslim empires have with Europeans, and how was each empire affected by that contact?
- What role did women play in each of the Muslim empires?
- How did each of the great Muslim empires come into existence, and why did they ultimately decline?

One of the primary objectives of European leaders in seeking a route to the Spice Islands was to lessen the political and economic power of Islam by reducing the Muslims' strong position in the global trade network. As we saw in Chapter 14, Portuguese fleets, followed by those of the Spanish, the English, and the Dutch, had some success in wresting control over the spice trade from Muslim shippers, although the latter were never totally driven out of the business. By the eighteenth century, the Indian Ocean had ceased to be an Arab preserve and had become, in some respects, a European lake.

Thus the European dream of controlling global trade markets had become a reality. But in the broader scheme of things, the goal of crippling the power of Islam was not entirely realized, for Europe's success had not been achieved by the collapse of its great rival. To the contrary, the Muslim world, which appeared to have entered a period of decline with the collapse of the Abbasid caliphate during the era of the Mongols, managed to revive in the shadow of Europe's Age of Exploration, a period that also saw the rise of three great Muslim empires. These powerful Muslim states—

of the Ottomans, the Safavids, and the Mughals—dominated the Middle East and the South Asia subcontinent and brought stability to a region that had been in turmoil for centuries.

This stability lasted for about two hundred years. By the end of the eighteenth century, much of India and the Middle East had come under severe European pressure and had returned to a state of anarchy, and the Ottoman Empire had entered a period of gradual decline. But that decline was due more to internal factors than to the challenge posed by a resurgent Europe. •

THE OTTOMAN EMPIRE

The Ottoman Turks were among the various Turkic-speaking peoples who had spread westward from Central Asia in the ninth, tenth, and eleventh centuries. The first to dominate were the Seljuk Turks, who initially attempted to revive the declining Abbasid caliphate in Baghdad. Later they established themselves in the Anatolian peninsula at the expense of the Byzantine Empire. Turks served as warriors or administrators, while the peasants who tilled the farmland were mainly Greek.

In the late thirteenth century, a new group of Turks under the tribal leader Osman (1280–1326) began to consolidate their power in the northwestern corner of the Anatolian peninsula. That land had been given to them by the Seljuk rulers as a reward for helping drive out the Mongols in the late thirteenth century. At first, the Osman Turks were relatively peaceful and engaged in pastoral pursuits, but as the Seljuk empire began to disintegrate in the early fourteenth century, they began to expand and founded the Osmanli (later to be known as Ottoman) dynasty.

A key advantage for the Ottomans was their location in the northwestern corner of the peninsula. From there they were able to expand westward and eventually control the Bosporus and the Dardanelles, between the Mediterranean and the Black Seas. The Byzantine Empire, of course, had controlled the area for centuries, serving as a buffer between the Muslim Middle East and the Latin West. The Byzantines, however, had been severely weakened by the sack of Constantinople in the Fourth Crusade (in 1204) and the Western occupation of much of the empire for the next half century. In 1345, Ottoman forces under their leader Orkhan I (1326–1360) crossed the Bosporus for the first time to support a usurper against the Byzantine emperor in Constantinople. Setting up their first European base at Gallipoli at the Mediterranean entrance to the Dardanelles, Turkish forces expanded gradually into the Balkans and allied with fractious Serbian and Bulgar forces against the Byzantines. In these unstable conditions, the Ottomans gradually established permanent settlements throughout the area, where Turkish beys (provincial governors in the Ottoman Empire; from the Turkish *beg*, "knight") drove out the previous landlords and collected taxes from the local Slavic peasants. The Ottoman leader now began to claim the title of sultan or sovereign of his domain.

In 1360, Orkhan was succeeded by his son Murad I, who consolidated Ottoman power in the Balkans, set up a capital at Edirne (modern Adrianople), and gradually reduced the Byzantine emperor to a vassal. Murad did not initially attempt to conquer Constantinople because his forces were composed mostly of the traditional Turkish cavalry and lacked the ability to breach the strong walls of the city. Instead, he began to build up a strong military administration based on the recruitment of Christians into an elite guard. Called Janissaries (from the Turkish *yeni cheri*, "new troops"), they were recruited from the local Christian population in the Balkans and then converted to Islam and trained as foot soldiers or administrators. One of the major advantages of the Janissaries was that they were directly subordinated to the sultanate and therefore owed their loyalty to the person of the sultan. Other military forces were organized by the beys and were thus loyal to their local tribal leaders.

The Janissary corps also represented a response to changes in warfare. As the knowledge of firearms spread in the late fourteenth century, the Turks began to master the new technology, including siege cannons and muskets. The traditional nomadic cavalry charge was now outmoded and was superseded by infantry forces armed with muskets. Thus the Janissaries provided a well-armed infantry who served both as an elite guard to protect the palace and as a means of extending Turkish control in the Balkans. With his new forces, Murad defeated the Serbs at the famous Battle of Kosovo in 1389 and ended Serbian hegemony in the area.

Under Murad's successor, Bayazid I (1389–1402), the Ottomans advanced northward, annexed Bulgaria, and slaughtered the flower of French cavalry at a major battle on the Danube. A defeat at the hands of the Mongol warrior Tamerlane (see Chapter 9) in 1402 proved to be only a temporary setback. When Mehmet II (1451–1481) succeeded to the throne, he was determined to capture Constantinople. Already in control of the Dardanelles, he ordered the construction of a major fortress on the Bosporus just north of the city, which put the Turks in a position to strangle the Byzantines.

The last Byzantine emperor desperately called for help from the Europeans, but only the Genoese came to his defense. With eighty thousand troops ranged against only seven thousand defenders, Mehmet laid siege to Constantinople in 1453. In their attack on the city, the Turks made use of massive cannons with 26-foot barrels that could launch stone balls weighing up to 1,200 pounds each. The Byzantines stretched heavy chains across the Golden Horn, the inlet that forms the city's harbor, to

THE FALL OF CONSTANTINOPLE

ew events in the history of the Ottoman Empire are more dramatic than the conquest of Constantinople in 1453. In this excerpt, the conquest is described by Kritovoulos, a Greek who later served in the Ottoman administration. Although the author did not witness the conquest itself, he was apparently well informed about the event and provides us with a vivid description.

KRITOVOULOS, *LIFE OF MEHMED THE CONQUEROR*

So saying, he [the Sultan] led them himself. And they, with a shout on the run and with a fearsome yell, went on ahead of the Sultan, pressing on up to the palisade. After a long and bitter struggle they hurled back the Romans [Byzantines] from there and climbed by force up the palisade. They dashed some of their foe down into the ditch between the great wall and the palisade, which was deep and hard to get out of, and they killed them there. The rest they drove back to the gate.

He had opened this gate in the great wall, so as to go easily over to the palisade. Now there was a great struggle there and great slaughter among those stationed there, for they were attacked by the heavy infantry and not a few others in irregular formation, who had been attracted from many points by the shouting. There the Emperor Constantine [Constantine XIII Paleologus], with all who were with him, fell in gallant combat.

The heavy infantry were already streaming through the little gate into the City, and others had rushed in through the breach in the great wall. Then all the rest of the army, with a rush and a roar, poured in brilliantly and scattered all over the City. And the Sultan stood before the great wall, where the standard also was and the ensigns, and watched the proceedings. The day was already breaking. . . .

The soldiers fell on them [the citizens] with anger and great wrath. For one thing, they were actuated by the hardships of the siege. For another, some foolish people had hurled taunts and curses at them from the battlements all through the siege. Now, in general they killed so as to frighten all the City, and to terrorize and enslave all by the slaughter.

When they had had enough of murder, and the City was reduced to slavery, some of the troops turned to the mansions of the mighty, by bands and companies and divisions, for plunder and spoil. Others went to the robbing of churches, and others dispersed to the simple homes of the common people, stealing, robbing, plundering, killing, insulting, taking and enslaving men, women, and children, old and young, priests, monks—in short, every age and class. . . .

After this the Sultan entered the City and looked about to see its great size, its situation, its grandeur and beauty, its teeming population, its loveliness, and the costliness of its churches and public buildings and of the private houses and community houses and those of the officials. . . . When he saw what a large number had been killed, and the ruin of the buildings, and the wholesale ruin and destruction of the City, he was filled with compassion and repented not a little at the destruction and plundering. Tears fell from his eyes as he groaned deeply and passionately: "What a city we have given over to plunder and destruction." . . .

As for the great City of Constantine, raised to a great height of glory and dominion and wealth in its own times, overshadowing to an infinite degree all the cities around it, renowned for its glory, wealth, authority, power, and greatness, and all its other qualities, it thus came to its end.

prevent a naval attack from the north and prepared to make their final stand behind the 13-mile-long wall along the western edge of the city. But Mehmet's forces seized the tip of the peninsula north of the Golden Horn and then dragged their ships overland across the peninsula from the Bosporus and put them into the water behind the chains. Finally, the walls were breached; the Byzantine emperor died in the final battle (see the box above). Mehmet II, standing before the palace of the emperor, paused to reflect on the passing nature of human glory. But it was not long before he and the Ottomans were again on the march.

The Fall of Constantinople, 1453

Expansion of the Empire

With their new capital at Constantinople, renamed Istanbul, the Ottoman Turks were now a dominant force in the Balkans and the Anatolian peninsula. They now began to advance to the east against the Shi'ite kingdom of the Safavids in Persia (see "The Safavids" later in this chapter), which had been promoting rebellion among the Anatolian tribal population and disrupting Turkish trade through the Middle East. After defeating the Safavids at a major battle in 1514, Emperor Selim I (1512–1520) consolidated Turkish control over Mesopotamia and then turned his

➤ **MEHMET II, CONQUEROR OF CONSTANTINOPLE.**
Identified with the seizure of Constantinople from the Byzantine Empire in 1453, Mehmet II was one of the most illustrious Ottoman sultans. This Turkish miniature portrays Mehmet II with his handkerchief, a symbol of the supreme power of the Ottoman ruler. He is also smelling a rose, representing his cultural interests, especially as patron of the arts.

➤ **THE TURKISH CONQUEST OF CONSTANTINOPLE.**
Mehmet II put a stranglehold on the Byzantine capital of Constantinople with a surprise attack by Turkish ships, which were dragged overland and placed in the water behind the enemy's defense lines. In addition, the Turks made use of massive cannons that could launch stone balls weighing up to 1,200 pounds each. The heavy bombardment of the city walls presaged the beginning of a new era of warfare in Europe. Notice the fanciful Gothic interpretation of the city in this contemporary French miniature of the siege of Constantinople.

attention to the Mamluks in Egypt, who had failed to support the Ottomans in their struggle against the Safavids. The Mamluks were defeated in Syria in 1516; Cairo fell a year later. Now controlling several of the holy cities of Islam, including Jerusalem, Mecca, and Medina, Selim declared himself to be the new caliph, or succes-

sor to Muhammad. During the next few years, Turkish armies and fleets advanced westward along the African coast, occupying Tripoli, Tunis, and Algeria and eventually penetrating almost to the Strait of Gibraltar (see Map 15.1). In their advance, the invaders had taken advantage of the progressive disintegration of the Nasrid dynasty in Morocco, which had been in decline for decades and had lost its last foothold on the European continent when Granada fell to the rising power of Spain in 1492.

The impact of Turkish rule on the peoples of North Africa was relatively light. Like their predecessors, the Turks were Muslims, and they preferred where possible to administer their conquered regions through local rulers. Central government direction was achieved through appointed *pashas* who collected taxes (and then paid a

MAP 15.1   The Ottoman Empire   This map shows the territorial growth of the Ottoman Empire from the eve of the conquest of Constantinople in 1453 to the end of the seventeenth century, when a defeat at the hands of Austria led to the loss of a substantial portion of central Europe. ➤ *Where did the Ottomans come from?*

fixed percentage as tribute to the central government), maintained law and order, and were directly responsible to Istanbul. The Turks ruled from coastal cities like Algiers, Tunis, and Tripoli and made no attempt to control the interior beyond maintaining the trade routes through the Sahara to the trading centers along the Niger River. Meanwhile, local pirates along the Barbary Coast—the northern coast of Africa from Egypt to the Atlantic Ocean—competed with their Christian rivals in raiding the shipping that passed through the Mediterranean.

By the seventeenth century, the links between the imperial court in Istanbul and its appointed representatives in the Turkish regencies in North Africa had begun to decline. Some of the pashas were dethroned by local elites, while others, such as the bey of Tunis, became hereditary rulers. Even Egypt, whose agricultural wealth and control over the route to the Red Sea made it the most important country in the area to the Turks, gradu-

ally became autonomous under a new official class of Janissaries. Many of them became wealthy landowners by exploiting their official function to collect tax revenues far in excess of what they had to remit to Istanbul. In the early eighteenth century, the Mamluks returned to power, although the Turkish government managed to retain some control by means of a viceroy appointed from Istanbul.

TURKISH EXPANSION IN EUROPE

After their conquest of Constantinople in 1453, the Ottoman Turks tried to complete their conquest of the Balkans, where they had been established since the fourteenth century. Although they were successful in taking the Romanian territory of Wallachia in 1476, the resistance of the Hungarians initially kept the Turks from advancing up the Danube valley. From 1480 to 1520, inter-

A PORTRAIT OF SULEYMAN THE MAGNIFICENT

Suleyman the Magnificent was perhaps the greatest of all Ottoman sultans. Like King Louis XIV of France and Emperor Kangxi of China, he presided over his domain at the peak of its military and cultural achievement. This description of him was written by Ghislain de Busbecq, the Habsburg ambassador to Constantinople. Busbecq observed Suleyman at first hand and, as this excerpt indicates, was highly impressed by the Turkish ruler.

GHISLAIN DE BUSBECQ, *THE TURKISH LETTERS*

The Sultan was seated on a rather low sofa, no more than a foot from the ground and spread with many costly coverlets and cushions embroidered with exquisite work. Near him were his bow and arrows. His expression, as I have said, is anything but smiling, and has a sternness which, though sad, is full of majesty. On our arrival we were introduced into his presence by his chamberlains, who held our arms—a practice which has always been observed since a Croatian sought an interview and murdered the Sultan Amurath in a revenge for the slaughter of his master, Marcus the Despot of Serbia. After going through the pretense of kissing his hand, we were led to the wall facing him backwards, so as not to turn our backs or any part of them toward him. He then listened to the recital of my message, but, as it did not correspond with his expectations (for the demands of my imperial master [the Habsburg emperor Ferdinand I] were full of dignity and independence, and, therefore, far from acceptable to one who thought that his slightest wishes ought to be obeyed) he assumed an expression of disdain, and merely answered "Giusel, Giusel," that is, "Well, Well." We were then dismissed to our lodging. . . .

You will probably wish me to describe the impression which Suleyman made upon me. He is beginning to feel the weight of years, but his dignity of demeanor and his general physical appearance are worthy of the ruler of so vast an empire. He has always been frugal and temperate, and was so even in his youth, when he might have erred without incurring blame in the eyes of the Turks. Even in his earlier years he did not indulge in wine or in those unnatural vices to which the Turks are often addicted. Even his bitterest critics can find nothing more serious to allege against him than his undue submission to his wife and its result in his somewhat precipitate action in putting Mustapha [his firstborn son, by another wife] to death, which is generally imputed to her employment of love potions and incantations. It is generally agreed that, ever since he promoted her to the rank of his lawful wife, he has possessed no concubines, although there is no law to prevent his doing so. He is a strict guardian of his religion and its ceremonies, being not less desirous of upholding his faith than of extending his dominions. For his age—he has almost reached his sixtieth year—he enjoys quite good health, though his bad complexion may be due to some hidden malady; and indeed it is generally believed that he has an incurable ulcer or gangrene on his leg. This defect of complexion he remedies by painting his face with a coating of red powder, when he wishes departing ambassadors to take with them a strong impression of his good health; for he fancies that it contributes to inspire greater fear in foreign potentates if they think that he is well and strong. I noticed a clear indication of this practice on the present occasion; for his appearance when he received me in the final audience was very different from that which he presented when he gave me an interview on my arrival.

---

nal problems and the need to consolidate their eastern frontiers kept the Turks from any further attacks on Europe.

Suleyman I the Magnificent (1520–1566; see the box above), however, brought the Turks back to Europe's attention. Advancing up the Danube, the Turks seized Belgrade in 1521 and won a major victory over the Hungarians at the Battle of Mohács on the Danube in 1526. Subsequently, the Turks overran most of Hungary, moved into Austria, and advanced as far as Vienna, where they were finally repulsed in 1529. At the same time, they extended their power into the western Mediterranean and threatened to turn it into a Turkish lake until a large Turkish fleet was destroyed by the Spanish at Lepanto in 1571. Despite the defeat, the Turks continued to hold nominal suzerainty over the southern shores of the Mediterranean.

Although Europeans frequently called for new Christian Crusades against the "infidel" Turks, the Ottoman Empire was by the beginning of the seventeenth century being treated like any other European power by European rulers seeking alliances and trade concessions. During the first half of the seventeenth century, the Ottoman Empire was a "sleeping giant." Involved in domestic bloodletting and heavily threatened by a challenge from Persia, the Ottomans were content with the status quo in eastern Europe. But under a new line of grand vezirs in the second half of the seventeenth century, the Ottoman Empire again took the offensive. By mid-1683, the Ottomans had marched through the Hungarian plain and laid siege to Vienna. Repulsed by a mixed army of Austrians, Poles, Bavarians, and Saxons, the Turks retreated and were pushed out of Hungary by a new European coalition. Although they

© Sonia Halliday Photographs

⇒ **THE SIEGE OF VIENNA.** After seizing the Byzantine capital of Constantinople in 1453, Turkish forces began advancing into southern Europe to extend the borders of the Ottoman Empire. By 1529, they had reached the gates of Vienna, capital of the Habsburg Empire, which they placed under siege. In this contemporary painting from the Topkapi Palace in Istanbul, Turkish forces across the Danube River have besieged the walled city, shown in the background. Despite the use of cannons, first introduced to the West by Ottoman forces during this campaign, the siege was unsuccessful.

system was the sultan, who was the supreme authority in both a political and a military sense. The origins of this system can be traced back to the bey, who was only a tribal leader, a first among equals, who could claim loyalty from his chiefs so long as he could provide booty and grazing lands for his subordinates. Disputes were settled by tribal law, while Muslim laws were secondary. Tribal leaders collected taxes—or booty—from areas under their control and sent one-fifth on to the bey. Both administrative and military power were centralized under the bey, and the capital was wherever the bey and his administration happened to be.

But the rise of empire brought about changes and an adaptation to Byzantine traditions of rule. The status and prestige of the sultan now increased relative to the subordinate tribal leaders, and the position took on the trappings of imperial rule. Court rituals were inherited from the Byzantines and Persians, and a centralized administrative system was adopted that increasingly isolated the sultan in his palace. The position of the sultan was hereditary, with a son, although not necessarily the eldest, always succeeding the father. This practice led to chronic succession struggles upon the death of individual sultans, and the losers were often executed (strangled with a silk bowstring) or later imprisoned. Heirs to the throne were assigned as provincial governors to provide them with experience.

The heart of the sultan's power was in the Topkapi Palace in the center of Istanbul. Topkapi (meaning "cannon gate") was constructed in 1459 by Mehmet II and

retained the core of their empire, the Ottoman Turks would never again be a threat to Europe. Although the Turkish empire held together for the rest of the seventeenth and the eighteenth centuries, it would be faced with new challenges from the ever growing Austrian Empire in southeastern Europe and the new Russian giant to the north.

The Nature of Turkish Rule

Like other Muslim empires in Persia and India, the Ottoman political system was the result of the evolution of tribal institutions into a sedentary empire. At the apex of the Ottoman served as an administrative center as well as the private residence of the sultan and his family. Eventually, it had a staff of twenty thousand employees. The private domain of the sultan was called the harem ("sacred place"). Here he resided with his concubines. Normally, a sultan did not marry but chose several concubines as his favorites; they were accorded this status after they gave birth to sons. When a son became a sultan, his mother became known as the queen mother and served as adviser to the throne. This tradition, initiated by the influential wife of Suleyman the Magnificent, often resulted in considerable authority for the queen mother in the affairs of state.

Members of the harem, like the Janissaries, were often of slave origin and formed an elite element in Ottoman society. Since the enslavement of Muslims was forbidden, slaves were taken among non-Islamic peoples. Some concubines were prisoners selected for the position, while others were purchased or offered to the sultan as a gift. They were then trained and educated like the Janissaries in a system called *devshirme* ("collection"). *Devshirme* had originated in the practice of requiring local clan leaders to provide prisoners to the sultan as part of their tax obligation. Talented males were given special training for eventual placement in military or administrative positions, while their female counterparts were trained for service in the harem, with instruction in reading, the Koran, sewing and embroidery, and musical performance. They were ranked according to their status, and some were permitted to leave the harem to marry officials. If they were later divorced, they were sometimes allowed to return to the harem.

Unique to the Ottoman Empire from the fifteenth century onward was the exclusive use of slaves to reproduce its royal heirs. Contrary to myth, few of the women of the imperial harem were used for sexual purposes, as the majority were relatives of the sultan's extended family—sisters, daughters, widowed mothers, and in-laws, with their own personal slaves and entourage. Contemporary European observers compared the atmosphere in the Topkapi harem to a Christian nunnery, with its hierarchical organization, enforced chastity, and rule of silence.

Because of their proximity to the sultan, the women of the harem often wielded so much political power that the era has been called "the sultanate of women." Queen mothers administered the imperial household and engaged in diplomatic relations with other countries while controlling the marital alliances of their daughters with senior civilian and military officials or members of other royal families in the region. One princess was married seven separate times from the age of two after her previous husbands died either in battle or by execution.

The sultan ruled through an imperial council that met four days a week and was chaired by the chief minister known as the grand vezir (*wazir*, sometimes rendered in English as *vizier*). The sultan often attended behind a screen, whence he could privately indicate his desires to the grand vezir. The latter presided over the imperial bureaucracy. Like the palace guard, the bureaucrats were not an exclusive group but were chosen at least partly by merit from a palace school for training officials. Most officials were Muslims by birth, but some talented Janissaries became senior members of the bureaucracy, and almost all the later grand vezirs came from the *devshirme* system.

Local administration during the imperial period was a product of Turkish tribal tradition and was similar in some respects to fief-holding in Europe. The empire was divided into provinces and districts governed by officials who, like their tribal predecessors, combined both civil and military functions. They were assisted by bureaucrats trained in the palace school in Istanbul. Senior officials were assigned land in fief by the sultan and were then responsible for collecting taxes and supplying armies to the empire. These lands were then farmed out to the local cavalry elite called the *sipahis*, who exacted a tax from all peasants in their fiefdoms for their salary. These local officials were not hereditary aristocrats, but sons often inherited their fathers' landholdings, and the vast majority were descendants of the tribal beys who had served as a tribal elite during the preimperial period.

Religion and Society in the Ottoman World

Like most Turkic-speaking peoples in the Anatolian peninsula and throughout the Middle East, the Ottoman ruling elites were Sunni Muslims. Ottoman sultans had claimed the title of caliph ("defender of the faith") since the early sixteenth century and thus theoretically were responsible for guiding the flock and maintaining Islamic law, the *Shari'a*. In practice, the sultan assigned these duties to a supreme religious authority, who administered the law and maintained a system of schools for educating Muslims.

Islamic law and customs were applied to all Muslims in the empire. Like their rulers, most Turkic-speaking people were Sunni Muslims, but some communities were attracted to Sufism (see Chapter 7) or other heterodox doctrines. The government tolerated such activities so long as their practitioners remained loyal to the empire, but in the early sixteenth century, unrest among these groups—some of whom converted to the Shi'ite version of Islamic doctrine—outraged the conservative *ulama* and eventually led to war against the Safavids (see "The Safavids" later in this chapter).

Non-Muslims—mostly Orthodox Christians (Greeks and Slavs), Jews, and Armenian Christians—formed a significant minority within the empire, which treated them with relative tolerance. Non-Muslims were compelled to pay a head tax (because of their exemption from military service), and they were permitted to practice their religion or convert to Islam, although Muslims were prohibited from adopting another faith. Most of the population in European areas of the empire remained Christian, but in some places, such as the territory now called Bosnia, substantial numbers converted to Islam.

Each religious group within the empire was organized as an administrative unit called a *millet* ("nation" or "community"). Each group, including the Muslims themselves, had its own patriarch or grand rabbi who dealt as an intermediary with the government and administered the community according to its own laws. The leaders of the individual nations were responsible to the sultan and his officials for the behavior of the subjects under their care and collected taxes for transmission to the government. Each nation established its own system of justice, set its own educational policies, and provided welfare for the needy.

Technically, women in the Ottoman Empire were subject to the same restrictions that afflicted their counterparts in other Muslim societies, but their position was ameliorated to some degree by various factors. In the first place, non-Muslims were subject to the laws and customs of their own religions; thus Orthodox Christian, Jewish, and Armenian Christian women were spared some of the restrictions applied to their Muslim sisters. In the second place, Islamic laws as applied in the Ottoman Empire defined the legal position of women comparatively tolerantly. Women were permitted to own and inherit property, including their dowries. They could not be forced into marriage and in certain cases were permitted to seek a divorce. As we have seen, women often exercised considerable influence in the palace and in a few instances even served as senior officials, such as governors of provinces. The relatively tolerant attitude toward women in Ottoman-held territories has been ascribed by some to Turkish tribal traditions, which took a more egalitarian view of sex roles than the sedentary societies of the region did.

The Ottomans in Decline

The Ottoman Empire reached its zenith under Suleyman the Magnificent, often known as Suleyman Kanuni, or "the lawgiver," who launched the conquest of Hungary. But Suleyman also sowed the seeds of the empire's eventual decline. He executed his two most able sons on suspicion of factionalism and was succeeded by Selim II (the Sot, or "the drunken sultan"), the only surviving son.

By the seventeenth century, signs of internal rot had begun to appear, although the first loss of imperial territory did not occur until 1699, at the Battle of Carlowitz. Apparently, a number of factors were involved. In the first place, the administrative system inherited from the tribal period began to break down. Although the *devshirme* system of training officials continued to function, *devshirme* graduates were now permitted to marry and inherit property and to enroll their sons in the palace corps. Thus they were gradually transformed from a meritocratic administrative elite into a privileged and often degenerate hereditary caste. Local administrators were corrupted and taxes rose as the central bureaucracy lost its links with rural areas. The imperial treasury was depleted by constant wars, and transport and communications were neglected. Interest in science and technology, once a hallmark of the Arab empire, was in decline. In addition, the empire was increasingly beset by economic difficulties, caused by the diversion of trade routes away from the eastern Mediterranean and the price inflation brought about by the influx of cheap American silver.

Another sign of change within the empire was the increasing degree of material affluence and the impact of Western ideas and customs. Sophisticated officials and merchants began to mimic the habits and lifestyles of their European counterparts, dressing in the European fashion, purchasing Western furniture and art objects, and ignoring Muslim strictures against the consumption of alcohol and sexual activities outside marriage. During the sixteenth and early seventeenth centuries, coffee and tobacco were introduced into polite Ottoman society, and cafés for the consumption of both began to appear in the major cities (see the box on p. 423). One sultan in the early seventeenth century issued a decree prohibiting the consumption of both coffee and tobacco, arguing (correctly, no doubt) that many cafés were nests of antigovernment intrigue. He even began to wander incognito through the streets of Istanbul at night. Any of his subjects detected in immoral or illegal acts were summarily executed and their bodies left on the streets as an example to others.

There were also signs of a decline in competence within the ruling family. Whereas the first sultans reigned twenty-seven years on average, later ones averaged only thirteen years. The throne now went to the oldest surviving male, while his rivals were kept secluded in a latticed cage and thus had no governmental experience if they succeeded to rule. Later sultans also became less involved in government, and more power flowed to the office of the grand vezir (called the Sublime Porte) or to eunuchs and members of the harem. Palace intrigue increased as a result.

Ottoman Art

The Ottoman sultans were enthusiastic patrons of the arts and maintained large ateliers of artisans and artists, primarily at the Topkapi Palace in Istanbul but also in other important cities of the vast empire. The period from Mehmet II in the fifteenth century to the early eighteenth century witnessed the flourishing of pottery, rugs, silk and other textiles, jewelry, arms and armor, and calligraphy. All adorned the palaces of the new rulers, testifying to their opulence and exquisite taste. The artists came from all parts of the realm and beyond. Besides Turks, there were Persians, Greeks, Armenians, Hungarians, and Italians, all vying for the esteem and generous rewards of the sultans and fearing that losing favor might mean losing their heads! In the second half of the sixteenth century, Istan-

A TURKISH DISCOURSE ON COFFEE

Coffee was first introduced to Turkey from the Arabian peninsula in the mid-sixteenth century and allegedly came to Europe during the Turkish seige of Vienna in 1527. The following account was written by Katib Chelebi, a seventeenth-century Turkish author who, among other things, compiled an extensive encyclopedia and bibliography. Here, in The Balance of Truth, he describes how coffee entered the empire and the problems it caused for public morality. (In the Muslim world, as in Europe and later in colonial America, the drinking of coffee was associated with coffeehouses, where rebellious elements often gathered to promote antigovernment activities.) Chelebi died in Istanbul in 1657, reportedly while drinking a cup of coffee.

KATIB CHELEBI, *THE BALANCE OF TRUTH*

[Coffee] originated in Yemen and has spread, like tobacco, over the world. Certain sheikhs, who lived with their dervishes in the mountains of Yemen, used to crush and eat the berries . . . of a certain tree. Some would roast them and drink their water. Coffee is a cold dry food, suited to the ascetic life and sedative of lust. . . .

It came to Asia Minor by sea, about 1543, and met with a hostile reception, fetwas [decrees] being delivered against it. For they said, Apart from its being roasted, the fact that it is drunk in gatherings, passed from hand to hand, is suggestive of loose living. It is related of Abul-Suud Efendi that he had holes bored in the ships that brought it, plunging their cargoes of coffee into the sea. But these strictures and prohibitions availed nothing. . . . One coffeehouse was opened after another, and men would gather together, with great eagerness and enthusiasm, to drink. Drug addicts in particular, finding it a life-giving thing, which increased their pleasure, were willing to die for a cup.

Storytellers and musicians diverted the people from their employments, and working for one's living fell into disfavor. Moreover the people, from prince to beggar, amused themselves with knifing one another. Toward the end of 1633, the late Ghazi Gultan Murad, becoming aware of the situation, promulgated an edict, out of regard and compassion for the people, to this effect: Coffeehouses throughout the Guarded Domains shall be dismantled and not opened hereafter. Since then, the coffeehouses of the capital have been as desolate as the heart of the ignorant. . . . But in cities and towns outside Istanbul, they are opened just as before. As has been said above, such things do not admit of a perpetual ban.

---

bul alone listed over 150 craft guilds, ample proof of the artistic activity of the era.

By far the greatest contribution of the Ottoman Empire to world art was its architecture, especially the magnificent mosques of the second half of the sixteenth century. Traditionally, prayer halls in mosques were subdivided by numerous pillars that supported small individual domes, creating a private, forestlike atmosphere. The Turks, however, modeled their new mosques on the open floor plan of the Byzantine church of Santa Sophia (completed in 537), which had been turned into a mosque by Mehmet II, and began to push the pillars toward the outer wall to create a prayer hall with an uninterrupted central area under one large dome. With this plan, large numbers of believers could worship in unison in accordance with Muslim preference. By the mid-sixteenth century, the greatest of all Ottoman architects, Sinan, began erecting the first of his eighty-one mosques with an uncluttered prayer area. Each was topped by an imposing dome, and often, as at Edirne, the entire building was framed with four towering narrow minarets. By emphasizing its vertical lines, the minarets camouflaged the massive stone bulk of the structure and gave it a feeling of incredible lightness. These four graceful minarets would find new expression sixty years later in India's white marble Taj Mahal (see "Mughal Culture" later in this chapter).

The lightness of the exterior was reinforced in the mosque's interior by the soaring height of the dome and the numerous windows. Added to this were delicate plasterwork and tile decoration that transformed the mosque into a monumental oasis of spirituality, opulence, and power. Sinan's masterpieces, such as the Suleymaniye and the Blue Mosque of Istanbul, were always part of a large socioreligious compound that included a library, school, hospital, mausoleums, and even bazaars, all of equally magnificent construction.

Earlier, the thirteenth-century Seljuk Turks of Anatolia had created beautiful tile decorations with two-color mosaics. Now Ottoman artists invented a new glazed tile art with painted flowers and geometrical designs in brilliant blue, green, yellow, and their own secret "tomato red." Entire walls, both interior and exterior, were covered with the painted tiles, which adorned palaces as well as mosques. Produced at Iznik (the old Nicaea), the distinctive tiles and pottery were in great demand; the city's ateliers boasted more than three hundred artisans in the late sixteenth century.

The sixteenth century also witnessed the flourishing of textiles and rugs. The Byzantine emperor Justinian had introduced the cultivation of silkworms to the West in the sixth century, and the silk industry resurfaced under the Ottomans. Its capital was at Bursa, where factories produced silks for wall hangings, soft covers, and especially court costumes. Perhaps even more famous than Turkish silk are the rugs. But whereas silks were produced under the patronage of the sultans, rugs were a peasant industry. Each village boasted its own distinctive design and

THE BLUE MOSQUE, ISTANBUL.   The magnificent mosques built under the patronage of Suleyman the Magnificent are a great legacy of the Ottoman Empire and a fitting supplement to Santa Sophia (Hagia Sophia) Cathedral, built by the Byzantine emperor Justinian in the sixth century C.E. Towering under a central dome, these mosques seem to defy gravity, and, like European Gothic cathedrals, convey a sense of weightlessness. The Blue Mosque, so called for the blue tiles in its interior, is one of the most impressive and most graceful in Istanbul. A far cry from the seventh-century desert mosques constructed of palm trunks, the Ottoman mosques stand among the architectural wonders of the world.

color scheme for the rugs it produced. Common to all the rugs, however, was the use of the knot from the Gordes region—hence the term "Gordian knot."

THE SAFAVIDS

After the collapse of the empire of Tamerlane in the early fifteenth century, the area extending from Persia into Central Asia lapsed into anarchy. The Uzbeks, Turkic-speaking peoples from Central Asia, were the chief political and military force in the area. From their capital at Bokhara, they maintained a semblance of control over the highly fluid tribal alignments until the emergence of the Safavid dynasty in Persia at the beginning of the sixteenth century.

The Safavid dynasty was founded by Shah Ismail (1487–1524), the descendant of a sheikh called Safi al-Din (thus the name Safavid), who traced his origins to Ali, the fourth imam of the Muslim faith. In the early fourteenth century, Safi had been the leader of a community of Turkic-speaking tribespeople in Azerbaijan, near the Caspian Sea. Safi's community was only one of many Sufi mystical religious groups throughout the area. In time the doctrine spread among nomadic groups throughout the Middle East and was transformed into the more activist Shi'i heresy. Its adherents were known as "red heads" because of their distinctive red cap with twelve folds, meant to symbolize allegiance to the twelve imams of the Shi'i faith.

In 1501, Ismail's forces seized much of Iran and Iraq, and he called himself the shah of a new Persian state.

Baghdad was subdued in 1508 and the Uzbeks in Bokhara shortly thereafter. Ismail now sent Shi'ite preachers into Anatolia to proselytize and promote rebellion among Turkish tribal peoples in the Ottoman Empire. In retaliation, the Ottoman sultan, Selim I, advanced against the Safavids in Iran and won a major battle near Tabriz in 1514. But Selim could not maintain control of the area, and Ismail regained Tabriz a few years later.

The Ottomans returned to the attack in the 1580s and forced the new Safavid shah, Abbas I (1587–1629), to sign a punitive peace in which much territory was lost. The capital was subsequently moved from Tabriz in the northwest to Isfahan in the south. Still, it was under Shah Abbas that the Safavids reached the zenith of their glory. He established a system similar to the Janissaries in Turkey to train administrators to replace the traditional warrior elite. He also used the period of peace to strengthen his army, now armed with modern weapons, and in the early seventeenth century he attempted to regain the lost territories. Although he had some initial success, war resumed in the 1620s, and a lasting peace was not achieved until 1638 (see Map 15.2).

Abbas the Great had managed to strengthen the dynasty significantly, and for a time after his death in 1629, it remained stable and vigorous. But succession conflicts plagued the dynasty. Partly as a result, the power of the more militant Shi'ites began to increase at court and in Safavid society at large. The intellectual freedom that had characterized the empire at its height was curtailed under the pressure of religious orthodoxy, and Iranian women, who had enjoyed considerable freedom and influence during the early empire, were forced to withdraw into seclusion and behind the veil. Meanwhile, attempts to suppress the religious beliefs of minorities led to increased popular unrest. In the early eighteenth century, Afghan warriors took advantage of local revolts to seize the capital of Isfahan, forcing the remnants of the Safavid ruling family to retreat to Azerbaijan, their original homeland. The Ottomans seized territories along the western border. Eventually, order was restored by the military adventurer Nadir Shah Afshar, who launched an extended series of campaigns that restored the country's borders and even occupied the Mughal capital of Delhi (see "Twilight of the Mughals" later in this chapter). After his death, the Zand dynasty ruled until the end of the eighteenth century.

MAP 15.2 The Ottoman and Safavid Empires, c. 1683. During the seventeenth century, the two empires contested vigorously for hegemony in the eastern Mediterranean and the Middle East. This map shows the territories controlled by each state in the late seventeenth century. ➤ *What were the key cities in the two empires?*

THE RELIGIOUS ZEAL OF
SHAH ABBAS THE GREAT

Shah Abbas I, probably the greatest of the Safavid rulers, expanded the borders of his empire into areas of the southern Caucasus inhabited by Christians and other non-Muslim peoples. After Persian control was assured, he instructed that the local population be urged to convert to Islam for its own protection and the glory of God. In this passage, his biographer, the Persian historian Eskander Beg Monshi, recounts the story of that effort.

THE CONVERSION OF A NUMBER OF CHRISTIANS TO ISLAM

This year the Shah decreed that those Armenians and other Christians who had been settled in [the southern Caucasus] and had been given agricultural land there should be invited to become Muslims. Life in this world is fraught with vicissitudes, and the Shah was concerned lest, in a period when the authority of the central government was weak, these Christians . . . might be subjected to attack by the neighboring Lor tribes (who are naturally given to causing injury and mischief), and their women and children carried off into captivity. In the areas in which these Christian groups resided, it was the Shah's purpose that the places of worship which they had built should become mosques, and the muezzin's call should be heard in them,

so that these Christians might assume the guise of Muslims, and their future status accordingly be assured. . . .

Some of the Christians, guided by God's grace, embraced Islam voluntarily; others found it difficult to abandon their Christian faith and felt revulsion at the idea. They were encouraged by their monks and priests to remain steadfast in their faith. After a little pressure had been applied to the monks and priests, however, they desisted, and these Christians saw no alternative but to embrace Islam, though they did so with reluctance. The women and children embraced Islam with great enthusiasm, vying with one another in their eagerness to abandon their Christian faith and declare their belief in the unity of God. Some five thousand people embraced Islam. As each group made the Muslim declaration of faith, it received instruction in the Koran and the principles of the religious law of Islam, and all bibles and other Christian devotional material were collected and taken away from the priests.

In the same way, all the Armenian Christians who had been moved to [the area] were also forcibly converted to Islam. . . . Most people embraced Islam with sincerity, but some felt an aversion to making the Muslim profession of faith. True knowledge lies with God! May God reward the Shah for his action with long life and prosperity!

Safavid Politics and Society

Like the Ottoman Empire, Iran under the Safavids was a mixed society. The Safavids had come to power with the support of nomadic Turkic-speaking tribal groups, and leading elements from those groups retained considerable influence within the empire. But the majority of the population were Iranian; most of them were farmers or townspeople, with attitudes inherited from the relatively sophisticated and urbanized culture of pre-Safavid Iran. Faced with the problem of integrating unruly Turkic-speaking tribal peoples with the sedentary Persian-speaking population of the urban areas, the Safavids used the Shi'ite faith as a unifying force (see the box above). The shah himself acquired an almost divine quality and claimed to be the spiritual leader of all Islam. Shi'ism was declared the state religion.

Although there was a landed aristocracy, aristocratic power and influence were firmly controlled by strong-minded shahs, who confiscated aristocratic estates when possible and brought them under the control of the crown. Appointment to senior positions in the bureaucracy was by merit rather than birth. To avoid encouraging compe-

tition between Turkish and non-Turkish elements, Shah Abbas I hired a number of foreigners from neighboring countries for positions in his government.

The Safavid shahs took a direct interest in the economy and actively engaged in commercial and manufacturing activities, although there was also a large and affluent urban bourgeoisie. Like the Ottoman sultan, one shah regularly traveled the city streets incognito to check on the honesty of his subjects. When he discovered that a baker and butcher were overcharging for their products, he had the baker cooked in his own oven and the butcher roasted on a spit.

At its height, Safavid Iran was a worthy successor to the great Persian empires of the past, although it was probably not as wealthy as its Mughal and Ottoman neighbors to the east and west. Hemmed in by the sea power of the Europeans to the south and by the land power of the Ottomans to the west, the early Safavids had no navy and were forced to divert overland trade with Europe through southern Russia to avoid an Ottoman blockade. In the early seventeenth century, the situation improved when Iranian forces, in cooperation with the English, seized the island of Hormuz from Portugal and established a new sea-

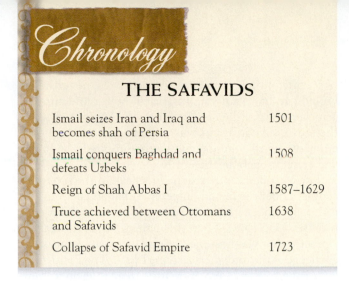

Chronology

THE SAFAVIDS

Ismail seizes Iran and Iraq and becomes shah of Persia	1501
Ismail conquers Baghdad and defeats Uzbeks	1508
Reign of Shah Abbas I	1587–1629
Truce achieved between Ottomans and Safavids	1638
Collapse of Safavid Empire	1723

port on the southern coast at Bandar Abbas. As a consequence, commercial ties with Europe began to increase.

Safavid Art and Literature

Persia witnessed an extraordinary flowering of the arts during the reign of Shah Abbas I. His new capital of Isfahan was a grandiose planned city with wide visual perspectives and a sense of order almost unique in the region. Shah Abbas ordered his architects to position his palaces,

mosques, and bazaars around the Maydan-i-Shah, a massive rectangular polo ground. Much of the original city is still in good condition and remains the gem of modern Iran. The immense mosques are richly decorated with elaborate blue tiles. The palaces are delicate structures with unusual slender wooden columns. These architectural wonders of Isfahan epitomize the grandeur, delicacy, and color that defined the Safavid golden age. To adorn the splendid buildings, Safavid artisans created imaginative metalwork, tile decorations, and original and delicate glass vessels. The ceramics of the period, imitating Chinese prototypes of celadon or blue-and-white Ming design, largely ignored traditional Persian designs.

The greatest area of productivity, however, was in textiles. Silk weaving based on new techniques became a national industry. The silks depicted birds, animals, and flowers in a brilliant mass of color with silver and gold threads. Above all, carpet weaving flourished, stimulated by the great demand for Persian carpets in the West. Still highly prized all over the world, these seventeenth-century carpets reflect the grandeur and artistry of the Safavid dynasty.

The long tradition of Persian painting continued in the Safavid era but changed from paintings to line drawings

THE ROYAL ACADEMY OF ISFAHAN. Along with institutions such as libraries and hospitals, theological schools were often included in the mosque compound. One of the most sumptuous was the Royal Academy of Isfahan, built by the shah of Iran in the early eighteenth century. This view shows the large courtyard surrounded by arcades of student rooms, reminiscent of the arrangement of monks' cells in European cloisters.

© George Holton/Photo Researchers, Inc.

✎ **ASCENSION OF THE PROPHET MUHAMMAD.** During the sixteenth century, exquisite illuminated manuscripts were produced by book workshops at the Safavid court in Tabriz. Shown here is an illustration of Muhammad's ascension to Heaven, as described in the Koran. Muhammad is veiled, in accordance with the accepted practice of not showing his facial features. Riding a celestial creature with the face of a woman, he arrives in Jerusalem to join Abraham, Jesus, and other prophets in prayer at the site of the Temple of Solomon. From there he ascends to Heaven to meet Allah, thus making the Dome of the Rock one of the sacred sites of the Muslim religion. Then Muhammad returned to Mecca, where he died in the year 632 C.E.

and from landscape scenes to portraits, mostly of young ladies, boys, lovers, or dervishes. Although some Persian artists studied in Rome, Safavid art was little influenced by the West. Riza-i-Abassi, the most famous artist of this period, created exquisite works on simple naturalistic subjects, such as an ox plowing, hunters, or lovers. Soft colors, delicacy, and flowing movement were the dominant characteristics of the painting of this era.

THE GRANDEUR OF THE MUGHALS

In retrospect, the period from the sixteenth to the eighteenth centuries can be viewed both as a high point of traditional culture in India and as the first stage of perhaps its greatest challenge. The era began with the creation of one of the subcontinent's greatest empires—that of the Mughals. Mughal rulers, although foreigners and Muslims

like many of their immediate predecessors, nevertheless brought India to a peak of political power and cultural achievement. For the first time since the Mauryan dynasty, the entire subcontinent was united under a single government, with a common culture that inspired admiration and envy throughout the entire region.

The Mughal Empire reached its peak in the sixteenth century under the famed Emperor Akbar and maintained its vitality under a series of strong rulers for another century (see Map 15.3). Then the dynasty began to weaken, a process that was hastened by the increasingly insistent challenge of the foreigners arriving by sea. The Portuguese, who first arrived in 1498, were little more than an irritant. Two centuries later, however, Europeans began to seize control of regional trade routes and to meddle in the internal politics of the subcontinent. By the end of the eighteenth century, nothing remained of the empire but a shell.

But some historians see the seeds of decay less in the challenge from abroad than in internal weakness—in the very nature of the dynasty itself, which was always more a heterogeneous collection of semiautonomous political forces than a centralized empire in the style of neighboring China. At its height, the dynasty was fully capable of fending off the demands of the Europeans. But after two centuries of expansion and consolidation, it began to lose its vitality, and by the end of the eighteenth century, it had lapsed into a mere shadow of its former self. Into the vacuum left by its final decrepitude stepped the British, who used a combination of firepower and guile to consolidate their power over the subcontinent.

The Mughal Dynasty: A "Gunpowder Empire"?

When the Portuguese fleet led by Vasco da Gama arrived at the port of Calicut in the spring of 1498, the Indian subcontinent was still divided into a number of Hindu and Muslim kingdoms. But it was on the verge of a new era of unity that would be brought about by a foreign dynasty called the Mughals. Like so many recent rulers of northern India, the founders of the Mughal Empire were not natives of India but came from the mountainous region north of the Ganges River. The founder of the dynasty, known to history as Babur (1483–1530), had an illustrious pedigree. His father was descended from the great Asian conqueror Tamerlane, his mother from the Mongol conqueror Genghis Khan.

Babur had inherited a fragment of Tamerlane's empire in an upland valley of the Syr Darya River. Driven south by the rising power of the Uzbeks and then the Safavid dynasty in Persia, Babur and his warriors seized Kabul in 1504 and, thirteen years later, crossed the Khyber Pass to India.

Following a pattern that we have seen before, Babur began his rise to power by offering to help an ailing dynasty against its opponents. Although his own forces were far

THE MUGHAL CONQUEST OF NORTHERN INDIA

Babur, the founder of the great Mughal dynasty, began his career by allying with one Indian prince against another and then turned on his ally to put himself in power, a tactic that had been used by the Ottomans and the Mongols before him (see Chapter 10). In this excerpt from his memoirs, Babur describes his triumph over the powerful army of his Indian enemy, the Sultan Ibrâhim.

BABUR, MEMOIRS

They made one or two very poor charges on our right and left divisions. My troops making use of their bows, plied them with arrows, and drove them in upon their center. The troops on the right and the left of their center, being huddled together in one place, such confusion ensued, that the enemy, while totally unable to advance, found also no road by which they could flee. The sun had mounted spear-high when the onset of battle began, and the combat lasted till midday, when the enemy were completely broken and routed, and my friends victorious and exulting. By the grace and mercy of Almighty God, this arduous undertaking was rendered easy for me, and this mighty army, in the space of half a day, laid in the dust. Five or six thousand men were discovered lying slain, in one spot, near Ibrâhim. We reckoned that the number lying slain, in different parts of this field of battle, amounted to fifteen or sixteen thousand men. On reaching Agra, we found, from the accounts of the natives of Hindustân, that forty or fifty thousand men had fallen in this field. After routing the enemy, we continued the pursuit, slaughtering, and making them prisoners. . . .

It was now afternoon prayers when Tahir Taberi, the younger brother of Khalîfeh, having found Ibrâhim lying dead amidst a number of slain, cut off his head, and brought it in. . . .

In consideration of my confidence in Divine aid, the Most High God did not suffer the distress and hardships that I had undergone to be thrown away, but defeated my formidable enemy, and made me the conqueror of the noble country of Hindustân. This success I do not ascribe to my own strength, nor did this good fortune flow from my own efforts, but from the fountain of the favor and mercy of God.

---

smaller than those of his adversaries, he possessed advanced weapons, including artillery, and used them to great effect. His use of mobile cavalry was particularly successful against the massed forces, supplemented by mounted elephants, of his enemy. In 1526, with only twelve thousand troops against an enemy force nearly ten times that size, Babur captured Delhi and established his power in the plains of northern India (see the box above). Over the next several years, he continued his conquests in northern India, until his early death in 1530 at the age of forty-seven.

Babur's success was due in part to his vigor and his charismatic personality, which earned him the undying loyalty of his followers. His son and successor Humayun (1530–1556) was, in the words of one British historian, "intelligent but lazy." Whether or not this is a fair characterization, Humayun clearly lacked the will to consolidate his father's conquests and the personality to inspire personal loyalty among his subjects. In 1540, he was forced to flee to Persia, where he lived in exile for sixteen years. Finally, with the aid of the Safavid shah of Persia, he returned to India and reconquered Delhi in 1555 but died the following year in a household accident, reportedly from injuries suffered in a fall after smoking a pipeful of opium.

Humayun was succeeded by his son Akbar (1556–1605). Born while his father was living in exile, Akbar was only fourteen when he mounted the throne. Illiterate but highly intelligent and industrious, Akbar set out to extend his domain, then limited to Punjab and the upper Ganges River valley. "A monarch," he remarked, "should be ever intent on conquest, otherwise his neighbors rise in arms against him. The army should be exercised in warfare, lest from want of training they become self-indulgent."[1] By the end of his life, he had brought Mughal rule to most of the subcontinent, from the Himalaya Mountains to the Godavari River in central India and from Kashmir to the mouths of the Brahmaputra and the Ganges. In so doing, Akbar had created the greatest Indian empire since the Mauryan dynasty nearly two thousand years earlier. Some historians believe Akbar's success was due to the use of heavy artillery, which enabled his armies to besiege and subdue the traditional stone fortresses of his rivals. This "gunpowder empire" thesis has been challenged by the historian Douglas Streusand, who argues that the Mughals used "the carrot and the stick" to extend their authority relying not just on heavy artillery but also on other forms of siege warfare and the offer of negotiations. Whatever the case, the end result was an empire that appeared highly centralized from the outside but was actually a collection of semiautonomous principalities ruled by provincial elites and linked together by the overarching majesty of the Mughal emperor.

Akbar and Indo-Muslim Civilization

Although Akbar was probably the greatest of the conquering Mughal monarchs, like his famous predecessor Asoka, he is best known for the humane character of his

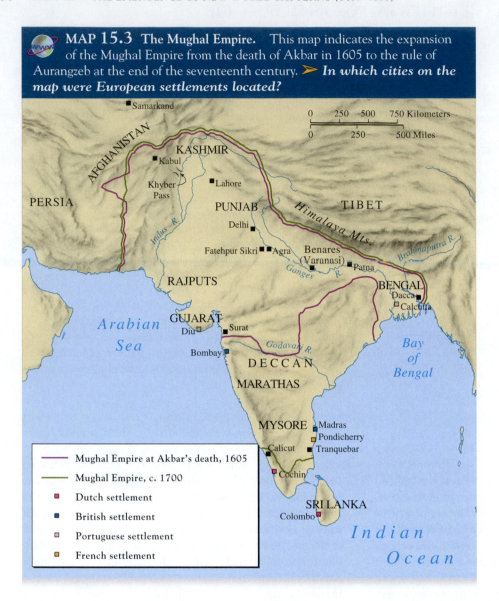

MAP 15.3 The Mughal Empire. This map indicates the expansion of the Mughal Empire from the death of Akbar in 1605 to the rule of Aurangzeb at the end of the seventeenth century. ➤ *In which cities on the map were European settlements located?*

Mughal Empire at Akbar's death, 1605

Mughal Empire, c. 1700

■ Dutch settlement

■ British settlement

□ Portuguese settlement

□ French settlement

rule. Above all, he accepted the diversity of Indian society and took steps to reconcile his Muslim and Hindu subjects.

Though raised an orthodox Muslim, Akbar had been exposed to other beliefs during his childhood and had little patience with the pedantic views of Muslim scholars at court. As emperor, he displayed a keen interest in other religions, not only tolerating Hindu practices in his own domains but also welcoming the expression of Christian views by his Jesuit advisers. Akbar put his policy of religious tolerance into practice by taking a Hindu princess as one of his wives, and the success of this marriage may well have had an effect on his religious convictions. He patronized classical Indian arts and architecture and abolished many of the restrictions faced by Hindus in a Muslim-dominated society.

During his later years, Akbar became steadily more hostile to Islam. To the dismay of many Muslims at court, he sponsored a new form of worship called the Divine

Faith (*Din-i-Ilahi*), which combined characteristics of several religions with a central belief in the infallibility of all decisions reached by the emperor. Some historians have maintained that Akbar totally abandoned Islam and adopted a Persian model of imperial divinity. But others have pointed out that the emperor was claiming only divine guidance, not divine status, and suggest that the new ideology was designed to cement the loyalty of officials to the person of the monarch. Whatever the case, the new faith aroused deep hostility in Muslim circles and rapidly vanished after his death.

Akbar also extended his innovations to the empire's administration. Although the upper ranks of the government continued to be dominated by nonnative Muslims, a substantial proportion of lower-ranking officials were Hindus, and a few Hindus were appointed to positions of importance. At first, most officials were paid salaries, but later they were ordinarily assigned sections of agricultural

THE POWER BEHIND THE THRONE

During his reign as Mughal emperor, Jahangir (1605–1628) was addicted to alcohol and opium. Because of his weakened condition, his Persian wife Nur Jahan began to rule on his behalf. She also groomed his young son Khurram to rule as the future emperor Shah Jahan and arranged for him to marry her own niece Mumtaz Mahal, thereby cementing her influence over two successive Mughal rulers. During this period, Nur Jahan was the de facto ruler of India, exerting her influence in both internal and foreign affairs during an era of peace and prosperity. Although the extent of her influence was often criticized at court, her performance impressed many European observers, as these remarks by two English visitors attest.

NUR JAHAN, EMPRESS OF MUGHAL INDIA

If anyone with a request to make at Court obtains an audience or is allowed to speak, the King hears him indeed, but will give no definite answer of Yes or No, referring him promptly to Asaf Khan, who in the same way will dispose of no important matter without communicating with his sister, the Queen, and who regulates his attitude in such a way that the authority of neither of them may be diminished. Anyone then who obtains a favour must thank them for it, and not the King. . . .

Her abilities were uncommon; for she rendered herself absolute, in a government in which women are thought incapable of bearing any part. Their power, it is true, is sometimes exerted in the haram; but, like the virtues of the magnet, it is silent and unperceived. Nur Jahan stood forth in public; she broke through all restraint and custom, and acquired power by her own address, more than by the weakness of Jahangir. . . .

Her former and present supporters have been well rewarded, so that now most of the men who are near the King owe their promotion to her, and are consequently under . . . obligations to her. . . . Many misunderstandings result, for the King's orders or grants of appointments, etc., are not certainties, being of no value until they have been approved by the Queen.

---

land for their temporary use; they kept a portion of the taxes paid by the local peasants in lieu of a salary. These local officials, known as *zamindars*, were expected to forward the rest of the taxes from the lands under their control to the central government. *Zamindars* often recruited a number of military and civilian retainers and accumulated considerable power in their localities.

The same tolerance that marked Akbar's attitude toward religion and administration extended to the Mughal legal system. While Muslims were subject to the Islamic codes (the *Shari'a*), Hindu law (the *Dharmashastra*) applied to areas settled by Hindus, who after 1579 were no longer required to pay the hated *jizya*, or poll tax on non-Muslims. Punishments for crime were relatively mild, at least by the standards of the day, and justice was administered in a relatively impartial and efficient manner.

Overall, Akbar's reign was a time of peace and prosperity. Although all Indian peasants were required to pay about one-third of their annual harvest to the state through the *zamindars*, the system was applied fairly, and when drought struck in the 1590s, the taxes were reduced or even suspended altogether. Thanks to a long period of relative peace and political stability, commerce and manufacturing flourished. Foreign trade, in particular, thrived as Indian goods, notably textiles, tropical food products, spices, and precious stones, were exported in exchange for gold and silver. Tariffs on imports were low. Much of the foreign commerce was handled by Arab traders, since the Indians, like their Mughal rulers, did not care for travel by sea. Internal trade, however, was dominated by large merchant castes, who also were active in banking and handicrafts.

Twilight of the Mughals

Akbar died in 1605 and was succeeded by his son Jahangir (1605–1628). During the early years of his reign, Jahangir continued to strengthen central control over the vast empire. Eventually, however, his grip began to weaken (according to his memoirs, he "only wanted a bottle of wine and a piece of meat to make merry"), and the court fell under the influence of one of his wives, the Persian-born Nur Jahan (see the box above). The empress took advantage of her position to enrich her own family and arranged for her niece Mumtaz Mahal to marry her husband's third son and ultimate successor, Shah Jahan. When Shah Jahan succeeded to the throne in 1628, he quickly demonstrated the single-minded quality of his grandfather (albeit in a much more brutal manner), ordering the assassination of all of his rivals in order to secure his position.

During a reign of three decades, Shah Jahan maintained the system established by his predecessors while expanding the boundaries of the empire by successful campaigns in the Deccan Plateau and against Samarkand, north of the Hindu Kush. But Shah Jahan's rule was marred by his failure to deal with the growing domestic problems. He had inherited a nearly empty treasury because of Empress Nur Jahan's penchant for luxury and ambitious charity projects. Though the majority of his subjects lived in grinding poverty, Shah Jahan's frequent military campaigns and expensive building projects put a heavy strain on the imperial finances and compelled him to raise taxes. At the same time, the government did little to improve rural conditions. In a country where transport was primitive (it often took three months to travel the 600 miles between Patna, in the middle of the Ganges River valley, and Delhi) and drought conditions frequent, the dynasty made few efforts to increase agricultural efficiency or to improve the roads or the irrigation network. A Dutch merchant in Gujarat described conditions during a famine in the mid-seventeenth century:

> As the famine increased, men abandoned towns and villages and wandered helplessly. It was easy to recognize their condition: eyes sunk deep in head, lips pale and covered with slime, the skin hard, with the bones showing through, the belly nothing but a pouch hanging down empty, knuckles and kneecaps showing prominently. One would cry and howl for hunger, while another lay stretched on the ground dying in misery; wherever you went, you saw nothing but corpses.[2]

In 1648, Shah Jahan moved his capital from Agra to Delhi and built the famous Red Fort in his new capital city. But he is best known for the Taj Mahal in Agra, widely considered to be the most beautiful building in India, if not in the entire world. The story is a romantic one—that the Taj was built by the emperor in memory of his wife Mumtaz Mahal, who had died giving birth to her thirteenth child at the age of thirty-nine. But the story has a less attractive side: the expense of the building, which employed twenty thousand masons over twenty years, forced the government to raise agricultural taxes, further impoverishing many Indian peasants.

Succession struggles returned to haunt the dynasty in the mid-1650s when Shah Jahan's illness led to a struggle for power between his sons Dara Shikoh and Aurangzeb. Dara Shikoh was described by his contemporaries as progressive and humane, although possessed of a violent temper and a strong sense of mysticism. But he apparently lacked political acumen and was outmaneuvered by Aurangzeb (1658–1707), who had Dara Shikoh put to death and then imprisoned his father in the fort at Agra.

Aurangzeb is one of the most controversial individuals in the history of India. A man of high principle, he attempted to eliminate many of what he considered to be India's social evils, prohibiting the immolation of widows on their husband's funeral pyre (*sati*), the castration of eunuchs, and the exaction of illegal taxes. With less success, he tried to forbid gambling, drinking, and prostitution. But Aurangzeb, a devout and somewhat doctrinaire Muslim, also adopted a number of measures that reversed the policies of religious tolerance established by his predecessors. The building of new Hindu temples was prohibited and the Hindu poll tax was restored. Forced conversions to Islam were resumed, and non-Muslims were driven from the court. Aurangzeb's heavy-handed religious policies led to considerable domestic unrest and to a revival of Hindu fervor during the last years of his reign. A number of revolts also broke out against imperial authority.

During the eighteenth century, Mughal power was threatened from both within and without. Fueled by the growing power and autonomy of the local gentry and merchants, rebellious groups in provinces throughout the empire, from the Deccan to the Punjab, began to reassert local authority and reduce the power of the Mughal emperor to that of a "tinsel sovereign." Increasingly divided, India was vulnerable to attack from abroad. In 1739, Delhi was sacked by the Persians, who left it in ashes and carried off its splendid Peacock Throne.

A number of obvious reasons for the virtual collapse of the Mughal Empire can be identified, including the draining of the imperial treasury and the decline in competence of the Mughal rulers. But it should also be noted that even at its height under Akbar, the empire was a loosely knit collection of heterogeneous principalities held together by the authority of the throne, which tried to combine Persian concepts of kingship with the Indian tradition of decentralized power. Decline set in when centrifugal forces gradually began to predominate over centripetal ones.

Ironically, one element in this process was the very success of the system, which led to the rapid expansion of wealth and autonomous power at the local level. As local elites increased their wealth and influence, they became less willing to accept the authority and financial demands from Delhi. The reassertion of Muslim orthodoxy under Aurangzeb and his successors simply exacerbated the problem. This process was hastened by the growing European military and economic presence along the periphery of the empire.

The Impact of Western Power in India

As we have seen, the first Europeans to arrive were the Portuguese. Although they established a virtual monopoly over regional trade in the Indian Ocean, they did not aggressively seek to penetrate the interior of the subcontinent. The situation changed at the end of the sixteenth century, when the English and the Dutch entered the scene. Soon both powers were in active competition with Portugal, and with each other, for trading privileges in the region (see the box on p. 433).

Penetration of the new market was not easy. When the first English fleet arrived at Surat, a thriving port on the northwestern coast of India, in 1608, their request for trading privileges was rejected by Emperor Jahangir, at the suggestion of the Portuguese advisers already in residence at the imperial court. Needing lightweight Indian cloth to trade for spices in the East Indies, the English persisted, and in 1616, they were finally permitted to install their own ambassador at the imperial court in Agra. Three years later, the first English factory was established at Surat.

During the next several decades, the English presence in India steadily increased while Mughal power gradually waned. By mid-century, additional English factories had been established at Fort William (now the great city of Calcutta) on the Hoogly River near the Bay of Bengal and at Madras on the southeastern coast. From there English ships carried Indian-made cotton goods to the East Indies, where they were bartered for spices, which

THE USES OF THE COCONUT

*T*he Portuguese traveler Duarte Barbosa was one of the most astute observers of the lands that he visited as an official of the Portuguese crown in the early sixteenth century. Here, in a section devoted to the lands of Malabar, on the southwestern coast of India, he writes of the many uses that the local population made of the coconut palm. Many peoples of Asia still use the coconut in similar ways in our own day.

DUARTE BARBOSA, *THE BOOK OF DUARTE BARBOSA*

This land, or rather the whole land of Malabar, is covered along the strand with palm trees as high as lofty cypresses, the trunk whereof is extremely clean and smooth, and on the top a crown of branches among which grows a great fruit which they call *cocos*, it is a fruit of which they make great profit, and whereof they load many cargoes yearly. They bear their fruit every year without fail, never either more or less. All the folk of Malabar have these palms, and by their means they are free from any dearth, even though other food be lacking, for they produce ten or twelve things all very needful for the service of man, by which they help and profit themselves greatly, and everything is produced in every month of the year.

In the first place they produce these cocos, a very sweet and grateful fruit when green; from them is drawn milk like that of almonds, and each one when green, has within it a pint of a fresh and pleasant water, better than that from a spring. When they are dry this same water thickens within them into a white fruit as large as an apple which also is very sweet and dainty. The coco itself after being dried is eaten, and from it they get much oil by pressing it, as we do. And from the shell which they have close to the kernel is made charcoal for the goldsmiths, who work with no other kind. And from the outer husk which throws out certain threads, they make all the cord which they use, a great article of trade in many parts. And from the sap of the tree itself they extract a *must*, from which they make wine, or properly speaking a strong water, and that in such abundance that many shops are laden with it, for export. From this same *must* they make very good vinegar, and also a sugar of extreme sweetness which is much sought after in India. From the leaf of the tree they make many things, in accordance with the size of the branch. They thatch the houses with them, for as I have said above, no house is roofed with tiles, save the temples or the palaces; all others are thatched with palm leaves. From the same tree they get timber for their houses and firewood as well, and all this in such abundance that ships take in cargoes thereof for export.

Other palm trees there are of a lower kind whence they get the leaves on which the Heathen write; it serves as paper. There are other very slender palms the trunks of which are of extreme height and smoothness; these bear a fruit as large as walnuts which they call Areca, which they eat with betel. Among them it is held in high esteem. It is very ugly and disagreeable in taste.

---

were shipped back to England. Tensions between local authorities and the English over the payment of taxes led to a short war in 1686. The English were briefly expelled, but after differences were patched up, Aurangzeb permitted them to return.

English success in India attracted rivals, including the Dutch and the French. The Dutch abandoned their interests to concentrate on the spice trade in the middle of the seventeenth century, but the French were more persistent and established factories of their own. For a brief period,

Courtesy of William J. Duiker

THE CHINESE NETS AT COCHIN. Cochin, one of the port cities visited by Vasco da Gama during his first visit to India in 1498, had long been a major stopover on the trade routes across the Indian Ocean. Nearly a century previously, it had been visited by Chinese fleets en route to Africa. These voyages, to be discussed in the next chapter, left their own legacy, as Indian fishers learned from Chinese sailors how to place large nets in the water of the harbor to catch fish. After the arrival of the Portuguese, much of the local population was converted to Christianity. Shown here are the "Chinese nets" of Cochin, which are still in use. A few yards away is the first Christian church erected in India. An old synagogue, which perhaps dates back to the pre-European era, is located a mile away.

Chronology

THE MUGHAL ERA

Arrival of Vasco da Gama at Calicut	1498
Babur seizes Delhi	1526
Death of Babur	1530
Humayun recovers throne in Delhi	1555
Death of Humayun and accession of Akbar	1556
First Jesuit mission to Agra	1580
Death of Akbar and accession of Jahangir	1605
Arrival of English at Surat	1608
Reign of Emperor Shah Jahan	1628–1657
Foundation of English fort at Madras	1639
Aurangzeb succeeds to the throne	1658
Bombay ceded to England	1661
Death of Aurangzeb	1707
French capture Madras	1746
Battle of Plassey	1757

under the ambitious empire builder Joseph François Dupleix, the French competed successfully with the British. But the military genius of Sir Robert Clive, an aggressive British administrator and empire builder who eventually became the chief representative of the East India Company in the subcontinent, and the refusal of the French government to provide financial support for Dupleix's efforts eventually left the French with only their fort at Pondicherry and a handful of small territories on the southeastern coast.

In the meantime, Clive began to consolidate British control in Bengal, where the local ruler had attacked Fort William and imprisoned the local British population in the infamous Black Hole of Calcutta (an underground prison for holding the prisoners, many of whom died in captivity). In 1757, a small British force numbering about three thousand defeated a Mughal-led army over ten times that size in the Battle of Plassey. As part of the spoils of victory, the British East India Company exacted from the now-decrepit Mughal court the authority to collect taxes from extensive lands in the area surrounding Calcutta. Less than ten years later, British forces seized the reigning Mughal emperor in a skirmish at Buxar, and the British began to consolidate their economic and administrative control over Indian territory through the surrogate power of the now powerless Mughal court (see Map 15.4).

To officials of the East India Company, the expansion of their authority into the interior of the subcontinent probably seemed like a simple commercial decision, a move designed to seek guaranteed revenues to pay for the increasingly expensive military operations in India. To historians, it marks a major step in the gradual transfer of all of the Indian subcontinent to the British East India Company and later, in 1858, to the British crown. The process was more haphazard than deliberate. Under a new governor general, Warren Hastings, the British attempted to consolidate areas under their control and defeat such rivals as the rising Hindu Marathas, who exploited the decline of the Mughals to expand their own empire in Maharashtra.

The company's takeover of vast landholdings, notably in the eastern Indian states of Orissa and Bengal, may have been a windfall for enterprising British officials, but it was a disaster for the Indian economy. In the first place, it resulted in the transfer of capital from the local Indian aristocracy to company officials, most of whom sent their profits back to Britain. Second, it hastened the destruction of once healthy local industries, because British goods such as machine-made textiles were imported duty-free into India to compete against local products. Finally, British expansion hurt the peasants. As the British took over the administration of the land tax, they also applied British law, which allowed the lands of those unable to pay the tax to be confiscated. In the 1770s, a series of massive famines led to the death of an estimated one-third of the population in the areas under company administration. The British government attempted to resolve the problem by assigning tax lands to the local revenue collectors (zamindars) in the hope of transforming them into English-style rural gentry, but many collectors themselves fell into bankruptcy and sold their lands to absentee bankers while the now landless peasants remained in abject poverty. It was hardly an auspicious beginning to "civilized" British rule.

As a result of such problems, Britain's rise to power in India did not go unchallenged. Astute Indian commanders avoided pitched battles with the well-armed British troops but harassed and ambushed them in the manner of guerrillas in our time. Said Haidar Ali, one of Britain's primary rivals for control in southern India:

> You will in time understand my mode of warfare. Shall I risk my cavalry which cost a thousand rupees each horse, against your cannon ball which cost two pice? No! I will march your troops until their legs swell to the size of their bodies. You shall not have a blade of grass, nor a drop of water. I will hear of you every time your drum beats, but you shall not know where I am once a month. I will give your army battle, but it must be when I please, and not when you choose.[3]

Unfortunately for India, not all its commanders were as astute as Haidar Ali. In the last years of the eighteenth century, when the East India Company's authority came into the capable hands of Lord Cornwallis and his successor, Lord Mornington, the future marquess of Wellesley, the stage was set for the final consolidation of British rule over the subcontinent.

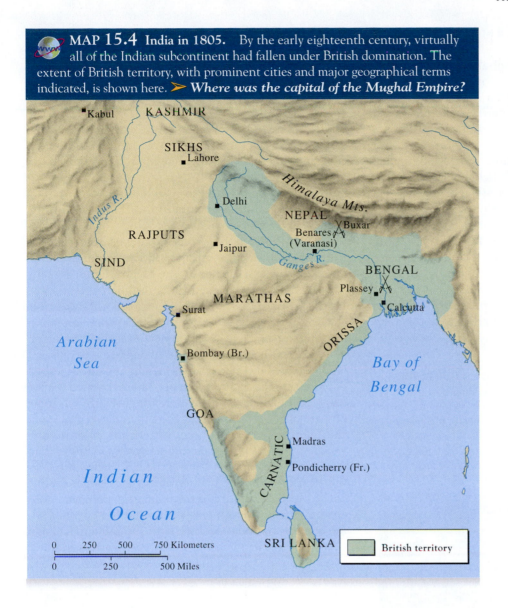

MAP 15.4 India in 1805. By the early eighteenth century, virtually all of the Indian subcontinent had fallen under British domination. The extent of British territory, with prominent cities and major geographical terms indicated, is shown here. ➤ *Where was the capital of the Mughal Empire?*

Society and Culture Under the Mughals

The Mughals were the last of the great traditional Indian dynasties. Like so many of their predecessors since the fall of the Guptas nearly a thousand years before, the Mughals were Muslims. But like the Ottoman Turks, the best Mughal rulers did not simply impose Islamic institutions and beliefs on a predominantly Hindu population; they combined Muslim with Hindu and even Persian concepts and cultural values in a unique social and cultural synthesis that still today seems to epitomize the greatness of Indian civilization.

DAILY LIFE

Whether Mughal rule had much effect on the lives of ordinary Indians seems somewhat problematic. The treatment of women is a good example. Women had tradi-

tionally played an active role in Mongol tribal society—many actually fought on the battlefield alongside the men—and Babur and his successors often relied on the women in their families for political advice. Women from aristocratic families were often awarded honorific titles, received salaries, and were permitted to own land and engage in business. Women at court sometimes received an education, and Emperor Akbar reportedly established a girls' school at Fatehpur Sikri to provide teachers for his own daughters. Aristocratic women often expressed their creative talents by writing poetry, painting, or playing music. Women of all castes were adept at spinning thread, either for their own use or to sell to weavers to augment the family income. Weaving was carried out in home production units by all the members of the subcaste weaving families. They sold simple cloth to local villages and fine cottons, silks, and wool to the Mughal court. By Akbar's rule, in fact, the textile manufacturing was of such high quality and so well established that India sold cloth to much of the world: Arabia, the coast of East Africa, Egypt, Southeast Asia, and Europe.

To a certain degree, these Mughal attitudes toward women may have had an impact on Indian society. Women were allowed to inherit land, and some even possessed *zamindar* rights. Women from mercantile castes sometimes took an active role in business activities. At the same time, however, as Muslims, the Mughals subjected women to certain restrictions under Islamic law. On the whole, these Mughal practices coincided with and even accentuated existing tendencies in Indian society. The Muslim practice of isolating women and preventing them from associating with men outside the home (*purdah*) was adopted by many upper-class Hindus as a means of enhancing their status or protecting their women from unwelcome advances by Muslims in positions of authority. In other ways, Hindu practices were unaffected. The custom of *sati* continued to be practiced despite efforts by the Mughals to abolish it,

🔸 **THE PALACE OF THE WINDS AT JAIPUR.**   Built by the maharaja of Jaipur in 1799, this imposing building, part of a palace complex, is today actually only a facade. Behind the intricate pink sandstone window screens, the women of the palace were able to observe city life while at the same time remaining invisible to prying eyes. The palace, like most of the buildings in the city of Jaipur, was constructed of sandstone, a product of the nearby desert of Rajasthan.

© SEF/Art Resource, NY

and child marriage (most women were betrothed before the age of ten) remained common. Women were still instructed to obey their husbands without question and to remain chaste.

For their part, Hindus sometimes attempted to defend themselves and their religious practices against the efforts of some Mughal monarchs to impose the Islamic religion and Islamic mores on the indigenous population. In some cases, despite official prohibitions, Hindu men forcibly married Muslim women and then converted them to the native faith, while converts to Islam normally lost all of their inheritance rights within the Indian family. Government orders to destroy Hindu temples were often ignored by local officials, sometimes as the result of bribery or intimidation. Sometimes Indian practices had an influence on the Mughal elites, as many Mughal chieftains married Indian women and adopted Indian forms of dress.

Long-term stability led to increasing commercialization and the spread of wealth to new groups within Indian society. The Mughal era saw the emergence of an affluent landed gentry and a prosperous merchant class. Members of prestigious castes from the pre-Mughal period reaped many of the benefits of the increasing wealth, but some of these changes transcended caste boundaries and led to the emergence of new groups who achieved status and wealth on the basis of economic achievement rather than traditional kinship ties. During the late eighteenth century, this economic prosperity was shaken by the decline of the Mughal Empire and the increasing European presence. But many prominent Indians reacted by establishing commercial relationships with the foreigners. For a time, that relationship often worked to the Indians' benefit. Later, as we shall see, they would have cause to regret the arrangement.

MUGHAL CULTURE

The era of the Mughals was one of synthesis in culture as well as in politics and religion. The Mughals combined Islamic themes with Persian and indigenous motifs to produce a unique style that enriched and embellished Indian art and culture. The Mughal emperors were zealous patrons of the arts and enticed painters, poets, and artisans from as far away as the Mediterranean. Apparently, the generosity of the Mughals made it difficult to refuse a trip to India. It was said that they would reward a poet with his weight in gold.

Undoubtedly, the Mughals' most visible achievement was in architecture. Here they integrated Persian and Indian styles in a new and sometimes breathtakingly beautiful form best symbolized by the Taj Mahal, built by the emperor Shah Jahan in the mid-seventeenth century. Although the human and economic cost of the Taj tarnishes the romantic legend of its construction, there is no denying the beauty of the building. It had evolved

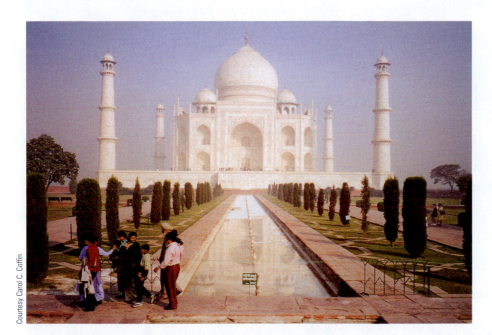

Courtesy Carol C. Coffin

➤ **THE TAJ MAHAL.** The Taj Mahal was completed in 1653 by Emperor Shah Jahan as a tomb to glorify the memory of his beloved wife. Raised on a marble platform above the Jumna River, the Taj is dramatically framed by contrasting twin red sandstone mosques, magnificent gardens, and a long reflecting pool that mirrors and magnifies its beauty. The effect is one of monumental size, near blinding brilliance, and delicate lightness, a startling contrast to the heavier and more masculine Baroque style then popular in Europe.

from a style that originated several decades earlier with the tomb of Humayun, which was built by his widow in Agra in 1565 during the reign of Akbar.

Humayun's mausoleum had combined Persian and Islamic motifs in a square building finished in red sandstone and topped with a dome. The style was repeated in a number of other buildings erected throughout the empire, but the Taj brought the style to perfection. Working with a model created by his Persian architect, Shah Jahan raised the dome and replaced the red sandstone with brilliant white marble. The entire exterior and interior surface is decorated with cut-stone geometrical patterns, delicate black stone tracery, or intricate inlay of colored precious stones in floral and Koranic arabesques. The technique of creating dazzling floral mosaics of lapis lazuli, malachite, carnelian, turquoise, and mother of pearl may have been introduced by Italian artists at the Mughal court. Shah Jahan had intended to erect a similar building in black marble across the river for his own remains, but the plans were abandoned after he was deposed by his son Aurangzeb. Shah Jahan spent his last years imprisoned in a room in the Red Fort at Agra; from his windows, he could see the beautiful memorial to his beloved wife.

The Taj was by no means the only magnificent building erected during the Mughal era. Akbar, who, in the words of a contemporary, "dresses the work of his mind and heart in the garment of stone and clay," was the first of the great Mughal builders. His first palace at Agra, the Red Fort, was begun in 1565. A few years later, he ordered the construction of a new palace at Fatehpur Sikri, 26 miles west of Agra. The new palace was built in honor of a Sufi mystic who had correctly forecast the birth of a son to the emperor. In gratitude, Akbar decided to build a new capital city and palace on the site of the mystic's home

in the village of Sikri. Over a period of fifteen years, from 1571 to 1586, a magnificent new city in red sandstone was constructed. Although the city was abandoned before completion and now stands almost untouched, it is a popular destination for tourists and pilgrims.

Central India Under the Mughals

The other major artistic achievement of the Mughal period was painting. Painting had never been one of the great attainments of Indian culture due in part to a technological difficulty. Paper was not introduced to India from Persia until the latter part of the fourteenth century, so traditionally painting had been done on palm leaves, which had severely hampered artistic creativity. By the fifteenth century, Indian painting had made the transition from palm leaf to paper, and the new medium eventually stimulated a burst of creativity, particularly in the genre of miniatures, or book illustrations.

As in so many other areas of endeavor, painting in Mughal India resulted from the blending of two cultures. While living in exile, Emperor Humayun had learned to admire Persian miniatures. On his return to India in 1555, he invited two Persian masters to live in his palace and introduce the technique to his adopted land. His successor, Akbar, appreciated the new style and popularized it with his patronage. He established a state workshop at Fatehpur Sikri for two hundred artists, mostly Hindus, who worked under the guidance of the Persian masters to create the Mughal school of painting.

© Orde Eliason/Link India

FATEHPUR SIKRI.   In gratitude to a Sufi mystic who had correctly forecast the birth of his son, Akbar chose the mystic's village of Sikri as the site for his new palace and capital city. Completed at great speed in 1586, the splendid city, which was built of red sandstone and measured 2 miles long and a mile wide, was soon abandoned because of an inadequate water supply. Its elaborate palaces, mosque, reflecting pools and courtyards, harems, and impressive victory gate all symbolize the elegance and greatness of Akbar's reign.

The "Akbar style" combined Persian with Indian motifs, such as the use of extended space and the portrayal of physical human action, characteristics not usually seen in Persian art. Akbar also apparently encouraged the imitation of European art forms, including the portrayal of Christian subjects, the use of perspective, lifelike portraits, and the shading of colors in the Renaissance style. The depiction of the human figure in Mughal painting outraged orthodox Muslims at court, but Akbar argued that the painter, "in sketching anything that has life . . . must come to feel that he cannot bestow individuality upon his work, and is thus forced to think of God, the Giver of Life, and will thus increase in knowledge."[4]

Painting during Akbar's reign followed the trend toward realism and historical narrative that had originated in the Ottoman Empire. For example, Akbar had the illustrated *Book of Akbar* made to record his military exploits and court activities. Many of these paintings of Akbar's life portray him in action in his real world. After his death, his son and grandson continued the patronage of the arts.

The development of Indian literature was held back by the absence of printing, which was not introduced until the end of the Mughal era. Literary works were inscribed by calligraphers, and one historian has estimated that the library of Agra contained more than 24,000 volumes. Poetry, in particular, flourished under the Mughals, who established poet laureates at court. Poems were written in the Persian style and in the Persian language. In fact, Persian became the official language of the court until the sack of Delhi in 1739. At the time, the Indians' anger at their conquerors led them to adopt Urdu as the new language for the court and for poetry. By that time, Indian verse on the Persian model had already lost its original vitality and simplicity and had become more artificial in the manner of court literature everywhere.

Another aspect of the long Mughal reign was a Hindu revival of devotional literature, much of it dedicated to Krishna and Rama. The retelling of the Ramayana in the vernacular, beginning in the southern Tamil languages in the eleventh century and spreading slowly northward, culminated in the sixteenth-century Hindi version by the great poet Tulsidas (1532–1623). His *Ramcaritmanas* presents the devotional story with a deified Rama and Sita. Tulsidas's genius was in combining the conflicting cults of

➤ THE CONSTRUCTION OF FATEHPUR SIKRI. In this contemporary Mughal painting, artisans are completing construction of the Elephant Gate at Akbar's new capital of Fatehpur Sikri. Since both the Ottoman Empire and Mughal India used Persian as their court language, they learned to appreciate the illuminated manuscript techniques produced by Safavid workshops in Persia and adapted them to their own cultural heritage. Emperor Akbar, the greatest Mughal ruler, enthusiastically embraced the art of bookmaking, peopling his royal workshops with more than one hundred artists. The illustrated manuscripts from Mughal India rival those of Safavid Persia in brilliance and imagination and provide fascinating historical details of military campaigns and court ceremonies, as well as scenes from daily life.

Vishnu and Siva into a unified and overwhelming love for the divine, which he expressed in some of the most moving of all Indian poetry. The *Ramcaritmanas* has eclipsed its two-thousand-year-old Sanskrit ancestor in popularity and even became the basis of an Indian television series in the late 1980s.

CONCLUSION

The three empires that we have discussed in this chapter exhibit a number of striking similarities. First of all, they were Muslim in their religious affiliation, although the Safavids were Shi'ite rather than Sunni, a distinction that often led to mutual tensions and conflict. More important, perhaps, they were all of nomadic origin, and the political and social institutions that they adopted carried the imprint of their preimperial past. Once they achieved imperial power, however, all three ruling dynasties displayed an impressive capacity to administer a large empire and brought a degree of stability to peoples who had all too often lived in conditions of internal division and war.

Another similarity is that the mastery of the techniques of modern warfare, including the use of firearms, played a central role in all three empires' ability to overcome their rivals and rise to regional hegemony. Some scholars have therefore labeled them "gunpowder empires" in the belief that technical prowess in the art of warfare was a key element in their success. Although that is undoubtedly true, we should not forget that other factors, such as dynamic leadership, political acumen, and the possession of an ardent following motivated by religious zeal, were equally if not more important in their drive to power and ability to retain it. Weapons by themselves do not an empire make.

The rise of these powerful Muslim states coincided with the opening period of European expansion at the end of the fifteenth century and the beginning of the sixteenth. The military and political talents of these empires helped protect much of the Muslim world from the resurgent forces of Christianity. To the contrary, the Ottoman Turks carried their empire into the heart of Christian Europe and briefly reached the gates of the great city of Vienna. By the end of the eighteenth century, however, the Safavid dynasty had imploded, and the powerful Mughal Empire was in a state of virtual collapse. Only the Ottoman Empire was still functioning. Yet it too had lost much of its early expansionistic vigor and was showing signs of internal decay.

The reasons for the decline of these empires have inspired considerable debate among historians. One factor was undoubtedly the expansion of European power into the Indian Ocean and the Middle East. But internal causes were probably more important in the long run. All three empires experienced growing factionalism within the ruling elite, incompetence within the palace, and the emergence of divisive forces in the empire at large—factors that have marked the passing of traditional empires since early times. Climatic change (the region was reportedly hotter and drier after the beginning of the seventeenth century) may have been a hidden reason. Paradoxically, one of the greatest strengths of these empires—their mastery of gunpowder—may have simultaneously been a serious weakness in that it allowed them to develop a complacent sense of security. With little incentive to turn their attention to new developments in science and technology, they were increasingly vulnerable to attack by the advanced nations of the West. The weakening of the gunpowder empires created a political vacuum into which the dynamic and competitive forces of European capitalism were quick to enter.

The gunpowder empires, however, were not the only states in the Old World that were able to resist the first outward thrust of European expansion. Farther to the east, the mature civilizations in China and Japan successfully faced a similar challenge from Western merchants and missionaries. Unlike their counterparts in South Asia and the Middle East, as the nineteenth century dawned, they continued to thrive.

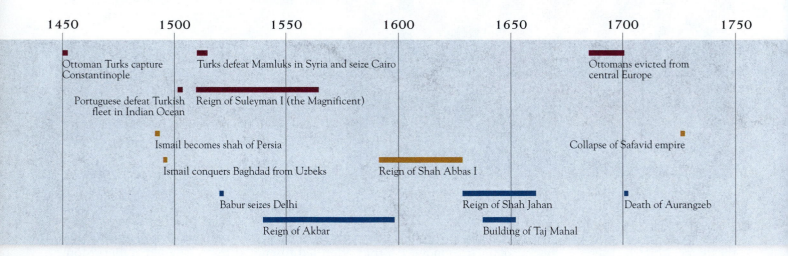

| 1450 | 1500 | 1550 | 1600 | 1650 | 1700 | 1750 |

Ottoman Turks capture Constantinople

Turks defeat Mamluks in Syria and seize Cairo

Ottomans evicted from central Europe

Portuguese defeat Turkish fleet in Indian Ocean

Reign of Suleyman I (the Magnificent)

Ismail becomes shah of Persia

Collapse of Safavid empire

Ismail conquers Baghdad from Uzbeks

Reign of Shah Abbas I

Babur seizes Delhi

Reign of Shah Jahan

Death of Aurangzeb

Reign of Akbar

Building of Taj Mahal

CHAPTER NOTES

1. Vincent A. Smith, *The Oxford History of India* (Oxford, 1967), p. 341.
2. Quoted in Michael Edwardes, *A History of India: From the Earliest Times to the Present Day* (London, 1961), p. 188.
3. Quoted in Edwardes, *History of India,* p. 220.
4. Quoted in Roy C. Craven, *Indian Art: A Concise History* (New York, 1976), p. 205.

SUGGESTED READING

The most complete general survey of the Ottoman Empire is S. J. Shaw, *History of the Ottoman Empire and Modern Turkey* (Cambridge, 1976). Shaw is difficult reading but informative on administrative matters. A more readable albeit less definitive account is Lord Kinross, *The Ottoman Centuries: The Rise and Fall of the Ottoman Empire* (New York, 1977), which is larded with human-interest stories. Also of interest is B. Lewis, *Istanbul and the Civilization of the Ottoman Empire* (Norman, Okla., 1963), written by a veteran Arabist.

For a dramatic account of the conquest of Constantinople in 1453, see S. Runciman, *The Fall of Constantinople, 1453* (Cambridge, 1965). The life of Mehmet II is chronicled in F. Babinger, *Mehmed the Conqueror and His Time*, trans. R. Manheim (Princeton, N.J., 1979). On Suleyman the Magnificent, see R. Merriman, *Suleiman the Magnificent, 1520–1566* (Cambridge, 1944). On the Safavids, see R. M. Savory, *Iran Under the Safavids* (Cambridge, 1980), and E. B. Monshi, *History of Shah Abbas the Great*, 2 vols. (Boulder, Colo., 1978).

For a concise introduction to Ottoman art, consult D. T. Rice, *Islamic Art* (London, 1975); E. J. Grube, *The World of Islam* (New York, 1967); and J. Bloom and S. Blair, *Islamic Arts* (London, 1997).

For an overview of the Mughal era, see S. Wolpert, *New History of India* (New York, 1989). A more dramatic account for the general reader is W. Hansen, *The Peacock Throne: The Drama of Mogul India* (New York, 1972).

There are a number of specialized works on various aspects of the period. For a treatment of the Mughal era in the context of Islamic rule in India, see S. M. Ikram, *Muslim Civilization in India* (New York, 1964). The concept of "gunpowder empires" is persuasively analyzed in D. E. Streusand, *The Formation of the Mughal Empire* (Delhi, 1989). Economic issues predominate in much recent scholarship. For example, S. Subrahmanyan, *The Political Economy of Commerce: Southern India, 1500–1650* (Cambridge, 1990), focuses on the interaction between internal and external trade in southern India during the early stages of the period. The Mughal Empire is analyzed in a broad Central Asian context in R. C. Foltz, *Mughal India and Central Asia* (Karachi, 1998). Finally, K. N. Chaudhuri, *Trade and Civilization in the Indian Ocean: An Economic History from the Rise of Islam to 1750* (Cambridge, 1985), views Indian commerce in the perspective of the regional trade network throughout the Indian Ocean.

Personal accounts of the period are numerous, although most are by European visitors. For some examples, see R. C. Temple, ed., *The Travels of Peter Mundy, in Europe and Asia, 1608–1667* (Cambridge, 1907–1936); J. B. Tavernier, *Travels in India* (London, 1925); T. Roe, *The Embassy of Sir Thomas Roe, 1615–1619* (London, 1926); and F. Bernier, *Travels in the Mogul Empire, 1656–1668* (London, 1968). For an inside look, see J. Leyden and W. Erskine, trans., *Memoirs of Zehir-ed-Din Muhammad Babur* (London, 1921).

Standard works on Mughal art and culture include A. L. Basham, *A Cultural History of India* (Oxford, 1975); R. C. Craven, *Indian Art: A Concise History* (New York, 1976); and M. C. Beach, *The Imperial Image* (Washington, D.C., 1981).

For treatments of all three Muslim empires in a comparative context, see J. J. Kissling et al., *The Last Great Muslim Empires* (Princeton, N.J., 1996), and M. G. S. Hodgson, *Rethinking World History: Essays on Europe, Islam, and World History* (Cambridge, 1993).

For an introduction to the women of the Ottoman Empire and those of the Mughal Empire, see S. Hughes and B. Hughes, *Women in World History*, vol. 2 (Armonk, N.Y., 1997). For a more detailed presentation of women in the imperial harem, consult L. P. Peirce, "Beyond Harem Walls: Ottoman Royal Women and the Exercise of Power," in *Gendered Domains: Rethinking Public and Private in Women's History*, ed. D. O. Helly and S. M. Reverby (Ithaca, N.Y., 1992), and L. P. Peirce, *The Imperial Harem: Women and Sovereignty in the Ottoman Empire* (Oxford, 1993). The fascinating story of the royal woman who played an important role behind the scenes is found in E. B. Findly, *Nur Jahan: Empress of Mughal India* (Oxford, 1993).

INFOTRAC COLLEGE EDITION

For additional reading, go to InfoTrac College Edition, your online research library at
http://web1.infotrac-college.com

Enter the search term "Islam" using the Subject Guide.

Enter the search terms "Ottoman Empire" using Keywords.

Enter the search term "Safavid" using Keywords.

Enter the search term "Mughal" using Keywords.

Chapter 16

Gift of James A. Michener, Honolulu Academy of Arts

THE EAST ASIAN WORLD

CHAPTER OUTLINE

- CHINA AT ITS APEX
- TOKUGAWA JAPAN
- KOREA: THE HERMIT KINGDOM
- CONCLUSION

FOCUS QUESTIONS

- Why were the Manchus so successful at establishing a foreign dynasty in China, and what were the main characteristics of their rule?
- How did China and Japan respond to the coming of the Europeans, and what impact did the Europeans have on these East Asian civilizations in the sixteenth through eighteenth centuries?
- How did the unification of Japan come about, and how did the Tokugawa rulers maintain that unity?
- How did the economy and society of Japan change during the Tokugawa era, and how did Japanese culture reflect those changes?
- ➤ How did the economy and society of China change during the Ming and Qing eras, and to what degree did these changes seem to be leading toward an industrial revolution on the Western model?

*I*n December 1717, the emperor Kangxi returned from a hunting trip north of the Great Wall and began to suffer from dizzy spells. Conscious of his approaching date with mortality—he was now nearly seventy years of age—the emperor called together his sons and leading government officials in the imperial palace and issued the following edict:

> *The rulers of the past all took reverence for Heaven's laws and reverence for their ancestors as the fundamental way in ruling the country. To be sincere in reverence for Heaven and ancestors entails the following: Be kind to men from afar and keep the able ones near, nourish the people, think of the profit of all as being the real profit and the mind of the whole country as being the real mind, be considerate to officials and act as the father to the people, protect the state before danger comes and govern well before there is any disturbance, be always diligent and always careful, and maintain the balance between leniency and strictness, between principle and expediency, so that long-range plans can be made for the country: That's all there is to it.*[1]

442

THE EAST ASIAN WORLD • CHAPTER 16

As a primer for political leadership, the emperor's edict reflects the genius of Confucian philosophy at its best and has a timeless quality that applies to our age as well as to the Golden Age of the Qing dynasty.

Kangxi reigned during one of the most glorious eras in the long history of China. Under the Ming (1369–1644) and the early Qing (1644–1911) dynasties, the empire expanded its borders to a degree not seen since the Han and the Tang. Chinese culture was the envy of its neighbors and earned the admiration of many European visitors, including Jesuit priests and Enlightenment philosophes.

On the surface, China appeared to be an unchanging society patterned after the Confucian vision of a "golden age" in the remote past. This indeed was the image presented by China's rulers, who referred constantly to tradition as a model for imperial institutions and cultural values. Although few observers could have been aware of it at the time, however, China was changing—and rather rapidly.

A similar process was under way in neighboring Japan. A vigorous new shogunate called the Tokugawa rose to power in the early seventeenth century and managed to revitalize the traditional system in a somewhat more centralized form that enabled it to survive for another 250 years. But major structural changes were taking place in Japanese society, and by the nineteenth century, tensions were growing as the gap between theory and reality widened.

One of the many factors involved in the quickening pace of change in both countries was contact with the West, which began with the arrival of Portuguese ships in Chinese and Japanese ports in the first half of the sixteenth century. The Ming and the Tokugawa initially opened their doors to European trade and missionary activity. Later, however, Chinese and Japanese rulers became concerned about the corrosive effects of Western ideas and practices and attempted to protect their traditional societies from external intrusion. But neither could forever resist the importunities of Western trading nations, and when the doors to the West were finally reopened in the mid-nineteenth century, both societies were ripe for radical change. •

CHINA AT ITS APEX

In 1514, a Portuguese fleet dropped anchor off the coast of China, just south of the Pearl River estuary and present-day Hong Kong. It was the first direct contact between the Chinese Empire and the West since the arrival of the Venetian adventurer Marco Polo two centuries earlier, and it opened an era that would eventually change the face of China and, indeed, all the world.

From the Ming to the Qing

Marco Polo had reported on the magnificence of China after visiting Beijing during the reign of Khubilai Khan, the great Mongol ruler. By the time the Portuguese fleet arrived off the coast of China, of course, the Mongol Empire had long since disappeared. It had gradually weakened after the death of Khubilai Khan and was finally overthrown in 1368 by a massive peasant rebellion under the leadership of Zhu Yuanzhang, who had declared himself the founding emperor of a new Ming (Bright) dynasty and assumed the reign title of Ming Hongwu (Ming Hung Wu, or Ming Martial Emperor). The Ming inaugurated a new era of greatness in Chinese history. Under a series of strong rulers, China extended its rule into Mongolia and Central Asia. The Ming even briefly reconquered Vietnam, which, after a thousand years of Chinese rule, had reclaimed its independence following the collapse of the Tang dynasty in the tenth century. Along the northern frontier, the Emperor Yongle (Yung Lo; 1402–1424) strengthened the Great Wall and pacified the nomadic tribespeople who had troubled China in previous centuries. A tributary relationship was established with the Yi dynasty in Korea.

The internal achievements of the Ming were equally impressive. When they replaced the Mongols in the fourteenth century, the Ming turned to traditional Confucian institutions as a means of ruling their vast empire. These included the six ministries at the apex of the bureaucracy, the use of the civil service examinations to select members of the bureaucracy, and the division of the empire into provinces, districts, and counties. As before, Chinese villages were relatively autonomous, and local councils of elders continued to be responsible for adjudicating disputes, initiating local construction and irrigation projects, mustering a militia, and assessing and collecting taxes.

The society that was governed by this vast hierarchy of officials was a far cry from the predominantly agrarian society that had been ruled by the Han. In the burgeoning ping on the way at ports in South Asia. The size of the fleet was impressive: it included nearly 28,000 sailors on sixty-two ships, some of them junks larger by far than any other oceangoing vessels the world had yet seen. China seemed about to become a direct participant in the vast trade network that extended as far west as the Atlantic Ocean, thus culminating the process of opening China to the wider world that had begun with the Tang dynasty.

Why the expeditions were undertaken has been a matter of some debate. Some historians assume that economic profit was the main reason. Others point to Yongle's native curiosity and note that the voyage—and the six others that followed it—returned not only with goods but also with a plethora of information about the outside world as well as with some items unknown in China (the emperor was especially intrigued by the giraffes and placed them in the imperial zoo, where they were identified by soothsayers with the coming of good government). Others speculate that the emperor was seeking to ascertain the truth of rumors that his immediate predecessor, Emperor Jianwen or Chien Wen (1398–1402), had escaped to Southeast Asia to live in exile.

Whatever the case, the voyages resulted in a dramatic increase in Chinese knowledge about the world and the nature of ocean travel. It also brought massive profits for their sponsors, including individuals connected with Admiral Zhenghe at court. This aroused resentment among conservatives within the bureaucracy, some of whom viewed commercial activities with a characteristic measure of Confucian disdain. One commented that an end to the voyages would provide the Chinese people with a respite "so that they can devote themselves to husbandry [agriculture] and schooling."

Shortly after Yongle's death, the voyages were discontinued, never to be revived. An early European visitor reported that "no one sails the sea from north to south; it is prohibited by the king, in order that the country may not become known."[2] The decision had long-term consequences and in the eyes of many modern historians marks a turning inward of the Chinese state, away from commerce and toward a more traditional emphasis on agriculture, away from the exotic lands to the south and toward the heartland of the country in the Yellow River valley.

Ironically, the move toward the Yellow River had been initiated by Yongle himself when he had decided to move the Ming capital from Nanjing, in central China, where the ships were built and the voyages launched, back to Beijing, where official eyes were firmly focused on the threat from beyond the Great Wall to the north. As a means of reducing that threat, Yongle ordered the resettlement of thousands of families from the rich Yangtze valley. The emperor had presumably not intended to set forces in motion that would divert the country from its growing contacts with the external world. After all, he had been the driving force behind Zhenghe's voyages. But the end result was a shift in the balance of power from central China, where it had been since the southern Song dynasty,

Courtesy of William J. Duiker

THE GREAT WALL OF CHINA   Although the Great Wall is popularly believed to be over two thousand years old, the part of the wall that is most frequently visited by tourists was a reconstruction undertaken during the early Ming dynasty as a means of protection against invasion from the north. Part of that wall, which was built to protect the imperial capital of Beijing, is shown here.

cities near the coast and along the Yangtze River valley, factories and workshops were vastly increasing the variety and output of their manufactured goods. The population had doubled, and new crops had been introduced, greatly expanding the food output of the empire.

In 1405, in a splendid display of Chinese maritime might, Yongle sent a fleet of Chinese trading ships under the eunuch admiral Zhenghe (Cheng Ho) through the Strait of Malacca and out into the Indian Ocean; there they traveled as far west as the east coast of Africa, stop-back to northern China, where it had originated and would remain for the rest of the Ming era. China would not look outward again for over four centuries.

FIRST CONTACTS WITH THE WEST

Despite the Ming's retreat from active participation in the maritime trade, when the Portuguese arrived in 1514, China was in command of a vast empire that stretched from the steppes of Central Asia to the China Sea, from the Gobi Desert to the tropical rain forests of Southeast Asia. From the lofty perspective of the imperial throne in Beijing, the Europeans could only have seemed like an unusually exotic form of barbarian to be placed within the familiar framework of the tributary system, the hierarchical arrangement in which rulers of all other countries were regarded as "younger brothers" of the Son of Heaven. Indeed, the bellicose and uncultured behavior of the Portuguese so outraged Chinese officials that they expelled the Europeans, but after further negotiations, the Portuguese were permitted to occupy the tiny territory of Macao, a foothold they would retain until the end of the twentieth century.

Initially, the arrival of the Europeans did not have much impact on Chinese society. Direct trade between Europe and China was limited, and Portuguese ships became involved in the regional trade network, carrying silk to Japan in return for Japanese silver. Eventually, the Spanish also began to participate, using the Philippines as an anchor in the galleon trade between China and the great silver mines in the Americas.

More influential than trade, perhaps, were the ideas introduced by Christian missionaries. Among the most active and the most effective were highly educated Jesuits, who were familiar with European philosophical and scientific developments. Recognizing the Chinese pride in their own culture, the Jesuits attempted to draw parallels between Christian and Confucian concepts (for example, they identified the Western concept of God with the Chinese character for Heaven) and to show the similarities between Christian morality and Confucian ethics. European inventions such as the clock, the prism, and various astronomical and musical instruments impressed Chinese officials, hitherto deeply imbued with a sense of the superiority of Chinese civilization, and helped Western ideas win acceptance at court. An elderly Chinese scholar expressed his wonder at the miracle of eyeglasses:

> White glass from across the Western Seas
> Is imported through Macao:
> Fashioned into lenses big as coins,
> They encompass the eyes in a double frame.
> I put them on—it suddenly becomes clear;
> I can see the very tips of things!
> And read fine print by the dim-lit window
> Just like in my youth.[3]

For their part, the missionaries were much impressed with many aspects of Chinese civilization, and reports of their experiences heightened European curiosity about this great society on the other side of the world (see the box on p. 446).

THE MING BROUGHT TO EARTH

During the late sixteenth century, the Ming began to decline as a series of weak rulers led to an era of corruption, concentration of land ownership, and ultimately peasant rebellions and tribal unrest along the northern frontier. The inflow of vast amounts of foreign silver led to an alarming increase in inflation. Then the arrival of the English and the Dutch disrupted the silver trade; silver imports plummeted, severely straining the Chinese economy by raising the value of the metal relative to that of copper. Crop yields declined due to harsh weather—linked to the "little ice age" of the early seventeenth century—and the resulting scarcity reduced the ability of the government to provide food in times of imminent starvation. High taxes, provoked in part by increased official corruption, led to peasant unrest and worker violence in urban areas. A folk song of the period, addressed to the "Lord of Heaven," complained,

> Old skymaster,
> You're getting on, your ears are deaf, your eyes are gone.
> Can't see people, can't hear words.
> Glory for those who kill and burn;
> For those who fast and read the scriptures,
> Starvation.
> Fall down, old master sky, how can you be so high?
> How can you be so high? Come down to earth.[4]

As always, internal problems were accompanied by unrest along the northern frontier. Following long precedent, the Ming had attempted to pacify the frontier tribes by forging alliances with them, arranging marriages between them and the local aristocracy, and granting trade privileges. One of the alliances was with the Manchus (also known as the Jurchen), the descendants of peoples who had briefly established a kingdom in northern China during the early thirteenth century. The Manchus, a mixed agricultural and hunting people, lived northeast of the Great Wall in the area known today as Manchuria.

At first the Manchus were satisfied with consolidating their territory and made little effort to extend their rule south of the Great Wall. But during the first decades of the seventeenth century, the problems of the Ming dynasty began to come to a head. A major epidemic devastated the population in many areas of the country. The suffering brought on by the epidemic helped spark a vast peasant revolt led by Li Zicheng (Li Tzu-ch'eng, 1604–1651). Li was a postal worker in central China who had been dismissed from his job as part of a cost-saving measure by the imperial court, now increasingly preoccupied by tribal

THE ART OF PRINTING

Europeans obtained much of their early information about China from the Jesuits who served at the Ming court in the sixteenth and seventeenth centuries. Clerics such as the Italian Matteo Ricci (1552–1610) found much to admire in Chinese civilization. Here Ricci expresses a keen interest in Chinese printing methods, which at that time were well in advance of the techniques used in the West.

MATTEO RICCI, *THE DIARY OF MATTHEW RICCI*

The art of printing was practiced in China at a date somewhat earlier than that assigned to the beginning of printing in Europe, which was about 1405. It is quite certain that the Chinese knew the art of printing at least five centuries ago, and some of them assert that printing was known to their people before the beginning of the Christian era, about 50 B.C. Their method of printing differs widely from that employed in Europe, and our method would be quite impracticable for them because of the exceedingly large number of Chinese characters and symbols. . . .

Their method of making printed books is quite ingenious. The text is written in ink, with a brush made of very fine hair, on a sheet of paper which is inverted and pasted on a wooden tablet. When the paper has become thoroughly dry, its surface is scraped off quickly and with great skill, until nothing but a fine tissue bearing the characters remains on the wooden tablet. Then, with a steel graver, the workman cuts away the surface following the outlines of the characters until these alone stand out in low relief. From such a block a skilled printer can make copies with incredible speed, turning out as many as fifteen hundred copies in a single day. . . . This scheme of engraving wooden blocks is well adapted for the large and complex nature of the Chinese characters, but I do not think it would lend itself very aptly to our European type, which could hardly be engraved upon wood because of its small dimensions.

Their method of printing has one decided advantage, namely, that once these tablets are made, they can be preserved and used for making changes in the text as often as one wishes. Additions and subtractions can also be made as the tablets can be readily patched. . . . We have derived great benefit from this method of Chinese printing, as we employ the domestic help in our homes to strike off copies of the books on religious and scientific subjects which we translate into Chinese from the languages in which they were written originally. In truth, the whole method is so simple that one is tempted to try it for himself after once having watched the process. The simplicity of Chinese printing is what accounts for the exceedingly large numbers of books in circulation here and the ridiculously low prices at which they are sold.

---

attacks along the frontier (see Map 16.1). In the 1630s, Li managed to extend the revolt throughout the country and finally occupied the capital of Beijing in 1644. The last Ming emperor committed suicide by hanging himself from a tree in the palace gardens.

But Li was unable to hold his conquest. The overthrow of the Ming dynasty presented a great temptation to the Manchus. With the assistance of many military commanders who had deserted from the Ming, they conquered Beijing on their own. Li Zicheng's army disintegrated, and the Manchus declared the creation of a new dynasty with the reign title of the Qing (Ch'ing, or Pure). Once again, China was under foreign rule.

The Greatness of the Qing

The accession of the Manchus to power in Beijing was not universally applauded. Their ruthless policies and insensitivity to Chinese customs soon provoked resistance. Some Ming loyalists fled to Southeast Asia, but others continued their resistance to the new rulers from inside the country. To make it easier to identify the rebels, the government ordered all Chinese to adopt Manchu dress and hairstyles. All Chinese males were to shave their foreheads and braid their hair into a queue; those who refused were to be executed. As a popular saying put it, "Lose your hair or lose your head."[5]

But the Manchus eventually proved to be more adept at adapting to Chinese conditions than their predecessors, the Mongols. Unlike the latter, who had tried to impose their own methods of ruling, the Manchus adopted the Chinese political system (although, as we shall see, they retained their distinct position within it) and were gradually accepted by most Chinese as the legitimate rulers of the country.

Like all of China's great dynasties, the Qing was blessed with a series of strong early rulers who pacified the country, rectified many of the most obvious social and economic inequities, and restored peace and prosperity. For the Ming dynasty, these strong emperors had been Hongwu and Yongle; under the Qing, they would be Kangxi (K'ang Hsi) and Qianlong (Ch'ien Lung). The two Qing monarchs ruled China for well over a century, from the middle of the seventeenth century to the end of the eighteenth, and were responsible for much of the greatness of Manchu China.

Kangxi (1661–1722) was arguably the greatest ruler in Chinese history. Ascending to the throne at the age of seven, he was blessed with diligence, political astuteness, and a strong character and began to take charge of Qing administration while still an adolescent. During the six decades of his reign, Kangxi not only stabilized impe-

MAP 16.1   China and Its Enemies During the Late Ming Era.   During the seventeenth century, the Ming dynasty faced challenges on two fronts, from China's traditional adversaries—nomadic groups north of the Great Wall—and from new arrivals—European merchants—who had begun to press for trading privileges along the southern coast. ➤ *How do these threats differ from those faced by previous dynasties in China?*

rial rule by pacifying the restive peoples along the northern and western frontiers but also managed to make the dynasty acceptable to the general population. As an active patron of arts and letters, he cultivated the support of scholars through a number of major projects.

During Kangxi's reign, the activities of the Western missionaries, Dominicans and Franciscans as well as Jesuits, reached their height. The emperor was quite tolerant of the Christians, and several Jesuit missionaries became influential at court. Several hundred court officials converted to Christianity, as did an estimated 300,000 ordinary Chinese. But the Christian effort was ultimately undermined by squabbling among the Western religious orders over the Jesuit policy of accommodating local beliefs and practices in order to facilitate conversion. The Jesuits had acquiesced to the emperor's insistence that traditional Confucian rituals such as ancestor worship were civil ceremonies and thus could be undertaken by Christian converts. Jealous Dominicans and Franciscans complained to the pope, who issued an edict ordering all missionaries and converts to conform to the official orthodoxy set forth in Europe. At first, Kangxi attempted to resolve the problem by appealing directly to the Vatican, but the pope was uncompromising. After Kangxi's death, his successor began to suppress Christian activities throughout China.

Kangxi's achievements were carried on by his successors, Yongzheng (Yung Cheng, 1722–1736) and Qianlong (1736–1795). Like Kangxi, Qianlong was known for his diligence, tolerance, and intellectual curiosity, and he too combined vigorous military action against the unruly tribes along the frontier with active efforts to promote economic prosperity, administrative efficiency, and scholarship and artistic excellence. The result was continued growth for the Manchu Empire throughout much of the eighteenth century.

QING POLITICS

One reason for the success of the Manchus was their ability to adapt to their new environment. They retained the Ming political system with relatively few changes. They also tried to establish their legitimacy as China's rightful rulers by stressing their devotion to the principles of Confucianism. Emperor Kangxi ostentatiously studied the sacred Confucian classics and issued a "sacred edict" that proclaimed

SIXTEEN CONFUCIAN COMMANDMENTS

Although the Qing dynasty was of foreign origin, its rulers found Confucian maxims convenient for maintaining the social order. In 1670, the great emperor Kangxi issued the Sacred Edict to popularize Confucian values among the common people. The edict was read publicly at periodic intervals in every village in the country and set the standard for behavior throughout the empire. Note the similarities and differences with the Japanese decree on p. 463 later in this chapter.

KANGXI'S SACRED EDICT

1. Esteem most highly filial piety and brotherly submission, in order to give due importance to the social relations.
2. Behave with generosity toward your kindred, in order to illustrate harmony and benignity.
3. Cultivate peace and concord in your neighborhoods, in order to prevent quarrels and litigations.
4. Recognize the importance of husbandry and the culture of the mulberry tree, in order to ensure a sufficiency of clothing and food.
5. Show that you prize moderation and economy, in order to prevent the lavish waste of your means.
6. Give weight to colleges and schools, in order to make correct the practice of the scholar.
7. Extirpate strange principles, in order to exalt the correct doctrine.
8. Lecture on the laws, in order to warn the ignorant and obstinate.
9. Elucidate propriety and yielding courtesy, in order to make manners and customs good.
10. Labor diligently at your proper callings, in order to stabilize the will of the people.
11. Instruct sons and younger brothers, in order to prevent them from doing what is wrong.
12. Put a stop to false accusations, in order to preserve the honest and good.
13. Warn against sheltering deserters, in order to avoid being involved in their punishment.
14. Fully remit your taxes, in order to avoid being pressed for payment.
15. Unite in hundreds and tithing, in order to put an end to thefts and robbery.
16. Remove enmity and anger, in order to show the importance due to the person and life.

to the entire empire the importance of the moral values established by the master (see the box above).

Still, the Manchus, like the Mongols, were ethnically, linguistically, and culturally distinct from their subject population. The Qing attempted to cope with this reality by adopting a two-pronged strategy. On the one hand, the Manchus, representing less than 2 percent of the entire population, were legally defined as distinct from everyone else in China. The Manchu nobles retained their aristocratic privileges, while their economic base was protected by extensive landholdings and revenues provided from the state treasury. Other Manchus were assigned farmland and organized into military units, called banners, which were stationed as separate units in various strategic positions throughout China. These "bannermen" were the primary fighting force of the empire. Ethnic Chinese were prohibited from settling in Manchuria and were still compelled to wear their hair in a queue as a sign of submission to the ruling dynasty.

But while the Qing attempted to protect their distinct identity within an alien society, they also recognized the need to bring ethnic Chinese into the top ranks of imperial administration. Their solution was to create a system, known as dyarchy, in which all important administrative positions were shared equally by Chinese and Manchus. Of the six members of the grand secretariat, three were Manchu and three were Chinese. Each of the six ministries had an equal number of Chinese and Manchu members, and Manchus and Chinese also shared responsibilities at the provincial level.

Below the provinces, Chinese were dominant. Although the system did not work perfectly, the Manchus' willingness to share power did win over the allegiance of many Chinese. Meanwhile, the Manchus themselves, despite official efforts to preserve their separate language and culture, were increasingly assimilated into Chinese civilization.

The new rulers also tinkered with the civil service examination system. In an effort to make it more equitable, quotas were established for each major ethnic group and each province to prevent the positions from being monopolized by candidates from certain provinces in central China that had traditionally produced large numbers of officials. In practice, however, the examination system probably became less equitable during the Manchu era because increasingly positions were assigned to candidates who had purchased their degree rather than competing through the system. Moreover, positions were becoming harder to obtain because their number did not rise fast enough to match the unprecedented increase in population under Qing rule.

CHINA ON THE EVE OF THE WESTERN ONSLAUGHT

In some ways, China was at the height of its power and glory in the mid-eighteenth century. But it was also under Qianlong that the first signs of the internal decay of the Manchu dynasty began to appear. The clues were familiar ones. Qing military campaigns along the frontier were expensive and placed heavy demands on the imperial treasury. As the emperor aged, he became less astute in selecting his subordinates and fell under the influence of corrupt elements at court, including the notorious Manchu official Heshen (Ho Shen). Funds officially destined for military or other official use were increasingly siphoned off to Heshen or his favorites, arousing resentment among military and civilian officials.

Corruption at the center led inevitably to unrest in rural areas, where higher taxes, bureaucratic venality, and rising pressure on the land because of the growing population had produced economic hardship. The heart of the unrest was in central China, where discontented peasants who had recently been settled on infertile land launched a revolt known as the White Lotus Rebellion (1796–1804). The revolt was eventually suppressed but at great expense.

Unfortunately for China, the decline of the Qing dynasty occurred just as China's modest relationship with the West was about to give way to a new era of military confrontation and increased pressure for trade. The first problems came in the north, where Russian traders seek-

ing skins and furs began to penetrate the region between Siberian Russia and Manchuria. Earlier the Ming dynasty had attempted to deal with the Russians by the traditional method of placing them in a tributary relationship and playing them off against other non-Chinese groups in the area. But the tsar refused to play by Chinese rules. His envoys to Beijing ignored the tribute system and refused to perform the kowtow (the ritual of prostration and knocking the head on the ground performed by foreign emissaries before the emperor), the classical symbol of fealty demanded of all foreign ambassadors to the Chinese court. Formal diplomatic relations were finally established in 1689, when the Treaty of Nerchinsk (negotiated with the aid of Jesuit missionaries resident at the Qing court) settled the boundary dispute and provided for regular trade between the two countries. Through such arrangements, the Manchus were able not only to pacify the northern frontier but also to extend their rule over Xinjiang and Tibet to the west and southwest (see Map 16.2). In the meantime, tributary relations were established with such

MAP 16.2   The Qing Empire in the Eighteenth Century.   The boundaries of the Chinese Empire at the height of the Qing dynasty in the eighteenth century are shown on this map. ➤ *What areas were linked in tributary status to the Chinese empire?*

The Art Archive/Marine Museum Stockholm/Dagli Orti (A)

➤ **EUROPEAN WAREHOUSES AT CANTON.**   Aggravated by the growing presence of foreigners in the
eighteenth century, the Chinese court severely restricted the movement of European traders in China.
They were permitted to live only in a compound near Canton during the seven months of the trading
season and could go into the city only three times a month. In this painting, the Dutch and British flags
fly over the warehouses and residences of the foreign community, while Chinese sampans and junks sit
anchored in the river.

neighboring countries as Korea, Burma, Vietnam, and
Ayuthaya.

Dealing with the foreigners who arrived by sea
was more difficult. By the end of the seventeenth
century, the English had replaced the Portuguese as
the dominant force in European trade. Operating through
the East India Company, which served as both a trading
unit and the administra-
tor of English territories
in Asia, the English
established their first
trading post at Canton
in 1699. Over the next
decades, trade with
China, notably the
export of tea and silk
to England, increased
rapidly. To limit contact
between Chinese and
Europeans, the Qing
licensed Chinese trading

Canton in the Eighteenth Century

Canton

Pearl River

EUROPEAN FACTORIES

firms at Canton to be the exclusive conduit for trade with
the West. Eventually, the Qing confined the Europeans
to a small island just outside the city walls and permitted them to reside there only from October through
March.

For a while, the British tolerated this system, which
brought considerable profit to the East India Company and
its shareholders. But by the end of the eighteenth century,
the British had begun to demand access to other cities
along the Chinese coast and that the country be opened
to British manufactured goods. The British government
and traders alike were restive at the uneven balance of
trade between the two countries, which forced the British
to ship vast amounts of silver bullion to China in exchange
for its silks, porcelains, and teas. In 1793, a mission under
Lord Macartney visited Beijing to press for liberalization
of trade restrictions. A compromise was reached on the
kowtow (Macartney was permitted to bend on one knee
as was the British custom), but Qianlong expressed no
interest in British manufactured products (see the box
on p. 451). An exasperated Macartney compared the

THE TRIBUTE SYSTEM IN ACTION

In 1793, the British emissary Lord Macartney visited the Qing Empire to request the opening of formal diplomatic and trading relations between his country and China. Emperor Qianlong's reply, addressed to King George III of Britain, illustrates how the imperial court in Beijing viewed the world. King George could not have been pleased. The document provides a good example of the complacency with which the Celestial Empire viewed the world beyond its borders.

A DECREE OF EMPEROR QIANLONG

An Imperial Edict to the King of England: You, O King, are so inclined toward our civilization that you have sent a special envoy across the seas to bring to our Court your memorial of congratulations on the occasion of my birthday and to present your native products as an expression of your thoughtfulness. On perusing your memorial, so simply worded and sincerely conceived, I am impressed by your genuine respectfulness and friendliness and greatly pleased.

As to the request made in your memorial, O King, to send one of your nationals to stay at the Celestial Court to take care of your country's trade with China, this is not in harmony with the state system of our dynasty and will definitely not be permitted. Traditionally people of the European nations who wished to render some service under the Celestial Court have been permitted to come to the capital. But after their arrival they are obliged to wear Chinese court costumes, are placed in a certain residence, and are never allowed to return to their own countries. This is the established rule of the Celestial Dynasty with which presumably you, O King, are familiar. Now you, O King, wish to send one of your nationals to live in the capital, but he is not like the Europeans who come to Peking as Chinese employees, live there, and never return home again, nor can he be allowed to go and come and maintain any correspondence. This is indeed a useless undertaking.

Moreover the territory under the control of the Celestial Court is very large and wide. There are well-established regulations governing tributary envoys from the outer states to Peking [Beijing], giving them provisions (of food and traveling expenses) by our post-houses and limiting their going and coming. There has never been a precedent for letting them do whatever they like. Now if you, O King, wish to have a representative in Peking, his language will be unintelligible and his dress different from the regulations; there is no place to accommodate him. . . .

The Celestial Court has pacified and possessed the territory within the four seas. Its sole aim is to do its utmost to achieve good government and to manage political affairs, attaching no value to strange jewels and precious objects. The various articles presented by you, O King, this time are accepted by my special order to the office in charge of such functions in consideration of the offerings having come from a long distance with sincere good wishes. As a matter of fact, the virtue and prestige of the Celestial Dynasty having spread far and wide, the kings of the myriad nations come by land and sea with all sorts of precious things. Consequently there is nothing we lack, as your principal envoy and others have themselves observed. We have never set much store on strange or ingenious objects, nor do we need any more of your country's manufactures. . . .

Chinese Empire to "an old, crazy, first-rate man-of-war" that had once awed its neighbors "merely by her bulk and appearance" but was now destined under incompetent leadership to be "dashed to pieces on the shore."[6] With his contemptuous dismissal of the British request, the emperor had inadvertently sowed the seeds for a century of humiliation.

Changing China

During the Ming and Qing dynasties, China remained a predominantly agricultural society; nearly 85 percent of its people were farmers. But although most Chinese still lived in rural villages, the economy was undergoing a number of changes that have led some historians to suggest that China, under other circumstances, might have experienced an industrial revolution as in the West. In this view, the arrival of Western imperialism in the nineteenth century not only failed to stimulate economic change but may actually have hindered it.

THE POPULATION EXPLOSION

In the first place, the center of gravity was continuing to shift steadily from the north to the south. In the early centuries of Chinese civilization, the bulk of the population had been located along the Yellow River. Smaller settlements were located along the Yangtze and in the mountainous regions of the south, but the administrative and economic center of gravity was clearly in the north. By the Song period, however, that emphasis had already begun to shift drastically as a result of climatic changes, deforestation, and continuing pressure from nomads in the Gobi Desert. By the early Qing, the economic breadbasket of China was located along the Yangtze River or in the mountains to the south. One concrete indication of this shift occurred during the Ming dynasty, when Emperor Yongle ordered the renovation of the Grand Canal to facilitate the shipment of rice from the Yangtze delta to the food-starved north.

Moreover, the population was beginning to increase rapidly. For centuries, China's population had remained

Chronology

CHINA DURING THE EARLY MODERN ERA

Rise of Ming dynasty	1369
Voyages of Zhenghe	1405–1433
Portuguese arrive in southern China	1514
Matteo Ricci arrives in China	1601
Li Zicheng occupies Beijing	1644
Manchus seize China	1644
Reign of Kangxi	1661–1722
Treaty of Nerchinsk	1689
First English trading post at Canton	1699
Reign of Qianlong	1736–1795
Lord Macartney's mission to China	1793
White Lotus Rebellion	1796–1804

within a range of 50 to 100 million, rising in times of peace and prosperity and falling in periods of foreign invasion and internal anarchy. During the Ming and the early Qing, however, the population increased from an estimated 70 to 80 million in 1390 to over 300 million at the end of the eighteenth century. There were probably several reasons for this population increase: the relatively long period of peace and stability under the early Qing; the introduction of new crops from the Americas, including peanuts, sweet potatoes, and maize; and the planting of a new species of faster-growing rice from Southeast Asia.

Of course, this population increase meant much greater population pressure on the land, smaller farms, and a razor-thin margin of safety in case of climatic disaster. The imperial court attempted to deal with the problem through a variety of means, most notably by preventing the concentration of land in the hands of wealthy landowners. Nevertheless, by the eighteenth century, almost all the land that could be irrigated was already under cultivation, and the problems of rural hunger and landlessness became increasingly serious.

SEEDS OF INDUSTRIALIZATION

Another change that took place during the early modern period in China was the steady growth of manufacturing and commerce. Taking advantage of the long era of peace and prosperity, merchants and manufacturers began to expand their operations beyond their immediate provinces. Commercial networks began to operate on a regional and sometimes even a national basis, as trade in silk, metal and wood products, porcelain, cotton goods, and cash crops like cotton and tobacco developed rapidly.

Foreign trade also expanded as Chinese merchants set up extensive contacts with countries in Southeast Asia.

Although this rise in industrial and commercial activity resembles the changes occurring in western Europe, China and Europe differed in several key ways. In the first place, members of the bourgeoisie in China were not as independent as their European counterparts. In China, trade and manufacturing remained under the firm control of the state. In addition, political and social prejudices against commercial activity remained strong. Reflecting an ancient preference for agriculture over manufacturing and trade, the state levied heavy taxes on manufacturing and commerce while attempting to keep agricultural taxes low.

One of the consequences of these differences was a growing technological gap between China and Europe. The Chinese reaction to European clockmaking techniques provides an example. In the early seventeenth century, the Jesuit Matteo Ricci introduced advanced European clocks driven by weights or springs. The emperor was fascinated and found the clocks more reliable than Chinese methods of keeping time. Over the next decades, European timepieces became a popular novelty at court, but the Chinese expressed little curiosity about the technology involved, provoking one European to remark that playthings like cuckoo clocks "will be received here with much greater interest than scientific instruments or *objets d'art*."[7]

Daily Life in Qing China

Despite the changes in the economy, daily life in China under the Ming and early Qing dynasties continued to follow traditional patterns. As in earlier periods, Chinese society was organized around the family. As in earlier times, the ideal family unit in Qing China was the joint family, in which as many as three or even four generations lived under the same roof. When sons married, they brought their wives to live with them in the family homestead. Prosperous families would add a separate section to the house to accommodate the new family unit. Unmarried daughters would also remain in the house. Aging parents and grandparents remained under the same roof until they died and were cared for by younger members of the household. This ideal did not always correspond to reality, however, since many families did not possess sufficient land to support a large household. One historian has estimated that only about 40 percent of Chinese families actually lived in joint families.

The family continued to be important in early Qing times for much the same reasons as in earlier times. As a labor-intensive society based primarily on the cultivation of rice, China needed large families to help with the harvest and to provide security for parents too old to work in the fields. Sons were particularly prized, not only because they had strong backs but also because they would raise their own families under the parental roof. With few opportunities for employment outside the family, sons had little choice but to remain with their parents and help on the land. Within the family, the oldest male was king, and his wishes theoretically had to be obeyed by all family members. These values were reiterated in Emperor Kangxi's Sacred Edict, which listed filial piety and loyalty to the family as its first two maxims (see the box on p. 448).

For many Chinese, the effects of these values were most apparent in the choice of a marriage partner. Marriages were normally arranged for the benefit of the family, often by a go-between, and the groom and bride were usually not consulted. Frequently, they did not meet until the marriage ceremony. Under such conditions, love was clearly a secondary consideration. In fact, it was often viewed as detrimental, since it inevitably distracted the attention of the husband and wife from their primary responsibility to the larger family unit.

Although this emphasis on filial piety might seem to represent a blatant disregard for individual rights, the obligations were not all on the side of the children. The father was expected to provide support for his wife and children and, like the ruler, was supposed to treat those in his care with respect and compassion. All too often, however, the male head of the family was able to exact his privileges without performing his responsibilities in return.

Beyond the joint family was the clan. Sometimes called a lineage, a clan was an extended kinship unit consisting of dozens or even hundreds of joint and nuclear families linked together by a clan council of elders and a variety of other common social and religious functions. The clan served a number of useful purposes. Some clans possessed lands that could be rented out to poorer families, or richer families within the clan might provide land for the poor. Since there was no general state-supported educational system, sons of poor families might be invited to study in a school established in the home of a more prosperous relative. If the young man succeeded in becoming an official, he would be expected to provide favors and prestige for the clan as a whole.

Like joint families, clans were not universal, and millions of Chinese had none. The clans apparently originated in the great landed families of the Tang period and managed to survive despite periodic efforts by the imperial court to weaken and destroy them. In many cases, clan solidarity was weakened by intralineage conflicts or differing levels of status and economic achievement. Nevertheless, in the early modern period, they were still an influential force at the local level and were particularly prevalent in the south.

THE ROLE OF WOMEN

In traditional China, the role of women had always been inferior to that of men. A sixteenth-century Spanish visitor to South China observed that Chinese women were "very secluded and virtuous, and it was a very rare thing for us to see a woman in the cities and large towns, unless it was an old crone." Women were more visible, he said, in rural areas, where they frequently could be seen working in the fields.[8]

The concept of female inferiority had deep roots in Chinese history. This view was embodied in the belief that only a male would carry on sacred family rituals and that men alone had the talent to govern others. Only males could aspire to a career in government or scholarship. Within the family system, the wife was clearly subordinated to the husband. Legally, she could not divorce her husband or inherit property. The husband, however, could divorce his wife if she did not produce male heirs, or he could take a second wife as well as a concubine for his pleasure. A widow suffered especially, because she had to either raise her children on a single income or fight off her former husband's greedy relatives, who would coerce her to remarry since, according to the law, they would then inherit all of her previous property and her original dowry.

Female children were less desirable because of their limited physical strength and because their parents would be required to pay a dowry to the parents of their future husband. Female children normally did not receive an education, and in times of scarcity when food was in short supply, daughters might even be put to death.

Though women were clearly inferior to men in theory, this was not always the case in practice. Capable women often compensated for their legal inferiority by playing a strong role within the family. Women were often in charge of educating the children and handled the family budget. Some privileged women also received training in the Confucian classics, although their schooling was generally for a shorter time and less rigorous than that of their male counterparts. A few produced significant works of art and poetry (see the box on p. 454).

All in all, however, life for women in traditional China was undoubtedly difficult. In Chinese novels, women were treated as scullery maids or love objects. They were frequently under the domination of both their husband and their mother-in-law, and in some cases the bullying was so brutal that suicide seemed to be the only way out.

Cultural Developments

During the late Ming and the early Qing dynasties, traditional culture in China reached new heights of achievement. With the rise of a wealthy urban class, the demand for art, porcelain, textiles, and literature was at a premium.

THE RISE OF THE CHINESE NOVEL

During the Ming dynasty, a new form of literature arose that eventually evolved into the modern Chinese novel. Although considered less respectable than poetry and

A CHINESE WOMAN ARTIST

During the early Qing era, some women from gentry families became skilled painters, studying in the privacy of their homes, as they were not expected to practice their art in public. Some were taught by other family members or by distant relatives, who were referred to as the "teachers of the inner chambers." Often a shared interest in art created a strong bond between a married couple, as witnessed here in this son's account of his mother's artistic venture.

VIEW FROM THE JADE TERRACE

As a child she learned to read by asking the boys of her clan to pass along what they learned in school. Her strict mother initially frowned on such unfeminine conduct and forbade her to take time away from her needlework to practice with the brush. Undeterred, Chen Shu one day made a copy of a famous painting hanging on the wall of her father's study. For this she was beaten, but a god intervened by appearing to her mother in a dream and saying: "I have given your daughter a brush. Someday she will be famous. How can you forbid it?" This tale served to underscore the idea that Chen Shu was destined for great achievement and perhaps was used to explain her devotion to pursuits regarded by some as unnecessary, even undesirable, for women.

Chen Shu married into the Qian family . . . becoming the second wife of Qian Lunguang. Qian did not distinguish himself as an official, but he did earn a modest reputation as a calligrapher and poet. Shared artistic interests were a part of the couple's relationship, and Qian occasionally added poetic inscriptions to Chen's paintings. . . .

The Qian family associated with some of the leading scholars of the area and took pleasure in entertaining guests, evidently in a manner beyond the family's means. To defray the costs of these gatherings, Chen Shu pawned her clothing and sold her jewelry and paintings. . . .

The shape of Chen Shu's artistic career was determined by her primary roles as wife and mother. From the 1680s through the first decade of the seventeenth century, much of her time was devoted to caring for her four children . . . , parents-in-law, and mother. . . . Chen Shu undoubtedly continued to paint during these busy years, but her last three decades seem to have been her most productive; her surviving dated paintings were executed between 1700 and 1735.

In 1721 Qian Chenqun, her eldest son, . . . received an appointment to the Hanlin Academy. . . . When her son asked the [imperial] court's permission to visit her in 1735, she nobly insisted that he stay at his post and . . . set out to join him in the capital. . . . She was then seventy-five years old. . . . Late in the spring of the following year she died in Beijing. . . .

In the course of his successful career under the Qianlong emperor, Qian Chenqun frequently presented paintings by his mother to the throne. The emperor received Chen Shu's works with pleasure and wrote on many of them with his characteristic lack of restraint.

---

nonfiction prose, these groundbreaking works (often written anonymously or under pseudonyms) were enormously popular, especially among well-to-do urban dwellers.

Written in a colloquial style, the new fiction was characterized by a realism that resulted in vivid portraits of Chinese society. Many of the stories sympathized with society's downtrodden—often helpless maidens—and dealt with such crucial issues as love, money, marriage, and power. Adding to the realism were sexually explicit passages that depicted the private side of Chinese life. Readers delighted in sensuous tales that, no matter how pornographic, always professed a moral lesson; the villains were punished and the virtuous rewarded. During the more puritanical Qing era, a number of the more erotic works were censored or banned and found refuge in Japan, where several have recently been rediscovered by scholars.

Gold Vase Plum, known in English translation as *The Golden Lotus,* presents a cutting exposé of the decadent aspects of late Ming society. Considered by many the first realistic social novel—preceding its European counterparts by two centuries—*The Golden Lotus* depicts the depraved life of a wealthy landlord who cruelly manipulates those around him for sex, money, and power. In a rare exception

in Chinese fiction, the villain is not punished for his evil ways; justice is served instead by the misfortunes that befall his descendants.

The Dream of the Red Chamber is generally considered China's most distinguished popular novel. Published in 1791, some 150 years after *The Golden Lotus,* it tells of the tragic love between two young people caught in the financial and moral disintegration of a powerful Chinese clan. The hero and the heroine, both sensitive and spoiled, represent the inevitable decline of the Chia family and come to an equally inevitable tragic end, she in death and he in an unhappy marriage to another.

THE ART OF THE MING AND THE QING

During the Ming and the early Qing, China produced its last outpouring of traditional artistic brilliance. Although most of the creative work was modeled on past examples, the art of this period is impressive for its technical perfection and breathtaking quantity.

In architecture, the most outstanding example is the Imperial City in Beijing. Building on the remnants of the palace of the Yuan dynasty, the Ming emperor Yongle

⚜ **THE TEMPLE OF HEAVEN.**   This temple, located in the capital city of Beijing, is one of the most important historical structures in China. Built in 1420 at the order of the Ming emperor Yongle, it served as the location for the emperor's annual ceremony appealing to Heaven for a good harvest. Yongle's temple burned to the ground in 1889 but was immediately rebuilt according to the original design.

ordered renovations when he returned the capital to Beijing in 1421. Succeeding emperors continued to add to the palace, but the basic design has not changed since the Ming era. Surrounded by high walls, the immense compound is divided into a maze of private apartments and offices and an imposing ceremonial quadrangle with a series of stately halls for imperial audiences and banquets. The grandiose scale, richly carved marble, spacious gardens, and graceful upturned roofs also contribute to the splendor of the "Forbidden City."

The decorative arts flourished in this period, especially the intricately carved lacquerware and the boldly shaped and colored cloisonné, a type of enamelwork in which colored areas are separated by thin metal bands. Silk production reached its zenith, and the best-quality silks were highly prized in Europe, where chinoiserie, as Chinese art of all kinds was called, was in vogue. Perhaps the most famous of all the achievements of the Ming era was its blue-and-white porcelain, still prized by collectors throughout the world. One variety caused such a sensation in the Netherlands that the Dutch began to manufacture their own blue-and-white porcelain at a new factory set up in Delft.

During the Qing dynasty, artists produced great quantities of paintings, mostly for home consumption. The wealthy city of Yangzhou on the Grand Canal emerged as an active artistic center. Inside the Forbidden City in Beijing, court painters worked alongside Jesuit artists and experimented with Western techniques. European art, however, did not greatly influence Chinese painting at this time; some dismissed it as mere "craftsmanship." Scholarly painters and the literati totally rejected foreign techniques

Beijing Under the Ming and the Manchus, 1400–1911

City wall

INNER CITY

Imperial City

Palace

OUTER CITY

Temple of Heaven

© Dean Conger/National Geographic Image Collection

⧉ **THE IMPERIAL CITY IN BEIJING.**   During the fifteenth century, the Ming dynasty erected an immense imperial city on the remnants of the palace of Khubilai Khan in Beijing. Surrounded by $6\frac{1}{2}$ miles of walls, the enclosed compound is divided into a maze of private apartments and offices; it also includes an imposing ceremonial quadrangle with stately halls for imperial audiences and banquets. Because it was off-limits to commoners, the compound was known as the Forbidden City.

⧉ **WORLD-CLASS CHINA WARE.**   Ming porcelain was noted throughout the world for its delicate blue-and-white floral decorations. The blue coloring was produced with cobalt that had originally been brought from the Middle East along the Silk Road and was known in China as "Mohammedan blue." In the early seventeenth century, the first Ming ware arrived in the Netherlands, where it was called *kraak* because it had been loaded on two Portuguese carracks seized by the Dutch fleet. It took Dutch artisans over a century to learn how to produce a porcelain as fine as the examples brought from China.

Percival David Foundation of Chinese Art

and became obsessed with traditional Chinese styles. As a result, Qing painting became progressively more repetitive and stale. Ironically, the Qing dynasty thus represents the apogee of traditional Chinese art and the beginning of its decline.

🎴 TOKUGAWA JAPAN

At the end of the fifteenth century, the traditional Japanese system was at a point of near anarchy. With the decline in the authority of the Ashikaga shogunate at Kyoto, clan rivalries had exploded into an era of warring states similar to the period of the same name in Zhou dynasty China. Even at the local level, power was frequently diffuse. The typical daimyo (great lord) domain had often become little more than a coalition of fief-holders held together by a loose allegiance to the manor lord. Prince Shotoku's dream of a united Japan appeared to be only a distant memory (see Chapter 11). In actuality, Japan was on the verge of an extended era of national unification and peace under the rule of its greatest shogunate—the Tokugawa.

The Three Great Unifiers

The process began in the mid-sixteenth century with the emergence of three very powerful political figures, Oda Nobunaga (1568–1582), Toyotomi Hideyoshi

(1582–1598), and Tokugawa Ieyasu (1598–1616). In 1568, Oda Nobunaga, the son of a samurai and a military commander under the Ashikaga shogunate, seized the imperial capital of Kyoto and placed the reigning shogun under his domination. During the next few years, the brutal and ambitious Nobunaga attempted to consolidate his rule throughout the central plains by defeating his rivals and suppressing the power of the Buddhist estates, but he was killed by one of his generals in 1582 before the process was complete. He was succeeded by Toyotomi Hideyoshi, a farmer's son who had worked his way up through the ranks to become a military commander. Originally lacking a family name of his own, he eventually adopted the name Toyotomi ("abundant provider") to embellish his reputation for improving the material standards of his domain. Hideyoshi located his capital at Osaka, where he built a castle to accommodate his headquarters, and gradually extended his power outward to the southern islands of Shikoku and Kyushu (see Map 16.3). By 1590, he had persuaded most of the daimyo on the Japanese islands to accept his authority and created a national currency. Then he invaded Korea in an abortive effort to export his rule to the Asian mainland.

Despite their efforts, however, neither Nobunaga nor Hideyoshi was able to eliminate the power of the local daimyo. Both were compelled to form alliances with some daimyo in order to destroy other more powerful rivals.

At the conclusion of his conquests in 1590, Toyotomi Hideyoshi could claim to be the supreme proprietor of all registered lands in areas under his authority. But he then reassigned those lands as fiefs to the local daimyo, who declared their allegiance to him. The daimyo in turn began to pacify the countryside, carrying out extensive "sword hunts" to disarm the population and attracting samurai to their service. The Japanese tradition of decentralized rule had not been overcome.

After Hideyoshi's death in 1598, Tokugawa Ieyasu, the powerful daimyo of Edo (modern Tokyo), moved to fill the vacuum. Neither Hideyoshi nor Oda Nobunaga had claimed the title of shogun, but Ieyasu named himself shogun in 1603, initiating the most powerful and long-lasting of all Japanese shogunates. The Tokugawa rulers completed the restoration of central authority begun by Nobunaga and Hideyoshi and remained in power until 1868, when a war dismantled the entire system. As a contemporary phrased it, "Oda pounds the national rice cake, Hideyoshi kneads it, and in the end Ieyasu sits down and eats it."[9]

Opening to the West

The unification of Japan took place almost simultaneously with the coming of the Europeans. Portuguese traders sailing in a Chinese junk that may have been

THE SIEGE OF OSAKA CASTLE.   After the death of Toyotomi Hideyoshi in 1598, titular authority in Japan passed on to his infant son, Hideyori, whose supporters located their headquarters at Osaka Castle in central Japan. In 1615, the powerful warlord Tokugawa Ieyasu seized the castle, as shown here, and scattered Hideyori's supporters. The family's control over Japan lasted nearly 250 years. Note the presence of firearms, introduced by the Europeans half a century earlier.

A PRESENT FOR LORD TOKITAKA

The Portuguese introduced firearms to Japan in the sixteenth century, and Japanese warriors were quick to explore the possibilities of these new weapons. In this passage, the daimyo of a small island off the southern tip of Japan receives an explanation of how to use the new weapons and is fascinated by the results. Note how Lord Tokitaka attempts to understand the procedures in terms of traditional Daoist beliefs.

THE JAPANESE DISCOVER FIREARMS

"There are two leaders among the traders, the one called Murashusa, and the other Christian Mota. In their hands they carried something two or three feet long, straight on the outside with a passage inside, and made of a heavy substance. The inner passage runs through it although it is closed at the end. At its side there is an aperture which is the passageway for fire. Its shape defies comparison with anything I know. To use it, fill it with powder and small lead pellets. Set up a small . . . target on a bank. Grip the object in your hand, compose your body, and closing one eye, apply fire to the aperture. Then the pellet hits the target squarely. The explosion is like lightning and the report like thunder. Bystanders must cover their ears. . . . This thing with one blow can smash a mountain of silver and a wall of iron. If one sought to do mischief in another man's domain and he was touched by it, he would lose his life instantly. Needless to say this is also true for the deer and stag that ravage the plants in the fields."

Lord Tokitaka saw it and thought it was the wonder of wonders. He did not know its name at first nor the details of its use. Then someone called it "iron-arms," although it was not known whether the Chinese called it so, or whether it was so called only on our island. Thus, one day, Tokitaka spoke to the two alien leaders through an interpreter: "Inca-

pable though I am, I should like to learn about it." Whereupon, the chiefs answered, also through an interpreter: "If you wish to learn about it, we shall teach you its mysteries." Tokitaka then asked, "What is its secret?" The chief replied: "The secret is to put your mind aright and close one eye." Tokitaka said: "The ancient sages have often taught how to set one's mind aright, and I have learned something of it. If the mind is not set aright, there will be no logic for what we say or do. Thus, I understand what you say about setting our minds aright. However, will it not impair our vision for objects at a distance if we close an eye? Why should we close an eye?" To which the chiefs replied: "That is because concentration is important in everything. When one concentrates, a broad vision is not necessary. To close an eye is not to dim one's eyesight but rather to project one's concentration farther. You should know this." Delighted, Tokitaka said: "That corresponds to what Lao Tzu has said, 'Good sight means seeing what is very small.' "

That year the festival day of the Ninth Month fell on the day of the Metal and the Boar. Thus, one fine morning the weapon was filled with powder and lead pellets, a target was set up more than a hundred paces away, and fire was applied to the weapon. At first the people were astonished; then they became frightened. But in the end they all said in unison: "We should like to learn!" Disregarding the high price of the arms, Tokitaka purchased from the aliens two pieces of the firearms for his family treasure. As for the art of grinding, sifting, and mixing of the powder, Tokitaka let his retainer, Shinokawa Shoshiro, learn it. Tokitaka occupied himself, morning and night, and without rest in handling the arms. As a result, he was able to convert the misses of his early experiments into hits—a hundred hits in a hundred attempts.

blown off course by a typhoon had landed on the islands in 1543. Within a few years, Portuguese ships were stopping at Japanese ports on a regular basis to take part in the regional trade between Japan, China, and Southeast Asia. The first Jesuit missionary, Francis Xavier, arrived in 1549.

Initially, the visitors were welcomed. The curious Japanese (the Japanese were "very desirous of knowledge," said Francis Xavier) were fascinated by tobacco, clocks, spectacles, and other European goods, and local daimyo were interested in purchasing all types of European weapons and armaments (see the box above). Oda Nobunaga and Toyotomi Hideyoshi found the new firearms helpful in defeating their enemies and unifying the islands. The effect on Japanese military architecture was particularly striking as local lords began to erect castles on the European model. Many of these castles, such as Hideyoshi's castle at Osaka, still exist today.

The missionaries also had some success. Though confused by misleading translations of sacred concepts in both cultures (Francis Xavier was notoriously poor at learning foreign languages), they converted a number of local daimyo, some of whom may have been motivated in part by the desire for commercial profits. By the end of the sixteenth century, thousands of Japanese in the southernmost islands of Kyushu and Shikoku had become Christians. One converted daimyo ceded the superb natural harbor of the modern city of Nagasaki to the Society of Jesus, which proceeded to use the new settlement for both missionary and trading purposes. But papal claims to the loyalty of all Japanese Christians and the European habit of intervening in local politics soon began to arouse suspicion in official circles. Missionaries added to the problem by deliberately destroying local idols and shrines and turning some temples into Christian schools or churches.

TOYOTOMI HIDEYOSHI EXPELS
THE MISSIONARIES

When Christian missionaries in sixteenth-century Japan began to interfere in local politics and criticize traditional religious practices, Toyotomi Hideyoshi issued an edict calling for their expulsion. In this letter to the Portuguese viceroy in Asia, Hideyoshi explains his decision. Note his conviction that Buddhists, Confucianists, and followers of Shinto all believe in the same God and his criticism of Christianity for rejecting all other faiths.

TOYOTOMI HIDEYOSHI, LETTER TO THE VICEROY OF THE INDIES

Ours is the land of the Gods, and God is mind. Everything in nature comes into existence because of mind. Without God there can be no spirituality. Without God there can be no way. God rules in times of prosperity as in times of decline. God is positive and negative and unfathomable. Thus, God is the root and source of all existence. This God is spoken of by Buddhism in India, Confucianism in China, and Shinto in Japan. To know Shinto is to know Buddhism as well as Confucianism.

As long as man lives in this world, Humanity will be a basic principle. Were it not for Humanity and Righteousness, the sovereign would not be a sovereign, nor a minister of a state a minister. It is through the practice of Humanity and Righteousness that the foundations of our relationships between sovereign and minister, parent and child, and husband and wife are established. If you are interested in the profound philosophy of God and Buddha, request an explanation and it will be given to you. In your land one doctrine is taught to the exclusion of others, and you are not yet informed of the [Confucian] philosophy of Humanity and Righteousness. Thus there is no respect for God and Buddha and no distinction between sovereign and ministers. Through heresies you intend to destroy the righteous law. Hereafter, do not expound, in ignorance of right and wrong, unreasonable and wanton doctrines. A few years ago the so-called Fathers came to my country seeking to bewitch our men and women, both of the laity and clergy. At that time punishment was administered to them, and it will be repeated if they should return to our domain to propagate their faith. It will not matter what sect or denomination they represent—they shall be destroyed. It will then be too late to repent. If you entertain any desire of establishing amity with this land, the seas have been rid of the pirate menace, and merchants are permitted to come and go. Remember this.

Inevitably, the local authorities reacted. In 1587, Toyotomi Hideyoshi issued an edict prohibiting further Christian activities within his domains. Japan, he declared, was "the land of the Gods," and the destruction of shrines by the foreigners was "something unheard of in previous ages." To "corrupt and stir up the lower classes" to commit such sacrileges, he declared, was "outrageous."[10] The parties responsible (the Jesuits) were ordered to leave the country within twenty days. Hideyoshi was careful to distinguish missionary from trading activities, however, and merchants were permitted to continue their operations (see the box above).

The Jesuits protested the expulsion, and eventually Hideyoshi relented, permitting them to continue proselytizing so long as they were discreet. But he refused to repeal the edicts, and when the aggressive activities of newly arrived Spanish Franciscans aroused his ire, he ordered the execution of nine missionaries and a number of their Japanese converts. When the missionaries continued to interfere in local politics (some even tried to incite the daimyo in the southern islands against the shogunate government in Edo), Tokugawa Ieyasu completed the process by ordering the eviction of all missionaries in 1612. The persecution of Japanese Christians intensified, leading to an abortive revolt by Christian peasants on the island of Kyushu in 1637, which was bloodily suppressed.

At first, Japanese authorities hoped to maintain commercial relations with European countries even while suppressing the Western religion, but eventually they decided to prohibit foreign trade altogether and closed the two major foreign factories on the island of Hirado and at Nagasaki. The sole remaining opening to the West was at Deshima Island in Nagasaki harbor, where a small Dutch community was permitted to engage in limited trade with Japan (the Dutch, unlike the Portuguese and the Spanish, had not allowed missionary activities to interfere with their commercial interests). Dutch ships were permitted to dock at Nagasaki harbor only once a year and, after close inspection, were allowed to remain for two or three months. Conditions on the island of Deshima itself were quite confining: the Dutch physician Engelbert Kaempfer complained that the Dutch lived in "almost

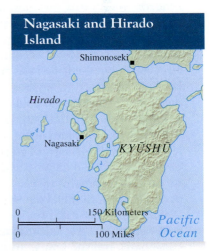

Nagasaki and Hirado Island

Shimonoseki
Hirado
Nagasaki
KYŪSHŪ
0   150 Kilometers
0   100 Miles
Pacific Ocean

THE PORTUGUESE ARRIVE AT NAGASAKI. Portuguese traders landed in Japan by accident in 1543. In a few years, they arrived regularly, taking part in a regional trade network between Japan, China, and Southeast Asia. In these panels done in black lacquer and gold leaf, we see a late-sixteenth-century Japanese interpretation of the first Portuguese landing at Nagasaki.

perpetual imprisonment."[11] Nor were the Japanese free to engage in foreign trade. A small amount of commerce took place with China, but Japanese subjects of the shogunate were forbidden to leave the country on penalty of death.

The Tokugawa "Great Peace"

Once in power, the Tokugawa attempted to strengthen the system that had governed Japan for over three hundred years. They followed precedent in ruling through the *bakufu*, composed now of a coalition of daimyo, and a council of elders. But the system was more centralized than it had been previously. Now the shogunate government played a dual role. It set national policy on behalf of the emperor in Kyoto while simultaneously governing the shogun's own domain, which included about one-quarter of the national territory as well as the three great cities of Edo, Kyoto, and Osaka. As before, the state was divided into separate territories, called domains (*han*), which were ruled by a total of about 250 individual daimyo lords. The daimyo were themselves divided into two types: the *fudai* (inside) daimyo, who were mostly small daimyo directly subordinate to the shogunate, and the *tozama* (outside) daimyo, who were larger and more independent lords usually more distant from the center of shogunate power in Edo.

In theory, the daimyo were essentially autonomous, since they were able to support themselves from taxes on their lands (the shogunate received its own revenues from its extensive landholdings). In actuality, the shogunate was able to guarantee daimyo loyalties by compelling daimyo lords to maintain two residences, one in their own domains and the other at Edo, and to leave their families in Edo as hostages for the daimyo's good behavior. Keeping up two residences also placed the Japanese nobility in a difficult economic position. Some were able to defray the high costs by concentrating on cash crops such as sugar, fish, and forestry products, but most were rice producers, and their revenues remained roughly the same throughout the period. The daimyo were also able to protect their economic interests by depriving their samurai retainers of their proprietary rights over the land and transforming them into salaried officials. The fief thus became a stipend, and the personal relationship between the daimyo and his retainers gradually gave way to a bureaucratic authority.

The Tokugawa also tinkered with the social system by limiting the size of the samurai class and reclassifying samurai who supported themselves by tilling the land as commoners. In fact, with the long period of peace brought about by Tokugawa rule, the samurai gradually ceased to be a warrior class and were required to live in the castle towns. As a gesture to their glorious past, samurai were still permitted to wear their two swords, and a rigid separation was maintained between persons of samurai status and the nonaristocratic segment of the population. Jesuit missionary Francis Xavier observed that "on no account would a poverty-stricken gentleman marry with someone outside the gentry, even if he were given great sums to do so."[12]

MAP 16.3 Tokugawa Japan. This map shows the Japanese islands during the long era of the Tokugawa shogunate. Key cities, including the shogun's capital of Edo, are shown.

➤ *Where was the location of the imperial court?*

SEEDS OF CAPITALISM

The long period of peace under the Tokugawa shogunate made possible a dramatic rise in commerce and manufacturing, especially in the growing cities of Edo, Kyoto, and Osaka. By the mid-eighteenth century, Edo, with a population of more than one million, was one of the largest cities in the world. The growth of trade and industry was stimulated by a rising standard of living—driven in part by technological advances in agriculture and an expansion of arable land—and the voracious appetites of the aristocrats for new products. The daimyo's need for income also contributed as many of them began to promote the sale of local goods from their domains, such as textiles, forestry products, sugar, and sake (fermented rice wine).

Most of this commercial expansion took place in the major cities and the castle towns, where the merchants and artisans lived along with the samurai, who were clustered in neighborhoods surrounding the daimyo's castle. Banking flourished and paper money became the normal medium of exchange in commercial transactions. Merchants formed guilds not only to control market conditions but also to facilitate government control and the collection of taxes. Under the benign if somewhat contemptuous supervision of Japan's noble rulers, a Japanese merchant class gradually began to emerge from the shadows to play a significant role in the life of the Japanese nation. Some historians view the Tokugawa era as the first stage in the rise of an indigenous form of capitalism.

Eventually, the increased pace of industrial activity spread beyond the cities into rural areas. As in Great Britain, cotton was a major factor. Cotton had been introduced to China during the Song dynasty and had spread to Korea and Japan shortly thereafter. Traditionally, however, cotton cloth had been too expensive for the common people, who instead wore clothing made of hemp. Imports increased during the sixteenth century, however, when cotton cloth began to be used for uniforms, matchlock fuses, and sails. Eventually, technological advances reduced the cost, and specialized communities for producing cotton cloth began to appear in the countryside and were gradually transformed into towns. By the eighteenth century, cotton had firmly replaced hemp as the cloth of choice for most Japanese.

Not everyone benefited from the economic changes of the seventeenth and eighteenth centuries, however, notably the samurai, who were barred by tradition and prejudice from commercial activities. Although some profited from their transformation into a managerial class on the daimyo domains, most still relied on their revenues from rice lands, which were often insufficient to cover their rising expenses; consequently, they fell heavily into debt. Others were released from servitude to their lord and became "masterless samurai." Occasionally, these unemployed warriors (known as *ronin*, or "wave men") revolted or plotted against the local authorities. In one episode, made famous in song and story as the "Forty-Seven Ronin," the masterless samurai of a local lord who had been forced to commit suicide by a shogunate official later assassinated the official in revenge. Although their act received wide popular acclaim, the *ronin* were later forced to take their own lives.

The effects of economic developments on the rural population during the Tokugawa era are harder to estimate. Some farm families benefited by exploiting the growing demand for cash crops. But not all prospered. Most peasants continued to rely on rice cultivation and were whipsawed between declining profits and rising costs and taxes (as daimyo expenses increased, land taxes often took up to 50 percent of the annual harvest). Many were forced to become tenants or to work as wage laborers on the farms of wealthy neighbors or in village industries. When rural conditions in some areas became desperate, peasant revolts erupted. According to one estimate, nearly seven thousand disturbances took place during the Tokugawa era. In general, though, the rural unrest was probably motivated less by a decline in the standard of living than by local factors and a new sense of peasant assertiveness. Peasant disturbances became a more or less routine means of protesting against rising taxes and official corruption or of demanding "benevolence" from the manor lord in times of climatic disaster.

Some Japanese historians, influenced by a Marxist view of history, have interpreted such evidence as an indication that the Tokugawa economic system was highly exploitative,

Chronology

JAPAN AND KOREA DURING THE EARLY MODERN ERA

First phonetic alphabet in Korea	Fifteenth century
Portuguese merchants arrive in Japan	1543
Francis Xavier arrives in Japan	1549
Rule of Oda Nobunaga	1568–1582
Seizure of Kyoto	1568
Rule of Toyotomi Hideyoshi	1582–1598
Edict prohibiting Christianity in Japan	1587
Invades Korea	1592
Death of Toyotomi Hideyoshi and withdrawal of army from Korea	1598
Rule of Tokugawa Ieyasu	1598–1616
Creation of Tokugawa shogunate	1603
Dutch granted permission to trade at Nagasaki	1609
Order evicting Christian missionaries	1612
Yi dynasty of Korea declares fealty to China	1630s
Christian uprising suppressed	1637
Dutch post at Nagasaki transferred to Hirado	1641

with feudal aristocrats oppressing powerless peasants. Recent scholars, however, have tended to adopt a more balanced view, maintaining that both agriculture and manufacturing and commerce experienced extensive growth. Some point out that although the population doubled in the seventeenth century, a relatively low rate for the time period, so did the amount of cultivable land, while agricultural technology made significant advances.

The relatively low rate of population growth probably meant that Japanese peasants were spared the kind of land hunger that many of their counterparts in China faced. Recent evidence indicates that the primary reasons for the relatively low rate of population growth were late marriage, abortion, and infanticide. As Honda Toshiaki, a late-eighteenth-century demographer, described:

> Aware that if they have many children they will not have any property to leave them, [husbands and wives] confer and decide that rather than rear children who in later years will have great difficulty in making a decent living, it is better to take precautions before they are born and not add another mouth to feed. If they do have a child, they secretly destroy it, calling the process by the euphemism of "thinning out."[13]

KEEPING TO THE STRAIGHT AND NARROW IN TOKUGAWA JAPAN

ike the Qing dynasty in China, the Tokugawa shoguns attempted to keep their subjects in line with decrees that carefully prescribed all kinds of behavior. As this decree, which was circulated in all Japanese villages, shows, the bakufu sought to be the moral instructor as well as the guardian and protector of the Japanese people. Compare and contrast this decree with Emperor Kangxi's Sacred Edict in the box earlier in this chapter.

MAXIMS FOR PEASANT BEHAVIOR

1. Young people are forbidden to congregate in great numbers.
2. Entertainments unsuited to peasants, such as playing the samisen or reciting ballad dramas, are forbidden.
3. Staging sumo matches is forbidden for the next five years.
4. The edict on frugality issued by the *han* at the end of last year must be observed.
5. Social relations in the village must be conducted harmoniously.
6. If a person has to leave the village for business or pleasure, that person must return by ten at night.
7. Father and son are forbidden to stay overnight at another person's house. An exception is to be made if it is to nurse a sick person.
8. Corvée [obligatory labor] assigned by the *han* must be performed faithfully.
9. Children who practice filial piety must be rewarded.
10. One must never get drunk and cause trouble for others.
11. Peasants who farm especially diligently must be rewarded.
12. Peasants who neglect farm work and cultivate their paddies and upland fields in a slovenly and careless fashion must be punished.
13. The boundary lines of paddy and upland fields must not be changed arbitrarily.
14. Recognition must be accorded to peasants who contribute greatly to village political affairs.
15. Fights and quarrels are forbidden in the village.
16. The deteriorating customs and morals of the village must be rectified.
17. Peasants who are suffering from poverty must be identified and helped.
18. This village has a proud history compared to other villages, but in recent years bad times have come upon us. Everyone must rise at six in the morning, cut grass, and work hard to revitalize the village.
19. The punishments to be meted out to violators of the village code and gifts to be awarded the deserving are to be decided during the last assembly meeting of the year.

Life in the Village

The changes that took place during the Tokugawa era had a major impact on the lives of ordinary Japanese. In some respects, the result was an increase in the power of the central government at the village level. The shogunate increasingly relied on Confucian maxims advocating obedience and hierarchy to enhance its authority with the general population. Decrees from the *bakufu* instructed the peasants on all aspects of their lives, including their eating habits and their behavior (see the box above). At the same time, the increased power of the government led to more autonomy from the local daimyo for the peasants. Villages now had more control over their local affairs and were responsible to the central government as much as to the nearby manor lord, although land taxes were still paid to the daimyo.

At the same time, the Tokugawa era saw the emergence of the nuclear family (*ie*) as the basic unit in Japanese society. In previous times, Japanese peasants had few legal rights. Most were too poor to keep their conjugal family unit intact or to pass property on to their children. Many lived at the manorial residence or worked as servants in the households of more affluent villagers. Now, with farm income on the rise, the nuclear family took on the same form as in China, although without the joint family concept. The Japanese system of inheritance was based on primogeniture. Family property was passed on to the eldest son, although younger sons often received land from their parents to set up their own families after marriage.

Another result of the changes under the Tokugawa was that women were somewhat more restricted than they had been previously. The rights of females were especially restricted in the samurai class, where Confucian values were highly influential. Male heads of households had broad authority over property, marriage, and divorce; wives were expected to obey their husbands on pain of death. Males often took concubines or homosexual partners, while females were expected to remain chaste. The male offspring of samurai parents studied the Confucian classics in schools established by the daimyo, while females were reared at home, where only the fortunate might receive a rudimentary training in reading and writing Chinese characters. Some women, however, became accomplished poets and painters since, in aristocratic circles, female literacy was prized for enhancing the refinement, social graces, and moral virtue of the home. Under the Tokugawa, it was the obligation of the wife in elite families to reflect her husband's rank and status through a strict code of comportment and dress.

Women were similarly at a disadvantage among the common people. Marriages were arranged, and as in China, the new wife moved in with the family of her husband. A wife who did not meet the expectations of her spouse or his family was likely to be divorced. Still, gender relations were more egalitarian than among the nobility. Women were generally valued as childbearers and homemakers, and both sexes worked in the fields. Coeducational schools were established in villages and market towns, and about one-quarter of the students were female. Poor families, however, often put infant daughters to death or sold them into prostitution and the "floating world" of entertainment (see "The Literature of the New Middle Class" later in this chapter). During the late Tokugawa era, peasant women became more outspoken and active in social protests and in some cases played a major role in provoking demonstrations against government exactions or exploitative acts by landlords or merchants.

Such attitudes toward women operated within the context of the increasingly rigid stratification of Japanese society. Deeply conservative in their social policies, the Tokugawa rulers established strict legal distinctions between the four main classes in Japan (warriors, artisans, peasants, and merchants). Intermarriage between classes was forbidden in theory, although sometimes the prohibitions were ignored in practice. Below these classes were Japan's outcasts, the *eta*. Formerly, they were permitted to escape their status, at least in theory. The Tokugawa made their status hereditary and enacted severe discriminatory laws against them, regulating their place of residence, their dress, and even their hairstyles.

Tokugawa Culture

Under the Tokugawa, the tensions between the old society and the emerging new one were starkly reflected in the arena of culture. On the one hand, the classical culture, influenced by Confucian themes, Buddhist quietism, and the samurai warrior tradition, continued to flourish under the patronage of the shogunate. On the other, a vital new set of cultural values began to appear, especially in the cities. This innovative era witnessed the rise of popular literature written by and for the townspeople. With the development of woodblock printing in the early seventeenth century, literature became available to the common people, literacy levels rose, and lending libraries increased the accessibility of the printed word. In contrast to the previous mood of doom and gloom, the new prose was cheerful and even frivolous, its primary aim being to divert and amuse.

THE LITERATURE OF THE NEW MIDDLE CLASS

The best examples of this new urban fiction are the works of Saikaku (1642–1693), considered one of Japan's finest novelists. Saikaku's greatest novel, *Five Women Who Loved Love*, relates the amorous exploits of five women of the merchant class. Based partly on real-life experiences, it broke from the Confucian ethic of wifely fidelity to her husband and portrayed women who were willing to die for love—and all but one eventually did. Despite the tragic circumstances, the tone of the novel is upbeat and sometimes comic, and the author's wry comments prevent the reader from becoming emotionally involved with the heroines' misfortunes. In addition to heterosexual novels for the merchant class, Saikaku wrote of homosexual liaisons among the samurai.

In the theater, the rise of *Kabuki* threatened the long dominance of the *No* play, replacing the somewhat restrained and elegant thematic and stylistic approach of the classical drama with a new emphasis on violence, music, and dramatic gestures. Significantly, the new drama emerged not from the rarefied world of the court but from the new world of entertainment and amusement. Its very commercial success, however, led to difficulties with the government, which periodically attempted to restrict or even suppress it. Early *Kabuki* was often performed by prostitutes, and shogunate officials, fearing that such activities could have a corrupting effect on the nation's morals, prohibited women from appearing on the stage; at the same time, they attempted to create a new professional class of male actors to impersonate female characters on stage. The decree had a mixed effect, however, because it encouraged homosexual activities, which had been popular among the samurai and in Buddhist monasteries since medieval times. Yet the use of male actors also promoted a greater emphasis on physical activities such as acrobatics and swordplay and furthered the evolution of *Kabuki* into a mature dramatic art.

In contrast to the popular literature of the Tokugawa period, poetry persevered in its more serious tradition. Although linked verse, so popular in the fourteenth and fifteenth centuries, found a more lighthearted expression in the sixteenth century, the most exquisite poetry was produced in the seventeenth century by the greatest of all Japanese poets, Basho (1644–1694). He was concerned with the search for the meaning of existence and the poetic expression of his experience. Basho's genius lies in his sudden juxtaposition of a general or eternal condition with an immediate perception, an electrical spark that instantly reveals a moment of truth. With his love of Daoism and Zen Buddhism, Basho found answers to his quest for the meaning of life in nature, and his poems are grounded in seasonal imagery. The following are among his most famous poems:

The ancient pond
A frog leaps in
The sound of the water.

On the withered branch
A crow has alighted—
The end of autumn.

His last poem, dictated to a disciple only three days prior to his death, succinctly expressed his frustration with the unfinished business of life:

On a journey, ailing—
my dreams roam about
on a withered moor.

Like all great artists, Basho made his poems seem effortless and simple. He speaks directly to everyone, everywhere.

TOKUGAWA ART

Art also reflected the dynamism and changes in Japanese culture under the Tokugawa regime. The shogun's order that all daimyo and their families live every other year in Edo set off a burst of building as provincial rulers competed to erect the most magnificent mansion. Furthermore, the shoguns themselves constructed splendid castles adorned with sumptuous, almost ostentatious decor and furnishings. And the prosperity of the newly rising merchant class added fuel to the fire. Japanese paintings, architecture, textiles, and ceramics all flourished during this affluent era.

Court painters filled magnificent multipaneled screens with gold foil, which was also used to cover walls and even ceilings. This lavish use of gold foil mirrored the grandeur of the new Japanese rulers but also served a practical purpose: it reflected light in the dark castle rooms, where windows were kept small for defensive purposes. In contrast to the almost gaudy splendors of court painting, however, some Japanese artists of the late sixteenth century returned to the tradition of black ink wash. No longer copying the Chinese, these masterpieces expressed Japanese themes and techniques. In *Pine Forest* by Tohaku, a pair of six-panel screens depicting pine trees, 85 percent of the paper is left blank, suggesting mist and the quiet of an autumn dawn.

Although Japan was isolated from the Western world during much of the Tokugawa era, Japanese art was enriched by ideas from other cultures. Japanese pottery makers borrowed both techniques and designs from Korea to produce handsome ceramics. The passion for "Dutch learning" inspired Japanese to study Western medicine, astronomy, and languages and also led to experimentation with oil painting and Western ideas of perspective and the interplay of light and dark. Some painters depicted the "southern barbarians," with their strange ships and costumes, large noses, and plumed hats. Europeans desired Japanese lacquerware and metalwork, inlaid with ivory and mother-of-pearl, and especially the ceramics, which were now as highly prized as those of the Chinese.

Courtesy of William J. Duiker

A JAPANESE CASTLE.   In imitation of European castle architecture, the Japanese perfected a new type of fortress-palace in the early seventeenth century. Strategically placed high on a hilltop, constructed of heavy stone with tiny windows and fortified by numerous watchtowers and massive walls, these strongholds were impregnable to arrows and catapults. They served as a residence for the local daimyo, while the castle compound also housed his army and contained the seat of the local government. Himeji Castle, shown here, is one of the most beautiful in Japan.

Perhaps the most famous of all Japanese art of the Tokugawa era is the woodblock print. Genre painting, or representations of daily life, began in the sixteenth century and found its new mass-produced form in the eighteenth-century woodblock print. The now literate mercantile class was eager for illustrated texts of the amusing and bawdy tales that had circulated in oral tradition. At first, these prints were done in black and white, but later they included vibrant colors. The self-confidence of the age is dramatically captured in these prints, which represent a collective self-portrait of the late Tokugawa urban classes. Some prints depict entire city blocks filled with people, trades, and festivals, while others show the interiors of houses; thus they provide us with excellent visual documentation of the times. Others portray the "floating world" of the entertainment quarter, with scenes of carefree revelers enjoying the pleasures of life.

One of the most renowned of the numerous block-print artists was Utamaro (1754–1806), who painted erotic and sardonic women in everyday poses, such as walking down the street, cooking, or drying their bodies after a bath.

Hokusai (1760–1849) was famous for *Thirty-Six Views of Mount Fuji,* a new and bold interpretation of the Japanese landscape. Finally, Ando Hiroshige (1797–1858) developed the genre of the travelogue print in his *Fifty-Three Stations of the Tokaido Road,* which presented ordinary scenes of daily life, both in the country and in the cities, all enveloped in a lyrical, quiet mood.

Why did a new popular culture begin to appear in Tokugawa Japan while traditional values continued to prevail in neighboring China? One factor was the rapid growth of the cities as the main point of convergence for all the dynamic forces taking place in Japanese society. But other factors may have been at work as well. Despite the patent efforts of the Tokugawa rulers to promote traditional Confucian values, Confucian doctrine had historically occupied a relatively weak position in Japanese society. In China, the scholar-gentry class served as the traditional defenders and propagators of traditional orthodoxy, but the samurai, who were steeped in warrior values and had little exposure to Confucian learning, did not play a similar role in Japan. Tokugawa policies also contributed. Whereas the scholar-gentry class in Qing China continued to reside in the villages, serving as members of the local council or as instructors in local schools, the samurai class in Japan was deliberately isolated from the remainder of the population by government fiat and class privilege. The result was an ideological and cultural vacuum that would eventually be filled by the growing population of merchants and artisans in the major cities.

➤ **THE FLOATING WORLD OF EDO.** In eighteenth-century Japan, the self-confidence of the newly affluent bourgeoisie expressed itself in the woodblock print. Many prints portrayed the "floating world," as the pleasure district in Edo was called. Seen here are courtesans, storytellers, jesters, and various other entertainers. Like their counterparts in Europe, city-dwellers in Japan were beginning to create a new popular culture distinct from the elite culture of the nobility as reflected by the growing popularity of *Kabuki* drama.

KOREA: THE HERMIT KINGDOM

While Japan was gradually moving away from its agrarian origins, the Yi dynasty in Korea was attempting to pattern its own society on the Chinese model. The dynasty had been founded by the military commander Yi Song Gye in the late fourteenth century and immediately set out to establish close political and cultural relations with the Ming dynasty. From their new capital at Seoul, located on the Han River in the center of the peninsula, the Yi rulers accepted a tributary relationship with their powerful neighbor and engaged in the wholesale adoption of Chinese institutions and values. As in China, the civil service examinations tested candidates on their knowledge of the Confucian classics, and success was viewed as an essential step toward upward mobility.

There were differences, however. As in Japan, the dynasty continued to restrict entry into the bureaucracy to members of the aristocratic class, known in Korea as the *yangban* (or "two groups," the civilian and military). At the same time, the peasantry remained in serflike conditions, working on government estates or on the manor holdings of the landed elite. A class of slaves (*chonmin*) labored on government plantations or served in certain occupations, such as butchers and entertainers, considered beneath the dignity of other groups in the population.

Eventually, Korean society began to show signs of independence from Chinese orthodoxy. In the fifteenth century, a phonetic alphabet for writing the Korean spoken language (*hangul*) was devised. Although it was initially held in contempt by the elites and used primarily as a teaching device, eventually it became the medium for private correspondence and the publishing of fiction for a popular audience. At the same time, changes were taking place in the economy, where rising agricultural production contributed to a population increase and the appearance of a small urban industrial and commercial sector, and in society, where the long domination of the *yangban* class began to weaken. As their numbers increased and their power and influence declined, some *yangban* became merchants or even moved into the ranks of the peasantry, further blurring the distinction between the aristocratic class and the common people.

In general, Korean rulers tried to keep the country isolated from the outside world, but they were not always successful. The Japanese invasion under Toyotomi Hideyoshi in the late sixteenth century had a disastrous impact on Korean society. A Manchu force invaded northern Korea in the 1630s and eventually compelled the Yi dynasty to grant allegiance to the new imperial government in Beijing. Korea was relatively untouched by the arrival of European merchants and missionaries, although information about Christianity was brought to the peninsula by Koreans returning from tribute missions to China, and a small

> **ONE OF THE FIFTY-THREE STATIONS ALONG THE TOKAIDO ROAD.** This block print by the famous Japanese artist Hiroshige shows the movement of goods along the main trunk road stretching from Kyoto to Edo in mid-nineteenth-century Japan. With gentle humor, Hiroshige portrayed in a series of color paintings the customs of travelers passing through various post stations along the east coast road. These romantic and somewhat fanciful scenes, very popular at the time, evoke an idyllic past, filling today's viewer with nostalgia for the old Japan.

Catholic community was established there in the late eighteenth century.

CONCLUSION

When Christopher Columbus sailed from southern Spain in his three ships in August 1492, he was seeking a route to China and Japan. He did not find it, but others soon did. In 1514, Portuguese ships arrived on the coast of southern China. Thirty years later, a small contingent of Portuguese merchants became the first Europeans to set foot on the islands of Japan.

At first the new arrivals were welcomed, if only as curiosities. Eventually, several European nations estab-

> **SEOUL PALACE PAGODA.** When the Yi dynasty came into power in the late fourteenth century, it established its capital at Seoul on the Han River. There it constructed a new palace. Korean public architecture was highly influenced by the Chinese classical model, as the multitiered pagoda on the palace grounds attests.

lished trade relations with China and Japan, and Christian missionaries of various religious orders were active in both countries and in Korea as well. But their success was short-lived. Europeans eventually began to be perceived as detrimental to law and order, and during the seventeenth century, the majority of the foreign merchants and missionaries were evicted from all three countries. From that time until the middle of the nineteenth century, China, Japan, and Korea were relatively little affected by events taking place beyond their borders.

That fact deluded many observers into the assumption that the societies of East Asia were essentially stagnant, characterized by agrarian institutions and values reminiscent of those of the feudal era in Europe. As we have seen, however, that picture is misleading, for all three countries were changing and by the early nineteenth century were quite different from what they had been three centuries earlier.

Ironically, these changes were especially marked in Tokugawa Japan, an allegedly "closed country," where traditional classes and institutions were under increasing strain, not only from the emergence of a new merchant class, but also from the centralizing tendencies of the powerful Tokugawa shogunate. Some historians have seen strong parallels between Tokugawa Japan and early modern Europe, which gave birth to centralized empires and a strong merchant class during the same period. The image of the monarchy is reflected in a song sung at the shrine of Toyotomi Hideyoshi in Kyoto:

> Who's that
> Holding over four hundred provinces
> In the palm of his hand
> And entertaining at a tea-party?
> It's His Highness
> So mighty, so impressive![14]

By the beginning of the nineteenth century, then, powerful tensions, reflecting a growing gap between ideal and reality, were at work in both Chinese and Japanese society. Under these conditions, both countries were soon forced to face a new challenge from the aggressive power of an industrializing Europe.

	1400	1450	1500	1550	1600	1650	1700	1750	1800

China
Rise of Ming dynasty
Voyage of Zhenghe
Portuguese arrive in southern China
Manchus seize China
Reign of Kangxi
First English trading post at Canton
Reign of Qianlong
White Lotus Rebellion

Japan
Rule of Oda Nobunaga
Rule of Toyotomi Hideyoshi
Portuguese sailors land in Japan
Rule of Tokugawa Ieyasu
Christian uprising suppressed
Christian missionaries expelled from Japan

Korea
Phonetic alphabet for Korean language devised
European post established in Korea

CHAPTER NOTES

1. From Jonathan D. Spence, *Emperor of China: Self-Portrait of K'ang Hsi* (New York, 1974), pp. 143–144.
2. Quoted in J. H. Parry, ed., *The European Reconnaissance: Selected Documents* (New York, 1968), p. 129.
3. Richard Strassberg, *The World of K'ang Shang-jen: A Man of Letters in Early Ch'ing China* (New York, 1983), p. 275.
4. Quoted in Frederick Wakeman Jr., *The Great Enterprise: The Manchu Reconstruction of Imperial Order in Seventeenth-Century China* (Berkeley, Calif., 1985), p. 16.
5. Lynn Struve, *The Southern Ming, 1644–1662* (New Haven, Conn., 1984), p. 61.
6. J. L. Cranmer-Byng, *An Embassy to China: Lord Macartney's Journal, 1793–1794* (London, 1912), p. 340.
7. Daniel J. Boorstin, *The Discoverers: A History of Man's Search to Know His World and Himself* (New York, 1983), p. 63.
8. C. R. Boxer, ed., *South China in the Sixteenth Century* (London, 1953), p. 265.
9. Chie Nakane and Sinzaburo Oishi, eds., *Tokugawa Japan* (Tokyo, 1990), p. 14.
10. Quoted in Jurgis Elisonas, "Christianity and the Daimyo," in John Whitney Hall, ed., *The Cambridge History of Japan*, vol. 4 (Cambridge, 1991), p. 360.
11. Engelbert Kaempfer, *The History of Japan: Together with a Description of the Kingdom of Siam, 1690–1692*, vol. 2 (Glasgow, 1906), pp. 173–174.
12. Parry, *European Reconnaissance*, p. 144.
13. Quoted in Donald Keene, *The Japanese Discovery of Europe, 1720–1830*, rev. ed. (Stanford, Calif., 1969), p. 114.
14. Quoted in Ryusaku Tsunda et al., *Sources of Japanese Tradition* (New York, 1964), p. 313.

SUGGESTED READING

For a general overview of this period in East Asian history, see volumes 8 and 9 of F. W. Mote and D. Twitchett, eds., *The Cambridge History of China* (Cambridge, 1976), and J. W. Hall, ed., *The Cambridge History of Japan*, vol. 4 (Cambridge, 1991).

For information on Chinese voyages into the Indian Ocean, see P. Snow, *The Star Raft: China's Encounter with Africa* (Ithaca, N.Y., 1988). Also see Ma Huan, *Ying-hai Sheng-lan: The Overall Survey of the Ocean's Shores* (Bagkok, 1996), an ocean survey by a fifteenth-century Chinese cataloger. Early documents on European activities can be found in J. H. Parry, *The European Reconnaissance: Selected Documents* (New York, 1968).

On the late Ming, see J. D. Spence, *The Search for Modern China* (New York, 1990), and L. Struve, *The Southern Ming, 1644–1662* (New Haven, Conn., 1984). On the rise of the Qing, see F. Wakeman Jr., *The Great Enterprise: The Manchu Reconstruction of Imperial Order in Seventeenth-Century China* (Berkeley, Calif., 1985). On Kangxi, see J. D. Spence, *Emperor of China: Self-Portrait of K'ang Hsi* (New York, 1974). Social issues are discussed in S. Naquin and E. Rawski, *Chinese Society in the Eighteenth Century* (New Haven, Conn., 1987). Also see J. D. Spence and J. Wills, eds., *From Ming to Ch'ing* (New Haven, Conn., 1979). For a very interesting account of Jesuit missionary experiences in China, see L. J. Gallagher, ed. and trans., *China in the Sixteenth Century: The Journals of Matthew Ricci, 1583–1616* (New York, 1953). For brief biographies of Ming-Qing luminaries such as Wang Yangming, Zheng Chenggong, and Emperor Qianlong, see J. E. Wills Jr., *Mountains of Fame: Portraits in Chinese History* (Princeton, N.J., 1994).

The best surveys of Chinese literature are Liu Wu-chi, *An Introduction to Chinese Literature* (Bloomington, Ind., 1966); S. Owen, *An Anthology of Chinese Literature: Beginnings to 1911* (New York, 1996);

and V. Mair, *The Columbia Anthology of Traditional Chinese Literature* (New York, 1994). For a concise and comprehensive introduction to the Chinese art of this period, see M. Sullivan, *The Arts of China,* 4th ed. (Berkeley, Calif., 1999); C. Clunas, *Art in China* (Oxford, 1997); and M. Tregear, *Chinese Art,* rev. ed. (London, 1997). For the best introduction to the painting of this era, see J. Cahill, *Chinese Painting* (New York, 1977), and Yang Xin et al., *Three Thousand Years of Chinese Paintings* (New Haven, Conn., 1997).

On Japan before the rise of the Tokugawa, see J. W. Hall et al., eds., *Japan Before Tokugawa: Political Consolidation and Economic Growth* (Princeton, N.J., 1981), and G. Elison and B. L. Smith, eds., *Warlords, Artists, and Commoners: Japan in the Sixteenth Century* (Honolulu, 1981). See also M. E. Berry, *Hideyoshi* (Cambridge, Mass., 1982), the first biography of this fascinating figure in Japanese history. On the first Christian activities, see G. Elison, *Deus Destroyed: The Image of Christianity in Early Modern Japan* (Cambridge, Mass., 1973), and C. R. Boxer, *The Christian Century in Japan, 1549–1650* (Berkeley, Calif., 1951). Buddhism is dealt with in N. McMullin, *Buddhism and the State in Sixteenth Century Japan* (Princeton, N.J., 1984).

On the Tokugawa era, see H. Bolitho, *Treasures Among Men: The Fudai Daimyo in Tokugawa Japan* (New Haven, Conn., 1974), and R. B. Toby, *State and Diplomacy in Early Modern Japan: Asia in the Development of the Tokugawa Bakufu* (Princeton, N.J., 1984). See also R. N. Bellah, *Tokugawa Religion: The Values of Pre-Industrial Japan* (New York, 1957), and C. I. Mulhern, ed., *Heroic with Grace: Legendary Women of Japan* (Armonk, N.Y., 1991). Three other worthwhile studies are S. Vlastos, *Peasant Protests and Uprisings in Tokugawa Japan* (Berkeley, Calif., 1986); H. Ooms, *Tokugawa Ideology: Early Constructs, 1570–1680* (Princeton, N.J., 1985); and C. Nakane, ed., *Tokugawa Japan: The Social and Economic Antecedents of Modern Japan* (Tokyo, 1990).

For a brief introduction to women in the Ming and Qing dynasties as well as the Tokugawa era, see S. Hughes and B. Hughes, *Women in World History,* vol. 2 (Armonk, N.Y., 1997). To witness Chinese village life in 1670, consult the classic J. D. Spence, *The Death of Woman Wang* (New York, 1978). For women's literacy in seventeenth-century China, see J. Handlin, "Lu K'un's New Audience: The Influence of Women's Literacy on Sixteenth-Century Thought," in *Women in Chinese Society,* eds. M. Wolf and R. Witke (Stanford, Calif., 1975), and D. Ko, *Teachers of the Inner Chambers: Women and Culture in Seventeenth Century China* (Stanford, Calif., 1994). Most valuable is the collection of articles edited by G. L. Bernstein, *Re-Creating Japanese Women, 1600–1945* (Berkeley, Calif., 1991).

Of specific interest to Japanese literature of the Tokugawa era are D. Keene, *World Within Walls: Japanese Literature of the Pre-Modern Era, 1600–1867* (New York, 1976). Of special value for the college student are D. Keene's *Anthology of Japanese Literature* (New York, 1955), *The Pleasures of Japanese Literature* (New York, 1988), and *Japanese Literature: An Introduction for Western Readers* (London, 1953). For an introduction to Basho's life, poems, and criticism, consult the stimulating *Basho and His Interpreters: Selected Hokku with Commentary* (Stanford, Calif., 1991), by M. Ueda.

For the most comprehensive and accessible overview of Japanese art, see P. Mason, *Japanese Art* (New York, 1993). For a concise introduction to Japanese art of the Tokugawa era, see J. Stanley-Baker, *Japanese Art* (London, 1984). For magnificent photographs and stimulating interpretation, consult D. Elisseeff and V. Elisseeff, *Art of Japan* (New York, 1985), and J. E. Kidder Jr., *The Art of Japan* (London, 1985).

INFOTRAC COLLEGE EDITION

For additional reading, go to InfoTrac College Edition, your online research library at
http://web1.infotrac-college.com

Enter the search terms "Ming China" using Keywords.

Enter the search terms "China history" using Keywords.

Enter the search terms "Japan history" using Keywords.

Enter the search term "Tokugawa" using Keywords.

Enter the search term "Qing" using Keywords.

©Réunion des Musées Nationaux/Art Resource, NY

Chapter 17

THE WEST ON THE EVE OF A NEW WORLD ORDER

CHAPTER OUTLINE

- THE ENLIGHTENMENT
- ECONOMIC CHANGES AND THE SOCIAL ORDER
- CHANGING PATTERNS OF WAR: GLOBAL CONFRONTATION
- COLONIAL EMPIRES AND REVOLUTION IN THE WESTERN HEMISPHERE
- TOWARD A NEW POLITICAL ORDER: ENLIGHTENED ABSOLUTISM
- THE FRENCH REVOLUTION
- THE AGE OF NAPOLEON

FOCUS QUESTIONS

- Who were the leading figures of the Enlightenment, and what were their main contributions?
- What changes occurred in the European economy in the eighteenth century, and to what degree were these changes reflected in social patterns?
- How did Spain and Portugal administer their American colonies, and what were the main characteristics of Latin American society in the eighteenth century?
- What do historians mean by the term *enlightened absolutism*, and to what degree did eighteenth-century Prussia, Austria, and Russia exhibit its characteristics?
- What were the causes, the main events, and the results of the American Revolution and the French Revolution? Which aspects of the French Revolution did Napoleon preserve, and which did he destroy?
- ➤ In what ways were the American Revolution, the French Revolution, and the seventeenth-century English revolutions alike? In what ways were they different?

*H*istorians have often portrayed the eighteenth century as the final phase of Europe's old order, before the violent upheaval and reordering of society associated with the French Revolution. The old order—still largely agrarian, dominated by kings and landed aristocrats, and grounded in privileges for nobles, clergy, towns, and provinces—seemed to continue a basic pattern that had prevailed in Europe since medieval times. However, just as a new intellectual order based on rationalism and secularism was emerging in Europe, demographic, economic, social, and political patterns were beginning to change in ways that proclaimed the emergence of a modern new order.

A key factor in the emergence of the new world order was the French Revolution. On the morning of July 14, 1789, a Parisian mob of some eight thousand men and women in search of weapons streamed toward the Bastille, a royal armory filled with arms and ammunition. The Bastille was also a state prison, and although it held only seven prisoners at the time, in the eyes of these angry Parisians, it was a glaring symbol of the government's despotic policies. It was defended by the marquis de Launay and a small garrison of 114 men. The attack on the Bastille began in earnest in the early afternoon, and after three hours of fighting, de Launay and the garrison surrendered. Angered by the loss of ninety-eight protesters, the victors beat de Launay to death, cut off his head, and carried it aloft in triumph through the streets of Paris. When King Louis XVI was told the news of the fall of the Bastille by the duc de La Rochefoucauld-Liancourt, he exclaimed, "Why, this is a revolt." "No, Sire," replied the duke. "It is a revolution."

The French Revolution has been portrayed as a major turning point in European political and social history, as a time when the institutions of the old regime were destroyed and a new order was created based on individual rights, representative institutions, and a concept of loyalty to the nation rather than the monarch. The revolutionary upheavals of the era, especially in France, did create new liberal and national political ideals, summarized in the French revolutionary slogan, "Liberty, Equality, Fraternity," that transformed France and then spread to other European countries and the rest of the world. •

THE ENLIGHTENMENT

The impetus for political and social change in the eighteenth century stemmed in part from the Enlightenment. The Enlightenment was a movement of intellectuals who were greatly impressed with the accomplishments of the Scientific Revolution. When they used the word *reason*—one of their favorite words—they were advocating the application of the scientific method to the understanding of all life. All institutions and all systems of thought were subject to the rational, scientific way of thinking if people would only free themselves from the shackles of past, worthless traditions, especially religious ones. If Isaac Newton could discover the natural laws regulating the world of nature, they too, by using reason, could find the laws that governed human society. This belief in turn led them to hope that they could make progress toward a better society than the one they had inherited. *Reason, natural law, hope, progress*—these were the buzzwords in the heady atmosphere of eighteenth-century Europe.

The Path to Enlightenment

The seventeenth century had witnessed a growing skepticism about religion and an increasing secularization of thought. Skepticism about both Christianity and European culture was nourished by the reports of world travelers. Traders, missionaries, and explorers began to publish books that gave accounts of many different cultures. The great geographical adventures of the eighteenth century, especially the discovery of the Pacific island of Tahiti and of New Zealand and Australia by James Cook, also aroused much enthusiasm in Europe. Cook's *Travels*, an account of his journey, became a best-seller.

For some European intellectuals, the existence of exotic peoples, such as the natives of Tahiti, presented an image of a "natural man" who was far happier than many Europeans. One such intellectual wrote:

> The life of savages is so simple, and our societies are such complicated machines! The Tahitian is close to the origin of the world, while the European is closer to its old age. . . . They understand nothing about our manners or our laws, and they are bound to see in them nothing but shackles disguised in a hundred different ways. Those shackles could only provoke the indignation and scorn of creatures in whom the most profound feeling is a love of liberty.[1]

The idea of the "noble savage" would play an important role in the political work of some eighteenth-century intellectuals.

The travel literature of the seventeenth and eighteenth centuries also led to the realization that there were highly developed civilizations with different customs in other parts of the world. China was especially singled out. One German university professor praised Confucian morality as superior to the intolerant attitudes of Christianity. Some European intellectuals began to evaluate their own civilization relative to others. What had seemed to be practices grounded in reason now appeared to be matters of custom.

NEWTON AND LOCKE

Major sources of inspiration for the Enlightenment were two Englishmen, Isaac Newton and John Locke. Newton contended that the world and everything in it worked like a giant machine. Enchanted by the grand design of this world-machine, the intellectuals of the Enlightenment were convinced that by following Newton's rules of reasoning, they could discover the natural laws that governed politics, economics, justice, and religion.

John Locke's theory of knowledge also made a great impact. In his *Essay Concerning Human Understanding,* written in 1690, Locke denied the existence of innate ideas and argued instead that every person was born with a *tabula rasa,* a blank mind:

> Let us then suppose the mind to be, as we say, white paper, void of all characters, without any ideas. How comes it to be furnished? Whence comes it by that vast store which the busy and boundless fancy of man has painted on it with an almost endless variety? Whence has it all the materials of reason and knowledge? To this I answer, in one word, from experience. . . . Our observation, employed either about external sensible objects or about the internal operations of our minds perceived and reflected on by ourselves, is that which supplies our understanding with all the materials of thinking.[2]

By denying innate ideas, Locke's philosophy implied that people were molded by their environment, by whatever they perceived through their senses from their surrounding world. By changing the environment and subjecting people to proper influences, they could be changed and a new society created. And how should the environment be changed? Newton had paved the way: reason enabled enlightened people to discover the natural laws to which all institutions should conform.

The Philosophes and Their Ideas

The intellectuals of the Enlightenment were known by the French term *philosophes,* although they were not all French and few were philosophers in the strict sense of the term. They were literary people, professors, journalists, economists, political scientists, and above all, social reformers. They came from both the nobility and the middle class, and a few even stemmed from lower-middle-class origins. Although it was a truly international and cosmopolitan movement, the Enlightenment also enhanced the dominant role being played by French culture; Paris

was its recognized capital. Most of the leaders of the Enlightenment were French. The French philosophes, in turn, affected intellectuals elsewhere and created a movement that touched the entire Western world, including the British and Spanish colonies in America (see Map 17.1).

To the philosophes, the role of philosophy was not just to discuss the world but to change it. As one writer said, the philosophe "applies himself to the study of society with the purpose of making his kind better and happier." To the philosophes, reason was a scientific method, and it relied on an appeal to facts. A spirit of rational criticism was to be applied to everything, including religion and politics.

Spanning almost a century, the Enlightenment evolved with each succeeding generation, becoming more radical as new thinkers built on the contributions of their predecessors. A few individuals, however, dominated the landscape so completely that we can gain insight into the core ideas of the philosophes by focusing on the three French giants—Montesquieu, Voltaire, and Diderot.

MONTESQUIEU

Charles de Secondat, the baron de Montesquieu (1689–1755), came from the French nobility. His most famous work, *The Spirit of the Laws,* was published in 1748. In this comparative study of governments, Montesquieu attempted to apply the scientific method to the social and political arena to ascertain the "natural laws" governing the social and political relationships of human beings. Montesquieu distinguished three basic kinds of governments: republics, which are suitable for small states and based on citizen involvement; monarchy, appropriate for middle-sized states and grounded in the ruling class's adherence to law; and despotism, apt for large empires and relying on fear to inspire obedience. Montesquieu used England as an example of monarchy, and it was his analysis of England's constitution that led to his most lasting contribution to political thought—the importance of checks and balances achieved by means of a separation of powers. He believed that England's system, with its separate executive, legislative, and judicial powers that served to limit and control each other, provided the greatest freedom and security for a state. The translation of his work into English two years after publication ensured its being read by American political leaders, who eventually incorporated its principles into the U.S. Constitution.

VOLTAIRE

The greatest figure of the Enlightenment was François-Marie Arouet, known simply as Voltaire (1694–1778). Son of a prosperous middle-class family from Paris, he studied

THE ATTACK ON RELIGIOUS INTOLERANCE

Although Voltaire's ideas on religion were in no way original, his lucid prose, biting satire, and clever wit caused his works to be widely read and all the more influential. These two selections present different sides of Voltaire's attack on religious intolerance. The first is from his straightforward treatise The Ignorant Philosopher, *and the second is from his only real literary masterpiece, the novel* Candide, *where he uses humor to make the same fundamental point about religious intolerance.*

VOLTAIRE, *THE IGNORANT PHILOSOPHER*

The contagion of fanaticism then still subsists. . . . The author of the Treatise upon Toleration has not mentioned the shocking executions wherein so many unhappy victims perished in the valleys of Piedmont. He has passed over in silence the massacre of six hundred inhabitants of Valtelina, men, women, and children, who were murdered by the Catholics in the month of September, 1620. I will not say it was with the consent and assistance of the archbishop of Milan, Charles Borome, who was made a saint. Some passionate writers have averred this fact, which I am very far from believing; but I say, there is scarce any city or borough in Europe where blood has not been spilt for religious quarrels; I say, that the human species has been perceptibly diminished because women and girls were massacred as well as men; I say, that Europe would have had a third larger population if there had been no theological disputes. In fine, I say, that so far from forgetting these abominable times, we should frequently take a view of them, to inspire an eternal horror for them; and that it is for our age to make reparation by toleration, for this long collection of crimes, which has taken place through the want of toleration, during sixteen barbarous centuries.

Let it not then be said, that there are no traces left of that shocking fanaticism, of the want of toleration; they are still everywhere to be met with, even in those countries that are esteemed the most humane. The Lutheran and Calvinist preachers, were they masters, would, perhaps, be as little inclined to pity, as obdurate, as insolent as they upbraid their antagonists with being.

VOLTAIRE, *CANDIDE*

At last [Candide] approached a man who had just been addressing a big audience for a whole hour on the subject of charity. The orator peered at him and said:

"What is your business here? Do you support the Good Old Cause?"

"There is no effect without a cause," replied Candide modestly. "All things are necessarily connected and arranged for the best. It was my fate to be driven from Lady Cunégonde's presence and made to run the gauntlet, and now I have to beg my bread until I can earn it. Things could not have happened otherwise."

"Do you believe that the Pope is Antichrist, my friend?" said the minister.

"I have never heard anyone say so," replied Candide; "but whether he is or he isn't, I want some food."

"You don't deserve to eat," said the other. "Be off with you, you villain, you wretch! Don't come near me again or you'll suffer for it."

The minister's wife looked out of the window at that moment, and seeing a man who was not sure that the Pope was Antichrist, emptied over his head a chamber pot, which shows to what lengths ladies are driven by religious zeal.

---

law, although he achieved his first success as a playwright. Voltaire was a prolific author and wrote an almost endless stream of pamphlets, novels, plays, letters, philosophical essays, and histories. His writings brought him both fame and wealth.

Voltaire was especially well known for his criticism of traditional religion and his strong attachment to the ideal of religious toleration (see the box above). As he grew older, Voltaire became ever more strident in his denunciations. "Crush the infamous thing," he thundered repeatedly—the infamous thing being religious fanaticism, intolerance, and superstition.

Throughout his life, Voltaire championed not only religious tolerance but also deism, a religious outlook shared by most other philosophes. Deism was built on the Newtonian world-machine, which implied the existence of a mechanic (God) who had created the universe. To Voltaire and most other philosophes, the universe was like a clock, and God was the clockmaker who had created it, set it in motion, and allowed it to run according to its own natural laws.

DIDEROT

Denis Diderot (1713–1784) was the son of a skilled craftsman from eastern France who became a freelance writer so that he could be free to study and read in many subjects and languages. One of Diderot's favorite topics was Christianity, which he condemned as fanatical and unreasonable. As he

MAP 17.1   The Enlightenment in Europe. "Have the courage to use your own intelligence!" Immanuel Kant's words epitomize the role of the individual in using reason to understand all aspects of life—the natural world and the sphere of human nature, behavior, and institutions. ➤ *Which countries or regions were at the center of the Enlightenment, and what reasons could account for peripheral regions' being less involved?*

Legend:
- Palaces modeled after Versailles
- Important universities
- Famous European academic centers
- Publication of scientific or philosophical journals
- Location of observatories

Map labels: Arctic Ocean; North Sea; Atlantic Ocean; Mediterranean Sea; Uppsala; Stockholm; Saint Petersburg; Glasgow; Edinburgh; Copenhagen; Danzig; Warsaw; Cambridge; London; Amsterdam; Leiden; Göttingen; Berlin; Greenwich; Halle; Leipzig; Paris; Versailles; Strasbourg; Vienna; Geneva; Turin; Venice; Bologna; Pisa; Florence; Rome; Naples; Lisbon; Madrid; Corsica; Sardinia; Sicily; Balearic Islands; Danube R.; Loire R.; Ebro R.

Scale: 0 300 600 900 Kilometers; 0 300 600 Miles

grew older, his literary attacks on Christianity grew more vicious. Of all religions, Christianity, he averred, was the worst, "the most absurd and the most atrocious in its dogma."

Diderot's most famous contribution to the Enlightenment was the *Encyclopedia, or Classified Dictionary of the Sciences, Arts, and Trades,* a twenty-eight-volume compendium of knowledge that he edited and referred to as the "great work of his life." Its purpose, according to Diderot, was to "change the general way of thinking." It did precisely that in becoming a major weapon of the philosophes' crusade against the old French society. The contributors included many philosophes who attacked religious intolerance and advocated a program for social, legal, and political improvements that would lead to a society that was more cosmopolitan, more tolerant, more humane, and more reasonable. The *Encyclopedia* was sold to doctors, clergymen, teachers, lawyers, and even military officers, thus spreading the ideas of the Enlightenment.

TOWARD A NEW "SCIENCE OF MAN"

The Enlightenment belief that Newton's scientific methods could be used to discover the natural laws underlying all areas of human life led to the emergence in the eighteenth century of what the philosophes called a "science of man," or what we would call the social sciences. In a number of areas, such as economics, politics, and education, the philosophes arrived at natural laws that they believed governed human actions.

The Physiocrats and Adam Smith have been viewed as founders of the modern discipline of economics. The leader of the Physiocrats was François Quesnay (1694–1774), a highly successful French doctor. Quesnay and the Physiocrats claimed they would discover the natural economic laws that governed human society. Their major "natural law" of economics was that individuals should be left free to pursue their own economic self-interest. Through the actions of these individuals, all society would ultimately benefit. Consequently, they argued that the state should in no way interrupt the free play of natural economic forces by government regulations on the economy, but should leave it alone, a doctrine that subsequently became known as *laissez-faire* (French for "leave it alone").

The best statement of *laissez-faire* was made in 1776 by a Scottish philosopher, Adam Smith (1723–1790), in his famous work *The Wealth of Nations*. Like the Physiocrats, Smith believed that the state should not interfere in economic matters; indeed, he gave to government only three basic functions: it should protect society from invasion (army), defend its citizens from injustice (police), and keep up certain public works, such as roads and canals that private individuals could not afford.

THE LATER ENLIGHTENMENT

By the late 1760s, a new generation of philosophes who had grown up with the worldview of the Enlightenment began to move beyond their predecessors' beliefs. Most famous was Jean-Jacques Rousseau (1712–1778), whose political beliefs were presented in two major works. In his *Discourse on the Origins of the Inequality of Mankind*, Rousseau argued that people had adopted laws and governors in order to preserve their private property. In the process, they had become enslaved by government. What, then, should people do to regain their freedom? In his celebrated treatise *The Social Contract*, published in 1762, Rousseau found an answer in the concept of the social contract. In a social contract, an entire society agreed to be governed by its general will. Each individual might have a particular will contrary to the general will, but if the individual put his particular will (self-interest) above the general will, he should be forced to abide by the general will. "This means nothing less than that he will be forced to be free," said Rousseau, because the general will was not only political but also ethical; it represented what the entire community ought to do.

Another influential treatise by Rousseau was his novel *Émile*, one of the Enlightenment's most important works on education. Rousseau's fundamental concern was that education should foster, rather than restrict, children's natural instincts. Rousseau's own experiences had shown him the importance of the emotions. What he sought was a balance between heart and mind, between emotion and reason.

A LONDON COFFEEHOUSE. Coffeehouses had first appeared in the major cities of the Ottoman Empire in the sixteenth century, where they were often associated with antigovernment activity. Coffeehouses spread quickly throughout Europe by the beginning of the eighteenth century and became a means for spreading Enlightenment ideas. In addition to drinking coffee, patrons of coffeehouses could read magazines and newspapers, exchange ideas, play chess, smoke, and even engage in business transactions. In this scene from a London coffeehouse of 1705, well-attired gentlemen make bids on commodities. Bidding went on until pins, which had been placed in lit candles, fell to the table. Thus bidding stopped when patrons could "hear a pin drop."

THE RIGHTS OF WOMEN

Mary Wollstonecraft responded to an unhappy childhood in a large family by seeking to lead an independent life. Few occupations were available for middle-class women in her day, but she survived by working as a teacher, chaperone, and governess to aristocratic children. All the while, she wrote and developed her ideas on the rights of women. This excerpt was taken from her Vindication of the Rights of Woman, *written in 1792. This work led to her reputation as the foremost British feminist thinker of the eighteenth century.*

MARY WOLLSTONECRAFT, *VINDICATION OF THE RIGHTS OF WOMAN*

It is a melancholy truth—yet such is the blessed effect of civilization—the most respectable women are the most oppressed; and, unless they have understandings far superior to the common run of understandings, taking in both sexes, they must, from being treated like contemptible beings, become contemptible. How many women thus waste life away the prey of discontent, who might have practiced as physicians, regulated a farm, managed a shop, and stood erect, supported by their own industry, instead of hanging their heads surcharged with the dew of sensibility, that consumes the beauty to which it at first gave luster. . . .

Proud of their weakness, however, [women] must always be protected, guarded from care, and all the rough toils that dignify the mind. If this be the fiat of fate, if they will make themselves insignificant and contemptible, sweetly to waste "life away," let them not expect to be valued when their beauty fades, for it is the fate of the fairest flowers to be admired and pulled to pieces by the careless hand that plucked them. In how many ways do I wish, from the purest benevolence, to impress this truth on my sex; yet I fear that they will not listen to a truth that dear-bought experience has brought home to many an agitated bosom, nor willingly resign the privileges of rank and sex for the privileges of humanity, to which those have no claim who do not discharge its duties. . . .

Would men but generously snap our chains, and be content with rational fellowship instead of slavish obedience, they would find us more observant daughters, more affectionate sisters, more faithful wives, and more reasonable mothers—in a word, better citizens. We should then love them with true affection, because we should learn to respect ourselves; and the peace of mind of a worthy man would not be interrupted by the idle vanity of his wife.

But Rousseau did not necessarily practice what he preached. His own children were sent to orphanages, where many children died at a young age. Rousseau also viewed women as "naturally" different from men. In Rousseau's *Émile,* Sophie, Émile's intended wife, was educated for her role as wife and mother by learning obedience and the nurturing skills that would enable her to provide loving care for her husband and children. Not everyone in the eighteenth century, however, agreed with Rousseau.

THE "WOMAN QUESTION" IN THE ENLIGHTENMENT

For centuries, many male intellectuals had argued that the nature of women made them inferior to men and made male domination of women necessary and right. Female thinkers in the eighteenth century, however, provided suggestions for improving the conditions of women. The strongest statement for the rights of women was advanced by the English writer Mary Wollstonecraft (1759–1797), viewed by many as the founder of modern European feminism.

In her *Vindication of the Rights of Women,* written in 1792, Wollstonecraft pointed out two contradictions in the views of women held by such Enlightenment thinkers as Rousseau. To argue that women must obey men, she said, was contrary to the beliefs of the same individuals that a system based on the arbitrary power of monarchs over their subjects or slave owners over their slaves was wrong. The subjection of women to men was equally wrong. In addition, she argued that the Enlightenment was based on an ideal of reason innate in all human beings. If women have reason, then they too are entitled to the same rights that men have. Women, Wollstonecraft declared, should have equal rights with men in education and in economic and political life as well (see the box above).

Culture in an Enlightened Age

Although the Baroque style that had dominated the seventeenth century continued to be popular, by the 1730s, a new style affecting decoration and architecture known as Rococo had spread throughout Europe. Unlike the Baroque, which stressed power, grandeur, and movement, Rococo emphasized grace, charm, and gentle action. Rococo rejected strict geometrical patterns and had a fondness for curves; it liked to follow the wandering lines of natural objects, such as seashells and flowers. It made much use of interlaced designs colored in gold with delicate contours and graceful arcs. Highly secular, its lightness and charm spoke of the pursuit of pleasure, happiness, and love.

Some of Rococo's appeal is evident already in the work of Antoine Watteau (1684–1721), whose lyrical views of aristocratic life, refined, sensual, and civilized, with gen-

⚹ **ANTOINE WATTEAU, *THE PILGRIMAGE TO CYTHERA*.** Antoine Watteau was one of the most gifted painters in eighteenth-century France. His portrayal of aristocratic life reveals a world of elegance, wealth, and pleasure. In this painting, Watteau depicts a group of aristocratic pilgrims about to depart the island of Cythera, where they have paid homage to Venus, the goddess of love.

tlemen and ladies in elegant dress, revealed a world of upper-class pleasure and joy. Underneath that exterior, however, was an element of sadness as the artist revealed the fragility and transitory nature of pleasure, love, and life.

Another aspect of Rococo was that its decorative work could easily be paired with Baroque architecture. The palace at Versailles had made an enormous impact on Europe. "Keeping up with the Bourbons" became important as European rulers built grandiose palaces. While imitating Versailles in size, they were not so much modeled after the French classical style as they were after the seventeenth-century Italian Baroque, as modified by a series of brilliant German and Austrian sculptor-architects. This Baroque-Rococo architectural style typified eighteenth-century palaces and church buildings, and often the same architects designed both. This is evident in the work of one of the greatest architects of the eighteenth century, Balthasar Neumann (1687–1753). One of Neumann's masterpieces was the pilgrimage church of the Vierzehnheiligen (The Fourteen Saints) in southern Germany. Secular and spiritual merge in its lavish and fanciful ornamentation; light, bright colors; and elaborate, rich detail.

⚹ **VIERZEHNHEILIGEN, EXTERIOR VIEW.** Balthasar Neumann, one of the most prominent architects of the eighteenth century, used the Baroque-Rococo style of architecture to design some of the most beautiful buildings of the century. Pictured here is the exterior of his pilgrimage church of the Vierzehnheiligen (Fourteen Saints), located in southern Germany. Although as monumental in size as the Taj Mahal, completed in seventeenth-century India (see page 437), the Vierzehnheiligen possesses a sense of heaviness that differs considerably from the delicate lightness of the Indian architectural masterpiece.

MUSIC

The eighteenth century was unsurpassed in the history of European music. In the first half of the century, two composers—Handel and Bach—stand out as musical geniuses. Johann Sebastian Bach (1685–1750) came from a family of musicians. During his tenure as director of church music

THE WEST ON THE EVE OF A NEW WORLD ORDER • CHAPTER 17   **477**

at the church of Saint Thomas in Leipzig in 1723, Bach composed his Mass in B Minor, his St. Matthew's Passion, and the cantatas and motets that have established his reputation as one of the greatest composers of all time. For Bach, music was above all a means to worship God; his task in life, he said, was to make "well-ordered music in the honor of God."

George Frederick Handel (1685–1759) was, like Bach, born in Saxony in Germany and in the same year. Unlike Bach, however, he was profoundly secular in temperament. He began his career by writing operas in the Italian manner and thereafter remained faithful to the Italian Baroque style. Although he wrote much secular music, Handel is best known for his religious music. Handel's *Messiah* has been called "one of those rare works that appeal immediately to everyone, and yet is indisputably a masterpiece of the highest order."[3]

Bach and Handel perfected the Baroque musical style with its monumental and elaborate musical structures. Two geniuses of the second half of the eighteenth century—Haydn and Mozart—were innovators who wrote music known today as classical.

Franz Joseph Haydn (1732–1809) spent most of his adult life as musical director for the Esterhazy brothers, wealthy Hungarian princes. Haydn was incredibly prolific, composing 104 symphonies in addition to string quartets, concerti, songs, oratorios, and Masses. His visits to England in 1790 and 1794 introduced him to another world, where musicians wrote for public concerts rather than princely patrons. This "liberty," as he called it, induced him to write his two great oratorios, *The Creation* and *The Seasons*, both of which were dedicated to the common people.

Wolfgang Amadeus Mozart (1756–1791) was a child prodigy who gave his first harpsichord concert at six and wrote his first opera at twelve. He, too, sought a patron, but his discontent with the overly demanding archbishop of Salzburg forced him to move to Vienna, where his failure to achieve a permanent patron made his life miserable. Nevertheless, he wrote music prolifically and passionately: string quartets, sonatas, symphonies, concerti, and operas. *The Marriage of Figaro*, *The Magic Flute*, and *Don Giovanni* are three of the world's greatest operas. Mozart composed with an ease of melody and a blend of grace and precision that arguably no one has ever excelled.

HIGH CULTURE

Historians have grown accustomed to distinguishing between a civilization's high culture and its popular culture. High culture is the literary and artistic culture of the educated and wealthy ruling classes; popular culture is the written and unwritten culture of the masses, most of which has traditionally been passed down orally. By the eighteenth century, European high culture reflected the learned tastes of theologians, scientists, philosophers, intellectuals, poets, and dramatists, for all of whom Latin remained a truly international language.

Especially noticeable in the eighteenth century was an expansion of both the reading public and publishing. Whereas French publishers issued three hundred titles in 1750, about sixteen hundred were being published yearly in the 1780s. Although many of these titles were still geared for small groups of the educated elite, many were also directed to the new reading public of the middle classes, which included women and even urban artisans.

An important aspect of the growth of publishing and reading in the eighteenth century was the development of magazines for the general public. Great Britain saw 25 different periodicals published in 1700, 103 in 1760, 158 in 1780. Along with magazines came daily newspapers. The first was printed in London in 1702, but by 1780, thirty-seven other English towns had their own newspapers.

POPULAR CULTURE

The distinguishing characteristic of popular culture is its collective nature. Group activity was especially common in the festival, a broad name used to cover a variety of celebrations: community festivals in Catholic Europe that celebrated the feast day of the local patron saint; annual festivals, such as Christmas and Easter, that go back to medieval Christianity; and Carnival, which was celebrated in the Mediterranean world of Spain, Italy, and France as well as in Germany and Austria. All of these festivals shared common characteristics. They were special occasions on which people ate, drank, and celebrated to excess. In traditional societies, festival was a time of play, since much of the rest of the year consisted of unrelieved work. As the poet Thomas Gray in 1739 said of Carnival in Turin: "One half of the remaining part of the year is passed in remembering the last [Carnival], the other in expecting the future Carnival."[4]

Indeed, the ultimate festival was Carnival, which began after Christmas and lasted until the start of Lent, the forty-day period of fasting and purification leading up to Easter. Because during Lent people were expected to abstain from meat, sex, and most recreations, Carnival was a time of great indulgence when heavy consumption of food and drink were the norm. It was a time of intense sexual activity as well. Songs with double meanings that would ordinarily be considered offensive could be sung publicly at this time of year. A float of Florentine "keymakers," for example, sang this ditty to the ladies: "Our tools are fine, new and useful. We always carry them with us. They are good for anything. If you want to touch them, you can."

ECONOMIC CHANGES AND THE SOCIAL ORDER

The eighteenth century in Europe witnessed the beginning of economic changes that ultimately had a strong impact on the rest of the world.

New Economic Patterns

Europe's population began to grow around 1750 and continued to increase steadily. The total European population was probably around 120 million in 1700, 140 million in 1750, and 190 million in 1790. A falling death rate was perhaps the most important reason for this population growth. Of great significance in lowering death rates was the disappearance of bubonic plague, but so was diet. More plentiful food and better transportation of food supplies led to improved nutrition and relief from devastating famines.

More plentiful food was in part a result of improvements in agricultural practices and methods in the eighteenth century, especially in Britain, parts of France, and the Low Countries. Food production increased as more land was farmed, yields per acre increased, and climate improved. Also important to the increased yields was the cultivation of new vegetables, including two important American crops, the potato and maize (Indian corn). Both had been brought to Europe from the Americas in the sixteenth century.

In European industry in the eighteenth century, the most important product was textiles, most of which were still produced by master artisans in guild workshops. But a shift in textile production to the countryside was spreading to many rural areas of Europe by the "putting-out" or "domestic" system in which a merchant-capitalist entrepreneur bought the raw materials, mostly wool and flax, and "put them out" to rural workers who spun the raw material into yarn and then wove it into cloth on simple looms. Capitalist-entrepreneurs sold the finished product, made a profit, and used it to purchase materials to manufacture more. This system became known as the "cottage industry" because the spinners and weavers did their work on spinning wheels and looms in their own cottages.

In the eighteenth century, overseas trade boomed. Some historians speak of the emergence of a true global economy, pointing to the patterns of trade that interlocked Europe, Africa, the Far East, and the Americas (see Map 17.2). One such pattern involved the influx of gold and silver into Spain from its colonial American empire. Much of this gold and silver made its way to Britain, France, and the Netherlands in return for manufactured goods. British, Dutch, and French merchants in turn used their profits to buy tea, spices, silk and cotton goods from China and India

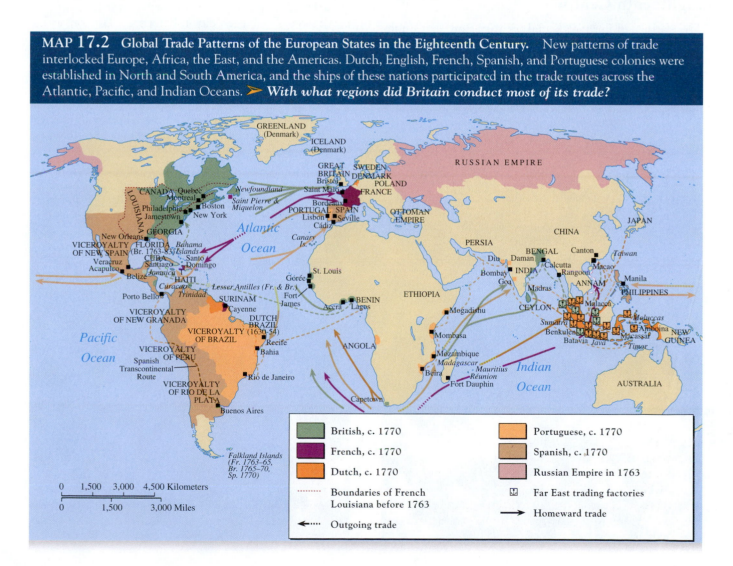

MAP 17.2   Global Trade Patterns of the European States in the Eighteenth Century.   New patterns of trade interlocked Europe, Africa, the East, and the Americas. Dutch, English, French, Spanish, and Portuguese colonies were established in North and South America, and the ships of these nations participated in the trade routes across the Atlantic, Pacific, and Indian Oceans. ➤ **With what regions did Britain conduct most of its trade?**

to sell in Europe. Another important source of trading activity involved the plantations of the Western Hemisphere. The plantations were worked by African slaves and produced tobacco, cotton, coffee, and sugar, all products in demand by Europeans. In a third pattern of trade, British merchant ships carried British manufactured goods to Africa, where they were traded for a cargo of slaves, which were then shipped to Virginia and paid for by tobacco, which was in turn shipped back to Britain, where it was processed and then sold in Germany for cash.

Commercial capitalism created enormous prosperity for some European countries. By 1700, Spain, Portugal, and the Dutch Republic, which had earlier monopolized overseas trade, found themselves increasingly overshadowed by France and England, which built enormously profitable colonial empires in the course of the eighteenth century. After the French lost the Seven Years' War in 1763, Britain emerged as the world's strongest overseas trading nation, and London became the world's greatest port.

European Society in the Eighteenth Century

The pattern of Europe's social organization, first established in the Middle Ages, continued well into the eighteenth century. Society was still divided into the traditional "orders" or "estates" determined by heredity. Governments helped maintain these divisions. In Prussia, for example, a law of 1794 forbade marriage between noble males and middle-class females.

Because society was still mostly rural in the eighteenth century, the peasantry constituted the largest social group, about 85 percent of Europe's population. There were rather wide differences within this group, however, especially between free peasants and serfs. In eastern Germany, eastern Europe, and Russia, serfs remained tied to the lands of their noble landlords. In contrast, peasants in Britain, northern Italy, the Low Countries, Spain, most of France, and some areas of western Germany were largely free.

The nobles, who constituted only 2 to 3 percent of the European population, played a dominating role in society. Being born a noble automatically guaranteed a place at the top of the social order, with all its attendant special privileges and rights. Nobles, for example, were exempt from many forms of taxation. Since medieval times, landed aristocrats had functioned as military officers, and eighteenth-century nobles held most of the important offices in the administrative machinery of state and controlled much of the life of their local districts.

Townspeople were still a distinct minority of the total population except in the Dutch Republic, Britain, and parts of Italy. At the end of the eighteenth century, about one-sixth of the French population lived in towns of two thousand people or more. The biggest city in Europe was London, with a million inhabitants; Paris was a little more than half that size.

Many cities in western and even central Europe had a long tradition of patrician oligarchies that continued to control their communities by dominating town and city councils. Just below the patricians stood an upper crust of the middle classes: nonnoble officeholders, financiers and bankers, merchants, wealthy *rentiers* who lived off

➤ **THE ARISTOCRATIC WAY OF LIFE.** The eighteenth-century country house in Britain fulfilled the desire of aristocrats for both elegance and greater privacy. The painting below by Richard Wilson shows a typical English country house of the eighteenth century, surrounded by a simple and serene landscape. Thomas Gainsborough's *Conversation in the Park,* shown at right, captures the relaxed life of two aristocrats in the park of their country estate.

© Erich Lessing/Art Resource, NY

Collection of the Earl of Pembroke, Wilton House, Wilts., UK/Bridgeman Art Library

their investments, and important professionals, including lawyers. Another large urban group was the lower middle class, made up of master artisans, shopkeepers, and small traders. Below them were the laborers or working classes and a large group of unskilled workers who served as servants, maids, and cooks at pitifully low wages.

CHANGING PATTERNS OF WAR: GLOBAL CONFRONTATION

The philosophes condemned war as a foolish waste of life and resources in stupid quarrels of no value to humankind. Despite their words, the rivalry among states that led to costly struggles remained unchanged in the European world of the eighteenth century. Europe consisted of a number of self-governing, individual states that were chiefly guided by the self-interest of the ruler. And as Frederick the Great of Prussia said, "The fundamental rule of governments is the principle of extending their territories."

In 1740, a major conflict erupted over the succession to the Austrian throne. After the death of the Habsburg emperor Charles VI, King Frederick II of Prussia took advantage of the succession of a woman, Maria Theresa (1740–1780), to the throne of Austria by invading Austrian Silesia. The vulnerability of Maria Theresa encouraged France to enter the war against its traditional enemy Austria; in turn, Maria Theresa allied with Great Britain, which feared French domination of Continental affairs.

The War of the Austrian Succession (1740–1748) was fought in three areas of the world. In Europe, Prussia seized Silesia from Austria while France occupied the Austrian Netherlands. In Asia, France took Madras in India from the British, and in North America, the British captured the French fortress of Louisbourg at the entrance to the Saint Lawrence River. By 1748, all parties were exhausted and agreed to a peace treaty that guaranteed the return of all occupied territories to their original owners, with the exception of Silesia.

The Seven Years' War: A Global War

Maria Theresa refused to accept the loss of Silesia and prepared for its return by working diplomatically to separate Prussia from its chief ally, France. In 1756, Austria achieved a diplomatic revolution. French-Austrian rivalry had existed since the late sixteenth century. But two new rivalries now replaced the old one: the rivalry of Britain and France over colonial empires and the rivalry of Austria and Prussia over Silesia. France abandoned Prussia and allied with Austria. Russia, which saw Prussia as a major hindrance to Russian goals in central Europe, joined the new alliance. In turn, Great Britain allied with Prussia. These new alliances now led to another worldwide war.

Again there were three major areas of conflict: Europe, India, and North America (see Map 17.3). In Europe, the British and Prussians fought the Austrians, Russians, and French. With his superb army and military skill, Frederick the Great of Prussia was able for some time to defeat the Austrian, French, and Russian armies. Eventually, however, his forces were gradually worn down and faced utter defeat until a new Russian tsar, Peter III, withdrew Russian troops from the conflict. A stalemate ensued, ending the European conflict in 1763. All occupied territories were returned, and Austria officially recognized Prussia's permanent control of Silesia.

The struggle between Britain and France in the rest of the world had more decisive results. In India, the French had returned Madras to Britain after the War of the Austrian Succession, but the struggle continued. Ultimately, the British under Robert Clive won out, not because they had better forces but because they were more persistent. By the Treaty of Paris in 1763, the French withdrew and left India to the British.

➤ ROBERT CLIVE IN INDIA.   Robert Clive was the leader of the army of the British East India Company. He had been commanded to fight the ruler of Bengal in order to gain trading privileges. To make his job easier, Clive arranged a meeting with Mir Jaffier, the commander of Bengal's army, in order to win him over to the British side. Although not present at the meeting, British artist Francis Hayman imaginatively re-created the scene in this 1760 painting.

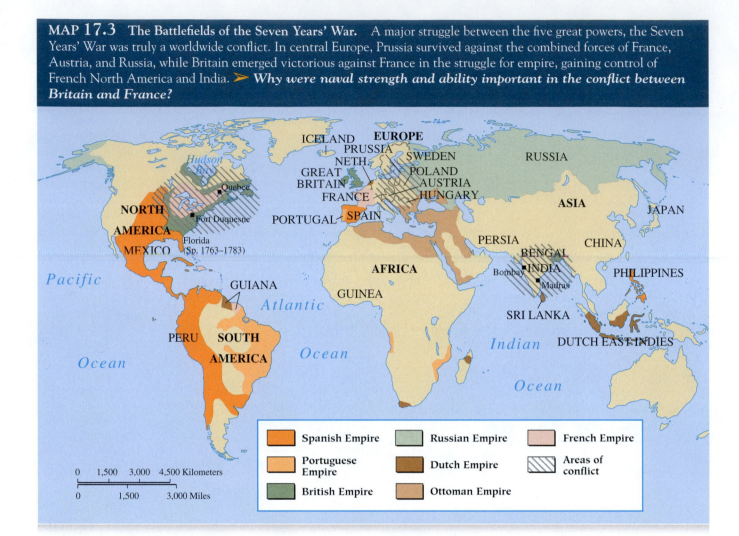

MAP 17.3 The Battlefields of the Seven Years' War.   A major struggle between the five great powers, the Seven Years' War was truly a worldwide conflict. In central Europe, Prussia survived against the combined forces of France, Austria, and Russia, while Britain emerged victorious against France in the struggle for empire, gaining control of French North America and India. ➤ *Why were naval strength and ability important in the conflict between Britain and France?*

By far the greatest conflicts of the Seven Years' War took place in North America. French North America (Canada and Louisiana) was thinly populated and run by the French government as a vast trading area. British North America had come to consist of thirteen colonies on the eastern coast of the present United States. They were thickly populated, containing about 1.5 million people by 1750, and were also prosperous.

British and French rivalry in North America led to two primary areas of contention. One consisted of the waterways of the Gulf of Saint Lawrence, protected by the fortress of Louisbourg and by forts near the Great Lakes and Lake Champlain that protected French Quebec and French traders. The other was the unsettled Ohio River valley. The French began to move down from Canada and up from Louisiana to establish forts in the Ohio River valley. To British settlers in the thirteen colonies, French activity threatened to cut off this vast area for their exploitation.

Despite initial French successes, British fortunes revived. The French had more troops in North America but less naval support. The defeat of French fleets in 1759 left the French unable to reinforce their garrisons. In 1759, British forces under General Wolfe defeated the French under General Montcalm on the Plains of Abraham, outside Quebec. The British went on to seize Montreal, the Great Lakes area, and the Ohio valley. The French were forced to make peace. By the Treaty of Paris, they ceded Canada and the lands east of the Mississippi to England. Their ally Spain transferred Spanish Florida to British control; in return, the French gave their Louisiana territory to the Spanish. By 1763, Great Britain had become the world's greatest colonial power.

COLONIAL EMPIRES AND REVOLUTION IN THE WESTERN HEMISPHERE

The colonial empires in the Western Hemisphere were an integral part of the European economy in the eighteenth century and became entangled in the conflicts of the European states. Nevertheless, the colonies of Latin America and British North America were developing along lines that sometimes differed significantly from those of Europe.

The Society of Latin America

In the sixteenth century, Portugal came to dominate Brazil while Spain established a colonial empire in the New World that included Central America, most of South America, and parts of North America. Within the lands of Central and South America, a new civilization arose that we have come to call Latin America (see Map 17.4).

Latin America was a multiracial society. Already by 1501, Spanish rulers allowed intermarriage between Europeans and native American Indians, whose offspring became known as *mestizos*. In addition, over a period of three centuries, possibly as many as eight million African slaves were brought to Spanish and Portuguese America to work the plantations. Mulattoes—the offspring of Africans and whites—joined mestizos and descendants of whites, Africans, and native Indians to produce a unique society in Latin America. Unlike Europe, and unlike British North America, which remained a largely white offshoot of Europe, Latin America developed a fairly well integrated multiracial society.

MAP 17.4 Latin America in the Eighteenth Century. In the eighteenth century, Latin America was largely the colonial preserve of the Spanish, although Portugal continued to dominate Brazil. The Latin American colonies supplied the Spanish and Portuguese with gold, silver, sugar, tobacco, cotton, and animal hides. ➤ *How do you explain the ability of Europeans to dominate such large areas of Latin America?*

Legend:
- Portuguese colonized by 1640
- Portuguese colonized by 1750
- Portuguese frontier lands, 1750
- Spanish colonized by 1640
- Spanish colonized by 1750
- Spanish frontier lands, 1750
- French colonies
- Dutch colonies
- English colonies
- Jesuit mission states
- Routes of colonial trade
- Extent of Inca Empire in 1525

THE ECONOMIC FOUNDATIONS

Both the Portuguese and the Spanish sought to profit from their colonies in Latin America. One source of wealth came from the abundant supplies of gold and silver. The Spaniards were especially successful, finding supplies of gold in the Caribbean and New Granada (Colombia) and silver in Mexico and the viceroyalty of Peru. Most of the gold and silver was sent to Europe, and little remained in the New World to benefit the people whose labor had produced it.

Although the pursuit of gold and silver offered prospects of fantastic financial rewards, agriculture proved to be a more abiding and more rewarding source of prosperity for Latin America. A noticeable feature of Latin American agriculture was the dominant role of the large landowner. Both Spanish and Portuguese landowners created immense estates, which left the Indians either to work as peons—native peasants permanently dependent on the landowners—on their estates or as poor farmers on marginal lands. This system of large landowners and dependent peasants has remained one of the persistent features of Latin American society. By the eighteenth century, both Spanish and Portuguese landowners were producing primarily for sale abroad.

Trade was another avenue for the economic exploitation of the American colonies. Latin American colonies became sources of raw materials for Spain and Portugal as gold, silver, sugar, tobacco, diamonds, animal hides, and a number of other natural products made their way to Europe. In turn, the mother countries supplied their colonists with manufactured goods. Both Spain and Portugal closely regulated the trade of their American colonies to keep others out, but both the British and the French became too powerful to be excluded from this lucrative Latin American market.

THE STATE AND THE CHURCH IN COLONIAL LATIN AMERICA

Portuguese Brazil and Spanish America were colonial empires that lasted over three hundred years. The difficulties of communication and travel between the New World and Europe made the attempts of the Spanish and Portuguese monarchs to provide close regulation of their empires virtually impossible, which left colonial officials in Latin America with much autonomy in implementing imperial policies. However, the Iberians tried to keep the most important posts of colonial government in the hands of Europeans.

Beginning in the mid-sixteenth century, the Portuguese monarchy began to assert its control over Brazil by establishing the position of governor-general. The governor-general (later called a viceroy) developed a bureaucracy but had at best only loose control over the captains-general, who were responsible for governing the districts into which Brazil was divided.

To rule his American empire, the king of Spain appointed a viceroy, the first of which was established for New Spain (Mexico) in 1535. Another viceroy was appointed for Peru in 1543. In the eighteenth century, two additional viceroyalties—New Granada and La Plata—were added. Viceroyalties were in turn subdivided into smaller units. All of the major government positions were held by Spaniards. For creoles—American-born whites—the chief opportunity to hold a government post was in city councils.

From the beginning of their conquest of the New World, Spanish and Portuguese rulers were determined to Christianize the native peoples. This policy gave the Catholic church an important role to play in the New World—a role that added considerably to church power. Catholic missionaries fanned out to different parts of the Spanish Empire. To facilitate their efforts, missionaries brought Indians together into villages where the natives could be converted, taught trades, and encouraged to grow crops (see the box on p. 485). Their missions enabled missionaries to control the lives of the Indians and keep them docile.

The Catholic church constructed hospitals, orphanages, and schools, which instructed Indian students in the rudiments of reading, writing, and arithmetic. The church also provided outlets for women other than marriage. Nunneries were places of prayer and quiet contemplation, but women in religious orders, many of them of aristocratic background, often lived well and operated outside their establishments by running schools and hospitals. Indeed, one of these nuns, Sor Juana Inés de la Cruz (1651–1695), was one of seventeenth-century Latin America's best-known literary figures. She wrote poetry and prose and urged that women be educated.

SOR JUANA INÉS DE LA CRUZ.   Nunneries in colonial Latin America gave women—especially upper-class women—some opportunity for intellectual activity. As a woman, Juana Inés de la Cruz was denied admission to the University of Mexico. Consequently, she entered a convent, where she wrote poetry and plays until her superiors forced her to focus on less worldly activities.

THE MISSION

In 1609, two Jesuit priests embarked on a missionary calling with the Guaraní Indians in eastern Paraguay. Eventually, the Jesuits established more than thirty missions in the region. Well organized and zealous, the Jesuits transformed their missions into profitable business activities. This description of a Jesuit mission in Paraguay was written by Félix de Azara, a Spanish soldier and scientist.

FÉLIX DE AZARA, *DESCRIPTION AND HISTORY OF PARAGUAY AND RIO DE LA PLATA*

Having spoken of the towns founded by the Jesuit fathers, and of the manner in which they were founded, I shall discuss the government which they established in them. . . . In each town resided two priests, a curate and a subcurate, who had certain assigned functions. The subcurate was charged with all the spiritual tasks, and the curate with every kind of temporal responsibility. . . .

The curate allowed no one to work for personal gain; he compelled everyone, without distinction of age or sex, to work for the community, and he himself saw to it that all were equally fed and dressed. For this purpose the curates placed in storehouses all the fruits of agriculture and the products of industry, selling in the Spanish towns their surplus of cotton, cloth, tobacco, vegetables, skins, and wood, transporting them in their own boats down the nearest rivers, and returning with implements and whatever else was required.

From the foregoing one may infer that the curate disposed of the surplus funds of the Indian towns, and that no Indian could aspire to own private property. This deprived them of any incentive to use reason or talent, since the most industrious, able, and worthy person had the same food, clothing, and pleasures as the most wicked, dull, and indolent. It also follows that although this form of government was well designed to enrich the communities it also caused the Indian to work at a languid pace, since the wealth of his community was of no concern to him.

It must be said that although the Jesuit fathers were supreme in all respects, they employed their authority with a mildness and a restraint that command admiration. They supplied everyone with abundant food and clothing. They compelled the men to work only half a day, and did not drive them to produce more. Even their labor was given a festive air, for they went in procession to the fields, to the sound of music . . . and the music did not cease until they had returned in the same way they had set out. They gave them many holidays, dances, and tournaments, dressing the actors and the members of the municipal councils in gold or silver tissue and the most costly European garments, but they permitted the women to act only as spectators.

They likewise forbade the women to sew; this occupation was restricted to the musicians, sacristans, and acolytes. But they made them spin cotton; and the cloth that the Indians wove, after satisfying their own needs, they sold together with the surplus cotton in the Spanish towns, as they did with the tobacco, vegetables, wood, and skins. The curate and his companion, or subcurate, had their own plain dwellings, and they never left them except to take the air in the great enclosed yard of their college. They never walked through the streets of the town or entered the house of any Indian or let themselves be seen by any woman—or indeed, by any man, except for those indispensable few through whom they issued their orders.

British North America

In the eighteenth century, Spanish power in the New World was increasingly challenged by the British. (The United Kingdom of Great Britain came into existence in 1707, when the governments of England and Scotland were united; the term *British* came into use to refer to both English and Scots.) In eighteenth-century Britain, the king or queen and Parliament shared power, with Parliament gradually gaining the upper hand. The monarch chose ministers who were responsible to the crown and who set policy and guided Parliament. Parliament had the power to make laws, levy taxes, pass budgets, and indirectly influence the monarch's ministers.

The eighteenth-century British Parliament was dominated by a landed aristocracy divided into two groups: the upper aristocracy or peers, who sat for life in the House of Lords, and the landed gentry, who were elected to the House of Commons. The two groups had much in common; both were landowners, and they frequently intermarried. The deputies to the House of Commons were chosen from the towns and counties not by popular vote but by holders of property.

In 1714, a new dynasty—the Hanoverians—was established when the last Stuart ruler, Queen Anne (1702–1714), died without an heir. The crown was offered to the nearest relatives, Protestant rulers of the German state of Hanover. Because the first Hanoverian king (George I) did not speak English and neither the first nor the second George had much familiarity with the British system, their chief ministers were allowed to handle Parliament. Robert Walpole served as prime minister from 1721 to 1742 and pursued a peaceful foreign policy. But growing trade and industry led to a growing middle class that favored expansion of trade and world empire. These people found a spokesman in William Pitt the Elder, who became prime minister in 1757 and expanded the British Empire by acquiring Canada and India in the Seven Years' War.

THE AMERICAN REVOLUTION

At the end of the Seven Years' War in 1763, Great Britain had become the world's greatest colonial power. In North America, Britain controlled Canada and the lands east of the Mississippi. After the Seven Years' War, British policymakers sought to obtain new revenues from the colonies to pay for British army expenses in defending the colonists. An attempt to levy new taxes by the Stamp Act of 1765 led to riots and the law's quick repeal.

The Americans and British had different conceptions of empire. The British envisioned a single empire with Parliament as the supreme authority throughout. The Americans, in contrast, had their own representative assemblies. They believed that neither king nor Parliament should interfere in their internal affairs and that no tax could be levied without the consent of their own assemblies.

Crisis followed crisis in the 1770s until 1776, when the colonists decided to declare their independence from the British Empire. On July 4, 1776, the Second Continental Congress approved a declaration of independence written by Thomas Jefferson. A stirring political document, the Declaration of Independence affirmed the Enlightenment's natural rights of "life, liberty, and the pursuit of happiness" and declared the colonies to be "free and independent states absolved from all allegiance to the British crown." The war for American independence had formally begun.

Of great importance to the colonies' cause was their support by foreign countries who were eager to gain revenge for earlier defeats at the hands of the British. French officers and soldiers served in the American Continental Army under George Washington as commander in chief. When the army of General Cornwallis was forced to surrender to a combined American and French army and French fleet under Washington at Yorktown in 1781, the British decided to call it quits. The Treaty of Paris, signed in 1783, recognized the independence of the American colonies and granted the Americans control of the territory from the Appalachians to the Mississippi River.

BIRTH OF A NEW NATION

The thirteen American colonies had gained their independence, but a fear of concentrated power and concern for their own interests caused them to have little enthusiasm for establishing a united nation with a strong central government, and so the Articles of Confederation, ratified in 1781, did not create one. A movement for a different form of national government soon arose. In the summer of 1787, fifty-five delegates attended a convention in Philadelphia to revise the Articles of Confederation. The convention's delegates—wealthy, politically experienced, and well educated—rejected revision and decided instead to devise a new constitution.

The proposed United States Constitution established a central government distinct from and superior to governments of the individual states. The national government was given the power to levy taxes, raise a national army, regulate domestic and foreign trade, and create a national currency. The central or federal government was divided into three branches, each with some power to check the functioning of the others. A president would serve as the chief executive with the power to execute laws, veto the legislature's acts, supervise foreign affairs, and direct military forces. Legislative power was vested in the second branch of government, a bicameral legislature composed of the Senate, elected by the state legislatures, and the House of Representatives, elected directly by the people. A supreme court and other courts "as deemed necessary" by Congress provided the third branch of government. They would enforce the Constitution as the "supreme law of the land."

The Constitution was approved by the states—by a slim margin. Important to its success was a promise to add a bill of rights to the Constitution as the new government's first piece of business. Accordingly, in March 1789, the new Congress enacted the first ten amendments to the Constitution, ever since known as the Bill of Rights. These guaranteed freedom of religion, speech, press, petition, and assembly, as well as the right to bear arms, protection against unreasonable searches and arrests, trial by jury, due process of law, and protection of property rights. Many of these rights were derived from the natural rights philosophy of the eighteenth-century philosophes and the American colonists. Is it any wonder that many European intellectuals saw the American Revolution as the embodiment of the Enlightenment's political dreams?

TOWARD A NEW POLITICAL ORDER: ENLIGHTENED ABSOLUTISM

There is no doubt that Enlightenment thought had some impact on the political development of European states in the eighteenth century. The philosophes believed in natural rights, which were thought to be inalienable privileges that ought not to be withheld from any person. These natural rights included equality before the law, freedom of religious worship, freedom of speech and press, and the right to assemble, hold property, and pursue happiness.

But how were these natural rights to be established and preserved? Most philosophes believed that people needed to be ruled by an enlightened ruler. What, however, made rulers enlightened? They must allow religious toleration, freedom of speech and press, and the rights of private property. They must foster the arts, sciences, and education. Above all, they must obey the laws and enforce them fairly for all subjects. Only strong monarchs seemed capable of overcoming vested interests and effecting the reforms society needed. Reforms then should come from above (from absolute rulers) rather than from below (from the people).

Many historians once assumed that a new type of monarchy emerged in the later eighteenth century, which they called "enlightened despotism" or "enlightened absolutism." Monarchs such as Frederick II of Prussia, Catherine the Great of Russia, and Joseph II of Austria supposedly followed the advice of the philosophes and ruled by enlightened principles. Recently, however, scholars have questioned the usefulness of the concept of "enlightened absolutism." We can determine the extent to which it can be applied by examining the major "enlightened absolutists" of the later eighteenth century.

Prussia: The Army and the Bureaucracy

Two able Prussian kings in the eighteenth century, Frederick William I and Frederick II, made Prussia into a major European power in the eighteenth century. Frederick William I (1713–1740) strove to maintain a highly efficient bureaucracy of civil service workers. The bureaucracy had its own code in which the supreme values were obedience, honor, and service to the king as the highest duty.

Frederick William's other major concern was the army. By the end of his reign, he had nearly doubled the army's size from 45,000 to 83,000 men. Although tenth in physical size and thirteenth in population in Europe, Prussia had the fourth-largest army (after France, Russia, and Austria). The nobility or landed aristocracy known as Junkers, who owned large estates with many serfs, were the officers in the Prussian army. These officers, too, had a strong sense of service to the king or state. As Prussian nobles, they believed in duty, obedience, and sacrifice. The Prussian army, because of its size and excellent reputation, was the most important institution in the state.

Frederick II, known as Frederick the Great (1740–1786), was one of the best-educated and most cultured monarchs in the eighteenth century. He was well versed in Enlightenment thought and even invited Voltaire to live at his court for several years. A believer in the king as the "first servant of the state," Frederick the Great was a conscientious ruler who enlarged the Prussian army (to 200,000 men) and kept a strict watch over the bureaucracy.

For a time, Frederick seemed quite willing to make enlightened reforms. He abolished the use of torture except in treason and murder cases and also granted limited freedom of speech and press, as well as complete religious toleration. However, he kept Prussia's rigid social structure and serfdom intact and avoided any additional reforms.

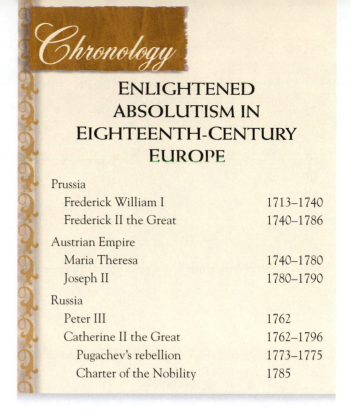

Chronology

ENLIGHTENED ABSOLUTISM IN EIGHTEENTH-CENTURY EUROPE

Prussia	
Frederick William I	1713–1740
Frederick II the Great	1740–1786
Austrian Empire	
Maria Theresa	1740–1780
Joseph II	1780–1790
Russia	
Peter III	1762
Catherine II the Great	1762–1796
Pugachev's rebellion	1773–1775
Charter of the Nobility	1785

The Austrian Empire of the Habsburgs

The Austrian Empire had become one of the great European states by the beginning of the eighteenth century. Yet it was difficult to rule because it was a sprawling empire composed of many different nationalities, languages, religions, and culture (see Map 17.5). Empress Maria Theresa (1740–1780) managed to make administrative reforms that helped centralize the Austrian Empire, but they were done for practical reasons—to strengthen the power of the Habsburg state—and were accompanied by an enlargement and modernization of the armed forces. Maria Theresa remained staunchly conservative and was not open to the wider reform calls of the philosophes. But her successor was.

Joseph II (1780–1790) was determined to make changes. He believed in the need to sweep away anything standing in the path of reason. As he said, "I have made Philosophy the lawmaker of my empire, her logical applications are going to transform Austria." Joseph's reform program was far-reaching. He abolished serfdom, abrogated the death penalty, and established the principle of equality of all before the law. Joseph produced drastic religious reforms as well, including complete religious toleration. Altogether, Joseph II issued six thousand decrees and eleven thousand laws in his effort to transform Austria.

Joseph's reform program proved overwhelming for Austria, however. He alienated the nobility by freeing the serfs and alienated the church by his attacks on the monastic establishment. Even the serfs were unhappy, unable to comprehend the drastic changes inherent in Joseph's policies. Joseph realized his failure when he wrote the epitaph for his own gravestone: "Here lies Joseph II, who was unfortunate in everything that he undertook." His successors undid many of his reforms.

Russia Under Catherine the Great

In Russia, Peter the Great was followed by six weak successors who were put in power and deposed by the palace guard. After a faction of nobles murdered the last of these, Peter III, his German widow emerged as autocrat of all the Russians. Catherine II the Great (1762–1796) was an intelligent woman who was familiar with the works of the philosophes and seemed to favor enlightened reforms. She invited the French philosophe Diderot to Russia and, when he arrived, urged him to speak frankly "as man to man." He did, outlining a far-reaching program of political and financial reform. But Catherine was skeptical about impractical theories, which, she said, "would have turned everything in my kingdom upside down." She did consider the idea of a new law code that would recognize the principle of the equality of all people in the eyes of the law. But in the end she did nothing, knowing that her success depended on the support of the Russian nobility. In 1785, she gave the nobles a charter that exempted them from taxes.

❧ **CATHERINE THE GREAT.**   Autocrat of Russia, Catherine was an intelligent ruler who favored reform. She found it expedient, however, to retain much of the old system in order to keep the support of the landed nobility. This portrait by Dmitry Levitsky shows her in legislative regalia in the Temple of Justice in 1783.

© Scala/Art Resource, NY

Catherine's policy of favoring the landed nobility led to even worse conditions for the Russian peasants and a rebellion. Led by an illiterate Cossack, Emelyan Pugachev, the rebellion spread across southern Russia. But the rebellion soon faltered. Pugachev was captured, tortured, and executed. The rebellion collapsed completely, and Catherine responded by even greater measures against the peasantry.

Above all, Catherine proved a worthy successor to Peter the Great in her policies of territorial expansion westward into Poland and southward to the Black Sea. Russia spread southward by defeating the Turks. Russian expansion westward occurred at the expense of neighboring Poland. In three partitions of Poland, Russia gained about 50 percent of Polish territory.

Of the rulers we have discussed, only Joseph II sought truly radical changes based on Enlightenment ideas. Both Frederick II and Catherine II liked to talk about enlightened reforms, and they even attempted some. But the policies of neither seemed seriously affected by Enlightenment thought. Necessities of state and maintenance of the existing system took precedence over reform. Indeed, many historians maintain that Joseph, Frederick, and Catherine were all primarily guided by a concern for the power and well-being of their states. In the final analysis, heightened state power was used to create armies and wage wars to gain more power.

It would be foolish, however, to overlook the fact that the ability of enlightened rulers to make reforms was also limited by political and social realities. Everywhere in Europe, the hereditary aristocracy was still the most powerful class in society. Enlightened reforms were often limited to administrative and judicial measures that did not seriously undermine the powerful interests of the European nobility. As the chief beneficiaries of a system based on traditional rights and privileges for their class, they were not willing to support a political ideology that trumpeted the principle of equal rights for all. The first serious challenge to their supremacy would come in the French Revolution, an event that blew open the door to the modern world of politics.

THE FRENCH REVOLUTION

The year 1789 witnessed two far-reaching events, the beginning of a new United States of America under its revamped Constitution and the eruption of the French Revolution. Compared to the American Revolution a decade earlier, the French Revolution was more complex, more violent, and far more radical in its attempt to reconstruct both a new political and a new social order.

Background to the French Revolution

The root causes of the French Revolution must be sought in the condition of French society. Before the Revolution, France was a society grounded in privilege and

MAP 17.5 Europe in 1763. By the middle of the eighteenth century, five major powers dominated Europe— Prussia, Austria, Russia, Britain, and France. Each sought to enhance its power both domestically, through a bureaucracy that collected taxes and ran the military, and internationally, by capturing territory or preventing other powers from capturing territory. ➤ *Given the distribution of Prussian and Habsburg holdings, in what areas of Europe were they most likely to compete for land and power?*

inequality. Its population of 27 million was divided, as it had been since the Middle Ages, into three orders or estates.

SOCIAL STRUCTURE OF THE OLD REGIME

The first estate consisted of the clergy and numbered about 130,000 people who owned approximately 10 percent of the land. Clergy were exempt from the *taille*, France's chief tax. Clergy were also radically divided: the higher clergy, stemming from aristocratic families, shared the interests of the nobility, while the parish priests were often poor and from the class of commoners.

The second estate was the nobility, composed of about 350,000 people who owned about 25 to 30 percent of the land. The nobility had continued to play an important and even crucial role in French society in the eighteenth century, holding many of the leading positions in the government, the military, the law courts, and the higher church offices. The nobles sought to expand their power

at the expense of the monarchy and to maintain their control over positions in the military, church, and government. Moreover, the possession of privileges remained a hallmark of the nobility. Common to all nobles were tax exemptions, especially from the *taille*.

The third estate, or the commoners of society, constituted the overwhelming majority of the French population. They were divided by vast differences in occupation, level of education, and wealth. The peasants, who alone constituted 75 to 80 percent of the total population, were by far the largest segment of the third estate. They owned about 35 to 40 percent of the land, although their landholdings varied from area to area and over half had little or no land on which to survive. Serfdom no longer existed on any large scale in France, but French peasants still had obligations to their local landlords that they deeply resented. These "relics of feudalism," or aristocratic privileges, were obligations that survived from an earlier age and included the payment of fees for the use of village facilities, such as the flour mill, community oven, and winepress.

Another part of the third estate consisted of skilled craftspeople, shopkeepers, and other wage earners in the cities. In the eighteenth century, a rise in consumer prices greater than the increase in wages left these urban groups with a noticeable decline in purchasing power. Their daily struggle for survival led many of these people to play an important role in the Revolution, especially in Paris.

About 8 percent of the population, or 2.3 million people, constituted the bourgeoisie or middle class, who owned about 20 to 25 percent of the land. This group included merchants, industrialists, and bankers who controlled the resources of trade, manufacturing, and finance and benefited from the economic prosperity after 1730. The bourgeoisie also included professional people—lawyers, holders of public offices, doctors, and writers. Many members of the bourgeoisie had their own set of grievances because they were often excluded from the social and political privileges monopolized by nobles. At the same time, remarkable similarities existed at the upper levels of society between the wealthier bourgeoisie and the nobility. By obtaining public offices, wealthy middle-class individuals could enter the ranks of the nobility. During the eighteenth century, 6,500 new noble families were created.

Moreover, the new political ideas of the Enlightenment proved attractive to both the aristocracy and the bourgeoisie. Both elites, long accustomed to a new socioeconomic reality based on wealth and economic achievement, were increasingly frustrated by a monarchical system resting on privileges and on an old and rigid social order based on the concept of estates. The opposition of these elites to the old order led them ultimately to drastic action against the monarchical regime. In a real sense, the Revolution had its origins in political grievances.

OTHER PROBLEMS FACING THE FRENCH MONARCHY

The inability of the French monarchy to deal with new social realities was exacerbated by specific problems in the 1780s. Although France had enjoyed fifty years of economic expansion, bad harvests in 1787 and 1788 and the beginnings of a manufacturing depression resulted in food shortages, rising prices for food and other goods, and unemployment in the cities. The number of poor, estimated at almost one-third of the population, reached crisis proportions on the eve of the Revolution.

The immediate cause of the French Revolution was the near collapse of government finances. Costly wars and royal extravagance drove French governmental expenditures ever higher. On the verge of a complete financial collapse, the government of Louis XVI (1774–1792) was finally forced to call a meeting of the Estates-General, the French parliamentary body that had not met since 1614. The Estates-General consisted of representatives from the three orders of French society. In the elections for the Estates-General, the government had ruled that the third estate should get double representation (it did, after all, constitute 97 percent of the population). Consequently, while both the first estate (the clergy) and the second estate (the nobility) had about three hundred delegates each, the third estate had almost six hundred representatives, most of whom were lawyers from French towns. To fix France's financial problems, most members of the third estate wanted to set up a constitutional government that would revoke the fiscal privileges of the church and the nobility.

From Estates-General to National Assembly

The Estates-General opened at Versailles on May 5, 1789. It was troubled from the start with the question of whether voting should be by order or by head (each delegate having one vote). Traditionally, each order would vote as a group and have one vote. That meant that the first and second estates could outvote the third estate two to one. The third estate demanded that each deputy have one vote. With the assistance of liberal nobles and clerics, that would give the third estate a majority. When the first estate declared in favor of voting by order, the third estate responded dramatically. On June 17, 1789, the third estate declared itself the "National Assembly" and decided to draw up a constitution. This was the first step in the French Revolution because the third estate had no legal right to act as the National Assembly. But this audacious act was soon in jeopardy, as the king sided with the first estate and threatened to dissolve the Estates-General. Louis XVI now prepared to use force.

The common people, however, saved the third estate from the king's forces. On July 14, a mob of Parisians stormed the Bastille, a royal armory, and proceeded to dismantle it, brick by brick. Louis XVI was soon informed that the royal troops were unreliable. Louis's acceptance of that reality signaled the collapse of royal authority; the king could no longer enforce his will. The fall of the Bastille had saved the National Assembly.

At the same time, popular revolts broke out throughout France, both in the cities and in the countryside. Behind the popular uprising was a growing resentment of the entire landholding system, with its fees and obligations. The fall of the Bastille and the king's apparent capitulation to the demands of the third estate now led peasants to take matters into their own hands. Peasant rebellions occurred throughout France, serving as a backdrop to the Great Fear, a vast panic that spread like wildfire through France between July 20 and August 6. The greatest impact of the agrarian revolts and Great Fear was on the National Assembly meeting in Versailles.

✦ **STORMING OF THE BASTILLE.**   Louis XVI planned to use force to dissolve the Estates-General, but a number of rural and urban uprisings by the common people prevented this action. The fall of the Bastille, pictured here in a painting by an unknown artist, is perhaps the most famous of the urban uprisings.

Destruction of the Old Regime

One of the first acts of the National Assembly was to destroy the relics of feudalism and aristocratic privilege. On the night of August 4, 1789, the National Assembly voted to abolish the rights of landlords and the fiscal exemptions of nobles, clergy, towns, and provinces. On August 26, the National Assembly adopted the Declaration of the Rights of Man and the Citizen (see the box on p. 492). This charter of basic liberties affirmed the demise of aristocratic privileges by proclaiming an end to exemptions from taxation, freedom and equal rights for all men, and access to public office based on talent. All citizens were to have the right to take part in the legislative process. Freedom of speech and the press were coupled with the outlawing of arbitrary arrests.

The declaration also raised another important issue. Did its ideal of equal rights for all men also include women? Many deputies insisted that it did, provided that, as one said, "women do not hope to exercise political rights and functions." Olympe de Gouges, a playwright, refused to accept this exclusion of women from political rights. Echoing the words of the official declaration, she penned the Declaration of the Rights of Woman and the Female Citizen, in which she insisted that women should have all the same rights as men (see the box on p. 493). The National Assembly ignored her demands.

In the meantime, Louis XVI, who had remained inactive at Versailles, refused to accept the decrees on the abolition of feudalism and the declaration of rights. On October 5, thousands of Parisian women, described by one

DECLARATION OF THE RIGHTS OF MAN AND THE CITIZEN

One of the important documents of the French Revolution, the Declaration of the Rights of Man and the Citizen was adopted in August 1789 by the National Assembly. The declaration affirmed that "men are born and remain free and equal in rights," that governments must protect these natural rights, and that political power is derived from the people.

DECLARATION OF THE RIGHTS OF MAN AND THE CITIZEN

The representatives of the French people, organized as a national assembly, considering that ignorance, neglect, and scorn of the rights of man are the sole causes of public misfortunes and of corruption of governments, have resolved to display in a solemn declaration the natural, inalienable, and sacred rights of man, so that this declaration, constantly in the presence of all members of society, will continually remind them of their rights and their duties. . . . Consequently, the National Assembly recognizes and declares, in the presence and under the auspices of the Supreme Being, the following rights of man and citizen:

1. Men are born and remain free and equal in rights; social distinctions can be established only for the common benefit.

2. The aim of every political association is the conservation of the natural and imprescriptible rights of man; these rights are liberty, property, security, and resistance to oppression.

3. The source of all sovereignty is located in essence in the nation; no body, no individual can exercise authority which does not emanate from it expressly.

4. Liberty consists in being able to do anything that does not harm another person. . . .

6. The law is the expression of the general will; all citizens have the right to concur personally or through their representatives in its formation; it must be the same for all, whether it protects or punishes. All citizens being equal in its eyes are equally admissible to all honors, positions, and public employments, according to their capabilities and without other distinctions than those of their virtues and talents.

7. No man can be accused, arrested, or detained except in cases determined by the law, and according to the forms which it has prescribed. . . .

10. No one may be disturbed because of his opinions, even religious, provided that their public demonstration does not disturb the public order established by law.

11. The free communication of thoughts and opinions is one of the most precious rights of man: every citizen can therefore freely speak, write, and print. . . .

12. The guaranteeing of the rights of man and citizen necessitates a public force; this force is therefore instituted for the advantage of all, and not for the private use of those to whom it is entrusted. . . .

14. Citizens have the right to determine for themselves or through their representatives the need for taxation of the public, to consent to it freely, to investigate its use, and to determine its rate, basis, collection, and duration.

15. Society has the right to demand an accounting of his administration from every public agent.

16. Any society in which guarantees of rights are not assured nor the separation of powers determined has no constitution.

17. Property being an inviolable and sacred right, no one may be deprived of it unless public necessity, legally determined, clearly requires such action, and then only on condition of a just and prior indemnity.

---

eyewitness as "detachments of women . . . armed with broomsticks, lances, pitchforks, swords, pistols and muskets," marched to Versailles and forced the king to accept the new decrees. The crowd now insisted that the royal family return to Paris. On October 6, the king complied. As a goodwill gesture, he brought along wagonloads of flour from the palace stores, escorted by women armed with pikes (some of which held the severed heads of the king's guards) singing, "We are bringing back the baker, the baker's wife, and the baker's boy" (the king, queen, and their son). The king became virtually a prisoner in Paris.

Because the Catholic church was seen as an important pillar of the old order, it too was reformed. Most of the lands of the church were seized. The new Civil Constitution of the Clergy was put into effect. Both bishops and priests were to be elected by the people and paid by the state. The Catholic church, still an important institution in the life of the French people, now became an enemy of the Revolution.

By 1791, the National Assembly had finally completed a new constitution that established a limited constitutional monarchy. There was still a monarch (now called "king of the French"), but the new Legislative Assembly was to make the laws. The Legislative Assembly, in which sovereign power was vested, was to sit for two years and consist of 745 representatives chosen by an indirect system of election that preserved power in the hands of the more affluent members of society. Only active citizens (men over the age of twenty-five paying in taxes the equivalent of three days' unskilled

DECLARATION OF THE RIGHTS OF WOMAN AND THE FEMALE CITIZEN

O *lympe de Gouges (a pen name for Marie Gouze) was a butcher's daughter who wrote plays and pamphlets. She argued that the Declaration of the Rights of Man and the Citizen did not apply to women and composed her own Declaration of the Rights of Woman.*

DECLARATION OF THE RIGHTS OF WOMAN AND THE FEMALE CITIZEN

Mothers, daughters, sisters and representatives of the nation demand to be constituted into a national assembly. Believing that ignorance, omission, or scorn for the rights of woman are the only causes of public misfortunes and of the corruption of governments, the women have resolved to set forth in a solemn declaration the natural, inalienable, and sacred rights of woman in order that this declaration, constantly exposed before all the members of the society, will ceaselessly remind them of their rights and duties. . . .

Consequently, the sex that is as superior in beauty as it is in courage during the sufferings of maternity recognizes and declares in the presence and under the auspices of the Supreme Being, the following Rights of Woman and of Female Citizens.

1. Woman is born free and lives equal to man in her rights. Social distinctions can be based only on the common utility.

2. The purpose of any political association is the conservation of the natural and imprescriptible rights of woman and man; these rights are liberty, property, security, and especially resistance to oppression.

3. The principle of all sovereignty rests essentially with the nation, which is nothing but the union of woman and man; no body and no individual can exercise any authority which does not come expressly from [the nation].

4. Liberty and justice consist of restoring all that belongs to others; thus, the only limits on the exercise of the natural rights of woman are perpetual male tyranny; these limits are to be reformed by the laws of nature and reason. . . .

6. The law must be the expression of the general will; all female and male citizens must contribute either personally or through their representatives to its formation; it must be the same for all: male and female citizens, being equal in the eyes of the law, must be equally admitted to all honors, positions, and public employment according to their capacity and without other distinctions besides those of their virtues and talents.

7. No woman is an exception; she is accused, arrested, and detained in cases determined by law. . . .

10. No one is to be disquieted for his very basic opinions; woman has the right to mount the scaffold; she must equally have the right to mount the rostrum, provided that her demonstrations do not disturb the legally established public order.

11. The free communication of thoughts and opinions is one of the most precious rights of woman, since that liberty assured the recognition of children by their fathers. . . .

12. The guarantee of the rights of woman and the female citizen implies a major benefit; this guarantee must be instituted for the advantage of all, and not for the particular benefit of those to whom it is entrusted. . . .

14. Female and male citizens have the right to verify, either by themselves or through their representatives, the necessity of the public contribution. This can only apply to women if they are granted an equal share, not only of wealth, but also of public administration, and in the determination of the proportion, the base, the collection, and the duration of the tax.

15. The collectivity of women, joined for tax purposes to the aggregate of men, has the right to demand an accounting of his administration from any public agent.

16. No society has a constitution without the guarantee of rights and the separation of powers; the constitution is null if the majority of individuals comprising the nation have not cooperated in drafting it.

17. Property belongs to both sexes whether united or separate; for each it is an inviolable and sacred right; no one can be deprived of it, since it is the true patrimony of nature.

---

labor) could vote for electors (men paying taxes equal in value to ten days' labor). This relatively small group of fifty thousand electors then chose the deputies.

By 1791, the old order had been destroyed. However, many people—including Catholic priests, nobles, lower classes hurt by a rise in the cost of living, peasants who remained opposed to dues that had still not been abandoned, and political clubs like the Jacobins who offered more radical solutions to France's problems—opposed the new order. The king also made things difficult for the new government when he sought to flee France in June 1791 and almost succeeded before being recognized, captured, and brought back to Paris. In this unsettled situation, under a discredited and seemingly disloyal monarch, the new Legislative Assembly held its first session in October 1791. France's relations with the rest of Europe soon led to Louis's downfall.

On August 27, 1791, the monarchs of Austria and Prussia, fearing that revolution would spread to their countries, invited other European monarchs to use force to reestablish monarchical authority in France. Insulted by this threat, the Legislative Assembly declared war on Austria on April 20, 1792. The French fared badly in the initial fighting, and a frantic search for scapegoats began. As one observer noted, "Everywhere you hear the cry that the king is betraying us, the generals are betraying us, that nobody is to be trusted; . . . that Paris will be taken in six weeks by the Austrians. . . . We are on a volcano ready to spout flames."[5] Defeats in war coupled with economic shortages in the spring led to renewed political demonstrations, especially against the king. In August 1792, radical political groups in Paris took the king captive and forced the Legislative Assembly to suspend the monarchy and call for a national convention, chosen on the basis of universal male suffrage, to decide on the future form of government. The French Revolution was about to enter a more radical stage.

The Radical Revolution

In September 1792, the newly elected National Convention began its sessions. Dominated by lawyers and other professionals, two-thirds of its deputies were under forty-five, and almost all had gained political experience as a result of the Revolution. Almost all distrusted the king. As a result, the convention's first step on September 21 was to abolish the monarchy and establish a republic. On January 21, 1793, the king was executed, and the destruction of the old regime was complete. There could be no turning back. But the execution of the king created new enemies for the Revolution both at home and abroad while strengthening those who were already its enemies.

In Paris, the local government, known as the Commune, whose leaders came from the working classes, favored radical change and put constant pressure on the convention, pushing it to ever more radical positions. Moreover, the National Convention still did not rule all of France. Peasants in the west and inhabitants of France's major provincial cities refused to accept the authority of the convention.

A foreign crisis also loomed large. By the beginning of 1793, after the king had been executed, most of Europe— an informal coalition of Austria, Prussia, Spain, Portugal, Britain, the Dutch Republic, and even Russia— aligned militarily against France. Grossly overextended, the French armies began to experience reverses, and by late spring France was threatened with invasion. If successful, both the Revolution and the revolutionaries would be destroyed and the old regime reestablished.

A NATION IN ARMS

To meet these crises, the convention gave broad powers to an executive committee of twelve known as the Committee of Public Safety, which came to be dominated by Maximilien Robespierre. For a twelve-month period, from 1793 to 1794, the Committee of Public Safety took control of France. To save the Republic from its foreign foes, the committee decreed a universal mobilization of the nation on August 23, 1793:

> Young men will fight, young men are called to conquer. Married men will forge arms, transport military baggage and guns and will prepare food supplies. Women, who at long last are to take their rightful place in the revolution and follow their true destiny, will forget their futile tasks: their delicate hands will work at making clothes for soldiers; they will make tents and

⇨ WOMEN PATRIOTS. Women played a variety of roles in the events of the French Revolution. This picture shows a women's patriotic club discussing the decrees of the National Convention, an indication that some women became highly politicized by the upheavals of the Revolution.

JUSTICE IN THE REIGN OF TERROR

The Reign of Terror created a repressive environment in which revolutionary courts often acted quickly to condemn traitors to the revolutionary cause. In this account, an English visitor describes the court, the procession to the scene of execution, and the final execution procedure.

J. G. MILLIGEN, *THE REVOLUTIONARY TRIBUNAL* (PARIS, OCTOBER 1793)

In the center of the hall, under a statue of Justice, holding scales in one hand, and a sword in the other, sat Dumas, the President, with the other judges. Under them were seated the public accuser, Fourquier-Tinville, and his scribes. . . . To the right were benches on which the accused were placed in several rows, and *gendarmes* with carbines and fixed bayonets by their sides. To the left was the jury.

Never can I forget the mournful appearance of these funereal processions to the place of execution. The march was opened by a detachment of mounted *gendarmes*—the carts followed; they were the same carts as those that are used in Paris for carrying wood; four boards were placed across them for seats, and on each board sat two, and sometimes three victims; their hands were tied behind their backs, and the constant jostling of the cart made them nod their heads up and down, to the great amusement of the spectators. On the front of the cart stood Samson, the executioner, or one of his sons or assistants; *gendarmes* on foot marched by the side; then followed a hackney, in which was the reporting clerk, whose duty it was to witness the execution, and then return to the public accuser's office to report the execution of what they called the law.

The process of execution was also a sad and heart-rending spectacle. In the middle of the Place de la Revolution was erected a guillotine, in front of a colossal statue of Liberty, represented seated on a rock, a cap on her head, a spear in her hand, the other reposing on a shield. On one side of the scaffold were drawn out a sufficient number of carts, with large baskets painted red, to receive the heads and bodies of the victims. Those bearing the condemned moved on slowly to the foot of the guillotine; the culprits were led out in turn, and if necessary, supported by two of the executioner's assistants, but their assistance was rarely required. Most of these unfortunates ascended the scaffold with a determined step—many of them looked up firmly on the menacing instrument of death, beholding for the last time the rays of the glorious sun, beaming on the polished axe: and I have seen some young men actually dance a few steps before they went up to be strapped to the perpendicular plane, which was then tilted to a horizontal plane in a moment, and ran on the grooves until the neck was secured and closed in by a moving board, when the head passed through what was called, in derision, "the republican toilet seat"; the weighty knife was then dropped with a heavy fall; and, with incredible dexterity and rapidity, two executioners tossed the body into the basket, while another threw the head after it.

---

they will extend their tender care to shelters where the defenders of the *Patrie* [nation] will receive the help that their wounds require. Children will make lint of old cloth. It is for them that we are fighting: children, those beings destined to gather all the fruits of the revolution, will raise their pure hands toward the skies. And old men, performing their missions again, as of yore, will be guided to the public squares of the cities where they will kindle the courage of young warriors and preach the doctrines of hate for kings and the unity of the Republic.[6]

In less than a year, the French revolutionary government had raised an army of 650,000; by September 1794, it numbered 1,169,000. The Republic's army was the largest ever seen in European history. It now pushed the allies back across the Rhine and even conquered the Austrian Netherlands.

The French revolutionary army was an important step in the creation of modern nationalism. Previously, wars had been fought between governments or ruling dynasties by relatively small armies of professional soldiers. The new French army was the creation of a "people's" government; its wars were now "people's" wars. The entire nation was to be involved in the war. But when dynastic wars became people's wars, warfare increased in ferocity and lack of restraint. The wars of the French revolutionary era opened the door to the total war of the modern world.

REIGN OF TERROR

To meet the domestic crisis, the National Convention and the Committee of Public Safety launched the "Reign of Terror." Revolutionary courts were instituted to protect the Republic from its internal enemies. In the course of nine months, sixteen thousand people were officially killed under the blade of the guillotine—a revolutionary device for the quick and efficient separation of heads from bodies (see the box above). Most of the Terror's executions occurred in places that had rebelled against the authority of the National Convention. The Committee of Public Safety held that this bloodletting was only temporary. Once the war and the domestic emergency were over, they would be succeeded by a "republic of virtue" in which the Declaration of the Rights of the Man and the Citizen would be fully implemented.

Revolutionary armies were set up to bring recalcitrant cities and districts back under the control of the National Convention. The Committee of Public Safety decided to make an example of Lyons, which had defied the authority of the National Convention. By April 1794, some 1,880 citizens of Lyons had been executed. When the guillotine proved too slow, cannon fire was used to blow condemned men into open graves. A German observed:

> Whole ranges of houses, always the most handsome, burnt. The churches, convents, and all the dwellings of the former patricians were in ruins. When I came to the guillotine, the blood of those who had been executed a few hours beforehand was still running in the street. . . . I said to a group of sansculottes [radicals] that it would be decent to clear away all this human blood. Why should it be cleared? one of them said to me. It's the blood of aristocrats and rebels. The dogs should lick it up.[7]

The National Convention also pursued a policy of dechristianization. A new calendar was instituted in which years were no longer numbered from the birth of Christ but from September 22, 1792, the first day of the French Republic. The new calendar also eliminated Sundays and church holidays. In Paris, the cathedral of Notre-Dame was designated the Temple of Reason; in November 1793, a public ceremony dedicated to the worship of reason was held in the former cathedral in which patriotic maidens adorned in white dresses paraded before a "temple of reason" where the high altar once stood.

EQUALITY AND SLAVERY

Early in the French Revolution, the desire for equality led to a discussion of what to do about slavery. A club called Friends of the Blacks advocated the abolition of slavery, which was achieved in France in September 1791. However, French planters in the West Indies, who profited greatly from the use of slaves on their sugar plantations, opposed the abolition of slavery in the French colonies. When the National Convention came into power, the issue was revisited, and on February 4, 1794, guided by ideals of equality, the government abolished slavery in the colonies.

In one French colony, slaves had already rebelled for their freedom. In 1791, black slaves in the French sugar colony of Saint Domingue (the western third of the island of Hispaniola), inspired by the ideals of the revolution occurring in France, revolted against French plantation owners. Led by Toussaint L'Ouverture (1746–1803), a son of African slaves, over 100,000 black slaves rose in revolt and seized control of all of Hispaniola. Later, an army sent by Napoleon captured L'Ouverture, who died in captivity in France. But the French soldiers, weakened by disease, soon succumbed to the slave forces. On January 1, 1804, the western part of Hispaniola, now called Haiti, announced its freedom and became the first independent state in Latin America. One of the French revolutionary ideals had triumphed abroad.

Revolt in Saint Domingue

Chronology

THE FRENCH REVOLUTION

1789	
Meeting of Estates-General	May 5
Formation of National Assembly	June 17
Fall of the Bastille	July 14
Great Fear	Summer
Abolition of feudalism	August 4
Declaration of the Rights of Man and the Citizen	August 26
March to Versailles; king's return to Paris	October 5–6
1790	
Civil Constitution of the Clergy	July 12
1791	
Flight of the king	June 20–21
1792	
France declares war on Austria	April 20
Attack on the royal palace	August 10
Abolition of monarchy	September 21
1793	
Execution of the king	January 21
Levy-in-mass	August 23
1794	
Execution of Robespierre	July 28
1795	
Adoption of Constitution of 1795—the Directory	August 22

Reaction and the Directory

By the summer of 1794, the French had been successful on the battlefield against their foreign foes, making the Terror less necessary. But the Terror continued because Robespierre, who had become a figure of power and authority, became obsessed with purifying the body politic of all the corrupt. Many deputies in the National Convention were fearful, however, that they were not safe while Robespierre was free to act and gathered enough votes to condemn him. Robespierre was guillotined on July 28, 1794.

After the death of Robespierre, a reaction set in as more moderate middle-class leaders took control. The Reign of Terror came to a halt, and the National Convention reduced the power of the Committee of Public Safety. Churches were allowed to reopen for public worship. In

NAPOLEON AND PSYCHOLOGICAL WARFARE

In 1796, at the age of twenty-seven, Napoleon Bonaparte was given command of the French army in Italy, where he won a series of stunning victories. His use of speed, deception, and surprise to overwhelm his opponents is well known. In this selection from a proclamation to his troops in Italy, Napoleon also appears as a master of psychological warfare.

NAPOLEON BONAPARTE, PROCLAMATION TO FRENCH TROOPS IN ITALY (APRIL 26, 1796)

Soldiers:

In a fortnight you have won six victories, taken twenty-one standards [flags of military units], fifty-five pieces of artillery, several strong positions, and conquered the richest part of Piedmont [in northern Italy]; you have captured 15,000 prisoners and killed or wounded more than 10,000 men. . . . You have won battles without cannon, crossed rivers without bridges, made forced marches without shoes, camped without brandy and often without bread. Soldiers of liberty, only republican troops could have endured what you have endured. Soldiers, you have our thanks! The grateful Patrie [nation] will owe its prosperity to you. . . .

The two armies which but recently attacked you with audacity are fleeing before you in terror; the wicked men who laughed at your misery and rejoiced at the thought of the triumphs of your enemies are confounded and trembling.

But, soldiers, as yet you have done nothing compared with what remains to be done. . . . Undoubtedly the greatest obstacles have been overcome; but you still have battles to fight, cities to capture, rivers to cross. Is there one among you whose courage is abating? No. . . . All of you are consumed with a desire to extend the glory of the French people; all of you long to humiliate those arrogant kings who dare to contemplate placing us in fetters; all of you desire to dictate a glorious peace, one which will indemnify the Patrie for the immense sacrifices it has made; all of you wish to be able to say with pride as you return to your villages, "I was with the victorious army of Italy!"

---

addition, a new constitution was created in August 1795 that reflected the desire for a stability that did not sacrifice the ideals of 1789. Five directors—the Directory—acted as the executive authority.

The period of the Revolution under the government of the Directory (1795–1799) was an era of stagnation and corruption, a materialistic reaction to the sacrifices that had been demanded in the Reign of Terror. At the same time, the government of the Directory faced political enemies from both the left and the right of the political spectrum. On the right, royalists who wanted to restore the monarchy continued their agitation. On the left, radical hopes of power were revived by continuing economic problems. Battered from both sides, unable to solve the country's economic problems, and still carrying on the wars inherited from the Committee of Public Safety, the Directory increasingly relied on the military to maintain its power. This led to a coup d'état in 1799 in which the popular military general Napoleon Bonaparte seized power.

THE AGE OF NAPOLEON

Napoleon dominated both French and European history from 1799 to 1815. He was born in 1769 in Corsica shortly after France had annexed the island. The young Napoleon was sent to France to study in one of the new military schools and was a lieutenant when the Revolution broke out in 1789. The Revolution and the European war that followed gave him new opportunities, and Napoleon rose quickly through the ranks. In 1794, at the age of only twenty-five, he was made a brigadier general by the Committee of Public Safety. Two years later, he commanded the French armies in Italy, where he won a series of victories and returned to France as a conquering hero (see the box above). After a disastrous expedition to Egypt, Napoleon returned to Paris, where he participated in the coup that gave him control of France. He was only thirty years old.

After the coup of 1799, a new form of the Republic—called the Consulate—was proclaimed in which Napoleon, as first consul, controlled the entire executive authority of government. He had overwhelming influence over the legislature, appointed members of the administrative bureaucracy, commanded the army, and conducted foreign affairs. In 1802, Napoleon was made consul for life, and in 1804, he returned France to monarchy when he had himself crowned as Emperor Napoleon I.

Domestic Policies

One of Napoleon's first domestic policies was to establish peace with the oldest and most implacable enemy of the Revolution, the Catholic church. In 1801, Napoleon arranged a concordat with the pope that recognized Catholicism as the religion of a majority of the French people. In return, the pope agreed not to raise the question of the church lands confiscated in the Revolution. As a result of the concordat, the Catholic church was no longer an enemy of the French government, and those

THE CORONATION OF NAPOLEON.   In 1804, Napoleon restored monarchy to France when he had himself crowned as emperor. In the coronation scene painted by Jacques-Louis David, Napoleon is shown crowning his wife, the empress Josephine, while the pope looks on. The painting shows Napoleon's mother seated in the box in the background, even though she was not at the ceremony.

who had acquired church lands during the Revolution were assured that they would not be stripped of them, an assurance that made them supporters of the Napoleonic regime.

Napoleon's most enduring domestic achievement was his codification of the laws. Before the Revolution, France had some three hundred local legal systems. During the Revolution, efforts were made to prepare a single code of laws for the entire nation, but it remained for Napoleon to bring the work to completion in the famous Civil Code. This preserved most of the revolutionary gains by recognizing the principle of the equality of all citizens before the law, the abolition of serfdom and feudalism, and religious toleration. Property rights were protected, and the interests of employers were safeguarded by outlawing trade unions and strikes.

At the same time, the Civil Code strictly curtailed the rights of some people. During the radical phase of the French Revolution, new laws had made divorce an easy process for both husbands and wives and allowed sons and daughters to inherit property equally. Napoleon's Civil Code undid these laws. Divorce was still allowed but was made more difficult for women to obtain. Women were now "less equal than men" in other ways as well. When they married, their property came under the control of their husbands, and in lawsuits, they were treated as minors.

Napoleon also developed a powerful, centralized administrative machine and worked hard to develop a bureaucracy of capable officials. Early on, the regime showed that it cared little whether the expertise of officials had been acquired in royal or revolutionary bureaucracies. Promotion, whether in civil or military offices, was to be based not on rank or birth but on ability only. This principle of a government career open to talent was, of course, what many bourgeois had wanted before the Revolution.

In his domestic policies, then, Napoleon both destroyed and preserved aspects of the Revolution. Liberty had been replaced by an initially benevolent despotism that grew increasingly arbitrary as the demands of war overwhelmed Napoleon and the French. The Civil Code, however, preserved the equality of all citizens before the law. The concept of careers open to talent was also a gain of the Revolution that Napoleon preserved.

Napoleon's Empire and the European Response

When Napoleon became consul in 1799, France was at war with a second European coalition of Russia, Great Britain, and Austria. Napoleon realized the need for a pause and made a peace treaty in 1802. But war was renewed in 1803 with Britain, who was soon joined by Austria, Russia, and Prussia in the Third Coalition. In a series of battles from 1805 to 1807, Napoleon's Grand Army defeated the Austrian, Prussian, and Russian armies,

giving Napoleon the opportunity to create a new European order.

THE GRAND EMPIRE

From 1807 to 1812, Napoleon was the master of Europe. His Grand Empire was composed of three major parts: the French Empire, dependent states, and allied states (see Map 17.6). The French Empire, the inner core of the Grand Empire, consisted of an enlarged France extending to the Rhine in the east and including the western half of Italy north of Rome. Dependent states were kingdoms under the rule of Napoleon's relatives; these came to include Spain, the Netherlands, the kingdom of Italy, the Swiss Republic, the Grand Duchy of Warsaw, and the

MAP 17.6 Napoleon's Grand Empire. Napoleon's Grand Army won a series of victories against Britain, Austria, Prussia, and Russia that gave the French emperor full or partial control over much of Europe by 1807. ➤ *On the Continent, what is the overall relationship between distance from France and degree of French control, and how can you account for this?*

French Empire

Under French control

Allied to France

→ Napoleon's route, 1812

🔫 Battle site

Confederation of the Rhine (a union of all German states except Austria and Prussia). Allied states were those defeated by Napoleon and forced to join his struggle against Britain; these included Prussia, Austria, Russia, and Sweden.

Within his empire, Napoleon sought acceptance of certain revolutionary principles, including legal equality, religious toleration, and economic freedom. As he explained to his brother Jerome after he had made him king of the new German state of Westphalia:

> What the people of Germany desire most impatiently is that talented commoners should have the same right to your esteem and to public employments as the nobles, that any trace of serfdom and of an intermediate hierarchy between the sovereign and the lowest class of the people should be completely abolished. The benefits of the Code Napoléon, the publicity of judicial procedure, the creation of juries must be so many distinguishing marks of your monarchy. . . . What nation would wish to return under the arbitrary Prussian government once it had tasted the benefits of a wise and liberal administration? The peoples of Germany, the peoples of France, of Italy, of Spain all desire equality and liberal ideas. I have guided the affairs of Europe for many years now, and I have had occasion to convince myself that the buzzing of the privileged classes is contrary to the general opinion. Be a constitutional king.[8]

In the inner core and dependent states of his Grand Empire, Napoleon tried to destroy the old order. Nobility and clergy everywhere in these states lost their special privileges. He decreed equality of opportunity with offices open to talent, equality before the law, and religious toleration. This spread of French revolutionary principles was an important factor in the development of liberal traditions in these countries.

Napoleon hoped that his Grand Empire would last for centuries; it collapsed almost as rapidly as it had been formed. Two major reasons explain this: Great Britain and nationalism. As long as Britain ruled the waves, it was not subject to military attack. Napoleon hoped to invade Britain, but he could not overcome the British navy's decisive defeat of a combined French-Spanish fleet at Trafalgar in 1805. To defeat Britain, Napoleon turned to his Continental System. Put into effect between 1806 and 1808, it attempted to prevent British goods from reaching the European continent in order to weaken Britain economically and destroy its capacity to wage war. But the Continental System failed. Allied states resented it; some began to cheat and others to resist. New markets in the Middle East and in Latin America gave Britain new outlets for its goods. Indeed, by 1809, British overseas exports were at near-record highs.

The second important factor in the defeat of Napoleon was nationalism. This political creed had arisen during the French Revolution in the French people's emphasis on solidarity against other peoples. Nationalism involved the

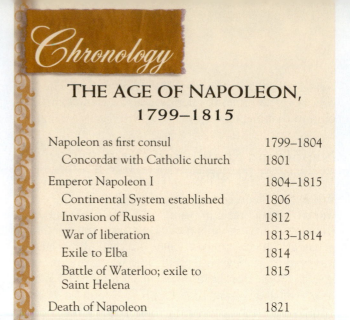

unique cultural identity of a people based on common language and national symbols. French nationalism had made possible the mass armies of the revolutionary and Napoleonic eras. But Napoleon's conquests aroused nationalism in two ways: by making the French hated oppressors and thus arousing the patriotism of others in opposition to French nationalism and by showing the people of Europe what nationalism was and what a nation in arms could do. It was a lesson not lost on other peoples and rulers. A Spanish uprising against Napoleon's rule, aided by British support, kept a French force of 200,000 pinned down for years.

THE FALL OF NAPOLEON

The beginning of Napoleon's downfall came in 1812 with his invasion of Russia. The refusal of the Russians to remain in the Continental System left Napoleon with little choice. Although aware of the risks in invading such a huge country, he also knew that if the Russians were allowed to challenge the Continental System unopposed, others would soon follow suit. In June 1812, he led his Grand Army of more than 600,000 men into Russia. Napoleon's hopes for victory depended on quickly defeating the Russian armies, but the Russian forces retreated and refused to give battle, torching their own villages and countryside to keep Napoleon's army from finding food. When the Russians did stop to fight at Borodino, Napoleon's forces won an indecisive and costly victory. When the remaining troops of the Grand Army arrived in Moscow, they found the city ablaze. Lacking food and supplies, Napoleon abandoned Moscow late in October and made a retreat across Russia in terrible winter conditions. Only 40,000 of the original 600,000 men managed to arrive back in Poland in January 1813.

This military disaster led other European states to rise up and attack the crippled French army. Paris was captured in March 1814, and Napoleon was sent into exile on the island of Elba, off the coast of Italy. Meanwhile, the Bourbon monarchy was restored in the person of Louis XVIII, the Count of Provence, brother of the executed king. Louis XVII, son of Louis XVI, had died in prison at age 10. Napoleon, bored on Elba, slipped back into France. When troops were sent to capture him, Napoleon opened his coat and addressed them: "Soldiers of the 5th regiment, I am your Emperor. . . . If there is a man among you would kill his Emperor, here I am!" No one fired a shot. Shouting "Vive l'Empereur! Vive l'Empereur," the troops went over to his side, and Napoleon entered Paris in triumph on March 20, 1815.

The powers that had defeated him pledged once more to fight him. Having decided to strike first at his enemies, Napoleon raised yet another army and moved to attack the allied forces stationed in what is now Belgium. At Waterloo on June 18, Napoleon met a combined British and Prussian army under the duke of Wellington and suffered a bloody defeat. This time, the victorious allies exiled him to Saint Helena, a small, forsaken island in the South Atlantic. Only Napoleon's memory continued to haunt French political life.

CONCLUSION

Everywhere in Europe at the beginning of the eighteenth century, the old order remained strong. Nobles, clerics, towns, and provinces all had privileges. Everywhere in the eighteenth century, monarchs sought to enlarge their bureaucracies to raise taxes to support the large standing armies that had originated in the seventeenth century. The existence of five great powers, with two of them (France and England) embattled in the East and in the Western Hemisphere, ushered in a new scale of conflict; the Seven Years' War can legitimately be viewed as the first world war. Although the wars changed little on the European continent, British victories enabled Great Britain to emerge as the world's greatest naval and colonial power. Everywhere

in Europe, increased demands for taxes to support these conflicts led to attacks on the privileged orders and a desire for change not met by the ruling monarchs. At the same time, sustained population growth and dramatic changes in finance, trade, and industry created tensions that undermined the traditional foundations of the old order. The inability of that old order to deal meaningfully with these changes led to a revolutionary outburst at the end of the eighteenth century that brought the old order to an end.

The revolutionary era of the late eighteenth century was a time of dramatic political transformations. Revolutionary upheavals, beginning in North America and continuing in France, spurred movements for political liberty and equality. The documents promulgated by these revolutions, the Declaration of Independence and the Declaration of the Rights of Man and the Citizen, embodied the fundamental ideas of the Enlightenment and created a liberal political agenda based on a belief in popular sovereignty—the people as the source of political power—and the principles of liberty and equality. Liberty meant, in theory, freedom from arbitrary power as well as the freedom to think, write, and worship as one chose. Equality meant equality in rights and equality of opportunity based on talent rather than wealth or status at birth. In practice, equality remained limited; property owners had greater opportunities for voting and officeholding, and women were still not treated as the equals of men.

The French Revolution set in motion a modern revolutionary concept. No one had foreseen or consciously planned the upheaval that began in 1789, but thereafter, radicals and revolutionaries knew that mass uprisings by the common people could overthrow unwanted elitist governments. For these people, the French Revolution became a symbol of hope; for those who feared such changes, it became a symbol of dread. The French Revolution became the classical political and social model for revolution. At the same time, the liberal and national political ideals created by the Revolution dominated the political landscape for well over a century. A new era had begun, and the world would never be the same.

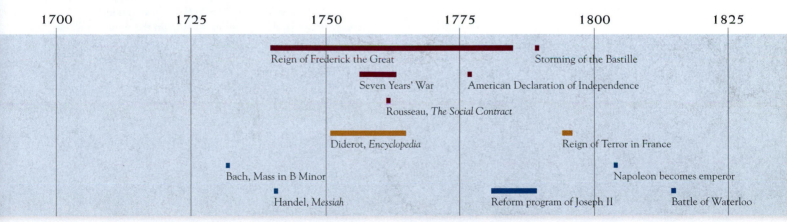

1700	1725	1750	1775	1800	1825

Reign of Frederick the Great

Storming of the Bastille

Seven Years' War

American Declaration of Independence

Rousseau, *The Social Contract*

Diderot, *Encyclopedia*

Reign of Terror in France

Bach, Mass in B Minor

Napoleon becomes emperor

Handel, *Messiah*

Reform program of Joseph II

Battle of Waterloo

CHAPTER NOTES

1. Quoted in Dorinda Outram, *The Enlightenment* (Cambridge, 1995), p. 67.
2. John Locke, *An Essay Concerning Human Understanding* (New York, 1964), pp. 89–90.
3. Kenneth Clark, *Civilization* (New York, 1969), p. 231.
4. Quoted in Peter Burke, *Popular Culture in Early Modern Europe* (New York, 1978), p. 179.
5. Quoted in William Doyle, *The Oxford History of the French Revolution* (Oxford, 1989), p. 184.
6. Quoted in Leo Gershoy, *The Era of the French Revolution* (Princeton, N.J., 1957), p. 157.
7. Quoted in Doyle, *Oxford History of the French Revolution*, p. 254.
8. Quoted in J. Christopher Herold, ed., *The Mind of Napoleon* (New York, 1955), pp. 74–75.

SUGGESTED READING

Two sound, comprehensive surveys of eighteenth-century Europe are I. Woloch, *Eighteenth-Century Europe* (New York, 1982), and M. S. Anderson, *Europe in the Eighteenth Century* (London, 1987).

Good introductions to the Enlightenment can be found in N. Hampson, *A Cultural History of the Enlightenment* (New York, 1968); U. Im Hof, *The Enlightenment* (Oxford, 1994); D. Goodman, *The Republic of Letters: A Cultural History of the French Enlightenment* (Ithaca, N.Y., 1994); and D. Outram, *The Enlightenment* (Cambridge, 1995). A more detailed synthesis can be found in the two volumes by P. Gay, *The Enlightenment: An Interpretation* (New York, 1966–1969). For a short, popular survey on the French philosophes, see F. Artz, *The Enlightenment in France* (Kent, Ohio, 1968). On women in the eighteenth century, see N. Z. Davis and A. Farge, eds., *A History of Women: Renaissance and Enlightenment Paradoxes* (Cambridge, Mass., 1993), and O. Hufton, *The Prospect Before Her: A History of Women in Western Europe, 1500–1800* (New York, 1998).

A readable general survey on the arts and literature is M. Levy, *Rococo to Revolution* (London, 1966). An important study on popular culture is P. Burke, *Popular Culture in Early Modern Europe* (New York, 1978).

On the European nobility in the eighteenth century, see J. Dewald, *The European Nobility 1400–1800* (Cambridge, 1996), and H. M. Scott, *The European Nobility in the Seventeenth and Eighteenth Centuries* (London, 1995). On European cities, see J. de Vries, *European Urbanization, 1500–1800* (Cambridge, Mass., 1984). The warfare of this period is examined in M. S. Anderson, *War and Society in Europe of the Old Regime, 1615–1789* (New York, 1988).

For a brief survey of Latin America, see E. B. Burns, *Latin America: A Concise Interpretive History*, 4th ed. (Englewood Cliffs, N.J., 1986). More detailed works on colonial Latin American history include S. J. Stein and B. H. Stein, *The Colonial Heritage of Latin America* (New York, 1970), and J. Lockhardt and S. B. Schwartz, *Early Latin America: A History of Colonial Spanish America and Brazil* (New York, 1983). A history of the revolutionary era in America can be found in R. Middlekauff, *The Glorious Cause: The American Revolution, 1763–1789* (New York, 1982), and C. Bonwick, *The American Revolution* (Charlottesville, Va., 1991). The importance of ideology is treated in G. Wood, *The Radicalism of the American Revolution* (New York, 1992). For an interesting comparative study, see the stimulating work by P. Higonnet, *Sister Republics: Origins of the French and American Revolutions* (Cambridge, Mass., 1988).

On enlightened absolutism, see H. M. Scott, ed., Enlightened *Absolutism: Reform and Reformers in Late Eighteenth-Century Europe* (Ann Arbor, Mich., 1990). Good biographies of some of Europe's monarchs include R. Asprey, *Frederick the Great: The Magnificent Enigma* (New York, 1986); I. De Madariaga, *Catherine the Great: A Short History* (New Haven, Conn., 1990); and T. C. W. Blanning, *Joseph II* (New York, 1994).

A well written, up-to-date introduction to the French Revolution can be found in W. Doyle, *The Oxford History of the French Revolution* (Oxford, 1989). For the entire revolutionary and Napoleonic eras, see O. Connelly, *The French Revolution and Napoleonic Era*, 3d ed. (Fort Worth, Tex., 2000), and D. M. G. Sutherland, *France, 1789–1815: Revolution and Counter-Revolution* (London, 1985). Two brief works are A. Forrest, *The French Revolution* (Oxford, 1995), and J. M. Roberts, *The French Revolution*, 2d ed. (New York, 1997).

The origins of the French Revolution are examined in W. Doyle, *Origins of the French Revolution* (Oxford, 1988). On the early years of the Revolution, see T. Tackett, *Becoming a Revolutionary* (Princeton, N.J., 1996), and N. Hampson, *Prelude to Terror* (Oxford, 1988). Important works on the radical stage of the French Revolution include N. Hampson, *The Terror in the French Revolution* (London, 1981); R. R. Palmer, *Twelve Who Ruled* (Princeton, N.J., 1941); and R. Cobb, *The People's Armies* (London, 1987). The importance of the revolutionary wars in the radical stage of the Revolution is underscored in T. C. W. Blanning, *The French Revolutionary Wars, 1787–1802* (New York, 1996). On the Directory, see M. Lyons, *France Under the Directory* (Cambridge, 1975). On the role of women in revolutionary France, see O. Hufton, *Women and the Limits of Citizenship in the French Revolution* (Toronto, 1992), and J. Landes, *Women and the Public Sphere in the Age of the French Revolution* (Ithaca, N.Y., 1988). The best brief biography of Napoleon is F. Markham, *Napoleon* (New York, 1963). Also valuable are M. Lyons, *Napoleon Bonaparte and the Legacy of the French Revolution* (New York, 1994); G. J. Ellis, *Napoleon* (New York, 1997); and the massive biographies by F. J. McLynn, *Napoleon: A Biography* (London, 1997), and A. Schom, *Napoleon Bonaparte* (New York, 1997).

INFOTRAC COLLEGE EDITION

For additional reading, go to InfoTrac College Edition, your online research library at
http://web1.infotrac-college.com

Enter the search term "Enlightenment" using the Subject Guide.

Enter the search term "Rousseau" using Keywords.

Enter the search terms "John Locke" using Keywords.

Enter the search terms "American Revolution" using Keywords.

Enter the search terms "French Revolution" using Keywords.

Enter the search term "Napoleon" using Keywords.

Enter the search terms "Napoleonic Wars" using Keywords.

THE EMERGENCE OF NEW WORLD PATTERNS (1400–1800)

*H*istorians often refer to the period from the fifteenth to the eighteenth centuries as the early modern era. During these years, several factors were at work that created the conditions of our own time.

From a global perspective, perhaps the most noteworthy event of the period was the extension of the maritime trade network throughout the entire populated world. The Chinese had inaugurated the process with their groundbreaking voyages to East Africa in the early fifteenth century, but the primary instrument of that expansion was a resurgent Europe, which exploded onto the world scene with the initial explorations of the Portuguese and the Spanish at the end of the fifteenth century and then gradually came to dominate shipping on international trade routes during the next three centuries.

Some contemporary historians argue that it was this sudden burst of energy from Europe that created the first truly global economic network. According to Immanuel Wallerstein, one of the leading proponents of this theory, the Age of Exploration led to the creation of a new "world system" characterized by the emergence of global trade networks dominated by the rising force of European capitalism, which now began to scour the periphery of the system for access to markets and cheap raw materials.

In the view of other contemporary historians, however, Wallerstein's view must be qualified. Some, for example, point to the Mongol expansion beginning in the thirteenth century, or even to the rise of the Arab empire in the Middle East a few centuries earlier, as signs of the creation of a global communications network enabling goods and ideas to travel from one end of the Eurasian supercontinent to the other.

Whatever the truth of this debate, there are still many reasons for considering the end of the fifteenth century as a crucial date in world history. In the most basic sense, it marked the end of the long isolation of the Western Hemisphere from the rest of the inhabited world. In so doing, it led to the creation of the first truly global network of ideas and commodities, which would introduce plants, ideas, and (unfortunately) many new diseases to all humanity (see the box on p. 505). Second, the period gave birth to a stunning increase in trade and manufacturing that stimulated major economic changes not only in Europe but in other parts of the world as well.

The period from 1400 to 1800, then, was an incubation period for the modern world and the launching pad for an era of Western domination that would reach fruition in

the nineteenth century. To understand why the West emerged as the leading force in the world at that time, it is necessary to grasp what factors were at work in Europe and why they were absent in other major civilizations around the globe.

Historians have identified improvements in navigation, shipbuilding, and weaponry that took place in Europe in the early modern era as essential elements in the Age of Exploration. As we have seen, many of these technological advances were based on earlier discoveries that had taken place elsewhere—in China, India, and the Middle East—and had then been brought to Europe on Muslim ships or along the trade routes through Central Asia. But it was the capacity and the desire of the Europeans to enhance their wealth and power by making practical use of the discoveries of others that was the significant factor in the equation and enabled them to dominate international sea lanes and create vast colonial empires in the New World.

But technological innovations by themselves cannot provide the final answer to the question of why at this time in history Europe suddenly became the engine for rapid global change. Another factor, certainly, was the change in the European worldview, the shift from a metaphysical to a materialist perspective and the growing inclination among European intellectuals to question first principles. Whereas in China, for example, the "investigation of things" had been put to the use of analyzing and confirming principles first established by Confucius during the Chinese "Golden Age," in early modern Europe, empirical scientists rejected received religious ideas, developed a new conception of the universe, and sought ways to improve material conditions around them.

Why were European thinkers more interested in practical applications for their discoveries than their counterparts elsewhere? One explanation perhaps lies in the growing strength of the urban bourgeoisie in many areas of early modern Europe and the deliberate appeal that scientists made to European mercantile elites when they showed how the new scientific ideas could be applied directly to specific technological needs.

A final factor can be attributed to political changes that were beginning to take place in Europe during this period. The breakup of the world of Christendom, a consequence of the religious wars of the sixteenth and seventeenth centuries, helped give birth to independent and relatively centralized monarchies in many areas of Europe. In the eighteenth century, this process continued as most European states enlarged their bureaucratic machinery

THE COLUMBIAN EXCHANGE

In the Western world, the discovery of the Americas has traditionally been viewed essentially in a positive sense, as the first step in a process that expanded the global trade network and eventually led to economic well-being and political democracy in societies throughout the world. That view has come under sharp attack from some observers, however, who claim that for the peoples of the New World, the primary legacy of the European conquest was not improved living standards but harsh colonial exploitation and the spread of pestilential diseases that decimated the local population. In recent years, the brunt of such criticism has been directed at Christopher Columbus, one of the chief initiators of the discovery and conquest of the Americas. Taking issue with the prevailing image of Columbus as a heroic figure in world history, critics view him as a symbol of Spanish colonial repression and a prime mover in the virtual extinction of the peoples and cultures of the New World.

There is no doubt that the record of the European conquistadors in the Western Hemisphere leaves much to be desired, and certainly the voyages of Columbus were not of universal benefit to his contemporaries or to the generations later to come. But to focus solely on the evils that were committed in the name of exploration and the propagation of Christianity distorts the historical realities of the era. The

MASSACRE OF THE INDIANS. This sixteenth-century engraving is an imaginative treatment of what was probably an all-too-common occurrence as the Spanish attempted to enslave the American peoples and convert them to Christianity.

age of European expansion that began with Prince Henry the Navigator and Christopher Columbus was only the latest in a series of population movements that included the spread of nomadic peoples across Central Asia and the expansion of Islam from the Middle East after the death of the prophet Muhammad. In fact, the migration of peoples in search of survival and a better livelihood has been a central theme in the evolution of the human race since the dawn of prehistory.

Even more important, it seems clear that the consequences of such population movements are too complex to be summed up in moral or ideological simplifications. The European expansion into the Americas, for example, not only brought the destruction of cultures and dangerous new diseases but also initiated the exchange of plant and animal species that have ultimately been of widespread benefit to peoples throughout the globe. The introduction of the horse, cow, and various grain crops vastly increased food productivity in the New World. The cultivation of corn, manioc, and the potato have had the same effect in Asia, Africa, and Europe. Whether Christopher Columbus was a hero or a villain is a matter of debate. That he and his contemporaries played a key role in the emergence of the modern world is a matter on which there can be no doubt.

and consolidated their governments in order to collect the revenues and amass the armies they needed to compete militarily with rivals. In this highly competitive environment, political leaders desperately sought ways to enhance their wealth and power and grasped eagerly at whatever tools were available to guarantee their survival and prosperity.

European expansion was not fueled solely by economic considerations, however. As had been the case with the rise of Islam in the seventh and eighth centuries, religion played a major role in motivating the European Age of Exploration in the early modern era. Although Christianity was by no means a new religion in the fifteenth century (as Islam had been at the moment of Arab expansion), the world of Christendom was in the midst of a major period of conflict with the forces of Islam, a rivalry that had been exacerbated by the conquest of the Byzantine Empire by the Ottoman Turks in 1453.

Although the claims of Portuguese and Spanish adventurers that their activities were motivated primarily by a desire to bring the word of God to non-Christian peoples undoubtedly included a considerable measure of self-delusion and hypocrisy, there seems no reason to doubt that religious motives played a meaningful part in the European Age of Exploration. Religious motives were perhaps less evident in the activities of the non-Catholic powers that entered the competition beginning in the seventeenth century. English and Dutch merchants and officials were more inclined to be motivated purely by the pursuit of economic profit or by the prevailing "beggar thy neighbor" mercantile philosophy of the day.

Conditions in many areas of Asia were less conducive to these economic and political developments. In China, after Yongle's brief experiment in maritime exploration was abandoned, a centralized monarchy continued to rely on a prosperous agricultural sector as the economic foundation of the empire. In Japan, power was centralized under the powerful Tokugawa shogunate, and the era of peace and stability that ensued saw an increase in manufacturing and commercial activity. But Japanese elites, after initially expressing interest in the outside world, abruptly shut the door on European trade and ideas in an effort to protect the "land of the gods" from external contamination.

In India and the Middle East, commerce and manufacturing had played a vital role in the life of societies since the emergence of the Indian Ocean trade network in the first centuries C.E. But beginning in the eleventh century, the area had suffered through an extended period of political instability, marked by invasions by nomadic peoples from Central Asia. The violence of the period and the local rulers' lack of experience in promoting maritime commerce had a severe depressing effect on urban manufacturing and commerce.

In the early modern era, then, Europe was best placed to take advantage of the technological innovations that had become increasingly available throughout the Old World. It possessed the political stability, the capital, and what today might be called the "modernizing elite" that provided the spur to active efforts to take advantage of new conditions for their own benefit. Where other regions were still beset by internal obstacles or had deliberately "turned inward" to seek their destiny, Europe now turned outward to seek a new and dominant position in the world. This should not blind us to the facts that significant changes were taking place in other parts of the world as well and that many of these changes had relatively little to do with the situation in the West (see the box on p. 507). As we have seen, the impact of European expansion on the rest of the world was still limited at the end of the eighteenth century. While European political authority was firmly established in a few key areas, such as the Spice Islands and Latin America, in most regions of Africa and Asia traditional societies remained relatively intact. And processes at work in these societies were often operating independently of events in Europe and would later give birth to forces that acted to restrict or shape the Western impact.

One of these forces was the progressive emergence of centralized states, some of them built on the concept of ethnic unity. In Japan, the Tokugawa shogunate had asserted an unprecedented degree of political and cultural authority. In India, a centralized empire had been created for the first time since the fall of the Mauryas in the era of antiquity. In mainland Southeast Asia, organized states emerged in Burma, Thailand, and Vietnam that were broadly based on rising ethnic consciousness. This trend was somewhat less apparent in the Middle East, where the Ottoman Empire still laid claim to universal hegemony over the entire eastern Mediterranean and Mesopotamia, and in sub-Saharan Africa, where the forces of state building were still in an embryonic stage.

Within these centralized states, the steady growth of a commercial and manufacturing sector was beginning to create the conditions for a future industrial revolution. A number of Asian societies made technological advances during this period and witnessed the emergence of a more visible and articulate urban bourgeoisie. For the moment, however, such forces were mere portents for the future, not signs of an imminent industrial revolution. At the beginning of the nineteenth century, the primary fact of life for most Asian and African societies was the expansionist power of an industrializing and ever more aggressive Europe. The power and ambition of the West provided an immediate challenge to the independence and destiny of societies throughout the rest of the world. The nature of that challenge will be the subject of our next section.

Timeline, 1400–1650

	1400	1450	1500	1550	1600	1650
Africa		Portuguese ships explore West African coast	First Portuguese sugar plantation at São Tomé / First boatload of African slaves to the New World			
India and the Middle East			Vasco de Gama arrives at Calicut / Babur seizes Delhi / Reign of Suleyman the Magnificent	Reign of Akbar		
East and Southeast Asia			Portuguese seize Malacca		Tokugawa Ieyasu seizes power in Japan / Dutch establish port at Batavia	Founding of Qing dynasty
Europe and the Western Hemisphere	The Renaissance in Italy		Protestant and Catholic Reformations	Wars of Religion		

POPULATION EXPLOSION

Between 1700 and 1800, Europe, China, and to a lesser degree India and the Ottoman Empire experienced a dramatic growth in population. In Europe, the population grew from 120 million people to almost 200 million by 1800; China, from less than 200 million to 300 million during the same period.

Four factors were important in causing this population explosion. First, better growing conditions, made possible by an improvement in climate, affected wide areas of the world and enabled people to produce more food. Summers in both China and Europe were warmer beginning in the early eighteenth century. Second, by the eighteenth century, people had begun to develop immunities to the epidemic diseases that had caused such widespread loss of life between 1500 and 1700. The spread of people by ship after 1500 had led to devastating epidemics. For example, the arrival of Europeans in Mexico led to smallpox, measles, and chickenpox among a native population that had no immunities to European diseases. In 1500, between 11 and 20 million people lived in the area of Mexico; by 1650, only 1.5 million remained. Gradually, however, people developed immunities to these diseases.

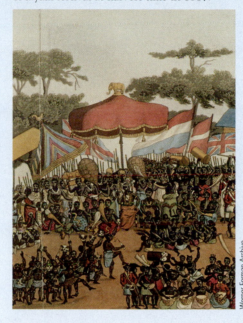

FESTIVAL OF THE YAM. The spread of a few major food crops made possible new sources of nutrition to feed more people. The importance of the yam to the Ashanti people of West Africa is evident in this celebration of a yam festival at harvest time in 1817.

Werner Forman Archive

A third factor in the population increase came from new food sources. As a result of the Columbian exchange (see the box on p. 505) American food crops—such as corn, potatoes, and sweet potatoes—were brought to other parts of the world, where they became important food sources. China had imported a new species of rice from Southeast Asia that had a shorter harvest cycle than that of existing varieties. These new foods provided additional sources of nutrition that enabled more people to live for a longer time. At the same time, land development and canal building in the eighteenth century also enabled government authorities to move food supplies to areas threatened with crop failure and famine.

Finally, the use of new weapons based on gunpowder allowed states to control larger territories and ensure a new degree of order. The early rulers of the Qing dynasty, for example, pacified the Chinese Empire and ensured a long period of peace and stability. Absolute monarchs achieved similar goals in a number of European states. Less violence led to fewer deaths at the same time that an increase in food supplies and a decrease in death from diseases were occurring, thus making possible in the eighteenth century the beginning of the world population explosion that persists to this day.

1650	1700	1750	1800

- Dutch way station established at Cape of Good Hope
- Founding of the kingdom of Ashanti
- Portuguese expelled from Mombasa

- Collapse of Safavids
- Battle of Plassey

- Reign of Kangxi
- Lord Macartney's mission to China

- Development of absolutism—Reign of Louis XIV
- Enlightened absolutism
- American Revolution
- French Revolution

GLOSSARY

absolutism a form of government where the sovereign power or ultimate authority rested in the hands of a monarch who claimed to rule by divine right and was therefore responsible only to God.

Agricultural (Neolithic) Revolution the shift from hunting animals and gathering plants for sustenance to producing food by systematic agriculture that occurred gradually between 10,000 and 4000 B.C. (the Neolithic or "New Stone" Age).

agricultural revolution the application of new agricultural techniques that allowed for a large increase in productivity in the eighteenth century.

anarchism a political theory that holds that all governments and existing social institutions are unnecessary and advocates a society based on voluntary cooperation.

ANC the African National Congress. Founded in 1912, it was the beginning of political activity by South African blacks. Banned by politically dominant European whites in 1960, it was not officially "unbanned" until 1990. It is now the official majority party of the South African government.

Analects the body of writing containing conversations between Confucius and his disciples that preserves his worldly wisdom and pragmatic philosophies.

anti-Semitism hostility toward or discrimination against Jews.

appeasement the policy, followed by the European nations in the 1930s, of accepting Hitler's annexation of Austria and Czechoslovakia in the belief that meeting his demands would assure peace and stability.

Arianism a Christian heresy that taught that Jesus was inferior to God. Though condemned by the Council of Nicaea in 325, Arianism was adopted by many of the Germanic peoples who entered the Roman Empire over the next centuries.

aristocracy a class of hereditary nobility in medieval Europe; a warrior class who shared a distinctive lifestyle based on the institution of knighthood, although there were social divisions within the group based on extremes of wealth.

Arthasastra an early Indian political treatise that sets forth many fundamental aspects of the relationship of rulers and their subjects. It has been compared to Machiavelli's well-known book, *The Prince*, and has provided principles upon which many aspects of social organization have developed in the region.

Aryans Indo–European-speaking nomads who entered India from the Central Asian steppes between 1500 and 1000 B.C.E. and greatly affected Indian society, notably by establishing the caste system. The term was later adopted by German Nazis to describe their racial ideal.

ASEAN the Association for the Southest Asian Nations formed in 1967 to promote the prosperity and political stability of its member nations. Currently Brunei, Indonesia, Laos, Malaysia, Myanmar, the Philippines, Singapore, Thailand, and Vietnam are members. Other countries in the region participate as "observer" members.

Ausgleich the "Compromise" of 1867 that created the dual monarchy of Austria-Hungary. Austria and Hungary each had its own capital, constitution, and legislative assembly, but were united under one monarch.

authoritarian state a state that has a dictatorial government and some other trappings of a totalitarian state, but does not demand that the masses be actively involved in the regime's goals as totalitarian states do.

auxiliaries troops enlisted from the subject peoples of the Roman Empire to supplement the regular legions composed of Roman citizens.

bakufu the centralized government set up in Japan in the twelfth century. *See* shogunate system.

balance of power a distribution of power among several states such that no single nation can dominate or interfere with the interests of another.

Bao-jia system the Chinese practice, reportedly originated by the Qin dynasty in the third century B.C.E., of organizing families into groups of five or ten to exercise mutual control and surveillance and reduce loyalty to the family.

Baroque a style that dominated Western painting, sculpture, architecture and music from about 1580 to 1730, generally characterized by elaborate ornamentation and dramatic effects. Important practitioners included Bernini, Rubens, Handel, and Bach.

Bedouins nomadic tribes originally from northern Arabia, who became important traders after the domestication of the camel during the first millennium B.C.E. Early converts to Islam, their values and practices deeply affected Muhammad.

benefice in the Christian church, a position, such as a bishopric, that consisted of both a sacred office and the right of the holder to the annual revenues from the position.

bhakti in Hinduism, devotion as a means of religious observance open to all persons regardless of class.

bicameral legislature a legislature with two houses.

Black Death the outbreak of plague (mostly bubonic) in the mid-fourteenth century that killed from 25 to 50 percent of Europe's population.

Blitzkrieg "lightning war." A war conducted with great speed and force, as in Germany's advance at the beginning of World War II.

bodhisattvas in some schools of Buddhism, individuals who have achieved enlightenment but, because of their great compassion, have chosen to renounce Nirvana and to remain on earth in spirit form to help all human beings achieve release from reincarnation.

Bolsheviks a small faction of the Russian Social Democratic Party who were led by Lenin and dedicated to violent revolution; seized power in Russia in 1917 and were subsequently renamed the Communists.

boyars   the Russian nobility.

Brezhnev Doctrine   the doctrine, enunciated by Leonid Brezhnev, that the Soviet Union had a right to intervene if socialism was threatened in another socialist state; used to justify the use of Soviet troops in Czechoslovakia in 1968.

caliph   the secular leader of the Islamic community.

calpulli   In Aztec society, a kinship group, often of a thousand or more, which served as an intermediary with the central government, providing taxes and conscript labor to the state.

capital   material wealth used or available for use in the production of more wealth.

caste system   a system of rigid social hierarchy in which all members of that society are assigned by birth to specific "ranks," and inherit specific roles and privileges.

cartel   a combination of independent commercial enterprises that work together to control prices and limit competition.

Cartesian dualism   Descartes's principle of the separation of mind and matter (and mind and body) that enabled scientists to view matter as something separate from themselves that could be investigated by reason.

caudillos   strong leaders in nineteenth-century Latin America, who were usually supported by the landed elites and ruled chiefly by military force, though some were popular; they included both modernizers and destructive dictators.

censorate   one of the three primary Chinese ministries, originally established in the Qin dynasty, whose inspectors surveyed the efficiency of officials throughout the system.

chaebol   a South Korean business structure similar to the Japanese keiretsu.

chansons de geste   a form of vernacular literature in the High Middle Ages that consisted of heroic epics focusing on the deeds of warriors.

chivalry   the ideal of civilized behavior that emerged among the nobility in the eleventh and twelfth centuries under the influence of the church; a code of ethics knights were expected to uphold.

Christian (northern) humanism   an intellectual movement in northern Europe in the late fifteenth and early sixteenth centuries that combined the interest in the classics of the Italian Renaissance with an interest in the sources of early Christianity, including the New Testament and the writings of the church fathers.

civic humanism   an intellectual movement of the Italian Renaissance that saw Cicero, who was both an intellectual and a statesman, as the ideal and held that humanists should be involved in government and use their rhetorical training in the service of the state.

civil rights   the basic rights of citizens including equality before the law, freedom of speech and press, and freedom from arbitrary arrest.

civil service examination   an elaborate Chinese system of selecting bureaucrats on merit, first introduced in 165 B.C.E., developed by the Tang dynasty in the seventh century C.E. and refined under the Song dynasty; later adopted in Vietnam and with less success in Japan and Korea. It contributed to efficient government, upward mobility, and cultural uniformity.

class struggle   the basis of the Marxist analysis of history, which says that the owners of the means of production have always oppressed the workers and predicts an inevitable revolution. *See* Marxism.

Cold War   the ideological conflict between the Soviet Union and the United States after World War II.

collective farms   large farms created in the Soviet Union by Stalin by combining many small holdings into one large farm worked by the peasants under government supervision.

collective security   the use of an international army raised by an association of nations to deter aggression and keep the peace.

coloni   free tenant farmers who worked as sharecroppers on the large estates of the Roman Empire (singular: *colonus*).

Comintern   a worldwide organization of Communist parties, founded by Lenin in 1919, dedicated to the advancement of world revolution; also known as the Third International.

common law   law common to the entire kingdom of England; imposed by the king's courts beginning in the twelfth century to replace the customary law used in county and feudal courts that varied from place to place.

commune   in medieval Europe, an association of townspeople bound together by a sworn oath for the purpose of obtaining basic liberties from the lord of the territory in which the town was located; also, the self-governing town after receiving its liberties.

conciliarism   a movement in fourteenth- and fifteenth-century Europe that held that final authority in spiritual matters resided with a general church council, not the pope; emerged in response to the Avignon papacy and the Great Schism and used to justify the summoning of the Council of Constance (1414–1418).

condottieri   leaders of bands of mercenary soldiers in Renaissance Italy who sold their services to the highest bidder.

Confucianism   a system of thought based on the teachings of Confucius (551–479 B.C.E.) that developed into the ruling ideology of the Chinese state. *See* Neo-Confucianism.

conquistadors   "conquerors." Leaders in the Spanish conquests in the Americas, especially Mexico and Peru, in the sixteenth century.

conscription   a military draft.

conservatism   an ideology based on tradition and social stability that favored the maintenance of established institutions, organized religion, and obedience to authority and resisted change, especially abrupt change.

consuls   the chief executive officers of the Roman Republic. Two were chosen annually to administer the government and lead the army in battle.

consumer society   a term applied to Western society after World War II as the working classes adopted the consumption patterns of the middle class and installment plans, credit cards, and easy credit made consumer goods such as appliances and automobiles widely available.

Continental System   Napoleon's effort to bar British goods from the Continent in the hope of weakening Britain's economy and destroying its capacity to wage war.

cosmopolitanism   the quality of being sophisticated and having wide international experience.

cottage industry   a system of textile manufacturing in which spinners and weavers worked at home in their cottages using raw materials supplied to them by capitalist entrepreneurs.

cultural relativism   the belief that no culture is superior to another because culture is a matter of custom, not reason, and derives its meaning from the group holding it.

cuneiform   "wedge-shaped." A system of writing developed by the Sumerians that consisted of wedge-shaped impressions made by a reed stylus on clay tablets.

daimyo   prominent Japanese families who provided allegiance to the local shogun in exchange for protection; similar to vassals in Europe.

decolonization   the process of becoming free of colonial status and achieving statehood; occurred in most of the world's colonies between 1947 and 1962.

deism   belief in God as the creator of the universe who, after setting it in motion, ceased to have any direct involvement in it and allowed it to run according to its own natural laws.

demesne   the part of a manor retained under the direct control of the lord and worked by the serfs as part of their labor services.

depression   a very severe, protracted economic downturn with high levels of unemployment.

destalinization   the policy of denouncing and undoing the most repressive aspects of Stalin's regime; begun by Nikita Khrushchev in 1956.

détente   the relaxation of tension between the Soviet Union and the United States that occurred in the 1970s.

dharma   in Hinduism and Buddhism, the law that governs the universe, and specifically human behavior.

dialectic   logic, one of the seven liberal arts that made up the medieval curriculum. In Marxist thought, the process by which all change occurs through the clash of antagonistic elements.

Diaspora   the scattering of Jews throughout the ancient world after the Babylonian captivity in the sixth century B.C.E.

dictator   in the Roman Republic, an official granted unlimited power to run the state for a short period of time, usually six months, during an emergency.

diocese   the area under the jurisdiction of a Christian bishop; based originally on Roman administrative districts.

direct representation   a system of choosing delegates to a representative assembly in which citizens vote directly for the delegates who will represent them.

divination   the practice of seeking to foretell future events by interpreting divine signs, which could appear in various forms, such as in entrails of animals, in patterns in smoke, or in dreams.

divine-right monarchy   a monarchy based on the belief that monarchs receive their power directly from God and are responsible to no one except God.

domino theory   the belief that if the Communists succeeded in Vietnam, other countries in Southeast and East Asia would also fall (like dominoes) to communism; a justification for the U.S. intervention in Vietnam.

dualism   the belief that the universe is dominated by two opposing forces, one good and the other evil.

dynastic state   a state where the maintenance and expansion of the interests of the ruling family is the primary consideration.

economic imperialism   the process in which banks and corporations from developed nations invest in underdeveloped regions and establish a major presence there in the hope of making high profits; not necessarily the same as colonial expansion in that businesses invest where they can make a profit, which may not be in their own nation's colonies.

empiricism   the practice of relying on observation and experiment.

enclosure movement   in the eighteenth century, the fencing in of the old open fields, combining many small holdings into larger units that could be farmed more efficiently.

encomienda system   the system by which Spain first governed its American colonies. Holders of an encomienda were supposed to protect the Indians as well as using them as laborers and collecting tribute but in practice exploited them.

encyclical   a letter from the pope to all the bishops of the Roman Catholic church.

enlightened absolutism   an absolute monarchy where the ruler follows the principles of the Enlightenment by introducing reforms for the improvement of society, allowing freedom of speech and the press, permitting religious toleration, expanding education, and ruling in accordance with the laws.

Enlightenment   an eighteenth-century intellectual movement, led by the philosophes, that stressed the application of reason and the scientific method to all aspects of life.

entrepreneur   one who organizes, operates, and assumes the risk in a business venture in the expectation of making a profit.

Epicureanism   a philosophy founded by Epicurus in the fourth century B.C. that taught that happiness (freedom from emotional turmoil) could be achieved through the pursuit of pleasure (intellectual rather than sensual pleasure).

equestrians   a group of extremely wealthy men in the late Roman Republic who were effectively barred from high office, but sought political power commensurate with their wealth; called equestrians because many had gotten their start as cavalry officers (*equites*).

ethnic cleansing   the policy of killing or forcibly removing people of another ethnic group; used by the Serbs against Bosnian Muslims in the 1990s.

eucharist   a Christian sacrament in which consecrated bread and wine are consumed in celebration of Jesus' Last Supper; also called the Lord's Supper or communion.

evolutionary socialism   a socialist doctrine espoused by Eduard Bernstein who argued that socialists should stress cooperation and evolution to attain power by democratic means rather than by conflict and revolution.

fascism   an ideology or movement that exalts the nation above the individual and calls for a centralized government with a dictatorial leader, economic and social regimentation, and forcible suppression of opposition; in particular, the ideology of Mussolini's Fascist regime in Italy.

feminism   the belief in the social, political, and economic equality of the sexes; also, organized activity to advance women's rights.

fief   a landed estate granted to a vassal in exchange for military services.

Final Solution   the physical extermination of the Jewish people by the Nazis during World War II.

five pillars of Islam   the core requirements of the faith, observation of which would lead to paradise: belief in Allah and his Prophet Muhammad; prescribed prayers; observation of Ramadan; pilgrimage to Mecca; and giving alms to the poor.

folk culture   the traditional arts and crafts, literature, music, and other customs of the people; something that people make, as opposed to modern popular culture, which is something people buy.

four modernizations   the slogan for radical reforms of Chinese industry, agriculture, technology, and national defense, instituted by Deng Xiaoping after his accession to power in the late 1970s.

free trade   the unrestricted international exchange of goods with low or no tariffs.

fundamentalism   a movement that emphasizes rigid adherence to basic religious principles; coined to describe Evangelical Christianity, it is often used to characterize Islamic conservatives.

general strike   a strike by all or most workers in an economy; espoused by Georges Sorel as the heroic action that could be used to inspire the workers to destroy capitalist society.

gentry   well-to-do English landowners below the level of the nobility; played an important role in the English Civil War of the seventeenth century.

geocentric theory   the idea that the earth is at the center of the universe and that the sun and other celestial objects revolve around the earth.

glasnost   "openness." Mikhail Gorbachev's policy of encouraging Soviet citizens to openly discuss the strengths and weaknesses of the Soviet Union.

Gleichschaltung   the coordination of all government institutions under Nazi control in Germany from 1933.

global civilization   human society considered as a single world-wide entity, in which local differences are less important than overall similarities.

good emperors   the five emperors who ruled from 96 to 180 (Nerva, Trajan, Hadrian, Antoninus Pius, and Marcus Aurelius), a period of peace and prosperity for the Roman Empire.

Great Schism   the crisis in the late medieval church when there were first two and then three popes; ended by the Council of Constance (1414–1418).

guest workers   foreign workers working temporarily in European countries.

guild   an association of people with common interests and concerns, especially people working in the same craft. In medieval Europe, guilds came to control much of the production process and to restrict entry into various trades.

gymnasium   in classical Greece, a place for athletics; in the Hellenistic Age, a secondary school with a curriculum centered on music, physical exercise, and literature.

Hegira   the flight of Muhammad from Mecca to Medina in 622, which marks the first date on the official calendar of Islam.

heliocentric theory   the idea that the sun (not the earth) is at the center of the universe.

Hellenistic   literally, "to imitate the Greeks"; the era after the death of Alexander the Great when Greek culture spread into the Near East and blended with the culture of that region.

helots   serfs in ancient Sparta, who were permanently bound to the land that they worked for their Spartan masters.

heresy   the holding of religious doctrines different from the official teachings of the church.

Hermeticism   an intellectual movement beginning in the fifteenth century that taught that divinity is embodied in all aspects of nature; included works on alchemy and magic as well as theology and philosophy. The tradition continued into the seventeenth century and influenced many of the leading figures of the Scientific Revolution.

hetairai   highly sophisticated courtesans in ancient Athens who offered intellectual and musical entertainment as well as sex.

hieroglyphics   a highly pictorial system of writing most often associated with ancient Egypt. Also used (with different "pictographs") by other ancient peoples such as the Mayans.

high culture   the literary and artistic culture of the educated and wealthy ruling classes.

Hinduism   the main religion in India, it emphasizes reincarnation, based on the results of the previous life, and the desirability of escaping this cycle. Its various forms feature both asceticism and the pleasures of ordinary life, and encompass a multitude of gods as different manifestations of one ultimate reality.

Holocaust   the mass slaughter of European Jews by the Nazis during World War II.

Hopewell culture   a Native American society that flourished from about 200 B.C.E. to 400 C.E., noted for large burial mounds and extensive manufacture. Largely based in Ohio, its traders ranged as far as the Gulf of Mexico.

hoplites   heavily armed infantry soldiers used in ancient Greece in a phalanx formation.

Huguenots   French Calvinists.

humanism   an intellectual movement in Renaissance Italy based upon the study of the Greek and Roman classics.

Hundred Schools   (of philosophy) in China around the third century B.C.E., a wide-ranging debate over the nature of human beings, society, and the universe. The Schools included Legalism and Daoism, as well as Confucianism.

iconoclasm   an eighth-century Byzantine movement against the use of icons (pictures of sacred figures), which was condemned as idolatry.

ideology   a political philosophy such as conservatism or liberalism.

imperialism   the policy of extending one nation's power either by conquest or by establishing direct or indirect economic or cultural authority over another. Generally driven by economic self-interest, it can also be motivated by a sincere (if often misguided) sense of moral obligation.

imperium   "the right to command." In the Roman Republic, the chief executive officers (consuls and praetors) possessed the *imperium;* a military commander was an *imperator.* In the Roman Empire, the title *imperator,* or emperor, came to be used for the ruler.

indirect representation a system of choosing delegates to a representative assembly in which citizens do not choose the delegates directly but instead vote for electors who choose the delegates.

individualism emphasis on and interest in the unique traits of each person.

indulgence the remission of part or all of the temporal punishment in purgatory due to sin; granted for charitable contributions and other good deeds. Indulgences became a regular practice of the Christian church in the High Middle Ages, and their abuse was instrumental in sparking Luther's reform movement in the sixteenth century.

infanticide the practice of killing infants.

inflation a sustained rise in the price level.

intendants royal officials in seventeenth-century France who were sent into the provinces to execute the orders of the central government.

intervention, principle of the idea, after the Congress of Vienna, that the great powers of Europe had the right to send armies into countries experiencing revolution to restore legitimate monarchs to their thrones.

isolationism a foreign policy in which a nation refrains from making alliances or engaging actively in international affairs.

jihad In Islam, "striving in the way of the Lord." The term is ambiguous and has been subject to varying interpretations, from the practice of conducting raids against local neighbors to the conduct of "holy war" against unbelievers.

joint-stock company a company or association that raises capital by selling shares to individuals who receive dividends on their investment while a board of directors runs the company.

joint-stock investment bank a bank created by selling shares of stock to investors. Such banks potentially have access to much more capital than do private banks owned by one or a few individuals.

Jomon the earliest known Neolithic inhabitants of Japan, named for the cord pattern of their pottery.

justification by faith the primary doctrine of the Protestant Reformation; taught that humans are saved not through good works, but by the grace of God, bestowed freely through the sacrifice of Jesus.

kami spirits who were worshiped in early Japan, and resided in trees, rivers and streams. *See* Shinto.

keiretsu a type of powerful industrial or financial conglomerate that emerged in post-World War II Japan following the abolition of zaibatsu.

kolkhoz a collective farm in the Soviet Union, in which the great bulk of the land was held and worked communally. Between 1928 and 1934, 250,000 kolkhozes replaced 26 million family farms.

laissez-faire "to let alone." An economic doctrine that holds that an economy is best served when the government does not interfere but allows the economy to self-regulate according to the forces of supply and demand.

latifundia large landed estates in the Roman Empire (singular: *latifundium*).

lay investiture the practice in which a layperson chose a bishop and invested him with the symbols of both his temporal office and his spiritual office; led to the Investiture Controversy, which was ended by compromise in the Concordat of Worms in 1122.

Lebensraum "living space." The doctrine, adopted by Hitler, that a nation's power depends on the amount of land it occupies; thus, a nation must expand to be strong.

Legalism a Chinese philosophy that argued that human beings were by nature evil and would follow the correct path only if coerced by harsh laws and stiff punishments. Adopted as official ideology by the Qin dynasty, it was later rejected but remained influential.

legitimacy, principle of the idea that after the Napoleonic wars peace could best be reestablished in Europe by restoring legitimate monarchs who would preserve traditional institutions; guided Metternich at the Congress of Vienna.

Leninism Lenin's revision of Marxism that held that Russia need not experience a bourgeois revolution before it could move toward socialism.

liberal arts the seven areas of study that formed the basis of education in medieval and early modern Europe. Following Boethius and other late Roman authors, they consisted of grammar, rhetoric, and dialectic or logic (the *trivium*) and arithmetic, geometry, astronomy, and music (the *quadrivium*).

liberalism an ideology based on the belief that people should be as free from restraint as possible. Economic liberalism is the idea that the government should not interfere in the workings of the economy. Political liberalism is the idea that there should be restraints on the exercise of power so that people can enjoy basic civil rights in a constitutional state with a representative assembly.

limited liability the principle that shareholders in a joint-stock corporation can be held responsible for the corporation's debts only up to the amount they have invested.

limited (constitutional) monarchy a system of government in which the monarch is limited by a representative assembly and by the duty to rule in accordance with the laws of the land.

lineage group the descendants of a common ancestor; relatives, often as opposed to immediate family.

Mahayana a school of Buddhism that promotes the idea of universal salvation through the intercession of bodhisattvas; predominant in north Asia.

mandates a system established after World War I whereby a nation officially administered a territory (mandate) on behalf of the League of Nations. Thus, France administered Lebanon and Syria as mandates, and Britain administered Iraq and Palestine.

manor an agricultural estate operated by a lord and worked by peasants who performed labor services and paid various rents and fees to the lord in exchange for protection and sustenance.

Marshall Plan the European Recovery Program, under which the United States provided financial aid to European countries to help them rebuild after World War II.

Marxism the political, economic, and social theories of Karl Marx, which included the idea that history is the story of class struggle and that ultimately the proletariat will overthrow the bourgeoisie and establish a dictatorship en route to a classless society.

mass education a state-run educational system, usually free and compulsory, that aims to ensure that all children in society have at least a basic education.

mass leisure forms of leisure that appeal to large numbers of people in a society including the working classes; emerged at the end of the nineteenth century to provide workers with amusements after work and on weekends; used during the twentieth century by totalitarian states to control their populations.

mass politics a political order characterized by mass political parties and universal male and (eventually) female suffrage.

mass society a society in which the concerns of the majority—the lower classes—play a prominent role; characterized by extension of voting rights, an improved standard of living for the lower classes, and mass education.

materialism the belief that everything mental, spiritual, or ideal is an outgrowth of physical forces and that truth is found in concrete material existence, not through feeling or intuition.

megaliths large stones, widely used in Europe from around 4000 to 1500 B.C.E. to create monuments, including sophisticated astronomical observatories.

Meiji Restoration the period during the late 19th and early 20th century in which fundamental economic and cultural changes occured in Japan, tranforming it from a feudal and agrarian society to an industrial and technological society.

mercantilism an economic theory that held that a nation's prosperity depended on its supply of gold and silver and that the total volume of trade is unchangeable; therefore, advocated that the government play an active role in the economy by encouraging exports and discouraging imports, especially through the use of tariffs.

Mesolithic Age the period from 10,000 to 7000 B.C., characterized by a gradual transition from a food-gathering/hunting economy to a food-producing economy.

mestizos the offspring of intermarriage between Europeans, originally Spaniards, and native American Indians.

metics resident foreigners in ancient Athens; not permitted full rights of citizenship but did receive the protection of the laws.

militarism a policy of aggressive military preparedness; in particular, the large armies based on mass conscription and complex, inflexible plans for mobilization that most European nations had before World War I.

ministerial responsibility a tenet of nineteenth-century liberalism that held that ministers of the monarch should be responsible to the legislative assembly rather than to the monarch.

Modernism the new artistic and literary styles that emerged in the decades before 1914 as artists rebelled against traditional efforts to portray reality as accurately as possible (leading to Impressionism and Cubism) and writers explored new forms.

monotheistic/monotheism having only one god; the doctrine or belief that there is only one god.

mulattoes the offspring of Africans and Europeans, particularly in Latin America.

mutual deterrence the belief that nuclear war could best be prevented if both the United States and the Soviet Union had sufficient nuclear weapons so that even if one nation launched a preemptive first strike, the other could respond and devastate the attacker.

mystery religions religions that involve initiation into secret rites that promise intense emotional involvement with spiritual forces and a greater chance of individual immortality.

nationalism a sense of national consciousness based on awareness of being part of a community—a "nation"—that has common institutions, traditions, language, and customs and that becomes the focus of the individual's primary political loyalty.

nationalities problem the dilemma faced by the Austro-Hungarian Empire in trying to unite a wide variety of ethnic groups including, among others, Austrians, Hungarians, Poles, Croats, Czechs, Serbs, Slovaks, and Slovenes in an era when nationalism and calls for self-determination were coming to the fore.

nationalization the process of converting a business or industry from private ownership to government control and ownership.

nation in arms the people's army raised by universal mobilization to repel the foreign enemies of the French Revolution.

nation-state a form of political organization in which a relatively homogeneous people inhabits a sovereign state, as opposed to a state containing people of several nationalities.

NATO the North Atlantic Treaty Organization; a military alliance formed in 1949 in which the signatories (Belgium, Canada, Denmark, France, Great Britain, Iceland, Italy, Luxembourg, the Netherlands, Norway, Portugal, and the United States) agreed to provide mutual assistance if any one of them was attacked; later expanded to include other nations, including former members of the Warsaw Pact—Poland, the Czech Republic and Hungary.

natural laws a body of laws or specific principles held to be derived from nature and binding upon all human society even in the absence of positive laws.

natural rights certain inalienable rights to which all people are entitled; include the right to life, liberty, and property, freedom of speech and religion, and equality before the law.

natural selection Darwin's idea that organisms that are most adaptable to their environment survive and pass on the variations that enabled them to survive, while other, less adaptable organisms become extinct; "survival of the fittest."

Nazi New Order the Nazis' plan for their conquered territories; included the extermination of Jews and others considered inferior, ruthless exploitation of resources, German colonization in the east, and the use of Poles, Russians, and Ukrainians as slave labor.

negritude   a philosophy shared among African blacks that there exists a distinctive "African personality" that owes nothing to Western values and provides a common sense of purpose and destiny for black Africans.

Neo-Confucianism   the dominant ideology of China during the second millennium C.E., it combined the metaphysical speculations of Buddhism and Daoism with the pragmatic Confucian approach to society, maintaining that the world is real, not illusory, and that fulfillment comes from participation, not withdrawal. It encouraged an intellectual environment that valued continuity over change and tradition over innovation.

Neoplatonism   a revival of Platonic philosophy; in the third century A.D., a revival associated with Plotinus; in the Italian Renaissance, a revival associated with Marsilio Ficino who attempted to synthesize Christianity and Platonism.

New Course   a short-lived, liberalizing change in Soviet policy to its Eastern European allies instituted after the death of Stalin in 1953.

New Culture Movement   a protest launched at Peking University after the failure of the 1911 revolution, aimed at abolishing the remnants of the old system and introducing Western values and institutions into China.

New Democracy   the initial program of the Chinese Communist government, from 1949 to 1955, focusing on honest government, land reform, social justice, and peace rather than on the utopian goal of a classless society.

New Economic Policy   a modified version of the old capitalist system introduced in the Soviet Union by Lenin in 1921 to revive the economy after the ravages of the civil war and war communism.

new imperialism   the revival of imperialism after 1880 in which European nations established colonies throughout much of Asia and Africa.

new monarchies   the governments of France, England, and Spain at the end of the fifteenth century, where the rulers were successful in reestablishing or extending centralized royal authority, suppressing the nobility, controlling the church, and insisting upon the loyalty of all peoples living in their territories.

Nirvana   in Buddhist thought, enlightenment, the ultimate transcendence from the illusion of the material world; release from the wheel of life.

nobiles   "nobles." The small group of families from both patrician and plebeian origins who produced most of the men who were elected to office in the late Roman Republic.

Nok culture   in northern Nigeria, one of the most active early ironworking societies in Africa, artifacts from which date back as far as 500 B.C.E.

nuclear family   a family group consisting only of father, mother, and children.

old regime/old order   the political and social system of France in the eighteenth century before the Revolution.

oligarchy   rule by a few.

Open Door notes   a series of letters sent in 1899 by U.S. Secretary of State John Hay to Great Britain, France, Germany, Italy, Japan and Russia, calling for equal economic access to the China market for all states and for the maintenance of the territorial and administrative integrity of the Chinese Empire.

optimates   "best men." Aristocratic leaders in the late Roman Republic who generally came from senatorial families and wished to retain their oligarchical privileges.

opium trade   the sale of the addictive product of the poppy, specifically by British traders to China in the 1830s. Chinese attempts to prevent it led to the Opium War of 1839–1842, which resulted in British access to Chinese ports and has traditionally been considered the beginning of modern Chinese history.

orders/estates   the traditional tripartite division of European society based on heredity and quality rather than wealth or economic standing, first established in the Middle Ages and continuing into the eighteenth century; traditionally consisted of those who pray (the clergy), those who fight (the nobility), and those who work (all the rest).

organic evolution   Darwin's principle that all plants and animals have evolved over a long period of time from earlier and simpler forms of life.

Organization of African Unity   founded in Addis Ababa in 1963, it was intended to represent the interests of all the newly independent countries of Africa and provided a forum for the discussion of common problems until 2001, when it was replaced by the African Union.

Paleolithic Age   the period of human history when humans used simple stone tools (c. 2,500,000–10,000 B.C.).

pan-Africanism   the concept of African continental unity and solidarity in which the common interests of African countries transcend regional boundaries.

pantheism   a doctrine that equates God with the universe and all that is in it.

paterfamilias   the dominant male in a Roman family whose powers over his wife and children were theoretically unlimited, though they were sometimes circumvented in practice.

patriarchal/patriarchy   a society in which the father is supreme in the clan or family; more generally, a society dominated by men.

patriarchal family   a family in which the husband/father dominates his wife and children.

patricians   great landowners who became the ruling class in the Roman Republic.

patronage   the practice of awarding titles and making appointments to government and other positions to gain political support.

Pax Romana   "Roman peace." A term used to refer to the stability and prosperity that Roman rule brought to the Mediterranean world and much of western Europe during the first and second centuries A.D.

peaceful coexistence   the policy adopted by the Soviet Union under Khrushchev in 1955, and continued by his successors, that called for economic and ideological rivalry with the West rather than nuclear war.

Pentateuch   the first five books of the Hebrew Bible (Genesis, Exodus, Leviticus, Numbers, and Deuteronomy).

peoples' democracies   a term invented by the Soviet Union to define a society in the early stage of socialist transition, applied to Eastern European countries in the 1950s.

perestroika   "restructuring." A term applied to Mikhail Gorbachev's economic, political, and social reforms in the Soviet Union.

permissive society   a term applied to Western society after World War II to reflect the new sexual freedom and the emergence of a drug culture.

Petrine supremacy   the doctrine that the bishop of Rome—the pope—as the successor of Saint Peter (traditionally considered the first bishop of Rome) should hold a preeminent position in the church.

phalanx   a rectangular formation of tightly massed infantry soldiers.

philosophes   intellectuals of the eighteenth-century Enlightenment who believed in applying a spirit of rational criticism to all things, including religion and politics, and who focused on improving and enjoying this world, rather than on the afterlife.

plebeians   the class of Roman citizens who included nonpatrician landowners, craftspeople, merchants, and small farmers in the Roman Republic. Their struggle for equal rights with the patricians dominated much of the Republic's history.

pluralism   the practice in which one person holds several church offices simultaneously; a problem of the late medieval church.

pogroms   organized massacres of Jews.

polis   an ancient Greek city-state encompassing both an urban area and its surrounding countryside; a small but autonomous political unit where all major political and social activities were carried out in a central location.

political democracy   a form of government characterized by universal suffrage and mass political parties.

politiques   a group who emerged during the French Wars of Religion in the sixteenth century; placed politics above religion and believed that no religious truth was worth the ravages of civil war.

polygyny   the state or practice of having more than one wife at a time.

polytheistic/polytheism   having many gods; belief in or the worship of more than one god.

popular culture   as opposed to high culture, the unofficial, written and unwritten culture of the masses, much of which was passed down orally; centers on public and group activities such as festivals. In the twentieth century, refers to the entertainment, recreation, and pleasures that people purchase as part of mass consumer society.

populares   "favoring the people." Aristocratic leaders in the late Roman Republic who tended to use the people's assemblies in an effort to break the stranglehold of the *nobiles* on political offices.

popular sovereignty   the doctrine that government is created by and subject to the will of the people, who are the source of all political power.

praetorian guard   the military unit that served as the personal bodyguard of the Roman emperors.

praetors   the two senior Roman judges, who had executive authority when the consuls were away from the city and could also lead armies.

predestination   the belief, associated with Calvinism, that God, as a consequence of his foreknowledge of all events, has predetermined those who will be saved (the elect) and those who will be damned.

price revolution   the dramatic rise in prices (inflation) that occurred throughout Europe in the sixteenth and early seventeenth centuries.

primogeniture   an inheritance practice in which the eldest son receives all or the largest share of the parents' estate.

principate   the form of government established by Augustus for the Roman Empire; continued the constitutional forms of the Republic and consisted of the *princeps* ("first citizen") and the senate, although the *princeps* was clearly the dominant partner.

proletariat   the industrial working class. In Marxism, the class who will ultimately overthrow the bourgeoisie.

purdah   the Indian term for the practice among Muslims and some Hindus of isolating women and preventing them from associating with men outside the home.

Puritans   English Protestants inspired by Calvinist theology who wished to remove all traces of Catholicism from the Church of England.

querelles des femmes   "arguments about women." A centuries-old debate about the nature of women that continued during the Scientific Revolution as those who argued for the inferiority of women found additional support in the new anatomy and medicine.

rationalism   a system of thought based on the belief that human reason and experience are the chief sources of knowledge.

realism   in medieval Europe, the school of thought that, following Plato, held that the individual objects we perceive are not real but merely manifestations of universal ideas existing in the mind of God. In the nineteenth century, a school of painting that emphasized the everyday life of ordinary people, depicted with photographic realism.

Realpolitik   "politics of reality." Politics based on practical concerns rather than theory or ethics.

real wages/income/prices   wages/income/prices that have been adjusted for inflation.

reason of state   the principle that a nation should act on the basis of its long-term interests and not merely to further the dynastic interests of its ruling family.

reincarnation   the idea that the individual soul is reborn in a different form after death; in Hindu and Buddhist thought, release from this cycle is the objective of all living souls.

relativity theory   Einstein's theory that holds, among other things, that (1) space and time are not absolute but are relative to the observer and interwoven into a four-dimensional space-time continuum and (2) matter is a form of energy ($E = mc^2$).

Renaissance   the "rebirth" of classical culture that occurred in Italy between c. 1350 and c. 1550; also, the earlier revivals of classical culture that occurred under Charlemagne and in the twelfth century.

rentier   a person who lives on income from property and is not personally involved in its operation.

reparations   payments made by a defeated nation after a war to compensate another nation for damage sustained as a result of the war; required from Germany after World War I.

revisionism   a socialist doctrine that rejected Marx's emphasis on class struggle and revolution and argued instead that workers should work through political parties to bring about gradual change.

revolution   a fundamental change in the political and social organization of a state.

revolutionary socialism   the socialist doctrine espoused by Georges Sorel who held that violent action was the only way to achieve the goals of socialism.

rhetoric   the art of persuasive speaking; in the Middle Ages, one of the seven liberal arts.

Rococo   a style, especially of decoration and architecture, that developed from the Baroque and spread throughout Europe by the 1730s. While still elaborate, it emphasized curves, lightness, and charm in the pursuit of pleasure, happiness, and love.

sacraments   rites considered imperative for a Christian's salvation. By the thirteenth century consisted of the eucharist or Lord's Supper, baptism, marriage, penance, extreme unction, holy orders, and confirmation of children; Protestant reformers of the sixteenth century generally recognized only two—baptism and communion (the Lord's Supper).

samurai   literally "retainer"; similar to European knights. Usually in service to a particular shogun, these warriors lived by a strict code of ethics and duty.

sans-culottes   the common people who did not wear the fine clothes of the upper classes (sans-culottes means "without breeches") and played an important role in the radical phase of the French Revolution.

sati   the Hindu ritual requiring a wife to throw herself upon her her deceased husband's funeral pyre.

satrap/satrapy   a governor with both civil and military duties in the ancient Persian Empire, which was divided into satrapies, or provinces, each administered by a satrap.

scholasticism   the philosophical and theological system of the medieval schools, which emphasized rigorous analysis of contradictory authorities; often used to try to reconcile faith and reason.

scientific method   a method of seeking knowledge through inductive principles; uses experiments and observations to develop generalizations.

Scientific Revolution   the transition from the medieval worldview to a largely secular, rational, and materialistic perspective; began in the seventeenth century and was popularized in the eighteenth.

secularization   the process of becoming more concerned with material, worldly, temporal things and less with spiritual and religious things.

self-determination   the doctrine that the people of a given territory or a particular nationality should have the right to determine their own government and political future.

self-strengthening   a late-nineteenth-century Chinese policy, by which Western technology would be adopted while Confucian principles and institutions were maintained intact.

senate/senators   the leading council of the Roman Republic; composed of about 300 men (senators) who served for life and dominated much of the political life of the Republic.

serf   a peasant who is bound to the land and obliged to provide labor services and pay various rents and fees to the lord; considered unfree but not a slave because serfs could not be bought and sold.

Shinto   a kind of state religion in Japan, derived from beliefs in nature spirits and until recently linked with belief in the divinity of the emperor and the sacredness of the Japanese nation.

shogunate system   the system of government in Japan in which the emperor exercised only titular authority while the shogun (regional military dictators) exercised actual political power.

skepticism   a doubtful or questioning attitude, especially about religion.

Social Darwinism   the application of Darwin's principle of organic evolution to the social order; led to the belief that progress comes from the struggle for survival as the fittest advance and the weak decline.

socialism   an ideology that calls for collective or government ownership of the means of production and the distribution of goods.

social security/social insurance   government programs that provide social welfare measures such as old age pensions and sickness, accident, and disability insurance.

Socratic method   a form of teaching that uses a question-and-answer format to enable students to reach conclusions by using their own reasoning.

Sophists   wandering scholars and professional teachers in ancient Greece who stressed the importance of rhetoric and tended toward skepticism and relativism.

soviets   councils of workers' and soldiers' deputies formed throughout Russia in 1917; played an important role in the Bolshevik Revolution.

sphere of influence   a territory or region over which an outside nation exercises political or economic influence.

stateless societies   the pre-Columbian communities in much of the Americas who developed substantial cultures without formal nation states.

Stoicism   a philosophy founded by Zeno in the fourth century B.C. that taught that happiness could be obtained by accepting one's lot and living in harmony with the will of God, thereby achieving inner peace.

subinfeudation   the practice in which a lord's greatest vassals subdivided their fiefs and had vassals of their own, and those vassals, in turn, subdivided their fiefs and so on down to simple knights whose fiefs were too small to subdivide.

suffrage   the right to vote.

suffragists   those who advocate the extension of the right to vote (suffrage), especially to women.

surplus value   in Marxism, the difference between a product's real value and the wages of the worker who produced the product.

Swahili   a mixed African-Arabian culture that developed by the twelfth century along the east coast of Africa; also, the national language of Kenya and Tanzania.

syncretism   the combining of different forms of belief or practice, as, for example, when two gods are regarded as different forms of the same underlying divine force and are fused together.

Taika reforms   the seventh-century "great change" reforms that established the centralized Japanese state.

taille   a French tax on land or property, developed by King Louis XI in the fifteenth century as the financial basis of the monarchy. It was largely paid by the peasantry; the nobility and the clergy were exempt.

tariffs   duties (taxes) imposed on imported goods; usually imposed both to raise revenue and to discourage imports and protect domestic industries.

tetrarchy   rule by four; the system of government established by Diocletian (284–305) in which the Roman Empire was divided into two parts, each ruled by an "Augustus" assisted by a "Caesar."

theocracy   a government ruled by a divine authority.

Theravada   a school of Buddhism that stresses personal behavior and the quest for understanding as a means of release from the wheel of life, rather than the intercession of bodhisattvas; predominant in Sri Lanka and Southeast Asia.

three-field system   in medieval agriculture, the practice of dividing the arable land into three fields so that one could lie fallow while the others were planted in winter grains and spring crops.

three kingdoms   Koguryo, Paekche, and Silla, rivals but all under varying degrees of Chinese influence, which together controlled virtually all of Korea from the fourth to the seventh centuries.

three obediences   the traditional duties of Japanese women, in permanent subservience: child to father, wife to husband, and widow to son.

tithe   a tenth of one's harvest or income; paid by medieval peasants to the village church.

Tongmenghui   the political organization—"Revolutionary Alliance"—formed by Sun Yat-sen in 1905, which united various revolutionary factions and ultimately toppled the Manchu dynasty.

Torah   the body of law in Hebrew Scripture, contained in the Pentateuch (the first five books of the Hebrew Bible).

totalitarian state   a state characterized by government control over all aspects of economic, social, political, cultural, and intellectual life, the subordination of the individual to the state, and insistence that the masses be actively involved in the regime's goals.

total war   warfare in which all of a nation's resources, including civilians at home as well as soldiers in the field, are mobilized for the war effort.

trade union   an association of workers in the same trade, formed to help members secure better wages, benefits, and working conditions.

transubstantiation   a doctrine of the Roman Catholic church that teaches that during the eucharist the substance of the bread and wine is miraculously transformed into the body and blood of Jesus.

trench warfare   warfare in which the opposing forces attack and counterattack from a relatively permanent system of trenches protected by barbed wire; characteristic of World War I.

tribute system   an important element of Chinese foreign policy, by which neighboring states paid for the privilege of access to Chinese markets, received legitimation and agreed not to harbor enemies of the Chinese Empire.

Truman Doctrine   the doctrine, enunciated by Harry Truman in 1947, that the United States would provide economic aid to countries that said they were threatened by Communist expansion.

twice-born   the males of the higher castes in traditional Indian society, who underwent an initiation ceremony at puberty.

tyrant/tyranny   in an ancient Greek *polis* (or an Italian city-state during the Renaissance), a ruler who came to power in an unconstitutional way and ruled without being subject to the law.

ulama   a convocation of leading Muslim scholars, the earliest of which shortly after the death of Muhammad drew up a law code, called the Shari'a, based largely on the Koran and the sayings of the Prophet, to provide believers with a set of prescriptions to regulate their daily lives.

umma   the Muslim community, as a whole.

uncertainty principle   a principle in quantum mechanics, posited by Heisenberg, that holds that one cannot determine the path of an electron because the very act of observing the electron would affect its location.

unconditional surrender   complete, unqualified surrender of a belligerent nation.

untouchables   the lowest level of Indian society, technically outside the caste system and considered less than human; renamed harijans ("children of God") by Gandhi and later dalits, they remain the object of discrimination despite affirmative action programs.

utopian socialists   intellectuals and theorists in the early nineteenth century who favored equality in social and economic conditions and wished to replace private property and competition with collective ownership and cooperation; deemed impractical and "utopian" by later socialists.

varna   Indian classes, or castes. *See* caste system.

vassal   a person granted a fief, or landed estate, in exchange for providing military services to the lord and fulfilling certain other obligations such as appearing at the lord's court when summoned and making a payment on the knighting of the lord's eldest son.

vernacular   the everyday language of a region, as distinguished from a language used for special purposes. For example, in medieval Paris, French was the vernacular, but Latin was used for academic writing and for classes at the University of Paris.

volkish thought   the belief that German culture is superior and that the German people have a universal mission to save Western civilization from inferior races.

war communism   Lenin's policy of nationalizing industrial and other facilities and requisitioning the peasants' produce during the civil war in Russia.

War Guilt Clause   the clause in the Treaty of Versailles that declared that Germany (and Austria) were responsible for starting World War I and ordered Germany to pay reparations for the damage the Allies had suffered as a result of the war.

Warsaw Pact   a military alliance, formed in 1955, in which Albania, Bulgaria, Czechoslovakia, East Germany, Hungary, Poland, Romania, and the Soviet Union agreed to provide mutual assistance. Dissolved in 1991, some former members joined NATO.

welfare state   a social/political system in which the government assumes the primary responsibility for the social welfare of its citizens by providing such things as social security, unemployment benefits, and health care.

wergeld   "money for a man." In early Germanic law, a person's value in monetary terms, which was paid by a wrongdoer to the family of the person who had been injured or killed.

world-machine   Newton's conception of the universe as one huge, regulated, and uniform machine that operated according to natural laws in absolute time, space, and motion.

Young Turks   a successful Turkish reformist group in the late nineteenth and early twentieth centuries.

zaibatsu   powerful business cartels formed in Japan during the Meiji era and outlawed following World War II.

zamindars   Indian tax collectors, who were assigned land, from which they kept part of the revenue; the British revived the system in a misguided attempt to create a landed gentry.

Zen Buddhism   (in Chinese, Chan or Ch'an) a school of Buddhism particularly important in Japan, some of whose adherents stress that enlightenment (satori) can be achieved suddenly, though others emphasize lengthy meditation.

ziggurat   a massive stepped tower upon which a temple dedicated to the chief god or goddess of a Sumerian city was built.

Zionism   an international movement that called for the establishment of a Jewish state or a refuge for Jews in Palestine.

Zoroastrianism   a religion founded by the Persian Zoroaster in the seventh century B.C.; characterized by worship of a supreme god Ahuramazda who represents the good against the evil spirit, identified as Ahriman.

PRONUNCIATION GUIDE

Abbasid   AB-uh-sid or a-BA-sid
Abu Bakr   a-BOO BAH-ker
Achaemenid   a-KEE-muh-nid
Adenauer, Konrad   AD-n'our-er
Aeschylus   ESS-kuh-lus
Afrikaners   a-fri-KAH-ners
Agamemnon   ag-uh-MEM-nahn
Agincourt   AJ-in-kor
Ahuramazda   ah-HOOR-ah-MAHZ-duh
Akhenaten   ah-kuh-NAH-tun
Akkadian   a-KAY-dee-un
al-Mas'udi   al-ma-SOO-dee
Albigensian   al-bi-GEN-see-un
Albuquerque, Afonso de   AL-buh-kur-kee, ah-FON-soh d'
Allah   AH-luh or AL-uh
Allende, Salvador   ah-YEN-day, SAL-vuh-DOR
al-Ma'mun   al-MAH-moon
al-Rahman, Abd   al-RAH-mun, abd
Amenhotep   ah-mun-HOE-tep
Andropov, Yuri   an-DROP-ov, YOOR-ee
Antigonid   an-TIG-oh-nid
apella   a-PELL-uh
Apennines   A-puh-NINES
Aquinas, Thomas   uh-KWIGH-nus
Archimedes   are-kuh-MEE-deez
Aristotle   ar-i-STAH-tul
Aristophanes   ar-i-STAH-fuh-neez
Arthasastra   ar-tuh-SAHS-tra
Ashkenazic   ash-kuh-NAH-zic
Ashurnasirpal   ah-shoor-NAH-suh-pul
Asoka   a-SHOH-kuh or a-SOH-kuh
assignat   as-seen-YAH or AS-sig-nat
Assyrians   uh-SEER-ee-uns
Attalid   AT-a-lid
Augustine   AW-gus-STEEN
Auschwitz-Birkenau   OUSH-vitz-BUR-kuh-now
Ausgleich   OUS-glike
Avicenna   av-i-SEN-uh
Avignon   ah-veen-YONE
Axum   OX-oom
Bach, Johann Sebastian   BAHK, yoh-HAHN
  suh-BASS-chen
Barbarossa   bar-buh-ROH-suh
Baroque   buy-ROHK
Bastille   ba-STEEL
Beauvoir, Simone de   boh-VWAH, see-MOAN duh
Belisarius   bell-i-SAR-ee-us

benefice   BEN-uh-fiss
Bhagavadgita   bog-ah-vahd-GEE-ta
Blitzkrieg   BLITZ-kreeg
Boeotia   bee-OH-shuh
Boer   BOHR
Boleyn, Anne   BUH-lin
Bólivar, Simón   BOH-luh-VAR, see-MOAN
Bologna   buh-LOHN-yuh
Brandt, Willy   BRAHNT, VIL-ee
Brétigny   bray-tee-NYEE
Brezhnev, Leonid   BREZH-nef, lyi-on-YEET
Briand, Aristide   bree-AHN, a-ree-STEED
Bulganin, Nilolai   bul-GAN-in, nyik-uh-LYE
Bund deutscher Mädel   BUNT DOICHer MAIR-del
Burschenschaften   BOOR-shen-shaft-un
Buthelezi, Mangosuthu   boo-teh-LAY-zee, man-go-SOO-tu
Calais   ka-LAY
caliph/caliphate   KAY-lif/KAY-li-FATE
Cambyses   kam-BY-seez
Camus, Albert   kuh-MOO, al-BEAR
Canaanites   KAY-nuh-nites
Cao Cao   tsau tsau
Capet/Capetian   ka-PAY or KAY-put/kuh-PEE-shun
Carolingian   kar-oh-LIN-jun
carruca   ca-ruh-kuh
Carthage/Carthaginian   KAR-thij/KAR-thuh-JIN-ee-un
Castlereagh, Viscount   KAS-ul-RAY
Castiglione, Baldassare   kass-teel-YOHnay, bahl-dah-SAR-ay
Çatal Hüyük   CHAH-tul HOO-YOOK
Catharism   KA-tha-ri-zem
Catullus   ka-TULL-us
caudillos   kow-THEE-yohz (TH as in the)
Cavendish, Margaret   KAV-un-dish
Cavour, Camillo di   ka-VOOR, kah-MIL-oh
Chaeronea   ker-oh-NEE-uh
Chaldean   kal-DEE-un
Charlemagne   SHAR-luh-mane
Chernenko, Konstantin   cher-NYEN-koh, kon-stun-TEEN
Chiang Kai-Shek   CHANG KIGH-shek
Chirac, Jacques   SHE-RAHK, ZHAHK
Chulalongkorn   CHOO-LAH-LONG-KON
Cicero   SIS-uh-roh
Cistercians   si-STIR-shuns
Cixi   TSE-she
Cleisthenes   KLISE-thuh-neez
Clemenceau, Georges   klem-un-SOH, ZHORZH
Clovis   KLOH-vis

Colbert, Baptiste   kahl-BEHR, buh-TEEST

Comneni   kahm-NEE,nee

Concordat of Worms   kon-KOR-dat of WURMZ or VAWRMZ

condottieri   kon-dah-TEE-AIR-ee

consul   KON-sul

Copernicus, Nicolaus   koh-PURR-nuh-kus, nee-koh-LAH-us

Corinth   KOR-inth

Cortés, Hernán   kor-TEZ, er-NAHN

Courbet, Gustave   koor-BAY, guh-STAWV

Crassus   KRASS-us

Crécy   kray-SEE

Croesus   KREE-suhs

Cruz, Juana Ines de la   KROOZ, WAHN-uh ee NAYS de lah

Curie, Marie   kyoo-REE, muh-REE

d'Este, Isabella   ES-tay

Daimyo   die-AIM-yo

Dao De Jing   dow duh JING

Darius   duh-RYE-us

dauphin   DAW-fin

de Gaulle, Charles   duh GOLL, SHARL

Delacroix, Eugène   del-uh-KWAW, yoo-ZHAHN

Deng Xiaoping   DUNG shee-ow-ping

Descartes, René   day-KART, ruh-NAY

Dias, Bartholomeu   DEE-us, bar-too-loo-MAY

Diaspora   die-AS-pur-uh

Díaz, Porfirio   DEE-ahz, pah-FEER-yoh

Diderot, Denis   DEE-duh-roh, duh-NEE

Diem, Ngo Dinh   dzee-EM, NGOH Den

Diocletian   die-uh-KLEE-shun

Dorians   DOR-ee-uns

Douhet, Giulio   doo-EE, JOOL-yoh

Duma   DOO-muh

Echeverria, Luis   ah-chuh-vuh-REE-uh, loo-EES

Einsatzgruppen   INE-zats-groo-pen

encomienda   en-koh-mee-EN-dah

Engels, Friedrich   ENG-ulz, FREE-drik

Entente Cordiale   ahn-TAHNT kor-DYALL

ephor   EF-or

Epicurus/Epicureanism   EP-i-KYOOR-us/EP-i-kyoo-REE-uh-ni-zem

Erasmus, Desiderius   i-RAZZ-mus, des-i-DIR-ee-us

Erhard, Ludwig   AIR-hart

Etruscan   i-TRUSS-kuhn

Euripides   yoo-RIP-i-deez

exchequer   EX-chek-ur

Fa Xian   fa SHIEN

fasces   FASS-eez

Fascio di Combattimento   FASH-ee-oh di com-BATT-ee-men-toh

Fatimid   FAT-i-mid

Flaubert, Gustave   floh-BEAR, guh-STAWV

Friedan, Betty   fri-DAN

Friedrich, Caspar David   FREE-drik, KASS-par DAHV-eet

Frimaire   free-MARE

Fronde   FROND

Führer   FYOOR ur

gabelle   gah-BELL

Garibaldi, Giuseppe   gar-uh-BAWL-dee, joo-ZEP-pay

Gaugamela   gaw-guh-MEE-luh

gerousia   juh-ROO-see-uh

Gierek, Edward   GYER-ek

Gilgamesh   GILL-guh-mesh

glasnost   GLAZ-nohst

Gleichschaltung   GLIKE-shalt-ung

Gomulka, Wladyslaw   goh-MOOL-kuh, vla-DIS-lawf

Gorbachev, Mikhail   GOR-buh-chof, meek-HALE

Gracchus   GRA-kus

Gropius, Walter   GROH-pee-us, VAHL-ter

Grossdeutsch   gross-DOICH

Guevara, Ernesto "Che"   gay-VAR-uh, er-NAY-stoh "CHAY"

Habsburg   HAPS-burg

Hadrian   HAY-dree-un

Hagia Sophia   HAG-ee-uh soh-FEE-uh

hajj   HAJ

Hammurabi   ham-uh-RAH-bee

Han Gaozu   HAHN GOW-ZOO

Hannibal   HAN-uh-bul

Harappan   har-RAP-an

harijans   har-uh-JAHNS

Harun al-Rashid   huh-ROON al-ra-SHEED

Hatshepsut   hat-SHEP-soot

Havel, Vaclav   HAH-vuhl, VAHT-slaf

Haydn, Franz Joseph   HIDE-n, FRAHNTS

hegemon   HEJ-uh-mon

Hegira   huh-JIGH-ruh

Hellenistic   hell-uh-NIS-tik

helots   HELL-uts

Herzl, Theodor   HERT-sul, TAY-oh-dor

Heydrich, Reinhard   HIGH-drik, RINE-hart

Hidalgo y Castilla, Miguel   hi-DAL-goh ee cahs-TEEL-yuh, mee-GEL

hieroglyph   HIGH-ur-oh-glif

Hitler Jugend   JOO-gunt

Ho Chi Minh   HOE CHEE MIN

Höch, Hannah   HOKH

Hohenstaufen   HOE-un-SHTAU-fun

Hohenzollern   HOE-un-ZAHL-lurn

Homo erectus   HOH-MOH i-RECK-tuhs

Homo habilis   HOH-MOH HAB-uh-lus

Homo sapiens   HOH-MOH SAY-pee-enz

hoplites   HOP-lites

Horace   HOR-us

Höss, Rudolf   HAHSS, roo-DAHLF

Huguenots   HYOO-guh-nots

Husak, Gustav   HOO-sahk, guh-STAHV

Hydaspes   high-DASS-peez

Hyksos   hik-SAHS or hik-SOHS

Ibn Khaldun   ib-en-kal-DOON

Ibn Sina   ib-en SEE-nuh

Ieyasu, Tokugawa   ee-eye-AY-soo, toe-koo-GAH-wah

Ignatius of Loyola   ig-NAY-shus of loi-OH-luh

Il Duce   eel DOO-chay

imperator   im-puh-RAH-tor

imperium   im-PIER-ee-um

intendant   in-TEN-duhnt

Inukai Tsuyoshi   EE-NUH-KIGH TSOO-yah-shee

Isis   EYE-sis

Issus   ISS-us

Jacobin   JAK-uh-bin

Jagiello   yah-GYELL-oh

Jaruzelski, Wojciech   yahr-uh-ZEL-skee, VOI-chek

Jiang Qing   JIANG CHING

jihad   ji-HAHD

Jinnah, Mohammed Ali   JEE-nah, moe-HA-mud a-LEE

Judaea   joo-DEE-uh

Junkers   YOONG-kers

Justinian   juh-STIN-ee-un

Juvenal   JOO-vuh-nul

Ka'aba stone   KAH-BAH

Kadar, Janos   KAY-dahr, YAHN-us

Kadinsky, Vassily   kan-DIN-skee, vus-YEEL-yee

kamikaze   kah-mi-KAH-zee

Kangxi   KANG-she

Keiretsu business arrangement   kai-RET-su

Kerensky, Alexander   kuh-REN-skee

Keynes, John Maynard   KAYNZ

Khan, Khubilai   KHAN, KOO-bil-eye

Khatemi, Mohammed   KHAH-tee-mee

Khayyam, Omar   kigh-YAHM, oh-MAR

Khmer Rouge   ka-MEHR roozh

Khoisan   KOY-SAN

Khrushchev, Nikita   KROOSH-chef, nuh-KEE-tuh

Khufu   KOO-FOO

Kita, Ikki   KEE-tah EEk-EE

Knossos   NAH-sus

Koguryo   ko-GOOR-yo

Kohl, Helmut   KOLE, HELL-mut

Kolkhoz   kahl-KAWZ

Kollantai, Alexandra   kawl-un-TIE

Kosovo   kah-suh-VOH

Kraft durch Freude   CRAFT durch FROI-duh

Kristallnacht   KRIS-tal-NAHCHT

Kshatriya   kuh-SHOT-ria

Kuchuk-Kainarji   koo-CHOOK-kigh-NAR-jee

kulaks   koo-LAKS

kulturkampf   kool-TOOR-kahmf

Kundera, Milan   KOON-de-rah, MIL-ahn

Kwasniewski, Aleksander   KWAHS-noo-skee, ah-lek-SAHN-der

laissez-faire   les-ay-FAIR

Lao Tzu   LAUW DZU

latifundia   lat-uh-FUN-dee-uh

Latium   LAY-shee-um

Laurier, Wilfred   LOR-ee-ay

Lebensraum   LAY-benz-roum

Lee Kuan-yew   LEE KWAN YEW

Lévesque, René   luh-VEK, ruh-NAY

Lin Zexu   LIN DZUH-shoo

Livy   LIV-ee

López Portillo, José   LOH-pez por-TEE-yoh, hoh-ZAY

Luddites   LUD-ites

Ludendorff, Erich   LOOD-un-dorf

Luftwaffe   LUFT-vaf-uh

l'uomo universale   l'oo-OH-moh oo-nee-vehr-SAH-leh

Lycurgus   ligh-KUR-gus

Machiavelli, Niccolò   mak-ee-uh-VELL-ee, nee-koh-LOH

Machu Picchu   MAH-CHOO PEEK-SHOO

Madero, Francisco   muh-der-oh, fran-CIS-koh

Magyars   MAG-yars

Mahabharata   MA-HA-bah-rah-tah

Majapahit   mah-ja-PAH-heet

Malleus Maleficarum   mall-EE-us mal-uh-FIK-ar-um

Manchukuo   man-CHOO-KWOH

Manetho   MAN-uh-THOH

Mao Zedong   mau zee-DONG

Marie Antoinette   muh-REE an-twuh-NET

Marius   MAR-ee-us

Marquez, Gabriel Garcia   MAR-kays, gab-ree-ELL gar-SEE-uh

Massaccio   muh-ZAHCH-ee-OH

Mbecki, Thabo   mu-BEK-ee, TYE-bo

Meiji   MAY-jee

Mein Kampf   mine KAHMF

Menander   me-NAN-der

Mendeleyev, Dmitri   men-duh-LAY-ef, di-MEE-tri

Meroë   mer-OH-ee

Mesopotamia   mess-oh-poh-TAME-ee-uh

mestizos   me-STEE-zohs

Metternich, Klemens von   MET-er-nik, KLAY-mens

Michelangelo   my-kell-AN-juh-loh

Mieszko   MYESH-koh

Millet, Jean-François   mi-LAY, ZHAHN-FRAN-swah

Milosevic, Slobodan   mi-LOH-suh-vich, slaw-BAW-dahn

Miltiades   mil-TIGH-uh-DEEZ

missi dominici   MISS-ee doe-MIN-ee-chee

Mitterrand, Francois   mee-ter-AHN, FRAN-swah

Moche   MO-chay

Moctezuma   mahk-tuh-ZOO-muh

Moldavia   mahl-DAY-vee-uh

Monet, Claude   moh-NAY, KLODE

Montesquieu   MONT-ess-skyoo

Montessori, Maria   mon-ti-SOR-ee

Morisot, Berthe   mor-ee-ZOH, BERT

Mozart, Wolfgang Amadeus   MOHT-sart, volf-GANG ah-muh-DAY-us

Muawiyah   moo-AH-wee-yah

Mughal   MOO-gahl

Muhammad   moe-HA-mud

mulattoes   muh-LA-tohs

Muslim   MUZ-lum

Mutsuhito   moo-tsoo-HEE-toe

Mwene Metapa   MWAHN-uh muh-TAH-puh

Mycenaean   my-suh-NEE-un

Nagy, Imry   NAHJD, IM-re

Nebuchadnezzar   neb-uh-kad-NWZZ-ar

Nehru, Jawaharlal   NAY-roo, jah-WAH-har-lahl

Nero   NEE-roh

Neumann, Balthasar   NOI-mahn, BAHL-tah-zar

Nevsky, Alexander   NEW-skee

Ngo Dinh Diem   NGOH din dee-EM

Ngugi Wa Thiong'o   en-GU-ji WA THIE-ong-oh

Nimwegen   NIM-vay-gun

Nkrumah, Kwame   en-KRU-may, KWA-may

Novotny, Antonin   noh-VOT-nee, AN-ton-yeen

Nyerere, Julius   nyay-RARE-ee

Nystadt   nee-STAHD

Octavian   ok-TAY-vee-un

optimates   opp-tuh-MAH-tays

Osiris   oh-SIGH-ris

Ovid   OV-id

Pachakuti   PAH-chah-koo-tee

Pahlavi dynasty   pah-LAH-vee

Palenque   pah-LENG-kay

Paleologus   pay-lee-OHL-uh-gus

Pankhurst, Emmeline   PANK-herst, em-uh-LINE

papal curia   PAY-pul KOOR-ee-uh

Parlement   par-luh-MAHN

paterfamilias   pay-ter-fuh-MILL-ee-us

Peloponnesus   pe-luh-puh-NEE-sus

Pentateuch   PEN-tuh-tuke

perestroika   pair-ess-TROY-kuh

Pericles   PER-i-kleez

Perón, Juan   pay-ROHN, WAHN

Pétain, Henri   pay-TAN, AHN-ree

Petrarch   PE-trark

philosophe   fee-luh-ZAWF

Phoenicians   fi-NISH-uns

Picasso, Pablo   pi-KAW-soh

Pinochet, Augusto   PEE-noh-shay, aw-GOO-stoh

Pisistratus   pi-SIS-truh-tus

Pissaro, Camille   pi-SARR-oh, kah-MEEYL

Pizarro, Francesco   pi-ZARR-oh, frahn-CHASE-koh

Planck, Max   PLAHNK

Plantagenet   plan-TA-juh-net

Plato   PLAY-toe

Poincaré, Raymond   pwan-kah-RAY, re-MOAN

polis   POE-lis

politiques   puh-lee-TEEKS

Polybius   poe LIB-ee-us

Pompey   POM-pee

pontifex maximus   PON-ti-feks MAK-suh-mus

populares   POP-yoo-lar-ays

praetor   PREE-ter

princeps   PRIN-seps

procurator   PROK-yuh-ray-ter

Ptolemy/Ptolemaic   TOL-uh-mee/TOL-uh-MAY-ik

Punic   PYOO-nik

Pugachev, Emelyan   poo-guh-CHEF, em-ELL-yun

Pyrrhus/Pyrrhic   PIR-us/PIR-ik

Qadhafi, Muammar   gah-DAH-fee, myoo-am-MAR

Qianlong   chee-UN-LUNG

Qin Shi Huangdi   chin SHE hwang-DEE

Qing dynasty   CHING

Quesnay, François   kay-NAY, FRAN-swah

Quetzalcoatl   ket-SAHL-koh-AHT-ul

Quipu   KEE-poo

Quran   kuh-RAN

Rameses   RAM-i-seez

Raphael   RAFF-ee-ul

Rasputin   rass-PYOO-tin

Realpolitik   ray-AHL-poe-li-teek

Reichsrat   RIKES-raht

Ricci, Matteo   REECH-ee, mah-TAY-oh

risorgimento   ree-SOR-jee-men-toe

Robespierre, Maximilien   ROHBZ-pee-air, mak-SEE-meel-yahn

Rococo   ro-KOH-koh

Rosas, Juan Manuel de   ROH-sahs, WAHN mahn-WELL duh

Rousseau, Jean-Jacques   roo-SOH ZHAHN-ZHAHK

Sadducees   SA-juh-seez

Sadi   sah-DEE

Safavids   suh-FAH-weedz

Sakharov, Andrei   SAH-kuh-rof, ahn-DRAY

Saladin   SAL-uh-din

Sallust   SALL-ust

San Martin, José   SAN mar-TEEN, hoh-ZAY

Sartre, Jean-Paul   SAR-truh, ZHAHN-PAUL

satrap/satrapy   SAY-trap/SAY-truh-pee

Schleswig-Holstein   SCHLES-vig-HOLE-stine

Schlieffen   SHLEE-fun

Schmidt, Helmut   SHMIT, HELL-mut

Schroeder, Gerhard   SHROH-der, ger-HART

Schönberg, Arnold   SHURN-burg, ARR-nawlt

Schutzstaffel   SHOOTS-shah-ful

Seleucus/Seleucid   si-LOO-kus/si-LOO-sid

Seljuk Turks   SELL-juke

Seneca   SEN-i-kuh

Sephardic   suh-FAR-dik

sesterces   SES-ters-eez

Sforza   SFORT-zuh

Shari'a   shay-REE-uh

Shari'ya   shay-REE-uh

Sheikh   SHEEK or SHAYK

Shi'ite   SHE-ite

Shotoku Taishi   show-TOE-koo tie-ISH-ee

Siddhartha Gautama   sid-AR-tha guh-TAW-mah

Sieveking, Amalie   SEEVE-king

Sima Qian   suh-MAH chee-AHN or chee-YEN

Sjahrir Sutan   SYAH-rir, soo-TAN

Socrates   SOK-ruh-teez

Solon   SOH-lun

Solzhenitsyn, Alexander   SOLE-zhuh-NEET-sin

Somoza, Anastasio   suh-MOH-zuh, ahn-ash-TAHS-yoh

Sophocles   SOF-uh-kleez

Soyinka, Wole   shah-YIN-kuh, WAH-lay

Spartacus   SPAR-tuh-kus

Speer, Albert   SHPIER

squadristi   sqah-DREES-tee

Sri Lanka   SREE-LAHN-kuh

Srivijaya   sree-vee-JAH-ya

Stoicism   STOH-i-siz-um

Stravinsky, Igor   struh-VIN-skee, EE-gor

Stresemann, Gustav   SHTRAY-zuh-mahn, GUS-tahf

Sturmabteilung   SHTOORM-AP-ti-loong

Sudetenland   soo-DAYT-un-LAND

Suger, Abbot   soo-ZHER

Suleyman I the Magnificent   soo-lee-MAHN

Sumerian   soo-MER-ee-un

Suttner, Bertha von   ZOOT-ner

Tacitus   TASS-i-tus

taille   TAH-yuh or TIE

Tang Taizong   TANG TYE-zawng

Tanzania   tan-zah-NEE-ah

Tenochtitlán   tay-NAWCH-teet-LAHN

Teotihuacán   TAY-oh-tee-WAH-kahn

Tertullian   tur-TULL-yun

Theocritus   thee-OCK-ri-tus

Thermidor   ter-mee-DOR

Thermopylae   thur-MOP-uh-lee

Thucydides   thoo-SID-uh-deez

Thutmosis   thoot-MOH-sus

Tiberius   tie-BIR-ee-us

Tito   TEE-toh

Tlaxcala   tlah-SKAHL-uh

Torah   TOR-uh

Tordesillas   tor-duh-SEE-yus

Toussaint L'Ouverture   too-SAN loo-vur-TOOR

Trajan   TRAY-jun

Trevithick, Richard   TREV-uh-thik

Trudeau, Pierre   TROO-doh, pee-YEHR

Tuthankhamun   tuh-tan-KAH-muhn

Tzara, Tristan   TSAH-rah, tri-STAN

Uighur   yu-EE-gur

ulama   oo-lah-MAH

Ulbricht, Walter   UL-brikt, VAHL-ter

Umayyads   oo-MY-ads

Unam Sanctam   OON-ahm SANK-tahm

universitas   yoo-ni-VER-si-tahs

Vaisya   VIGHSH-yuh

Valois   VAL-wah

van Eyck, Jan   van IKE

van Gogh, Vincent   van GOE

Vargas, Getúlio   VAR-gus, zhuh-TOOL-yoo

Venetia   vuh-NEE-shee-uh

Vesalius, Andreas   vi-SAY-lee-us, ahn-DRAY-us

Vespucci, Amerigo   ves-POO-chee, ahm-ay-REE-goe

Vierzenheiligen   feer-tsun-HILE-i-gun

Virgil   VUR-jul

vizier   vuy-ZEER

Volkschulen   FOLK-shool-un

Voltaire   vole-TAIR

Walesa, Lech   va-WENZ-uh, LEK

Wallachia   wah-lay-KEE-uh

Watteau, Antoine   wah-TOE, AHN-twahn

Weizsäcker, Richard von   VITS-zek-er, RIK-art

wergeld   wur-GELD

Winkelmann, Maria   VING-kul-mun

Xerxes   ZURK-seez

Xhosa   KOH-suh

Xinjiang   shin-JI-ang

Xiongnu (Hsiung-nu)   she-ONG-noo

Xuan Zang   SHYAHN ZAHNG

Yahweh   YAH-wah

Yeltsin, Boris   YELT-sun

Yi Song-gye   YEE sohn-GEE

yishuv   YISH-uv

Zapata, Emiliano   zuh-PAH-tuh, ay-mel-YAHN-oh

zemstvos   ZEMPST-voh

Zeno   ZEE-noh

Zhang Xueliang   JANG shwee-lee-ONG

Zhengke   JUNG-huh

Zhou   JOE

Zhu Xi   JOO SHEE

Zhu Yuanzhang   jew whan-JANG

ziggurat   ZIG-guh-rat

Zimbabwe   zim-BAH-bway

Zola, Emile   ZOH-luh, ay-MEEL

zollverein   TSOL-fuh-rine

Zoroaster   ZOR-oh-as-ter

MAP CREDITS

The authors wish to acknowledge their use of the following books as reference in preparing the maps listed here:

SPOT MAP, PAGE 38   Geoffrey Barraclough, ed., *Times Atlas of World History*, (Maplewood, N.J.: Hammond Inc., 1978), p. 65.

MAP 3.2   Geoffrey Barraclough, ed., *Times Atlas of World History*, (Maplewood, N.J.: Hammond Inc., 1978), p. 63.

MAP 3.3   Conrad Schirokauer, *A Brief History of Chinese and Japanese Civilizations*, 2d ed. (San Diego: Harcourt Brace Jovanovich, 1989), p. 52.

MAP 3.4   Hammond Past Worlds: *The Times Atlas of Archeology*, (Maplewood, N.J.: Hammond Inc. 1988), pp. 190–191.

MAP 6.2   Michael Coe, Dean Snow and Elizabeth Benson, *Atlas of Ancient America* (New York: Facts on File, 1988), p. 144.

MAP 6.3   Geoffrey Barraclough, ed., *Times Atlas of World History*, (Maplewood, N.J.: Hammond Inc., 1978), p. 47.

MAP 6.4   Phillipa Fernandez-Arnesto, *Atlas of World Exploration*, (New York: Harper Collins, 1991), p. 35.

MAP 6.5   Geoffrey Barraclough, ed., *Times Atlas of World History*, (Maplewood, N.J.: Hammond Inc., 1978), p. 47.

MAP 7.3   Geoffrey Barraclough, ed., *Times Atlas of World History*, (Maplewood, N.J.: Hammond Inc., 1978), pp. 134–135.

MAP 7.4   Geoffrey Barraclough, ed., *Times Atlas of World History*, (Maplewood, N.J.: Hammond Inc., 1978), p. 135.

MAP 8.1   Geoffrey Barraclough, ed., *Times Atlas of World History*, (Maplewood, N.J.: Hammond Inc., 1978), pp. 44–45.

MAP 8.4   Geoffrey Barraclough, ed., *Times Atlas of World History*, (Maplewood, N.J.: Hammond Inc., 1978), pp. 136–137.

MAP 9.1   Michael Edwardes, *A History of India* (London: Thames and Hudson, 1961), p. 79.

MAP 10.1   John K. Fairbank, Edwin O. Reischauer, and Albert M. Craig, *East Asia: Tradition and Transformation* (Boston: Houghton Mifflin, 1973), p. 103.

SPOT MAP, PAGE 266   Albert Hermann, *An Historical Atlas of China* (Chicago: Aidine, 1966), p. 13.

MAP 11.1   John K. Fairbank, Edwin O. Reischauer, and Albert M. Craig, *East Asia: Tradition and Transformation* (Boston: Houghton Mifflin, 1973), p. 363.

MAP 14.1   Geoffrey Barraclough, ed., *Times Atlas of World History*, (Maplewood, N. J.:Hammond, Inc. 1978), p. 160.

MAP 15.3   Geoffrey Barraclough, ed., *Times Atlas of World History*, (Maplewood, N. J.: Hammond, Inc. 1978), p. 173.

MAP 16.1   Jonathan Spence, *The Search for Modern China*, (New York: W. W. Norton, 1990), p. 19.

MAP 16.2   Conrad Schirokauer, *A Brief History of Chinese and Japanese Civilizations*, 2d ed., (San Diego: Harcourt Brace Jovanovich, 1989), p. 330.

MAP 16.3   John K. Fairbank, Edwin O. Reischauer, and Albert M. Craig, *East Asia: Tradition and Tranformation*, (Boston: Houghton Mifflin, 1973), pp. 402–403.

MAP 17.1   *Atlas of World History*, (New York: Harper & Row Publishers, 1987), p. 187.

MAP 20.4   Geoffrey Barraclough, ed., *Times Atlas of World History*, (Maplewood, N. J.: Hammond, Inc. 1978), p. 235.

MAP 21.1   John K. Fairbank, Edwin O. Reischauer, and Albert M. Craig, *East Asia: Tradition and Transformation*, (Boston: Houghton Mifflin, 1973), p. 451.

MAP 21.4   Geoffrey Barraclough, ed., *Times Atlas of World History*, (Maplewood, N. J.: Hammond, Inc. 1978), p. 243.

INDEX

Note: Page references in italics refer to maps and figures.